Somadeva's

Yaśastilaka

Aspects of
Jainism, Indian Thought and Culture

By the same Author

Pravarasena's *Setubandha* :
Translated from Prākrit into English with extracts from unpublished commentaries and an Introduction

Somadeva's

Yaśastilaka

Aspects of Jainism, Indian Thought and Culture

by

Krishna Kanta Handiqui

Rashtriya Sanskrit Sansthan
New Delhi

D.K. Printworld (P) Ltd.
New Delhi

Cataloging in Publication Data — DK
[Courtesy: D.K. Agencies (P) Ltd. <docinfo@dkagencies.com>]

Handiqui, Krishna Kanta.
Somadeva's Yaśastilaka : aspects of Jainism, Indian thought and culture / by Krishna Kanta Handiqui.
p. cm.
Reprint.
Includes bibliographical references and indexes.
ISBN 13: 9788124606001

1. Somadeva Sūri, 10th cent. Yaśastilaka. 2. Jainism — India. 3. Philosophy, Indic. 4. Philosophy, Medieval. 5. Jaina literature — India — History and criticism. I. Title.

DDC 891.3 22

ISBN 13: 978-81-246-0600-1 ISBN 10: 81-246-0600-5

First published in 1949 by Jain Saṁskṛti Saṁrakshaka Sangha, Sholapur as no. 2 of Jīvarāja Jaina Granthamālā under the title: Yaśastilaka and Indian Culture.

Second edition published in 1968

Reprinted in 2011

Published by:
RASHTRIYA SANSKRIT SANSTHAN
56-57, Institutional Area, Janakpuri, New Delhi – 110 058
Phones: (011) 2852 4993, 2852 1994, 2852 4995
E-mail: rsks@nda.vsnl.net.in
Website: www.sanskrit.nic.in

and

D.K. PRINTWORLD (P) LTD.
Regd. Office: 'Vedaśrī', F-395, Sudarshan Park
Ramesh Nagar Metro Station, New Delhi – 110 015-11
Phones: (011) 2545 3975; 2546 6019; *Fax*: (011) 2546 5926
E-mail: indology@dkprintworld.com
Website: www.dkprintworld.com

Printed by: D.K. Printworld (P) Ltd, New Delhi.

FOREWORD

Sanskrit has been a perennial source of wisdom and intellectual discourse. The literature of this language has also served as a vibrant storehouse of knowledge-systems and information on cultural achievements. In fact, the study of this literature is an essential prerequisite for understanding the development of Indian society and culture.

In his *History of Dharmaśāstra*, Mahāmahopādhyāya Purushottam Vaman Kane presented a most monumental work on ancient texts of law as sourcebooks for Indian culture. Prof. V.S. Agrawal, in his *India as Known to Paṇini*, established the paradigms of the cultural study of a Śāstric work in Sanskrit — the Aṣṭādhyāyī — a text that is definitely one of the most miraculous intellectual accomplishments in the history of human race. Prof. B.S. Upadhyaya and some other scholars have attempted studies of the works of Kālidāsa and other poets as sourcebooks for Indian culture and civilisation, still others have taken up similar studies of the texts by Yāska and Patañjali. However, Sanskrit classics produced in first two millenniums of ACE have remained by and large unexplored from the point of view of cultural studies. Prof. K.K. Handiqui, one of the most distinguished Sanskrit scholars of modern times, not only made a fruitful attempt to bridge a gap in the cultural studies of Sanskrit texts in his *Yaśastilaka and Indian Culture*, he also joined the glorious line of stalwarts like Mahāmahopādhyāya Purushottam Vaman Kane and Prof. V.S. Agrawal by presenting another landmark of the study in Sanskrit literature as source for cultural history. In fact, *Yaśastilaka* of Somadeva, a *campū kāvya* composed in tenth century ACE, is really the *Yaśastilaka* — auspicious mark on the forehead — of India's culture. It establishes Indian culture as a vibrant continuum enriched by numerous tributaries. A cultural study of *Yaśastilaka* becomes especially significant considering the fact that this text by Somadeva belongs to the other traditions — the traditions of Jainism and the *śramaṇas*, that have made equally enormous contribution to the growth of Indian culture.

A scholar of extraordinary accomplishments from Assam, Prof. K.K. Handiqui here presents a remarkable study of work of Somadeva — an author — who flourished in the southern parts of our country nearly one thousand years back. The work not only provides a first-hand knowledge of cultural organisations and genesis of various systems of law, administration and governance, it has really become an encyclopaedia of ancient Indian traditions and the milieu.

In the eighteen chapters of this book, Prof. Handiqui has covered all the aspects of Indian culture as visualised through Somadeva's *magnum opus* — historical, geographical, religious, philosophical and archaeological; he also interprets various cults, customs and beliefs that prevailed during Somadeva's period, providing us an authentic account of the life and times of the author under study. Prof. Handiqui not only presents a revision of paradigms for the cultural study of an ancient text, his work also provides a literary analysis of *Yaśastilaka* as a prose romance, bringing out Somadeva's excellence as a poet. This study is marked with a vivid account of moral dilemmas and intellectual dialogues and debates between various philosophical systems not only of a century but of the first millennium ACE.

Marked with an amazing accuracy and analytical acumen, studies by Prof. Handiqui present correct documentations of institutions and systems related to the culture of an era. His analysis of inspirations and other records is epigraphically validated. In his note on the 'Kālāmukha' Prof. Handiqui discovers an important and unknown sect, and with his authentic study of Cāḷukyan temples, brings out salient features of temple architecture and sculptures with illustrations. As a critique on Indian culture, this study brings out both glories and achievements of our ancestors, and it unhesitatingly takes notice of shortcomings and drawbacks as well.

Through this study, Prof. K.K. Handiqui has successfully established Somadeva's times as one of the most flourishing periods in the literary, social and cultural history of India, and his analysis of various facets of Indian culture as envisaged through *Yaśastilaka* presents issues that are still relevant. In fact, *Yaśastilaka* of Somadeva also presents a study in human psychology and the contradictions of Indian society that have wrecked the age. It is interesting to note that Girish Karnad, a celebrated Kannad author of our times, has based one of his well-known plays on Somadeva's work.

I am happy to present this brilliant exposition of *Yaśastilaka* and one of the most voluminous works on cultural study of a Sanskrit text by Prof. K.K. Handiqui. The first edition of this work was brought out by Prof. A.N. Upadhye, a veteran scholar himself, through the Jain Sanskrit Samrakshaka Samgha of Sholapur. The second edition appeared in 1968. The work has not been easily available for so many years, and this publication will hopefully fulfill a long-felt demand in the scholarly world.

I am extremely grateful to Mrs. Ahalya Gogoi for having taken pains to make this work available to Rashtriya Sanskrit Sansthan and giving us permission to produce this new edition. I specially want to thank Shri Susheel Mittal and the D.K. Printworld for collaborating with the Rashtriya Sanskrit Sansthan in bringing out this important treatise and for their meticulousness in carrying out the printing work. I am confident that the publication of this work will further stimulate the study of Sanskrit literature as source for history and culture.

Radhavallabh Tripathi
Vice-Chancellor
Rashtriya Sanskrit Sansthan

CONTENTS

AUTHOR'S PREFACE

(*Second Edition*)

The present edition is a reprint of the first edition published about twenty years ago. Circumstances have prevented me from undertaking a revision, but I have added supplementary notes incorporating the results of recent studies on the relations of the Lemulavāḍa or Vemulavāḍa Cālukyas with Somadevasūri and the locality in which he wrote his masterpiece *Yaśastilaka* and other works. A brief note on the Eastern Cālukyan temples, based on Dr. M. RAMA RAO's interesting monograph on the subject, has also been added to supplement the information brought together in Appendix III.

The early publication of this edition is entirely due to the enthusiasm and keen interest of my esteemed friend Dr. A.N. UPADHYE. I offer my sincere thanks to Dr. B. RAMA RAJU of Hyderabad for sending me information about some of the places dealt with in the supplementary notes and drawing my attention to Sri. S. GOPALAKRISHNA MURTHY's monograph *Jain Vestiges in Andhra.*

K. K. Handiqui

Jorhat (Assam),
8-1-68

AUTHOR'S PREFACE

Somadeva's *Yaśastilaka* was composed in 959 A. D. somewhere in the area corresponding to modern Dharwar and the westernmost districts of Hyderabad State. It is a Jaina religious romance written in Sanskrit prose and verse, but more important as an encyclopedic record of literary, socio-political, religious and philosophical data, valuable for the study of the cultural history of India, and particularly of the Deccan, in the tenth century and thereabouts, when the Rāṣṭrakūṭa empire still held sway in that part of the country. The object of the present volume is a critical study of the work; and if we have often gone far outside the limits of the text, it was only to give a more comprehensive picture of the life and thought of the times with reference to antecedent and subsequent factors in Indian cultural development.

The Sanskrit text was published long ago by the Nirnaya Sagar press in two volumes of a little over a thousand pages with the commentary of Śrutasāgara. The second volume of the work appeared in 1903, and the second edition of the first volume in 1916. A voluminous Jaina text composed in a difficult style could hardly be expected to be popular even with advanced students of Indian literature. To add to our difficulties, the commentary, which is our only guide to the work, breaks off at p. 244 of the second volume; and the printed text was found to be far too defective to admit of a critical study of the work.

To obviate these difficulties, I have utilized the following manuscripts of the text kindly lent by the Bhandarkar Oriental Research Institute, Poona : 1) MS. A : No. 230 of 1902-07, folios 434; 2) MS. B : No. 752 of 1886-92, folios 391; 3) MS. C : No. 274 of A. 1883-84, folios 341; and 4) another incomplete manuscript of the work. Of these MS. A is the most important. It is not only correct but contains valuable marginal notes which have been of great use in studying the text, specially the portion dealing with Jaina doctrines, on which the commentary is not available. Notes from MS. A have been incorporated in the present work; and, here and there, a line or a verse omitted in the printed text has been added from the manuscripts in the footnotes. In fact, nearly all the quotations from Somadeva's *Yaśastilaka* in the present volume have been collated with the manuscripts, especially A.

I am grateful to Dr. A. N. Upadhye, Kolhapur, for his generous and voluntary offer to publish this work on behalf of the Jaina Saṁskṛti Saṁrakṣaka Saṁgha of

Sholapur. The munificence of the Saṁgha has made the publication possible in a comparatively short time, but the work would not have appeared in a presentable form without Dr Upadhye's tireless efforts.

Dr. V. Raghavan of Madras University was kind enough to send me an offprint of his interesting paper *Gleanings from Somadevasūri's Yaśastilaka Campū* published in *Ganganatha Jha Research Institute Journal* (February-August, 1944). Dr. Raghavan refers in his paper to the unpublished commentary of Śrīdeva on the text. It is a fragment of 34 leaves preserved in the Bhandarkar Oriental Research Institute, and its existence was not known to me at the time of borrowing the manuscripst mentioned above.

I am indebted to my friend Prof. P. K. Gode, Curator, Bhandarkar Oriental Research Institute, for help in connection with manuscripts, and especially for carefully made copies of articles and papers otherwise inaccessible to me. The photographs of the sculptures relating to the ancient Jaina Stūpa of Mathura were a gift from Dr. Vasudev Agrawala when he was Curator of the Provincial Museum, Lucknow. The Śaiva sculpture preserved in the Rajputana Museum, Ajmer, is reproduced in this book with the kind permission of the Archaeological Survey of India. My sincere thanks are due to Sj. Brajendra Kumar Acharya, Lecturer in Bengali, Cotton College, for compiling the General Index.

GAUHATI,
April, 1949.

K K. HANDIQUI

SUPPLEMENTARY NOTES

(I)

The Vemulavāḍa Cālukyas and Somadevasūri.

Recent studies have conclusively shown that the Cālukya family during whose rule Somadeva lived and worked held the territory corresponding to Karimnagar district of former Hyderabad State, now included in Andhra.[1] These chiefs were feudatories of the Rāṣṭrakūṭas; and Yuddhamalla I, the founder of the family, has been assigned to about the middle of the eighth century. We are concerned here with the last three rulers Arikesarin II, Vadyaga or Baddega and Arikesarin III.[2]

Arikesarin II ruled in the second quarter of the tenth century, and was the patron of Pampa who wrote his famous poems *Ādipurāṇa* and *Vikramārjunavijaya* in Kannaḍa in 941 A. D.[3] According to the Parbhani plates, Arikesarin II was succeeded by his son Bhadradeva (II), also called Vadyaga, the father of Arikesarin III. Somadeva tells us in the colophon to his *Yaśastilaka* that he wrote the work in 959 A. D. during the reign of a prince who was the eldest son of Arikesarin (II), and who, as we have pointed out on p. 4, is variously called Vāgarāja, Vādyarāja, and Vadyagarāja in the manuscripts. The name Vadyaga is considered to be a variant of Baddiga, which occurs as the name of an earlier chief in the genealogy given in the Parbhani plates, and appears also as Baddega in the Vemulavāḍa pillar inscription of Arikesarin II.[4]

Baddega is said to have built a Jina temple for his teacher Somadevasūri in an inscription on the pedestal of an image of Pārśvanātha found at Vemulavāḍa in

---

1. See VENKATARAMANAYYA : *The Chālukyas of L (V) emulavāḍa*, Hyderabad, 1953; and specially N. LAKSHMINARAYAN RAO's paper The Family of Arikesarin, Patron of Pampa in the *Quarterly Journal of the Mythic Society*, Vol. XLV.
2. There is a confusion in the genealogy given on p. 4 of this book. The last two names should be omitted.
3. RICE : *A History of Kanarese Literature*, p. 30.
4. Baddega is called Baddega III by RAO op. cit., obviously because among the earlier chiefs there was another Baddega and another Bhadradeva (same as Baddega, being a Sanskrit variant of the name). But the first Bhadradeva is not mentioned in the Vemulavāḍa Pillar inscription, and if he did not actually rule, as seems probable, our Baddega might be called Baddega II.

Karimnagar district.[5] This is confirmed by the Parbhani plates issued in 966 A. D. by his son Arikesarin III, which state that the village of Vanikaṭupulu[6] was granted by him to Somadevasūri for the repairs and upkeep of a temple called Śubhadhāma-jinālaya built by his father Vadyaga in the capital city of Leṁbulapāṭaka, identified with the village of Lemulavāḍa or Vemulavāḍa mentioned above. Close to it was the prosperous town of Gaṅgadhārā where Somadeva says he composed his romance. The manner in which he refers to this town in the colophon to the work would seem to indicate that it enjoyed the bountiful patronage of the reigning chief Vadyaga or Baddega.[7]

Leṁbulapāṭaka[8] figures also in the Vemulavāḍa pillar inscription of Arikesarin II, which records a grant of land in a corner of the city for the maintenance of a Sun temple built by Peddaṇārya, a high official (*tantrapāla*) in the service of the ruling chief. Three other temples dedicated to Śiva (Rājeśvara, Baddegeśvara and Nagareśvara) are mentioned in the record, which shows that the place was a stronghold of Śaivism. Even today Vemulavāḍa is an important centre of pilgrimage in Telingana.[9]

Arikesarin II seems to have been a follower of the orthodox religion, but he was catholic in his sympathies, as shown by the fact that his court poet Pampa was a Jaina and wrote on Jaina themes. His son and successor Baddega came under the influence of Somadevasūri, who is described in the Parbhani plates as being held in great esteem and veneration by kings and powerful feudatory chiefs. He not only built a temple in the capital for the great teacher but seems to have adopted the Jaina creed under his guidance. It is noteworthy that the Parbhani inscription issued by his son Arikesarin III opens with a verse which extols the glory and the beneficent mission of the Jaina faith.

---

5. Rao op. cit., p. 216; Venkataramanayya op. cit., p. 45.
6. This and some other villages are said to exist almost under the same names in Sirsilla *tāluk* of Karimnagar district. Rao op. cit., p. 223.
7. Pt. Premi's manuscript gives this portion of the colophon in a more correct form than the printed edition : श्रीमद्वद्यगराजस्य लक्ष्मीप्रवर्धमानवसुधारायां गंगधारायां. Rao (op cit, p. 223) says that Gaṅgadhārā still exists under the same name near Vemulavāḍa. I am informed by Dr. B. Rama Raju of Hyderabad that it is in Jagtiyal *taluk* of Karimnagar district, ten miles from Vemulavāḍa.
8. The Parbhani plates and the revised text of the Vemulavāḍa pillar inscription of Arikesarin II in Rao *op. cit.* have -pāṭaka. The text of the latter record reproduced by Venkataramanayya (p. 91) has *-vāṭaka*.
9. Several Śaiva temples are shown on the site plan of Lemulavāda village in Venkataramanayya's monograph.

The Jaina relics at Vemulavāḍa have been surveyed,[10] but no trace exists of any Jaina structure or temple. The image of Pārśvanātha with the inscription mentioned above may have once belonged to the Śubhadhāma temple built by Baddega. There are as many as a dozen figures of Jaina Tīrthaṃkaras scattered in the precincts of the Hindu temples in the area besides a few other interesting Jaina sculptures. Vemulavāḍa may have had more than one Jaina temple, and was in any case a notable centre of Jainism during the reigns of the last two Cālukya chiefs in the third quarter of the tenth century. The rule of the Vemulavāḍa Cālukyas seems to have terminated with that of their overlords, the Rāṣṭrakūṭas; and soon afterwards Telingana came under the sway of the Cālukyas of Kalyāni. Jainism may have flourished for some time more, but it is probable that with the loss of royal patronage it declined and ultimately disappeared from the area. It is in the heyday of its glory at Vemulavāḍa that we see Somadevasūri as an honoured and influential exponent of the Jaina faith.

(II)

No attempt can be made here to fill the lacunae in Appendix III on the geographical distribution of the Śaiva temples, but a reference may be made to the Eastern Cālukyan temples by way of illustrating the dominant position of Śaivism in Andhra.[11] Most of these temples are dedicated to Śiva, and the more important ones are assigned to the ninth century, covering the reigns of Narendramṛgarāja Vijayāditya (806–46), Guṇaga Vijayāditya (848–891), and Cālukya Bhīma I (892-922). The first king is said to have built one hundred eight Śiva temples; while several such temples in the village of Bikkavolu in East Godavary district are attributed to the reign of Guṇaga Vijayāditya. The next king Cālukya Bhīma I was a great builder. He built three important temples known as Bhīmeśvara at Drākṣārāma, a township in Ramachandrapuram *taluk* of East Godavary district; at Cālukya-bhīmavaram, a village near Sāmalkot in the same district; and at Chebrolu in Bāpatla *taluk* of Guntur district. Other Eastern Cālukyan temples of the same period are the Rāmaliṅgeśvara at Pālakollu in West Godavary district; the Someśvara at Somārāma (now Somavaram forming part of the village of Bhīmavaram in the same district); and the Amareśvara at Amarāvati on the southern bank of the Krishnā in Guntur district. Most of these structures are two-storied and the shrine at Drākṣārāma with its elaborate sculptures is the most famous among the temples of

10. MURTHY : *Jain Vestiges in Andhra* (Andhra Pradesh Government Archaeological Series No. 12). Hyderabad, 1963.

11. See M. RAMA RAO : *Eastern Cālukyan* Temples of Andhra Deśa (Andhra Pradesh Government Archaeological Series, No. 19). Hyderabad, 1964.

Andhra. The development of Eastern Cālukyan temple architecture in the second half of the ninth century was coeval with the transition from the Pallava to the Cola style of temple building in the Tamil country during the reigns of Vijayālaya and Āditya I.

It is noteworthy that the temples named above with the exception of the one at Chebrolu are located at the five traditional Śaiva centres of Andhra, collectively known as Pañcārāma namely, Dakṣārāma (modern Drākṣārāma), Kumārārāma (Cālukya-bhīmavaram), Kṣīrārāma (Pālakollu), Somārāma (Somavaram) and Amarārāma (Amarāvati). Of these Amarāvati and Pālakollu are popular centres of Śaiva pilgrimage.

(III)

It may be noted that some of the verses cited by Somadeva in the *Yaśastilaka* in illustration of Buddhist doctrines (see pp. 188-9 & 457 of this book) are taken from the *Pramāṇavārttika* of Dharmakīrti (*circa* 600 *A. D.*). The two verses *yaḥ paśyaty ātmānaṃ* and *ātmani sati parasaṃjñā* occur in the *pramāṇa-siddhi* chapter of that work (see *Pramāṇavārttika* with the commentary of Manorathanandin, pp. 86-7; and *Pramāṇavārttikabhāṣyam* of Prajñākaragupta, pp. 146-7, Patna, 1953). The verse *vedaprāmāṇyaṃ kasyacit kartṛvādaḥ* occurs at the end of Dharmakīrti's own *vṛtti* on the *svārthānumāna* chapter of the above work. Karṇakagomin in his commentray on the *vṛtti*, however, reads *dhvastaprajñāne* for °*prajñānaṃ*, and says *pramāṇāvalambijñānaṃ prajñānaṃ, tad dhvastaṃ yasmin jāḍye tattathoktaṃ, nyāyānusārijñānarahita ityarthaḥ*. See *Pramāṇavārttikam*, p. 619, Allahabad edition.

(IV)

(Addendum by the General Editor : A. N. U.)

Lately an inscription is discovered on the hill Bommalaguṭṭa in the vicinity of the village Gaṅgādharam (Gaṅgadhārā ?) in the Karimnagar district of former Hyderabad State, now included in Andhra Pradesh. It was got carved by Jinavallabha, brother of Pampa. It is partly in prose and verses, and in three languages, Kannaḍa, Sanskrit and Telugu. It gives good many details about Pampa, his parentage and provenance. Arikesari donated the village Dharmapura to Pampa when the latter completed his Kannaḍa poem *Vikramārjunavijaya* (see p. 6 of this book and Note I above); and it is this event that is commemorated by Pampa's brother in this record. (See the Telugu Magazine *Bhāratī* for March 1967; *Journal of the Karnatak University*, Humanities No., Vol. XI 1967, pp. 73 f., 107f., also *Kannaḍa Nuḍi* March 1968, pp. 9f.)

The Achievements of Prof. Krishna Kanta Handiqui

Prof. Mukund Madhab Sharma

PROFESSOR Krishna Kanta Handiqui is one of the greatest Sanskritists and one of the greatest Indologists of the world, an educationist with uncommon ability and vision, a great philanthropist and, above all, a great man with certain highly commendable traits of personality. Although he is already highly celebrated in the world of letters for the last 66 years, yet his image was obviously more familiar to the scholars, and the other persons in general could not be expected to know him more intimately. Hence, on the present occasion of an AWARD being given in his memory to another luminary of the firmament of learning in the person of Professor R.N. Dandekar, we want to present a profile of Professor Handiqui in brief for the pleasure of the general run of admirers.

Handiqui is his family name. It appears to be an Anglicised form of the Assamese word *sandikai,* pronounced in Assamese as *xandikai* or *handikai.* The word is however derived from the Ahom (Tai) language. < *hun* (bridge) *dikai* (to lay or to place).

Professor Handiqui was born at Jorhat in upper Assam in July 1898, in an aristocratic Ahom family of traditional administrators connected with the Ahom monarchs of medieval Assam who ruled over the kingdom of Assam for 600 years at a stretch till 1826 when the kingdom got annexed to the territory under the sway of the East India Company. Krishna Kanta was the eldest son of his parents Radha Kanta Handikai and Narayani Handikai. His mother Narayani was a sister of another illustrious son of Assam, viz. Padma Nath Gohain Baruah, a great novelist and the first president of the Asom Xahitya Xabha. Radha Kanta Handikai who came in very close contact with the British administrators of those days and retired from the government service as an Asstt. Director of Land Records, had a highly Westernised way of life. Yet Krishna Kanta was destined to be a doyen of Indian culture and tradition, more particularly, even after his stay in European countries for long seven years beginning from the date of his attaining the age of "sweet two and twenty". It may not be unjustified to presume that this marvel could happen because of the training he received in India as a student of Sanskrit. Handiqui got a first class in B.A. Honours in Sanskrit securing Prasanna Kumar Sarbadhikari gold medal as a student of Calcutta Sanskrit College in 1917 at the age of 19 and a first class in M.A. Sanskrit of Calcutta University with special papers on Vedic literature in 1919. It may be noted that Vedic literature is the most traditional element among what we have in Sanskrit as a whole. In the M.A. class Handiqui had the privilege of studying as the only student of the Vedic group in that batch under a great scholar as Mahāmahopādhyāya Sitarama Shastri. The Mahāmahopādhyāya hailed from Maharashtra; he had only traditional education and he used to teach only through the medium of Sanskrit. He had a shaven head with a pigtail, and he used to put on only the *dhotī* and a *chaddar* for his dress and nothing else. With this thoroughly classical and traditional background Handiqui proceeded to England in 1920 and did his M.A. in Oxford University with Honours in Modern History in 1923. He then spent four more years in France and Germany, and during his seven years' stay in Europe he studied and learnt many a language like Latin, Greek, French, German, Russian, Italian and Spanish. Instead of going for higher degrees he considered it worthwhile to learn as much of European literature and as many of European languages as he could, and as a result of this love for learning languages Professor Handiqui had the distinction of knowing as many as 13 languages including his mother tongue, Assamese. Thanks to his well-meaning and well-to-do father, Krishna Kanta never had any financial stringency. Yet during his long stay in Europe he remained so much engrossed in his studies, so much busy in his movement from one library to another that he did not find any time to enjoy the ordinary pleasures of the Western life, nor did he have any taste for colourful luxuries of life.

In 1927 Handiqui came back to Assam with a huge personal collection of books, purchased during his stay in Europe. Within one year of his return from abroad Handiqui got married with Hemalata, and for three years up to 1930 he looked after the management of the family Tea Estate located at Tirual near Jorhat. To be the owner of a Tea Estate means belonging to the most affluent strata of the Assamese society. Handiqui paid full attention to his managerial assignment as well. From 1930 to 1948 he served as the founder Principal and Senior Professor of History of the Jorhat Jagannath Borooah College. From 1948 to 1957 Handiqui served as the founder Vice-Chancellor of the Gauhati University. Prof. Handiqui must be reckoned as one of the foremost educationists of India, because, as the founder Principal of the J.B. College, which was the first non-government degree college of the entire North-East region of

India, he gave this nascent institution a very firm footing. As the founder Vice-Chancellor of the University of Gauhati, the oldest university of the entire North-East region of India, he played the role in such a way that this institution also grew up from strength to strength. Subsequently in 1962 he started the Hemalata Handiqui Memorial Institute, a Higher Secondary English medium school with his innovative and constructive ideas, with a donation of more than Rs. 5 lakh. This institution is also enjoying a high degree of reputation as an ideal institute. After retiring from Gauhati University as Vice-Chancellor in 1957 Prof. Handiqui stayed in Jorhat being fully preoccupied with his literary activities till he retired to his heavenly abode on 7 June 1982.

Handiqui as a Scholar

To make a short survey of his contributions to the field of letters we have to mention the three monumental works, viz. the English translation of Śrīharṣa's *Naiṣadhacarita, Yaśastilaka and Indian Culture,* and the English translation of Pravarasena's *Setubandha.* Besides these Prof Handiqui wrote 31 learned articles on various aspects of Assamese, Sanskrit and European Literature for such standard journals like the *Indian Antiquary* and the *Indian Historical Quarterly.* He also wrote *Forewords* for some half a dozen learned works of other authors. We have also to take note of fifteen *Book Reviews* published in the *Oriental Literary Digest* published from Poona in 1937 and 1938.

(1) The translation of *Naiṣadhacarita,* published in 1934 as the first ever English translation immediately made him known to the whole world. The second and third editions were published by Deccan College, Poona, in 1956 and 1965. *Naiṣadhacarita of Śrīharṣa* in 22 cantos is the toughest of all the Sanskrit epics. It is so full of intellectual references and its diction is so difficult, that it is called "a medicine for the learned" — *naiṣadhaṁ vidvad auṣadham"* —, as the saying goes. Handiqui's book has been very well received by a whole host of eminent scholars from all parts of the globe. Some comments are quoted below:

> The poem is far from easy, and the translation has distinct merit. The extracts from commentaries hitherto unpublished add greatly to the utility of the work, while the appendices dealing with philosophical allusions contain much helpful matter, and prove the translator's familiarity with the leading exponents of Indian speculative thought. Special value attaches to the most important vocabulary, which is rich in contribution to Sanskrit lexicography. I note with pleasure that the translator is to publish another work dealing with Kāvya literature as a whole, a task for which he is clearly well qualified.
>
> — Prof. A.B. Keith, Edinburgh

The Translation will be a great help to readers of this difficult Māhākāvya. The critical notes and the extracts from the unpublished commentaries are very important for the restoration of the text and its interpretation. The vocabulary is a highly valuable contribution to Sanskrit lexicography.

— Prof. M. Winternitz, Prague

The rendering of a stiff Sanskrit poem like the great work of Śrīharṣa into elegant English was by no means an easy task. The importance of the publication has been further enhanced by the valuable Introduction and notes, and more particularly by the scholarly appendices and the vocabulary. Every portion of the book bears upon it the stamp of great erudition and wide research . . . remarkable production.

— Mahāmahopādhyāya G.N. Kaviraj,
Principal, Government Sanskrit College, Benares

The translation is literal but idiomatic, concise and yet exhaustive, happily worded, and it brings out the beauties of the original as far as a translation can. — *The Hindu*, Madras

The philosophical notes read more like researches in Indian philosophy, and may profitably be read even by people who are not interested in *Naiṣadha*. — *Indian Culure*

I am glad to be able to say that your rendering in English is accurate and faithful to the original. Your notes are copious, critical and scholarly. The *Naiṣadhacarita* is a great Śāstra Kāvya teeming with hundreds of Śāstraic allusions and it requires a rare combination of scholarly courage and indefatigable energy to produce an acceptable English rendering of that Śāstra Kāvya. Kindly permit me to say that you have succeeded in accomplishing this difficult task admirably well."

— Mahāmahopādhyāya S. Kuppuswami Sastri, M.A., I.E.S. (Retd.)

The Introduction is very scholarly and instructive. The translation is very accurate and brings out the meaning of the original quite clearly. Considering the toughness of the original, I must say that this is a real achievement of which anyone may be proud.

— Dr. C. Kunhan Raja,
Head of the Department of Sanskrit, Madras University

. . . Placed all Sanskrit scholars under heavy obligation by presenting in an English garb the difficult and all but unintelligible Mahākāvya of Śrīharṣa and furnishing your translation with many learned and valuable explanatory notes, which help the understanding of the curious and complicated but withal interesting fancies of the author. Extremely valuable are your notes and extracts from the commentaries, as well as your appendices on the philosophical allusions and other minor allusions, not to speak of the vocabulary with the illustration achieved a difficult and exacting piece of work for which Sanskrit scholars will be most grateful.

— Dr. V. Sukthankar, Ph.D., General Editor, *Mahabharata*

(2) Regarding the second monumental work *Yaśastilaka and Indian Culture,* we would like to quote the following passage from an article written by Abdus Sattar, Handiqui's biographer (in *K.K. Handiqui Felicitation Volume,* 1983, ed. by the present author, pp. 25f):

The Sanskrit work *Yaśastilaka* was originally written in prose and verse by Somadeva in the tenth century dealing with aspects of Jainism and Indian thought and culture. Prof. Handiqui's book was published in the year 1949 by Jaina Saṁskṛti Saṁrakṣaka Saṅgha of Sholapur, and the 2nd edition came out in the year 1968.

This book has been published under the supervision of two eminent scholars, Dr. A. N. Upadhye and Dr. H.L. Jain as General Editors. They have observed in the preface:

"His dissertation on the *Yaśastilaka* has been a pioneer and scholarly exploration in a more or less neglected religious romance based on domestic tragedy of a medieval author of encyclopaedic learning. Somadeva was fortunate that his Campū came to be studied by a worthy scholar of great literary acumen and historical perspective. In fact, Sanskrit studies have become richer by Professor Handiqui's contributions on the *Naiṣadhacarita* and *Yaśastilaka*. . . . Obviously his zest (even at the age of seventy) for Indian learning is a part of his personality; and his devoted self-training in Western universities has equipped him with the knowledge of many European languages, catholic taste and critical outlook."

They have also rightly remarked regarding Prof. Handiqui as follows:

"He leads the life of a true 'Vānaprastha' scholar whose entire time is spent in fruitful study and quiet research. Prof. Handiqui shuns publicity and is shy of positions: *vidyā vinayena śobhate*. He is an academic *ṛṣi*; and his dedication to learning should be an inspiring example for the younger generation. His detached pursuit of knowledge is characterised by generous instincts, rare indeed, these days."

Prof. Handiqui has given the copyright of this book as a gift to the "Saṅgha". Regarding this work *Yaśastilaka and Indian Culture,* eminent Italian scholar Oscar Botto has described it as ". . . il dottissimo lavoro di K.K. Handiqui", Which means "The most learned work of K.K. Handiqui." The late Prof. L. Renou, Professor of Sanskrit in Paris University, wrote as follows in French in the Journal of the *Academic des Inscriptions et Belles Lettres*: "Except for a note by Peterson, nothing had been written on *Yaśastilaka*. It required the remarkable zeal of Mr. Handiqui, which had already found expression fifteen years ago in a vastly learned work on Śrīharṣa's *Naiṣadhacarita,* to incorporate the *Yaśastilaka* in the general current of Hinduism. This is now an acquisition."

Dr. V. Raghavan, Retired Prof, of Sanskrit in the Madras University, opined that "It must be accepted that in the hands of Prof. Handiqui, the work *Yaśastilaka and Indian Culture,* like Somadeva's original, has become a mine of information, literary, historical, social, religious and archaeological, the collection of which must have involved prodigious labour." (Presidential address, the 15th All India Oriental Conference, Bomhay, 1949, Classical Sanskrit Section.)

Prof. A.L. Basham, Head of the Department of Asian Civilizations, the Australian National University, in a letter to the present author (dated. 24.9.1979) wrote about Prof. Handiqui as follows:

> Professor Handiqui's career has been exceptional in that he has succeeded in combining scholarly research and publication with academic administration at the highest level. His studies of Sanskrit texts can hardly be bettered, and it is hardly believable that he could have produced such masterly works as *Yaśastilaka and Indian Culture,* while directing first a young college and then an even younger university. The flourishing state of Gauhati University at present is in large measure due to this fine scholar who was its founder Vice-Chancellor. (Vide, *K.K. Handiqui Felicitation Volume,* p. xviii)

Prof. Madam Colette Caillat of Pare Eiffel, F 92310 Sèvres, France, in a letter dated 9.10.79 wrote to the present author as follows:

> Dear Dr. Sharma,
>
> It was very kind of you to invite me to send a contribution for the Felicitation Volume to Professor K.K. Handiqui, at the occasion of the celebrations of the Golden Jubilee of Jorhat J.B. College. I know what this institution has meant, and all the achievements of Professor Handiqui; I also remember how much Dr. Upadhye appreciated Professor Handiqui's scholarship and kindness. (Ibid, p. xvii)

Professor J. Gonda of the Utrecht University of Netherlands recognises Prof. Handiqui as a great Indologist with the following piece of encomium:

> I am very glad to learn that on the auspicious occasion of the golden jubilee of the Jorhat Jagannath Borooah College the Jubilee Celebrations Committee proposes to present a Felicitation Volume to Professor K.K. Handiqui. I cordially welcome this project and the idea to honour this eminent scholar by publishing a special volume. In his long life Professor Handiqui has rendered yeoman service to the study of Indology. . . . I hope that the Felicitation Volume will be a worthy and successful recognition of the great contribution to scholarship made by Professor Handiqui. (Ibid., p. xv)

(3) The third monumental work *Pravarasena's Setubandha* (published as Prakrit Text Series XX, in 1976, from Ahmedabad under the General Editorship of Professor H.C. Bhayani), is a

> Critical translation of Pravarasena's *Setubandha,* which is one of the few works that mark the highest achievement in the major literary *genre* of Mahākāvya. No recent work of Prākṛt literary scholarship matches the present work in richness of the exegetical materials culled after a meticulous scanning of numerous commentaries so as not to miss any significant detail. The *Setubandha* can fairly compare with the *Saptaśataka* of Hāla in points of age, importance and a continuous tradition of high literary esteem. The latter work had quite early received thorough attention it deserved from a scholar of Weber's stature; the *Setubandha,* it seems, was reserved for Prof. Handiqui's mature scholarship. (Vide General Editor's Foreword)

The salient features of all of Prof Handiqui's works may be enumerated as profound erudition and pinpoint accuracy. For the sake of these two elements the author is required to pursue every detail of a subject with an unswerving zeal and patience. This is why Prof. Handiqui presumably had to take apparently a longer time for bringing out each of his monumental works. Thus he started the work of the third book in 1960 and after long 16 years got the same published in 1976. We can have a clear idea about the amount of pain taken by him in respect of the work on *Setubandha* from the Preface, as Prof Handiqui wrote,

> . . . the book has been in the press for several years, and had to be printed at different places under difficult conditions. . . . Dr. A.N. Upadhye at whose suggestion I had undertaken this work, passed away to my great sorrow shortly before the publication of the volume. Without his help and encouragement it would have been difficult for me to complete the task in my declining years marked by ill health and bereavement."

The remaining part of Prof. H.C. Bhayani's Foreword which we quote below also deserves to be perused carefully in this very context:

> The difficult task set to himself by Prof. Handiqui was primarily to recover and ascertain the original meaning and implication of Pravarasena's verses. The enormity of the effort involved in such an undertaking can be figured out by considering the fact that for this purpose one is required to deal with a thousand year's textual confusion and wild overgrowth on divergent interpretations. Moreover, the earlier Commentaries are lost. All the preserved Commentaries are removed from the original by several centuries, and they were written during the period when Prākṛt had lost its earlier vigour and vitality, so that a considerable number of forms and expressions had become obscure or altogether incomprehensible. This made it quite difficult for the commentators in numerous cases to spot scribal errors, decide genuineness of a reading and give the correct meaning of an expression without indulging in guess-work. Prof Handiqui in spite of his advanced age and failing health has spared no pains in making available profuse extracts from various unpublished commentaries, thereby presenting very valuable data for the exegetical and textual history of the *Setubandha*. His translation is based on a critical consideraton of the numerous alternatives offered by the vast and varied exegetical materials. His notes to the translation are sure to prove a feast for the students of Prākṛt.
>
> The elaborate Introduction deals with all the important aspects of the poem like authorship, date, source and influence, form, cultural and geographical background, language, metre, literary worth, commentarial tradition and

> textual recensions. The detailed outline of the contents of the poem, spotlighting passages of significance, will be found very useful. The problem of exactly characterising the Prākr̥t of the *Setubandha* is highly complicated. What features were considered in the indigenous grammatical tradition as characteristic (exclusive or commonly shared by other literary Prākr̥ts) for Mahārāṣṭrī; what was the relationship of the stylised literary Mahārāṣṭrī with the colloquial speech of the Maharashtra region during the early centuries of the Christian era; what recension or recensions of the *Setubandha* provided basis for the rules and observations of the Prākr̥t grammarians; which of the readings found in different commentaries and Alaṁkāra works are old and original : such problems shall have to be tackled before we can arrive at tenable conclusions in this regard. In the section on the language of the *Setubandha* Prof. Handiqui has provided us with much food for thought concerning this problem.
>
> Numerous commentaries on the *Setubandha* composed in the south, the *Setutattvacandrikā* from Bengal, the *Rāmasetupradīpa* of Rāmadāsa of Rajasthan, etc. evidence a revival of Prākr̥t studies in the second millennium of the Christian era. The commentarial extracts given by Prof. Handiqui will be very useful also for the later history of Prākr̥t studies.
>
> It is quite evident that the future scholars working to settle various recensions and prepare a critical text of the *Setubandha* shall have to build on the foundations laid by Prof. Handiqui. The readers will no doubt welcome this translation and study of the *Setubandha* with several years' painstaking and careful work at their back, and appreciate them as a major contribution in the field of Prākr̥t philology. The Prakrit Text Society is not only extremely glad to publish this work, but it is also grateful to Prof. Handiqui for very generously bearing the publication cost of the work and donating it to the Society.

With regard to Prof. Handiqui's mode of approach to scholarly issues we have observed as follows in a Foreword to a work by Prof. Handiqui's younger daughter Ms. Ahalya Gogoi, viz. *Krishna Kanta Handikai* (Part I) Āru *Naiṣadhacaritar Jiliṅgani*:

> In passing it may be noted that even while dealing with scholarly issues Handiqui's approach is unlike that of many others. His method was to explain a dogma as clearly as possible and to present as much of relevant

information on the basis of an extensive survey of the connected literature for the convenience of the reader to arrive at a convincing conclusion through the process of comparison. This required a deep penetration and extensive exploration and an indomitable urge for perfection. At the cost of his own strain he wanted to be as helpful to the reader as possible. This is the reason why all the three masterpieces of Handiqui were so warmly accepted by one and all and acclaimed as the best model to be followed by others. It is to be noted that whatever was written by Handiqui stands unchallenged till this date. In case of other scholars a lot of controversies crop up. In case of Handiqui it has never happened like that. Moreover, other scholars generally indulge in refuting the views of fellow scholars. It is very strange that in none of his works he has ever entered into any argument with any other scholar. And this is how Handiqui has become what he is. Only in the addresses he has put forward his counsels with an expression of conviction, a degree of assertion and the force of a prophecy.

(4) Learned articles are as follows:

ASSAMESE

1913 "Ātma-bicār", *Bānhī.*

1914 "Amar-prakāśa", *Bānhī.*

1915 "Sāṁkhya-darśana", *Ālocanī.*

"Saraswatir Bar", *Akan.*

1916 "Bhāratīya-cintā", *Sanmilan Pravandhāvalī,* 1st series.

1918 "Bhūmikā", *Sanmilan Pravandhāvalī* (1st series), A.S.L. Club, Calcutta.

1919 "Prācīn Bebilanar Veda", *Sanmilan Pravandhāvalī* (3rd series).

1921 "Anubādar Kathā", *Cetanā.*

1922 "Europar bhāṣā āru sāhitya", *Cetanā*

1926 "Rus abhinaya", *Bānhī*

"Greek bhāṣā", *Bānhī*

"Germanir jñān-sādhanā", *Milan.*

"Socreticar mate kavir pratibhā", *Asom Sāhitya Sabhā Patrikā,*

1929 "Spanish sāhityar Romeo-Juliet", *Āwāhan.*

"Presidential Address", *Asom Chātra Sanmilan,* 14th Session, Golaghat.

1933 "German sāhityar sapon nātak", *Āwāhan.*

1936 "Naiṣadhacarita āru Bhāratiya citrakalā" *Āwāhan.*

1936 "Greek nātakar gān", *Āwāhan.*

1937 "Presidential Address", *Asom Sāhitya Sabhā,* 17th Session, Guwahati.

1974 "Campāvati nātakar duti caritra", *Hāzarikar sāhitya pratibhā.*

ENGLISH

1918 "The Word Swarāj in the R̥gveda", *The Modern Review,* Calcutta.

1920 "Women Poets of the R̥gveda", *The Indian Antiquary,* Bombay.

1928 "German Academic Ideals', *Forward.*

1936 "The Naiṣadhacarita and Rajput Painting", *Indian Historical Quarterly.*

1938 "An Indian Prince in a Greek Prose Romance", *The New Indian Antiquary,* Bombay.

1947 "Religion and the Language of the People", *J.B. College Magazine,* Jorhat.

1948 "Academic Standard", *The Assam Tribune,* Gauhati.

1951 "Vice-Chancellor's Address", 1st Convocation, Gauhati University, Gauhati, "Presidential Address", All India Oriental Conference (Classical Sanskrit Section), 16th Session, Lucknow.

1955 "Vice-Chancellor's Address', 2nd Convocation, Gauhati University, Gauhati.

1962 "Classical Sanskrit as a Vehicle of Indian Culture", *The Cultural Heritage of India,* vol. II, Ramakrishna Mission, Calcutta.

1982 "Remembering J.B. College", *J.B. College Golden Jubilee Volume.*

(5) In the form of forewords or prefaces Prof. Handiqui made the following contributions:

(a) A scholarly Preface in English to the *Citra Bhāgavata,* ed. Harinarayan Dutta Barua.

(b) Another Preface in English to Sanskrit *Jivandhara-Campū,* Bhāratiya Jñānpīth.

(c) Preface in Assamese to *Sati Jaymati Kāvya* in Sanskrit by Pandit Bhavadeva Bhagawati.

(d) Preface in Assamese to *Śakuntalā* (an Assamese Drama) by Atul Chandra Hazarika.

(e) Preface in Assamese to *Prasaṅga Kośa* by Abdus Sattar.

(f) Preface in Assamese to *Sandhiyār Sur* (Collection of Assamese Poems) by Nalinibala Devi.

(g) Preface in Assamese to the Assamese rendering of Anundoram Barooah's *Bhavabhuti and his Place in Sanskrit Literature* by Mukunda Madhava Sharma (present author)

(6) **Book Reviews**: So far as it could be gathered between 1937-38, Prof. Handiqui wrote book reviews for as many as fifteen different books in four issues of *Oriental Literary Digest* which used to be brought out every month from Poona. It is also gathered that the said digest was edited by Dr. S.M. Katre in collaboration with Prof. K.C. Chatterji, M.A.; Prof. N.G. Damle, M.A.; Dr. S.K. De, M.A., D.Litt; Prof. P.K. Gode, M.A.; Prof. K.K. Handiqui, M.A.; Prof. A.N. Krishna Aiyangar, M.A.; L.T.; Dr. V. Raghavan, M.A.; Ph.D.; Dr. B.A. Saletore, M.A., Ph.D., D. Phil.; Dr. V.S. Sukthankar, M.A., Ph.D.; Prof. A.N. Upadhye, M.A. & Prof. B.D. Verma, M.A.

A long list of scholars is given above to give the impression as to who were the leading Indologists of those days and what company Prof. Handiqui kept; for, there goes the adage, "Tell me what company you keep, I will tell you what you are".

Prof. Handiqui as an Administrator

Shri S.K. Dutta, formerly Chief Justice of the High Court of Assam and Nagaland and Ex-Vice-Chancellor of the Kurukshetra University, says as follows with regard to the dignified personality and the administrative ability of Prof. Handiqui:

> I have had the honour and happiness of enjoying the friendship of Shri K.K. Handiqui for more than four decades. As I worked as the Dean of the faculty of Law and the Secretary of the university classes of the Gauhati University for nearly three years since its inception, with Shri Handiqui as the Vice-Chancellor, I came in close contact with him. Apart from his scholastic attainments, his simplicity highly impressed me. This was the excellence of his character and was evident in his

dress, style, manners and way of life. Yet he was an astute administrator and a hard task-master. He discussed the various university problems with me and I found that he had a thorough grasp of every problem. He was, however, not the type of man to be guided by anybody. A sound head and an honest heart were his only guides.

The Gauhati University was lucky to have Shri Handiqui as its first Vice-Chancellor. He adopted the same recruitment policy as Sir Ashutosh Mookherjee did in the Calcutta University, viz. to recruit the best qualified persons as teachers from any part of India, irrespective of caste, creed or community. This put the university not only on a sound footing but also enhanced its prestige and spread its reputation.

Shri Handiqui was well known as a profound Sanskrit scholar and his English translation of the great Mahākāvya *Naiṣadhacarita of Śrī Harṣa* in twenty-two cantos is an invaluable contribution to Sanskrit literature. But many perhaps do not know that the subject in which he graduated in Oxford was "Modern History". Thus Shri Handiqui was on the one hand a Sanskrit *puṇḍit*, on the other hand, an Oxford Don. There was a beautiful blend of oriental and occidental cultures in him.

Munificence of Prof. Handiqui

Krishna Kanta's father Radha Kanta was extremely benevolent and is fondly referred to as a Dānavīra. Because of Dānavīra's donations we have in Guwahati the Handiqui Girls' College, the Narayani Handiqui Bhawan for housing the Deptt. of Historical and Antiquarian Studies and in Jorhat the Chandra Kanta Handikai Bhawan as the headquarters of Asom Sahitya Sabha, the largest literary organisation of Assam. The Dānvīra donated substantially also for the preparation and publication of the Assamese Chandra Kanta Abhidhana in memory of one of his late lamented sons Chandra Kanta and also a book of History of Assam in memory of yet another late lamented son Indra Kanta. Dānvīra's eldest son Krishna Kanta also kept up this laudable tradition from beginning to end in a commendable way. And the third generation from the Dānavīra has also not lagged behind. Krishna Kanta's donation for Hemalata Handiqui Memorial Institute has already been mentioned. He donated liberally for the publication of the subsequent editions of the *Chandra Kanta Abhidhan* and the maintenance and expansion of the Chandra Kanta Bhawan at Jorhat. He had bequeathed his fabulously rich personal library to the Gauhati University Library, which is now rechristened as Krishna Kanta Handiqui Library. A large number of authors such as Nalinibala Devi, Atul Chandra Hazarika, Kavi Chandra Mahanta and Abdus Sattar received donation from Prof Handiqui for getting their books published. Handiqui donated to the J.B. College, the whole amount that was due to him as his salary. He also gave the copyright of all three books of his, which are indeed exceptionally monumental works, to respective publishers, viz. Deccan College, the Jain Saṁskṛti Saṁrakṣaka Saṅgha and the Prakrit Text Society.

In appreciation of Handiqui's benign personality his biographer Abdus Sattar observes as follows:

> Prof. Handiqui shuns publicity and leads a secluded life. During my long association with him as his biographer I have noted that his life is governed by certain deeply felt convictions. He attaches greater importance to moral excellence than to the cultivation of the intellect. Ibsen's dictum: "Innocence is the source of all joy and happiness" is the motto of his life. He is totally indifferent to name and fame. Dante's beautiful line: "Non e il mondan romore altro che un fiato di vento" (Worldly fame is nothing but a breath of wind) is enshrined in his memory. He hates flattery and takes no heed of praise or blame. He reveres all religions and is cosmopolitan in his religious views.

Such is the scholar Prof. Handiqui who was honoured by Deccan College as Honorary Fellow in the year 1968. I have already mentioned above that it is a rare honour for a scholar of outstanding merit. Only five or six scholars have so far been awarded Honorary Fellowship of Deccan College. They are:

(1) Prof. R.L. Turner, Ex-Director, London School of Oriental Studies.

(2) Mahāmahopādhyāya Prof. P.V. Kane, Ex-Vice-Chancellor, Bombay University.

(3) Dr. C.D. Deshmukh, Ex-Chairman, U.G.C. and Ex-Finance Minister, Govt. of India.

(4) Prof. K.K. Handiqui, Ex-Vice-Chancellor, Gauhati University.

(5) Prof. Norman Brown. Professor of Sanskrit, John Hopkins University, U.S.A.

Sattar also observes:

> While he was the Vice-Chancellor of Gauhati University he always thought of getting quality rather than quantity. The following para is quoted from his first Convocation address:

"To the graduates of the university who will take their degrees today I offer cordial greetings and the best wishes of the university for their success and welfare in life. I need not remind them of their nascent responsibilities and the great tradition they have to carry forward as worthy citizens of India. They must remember that it is not degrees, but character and purity of the heart that will entitle them to the degnity of man. In a world full of temptations they have to keep their balance and resist the forces of evil."

Laurels Earned by Prof. Handiqui

Although Prof. Handiqui did not seek publicity and did not bother about fame, laurels deservedly came to him in a big way. He became the President, Asom Chatra Sammelan in 1929; President, Asom Xahitya Xabha in 1937 at the age of only 39; President, Classical Sanskrit Section, XVI AIOC, Lucknow, in 1951, and was elected to be the general president of the Srinagar session of AIOC in 1961, which he could not attend. He presided over the Inter University Board at Madras in 1952, received Padmashri in 1955 and Padmabhusan in 1967, Honorary Fellowship of the Deccan College, Poona in 1968, Honorary D. Litt degree of Gauhati Univerisity in 1968 and Honorary D. Litt degree of Dibrugarh University in 1972.

In 1984 Sahitya Academy Award was presented to Prof. Handiqui posthumously for the volume comprising his literary works in Assamese, viz. *Krishnakanta Handiqui Rachana-Sambhar,* compiled by Prof. J.N. Goswami and published by Asom Xahitya Xabha in 1984.

Prof. Handiqui also became the first *Sadasya Mahiyan* of Asom Xahitya Xabha. *Abhinandana Bharati : Professor K.K. Handiqui Felicitation Volume,* edited by Biswanarayan Shastri and Pratap Ch. Choudhury for the Kamrup Anusandhan Samity, Guwahati (1982) and *Professor Krishna Kanta Handiqui Felicitation Volume* edited by Mukunda Madhava Sharma and published by Radha Bora for Jorhat J.B. College Golden Jubilee Celebration Committee, Guwahati and *Prācyavidyārṇava Krishna Kanta* edited by Abdus Sattar for Asom Xahitya Xabha are also very significant tokens of love, respect and admiration of a host of scholars and connoisseurs from home and abroad. Handiqui is befittingly referred to as *Prācyavidyārṇava* (an ocean of oriental learning) which carries a persistent flavour of Indian tradition. The various monuments and memorial objects and activities also deserve to be reckoned as laurels for the Great Soul. To name a few of such memorials:

1. K.K. Handiqui Library of Gauhati University.

2. K.K. Handiqui Govt. Sanskrit College, Guwahati.
3. K.K. Handiqui Award for Indology.
4. K.K. Handiqui Sanskrit Talent Award for Students.
5. K.K. Handiqui Literary Award of Asom Xahitya Xabha.
6. K.K. Handiqui Bijñān Bhavan of J.B. College, Jorhat.
7. A commemorative stamp in honour of Prof. Krishna Kanta Handiqui by the Deptt. of Post & Telegraph on 7.10.1983.

The Message of the Great Indologist

One who knows well the facts and figures relating to the history of India and more particularly Inida's cultural history, is an Indologist. But one who, besides knowing the facts and figures, also can realise the true message of the Indian culture and tradition and appreciate the same and can make that message a part of his personality, is a great Indologist. To our mind Handiqui is such a great Indologist. Only a few stray statements of Prof. Handiqui should suffice to stand on our side.

(1) Handiqui was of the opinion that India has a cultural heritage, which deserves to be appreciated also in the modern world, and with that opinion Handiqui in his address as the president of the Classical Sanskrit Section of the All India Oriental Conference, Lucknow Session of 1951, stated as follows:

> Comprehensive and analytic study of Sanskrit texts, many of them vast and elaborate, is essential for the proper understanding and appraisal of old Indian writers and their cultural background. . . . But as students of Sanskrit we may ask ourselves whether our studies are to remain scholastic and antiquarian in character, and whether or not we have also a cultural mission, an obligation to interpret our cultural heritage in a manner intelligible to the modern world.

Handiqui himself took it as a mission and as an obligation to make the Indian heritage more easily intelligible to those who do not understand ancient languages like Sanskrit and Prākṛt. It was the reason why he paid more attention to translations with adequate amount of explanation.

(2) It is noteworthy that the majority of his three masterpieces, i.e. two out of three of his monumental works, are translations, viz. translation of the *Naiṣadhacarita* and translation of the *Setubandha*. Handiqui was guided by a specific philosophy

and conviction that "beauties and the basic ideas of Sanskrit literature" should be made easily available and intelligible to the younger generation, as it has been so convincingly stated in his AIOC Lucknow Session classical Sanskrit section Presidential Address, cf.

> There are many who wihout being students of Sanskrit take a keen interest in Sanskrit literature and Indian thought and culture. In the educational sphere it is necessary to implant and develop such an attitude in the younger generation and ensure that a knowledge of the beauties and the basic ideas of Sanskrit literature do not remain confined within the narrow circle of Sanskrit scholars. In the various courses in literature at the University stage it should not be difficult to include the study of selected Sanskrit classics in translation and that of Indian poetical and aesthetic theories and the main currents in the history of Sanskrit literature.

It may be noted that Professor Handiqui got some elements of Sanskrit literature included in the Assamese language and literature courses of his own university, i.e. Gauhati University, and that tradition still persists.

(3) In the same Presidential Address Prof Handiqui says:

> In estimating the cultural contribution of Sanskrit literature we must not forget the services rendered by Jainism and Buddhism. This statement conveys the message that the traditional Indian culture consists not only of the values of Vedic religion and Purāṇic Hinduism, but also of Jainism and Buddhism. As such a study and appreciation of traditional Indian culture should include all the faiths like Jainism, Buddhism and Hinduism as inseparable components of a large composite Indian culture, which again is intimately connected with the Chinese and Japanese cultures.

(4) In our opinion what makes Prof. Handiqui a great Indologist is his conviction that Indian civilisation has spiritual values and the ideals of ancient Indian culture provide the bedrock for a higher morality. Hence, cf.:

> But the classics have also a higher significance. In an address given to the Classical Association, Lord Greene has rightly observed that "the service of science whether pure or applied, cannot of itself lead to a complete and happy life, but, on the contrary, if followed to the exclusion of the humanities, tends to enslave the spirit and keep the eyes directd to the ground instead of raising them to the skies". For us the supreme importance of the study of Sanskrit lies in the fact that it must help us to preserve the

spiritual values of our civilisation and strive after a higher morality based on the ideals of ancient Indian culture. (Presidential Address)

In fine we cannot resist the urge to opine that for us Professor Krishna Kanta Handiqui was, and still remains, the very embodiment of spiritual values and higher morality.

भारतीप्रेष्ठपुत्राय ज्येष्ठपुत्राय च श्रियः।
नितान्तशुद्धचित्ताय ज्ञानवित्ताय धीमते।।
दिविसद्गुरवे ज्ञाने दाने कर्णसमाय च।
ध्याने सुगततुल्याय महावीरसमाय च।।
ऋषिकल्पाय पूज्याय सततं मितभाषिणे।
बोधिद्रुमस्वरूपाय लोकोपकारकारिणे।।
पुण्यश्लोकाय प्राज्ञाय प्राच्यविद्यार्णवाय वै।
पाश्चात्यज्ञानसिन्धोश्च नितान्तं पारदर्शिने।।
हन्दिकैकुलरत्नाय देवाय क्षणजन्मने।
नमस्तस्मै नमस्तस्मै कृष्णकान्तमहात्मने।। इति शम्।।

bharatīpreṣṭhaputrāya jyeṣṭhaputrāya ca śriyaḥ ।
nitāntaśuddhacittāya jñānavittāya dīmate ।।
divisadgurave jñāne dāne karṇasamāya ca ।
dhyāne sugatatulyāya mahāvīrasamāya ca ।।
r̥ṣikalpāya pūjyāya satataṁ mitabhāṣiṇe ।
bodhidrumasvarūpāya lokopakārkāriṇe ।।
puṇyaślokāya prājñāya prācyavidyārṇavāya vai ।
pāścātyajñānasindhośca nitāntaṁ pāradarśine ।।
handikaikularatnāya devāya kṣaṇajanmane ।
namastasmai namastasmai kr̥ṣṇakāntamahātmane ।। *iti śam* ।।

CHAPTER I

SOMADEVA AND HIS AGE

Two works of Somadeva are extant: *Yaśastilaka*[1] and *Nītivākyāmṛta.*[2] The former, called also *Yaśodhara-mahārāja-carita,* deals with the pathetic story of Prince Yaśodhara in prose and verse in eight Books called Āśvāsas. The latter work is a treatise on polity, divided into thirty-two chapters consisting of aphorisms on the various topics dealt with. *Nītivākyāmṛta* seems to have been written after *Yaśastilaka.*

Somadeva gives a fair amount of information about himself at the end of his *Yaśastilaka.* He belonged to an order of Jaina monks known as Devasaṁgha, and was the disciple of Nemideva who was the disciple of Yaśodeva.[3] The colophon to *Nītivākyāmṛta* tells us that Somadeva was the younger brother of Mahendradeva, and had the following honorific titles: Syādvādâcalasiṁha 'A lion on the mountain of Syādvāda', Tārkika-cakravartin 'The Lord of the logicians', Vādībha-pañcānana 'A lion to the elephants, to wit, the disputants', Vākkallola-payonidhi 'An ocean of the waves of eloquence', and Kavikularāja 'The king of the poets'. We are also told that Somadeva was the author of *Yaśodhara-mahārāja-carita, Ṣaṇṇavati-prakaraṇa, Mahendra-mātali-saṁjalpa* and *Yukticintāmaṇisūtra.* There is some doubt about the title of the last work, as a manuscript of *Nītivākyāmṛta* written in Saṁvat 1290, and preserved in one of the Jaina Bhaṇḍārs at Pattan, gives it as Yukticintāmaṇistava[4].

In one of the concluding verses of *Yaśastilaka* Somadeva tells us that the work was copied by a celebrated scribe named Racchuka, who was called Lekhaka-śikhāmaṇi, and whose calligraphy seems to have been utilized by the fair sex for their love-letters.[5] All trace of this first copy of the original manuscript seems to have been lost.

---

1 Kāvyamālā 70, Parts I & II, Bombay 1901.

2 Māṇikachandra D. Jaina Granthamālā 22, Bombay 1922.

3 श्रीमान्नस्ति स देवसंघतिलको देवो यशःपूर्वकः, शिष्यस्तस्य बभूव सद्गुणनिधिः श्रीनेमिदेवाह्वयः। तस्याश्चर्यतपःस्थितेस्त्रिनवतेर्जेतुर्महावादिनां, शिष्योऽभूदिह सोमदेव इति यस्तस्यैष काव्यक्रमः॥ *Yaśastilaka,* part II, p. 418.

4 *Descriptive Catalogue of Manuscripts in the Jain Bhandars at Pattan,* Vol. I, p. 31.

5 विद्याविनोदवनवासितहृच्छुकेन, पुस्तं व्यलेखि विलसल्लिपि रच्छुकेन। श्रीसोमदेवरचितस्य यशोधरस्य, सल्लोकमान्यगुणरत्नमहीधरस्य॥ अपि च। यस्याक्षरावलिरधीरविलोचनाभिराकाङ्क्ष्यते मदनशासनलेखनेषु। तस्मै विवेकिषु न यच्छति रच्छुकाय, को नाम लेखकशिखामणिनामधेयम्॥

Somadeva goes on to say that the Kāvya, that is, *Yaśastilaka* was composed in Śaka 881 (959 A. D.), the cyclic year being Siddhārtha, on the Madana-trayodaśī day of the month of Caitra, when Kṛṣṇarājadeva was extending his sway at Melpāṭī, after having vanquished the Pāṇḍya, Cola, Cerama (i. e. Cera), Ceylonese and other kings.[1] Somadeva's statement is remarkable for its historical accuracy, as it is corroborated by the Karhāḍ plates of the great Rāṣṭrakūṭa emperor Kṛṣṇa III, issued on the 9th March, 959 A. D., at Melpāṭī, a few weeks earlier than the completion of Somadeva's *Yaśastilaka.*[2] The subject of the inscription is the grant of a village in Karahāṭa (Karhāḍ in Satara district) to a Śaiva ascetic, but the record was issued at Melpāṭī (Melpāḍi in North Arcot district), where the emperor was encamped with his victorious army 'for establishing his followers in the southern provinces, for taking possession of the estates of the provincial chiefs and for constructing certain temples'.[3] The inscription, like Somadeva, refers to Kṛṣṇa III's victories over the Colas and the kings of the Ceranma (i. e. Cera), Pāṇḍya and other countries as well as Ceylon, and tells us, besides, that he erected a pillar of victory at Rāmeśvara.[4] The emperor states in the record that he issues the order, 'having established his victorious camp at Melpāṭī' (*melpāṭī-samāvāsita-śrīmadvijaya-kaṭakena mayā*).

The victory over the Colas was the most important, as Kṛṣṇa III is known to have occupied Toṇḍaimaṇḍalam (to the north of the Kāverī), and appears to have annexed the northern part of the Cola dominions to his empire, sometime after the decisive battle of Takkolam in 949 A. D., when the Cola crown-prince Rājāditya, the son of Parāntaka I, was killed on the battlefield by Kṛṣṇa's tributary and ally, the Gaṅga ruler Būtuga II.[5] The Karhāḍ grant of 959 A. D. shows the Rāṣṭrakūṭa emperor in his camp at Melpāṭī at the close of his victorious southern campaigns. As a recent authority on Cola history says, "there can be no question that the effect on the Cola empire was ruinous, and that as a consequence of the blow in

---

1 'शकनृपकालातीतसंवत्सरशतेष्वष्टस्वेकाशीत्यधिकेषु गतेषु (अङ्कतः ८८१) सिद्धार्थसंवत्सरान्तर्गतचैत्रमासमदनत्रयोदश्यां……मेल्पाटीप्रवर्धमानराज्यप्रभावे श्रीकृष्णराजदेवे सति ।'.

2 *Epigraphia Indica*, Vol. IV, parts VI and VII. "The date of the grant was Wednesday, the thirteenth *tithi* of the dark fortnight of Phālguṇa of the cyclic year Kālayukta, the Śaka year being 880 *past* (l. 56 f.)."

3 Ibid., p. 281.

4 Somadeva says: पाण्ड्यसिंहलचोलचेरमप्रभृतीन् महीपतीन् प्रसाध्य. The inscription says: कृत्वा दक्षिणदिग्जयोद्यतधिया चोलान्वयोन्मूलनं, तद्भूमिं निजभृत्यवर्गपरितश्चेरन्मपाण्ड्यादिकान् । येनोच्चैः सह सिंहलेन करदान् सन्मण्डलाधीश्वरान्, न्यस्तः कीर्तिलतांकुरप्रतिकृतिस्तम्भश्च रामेश्वरे ॥.

5 Altekar: *The Rāṣṭrakūṭas and their times*, p. 117 ff., Poona 1934.

the north, much of the south also slipped out of Parāntaka's hands. The Cola empire was no more; it had to be built up all over again".[1]

It is interesting to note that the Melpāṭī camp of Kṛṣṇa III is mentioned also by Puṣpadanta in his *Mahāpurāṇa*, a voluminous work in Apabhraṁśa verse on the lives of the sixty-three heroes (*śalākā-puruṣas*) of the Jaina faith, commenced in 959 A. D., that is, in the year of the completion of Somadeva's *Yaśastilaka*, and finished in 965 A. D.[2] Puṣpadanta says in his *Mahāpurāṇa* 1. 3—

तं कहमि पुराणु पसिद्धणामु सिद्धत्थवरिसि भुवणाहिरामु ।
उव्वद्धजूडु भूभंगभीसु तोडेप्पिणु चोडहो तणउ सीसु ।
भुवणेक्करामु रायाहिराउ जहिं अच्छइ तुडिगु महाणुभाउ ।
तं दीणदिण्णधणकंणयपयरु महि परिभमंतु मेपाडिणयरु ।

Puṣpadanta means to say that he commenced his Purāṇa in the cyclic year Siddhārtha (the same as that mentioned by Somadeva) when 'the lord of kings', Tuḍiga, explained in the gloss as Kṛṣṇarāja, was in the city of Mepāḍī, identified in the gloss with Melapāṭīya-nagara, that is, Melpāṭī, after having severed the Cola prince's head 'with the hair tied up'. This is obviously a reference to Rājāditya's death in the battle of Takkolam; the memory of which was still fresh in 959. Puṣpadanta describes the town of Melpāṭī as 'rolling in festivities', and as a place where presents of money and gold had been given to the poor. It is natural to surmise that Kṛṣṇa III was celebrating his southern victories at Melpāṭī that year, and the town was in a gay mood on account of the celebrations. The year 959 A. D. was indubitably a year of political and cultural importance in the history of the Dekkan, as it not only saw the consummation of Rāṣṭrakūṭa hegemony in the south, but the commencement and completion respectively of two monumental works of Indian literature.

Although Somadeva was a contemporary of Kṛṣṇa III, his work was not composed at Mānyakheṭa, the Rāṣṭrakūṭa capital, but at an obscure place called Gaṅgadhārā, which seems to have been the capital of a prince named Vāgarāja, the eldest son of a Cālukya chief named Arikesarin, a tributary of Kṛṣṇarāja.[3] The Arikesarin mentioned by Somadeva belonged to an obscure

1 Nilakanta Sastri: *The Colas*, Vol. I, p. 162.

2 Vaidya: Introduction to *Jasaharacariu*, p. 20, Poona 1931.

3 '...श्रीकृष्णराजदेवे सति तत्पादपद्मोपजीविनः......चालुक्यकुलजन्मनः सामन्तचूडामणेः श्रीमदरिकेसरिणः प्रथमपुत्रस्य श्रीमद्वागराजप्रवर्धमानवसुधारायां गङ्गधारायां विनिर्मापितमिदं काव्यमिति ।' *Yaśastilaka*, Book VIII, part II, p. 419. Ms. A reads गङ्गधरायां. This is omitted altogether in Mss. B and C. Ms. B, however, reads वसुधरायां, and in Ms. C वसुधारायां seems to be corrected into वसुधरायां.

branch of the Cālukya dynasty, which ruled over a province called Jola, a portion of which is said to have been included in the modern district of Dhārwār in Bombay Presidency.[1] Nothing is known about Gaṅgadhārā, but it seems to have been somewhere in or around Dharwar District. It may perhaps be identified with Gangawati in the south-western corner of Hyderabad State in Raichur District, quite near Dharwar. There is also a river named Gangawali in the North Kanara District south-west of Dharwar.[2]

As regards the prince during whose reign Somadeva composed his romance, there is some doubt about the reading of the name Vāgarāja found in the printed text of *Yaśastilaka*. Of the manuscripts of the work used by me, the well-written and correct A reads Vāgarāja as in the printed edition, but MSS. B and C read Vādyarāja, while a manuscript consulted by Pt. Nathuram Premi reads Vadyagarāja.[3] The correct name, as we shall see, seems to be Baddiga of which Vādyarāja and Vadyagarāja are Sanskritized variations.

A copper plate inscription in Sanskrit recently found at Parbhani in Hyderabad State[4] not only gives us a glimpse of Somadeva seven years after the composition of *Yaśastilaka* but furnishes a genealogy of the feudatory Cālukya chiefs in whose territory he lived and worked. The genealogy of these tributaries of the Rāṣṭrakūṭas, hitherto known to us from the Kanarese *Bhārata* composed by the Jaina poet Pampa in 941 A. D.,[5] is here carried to 966 A. D., the date of the inscription. The list of kings may be compiled as follows:

Yuddhamalla I, Arikesarin I, Narasiṁha I (+Bhadradeva), Yuddhamalla II, Baddiga I (defeated and captured Bhīma), Yuddhamalla III, Narasiṁha II, Arikesarin II (married a Rāṣṭrakūṭa princess named Lokāmbikā), Bhadradeva, Arikesarin III, Baddiga II (Vadyaga) and Arikesarin IV.

Of the kings mentioned Arikesarin II was the patron of Pampa who wrote his masterpieces in 941 A. D.; while Baddiga II or Vadyaga was the king during whose reign Somadeva completed his romance in the year 959 A. D., as recorded in the colophon. The inscription under discussion

1 Bhandarkar: *Early History of the Dekkan*, third edition, p. 137.

2 *The Imperial Gazetteer of India*, Vol. XXVI, Atlas, Plates 39 and 42.

3 Pt. Premi: *Jaina Sāhitya aura Itihāsa* p. 76, Bombay 1942.

4 Reproduced in the above work (p. 90 ff.) from the *Journal of the Bhārata Itihāsa Saṁśodhana Maṇḍala*, Poona, Vol. XIII, No. 3, published in Marāṭhī.

5 Bhandarkar: *Early History of the Dekkan*, p. 137 and Altekar: *The Rāṣṭrakūṭas and their times*, p. 129.

records the grant of a village to Somadeva by Vadyaga's son Arikesarin IV in Śaka 888 or 966 A. D. for the repairs and upkeep of a Jaina temple called Śubhadhāma-jinālaya, built by Vadyaga in the capital (Lem)bulapāṭaka. The name of the village granted to Somadeva was Vanikaṭupulu.[1]

It is clear from the above record that in 966 A. D. Somadeva was in charge of the Śubhadhāma temple, and seems to have carried on his literary activities undisturbed, as a hitherto unknown work *Syādvādopaniṣad* is here attributed to him in addition to *Yaśodharacarita*.[2] He was held in the highest esteem by his contemporaries, and kings and feudatory chiefs are described as reverently bowing at his feet.[3]

It may be noted in this connection that there are at least two puzzling factors in the inscription we are considering. Firstly, the Saṁgha to which Somadeva belonged is here called Gauḍasaṁgha: Yaśodeva, the *guru* of Somadeva's *guru* Nemideva, is assigned to this Saṁgha.[4] But, as we have seen, Somadeva himself describes Yaśodeva as belonging to the Devasaṁgha. Secondly, the capital of Arikesarin IV is stated to be (Lem)bulapāṭaka, about which nothing definite is known, although it might be somewhere in Hyderabad State. It is noteworthy that we have so far the names of three capitals of the Cālukya chiefs who ruled in the Jola territory. Arikesarin II, who was the patron of the famous Kannaḍa poet Pampa, ruled at Puligere (mod. Lakshmesvar in Dharwar District);[5] Vadyaga is described by Somadeva as ruling at Gaṅgadhārā; and his son Arikesarin IV calls (Lem)bulapāṭaka his capital. It may also be noted that just as Arikesarin, the father of Vadyaga, is described by Somadeva as a humble tributary of Kṛṣṇarāja (Kṛṣṇa III), similarly the present inscription describes Arikesarin, the son of Vadyaga, as a tributary of the same overlord in exactly similar terms.[6]

While Somadeva was a contemporary of Kṛṣṇa III and Vadyaga, it is not clear whether either of them was his patron; probably he had no

---

1 '(लें)बुलपाटकनामधेयनिजराजधान्यां निजपितुः श्रीमद्वद्यगस्य शुभधामजिनालयाख्यवस(तेः) खण्डस्फुटितनवसुधाकर्मबलिनिवेद्यार्थे शकाब्देष्वष्टाशीत्यधिकेष्वष्टशतेषु गतेषु……तेन श्रीमदरिकेसरिणा…श्रीमत्सोमदेवसूरये……वनिकटुपुलुनामा ग्रामः……दत्तः ॥'.

2 'विरचयिता यशोधरचरितस्य कर्त्ता स्याद्वादोपनिषदः कवि(वयि)ता चान्येषामपि सुभाषितानाम्……'.

3 'अखिलमहासाम(न्तसी)मन्तप्रान्तपर्यस्तोत्तंसस्रक्सुरभिचरणः सकलविद्वज्जनकर्णावतंसीभवद्यशःपुण्डरीकः सूर्य इव सकलावनिभृतां शिरःश्रेणिषु शिखण्डमण्डनायमानपादपद्मोऽभूत् ।'.

4 'श्रीगौडसंघे मुनिमान्यकीर्तिर्नाम्ना यशोदेव इति प्रजज्ञे ।' Pt. Premi (op. cit.) is inclined to identify this Gauḍa with the Gola or Golla kingdom of the South, mentioned in the Śravaṇa Belgola Inscriptions.

5 Rice: *Kanarese Literature*, p. 30.

6 'स्वस्त्यकालवर्षदेवश्रीपृथिवीवल्लभमहाराजाधिराजपरमेश्वरपरमभट्टारकश्रीमदमोघवर्षदेवपादानुध्यातप्रवर्द्धमानविजयराज्यश्रीकृष्णराजदेवपादपद्मोपजीविना ।'.

patron properly so called. Somadeva was a Jaina Ācārya and respectfully mentions his *guru*. He was, besides, a political thinker, and in his *Nītivākyāmṛta* pays homage to the state and not to any king.[1] It is, however, certain that he was intimately acquainted with court life, and may have passed some time in the Rāṣṭrakūṭa capital. The court life so minutely described by him in Book III of his *Yaśastilaka* does not apply to a petty feudatory chief like that of Gaṅgadhārā, and can be true only of a sovereign of imperial status, who receives embassies from foreign courts, declares war against refractory kings, and has at his disposal regiments drawn from different parts of Hindustan.[2] Somadeva, the author of *Nītivākyāmṛta*, was a patriotic citizen of the Rāṣṭrakūṭa empire, and gave much thought to the principles of state-craft and the well-being of the state, and in his great romance he gives a picture of the imperial court, besides throwing sidelights on the problems of government affecting war and peace.

The tenth century, like its predecessor, was a flourishing period of Jaina literature in Sanskrit and Prākrit, and in Kanarese as well. Confining ourselves to the epoch of Somadeva, we may safely assume it to coincide with the reign of Kṛṣṇa III from 939 to 968 A. D., and within these limits we come across several distinguished names in the annals of scholarship and literature. In 941 the famous Kanarese poet Pampa wrote his two poems, *Ādipurāṇa*, which relates the history of the first Tīrthaṁkara, and *Vikramārjuna-vijaya*, which tells the story of the Mahābhārata, or rather that of Arjuna. About the year 950 Pŏnna, the second great Kanarese poet of the century, wrote his *S'āntipurāṇa*, which relates the legendary history of the sixteenth Tīrthaṁkara, under the patronage of Kṛṣṇa III who gave the poet the honorific title of Ubhaya-kavi-cakravartin for his proficiency in Kanarese and Sanskrit.[3] Quite at the beginning of the reign of Kṛṣṇa III, Indranandin wrote in Sanskrit a work called *Jvālāmālinī-kalpa* dealing with a mystic fire-cult associated with the goddess Jvālāmālinī. The work was composed in 939 A. D. at Mānyakheṭa and refers to Kṛṣṇarāja.[4]

Among the immediate contemporaries of Somadeva we come across two distinguished names: Puṣpadanta and Muñjārya Vādighaṅghala Bhaṭṭa. We have already referred to the former, who commenced his *Mahāpurāṇa* in 959 A. D. under the patronage of Kṛṣṇa III's minister Bharata, and wrote two other works, *Jasaharacariu*, which, like Somadeva's *Yaśastilaka*, relates

---

1 'अथ धर्मार्थकामफलाय राज्याय नमः ।'

2 See below Chapters IV and V.

3 Rice: *Kanarese Literature.*

4 Hiralal: *Catalogue of Sanskrit and Prakrit Manuscripts in C. P. and Berar*, p. XXX.

the story of Yaśodhara, and *Nāyakumāracariu* or the story of Nāgakumāra, both under the patronage of Bharata's son and successor Nanna.[1] Puṣpadanta wrote in Apabhraṁśa verse, and is one of the most important Jaina poets in that language so far discovered; and his prodigious literary activity bears witness to the flourishing condition of Apabhraṁśa literature in the tenth century. Hariṣeṇa[2] who wrote his *Dharmaparīkṣā* in Apabhraṁśa in 988 A. D. mentions three distinguished Apabhraṁśa poets: Puṣpadanta, Svayaṁbhu and Caturmukha; and Puṣpadanta himself refers to Svayaṁbhu and Caturmukha in his *Mahāpurāṇa* 1.9.[3] The works of Svayaṁbhu—*Paümacariu* and *Riṭṭhaṇemicariu*—are available in manuscript, and his son Tribhuvana Svayaṁbhu was also a poet and made substantial additions to his father's poems.[4] Svayaṁbhu may be assigned to the eighth or ninth century, as he mentions Raviṣeṇa, the author of *Padmacarita* (seventh century), in his *Paümacariu*, and is himself mentioned by Puṣpadanta. Caturmukha is earlier than Svayaṁbhu, as the latter mentions him in his *Riṭṭhaṇemicariu* and other works. It is also noteworthy that a number of other Apabhraṁśa poets is cited by Svayaṁbhu in another work of his, a treatise on Prosody called *Svayaṁbhu-chanda*. There was thus a well-defined literary tradition in Apabhraṁśa in and before Somadeva's time; and there is no doubt that he was to some extent influenced by the prevailing current of Apabhraṁśa poetry, as he has used various Apabhraṁśa metres with considerable skill in a number of verses of his *Yaśastilaka*.[5] The use of Apabhraṁśa metres in Sanskrit verse is a novel experiment on the part of a writer who sets out to write classical Sanskrit in the style of Subandhu and Bāṇa, but it shows the wide range of Somadeva's literary equipment and his interest in the vernacular literature of the time. Further, in spite of the divergent character of the works of Somadeva and Puṣpadanta, they seem to have occasionally drawn on common sources for some at least of the literary material handled by them. The story of Yaśodhara itself is one such example; while the tale of Jamadagni and the two birds, and that of Śrībhūti and Bhadramitra related by Somadeva as independent stories in *Yaśastilaka*, Books VI and VII[6], occur in Puṣpadanta's *Mahāpurāṇa* (LXV. 13 ff. and LVII. 7 ff.) as part of a larger scheme of Jaina religious and mythological stories.

---

1 For details see the Introductions to the critical editions of these works. The first two are edited by Dr. Vaidya and the third by Prof. Jain.

2 *Annals* of the B. O. R. I., XXIII, 592–608; Pt. Premi's *Jaina Sāhitya aura Itihāsa*, p. 326.

3 चउमुहु सयंभु सिरिहरिसु दोणु णालोइउ कइ ईसाणु बाणु।

4 See Pt. Premi's article on Svayaṁbhu in his *Jaina Sāhitya aura Itihāsa*.

5 See below Chapter VII.

6 See below Chapter XVI.

Muñjāryya Vādighaṅghala Bhaṭṭa is known to us from the Kudlur plates of the Gaṅga king Mārasiṁha, dated 963 A. D.[1] Mārasiṁha was a tributary of Kṛṣṇa III, and the grant of a village to Vādighaṅghala Bhaṭṭa by the former forms the subject of the inscription, which eloquently describes the great Jaina teacher's attainments and influence. Vādighaṅghala Bhaṭṭa was a distinguished grammarian and seems to have propounded a system of grammar on a sure and sound basis.[2] He was an expert in Lokāyata, Sāṁkhya and Buddhist philosophy as well as Vedic interpretation,[3] a great master of Jaina doctrine, and an eminent poet. He was intimately connected with the Gaṅga king Būtuga II and Kṛṣṇa III and the Rāṣṭrakūṭa capital. We are told that his faultless and eloquent elucidation of literature (*sāhitya-vidyā*) made Gaṅga-Gāṅgeya (Būtuga II), 'a cuckoo in the pleasure-garden of learning', his pupil. He was honoured by the learned men of Vallabharāja's capital, who were enlightened by his exposition of all branches of political science,[4] and Vallabharāja seems to be no other than Kṛṣṇa III who is called Vallabhanarendradeva in the Karhāḍ grant, and Vallabhanarendra and Vallabharāya in Puṣpadanta's works.[5] Kṛṣṇa is, moreover, explicitly mentioned in the inscription, which declares that Kṛṣṇarājadeva, who with his tributaries honoured the master, conquered the regions by acting upon his counsel, which was 'sound in relation to the present as well as the future'.[6] It would thus appear that while Somadeva was preoccupied with the theoretical principles of state-craft, Vādighaṅghala Bhaṭṭa played the role of a practical statesman and acted as a political adviser to the Rāṣṭrakūṭa emperor. The glory and achievements of the empire seem to have opened new vistas before the thinking men of the age, and persons like Somadeva and Vādighaṅghala Bhaṭṭa, who in other times would probably have confined themselves to literature or speculative thought, took a deep interest in matters of vital importance to the state. The disruption of the Rāṣṭrakūṭa empire after Kṛṣṇa III must have been a rude shock to cultural possibilities in the Dekkan.

---

1 Text and translation in *Annual Report of the Mysore Archæological Department* for 1921.

2 'निःसंशयनिर्विवादव्युत्पादितव्याकरणप्रकारः' lines 159, 160.

3 'वेदार्थविचारचारुधिषणः' line 162.

4 'यस्य निरवद्यसाहित्यविद्याव्याख्याननिपुणधिषणानुगुणवाणीविशेषातिशयच्छात्रीभूतसकलविद्याविनोदारामकलकण्ठगङ्ग-गाङ्गेयभूपस्य, सकलराजविद्याप्रतिपादनप्रतिबुद्धबोधप्रबोधितवल्लभराजकटकानेकविद्वज्जनोपजनितपूजाप्रकटीकृतमहिमोन्नतिमहनीयविद्याविभवस्य', lines 165–169.

5 वल्लहणरिंदघरमहयरासु *Jasaharacariu* 1. 1. 3; वल्लहरायमहंतएण *Nāyakumāracariu* 1. 3. 2.

6 तदात्वायतिसुघटमन्त्रक्रमोपदेशानुष्ठानवशीकृताखिलदिगङ्गनासरभससंभोगसुखसंपन्नकृष्णराजदेवविहितवचनसंभावनाप्रभावोपनतसकलमण्डलिकसामन्तसंततिप्रसरस्य', lines 169–171.

Two important Jaina poets Vādirāja and Vādībhasiṁha are said to be Somadeva's disciples. Śrutasāgara in his commentary on *Yaśastilaka* 2. 126 quotes a statement which represents Somadeva as saying that both Vādirāja and Vādībhasiṁha are his disciples.[1] The statement cannot, however, be traced in the two extant works of Somadeva, and neither Vadirāja nor Vādībhasiṁha claims Somadeva as his *guru* in any of their works. Vādirāja says at the end of his *Pārśvanāthacarita*, a poem in 12 cantos, that his *guru* is Matisāgara; besides, he belonged to the Nandisaṁgha, while Somadeva belonged to the Devasaṁgha. Similarly, Vādībhasiṁha in his prose romance *Gadyacintāmaṇi* 1.6 gives expression to his deep obligations to his *guru* Puṣpasena. On the other hand, it is not chronologically impossible for Vādirāja and Vādībhasiṁha to be regarded as disciples of Somadeva. Vādirāja, according to his own statement, wrote his *Pārśvanāthacarita* in Śaka 947 (1025 A. D.) during the reign of the Western Cālukya king Jayasiṁha II who ruled from 1015 to 1042 A. D. As regards Vādībhasiṁha, he as well as Vādirāja is mentioned in the Belgāmve grant of Jayasiṁha II, dated 1036 A. D., which describes a Śaiva savant named Vādi-Rudraguṇa as having defeated in argument Vādībhasiṁha, Vādirāja and other scholars[2]; and the great king Rājarāja mentioned at the end of Vādībhasiṁha's poem *Kṣatracūḍāmaṇi*[3] might very well refer to the Cola king Rājarāja the Great who ruled from 985 to 1014 A. D. It will be thus seen that Vādirāja and Vādībhasiṁha flourished in the first quarter of the eleventh century; and assuming Śrutasāgara's statement to be correct and genuine, they may be regarded as having been Somadeva's disciples during their boyhood. But, nevertheless, it is strange that they should be so completely silent about their early *guru* Somadeva.

The epoch of Somadeva was preceded and followed by a considerable output of Jaina literature in various parts of India. Among his predecessors, from the beginning of the ninth century to the early part of the tenth, we find such names as Vīrasena (author of the *Dhavalā* commentary and part of the *Jayadhavalā*), Jinasena (completed the *Jayadhavalā* and wrote *Ādipurāṇa* and other works), Guṇabhadra (author of *Uttarapurāṇa* and *Ātmānuśāsana*), the Jaina Śākaṭāyana, Vidyānanda (author of *Aṣṭasahasrī*, *Tattvārthaślokavārtika* etc.), Siddharṣi (author of *Upamitibhavaprapañcā kathā*), and Hariṣeṇa (author of *Kathākośa*) and others; while among his immediate successors, from about the last quarter of the tenth century to the first quarter of the eleventh, we find Kanarese writers like Cāmuṇḍa-

1 स वादिराजोऽपि श्रीसोमदेवाचार्यस्य शिष्यः। 'वादीभसिंहोऽपि मदीयशिष्यः श्रीवादिराजोऽपि मदीयशिष्यः' इत्युक्तत्वाच्च।

2 See below Chapter XIII.

3 राजतां राजराजोऽयं राजराजो महोदयैः। तेजसा वयसा शूरः क्षत्रचूडामणिर्गुणैः॥.

rāya (wrote in prose *Cāmuṇḍarāya-purāṇa*), Ranna (wrote *Ajitapurāṇa* and *Gadāyuddha*), and Nāgavarma (author of the Kanarese version of Bāṇa's *Kādambarī*); philosophical writers like Nemicandra Siddhāntacakravartin (wrote in Prākrit *Gŏmmaṭasāra*, *Dravyasaṁgraha* and other works) and Prabhācandra (author of *Nyāyakumudacandra* and *Prameyakamalamārtaṇḍa*[1]); and poets and scholars like Vādirāja (wrote *Pārśvanāthacarita*, *Kākutsthacarita* and *Yaśodharacarita*), Vādībhasiṁha (wrote *Gadyacintāmaṇi* and *Kṣatracūḍāmaṇi*), Dhanapāla (author of *Tilakamañjarī*), Amitagati (author of *S'ubhāṣitaratnasaṁdoha*, *Dharmaparīkṣā* and other works), Asaga (author of *Vardhamānacarita*), Mahāsena (author of *Pradyumnacarita*), Vīranandin (author of *Candraprabhacarita*), and perhaps Kanakāmara (wrote *Karakaṇḍacariu* in Apabhraṁśa); and other writers like the grammarian Dayāpāla (author of *Rūpasiddhi* and contemporary of Vādirāja).

While Somadeva made substantial contributions to Jaina religious literature, his literary importance and achievement go beyond its narrow limits; and the value of his work can be assessed in relation to Sanskrit literature as a whole. He is one of the most versatile talents in the history of Indian literature, and his masterpiece *Yaśastilaka* reveals the manifold aspects of his genius. He is a master of prose and verse, a profound scholar with a well-stocked memory, an authority on Jaina dogma, and a critic of contemporary philosophical systems. He is a close student of the art of government, and in this respect his *Yaśastilaka* and *Nītivākyāmṛta* supplement each other. He is a redactor of ancient folktales and religious stories, and at times shows himself an adept in dramatic dialogue. Last but not least, he is a keen observer of men and manners. The position of Somadeva is, indeed, unique in Sanskrit literature.

Despite the fact that Somadeva's reputation rests on a prose romance and a treatise on polity, he was primarily a Jaina theologian; and nearly half of *Yaśastilaka* and presumably the lost works are devoted to the defence and exposition of the tenets of the Jaina faith. He acknowledges the fact himself and would have us believe that his poetry was a byproduct of his philosophical studies. He tells us in one of the opening verses of *Yaśastilaka* that just as a cow yields milk by eating grass, similarly his intellect produced the beautiful utterances of his poetical composition by feeding on the dry logical studies, to which he had devoted himself since his childhood.[2] Tarka or philosophical argumentation was Somadeva's true vocation, and his honorific titles Tārkikacakravartin and Vādībhapañcānana point to the fact that he, like many intellectuals of his age, spent a good

1 See Introduction (in Hindi) to *Nyāyakumudacandra*, p. 121, Bombay 1938.

2 आजन्मसमभ्यस्ताच्छुष्कात्तर्कात्तृणादिव ममास्याः । मतिसुरभेरभवदिदं सूक्तिपयः सुकृतिनां पुण्यैः ॥.

deal of his energy in engaging in controversy influential disputants belonging to rival faiths. This was, in fact, a trait of the times, as can be seen from such peculiar but significant names as Vādirāja, Vadībhasiṁha, Vādigharaṭṭa, Vādighaṅghala, Paravādimalla, Vādikolāhala etc., found among the Jaina writers and scholars of the age. That this was a practice common to all the schools is evident from I-tsing's eloquent description of it in his account of education in India towards the end of the seventh century. "When they are refuting heretic doctrines", says the Chinese traveller, "all their opponents become tongue-tied and acknowledge themselves undone. Then the sound of their fame makes the five mountains (of India) vibrate, and their renown flows, as it were, over the four borders." "They oppose the heretics as they would drive beasts (deer) in the middle of a plain, and explain away disputations as boiling water melts frost. In this manner they become famous throughout Jambudvīpa (India), receive respect above gods and men, and serving under the Buddha and promoting His doctrine, they lead all the people (to Nirvāṇa)."[1]

The Praśasti verses of *Nītivākyāmṛta* emphasize Somadeva's activity as a controversialist, and proclaim his superiority to all prospective disputants. One of the verses, for instance, asks a disputant how he dares argue with Somadeva, not being an Akalaṅka in argumentation nor a Haṁsasiddhāntadeva in the knowledge of traditional lore nor a Pūjyapāda in eloquence.

सकलसमयतर्के नाकलङ्कोऽसि वादी न भवसि समयोक्तौ हंससिद्धान्तदेवः ।
न च वचनविलासे पूज्यपादोऽसि तत्त्वं वदसि कथमिदानीं सोमदेवेन सार्धम् ॥

The final verse trumpets Somadeva's eloquence which strikes terror into the hearts of all disputants, and claims that even Bṛhaspati cannot hold his own in argument with him.[2]

While these boasts and eulogies are of a conventional character, they reveal one aspect of Somadeva's intellectual equipment; and he was perhaps as assiduous in his polemical activity as any of his contemporaries. This, however, should not blind us to the fact that poetry and literature must have made heavy claims on his time and intellectual effort, as the composition of an extensive work like *Yaśastilaka* in prose and verse was bound to presuppose long and careful preparation, involving laborious study of the secular branches of study and fervent devotion to the art of poetry. His statement that he had studied Tarka since his childhood shows that he began his career as a student of logic, metaphysics and allied subjects,

1 *A Record of the Buddhist Religion* by I-Tsing. Trans. by Takakusu, pp. 178, 181.

2 दर्पान्धबोधबुधसिन्धुरसिंहनादे,वादिद्विपोद्दलनदुर्धरवाग्विवादे । श्रीसोमदेवमुनिपे वचनारसाले, वागीश्वरोऽपि पुरतोऽस्ति न वादकाले ॥

and seems to have taken to poetry late in his life. But his devotion to his second love was no less sincere, and apparently he came to realise that poetry was an exacting mistress. As he says at the beginning of his work,

निद्रां विदूरयसि शास्त्ररसं रुणत्सि सर्वेन्द्रियार्थमसमर्थविधिं विधत्से ।
चेतश्च विभ्रमयसे कविते पिशाचि लोकस्तथापि सुकृती त्वदनुग्रहेण ॥ 1. 41.

'Thou Muse, thou evil genius, thou dost dismiss sleep, hinder delight in the Śāstras, reduce all the senses to impotence, and bewilder the mind. Yet men are lucky if they obtain thy favour.'

The combination of Tarka and Poetry, so prominent in the case of Somadeva, is not an isolated phenomenon in Indian literary history. Śrīharṣa, the author of *Naiṣadhacarita* and *Khaṇḍanakhaṇḍakhādya*, is a classic example of this tendency, which is also observed occasionally in lesser known poets. We may refer, for example, to Trailokya who flourished in Kashmir in the first half of the twelfth century, and is mentioned by Maṅkhaka in *S'rīkaṇṭhacarita* 25. 65, 66.[1] It is noteworthy that Maṅkhaka compares Trailokya to Tutātita or Kumārila, who is also supposed to have been a Tārkika as well as a Kavi, although no poem composed by him has come down to us.

It may be safely assumed that *Yaśastilaka* was the product of that period of Somadeva's life when his poetic power had reached its full maturity. The author makes certain claims for his work which will bear the scrutiny of investigation.

First, he says that he composed his work without aid from any source and without any model before him, and therefore compares it to a gem produced by the ocean.

असहायमनादर्शं रत्नं रत्नाकरादिव । मत्तः काव्यमिदं जातं सतां हृदयमण्डनम् ॥ 1. 14.

The claim of originality, like all such claims, may be admitted only in a limited sense. Somadeva cannot claim any originality regarding the plot, but there are some novel features in regard to the form and contents of the romance, which distinguish it from other versions of the story of Yaśodhara and, indeed, from other prose romances extant in Prakrit or Sanskrit. It may be added that the claim of originality is in conformity with Somadeva's idea that a poet should rely upon his own efforts and not imitate or borrow from others. He declares that the poet, who keeps before him the works of his predecessors and consults them again and again and expresses himself in the same manner or differently, is a plagiarist ('poetry thief') and a sinner.

---

1 दृढोऽपि तर्ककार्कश्ये प्रगल्भः कविकर्मणि । यः श्रीतुतातितस्येव पुनर्जन्मान्तरग्रहः ॥
तं श्रीत्रैलोक्यमालोक्य गण्यं सत्कर्मिणां धुरि । ययौ मुहुरधिज्यस्य कार्मुकस्य सधर्मताम् ॥.
Jonarāja remarks in his commentary: तुतातितः कुमारिलः । स हि तार्किकः कविश्चासीत् ।.

कृत्वा कृतीः पूर्वकृताः पुरस्तात् प्रत्यादरं ताः पुनरीक्षमाणः ।
तथैव जल्पेदथ योऽन्यथा वा स काव्यचोरोऽस्तु स पातकी च ॥ 1. 13.

It is, however, conceded that occasional similarity with other writers in ideas or expression cannot detract from the merits of a poet who is not in the habit of looking into the works of others.

कृतीः परेषामविलोकमानस्तदुक्तिवक्तापि कविर्न हीनः । 1. 12.

Somadeva's theory of poetical self-sufficiency is no doubt exaggerated and belied by literary history, but we may be certain that he relied mainly upon his own resources in the composition of his encyclopedic work.

Secondly, Somadeva says that he who has the curiosity to go through his work can avail himself of poetic utterances, appropriate dicta, and *the tenets of all the S'āstras.*

उक्तयः कविताकान्ताः सूक्तयोऽवसरोचिताः । युक्तयः सर्वशास्त्रान्तास्तस्य यस्यात्र कौतुकम् ॥ 1. 15.

This is not an empty boast or arrogant self-assertion. Poetic merits apart, *Yaśastilaka* is, indeed, a storehouse of information concerning the tenets of various Śāstras and schools of thought; and this aspect of the work conforms to the theory of Vyutpatti held by Somadeva himself and the writers on poetics. Somadeva tells us that there is one type of Kāvya, 'sweet to the ears' and eloquent with descriptions, and another type which charms the heart, being replete with meaning: no wise man will find fault with either of these, but proper and fit is that kind of composition which contributes to the all-round *vyutpatti* or scholarly instruction of the author himself and others.

किंचित् काव्यं श्रवणसुभगं वर्णनोदीर्णवर्णं, किंचिद्वाच्योचितपरिचयं हृच्चमत्कारकारि ।
अत्रासूयेत् क इह सुकृती किंतु युक्तं तदुक्तं, यद्व्युत्पत्त्यै सकलविषये स्वस्य चान्यस्य च स्यात् ॥ 1. 16.

The Vyutpatti mentioned by Somadeva has two aspects. The Vyutpatti of the poet is his scholarly training; and the idea of it appears in a systematic form in most writers on poetics, who lay stress on the importance of Vyutpatti as a supplementary discipline reinforcing Śakti or Pratibhā, or natural genius; while, among poets, Maṅkhaka emphasizes the value of Vyutpatti or Pāṇḍitya in his *S'rīkaṇṭhacarita* (2. 5, 27, 45–48). Certain writers, e. g., Mammaṭa, and especially Rājaśekhara[1] who is closely followed by Hemacan-

1 Rājaśekhara in *Kāvyamīmāṁsā*, chap 8, envisages a wide range of intellectual equipment for a poet, and enumerates twelve recognised sources of poetry: Śruti; Smṛti; Itihāsa; Purāṇa; Pramāṇavidyā or the philosophical systems; Samayavidyā or sectarian systems like those of the Śaivas, the Pāñcarātras, and the Buddhists, popularly called Āgama; the three Rājasiddhāntas consisting of Polity, Erotics, and Dramaturgy; Loka or a knowledge of the world, its geography and customs; Viracanā or fanciful stories and conceits; and Prakīrṇaka or miscellaneous subjects like the science of elephants, the Dhanurveda, the science of gems, treatises on Yoga etc.

dra, and Vāgbhaṭa, the author of *Kāvyānuśāsana,* and Kṣemendra, in his *Kavikaṇṭhābharaṇa,* who employs the term Paricaya for Vyutpatti, clearly enumerate the various branches of learning, with all or some of which the poet is expected to show his acquaintance. Considered from this standpoint, Somadeva's statement that his Kāvya is a repertory of all the Śāstras is corroborated to a large extent by an examination of the contents of the work, and there are few works in Kāvya literature which fulfil the conditions of Vyutpatti so completely as Somedeva's *Yaśastilaka.*

The Vyutpatti of 'others', that is, of the readers of a poem refers to their instruction in the topics of the Śāstras, so that a Kāvya is viewed as a kind of introduction to the learned branches of study. Somadeva's view of this aspect of Vyutpatti may be correlated with the opinion of Bhāmaha, who says in his *Kāvyālaṅkāra* (chap. V) that the Śāstras are, as a rule, difficult to understand and shunned by the untalented, who, however, enjoy them when mixed with the sweet potion of poetry, just as people take an unpalatable dose of medicine after tasting honey.[1] In other words, the *śāstric* pill is to be sugared with poetry for the benefit of those who are unable to swallow it as it is. The difficult topics of the Śāstras should be made interesting and popular through poetry, and this the poet can do by expounding or referring to them in the course of his Kāvya. Bhāmaha, accordingly, goes on to say that there is no topic—no word, no meaning, no principle of logic, and no art or science—which does not serve as an element in poetical composition, and the poet's burden is undoubtedly great.[2] It will be thus seen that the idea that a Kāvya should be a medium of instruction for its readers was prevalent long before the tenth century, and this idea no doubt greatly influenced the scope and composition of Somadeva's *Yaśastilaka.*

Somadeva speaks of the great transmuting power of poetry. The true poets are those whose words make familiar things unfamiliar and unfamiliar things familiar.

त एव कवयो लोके येषां वचनगोचरः । सपूर्वोऽपूर्वतामर्थो यात्यपूर्वः सपूर्वताम् ॥ 1. 25.

This somehow reminds us of certain lines of Wordsworth on the contemplation of Nature:

Familiar things and awful, the minute
And grand, are destined here to meet......[3]

---

1 प्रायेण दुर्बोधतया शास्त्राद् बिभ्यत्यमेधसः । तदुपच्छन्दनायैष हेतुन्यायलवोच्चयः ॥ स्वादुकाव्यरसोन्मिश्रं शास्त्रमप्युपयुञ्जते । प्रथमालीढमधवः पिबन्ति कटु भेषजम् ॥.

2 न स शब्दो न तद्वाच्यं न स न्यायो न सा कला । जायते यन्न काव्याङ्गमहो भारो महान् कवेः ॥.

3 Herbert Read: *Wordsworth*, p 193. The lines occur in the first draft of a passage intended as an alternative for some lines in Book VIII of the *Prelude*.

But it is obviously the genius of the poet, working on a broader canvas, that makes the familiar awful and the awful familiar.

Somadeva asserts that even the animals are thrilled with joy when they hear the utterances of a good poet.[1] This is an exaggeration, but he may have in mind the musical effect of lyric poetry.

The question of appreciation of poetry is considered by Somadeva from the standpoint of poets in several verses. The poets are said to be fond of people who may not be learned, but who can grasp the trend of the spoken word. In other words, learning is not necessary for the appreciation of poetry: the excellence of gold is, for instance, demonstrated by the touchstone which is of inferior value.[2] The ability of laymen to judge the merits of poetry, although they are not poets themselves, is set forth by citing the example of the man who can discern the flavour of sweets while eating, although he is ignorant of the process of boiling sugar.[3] As for princes, poetical efforts are useless when a king lacks in judgment; it is no use putting rich fare before an animal who feeds on grass.[4] The populace also lacks in judgment and delights in a poem, simply because it is reputed to be good; it often happens that literary works are held in esteem solely on account of their being accepted as good by others, just as a woman acquires a reputation for beauty when she becomes someone's mistress.[5] In matters affecting poetry, one should appeal to the judgment only of those who, like the ocean, 'keep within' (i. e. bear in mind) what is good, and throw out what is bad; that is, the true critic is one who appreciates the merits of a poem, ignoring the defects.[6] Further, a thing ought to be judged on its own merits and not in relation to a type to which it does not belong; it is futile to look for the sheen of gold while testing silver. In other words, poetry must be judged as poetry, and the critic must not expect to find in it what does not properly fall within the province of poetry.[7] Those who are blind to merits, being intent on fault-finding, and try to pass off blemishes as merits are unfit to study poetry: being the enemies of the goddess of learning, they have indeed no right to study it.[8] Finally, it is useless to argue whether any one

1 ता एव सुकवेर्वाचस्तिरश्चामपि याः श्रुताः । भवन्त्यानन्दनिष्यन्दामन्दरोमाञ्चहेतवः ॥ 1. 26.
2 अबुधेऽप्युक्तियुक्तिज्ञे कवीनामुत्सवो महान् । गुणाः किं न सुवर्णस्य व्यज्यन्ते निकषोपले ॥ 1. 28.
3 अवक्तापि स्वयं लोकः कामं काव्यपरीक्षकः । रसपाकानभिज्ञोऽपि भोक्ता वेत्ति न किं रसम् ॥ 1. 29.
4 वृथा वक्तुः श्रमः सर्वो निर्विचारे नरेश्वरे । प्राज्यभोज्यविधिः कः स्यात्तृणस्वादिनि देहिनि ॥ 1. 30.
5 अङ्गनावद्गिरो गण्याः प्रायेणान्यपरिग्रहात् । स्वयं विचारशून्यो हि प्रसिद्ध्या रज्यते जनः ॥ 1. 32.
6 काव्यकथासु त एव हि कर्तव्याः साक्षिणः समुद्रसमाः । गुणगणमन्तर्निदधति दोषमलं ये बहिश्च कुर्वन्ति ॥ 1. 36.
7 आत्मस्थितेर्वस्तु विचारणीयं न जातु जात्यन्तरसंश्रयेण । दुर्वर्णनिर्वर्णविधौ बुधानां सुवर्णवर्णस्य मुधानुबन्धः ॥ 1. 37.
8 गुणेषु ये दोषमनीषयान्धा दोषान् गुणीकर्तुमथेशते वा । श्रोतुं कवीनां वचनं न तेऽर्हाः सरस्वतीद्रोहिषु कोऽधिकारः ॥ 1. 38.

is a poet or not, since in the ultimate resort the ears and minds of the readers are capable of discerning the true nature of the spoken word and its significance respectively.[1]

Somadeva exploited to the full the resources of the Sanskrit language, and has an undisputed claim to rank as a classical writer; but he could not altogether escape the influence of Jaina literary usage in handling Sanskrit prose and verse. A glaring instance is his use of *imaiḥ* for *ebhiḥ*[2], a Prākritism found also in some other Jaina Sanskrit writers. He writes also *kleśa-bhājanaḥ* more than once (e. g., in 3. 388 and towards the end of Book VI), which is clearly against classical usage. A serious grammatical mistake occurs in 3. 480.

सुरपतिवधूहासोल्लासश्रियं श्रयदाकृतिः । प्रथमसमये चन्द्रोद्द्योतस्तवास्तु मुदे सदा ॥

Here *śrayat*, although it forms part of a Bahuvrīhi compound, is made to govern *śriyaṁ*. The editors of the N. S. edition of *Yaśastilaka* propose to read '*cchaviśraya*', but not only the printed text but the three manuscripts used by me have the incorrect form. An instance of loose construction is *kīnāśa-kelim anavāpta-dhiyaḥ* in 2. 130. The commentator explains the phrase by supposing *prati* to be understood between the two compounds: कीनाशकेलिं यमक्रीडां प्रति अनवाप्तधियः अप्राप्तबुद्धयः यावन्मरणं नायातीत्यर्थः Such irregularities are, however, few and far-between, and perhaps negligible considering the bulk of the work.

One of the most conspicuous characteristics of Somadeva as a writer is his use of numerous rare and unfamiliar words, many of which are not found elsewhere in Sanskrit literature. The command of vocabulary makes *Yaśastilaka* an exceptionally fruitful source of Sanskrit lexicography, but the use of far-fetched words sometimes gives a pedantic air to the work. Somadeva is not, indeed, the word-hunter ridiculed by Athenaeus[4]; he is rather the learned researcher who tries to bring into use obsolete words. As a matter of fact, he distinctly refers to this aspect of his literary effort, when he says at the end of Book V that he has resuscitated words that had been swallowed by the crooked monster of Time.

अरालकालव्यालेन ये लीढाः सांप्रतं तु ते । शब्दाः श्रीसोमदेवेन प्रोत्थाप्यन्ते किमद्भुतम् ॥

While Somadeva thus claims to have rescued long-forgotten words from oblivion, he also states that he has recovered words lying hidden at the bottom of the ocean of the Śāstras, and that with these gems of words he has made an ornament for the Goddess of speech.

---

1 अयं कविर्नैष कविः किमत्र हेतुप्रयुक्तिः कृतिभिर्विधेया । श्रोत्रं मनश्चात्र यतः समर्थं वागर्थयो रूपनिरूपणाय ॥ 1. 39.

2 विहितानन्दमहोत्सवः कुलवधूगीतप्रसाधैरिमैः । 2. 229 ; किं वेदोक्तैरिमैः सूक्तैरेत पिङ्गानुपास्महे Book IV, p. 118.

3 See Jacobi's Preface to *Upamitibhavaprapañcā Kathā*, p. XX.

4 *Deipnosophistae*, III. 98.

उद्धृत्य शास्त्रजलधेर्नितले निमग्नैः पर्यागतैरिव चिराद्भिधानरत्नैः ।
या सोमदेवविदुषा विहिता विभूषा वाग्देवता वहतु संप्रति तामनर्घाम् ॥

In the latter verse Somadeva evidently refers to the unfamiliar words and the technical terms of the Śāstras which he has used in his Kāvya. This was, in fact, a trait of Kāvya literature, especially of the later period, but Somadeva seems in this respect to have gone further than any other writer of the age.

Somadeva, like Bhavabhūti, sometimes gives expression to a sense of over-confidence in his own powers, and claims something like a monopoly of poetical talents (End of Book IV).

मया वागर्थसंभारे भुक्ते सारस्वते रसे । कवयोऽन्ये भविष्यन्ति नूनमुच्छिष्टभोजनाः ॥

In another place he says that if there are any honest people efficient in the art of poetry and the knowledge of the world, they should make it a point to study the utterances of the poet Somadeva.

लोकवित्त्वे कवित्वे वा यदि चातुर्यचञ्चवः । सोमदेवकवेः सूक्तीः समभ्यस्यन्तु साधवः ॥ 3. 513.

That Somadeva himself was conversant with the art of poetry as well as the way of the world, that he was a *kavi* as well as a *lokavid*, a shrewd observer of contemporary society, is apparent from his works, and that is the highest compliment we can pay him. That this was considered high praise even in those times is shown by the fact that Jinasena in his *Ādipurāṇa* I. 56 attributes these qualifications to his *guru* Vīrasena, the celebrated author of the Dhavalā commentary.[1]

Somadeva's self-assertion is in marked contrast to the modesty of an author like Siddharṣi, who wrote his great allegorical romance about half a century before *Yaśastilaka* was written.[2] But it is noteworthy that in the opening verses of *Yaśastilaka* Somadeva makes only modest claims in behalf of his work. He begins by saying that there is nothing that has not been visualized by the all but omniscient poets of old; and it is a miracle when a present-day poet, however sharp in intellect he may be, happens to make any utterance comparable to theirs (1. 11).[3] As regards his own Kāvya, he opines that it will create fun among the wicked, but will contribute towards the intellectual growth of the wise, while those who are impartial will not remain silent about the work. He hopes that the wise, whose sensibility has been made extremely dull by partaking of the excessive sweetness of

---

1 लोकवित्त्वं कवित्वं च स्थितं भट्टारके द्वयम् । वाग्मिता वाग्मिनो यस्य वाचा वाचस्पतेरपि ॥

2 In 908 A. D. See Jacobi's Preface to his ed. of *Upamitibhavaprapañcā kathā*, p. xxi.

3 सर्वज्ञकल्पैः कविभिः पुरातनैरवीक्षितं वस्तु किमस्ति संप्रति । ऐदंयुगीनस्तु कुशाग्रधीरपि प्रवक्ति यत्तत्सदृशं स विस्मयः ॥

the works of the meritorious poets, might have a liking for the utterances of poets like himself, just as they would relish Neem leaves after excessive indulgence in sweets (1. 22-3).

दुर्जनानां विनोदाय बुधानां मतिजम्मने । मध्यस्थानां न मौनाय मन्ये काव्यमिदं भवेत् ॥
सुकविकथामाधुर्यप्रबन्धसेवातिवृद्धजाड्यानाम् । पिचुमन्दकन्दलीष्विव भवतु रुचिर्मद्विधोक्तिषु बुधानाम् ॥

Despite the all-round importance of Somadeva as a writer, he seems to have exercised very little influence in any department of thought outside the sphere of Jaina religious literature. He was completely ignored by the non-Jaina *literati*, and his literary rehabilitation is due to the interest taken in him by modern research. He seems to have found only one commentator for his *Yaśastilaka*, the Jaina Śrutasāgara Sūri who wrote his works early in the 16th century.[1] As regards *Nītivākyāmṛta*, there is an anonymous commentary extant on the work, of unknown date: it is, however, full of quotations from ancient writers on Smṛti and polity, and its author was a non-Jaina as he salutes Hari at the beginning of the work.[2]

The literary fortunes of Somadeva are a sad commentary on how the achievement of a writer of genius can be neutralized by sectarian indifference and religious prejudices; but, as we shall see, Somadeva himself was imbued with such influences, and could hardly expect recognition outside the circle of his co-religionists. On matters relating to Jaina dogma he has always been recognised as an authoritative writer, and it is noteworthy that, in a number of verses quoted by Śrutasāgara in his commentary on Kundakunda's *Bhāvapāhuḍa* (V. 34), Somadeva is mentioned among the great teachers of Jainism:

अथ के ते आचार्या यैः कृतं शास्त्रं प्रमाणीक्रियते इत्याह—
श्रीभद्रबाहुः श्रीचन्द्रो जिनचन्द्रो महामतिः । गृध्रपिच्छगुरुः श्रीमान् लोहाचार्यो जितेन्द्रियः ॥
एलाचार्यः पूज्यपादः सिंहनन्दी महाकविः । वीरसेनो जिनसेनो गुणनन्दी महातपाः ॥
समन्तभद्रः श्रीकुम्भः शिवकोटिः शिवंकरः । शिवायनो विष्णुसेनो गुणभद्रो गुणाधिकः ॥
अकलङ्को महाप्राज्ञः सोमदेवो विदांवरः । प्रभाचन्द्रो नेमिचन्द्र इत्यादिमुनिसत्तमैः ॥
यच्छास्त्रं रचितं नूनं तदेवादेयमन्यकैः । विसंघै रचितं नैव प्रमाणं साध्वपि स्फुटम् ॥

Citations from *Yaśastilaka* are often found in later Jaina literature, e. g., in Padmaprabha's commentary on *Niyamasāra* (v. 101), Āśādhara's commentary on his *Anagāra-dharmāmṛta* (2. 75, 9. 81, 98), Brahmadeva's commentary on Yogīndudeva's *Paramātmaprakāśa* (2. 15), and frequently in

---

1 Pt. Premi: *Jaina Sāhitya aura Itihāsa*, p. 410.

2 On the quotations in the Commentary, see O. Stein's paper in the Ātmānanda Centenary Commemoration Volume, Bhavangar 1936, pp. 150–67. A commentary on *Nītivākyāmṛta* in Kannada by a Jaina author is known to exist. It was composed by Nemināṭha about the middle of the twelfth century A. D. See Pt. Premi (op. cit.), p. 80.

Śrutasāgara's commentary on the *Prābhṛtas* of Kundakunda.[1] The following verse of *Yaśastilaka* (VIII. 34) is found with a slight variation in Śivakoṭi's *Ratnamālā*,[2] this writer being different from the ancient author of that name.

सर्व एव हि जैनानां प्रमाणं लौकिको विधिः । यत्र सम्यक्त्वहानिर्न यत्र न व्रतदूषणम् ॥

The following three verses are cited from *Yaśastilaka* VI. 1 in Śubhacandra's *Jñānārṇava* (under 4. 27).

ज्ञानहीने क्रिया पुंसि परं नारभते फलम् । तरोश्छायेव किं लभ्या फलश्रीर्नष्टदृष्टिभिः ॥
ज्ञानं पङ्गौ क्रिया चान्धे निःश्रद्धे नार्थकृद्द्वयम् । ततो ज्ञानं क्रिया श्रद्धा त्रयं तत्पदकारणम् ॥
हतं ज्ञानं क्रियाशून्यं हता चाज्ञानिनः क्रिया । धावन्नप्यन्धको नष्टः पश्यन्नपि च पङ्गुकः ॥

It may be noted that the third verse does not belong to Somadeva, as it appears in his work as a quotation introduced by the phrase *uktaṁ ca*. Another verse of Somadeva occurring in *Yaśastilaka* VI. 21 is quoted in *Jñānārṇava* (under 6. 8): *uktaṁ ca granthāntare*:

मूढत्रयं मदाश्चाष्टौ तथानायतनानि षट् । अष्टौ शङ्कादयश्चेति दृग्दोषाः पञ्चविंशतिः ॥[3]

Somadeva's verse

कर्ता न तावदिह कोऽपि धियेच्छया वा दृष्टोऽन्यथा कटकृतावपि स प्रसंगः ।
कार्यं किमत्र सदनादिषु तक्षकाद्यैराहत्य चेत् त्रिभुवनं पुरुषः करोति ॥ (*Yaśastilaka* 2. 139)

is quoted anonymously in *Sarvadarśanasaṁgraha* in the chapter on Jaina philosophy. A verse occurring in *Yaśastilaka* in the philosophical dialogue towards the end of Book V (p. 257) is quoted as follows in Anantavīrya's commentary on *Parīkṣāmukhasūtra* (Viṣayasamuddeśa): *tathā coktam*

तदहर्जस्तनेहातो रक्षोदृष्टेर्भवस्मृतेः । भूतानन्वयनात् सिद्धः प्रकृतिज्ञः सनातनः ॥ इति ।

Hiralal says in his *Catalogue of Sanskrit and Prakrit manuscripts in C. P. and Berar* (P. XXXII) that 'in the *Stotracatuṣṭayaṭīkā* Vidyānanda makes frequent references to and quotations from *Dhyāna-paddhati* of Somadeva Sūri. This may be another work by our author.' It is, however, possible that this *Dhyāna-paddhati* is not an independent work; but may turn out to be the elaborate discourse on meditation (Dhyānavidhi) in *Yaśastilaka* VIII. 39.

As a poet, Somadeva's contribution to Kāvya literature is substantial enough to justify his claim to be regarded as a worthy successor of Māgha. The poetry of *Yaśastilaka* has been analysed elsewhere[1], and it

1 *Saṭprābhṛtādi-saṁgrahaḥ*, Māṇikacandra Digambara Jaina Granthamālā, 17.

2 Included in *Siddhāntasārādi-saṁgrahaḥ*, Ibidem 22.

3 It is uncertain whether the verses are actually quoted by the author of *Jñānārṇava* or merely occur in the manuscripts of the work. The *Jñānārṇava* is an original composition in fluent Sanskrit verse dealing with certain aspects of Jaina doctrine. A careful examination of the available manuscripts of the work will help to decide whether the quotations are genuine.

will be seen that Somadeva not only deals with the usual themes of Kāvya but adds to the rich fund of Sanskrit poetry by his treatment of topics not usually dealt with in Kāvya literature. He gives us vivid and intimate pictures of court life not found elsewhere, and their accuracy is apparently due to the fact that they are drawn from personal observation and experience. He depicts also other aspects of life, and among his most notable verses may be included those on child life, the cremation ground, and the goddess Caṇḍamārī. He is a sympathetic observer of animals, and some of his verses on animal life are among the best of their kind in Sanskrit literature. He has introduced Jaina religious themes into Kāvya poetry, and his verses on the Anuprekṣās are an important contribution to the literature on the subject. The use of Prākrit metres in Sanskrit verse is also a noteworthy experiment; and Somadeva has in this connection made a lyrical effort which merits attention as being anterior to the composition of Jayadeva's *Gītagovinda*.

Perhaps the most interesting body of verse in *Yaśastilaka* is that dealing with the vices and foibles of the ministers of kings, and the verses in question, varied and extensive as they are, constitute the first systematic attempt at political satire in Sanskrit poetry, and remind us of the satirical verse of Kṣemendra, who in his *Narmamālā* attacks the Kāyastha or the official caste of Kashmir. The later poet writes in a lighter vein, but his work is richer in concrete details, and covers a wider ground than the corresponding verses of Somadeva. The object of the latter is edification rather than entertainment, but from a historical point of view the observations of both the writers are important as throwing light on some of the abuses of the times. Somadeva may be said to have introduced in this respect a new theme in Sanskrit poetry, which was later developed with ampler details by Kṣemendra.

Somadeva is not a great inspired poet : he is sometimes artificial and suffers from verbosity and repetition of ideas. But his verse often throbs with the currents of contemporary life, and he ranks supreme among the Jaina Sanskrit poets who have adopted the *kāvya* style as a vehicle of expression. He has, besides, given effective expression to some of the noble teachings of Jainism in Sanskrit verse. The subject has been treated in another chapter, but we may cite here a notable verse which enshrines the idea of returning good for evil.

अज्ञानभावादशुभाशयाद्वा कुर्वीत चेत् कोऽपि जनः खलत्वम् ।
तथापि सद्भिः प्रियमेव चिन्त्यं न मथ्यमानेऽप्यमृते विषं हि ॥

---

1 See Chapter VII.

'Even if any one resorts to villainy from ignorance or evil motives, the good should think of doing only good. Nectar never becomes poison even when it is churned' (*Yaśastilaka*, 1. 151).

This is, indeed, not a new idea in Indian literature; and we may cite, for instance, the ancient Buddhist dictum: Enmity is not calmed by enmity (*na vaireṇa vairāṇi śāmyante*).[1] Nevertheless it represents one of the cardinal teachings of Jainism, and the exhortation is in harmony with the love for all creatures inculcated elsewhere in Somadeva's *Yaśastilaka*.[2]

CHAPTER II

Synopsis of Yaśastilaka

Book I

In the Yaudheya country there was a beautiful city named Rājapura, adorned with magnificent temples and lofty mansions belonging to the wealthy. Here reigned Māradatta, son of Caṇḍamahāsena, a powerful Prince who surpassed in valour such kings of old as Nṛga, Nala, Nahuṣa, Bharata, Bhagīratha and Bhagadatta. Ascending the throne while still quite young, he embarked on a wild career of reckless adventure along with companions who had passions and traits of character similar to his own. Sometimes, putting on his armour, he would play with rogue elephants, 'who had broken their chains like lotus fibres, flung away the pegs like sprouts of Vīraṇa grass, torn the ropes to pieces like branching creepers, and smashed the posts like reeds'. Sometimes he would pet vicious wild horses. Sometimes he would plunge into lakes and grapple crocodiles. Sometimes he would kill tigers with the force of his arms, and wander in the woods echoing with the uncanny screeching of owls in their mountain resort. Sometimes he would betake himself at night to cremation grounds, 'terrible with the sound of the loud drums in the hands of the female goblins', and engage in duels with powerful spirits and overthrow them in the encounter. But there was also a lighter side to his activities. Like a veritable god of love, he enjoyed the company of the women of different nationalities, to wit, Andhra, Cola, Kerala, Siṁhala, Karṇāṭa, Surāṣṭra, Kamboja, Pallava

1 *Mahāvastu*, Vol. I, p 132, etc.

2 'सर्वसत्त्वेषु मैत्री' Book VIII, section 36. For the verse in question See Chap. XI. The idea of returning good for evil was advocated by Lao-tzu in ancient China: it was disapproved and modified by the more practical Confucius. Soothill: *The Three Religions of China*, pp. 33, 205.

and Kaliṅga. Sometimes he dallied with young women in pleasure gardens, and, on other occasions, indulged in water-sports, surrounded by beautiful women, in artificial lakes, perfumed and abounding in flowers, with emerald floors, crystal embankments, golden steps and islets of pearls. Although reckless and self-willed, and addicted to wine, hunting, and courtesans, Māradatta was free from dangers and calamities, and considered himself akin to the gods.

One day a Tantric teacher named Vīrabhairava told him that he would obtain a miraculous sword with which he could conquer the realm of the Vidyādharas, if only creatures of all kinds were sacrificed in the temple of the goddess Caṇḍamārī in his capital, and if at the same time he killed with his own hands a couple of human beings possessing all auspicious physical characteristics. Hearing this, Māradatta summoned the entire population to the temple of the dread goddess under the pretext of celebrating the Mahānavamī festival, although it was not the proper season for it, and himself repaired to the shrine and ordered the guards to fetch the required couple of human beings for the purpose of sacrifice.

The temple of Caṇḍamārī was a horrid place, frequented by the terrible female spirits known as the Mahāyoginīs, and a crowd of fanatical votaries, engaged in outrageous forms of self-torture. Certain devotees were burning Guggula incense on their heads; some, extremely ferocious, were burning their arteries, like lights; while others, exceedingly bold, were trying to please Śiva by drinking their own blood. In one corner, Kāpālikas were selling for a price pieces of flesh cut off from their own bodies,[1] and at another place certain fanatics were worshipping the Mothers by swinging from their intestines, extracted with their own hands. Elsewhere certain grim men were offering their own flesh as an oblation in the sacred fire. Such was the temple of Caṇḍamārī, terrifying to Death himself.

Meanwhile, the Jaina sage Sudatta, famous for his austerities, and unaffected by the rigours of the winter and the summer and the monsoon, was approaching Rājapura with a large number of disciples. Avoiding the city in view of the impending slaughter, and turning to the east, he saw a beautiful pleasure garden where young men were disporting themselves with beautiful damsels, adorned with floral ornaments. But he said to himself thus:

ब्रह्मस्तम्बनितम्बिनीरतिकथाप्रारम्भचन्द्रोदयाः, कामं कामरसावतारविषयव्यापारपुष्पाकराः ।
प्रायः प्राप्तसमाधिशुद्धमनसोऽप्येते प्रदेशाः क्षणात्, स्वान्तध्वान्तकृतो भवन्ति तदिह स्थातुं न युक्तं यतेः ॥ 1. 71.

1 See Chap. XIII.

"Such places, like the hours of moonrise, occasion gossip about the amours of the beautiful women of all the world. Like the spring, they provide free scope for mundane joys in which the sentiment of love prevails. Such places, as a rule, delude in a moment the heart even of one whose mind is purified by deep concentration. So it is not meet for an ascetic to remain here."

Going a few steps further, the sage saw a cremation ground with the funeral pyres fiercely burning; and the gruesome scene of desolation awakened diverse thoughts in his mind. He moved further away, and came to a hill not far from Rājapura. Here he fixed his camp and ordered the monks to beg for alms in the neighbouring villages.

Among the disciples of Sudatta were two young ascetics, a boy and a girl, brother and sister, named Abhayaruci and Abhayamati respectively, who, unlike the others, were directed to beg in the city. They were the twin children of Kusumāvalī, sister of Māradatta, and chief queen of Yaśomati, son of Yaśodhara Mahārāja, and had taken the monastic vow in early childhood and wandered with the sage Sudatta. On their way to the city they were encountered by the guards, who had been sent in quest of a couple of human victims for the impending sacrifice. Careful not to frighten the young persons, the guards told them in a friendly manner that a great teacher, who had been apprised of their arrival, was waiting to see them in the temple of Bhavānī. Their frightful appearance, however, betrayed their real purpose; and the boy and the girl, resigning themselves to their fate, followed them to the temple of the goddess.

The temple of Caṇḍamārī, which was known as Mahābhairava, presented a strange spectacle, being full of the victims of all kinds brought there for sacrifice, and held fast by armed guards resembling the attendants of Śiva. There could be seen sheep, buffaloes, camels, elephants and horses frightened by the half-brandished swords of the keepers. There were aquatic animals like crocodiles, alligators, frogs, crabs, tortoises, and Pāṭhīna fish, all trembling with fear at the sight of the spirits waiting to drink their blood. The keepers were at pains to hold together the numerous birds, scared by the movements of the circular sacrificial blade, and the other victims such as antelopes, tigers, lions, wolves, boars and apes. The mass slaughter of the animals was to take place after the king had sacrificed the first victims.

The young ascetics saw before them the grim figure of Māradatta. Standing on the floor of the temple, with drawn sword, he looked like a mountain in the middle of a river, with a serpent with raised hood on its slope. The king 'seemed to be aflame with his valour flaring up in his inner being, and burn everything with his angry look. He was extremely ferocious like a venomous serpent, and seemed to consume everything with the fury of his deportment. The aspect and character of the goddess were still more terrible.

दंष्ट्राकोटिनिविष्टदृष्टिकुटिलव्यालोकविस्फारितभ्रूभङ्गोद्भटभावभीषणमुखत्रस्यत्रिलोकीपति ।
लालाटोल्बणलोचनानलमिलज्ज्वालाकरालाम्बरप्लुष्टद्विष्टपुरत्रयं विजयते यस्याः प्रचण्डं वपुः ॥ 1. 136.

The young ascetics whose minds were bent on the highest beatitude were not in the least afraid of the danger before them, and never lost their balance and composure when ushered into the presence of the king in the grim setting of the temple of Caṇḍamārī. They encouraged each other to be firm and resolute, scorn death, and regard salvation as the highest object of human endeavour. Māradatta's heart softened at the sight of the tender boy and the girl; and although he could not recognise them to be his own nephew and niece, he felt the kindly influence of their presence, and said to himself (p. 156):

"कथं नामैतद्दर्शनादाचान्तामृतमिव नृशंसाशयबहलकालुष्यमपि मुहुः प्रशान्तं मे चेतः, चक्षुः पुनः कुलिशकीलितमिव कथं न विषयान्तरमवगाहते, चिरप्रवसितप्रणयिजनावलोकनादिव कथमयमात्मा परमन्तर्मोदते, चित्तमपि चेदं चिरायाचरितपरिचयमिव कथमतीवानन्दथुमन्थरम्, किं नु खलु तदेतन्न स्यान्मम भागिनेययमलम्, आचकर्ण चापरेद्युरेव रेवतकनामप्रसिद्धात् कुलवृद्धादेतस्य बालकाल एवाश्चर्यायं तपश्चर्यापर्यायम्, भवन्ति ह्रीमानीन्द्रियाण्यदृष्टपूर्वेष्वपि प्रियजनेषु प्रायेण प्रातस्तपनतेजांसीव रागोल्बणवयांसि ।"

"How is it that, at the sight of these two, my heart, though heavily tainted by cruel thoughts, has become absolutely calm, as if it had partaken of nectar; and my eyes turn to no other object, as if because riveted upon them with the force of thunder? Why is my soul in an ecstasy of joy, as if at the sight of beloved friends who have been long abroad? Why is my heart steeped in joy, as if it were long familiar with them? Are they not possibly my own nephew and niece? Only the other day I heard from one of the elders of my family, Revataka by name, the amazing story of their religious austerities even in childhood. At the sight of beloved persons, though never seen before, the senses become suffused with youth in an ecstasy of love, like the rays of the morning sun."

Observing the change in the attitude of the king, a bard recited two verses and appealed to him to lay aside his sword.

नासन्ना रिपवो न चापि भवतः कश्चिन्निदेशावशः श्रीरेषा तव देव या प्रणयिनी तस्यै न कोऽपीर्ष्यति ।
गाढं मुष्टिनिपीडनश्रमभरप्रोद्भ्रान्तधाराजलां मुञ्चस्वाहवकेलिदोःसहचरीं तत्खड्गयष्टिं भवान् ॥ 1. 148.

'No enemies are near at hand; none transgresses thy command. Sire, the goddess of prosperity is devoted to thee, and no one is jealous of her. Do thou therefore discard thy sword, the companion of thy arm in the sport of war: its blade doth emit its lustre under the pressure of thy powerful grip!"

Māradatta listened to the verses recited by the bard, and laid down his sword at the feet of the goddess. Then imposing silence on the noisy crowd of spectators with his raised hand, he offered a seat to the ascetic boy and the girl, who now recited, one after the other, a series of panegyrics in honour of the king in the conventional style of court poetry.

The purpose of the ascetic boy was to convert the king to the Jaina faith; but he thought it advisable to proceed slowly and cautiously in the matter, and reflected within himself (p. 176):

"रजस्तमोबहुलेषु च प्राणिषु प्रथमतरमेव धर्मोपदेशः करोति महतीं शिरःशूलव्यथाम्, भवति चावधीरणाय वक्तुः, तदेनमभ्यस्तरसप्रसरैरेव वचोभिरुल्लासयामि, नयवेदिनो हि वनगज इव स्वादुकफलप्रलोभनमविदिततत्त्वे पुंसि छन्दानुवर्तनमपि भवत्यायत्यामभिमतावाप्तये।"

"Preaching of religion at the very outset to persons, dominated by passion and ignorance, only gives them a severe headache, and brings the speaker into contempt. So I will cheer him with words enlivened by such sentiments as are familiar to him. A sagacious person ultimately obtains the desired result with regard to one who is ignorant of the truth, even by humouring him, just as one subdues a wild elephant by alluring him with delicious fruits."

The ascetic boy, followed by his companion, again praised the king in a series of lyrical verses; and the latter now questioned them about their native place and origin. The boy promised to satisfy the king's curiosity and addressed to him a benedictory verse.

Book II

The ascetic boy Abhayaruci, addressing Māradatta, now begins the story of his previous births, an autobiographical record, which incidentally throws interesting light on medieval court life in India.

There is a prosperous country named Avanti, hospitable with its fruit-trees, lotus-pools and vernal bowers.

मार्गोपान्तवनद्रुमावलिदलच्छायापनीतातपाः पूर्णाभ्यर्णसरोऽवतीर्णपवनव्याधूतदेहश्रमाः।
पुष्पैर्मन्दमुदः फलैर्भृतधियस्तोयैः कृतक्रीडनाः पान्था यत्र वहन्ति केलिकमलव्यालोलहारश्रियः॥ 2. 12.

"There the travellers wear beautiful unsteady wreaths of toy-lotus blossoms, and are protected from the sun by the shade of the leaves of the woodland trees alongside the roads. Their fatigue is removed by the breezes coming from the neighbouring pools of water, full to the brim; and delighted with the flowers, and contented with the fruits, they indulge in sports in the waters."

In that country was the famous city of Ujjayinī where reigned a great king named Yaśorgha. "The Mandara mountain gave him the quality of firmness, the ocean gave him depth, the god of love gave him beauty, Bṛhaspati gave him mastery of traditional lore, the Kalpa tree made him accessible to suppliants, the Earth gave him the virtue of forbearance, and the sky gave him dignity. The goddess of speech gave him eloquence, the goddess of wealth gave him success in the art of commanding, the Cintāmaṇi gem gave him intellectual power, and the family goddess gave him physical fitness, while the god of death gave him the power of bringing all men under his control. In this way, other deities, too, such as Varuṇa and Kubera, gave him their essential qualities, like ancestral wealth (p. 218)."

Candramati was the consort of Yaśorgha, and is no other than the ascetic girl Abhayamati in her present birth. Yaśodhara was the son of Yaśorgha and Candramati, and is no other than the ascetic boy himself in his present birth.[1] One day king Yaśorgha happened to see a growth of grey hair on his head, and immediately his thoughts turned to renunciation of worldly ties; and he revolved in his mind the twelve topics of meditation prescribed by the Jaina faith, commonly known as the Anuprekṣās. Thereafter the king gave orders for the marriage and coronation of his son Yaśodhara, and himself renounced the world and took the monastic vow under the direction of a learned sage named Saṁyamadhara. Pratāpavardhana, the chief of the army, with the help of an architect, made the requisite preparations for the coronation. A branch city with spacious avenues was built on the bank of the Siprā as well as a bejewelled pavilion, protected from the sun by beautiful curtains, and equipped with numerous gates, towers, altars and apartments. Round about were the camps of the princes who had come to witness the festival.

The selection of a suitable elephant and a horse for the new king was the next important item preliminary to the coronation. Under instructions from Pratāpavardhana, a committee of experts selected an elephant named Udayagiri from among those sent by the king of Kaliṅga as part of his annual tribute, and the chief keeper of the royal elephants communicated to Yaśodhara the findings of the experts, an elaborate report

1 What follows may be termed the STORY OF YAŚODHARA. Throughout the narrative Abhayaruci identifies himself with Yaśodhara and speaks in the first person. YAŚASTILAKA is another name of Abhayaruci.

on the characteristics of the chosen animal, full of technical details. Meanwhile, a bard named Karikalabha recited a number of verses in praise of elephants. Similarly, a notable white charger of Kamboja was selected by another committee of experts, whose report was likewise communicated to the Prince by the keeper of the royal stable, Śālihotra, after which a bard named Vājivinodamakaranda recited some verses in praise of horses.

The astrologers then reported to Yaśodhara that the coronation might follow the marriage rites, or the marriage rites the coronation, or if the time was favourable, both the functions might take place together; just as an idol could be installed after the building of a temple, or a temple built after the installation of an idol, or if one's resources permitted, the building and the installation could proceed together. The astrologers described in detail the time and hour technically favourable for both the coronation and the marriage rites.

Yaśodhara proceeded to the coronation pavilion where gold and silver pitchers, various herbs and Kuśa blades, and water from ocean-going rivers were kept ready. The royal throne, the white umbrella, and the fly-whisks added to the beauty of the structure, and the arms and the family treasures were carefully arranged near the idol of the tutelary goddess. Auspicious utterances were made by gay women, and crowds kept at a distance by trustworthy officers. Here, to the accompaniment of music, the sacred water was poured over Yaśodhara by a bevy of courtesans, while a bard named Jalakelivilāsa recited verses celebrating the ceremonial bath.

The ceremonial bath was followed by the marriage rites. Attended by the family priest, Yaśodhara worshipped the blazing Fire with butter mixed with curds, and curds mixed with boiled milk, while other priests offered oblations in the fire and uttered blessings with appropriate formulas. The marriage of Yaśodhara and Amṛtamati was celebrated in prose and verse by the bard Manojakuñjara.

Next came the ceremony of coronation, of which the principal feature was the presentation of the royal insignia to the prince, while relevant verses were uttered by the bards. The white umbrella was presented first, and Yaśodhara was asked to ascend the throne. Then followed the presentation of the royal turban and the sword.

After the coronation, Yaśodhara and his bride mounted the elephant Udayagiri, and the royal procession started from the bank of the Siprā on its way to the capital. Trustworthy followers, equipped with armour, and others armed with swords guarded the king, while attendants, wielding various weapons, cleared the road and removed inauspicious persons such as women in periods, eunuchs, men with deformities, Cāṇḍālas and the like. The elders recited congratulatory verses, and women sang to the flute and the lyre. The neighing of horses and the trumpeting of elephants mingled with the sound of drums.

The procession passed through the streets of the decorated city, the terraces and windows of the buildings being crowded with women eager to have a look at the royal pair. Meanwhile, in the palace, the aged lady superintendents of the royal household were stirring up the maids and attendants with admonitions and directions preparatory to the reception of the king. The frivolous maid Vasantikā was, for instance, asked to have done with the gamblers and make garlands of Bakula buds. Lavaṅgī was ordered not to join her playmates, but to get busy in making 'ornamental designs on the floor' (*raṅgavalli*).[1] Madanā was asked if she was sleeping even at that hour, and told to make preparations for the ceremonial waving of lights. Kuraṅgī was ordered to prepare cosmetics, and Mālatī to decorate the throne; while Kalahaṁsī was urged to get the betel-stand ready, and Madhukarī the flywhisks. The eunuch was advised to step aside, the Kirāta to remain indoors, the hunchback to do auspicious acts, the dwarf to indulge in sports, and the chamberlain to set about his business in right earnest; and even the tame birds were asked to put forth joyous notes. On arrival at the palace, bedecked with white flags, the king was welcomed by the bard Kīrtisāhāra with a poetical description of the noble edifice.

Book III

The narrative continues in the form of an autobiographical record and describes Yaśodhara's life as a king; but it is by no means a continuous account, being rather a series of episodes incidental to the routine of a medieval court. They are here enumerated in the order in which they occur in the text.

a) Yaśodhara is awakened from sleep by bards reciting verses descriptive of the morning scenery, after which the king goes to his durbar to dispense justice with the help of learned and impartial judges, while erudite scholars expound the law-books.

---

1 Called also *raṅgāvali* and *raṅgarekhā*, and made with coloured powder, also with camphor dust, and even with pulverized pearls and gems. Cf. अनल्पकर्पूरपरागपरिकल्पित-रङ्गावलिविधानम् Book III; रङ्ग(ा)वलिमणीन् Book IV; मण्ड्यन्तां मसृणमुक्ताफलक्षोदरङ्गावलीभिः प्राङ्गणानि *Nalacampū* Book VI; चूर्णितकर्पूररङ्गरेखाभाजि......विनोदमण्डपे Ibid. Book VII; मुक्ताफलरन्चित-तरङ्गरन्ध्वरङ्गरेखाराजिराजिताजिरम् Ibid.

b) The relative merits of fate and personal endeavour form the subject of an academical discussion in the council-chamber, in which the ministers maintain different points-of-view, and the deliberation ends with a discourse on the principles which ought to govern the relations of a king with other kings.

c) An arrogant message in verse summoning rival princes to accept the suzerainty of Yaśodhara is read out to the envoy in charge of the mission by the royal clerk under the king's direction.

d) The chief of the secret police reports to Yaśodhara that the spy Śaṅkhanaka has returned after gathering information about various people in the country and abroad. Yaśodhara summons the spy to his presence and spends some time, jesting with him. Questioned by the king about the absence of his former corpulence, Śaṅkhanaka replies that poor men like himself can hardly expect to have protuberant bellies. It is, of course, otherwise with men like Yaśodhara and the idle rich, who daily gorge themselves with luxurious food, such as rice white and clear like the glances of beautiful women; broths of the colour of gold; butter fragrant as the mouth of a beloved woman; curries charming as the graceful movements of nautch girls; well-cooked dishes, savoury like a beloved woman's lips; curds well-shaped and hard like the breasts of a young woman; milk sweet as the glances of one's beloved; sugared preparations of milk-rice, delicious as the first union with a newly-married bride; and water perfumed with camphor, refreshing as the mysteries of love!

Addressed by the king as 'the lord of the rams,' and asked whether he has had anything to eat, Śaṅkhanaka replies that he has been in a way entertained by a miserly, penniless and greedy fellow named Kiliñjaka, the righthand man of the Chief of the Secret Agents, Viśvāvasu, a native of the Deccan. The meal consisted of boiled rice grown stale, and full of husk and gravel; some rotten beans; a few drops of rancid Atasī oil; slices of half-cooked gourds and certain badly cooked vegetables as well as some raw fruits and overburnt brinjals thrown in. The meal ended with sour gruel mixed with plenty of mustards, and the beverage was some alkaline fluid with a taste like that of the water of a salt-mine. Śaṅkhanaka pitifully relates that he could eat nothing and remained hungry; and his only subsistence was a quantity of boiled Śyāmāka rice mixed with whey, which the miser's wife had the goodness to serve, unseen by her husband.

Yaśodhara once asked the spy for particulars about a minister named Pāmarodāra, entrusted with the administration of a province, and famous for his piety, wisdom and spotless character. This brings us to what may be termed a detailed report of the spy on the doings of the minister.

Śaṅkhanaka promises to speak the truth, but warns the king that what he is going to relate will to some extent put a slur upon him as well. It is the master's fault if his servants do as they like through a sense of their own power and influence.

The spy goes on to quote a large number of verses on the evil ways of ministers, composed by various poets by way of criticizing the king's failure to investigate the misdeeds of Pāmarodāra. The verses are mostly general in character, but a few directly attack the offending minister.

Śaṅkhanaka gives an idea of Pāmarodāra's administration by saying that the latter demands unpaid labour when the people are busy sowing, and collects taxes before the corn is ripe, while the harvest is spoilt by the unlicensed movements of the soldiery.

The revelation of the spy is a rude shock to Yaśodhara who is unwilling to believe his allegations, but Śaṅkhanaka replies that, in all matters beyond the range of direct perception, a king must depend upon spies as well as his own judgment, as if they were his eyes. He quotes a verse to the effect that when a king does not employ spies nor exercise his own judgment, his kingdom is at the mercy of his ministers, just as the milk belonging to a blind man becomes the prey of cats.

The low origin of Pāmarodāra is described as the cause of his overweening pride. His father was an oilman and mother a low-born woman, while his wife has had five husbands! The respect shown to such a man on account of his rank was bound to make him proud and overbearing. The spy then illustrates by various examples the danger to kings from elevating low-born persons to high positions in the state.

Describing Pāmarodāra as a monster of corruption, to wit, bribery and extortion, the spy tells Yaśodhara that the minister, after cheating him, as he did the former kings, will one day go over to some other king, like a trumpeter who serves any one employing him:

अपि त्वामतिवाह्यैष यथातीतान् महीपतीन् । तूरीवान्याश्रयस्थायी लञ्चालुञ्चानिशाचरः ॥ 3. 185.

Pāmarodāra's 'valour' is next described. He is brave and valiant in the presence of merchants, physicians, the weak and the deformed, but, like an ape, maintains a discreet silence in the presence of warriors and desperadoes:

वणिजि च भिषजि च शूरः शौण्डीरो दुर्बले च विकले च। कपिरिव निभृतस्तिष्ठति रणशौण्डे चण्डदण्डे च॥ 3. 190.

Speaking of the origin of villains, Śaṅkhanaka relates that, in days of yore, there came into being fourteen, or rather eighteen, groups of them. He declares that the king's minister combines in himself the vices of all the categories of villains enumerated by him.

After quoting some verses attributed to different poets, and containing reflections on Pāmarodāra's character, the spy represents him as an enemy of religion. He misappropriates money donated for the worship of the gods, and breaks or melts down valuable idols and replaces them by others of lesser value. Sometimes he would sell an idol, and, with the proceeds, celebrate a religious festival. It is also his habit to rob people by employing the methods of *thugs*, and give the money to worthy Brāhmanas. Besides, he confiscates villages and property endowed for the purpose of maintainiag the worship of the gods[1]:

देवद्रविणादाता देवद्रोहाच्च देवनिर्माता । अहह खरः खलु संप्रति धर्मपरः पामरोदारः ॥ 3. 227.

विक्रीय देवं विदधाति यात्रां तद्रालनादेष परांश्च देवान् ।

प्रमुष्य लोकं ठकवृत्तिभावैर्ददाति दानं द्विजपुंगवेभ्यः ॥ 3. 235.

अग्रहारग्रहः साक्षाद्देवभोगभुजंगमः । शिष्टविष्टपसंहारप्रलयानलमानसः ॥ 3. 236.

Crime and irreligion play their part in a more serious charge brought against the minister. The latter had employed five Cāṇḍālas, knowing them to be such, in his household for cooking and drawing water; but this violation of the caste-rules gave rise to a scandal, and one night he murdered them all while they were fast asleep. When it was suggested by some distinguished person that he should perform purificatary rites to expiate the crime, he ridiculed the idea by putting forward heterodox opinions, commonly associted with the Cārvākas:

रविरश्मिरत्नपावकमाहेयीवायवोऽन्त्यजैः स्पृष्टाः । न हि दुष्टास्तद्वदहं प्रकृतिशुचिर्मालमध्येऽपि ॥

आत्मा स्वभावशुद्धः कायः पुनरशुचिरेष च निसर्गात् । प्रायश्चित्तविधानं कस्येति विचिन्त्यतां जगति ॥

वर्णाश्रमजातिकुलस्थितिरेषा देव संवृतिर्नान्या । परमार्थतश्च नृपते को विप्रः कश्च चाण्डालः॥ 3. 232-4

"The rays of the sun, jewels, fire, cows and air are not polluted when touched by Cāṇḍālas. Similarly, being pure by nature, I could not be contaminated even in the midst of Cāṇḍālas. The soul is pure by nature, while the body is naturally impure. Think over the matter. To whom, in the world, does the process of purification apply? Sire, the regulation of castes and orders of society and birth and family is a matter of convention and nothing more. In reality, O king, there is neither Brāhmaṇa nor Cāṇḍāla."

Further charges against Pāmarodāra are contained in a verse which describes the harm done by the minister to certain scholars and poets. He destroyed the livelihood of a scholar named Tridaśa, and caused financial loss to (the poet) Kohala. He insulted the poet Gaṇapati, and brought about the ruin of (the scholar) Śaṁkara. He outraged the religious

1 See Chap. V.

susceptibilities of the scholar Kumuda, and compelled (the poet) Kekaṭi to leave the country.

The spy concludes by saying that the religious merit of a king and the joy and happiness of his friends and servants depend upon the removal of wicked ministers; but we are left in the dark about what steps, if any, were taken against Pāmarodāra.

e) Yaśodhara reviews his army on the eve of an expedition, and the different regiments recruited from various parts of India are described to him by the military commanders.[1]

f) The Sandhivigrahins or Secretaries for peace and war announce in verse the arrival of the envoys of various monarchs at the court of Yaśodhara. *g*) Utterances of the court jester. *h*) Yaśodhara discusses Arthaśāstra verses. *i*) Yaśodhara says that he sometimes witnessed exhibitions of dances in dancing halls in the company of connoisseurs of the art. We have in this connection a hymn to Sarasvatı forming part of the Pūrvaraṅga ceremony. *j*) Yaśodhara wounds the vanity of a tactless and self-conceited poet. *k*) Yaśodhara takes part in philosophical discussions. *l*) Stick in hand, Yaśodhara trains elephants; and while in training, the animal is addressed in prose and verse, the elaborate prose invocations ending with the words *he he hala divyasāmaja mātrāśataṁ tistha tistha.* The following is one of the verses containing the instructions of the trainer (3. 282):

गात्रैस्तिष्ठ समैः पुरोनखसमं हस्तं निधेहि क्षितौ दृष्टिं देहि कराग्रतः स्थिरमनाः कर्णौ गजाश्लेषय ।
वालं धारय वत्स यावदचिरान्मौन्यामहं कल्पये मात्राणां शतमास्स्व तावदचलस्त्वं योगिकल्पाकृतिः ॥

"Stand with thy limbs in equipoise. Place the trunk on the ground on a level with the claws. Fix thy look on the tip of the trunk. Tusker, hold thy ears motionless, with a steady mind. Move not the tail. Child, keep still, like a sage in meditation, for a space of time equal to a hundred *mātrās*, while I quickly devise (another) posture (for thee)."

m) Yaśodhara reports that once during an inspection of different categories of elephants, a military commander enumerated to him the various states of intoxication in which rutting elephants are found. It was also his custom to witness the sports of elephants from a special pavilion in the race-course, accompanied by experts conversant with the different methods of treating elephants during their period of frenzy. On such occasions keepers used to delight him by reciting verses in praise of the animals. Sometimes, again, he supervised the process of armouring the tusks of his war-elephants with protective sheaths of iron. *n*) Yaśodhara listens to a lecture on health and dietetics.

1 See Chap. IV.

o) Yaśodhara says that he passed the hours of noon in the hot summer days in amorous sports in his garden called Madanamadavinoda 'The Frenzied gaiety of love', and indulged in water-sports with his mistresses in the Hall of Mechanical Showers (*yantradhārāgṛha*), 'cooler than the Himālayas'. We find here 'watery beds' on the raised floor of pavilions erected on islets on the surface of pools for water-sports; vessels of gold, gems and silver containing scented water; ground lotus-beds watered by showers from 'mechanical clouds'; streams of water gushing from the mouths of the statues of various wild animals; currents of water issuing from the holes of artificial lotus-stalks made of moonstones; sprays emitted by the trunks of artificial elephants; fountains rising from the mouths of artificial alligators; and water let loose from the mouths of artificial monkeys placed in creepery recesses. What seems to be a statuary group represents water-deities quarrelling in the course of their water-sports, the sage Nārada dancing in joy at the sight, and the Seven Sages hurrying to the scene, the figures of the latter spouting a copious flood of water. We see also handfuls of water thrown up by the statues of nymphs, seated on the trunks of artificially made Celestial Trees, while water for bath comes pouring from the bosoms of mechanical 'cloud-puppets'. Another mechanical device is the decorated figure of a woman, which discharges streams of liquid sandal when pressed on different parts of the body (3. 375):

हस्ते स्पृष्टा नखान्तैः कुचकलशतटे चूचुकप्रक्रमेण वक्त्रे नेत्रान्तराभ्यां शिरसि कुवलयेनावतंसार्पितेन ।
श्रोण्यां काञ्चीगुणाग्रैस्त्रिवलिषु च पुनर्नाभिरन्ध्रेण धीरा यन्त्रस्त्री यत्र चित्रं विकिरति शिशिराश्चन्दनस्यन्दधाराः ॥

p) Once in the rainy season, while Yaśodhara was enjoying the beauty of the clouds from a palace on the slope of a pleasure hill, accompanied by his tributaries and warriors, the Sandhivigrahin ushered into his presence an envoy and a messenger from the court of Acala, the king of Pañcāla, with symbolic presents conveying a threat of war. This causes considerable excitement and commotion in the court of Yaśodhara, and ultimately a letter is sent to the king of Pañcāla, demanding submission.[1] *q*) At the advent of autumn, war is declared against the king of Pañcāla, and an expedition sent against him under the command of Vijayavardhana. Winter comes, and at the dead of night a spy arrives to announce to Yaśodhara the victory of his commander-in-chief and the defeat of Acala.

r) Spring arrives, and Yaśodhara participates in the festivities of the season. While the bards recite verses describing the glory of the spring and the vernal attire of the king and the gaily decorated swings in the royal household, Yaśodhara worships the god of love and celebrates the festival in his honour.

---

1) See Chap. V.

s) The spring festivities are followed by the Mahānavamī in the course of which the goddess Aparājitā is worshipped. Then comes the Festival of Light (*dīpotsava*). After this, Yaśodhara practises archery, while a bard recites verses in praise of his skill in shooting with bow and arrows. *t*) Moonrise and the gaiety of love.

Book IV

Yaśodhara now turns to his domestic affairs, and relates an episode of his married life, which is the pivotal point of the story.

One evening Yaśodhara visited his consort Amṛtamati to pass the night with her in her apartments on the top floor of a seven-storied palace About midnight the king, who was not quite asleep, noticed that the queen slipped away from his bed, and, furtively looking at him, discarded her ornaments, and, putting on the clothes of her maid, quickly went out of the chamber. The king's suspicion was aroused, and he at once followed her close on her heels, and saw her entering the hut of an elephant-driver named Aṣṭavaṅka, an ugly cripple, who was fast asleep in a miserable bed, resting his head on a pile of ropes. Amṛtamati sat down near him, and took hold of his hands, but he was furious at her delay in coming to him, and, dragging her by the hair with the left hand, gave her blows with the other. The queen was profuse in her apologies and confession of love, and swore by the goddess Kātyāyanī that she was thinking only of him even when in the company of Yaśodhara. The latter was observing the scene unseen, and was about to draw his sword to strike the guilty pair, but restrained himself, thinking of the resulting scandal and the grief the young prince Yaśomati would feel at the death of his mother. Yaśodhara then returned to the palace; and Amṛtamati, too, stealthily came and quietly lay down beside him as if nothing had happened.

Yaśodhara could hardly sleep, and was filled with anguish and disgust, and felt abhorrence not only for Amṛtamati but for women in general. He was puzzled at the queen's strange infatuation with a low-born elephant-driver, but remembered that the cripple was an expert singer, reputed to be able to make even withered trees put forth new shoots with the melody of his voice, and that songs had a ravishing effect upon women who were apt to be bewitched by a singer, however wretched or ugly he might be.

Yaśodhara continued to reflect on the conduct of Amṛtamati, and the more he brooded over it, the greater became his disgust for women and worldly pleasures; and he made up his mind to renounce the world, leaving the throne to his son Yaśomati. Next morning he appeared in court, and was there joined by his mother Candramati. A bard recited some verses which seemed to reflect the king's own thoughts at the moment (p. 84):

त्वं मन्दिरद्रविणदारतनूद्भवाद्यैस्तृष्णातमोभिरनुबन्धिभिरस्तबुद्धिः ।
क्लिश्नास्यहर्निशमिमं न तु चित्त वेत्सि दण्डं यमस्य निपतन्तमकाण्ड एव ॥

'Deluded by the ever-recurring darkness of desires such as those relating to home, wealth, wife and children, thou dost suffer day and night, o mind, but reckest not of the suddenly arriving scourge of Death!'

The bard recited another verse on the futility of trying to keep women under control; and it seemed to Yaśodhara as if the bard had come to know of the events of the previous night. Candramati also noticed the change in her son's demeanour, and had misgivings about his relations with Amṛtamati, who, she thought, had been given much more freedom than was good for a woman. She remembered also that a maid-servant had reported to her that her daughter-in-law was in the habit of casting affectionate glances at the elephant-driver. Nevertheless she asked Yaśodhara the reason of his dejection and restlessness, but he told her a concocted story about having seen a dream, in which he appeared to renounce the world and retire to the woods, after having put Prince Yaśomati on the throne. Candramati advised her son not to have any faith in dreams, and told him the story of the teacher, who had dreamt of his school as being full of sweetmeat balls, and, relying on his dream, invited the king to a luxurious repast! She further related that the maid-servant Vasantikā had just reported to her that in a dream seen by her she had turned into rice gruel, and was being eaten up by the Brāhmins invited to the *śrāddha* of her deceased mother! After thus demonstrating the fantastic character of dreams, Candramati suggested that, if Yaśodhara was really apprehensive of having seen an evil dream, he should seek a remedy by sacrificing all kinds of animals to the tutelary goddess, and perform the customary rites to counteract the evil.

Yaśodhara was shocked at the idea of sacrificing animals, and his heart revolted against the use of animal flesh in the worship of the gods. As he made no attempt to conceal his feeling of revulsion at the course of action suggested by his mother, the latter attributed his heterodox leanings to the insidious influence of the Jainas, and accused the courtiers of disloyalty and corruption for allowing her simple-minded son to associate with the Digambaras, who, like magicians, were so skilled in deluding the world! An animated discussion ensued between mother and son on such controversial topics as animal sacrifice and various other Brāhmanical tenets and practices, which were subjected to adverse criticism by Yaśodhara. While Candramati exhorted the latter to worship Śiva or Viṣṇu or the sun, he picked holes in the Brāhmanical religion, and sought to establish the antiquity and prestige of the Jaina faith by citing various texts in support of his thesis.

Candramati felt herself to be worsted in the argument, and ultimately persuaded Yaśodhara in the name of filial piety to accept a compromise, whereby he would sacrifice to the tutelary goddess a cock made out of flour, and partake of the offering, imagining it to be flesh. While orders were given to make such a cock and decorate the temple of the goddess, Amṛtamati came to know of the happenings at the court, and at once realised that the story of the dream was only a feint, and that she had been detected in her escapade of the previous night. She decided to act quickly, and made up her mind to strike Yaśodhara before he could strike her. Accordingly, she sent to him the minister Gaviṣṭhira with a message, declaring her willingness to sacrifice herself before the goddess in order to counteract the evil effect of the king's dream and ensure his safety. Furthermore, she begged that should the king decide to renounce the world, she might be permitted to accompany him to the woods, like the devoted wives of old, such as Sītā, Draupadī, Arundhatī and others. Meanwhile, she invited Yaśodhara and his mother to a banquet in her house after the worship of the goddess was over. Yaśodhara accepted the invitation and sent back the queen's minister.

The treachery and hypocrisy of Amṛtamati served only to deepen Yaśodhara's hatred of her, but still he decided to abide by his promise to eat in her house. Meanwhile, the sound of music accompanying the dance of courtesans in the streets announced to the citizens that Candramati and her retinue were on their way to the temple of Caṇḍikā, and Yaśodhara also started for the same place on the back of an elephant amidst a host of evil omens. Arriving at the temple, he severed the head of the cock made out of dough with a knife, according to the instructions of the priests, praying to the goddess that the offering might produce for him the same results as the actual killing of animals in sacrifices. He then sent the dough, from which the cock was fashioned, to the kitchen, as if it were the flesh of a real cock.

Next day, Yaśodhara, accompanied by his mother, son and daughter-in-law, dined in Amṛtamati's house. But she had mixed the food served out to her husband and mother-in-law with poison, which at once took effect and imperilled their lives. Physicians were sent for, and the inmates went about looking for medicine. Meanwhile, Amṛtamati cried aloud, and feigning to droop on Yaśodhara's bosom, strangled him to death. The mother also died.

Book V

The ascetic boy describes the rebirths of Yaśodhara and his mother Candramati after their tragic death.

a) Yaśodhara was reborn in a family of peacocks inhabiting a large tree in a well-watered valley to the north-east of the Suvela mountain. There he was caught by a hunter and presented to Yaśomati, who had ascended the throne after Yaśodhara's death. The peacock miraculously remembered the events of his former birth, and recognised the old scenes and associates as soon as he entered the city of Ujjayinī and saw the royal palace:

सैवेयं नगरी तदेव भवनं ता एव केलीधराः सैवैषा वनभूः स एव सरसीसारे विलासाचलः ।
सैवासौ वनिता स एव तनयस्ते चैव मे बान्धवाश्चित्रं केवलमेक एव हि कथं जातोऽहमन्याकृतिः ॥

Meanwhile, Candramati was reborn as a dog in a cowherd settlement in Karahāṭa, a country lying to the south of the Vindhya mountain. It so happened that the dog was also presented by the owner to the king, who was glad to receive so fine an animal for his hunting excursions.

One day the peacock wandered to the seventh floor of the royal palace, and discovered Amṛtamati dallying with her paramour, the cripple. The peacock became mad with rage and attacked the pair with his beak, wings and throat. The serving maids saw this, and raising a hue and cry, struck the bird with whatever they found ready to hand, caskets, canes, fans and shoes. The dog, too, came and rushed upon the bird and killed him. The king, who was playing a game of dice nearby, saw the dog attacking the peacock, and dealt a blow at the animal with the board, killing him outright.

b) In the next birth Yaśodhara became a stag and Candramati a serpent. On the very day of his birth, the former developed a taste for snake's flesh, and discovered the serpent while digging up ant-hills with his horns. He at once started to devour the reptile, but the hoarse sound emanating from his throat, gorged with snake's flesh, awakened a hyena asleep in a neighbouring grove of Kadamba trees, and the stag in his turn became the hyena's prey.

c) Yaśodhara was then reborn as a huge fish and Candramati as a crocodile in the Siprā. One day, during the water-sports of the women of Ujjayinī in the river, a maid of the royal household was seized by the crocodile, and Yaśomati, in anger, ordered the fishermen to destroy all dangerous animals in the river. They at once got into all kinds of fishing craft; and in the course of the operation, the crocodile was pierced in the throat by a spear, and the fish, too, caught in a net. Both of them were brought ashore, and ordered by the king to be made over to the cook of a hospice for Brāhmins. Everyday slices from their bodies were cooked and served to the inmates until they both expired after prolonged sufferings.

d) After this, Yaśodhara and Candramati were reborn as a pair of goats in a herd of sheep in the village of Kaṅkāhi, near Ujjayinī. One day, while the male goat (Yaśodhara) was covering the female, the herd got scared, and the leader of the rams attacked the billy-goat with his horns. The goat died, but was reborn in the womb of the she-goat. One day Yaśomati came there on a hunting expedition, accompanied by a large number of hunters; but unable to kill any game in the woods, he returned, angry and disgruntled, and while passing through the herd, hit the she-goat (Candramati) with an arrow, ripped open her belly, and found the kid in the womb.

The young goat was entrusted to the care of the chief cook, and passed a few months in the royal kitchen. There he saw Amṛtamati teaching the cooks how to roast meat, but she had been stricken with leprosy in consequence of her sins, and her loathsome body emitted so foul a smell that the attendants had to go about, covering their noses. Besides, the maids used to point at her mockingly, and tell passers-by how she had administered poison to her husband, the great and good Yaśodhara.

Meanwhile, the she-goat, after her death, was reborn as a buffalo in Kaliṅga. Purchased by the owner of a caravan, the animal came in course of time to Ujjayinī, and used to swim in the Siprā. One day he happened to meet Yaśomati's horse, and immediately made a murderous attack on the latter, owing to the innate mutual hostility of the two species of animals As a punishment, the buffalo was tortured to death under the orders of the king. The young goat, too, was killed for the table of Amṛtamati who was inordinately fond of meat.

e) Yaśodhara and his mother Candramati were next reborn as a cock and a hen, but there is a prelude to the story.

A sage named Manmathamathana was engaged in deep meditation on the Vijayārdha mountain. A Vidyādhara named Kandalavilāsa, who was going over the mountain in his aerial car, was ashamed to find that the motion of the vehicle was checked by the mystic force of the sage. By way of retaliation, the Vidyādhara decided to exercise his own magical powers to interrupt the meditation of the sage, and conjured up a scene of terror, by producing torrential rain, hail-stones and hurricanes, and a crowd of goblins, decked with serpents. Ratnaśikhaṇḍin, the king of the Vidyādharas, who was coming to worship the sage, was enraged to see the evil action of Kandalavilāsa, and cursed him, saying that as a result of his offence he would become a hangman in the city of Ujjayinī. Implored by the Vidyādhara for mercy, Ratnaśikhaṇḍin decreed that he would regain his former state and powers, if he ever had an opportunity of meeting the great sage Sudatta, and received religious instruction from him. Incidentally, the king of the Vidyādharas related that Sudatta was once the mighty king of Kaliṅga. One day a thief was produced before his court and accused of having murdered and robbed a barber in his sleep. The judges, consulted by the king, opined that the culprit should be subjected to various kinds of torture and maltreatment in such a way that he might expire in ten to twelve days. Hearing this verdict, Sudatta pondered over the dilemma of kings: if they served the cruel ends of justice, they were bound to incur sin; if they did not, there would be social disorder and imputation of cowardice. Failing to solve the problem of reconciling justice with mercy, Sudatta renounced his kingdom and became a Jaina monk.

In due course the Vidyādhara appeared in the role of a hangman in Ujjayinī, and Yaśodhara and Candramati were reborn as a cock and a hen in a Cāṇḍāla settlement in the vicinity of the city. One day the hangman who was known as Caṇḍakarman, happened to see the birds in the hands of a Cāṇḍāla boy, acquired them from him, and took them to Yaśomati. The latter was about to start for the garden of the Temple of the Thousand Spires, accompanied by a large retinue composed of boon companions and women of the harem, for the purpose of celebrating the worship of Makaradhvaja, the god of love. The king asked Caṇḍakarman to take the birds to the scene of the festival and give an exhibition of cock-fighting.

The temple garden was full of orange-coloured tents and rows of pavilions erected for the festival. Caṇḍakarman went there with the birds in a cage, accompanied by the augur Āsuri, a Bhāgavata; the astrologer Dhūmadhvaja, a Brāhmaṇa; the Śaiva Haraprabodha, an expert in divining underground treasure; and the Buddhist Sugatakīrti, a consummate cheat. There they saw Sudatta under an Aśoka tree, and severally expounded before the sage the philosophical tenets followed by each. Sudatta refuted all their doctrines, and explained that Ahiṁsā or non-injury to living creatures is the basis of Dharma, the sole means of attaining worldly happiness and final beatitude. In illustration of his point, he referred to the sufferings of the two birds in their various previous births as a result of obeying the law of violence, and briefly mentioned the circumstances of the death of Candramati and Yaśodhara and the succession of their births. Caṇḍakarman and his companions, chastened by the teachings of the sage, took the vow of Jaina laymen; and Caṇḍakarman himself, having fulfilled the conditions of the curse inflicted upon him, regained his former status and departed for the world of the Vidyādharas.

Meanwhile, Yaśomati was enjoying the company of his consort Kusumāvalī in a tent in the garden. Wishing to show her his skill in hitting invisible objects with arrows simply by hearing the sound, he shot an arrow which pierced and killed the cock and the hen left behind by Caṇḍakarman. Soon after, Kusumāvalī conceived, and the birds found their next birth in her womb. During the ante-natal period, the queen implored the king to proclaim protection from injury for all creatures and prohibit the sale of wine and the use of meat. Further, she expressed a keen desire to have teachings on kindness to living creatures expounded to her, and worship holy women noted for their self-control. The king was convinced that he was going to have a child with an innate leaning towards the Jaina religion, and tried his best to fulfil the wishes of the queen. In due course Kusumāvalī gave birth to a pair of twins, a boy and a girl, who were respectively called YAŚASTILAKA and Madanamati, better known as Abhayaruci and Abhayamati, on account of the mother's solicitude for *abhaya* or 'protection from injury' for all creatures during the period preceding their birth. The children grew up, and it was rumoured that Abhayaruci would soon be made crown-prince, and Abhayamati married to the king of Ahicchatra.

One day Yaśomati went hunting, and happened to see the sage Sudatta in the garden of the Temple of the Thousand Spires. Ajamāra, a boon companion of the king, suggested that the inauspicious sight of the naked ascetic augured ill for the hunt, and this annoyed the king and made him feel disgust for the sage. A merchant named Kalyāṇamitra, who had come to pay homage to Sudatta, entreated Yaśomati not to be disrespectful towards the saint, who was once the king of Kaliṅga and renounced his throne to practise religious austerities. The merchant and Yaśomati then both paid their respects to the sage, who greeted the king with a benedictory verse, and uttered a panegyric (p. 262):

स्वं धीरवैरिवनितानयनेन्दुकान्तनिष्यन्दसंपदि मतोऽसि नरेश राजा ।
आदित्य एव च भवान्नहिताङ्गनाङ्गनिस्तोकशोकतपनोपलदीपनेषु ॥

The affable conduct of the sage touched the king to the heart; and repenting that he should have ever harboured ill-feeling for so good a man, he resolved within himself to cut off his own head and lay it at the feet of the sage as an expiatory offering. The latter at once read Yaśomati's thoughts and forbade him to do such a thing. The miraculous power of the sage astonished the king, who now questioned him about the whereabouts of his departed parents and grand-parents after their death. The sage related that Yaśorgha, the king's grand-father, after practising religious austerities according to Jaina tenets, became after his death a divine sage, while his mother Amṛtamati went to the fifth hell in consequence of her sins. As for his father Yaśodhara and grand-mother Candramati, they had to undergo countless sufferings in many a birth owing to the sin of having sacrificed a cock made out of flour-paste in lieu of living animals, and have now been reborn as Yaśomati's own children, Abhayaruci and Abhayamati. The words of the sage made the king realise the enormity of his own sin on account of having killed numerous animals and partaken of their flesh since his early childhood. Disgusted with life, he made up his mind to follow the path of religion, but before renouncing the world, narrated to Abhayaruci and Abhayamati the story of their previous births.

The ascetic boy (Abhayaruci) now relates to Māradatta that he and his sister Abhayamati, on hearing their father's words, suddenly remembered their former births, and decided in their turn to renounce the world, although they were at that time only about eight years old. Owing to their tender age, they became religious apprentices under the sage Sudatta, and travelling in his company, had arrived at the outskirts of Ujjayinī, when they were arrested by Māradatta's men and produced before him.

The narrative of the ascetic boy visibly moved Māradatta, and the latter, having realised that worldly happiness is like a dream or a magic show, expressed his desire to enter the order as a novice. Abhayaruci advised him to see the sage Sudatta, and both set out to meet the great teacher.

Book VI

Sudatta, perceiving by his supernatural knowledge that Māradatta was coming to meet him, himself came to the king's court, and was received with honour. Abhayaruci introduced Māradatta to the sage as the son of king Caṇḍamahāsena, of the Yadu dynasty and the younger brother of his mother Kusumāvalī, and spoke about the prince's desire to be initiated into the religious life. Māradatta then questioned Sudatta about the nature of Dharma, the causes of salvation and the cycle of births, and the duties of householders and monks.

Sudatta now commences his great discourse on Jaina doctrines, starting with a brief résume and criticism of the theories of other schools, and an exposition of the doctrine of Samyaktva or right faith, that is, faith in the tenets of the Jaina religion. He then describes the four obstacles to the growth of Samyaktva as well as the four factors conducive to its growth, illustrating each of them with appropriate stories which occupy most of the

Chapter. This portion of the discourse ends with an enumeration of the different categories of Samyaktva and a brief difinition of Right knowledge and Right conduct, which with Samyaktva constitute the fundamental dogma of the Jaina faith.

Book VII

Continuing his discourse, Sudatta deals with certain essential features of Jaina religious practice, e. g., the prohibition of wine and meat. The stories are again prominent, and illustrate the evil results of drinking and flesh-eating and the merit of abstaining therefrom. Another series of stories illustrates in detail the bitter consequences of malevolence, theft or breach of trust, falsehood, lust and greed, abstention from which forms the keynote of the five primary vows known as Aṇuvratas.

Book VIII

The Jaina system of worship and devotions (*japa, dhyāna* etc.) is outlined in the remaining portion of Sudatta's elaborate discourse. His teachings have the desired effect, and Māradatta and the citizens are initiated into the Jaina religion. Abhayaruci and his sister, Māradatta who became an ascetic, the sage Sudatta, and Yaśomati, who had already renounced the world and taken the ascetic's vow, all became celestial beings after their death.

Somadeva sings the glory of the Jaina faith and acclaims the Goddess of Poetry at the end of the story (p. 418):

जयतु जगदानन्दस्पन्दी जिनोक्तिसुधारसस्तदनु जयतात् कामारामः सतां फलसंगमैः ।
जयतु कवितादेवी शश्वत्ततश्च यदाश्रयात् कृतिमतिरियं सूते सूक्तिं जगत्त्रयभूषणम् ॥

CHAPTER III

The Story of Yaśodhara and its Sources

It is not possible to determine how old the story of Yaśodhara is, but it is certain that it is much older than the 10th century. It is said that a *Yaśodharacarita* by Prabhañjana is mentioned in the unpublished Prākrit romance *Kuvalayamālā* composed by Uddyotanasūri in 777 A. D. at Jāvālipura, identified with Jhalor in Marwar[1]. This shows that the story must have been current long before the eighth century, and we find it

1 The relevant verse of *Kuvalayamālā* is cited by Pt. Nathuram Premi in his *Jaina Sāhitya aura Itihāsa*, p. 539. The verse describes Prabhañjana as a Rājarṣi, and says that he became famous in the country by virtue of his *Yaśodharacarita* which was probably composed in Prākrit. See also Introduction to Apabhraṁśa-kāvyatrayī (G. O. S.), p. 90, and Jinavijayaji Muni's articles on *Kuvalayamālā* in *Bhāratīya Vidyā*, Vol. II, Parts I and II.

incorporated also in Haribhadra's Prākrit romance *Samarāiccakahā*. Haribhadra was one of the *gurus* of Uddyotana, and his literary activity is assigned to the middle of the eighth century.

HARIBHADRA'S PRĀKRIT VERSION

The story of Yaśodhara occurs in the fourth *Bhava* of *Samarāiccakahā*[1] in connection with the story Dhana and Dhanaśrī. Haribhadra's version is a detailed narrative, and important as recording the story as it was current two hundred years before it was handled by Somadeva. Its most notable feature is the absence of the episode of Māradatta and the projected human sacrifice in the temple of Caṇḍamārī. It may be surmised, although we cannot be sure on the point, that this was a later addition to the story of Yaśodhara. Apart from this and certain other minor divergences, the Prākrit version does not materially differ from the story as we have it in Somadeva's *Yaśastilaka*. Another noteworthy feature is that the names of the principal characters differ in the earlier version, and the name Yaśodhara occurs only at the end. As in Somadeva's romance, the narrative is in the form of an autobiographical record, and related by the monk Yaśodhara to Dhana, the hero of the fourth *Bhava* of *Samarāiccakahā*. The story as told by Haribhadra may be summarized as follows.

Surendradatta was the son of Amaradatta, the king of Viśālā. Yaśodharā was his mother and Nayanāvalī his wife. Surendradatta succeeded his father on the throne, and on a certain occasion made up his mind to renounce the world on discovering a white hair on his head, saying that the messenger of Dharma had arrived. On the eve of his departure from worldly life, he passed a night with his consort Nayanāvalī in her mansion, and was surprised to see her slink away from his side at the dead of night. Fearing that she might have gone out to commit suicide in her grief at the impending separation from him, he followed her footsteps, sword in hand, and was amazed to see her in the embrace of a hunchback, who was employed as a watchman at the palace. The king, who observed them unseen, drew his sword and was about to kill the guilty pair, but restrained himself, thinking of his past affection for the queen, the follies of women, and the young prince Guṇadhara, his son. He then returned to bed and feigned to be asleep, and was shortly afterwards joined by the queen, who quietly laid herself to rest by his side.

Next night the king saw in a dream that he was sitting on a throne on the top of the palace, but was thrown to the ground by his mother Yaśodharā, speaking something that was contrary to his wishes. He went

1 Ed. by Jacobi, Bibliotheca Indica, No. 169, Calcutta 1926.

rolling to the seventh floor below, followed by his mother who also rolled down after him, but he managed somehow to rise and climb up the Mandara mountain. The dream was unpleasant in the beginning, but pleasant towards the end, and the king could not guess its significance; yet he remained indifferent, bent as he was on the conquest of the life beyond.

Next morning the king appeared in court, and his mother also joined him there, but he gave her a different version of the dream with a view to making her more readily consent to his idea of renouncing the world. He spoke of having dreamt that he had transferred the kingdom to prince Guṇadhara and become a monk and fallen from the top of the palace. The mother, who was an adept in the science of dreams, at once suggested that, in order to counteract the evil effect of the vision, he should assume the garb of a monk for a few days, and sacrifice different kinds of animals at the altar of the tutelary goddess. The king was horrified at the idea of killing animals, as he held *ahiṁsā* to be the basis of Dharma. The mother, however, persisted in her demand; and the king, finding it impossible to reconcile his religious principles with obedience to his mother, drew his sword to kill himself and asked her to worship the tutelary goddess with his blood. This led to a commotion among those present at the court, and the mother got frightened and deterred her son from the attempt. At this moment a cock crowed, and the old lady suggested that he should sacrifice before the goddess not a live cock, but one made out of paste. The king agreed and 'killed' with his sword an artificial cock in the shrine of the goddess, while the mother prayed for his longevity and health. The paste model was then roasted as if it were a real cock, and despite the objection of the king to the eating of meat, he was induced by his mother to partake of the sacrificial offering, on the plea that it was not real meat that he had been asked to eat.

Next day the young prince Guṇadhara was installed on the throne, and preparations were made for the king's departure as a religious mendicant. The queen Nayanāvalī now thought if she did not accompany the king and share in his ascetic life, it would cause a great scandal; on the other hand, if he died, it would be possible for her to abstain from *suttee* on the plea that she would have to act as regent during her son's minority. Accordingly she decided to murder her husband by poisoning.

The hour of dinner arrived, and Nayanāvalī took her meal with the king. She had, however, secretly mixed poison with a digestive pill, and gave it to her husband at the end of the meal after the withdrawal of the guards. The king, suspecting nothing, took the pill and retired to his chamber and at once showed symptoms of poisoning. A hue and cry was raised by the doorkeeper, and physicians were sent for; but Nayanāvalī, thinking that medical consultation would not be to her advantage, cried aloud and rushed upon the king, and weeping without tears, strangled him to death. Yaśodharā also died the same day as her son.

The births and rebirths which the king and his mother undergo after their death are practically same in both the versions of the story until we come to the birth of Abhayaruci and Abhayamati, these names being common to the two versions. In Haribhadra's version Abhayaruci and Adhayamati are not brought to the temple of Caṇḍamārī for sacrifice, but are reborn as gods in the Sahasrāra heaven. On the termination of their life in heaven, Abhayaruci is born as the son of Vinayandhara, the king of Ayodhyā, and named Yaśodhara; while Abhayamati is born as the daughter of Īśānasena, the king of Pāṭaliputra, and named Vinayamati. When they were grown up, Vinayamati was sent to Ayodhyā with a great retinue as *svayaṁvarā* bride for Yaśodhara, and preparations were at once made by the latter's father for the wedding of the young couple. But, on the day fixed for the marriage, while Yaśodhara was going in a procession on the back of a white elephant to the bride's quarters, he happened to see a monk begging at a merchant's house, which at once revived the memories of his previous births, and he fell into a swoon. The trouble was thought to be due to the toxic effect of betel, and sandal-water was sprinkled over the prince, who soon regained consciousness, opened his eyes, and felt a deep disgust for the world. Yaśodhara then asked his father to call the queens and the notables; and when they were all assembled in a road-side pavilion, he related the long story of his previous existences beginning with his birth as Surendradatta, king of Ujjain. He spoke about the terrible consequences of sin and his own indifference to the prison of the world, and finally declared his unwillingness to proceed with the marriage. The remonstrances of his father were of no avail; and a priest was at last sent to the bride to intimate to her the decision of the prince and his desire to renounce the world. The priest went on his mission and began to relate the story of Yaśodhara's previous birth, but as soon as the princess heard the names Surendradatta, Yaśodharā and Nayanāvalī, she in her turn remembered her past lives and fell into a swoon. Regaining consciousness, Vinayamati bewailed the strange way of the world, and declared that she was no other than Yaśodharā, the mother of Surendradatta. She, too, expressed her desire to renounce the world and asked for permission to do so.

Yaśodhara's father was deeply moved by these happenings, and became convinced of the illusory nature of life; and the queens, too, realised the transient character of the world resembling a troop of actors. Yaśodhara's younger brother Yaśovardhana was then installed on the throne; while Yaśodhara, his father, Vinayamati, the queens, and the chief notables renounced the world and took the monastic vow under a celebrated teacher named Indrabhūti. Thus ends the story of the monk Yaśodhara, as related by him to the merchant Dhana.

It will be seen that the sequel of Hraibhadra's version differs completely from that of the story as found in Somadeva's *Yaśastilaka*. A comparison of the two versions reveals certain other points of difference in the treatment of the story.

Firstly, Somadeva does not pay much attention to Amṛtamati after the murder of Yaśodhara beyond the fact that she appears occasionally in certain episodes, according to the requirements of the story; and we are told at the end that she went to hell. Haribhadra, on the other hand, gives a more detailed picture of the guilty woman after her crime. The prose description of Nayanāvalī's affliction with leprosy is followed by several verses, in which her former beauty is contrasted with the physical havoc wrought by her dreadful disease. This reminds us of certain verses in Somadeva's description of the cremation ground in which he contrasts the decaying corpse of a courtesan with her former beauty and charms.[1] Haribhadra says, for instance (p. 262):

वयणेण थणहरेणं चरणेहि य जीए निज्जिया आसि । सव्वविलयाणमहियं सोहा ससिकलसकमलाणं ॥
तीए च्चिय पेच्छ कहं अंगुलिविगमखयसंगमेहिं च । ते चेव हंदि देसा धणियं उव्वेवया जाया ॥

Haribhadra touches also the subject of Nayanāvalī's redemption. Abhayaruci begs the sage Sudatta to give her religious instruction and initiate her into the Jaina religion. The sage replies that she is beyond the scope of religious instruction, that her disease of Karma has been aggravated by her misdeeds acting like prohibited food, and that she is doomed to hell and unfit to receive the blessings of Jainism on account of her great delusion.[2]

Secondly, the motive of the murder is not the same in the two versions. Somadeva represents Amṛtamati as acting in self-defence[3], while in Haribhadra's version Nayanāvalī murders her husband just to avoid taking the monastic vow. This is a weak point in Haribhadra's treatment of the story. The delineation of Amṛtamati by Somadeva is far more complex, involving as it does a study of character and analysis of motives.

---

1 1. 95ff. See Chapter VII.

2 'अविसओ खु एसा धम्मकहाए। संतप्पिओ इमीए अकज्जायरणापच्छासेवणाए कम्मवाही, बुद्धं च तच्चपुढवीए परभवाउयं, अओ पावियव्वमवस्सं तीए नारयत्तणं, न पवज्जइ य एसा महामोहओ जिणधम्मरयणं ति।' p. 278.

3 See below.

Thirdly, there is hardly any theological bias in Haribhadra's version. Somadeva employs the dialogue between Yaśodhara and his mother in Book IV on the subject of animal sacrifice as a vehicle for launching a series of attacks on Hinduism; and the aim of the writer is also to establish the claim of Jainism to greater consideration than it seems to have received among his non-Jaina cantemporaries.[1] In Haribhadra's version, the mother, indeed, asks her son to sacrifice animals 'according to the Vedic procedure', but the latter confines himself to pointing out that a propitiatory rite is not compatible with the killing of animals, and that he best performs a *śāntikarma* who regards all living beings with the same consideration as himself (p. 246):

इहलोए परलोए य संतियम्मं अणुत्तरं तस्स । जह पेच्छइ अप्पाणं तह जो सव्वे सया जीवे ॥

As regards the mother's contention that it is permissible to commit sin for the sake of health, the son asserts that it is rather on account of the protection given to living creatures that a man acquires longevity, beauty and health, besides winning universal admiration in the life to come (p. 247):

दीहाउओ सुरूवो नीरोगो होइ अभयदाणेणं । जम्मंतरे वि जीवो सयलजणसलाहणिज्जो य ॥

The controversy between the king and his mother, in Haribhadra's version, comes to an end with a declaration by the former of the evils of flesh-eating and the benefits of abstention therefrom. Throughout the episode the Jaina standpoint is stressed, but attacks on the Brahmanical religion are entirely absent. It is obviously far from the intention of Haribhadra to make the mother and the son protagonists of two rival faiths, as is done by the author of *Yaśastilaka*.

Thoughts on the treachery of women are common to both the versions, and that of Haribhadra contains besides a condemnation of marriage in the episode of Yaśodhara and Vinayamati. Most of the birth stories generally agree in the two versions, but there are certain episodes which Haribhadra with his lucid and simple style treats in a more realistic fashion. The torture of the buffalo that killed the king's favourite horse, is, for example, repulsive enough in Somadeva,[2] but it is more so in the detailed picture of refined cruelty which Haribhadra presents before his readers. On the whole, the latter's version of the story of Yaśodhara is a well-balanced narrative with qualities which we miss in the intricate prose of Somadeva's *Yaśastilaka*.

---

1 See Chapter XIII.

2 Book V.

ANALOGOUS STORIES

Considered as a folk-tale, the story of Yaśodhara is of considerable interest, although the *motif* of adultery is quite common in folklore and legend. The chief interest centres round the character of Amṛtamati, who represents a type recognised very early in Indian literature. An ancient Buddhist text, for example, speaking of the seven kinds of wives, refers to the first variety as *vadhakā* 'murderess' and describes her thus:

पदुट्ठचित्ता अहितानुकंपिनी अञ्ञेसु रत्ता अतिमञ्ञते पतिं ।
धनेन कीतस्स वधाय उस्सुका या एवरूपा पुरिसस्स भारिया ॥
वधका च भारिया ति च सा पवुच्चति—Aṅguttaranikāya (Sattakanipāta LIX).

The *vadhakā* wife, we are told, is corrupt in mind and addicted to evil; she despises her husband and reserves her affection for others; she is bent on murder, and may be purchased by wealth. Guilty of adultery and murder, Amṛtamati is *vadhakā*, but the characteristic thing about her is that she, a woman of high rank, has a lowborn paramour.

The closest parallel to the tale of Yaśodhara and Amṛtamati is found in another Jaina story, that of Devarati and Raktā. Devarati was the king of Ayodhyā and Raktā his queen. It is said that Raktā had a paramour in the person of a lame gardener, and got rid of the king by murdering him and throwing the corpse into a river. The story of Devarati and Raktā seems to be as old as the Yaśodhara story, as it is referred to in *Jasaharacariu* (II. 10) of Puṣpadanta[1], who, like Somadeva, belongs to the tenth century. The story is mentioned also in *Anagāradharmāmṛta* (4. 77) of Āśādhara who wrote about the middle of the thirteenth century.[2]

Jaina narrative literature acquaints us with the existence of Amṛtamatis in middle-class society as well. In the story of the wealthy young merchant Dhana and his wife Dhanaśrī, occurring in the fourth Book of Haribhadra's *Samarāiccakahā*, Dhanaśrī has a paramour in the person of her servant Nandaka, administers poison to her husband, throws him overboard during a sea-voyage, and succeeds in killing him even after he has escaped and become a monk. In the similar story in the sixth Book of the same work, Lakṣmī, the wife of the young and wealthy

1 णइसंगमि दुट्ठइ वइरिणिए उवयारविमुक्कइ सइरिणिए ।
उज्झाहिउ देवरइ त्ति मूढु पंगुलणिमित्तु रत्ताइ छूढु ।

2 The story of Devarati is referred to in the Bhagavatī Ārādhanā of Śivārya; and it is given, in short or eleborately, in different Kathākośas. See Bṛhatkathākośa (ed. A. N. Upadhye, Bombay 1943), Intro. p. 76, Story No. 85, Notes p. 388.

merchant Dharaṇa, is no better than Dhanaśrī: she first prefers a robber and then a merchant from China to her husband whom she attempts to murder. Two other women Gopavatī and Vīravatī give evidence of similar propensities in stories which seem to be drawn from the life of the common people. Both the stories are mentioned in *Jasaharacariu* of Puṣpadanta (II. 9) and in *Anagāradharmāmṛta* of Āśādhara (op. cit.), who alludes to Raktā, Gopavatī and Vīravatī together, showing that the three women were notorious in Jaina tradition for their treachery and crimes.[1] It may be mentioned that *Daśakumāracarita* (Book VI) and *Kathāsaritsāgara* 10. 9 also contain a popular tale in which a woman attempts to murder her husband for the sake of a mutilated wretch, the two versions showing variations in details.

The placid complacence of Yaśodhara after the discovery of his consort's crime is a noteworthy feature of our story and seems to go beyond the ordinary limits of forbearance. But the pardoning of the guilty wife is a trait that fits in with the religious character of the story; and the *motif* occurs also in the ancient Buddhist tale in which the Bodhisattva, while a king, once pardoned his chief queen, who had been found guilty of a serious offence and taken to the place of execution.[2] Kings are not, however, always lenient in regard to their guilty wives; and Jaina tradition records stories of how some of them dealt with their adulterous queens. The *Vivāgasuya*, the eleventh Aṅga of the Jaina canon, records the story of the young priest Bahassaïdatta, who is surprised by king Udāyaṇa of Kosambī in the inner apartments of his palace in the queen's company, and in consequence arrested and sentenced to death. Another story occurs in Hemacandra's *Pariśiṣṭaparvan* (2. 547 ff.), in which one of the wives of a king pays a nocturnal visit to an elephant-driver, as in the story of Yaśodhara, but is discovered; and a dreadful sentence is passed on the guilty pair.

Popularity of the Story of Yaśodhara

The popularity of the story of Yaśodhara with Jaina writers seems to date from the tenth century. Puṣpadanta who told the story in Apabhraṁśa verse in his *Jasaharacariu* in four Cantos was a contemporary of Somadeva, the author of *Yaśastilaka*. The story was next narrated in

1 रक्ता देवरतिं सरित्यवनिपं रक्ताऽक्षिपत् पङ्कुके, कान्तं गोपवती द्रवन्तमवधीच्छित्त्वा सपत्नीशिरः। शूलस्थेन मलिम्लुचेन दलितं स्वोष्ठं किलाख्यत् पतिच्छिन्नं वीरवतीति चिन्त्यमबलावृत्तं सुवृत्तैः सदा ॥ IV. 77. See also Bhagavatī Ārādhanā, 949–51, and Bṛhatkathākośa, story Nos. 85–87.

2 'इमिना एव च भगवता राज्ञा सता अग्रमहिष्याः महापराधापराद्धाया वध्यस्थानप्राप्तायाः याचिन्त्या अभयं दत्तं' Mahāvastu, Vol. I, p. 132.

Sanskrit verse by Vādirāja who wrote a *Yaśodharacarita* in four Cantos. Vādirāja is said to have been a pupil of Somadeva[1] and wrote his *Pārśvanāthacarita*, a Sanskrit Kāvya, in twelve Cantos, according to his own statement, in Śaka 947 or 1025 A. D. After Vādirāja may be mentioned Vāsavasena, who wrote a *Yaśodharacarita* in Sanskrit in eight Cantos, and Vatsarāja who also composed a poem on the subject. Vāsavasena and Vatsarāja are earlier than the fourteenth century, as the poet Gandharva who made certain additions to the *Jasaharacariu* of Puṣpadanta in 1308 A. D. refers to both of them as his sources for certain episodes in the story of Yaśodhara.[2] Vāsavasena, too, mentions in his work two earlier poets who handled the story of Yaśodhara, viz., Prabhañjana and Hariṣeṇa[3]. Prabhañjana, as we have seen, is earlier than the eighth century, and one of the earliest writers who narrated the tale of Yaśodhara. We know nothing about Hariṣeṇa's work, but he may perhaps be identified with Hariṣeṇa who wrote his *Kathākośa* in Sanskrit verse in 931 A. D. at Wadhwan in Kathiawar.[4] There is however more than one Hariṣeṇa, and the identification must await further evidence.

The widespread popularity of the tragic story of Yaśodhara is shown by the fact that numerous other poems dealing with the subject were composed in the succeeding centuries not only in Sanskrit but in Old Gujarati, Old Hindi, Tamil and Kannaḍa; while a prose version of the story in Sanskrit was produced by Kṣamākalyāṇa as late as the 18th century. A comprehensive list of these works has been compiled by Dr. Vaidya in the Introduction to his edition of Puṣpadanta's *Jasaharacariu*.

The Character of Amṛtamati

Somadeva's *Yaśastilaka*, composed in prose and verse, is entirely different from the other versions of the story of Yaśodhara inasmuch as it is also a great socio-political study and a learned compendium of philosophy, theology and religion. Even in the treatment of the story proper, Somadeva is not without some originality, following as he does his own method in dealing with some of the principal episodes. But his most important contribution to the narrative is his portrayal of Amṛtamati's character. He, of course, regards her as a sinner, but takes care to analyse her motives, explain her conduct, and exhibit her point of view. Thus Yaśodhara,

---

1 See Chapter I.

2 Vaidya: Introduction to *Jasaharacariu*, p. 18.

3 Ibid., p. 25.

4 Now edited by Dr. A. N. Upadhye (Singhī Jaina Series, 17, Bombay 1943) who kindly supplied these details. See Intro. pp. 117-18.

in the course of his long and bitter tirade against women, tries to discover the cause of the queen's strange infatuation with the deformed elephant-driver, and attributes it to his melodious singing. He says: "The preceptors declare singing to be the greatest of the arts. A well-sung song makes even a man, wretched by nature, the resort of the eyes of young women as of their minds. A singer, though ugly in appearance, is more beautiful in the eyes of women than even the god of love. Even women, not easily visible, are deeply attracted by song, as if dragged by a halter. Singing done by expert singers does away with the obstinate pride of proud women, and produces in them an anguish that cannot be remedied by others."[1] This at least partially explains the queen's undignified passion for a paramour of humble station.

Further, it is apparent from the words put in the mouth of Amṛtamati, after the discovery of her infidelity, that her married life was an unhappy one, and she had come to Yaśodhara as an unwilling bride. This seems to be the meaning of her assertion that Yaśodhara and others like him can only be the masters of the bodies of their wives, sold to them by their parents in the presence of the gods, the Brāhmaṇas, and the Fire, but not of their hearts: the lord of one's heart is he who is the object of one's undivided love, 'the haven of confidence.'[2] Less cogent is her appeal to the example of certain wives of legend, who, it is hinted, acted like her, the reference being to the relations of Gaṅgā with Śiva, of Rādhā with Kṛṣṇa, of Tārā, wife of Bṛhaspati, with the Moon-god, and of Tārā, wife of Sugrīva, with Vāli. The appeal to antiquity reminds one of that in the nurse's speech in the *Hippolytus* of Euripides (vv. 451 *sq.*), and does not improve Amṛtamati's case; it is rather an admission of her moral weakness. It is, however, certain that Amṛtamati was thoroughly disgusted with her married life with Yaśodhara. As she says,[3] there is nothing in the world which men of fortitude cannot do except the reawakening of love in a heart filled with disgust: who can, indeed, unite two hearts that are like two iron balls, the one hot and the other

---

1 'गृणन्ति च कलासु गीतस्यैव परं महिमानमुपाध्यायाः। सुप्रयुक्तं हि गीतं स्वभावदुर्भगमपि नरं करोति युवतीनां नयनमनोविश्रामस्थानम्। भवति कुरूपोऽपि गायनः कामदेवादपि कामिनीनां प्रियदर्शनः। गानेन हि दुर्दर्शा अपि योषितः पाशेनाकृष्टा इव सुतरां संगच्छन्ते। कुशलैः कृतप्रयोगं हि गेयमपनीय मानग्रहमपरमेव कंचिदनन्यजनसाध्यमाधिमुत्पादयति मनस्विनीनाम्।' Book IV, p. 55. The idea goes as far back as the Yajurveda. Cf. Taittirīyasaṁhitā VI. 1. 6: गायन्तं स्त्रियः कामयन्ते.

2 'कुलवधूनां ह्ययमन्यश्च देवद्विजाग्निसमक्षं मातापितृविक्रीतस्य कायस्यैव भर्तीश्वरः न मनसः। तस्य पुनः स एव स्वामी यत्रायमसाधारणः प्रवर्तते परं विश्रम्भविश्रमाश्रयः प्रणयः।' Ibid., p. 141.

3 'महासत्त्वेषु हि जगति न किंचिद्दुष्करमस्ति अन्यत्र विरक्ते चेतसि रागप्रत्यानयनात्। को हि नामायःपिण्ड इव तप्तातप्ते मनसी संधातुमर्हति।' Ibid., p. 142.

cold? Further, she accuses Yaśodhara of jealousy when she says that only an intelligent person, free from jealousy, can be happy with women; one who behaves otherwise runs the risk of losing his life, like a worshipper of the evil spirit Kṛtyā, or at least incurs a woman's hatred.[1] Amṛtamati's plea for reciprocity of love as an essential condition of conjugal harmony cannot, of course, absolve her from moral responsibility as wife and mother. But she says enough to convince us of the misery of her married life, and we may feel inclined to look upon her failure as a wife as a domestic tragedy rather than as an inveterate case of moral depravity.

The next episode, the murder of Yaśodhara, can be regarded only as a premeditated crime without any redeeming feature; but even here, as already pointed out, Somadeva represents Amṛtamati as acting in self-defence. She regards the story of Yaśodhara's dream and his plan to renounce the world as a feint[2], that is, as a device to take her unawares, and resolves to act quickly: 'Before he lets loose the poison of his wrath on me, I will let it loose on him!"[3] She opines that a person who is honest in his dealings with cheats and villains, the wily and the selfish, and those who lack in self-respect, is a fool and becomes the dupe of all.[4] So she decides to follow 'the policy of deceit for deceit' (*śaṭhaprati-śaṭhanyāya*), and pay Yaśodhara in his own coin. The plea of self-defence is, however, hardly convincing, as there is nothing in Yaśodhara's attitude to justify any suspicion of revengeful action on his part. Somadeva is well aware of this, and does not, in fact, try to palliate Amṛtamati's crime. But he depicts her as a weakling who cannot help her instincts, and lacks the moral strength to resist their power over her life. He analyses her motives and examines her conduct from different points of view, and seeks to preserve to some extent our sympathy for the guilty woman. In the succeeding portion of the story Somadeva does not add anything important to the traditional presentation of Amṛtamati's career, and seems rather to lose interest in her and lets her appear according to the exigencies of the story. But, on the whole, Amṛtamati in Somadeva's romance is a remarkable piece of characterization showing originality and skill, and reveals an aspect of the author's genius all but obscured by the wealth of scholarship and learning exhibited in the work.

---

1 'किंच परमकुहन एव पुरंध्रीषु बुद्धिमानवाप्नोति स्वश्रेयसम् । अन्यथा कृत्याराधक इव ध्रुवं पञ्चजनः पञ्चतामश्नुवीत । भवेद्वावश्यमक्षिगतः ।' p. 142. Śrutasāgara says परं केवलमकुहन एव ईर्ष्यारहित एव । Ibid.

2 'न खलु मे यामिनीसमाचरितसाहसादस्य वसुमतीपतेरपरमेवंविधकूटकपटानुष्ठानमस्ति ।' Ibid. p. 141.

3 'तदेष यावन्न मयि रोषविषं वर्षति तावदहमेवास्य तद्वर्षामि ।' Ibid., p. 142.

4 धूर्तेषु मायाविषु दुर्जनेषु स्वार्थैकनिष्ठेषु विमानितेषु । वर्तेत यः साधुतया स लोके प्रतार्यते मुग्धमतिर्न केन ॥ Ibid., p. 145.

CHAPTER IV

Yaśastilaka as a Prose Romance

The history of Sanskrit prose romances shows a lamentable gap after the masterpieces of Bāṇa and Subandhu; and when prose romances reappear two centuries later, they bear the impress of new influences and point to a somewhat different literary environment. In the first place, most of the Sanskrit prose romances of the tenth and eleventh centuries were composed by Jaina writers, who were eager to expound and glorify their religion, and may be said to have introduced a religious element into this branch of literary composition. In the second place, there is an increased tendency to mix prose with verse, and the two earliest extant Campūs were, in fact, composed in the tenth century.

Somadeva's *Yaśastilaka* owes a good deal to Bāṇa and Subandhu in the matter of style and the treatment of conventional topics, but it differs from all other Sanskrit prose romances in so many respects that it may be said to stand in a class by itself. Apart from its special characteristics as a prose narrative, *Yaśastilaka* combines features which bring it into relation with diverse branches of Sanskrit literature. It is not only a Jaina romance in prose and verse but a learned compendium of Jaina and non-Jaina philosophical and religious doctrines, a manual of statecraft, and a great repository of Kāvya poetry, ancient tales, citations and references, and numerous rare words of lexical interest. Somadeva's *Yaśastilaka* is a work of massive scholarship enlivened by occasional flashes of literary genius and poetic feeling.

Among his predecessors in the field of prose romances, Somadeva mentions Bāṇa in *Yaśastilaka*, Book IV, and shows some acquaintance with his works, especially the *Kādambarī*. He clearly refers to the deprecation of the life of the Śabara hunters uttered by the parrot in Bāṇa's romance, and quotes a phrase from the passage in question.[1] Somadeva's claim that the religion of the Arhat enjoys great renown in the works of Bāṇa among others should, however, be taken with a grain of salt. Bāṇa, indeed, refers to Jaina mendicants carrying peacock feathers in *Kādambarī* as well as *Harṣacarita*[2], and in the former work describes Vilāsavatī as respectfully offering food to naked Jaina mendicants called Siddhas and asking them questions about the future.[3] The Jinadharma, compassionate to living

1 'आहारः साधुजननिन्दितो मधुमांसादिरिति कथं चेदं मृगयोपयोगानन्दं शबरवृन्दं निन्दतावादि बाणेन ।'.

2 'कैश्चित् क्षपणकैरिव मयूरपिच्छधारिभिः' *Kādambarī*; 'शिक्षितक्षपणकवृत्तय इव वनमयूरपिच्छचंयानुचिन्वन्तः' *Harṣacarita*, Book II.

3 'स्वयमुपहृतपिण्डपात्रान् भक्तिप्रवणेन मनसा सिद्धादेशान् नग्नक्षपणकान् पप्रच्छ ।'.

creatures, is mentioned in *Kādambarī*.[1] But the sight of a naked and unwashed Jaina mendicant with his peacock feathers is mentioned among certain evil omens enumerated in *Harṣacarita*, Book V.[2]

Somadeva is not only influenced by Bāṇa and Subandhu in the conventional descriptions such as those of the seasons, morning and evening scenery, mountains, kings and countries etc., but also borrows an idea here and there from the earlier writers. The description of the different categories of villains and their origin in *Yaśastilaka*, Book III, is obviously suggested by that of the fourteen families of nymphs and their origin in *Kādambarī*. The famous advice of Śukanāsa to Candrāpīḍa has its counterpart in *Yaśasatilaka*, Book II. The conglomeration of picturesque names of women in brief sentences occurring towards the end of the same Book is a device already found in *Kādambarī*, *Harṣacarita* and *Vāsavadattā*. The enumeration of evil omens in *Yaśastilaka*, Book IV, may be compared with the similar lists in *Harṣacarita*, Books V and VI. Dust in Kāvya literature is not as trifling a thing as one might suppose, and the description of the battle scene and the resulting dust in *Yaśastilaka*, Book III, is forestalled in *Vāsavadattā*; while Bāṇa in *Kādambarī* pays attention to the dust raised by Candrāpīḍa's expedition. A brief description of a cremation ground occurs in Subandhu's work; but the similar account in *Yaśastilaka*, Book I, is in verse and far more elaborate and serves a different purpose.

These and other similarities between *Yaśastilaka* and the romances of Bāṇa and Subandhu would appear to be superficial in face of the essential differences in style, outlook, and the character of the respective stories. The style of Bāṇa and Subandhu, though by no means simple, is simpler than that of Somadeva's prose; and the Jaina narrative shows, on the whole, a greater elaboration of details than is found in *Kādambarī* and *Vāsavadattā*. It is noteworthy that Somadeva has chosen to employ the involved style even in the moral and religious tales narrated in *Yaśastilaka*, Books VI and VII; and one of the factors which makes his prose less attractive than that of Bāṇa and Subandhu is the use of rare and obsolete words, which, though valuable from a philological point of view, makes *Yaśastilaka* a far more difficult work than the earlier prose romances. Many of the descriptive passages are undoubtedly more complicated and artificial than those of *Kādambarī*. One may contrast, for example, the portrait of Jābāli with that of Sudatta in *Yaśastilaka*, Book I; the picture of the Śālmali tree in the Vindhya forest in Bāṇa's

1 'जिनधर्मेणेव जीवानुकम्पिना'.

2 'कज्जलमय इव बहुदिवससमुपचितबहलमलपटलमलिनितततनुरभिमुखमाजगाम शिखिपिच्छलाञ्छनो नग्नाटकः।'.

romance with the unwieldy description of the huge tree in the valley of the Suvela mountain towards the beginning of *Yaśastilaka*, Book V; and Bāṇa's beautiful portrayal of the trees around the Śiva temple where Mahāśvetā worshipped with the Jaina author's laboured description of the pleasure garden in *Yaśastilaka*, Book I. Similarly, the enumeration of different varieties of plants illustrated in Subandhu's description of the sea-shore in *Vāsavadattā* is overdone in Somadeva's picture of the great forest in *Yaśastilaka*, Book V. It may be said, on the whole, that in natural descriptions Somadeva is far excelled by Bāṇa and Subandhu; and there is nothing in *Yaśastilaka* which will bear comparision with the serene picture of the rule of concord and harmony governing the life of animals and human beings in Jābāli's hermitage, as described in Bāṇa's *Kādambarī*. Lengthy and detailed descriptions of female beauty, so wearisome to readers of Sanskrit prose romances, are practically absent in *Yaśastilaka* owing to the very nature of the subject-matter.

More important than the question of style is the fundamental difference between the story of Yaśodhara and the romantic tales of Kādambarī and Vāsavadattā. The salient feature of the story of Yaśodhara is that it is a realistic tale based on a domestic tragedy, even an unpleasant incident of domestic life, around which is woven a story of moral and religious edification. It was a daring experiment on the part of Somadeva to have composed a romance, of which adultery and murder were two prominent features, in the grand style of Bāṇa and Subandhu; and *Yaśastilaka*, is, as a matter of fact, the only considerable Sanskrit prose romance which deals with tragic incidents of conjugal life, eschewing romantic love in favour of grim realities and the workings of fate. From this standpoint *Yaśastilaka* may be described as a realistic novel, and the note of realism is accentuated by the complete absence of the miraculous except in a few minor episodes independent of the main story. This appears to be a noteworthy characteristic of Somadeva's work when we remember the part played by the miraculous in all other Sanskrit prose romances from *Kādambarī* to *Gadyacintāmaṇi*.

Two other characteristic features of *Yaśastilaka* may be emphasized: it is a vivid picture of certain aspects of contemporary life and society as well as a great religious romance; and in both respects it differs widely not only from *Kādambarī* and *Vāsavadattā* but from the remaining Sanskrit prose romances. These points have been dealt with in subsequent chapters, and we may here attempt a somewhat detailed treatment of Somadeva's prose as far as it is represented in his *Yaśastilaka*.

As is usual in Sanskrit prose romances, long-winding descriptions preponderate in *Yaśastilaka* to the detriment of the narrative, and are often complicated by conglomerations of intricate and loosely constructed compounds of considerable length. There is, however, no doubt that Somadeva has at his command a rich variety of details, and shows an intimate knowledge of diverse phases of the life of his times. The conventional descriptions are mostly involved and artificial, but there are others simpler and more effective, mostly dealing with topics peculiar to the romance, and by no means frequent in Kāvya literature. We may start, for example, with the picture of the dread goddess Caṇḍamārī in Book I (p. 150):

यस्याः कपालमालाः शिखण्डमण्डनानि, शवशिशवः श्रवणावतंसाः, प्रमितप्रकोष्ठाः कर्णकुण्डलानि, परेतकीकसमणयः कण्ठभूषणानि, परासुनलरसाः शरीरवर्णकानि, गतजीवितकरङ्काः करक्रीडाकमलानि, सीधुसिन्धवः संध्याचमनकुल्याः, पितृवनानि विहारभूमयः, चिताभसितानि चन्द्रकवलाः, चण्डातकमार्द्रचर्माणि, सारसनं मृतकान्त्रच्छेदाः, प्रनर्तनप्रदेशः संस्थितोरःस्थलानि, कन्दुकविनोदः स्तभोत्तमाङ्गैः, जलकेलयः शोणितदीर्घिकाभिः, निशावलिप्रदीपाः श्मशानकृशानुकीलाभिः, प्रत्यवसानोपकरणानि नरशिरःकरोटिभिः, महान्ति दोहदानि च सर्वसत्त्वोपहारेण ।

"Garlands of human skulls are her head-ornament. Corpses of children are her ear-ornament. The elbows of dead men are her earrings. Balls made from the bones of dead bodies form her necklaces. The oozings from the leg-bones of corpses serve as her cosmetics. Skeletons play the part of toy-lotuses in her hands. Rivers of wine are the streams wherein she performs her evening ablutions. Charnel-fields are her pleasure grounds. The ashes of funeral pyres are her face-ornament. Raw hides constitute her robe. The intestines of dead bodies form her girdle. The bosoms of dead men are her dancing floor. She plays with the heads of goats as with balls. Her water-sports take place in lakes of blood. The blazing fires of cremation-grounds serve as her votive lamps at night. Human skulls are the vessels she eats from. Her greatest pleasure is when living creatures of all kinds are sacrificed at her altar."

The description of the shrine of the goddess, the Mahābhairava temple, gives a good idea of a contemporary cult of savage character, and is perhaps the most elaborate picture of its kind in Sanskrit literature; and, although in this respect Somadeva is anticipated by Bāṇa in his description of the temple of Caṇḍikā in *Kādambarī*, and by Haribhadra in his verse description of the temple of Kādambarī or Caṇḍikā in *Samarāiccakahā* (Book VI), the corresponding account in *Yaśastilaka* preserves interesting details not recorded elsewhere.[1] The delineation of the surging crowd of the Mahāyoginīs in the temple, for example, although fantastic to some extent, graphically presents the grim aspect of these monstrous deities, "extremely ferocious and long-limbed like the Nights of universal destruction". "They were emerging with fury from the surface of the sky,

---

1 See Chap. II.

from the earth, from the depths of the nether regions, and from all the corners of the sky, like darkness at night." "The banners of the Sun's aerial car were singed by the flames issuing from the eye on their foreheads, being fanned by the gaspings of the hapless serpents, ruthlessly pressed in the tangled masses of their hair; while the Sun's rays were obstructed by the huge vultures hovering about the gruesome skulls decorating their heads; and the ornamental designs of blood painted on their cheeks were being lapped up by the snakes adorning their ears."[1]

A notable picture is the dramatic appearance of the spy of Yaśodhara in the streets of Ujjain with his grotesque dress and clamorous retinue (Chap. III, p. 397):

कृतकार्धचन्द्रचुम्बितचन्द्रकापीडविडम्बितमुण्डमण्डलः, तूलिनीकुसुमकुड्मलाकृतिजातुषोत्कर्षितकर्णकुण्डलः, कार्मणानेकजटाजातिजटितकण्ठिकावगुण्ठनजठरकण्ठनालः, चिरचेलचीरीचर्चितविचित्राप्रपदीनप्रालम्बजालः, कुवलीफलस्थूलत्रापुषमणिविनिर्मिताङ्गदसंपादितप्रकाण्डमण्डनः, कूर्परपर्यन्तप्रकोष्ठप्रकल्पितगवलवलयावरुण्डनः, काकनन्तिकाफलमालोपरचितवैकक्षकवक्षःस्थलः, कठोरकमठपृष्ठाष्ठीलस्थपुटपाणितलः, 'पटच्चरपर्याणगोणीगुह्यापिहितमेहनः, पुराणतरमन्दीरमेखलालंकृतनितम्बनिवेशनः, कंसहंसकरसितवाचालचरणचारचातुरीक्षोभितवीथीजनमनस्कारः, कातरेक्षगविषाणक्काणविनिवेदितनिशाबलिप्रचारः, किरातवेषस्य भगवतो विश्वमूर्तेरपरमेव कमप्याकल्पं बिभ्राणः, पुत्रभाण्डं बन्दिवृन्दारकस्य कटकाधिपतेः, जामिर्भोगावलीपाठिनः सुभटसौहार्दस्य, दौहित्रः श्रोत्रियकितवनाम्नो नर्मसचिवस्य, समाश्रयस्थानमवकीर्णिलोकानाम्, अखिलपुनर्भूविवाहकृतकशिपुवेतनसंबन्धः, सकलगोकुलालिखिततूवरसुरभिसैरिभीदायनिबन्धः, प्रचुरप्रतिकर्मविकृतगात्रैः सत्त्रिपुत्रैर्दण्डाजिनिकैश्च परिव्राजकैः 'एष खलु भगवान् संजातमहायोगिनीसंगतिरतीन्द्रियज्ञानोद्गतिः सिद्धः सामेभिकः संवननकर्मणा करिणीं केसरिणमपि संगमयति विद्वेषभेषजेन जननीमप्यात्मजेषु वैरिणीं विदधाति' इत्यावेद्यमानज्ञानमन्त्रतन्त्रप्रभावः।

"His head was adorned with a crown of peacock feathers surmounted by a crescent, and he was wearing earrings made of red lac and shaped like the flowers and buds of the silk-cotton tree. The neck was stiffened by the fastening of a necklace made out of many varieties of magic roots, and he was wearing a garland made from shreds of old rags, multicoloured, and reaching to the feet. The upper arms were decorated with armlets made of tin balls large as plums, and the forearms enveloped with buffalo-horn bracelets up to the elbows; while a garland of Guñja berries served the purpose of a *vaikakṣaka* wreath across the bosom. The hands were rugged like the bony frame of the carapace of a tortoise, and the privy parts were covered with the lower edge of an old saddle cloth. The waist was decorated with a girdle of worn out churning ropes and the attention of the passers-by was attracted by the nimble gait of his feet resounding with the brass anklets worn by him. He announced his nocturnal rites with the sound of his buffalo-horn; and he was, in fact,

1 'कपर्दनिर्दयसंमर्दनिर्मोदालगर्दगलगुहास्फुरत्फूत्कारस्फारितललाटलोचनानलज्वालाग्लपितादितिसुतनिकेतनपताकाभोगाभिः, शिखण्डमण्डनोड्डमरनरशिरःश्रेणिपर्यन्तभ्रान्तप्रवृद्धगृध्रनिरुद्धब्रध्नदीधितिप्रबन्धाभिः, श्रवणभूषणभुजङ्गजिह्वालिह्यमानकपोलतललिखितरक्तपत्राभिः' (p. 45).

dressed in an attire exactly like that of Lord Śiva disguised as the Kirāta hunter. He was the son of the chief panegyrist Kaṭakādhipati (Camp-commander), the son-in-law of the minstrel Subhaṭa-sauhārda (Friend of Warriors), the grandson of the jester Śrotriyakitava (Brāhmaṇa Gambler), and the refuge of all who had transgressed their vows. His food and emoluments were earned by arranging the nuptials of all the harlots[1], and he had endowments of hornless cows and she-buffaloes registered in his favour in all the dairy farms. The glory of his wisdom and knowledge of mystic formulas and rites was proclaimed in the following manner by religious mendicants[2], carrying sticks and deerskins, and acting as informers, with bodies made ugly by excessive decorations: 'Here is the Exalted One who has communed with the Mahāyoginīs and acquired supersensuous knowledge. He has attained spiritual perfection, and his utterances are unfailingly true. By his art of enchantment he can unite even a lion with an elephant, and by means of animosity-producing drugs he can make even a mother an enemy of her children!'

The picture of the elephant-driver in Book IV is a minute study in ugliness, which is emphasized in such a manner as to suggest the enormity of the queen's strange infatuation. He is described as sleeping on the floor of a thatched hut strewn with grass left over from the ration of elephants, resting his head on a heap of coiled up ropes serving as a pillow. His only clothing was a piece of rag used for rubbing elephants with oil. He had coarse thorn-like hair; ears like old shoes; eyes like the mouth of a bucket; lips like the fringe of a leather oil-flask gnawed off by rats; cheeks like the hollow of an age-worn tree; teeth protruding like an irregular row of cowries; a chin hardly visible, as he had a regular goat's beard;[3] a throat with the veins visible, resembling the trunk of a castor-oil plant; arms like a couple of dead serpents suspended from on high; a stomach bloated like inflated billows; and thighs like stakes damaged by fire. 'He was repulsive to sight like a mass of sins, and extremely disgusting like a charnel-field. He appeared to be a compact mass of iron rust in human shape, and fashioned by the Creator by combining all kinds of deformities.' The original passage runs as follows (Chap. IV, p. 42):

कटङ्करकुटीरके करिकवलावशिष्टयवसस्रस्तरिणि[4] अवगुण्ठितरज्जुपुञ्जपरिकल्पितशिरस्पदे निद्रायन्तम्, इभाभ्यङ्ग-कर्पटपिहितलज्जास्थानम् अतिकठिनकचकण्टकोड्डमरमुण्डमण्डलम्, अनवानुपदीनापटलसमश्रवसम्,...... उदञ्चनशुषिराति-शायिलोचनम्,...... उन्दुरविकर्तरितसंघाटतटतुलितोभयदशनवसनम्, अतिपुराणकुजकोटरप्रतिमल्लगल्लम्, असमस्थापितवराट-कविकटदन्तम्, अजश्मश्रुदुर्दर्शचिबुकमन्यम्. एरण्डकाण्डविडम्बिधमनीलगलनालम्,...... उल्लम्बितमृतगोनसानुकारिक्षिपस्ति-

---

1 Śrutasāgara says पुनर्भूणां पुंश्चलीनां संग्रहस्त्रीविधवानाम्.

2 Obviouly employed by the court.

3 'अजश्मश्रु Cf. the Greek phrase *pōgōn mala tragikos* (Lucian, *The Dream*, 10).

4 This is the reading of Ms. A. The printed text reads...प्रस्तरविस्तरिणि.

निर्गमम, अनिलभृतभस्त्राध्मातजठरम्,......अग्निलङ्घितस्थाणुगणनोरुकम्,......अघसंघातमिव दुर्रीक्ष्यम्, अमङ्गलस्थानमिव नितरामुद्वेजनीयम्, अखण्डमण्डूरकुलमिव मनुष्यरूपेण परिणतम्, अखिलमिव वैरूप्यमवचित्य वेधसा निष्पादितम्.......

The account of the regiments of Yaśodhara's army has more than a literary interest, and is full of important details throwing light on the composition of old Indian armies. It is one of the most remarkable descriptions not only in *Yaśastilaka* but in Sanskrit literature as a whole (chap. III, p. 461 etc.):

निटिलतटपट्टिकाप्रतानघटितोद्भटजूटम्, उत्कोशकिंशुकप्रसूनमञ्जरीजालजटिलविषाणविकटमेकशृङ्गमृगमण्डलमिव, कर्तरीमुखचुम्बितामूलश्मश्रुबालम्, उद्भिद्यमानमदतिलकितकपोलं पीलुकुलमिव, किर्मीरमणिविनिर्मितत्रिशरकण्ठिकं महामण्डलावगुण्ठितगलनालमान्यमीशानसैन्यमिव, आकुफणिकृतकालायसवलयकरालकराभोगं बालबिलेशयवेष्टितविटपभागं भद्रश्रियानोकहगहनमिव, आनाभिदेशोत्तम्भितासिधेनुकम् अहीश्वरानुबद्धमध्यमेखलं मन्थानकाचलमिव, आवङ्क्षणोत्क्षिप्तनिबिडनिवसनं सकौपीनं वैखानसवृन्दमिव, अनेकाङ्कनामसंभावनोद्ग्रीवाननम्, आत्मस्तवाडम्बरोड्डमरमागधोत्कर्णितवदनम्, ऊर्ध्वनखरेखालिखितदेहप्रासादं देव इदं विहितविविधायुधवर्तनौचित्यं दाक्षिणात्यं बलम्।

"Sire, this is the Deccan regiment practised in the use of diverse arms. The luxuriant tangle of the hair of the men is tied up with cloth bands around their foreheads. Conspicuous by the horns carried by them, entwined with sprays of fullblown Palāśa flowers, they look like a troop of rhinoceroses; and with the tips of their knives coming up to the roots of their beards, they resemble a troop of elephants with the cheeks dotted with flowing ichor. They are wearing triple necklaces made of many-coloured beads, and look like Śiva's troops, awful on account of their necks being enwrapped with Mahāmaṇḍala serpents. They have the forearms enveloped with iron bracelets worn up to the elbows and resemble a thicket of sandal trees with the branches entwined by young snakes. With their daggers fixed about the centre of the waist, they resemble the mountain wherewith the gods churned the ocean, with its central slope encircled by the lord of serpents (Vāsuki). With their thick loin-cloths tucked up as far as the thigh-joints, they look like a crowd of religious mendicants wearing *kaupīna*. They are looking up on hearing the many laudatory poems, and stand with upturned faces, as they listen to the minstrels loudly reciting exuberant panegyrics in their honour. Their bodies are scratched all over with upward lines of finger-nail marks."

इतश्च पर्यन्तखर्वितकुन्तलतयार्धमुष्टिमितमस्तकमध्यकेशम्, अतिप्रलम्बश्रवणदेशदोलायमानस्फारसुवर्णकर्णिकाकिरणकोटिकमनीयमुखमण्डलतया कपोलस्थलीपरिकल्पितप्रफुल्लकर्णिकारकाननमिव, समुत्कर्षितस्थूलचिबुकजङ्घाग्रभागरोमलोमशम्, अहरहःप्रमार्जितदशनप्रकाशपेशलवदनतया प्रदर्शितस्वकीययशःप्रसूतिक्षेत्रमिव, अनङ्गग्रहपरिवेषवर्तुलदन्तक्षतक्षपितभुजशिखरम्, अनवरतक्षरत्क्षपारसरागरक्तशितिशरीरतया कजकिंजल्ककलुषकालिन्दीकल्लोलकुलमिव, मायूरबर्हातपत्रप्रभाश्यामिकासंपादितगगनगारुडोपलकुट्टिमच्छायम्, दरदद्रवापाटलफलकान्तिकुटिलकल्पितटोल्लासलालसकरं संध्याभ्रगर्भविभ्रान्ताभ्रियसंदर्भनिर्भरं नभ इव, देव, इदमनेकदोलिकाविलं द्रामिलं बलम्।

"This, Sire, is the Tamil regiment provided with numerous litters. The men have a mere handful of hair on the crown of their heads owing to the hair all around being cropped short. They seem to have clusters of full-blown Karṇikāra blossoms attached to their cheeks on account of their countenances being lovely with the shooting rays of the large gold earrings swinging from their elongated ears. They are shaggy on account of the profuse growth of hair on the borders of the lips, the chins, and the frontal part of the legs. They seem to be displaying the source of their fame[1], their visage being beautiful with the lustre of their daily cleaned teeth. Their upper arms are dented with the marks of bites (given by their mistresses), round as the halo of a planet, to wit, the god of love. They look like the waves of the Yamunā blended with the filaments of lotus blossoms, their dark bodies being painted with fluid turmeric ceaselessly dripping. With the blue sheen of their parasols made of peacock feathers they have caused the sky to look like an emerald floor; and with their hands playfully moving along their curved loins shining with the lustre of their shields painted with liquid red lead, they look like the sky full of flashes of lightning playing in the bosom of the evening clouds."

इतश्चोत्तप्तकाञ्चनकान्तकायपरिकरम्, करोत्तम्भितकर्तरीकणयकृपाणप्रासपट्टिशबाणासनम् आसनविशेषवशातिविद्रुत-मितद्रवखुरक्षोभितकुम्भिनीभागम्, भागभागार्पितानेकवर्गवसनवेष्टितोष्णीषम्, अनवधिप्रकारप्रसवस्तबकचुम्बितशिखं विजयश्री-निवासवनमिवेदं, देव, तुरगवेगवर्णनोदीर्णं यथायथकथमौत्तरपथं बलम् ।

"Here, Sire, is the North Indian regiment of truthful speech, and elcquent in praise of the speed of horses. The men have bodies comely as heated gold; and held fast in their hands are knives, darts, daggers, spears, blades and bows. The surface of the earth is agitated by the hooves of their horses galloping at top speed on account of their particular mode of riding. They wear *puggrees*[2] made up with multicoloured scarves arranged in layers; and with the crown of their heads adorned with clusters of flowers of endless varieties, they look like the sylvan abode of the goddess of victory."

इतश्च············करिवरैस्तमालिताखिलाशावलयम् अनवरतचिपिटचर्वणदीर्गदशनाग्रदेशैर्गुवाकफलकषायित-वदनवृत्तिभिः स्वभावादेवातिकोपनहृदयैराप्रपदीनचोलकस्खलितगतिवैलक्ष्योत्क्षिप्तपर्यन्तजनदुर्वाग्विधिभिः प्रकामायामलोमचूडै-गौंडैराकुलितसकलसैनिकम्, विचित्रसूत्रगुम्फितस्फारफरकोत्करकर्बुरितसर्वदाक्षायणीदेशम्, ············आहवैकानुरागं, देव, इदं जलयुद्धबद्धक्रियाविशेषासक्तं तैरभुक्तं बलम् ।

"Here, Sire, is the Tirhut regiment, fond solely of war and devoted to manoeuvres incidental to naval combats[3]: it has darkened the entire horizon with its mighty elephants...............All the troops of this regiment are

---

1 Fame in Sanskrit poetry is always white.

2 A marginal note in Ms. A says उष्णीषः शिरोवेष्टकिरीटयोः । अत्र तु पाघडी मुडासा.

3 This seems to be a reference to river operations. The Deopara stone inscription of Vijayasena of Bengal (about the end of the eleventh century speaks of the royal fleet going up the entire course of the Ganges for the conquest of the western regions (पाश्चात्यचक्रजयकेलिषु यस्य यावद्गङ्गाप्रवाहमनुधावति नौवितानं). *Ep. Ind.*, Vol. I, p. 309.

disturbed by the Gauḍa soldiers with extremely long tufts of hair: the extremities of their teeth are worn out by constant chewing of flattened rice, and their mouths are tinged red with betel; they are by nature exceedingly irascible, and hurl abuse at the bystanders, being ashamed of stumbling on account of their cloaks reaching to the feet. The large shields of the regiment made from multicoloured cords have tinged the entire expanse of the sky with diverse hues."

इतश्चाजानुलम्बमाननिवसनम्, माहिषविषाणघटितमुष्टिकटारकोत्कटकटीभागम्, निरन्तरघनदीर्घदेहलोमकलापकल्पितसर्वाङ्गीणकङ्कटम्, अधस्तिर्यक्प्रबन्धप्रवृद्धकूर्चकेशतया क्रियानुमेयनाभिनासानयनश्रवणदेशम्, उभयांसोत्तम्भितभूरिभस्त्रतया त्रिशिरोनिशाचरानीकमिव, लघुदृढदुष्करदूरलक्ष्यादिपातादिपाटवापहसितकृपकृपधर्मकर्णार्जुनद्रोणद्रुपदभर्गभार्गवम्, धृताधिज्याजकावं, देव, इदं गौर्जरं बलम् ॥

"This, Sire, is the Gujarat regiment armed with strung up bows. The men are wearing cloaks reaching to the knees, and their loins are girt with daggers with buffalo-horn hilts. The close, dense and long hair of their bodies constitutes an all-enveloping armour; and the existence of certain portions of their bodies, the navel, the eyes and the ears, can only be inferred from their actions, owing to their beards expanding thickly downwards and sidewise. They look like a throng of three-headed monsters on account of the large quivers attached to both the shoulders. They surpass even Kṛpa, Kṛpadharma, Karṇa, Arjuna, Droṇa, Drupada, Bharga and Bhārgava in efficiency, in swift aiming, vigorous shooting, and hitting of difficult and distant targets."

The report of the spy against a minister of Yaśodhara and the account of the embassy sent by the king of Pañcāla to the latter's court, in Book III, are not only socio-political records of great value but interesting as good specimens of Somadeva's simpler style and businesslike prose. The account of the embassy has been reproduced elsewhere[1] and we may here give a few illustrative extracts from the former document. It is necessary to point out that the spy's report, comprehensive as it is, contains, besides specific charges against the minister in question, a satire in prose and verse against ministers in general, quasi-historical traditions, and observations on human traits.

Speaking of villains, the spy gives a fanciful account of their origin, classifying them into eighteen different groups. The first group originated from the Kālakūṭa poison in Śiva's throat; the second from serpents; the third from the ferocious beak of Garuḍa; the fourth from the moon of the fourth lunar day (believed to cause disputes); the fifth from the attendants

---

1 See Chap. V.

of Death; the sixth from the dust of a libertine's feet[1]; the seventh from fire; the eighth from hell; the ninth from the illusion created by Viṣṇu; the tenth from the jaws of the god of death; the eleventh from the evil ways taught by heretic schools; the twelfth from the sin of doubt and hesitation; the thirteenth from burning shame; and the fourteenth from the arts of deception. In addition to these, one group of villains originated from darkness, whence arose in the sky Rāhu, the enemy of the other planets. A second group originated from the quarrel of Brahmā and Viṣṇu at the time of the glorification of the Phallic Śiva[2], whence arose also the sage Nārada, the lover of disputes. A third group originated from the clash of thunder and lightning, whence arose also the submarine fiare. A fourth group of villains originated from Diti who gave birth to Tāraka, the demon who habitually cheated all pious people on the earth. This account of the origin of villains appears to be Somadeva's invention, and shows imagination and selective power, although in design he is indebted to the story of the fourteen families of nymphs and their origin in Bāṇa's *Kādambarī*. An indirect reference to this occurs in the passage in *Yaśastilaka* which runs as follows (Chap. III, p. 441):

देव, अप्सरसामिवामरेषु नरेष्वपि किल खलानां चतुर्दश कुलानि पुरा प्रादुर्बभूवुः । तत्र तावत् प्रथमं प्रमथनाथकण्ठालंकारनिकटात् कालकूटात् प्रादुरासीत्, द्वितीयं द्विजिह्वेभ्यः, तृतीयं तृक्षात्मजतुण्डचण्डतायाः.................

The irresistible and invariable character of the evil propensities of a man is illustrated with various examples. Addressing the king, the spy says: देव, मांसरसरतस्य पुंसः किमिव मांसव्रतम् । कपाले भुञ्जानस्य हि नरस्य क इव केशदर्शनादाशप्रत्यादेशः । पुरे प्रमोषदक्षस्य हि पुरुषस्य केव कान्तारेऽपेक्षा । निरम्बरनितम्बायामात्माम्बायां दाहोद्योगस्य हि जनस्य क इव पराम्बायामम्बरपरित्यागः । यतः

स्थितासुं ग्रसमानस्य गतासौ कीदृशी दया । परबाले कृपा कैव स्वबालेन बलिक्रिये ॥

"Sire, how can a man who is fond of the savour of meat undertake a vow of abstention from flesh eating? Does a man who eats from a skull stop eating on discovering the presence of hair in his food? Does a man who is expert in stealing in the city need a forest for his activities? How will a man whose passion is aroused at the sight of his naked mother react to the nudity of another's mother? Because, how can one who devours the living have pity on a corpse? How can one who sacrifices his own child be compassionate to that of another?" 3. 174.

1 'षष्ठं षट्प्रज्ञपादपरागात्'

2 This seems to be a reference to the quarrel of the two gods about the extent of the Phallus. See Chap. XVII. Somadeva says: खण्डपरश्वधायुधस्य साधनसमृद्धिसमये द्रुहिणदामोदरकन्दलात्. S'rutasāgara says: खण्डपरशोर्वशीकरणावसरे ब्रह्मविष्णुयुद्धात्.

देव, स्वभावजा हि दुस्त्यजा खलु प्रकृतिः। न खलु पोषितोऽप्यहिपोतो जहाति हिंसाध्यवसायम्, न खलु व्रतशीलोऽपि बिडालस्त्यजति क्रौर्यम्, न खलु प्रायोपवेशनवासिन्यपि कुट्टनी मुञ्चति परवञ्चनोचितां चिन्ताम्, न खलु कालकवलनिकटोऽपि किराटो रहति शाठ्यस्थितिम्। यतः

यः स्वभावो भवेद्यस्य स तेन खलु दुस्त्यजः। न हि शिक्षाशतेनापि कपिर्मुञ्चति चापलम्॥

"Sire, verily it is difficult to renounce one's natural propensities. A young snake, though nourished with food, does not renounce the effort to do harm. A cat, though he may practise religious observances, dose not give up his ferocity. A bawd, though she observes religious fasts, does not abandon the design of cheating others. A merchant[1] does not give up his art of deception even when he is on the verge of death. Because, verily, of whatever nature a person may be, it is hard for him to discard it. A monkey never forsakes his fickle habits even if he is given a hundred kinds of training." 3. 175.

The tirade against the ministers of kings in verse, forming part of the spy's report, has been summarized elsewhere; and there is also a satirical description of them in prose (Chap. III, p. 439):

देव, सरलस्वभावस्य देवस्यामात्यदैत्यानामाकल्पोदञ्चः प्रतिक्रियाप्रपञ्चश्च साधुतायोगेऽनुरागे च कारणम्। तत्र चामीषामेतत्तात्पर्यम्। तथा हि सत्पुरुषपृषतवधाय व्याधस्याखिलाङ्गसंवरणं यत्रावरणमिवामात्यजनस्य लम्बाञ्चलकं चोलकम्, मुग्धमीनबन्धनानायमिव महाकायः कूर्चकेशनिकायः, कपटबकोटपेटकघटनाय सर इवोदारमुदरम्, परव्यसनान्वेषणाय मृगधूर्तस्येव मन्दमन्दाचारः पादप्रचारः, कथमेते खलु पातालस्थाः करस्था मम भविष्यन्ति शेषशिखामणय इति लुण्टाकतयेव मुहुर्मुहुर्जलेषु निमज्जनम्, कदा ह्यमी गगनचराः कदनकन्दुकविनोदकरा मम भविष्यन्ति रविरथतुरङ्गा इत्यपजिहीर्षयेवादितिसुतोपासनम्, अरे हताश हुताश मयि सत्याश्रयाशे सर्वाशे च कथं नाम तन्नामवान् भवानितीर्ष्ययेवाहुतिमिषेण विषमरीचिताडनम्, सुप्रयुक्तस्य दम्भस्य ब्रह्माप्यन्तं न गच्छतीति मनीषया साधुजनशकुनिहननाय द्वीपिद्विजोद्दीपनमिव देवतार्चनम्, कियन्तो मया महान्तः प्रतारिताः कियन्तो नाद्यापि इति संभालनायेव जपव्यवसायः, कुशलशकुलाशनाय बकस्येव ध्यानपरता, चतुरवञ्चनाय ठकस्येव धर्मागमपाठः, परलोकगतिभङ्गाय निगलजालस्येव गुरुचरणोपचारः, शाकिनीजनस्येव सेवकेषु जीवितविनाशाय प्रियंवदता, अविज्ञातान्तस्तत्त्वस्य शुष्कसरःसेतोरिव क्लेशाय प्रियालोकता।

"Sire, the pomp of dress and flurry of remedial measures of those devils, the ministers of Your Majesty, straightforward as you are, are intended to give an impression of honesty and loyalty. Their real purpose is as follows: The flowing robes of ministers are like a hunter's cloak enveloping all his limbs, and designed to kill honest people, like deer. The huge mass of their beard and hair seems to be a drag-net for capturing ignorant fools, like fish. Their big bellies are like a pool for amassing tricks, like a flock of cranes. They walk slowly and slowly like jackals to look for the weak points of others. A minister makes very frequent ceremonial dips into waters, as if with a thievish purpose: 'How will indeed the crest-jewels of the serpent Ananta abiding in the nether regions come into my possession?' He worships the Sun, as if with motives of robbery: 'When will those

1 Ms. A explains किराट as वणिक्.

horses of the Sun's chariot, coursing in the sky, play the ball-game of war for me?' He strikes the Fire by way of offering oblations, as if out of spite, saying: 'Since it is I who destroy my own refuge or benefactor, and destroy also all and sundry, why dost thou, o wretched Fire assume the names *āśrayāśa* (one who consumes one's own refuge) and *sarvāśa* (one who consumes all)?' The worship of the gods by a minister is comparable to letting loose a bird of prey for killing honest people, like birds, with the idea that not even Brahmā sees through a well-devised trick.[1] The muttering of prayers by a minister seems to be a device for recalling how many great men he has cheated and how many still remain uncheated. The meditation of a minister is like that of a crane for the purpose of 'devouring' able men, like fish. The study of the Law Books by him is like that of a *thug* for the purpose of cheating the wise. His obeisance at the guru's feet looks like the spreading of a network of chains for obstructing the way to heaven. His sweet words, like those of a witch, serve only to ruin his followers. His amiable looks, like the pleasant aspect of the embankment of a dried up pool, bring distress to those who are ignorant of the inner truth."

The more important of the charges against Yaśodhara's minister bearing on contemporary conditions have been discussed in another chapter viz., Chap. V. Some of the observations of the spy on the ways of the minister provide interesting reading. The cultural pretensions of the man are severely criticized, his mean tricks exposed, and the secret of his fame explained. A healthy feature is the insistence on learning being independent of wealth procured by royal favour:

देव, प्रसादनादनात्मभाविन्योऽपि विभूतयः पतिंवरा इव खात् पतितस्यापि जनस्य भवन्ति, न पुनरायुःस्थितय इवानुपासितगुरुकुलस्य यत्नवत्योऽपि सरस्वत्यः । यतः

नृपकरुणायाः कामं द्रविणकणाः संचरन्ति शरणेषु । न त्वाभिजात्यमेतत् पाण्डित्यं वा नृणां भवति ॥

देव, तच्छून्येऽपि यत् क्वचित् पुंसि नभसि विद्युत इव विद्याविलसितम्, तद्धनस्य घनस्येव माहात्म्यान्नात्मनः । यतः

विद्यारसविहीनापि धीस्थली विभवातपात् । व्यलीकोक्तोत्तरङ्गेयं भवेन्मुग्धमृगप्रिया ।

यदपि क्वचित् क्वचित् कलासु पयसि पतितस्य तैलबिन्दोरिवान्तर्व्याप्तिशून्यस्याप्यस्योपन्याससाहसम्, तदपि लक्ष्मीलवलाभाशापाशस्खलितमतिमृगीप्रचारस्य दुर्भरजठरकुठारविनिर्भिन्नमानसारस्य हताहंकारस्य सरस्वतीपण्यपातकावसरस्य जनस्याजर्यान्न पुनर्बोधौदार्यात् । यतो देव, घटदासीनां हि वदनसौरभं स्वामिताम्बूलोद्गालान्न सौभाग्यबलात्, पवनस्य हि परिमलपेशलता प्रसूनवनसंसर्गान्न निसर्गात्, दारुणो हि दाहदारुणता बृहद्भानुभावान्न स्वभावात्, मण्डलस्य हि भण्डनकण्डूलताधिपतिसंनिधानवशान्न शौयावेशात्, उपलशकलस्य हि नमस्यता देवाकारानुभावान्न प्रकृतिभावात् । ·········यत् पुनः सेवकलोकदौरात्म्यं प्रचिख्यापयिषुः किमप्यणकपदबन्धेन भगवतीं सरस्वतीं विधमति, तत्र यो हि स्वयमेवं निकायति स कथं मम दुरात्मा स्यादिति परप्रतारणार्थम् । ··· ······वृत्तं पुनरस्य पिण्याकपण्याङ्गनाजनस्येवालोकान्तोत्सर्गैरनेकशोऽनेकपाखण्डिलिङ्गिसंसर्गविसर्गैरेव राजपथीकृतम् । यतः

त्रैदण्डिकाहितुण्डिककापालिककौशिकव्रतकैः । कीर्तिर्जगति प्रसृता खरपटदीक्षाधिकैरस्य ॥

---

1 i. e., the worship of the gods by a minister is a carefully planned show of piety, the real motive being to obtain their help in cheating and ruining honest people.

"Sire, riches, although they do not crop up of their own accord, may, like brides seeking a husband, come into the possession even of a man fallen from the sky, as a result of (royal) favour; but learning, like the span of life, never comes to a man, even though accompanied by efforts, unless he attends the lecture-hall of a teacher. Because, 'wealth there may be in plenty in men's homes as a result of a king's favour, but not nobility of birth nor scholarship' (3. 179). When, my lord, there is a show of learning in a man, although he is devoid of these two qualities, it is due not to his own ability but to that of wealth, just as a flash of lightning in the sky is due not to any potency of the sky itself but to the presence of clouds.

The field of the intellect, although devoid of the water of learning, may on account of the power of wealth undulate with falsehood, and prove attractive to those deer, the dunces (3. 180). Indeed, this minister (of yours) has the hardihood to hold forth on certain branches of art, although lacking in depth, just as a drop of oil spreads on water without penetrating below the surface; but even that is due not to any great measure of intelligence on his part, but to his association with people who commit the sin of prostituting their learning, being without any self-respect, with all sense of pride destroyed by the axe of chill penury,[1] and the antelope of their intelligence trapped in the snare of the hope of gaining an infinitesimal quota of wealth. Sire, the fragrance of the mouths of slave girls is due not to any luck but to their taking the remnants of the betel chewed by their masters. The lovely redolence of a breeze is due not to its natural qualities but to its contact with flower gardens. The fierce burning of wood is due not to its natural properties but to the action of fire. A dog is eager to fight not on account of his courage but on account of the presence of his master, and a piece of stone becomes an object of veneration not on account of its natural state but because it is shaped into the likeness of a god............

Further, the minister annoys the Exalted Goddess of Speech with his wretched verses, his purpose being to proclaim the villainy of his subordinates. This is meant to put outsiders off the scent, who would be led to think, 'How can a man who speaks thus (about the vices of his subordinates) be a villain himself?'...........

Then it is the associates of the many heretics, wandering in the world to its farthest limits, who have oftentimes given wide publicity to his way of life, similar to that of a spendthrift whore.

---

1 Lit, the axe of a stomach difficult to replenish.

His fame has been spread in the world by religious mendicants snake-charmers, Kāpālikas, jugglers and consummate thugs." 3 183.

The minister is then accused of various offences such as tyranny, disloyalty, usurpation of power and financial maladministration, all kinds of motives being attributed to him.

यस्तु स्वास्थ्यावसरेष्वपि समृद्धदेशो हि महीशः कीनाश इवावश्यं करोति कामपि विकृतिमिति धूमकेतुरिवानपराधमपि जनपदं पीडयति, प्रभूतपक्षबलो हि भूपालः शैल इव कस्य भवति वश इत्यनुरक्तमतीरपि प्रकृतीरसमञ्जसयति, कृशकोशको हि धरेशः क्षपितपक्षः पक्षीव भवेत् सुखसाध्य इति धनं निधनयति, व्यसनव्याकुलितो हि राजसुतो व्याधित इव न जातु विकुरुते पुरश्चारिष्विति द्विषतः प्रोत्कर्षयति, एकारक्षो हि क्षितिपतिः करिपतिरिव न स्यात् परेषां विषय इति न कमप्यभिजातं सहते, स किल प्राणप्रतीकारेषु स्वापतेयोपकारेषु वा विधुरेषु भवितोपकर्तेति को नाम श्रद्दधीत । यतः

स्वस्थावस्थायामपि योऽनर्थपरम्परार्थमीहेत । स कथं विधुरेषु पुनः स्वामिहिते चेष्टतेऽमात्यः ॥

"Like an outbreak of fire, he oppresses the innocent population even in peaceful times, because a king whose realm is prosperous is sure to do some harm (to his ministers), like the god of death. He creates disaffection among the loyal citizens, because a king with a large following is like a mountain and comes under no one's influence. He squanders public funds, because a king with a depleted treasury can be tackled with ease, like a bird whose wings are cut off. He consolidates your enemies, because a prince overwhelmed by peril is like an invalid, and gives no offence to his counsellors. He never tolerates any highborn person, thinking that a king in the grip of any particular individual is, like an elephant, unlikely to come under the influence of others. Who would believe that such a man would be of any help in the preservation of life or the protection of property in times of danger? Because, how can a minister who strives to do continuous harm even in easy circumstances exert himslf for the good of his master in times of peril?" 3. 184.

The minister is also accused of having banished various distinguished men whose presence was vital to the welfare of the state (Book III, p. 453):

ततोऽसौ यदि देवस्य परमार्थतो न कुप्यति, सत्पुरुषपरिषदिव मनसि मनागपि नाभ्यसूयति, तत् किमिति मनीषापौरुषाभ्यामशेषशिष्टशौण्डीरशिखामणीयमानमतिसमीक्षं पुण्डरीकाक्षम्, सिन्धुरप्रधानो हि विजयो विशामीशानामिति तत् किमिति समस्तसामजैतिह्यगृह्यमनःप्रभावं बन्धुजीवम्, महाकविसंग्रहान्महीपतीनामाचन्द्रार्कावकाशं यश इति तत् किमिति स भवत्कीर्तिलतालल्लनालापामृतसेवकसारं हारम्, 'यासु सन्तो न तिष्ठन्ति ता वृथैव विभूतयः' इति तत् किमिति स्वभावादेव देवस्य प्रसेदुषोऽपरानपि विदुषः पुरुषानमिषन्नगारान्तरापतितः कपोत इव निर्वास्य स्वयमेकैश्वर्ये वर्तते ।

"If then he really has no illwill towards Your Majesty, and if he, like an assembly of good men, bears not the slightest malice in his heart, why has he monopolized all power by banishing, like a dove flying into a house,[1] such men as Puṇḍarīkākṣa, whose intellect and insight were as

---

1 See Chap. XV for the superstition.

the crest-jewel of all cultured and spirited men by virtue of his talents and courage? The triumph of kings depends upon elephants; yet (why did he banish) Bandhujīva whose mental faculties were devoted to the mastery of all branches of elephant-lore? The fame of kings lasts as long as the sun and the moon owing to their patronage of great poets; yet (why did he banish) the poet Hāra, an excellent votary of the nectar of sweet utterances on the creeper of your fame? Wealth that does not support the good is of no use: knowing this, why did he, being intolerant, banish yet other learned men, friendly by nature to Your Majesty?"

Good examples of reflective prose are provided by the musings of Yaśodhara after the discovery of the misconduct of his consort. Pausing after his momentary resolve to kill her, Yaśodhara says (Chap IV, p. 48):

आः किमिदमहो कर्माहमनुष्ठातुं व्यवसितः। न खलु नार्य इव शुभमशुभं वा कर्म सहसैवारभन्ते विनीतमतयः, नापि विपदि संपदि वा कृपणप्रकृतय इवाशु विक्रियां गच्छन्ति महानुभावाः, न चाल्पमेधसामिव महीयसामुपपन्ना भवन्ति कामचारेण प्रवृत्तयः, न चैतद्गहनं किंतु प्रातर्मयैव लज्जावनतमस्तकेन शिरः पिधाय स्थातव्यम्। शोचितव्यं च मयैव प्रणयिनां पुरः पश्चात्तापदुःप्रतिष्ठानमिदमनुष्ठानम्। श्रोतव्या भविष्यन्ति मयैव कर्णकटुताकाराः पुरजनस्य धिक्काराः। सुष्ठु मलिनीकृतं स्यान्मयैवात्मीयं मामीय च कुलम्। सोढव्या मयैव स्वदुष्कृतनिरुत्तरविधाश्चित्तशल्यस्पृशः कुलवृद्धानामभिधाः। अहमेवोदाहरणं भविष्यामि दुर्बुद्धीनां कुटुम्बविघटने। कलुषतामेष्यत्येषैवास्थाने विनियोजिता खड्गलता। स्त्रीवधादयमजनि तपस्वीति मृतस्यापि मे न दुर्यशः प्रशान्तिमर्हति। शोकातङ्के पतिष्यति च सापराधसवित्रीमृतिदुःखितो युवराजः। परं च बह्वपराधे हि देहिनि क्षणमात्रव्यथाशरणं मरणमनुग्रह इव। यदि पुनरनवेक्षणमुपस्थितस्य, असंभाषणमासन्नस्य, उपेक्षणं विज्ञपयतः, अवधीरणमसमैः परिभूयमानस्य, आशाभङ्गकरणमर्थयतः, प्रीतिवितरणं तदनभिमतानाम्, अस्मरणं प्रियगोष्ठीषु, अनवेक्षणं तत्परिजनस्य, अपवार्य व्याहरणं स्वप्रकाशेष्वप्यालापेषु, अनवसरानुसरणमसंगभावेष्वपि प्रस्तावेषु क्रियेत, स्यात् प्रत्यानीतश्चिरमस्थाने कृतसमयः प्रणयः।

"Ah, what have I set myself to do? Certainly the wise never do anything good or bad, like women, on the spur of the moment, nor are the high-spirited quickly perturbed, like the weak-minded, in prosperity or danger, nor do arbitrary acts befit the great as they they do those who are poor in talents. This is by no means hard to comprehend. (If I kill her) it is I who will have to cover my head on the morrow, downcast with shame; it is I who will have to bewail my action, injudicious on account of repentance, in the presence of friends; it is I who will have to hear the reproaches of the citizens, harsh to the ear; it is I who will have tarnished my own family and that of my uncle; it is I who will have to bear the cutting remarks of the elders, without any means of reply on account of my misdeed. I will be cited as an example of how the foolish disrupt their own families. And this sword will be polluted, if applied to an unworthy object. 'He became a miserable wretch by murdering a woman'—this evil report concerning me will not subside even after my death. And the prince (Yaśomati), miserable at the death of his guilty mother, will be sorely afflicted with grief. Besides, death with its momentary

pain is as a favour to **one** who **has committed a grievous offence. On the other** hand, it is possible to repudiate long misdirected love if the person so loved is treated with contempt[1] even on isolated occasions; for example, if one does not take any notice of him when present; if one does not talk to him when near; if one ignores him when he makes a statement; if one neglects him when insulted by his inferiors; if one disappoints him when he asks for a favour; if one befriends those who are disliked by him; if one does not mention him in conversation with friends; if one does not look at his attendants; and if even in self-evident matters (requiring no deliberation) one dismisses him on the pretext of lack of leisure."

After recognising that the pageant of life loses its meaning without women, Yaśodhara dilates on their villainy and faithless character (p. 61):

इमा ह्यनिशमनुनीयमाना गृहमर्कटमिव विडम्बयन्ति पुरुषम्, उपचारैर्गृह्यमाणा दानदुर्भराः स मेष इत्यधिक्षिपन्ति, अपेक्ष्यमाणाः पशुमिव मन्यन्ते, हठादुपभुज्यमानाः श्मशानकुटमिव परिहरन्ति, सेर्ष्यमनुयुज्यमाना भुजङ्गा इव दशन्ति, गुणवद्भ्यो निम्बादिवोद्विजन्ते, शुचिक्रियेषु मृत्पिण्ड इवाभिनिविशन्ते, अनुरज्यन्त्य एव भवन्ति कारणमनर्थपरंपरायाः, हसन्त्य एव शल्ययन्त्यङ्गानि, पश्यन्त्य एव दहन्ति देहम्, आलपन्त्य एव स्खलन्ति मनसः स्थैर्यम्, आसजन्त्य एव कुर्वन्ति तृणादपि लघुतरं मनुष्यम्, आरक्ष्यमाणाः स्वच्छलेनैवारभन्ते दुष्कर्माणि । न चासामस्ति रक्षणोपायः ।

"Constantly pampered, they deride men as they would a tame monkey. They are never satisfied with presents, and when treated with marks of esteem, they mock at men as being sheep. When sought after, they look upon men as brutes. When enjoyed against their will, they forsake men like a water-pot used in a cremation ground. Jealously questioned, they bite like serpents. They shun those who are virtuous like the Neem tree (with the bitter leaves), and regard those who act from pure motives as clods of earth. Women become a source of perennial evil even while they profess love, pierce one's limbs even while they laugh, consume one's body even while they cast glances, undermine one's strength of mind even while they talk, and degrade a person even lower than a blade of grass by attaching themselves to him. When guarded, they commit misdeeds by resorting to their own devices, and there is in fact no means of effectively guarding them."

The disgruntled husband takes a pessimistic view of youth, wealth and the joys of life, all these being regarded as disturbing influences on the moral life. The observations are enlivened by a large number of illustrative similes (p. 66):

यौवनाविर्भावः पुनः कादम्बरीयोग इव परं मुमुक्षूणामपि नाविकार्य मनांसि विश्राम्यति । श्रीमदः सर्वेन्द्रियाणां जनुषान्धत्वमिवाप्रतीकारमुपघातकरणम् । अनङ्गसिद्धान्तः खलोपदेश इवानर्थभुजङ्गमानामुत्थापनदण्डः । कवयः पुनः पिशाचा इव विषयेषु विभ्रमयन्ति निसर्गादजिह्मान्यपि चित्तानि । डिण्डिमध्वनिरिव व्यसनव्यालप्रबोधनकरः कलानामभ्यासः । नियोगलाभ इवापातसुन्दरः प्रसह्योन्मादयति सुविदुषोऽपि पुरुषान् प्रणयिजनविलासो हृदयमुपनिपत्य दर्पयति च । याचितकमण्डनमिव

1 Ms. A remarks यदि अनवसरानुसरणं निरादरः क्रियेत तदा प्रणयः निराकृतः स्यात् । अनवसरानुसरणं किमिव अनवेक्षणमित्यादि क्रियेत·

छन्दानुवर्ती परिजनः । तदेतेष्वेकमप्यलमुपहन्तुं प्राणिनः, किं पुनरमीषां न समवायः ।............................. यस्यां पुनर्लक्ष्म्यामयं महानाग्रहो लोकस्य सा दैवात् करमुपागतापि सूतककणिकेव न भवति स्थिरा । खलमैत्रीव संगच्छमानापि जनयत्यवश्यं कांचिद्विपदम् । अपामार्गयवागूरिव लब्धापि न शक्यते परिणमयितुम् । प्रयत्नपरिपालितापि कुलटेव करोत्युपपतावभिलाषम् । अनुभूयमानापि मदिरेव मोहयत्यन्तःकरणम् । ग्रहोपरागलेखेव गताप्यसंतापयन्ती न व्यवतिष्ठते । साहसैरुपस्थितापि राक्षसीव छलयति केवलं महापुरुषेषु प्रतिष्ठां प्रत्यवसादयितुम् । दुर्जनेषु क्षणमात्रं सखीभावमुपयाति ।

"The advent of youth, like the drinking of wine, never fails to pervert the minds even of those who are bent on salvation. The pride of wealth, like birth-blindness, causes an incurable paralysis of all the senses. Erotic lore, like a villain's counsel, is a magic wand for raising serpents, the evils of life. The poets, like demons, bewilderingly divert the minds of men, although straightforward by nature, to mundane joys. The practice of the arts is like the sound of a drum, awakening the serpents of evil passions. The enjoyment of a beloved woman, charming only at the beginning, like an appointment newly obtained, forcibly intoxicates even very wise men, and taking possession of the heart, fills it with pride. The subservient attendants are like borrowed ornaments.[1] Not to speak of the combination of these evils, even one of them is sufficient to destroy sentient beings.

The Goddess of wealth, for whom the world has so great a longing, becomes fickle like a particle of mercury even when she comes into one's possession by chance. Like the friendship of villains, she is bound to cause some calamity even when she is one's associate. Like gruel made from the Apāmārga plant, she cannot be assimilated even when one has acquired her. Like a lewd woman, she longs for a paramour even when cherished with care. Like wine, she deludes the mind even while she is enjoyed. Like an eclipse, she never fails to cause distress even after she has vanished. Although she appears at the call of bravery, she practises deception, like a demoness, in order to destroy the eminence of the great. For a moment she befriends the villains."

The difficulty of controlling the mind is emphasized in Sudatta's reflections in Book I, similes being used as usual to give point to the remarks (p. 111):

तथा सकृच्चलितं च चेतः प्रासाद इव पुनः दुष्करमुद्धर्तुम्, दूरतरमुन्नतानि गिरिशिखराणीव शक्यन्ते शरीरिणां हृदयानि सुखेनैवाधस्तात् पातयितुमारोहयितुं न पुनर्दुःखेनापि । अस्ति च 'श्रेयांसि बहुविघ्नानि' इति विदुषां प्रवादः । श्रुताभ्यासश्च बिसतन्तुर्दन्तिनमिव प्रत्यवस्यन्तमात्मानमलं न भवति निवारयितुम्, तनुच्छद इवाधीरधीषु न जायते चलतश्चित्तस्य त्राणाय देहदाहकरागमः संयमः, बहिरुत्थावस्थितः पारदरस इव द्वन्द्वपरिगतः पुमान् क्षणमपि नास्ते प्रसंख्यानक्रियासु ।

"It is as difficult to steady the mind, once it has gone astray, as it is to restore a building shaken to its foundations. The hearts of men,

1 i. e. fickle, faithless. Borrowed ornaments denote the idea of instability as they are claimed back by their owners. The idea is fully explained in a Buddhist simile which compares the pleasures of sense to borrowed wealth. See *Majjhima Nikāya*, Potaliya Sutta (LIV): याचितकूपमा कामा.'

like extremely high mountain-peaks, can easily be flung to a lower level, but cannot be elevated even with difficulty. And there is a saying of the wise that the good is accompanied by many impediments. The study of the Scriptures cannot check the erring self, just as lotus fibres cannot hold back an elephant. Self-control, physically distressing as it is, cannot protect the unsteady minds of those who are fickle, just as an armour cannot fortify the wavering hearts of cowards. A man surrounded by distractions cannot concentrate even momentarily on meditative efforts, just as mercury placed over the fire does not last even for a moment."

A few homely pictures are provided by Somadeva's description of certain misers in *Yaśastilaka*. In the humorous prelude to the spy's report, the latter speaks of a fellow named Kiliñjaka described as 'the foremost of misers.' "He is to be counted first among the stingy. He is the exemplar of the penurious, and deserves to be called the chief of the untidy. He is the crest-jewel of the greedy, and his name can be mentioned only at the end of a meal." The spy gives a detailed account of the wretched meal to which he was treated by the miser (Book III, p. 404):

..................अर्धरद्धालाबूफलफालिप्रकारम्, ईषत्स्विन्नकर्कारुकर्कशच्छेदसारम्, अवालमालूरमूलकचक्रोपक्रमम्, अभृष्टचिर्भटिकाभक्षणभग्नभावक्रमम्, अपक्वार्काग्निदमनरिङ्गिणीफलाविरलविरचनम्, अगस्तिचूताम्रातकपिचुमन्दकन्दलसदनम्, अनेकदिवसवासार्थिताम्लखलकविस्तारम्, अतीवपाकोपहतबृहतीवार्ताकफलसोभाञ्जनकन्दसालनकावतारम्, एरण्डफलपलाण्डु-मुण्डिकाडम्बरम्, उच्छूनोद्वेल्लितवल्लकरालकक्कोकुन्दोड्डमरम्, अनल्पराजिकावर्जितावन्तिसोमावसानम्,..................

The description is of interest not only on account of the names of a large variety of fruits and vegetables but as providing detail of domestic life, and is a contrast to the rather empty rhetoric which sometimes characterizes Kāvya prose, including Somadeva's own writing. It reminds one of a similar but less complex account of poor men's fare preserved in an extract from the Greek comedian Alexis, cited by Athenaeus in *Deipnosophistae* II. 55.

Somadeva in *Yaśastilaka*, Book VII (section 32), gives another picture of a notorious miser, the wealthy merchant Sāgaradatta, who has rather queer notions of economy and resorts to ingenious devices to put them into practice. He does not, for instance, buy oil for lighting his courtyard, but hangs a mirror from the edge of the roof of his house, and allows the light from his neighbour's house to be reflected in the mirror. He would advise the boys of the household not to waste oil in massaging their bodies before bath, but to have contact with the oil-smeared bodies of the boys of the neighbourhood in a close fight with them. He would instruct his servants to purchase oil and salt and then return both as beihg bad, the particles adhering to the receptacle being sufficient for subsistence! He avoids washing expenses by selling his dirty linen, and never accepts an invitation to dinner lest he should be required to return the invitation; and his servants see what other people ate in their homes. It will be conceded that we have here a portrait worthy of Theophrastus.

Descriptions of female beauty so frequent in Sanskrit literature are rare in *Yaśastilaka*. A well-drawn picture is that of the beautiful daughters-in-law of Queen Celinī, followed by the pathetic figure of the wife of Puṣpadanta, grown ugly and emaciated after twelve years of separation from her husband who had taken the monastic vow.[1] The portrait of Māradatta in Book I is chiefly remarkable for the young king's love of dangerous exploits and strange rites; while the cumbrous description of king Yaśorgha in Book II may be contrasted with the simple one of Sudatta as king of Kaliṅga in Book V. The seasonal descriptions in Book I form the background of Sudatta's religious austerities which are briefly outlined. Not much interest attaches to the artificial description of Avanti in Book II and the pleasure garden in Book I.

Most of the natural descriptions are of the conventional type and often characterized by artificial conceits and commonplace images. There are, however, others enlivened by striking details illustrating the author's powers of observation. Mention may be made of the animated description, in Book V, of the prosperous dairy-farm of Karahāṭa, full of all kinds of cows, horses, mules, donkeys and sheep, 'a combination, as it were, of the oceans of curds, milk and clarified butter'. A variety of scenes common to life in a dairy-farm in medieval India is vividly described (p. 184):

क्वचिदुन्निगलमण्डलवालाकुलितबस्तवर्करकम्, क्वचिद्गोपालपोतपारिप्लवोपद्रूयमानवृद्धवृष्णिकम्, क्वचिद्वत्सेक्षणक्षरत्स्तनधेनुदुग्धधाराधाव्यमानधरापीठम्, क्वचित् कालशेयकलशराशिविश्राणनप्रीयमाणातिथिपेटम्, क्वचिद् वनविनिवृत्तनिचिकीनिटिलनिकटनिक्षिप्यमाणदधिदर्भदूर्वाक्षतप्रसवम्, क्वचिद्दलितदामदासेरकार्भकभ्रान्तिशङ्कितशक्वत्करिखुरक्षुद्यमानाध्मनिदेशपल्लवम्, क्वचित्तरुणतराभीरोद्गूर्णघनद्रुघणघोरघातघूर्ण्यमानरणरभसक्षोभसंधुक्षितरक्ताक्षकक्षम्, क्वचिदुन्माथनाथहरियूथयुद्धबाध्यमानप्रष्ठौहीपक्षम्, क्वचिद्बष्कयणीक्षीरप्रतीक्ष्यमाणगृहगृहावैग्रहणीगृहदेवताकुलम्, क्वचिद्गोमिथुनपरिणयोत्फुल्लपल्लवस्ववासिनीजनोच्चार्यमाणमङ्गलम्, क्वचिद्दधिमन्थमन्थामध्वनिविनर्त्यमानभवत्तबर्हिणम्, क्वचिन्माहेयीदोहव्याहाराहूयमानपयःपानपरपथिकगणम्, क्वचित् संदानदामनीच्युतचपलतरतर्णकक्षोदरुदितदारकदीयमानजरतीरक्षाविधानम् ....

"Somewhere in the farm the kids are harassed by the unchained young dogs, and elsewhere an old ewe is tormented by the pranks of a cow-boy. At one place the ground is drenched with milk streaming from a cow's udders at the sight of her calf; at another place guests are entertained with gifts of pitchers of buttermilk; and elsewhere curds, blades of *kuśa* and *dūrvā* grass, unbroken rice and flowers are placed on the forehead of a cow back from the woods. Here the tender leaves in the mangers are crushed by the hooves of

1 For the story see Chap. XVI.

calves frightened by the scamper of the young camels who have broken their chains; there the buffaloes stagger under the merciless blows dealt by the young Ābhīras with heavy sticks, and are infuriated by the violent commotion of the fight. At one place the resort of cows with young for the first time is disturbed by the combats of a herd of powerful bulls. At one place the tutelary deities presiding over the threshold of a house are worshipped with the milk of cows with grown up calves; and at another place women with husbands alive, carrying blossoming sprigs, sing auspicious songs at the nuptials of a bull and a cow; while elsewhere the domestic peacocks are made to dance by the sound of the churn-staff in the making of curds. Somewhere in the farm the sound of the milking of cows invites wayfarers eager to partake of milk; while elsewhere an old dame comes to the rescue of a boy weeping at being trampled on by a nimble calf that has broken away from the tether."

The elaborate description of the great forest in Book V is interesting chiefly for the vivid portrayal of a variety of wild animals in their natural surroundings (p. 198):

.........क्वचिदुपलम्बाप्रलम्बस्तम्बविलम्बमानजानकोत्त्रासितहरिणप्रयाणभरभीतभल्लूकनिकरम्, ...क्वचिदनवरतमृगमार्गमार्गणश्रमश्रान्तचिलातचेल्लिकोच्चुलुञ्चितचुरीवारिवीक्षणातुरतरक्षुचक्षुर्दुर्लक्ष्यनगनिम्नगापुलिनम्, क्वचिड्डामरिकनिकायसायकविद्धवृद्धवराहविरसविरसितस्रवत्कुरङ्गाङ्गनागर्भनिर्भरम्, क्वचिदुन्मदमहिषमण्डलारब्धरणविषाणसंघट्टोच्छलत्स्फुलिङ्गसंगशीर्यमाणागमाग्रपल्लवभरम्, ...क्वचिदविच्छिन्नविहारवानरनिकरविकीर्यमाणनीडक्रोडोड्डीनाण्डजच्छदच्छन्नाम्बरम्.........क्वचिद्घनघूकघोरघूत्कारघूर्ण्यमाणपुराणविटपिकोटरप्रसूतवायसीवर्गम्, क्वचिद्बलवद्बलालोन्मूलितद्रुमलाकुलकलभप्रचारम्,.........क्वचिच्चित्रककुलाघ्रातपृषतखुरखण्ड्यमानकदलीप्रवालान्तरङ्गम्, क्वचिदनन्यसामान्योदन्यानुद्रुतद्रवद्रङ्कुजिह्वावलिह्यमानमृगतृष्णिकातरङ्गम् क्वचित्प्रचण्डगण्डकवदनविदार्यमाणरुरुरुधिरदुरीक्षवृक्षानीकम्, क्वचिन्निःशल्यशल्लकशलाकाजालकील्यमानरल्लकलोकलोकम्.......

"Somewhere in the forest a pack of bears is scared by a herd of deer rushing past, being struck with terror at the sight of the wild oxen loitering among the clumps of spreading creepers......................At one place the islet of a mountain river looks terrible with the hyenas worried at the sight of the water of the sandy pools being drunk up by the Bhilla boys, exhausted by the constant search for the track of deer. A corner of the forest is covered with the embryos of hinds expelled by the shrill cries of the old boars pierced by the arrows of a band of robbers. At one place the extremities of the thick foliage of trees wither in contact with the sparks shooting up from the the clash of horns in the combats of frenzied buffaloes..............At one place the sky is covered with the feathers of birds flying away from their nests, being dispersed by a crowd of monkeys roaming at will........................At another place the female crows bring forth their young in the hollows of the old trees shaken by the horrible cries of the compact flocks of screech-owls. In one part of the forest, the movements of the elephant cubs are hampered by the clusters of trees uprooted by violent gales......................Another part of the forest is covered with the leaves of the banana plants cut up by the hooves of the bucks attacked by leopards. At one place antelopes, oppressed by an uncommon thirst, run and lap up the ripples of a mirage. At another place the trees are ghastly with the blood of stags pierced by the horn of some fierce rhinoceros, and all the Rallaka deer are transfixed by the spines of the porcupines moving about freely."

Similar delineation of the wild life of nature is found in the descripion of the Śiprā river in Book V (p. 208):

अन्योन्यापघनघनाघट्टकुपितकुम्भीरभयभ्राम्यत्ककुभकुहूत्कारमुखरम्, अवाग्चाटबकोटचेष्टितचकितकमल्मूलनिलीयमानपोताधानम्, अम्बुरुहकुहरविहरदवहारविघ्नितवैखानसकुसुमोञ्छनविधानम्, उदीर्णदर्पदीवि[1]तुमुलकलिकोलाहलावलोकमूकमूककलोकम्, उन्मत्तमकरकरास्फालनोत्ताललहरिकोत्तालितारविन्दकन्दरद्रवन्मकरन्दबिन्दुचन्द्रकावचयचटुलचञ्चरीकमेचकवीचिकानीकम्, उद्दामोदर्कद्विपदशनदश्यमानमृणालिनीशकलसारप्रसरम्, अतुच्छकच्छपाच्छोटमूर्छत्पाठीनपृष्ठपीठीलुठदुद्दण्डडिण्डीरपिण्डशिखण्डिताटनितटीनिकटकर्करम्[2].................

"The waters resound with the cries of the water-fowl hovering about in fear of the alligators enraged at the heavy clash of each other's bodies, and the young fish lie hidden under the lotus beds, scared by the movements of the silent cranes; while the gathering of flowers by anchorites is hampered by the water-snakes prowling inside the lotus beds. The frogs keep quiet on hearing the noise of the fierce fights of ferocious water-serpents; and the ripples are darkened by the bees briskly collecting the spreading honey drops oozing from the inner cavity of the lotus blossoms swayed by the surging waves caused by frenzied crocodiles splashing the water with their claws. The waters are overspread with fragments of lilies chewed by fierce hippopotami; and the contiguous rocks of the mountain slopes are fringed with heavy masses of foam floating on the broad backs of the Pāṭhīna fish, excited by the splash made by huge tortoises."

Among other descriptions of nature the oncoming darkness is described towards the end of Book III, and Book IV opens with an overwrought picture of sunset and the evening twilight. Elaborate descriptions of the seasons occur in Books I and III, and although the imagery is conventional, there are graphic touches; for example, in the portrayal of the flowers and plants of the rainy season when "the fields are uneven with dense masses of mushrooms; the horizon is pink with blossoms of water-pepper plants; the crevices of mountain rocks are delightfully fragrant with jasmine flowers; ....the hill tops are adorned with Girimallikā buds;............... the mountain bowers are gay with Sarja and Arjuna trees; and the leafy petals of the Ketakī flowers glisten, shaped like Cupid's darts." (Book III).

---

1 Ms. A reads दीवट for दीवि.

2 This is the reading of Ms. A. The printed text reads..........शिखण्डिततटिनीनिकटकर्करम्.

The prose hymns in Book VIII are an interesting experiment in Kāvya prose, and illustrate a Jaina literary genre. They are in the form of elaborate prayers addressed to the Pañca-Parameṣṭhins, the five supreme spiritual leaders of the Jaina church, and are in keeping with the character of *Yaśastilaka* as a Jaina religious romance composed in Kāvya style. The place of these prose invocations in the devotional scheme outlined by Somadeva has been indicated in a subsequent chapter, and it may here be pointed out that each invocation ends with a verse in the *anuṣṭup* metre. There are eight such groups, five addressed to the Parameṣṭhins (Arhat, Siddha, Ācārya, Upādhyāya and Sādhu), and three abstract ones addressed to the Jewels of Right Faith, Right Knowledge and Right Conduct. For example,

ॐ निखिलभुवनपतिविहितनिरतिशयसपर्यापरम्परस्य............................विरहितारिरजोरहःकुहकभावस्य समवसरणसरोऽवतीर्णजगत्त्रयपुण्डरीकखण्डमार्तण्डमण्डलस्य दुष्पाराजवञ्जवीभावजलनिमज्जज्जन्तुजातहस्तावलम्बपरमागमस्य भक्तिभरविनतविष्टपत्रयीपालमौलिमणिप्रभाभोगनभोविजृम्भमाणचरणनक्षत्रनिकुरुम्बस्य सरस्वतीवरप्रसादचिन्तामणेर्लक्ष्मीलता-निकेतकल्पानोकहस्य कीर्तिपोतिकाप्रवर्धनकामधेनोरवीचिपरिचयखलीकारकारणाभिधानमात्रमन्त्रप्रभावस्य सौभाग्यसौरभसंपादन-पारिजातप्रसवस्तबकस्य सौरूप्योत्पत्तिमणिमकरिकाघटनविकटाकारस्य[1] रत्नत्रयपुरःसरस्य भगवतोऽर्हत्परमेष्ठिनोऽष्टतयीमिष्टिं करोमीति स्वाहा। अपि च

नरोरगसुराम्भोजविरोचनरुचिश्रियम्। आरोग्याय जिनाधीशं करोम्यर्चनगोचरम्॥

"I perform the eightfold worship[2] of the Exalted Arhat Parameṣṭhin preceded by the Three Jewels. All hail! He is continuously worshipped with intense devotion by the lords of all the worlds......................He is free from the deception of Deluding, Knowledge- and Conation-obscuring and Obstructive Karmas.[3] He is a sun to the lotus-bed of the universe appearing in his great audience-hall as on a pool of water. He is the mighty support of the creatures submerged in the impassable waters of transmigration. His feet, like stars, shine in the firmament of the expansive radiance of the crown jewels of the lords of the three worlds, devoutly bowing in obeisance. He is as a wishing gem for obtaining the highest favours of the goddess of learning. He is a Kalpa tree, the support of the creeper of Prosperity. He is as the all-giving celestial cow in nourishing the nascent Fame (of his worshippers). The mere utterance of his name has the efficacy of a magic formula in destroying one's chance of going to hell. He is as a bunch of Pārijāta flowers radiating the fragrance of well-being. He is the imagemaker that creates the bejewelled figure of Beauty's rise. Further, I worship Lord Jina for health. His splendour doth produce

1 Ms. A explains विकटा as पुत्तलिका.

2 See Chap. X.

3 Ms. A says अरिर्मोहः। रजो ज्ञानदर्शनावरणद्वयम्। रहः अन्तरायः।

on men, gods and serpents an effect like that of the rays of the sun on lotus blossoms."

ॐ विदितवेदितव्यस्य बाह्याभ्यन्तराचरणकरणत्रयविशुद्धित्रिपथगापगाप्रवहनिर्मूलितमनोजकुजकुटुम्बाडम्बरस्य अमराम्बरचरनरनितम्बिनीकदम्बनदप्रादुर्भूतमदनमदमकरन्ददुर्दिनविनोदारविन्दचन्द्रायमाणोदितोदितव्रतव्रातापहसितार्वाचीनचरित्रच्युतविरिञ्चविरोचनादिवैखानसरसस्य अनेकशस्त्रिभुवनक्षोभविधायिभिर्ध्यानधैयावधूतविष्वक्प्रत्यूहव्यूहैरनन्यजनसामान्यवृत्तिभिर्मनोगोचरातिचरैराश्चर्यप्रभावभूमिभिरनवधारितविधानैस्तैस्तैर्मूलोत्तरगुणग्रामणीभिस्तपःप्रारम्भैः सकलैहिकसुखसाम्राज्यवरप्रदानावहितायातावधीरितविस्मितोपनतवनदेवतालकालिकुलविलुप्यमानचरणसरसिजपरागस्य निर्वाणपथनिष्ठितात्मनो रत्नत्रयपुरःसरस्य भगवतः सर्वसाधुपरमेष्ठिनोऽष्टतयीमिष्टिं करोमीति स्वाहा। अपि च

बोधापगाप्रवाहेण विध्यातानङ्गवह्नयः। विध्याराध्याङ्घ्रयः सन्तु साध्यबोध्याय साधवः ॥[1]

"I perform the eightfold worship of the Exalted, All-holy Sādhu Parameṣṭhin preceded by the Three Jewels, the Saint who has devoted himself to the path of salvation. All hail! He has comprehended all knowable things, and uprooted the luxuriant grove of passion with the Ganges flow of the purity of mind, body and speech in the external and internal spheres of activity. He has thrown into the shade the religious meditation of inferior and degenerate recluses such as Brahmā, Virocana and others, by dint of the multitude of his own ever-recurring vows, which, like the moon, wither up the honey-laden toy-lotus of frenzied passion, originating in the river of beautiful maids among the gods, men and the Vidyādharas. The dust of his lotus feet is wiped off by the bees in the shape of the hair of the sylvan deities, bowing to him in obeisance, who come to confer on him the boon of worldly happiness in its entire range, but are amazed at being ignored by him on account of his diverse austerities, headed by the vows comprising the Mūla- and the Uttara-guṇas; (austerities) that perturb the three worlds in diverse ways, and remove all obstacles with the strength of meditation, and are extraordinary in character, and beyond the range of thought, and inscrutable in their working, and productive of miraculous power! Further, may the saints whose feet are to be worshipped, according to the prescribed rule, help us to acquire perfect knowledge! They have extinguished the fire of passion with the current of the river of knowledge."

ॐ यत् सकललोकालोकावलोकनप्रतिबन्धकान्धकारविध्वंसनम्, अनवद्यविद्यामन्दाकिनीनिदानमेदिनीधरम्, अशेषसत्त्वोत्सवानन्दचन्द्रोदयम्, अखिलव्रतगुप्तिसमितिलतारामपुष्पाकरसमयम्, अनल्पफलप्रदायितपःकल्पद्रुमप्रसवभूमिमस्मयोपशमसौमनस्यवृत्तिधैर्यप्रधानैरनुष्ठीयमानमुशन्ति सद्धांधनाः परमपदप्राप्तेः प्रथममिव सोपानम्, तस्य पञ्चतयात्मनः सर्वक्रियोपशमातिशयावसानस्य सकलमङ्गलविधायिनः पञ्चपरमेष्ठिपुरःसरस्य भगवतः सम्यक्चारित्ररत्नस्याष्टतयीमिष्टिं करोमीति स्वाहा अपि च

धर्मयोगिनरेन्द्रस्य कर्मवैरिजयार्जने। शर्मकृत् सर्वसत्त्वानां धर्मधीर्वृत्तमाश्रये ॥

1 Ms. A says साध्यो बोध्य आत्मा यस्य तत् साध्यबोध्यं केवलज्ञानं तस्मै.

"I undertake the eightfold worship of the Exalted Jewel of Right Conduct, preceded by the five Parameṣṭhins, and fivefold in character[1] that produces all good, and culminates in the absolute cessation of all forms of activity. All hail! It destroys the darkness that obstructs the view of the entire universe. It is the Himālaya of unblemished knowledge; the moonrise of festive joy to all living creatures; and the springtime of the creepery grove of all the vows and modes of self-restraint[2] and vigilance[3]. It is the nursery of the Kalpa trees of religious austerities that vouchsafe mighty results, and it is practised by those who possess humility, mental calm, a kindly disposition and fortitude. The wise call this Jewel of Right Conduct the first step to the attainment of the supreme goal. Further, intent on Dharma, and for the purpose of vanquishing my enemy, Karma, I resort to the way of life of the Dharmayogin, the best of men. It doth bring happiness to all living creatures."

Somadeva's style is enlivened by the occasional use of popular maxims occurring chiefly in his prose and sometimes also in verses. For example, 'शिरो मुण्डयित्वा नक्षत्रप्रश्नः' (Book IV): *Enquiring as to an auspicious date for shaving one's head after one has already finished it.* As pointed out by Jacob, *Laukikanyāyāñjali*, Part II, this proverb occurs in the *Nyāyamañjarī* in the form मुण्डितशिरोनक्षत्रान्वेषणम्. The proverb 'श्रेयांसि बहुविघ्नानि' (Book I) occurs at the beginning of a popular verse cited, for example, by Haribhadra at the commencement of his own commentary on his *Anekāntajayapatākā:*

श्रेयांसि बहुविघ्नानि भवन्ति महतामपि । अश्रेयसि प्रवृत्तानां क्वापि यान्ति विनायकाः ॥

'इतस्तटमितो व्याघ्रः केनास्तु प्राणिनो गतिः' (Book IV): *On one side a precipice, on the other a tiger; how can a living creature pass?* To be between the devil and the deep sea. This and two other similar sayings are cited in *Nalacampū*, Book V: 'इतो व्याघ्र इतस्तटी, इतो दवाग्निरितो दस्यवः, इतो दुष्टदन्दशूक इतोऽप्यन्धकूपः' इति न्यायात् ।. 'नरकान्तं राज्यम्, बन्धनान्तो नियोगः, मरणान्तः स्त्रीषु विश्वासः, विपदन्ता खलेषु मैत्री' (Books VII & V): *Sovereignty leads to hell, employment to captivity, trust in women to death, and friendship with villains to danger.* 'गतोदके कः खलु सेतुबन्धः' occurs in a verse of Book IV. 'सर्वत्र हे पुत्र न षड्गुलानि' Ibid.[4] 'को नाम धीमाँल्लवणाम्बुराशेरुपायनार्थं लवणं नयेत' Ibid.

---

1 For the fivefold Cāritra (conduct) see Chap. XI (section on Cāritrabhakti).

2 Effective control over mind, body, and speech (कायगुप्ति, वाग्गुप्ति and मनोगुप्ति). *Tattvārthādhigama-sūtra* 9.4.

3 ईर्यासमिति (Proper care in walking), भाषासमिति (Proper care in speaking), एषणासमिति (Proper care in eating), आदाननिक्षेपसमिति (Proper care in lifting and depositing), and उत्सर्गसमिति (Proper care in excretion). Ibid.9.5.

4 See Chap. XII.

What wise man will carry salt for presenting it to the saltsea? 'इन्द्रयमस्थानं हि गुणदोषयोर्महीयपतः' इति नीतिवाक्यम्, Book VII, section 32. The sense, as far as can be judged from the context, seems to be that kings are as liberal as Indra in rewarding merit and as strict as Yama in punishing crime. 'राजपरिगृहीतं तृणमपि काञ्चनीभवति' Ibid.: *Even a blade of grass belonging to the king becomes as valuable as gold.* 'शठप्रतिशठन्यायेन' Book IV, 'अन्धकवर्तकीयम्' Book II, verse 153: The maxim of the blind man and the quail[1]. 'को नाम शैलमारोहेदर्के लब्धमधुः सुधीः' Book III, verse 73, is a variation of the wellknown maxim अर्के चेन्मधु विन्देत किमर्थं पर्वतं व्रजेत् discussed by Jacob (op. cit.), Part I. The following maxims bearing on the character of women occur in Book IV: स्त्रियः खलेषु रज्यन्ते दासहस्तिपकादिषु' इति, 'अपात्रे रमते नारी' इति वचनमस्ति। अत एवोशन्ति नीतिवेदिनः- 'तैरश्चोऽपि पुंयोगः स्त्रियो दूषयति, किं पुनर्न मानुषः'। The last of these maxims is also cited by Somadeva in *Nītivākyāmṛta*: स्त्रीणां दौत्यं स्त्रिय एव कुर्युस्तैरश्चोऽपि पुंयोगः।.

Somadeva has an eye for the grotesque, as exemplified in his description of the elephant driver in Book IV and the king's spy in Book III. His power to depict the strange and the terrible is illustrated not only in his remarkable picture of Caṇḍamārī and the Mahābhairava temple in Book I but in the description of the scenes of horror conjured up by a Vidyādhara to disturb the meditation of the sage Manmathamathana, in Book V, and the similar scenes created by two gods to test the steadfastness of Jinadatta and Padmaratha in their austerities, in the first story of Book VI. Disease and disgusting conditions are delineated in the story of Auddāyana in Book VI (section 9); while Amṛtamati, stricken with leprosy after her crime, is introduced in a verse of Book V. Curious examples of abusive language are found in the story of the Vidyādhara mentioned above, who is discovered in the act of molesting the sage Manmathamathana by the king of the Vidyādharas, and addressed by the latter thus:

अरे कदाचाराचार पराकदुरात्मन् खलपुरोभागिन् विद्याधराधम खेचरखेट विहायोगमयाप्य वियच्चरखेल हेठ नरकनिवास पापाचार बहुकुमतिभृतचित्त गुणमटह निहीन गन्धर्वलोकापसद मातरिपुरुष.............................

Similarly, in the story of Śrībhūti in Book VII (section 27), the dishonest priest is rebuked by the king in opprobrious language. The incorporation of the religious and moral tales in Books VI and VII gives the author an opportunity of presenting scenes not usually found in Sanskrit prose romances.

---

1 The translation of the verse in question in chapter XI follows Śrutasāgara's explanation of the maxim. Vardhamāna, on *Gaṇaratnamahodadhi* III. 195, explains it differently. See Jacob (p. cit.), Part I.

Frequent and sometimes felicitous use of similes is made by Somadeva in his narrative and descriptive prose. Vajrakumāra was, for instance, adorned by his youth, 'just as a desert path is adorned by a shady tree; just as a shady tree is adorned by a pool of water; just as a pool of water is adorned by a lotus-bed; just as a lotus-bed is adorned by a flock of swans; just as a flock of swans is adorned by the company of beautiful women; and just as the company of beautiful women is adorned by the graceful play of love'.[1] After the discovery of Amṛtamati's guilt, Yaśodhara's heart burnt like a tree enveloped by fire; he was furious like the ocean overflowing its shores; he changed countenance like the moon attacked by Rāhu, and trembled like creatures at the approach of death; his lips quivered like a leaf that is being cut to pieces; he frowned like Śiva intent on burning the Three Cities; and his bosom was aglow like a heated cauldron.[2] The guilty woman, after her transgression, crept back to her husband's bed and slept, clinging to his bosom, like as a female rogue elephant enters a grove of trees, just as a sheet of lightning plunges into a rain-cloud, just as a serpent enters a mountain cave, just as the messenger of death enters the world, just as a crocodile enters the ocean, or a female goblin the dense woods.[3] This may be contrasted with another series of similes, in which the conjugal harmony of Candramati and her consort Yaśorgha is likened to the relationship existing between wise policy and a kingdom, forbearance and religious austerities, modesty and learning, fame and life, the Flag of triumph and the god of love, mango blossoms and springtime, the Kalpa creeper and a tree of heaven, and a series of beneficial happenings and a sacred day of religious piety.[4] A long series of similes occurs also in Yaśodhara's reflections on women as an indispensable factor in the joys of life. Without women, a kingdom is like a forest, ornaments are like the decoration of a dead body, beauty paint is like smearing of clay, adornment of the body is like shampooing a man who is asleep, the flurry of fly-whisks and parasols is like the worship of evil spirits, the practice of the arts is like a device for wasting time, the study of poetry is like an attempt to remove the irritation of the mouth, deliberations in the council chamber are like possession by evil spirits, public audience is like entering a prison, music is like a loud sermon on the futility of life, the sound of drums is like a trumpet proclaiming the banishment of worldly happiness, mansions are

---

1 'मरुमार्ग इव छायापादपेन, छायापादप इव जलाशयेन, जलाशय इव कमलाकरेण' etc. Book VI, section 16.

2 'आशुशुक्षणिकक्षीकृतः क्षितिरुह इव दह्यमानान्तर्देहः, च्युतमर्यादमुद्रः समुद्र इवानिवार्यकोपप्रसरः' etc. Book IV.

3 'कुजनिकुञ्जमिव व्याली, पर्जन्योत्सङ्गमिव सौदामिनी, कुत्कीलकन्दरमिव भुजङ्गी' etc. Ibid.

4 'नीतिरिव राज्यस्य, क्षान्तिरिव तपसः, अनुत्सेकस्थितिरिव श्रुतस्य, कीर्तिरिव जीवितव्यस्य, विजयवैजयन्तीव मनसिजस्य' etc Book II.

like mountain caves, pleasure gardens are like charnel-fields, protecting one's subjects is like wage-earning, conciliation of the citizens is like the rounds of a city barber, execution of the six-fold policy is like the crossing of a dried up river, and the effort to acquire wealth is like dancing in the dark.[1]

Yaśodhara's disgust for the world and decision to renounce the world is brought into harmony with the morning scenery in a series of appropriate similes. "The east cleared up like my own decision. The stars vanished like my desire for sovereignty. The lunar orb grew dim like my passion of love. The day lotus beds blossomed forth like the disgust of my heart. The darkness of the night disappeared like my desire for worldly happiness. The glow of the early dawn melted away like the snare of my delusion."[2]

Rather bold and exaggerated similes are used to praise the Śiprā river in Book V. Its waters are bright as a stream of nectar and beautiful as the oozings from moonstones, and delight the world like the Supreme Light. Abstract similes are sometimes used to describe concrete objects, e. g., in the description of the great forest in Book V: it is impenetrable like the heart of a wicked man, dreadful like the hour of universal destruction, deep like the science of numbers, intricate like the character of a woman, infested with mischievous thorns like a period of anarchy, harmful like a villain's counsel, and inaccessible like the heart of a prince[3]. Some of the similes are marred by word-play, and a typical example is the comparison of the forest just mentioned to Raghu's family, simply because both happen to contain 'Māgadhī', which, applied to the forest, means a *pippalī* creeper; and applied to the family in question means Sudakṣiṇā, the consort of Dilīpa.[4] Simpler and more tolerable is the comparison of king Yaśorgha, also based on verbal similarity, to the autumn, the spring and the other seasons.[5] Similes based on paronomasia are in fact a common feature of the Kāvya style, and it is perhaps significant that Somadeva's romance opens with a long series of similes of this type (*śliṣṭopamā*).[6] They are used also in the description of the great tree in the valley of the Suvela mountain in Book V.[7]

---

1 'विना हि विलासिनीजनेनारण्यमिवेदं राज्यम्, मृतकमण्डनमिवाभरणम्, पङ्कोपदेह इव विलेपनम्, सुप्तसंवाहनमिव शरीरसंस्कारः, प्रकरणमिव चामरातपत्राडम्बरः, कालहरणोपाय इव कलानामभ्यासः, तुण्डकण्डूविनयनमिव काव्याध्ययनम्' etc. Book IV.

2 'मत्कार्यपरिच्छेदेनेव स्फुटितं पूर्वदिग्भागेन, मद्राज्याभिलाषेणेव विरलीभूतं तारकनिकरेण, मन्मनसिजविलासेनेव विच्छायितमिन्दुबिम्बेन, मद्वैराग्यमनसेव विकसितमरविन्दवृन्देन' etc. Book IV.

3 'दुर्जनहृदयमिव दुष्प्रवेशम्, प्रलयकालमिव भयानकम्, निगद्यागममिव गहनावसानम्, ······ वामेक्षणाचरितमिव स्वभावविषमम्' etc.

4 'रघुवंशमिव मागधीप्रभवम्'.

5 'शरत्समय इव प्रतापवर्धितमित्रमण्डलः' etc. Book II.

6 'यत्र महानृपतय इव गोमण्डलवन्तः, चक्रवर्तिश्रिय इव महिषीसमाकुलाः, भरतप्रयोगा इव सगन्धर्वाः ············ग्रामाः।'

7 'काकुत्स्थकथावतार इव कपिकुलविलुप्यमानपलाशप्रसरः, सत्रमण्डप इव द्विजराजविराजितः········ छन्दःप्रस्तार इव पादप्रबन्धावरुद्धवसुधः' etc.

Other examples of word-play are not very numerous considering the bulk of the romance. The device is aptly used in the satirical description of the wicked minister in Book III. The spy says, for instance, that the minister is indeed the *vardhana* or 'promoter' of the prosperity of the kingdom, but the word means also 'cutter', 'destroyer'. Similarly, he is the cause of *vibhūti* 'glory', but the word means also 'ashes'; and he is also the maker of a series of *maṅgalas*, which means both 'happy events' and 'potsherds'.[1] There is likewise a long series of compounds in Book II, which describes in identical language the condition of kings, both when they are favoured by Yaśorgha and when they incur his displeasure. When, for instance, the great king is displeased with them, their lot is *tīrthopāsana*, i. e. deprived of their kingdoms, they pass their days in sacred places for the practice of religion; but when Yaśorgha is favourable to them, they have *tīrthopāsana* of another kind, i. e. enjoy the loyalty of the various components of the state in full sovereignty of the realm[2]. Similarly, another series of compounds describes simultaneously a pleasure garden and a crowd of beautiful women in a description of the summer in Book III. Virodhābhāsas and Parisaṁkhyās, based on word-play, are also met with, but their number is not large. The description of the royal palace towards the end of Book II contains some highly artificial examples of Virodhābhāsa.

The most typical of the characteristics of the later Kāvya style is, however, exhibited by the use of Utprekṣās which are frequently employed in our work. A series of Utprekṣās is used, for example, in Book I, to describe a hill, which is fancied as the bosom of Dame Earth, as the play-ball of some sylvan deity, as a sweetmeat ball given to the boyish Regions of the sky by their mothers, as the hump of the Earth Bull, as a mound barring the entrance to the nether regions, and as the supporting roost of the Sky Bird[3]! Utprekṣās are generally used to give greater perspicuity to an image and make it more striking and graphic, but very often the effect produced is rather bizarre and grotesque, although there are numerous exceptions. Those employed, for instance, to describe Caṇḍamārī are quite in keeping with the dread character of the goddess, who is fancied as the younger sister of Yama, as the mother of Mahākāla-Śiva, as the messenger of the god of death, as the companion of the Kālāgni form of Śiva associated with the hour of universal

1 'देव, देवस्यायमेव राज्यलक्ष्मीवल्लीवर्धनः। देव, देवस्यायमेव मङ्गलपरम्परासंपादनः।………देव, देवस्यायमेव समरेषु जयविभूतिकारणम्।'.

2 'प्रथिततीर्थोपासनाविर्भवदाश्चर्यैश्वर्याः………स्वस्य रोषतोषयोः समतामानिन्यिरे भूमिभुजः।'

3 'स्तनाभोग इव महीमहिलायाः, क्रीडाकन्दुक इव वनदेवतायाः, मातृमोदक इव दिग्बालकलोकस्य' etc.

destruction, as the stewardess of the kitchen of the awful Mothers[1], as the nurse of the monsters, as the ground where the kinsmen of the god of death worship the Manes, and as the Night of destruction of all living creatures.[2] Not so successful is the attempt to reproduce the nasty spectacle of a serpent half buried in an anthill. The reptile is fancied as the intestines of the Earth Antelope, as the tail of the Earth Lioness, as the root of the Earth Creeper, as the stalk of the Earth Lily, and as the lock of hair of the Earth figured as a female monster.[3]

The constant desire to add new images tends to make Utprekṣās farfetched and artificial, and sometimes a good image is spoilt by juxtaposition with others less effective. As is to be expected, Utprekṣās occur mostly in descriptions; and some characteristic examples are provided by the natural descriptions in our romance. The Siprā river is, for example, fancied as a girdle of moonstones worn by the city of Ujjayinī like a graceful lady, as the pleasure tank of the mistresses of the king of Mālava, as a festive banner flying over the nether regions, as a nuptial garland for the wayside mountains, as a pearlstring worn by the Earth goddess, as a banner proclaiming the fame of the mountain from which the river rises, and as an irrigation canal for the gems in the ocean.[4] Similarly, in the rainy season the sky seems to be a shower-bath for the earth long scorched by heat; the mountains with the waters of the cascades streaming down their sides appear to have white banners covering their slopes; and the lakes, full to the brim, seem to be ceremonial vessels of water, a parental offering to the Summer dead and gone![5] Another series of Utprekṣās occurs in the description of the temples of Rājapura in Book I. The tall, white edifices are fancied as clusters of flowers of the Sky tree, as white lights of the firmament, as masses of lotus blossoms adorning the crest of the Sky Goddess, as places for the acquisition of vast

---

1 The seven Mātṛs are mentioned in the following verse quoted by Śrutasāgara: ब्रह्माणी च तथेन्द्राणी वाराही भैरवी तथा । चामुण्डा कर्णमोटी च चर्चा स्युः सप्त मातरः ॥. For other definitions, and the number of the Mothers, which is sometimes given as nine, see the English trans. of *Naiṣadhacarita*, Vocab. under अम्बिका.

2 'या च लघीयसी भगिनीव यमस्य, जननीव महाकालस्य, दूतिकेव कृतान्तस्य, सहचरीव कालाग्निरुद्रस्य, महानसिकीव मातृमण्डलस्य' etc.

3 'पुरीतत्प्रतानमिव मेदिनीकुरङ्गिकायाः, लाङ्गूलमिव महीसिंहिकायाः' etc. Book V.

4 'इन्दुमणिमेखलेव पद्मावतीविलासिन्याः, जलकेलिदीर्घिकेव मालवावनीपालविलासिनीनाम्, नित्योत्सवपताकेव भुजङ्गमलोकस्य, वरणमालेव मार्गमहीधराणाम्' etc. Ibid.

5 'चिरतरातपसंतापदुःस्थितायाः क्षितेर्यन्त्रधारागारलीलामिव बिभ्रति गगनमण्डले..............निदाघनिवापजलसरावेष्विव निर्भराम्भःसंभृतेषु सरःसु' Book III.

religious merit by the pious of the three worlds, as expanses of the foam of the atmospheric ocean, as gleams of the loud laugh of Śiva incarnate as the sky, as crystal pleasure hills of the planetary world, and as elephant cubs of the Sky Forest belonging to the (white) Airāvata family.[1]

Accumulations of Rūpakas are occasionally met with, for example, in the description of Māradatta as the lover of women of different nationalities.[2] The lengthy series of epithets, mostly Rūpakas, applied to Yaśodhara in the letter despatched to a rival,[3] illustrates a current practice in royal correspondence and inscriptional records of grants and endowments. Some of the epithets are as follows: "The Sunrise of prowess; Brahman himself in wisdom; an ocean of discernment; a swan participating in the joyful sports of the goddess of learning; the beloved consort of poetic speech; a Vidyādhara in the game of ball-throwing; an Indra in playing with rutting elephants; an Aruṇa in chariot-driving; a Garuḍa in fighting on foot; a Gandharva king in singing; a Bṛhaspati in the science of instrumental music; a Bharata in the art of dancing;................................. a Paraśurāma in self-sacrifice; an axe in the jungle of hostilities; a lion to the 'fawn' of Kalinga[4]; a blaze to the 'bamboo clump' of Aśmaka; a fire to the 'moth' of the Śaka country; a flame consuming the king of Krathakaiśika; the crest-jewel of the Kṣatriyas of Ahicchatra; Deathknell to the insubordination of the king of Pañcāla; a thunder-bolt to the royal dynasty of Kerala; lightning-fire to the Yavana Tree;[5] the subject of pleasant disputes among the beautiful women of Cedi; the luxury mirror of the women of Magadha; a tender leaf on the plump bosoms of the ladies of Kāñcī; a love-god to the youthful Ratis of Māhiṣmatī; the beauty-paint of the ruddy lips of the fair women of Kauśāmbī; the ear-ornament of the women of Daśārṇa; the passionate lover of the courtesans of Pāṭaliputra; a bee enjoying the graceful gestures of the beautiful women of Valabhī; the perfumed ornamental dot on the foreheads of the women of Ayodhyā." A reference to the original will show that most of these epithets are used with an eye to verbal effect, to which Kāvya poets paid considerable attention.

---

1 'प्रफुल्लस्तवकैरिवान्तरिक्षवृक्षस्य, श्वेतदीपसृष्टिभिरिव रोदःकोटरस्य' etc.

2 'आन्ध्रीणामलकवल्लरीविजृम्भणजलधरः, चोलीषु भ्रूलतानर्तनमलयानिलः, केरलीनां नयनदीर्घिकाकेलिकलहंसः, सिंहलीषु मुखकमलमकरन्दपानमधुकरः, कर्णाटीनां कुचकलशविलासपल्लवः, सौराष्ट्रीषु वलिवाहिनीविनोदकुञ्जरः, कम्बोजीनां नाभिवलभिगर्भसंभोगभुजङ्गः, पल्लवीषु नितम्बस्थलीखेलनकुरङ्गः, कलिङ्गीनां चलनकिसलयोत्सवपुष्पाकरः ।'.

3 See chap. V.

4 'Fawn', 'Bamboo clump' and 'Moth' are contemptuous references to the kings of the respective countries.

5 i.e. the Yavana king.

The Rūpakas used are not, all of them, equally successful. The courtesan whose dead body forms the subject of the verse description in Book I was 'the pleasure resort of the apish minds of all who are henchmen of the god of love'.[1] The nights of the rainy season are 'the female buffaloes who nourish the child minds of the women going out to meet their lovers'.[2] A young man who took the help of a nurse in his love affairs is described as having made her a field for the growth of the woodland of his project.[3] A certain sage is called 'an elephant engaged in water-sports in the river of learning.[4] A particularly bad example is the description of another sage as 'an enclosure for the capture of the elephant herd of religious merit'.[5]

Neglect of proportion is a common characteristic of later Kāvya style, and overelaboration of details often leads to the use of artificial conceits and hyperboles. Somadeva, for instance, devotes no less than twenty elaborate and mostly far-fetched epithets to Māradatta's sword (Book I, p. 161), and an almost equal number is applied to the dust raised by Yaśodhara's troops (Book II, p. 337). The particles of dust are incidentally likened in an elaborate fashion to lovers enjoying the company of their beloved, because they enshroud and cling to the various limbs of the women accompanying the procession.[6] The height of the temples of Rājapura is conveyed by saying that 'the showers of water streaming from the conduits made of moonstones, emitting moisture in contact with the rays of the moon, drench the bodies of the nymphs of heaven, withered by the fire of separation from their lovers'.[7] Sometimes a conceit employed is exaggerated to the extent of producing something like a comic effect. In the description of the great hospitable tree in Book V, for example, the tree is fancied as mockingly addressing other trees in the forest on the subject of their being barren and useless for wayfarers.[8]

---

1 'चेतोभवानुचरमानवमनोमर्कटक्रीडावनविहारवसतिः'.

2 'अभिसारिकाजनमनोऽपत्यपोषणगवर्यैः शर्वर्यैः'.

3 'स्वकीयाकूतकान्तारप्रवर्धनधरित्रीमकरोत्' Book VII, section 31.

4 'सरस्वतीसरिज्जलकेलिकुञ्जरः' Book V.

5 'पुण्यद्विपयूथबन्धनवारिः' Book VI, section 19.

6 'ततः सैन्यसीमन्तिनीचरणप्रणिपातप्रणयिमानसाप्रणीतप्रसूतासंवाहनविनोदकर्माणः कृतनितम्बस्थलीखेलखेदाः संजनितना-भिदरकुहरविहरणाः ....समाचरितसीमन्तप्रान्तचुम्बनाः सूत्रितसुरतसमागमाः प्रियतमा इव..................बलसंचरणरेणवः।'.

7 'अमृतकरातपस्पर्शद्रवच्चन्द्रकान्तमयप्रणालोच्छलज्जलजालकासारसिच्यमानवियद्विहारिणीविरहवैश्वानरकर्ममर्मरशरीरयष्टिभिः'.

8 यश्चानवरतमखिलजनोपसेव्यमानसर्वस्वः पवनवशविकाशधरेण पल्लवाधरेणोपहसतीव प्रतिवेशितरून्। 'अस्मिन् दुःसंचारे कान्तारे दैवादवाप्यमानसमागमनस्यार्थिजनस्याविधाय कमप्युपकारमरे खदिर, किं तवान्तःसारतया। सरल, वृथेदं सरलत्वम् ....पूतीक, अर्थिजनाशाभङ्गाय मार्गावस्थितिः।'

One of the topics which makes later Sanskrit writers throw off all restraint is fame, usually the fame of kings. Apart from poetical descriptions of royal fame, Somadeva gives an elaborate picture of the fame of the sage Sudatta (Book I), which illustrates how Kāvya poets seek novelty in the treatment of conventional themes by introducing fanciful images and conceits. The description in question may be summarised thus. "The universe having been pervaded by Sudatta's fame, white as the foam of milk, Brahman is anxious lest the white things created by him should be merged in the general whiteness and lost to view. So he devises signs of recognition, and puts the submarine fire in the Ocean of Milk, masses of matted hair on Śiva's head, a dark spot in the form of a deer in the moon, protuberances on the heads of Airāvata and other divine elephants, mineral peaks on the Himālayas, Tamāla trees on the slopes of the Kailāsa mountain, the dark waters of the Yamunā in the course of the Ganges, and yellow filaments in white lotus blossoms; while he prescribes for the Pāñcajanya conch contact with the dark hands of Kṛṣṇa. Sudatta's fame is also represented as a maiden in her nuptial attire, wandering in the universe and rejecting various suitors for her hand on different grounds. She tells Brahman, for instance, that he is too old to accompany her in her travels; tells Agni, the god of fire, that he is hardly fit for marriage, suffering as he does from acute jaundice; and rejects Varuṇa, the lord of the ocean, because he is disabled by dropsy and hence debarred from the gaieties of love. Vāyu, the wind-god, is too fickle for her, and she tells Kubera, the god of wealth, that a confirmed drunkard like him[1] is not fit to converse with a maiden like her. Śiva who lives near funeral pyres is, of course, ruled out; and she warns the Moon that his life is in danger on account of his incurable consumption, and tells Viṣṇu that, being a baldpate with a scalp resembling an iron cauldron turned upside down, he is not worthy of her kisses.[2] Unable to accept any one of them, Maiden Fame continues to wander without abiding anywhere, like a doe deluded by a mirage, like the mind of a king who has lost his throne, like the intellect of a sage who has attained the inner vision." There is no doubt that this description of fame shows considerable ingenuity, but the reckless elaboration of a favourite theme all but makes it verge on the comic.[3]

---

1 'अनवरतमधुपानपरिच्युतमतिप्रकाश वित्तेश, न गोचरश्चतुरोक्तिसुधारसास्वादविस्फुरितश्रवणाञ्जलिपुटायाः सहालापगोष्ठीनाम्' इति नकूलबरपितरम्।

2 'अवतानकालायसतलिकाकृतिखलतिमस्तकदेश हृषीकेश, न समीपमदयकचग्रहग्रहिलविग्रहायाः कुटिलकुन्तलाविलविलोचनचुम्बनानाम्' इति मुकुन्दम्।

3 Certain other gods are also mentioned, including a vulgar reference to Indra.

An interesting example of Kāku-Vakrokti is found in Amṛtamati's fraudulent message to Yaśodhara, in which she begs to be allowed to accompany the king into wilderness after his proposed renunciation of the world. Yaśodhara, while listening to the message, interjects sarcastic remarks which appear to corroborate her statements, but really give them a different interpretation reflecting on her character. Portions of the message may be reproduced here, Yaśodhara's remarks being put within brackets. Amṛtamati says: 'I will accompany Your Majesty, just as the tide accompanies the ocean (That is why you are fickle); just as the image of the moon accompanies the sky (That is why you have a black spot[1]); just as the shade accompanies a tree (That is why you are enjoyed by others); just as the track accompanies a chariot (That is why you are 'full of dust'[2]); just as the flame accompanies a lamp (That is why you emit 'smoke'[3]); just as sylvan beauty accompanies the spring (That is why you are full of Cupid's lore); just as the Ganges is the companion of the Himālayas (That is why you seek a lower[4] level)'.[5]

Instances of Yamakas are occasionally found. A device used more than once is the Śṛṅkhalayamaka which consists in the continuous repetition of the last syllables of a series of compounds at the beginning of each succeeding compound. For example,

यः खल्वनेकविकिरकुलकामिनीनिशितशिखोल्लेखनखमुखविलिख्यमानशाखाभुजशिखरः, शिखरशिखाडम्बरित… कुपलपर्यन्तः, कुपलपर्यन्त………पल्लवपुटपटलः, पल्लवपुटपटलान्तराल……पथिकसार्थः, पथिकसार्थ…………… सहचरीनिचयः, सहचरीनिचय……छायाच्छन्नतलदेशः, छायाच्छन्नतलदेश………………

As pointed out by Jacobi, the Śṛṅkhalayamaka is used by Siddharṣi in *Upamitibhavaprapañcā kathā*, p. 752. Haribhadra too has used this device in verses in his *Samarāiccakahā*.[6]

The mixture of prose and verse is a salient feature of *Yaśastilaka* which is one of the two earliest extant Campūs, the first being Trivikrama's *Nalacampū* written during the reign of the Rāṣṭrakūṭa Emperor Indra

1 i. e. a blot on her character.

2 'a lewd woman'.

3 i. e. disgrace.

4 i. e. a paramour of lower rank.

5 'देवस्याहं सहचरी…………जलनिधेर्वेलेव अत एव चपलासि, नभसः शशिप्रतिमेव अत एव सकलङ्कासि, विटपिनश्छायेव अत एवान्योपभोग्यासि,…………रथस्य मार्गभूमिरिव अत एव पांशुलासि। प्रदीपस्य शिखेव अत एव मलिनोद्गारासि, वसन्तस्य वनलक्ष्मीरिव अत एव मन्मथकथासनाथासि………हिमगिरेर्गङ्गेव अत एव नीचानुगतासि ………'

6 See B. I. ed., pp. 79, 423-4, 449, etc.

III in the first quarter of the tenth century. It will be out of place to trace here the growth of Sanskrit narrative composition in mixed prose and verse, the origins of which go back to Vedic literature as well as Buddhist writings in Pāli and Sanskrit. There is, however, no doubt that this form of composition became popular in the Deccan in the tenth century in Sanskrit as well as Kanarese literature.[1] Apart from the romances of Trivikrama and Somadeva, the Kudlur grant of the Ganga king Mārasiṁha, elaborately composed in Sanskrit prose and verse, and containing a detailed account of the Ganga dynasty, was issued in 963 A. D. about five years after the composition of Somadeva's *Yaśastilaka*.[2] As regards Kanarese literature, Pampa wrote his famous works *Ādipurāṇa* and *Pampa Bhārata* in mixed prose and verse in 941 A. D., and the *campū* style continued to be popular in that literature for a long period after. Among notable later examples of the mixed style may be mentioned Nāgacandra's *Pampa Rāmāyaṇa* (*circa* 1105 A. D.) and Nemicandra's *Līlāvatī* (*circa* 1170 A. D.), 'the earliest known specimen of the Novel, or genuine work of fiction, of the Kanarese language'.[3] Somadeva wrote his *Yaśastilaka* less than two decades after the composition of Pampa's works; and being a native of Karṇāṭaka, he may have been influenced by the prevailing Kanarese literary style of his time. As we have already pointed out, Pampa was court-poet of Arikesarin II who reigned at Puligere (Lakshmesvar, Dharwar District), while Somadeva wrote at Gangadhārā during the reign of one of his successors. Another noteworthy point is that most of the Kanarese writers of the tenth century and after were Jainas, and it is highly probable that they as well as Somadeva were influenced by the example of the great Jaina Prākrit romances in mixed prose and verse, e. g., the *Samarāiccakahā* of Haribhadra and the *Kuvalayamālā* of Uddyotana[4] composed in the eighth century. The extensive allegorical novel *Upamitibhavaprapañcā kathā* of Siddharṣi composed in prose and verse in 906 A. D. is an early example of a Jaina romance written in Sanskrit under similar influences, though not in Kāvya style. Comprehensive Jaina narrative works in Prākrit using prose and verse indiscriminately continued to be written till long after the eighth century, e. g., Guṇacandra's *Mahāvīracarita* (1082 A. D.),[5] Somaprabha's *Kumārapālapratibodha* (1184

1 See Rice: *Kanarese Literature.*

2 *Annual Report of the Mysore Archaeological Department* for 1921.

3 Rice (op. cit.), p. 43.

4 For *Kuvalayamālā* see *Bhāratīya Vidyā*, Vol. II, p. 77

5 *Annals of the Bhandarkar O. R. Institute*, Vol. XVI, p.37.

A. D.) etc. While Somadeva's *Yaśastilaka,* like Trivikrama's *Nalacampū,* is essentially a work written in Sanskrit Kāvya style, its Jaina characterisitics and the probable influence exercised by the Jaina Prākrit romances on its style and composition cannot entirely be ignored.

Dialogues in prose and verse add to the interest of Somadeva's work. The controversial dialogue in Book IV has been dealt with elsewhere, and we may refer to the story of Padmā in Book VII, section 31, which is practically in the form of dialogues linked together by brief narrative passages. The story contains two main dialogues cast in a dramatic form which could be easily adapted to the stage. That between the bawd and Padmā is reproduced below: एकदा मुदा ......तां पुष्यकान्तामुद्दिश्य श्लोकमुदाहार्षीत्।

स्त्रीषु धन्यात्र गङ्गैव परभोगोपगापि या। मणिमालेव सोल्लासं ध्रियते मूर्ध्नि शंभुना ॥

भट्टिनी (स्वगतम्) — इत्वरीजनाचरणहर्म्यनिर्माणाय प्रथमसूत्रपात इवायं वाक्योपोद्घातः।....... .. (प्रकाशम्) आर्ये, किमस्य सुभाषितस्य ऐदंपर्यम्।

धात्री — परमसौभाग्यभागिनि भट्टिनि, जानासि एवास्य सुभाषितस्य कैंपर्यम्, यदि न वज्रघटितहृदयासि।

भट्टिनी — (स्वगतम्) सत्यं वज्रघटितहृदयाहम्, यदि भवत्प्रयुक्तोपघातघुणजर्जरितकाया न भविष्यामि। (प्रकाशम्) आर्ये, हृदयेऽभिनिविष्टमर्थं श्रोतुमिच्छामि।

धात्री — वत्से, कथयामि। किं तु

चित्तं द्वयोः पुरत एव निवेदनीयं ज्ञानाभिमानधनधन्यधिया नरेण।
यः प्रार्थितं न रहयत्यभियुज्यमानो यो वा भवेन्ननु जनो मनसोऽनुकूलः ॥

भट्टिनी — (स्वगतम्) अहो नभःप्रकृतिमपीयं पङ्कैरुपलेप्तुमिच्छति। (प्रकाशम्) आर्ये, उभयत्रापि समर्थाहं न चैतन्मदुपज्ञं भवदुपक्रमं वा।

धात्री — (स्वगतम्) अनुगुणेयं खलु कार्यपरिणतिः .... (प्रकाशम्) अत एव भद्रे, वदन्ति पुराणविदः—
विधुर्गुरोः कलत्रेण गोतमस्यामरेश्वरः। संतनोश्चापि दुश्चर्मा समगस्त पुरा किल ॥

भट्टिनी — आर्ये, एवमेव। यतः

स्त्रीणां वपुर्बन्धुभिरग्निसाक्षिकं परत्र विक्रीतमिदं न मानसम्।
स एव तस्याधिपतिर्मतः कृती विस्रम्भगर्भा ननु यत्र निर्वृतिः ॥

धात्री — पुत्रि, तर्हि श्रूयताम्। त्वं किलैकदा कस्यचित् कुसुमकिंसारुनिर्विशेषवपुषः:............................ प्रासादपरिसरविहारिणी वीक्षणपथानुसारिणी सती कौमुदीव हृदयचन्द्रकान्तानन्दस्यन्दसंपादिनी अभूः। तत्प्रभृति ननु तस्य मदनसुन्दरस्य यूनः.. प्रतिवासरं कार्श्यावतारः, स्मराराधनप्रणीतप्रणिधानस्येवेन्द्रियेषु सन्नता, प्राणेषु चायश्चीनपथा कथा। अपि च

अनवरतजलार्द्रान्दोलनस्यन्दमन्दैरतिसरसमृणालीकन्दलैश्चन्दनार्द्रैः।
अमृतरुचिमरीचिप्रौढितायां निशायां प्रियसखि सुहृदस्ते किंचिदासप्रबोधः ॥

भट्टिनी— आर्ये, किमित्यद्यापि गोपाय्यते ।

धात्री— (कर्णजाहमनुसृत्य) एवमेवम् ।

भट्टिनी—को दोषः ।

धात्री—कदा ।

भट्टिनी—यदा तुभ्यं रोचते ।

The above dialogue is of interest as presenting a lifelike picture of a procuress attempting to seduce a respectable married woman at the instance of a young man of high social standing. There is some resemblance between the Sanskrit dialogue and the first Mime of the *Mimiambi* of the Greek poet Herodas, a collection of Mimes or dramatic dialogues of a literary character, composed about the third century B. C.[1] In the Mime in question the bawd Gyllis visits Metriche, a well-to-do young lady, whose husband Mandris[2] has been away in Egypt for nearly a year, and tries to persuade her to accept a wealthy young man who has vehemently fallen in love with her, and employed the old woman as a go-between. Metriche politely but firmly rejects her proposal and dismisses her with a cheering cup of wine. In both the versions the bawd is an old woman, the husband is or expected to be away, and the passion of the admirer is eloquently described, but the mission ends in failure owing to the loyalty of the young wife. There are, however, important points of difference. The Sanskrit dialogue forms part of a moral and religious tale illustrating the evil consequences of unlawful love, while the Mime is a faithful representation of the seamy side of contemporary life. Further, the sequel is different in the Indian tale, as Padmā, the chaste wife of the priest, instead of dismissing the bawd in a friendly spirit, like Metriche, pretends to accept her proposal, and hatches a plot to trap the young libertine. The Mime is no doubt by far the more realistic in tone and expression; but the treatment, as dramatic dialogue, is no less vivid in the Sanskrit story. Obscure allusions occur in both the Sanskrit dialogue and the Greek Mime. Somadeva employs the ornate style of the Sanskrit drama in prose and verse; while Herodas uses only verse, but in an artificial dialect. The dramatic qualities of the dialogues in the story of Padmā are also present to a lesser extent in the dialogue between Yaśodhara and his mother in Book IV, though the importance of the latter is socio-religious rather than literary.

---

1 Text and Trans. in Otto Crusius: *Die Mimiamben des Herondas............umgearbeitet von Rudolf Herzog*, Leipzig, 1926; and Knox: *Herodes* etc. (*Loeb Classical Library*).

2 Korte (*Hellenistic Poetry, p.329*) thinks Mandris is Metriche's lover.

CHAPTER V

Yaśastilaka as a Socio-political Record

As we have already pointed out, *Yaśastilaka* throws considerable light on contemporary life and society, especially court life and administration; and the available data may be classed under three heads: court life, problems of statecraft and social conditions.

Court Life

A glance at the Synopsis and Chapter VII (the section on Court poetry) will show that Books II and III of *Yaśastilaka* contain valuable information on medieval court life; and the conditions described therein are chiefly applicable to an Imperial court, which, as suggested in a previous chapter, could be no other than that of the Rāṣṭrakūṭa emperors about the middle of the tenth century. Somadeva describes the ceremonies connected with the birth, nuptials and the coronation of the prince, and draws a series of vivid pictures of the various activities of the court. On the intellectual side we have weighty discussions of an academic character: sometimes the king listens to an elaborate debate on the guiding principles of policy;[1] sometimes he discusses important verses of the Arthaśāstra[2]; or participates in heated debates, winning the applause of the learned by his proficiency in the philosophical systems of Jina, Jaimini, Kapila, Kaṇāda, Cārvāka and Buddha.[3] Interludes in a lighter vein are not wanting. For example, on a certain occasion, while the king is discussing the poetical works of the Mahākavis, a poet named Paṇḍita-vaitaṇḍika (Scholar Sophist) comes along and recites an untimely panegyric in his honour, e. g. (3. 271),

हरगिरयन्ति महीध्राः क्षीरोदधयन्ति वार्धयः सर्वे । तव देव यशसि विसरति सौधन्ति जगन्ति च त्रीणि ॥

"Sire, by reason of the expansion of thy fame, mountains turn white like the Kailāsa; the seas turn white as the Ocean of milk, all of them; and the three worlds resemble palaces in lustre!" Finding the king inattentive, he asks discourteously how it is that the sovereign does not recognise a world-renowned poet like him![4] The king, however, wounds his vanity by asking him the purport of a difficult verse of Sanskrit poetics which proves to be beyond his comprehension.[5]

---

1 See Chap. VII.

2 See Chap. XVIII.

3 'कदाचित्……पण्डितप्रकाण्डमण्डलीमण्डनाडम्बरगीर्गुम्फसंरम्भेषु जिनजैमिनिकपिलकणचरचार्वाकशाक्यप्रणीतप्रमाण-संवीणतया विदुष्विणीनां परिषदां भित्तिभित्तिष्वात्मयशःप्रशस्तीरुल्लिलेख ।' Vol. I, p. 480.

4 सकलकविलोकचक्रप्रमर्दनः ख्यात एव भुवनेऽस्मिन् । कथमिह संप्रति भवता समागतो नावबुध्येऽहम् ॥ 3. 273.

5 For the verse in question see Chap. XVIII.

Court poets or rather panegyrists are very much in evidence, and recite appropriate verses on diverse occasions, marriage, coronation etc. Certain of them describe the morning and evening scenery, the beauties of the seasons and the gaiety of court festivals; recount the merits of horses and elephants, and recite panegyrics while the king practises archery in the gymnasium. One of the bards who recites the verses in praise of the rising moon is described as having been a fellow student with the king; and there is no doubt that the presence of these educated versifiers adds to the refinement and cultural atmosphere of the court.

Reference is made in Book II to Committees of Experts (*ācārya-pariṣad*) for the examination of horses and elephants and their representatives, the Mahāmātra and the Mahāsādhaka, the chief keepers of the royal elephants and horses respectively, who submit to the king detailed oral reports on the characteristics of the elephant and the horse selected for his use. The Mahāmātra appears to be a Brāhmaṇa, being introduced as belonging to the family of Paraśurāma; while the Mahāsādhaka is an experienced soldier, being described as having a body marked with the scars of wounds received in many a battle. Great attention seems to have been paid to elephants. The king himself takes part in the training and arming of elephants, and one of his favourite recreations is the witnessing of elephant-races in the race-courses (*pradhāva-dharaṇi*[1]).

The court jester (*narma-saciva*) does not appear in person in our work, but certain utterances attributed to him contain some home truths about the character of kings (3. 254–5):

समरभरः सुभटानां फलानि कर्णेजपैस्तु भोग्यानि। करिदशना इव नृपतेर्बाह्याः क्लेशाय खादनेऽन्तस्थाः ॥
स्रक्पुष्पमिव निसर्गाद्गुणेषु नृपतिः पराङ्मुखः प्रायः। कोश इवात्मविदारिणि निस्त्रिंशे संमुखो भवति ॥

"The warriors bear the brunt of the fighting, but it is the wirepullers who enjoy the results. Those serving a king from outside undergo all hardship, while those in the inner circle reap the benefits; just as the outer tusks of an elephant do the hard jobs, while the inner teeth are employed in eating. Kings, by nature, turn their backs at merits, just as the flowers of a wreath turn their backs at the string. They welcome the heartless who destroy them, even as a sheath receives the sword that cleaves it."

The minister, the physician, the chef and the priest are mentioned together in one of the morning verses (3. 11) recited by the bards, who announce their arrival at the court. The court physician seems to be well-read in medical literature, aud admonishes the king in a lengthy

1 Book III (प्रधावधरणिषु करिविनोदविलोकनदोहदं प्रासादमध्यास्य etc.).

discourse on matters connected with physical exercise, food and drink.[1] Astrologers are mentioned in Book II, and they are consulted on the eve of the coronation, and doubtless on many other occasions. The Sthapati or the architect appears in connection with the arrangements for the coronation and the construction of the magnificent pavilion on the bank of the Śiprā.[2]

The composition of the personnel of medieval courts seems to have been more or less similar in India and elsewhere. Nizami of Samarcand declared about 1155 that a properly constituted court should have four classes of educated men: secretaries of state, poets, astrologers and physicians, for "the business of kings cannot be conducted without competent secretaries; their triumphs and victories will not be immortalized without eloquent poets; their enterprises will not succeed unless undertaken at seasons adjudged propitious by sagacious astrologers; while health, the basis of all happiness and activity, can only be secured by the services of able and trustworthy physicians".[3] This is a fairly accurate description of the composition of medieval courts, whether oriental or occidental. We are told that "even in the West most courts had their astrologers[4] by the thirteenth century–the earl of Chester even in the twelfth–and the other three might well be found still earlier, but in a less bureaucratic form." The description is particularly true of the Sicilian court of the twelfth and thirteenth centuries with "its astrologers and poets, its Arab physicians and many-tongued secretaries"; and the entourage of the Indian court was not, we presume, materially different, to judge from Somadeva's circumstantial account. As regards secretaries and state officials, we may here refer to the Sandhivigrahins, who appear in our work in the role of secretaries of state, and can be accurately described as 'many-tongued', as will be seen later.

One of the functions of the Sandhivigrahins in our work is to announce the arrival at the imperial court of envoys from foreign courts with presents characteristic of their respective countries.[5] The poetical utterances of the Sandhivigrahins are reproduced below (3. 247–46):

दूताः केरलचोलसिंहलशकश्रीमालपञ्चालकैरन्यैश्चाङ्गकलिङ्गवङ्गपतिभिः प्रस्थापिताः प्राङ्गणे ।
तिष्ठन्त्यात्मकुलागताखिलमहीसारं गृहीत्वा करे देवस्यापि जगत्पतेरवसरः किं विद्यते वा न वा ॥

1 See below.

2 See Chap. II.

3 Haskins: *The Renaissance of the twelfth century*, p. 54.

4 'The court astrologer...became an indispensable adjunct of the 'Abbāsid throne. Hitti: *History of the Arabs*, p. 318.

5 The *ḥājib* or chamberlain of the Baghdad court was attached to the person of the caliph, and his duty consisted in introducing accredited envoys and dignitaries into the caliphal presence. Hitti (op. cit.).

अवलगति कलिङ्गाधीश्वरस्त्वां करीन्द्रैस्तुरगनिवह एष प्रेषितः सैन्धवैस्ते ।
अयमपि च समास्ते पाण्ड्यदेशाधिनाथस्तरलगुलिकहारप्राभृतव्यग्रहस्तः ॥

कश्मीरैः कीरनाथः क्षितिप मृगमदैरेष नेपालपालः कौशेयैः कोशलेन्द्रः शिशिरगिरिपतिर्ग्रन्थिपर्णैरुदीर्णैः ।
श्रीचन्द्रश्चन्द्रकान्तैर्विविधकुलधनैर्मागधः प्राभृतैस्त्वां द्रष्टुं द्वारे समास्ते यदिह समुचितं देव तन्मां प्रशाधि ॥

"The envoys, despatched by the kings of Kerala, Cola, Ceylon, the Śaka land, Śrīmāla and Pañcāla, and by the lords of Aṅga, Kaliṅga and Vaṅga as well as other kings, stand in the courtyard, holding in their hands the choicest products of all their dynastic possessions. (They may be told) whether Your Majesty, the lord of the earth, has the leisure to see them or not." "The lord of Kaliṅga comes to thee with mighty elephants, and the princes of the Indus region have sent thee yonder multitude of horses. Here, too, is the lord of the Pāṇḍya country, his hands full of wreaths of large pearls brought as presents." "Ruler of the earth, to see thee the lord of Kāśmīra is at the door with presents of saffron, the ruler of Nepāla with musk, the lord of Kośala with silks, the lord of the Himālayas with large Granthiparṇa[1] roots, the lord of Kailāsa with moonstones, and the king of Magadha with diverse heirlooms. Sire, command me to do what befits the occasion."

The challenge to various kings, demanding submission, intended to be delivered by Yaśodhara's envoy, is no more than a rhetorical exercise[2]; but interesting data on the reception of envoys from hostile courts and the declaration of war can be gleaned from the episode of the king of Pañcāla described in *Yaśastilaka*, Book III. The Sandhivigrahin enters and tells Yaśodhara: 'Sire, Dukūla, an envoy of Acala, king of Pañcāla, has arrived and is waiting at the gate.' Thus saying, he ushers in the envoy, and ordered by Yaśodhara, offers him a seat at the proper place after he has paid his respects to the king. The Sandhivigrahin then says: 'Envoy, show to yonder Lord the presents sent by your master. Messenger, deliver the letter;' and both the envoy (*dūta*) and the messenger (*śāsanahara*) carry out the instructions. The Sandhivigrahin had already been informed by a spy, living in Acala's capital in the guise of an ascetic under the name of Jābāla, that that king had a powerful force of elephants and planned to declare war against Yaśodhara before long The information supplied by the spy is corroborated by certain indications provided by the articles sent – an iron ball, the letter marked with the emblem of a sword on the outside, and the presents wrapped in four pieces of cloth; or according to another interpretation, an iron ball and the presents and the letter,

1 A fragrant root called गाथियन in Assamese, which is pounded by women to the accompaniment of sengs during the night on nuptial occasions among the Assamese people.

2 See Chap. VII.

both marked with the figure of a sword and four encircling lines.[1] In *Nītivākyāmṛta* (Chap. 13) Somadeva refers to these emblems as being present on letters from enemies.[2] Now, the iron ball symbolized the invulnerability of the sender; the fourfold wrappings or the four encircling lines the 'four-limbed' army consisting of cavalry, infantry, elephants, and chariots; and the sword, of course, the threat of war. It was apparently usual to despatch such symbolic gifts as a prelude to warlike measures; and that it was a very ancient custom, and not confined to India, is shown by the account of the gifts (a bird, a mouse, a frog and five arrows) sent by the Scythian kings to Darius under similar circumstances, as related by Herodotus, Book IV. 131.

Be that as it may, the Sandhivigrahin is convinced of the war-like intentions of the king of Pañcāla, and considers it useless to examine the insincere presents and the contents of the letter, which was only too likely to proclaim the enemy's glory. Accordingly he puts aside the letter and asks the envoy to deliver his message orally, at the same time threatening him with dire punishment for his unfriendly mission: the nose would be chopped off, the head shaved at random, Bilva fruits tied to the forelock, and a garland of potsherds hung round the neck; besides, he would have to ride a donkey.[3] Controlling himself, the Sandhivigrahin admits that no wise man should be angry with an envoy who is bound to report facts. Then addressing the envoy, a Brāhmaṇa, the royal official stresses the futility of further queries, and goes on to say: "The motives of your master are clear from your demeanour. The reason why His Majesty has so long connived at Acala, in spite of his having committed many an act of defiance, is that the kings of his line had long paid homage in the past to His Majesty's forbears. But, now, if Acala seeks for himself the fate of a moth in the flames of His Majesty's might, it would be like desiring to play with the manes of a lion, or decorate oneself with the crest-gems of deadly serpents, or scratch with one's finger-nails the tusks of a rutting elephant, or extinguish with one's hands the fire of the epoch of universal destruction, or swim across the ocean, or traverse the sky with

1 The first interpretation is found in a marginal note in Ms. A. Somadeva says प्राभृततन्त्रमेतत् पत्रं च प्राहिणोत् । तथाह्यनयोर्मण्डलाग्रमुद्राङ्कितो वेष्टनचतुष्टयानेष्टाङ्कितश्च बहिःप्रकाशः सनिवेशः। p. 550. Ms. A says अनयोर्लेखप्राभृतयोः संनिवेशः संस्थितिः यथासंख्यं लेखस्य संनिवेशः खड्गचिह्नसहितः युद्धं सूचयति । प्राभृतस्य संनिबेशः वेष्टनचतुष्टयमिष्टं वस्त्रचतुष्टयेन वेष्टितः सैन्यभयं दर्शयतीति भावः । 'चत्वारि वेष्टनानि खड्गमुद्रा च प्रतिपक्षलेखानाम्'।

2 The anonymous commentary says तेषामुपरि चत्वारि वेष्टनानि बन्धनानि भवन्ति·

3 नासोद्वासनमार्गमुण्डनशिखामालूरबन्धक्रमः कण्ठे शीर्णशरावदामकलनं कात्रेयकारोहणम् । दूतान्यश्च न ते निकारपरुषः कोऽप्यत्र कार्यो विधिस्तत्त्वस्थो वद वाचिकं निजपतेर्लेखस्त्वयं तिष्ठतु ॥ 3. 402.

a bound, or lift the Mandara mountain with one's hands, or use the axe of Śiva as a mirror, or extract the pearl embedded in the jaw of the Primeval Boar[1] for using it as an ornament." Acala, in fact, proud of his own power in destroying the petty enemies of his kingdom, does not even now realise the great king's valour, praised by Indra himself in talks about Kṣatriya heroes(3. 403):

वैकुण्ठः कुलकीर्तनं कमलभूर्दर्भप्रगल्भाङ्गुलिर्नं स्त्री नैव पुमानुमापतिरयं चन्द्रो निशासेवकः।
हेलिः केलिसरोजबन्धुरनिलः क्रीडाश्रमे चाटुमान् यस्येत्थं गणनामरेषु विजयी तस्याहवे कोऽपरः॥

"Who can conquer him in battle who is talked about among the gods thus: Viṣṇu is his panegyrist, and Brahman his priest, busily taking up Kuśa blades with the fingers; Śiva is the eunuch of his harem, and yonder Moon serves him at night; and the Sun is the friend of his toy lotuses, and the wind caresses him in the fatigue of his sports!"

The speech of the Sandhivigrahin arouses the martial ardour of the warriors present, each of whom, addressing himself to the envoy, utters a vehement challenge to the king of Pañcāla. Kodaṇḍamārtaṇḍa, for example, catching hold of the envoy's hand, says (3. 405–6):

श्रीपदं मित्रपक्षाणां खरदण्डं च विद्विषाम्। देवस्यास्य पदाम्भोजद्वयं शिरसि धार्यताम्॥
नो चेत् कोदण्डमार्तण्डकाण्डखण्डितमस्तकः। यास्यत्याजौ स ते स्वामी रुण्डताण्डवडम्बरम्॥

"Hold on thy head His Majesty's lotus feet, a source of prosperity to his allies, but grimly oppressive to his foes. Otherwise, thy master, decapitated by the arrows of Kodaṇḍa-mārtaṇḍa (The Sun of the Bow), will vehemently dance on the battlefield, a headless trunk." Karavālavīra declares, brandishing his sword (3. 409–10): अध्वग, साध्ववधार्यताम्।

अखर्वगर्वदुर्वारवीर्यपर्यस्तमानसः। मदीयस्वामिसेवासु यः कोऽपि हतसाहसः॥
विपक्षपक्षक्षयदक्षदीक्षः कौक्षेयको मामक एष तस्य। रक्षांसि वक्षःक्षतजैः क्षरद्भिः प्रतीक्षतेऽक्षुण्णतया रणेषु॥

"Wayfarer[2], know for certain, this my sword, consecrated to the task of destroying the foeman and his allies, amply gratifies the goblins on the battlefield with the blood gushing from the bosom of the man, who is slack in paying homage to my master, being perverted by a sense of overweening pride and irresistible might."

Certain of the champions ask the envoy to deliver threatening messages to the king of Pañcāla, of which the following are specimens, being communicated by Triśūla-bhairava and Asama-sāhasa respectivly (3. 416 and 320):

इदं त्रिशूलं तिसृभिः शिखाभिर्मार्गत्रयं वक्षसि ते विधाय। पातालमर्त्यत्रिदिवावतारां कर्ता रणे कीर्तिमिमां मदीयाम्॥

1 The Boar Incarnation of Viṣṇu.

2 i. e. the envoy.

"Three openings will this trident make in thy bosom with its three prongs, and spread my martial fame on earth, in heaven and in the nether regions!"

तुलारणे द्वन्द्वरणे दिवारणे निशारणे कूटरणे परत्र वा। यदि प्रवीरस्त्वमिहैधि मे पुरे न गर्जितैः शौर्यकलेषु कीर्तयः ॥

"If thou art strong in duels or in day-war or night-war or deceptive warfare or in other modes of fighting, do thou confront me in any of them. The fame of the valiant is not produced by empty roars."

Throughout this unseemly scene, insulting language is freely used, the king of Pañcāla being referred to as 'the meanest of all the villains'[1], and the envoy variously addressed as *Veda-vaivadhika* ('one to whom the Vedas are a burden'), *dvijāpasada, brahmabandhu, dvija-vaṁśapāṁsana*, or simply as 'Brāhmaṇa'. Happily the disorder is stopped by the intervention of the commander-in-chief who addresses the assembly: Ye wise men, useless are the shouts of men lacking in proper conduct. The brave and the timorous will be sorted out in war (3. 422). Therefore let every one of you control his wrath and desist from offensive language. You, too, Sandhi-vigrahin, eager to enhance the might of your master, should not give way to emotion. Examine the letter and draft a reply. Examine the presents and prepare counterpresents. Let due respect be shown to all the three (the envoy, the letter and the presents), for the kings speak through their envoys even when they take up arms against each other. Not to speak of the envoys, even their servants should not be insulted. Further, neither one's own failure nor the success of others depends upon the loud declamations of envoys. They are non-combatant intermediaries and speak as they like." (3. 423)

The letter is soon ready, and the Sandhivigrahin reads it out. It is extremely brief except for a lengthy conglomeration of epithets designed to glorify Yaśodhara; and, after a polite and formal prelude, communicates an arrogant message from the commander-in-chief, Vijayavardhana, calling upon the king of Pañcāla to submit, since there is no safety for him whether on the battlefield or in flight. The letter is reproduced in part below:

स्वस्ति। समस्तमहासामन्तशिखण्डमण्डनीभवच्चरणकमलः कमलाकरससेजसेव्यमानपादपल्लवः पल्लवपाण्ड्यचोलचेरमहर्म्यनिर्माणप्रकाश्यमानदिग्विजयवाहिनीप्रचारः चारचक्षुःसहस्रसाक्षात्कृतसकलभूपालमण्डलः मण्डलाग्रधाराजलनिमग्ननिखिलारातिसंतानः ··········पाटलिपुत्रपण्याङ्गनाभुजङ्गः वलभिरम्भोरुविभ्रमभ्रमरः पौरवपुरंध्रीरोध्रतिलकः सततवसुवितरणप्रीणितद्विजसमाजः श्रीयशोधरमहाराजः सकलप्रशस्तिसहितमचलमहीपतिमादिशति। श्रेयोऽन्यत्। कार्यं चैतदेव–यदुत विजयवर्धनः सेनापतिर्भवन्तमेवमामन्त्रयते··················

The episode of the embassy, divested of rhetoric, throws interesting sidelights on court practices in the tenth century, but even the rhetoric

1 'अहो दूत निवेदयेदं मद्वचनं तस्य सकलदुराचारलोकहेठस्य' etc.

cannot entirely be ignored, as it somehow always appears in the background of medieval court life. Diplomatic immunity seems to have been assured by time-honoured custom, but there was nothing to prevent an envoy being subjected to humiliation or open insult. Things were not far different in this respect in the contemporary Byzantine court, to judge from the *Legatio* of Liudprand, Bishop of Cremona, a Western contemporary of Somadeva, who gives an account of an embassy to Constantinople during the reign of the Emperor Nicephorus Phocas, undertaken on behalf of Otto the Great in 968 A. D. Not only was Liudprand compelled every now and then to swallow affront and offensive language at the Byzantine court, but he also describes how in the same year the envoys of the Pope were actually put in prison for bringing an improperly addressed letter to the emperor. The fulminations of the court officials against the Papal legates may be compared with the threats uttered by the Sandhivigrahin against the envoy of the king of Pañcāla: "............Would that one of them were a bishop and the other a marquess! Then we would sew them in a sack, and after giving them a sound beating with rods and plucking out their beards and hair we would throw them into the sea. As for these fellows, their lives may be spared;....................".[1]

The comprehensive report of the spy to the king in Book III is a unique document, to which we will return presently. The review of the army is an important incident of court life, and Somadeva's detailed account of it in the same Book gains in importance from the fact that he describes regiments of soldiers from different parts of India in the king's army.[2] Somadeva's picture is so minute and lifelike that he must have personally observed the ways of these soldiers, and may be supposed to have witnessed them, if anywhere, in the capital of the Rāṣṭrakūṭa emperors, who possibly included in their armies regiments composed of fighting men of different nationalities of India to meet the demands of their far-flung campaigns beyond the limits of the Deccan. Five regiments in all are described: the Deccan regiment; the Drāmila or South Indian regiment provided with litters; the North Indian regiment of cavalry; the Gurjara regiment of archers; and the Tirhut regiment, expert in naval warfare, and well-equipped with elephants, and containing an undisciplined Gauḍa element. The Tirhut, or the Tairabhukta regiment, as it is called, may be roughly described as the Behar and Bengal regiment, and it may

1 Liudprand:. *Works. Trans.* Wright, p. 264.

2 See Chap. IV. The King reviews the troops from a raised platform. Somadeva says सकलसैन्यसमालोकनोत्तुङ्गतमङ्गसंगतिकरेषु बलदर्शनावसरेषु । p. 461.

be noted in this connection that there is another reference to naval soldiers (*tarīcaranara*) elsewhere in the work.[1] It will be seen that most of the regiments described are those of foot-soldiers; and the description, on the whole, corresponds to Al Masudi's statement that the Balhara or the Rāṣṭrakūṭa king's 'horses and elephants were innumerable, but his troops were mostly infantry'.[2] It has, however, been rightly pointed out that the Rāṣṭrakūṭa cavalry cannot be overlooked, and "the lightning all-India movements of Dhruva, Govinda III and Indra III presuppose a strong cavalry".[3] Another noteworthy feature of Somadeva's description of the regiments is the absence of any reference to chariots, although he refers to their fighting qualities in his theoretical work *Nītivākyāmṛta*. This seems to corroborate the view that chariots as an instrument of war were no longer in use in the days of the Rāṣṭrakūṭas.[4]

The lighter side of court life is represented by dance exhibitions in the court theatre in connection with the Pūrvaraṅga ceremony accompanied by hymns to Sarasvatī. The king is described as witnessing these performances in company with expert dancers and well-trained exponents of the histrionic art.[5] As is to be expected, certain court festivals are also mentioned: the Mahānavamī, the Dīpotsava, the Spring carnival and the worship of Makaradhvaja, the god of love.[6]

It is hardly necessary to emphasize the documentary value of the second and third Books of *Yaśastilaka* as presenting before us a detailed and vivid picture of Indian court life about the middle of the tenth century. Yaśodhara, the hero of the story, is a legendary figure; but the setting of his court has a historical character and reflects the conditions prevailing in the writer's own time. It is a curious coincidence that not long before Somadeva composed his imaginative account of Indian court life, the Byzantine Emperor Constantine VII (912–59) wrote his *De cerimoniis aulae*, 'an account of the whole life of the Byzantine polity, with its hierarchy of lay and ecclesiastical officials,' and the traditional ceremonies and festivals, 'from the coronation and burial of an Emperor to the baptism of his son'.[7] The Indian writer would presumably have

1 'कदनमेदिनीषु नखरदविदारितारातिकरितुरगरथतरीचरनरनिकर……' Book III, p. 490.

2 Altekar: *The Rāṣṭrakūṭas and their times*, p. 248.

3 Ibid., p. 249.

4 Ibid., p. 248.

5 See Chap. XV.

6 See Chap. XV.

7 Hussey: *Church and Learning in the Byzantine Empire*, p. 28.

shared the emperor's idea that 'it is through its glorious ceremonial that the imperial majesty is increased in splendour'; and Somadeva was doubtless sufficiently impressed by the grandeur of contemporay court life, which partly explains his treatment of the theme as a pendent to the traditional story of Yaśodhara. But he does more: he deals with problems of administration, a subject in which he is deeply interested.

Problems of Statecraft

Side by side with the portrayal of court life, Somadeva lays down precepts and principles for the guidance of a monarch, and illustrates them where necessary by means of concrete examples and quasi-historical traditions. From this point of view, *Yaśastilaka* may be regarded as a sort of illustrative commentary on some of the topics dealt with in the formal treatises on the *nītiśāstra* including Somadeva's own *Nītivākyāmṛta.* The latter is a comprehensive work in the form of *sūtras* in thirtytwo chapters; and topics briefly touched in *Nītivākyāmṛta* are often treated in greater detail in *Yaśastilaka*, the two works supplementing each other, so far as problems of statecraft are concerned.

Somadeva lays great emphasis on the paramount influence of the monarch in moulding the character of his subjects, who implicitly follow his example whether it is good or bad. We are told that just as the day and the night cause light and darkness respectively, so is the example of the king the determining factor in the practice of virtue or sin by his subjects (Book IV, p. 95):

अहोरात्रं यथा हेतुः प्रकाशध्वान्तजन्मनि । तथा महीपतिर्हेतुः पुण्यपापप्रवर्तने ॥

Somadeva quotes in this connection a popular verse: उक्तं च—

राज्ञि धर्मिणि धर्मिष्ठाः पापे पापाः समे समाः । राजानमनुवर्तन्ते यथा राजा तथा प्रजाः ॥

A similar verse is found also in *S'ukranītisāra* 4. 1. 62:

सुपुण्यो यत्र नृपतिर्धर्मिष्ठास्तत्र हि प्रजाः । महापापी यत्र राजा तत्राधर्मपरो जनः ॥

The idea is indeed an old one, and occurs in Āryaśūra's *Jātakamālā* XIII. 39, wherein the subjects unhesitatingly following the king's example, good or bad, are compared to cows following the lead of an ox:

जिह्मं शुभं वा वृषभप्रचारं गावोऽनुगा यद्वदनुप्रयान्ति । उत्क्षिप्तशङ्काङ्कुशनिर्विघट्टं प्रजास्तथैव क्षितिपस्य वृत्तिम् ॥

It is interesting to note that the influence of the king's example on his subjects is likewise emphasized in St. John Damascene's *Barlaam and Ioasaph* (Chap. XXXIII) a religious romance of the eighth century to which we will have occasion to revert.

"And soothly, the king was a good example to all; and he inflamed and kindled the hearts of many to be of the same mind with himself.

For such is the nature of authority. Its subjects always conform to its likeness, and are wont to love the same objects, and to practise the pursuits which they perceive to be pleasing to their governor."[1]

Somadeva goes on to say: "Verily the habits and customs of men are based on those of the king. And the customary regulations of the different castes and orders of society, leading to religious merit and demerit, are subject to the king's control. The citizens do exactly what the kings do, good or bad, under the influence of passion or anger, or through ignorance."[2] Somadeva reinforces his remarks by pointing out how the bad example set by kings is responsible for the existence of evil customs among their subjects. For instance, the kings are to blame for the fact that the Brāhmaṇas of the Vaṅgī kingdom are in the habit of drinking wine, and the Persians commit incest with their mothers, and there is intermixture of castes in Ceylon.[3] It is difficult to adjudge the historical value of these statements. The Vaṅgī country is identified by Śrutasāgara in his commentary with Ratnapura, modern Ratanpur, which was the capital of Dakṣiṇa Kosala (Bilaspur District, C. P.), where reigned a branch of the Cedis of Tripuri.[4] The reference to the intermixture of castes in Ceylon may have something to do with the conversion of the island to Buddhism by Mahinda under the king Devānaṁpiya Tissa, a contemporary of Aśoka, as related in the *Mahāvaṁsa*. As regards the Persian custom, the Christian Apologist Tertullian (second century A. D.) says in his *Apology* IX. 16 that the Persians, according to Ctesias,[5] consort with their mothers.[6]

Be that as it may, Somadeva concludes his argument by declaring that just as a good king acquires the sixth part of the religious merit of those who practise virtue, so does a wicked one the sixth part of the sin of those who commit misdeeds:

यथैव पुण्यस्य सुकर्मभाजां षष्ठांशभागी नृपतिः सुवृत्तः । तथैव पापस्य कुकर्मभाजां षष्ठांशभागी नृपतिः कुवृत्तः ॥

1 Text and Trans. in *Loeb Classical Library*, p. 515.

2 'नृपतिप्रतिष्ठानि च खलु देहिनां व्यवहारतन्त्राणि वर्तन्ते । नृपत्यायत्ताः पुण्यपापहेतवो वर्णाश्रमाचारव्यवस्थाश्च । ते च नृपतयः कामक्रोधाभ्यामज्ञानेन वा यथैव शुभमशुभं वा कर्मारभन्ते तथैव जानपदा अपि ।' Book IV.

3 'श्रूयते हि—वङ्गीमण्डले नृपतिदोषाद्भूदेवेष्वासवोपयोगः, पारसीकेषु स्वसवित्रीसंयोगः, सिंहलेषु च विश्वामित्रसृष्टिप्रयोग इति ।' Ibid. p. 95.

4 Poussin: *Dynasties et Histoire de l' Inde*, p. 155.

5 Ctesias of Cnidus lived many years at the Persian court towards the end of the 5th century B. C., and wrote in the Ionic dialect a comprehensive work on the history of Persia.

6 *Persas cum suis matribus misceri Ctesias refert.*

The idea is not new. Yājñavalkya 1. 335 says that the king acquires the sixth part of the religious merit of the subjects as a result of governing them with justice;[1] while the *Agnipurāṇa* 223. 10 goes further and says that a king acquires the sixth part of both the merit and the demerit of his subjects.[2]

Somadeva lays great emphasis on the personal supervision of the affairs of the state by the king. He says: "A king inaccessible to his subjects is misled by those near him and baffled by his enemies. The employees, like faithless wives, have, as a rule, no other means of thriving than the troubles of their masters, nor has a master any other means of thriving than by checking the transgression of his employees, like that of his wives."[3] Somadeva has in this connection the following verses in *Yaśastilaka*, Book III (3. 23-26):

नियुक्तहस्तार्पितराज्यभारास्तिष्ठन्ति ये स्वैरविहारसाराः ।
बिडालवृन्दाहितदुग्धमुद्राः स्वपन्ति ते मूढधियः क्षितीन्द्राः ॥
ज्ञायेत मार्गः सलिले तिमीनां पतत्रिणां व्योम्नि कदाचिदेषः ।
अध्यक्षसिद्धेऽपि कृतावलोपा न ज्ञायतेऽमात्यजनस्य वृत्तिः ॥
व्याधिवृद्धौ यथा वैद्यः श्रीमतामाहितोद्यमः । व्यसनेषु तथा राज्ञः कृतयत्ना नियोगिनः ॥
नियोगिभिर्विना नास्ति राज्यं भूपे हि केवले । तस्मादमी विधातव्या रक्षितव्याश्च यत्नतः ॥

"Kings who enjoy pleasures at will, leaving the charge of the kingdom in the hands of officials, are foolish indeed. They might as well sleep, leaving the cats in charge of the milk. The movement of fish in the water and of birds in the sky might sometimes be known, but the conduct of ministers, inscrutable even in palpable matters, can never be known. Just as a physician exerts himself to aggravate ailments of wealthy patients, so do the officials of a king attempt to create troubles for him. There cannot be a kingdom with the king alone, without any officials; so they have to be created as well as guarded with care."

The necessity of strict control to be exercised by the king over his officials is emphasized also in Somadeva's *Nītivākyāmṛta* (Chaps. 17 and 18), and there is sometimes close verbal resemblance between the statements in the two works. For example, we read in *Nītivākyāmṛta* (17. 38-9, 44):

दुर्दर्शो हि राजा कार्याकार्यविपर्यासमासन्नैः कार्यतेऽतिसंधीयते च द्विषद्भिः । वैद्येषु श्रीमतां व्याधिवर्धनादिव नियोगिषु भर्तुर्व्यसनवर्धनादपरो नास्ति जीवनोपायः । मार्जारेषु दुग्धरक्षणमिव नियोगिषु विश्वासकरणम् ।

---

1 पुण्यात् षड्भागमादत्ते न्यायेन परिपालयन् । सर्वदानाधिकं यस्मात् प्रजानां परिपालनम् ॥

2 'राजा षड्भागमादत्ते सुकृताद्दुष्कृतादपि'.

3 'दुर्दर्शो हि राजा कार्याकार्यविपर्यासमासन्नैः कार्यतेऽतिसंधीयते च द्विषद्भिः । न हि नियोगिनामसतीजनानामिव भर्तुर्व्यसनादपरः प्रायेणास्ति जीवनोपायः । स्वामिनो वा नियुक्तानां स्त्रीणामिवातिप्रसरणनिवारणात् ।' Book III, p. 373.

It may also be noted in this connection that the verse 3. 24 quoted above is reminiscent of the following verses of Kauṭilya's *Arthaśāstra* II. 9:

मत्स्या यथान्तःसलिले चरन्तो ज्ञातुं न शक्याः सलिलं पिबन्तः ।
युक्तास्तथा कार्यविधौ नियुक्ता ज्ञातुं न शक्या धनमाददानाः ॥
अपि शक्या गतिर्ज्ञातुं पततां खे पतत्रिणाम् । न तु प्रच्छन्नभावानां युक्तानां चरतां गतिः ॥

Somadeva opines that the ministers of a king should be men of pure lives, loyal and well-versed in the science of government: they should be men of birth and natives of the country.[1] A king should not depend upon a single minister, the prosperity of one doing so being compared to a creeper climbing a tree with a single branch. Somadeva says in *Yaśastilaka* 3. 230:

एकामात्ये महीपाले नालं लक्ष्मीर्विजृम्भते । लतायास्तत्र का वृद्धिः शाखैका यत्र शाखिनि ॥

In *Nītivākyāmṛta* 10. 82 he expresses the same idea by saying that a tree with a single branch does not cast a large shadow.[2] In the same work (10. 71) he recommends that a king should have three, five or seven ministers. Yet the destiny of a king often depends upon the character of a single minister. Somadeva points out in *Yaśastilaka* 3. 242 that Duryodhana, though powerful, was ruined, because he had a wicked minister; while Candragupta, though without any resources, obtained a kingdom, because he had a good minister in Cāṇakya.

The primary duty of a minister is described thus: he should protect those of the citizens lacking in fighting spirit and resolution with courage, and take care of those who are poor by charitable actions; and by avoiding all cause of disaffection, he should secure the loyalty of the subjects, infected with sedition, whether latent or manifest in ineffectual outbursts.[3] The true minister of a king is one who is liked by the army and the allies, upright in matters relating to the country and the treasury, and above all devoted to the king (3. 200):

तन्त्रमित्रार्पितप्रीतिर्देशकोशोचितस्थितिः । यश्चात्मनि भवेद्भक्तः सोऽमात्यः पृथिवीपतेः ॥

The attitude of a minister towards the king should be governed by loyalty tempered with justice (3. 241):

यः कार्यार्थिनि भूपतावसमधीः कार्याय धत्ते धुरं यश्चार्थार्थिनि संनयोचितमतिश्चिन्तामणिर्जायते ।
भक्तौ भर्तरि मन्त्रिणामिदमहो दिव्यं द्वयं कीर्तितं न क्षोणीश महीयसां निरसनं राज्यस्य वा ध्वंसनम् ॥

---

1 शुचयः स्वामिनि स्निग्धा राजराद्धान्तवेदिनः । मन्त्राधिकारिणो राज्ञामभिजाताः स्वदेशजाः ॥ 3. 110.

2 'किमेकशाखस्य शाखिनो महती भवति च्छाया'.

3 'विग्रहावग्रहाभ्यां हीनानां दीनानां च प्रजानामवदानप्रदानाभ्यां रक्षणमवेक्षणं चान्तर्बहिरवान्तराटोपैः कोपैर्दुःस्थितावस्थितीनां प्रकृतीनां विरागकारणपरिहारेणैकमुखीकरणं च संक्षेपेण मन्त्रिणः कर्म ।' Book III, p. 445.

"Unequalled in wisdom, he undertakes the responsibility of executing a task when the king demands action, and acts like the Wishing gem, in conformity with justice, when the king is in need of funds. These are said to be the two divine factors governing the loyalty of ministers to their master, and not, o king, the expulsion of the great nor the extinction of the realm."

Those who are in constant fear of their lives (that is, fear the king), and have no motives of sordid gain in deliberations, are alone fit to be ministers of kings, and not those who are like blood-sucking leeches (Book IV, p. 155):

प्रतिक्षणं संशयितायुषो ये न येष्वपेक्षास्ति च कार्यवादे । त एव मन्त्रेऽधिकृता नृपाणां न ये जलौकासमवृत्तयश्च ॥

Further, a minister should exercise independence of judgment in expressing his views, and his aim should not merely be to please the king. Somadeva remarks (Ibid.):

प्रशास्ति यः श्रोतृवशेन धर्मं नृपेच्छया यो निगृणाति कार्यम् । अकल्पकामोपचयेन वैद्यस्त्रयस्त एते कालिकालपादाः ॥

"He who preaches religion according to the inclinations of his hearers, he who sets forth a project in conformity with the wishes of the king, and the physician who lives by ministering to the desires of his patients: these three are the pillars of the Kali Age!"

Ministers are, however, faced with a dilemma. If they followed the wishes of the king, the people might be ruined; while if they acted according to the wishes of the people, they might ruin their own position. Yet it is incumbent on ministers to speak the truth: this might only inolve their own ruin, but false counsel might bring about the ruin of the state, the king, and themselves as well (Book IV, pp. 155-6):

प्रजाविलोपो नृपतीच्छया स्यात्प्रजेच्छया चाचरिते स्वनाशः । न मन्त्रिणां वेधविधायिनीवत्सुखं सदैवोभयतः समस्ति ॥
यतो यथार्थं वदतां नराणामात्मक्षयः स्यात्परमेक एव । राष्ट्रस्य राज्ञो ध्रुवमात्मनश्च मिथ्योपदेशस्तु करोति नाशम् ॥

Somadeva speaks a good deal about ministerial corruption. The report of the spy in Book III is designed to show to what length the corruption of a single minister, placed in charge of a province, can possibly go; and it also gives occasion to a large number of verses, attributed to diverse poets, on the supposed villainy of ministers in general.[1] The author of *Yaśastilaka* seems to regard the proper control and supervision of the activities of the ministers by the king as the first and foremost requisite in the administration of a state. He opines that the evil ways of ministers cease only when the king is strict in determining issues of justice and

---

1 See Chap. VII.

injustice; if he is lenient, indolent and bent on the pleasures of the moment, the ministers are bound to prove insolent and disloyal (3. 196):

सचिवचरितं तत्रैवैतत् प्रशाम्यति भूपतौ भवति इह य न्यायान्यायप्रतर्कणकर्कशः ।
सदयहृदये मन्दोद्योगे तदात्वसुखोन्मुखे स्त्रिय इव नृपे दृप्ता भृत्याः कथं न विकुर्वते ॥

The evil consequences of ministerial corruption and misrule are summed up thus (3. 197):

प्रकृतिविकृतिः कोशोत्क्रान्तिः प्रजाप्रलयागतिः स्वजनविरतिर्मित्राप्रीतिः कुलीनजनास्थितिः ।
कुसचिवरते राजन्येतद्ध्रुवं ननु जायते तदनु स परैर्दायादैर्वा बलादवलुप्यते ॥

"Sedition among the citizens, depletion of the treasury, decimation of the population, disaffection of kinsmen, hostility of friends, and the emigration of the high-born: verily, this is sure to happen when a king is attached to a wicked minister. Thereafter the former is ousted by force by his enemies or by his kinsmen."

Magnanimity accompanied by pre-eminence is stated to be the sole cause of a king having honest persons to serve him. A king may be poor; but if he is magnanimous, he can have plenty of trustworthy servants: even when a pool of water is dried up, numerous trees grow under its bridge (3. 198):

अधनस्यापि महीशो महीयसो भवति भृत्यसंपत्तिः । शुष्कस्यापि हि सरसः पालितले पादपविभूतिः ॥

It is dangerous for kings to incur the displeasure of the people by favouring the unworthy and dishonouring the worthy. Several semi-legendary examples are cited by Somadeva to illustrate the point. A king of Kaliṅga named Anaṅga, who had made a barber his commander-in-chief, was pelted to death with clods of earth by the enraged citizens. Similarly, a king named Karāla was killed in the Kerala country for making a gambler his priest; king Maṅgala was killed in the country of Vaṅgāla for making an outcaste his minister; while in the country of Krathakaiśika a king named Kāma met with a similar fate for making the son of a courtesan the Crown prince. On the other hand, in Vaṅga a king named Sphuliṅga was assassinated for humiliating his honest and sincere minister; in Magadha a king named Makaradhvaja was murdered for despising his pious priest; in Kauṅga a king named Kuraṅga was killed for insulting his powerful commander-in-chief; and in Cedi king Nadīśa was similarly punished for removing his innocent eldest son from the position of heir-apparent.[1]

Danger to kings lurks also in presents sent by rival courts, which should be carefully scrutinized before acceptance. It is said that king

---

1 Book III, p. 431.

Dhiṣaṇa killed king Durdharṣa by presenting him with a jewel casket containing a deadly artificial serpent. Another king, Kaṇapa[1] by name, killed a rival named Kṛpaṇa by sending him a perfumed cloth for covering idols which was coated with a deadly poison.[2] These stories are also mentioned with slight variations in *Nītivākyāmṛta* (Chap. 13) wherein we are told that a king of Karahāṭa named Kaitabha killed king Vasu by presenting him with a marvellous cloth perfumed with a deadly poison, and a king named Karavāla killed king Karāla by sending him a jewel casket containing a venomous serpent.[3] Somadeva clearly says in the latter work that letters and presents sent by an enemy should not be accepted without being examined by trustworthy persons (13. 15).

A king should also be on his guard in his relations with women. This is, as a matter of fact, one of the lessons of the romance; and the subject is also treated in detail in *Nītivākyāmṛta* (Chap. 24). The direction given in the latter work (24. 32) that nothing coming from the ladies' apartments should be eaten by the king has a direct bearing on the story of Yaśodhara. Free and careless association with the inmates of the harem is held to be a source of danger to the king (Book IV, p. 153):

अन्तःपुरे भूमिपतिर्मदान्धः करोति यः संगतिमङ्गनाभिः । तस्य ध्रुवं स्यादचिरेण मृत्युर्बिलप्रवेशादिव दर्दुरस्य ॥

"Verily, the king who, blind with passion, associates with women in the inner apartments, soon loses his life, like a frog entering a serpent's hole." The idea occurs also in *Nītivākyāmṛta*—

दर्दुरस्य सर्पगृहप्रवेश इव स्त्रीगृहप्रवेशो राज्ञः । 24. 31.

Further, both works record a number of traditions, with slight variations, to illustrate how kings are sometimes assassinated by women with devices of their own. For instance, in the Yavana country a queen named Maṇikuṇḍalā killed king Ajarāja (Aṅgarāja) by giving him a mouthful of poisoned wine, in order to place her son on the throne. In the country of Śūrasena, Vasantamati killed king Suratavilāsa by kissing him with lips painted with poisoned red lac. In the Daśārṇa country Vṛkodarī killed king Madanārṇava with her girdle-jewel smeared with poison. In Magadha, Madirākṣī killed king Manmathavinoda with a sharp-edged mirror, and

1 Ibid. p. 550; Ms. A reads कणय.

2 'देवाङ्गवस्त्रवासनिषेकेण च स्पर्शविषेण'.

3 मणिकरण्डकविन्यस्तबपुषा कृत्रिमेणाशीविपत्रिपधरेण (*Yaśastilaka*); आशीविषविषधरोपेतरत्नकरण्डकप्राभृतेन (*Nītivākyāmṛta*). Envenomed gifts are familiar in Greek literature. In one version of the story of Medea she kills her rival Glauce by presenting her with a poisoned robe and crown. Cf. Euripides, *Medea*, 1116 *sqq.* and Diodorus Siculus, IV. 54. 6. The death of Heracles caused by 'the deadly robe' unwittingly sent by his aggrieved wife is the theme of the *Trachiniae* of Sophocles.

in the Pāṇḍya (Pāṇḍu) country Caṇḍarasā murdered king Muṇḍīra (Puṇḍarīka) with a dagger concealed in the lock of her hair.[1]

The danger from women is also illustrated by asserting that it is risky to educate them. Yaśodhara says in Book IV (p. 152):

इच्छन् गृहस्यात्मन एव शान्तिं स्त्रियं विदग्धां खलु कः करोति ।
दुग्धेन यः पोषयते भुजङ्गीं पुंसः कुतस्तस्य सुमङ्गलानि ॥

"Who doth ever make a woman excel in wisdom, desiring his domestic peace? How can a man, who nourishes a serpent with milk, profusely thrive?" This is not merely the opinion of a disillusioned husband. Somadeva makes a similar observation in *Nītivākyāmṛta* 24. 43: नातीव स्त्रियो व्युत्पादनीयाः स्वभावसुभगोऽपि शास्त्रोपदेशः स्त्रीषु शस्त्रीषु पयोलव इव विषमतां प्रतिपद्यते ।; and the statement, in fact, occurs also in *Yaśastilaka*, Book IV.[2]

Further, we are told that women may have as much freedom as they like in the discharge of their duties towards their husbands and children, but must not interfere in matters which properly belong to men's sphere, their minds being extremely fickle and superficial, like a drop of water on a lotus leaf. No one who accepts the participation of women in activities other than domestic duties can thrive for long, being like a tree fallen into the current of a river. And it is under a man's control that a woman can achieve her desired end, like a sword in the grip of a man.[3] These statements are put in the mouth of Yaśodhara, annoyed at the importunities of his mother in behalf of animal sacrifice, and remind one of the words of Eteocles, in Aeschylus' *Septem Contra Thebas* (200, 201), that 'outside affairs are men's business—let woman not advise thereon'. It may be added that the gist of what Yaśodhara says occurs also in *Nītivākyāmṛta* (Chap. 24).[4]

The narrow view of women's character and capacity to which Somadeva here gives expression should be considered in relation to what

---

1 *Yaśastilaka*, Book IV (P. 153) and *Nītivākyāmṛta* (chapter on राजरक्षा). The anonymous commentary on the latter work remarks that the stories in question are found in the *Bṛhatkathā*.

2 'स्वभावसुभगावेशोऽपि च शास्त्रोपदेशः स्त्रीषु शस्त्रीष्विव पयोलवः परं परोपघातायैव प्रभवति ।' P. 152.

3 स्त्रियो हि नाम भवन्तु भर्तृषु शय्याविषये पुत्रेषु च प्रतिपालनसमये प्रकामं निसृष्टार्था निरङ्कुशाचरणसमर्थाश्च, न पुनः पौरुषेयेषु कर्मसु । यस्मात् कमलिनीदलेषु जलकणस्येव नारीणां मनसश्चञ्चलतरत्वादतीव निःसारत्वाच्च । पुरुषोऽपि गृहकार्यादन्यत्र स्त्रियं प्रमाणयन् नदीप्रवाहपतितः पादप इव न चिरं नन्दति । स्त्री तु पुरुषमुष्टिस्थिता खड्गयष्टिरिव साधयत्यभिमतमर्थम् ।' P. 135.

4 'अपत्यपोषणे गृहकर्मणि शरीरसंस्कारे शयनावसरे स्त्रीणां स्वातंत्र्यं नान्यत्र' (39), 'स्त्रीवशपुरुषो नदीप्रवाहपतितपादप इव न चिरं नन्दति' (41); 'पुरुषमुष्टिस्था स्त्री खड्गयष्टिरिव कमुत्सवं न जनयति' (42).

is called *rājarakṣā* or protection of kings, and is in keeping with the precaution against familiarity with women recommended as a measure of self-defence. There are no adequate grounds for holding that Somadeva is ǎ misogynist. It is noteworthy that almost all the attacks on women in *Yaśastilaka* are put in the mouth of Yasodhara and the Jaina ascetic Sudatta, appropriately enough, it would seem. Somadeva refers also to the Digambara Jaina doctrine that women are unfit for salvation[1], but he declares in emphatic terms that women are superior to men in the intellectual field (1. 146):

देहायत्ते कर्मण्ययं नरः स्त्रीजनोऽयमिति भवति । चित्तायत्ते कर्मण्यधिका नारी तु मध्यमः पुरुषः ॥

"Discrimination between men and women is valid in respect of physical activity. But women are superior and men inferior in intellectual activity." It may also be noted that Somadeva as a practical thinker tells us in *Nītivākyāmṛta* that women are neither good nor bad: they are, like the Ocean of Milk, the source of poison as well as nectar (24. 10), and have neither any innate merit nor blemish, but become just like their husbands, as rivers assume the character of the ocean when they are merged therein (24. 25). The Jaina author's position with regard to women is, in fact, similar to that of Kalhaṇa as stated in a verse of his *Rājataraṅgiṇī* (VII. 856).

व्रजति रजनी त्यक्त्वा क्वापि क्षये क्षणदाकरं पदमुपगतस्यास्तं संध्या रवेरनुगच्छति ।
इति परिणतौ प्रेमण्युच्चावचे परिचिन्तति क्वचन नियमान्निन्द्या वन्द्या न वा सुधियां स्त्रियः ॥

The guiding principles of a king's policy in matters affecting peace and war, and, generally speaking, his relations with other kings are expounded in an academic discussion in verse in Book III.[2] The framework of the discussion is provided by an examination of the relative claims of *daiva* and *puruṣakāra*, a subject bearing on *rājadharma*, as already recognised in early texts like Yājñavalkya (1. 346 ff.). The king is also recommended to rule the kingdom, as a gardener looks after the garden (3. 107):

वृक्षान् कण्टकिनो बहिर्नियमयन् विश्लेषयन् संहितानुत्खातान् प्रतिरोपयन् कुसुमितांश्चिन्वंल्लघून् वर्धयन् ।
उच्चान् संनमयन् पृथूंश्च कृशयन्नत्युच्छ्रितान् पातयन् मालाकार इव प्रयोगनिपुणो राजन् महीं पालय ॥

"Skilled in devising ways and means, rule the earth, like a gardener, o king: expelling the petty enemies, like thorny plants; disuniting the united; replanting the uprooted; collecting dues from the well-to-do, as a gardener gathers flowers from the blossoming trees; elevating the lowly, as a gardener rears the smaller plants; humbling the high-born, as he bends the tall-growing ones; reducing the great, as he thins out the thick under-

1 *Yaśastilaka* 1. 145.

2 See Chap VII.

growths; and levelling the mighty, as he fells the lofty trees." No enemy, however small, should be neglected (3. 108):

स्वल्पादपि रिपोर्बीजादश्वत्थस्येव शाखिनि । भयं जायेत कालेन तस्मात् कस्तमुपेक्षते ॥

"Even from the tiny germ of an enemy there might be cause of fear in the course of time, just as there might be danger to other trees even from a small seed of the Pippal. Who can therefore neglect an enemy?"

The duties and qualifications of various officials of the king are dealt with by Somadeva in *Yaśastilaka* as well as *Nītivākyāmṛta*. The Dūta or envoy should be an aged Brāhmaṇa, learned, eloquent, forbearing in face of provocation and amiable: he should be efficient, courageous, pure, wise, bold and readywitted (3. 111). Even when an envoy is entrusted by his master with a provocative message, he should regulate his speech according to the temperament, character, or the resources of the king to whose court he is sent. To a proud enemy he should speak in conciliatory terms. To one well-versed in polity he should talk about principles. To one who is powerful he should speak about dissensions among his subjects; while to an enemy inferior in resources he should talk in terms of war. The responsibility of an envoy is shown by the fact that the prosperity of a king, however great, is endangered by the misconduct of envoys that are greedy and rough in the manner and content of their speech (3. 114-5):

संकीर्तयेत् साम रिपौ सदर्पे नयं सनीतौ बलिनि प्रभेदम् । मन्त्रेण तन्त्रेण च हीनवृत्तौ दण्डाश्रयोपायविधिं विधिज्ञः ॥

अन्यथा—वागर्थरूक्षलुब्धानां दूतानां दुःप्रवृत्तिभिः । श्रीः स्वामिनः प्रवृद्धापि क्रियते संशयाश्रया ॥

The commander-in-chief should be brave, experienced in the practice of arms and well-versed in the Arthaśāstra. He should be a skilled fighter, and well-provided with elephants, cavalry, infantry and chariots; and loyal to his master, and popular with the army (3. 245):

शूरोऽर्थशास्त्रनिपुणः कृतशस्त्रकर्मा संग्रामकेलिचतुरश्चतुरङ्गयुक्तः ।
भर्तुर्निदेशवशगोऽभिमतः स्वतन्त्रे सेनापतिर्नरपतेर्विजयागमाय ॥

The Sandhivigrahin, 'officer in charge of peace and war', may be called the Secretary of state for foreign affairs. He is an important court official with varied functions. In Somadeva's romance, as we have seen above, he receives the envoys of friendly courts and ushers them into the king's presence; and deals also with the envoy of a hostile court, addresses him, and drafts a threatening letter to the enemy. The Sandhivigrahin is thus in charge of matters affecting peace and war; and he seems to be in close attendance on the king, for we find Yaśodhara in

Book IV questioning the Sandhivigrahin about the sudden peals of music in the city.[1] In *Rājataraṅgiṇī* 4. 137–8 we have another glimpse of the functions of the Sandhivigrahin in the person of Mitraśarman, styled as the Sāndhivigrahika of Lalitāditya, king of Kashmir, who is present at the drafting of the treaty between Lalitāditya and Yaśovarman of Kanauj, and objects to the latter's name being recorded prior to his master's in the document in question.[2] In Bāṇa's *Harṣacarita* (Book VI) we find Harṣa, after his decision to punish the king of Gauḍa for treachery, dictating to his Sandhivigrahin Avanti, called Mahā-sandhi-vigrahādhikṛta, an arrogant proclamation calling upon all kings to accept his suzerainty or prepare for battle. It seems that there were sometimes more than one Sandhivigrahin in the same court: Somadeva, for instance, records what he calls 'the verses of the Sandhivigrahins' in the court of Yaśodhara.[3] The occasional addition of the epithet *Mahā* to the usual designation shows that there was sometimes a chief official of that class. Among the new offices created by Lalitāditya (first half of the eighth century), as related in *Rājataraṅgiṇī* 4. 142, mention is made of a Mahā-sandhi-vigraha, which is also the appellation of Harṣa's secretary for foreign affairs, as stated above. It may also be noted that one of the verses quoted from Vyāsa in Aparārka's commentary on Yājñavalkya 1. 319 refers to a Sandhi-vigraha-lekhaka, obviously the same as Sandhivigrahin; but his function is to draft records of grants of land made by the king. It would appear that the Sandhivigrahin was a Secretary of State whose functions were not confined to the conduct of foreign affairs. Somadeva tells us that he should be able to read, write, narrate and interpret all scripts and languages: he should be ready-witted and capable of gauging the relative strength of his own master and other princes (3. 250):

वाचयति लिखति कवते गमयति सर्वा लिपीश्च भाषाश्च । आत्मपरस्थितिकुशलः सप्रतिभः संधिविग्रही कार्यः ॥

The Ākṣapaṭalika or the keeper of the state records is mentioned in connection with the challenge to other kings (3. 112, 113) issued by Yaśodhara,[4] similar to the one issued by Harṣa in Bāṇa's romance (see above). The Ākṣapaṭalika is here commissioned to read out the message to the envoy who was expected to deliver it to the kings in question.[5] The

---

1 'इति बुधप्रबोधं संधिविग्रहिणमापृच्छमाने' P. 157.

2 श्रीयशोवर्मणः संधौ सांधिविग्रहिको न यत् । नयं नियमनालेखे मित्रशर्मास्य चक्षमे ॥ सोऽभूत् संधिर्यशोवर्मललितादित्ययोरिति । लिखितेनादिनिर्देशादनर्हत्वं विदन् प्रभोः ॥.

3 See above. 'संधिविग्रहिणां गीतीराकर्णयामास' Book III.

4 See Chap. II.

5 'दूतमाक्षपटलिकेन तमेव लेखार्थं श्रावयामास'.

Akṣapaṭala, to judge from certain references in the *Rājataraṅgiṇī*, was the royal archive containing the records of grants and deeds of gift, and the official who drafted the deeds of gift or made the necessary entries was called Paṭṭopādhyāya.[1] The same work (5. 301) mentions an Akṣapaṭalādhīśa, chief of the record office, obviously the same as Ākṣapaṭalika.

Great importance is attached to the rôle of spies in the king's government; and they are regarded as a sort of second sight for him.[2] The report of the spy in Book III provides a concrete example of the kind of information available to kings from this source, and gives us an idea of how minute and comprehensive such information could be. The importance of spies is stressed in the following verses of *Yaśastilaka* (3. 116–7):

सर्वचेतोगतानर्थान् द्रष्टुं येषां कुतूहलम् । ते भवन्तु परं चारैश्चक्षुष्मन्तः क्षितीश्वराः ॥
चारसंचारतो येषां नाध्यक्षा स्वपरस्थितिः । नियुक्तारातिसंपातात्तेषां नार्थो न चासवः ॥

"Let those kings, who have the curiosity to visualise what is in the mind of every one, have spies only for eyes. Those who are not aware of the situation of themselves and others, through the movements of spies, are deprived of both wealth and life by the action of their officials and foes."

The institution of spies is treated in great detail in all ancient works on Indian polity. Manu (7. 223) and Yājñavalkya (1. 330), for instance, lay down that the king should listen to the reports of spies after the evening ablutions, and, as Manu says, indoors, and the king should be armed while doing so. Yājñavalkya (1. 338–9) suggests what action should be taken by the king in regard to his officers on the reports of spies: those who take bribes, for instance, should be dispossessed and exiled. Espionage is dealt with in several chapters of Kauṭilya's *Arthaśāstra*, on which Somadeva's own treatment of the topic in *Nītivākyāmṛta* is based. In *Yaśastilaka*, too, he is indebted to Kauṭilya (Chap. XI) in the description of Yaśodhara's spy, disguised as a religious mendicant, and surrounded by disciples who proclaim his mystic powers.[3] The expression *siddhaḥ sāmedhikaḥ* occurring in *Yaśastilaka*, Book III, is taken from Kauṭilya (op. cit.); and the topic is, of course, elaborated in the romance. As regards the report of the spy on the corruption of one of the ministers of Yaśodhara, analysed elsewhere (Chap. II), its prototype may be found

---

1 Cf. राज्ञा प्रदत्ते रङ्गाय हेलुग्रामेऽग्रहारवत् । लिलेख पट्टोपाध्यायो न यदा दानपट्टकम् ॥ तदाक्षपटलं गत्वा रङ्गः कोपात् तमब्रवीत् । रङ्गस्स हेलु दिण्णेति दासीसुत न लिख्यते ॥ 5. 397–398. Kauṭilya deals with the organisation of the Akṣapatala in *Arthaśāstra* 2. 7; it was the Records and Accounts office combined.

2 *Yaśastilaka* 3. 173.

3 See Chap. IV.

in the *Mahābhārata* (*S'āntiparva,* chap. 82) in the story of the sage Kālakavṛkṣīya, who, taking with him a crow credited with the power of soothsaying, goes round the capital of the king of Kosala and observes the evil ways of his ministers, and later reports to him all details of their corruption and conspiracies.

Reference is made in Book III to the Chief of the secret agents called Variṣṭhaka[1], and it is he who reports to the king the arrival of the spy from his tour.[2] Śrutasāgara in his commentary seems to take Variṣṭhaka as a proper name, but in Book IV we find a Variṣṭhaka named Vaikuṇṭhamati, who brings, however, an ordinary message to the king.[3] The spy in his report mentions also a chief of the emissaries or couriers (*jaṅghācārika-nāyaka*).[4] Śrutasāgara and Ms. A, however, explain the term *jaṅghācārika* as a *cārapuruṣa, herika,* a spy.[5] The forms *jaṅghārika* and *jaṅghākarika* occur in *Arthaśāstra* II. I, but there the word is taken to mean 'messenger' or 'courier'.[6] It is difficult to determine the exact significance of these terms, but there is no doubt that the Criminal Intelligence Department had many ramifications, and was as important in the tenth century as it was in the days of Kauṭilya.

We have already referred to Somadeva's description of the regiments of Yaśodhara's army in connection with the review of troops, which is included by Yājñavalkya (1. 329) in the daily routine of the king. In *Nītivākyāmṛta* 22. 17 the king's neglect to review the troops personally is described as one of the causes of the disaffection of the army.

Elephants and horses were two principal components of old Indian armies; and a number of verses occurs on the importance of the military rôle of these animals (2. 176, 180):

भयेषु दुर्गाणि जलेषु सेतवो गृहाणि मार्गेषु रणेषु राक्षसाः ।
मनःप्रसादेषु विनोदवेधसो गजा इवान्यत् किमिहास्ति वाहनम् ॥

Elephants serve as fortresses in danger, as causeways in traversing waters, as houses on the wayside, and as monsters in battle. They give

1 See Chap. II.

2 'जनश्रुतिमादायागतः शङ्खनकनामा प्रणिधिरिति गूढपुरुषाधिष्ठायकाद्वरिष्ठकादाकर्ण्य' P. 400.

3 '………तदर्थं चैव नगरे पौराणामुद्यावोद्यमः । तत्र देवः कालविलम्बनमकृत्वा सज्जीभवतु मज्जनादिषु क्रियासु' इत्यागत्य वैकुण्ठमतिना वरिष्ठकेन विज्ञप्ते…… P. 158.

4 'जङ्घाचारिकनायकस्य विश्वावसोः'. Printed text reads नामकस्य which is incorrect. Ms. A reads नायकस्य.

5 Śrutasāgara says चारपुरुषप्रधानस्य.

6 See Shama Sastri's Translation and Word Index, and M. M. Ganapati Sastri s ed.

delight in moments of joy: what other vehicle is there in the world, comparable to them?

पुरः प्रत्यक्पक्षभ्रमिभिरभिहन्तुं व्यवसिते गतैः सव्यैर्गर्वात् समरसमये सिन्धुरपतौ ।
विदीर्णं मातङ्गैस्तुरगनिवहैश्चापि दलितं रथैः प्रास्तं पद्भैः पिशितकवलीभूतमचिरात् ॥

When, at the time of battle, a mighty elephant proudly begins to charge, stepping to and fro, and turning to the right and to the left, with all possible movements, the foeman's elephants are ere long pierced, the horses crushed, the chariots scattered, and the infantry reduced to pulp. The speed of elephants is praised in *Yaśastilaka* 3. 309, and Somadeva, the writer on polity, goes as far as to offer salutation to elephants (2. 169):

सामोद्भवाय शुभलक्षणलक्षिताय दिव्यात्मने सकलदेवनिकेतनाय ।
कल्याणमङ्गलमहोत्सवकारणाय तुभ्यं नमः करिवराय वराय नित्यम् ॥

A large number of technical terms appertaining to elephant lore is used in Books II and III. In the latter Book Somadeva enumerates the different methods of treatment applied to rutting elephants,[1] and gives the names of certain kinds of elephants and the particular states of intoxication to which they are subject. For example,

Names of elephants	States of intoxication
Vasumatītilaka	Saṁjāta-tilakā
Paṭṭavardhana	Ārdra-kapolikā
Uddhatāṅkuśa	Ādhonibandhinī
Paracakra-pramardana	Gandhacāriṇī
Ahitakula-kālānala	Krodhinī
Carcarīvataṁsa	Ativartinī
Vijayaśekhara	Saṁbhinna-madamaryādā

The above details are in our work reported to the king by an army commander; and elephant-lore, like the science of horses, was regarded as an auxiliary branch of statecraft in view of the important part played by elephants in warfare.

Like elephants, horses are also praised for their utility in war, and mention is made of various characteristics of efficient chargers. Particularly good are the well-trained ones with well-proportioned, symmetrical and compact limbs (2. 206).[2] Good horses have large foreheads, mouths depressed on the outside, smooth skins, stout shoulders, long

1 'सोत्सालब्बृंहणसंचयन्यास्तारमुखवर्धनकटवर्धनकटशोधनप्रतिभेदनपवंर्धनवर्णकरगन्धकरोद्दीपनहासभविनिवर्तनप्रभेदमदोपचारोपदेशविशारद·········' P. 495.

2 अन्यूनाधिकदेहाः समसुविभक्ताश्च वर्ष्मभिः सर्वैः। संहतघनाङ्गबन्धाः कृतविनयाः कामदास्तुरगाः ॥.

legs, broad backs and lean bellies (2. 203).[1] Their colours are like those of pearls, or blue lotuses, or gold, or filaments of flowers, or collyrium, or bees, or the rising sun, or Aśoka flowers, or parrots. The neighing of good horses is deep like the trumpeting of elephants, or the roar of lions, or the bellowing of oxen, or like the sound of trumpets, drums or clouds; and the smell of lotuses, blue lotuses, Mālatī flowers, clarified butter, honey, milk, or the perspiration of rutting elephants is present in their perspiration, mouths and ears (2. 197–9).

Questions of food and drink are discussed in relation to health and physical well-being in a large number of verses (3. 321–74) attributed to the court physician Sajjana, alias Vaidyavidyāvilāsa, to whose words the king listens at meal-time. Sajjana is also described as one who gives instruction in the art of producing sixty-three varieties of flavours by primary and secondary combinations of the usual six,[2] and Śrutasāgara in his commentary gives a formidable list of these combinations. Sound dietetics is a subject intimately connected with the welfare of the king, and accordingly given a place in Somadeva's discourse on the art of government.

Sajjana says many sensible things. Addressing the king, he remarks that just as food is not well cooked in a vessel that is neither covered nor stirred, so a man who has neither sleep nor exercise cannot digest what he eats (3.322). He who gorges himself with food gluttonously even when he is not hungry stirs up diseases, like dormant snakes, for his own ruin (3.329). All stale food with the exception of clarified butter and liquids, food containing hair or worms, and *réchauffés* should be avoided (3.344); and one should also abstain from overeating, undereating, eating of combinations of hygienic and unhygienic food, and eating immediately after eating (3.345).[3]

Certain kinds of food are recommended for particular reasons. In the autumn one should take sweet, bitter and astringent things; in the rainy season and the winter sweet, salty and sour things; in the spring pungent, bitter and astringent things; and in the summer mild preparations (3.349). Again, in the winter one should take fresh food, preparations of milk, pulses, and sugarcane, curds, and things prepared with ghee; and oil, too, is beneficial (3.350). In the spring one should take food consisting chiefly of barley and wheat, and containing little ghee, and avoid

1 विशालभाला बहिरानतास्याः सूक्ष्मत्वचः पीवरबाहुदेशाः । सुदीर्घजङ्घाः पृथुपृष्ठमध्यास्तनूदराः कामकृतस्तुरङ्गाः ॥

2 'रसानां गुरुसंसर्गभेदेन त्रिषष्टिव्यञ्जनोपदेशभाजः सज्जनभिषजः'.

3 'अत्यशनं लघ्वशनं समशनमध्यशनमत्र संत्याज्यम्'.

heavy, cold and sweet dishes (3.351). On hot days one should take Śāli rice, Moog soup containing ghee, lotus stalks, fresh shoots and bulbs, fried barley flour, sherbets, curds mixed with sugar and spices, coconut-milk, and water or milk with plenty of sugar (3.352). In the rainy season the food should be dry light, oily and warm; and preparations of old Śāli rice, wheat and barley should be taken (3.353). In the autumn the diet should consist of ghee, *moog*, Śāli rice, powdered wheat, preparations of milk, *paṭolas*, grapes, Āmalakī fruits, sugar, and sweet bulbs and leaves (3.354).[1] A number of vegetables including slices of fresh ginger is praised in 3.356[2], and the properties of ghee, curds, butter and milk are described in verses 3.360-63. We are also told that the constant eating of over-sweet dishes leads to indigestion, too much of salty food causes weakening of vision, extremely sour and pungent dishes lead to physical decay, and any unhygienic food causes loss of strength as soon as it is taken (3.364). Certain remedies are suggested for indigestion (3.366), and emphasis is laid on the proper use of water. Water is called both *amṛta* and *viṣa*; properly used, it is *amṛta*, nectar, and used without proper care, it is *viṣa*, poison (3.368). Transparent water without any taste and smell, and swept by wind and sunshine, is beneficial by nature; in all other cases water should be boiled before drinking. Water exposed to the rays of the sun and the moon should not be used longer than a day and a night; water boiled in daytime should not be taken at night, and water boiled at night should not be taken in daytime (3. 370-1).

Examination of food and detection of poison is dealt with in a number of verses; and the subject has, of course, an important bearing on the safety of the king, and is exhaustively dealt with in Kauṭilya's *Arthaśāstra* I. XXI. Speaking of poison, the court physician mentions certain phenomena indicating its presence in food. He observes that, at the sight of poison, crows and cuckoos cry in an unwonted fashion, mungooses and peacocks are overjoyed, the Krauñca bird sleeps, the cock crows in a harsh tone, the parrot vomits, and the monkey evacuates bowels; while the eyes of the Cakora bird lose colour, and the goose limps. Besides, flies do not settle on food containing poison (3. 338-9). Addressing the king, Sajjana further remarks that fire crackles in contact with food mixed with poison, as it does when a quantity of salt is thrown into it (3. 340).

---

1 घृतं मुद्गाः शालिः समिथविकृतिः क्षीरविधयः पटोलं मृद्वीकाः फलमिह च धात्र्याः समुचितम् । सिता शीतच्छाया मधुरसवशं कन्दकुपलं शरत्काले सेव्यं रजनिवदने चन्द्रकिरणाः ॥.

2 वालं वृन्ताकं कोहलं कारवेलं चिर्भी जीवन्ती वास्तुलस्तण्डुलीयः । सद्यः संभृष्टाः पर्पटाश्चिर्भटान्ताः किं स्वर्लोकैश्चेत् फालयश्चार्द्रकस्य ॥.

Certain kinds of food are forbidden under given circumstances, for example, germinating paddy, and ghee kept in a brass vessel for a period of ten days (3. 341). Further, bananas should not be taken with curds and butter-milk nor milk with salt..................nor broth of pulses with radishes; fried barley powder should not be taken when it becomes compact like curds, and all sesamum preparations are prohibited at night (3. 342–43).

The discourse on food and drink shows the importance attached by Somadeva to a proper understanding of dietetics for the safety and physical wellbeing of the king and the efficient discharge of his duties.[1] It shows also the Jaina teacher's keen interest in the secular branches of study.

It is evident that Somadeva in *Yaśastilaka* does not go over the entire range of topics dealt with in the *nītiśāstras*, but rather concentrates on problems affecting the king personally and the rôle played by him in the administration of the state. Considered from this point of view, the relevant portion of *Yaśastilaka* reminds one of the Mirrors or manuals of instruction for the guidance of kings, which were widely prevalent in the Middle Ages in the West, such as the book of Agapetos, the tutor of the Emperor Justinian (sixth century A. D.), and specially the famous *Secretum Secretorum* attributed to Aristotle, many versions of which are known to exist in different languages.[2] There are, for instance, Latin texts not earlier than the twelfth century, which 'in their turn rest on Arabic originals'. We may here refer to two English versions, the first from a shortened French source, the second from a Latin source made soon after 1400 A. D.[3] The Prologue to the first version tells us that the book was translated from Greek into Syriac, and thence into Arabic. It is interesting to find that although Somadeva's discourse is far more systematic and methodical, and more intimately connected with the actual problems of administration, there are certain noteworthy points of resemblance batween his work and the *Secretum Secretorum*. Firstly, as in *Yaśastilaka*, the king is warned in the *Secretum* never to trust a woman, and it is also pointed out that many kings have been poisoned, a woman's hate being the worst poison.[4] Secondly, both works treat of questions of health and food and drink; and proportionately speaking, the *Secretum* seems to attach even greater importance to the subject

1 Cf. the treatise on diet composed by Anthimus, a Byzantine doctor, for the Frank king Clovis (481–511 A. D.), to whom he had been sent by Theodoric the Great.

2 *J. R. A. S.* 1908, pp. 1065–1084.

3 See *Three Prose Versions of the Secreta Secretorum*. ed. Steele. Part I. Text an Glossary. (Early English Text Society).

4 Pp. 20, 64.

than our text. Both works deal with the seasons and the kinds of food appropriate to each of them;[1] and the *Secretum*, too, speaks of forbidden combinations of food, e. g., milk and flesh.[2] Thirdly, the qualities of secretaries, messengers, and counsellors are dealt with in the *Secretum* as in *Yaśastilaka*, although the subject is treated far more exhaustively by Somadeva with concrete details and illustrations. The opinion of the *Secretum* that the king should have five counsellors, or not less than three, if five are not available,[3] may be compared with Somadeva's recommendation in *Nītivākyāmṛta* that the number of ministers should be three or five or seven. On the other hand, the author of *Yaśastilaka* does not evince any interest in certain topics dealt with at length in the *Secretum* e. g., physiognomy, miraculous properties of plants, magic stones etc.

It is a noteworthy feature of Somadeva as a political thinker that he divests himself of his theological bias while treating of the problems of the state. For example, as an exponent of Jaina doctrines he severely condemns the Lokāyatika or materialistic view of life,[4] but in *Nītivākyāmṛta* 6. 33 he declares that a king conversant with the Lokāyatika system is capable of exterminating the malefactors of the state. Similarly, while emphasizing the importance of Dharma, he declares in the same work that he who solely devotes himself to Dharma, overriding the claims of Artha and Kāma, is like a man who tills a forest, abandoning a ripe cornfield (1. 44). It is also noteworthy that at the beginning of *Nītivākyāmṛta* Somadeva offers obeisance not to the Arhat but to the State (Rājya); and his method of approach to the problems of government is certainly not that of a Jaina theologian but that of an unbiassed thinker with considerable knowledge and experience of the affairs of the state. The non-theological attitude of the Jaina author in matters affecting the state may be contrasted with the outlook of certain Western political thinkers of the Carolingian age, who were Churchmen and 'approached the questions at issue through theology'.[5] The aim of writers like Smaragdus, Jonas and Sedulius, who paid attention to the problem of government in the first half of the ninth century, and wrote hortatory treatises, contrasting the good and the bad ruler, is, generally speaking, to produce, 'as it were, manuals of Christian ethics for Christian rulers'. Admonitions such as

---

1 Pp. 27, 72.

2 P. 76.

3 Pp. 98, 101.

4 See Chap. VIII.

5 Laistner: *Thought and Letters in Western Europe* (A. D. 500 to 900), p. 261.

that 'the Christian ruler must trust in divine aid rather than in his own courage and that of his troops' would have appeared highly incongruous to the Jaina thinker.

Somadeva's ideal of kingship is evident from his description of the life of Yaśodhara as a ruler. In presenting before us a picture of his activities, the author of *Yaśastilaka* does not attempt to make him a paragon of virtue or even a hero, but is content to depict him as a prince diligent in discharging the duties that devolve upon him as the ruler of the state. Yet he came to an untimely end, because of his failure to take precaution against a woman's perfidy; and his example is intended to be an object lesson for other kings to profit by. Yaśodhara, as represented by Somadeva, is very different from the Syrian king, mentioned by Dio Chrysostom,[1] who spent his life indoors with eunuchs and concubines without even a glimpse of army or war or assembly at all. It may be noted that Dio insists on virile pursuits for the king, and considers hunting to be the best recreation for him.[2] Yaśodhara does not indeed indulge in hunting, but we see him training elephants and armouring their tusks and practising archery. More questionable is his participation in the summer sports and the gaieties of moonrise in the company of young women, as described in *Yaśastilaka*, Book III; but this may be regarded as a concession to prevailing custom and the conventions of *kāvya* poetry, and is certainly contrary to Somadeva's considered opinion against the association of the king with the women of the harem.

Somadeva's discourse on the problems of government in *Yaśastilaka* is doubtless unparalleled in *kāvya* literature, but it should be remembered that earlier poets like Bhāravi, Māgha, Bhaṭṭi, and Ratnākara also deal with aspects of Nīti especially in relation to matters affecting peace and war; while Bāṇa's interest in the duties and responsibilities of kingship is revealed in Śukanāsa's advice to Candrāpīḍa. Further, Bāṇa, like Somadeva, records in *Harṣacarita*, Book VI, a large number of semi-legendary traditions illustrating the mortal danger to kings from carelessness and risky adventures and from the machinations of women. Somadeva and Bāṇa both seem to draw on earlier sources, as similar stories, for instance, those about women murdering kings, are also found in Kauṭilya's *Arthaśāstra* I. XX and Kāmandaka's Nītisāra 7. 11. 51 ff.

---

1 In the Fourth Discourse on Kingship. Dio was a Greek moralist of the first century A. D.

2 In the Third Discourse on Kingship.

SOCIAL DATA

The interesting data concerning religious conditions in the tenth century, preserved in our text, constitute a large mass of information which has been analysed in subsequent chapters; and we may here confine ourselves to Somadeva's references to social conditions proper.

The charges brought by the spy against the king's minister, a provincial governor, in Book III, point to certain potential abuses of the times, and similar incidents are mentioned also in *Rājataraṅgiṇī*. The spy, for instance, says (3. 172):

वापसमयेषु विष्टिः सिद्धायः क्षीरिकणिशकालेषु । लवनावसरेषु पुनः स्वच्छन्दः सैनिकाबाधः ॥

The minister is alleged to be responsible for three things: demanding unpaid labour at the time of sowing, collection of dues while the ears of corn are still unripe, and the unbridled movement of troops at the harvesting season. In *Nītivākyāmṛta* 19. 15, 16 Somadeva says that the collection of dues (*siddhādāya*) while the ears of corn are unripe depopulates a country, and the movement of troops at the time of harvest leads to famine.[1] As regards unpaid or forced labour (*viṣṭi*), it goes back to early times; and Kauṭilya says in *Arthaśāstra* II. I that the king should protect agriculture from the abuses of fines, *forced labour*, and taxation.[2] Forced labour seems to have been the poor man s terror as we learn from the parable of the foolish son in *Saddharmapuṇḍarīka*, wherein the vagrant youth comes after years to beg at the mansion of his wealthy father, and taking the latter for a king or a grandee, fears lest he should be detained to do forced labour, and slinks away in a hurry.[3] The grant of a village sometimes carried with it the right to unpaid labour within the area granted. A record of the Rāṣṭrakūṭa king Indra III, dated 915 A. D., grants, for instance, a village called Tenna to a Brāhmaṇa with the accompanying right to forced labour as occasion presents itself.[4] Somadeva, it should be noted, takes exception to forced labour only at the time of sowing.

It is also alleged by the spy that Yaśodhara's minister misappropriates *agrahāras* and *devabhogas*.[5] *Agrahāras* are villages granted to Brāhmaṇas, and *devabhogas* are temple endowments (villages, cornfields

---

1 'क्षीरिषु कणिशेषु सिद्धादायो जनपदमुद्वासयति', 'लवनकाले सेनाप्रचारो दुर्भिक्षमावहति ।'

2 'दण्डविष्टिकराबाधै रक्षेदुपहतां कृषिम्'.

3 'मा दानि दोषं पि लभेयमत्र गृह्वित्व वेष्टिं पि च कारयेयम्' IV. 17.

4 'सोत्पद्यमानविष्टिकः' *E. I.* Vol. IX (*Two grants of Indrarāja III*).

5 *Yaśastilaka* 3. 236 quoted in Chap. II (q. v.)

etc.); and the two terms are sometimes mentioned together, e. g., in the aforesaid grant of Indra III (verse 24). It was, of course, an abuse of power to rob the grantees of their legitimate rights, and similar instances are also recorded in the *Rājataraṅgiṇī*. For example, during the reign of Avantivarman (855-883 A. D.) a powerful feudal baron was beheaded under the orders of the minister Śūra for the crime of robbing the temple of Bhūteśa of villages (5. 52ff.). Some of the later kings of Kashmir were themselves notorious for such usurpations, notably Śaṁkaravarman (883-902 A. D.), Kalaśa (1063-89 A. D.), and Harṣa (1089-1101 A. D.). Kalhaṇa deplores the fact that Gauraka, the aged and virtuous minister of Harṣa, accepted the post of Arthanāyaka (Prefect of Wealth) for the confiscation of the villages and the entire property of all the temples of the gods (7. 1103-4).

The next charge against the minister is that he melts down the images of the gods and replaces them by those of lesser value; he also sells an image, and with the proceeds institutes a religious festival.[1] The motives of the minister are evidently not only cupidity but a show of piety Be that as it may, the practice of melting down images by greedy monarchs is wellknown in history and found not only in India but also elsewhere; it was a form of sacrilege akin to the plunder of temples practised by many kings for the treasury. The *Rājataraṅgiṇī* has a good deal to say about such practices being resorted to by the kings of Kashmir. Śaṁkaravarman plundered sixty-four temples of the gods (5. 169). Kalaśa removed the copper image of the Sun called Tāmrasvāmin, and carried away also the brass statues from the Vihāras (7. 696). The climax came during the reign of Harṣa, who, after plundering the treasures of the temples granted by former kings, turned his attention to the images, and appointed an officer called the Prefect for the uprooting of the gods (*devotpāṭana-nāyaka*), with the result that images of gods made of gold, silver and other metals rolled in filth in the streets, like faggots of wood (7. 1089 ff.). Another king of Kashmir Kṣemagupta (950-958 A. D.), a contemporary of Somadeva, used the brass from a statue of Buddha in building the shrine of Kṣema-Gaurīśvara, a show of piety comparable to that of Yaśodhara's minister (6. 172-3). Turning elsewhere, we find that towards the end of the twelfth century a prince of Gujarat, Prahlādanadeva, the author of *Pārthaparākrama Vyāyoga* and founder of Palanpur, melted a brass statue of Jina for making a bull for the Acaleśvara temple; and there is a legend that he was stricken with leprosy as a result of the sin, but cured himself by building a monastery

1 Ibid. 3. 227, 235 quoted in Chap. II (q. v.)

and setting up therein Jaina statues and shrines.[1] The references in *Yaśastilaka* would lead one to suppose that the melting down of images to meet financial needs was not unknown in the Deccan in the tenth century, and Somadeva's statements may be taken as a kind of protest against the practice being resorted to by provincial governors.[2] It may be mentioned in this connection that, elsewhere, during the reign of the Byzantine Emperor Alexius I Comnenus (1081–1118 A. D.), Leo, Bishop of Chalcedon, came to grief for protesting against the melting down of icons 'for purposes of filling the imperial treasury'.[3]

The spy in his report describes Yaśodhara's minister as a monster of financial corruption (*lañcā-luñcā-niśācaraḥ* 3. 185). *Lañcā* or *lañca* is bribery,[4] while *luñcā* is extortion; and the phrase is used in the sense of financial corruption in general. Somadeva deals with the subject in his *Nītivākyāmṛta* and describes *lañcaluñcā* as the source of all evils. Financial malpractice represents the seamy side of government, and Somadeva exhorts the king not to allow persons who come on business to become the victims of rapacious officials.[5]

Glimpses of economic prosperity are occasionally afforded by our work. The description of a prosperous dairy-farm of Karahāṭa occurring in Book V has been translated in the previous chapter. More interesting is the description of the mart owned and run by the trusted priest Śrībhūti in the story recounted in *Yaśastilaka*, Book VII, section 27. We are told that

1 See Dalal's *Introduction* to the play in *G. O. S.*

2 Classical antiquity provides instances of rapacious princes laying sacrilegious hands on costly images. Clement of Alexandria (second century A. D.) reports in his *Exhortation to the Greeks* (Chap. IV) that the tyrant Dionysius the younger stripped the statue of Zeus in Sicily of its golden cloak and ordered it to be clothed with a woolen one; while Antiochus of Cyzicus, a Greek city of Asia Minor, when he was in want of money, ordered the golden statue of Zeus, fifteen cubits high, to be melted down, and a similar statue of cheaper material covered with gold leaf to be set up in its place.

3 Hussey: *Church and Learning in the Byzantine Empire*, p. 94.

4 *Lañca*, 'bribe', is used in Pali, being peculiar to the Jātaka literature. See Rhys Davids: *Pali–English Dictionary*. Cf. Pali *lañcakhādaka*, 'bribe-eater'. The Bengali expression *ghuṣkhor* means the same thing. Compare also *lāca khāṇe* in Marāṭhī and *lañca tinnu* in Kannaḍa.

5 'कार्यार्थिनः पुरुषान् लञ्चलुञ्चानिशाचराणां भूतबलीन्न कुर्यात्'; 'लञ्चलुञ्चा हि सर्वपातकानामागमनद्वारम्'; 'मातुः स्तनमपि लुञ्चन्ति लञ्चोपजीविनः' etc. Śrutasāgara in his comm. on *Yaśastilaka* 3. 185 explains लञ्चालुञ्चानिशाचरः as उत्कोट(च ?)-त्रोटने राक्षसः. The anonymous comm. on *Nītivākyāmṛta* says लञ्चलुञ्चानिशाचराणां लुञ्चकशब्देन (लञ्चशब्देन ?) उत्कोचः लुञ्चाशब्देन बलात्कारः एत एव निशाचरा राक्षसाः. Farther on it says लञ्चेन बलात्कारग्रहणेन, also लञ्चेन कार्यकरणे बलात्कारेण हरणे. There is some confusion of meaning, but the expression as a whole signifies extortion or unlawful exactions by the king or his officials. Somadeva remarks in *Nītivākyāmṛta* (op. cit.): राज्ञो लञ्चेन कार्यकरणे कस्य नाम कल्याणम्.

the mart (*peṇṭhāsthāna*) was furnished with tents containing many compartments and large stores of merchandise, with stalls for cattle nearby. Water, fodder and fire-wood were easily available, and the establishment covered an area of about four miles. It was closely guarded by troops, and protected by moats, gates, walls and ramparts, and had avenues with arrangements for water-supply, eating houses, assembly halls, and warehouses for different classes of commodities. Gamblers, whoremongers, jesters and dancing masters were excluded from the precincts of the mart. Here merchants from many countries were allowed to carry on their business, the rates of toll and rent being extremely moderate.[1] The mart maintained by Śrībhūti seems to be entirely a private organisation, but in *Nītivākyāmṛta* 19. 21 Somadeva speaks of *pinṭhā* (*sic*) as a state organisation, and observes that a mart 'maintained with justice' is a source of endless profits to the king.[2] The commentary on the latter work explains *pinṭhā* as *śulkasthāna*, and quotes a verse from Śukra to the effect that toll should not be realised at excessive rates, and whatever is stolen by thieves from the mart should be restored to the merchants by the king from his own treasury.[3] The *pinṭhā* is described in *Nītivākyāmṛta* as *paṇyapuṭabhedinī*, explained in the commentary as containing diverse places for storing commodities,[4] and it seems to have had an elaborate organisation, to judge from the description in *Yaśastilaka*. The granting of proper facilities and protection to merchants was the chief aim of these emporiums, which were also an important source of revenue to the state.

References to the fine arts are few and far between in our work. An interesting statuary group is presented in the description of the Pavilion of mechanical showers in Book III.[5] The account of the Jaina temple in Book V is chiefly remarkable for its paintings, of which two categories are mentioned.[6] Firstly, there are portraits of wellknown figures of Jaina legend and mythology, viz. Bāhubali the warrior saint,[7] Pradyumna whose austerities

1 'स किल श्रीभूतिर्विश्वासरसनिर्विघ्नतया परोपकारनिघ्नतया च विभक्तानेकापवरकरचनाशालिनीभिर्महाभाण्डवाहिनीभिर्गोशालोपशल्याभिः कुंल्याभिः समन्वितम्, अतिसुलभजलयवसेन्धनप्रचारम्, भण्डनारम्भोद्भटभरीरपेटकपक्षरक्षासारम्, गोरुतप्रमाणं वप्रप्राकारप्रतोलिपरिखापरिसूत्रितत्राणं प्रपासत्रसभासनाथवीथिनिवेशनं पण्यपुटभेदनं विदूरितकितवविटविदूषकपीठमर्दावस्थानं पेण्ठास्थानं विनिर्माप्य नानादिग्देशोपसर्पणयुजां वणिजां प्रशान्तशुल्कभाटकभागहारव्यवहारमचीकरत्। p. 345.

2 'न्यायेन रक्षिता पण्यपुटभेदिनी पिण्ठा राज्ञां कामधेनुः'.

3 तथा च शुक्रः—ग्राह्यं नैवाधिकं शुल्कं चौरैर्यच्चाहृतं भवेत्। पिण्ठायां भूभुजा देयं वणिजां तत् स्वकोशतः॥

4 'पण्यानि वणिग्जनानां कुंकुमहिंगुवस्त्रादीनि क्रयाणकानि तेषां पुटाः स्थानानि भिद्यन्ते यस्यां सा पण्यपुटभेदिनी।'

5 See Chap. II.

6 'सुकविकृतिरिव चित्रबहुला' p. 246.

7 'विजयसेनेव बाहुबलिविदिता'.

are celebrated in Jaina legend,[1] the Tīrthaṁkara Supārśva,[2] and king Aśokacandra and his consort Rohiṇī, the woman who did not know how to weep.[3] Secondly, there are representations of most of the dreams of Ṛṣabha Jina's mother, e. g., the Airāvata elephant, a bull, a lion, the goddess Lakṣmī, the sun and the moon, a lotus-pool, the ocean, flames, a heap of jewels, and an aerial car.[4] Further, the temple is described as being marked with two fish, like the Mudrā of the Pāṇḍyan kings.[5] The figures of fish were apparently painted on the walls, a pair of fish being included among the eight auspicious objects of the Jainas. It may be noted in this connection that the fish appears also in early Christian art where it 'recalled the name of Jesus, as Christ, Son of God and Saviour'.[6] As regards the Pāṇḍyan *mudrā*, it might mean seal or coin or perhaps both. We know that "gold coins bearing the emblem universally adopted by the Pāṇḍyas in later times, viz. the fish have been attributed to a period from the 7th to the 10th century A. D."[7] It is extremely probable that Somadeva actually saw Pāṇḍyan coins with the double fish emblem.[8]

In the course of the description of the Jaina temple Somadeva refers to two technical terms of painting: *rūpaguṇanikā* 'the study of figures' and *pārśvāgata* 'the side view proper', being one of the nine different positions in which the figures may appear.[9] *Viṣṇudharmottara* 39. 1 (Part III) says, *nava sthānāni rūpāṇām.*[10]

Writing in ink on ivory slabs is mentioned in Book I.[11] In Book III Somadeva refers to a gold ring with the figure of Lakṣmī stamped on

---

1 'प्रकटरतिजीवितेशा'. Ms. A remarks प्रकटः कामो यत्र, प्रद्युम्नस्वामी चित्रलिखितो यत्र.

2 'सुपार्श्वागता'.

3 'अशोकरोहिणीपेशला'. For the story see the *Kathā* of Kanakakuśala.

4 'संनिहितैरावता......आसीनसौरभेया......निलीनोपकण्ठकण्ठीरवा......रमोपशोभिता' etc. Ms. A remarks चित्रलिखितस्वप्नावली.

5 'पाण्ड्यमुद्रेव शकुलियुगलाङ्किता'.

6 Foakes Jackson: *History of Christianity A. D. 590–1314*, p. 35.

7 Rapson: *Indian Coins*, p. 36.

8 Prof. K. A. Nilakanta Sastri writes to me that the Pāṇḍyan emblem was always a pair of fish—both *lāñchana* and *dhvája*. Jayanagara of E. Java (1309–28) who called himself Sundarapāṇḍyadevādhīśvara-nāma-rājābhiṣeka also had a pair of fish for his mark on his seal. Pāṇḍyan coins with fishes on them are noticed also by Hultzsch in *Indian Antiquary*, Vol. 21, p. 324 and by Codrington: *Ceylon coins and currency*, pp. 86–89.

9 'रूपगुणनिकेव सुपार्श्वगता', which refers also to the Tīrthaṁkara Supārśva by श्लेष.

10 See also Kramrisch: *Vishṇudharmottara*, p. 13.

11 'द्विरदरदफलकमषीलिखितलिपिस्पर्धीनि' p. 79.

it.[1] Glass bangles are mentioned in Book IV.[2] Shopfronts of garland-sellers,[3] stalls of dealers in perfumes,[4] and streets full of courtesans and women messengers[5] form part of the description of evening scenery at the beginning of Book IV. The gorgeous apartments of the queen are located on the top floor of a seven-storied palace,[6] and a Jaina shrine is described as being on the top floor of a seven-storied palace belonging to a wealthy merchant in a story in Book VI, section 12. Palaces whence elephant-races were witnessed are mentioned in Books III and VII, section 32.[7]

The prevalence of early marriage is attested both in *Yaśastilaka* and *Nītivākyāmṛta*. A speaker in a story in the former work (Book VI, section 19) identifies heaven with the mutual love of a maiden, twelve years of age, and a youth of sixteen[8]; while in *Nītivākyāmṛta* 31. 1 it is clearly said that a maiden and a youth of the age specified above are fit for marital relations.[9]

Certain details concerning crime and punishment are preserved in *Yaśastilaka*. In a story in Book VII, section 27, the priest Śrībhūti who is found guilty of breach of trust is given three choices by the king: he must either swallow three bowls of cow-dung or receive thirty-three blows to be given by powerful wrestlers, or forfeit his entire property. When he chooses the latter alternative, all his wealth is confiscated; and he is smeared with clay teeming with worms, and made to wear garlands of potsherds and abandoned platters, and expelled from the city seated on the back of a donkey. Similar treatment is meted out to Parvata by the enraged citizens in a story in Book VII, section 30. He is pelted with clods of earth and severely whipped and turned out of the city on the back of a donkey, clothed in rags from the cremation ground, and wearing a garland

---

1 'लक्ष्मीमुद्राङ्कां गाङ्गेयोर्मिकामिव' p. 394.

2 'को नु खलु विघटितं चेतः स्फटिकवलयमिव मुधापि संधातुमर्हति' p. 77.

3 'स्रगाजीविनामापणरङ्गभागेषु' p. 18.

4 'सौगन्धिकानां विपणिविस्तारेषु' p. 18.

5 'पण्याङ्गनासमितिभिः......संचारिकानिकायेन च समाकुलेषु...राजवीथीमण्डलेषु' p. 19.

6 'सप्ततलप्रासादोपरितनभागवर्तिनि......वासभवने' Book IV, p. 29. A partially ruined palace, known as the Kushk Mahal, at Chanderi, now in Gwalior state, has been identified as a seven-storied palace ordered to be built by Mahmud Shah of Malwa in 1445. Only the remains of four stories now exist. Percy Brown: *Indian Architecture*, Vol. II, p. 65.

7 'राजसिन्धुरप्रधावसंदर्शनप्रासादसंपादनाय'; 'प्रधावधरणिषु करिविनोदविलोकनदोहदं प्रासादमध्यास्य'. Vol. I, p. 495; Vol. II, 369.

8 'द्वादशवर्षा स्त्री षोडशवर्षः पुरुषः। तयोरन्योन्यमनन्यसामान्यस्नेहरसोत्सेकप्रादुर्भूतिः प्रीतिः......स्वर्गः।' p. 317.

9 'द्वादशवर्षा स्त्री षोडशवर्षः पुमान् प्राप्तव्यवहारौ भवतः'

of platters, with the head shaven at random with the blade held in the reverse direction, and Bilva fruits suspended from the tuft of hair on the crest of the head. As we have already seen, the envoy of the king of Pañcāla was threatened with humiliation of this nature on account of the hostility of his master to Yaśodhara. In another story in Book VII, section 31, the libertine Kaḍārapiṅga and his father, the minister Ugrasena, who connived at his adulterous adventure, are exiled by the king after indictment in the presence of all the people.[1] Public humiliation of the kind noticed here seems to have been reserved for respectable offenders, and is heard of in the annals of other countries as well. In the eighth century at Rome, for example, the deposed Pope Constantine, after he was blinded, 'was led in derision through the streets seated on a horse with a woman's saddle and heavy weights attached to his feet.' Somadeva refers also to the torture of thieves and the indignities heaped upon them. In *Yaśastilaka*, Book V, in the episode of king Sudatta, a thief accused of robbing and murdering a barber is condemned by the judges to 'picturesque imprisonment' (*citro bandhaḥ*) so that he might lose his life in ten or twelve days, the preliminary indignities to be inflicted on him being riding a donkey, and fastening round the neck a row of cast off earthen vessels.[2]

Certain details about cruelty to animals are recorded in our work. In one of the birth-stories in Book V, a buffalo is tortured to death with revolting cruelty for killing the king's horse; and the incident is described also in Haribhadra's *Samarāiccakahā*.[3] We are told that the feet of the animal were tied together, and burning coals heaped upon the body, while salt water was poured over the wounds, and he was allowed to drink water mixed with boiled extracts of peppers. On the other hand, the epitaphs on the dog and the peacock who were accidentally killed, as related in another story[4] in the same Book, bear testimony to the love of animals. It is interesting to note that a contemporary record, the Ātakūr inscription of the Gaṅga ruler Būtuga II, who took part in the battle of Takkolam in 949 A. D., tells us that Manālara who fought in front of him in the battle made a gift of land in memory of a hound, who had attacked and killed a boar, but was himself killed in the fight.[5]

---

1 'निखिलजनसमक्षमाक्षारणापूर्वकं प्रावासयत्' p. 366.

2 'तदस्य पाटच्चरस्य चर्क्रावदारोहणोच्छिष्टशालाजिरराजिबन्धविडम्बनपूर्वकश्चित्रो बन्धः कर्तव्यो यथायं नक्षत्रवाणिजो दशभिर्द्वादशभिर्वा दिवसैरसून् विसृजति ।' p. 245.

3 See Chap. III of this book.

4 See Chapters II and VII.

5 *Sources of Karṇāṭaka History*, Vol. I, p. 97.

CHAPTER VI

Yaśastilaka as a Religious Romance

As we have already remarked (Chap. IV), the Jaina writers of the tenth century and after, who composed prose romances in Sanskrit, introduced into them a religious element which was absent in the works of Daṇḍin, Bāṇa and Subandhu. Siddharṣi's *Upamitibhavaprapañcā Kathā* and Somadeva's *Yaśastilaka* are two outstanding examples of Jaina religious romance in the tenth century, and it is evident that the development of the religious novel is a comparatively late phenomenon in Sanskrit literary history. In Prākrit, on the other hand, we have comprehensive Jaina religious romances like Uddyotana's *Kuvalayamālā* and Haribhadra's *Samarāiccakahā* in prose and verse composed in the eighth century, while the extensive *Vasudevahiṇḍī* in prose is ascribed to about the seventh century, and the lost *Taraṅgavatī* of Pādalipta is much earlier.[1] Such religious romances are called *dhammakahā* (*dharmakathā*) in Prākrit; and Haribhadra, in fact, enumerates four varieties of *kathā* in the prologue to his *Samarāiccakahā*: *arthakathā*, *kāmakathā*, *dharmakathā* and the mixed *saṁkīrṇakathā*. Of these the *dharmakathā* is declared to be the highest type of narrative, illustrating as it does such qualities as forbearance, kindness, honesty, renunciation, austerities, self-restraint, truthfulness, purity, non-possession, and chastity, and the Aṇuvratas and the other vows; in fact, the entire code of Jaina ethics and religious discipline. Uddyotana in his *Kuvalayamālā* mentions four types of *dharmakathā*: *ākṣepiṇī* or pleasant, *vikṣepiṇī* or unpleasant, *saṁvegajananī* or leading to knowledge, and *nirvedajananī* or leading to detachment.[2] The purpose of the *dharmakathā* is clear from these definitions, and we may in this connection refer to another division of *kathā* into *cariya* and *kappiya* found in *Vasudevahiṇḍī*, Chap. X, which has a bearing on the character of the *dharmakathā*. The *cariya* deals with what is actually seen, heard or experienced in matters relating to *dharma*, *artha* and *kāma*; while the *kappiya* is a story modified and altered for the purpose of instruction, and narrated in one's own way:[3] it is obviously an imaginative tale with a didactic purpose, and may be correlated with a *dharmakathā*.

---

1 *Annals of the Bhandarkar Oriental Research Institute*, Vol XVI, p. 31.

2 'तत्राक्षेपिणी मनोऽनुकूला, विक्षेपिनी मनःप्रतिकूला, संवेगजननी ज्ञानोत्पत्तिकारणम्, निर्वेदजननी वैराग्यजनका।' Ratnaprabhasūri's Sanskrit summary of *Kuvalayamālā*.

3 दुविहा कहा—चरिया य कप्पिया य। तत्थ चरिया दुविहा—इत्थीए पुरिसस्स वा। धम्मत्थकामकज्जेसु दिट्ठं सुयमणुभूयं चरियं ति वुच्चति। जं पुण विवज्जासियं कुसलेहिं उवदेसियपुव्वं समतीए जुज्जमाणं कहिज्जइ तं कप्पियं।'

Judged by these standards, *Yaśastilaka* is clearly a *dharmakathā*. Apart from the fact that it is a comprehensive manual of Jaina moral and religious doctrines, its purpose is to illustrate the great doctrine of *ahiṁsā* and its manifold implications. Yaśodhara, it will be remembered, had to undergo grievous suffering in several births even for the sin of sacrificing the paste model of a cock with the idea of killing. This aspect of the story brings into relief certain moral and religious issues which throw interesting light on the Jaina view of *ahiṁsā*.

In the first place, the practice of sacrificing the effigy of an animal seems to have been an expedient favoured by those who were opposed to animal sacrifices as such, and instances of this are recorded not only in Indian but also Greek literature. It is stated, for example, in *Rājataraṅgiṇī* 3. 7 that during the reign of Meghavāhana, an ancient king of Kashmir, who prohibited animal slaughter in the kingdom, it was the custom to sacrifice butter models of animals in Vedic rites and those of paste in the Bhūtayajña offerings.[1] In later times Madhvācārya is said to have introduced a reform consisting in the substitution of similar models of rice-flour for live animals in Vedic ritual.[2] As regards Greek tradition, Philostratus likewise says in the *Life* of Apollonius of Tyana, the Greek saint and mystic of the first century A. D., that Empedocles of Acragas (in Sicily), made at Olympia a bull out of pastry (*pemma poiēsamenos*) and sacrificed it to the god, showing thereby that he approved of the sentiments of Pythagoras.[3] Apollonius himself, who was opposed to animal sacrifices, is said to have condemned blood offerings in the temple at Alexandria, and sacrificed in the fire, by way of contrast, a *plasma* interpreted as a frankincense model of a bull (V. XXV). It is interesting to note that Apollonius refers in this connection to Indian sentiments, perhaps Buddhist or Jain. When the Egyptian priest sneered at his disapproval of animal sacrifices by saying that no one was so clever as to make corrections in the rites of the

1 तस्य राज्ये जिनस्येव मारविद्वेषिणः प्रभोः । क्रतौ घृतपशुः पिष्टपशुर्भूतबलावभूत् ॥.

2 See *Indian Historical Quarterly*, Vol. XVI, p. 378.

3 Book I, chap. I (*Loeb Classical Library*). Philostratus wrote about 217 A. D. Diogenes Laertius VIII. 53 records a statement that Empedocles sacrificed a bull made out of honey and barley-meal in honour of the Sacred envoys. It may be noted that the early Egyptian king Amenhetep IV (fourteenth century B. C.) is said to have offered in his temple bloodless sacrifices, chiefly of incense. He suppressed the worship of Amen and of the old gods of Egypt, and led a short-lived religious revolution in favour of the god Aten, which represented a solar monotheism based on the worship of the disc of the sun. Budge: *Egypt*, p. 146. cf. Erman: *Handbook of Egyption Religion*, p. 63 ff. and Breasted: *Development of Religion and Thought in ancient Egypt*, p. 319 ff.

Egyptians, Apollonius is reported to have answered: "Anyone with a little wisdom, if only he comes from India". Be that as it may, the story of Yaśodhara makes it clear that so far as Jainism was concerned, it was opposed even to the sacrifice of lifeless models of animals; it rejected the very idea of animal sacrifices.

In the second place, the story of Yaśodhara is designed also to show that the resulting consequences might be quite out of proportion to the sin committed by an individual. The latter point is emphasized by Haribhadra in his version of the story.[1] He makes Yaśodhara declare that even a slight error is fraught with peril, as can be seen from the dire results produced even by the sacrifice of a cock made out of paste.[2]

Somadeva considers the problem of *ahiṁsā* in its relation to *abhiniveśa*, the decisive character of which is stressed in a notable discourse in Book IV. It is put in the mouth of Yaśodhara, who accepts a compromise on the subject of animal sacrifice, and agrees to sacrifice an artificial cock to Caṇḍikā with the object of attaining the results obtainable by sacrificing living creatures.[3] The idea of killing is thus present, although a lifeless model is substituted for a real cock. Somadeva emphasizes in this connection the importance of *abhiniveśa*, 'mental preoccupation or resolve', 'purpose or motive', or 'intention', and declares that "the wise speak of *abhiniveśa* as occupying the paramount place in all actions leading to virtue or sin. The external sense-organs, like the rays of the sun, are drawn equally to good as well as bad objects, but that alone does not make the agent liable to virtue or sin."[4] This is another way of saying that it is the intention and not the outward act which determines the moral validity of an action. The idea is implied in another statement which Somadeva makes elsewhere, that if a person, pure in thought and action, inflicts injury on any one, he cannot be regarded as having done any injury at all.[5] Somadeva illustrates the point further, using in this connection the term *abhidhyāna* in place of *abhiniveśa*. A fisherman, for example, although he does not actually kill the fish, is a sinner because his motive is *hiṁsā*;

1 See Chap. III.

2 'अहो दारुणविवागया अकज्जायरणाणं जमिह देवयानिमित्तं पिट्ठमयकुक्कुडवहो वि एवं परिणओ त्ति ।' 'दारुणो य विवाओ थेवस्स वि पमायचेट्ठियस्स जेण पिट्ठमयकुक्कुडवहो वि पेच्छ कहं परिणओ त्ति ।'.

3 'सर्वेषु सत्त्वेषु हतेषु यन्मे भवेत् फलं देवि तदत्र भूयात्' Book IV, p. 163.

4 'अभिनिवेशं च पुनः पापपुण्यक्रियासु प्रधानं निधानमामनन्ति मनीषिणः । बाह्यानीन्द्रियाणि तपनतेजांसीव शुभेष्वशुभेषु च वस्तुषु समं विनिपतन्ति । न चैतावता भवति तदधिष्ठातुः कुशलेन चादृष्टेन संबन्धः ।' Śrutasāgara says अदृष्टेन पापेन. p. 136.

5 शुद्धमार्गमतोद्योगः शुद्धचेतोवचोवपुः । शुद्धान्तरात्मसंपन्नो हिंसकोऽपि न हिंसकः ॥ Book VI, section 21, p. 335.

while a cultivator who happens to kill various creatures while tilling the ground incurs no sin, because he has no deleterious motive.[1]

Somadeva uses also the terms *saṁkalpa* and *abhisaṁdhi* in the same sense as *abhiniveśa*. *Abhisaṁdhi* is often used in this sense elsewhere, for example, in the *Praśastapāda Bhāṣya* on the Vaiśeṣika Sūtras.[2] With regard to *saṁkalpa*, Somadeva says that the profanation of stones invested with divinity and set up with the *saṁkalpa* or intention of worshipping them is (in the Jaina view) a grievous sin.[3] Similarly, it is the *saṁkalpa* which makes a householder an ascetic, and an ascetic a householder.[4] The householder Arhaddāsa continued his religious meditation even on hearing of the death of his wife and children; while the sage Puruhūta, formerly a king, although engaged in austerities, formed a warlike resolution as soon as he heard that his son was being attacked by enemies.[5] The respective *saṁkalpās* of Arhaddāsa and Puruhūta thus determined their moral outlook, regardless of their outward vocations. Somadeva lays emphasis also on the difficulty of purifying the mind once it is polluted by an evil intention, and says that the sum total of pious acts done over a long period is completely destroyed in a moment, like a house on fire, if marred by an evil intention even once through error.[6] Further, the bearing and conduct of different persons towards the same object are bound to vary according to the diversity of their intentions or mental attitude. A sage, a libertine and a vulture do not, for example, have the same attitude towards the body of a young woman.[7]

Somadeva points out that mental activity is the main spring of virtue and sin:

नरेषु संकल्पवशेन मन्मथो यथा प्रवर्तेत पयश्च धेनुषु। तथैव कर्माण्युभयानि मानसाद्धाति बोधाधिपतिर्विजृम्भितात् ॥

'Just as, under the stress of mental preoccupation, Love appears in men, and milk in cows (at the sight of the calf), similarly on account

---

1 सा क्रिया कापि नास्तीह यस्यां हिंसा न विद्यते। विशिष्येते परं भावावत्र मुख्यानुषङ्गिकौ ॥ अघ्नन्नपि भवेत् पापी निघ्नन्नपि न पापभाक्। अभिध्यानविशेषेण यथा धीवरकर्षकौ ॥ Book VII, section 26, p. 335.

2 'धर्मः.........पुरुषान्तःकारणसंयोगविशुद्धाभिसन्धिजः'.

3 'संकल्पोपपन्नप्रतिष्ठानि च देवसायुज्यभाञ्जि शिलाशकलानि किमत्यासादयन् पुरुषो न भवति लोके पञ्चमहापातकी।' Book IV, p. 136. There is a marginal note in Ms. A: आसातनां कुर्वन्, which we have followed.

4 संकल्पेन च भवन्ति गृहमेधिनोऽपि मुनयः। ....मुनयश्च गृहस्थाः।' Ibid.

5 उत्तरमथुरायां निशाप्रतिमास्थितस्त्रिदिवसूत्रितकलत्रपुत्रमित्रोपद्रवोऽप्येकत्वभावनमानसोऽर्हद्दासः।' 'कुसुमपुरे चरादाकर्णितसुतसमरस्थितिरतापनयोगयुतोऽपि पुरुहूतदेवर्षिः।' Ibid., p. 137.

6 'चिरेणापि च कालेन कृतः कल्याणकर्मणां प्रचयः प्रमादवशेन सकृदपि संजातविधिर्दुरभिसंधिः पावकनिक्षेपात् प्रासाद इव क्षणेन विनश्यत्यामूलतः।' Ibid., p. 136

7 'अस्ति च जगत्प्रसिद्धमिदमुदाहरणम्—एकस्मिन्नेव किल कामिनीकलेवरे मुनिकामिकुणपाशिनामभिनिवेशनिमित्तो विचित्रनिषेकः कर्मविपाक इति।' Ibid., p. 137.

of mental activity the Self acquires karma, good and bad (Book IV, p. 137). Thus, according to Somadeva, mental activity represented by *abhiniveśa* or *saṁkalpa* involves a process which gives rise to the physical act and determines its moral validity. And *ahiṁsā* is not merely abstention from killing, but presupposes the absence of the very idea of killing, the complete absence of any *saṁkalpa* that might have the remotest connection with injury to living creatures.

The insistence on *ahiṁsā* brought Jainism into conflict with diverse cults, and *Yaśastilaka* preserves a faithful record of the religious conflict of the times. Somadeva's romance is a notable protest not only against the Vedic sacrificial system but against the debased form of contemporary Kaula or Tantric cults involving human sacrifice, and contains also important data on the historic conflict between Śaivism and Jainism in the South. These topics have been dealt with in subsequent chapters, and we may here confine our remarks to the protest against Tantric and Vedic rites. It may be noted that such protests occur also in Jaina works outside Sanskrit literature, for example, in the poem *Neelakeśi*, one of the early Tamil classics,[1] which describes how the Jaina ascetic Municandrá puts a stop to blood offerings to Kālī, and foils the designs of the goddess and her chief Neelakeśī, who is ultimately converted to Jainism, and preaches the doctrine of *ahiṁsā*. The *Neelakeśi* is also a controversial work, like Somadeva's *Yaśastilaka*, directed against Buddhism and other systems, one chapter being devoted to the criticism of Vedavāda involving animal sacrifices.

It will be remembered that *Yaśastilaka* opens with the Māradatta episode which shows the Tantric cult in the darkest colours, and there is hardly any parallel to Somadeva's graphic description of the temple of Caṇḍamarī and its horrid atmosphere in the whole range of Sanskrit literature.[2] The human victims are brought to the temple, but not actually sacrificed; and this gives the author an opportunity of demonstrating the salutary influence of Jainism, which undoubtedly did good work by raising its voice against blood-thirsty cults like those of Caṇḍamārī or Caṇḍikā.[3] A somewhat similar episode occurs in Haribhadra's *Samarāiccakahā* (Book VI) in the story of Dharaṇa, who is brought by the Śabaras to the temple of Kādambarī or Caṇḍikā as an offering, but is not actually immolated;

1 See *Jaina Antiquary*, Vol. VI, No. 2 and Vol. VII, No. 1.

2 See Chap. II.

3 Compare the early Christian protest against human sacrifices, e. g. in Clement's *Exhortation to the Greeks* (second century). In that work he records a number of Pagan cults involving human sacrifice, and remarks that such sacrifice is murder and human butchery.

and the Śabara chief Kālasena partially at least accepts the principle of *ahiṁsā*, and agrees to worship the idol with flowers and perfumes instead of blood offerings. In our work Māradatta and his subjects are, of course, converted to Jainism at the end; and the conversion *motif* is an appropriate feature of a religious romance, and found, for example, in early Christian novels like *Xanthippe and Polyxena* attributed to about the fourth century,[1] and St. John Damascene's *Barlaam and Ioasaph etc.* Perhaps more striking is the calm and fearless attitude of the two young votaries of Jainism, who are brought to the temple of Caṇḍamārī as sacrificial victims. Their courage, equanimity and dignified bearing do credit to the faith; and it is they who give utterance to the great idea of returning good for evil.[2] As we have pointed out elsewhere (chap. I), the idea is common in Buddhist literature, and inherent in the doctrine of the Four Actions,[3] but it no doubt represents one of the noblest teachings of Jainism as well. The utter resignation of the young ascetics and their readiness for suffering and disregard of death, as expressed in their own utterances, clearly illustrate some of the best moral influences of the doctrine of the Arhat. For example,

सोढस्त्वत्प्रणयादनेन मनसा तद्दुःखदावानलः संसाराब्धिनिमज्जनादपि कृतं किंचित्त्वदानन्दनम् ।
त्वत्क्रीडागमकारणोचितमतेस्त्यक्तः श्रियः संगमो यद्यद्यापि विधे न तुष्यसि तदा तत्रापि सज्जा वयम् ॥

'Thou Fate, thanks to thy favour, this heart hath endured the intense fire of all that suffering (in previous lives). Thou hast even been gratified a little by our plunging into the ocean of worldly existence. Prosperity, apt to be the cause of thy sports, hath been discarded by us. If thou art not pleased even now, ready we are for suffering evermore.' (1. 132). The ascetic boy likewise says to his companion at the sight of the terrible goddess and the king and the crowd in her temple:

विशुद्धबोधं तप एव रक्षा ग्रामेष्वरण्येषु च संयतानाम् ।
अतः कृतान्तेऽपि समीपवृत्तौ मातर्मनो मा स्म कृथा निरीशम् ॥
जीवस्य सद्दर्शनरत्नभाजश्चारित्रयुक्तस्य समाहितस्य ।
आशंसितो मृत्युरुपप्रयातः परं प्रमोदस्य समागमाय ॥

'Austerities, based on pure knowledge, are the sole protection for those who have self-control, whether in human habitations or in the woods. Hence, o mother, never feel helpless even when Death is near. Death, ever expected, when it comes, causes only delight to the man who

1 Glover: *Life and Letters in the fourth century*, p. 376.

2 *Yaśastilaka* 1. 151.

3 According to the *Mūlasarvāstivādaikaśatakarman*, they are (1) not returning slander for slander; (2) not returning anger for anger; (3) not meeting insult with insult; (4) not returning blow for blow. See I-Tsing: *A Record of the Buddhist Religion*, translated by Takakusu, p. 56 (f. n. 2.).

possesses the Jewel of Right Faith, and is endowed with Right Conduct, and devoted to holy meditation.' (1. 139-40).

Without disparaging Somadeva's picture of the fortitude and equanimity of the young Jaina *munis*, we may here refer to the remarkable story of the young Buddhist novice Adhimutta in the *Theragāthā* (705 ff.), which depicts his dauntless courage and philosophic calm when he is seized by highwaymen as a suitable offering to their deity, apparently of the same type as the Caṇḍamārī figuring in our romance. Adhimutta declares, for example,

> This body irketh me; no seeker I
> To live. This mortal frame will broken be,
> And ne'er another from it be reborn.
> Your business with my body, come, that do
> E'en as ye will; and not on that account
> Will hatred or affection rise in me.[1]

The attack on Vedic and Smārta rites involving animal sacrifices occurs chiefly in the controversial dialogue between Yaśodhara and his mother, analysed elsewhere.[2] The Jaina condemnation of animal sacrifices is similar to that of the Buddhists, and reminds one of the attacks on Pagan sacrifices found in the writings of the Christian apologists of the second century such as Justin, Clement of Alexandria, Tertullian, and Tatian, and Arnobius (end of the third century) and others.[3] Arnobius, for example, says: "Lastly, what pleasure is it to take delight in the slaughter of harmless creatures,...........to see rivers of blood, the life fleeing away with the blood...........? Will any one believe that the gods, who are kind, beneficent and gentle, are delighted and filled with joy by the slaughter of cattle, if ever they fall and expire pitiably before their altars?"[4] Similar sentiments are found in *Yaśastilaka*, Book IV and other anti-Brahmanical writings.[5] Arnobius goes on to say: "..............is that foul smell, then, which is given forth and emitted by burning hides, by bones, by bristles,..............(is that) a favour and an honour to the deity?" This sounds like Somadeva's line (Book IV, p. 109):

सुधान्धसः स्वर्गसुखोचिताङ्गाः खादन्ति किं वह्निगतं निलिम्पाः ।

---

1 *Psalms of the Early Buddhists II*. Trans. by Mrs. Rhys Davids, p. 293.

2 See Chap. XII.

3 Details in Lietzmann: *Christliche Literatur*; Croiset: *Histoire de la Littérature Grecque*, Vol. V, p. 727 ff.; Schanz: *Geschichte der Römischen Litteratur*, Vol. III, p. 245 ff.) 3rd ed.); and Puech: *Histoire de la Littérature Grecque Chrétienne*.

4 *The Seven Books of Arnobius Adversus Gentes* VII. 4 (*Ante-nicene Library*).

5 See Chapters XII and XIII.

Similarly, the sarcastic verse, attributed in our work to an ox addressing a priest about to sacrifice him, in the story related by Yaśodhara in the dialogue with his mother,[1] has its counterpart in Arnobius VII. 9 in the elaborate speech imagined to be addressed to Jupiter by an ox on the iniquity of sacrificing him to appease the fury of the gods. But the Jaina view of *ahiṁsā* is far more comprehensive than the Christian objection to animal sacrifices, involving as it does complete abstinence from all kinds of flesh food. Arnobius, in fact, deeply regrets the necessity that compels men to kill animals for food, and we have what we may call his confession on the subject: "We half-savage men, nay rather..........., we savages, whom unhappy necessity and bad habit have trained to take these as food, are sometimes moved with pity for them...............".[2]

The condemnation of animal food and blood-shedding sacrifices is an important adjunct of the Jaina doctrine of *ahiṁsā*, and Somadeva's *Yaśastilaka* contains many interesting data on this aspect of Jainism. Buddhism was equally opposed to sacrifices, but the Jaina prohibition of animal food is far stricter than that of the Buddhists; and Somadeva, in fact, severely criticizes the latter for eating flesh[3], and similar criticism occurs also in the Tamil Jaina poem *Neelakeśi*.[4] It is noteworthy that it is in certain early Greek[5] and Jewish and Jewish-Christian[6] sects

1 Quoted in Chap. XII.

2 Arnobius (op. cit.) VII. 4.

3 See Chap. XIII.

4 *Jaina Antiquary*, Vol. VII, p. 3.

5 The early Pythagoreans do not seem to have been strict in abstinence from animal flesh. It is said that Pythagoras himself did not abstain from animal flesh in general, but only from that of the ploughing ox and the ram, although he is said to have refused to sacrifice on any but the oldest altar, that of Apollo the Father, where only bloodless sacrifices were allowed. It was the later Pythagoreans (fourth century B. C.), called also Akousmatics, who practised vegetarianism and complete abstinence from meat, fish, wine etc., and did not participate in the usual sacrifices. Diogenes Laertius, Book VIII; Burnet: *Early Greek Philosophy*, p. 93; Zeller: *Outlines of the History of Greek Philosophy*, p. 72. Still later, the Pythagorean rule of life embodying these principles was again preached by Apollonius of Tyana, as stated above. Empedocles of Akragas (fifth century B. C.), who as a religious teacher was guided by Pythagorean influence, also advocated abstinence from animal food and blood-offerings, which, as we have seen, were replaced by sacrificial cakes in animal form. Burnet (*op cit.*), p. 250; Zeller, p. 58.

6 The Essenes were a pre-Christian Jewish sect of Syria and Palestine, and followed, according to the historian Josephus, the Pythagorean mode of life, a significant phrase. Moore: *Judaism*, Vol. I, p. 457. They were communists, and the initiate, before he was allowed to share the common meal, was required to take an oath, among other things, "*never to injure anyone, either of his own accord or under compulsion*". The Essenes included the Therapeutae, who were to be found in Egypt,

and schools that we find a close parallel to the Jaina prohibition of animal food and sacrifices; and special reference may be made in tnis connection to the Pythagorean rule of life preached by Apolloinus of Tyana in the first century A. D., as recorded in the biography of the saint by Philostratus (VI. XI; VIII. VII etc.).

The dialogue between Yaśodhara and his mother in *Yaśastilaka*, Book IV, is highly interesting from the standpoint of comparative religion. In the first place, the attack on the Brahmanical deities, found also elsewhere in the work as well as in other Jaina texts, is comparable to the attack on the pagan deities found even in a more systematic form in early Christian apologetic literature, e. g., in Clement's *Exhortation to the Greeks*, *The Seven Books of Arnobius Adversus Gentes* etc. In the second place, it is noteworthy that in the dialogue in question Yaśodhara takes pains to prove the antiquity of Jainism in order to refute the charge that it is a modern creed, and cites in support of his thesis evidence that is not altogether convincing and reliable.[1] The anxiety of a minority faith to establish its ancient origin by all kinds of literary evidence at its disposal for the purpose of enhancing its prestige is inevitable in its struggle for recognition, and instances of this are found also in the literature of Christianity in the early period of its conflict with the Pagan cults. For example, Tertullian, who admits that the Christian community is rather modern, points out that it rests on the very ancient books of the Jews, and asserts that Moses is earlier than Danaus, "*Your* most ancient of men", about a thousand years ahead of the Trojan

and led the contemplative life of ascetics; their so-called feasts *where no flesh was served* 'were famous and formed a contrast to Greek revels.' *Encyclopedia Britannica, sub voce, fourteenth edition.* Next in importance for our purpose is the Jewish-Christian sect of the Ebionites (second century), or, strictly speaking, that section of the Ebionites who derived their tenets from contact with the Essenes and the Gnostics, and professed what is known as Essene or Gnostic Ebionism. These Ebionites denied the divinity of Jesus, and their discipline included abstinence from flesh and prohibition of blood-shedding sacrifices: the Pentateuch, specially where it requires sacrifice and the use of flesh, was to be rejected. Gnosticism has been described as a system of heathenish thought, adoptiug some Jewish and some Christian elements; and we are here concerned with the Syrian school whose inspiration was Oriental, and practice ascetic. Satornilus, or Saturninus, of Antioch and Tatian of Mesopotamia belong to the Syrian school (second century A. D.). Both of them condemned marriage and animal food, while the asceticism of Tatian was so thorough that his followers were called Encratites, or professors of an abstinence that was really total. Kidd: *A History of the Church*, vol. I, chapters IV and VIII. On the Essenes cf. Headlam: *The Life and teaching of Jesus the Christ*, pp. 110, 137, 162, fourth edition, 1940; Peters: *The Religion of the Hebrews*, p. 423.

1 See Chap. XIII.

war, and fifteen hundred years before Homer. As regards proofs, the task of setting them out in detail is "not difficult so much as endless, not an arduous task, but for the moment too long".[1] To the same category of presumptions belong Pontius Pilate's alleged report to Tiberius on the story of the resurrection of Christ[2], and spurious documents such as the letter of Marcus Aurelius to the Senate on the miraculous effect of the prayers of his Christian soldiers on the great drought in Germany, Abgar's letter to Christ and his reply thereto etc.[3] So far as Somadeva is concerned, he cannot indeed be accused of forgery, but only of misjudging the chronological value of some of the authorities cited by him.

It will also be seen that, in Yaśodhara's dialogue with his mother Candramati, he makes a serious attempt to refute the charges levelled against Jainism by her; and elsewhere in the work Somadeva justifies certain typical beliefs and practices of the Jaina faith.[4] It is, as a matter of fact, one of the objects of *Yaśastilaka* to remove misconceptions and prejudices concerning the religion of the Arhat, and establish its legitimate place among the recognised schools and systems of the land. In this respect also Somadeva's work reminds one of the literary efforts of the early Christian apologists, and we may besides refer in this connection to a work like *Against Apion* of the Jewish historian Josephus (first century A. D.), who sets out not only to demonstrate the great antiquity of the Jewish people and explain and eulogize their law but to rebut certain calumnies of the Greek writers on the subject.[5] The occasional similarities between Jaina and Christian polemical literature are not surprising, and may be attributed to a like cause, the religious conflicts of the Graeco-Roman world and of Ancient and Medieval India.[6] Apologetic literature is, however, apt to lose part of its interest after the storm and stress of controversy is over, and what has been said of the work of Josephus may also be applied to Somadeva's apology for Jainism in his romance. No one today doubts the antiquity of Jainism or considers the Digambaras

1 *Apology*, Ch. XIX, Trans. by Glover.

2 Ibid. Ch. XXI.

3 Eusebius: *Ecclesiastical History* I. XIII.

4 See Chaps. X and XIII.

5 Croiset (op. cit), p. 443.

6 Candramati's strictures on the Digambaras for their part in the conversion of Yaśodhara to Jainism reflect the feelings of a pious Hindu and indicate the spirit of the times. We are reminded of the attack of Celsus (second century) on converts from Judaism to Christianity, the main charge being that they have erred 'in consequence of their minds being led captive by Jesus; that they have been most ridiculously deceived' etc. Kidd: *A History of the Church*, Vol. I, p. 413. For similarity of language see Candramati's remarks cited in Chap. XII.

to be unworthy people, but the defence of Jainism in the dialogue in *Yaśastilaka*, Book IV, although a record of past prejudices, is important as reflecting contemporary conditions, and preserving for us a number of citations from works no longer extant and certain important references to little known authors.

The controversial dialogue is indeed a conspicuous feature of *Yaśastilaka* as a religious romance. In addition to the dialogue between Yaśodhara and his mother in Book IV, the episode of Caṇḍakarman in Book V contains a dialogue in which a follower of the Sāṁkhya system, a Mīmāṁsaka, a Cārvāka, a Śaiva and a Buddhist expound their respective tenets before the Jaina teacher Sudatta, who makes a summary reply, reserving for special attack the doctrines of the Śaivas.[1] Very unlike is the dialogue between Yaśodhara and his mother, which is a lively debate on questions at issue between Jainism and the Brahmanical religion. It is an interesting fact that, whenever there is a conflict of religions, the controversial dialogue or religious debate tends to appear in contemporary literature. In Jaina literature itself there are examples which might have served as models for later writers like Somadeva. For instance, in the *Sūtrakṛtāṅga Sūtra* II. 6 there is an important dialogue, in which Ārdraka, a follower of Mahāvīra, is the chief speaker, and refutes the views of the representatives of various schools: Gośāla, a Buddhist, a Vedāntin, a Vedic priest, and a Hastitāpasa.[2] Turning to Western literature, we may refer to such examples as the famous *Octavius* of Minucius Felix (*circa* 180 A. D.), which records a debate in Latin between two friends on the relative merits of Pagan and Christian beliefs; Justin's *Dialogue with the Jew Trypho* (2nd century) in Greek; and Aristo's lost *Dialogue between the Christian Jason and the Jew Papiscus*, also in Greek,[3] and composed about the same time. Amicable debates between exponents of Christianity and Islam are known to have been encouraged by certain Califs and Byzantine Emperors;[4] while the Emperor Manuel Palaeologus (1391-1425 A. D.) wrote a large number of polemical dialogues directed against Islam.[5] More interesting from our point of view is the debate on the validity and merits of Pagan beliefs and the Christian religion occurring in St. John Damascene's *Barlaam and Ioasaph*, a Greek religious novel of about the eighth century

---

1 See Chap. VIII.

2 Jacobi: *Jaina Sūtras*, Part II, p. 409 ff.

3 Croiset (op. cit.), p. 736 ff. cf. Glover: *Conflict of Religions in the early Roman Empire*, p. 176.

4 Runciman: *Byzantine Civilisation*, p. 131.

5 Montelatici: *Letteratura Bizantina*, p. 250.

A. D.[1] The discussion here is not in the form of a dialogue, but we have the speech of Nachor against the Pagan deities and in praise of the Christians; and the contest, as recorded in the work, provides, on the whole, a good example of a religious debate incorporated in a prose romance (Chap. XXVI ff.). Authorities are not cited as in *Yaśastilaka*, but the speech of Nachor itself is nothing but the *Apology* of Aristides, a philosopher of Athens of the second century A. D., 'fitted, with some deftness into its new context.' In the Jaina romance mother and son disagree on religious issues, while in the Greek story the disagreement is between father and son; but while in *Yaśastilaka* the disputants themselves carry on the debate, in *Barlaam and Ioasaph* orators are employed by both parties to plead their cause. Religion plays an important part in another medieval Greek romance of the tenth century, the Byzantine poem of *Digenis Akritas*, wherein Emir Mousour, a Muhammadan convert to Christianity, soon after his baptism enters into a discussion with his mother to make her renounce the religion of Islam, and argues like a veritable theologian.[2] Somadeva's *Yaśastilaka* is likewise a religious romance composed in an age of conflict, and as such shares some of the characteristics of works written at similar epochs.

The stories of rebirth in Book V are a typically Jaina feature, and similar stories are found in earlier romances like *Vasudevahiṇḍī*, *Samarāiccakahā* etc.; they are not without interest from the standpoint of comparative literature.[3] The sequence of Karma and rebirth, which

1 Text and Trans. in *Loeb Classical Library*.

2 Diehl: *Figures Byzantines*, Vol. II, p. 312.

3 As is well-known, Pythagoras and Empedocles taught the doctrine of Rebirth or transmigration, which the former may have learnt from the contemporary Orphics, For possible Indian influence on Pythagoras see Gomperz: *Greek Thinkers*, vol. I, p. 127. Empedocles says that he has not only been a human being, a boy and a maid. and a plant, but even a fish. Diogenes Laertius, VIII. 77. The Greek writer Lucian of Samosata (second century A. D.), in his pleasant satire *The Dream, or The Cock*, describes the bird as declaring to his master Micyllus the cobbler that, before being a cock, he was first Euphorbus who fought at Troy, then Pythagoras, then the courtesan Aspasia, then the Cynic Crates; after that, a king, then a poor man, and soon a satrap; then a horse, a jackdaw, a frog, and a thousand things besides: the cobbler admits that he can no longer call himself the master of such a bird. Traces of belief in metempsychosis are found in old Irish sagas (seventh century A. D. and earlier). For example, Tuan, son of Cairell, had been successively a man, a stag, a boar, a falcon, a salmon, and then again a man. Dottin: *L'Épopèe Irlandaise*, p. 9. The peculiarity of the Jaina stories is that each successive birth of an individual is narrated in detail so as to form a regular sequence designed to illustrate the vicissitudes brought about by the law of Karma. The period of development of these stories may be taken to be the same as

these stories illustrate, is also emphasized elsewhere in the romance, being represented as the *raison d' être* of Dharma and the antidote against materialism.

सत्यं न धर्मः क्रियते यदि स्याद् गर्भावसानान्तर एव जीवः ।

न चैवम् ।

जातिस्मराणामथ रक्षसां च दृष्टिः परं किं न समस्ति लोके ॥
स्वयं कृतं जन्तुषु कर्म नो चेत् समः समस्तः खलु किं न लोकः ।
भूतात्मकं चित्तमिदं च मिथ्या स्वरूपभेदात् पवनावनीव ॥

एवं चेदमपि संगच्छते—

यदुपचितमन्यजन्मनि शुभाशुभं तस्य कर्मणः प्राप्तिम् । व्यञ्जयति शास्त्रमेतत्तमसि द्रव्याणि दीप इव ॥

"Dharma need not, of course, be practised if the existence of the Self were limited to the period between birth and death. But that is not the case. Because, do we not see in the world people who can remember their past lives as well as those who become ghosts after death? If self-done Karma had no effect on sentient beings, would all creatures not be equal in status? It is also false to say that the mind is composed of matter, because mind and matter essentially differ, like earth and air. On these grounds the following statement turns out to be true. The science of astrology[1] reveals the consequences of good and bad Karma accumulated in another birth, just as a lamp reveals things in darkness." (Book IV, p. 92).

The romance of Yaśodhara has also a didactic purpose. It shows us the seamy side of a woman's character and warns against the grave consequences of conjugal infidelity. The idea that marriage entitles the husband to the body of a woman, 'sold by her parents in the presence of the gods, the Brāhmaṇas, and the Fire'[2] but not necessarily to her heart, occurs twice in our work, in Book IV, and in the story of Padmā in Book VII. We read in the latter context:

स्त्रीणां वपुर्बन्धुभिरग्निसाक्षिकं परत्र विक्रीतमिदं न मानसम् ।
स एव तस्याधिपतिर्मतः कृती विस्रम्भगर्भा ननु यत्र निर्वृतिः ॥

---

that of the Jaina Kathānaka literature. See Chap. XVI. It may be added that the doctrine of metempsychosis appears also in the system of the Elkasaites, a Jewish-Christian sect of the second century: 'for, though Christ was regarded as born in the ordinary way, His birth of Mary was held to be but one of many such experiences. He had been incarnate before and would be incarnate again.' Kidd (op. cit.), vol. I, p. 103. The literary history of metempsychosis is a subject which requires detailed treatment on comparative lines.

1 Śrutasāgara says in his commentary that the verse is written at the beginning of horoscopes. The evidence of astrrlogy is cited to prove the existence of Karma and rebirth.

2 See Chap. III.

'The body of a woman and not her heart is sold to another by her relations with Fire for witness. But he alone is the lucky lord of her heart, in whom she verily finds joy and bliss born of confidence.' (p. 363).

These ideas favourable to free love seem to have been current in Somadeva's time, and it is his purpose in *Yaśastilaka* to show that they cannot be put forward as an excuse for treachery much less for crime.

We have discussed elsewhere Somadeva's attitude towards women, and as is to be expected in a thinker like him, it takes into account diverse aspects of female character (Chap. V). There are, however, certain attacks on women, for example, those in Book I, attributed to the sage Sudatta, which may fittingly occur in a religious romance, particularly in one dealing with a Jaina theme. Similar attacks are also found, for example, in the Buddhist biographical romance *Lalitavistara* (Chap. 15). Disgust for women is only a form of that detachment and indifference to worldly pleasures which it is the purpose of a Jaina *dharmakathā* to inculcate. This is the moral and religious background of Sudatta's reflections on the decomposed body of a young woman in the cremation ground (1. 95–124), particular emphasis being laid on the contrast between the courtesan's once admired beauty and the miserable condition of her corpse.[1] The musings of the Jaina monk belong to the same category as the Buddhist *aśubha-bhāvanā*, the meditation on impurity, on the horrors of bodily disease, decay and corruption. The dead body of a young woman is a familiar object for such contemplation, and an early example of this is found in a psalm attributed to the Thera Rājadatta in the *Theragāthā* (315 ff.), which describes the monk's effort to meditate on the partially intact corpse of a courtesan slain and cast into the charnel-field.[2] It may also be noted that observation and contemplation of corpses in various stages of decomposition, and the realisation that one's own body is of like nature, form part of the discipline envisaged by the introspective process of *satipaṭṭhāna*, described in the *Dīghanikāya* XXII. 7 ff. and other Buddhist texts. Meditation of this type is known as *pratyūha* or *pratipakṣa-bhāvanā*, 'meditation counteracting attachment to worldly objects', in Brahmanical literature. Jayanta, discussing the subject in *Nyāyamañjarī* (Chap. 9), explains how

1 See Chap. VII

2 *Psalms of the Early Buddhists*, II. p. 189. Cf. *Majjhima-nikāya* XIII, *Mahā-dukkha-kkhandha Sutta*. Here the body of a young woman, lying dead in a charnel-field, and being devoured by animals and birds of prey, is described to illustrate the perils that attend visible forms and the satisfaction they give.

the Vivekin contemplates objects likely to produce *vairāgya*, and gives the same example of meditating on the body of a beautiful maiden mangled by birds of prey:

असौ तरलताराक्षी पीनोत्तुङ्गघनस्तनी ।
विलुप्यमाना कान्तारे विहगैरद्य दृश्यते ॥
विभाति बहिरेवास्याः पद्मगन्धनिभं वपुः ।
अन्तर्मज्जास्थिविण्मूत्रमेदःक्रिमिकुलाकुलम् ॥
व्यात्तानना विवृत्ताक्षी विवर्णा श्वासघुर्घुरा ।
कथमद्य न रागाय म्रियमाणा तपस्विनी ॥

Sudatta's verses on the corpse of the young woman in *Yaśastilaka*, Book I, may be called a poetic elaboration of a similar idea, and constitute an eloquent sermon on the emptiness of life.[1]

An idea of the place occupied by religious topics in *Yaśastilaka* may be had from the fact that, of its eight Books, the last three exclusively deal with Jaina doctrines; the comprehensive controversial dialogue between Yaśodhara and his mother occurs in Book IV, and Sudatta's dialogue with Caṇḍakarman and his companions containing the criticism of Śaiva doctrines in Book V; while the cult of Caṇḍamārī and the Jaina reaction to it are delineated in Book I. Only Book II and the lengthy Book III may be said to be free from religious topics as such.

---

1 Scenes from the burning ground, 'the vultures and their mates in flocks' and 'the skulls of the dead', are used to illustrate the essential vileness of the human frame in the *Nālaḍiyār* (Chap. V), one of the early Tamil classics, and believed to be of Jaina origin. Pope's translation, p. 29. He remarks that there is no chapter corresponding to this in the *Kurral*, but the same spirit is recognised in the Tamil Jaina epic *Jīvakacintāmaṇi* XIII. 162–201, 'very striking verses'. "Everything that can be said in disparagement of the 'body of humiliation' is heaped up there. This is a characteristic of Jaina works. In Śaiva books the standpoint is somewhat different." A foundation is laid in this and the preceding chapters for the doctrine of Renunciation, which is defined as 'the relinquishment of all attachment to worldly wealth without, and to the body within (the lusts of the flesh) in view of their impermanency.' pp. 30, 35.

CHAPTER VII

YAŚASTILAKA AS AN ANTHOLOGY OF SANSKRIT VERSE

The large number of verses interspersed in *Yaśastilaka* makes it a veritable anthology of Kāvya poetry in the tenth century. There are groups of verses on diverse topics as well as individual ślokas, which can be detached from the context without causing any appreciable break in the narrative, and form, so to speak, an independent body of verse valuable for the study of the poetry of the period. These verses, as a rule, are composed in a comparatively easy style more attractive than the intricate prose, in which Somadeva chose to recount his story.

I. COURT POETRY

A number of verse-groups forming part of the autobiographical record of Yaśodhara deals with aspects of medieval court life, with which the romance is so closely bound up, and often gives vivid pictures of scenes which Somadeva must have personally witnessed. The cultural value of these verses can hardly be overestimated, and the following specimens form a more or less consecutive series.

a) BIRTH OF YAŚODHARA

The festivities and the atmosphere of gaiety at the royal palace at Ujjayinī on the occasion of the birth of Yaśodhara are described in a dozen verses (2. 68–79).

नृत्यद्वृद्धपुरन्धिगेयसुभगाः सोल्लासहल्लाननाः खेलद्वामनकामिनीप्रियभुवः सानन्दधात्रीकुलाः ।
पिष्टापीडविडम्ब्यमानजरतीसीमन्तकान्ताङ्गणास्तूरोघावरवैः समं किल बभुः शुद्धान्तमध्यास्तदा ॥

At that hour the inner apartments, delightful with the songs of the old matrons dancing therein, rang with the festive notes of musical instruments, and the countenance of the attendants beamed with joy. The floor presented an amusing scene, dwarfish women indulging in sports. Groups of delighted nurses were about, and the forecourts were charming with the presence of old dames, their hair heavily laden with heaps of coloured powder (2. 68).

आनन्दवाद्यरवपूरितदिङ्मुखानि पौराङ्गनाजनविनोदमनोहराणि ।
आमुक्तकेतुरचितोत्सवतोरणानि कामं तदा शुशुभिरे नगरे गृहाणि ॥

At that time the mansions in the city brightly shone, with flags flying and decorative arches built for the occasion. Charming they were with the pleasantry of the women of the city, and filled the quarters with the gay notes of music (2. 75).

आखण्डलप्रतिमपुत्रवतां धुरीणः स्त्रीलोचनोत्पलविलासरसप्रवीणः ।
त्रैलोक्यपावनयशःकिरणोदयेन त्वं नन्दतात्तनयजन्ममहोत्सवेन ॥

धर्मः पल्लवितः श्रियः कुसुमिताः कामः फलैः श्लाघ्यते वंशस्ते क्षितिनाथ संप्रति परां छायां श्रितः कामपि ।
भूदेवी सकृतार्थतामुपगता मूलान्वयानां पुनश्चित्ते माति न देव सान्द्रितरसस्त्वत्पुत्रजन्मोत्सवः ॥

सानन्दं बन्दिवृन्दैः क्वचिदवनिपतिः स्तूयते प्रार्थितार्थैर्बन्धूनां तुष्टिदानैः क्वचिदतनुमुदः सौविदल्लास्त्वरन्ते ।
आकल्पं भर्तृलक्ष्मीमियमनुभवतात् पुत्रपौत्रैश्च सार्धं देवीत्येवं पुरोधाः क्वचिदपि च पठत्याशिषः कामितश्रीः ॥

स्वर्गः कल्पद्रुमैर्भूः कुलधरणिधरैर्गौरधाम्ना पयोधिर्द्यौः पूष्णा भोगिलोको भुजगपरिवृढेनाकरक्ष्मेव रत्नैः ।
देवस्तावच्चिराय प्रथितपृथुयशाः कीर्तिपृथ्वी तथेयं देवी च स्तात् प्रमोदावहदिवसवती पुत्रजन्मोत्सवेन ॥

At one place the bards, asking for various gifts, praised the king (Yaśorgha) in joy: "Thou art chief among those who possess sons like Indra. Thou dost delight in the amorous play of women's lotus eyes. Mayst thou rejoice in the birth of thy son, a mighty festival, the source of a world-purifying halo of fame! The tree of virtue has put forth leaves, riches have blossomed forth, and desire is crowned with success. Thy dynasty, o king, now attains a radiant glory beyond all words. The divine Earth has her crowning desire fulfilled. And, sire, the joy of thy ministers occasioned by the birth of thy child, knows no bounds, for it has deepened the affection of their hearts." At one place the chamberlains were hurrying to and fro, overjoyed at the gifts presented by their friends. Elsewhere the family priest, desiring wealth, recited blessings: "May the queen share for years the prosperity of her consort in company with her sons and grandsons! Just as heaven is delighted with the Kalpa trees, the ocean with the moon, and the nether regions with the lord of the serpents; similarly, may the king, with his fame spreading far and wide, long enjoy days of happiness on account of the joyous birth of this child! May the queen, too, be likewise happy, great in her renown; just as the earth is happy with the great mountain-ranges, the sky with the sun, and the bosom of the earth with its jewels!" (2. 76–79).

b) WEDDING AND CORONATION OF YAŚODHARA

The wedding and coronation of Yaśodhara give occasion to a series of verses recited by the court poets. A bard named Jalakelivilāsa announces the preliminary ceremonial bath (2. 202–13):

यत्राभूदमृतातपः सुरकरी कल्पद्रुमः कौस्तुभो लक्ष्मीरप्सरसां गणश्च सुधया सार्धं बुधानां मुदे ।
यद्भूयो भुवनोपकारिचरितैरासेव्यमानं घनैस्तद्रत्नाकरवारि मज्जनविधौ भूयात्तव श्रेयसे ॥

यन्नाकलोकमुनिमानसकल्मषाणां कार्श्यं करोति सकृदेव कृताभिषेकम् ।
प्रालेयशैलशिखराश्रमतापसानां सेव्यं च यत्तव तदम्बु मुदेऽस्तु गाङ्गम् ॥

"In the ceremony of thy bath, may the waters of the ocean bring good to thee, the waters whence emerged the moon and the Airāvata elephant and the Kalpa tree and the Kaustubha gem and the goddess of wealth, and the nymphs along with nectar for the pleasure of the gods! The clouds, benefactors of the world, frequent those waters again and again (2. 210). May the waters of the Ganges bring thee joy! Even a single dip in them destroys the mental impurities of the sages living in the celestial world. Those are the waters resorted to by the anchorites living in the hermitages on the Himalayan peaks." (2. 211).

यमुनानर्मदागोदाचन्द्रभागासरस्वती- । सरयूसिन्धुशोणोत्थैर्जलैर्देवोऽभिषिच्यताम् ॥

"Let the king be bathed with the water brought from the Yamunā, the Narmadā, the Godāvarī, the Candrabhāgā, the Sarasvatī, the Sarayū, the Indus and the Śoṇa!" (2. 213).

The ceremonial bath is described in the following verse spoken by Yaśodhara:

उल्लोलालकवीचिभिर्विचलितापाङ्गोत्पलश्रेणिभिः प्रक्षुभ्यत्कुचचक्रवाकमिथुनैर्व्यालोलनाभीह्रदैः ।
वारस्त्रीनिवहैः सतूर्यनिनदं जाताभिषेकोत्सवः कामं स्फारितकाञ्चिदेशपुलिनैः सिन्धुप्रवाहैरिव ॥

'The gay ceremony of my bath was performed by bevies of courtesans resembling river-streams, to the sound of music. The curls of their hair waved like ripples; the corners of the eyes moved like blue lotus beds; the bosoms heaved like pairs of red geese; the navels were agitated like pools of water; and the hips expanded freely like a river's sandy bank.' (2. 214).

The sacred bath is followed by the nuptial rites, and a bard named Manojakuñjara addresses felicitations to Yaśodhara and his bride Amṛtamati (2. 215–220). There is almost an ironic touch in these verses in view of the tragic sequel to the marriage, which at the moment augured so well for the future.

लक्ष्मीरियं त्वमपि माधव एव साक्षादेषा शची सुरपतिस्त्वमपि प्रतीतः ।
आशास्यते तदिह किं भवतोरिदानीं प्रीतिः परं रतिमनोभवयोरिवास्तु ॥
एषा हिमांशुमणिनिर्मितदेहयष्टिस्त्वं चन्द्रचूर्णरचितावयवश्च साक्षात् ।
एवं न चेत् कथमियं तव संगमेन प्रत्यङ्गनिर्गतजला सुतनुश्चकास्ति ॥

"She is the goddess of wealth and thou art Viṣṇu himself; she is Śacī and thou art the illustrious Indra. What blessings can now be given to you twain? Yet may mutual love be yours like that of Cupid and Rati! Her frame is verily made of moonstones, and thy limbs seem to be composed of particles of moonbeams. Otherwise how is it that the fair maiden shines in thy company, perspiring all over the body." (2. 215–216)[1].

---

1 Moonstones are supposed to emit moisture when exposed to the light of the moon.

The bard then adopts an impersonal tone and describes the deportment of a newly married bride, an erotic picture often met with in Kāvya literature.

उक्ता वक्ति न किंचिदुत्तरमियं नालोकितालोकते शय्यायां विहितागमा च विवशश्वासोल्बणं वेपते ।
नर्मालापविधौ सकोपहृदया गन्तुं पुनर्वाञ्छति प्रीतिं कस्य तथापि नो वितनुते बाला नवे संगमे ॥
किंचित् केकरवीक्षितं किमपि च भ्रूभङ्गलीलायितं किंचिन्मन्मनभाषितं किमपि च श्लेषाभिलाषेहितम् ।
इत्थं मुग्धतया बहिर्विलसितं वध्वा नवे संगमे चित्तस्थेन मनोभुवा बलवता नीवीखलत्वं कृतम् ॥

"When spoken to, she never replies; when looked at, she never glances. Coming to the bed, she trembles heavily, being out of breath. Offended by jesting, she desires to depart. Yet who is not charmed by a maiden in the first union with her? A slight side-glance, a gentle play of the eyebrows, a few indistinct words, and a faint desire and effort to embrace. Such is the deportment born of simplicity, manifested by a bride in her first union with her lover; while the powerful Cupid, abiding in her heart, plays the villain with the knot of her skirt!" (2. 218-219).

Then follow the coronation verses recited by the bards while the prince accepts the emblems of sovereignty:

अपहसितपुष्पदन्तं कुवलयकमलावबोधनाद्देव । अधरितसकलमहीधरमाभाति तवातपत्रमिदमेकम् ॥

"Sire, here shines the unique parasol. It hath brought under its shade all kings, and surpasses in grandeur the sun and the moon, for it illumines the earth and calls into activity the goddess of wealth."[1] (2. 222).

द्विषद्द्विपमदध्वंसाद्भूभृतां शिरसि स्थितः । आरोहतां क्षितीशानां सिंहः सिंहासनं नृपः ॥

"Let the prince ascend the throne. A lion among kings, he is above all rulers of the earth, having destroyed the pride of his enemies, elephants as it were." (2. 223).

मृगमदतिलकेऽस्मिन्नर्धचन्द्रावदाते जलनिधिरसनोर्वीभाजनैश्वर्यवर्ये ।
जनितसकललोकानल्पकल्पप्रमोदः क्षितिरमण ललाटे पट्टबन्धस्तवास्तु ॥[2]

---

1 *Kuvalaya* 'the earth' means also 'night lotus' which cannot be opened by the sun; and *Kamalā* 'the goddess of wealth' has to be construed also as *Kamala* 'day lotus' which cannot be opened by the moon.

2 Helen Johnson points out in *ABORI*, Vol. XXVII, p. 187, that there is a reference to *paṭṭabandha* in Hemacandra's Triṣaṣṭiśalākāpuruṣacarita 10. 11. In an account of the feud between Pradyota of Avanti and Udayana of Vītabhaya he describes the capture of Pradyota by Udayana who branded Pradyota's forehead with an insulting term. Subsequently they were reconciled and "Udayana made a *paṭṭabandha* which concealed the brand on Pradyota's forehead. From that time a *paṭṭabandha* indicated the majesty of kings. Formerly they wore a *kirīṭa* and nothing else as a head-ornament." Hemacandra thus meant by *paṭṭabandha* a 'fillet', 'diadem', worn around the forehead in contrast with a head-dress worn higher on the head.

"Sire, let the diadem be placed round thy forehead, causing delight to all the world for countless ages. Adorned with an ornamental mark of musk-paint, thy brow is bright as the half-moon, shining with the glory of sovereignty over the sea-girt earth!" (2. 224). खड्गश्च तवायम्

लक्ष्मीविनोदकुमुदाकरचन्द्रहासः संग्रामकेलिनलिनीवनसूर्यहासः ।
विद्विष्टदैत्यमदमान्ध्यहराट्टहासः कीर्तिस्त्रियास्त्रिभुवनोदयमोदहासः ॥

"And, this thy sword is verily the light of the moon, causing the bloom of the night lotus-bed, to wit, the joyous advent of prosperity. It is verily the light of the sun, causing the bloom of the day lotus-bed, to wit, the sport of war. It is verily the loud laugh of Śiva, reducing the pride of the demons, namely, thy enemies. It is verily the smile of Lady Fame, caused by the joy of her prosperous career through the world." (2. 226).

After the coronation, Yaśodhara is greeted by the elders of the family who recite a number of *puṇyaślokas* or verses conveying good wishes and blessings (2. 229–235):

यावद्द्यौरवनिः कुलावनिभृतः शेषः पयोराशयः सूर्यः शीतरुचिर्दिशः सुरपतिर्ब्रह्मा च सर्गैः सह ।
एतेषां द्विगुणीकृतोदयजयस्तत्साम्यभाजात्मना तावत्त्वं क्षितिपाल पालय महीं जातोत्सवः कामितैः ॥

"Rule thou the earth, o king, rejoicing in the fulfilment of thy desires as long as exist heaven and earth, the great mountain ranges, the serpent Ananta, the oceans, the sun and the moon, the regions of the sky, Indra and Brahman, and the created worlds : with a soul as exalted as any of these, but crowned with a glory twice as great as theirs!"

ब्रह्मन्नाहवजैत्रमन्त्रसुभगास्तूर्णं कुरु व्याहृतीर्द्रागिन्द्र प्रहिणु द्विषां विजितये दिव्यास्त्रतन्त्रं रथम् ।
दिक्पालाः पुनरेत सत्वरममी देवस्य सेवाविधावित्थं पार्थिवनाथ कत्थनपरः शङ्खध्वनिर्जृम्भताम् ॥

"King of kings, let the sound of conch proclaim this message: Recite quickly, o Brahman, Vedic verses charming with mystic formulas ensuring victory in battles! Send forthwith, o Indra, a chariot equipped with divine arms for vanquishing all foes! Come swiftly, ye guardians of the regions of the sky, to serve our king!" (2. 234).

The coronation over, Yaśodhara and his bride leave the river side pavilion and return to the city on the back of an elephant. Yaśodhara briefly recounts what he said to himself at the sight of the gaily decorated city (2. 236-239).

सौधाग्रभागेषु पुराङ्गनानां नीलोत्पलस्पर्धिभिरीक्षणैर्मे ।
आनन्दभावादियमम्बरश्रीः पुष्पोपहाराय कृतादरेव ॥

'The goddess embodying the beauty of yonder sky seems to be eager to shower flowers on me in her joy, using for the purpose the eyes, resembling blue lotus blossoms, of the women of the city, standing on the front terraces of the mansions.' (2. 237).

On arrival at the royal palace Yaśodhara is welcomed by a bard named Kīrtisāhāra.

लक्ष्मीं बिभ्रद् ध्वजौघैः क्वचिदनिलबलोल्लोलवीचेर्द्युनद्या-
श्छायां पुष्यत् सुमेरोः क्वचिदरुणतरैः स्वर्णकुम्भांशुजालैः ।
कान्तिं कुर्वत् सुधाब्धेः क्वचिदतिसितिमद्योतिभिर्भित्तिभागैः
शोभां श्लिष्यद्धिमाद्रेः क्वचिदिव गगनाभोगभाग्भिश्च कूटैः ॥

स्त्रीलीलाकमलं तवावनिपते साम्राज्यचिह्नं महत् कीर्त्युत्पत्तिनिकेतनं क्षितिवधूविश्रामधाम स्वयम् ।
लक्ष्मीविभ्रमदर्पणं कुलगृहं राज्याधिदेव्याः पुनः क्रीडास्थानमिदं विभाति भवनं वाग्देवताया इव ॥

"Thy palace, o king, sometimes looks beautiful as the Ganges with its wind-tossed ripples on account of the rows of flags flying over the top. Sometimes it looks beautiful as the mountain of the gods by virtue of the crimson lustre of its golden cupolas. Sometimes it reproduces the beauty of the ocean of nectar with its glistening white walls. Sometimes it resembles the Himālayas with its sky-touching domes. A mighty emblem of thy sovereignty, this palace is verily the toy-lotus of the goddess of wealth! It is the birth-place of Fame, and Dame Earth's own resting-place! It is the luxury mirror of the goddess of wealth, and the family mansion of the presiding goddess of the realm! It appears to be the play-ground of the goddess of learning!" (2. 242–243).

c) MORNING SONGS

Verses recited by bards in the morning to awaken the king form an important component of court poetry, and in our work there are two sets of verses recited by the *prabodha-maṅgala-pāṭhakas* and the *saukhaśāyanikas* respectively to arouse Yaśodhara from sleep (3. 3–13, 14–22). The bright morning scenery is the theme of these verses, and there is also a personal touch in them, containing as they do occasional references to the king and his court.

d) A DISCUSSION AT THE COURT

An interesting discussion takes place at the court of Yaśodhara on the relative merits of fate and personal endeavour as governing principles of human conduct, followed by a diversion on topics relating to state-craft. Pronouncements on the respective claims of *daiva* and *puruṣakāra* are as old as the Mahābhārata, but they assume here the character of a formal debate designed to give the king practical hints in shaping his policy.

The discussion is opened by a minister named Vidyāmahodadhi, who, after stressing the importance of maintaining the secrecy of deliberations in the council-chamber, proclaims the supremacy of fate[1], and recommends the policy of least resistance, free from warlike adventures, and aimed at the peaceful enjoyment of the fruits of prosperity and the cultivation of justice and virtue. The minister argues that man toils and suffers for nothing: what is written on the forehead will come about even if he remains inactive. Indra is the lord of heaven and the serpent Ananta the mainstay of the earth, not because of any personal exertion on their part, but because they are fated to be so:

एवमेव परं लोकः क्लिश्नात्यात्मानमात्मना । यदत्र लिखितं भाले तत् स्थितस्यापि जायते ॥
मघोनश्चिदिवैश्वर्ये शेषस्योद्धरणे भुवः । को नाम पौरुषारम्भस्तदत्र शरणं विधिः ॥ 3. 37-8.

As for warlike ventures, the very name of enemies is unpleasant, and their sight, too, hateful like that of serpents:

वार्तयापि हि शत्रूणां प्रक्षुभ्यति मनोऽम्बुधिः । कस्तान् दृष्टिपथे कुर्यान्नरः कुम्भीनसानिव ॥ 3. 40.

Fortifications and wise counsel are futile when fate decrees otherwise:

दुर्गं मन्दरकन्दराणि परिधिस्ते गोत्रधात्रीधराः खेयं सप्त पयोधयः स्वविषयः स्वर्गः सुराः सैनिकाः ।
मन्त्री चास्य गुरुस्तथाप्ययमगात् प्रायः परेषां वशं दैवाद्देवपतिस्तदत्र नृप किं तन्त्रेण मन्त्रेण वा ॥

The Mandara caves are Indra's forts. The great mountain-ranges are his ramparts. The seven oceans are his moat. Heaven is his realm, the gods are his soldiers, and Bṛhaspati his minister. Yet, by the decree of fate, he was oftentimes subjugated by his foes. Sire, of what avail is then army or counsel on earth? (3. 41).[2]

The king should, therefore, enjoy his great fortune in peace without forgetting the claims of virtue. The speaker concludes by saying:

धनं धर्मविलोपेन परभोगाय भूपतेः । पापं त्वात्मनि जायेत हरेर्द्विपवधादिव ॥

The wealth earned by a king by violating the right is enjoyed by others; he acquires only the sin for himself: just as a lion acquires sin by killing an elephant, while the other beasts feed on the flesh (3. 44).

The views of Vidyāmahodadhi are attacked by another minister described as a materialist, who regards personal endeavour as the sole guarantee of success. As a follower of Cārvāka doctrines, he cannot, of course, accept any unseen agency like fate, but his views in this respect do not materially differ from those of the *Yogavāśiṣṭha*, which, too, glorifies personal effort and denies the existence of fate,[3] although a Cārvāka would not certainly accept its theory that the so-called fate of popular imagination

1 The *Sūtrakṛtāṅga* 2. 1. 12 describes a heretical school which regards Fate as the cause of everything. See also Jacobi: *Jaina Sūtras* II (S. B. E.), p. 35.

2 Very similar verses occur in Guṇabhadra's *Ātmānuśāsana* and Bhartṛhari's *Nītiśataka*.

3 *Mumukṣuprakaraṇa*, chas. 6–9.

is nothing more than the sumtotal of the actions and desires of previous births.[1]

Arguing that all actions depend upon effort and not on passivity, the speaker goes on to show the futility of depending upon fate. Fate, for instance, is powerless to feed even a man who has food before him, but whose hands are tied. He who relies upon fate is bound to lose even the wealth he has acquired: fate never guards a traveller who carries with him a bundle of jewels, but falls asleep on the way.

नरस्य बद्धहस्तस्य पुरो भक्ते कृतेऽपि यत् । अशक्तं मुखनिक्षेपे तद्दैवं कः समाश्रयेत् ॥ 3. 47.
दैवावलम्बनवतः पुरुषस्य हस्तादासादितान्यपि धनानि भवन्ति दूरे ।
आनीय रत्ननिचयं पथि जातनिद्रे जागर्ति तत्र पथिके हि न जातु दैवम् ॥ 3. 49.

The minister then applies his theory to the policy to be followed by the king:

विहाय पौरुषं यो हि दैवमेवावलम्बते । प्रासादसिंहवत्तस्य मूर्ध्नि तिष्ठन्ति वायसाः ॥

Crows perch on the head of one who abandons effort and depends upon fate, just as they do on the head of a sculptured lion in a palace (3. 50).

तेजोहीने महीपाले स्वाः परे च विकुर्वते । निःशङ्कं हि न को धत्ते पदं भस्मन्यनूष्मणि ॥

When a king is devoid of vigour, both friend and foe prove disloyal. Who does not fearlessly tread on ashes that are cold?[2] (3. 51).

अहंकारविहीनस्य किं विवेकेन भूभुजः । नरे कातरचित्ते हि कः स्यादस्त्रपरिग्रहः ॥

Intellect is of no use to a king who lacks in pride. A coward has no use for arms (3. 52).

हर्षोऽमर्षश्च नो यस्य धनाय निधनाय च । को विशेषो भवेद्राज्ञस्तस्य चित्रगतस्य च ॥

What difference is there between a living king and a painted one, when his favour brings not riches nor his wrath destruction? (3. 53).

येषां बाहुबलं नास्ति येषां नास्ति मनोबलम् । तेषां चन्द्रबलं देव किं कुर्यादम्बरस्थितम् ॥

What, o king, can the power of the moon in the sky[3] do for those who have no strength in their arms nor any strength of mind? (3. 54).

The speaker, therefore, appeals to the king to exert his valour and triumph over his enemies. He urges valiant action and a resolute attempt to expand the existing prosperity, and concludes by saying:

लब्धाप्यनन्यसामान्यसाहसं नायकं विना । लक्ष्मीर्न निर्भराश्लेषा प्रमदेव जरत्पतौ ॥

Just as a woman does not closely embrace her decrepit husband, similarly

---

1 Cf. *Matsyapurāṇa* 221. 2: स्वमेव कर्म दैवाख्यं देहान्तरार्जितम्. The Jain Amitagati also identifies fate with the Karma of previous births, representing it as an all-powerful agency which none can escape. *Subhāṣitaratnasaṁdoha*, verses 343–374.

2 Cf. Bhāravi 2. 20.

3 i. e. planetary influence.

the goddess of wealth, though possessed by someone, does not closely adhere to him unless he is a hero of uncommon courage (3. 59).

The next speaker is a minister named Kavikulaśekhara who tries to effect a compromise between the views of the two previous speakers. He recognises both fate and effort as determining factors in the life of man, although he gives greater importance to effort, and his point of view is the same as that developed in the Mahābhārata (Anuśāsanaparva, chap. 6), which likewise admits the existence of fate, but lays by far the greater emphasis on personal endeavour.[1]

Kavikulaśekhara opines that when success comes without being deliberately aimed at, it is to be attributed to fate; in all other cases personal exertion must be held to be the determining cause. When a serpent comes in contact with a man in his sleep and he remains unhurt, his safety is to be attributed to fate, but when the reptile is seen and avoided, the determining factor is one's personal effort. Fate and personal effort often help each other, and their mutual relation is like that of medicine and the vitality of a patient (3. 61–63):

अप्रेक्षापूर्विका यत्र कार्यसिद्धिः प्रजायते । तत्र दैवं नृपान्यत्र प्रधानं पौरुषं भवेत् ॥
सुप्तस्य सर्पसंपर्के दैवमायुषि कारणम् । दृष्ट्वानुवञ्चिते सर्पे पौरुषं तत्र कारणम् ॥
परस्परोपकारेण जीवितौषधयोरिव । दैवपौरुषयोर्वृत्तिः फलजन्मनि मन्यताम् ॥

Nevertheless the speaker recognises personal endeavour as the governing principle of human activity and dismisses fate as something outside the range of sense experience[2] (3. 64):

तथापि पौरुषायत्ताः सत्त्वानां सकलाः क्रियाः । अतस्तच्चिन्त्यमन्यत्र का चिन्तातीन्द्रियात्मनि ॥

A youthful minister, Upāyasarvajña by name, protests against this theoretical discussion, declaring that the king's council-chamber is not a school nor is the time opportune for an academic controversy. He, therefore,

1 The *Matsyapurāṇa* (Chap. 221) admits a third factor, *kāla*, (दैवं पुरुषकारश्च कालश्च पुरुषोत्तम । त्रयमेतन्मनुष्यस्य पिण्डितं स्यात् फलावहम् ॥) but gives the palm to *puruṣakāra*. The *Sūtrakṛtāṅga* 1. 1. 2. 4 gives equal importance to fate and human exertion. See also Jacobi: *Jaina Sūtras*, II, p. 240. They are treated as mutually dependent in Haribhadra's *Viṁśativiṁśikā*, section 5.

2 Cf. *Yogavāśiṣṭha*, op. cit., 7. 6. The discussion of the ministers reminds one of the tenets of the early Jewish sects about destiny and free will. The Essenes exempted nothing from the sway of destiny. The Sadducees denied destiny altogether. The Pharisees 'held the middle ground—some things, but not all, are the work of destiny; some are in man's own power to determine whether they shall come to pass or not.' Moore: *Judaism*, Vol. I, p. 457. The Sadducees supposed that 'all our actions are in our own power.' The Pharisees ascribed everything to fate, and yet allowed that to do right or wrong is within the power of each individual, although fate does co-operate in his action. Peters: *The Religion of the Hebrews*, p. 421.

calls attention to matters of political import, confining himself to questions of foreign policy, which can be narrowed down to the problem of dealing with hostile or rival kings. Although the speaker is convinced of the might of his king, he recommends the utmost caution in adopting war as an expedient. In the first place, if the desired object can be attained by diplomacy, it is useless to resort to war: who, for instance, climbs a mountain in search of honey if he can get it on the Mandāra tree?

मन्त्रयुद्धाश्रितश्रीणां शस्त्रयुद्धेन किं फलम् । को नाम शैलमारोहेदर्के लब्धमधुः सुधीः ॥ 3. 73.

In the second place, a king should take up arms only when all other means, conciliation, gifts and sowing dissension, have been tried and found wanting. It is useless to take up arms when the desired result can be obtained by conciliation: who, for instance, administers poison when death can be caused with molasses?

साम्ना दानेन भेदेन यत् कार्यं नैव सिध्यति । तत्र दण्डः प्रयोक्तव्यो नृपेण श्रियमिच्छता ॥
सामसाध्येषु कार्येषु को हि शस्त्रं प्रयोजयेत् । मृतिहेतुर्गुडो यत्र कस्तत्र विषदायकः ॥ 3. 91, 92.

The speaker pertinently asks, how much can be achieved by the sword? A man has, after all, one body and two hands: there are enemies at every step, and even an insignificant foe can be extremely troublesome (3. 90):

एकं वपुरुभौ हस्तौ शत्रवश्च पदे पदे । दुःखकृत् कण्टकोऽपि स्यात् कियत् खड्गेन साध्यते ॥

When war is decided upon, it is the duty of a king to adopt defensive measures for his own realm: a king who neglects to do so is like a man who takes off his underwear to cover his head with:

अकृत्वा निजदेशस्य रक्षां यो विजिगीषते । स नृपः परिधानेन वृत्तमौलिः पुमानिव ॥ 3. 74.

There are three periods in the life of a king: that of superiority to an enemy, that of equality with an enemy, and that of inferiority to him. It is in the first of these that warlike operations should be undertaken. Fighting with a powerful enemy is like fighting with an elephant on foot; while a clash between two equals, like that of two raw vessels, leads to the destruction of both. A powerful enemy should be attacked, like a wild elephant, by a combination of forces; while an equal should be subdued by employing others against him, just as one captures an elephant with the help of other elephants (3. 81–3):

उदयः समता हानिस्त्रयः काला महीभुजाम् । तत्राद्य एव योद्धव्यं स्थातव्यमुभयोः पुनः ॥
पादयुद्धमिवेभेन भूयसा सह विग्रहः । तं संघातविघातेन साधयेद्वनहस्तिवत् ॥
आमभाजनवद्युद्धे समेनोभयतः क्षयः । एनं प्रबन्धयेदन्यैर्गजं प्रतिगजैरिव ॥

No enemy, however small, should be neglected; mighty elephants often meet with death at the hands of lion cubs. Sowing dissension among enemies is an important step: a king neglecting this is like a man who pulls at bamboos interlaced in tall clumps. A king without power is like a lame man, unable to use his intelligence; and a king without intelligence is like a blind man, unable to use his power:

अहं महानयं स्वल्पश्चिन्तेयं नृप मुच्यताम् । सिंहशावात् करीन्द्राणां मृत्युरत्र निदर्शनम् ॥ 3. 85.

अभित्वा शत्रुसंघातं यः पराक्रमते नृपः । स तुङ्गस्तम्बसंलग्नवीरणाकर्षकायते ॥ 3. 94.

शक्तिहीने मतिः कैव का शक्तिर्मतिवर्जिते । नृपस्य न्याय्यदृष्टान्तः पङ्गुरन्धश्च कथ्यताम् ॥ 3. 95.

Bravery and loyalty count more in an army than numbers. A brave, well-equipped and efficient army, though small, contributes to success, provided it is loyal; a mere conglomeration of heads serves no useful purpose. Loyalty is an important factor, and a king who causes disaffection among his loyal subjects is bound to come to grief like a man who awakens a sleeping cobra:

क्षत्रसारं भृतं शूरमस्त्रज्ञमनुरागि चेत् । अपि स्वल्पं श्रियै सैन्यं वृथेयं मुण्डमण्डली ॥ 3. 87.

स्वानुवर्तिषु लोकेषु यस्तु क्षोभाय चेष्टते । श्रेयांसि न चिरं तस्य सुप्तव्यालप्रबोधिवत् ॥ 3. 103.

In spite of the caution recommended by the speaker himself in matters affecting war, he ends by asking the king to send an expeditionary force against those whom a false sense of power has made overbearing and proud.

The chief minister Nītibṛhaspati approves the foregoing speech, and, for his part, gives some advice to the king. He asks the king to look after the kingdom as a gardener does a garden, and reiterates the warning not to despise enemies, however small.

e) A CHALLENGE TO OTHER KINGS

We have next a specimen of a challenge to various kings and peoples, which the royal clerk, ordered by the king, reads out to the envoy, entrusted with the message:

गर्वं बर्बर मुञ्च मा चरत रे पञ्चालकाश्चापलं केलिं केरल संहर प्रविश रे मद्रेश देशान्तरम् ।
मिथ्यैश्वर्यबलावलेपरभसभ्रश्यद्विवेकात्मनामित्थं वष्टिरिटिल्लितं न सहते देवः स दैवाश्रयः ॥
शौण्डीर्यशालिनि जगत्त्रयलब्धवर्णे देवे न यः प्रणतिभावमुपैति भूपः ।
तस्याहवेषु वयसां शिरसि प्रबन्धो यद्वाश्रमेषु परलोकधिया जटानाम् ॥

"Thou Barbara, renounce thy pride. Ye men of Pañcāla, be not wanton. Chief of Kerala, wind up thy amusements. King of Madra, take refuge in another land. The great king (Yaśodhara), who believes in his destiny, will not tolerate your misdemeanour. You have forthwith lost all · ver of discernment through a false pride of wealth and power. The king who does not submit to His Majesty, magnanimous and renowned in all the three worlds, shall have birds of prey pouncing on his head fallen on the battlefield, or have a tangled mass of hair on the head, passing his days in holy resorts, with his mind fixed on the world beyond[1]!" (3. 112–3).

Luckily this arrogant message does not seem to have been delivered, for the author says that, in spite of the king's order to deliver a message like this, an envoy should regulate his speech and conduct according to the temperament and resources of the court he visits.

f) VERSES AGAINST MINISTERS

The report of the spy against a wicked minister of Yaśodhara gives occasion to a poetical outburst against ministers in general, which is all the more interesting as the relevant verses are attributed to various poets whose names are clearly mentioned. It is difficult to say whether these names are fictitious or refer to real personages. The former alternative seems to be the more probable, as in the foregoing sections also various verses have been attributed to bards or speakers whose names are obviously fictitious, and seem to have been introduced to lend a graphic character to the narrative. It may, however, be pointed out that the section on ministers belongs to a somewhat different category, as the verses here are given in the form of a regular anthology, and look like quotations from different poets. It is not impossible that some of the names refer to poets who were Somadeva's contemporaries or obscure writers, now forgotten, but we cannot be certain on the point. It is also noteworthy that certain names, e. g., Mugdhāṅganā-keli-kutūhala, Vilāsinī-locana-kajjala, and Prauḍha-priyāpāṅga-navotpala are too artificial to be real, although, as a matter of fact, fantastic names of poets are not quite rare in the Sanskrit Anthologies.

The chief value of this collection of verses lies in the fact that it is the nearest approach to political satire that we have in Sanskrit literature before Kṣemendra. Treatment of questions relating to Nīti or public policy is constantly found in the Mahākāvyas, but we have here a body of satirical verse directed against the ministers of kings; and there is at the end a set of verses which have for target a particular minister, and constitute a personal attack on him.

Taruṇī-līlā-vilāsa is the author of a prelude to what he calls the drama of a minister's villainy.

चञ्चापञ्चजनाकृतिः क्षितिपतिर्यत्राभवन्नायकः पौरो भाग्यपुराणपालितमतिर्मंत्री धवित्रीसुतः ।
स प्रौढोक्तिबृहस्पतिश्च तरुणीलीलाविलासः कविस्तदुर्मन्त्रिदुरीहितं विजयते सूक्तोत्कटं नाटकम् ॥

The drama of a wicked minister's villainy thrives indeed well. It is full of excellent precepts. A king resembling a figure of straw is its hero.

1 i. e. defeat will cause him to renounce the world.

The citizens are nurtured on the myth of Fate, and the minister is the son of a blacksmith's wife. And there is a poet in the drama, Taruṇīlīlāvilāsa by name; he is Bṛhaspati himself in forceful composition (3. 125).

मृल्लोष्टचेष्टः क्षितिपः स्वभावात् सुदुष्टचेष्टः सचिवश्च यत्र ।
शुभाशयस्यापि सुमेधसोऽपि क्षेमः कुतस्तत्र भवेज्जनस्य ॥

'How can even a man, honest and intelligent, be happy in a realm where the king is, by nature, like a clod of earth, and the minister a perfect villain?' (3. 126).

शिष्टावासः कुतस्तत्र दुर्मैत्री यत्र भूपतौ । श्येनैश्वर्यं तरौ यत्र कुतस्तत्रापरे द्विजाः ॥

'How can the good live under a king with a wicked minister? How can small birds live on a tree where the mastery belongs to a hawk?' (3. 127).

दुर्मन्त्रिणो नृपसुतात् सुमहान् स लाभः प्राणैः समं भवति यन्न वियोगभावः ॥
सूनाकृतो गृहमुपेत्य ससारमेयं जीवन् मृगो यदि निरेति तदस्य पुण्यम् ॥

When a person is not deprived of his life by a prince with a wicked minister, it must be reckoned a mighty favour. When a stag comes out alive, after entering the dog-guarded house of a butcher, it must be due to his religious merit (3. 130).

Kavi-kaumudī-candra declares:

अहिवलयितमूलः पादपः केन सेव्यः श्रयति क इह शिष्टः शल्यसंगं तडागम् ।
विषकलुषितमन्धः कस्य भोज्याय जातं कुसचिवहतभूतिर्भूपतिः कैरुपास्यः ॥
अविवेकमतिर्नृपतिर्मन्त्री गुणवत्सु वक्रितग्रीवः । यत्र खलाश्च प्रबलास्तत्र कथं सज्जनावसरः ॥

Who can resort to a tree that has a serpent coiled round its trunk? What wise man enters a tank with thorns in it? Who ever partakes of poisoned food? Who can serve a king whose welfare is marred by a villain of a minister? How can the good have any scope in a realm where the king lacks in discernment, the minister turns his face away from those who have merit, and villians are in power? (3. 131–2).

Two verses are attributed to a poet named Vidagdhamugdha, but they depend for force upon *double entendre*, and can be appreciated only in the original.

पङ्केजवने लक्ष्मीर्विपिने विजयो हुताशने तेजः । तपने च परं मण्डलमवनिपतेर्भवति दुःसचिवात् ॥
खड्गेषु परं कोशः शेषायां तण्डुलाः करे पर्व । चतुरङ्गेषु च तत्रं दुर्मन्त्रिणि भवति भूपस्य ॥

Nītinetra mentions the characteristics of a wicked minister:

राज्यवृद्धिस्ततोऽमात्याद्यो न कुक्षिंभरिः स्वयम् । अत्ति स्थाल्येव चेदन्नं भोक्तुर्भुक्तिर्भवेत् कुतः ॥
यः स्याद्गुजगवद्भूयो बहिरीक्षितमोहितः । तं खादन्ति न किं नाम लञ्जिका इव सेवकाः ॥

The prosperity of a kingdom can be enhanced only by a minister who is not greedy. How can the owner eat if the cooking-vessel itself eats up the rice? Is not the king who is charmed by outward looks, like a libertine, ruined by his servants, like whores? (3. 135–6).

कोशोद्गासी प्रजाध्वंसी तन्त्रक्षोभविधायकः । यो विद्वेष्टा विशिष्टानां शत्रुर्मन्त्रिमिषादसौ ॥

An enemy he is in the guise of a minister, who empties the royal treasury, ruins the people, stirs up rebellion in the army, and does harm to the leading citizens (3. 138).

Mānadhanañjaya says:

नृपतिसुतः खलनिरतः सचिवजनो दुर्जनोऽधनः सुजनः । महतां मस्तकशूलं जातैश्वर्यः कदर्यश्च ॥

A prince devoted to villains and a wicked minister, and the virtuous poor, and the wealthy miser cause headache to the wise (3. 140).

Kavikovida dwells on the wiles of ministers:

यदीच्छसि वशीकर्तुं महीशं गुणय द्वयम् । बहुमायामयं वृत्तं चित्तं चाकरुणामयम् ॥

If you wish to bring a king under your control, cultivate two things, an extremely deceitful character and a cruel heart (3. 142).

बहिरलघुरसप्रभवैरन्तःशून्यार्थपाटवैः सचिवैः । मुग्धमृगाः प्रतिदिवसं वञ्च्यन्ते मरुमरीचिकाशङ्कैः ॥

Like a mirage in a desert, the ministers daily deceive those (thirsty) deer, the simpletons. Outwardly they have charming manners, but inwardly they are good for nothing (3. 143).

कार्ये स्वस्याभिमते सचिवः सिद्धिं करोति हठवृत्त्या । नृपतिरयं बहुसचिवः के वयमत्रेति भाषतेऽन्यस्य ॥

A minister executes a task even by violent means when it serves his purpose. But when it serves the purpose of another, he simply says: 'The king has so many ministers; what authority have I?' (3. 144).

Abhimāna-mahīdhara says:

यद्यपि विधे न सुविधिः काम्येऽर्थे याच्यसे तथापीदम् । कुरु मरणं माकार्षीः सुजनानां दुर्जनैः संगम् ॥

Albeit thou grantest not our desires, o Fate, we beg this favour of thee: inflict death upon us, but never cause the good to associate with villains (3. 148).

मन्त्रावसरे समरे विधुरे दारेषु वस्तुसारेषु । यो न व्यभिचरति नृपे स कथं तु न वल्लभस्तस्य ॥

He who is faithful to a king in deliberations, war and adversity, and in respect of his wife and treasures, is bound to be dear to him (3. 149).

Avyādhidurbala enumerates certain things that are not likely to happen:

क्षाराब्धौ सलिलस्य दुर्जनजने विद्याविनोदस्य च क्षुद्रे संभ्रमभाषितस्य कृपणे लक्ष्मीविलासस्य च ।
भूपे दुःसचिवागमस्य सुजने दारिद्र्यसंगस्य च ध्वंसः स्यादचिरेण यत्र दिवसे तं चिन्तयन् दुर्बलः ॥

I am tired of waiting for the day when the waters will forthwith cease to exist in the salt ocean, when villains will cease to profess love of learning, when mean fellows will cease to be addressed with respect, when misers will cease to have joy of wealth, when kings will cease to have wicked ministers, and when honest persons will cease to be poor (3. 150).

Kavikusumāyudha is rather emphatic in what he says:

यदि तव हृदयं सनयं विद्वन् स्वप्नेऽपि मा स्म सेविष्ठाः । सचिवजितं युवतिजितं खड्गिजितं खलजितं च राजानम् ॥
उपलः सलिलेषु तरेज्जलधिर्गाधेत मन्दरः प्रचरेत् । इति संभवति कदाचिन्नाखलभावः पुनः सचिवः ॥

If thou hast any sense of right, o wise man, never, even in a dream, resort to a king dominated by a minister or a young woman or a swordsman or a villain. A stone may float on water, the ocean may turn shallow, and the Mandara mountain may move, all this may one day happen, but never will there be a minister who is not a villain (3. 152–3).

Sujanajīvita is hard both on kings and ministers:

विश्वस्तं महिमास्तं सुजनं विजनं कुलीनमसुहीनम् । गुणिनं च दुःखकणिनं कुर्यादिति सचिवसिद्धान्तः ॥
कुमुदाकर इव दिनकृति विरमति नृपतिर्नरे सरागे हि । स लघु विरक्ते रज्यति रजनिरसश्चूर्णरजसीव ॥

'The faithful should be degraded, good men isolated, the highborn killed, and the virtuous made miserable': such is the doctrine of ministers. A king ceases to love a loyal person, just as a night lotus-bed ceases to bloom at the sight of the sun. He suddenly becomes attached to one who is disloyal, just as fluid turmeric sticks to pulverised lime (3. 156–7).

Mugdhāṅganā-kelikutūhala describes how ministers dissuade the king from helping good and pious men:

ज्वरार्त इव खिद्येत मन्त्री सत्सु धनव्यये । कृतार्थ इव मोदेत विट-वागूजीवनादिषु ॥
भस्मनि हुतमिव महते यद्दत्तं देव तदफलं सकलम् । उपयोगिने तु देयं नटाय विटपेटकायापि ॥
पिण्डीशूराः केवलममी हि सर्वस्वभक्षणे दक्षाः । न हि यामार्थं सन्तः स्वामिन् भटपेटिकार्थं वा ॥

A minister would be pained, like a man suffering from fever, if money were spent for the benefit of honest people. But he would rejoice like a man who has achieved success, if it were spent on libertines, panegyrists and the like. (He says to the king) 'Sire, what is given to the pious is all useless, like an oblation offered on ashes. Money should be given to those who serve an useful purpose, even to dancers and pimps. Those pious fellows are merely gluttons, expert in consuming their substance. Sire, they do not keep watch at night nor do they contribute to the maintenance of the warriors.' (3. 158–60).

Vilāsinīlocanakajjala refers to the misappropriation of public money by ministers:

यदल्पं दर्श्यतेऽमात्यैः फलमाकाशजं क्वचित् । तत्सर्वस्वापहाराय मुग्धेषु पुरधूर्तवत् ॥
संभावयत्यमात्योऽयं यत् स्वमेव महीभुजि । तदन्यस्माद्विवेकोऽस्य मा भून्मयि धनाशिनि ॥

If ministers sometimes show to ignorant kings a slight transitory profit from some investment, it is with a view to misappropriating the entire amount; just as certain jackals, showing to the lion a small portion of the game, ate all of it themselves![1] A minister creates an impression of his own honesty on the mind of the king lest the latter should find out the truth from another while he is misappropriating[2] public money (3. 162–3).[3]

Sārastanī-kaitava-kautuka, after pointing out that the evil accompanies the good, depicts a minister as a kind of monster:

औवोंऽखर्वः सुधाम्भोधौ भूपाले प्रबलाः खलाः । सदर्पाश्चन्दने सर्पा न रत्नमनुपद्रवम् ॥

The great submarine fire burns in the ocean of nectar; villains are in power in the court of a king; and fierce serpents are found on the sandal tree. No gem is there without some blemish (3. 165).

ग्रहो ग्रहाणामसुरोऽसुराणां यमो यमस्यापि नृपस्य मन्त्री ।
एवं न चेदेष कथं नु जीवेदकारणं कोविदकामकालः ॥
द्विजिह्वो जन्तूनां मृगपतिरिभानामिव कुले तडिद्दण्डोऽद्रीणामयमसमरोचिः क्षितिरुहाम् ।
हिमातानोऽब्जानां तपतपनकालश्च सरसामभूत् क्रूरः कोऽपि प्रकृतिखलभावेन महताम् ॥

The minister of a king is a planet among the harmful planets, a demon among demons, and death of death. If it is not so, how does he manage to exist without any justifying cause, he who frustrates the desires of all wise men? A minister is born among the great, savagely cruel by reason of his vile nature, like a serpent among the creatures, like a lion among the elephants, like a thunder-bolt over the mountains, like a fire among the trees, like a screen of frost over the lotuses, and like the hot summer among the pools of water (3. 166–7).

Prauḍha-priyāpāṅga-navotpala says:

तत्र कथं मनु सन्तो यत्रास्ते तच्चतुष्टयं युगपत् । कलिकालः खलकालो नृपकालः सचिवकालश्च ॥

How can the good live in a place where these four live simultaneously: the Death-like Kali Age, Death-like villains, a Death-like king, and a Death-like minister! (3. 169).

The verses of the remaining poets are directed against the wicked minister Pāmarodāra, and contain various charges against his character. The poet Aśvattha says:

---

1 See Śrutasāgara's commentary.

2 धनाशिन् means literally 'one who eats money.' 'Eating money' is the Assamese expression for 'misappropriation.' Compare also *rŏkka tinnu* in Kannaḍa and *paise khāṇẽ* in Marāṭhi.

3 "The emperor's councillors are swindlers," declares a chronicler speaking of the conditions in Germany on the eve of the Reformation; "they nearly all grow rich while the emperor grows poor." Quoted by Janssen: *History of the German People at the close of the Middle Ages*, ii. 84.

परमहिलाः कुलमहिलाः परिजनवनिता विनोदवनिताश्च । रतिरसभाण्डं रण्डास्तापस्यश्चास्य गृहदास्यः ॥

The wives of others are, as it were, his married wives. The wives of his relatives are his companions of joy. Whores are the object of his love and affection. Nuns are his serving maids (3. 206).

The young poet Bharata (Bharata-bāla-kavi), after accusing the minister of dishonesty and corruption, exposes his hypocrisy:

परवित्तरतः परदाररतः परवञ्चनवृत्तिचरित्ररतः । अधमध्वजवंशभवः सचिवः समभूत्तव देव तमःप्रभवः ॥

Sire, thy minister, belonging to a degenerate oilman's family was born as the source of sin. He is addicted to the wealth of others, addicted to the wives of others, and addictod to the habit of cheating others (3. 201).

करितुरगरथनरोत्करविहारसंहारिताखिलप्राणी । संचरति राष्ट्रमध्ये नादत्ते पादुकायुगलम् ॥
दलफुल्लफलानि तरोर्नोञ्छति किल तत्र जीवपीडेति । यम इव सकलांश्च पुनर्देवद्विजतापसान् ग्रसते ॥

'He travels in the kingdom, destroying numerous creatures by the reckless march of his elephants, horses, chariots and camp-followers, but does not wear a pair of shoes (for fear of hurting animal life)! He plucks no leaves, flowers, and fruits of trees lest he should hurt any sentient being; but, like the god of death, he destroys all gods (i. e. idols), Brāhmaṇas and hermits.' (3. 210–11).

Puruhūta gives the following estimate of Pāmarodāra's character:

मानवति मानदलनो गुणवति गुणगोपनः स्वतः परतः । कुलशीलशौर्यशालिषु विशेषतो नृषु च कीनाशः ॥
क्षारोदधिरिव सुधियां चण्डालजलाशयोपमः कृतिनाम् । मरुमालकूपकल्पः सतां च तव देव सांप्रतं सचिवः ॥
नटा विटाः किराटाश्च पटुवाचाटतोत्कटाः । सचिवे तव चेष्टन्तां कटके प्रकटश्रियः ॥

'He wounds the pride of those who are proud, and conceals the merit of those who are meritorious, either himself or with the help of others. He is Death particularly to those who are high-born, good-natured and brave. Sire, thy minister is at the moment like the salt ocean in his dealings with persons of talent. For the virtuous he is like a Caṇḍāla's tank. For the good he is like a rocky well in a desert. So long as thy minister is in office, may dancers, libertines, swindlers and glib tattlers thrive in thy camp!' (3. 216, 218, 220).

Paṇḍitavaitaṇḍika reports a conversation between Villainy and his mother Deceit bearing on the character of Pāmarodāra:

हे वत्स दौर्जन्य किमम्ब माये कः सांप्रतं नावुचितो निवासः ।
वदामि मातः शृणु सोऽस्ति नूनं यः पामरोदारगिराधराङ्कः ॥

(Deceit:) 'Child Villainy!' (Villainy:) 'What sayst thou, mother Deceit?' (Deceit:) 'What will now be our fitting abode?' (Villainy:) 'I say, mother, hear. There it is, a symbol of meanness, under the name Pāmarodāra!' (3. 224).

Sarasvatītuḍaga makes the final attack:

स्वयं कर्ता स्वयं हर्ता स्वयं वक्ता स्वयं कविः । स्वयं नटः स्वयं भण्डो मन्त्री विश्वाकृतिस्तव ॥

'Thy minister appears in an endless variety of rôles. He is himself creator and destroyer both. He is himself the speaker and the poet, the dancer and the clown!' (3. 225).

In addition to the verses attributed to various poets, a number of verses on the much hated ministers is interspersed in the report of the spy, the line of attack being very much the same.

बहिरविकृतवेषैर्मन्दमन्दप्रचारैर्निभृतनयनपातैः साधुताकारसारैः ।
निकृतिनयविनीतैश्चान्तरेतैरमात्यैस्तिमय इव बकोटैर्वञ्चिताः के न लोकाः ॥
दूराद्दीर्घमवेक्षणं सरभसः प्रीतिक्रमः संभ्रमः प्रत्यासन्नमथासनं प्रियकथाचारे महानादरः ।
बाह्योऽयं सचिवेषु चेष्टितविधिः कामं न कं मोदयेच्चित्तेहा तु न जातु मार्दवमयी मन्ये जनन्यामपि ॥

None there is who is not deceived by these ministers, as the fishes are by the cranes. They are immaculate in outward appearance and dress, walk slowly, and cast steadfast glances. A pretence of honesty is their asset, and they are trained in their inmost hearts in the art of deception (3. 191). They look intently at a visitor even from a distance, receive him with effusive courtesy and respect, offer him a seat near themselves, and cordially indulge in pleasant talks. Who is not supremely delighted by their outward deportment? But, methinks, they have no pity in their hearts even for their mothers (3. 193).

g) MINOR THEMES OF COURT POETRY

Among other verses incidental to court life may be mentioned those attributed to the Sandhivigrahins, announcing the arrival of the envoys of different princes at Yaśodhara's court (3. 246-9); the verses containing the challenge of his warriors to the king of Pañcāla (3. 405ff); and the eulogistic verses recited by the bard Mārgaṇamalla during Yaśodhara's archery practice (3. 466-72). There are also groups of verses which describe various court festivals. One such group is connected with the spring festival when the god of love is worshipped by the king. The latter is asked to put on vernal attire in a series of verses (3. 447-56), while the sport of swings which forms part of the festivities in honour of Cupid is described in the verses quoted below:

नवकिसलयपूगीपादपस्तम्भशोभाः सिततरुफलकान्ताशोकवल्लिप्रतानाः ।
मणिकुसुमदुकूलोल्लोचकेतुप्रकान्तास्तव नृपवर दोलाः कुर्वतां कामितानि ॥
वक्रं वक्त्रमुपैति यत्र नयने नेत्रप्रतिस्पर्धिनी वक्षः पीनपयोधराग्रकलनात् सोल्लासलीलान्तरम् ।
हस्तौ हस्तसमीपवृत्तिवलितौ जङ्घे च जङ्घाश्रिते दोलान्दोलनमङ्गनार्पितभरं तत् कस्य न प्रीतये ॥

'May the swings, o best of kings, fulfil thy desires! They are beautiful with poles of areca trees with fresh young leaves, and fitted with branching Aśoka creepers with camphor wood boards attached to the ends. Charming they are with canopies and banners of silk set with flower-shaped gems. Who is not delighted by the oscillation of the swings, the women adding their weight? During the sport, mouth comes near mouth; eyes meet eyes; the heart is enraptured at the contact of the partner's high projecting bosom; hands move close to hands; and legs are entwined with legs.' (3. 447, 458).

A bard named Śūnāsūkta recites a few verses (3. 462-464) describing to the king the Festival of Lights (*dīpotsava*):

द्यूतोन्मादितकामिनीजितधृतप्राणेशचाटूत्कटः क्रीडद्वारविलासिनीजनभवद्भूषाविकल्पोद्भटः ।
आतोद्यध्वनिमङ्गलारवभरव्याजृम्भिताशामुखः प्रीतिं पूर्णमनोरथस्य भवतः पुष्यात् प्रदीपोत्सवः ॥

'May the Festival of Lights bring delight to thee, whose desires are fulfilled! It is enlivened by the flattering words of lovers, defeated in gambling, and held fast by their mistresses, excited by the game. It is charming with the varied adornment of the courtesans, engaged in sports. The regions of the sky resound with the deep auspicious notes of instrumental music.' (3. 463).

The blessings of the goddess Aparājitā are invoked on the occasion of the Mahānavamī festival by a bard named Vijayajaitrāyudha for the victory of the king on the battlefield (3. 459-61):

खड्गे खड्गतनुस्थितिर्धनुषि च प्राप्ता धनुःसंहतिं बाणे बाणवपुर्भुजे भुजमयी गात्रे तनुत्राकृतिः ।
संग्रामेऽग्रजयाय चिन्तितविधौ चिन्तामणिर्भूभुजां या सा स्यादपराजिता तव मुहुर्जैत्राय धात्रीपते ॥

'May Aparājitā contribute to thy victory oft and anon, o king! In the sword of kings she is incarnate as a Sword, and in their bow she assumes the shape of a Bow. She is incarnate as Arrow in their arrows and as Arm in their arms, and assumes the form of an armour round their bodies: she is as a Wishing Gem in fulfilling their desire for triumph in battles.' (3. 459).

The blessings of Sarasvatī are similarly invoked during the Pūrvaraṅga ceremony in the court theatre on the occasion of dance performances, and we have here a specimen hymn to Sarasvati recited on such occasions (3. 261-268):

स्वर्गसदां वदनपद्मनिवासहंसी विद्याधरश्रवणमण्डनरत्नरेखा ।
भूवासमानसविभूषणहारयष्टिर्वाग्देवता नृप तवातनुतां हितानि ॥
संध्यासु प्रतिवासरं श्रुतिधृतिर्बद्ध्वा प्रणामाञ्जलिं योगस्वापमुपेत्य दुग्धजलधौ शेषाश्रितः श्रीपतिः ।
शंभुर्ध्यायति चाक्षसूत्रवलयं कृत्वा करेऽनन्यधीर्देवि त्वत्पदपङ्कजद्वयमिदं सर्वार्थकामप्रदम् ॥

'May the Goddess of speech confer benefits on thee, o king! She is a swan abiding in the lotus mouths of the gods; a spray of jewels adorning the ears of the Vidyādharas; a pearlstring embellishing the minds of mortals! Everyday at morn, noon and eve, Brahmā, Viṣṇu and Śiva intently contemplate thy lotus feet that grant all objects and desires, o goddess! Brahmā, by folding his hands in obeisance; Viṣṇu that lies on the serpent Ananta in the Ocean of Milk, by resorting to Yogic trance; and Śiva, by holding in his hand a rosary of Rudrākṣa beads!' (3. 264–5).

h) PANEGYRICS

Panegyrics are an essential feature of court poetry, and there are several of them in *Yaśastilaka.* The following specimens are from among the verses addressed to Māradatta by the ascetic boy and the ascetic girl:

कर्पूरद्रुमगर्भधूलिधवलं यत् केतकानां त्विषः श्वेतिम्ना परिभूय चन्द्रमहसा सार्धं प्रतिस्पर्धते ।
तत् पाकोन्मुखनालिकेरसलिलच्छायावदातं यशः प्रालेयाचलचूलिकासु भवतो गायन्ति सिद्धाङ्गनाः ॥

पुष्पश्रीर्यस्य ताराः फलममृतरुचिः पत्रलक्ष्मीर्द्युनद्याः कल्लोलाः स्कन्धबन्धो हरगिरिरमराम्भोधिरप्यालवालः ।
कन्दः शेषश्च शाखाः पुनरखिलदिगाभोग एवैष स स्तात्त्रैलोक्यप्रीतिहेतुः क्षितिप तव यशःपादपोऽनल्पकल्पम् ॥

रिपुकुलतिमिरनिकरदावानल जगति तनोषि मङ्गलं दिवि भुवि विदिशि दिशि च विबुधार्चित धाम दधासि संततम् ।
भुवनाम्भोजसरसि महतां मत दिशसि विबोधनश्रियं धर्मविनोद भूप तव भानुमतश्च न किंचिदन्तरम् ॥

'The wives of the semi-divine Siddhas sing thy fame on the Himalayan peaks. White as the inner dust of camphor trees, and bright as the lustre of the milk in mature coconuts, thy fame vies with moonbeams, surpassing in whiteness the radiance of Ketakas in bloom! (1. 155). Sire, may the tree of thy fame delight the universe for endless ages! The stars are its flowers, the moon is its fruit, the ripples of the celestial Ganges are its leaves, the mount of Kailāsa is its trunk, the Ocean of Milk is its watering basin, the serpent Ananta is its root, and all the regions of the sky are its branches! (1. 165). No difference is there between thee and the sun, o king, delighting in religious virtue. Thou who art a forest-fire in destroying the expanse of darkness, to wit, thy foes, thou dost good to the world. Thou who art honoured by the wise, ever dost thou radiate thy brilliance in heaven, on earth, and in the regions and corners of the sky Thou who art esteemed by the great, thou dost create the beauty of bloom in the lotuspool of the world!' (1. 169).

Battle-scenes, a favourite theme of Kāvya poetry, are described in *Yaśastilaka* (3. 437–441):

क्रोधावेशप्रधावोद्भटसुभटघटाविर्भवन्मूलबन्धस्तूर्णत्वङ्गत्तुरङ्गाननपवनवशावेशविस्तारसारः ।
आसीदत्स्यन्दनाग्रध्वजनिभृतभरः पर्यटत्कुञ्जरेन्द्रस्फारव्यापारकर्णाहतिविततशिखः पांसुरूर्ध्वं व्यधावीत् ॥

The dust of the battlefield sped high, originating from the multitudes of warriors vehemently rushing forward in a paroxysm of rage, and was spread far and wide by the pantings of the swiftly galloping chargers. Masses of it were held fast by the banners on the top of the advancing chariots, and its topmost layer was dispersed by the extensive flappings of the ears of the roving elephants (3. 437).

II. Scenes of Nature

Nature poetry is adequately represented in *Yaśastilaka*, some of the descriptions being put in the mouth of the bards of Yaśodhara's court and addressed to the king. While Somadeva's portrayal of natural scenery will not bear comparison with the classic descriptions of the earlier poets, it is not wanting in genuine touches which reveal the poet's sympathy with Nature and his accurate powers of observation. There are elaborate pictures of the seasons and morning and evening scenery as well as glimpses of animal life; and it may be said, on the whole, that the poet's verses on the subject often have rapidity of movement and show a comprehensive grasp of details.

A large number of verses is devoted to the seasons (1. 53-68 ; 3. 376–387, 389–401, 425–435, 442–446).

भास्वद्भास्वति दाहवाहिमरुति ज्वालोल्बणाशाकृति शुष्यद्भूभृति दीप्यमानवियति प्रेङ्खन्मुखाम्भोद्युति ।
संशुष्यत्सरिति क्वथत्तनुमति स्वान्तोद्भवोर्जाहृति ग्रीष्मेऽस्मिन् महति क्षयामयचिति प्राञ्चन् मृतिं गच्छति ॥

In the summer the sun shines bright, the winds radiate heat, the regions of the sky are made fierce like flames, the mountains wither, the sky is ablaze, and perspiration gleams on the visage of men. The rivers dry up, the creatures are scorched, Love loses its force, and the disease of consumption prevails. A wanderer at the height of summer meets with death (3. 377).

मार्तण्डश्चण्डतापस्तपति मरुभुवामग्निसात्त्वं दधानः कामं व्योमान्तराणि स्थगयति किमपि द्योति धावत् पुरस्तात् ।
ऊर्ध्वं निर्ध्यामवीचीचयमिव विसृजत्येतदाशान्तरालं मग्नाङ्गान् निम्नगानां पयसि च करिणः क्वाथयन् वाति वातः ॥

Fierce with heat, the sun doth shine, setting the deserts on fire. A mysterious luminosity, moving before the eyes, intensely pervades the regions of the sky. Yonder horizon seems to belch forth waves of vapour. The wind blows, scorching the elephants, immersed in the waters of rivers (1. 60).

The king is asked to resort to the refreshing shade of the gardens in the summer :

कृतकिसलयशय्याः प्रान्तचूतप्रतानाः स्तबकरचितकुड्यास्तत्प्रसूनोपहाराः ।
जलसरणिसमीरासारसाराः प्रियाणां कुचकलशविलासैर्निर्विशोद्यानभूमीः ॥

'Enjoy the gardens, delightful with breezes from the rivulets, accompanied by the graceful movements of the plump bosoms of thy mistresses. Beds of leaves are made in them, and mango groves are on the borders. The garden walls are made of clusters of flowers, and blossoms are strewn on the ground." (3. 378).

The effect of the summer heat on certain familiar birds and animals is described in the following verse:

मध्याह्नेऽह्नाय वाहाश्चटुलतरखुरास्तोयमार्गं त्यजन्ति स्थानायानेतुमीशाः पयसि कृतरतीन् हस्तिनी नैव मिण्ठाः ।
शोषोत्तुण्डः शिखण्डी विमृशति शिशिरान् कन्दरद्रोणिदेशान् स्वेच्छं कच्छेषु चेमाः कमलदलतलं वारलाः संश्रयन्ति ॥

At noon the horses quickly leave the channels of water with ever swift hooves. The keepers fail to bring home the elephants playing in the waters. The peacock, raising his beak from heat, seeks cool caves and valleys, and yonder female swans rest as they like under lotus leaves on the borders of streams (1. 61).

The rainy season is brought into special connection with love and described with gusto and enthusiasm:

उन्मार्गाम्भसि मेघमन्दनभसि छन्नांशुमत्तेजसि क्षुभ्यत्स्रोतसि रुद्धपान्थतरसि स्फूर्जत्तडिद्भूयसि ।
कंदर्पौकसि मत्तकेकिमनसि प्रेमोद्यते चेतसि काले यासि कथं च रूढवयसि प्रौढां प्रियां मुञ्चसि ॥

In the season when the waters overflow, the sky is overcast, the rays of the sun are obscured, the streams are in flood, the speed of wayfarers is checked, and flashes of lightning abound: in such a season, the resort of the god of love, when the peacocks' hearts are maddened, and thy own heart is eager for love, how canst thou leave thy youthful wife and go on thy travels, young as thou art! (3. 389).

उत्कूजच्छिखिनं नटत्करटिनं प्रादुर्भवच्छाखिनं क्रीडद्भेककुलं पतद्बहुजलं क्षुभ्यद्धरित्रीतलम् ।
पुष्यत्कामदं जयज्जनपदं सोत्सर्गसिन्धुस्यदं दृष्ट्वेमं मिहिरं जगत्प्रियकरं काभ्येति न स्त्री नरम् ॥

What woman doth not approach her lover at the sight of the rainclouds, delightful to the world? Now the peacocks sing, the elephants dance, the trees flourish, the frogs make merry, heavy showers come, and the earth is astir; the frenzy of love grows apace, the countryside thrives in glory, and the current of rivers gains in force (3. 390).

The monsoon breezes are described in several verses:

कुर्वाणाः प्रचलाकिनां कलरवैरुत्तालनृत्तक्रियां न्यस्यन्तो निचुलेषु कन्दलदलोल्लासावकाशश्रियः ।
एते चातकपोतपेयनिपतत्पाथःकणश्रेणयो वाता वान्ति निदाघलङ्घनघनोल्लाघाः प्रदीर्घागमाः ॥

Breezes blow, pervasive in their approach, and skilled in overcoming the summer heat. They dance wildly to the sweet notes of peacocks, and exhibit in Kadamba trees the beauty born of the rich array of shoots and leaves, and produce the raindrops the young Cātaka birds drink (3. 392).

स्फुटितकुटजराजिर्मल्लिकोल्लासहारी नवनिचुलविलासः कन्दलानन्दकारी ।
सरति घनसमीरः सीकरासारधारी कृतसमधिककान्तिः केतकीकाननानाम् ॥

A strong wind sweeps along, conveying sprays of water, and enhancing the beauty of the Ketakī groves. It makes the rows of Kuṭaja trees burst into bloom, and destroys the gaiety of Mallikā blossoms, and makes the young Kadamba trees gay, and brings joy to Kandala flowers (3. 393).

प्रोत्तालयन् करटिनां करपुष्कराणि रन्ध्रोद्धुरध्वनितकीचककाननान्तः ।
उद्गापयन् मधुकरीर्नवनीपलग्ना वातः प्रवाति शिखिताण्डवपूर्वरङ्गः ॥

The wind blows, a prelude to the dance of peacocks, making the bees, seated on the fresh Kadamba blossoms, sing. It quickens the movements of the fore-ends of elephants' trunks; and makes the interior of the bamboo groves echo with loud sounds coming through the holes (3. 394).

The pleasures of the rainy season are recounted again:

रामाः कामप्रकामाः सुकविकृतिकथादोहदा वाग्विवादाः सौधोत्सङ्गाः सभोगास्तरुणतरुदलोल्लासकान्ता दिगन्ताः ।
यस्मिंश्चासारवारिस्रवदणुकणश्रेणिसाराः समीराः सोऽयं मोदाय राजन्न भवति समयः कस्य पर्जन्यजन्यः ॥

Sire, who is not delighted by this season of rainclouds? Now the women burst with passion; literary quarrels take place centering round topics in the works of worthy poets; the palaces are equipped with the joys of life; the regions of the sky look charming with the gay beauty of the young leaves of trees; and the breezes are laden with thick sprays of water issuing from heavy showers (3. 401).

The plight of the animals in the deepening gloom of the rainy season with its floods and storms is touchingly described:

मेघोद्गीर्णपतत्कठोरकरकासारत्रसत्सिन्धुरे पूरप्लावितकूलपादपकुलक्षुभ्यत्सरित्पाथसि ।
अम्भश्चण्डसमीरणाश्रयशिवाफेत्कारताम्यन्मृगे काले सूचिमुखाग्रभेद्यतिमिरप्रायःक्षपासङ्गिनि ॥
भूयःपयःप्लवनिपातितशैलशृङ्गे पर्जन्यगर्जितवितर्जितसिंहपोते ।
सौदामनीद्युतिकरालितसर्वदिक्के कं देशमाश्रयतु डिम्भवती कुरङ्गी ॥

The elephants are frightened by showers of ever falling rough hailstones hurled by the clouds. The waters of the rivers heave with the trees on the banks swept away by the current. The deer languish as the jackals howl on account of violent rainstorms. In such a season when the nights are dark as pitch, where will the hind take shelter with her young? Now, the mountain peaks are hurled down by heavy floods; the lion cubs are frightened by the rumble of the rainclouds, and the regions of the sky made lurid by flashes of lightning (1. 65-6).

Winter scenery and the joys of the season are described in the following verses:

इक्षूल्लासिनि सस्यशालिनि खरं शेफालिकोत्फुल्लिनि क्रौञ्चोन्मादिनि कुन्दनन्दिनि घनाश्लेषाङ्गनापादिनि ।
भास्वन्मन्दिनि वातवाहिनि हिमासारावसन्नाङ्गिनि काले कामिनि दीर्घरात्रिघटिनि प्राटेत् कृती कोऽध्वनि ॥
यत्रैतत् स्वयमेव कामिषु निशि स्त्रीणां घनालिङ्गनं यत्रायं स्मरकेलिकामितसमायामत्रियामागमः ।
यत्रार्द्रार्द्रकफालिभिः परिचितः सद्यःस्रुतोऽसौ रसः प्रीत्यै कस्य न स क्षितीश्वरपते प्रालेयकालोऽधुना ॥

Beloved, what wise man would take the road in the season that prolongs the nights? It lessens the heat of the sun and lets loose winds, and the creatures are benumbed by snowstorms. This is the season that ripens the sugarcanes, and looks beautiful with the corn, and makes Śephālikā flowers abundantly bloom; maddens Krauñca birds, cheers up Kunda blossoms, and causes women to tighten their embrace (3.431). O lord of kings, who doth not delight in the winter now? In this season the women tightly embrace their lovers of their own accord at night; and the nights are long, like the cherished joys of the sports of love. Now is also served fresh sugarcane juice flavoured with slices of raw ginger (3. 435).

यैर्नीताः सौधमध्ये घनघुसृणरसालिप्तगात्रैः प्रकामं कान्तावक्षोजकुञ्जार्जनविजयिभुजैर्दीर्घयामास्त्रियामाः ।
विध्यातासन्नवह्निप्रसरितभसितापाण्डवः पिण्डशेषास्ते हेमन्ते नयन्ते तव नृप रिपवः शर्वरीं पर्वतेषु ॥

Lean and emaciated, thy enemies, o king, pass the winter nights on the mountains, their bodies whitened by the spreading ashes of the fires dying out near them. Once did they pass the long nights in their palaces, their bodies profusely smeared with thick saffron paint, with the hands gaily placed in the bower of the bosoms of their beloved! (3. 433).

The poet is fond of dilating on the severity of the winter cold and its benumbing effect on men and animals, and sets before our eyes a series of vivid little frosty scenes:

सिंहः संनिहितेऽपि सीदति गजे शीर्यत्क्रमस्पन्दनो मध्याह्नेऽपि न जातशष्पकवलः प्रायः कुरङ्गीपतिः ।
वत्सः कुण्ठितकण्ठनालवलनः पातुं न शक्तः स्तनं वक्त्रं नैति विभातकर्मकरणे पाणिर्द्विजानामपि ॥
हंसी चञ्चुपुटान्तरार्पितबिसच्छेदात् खरं खिद्यते भूमिन्यस्तकरा करेणुरवशक्षीरस्तनी ताम्यति ।
प्रातर्डिम्भविचेष्टितुण्डकलनान्नीहारकालागमे हस्तन्यस्तफलद्रवा च शबरी बाष्पातुरं रोदिति ॥
अह्नोऽर्धेऽपि तरङ्गवारि करिणो गृह्णन्ति रोधःस्थिता जिह्वाग्राद्गलनालमेति न पयः सिंहे सतृष्णेऽपि च ।
एणानामधरान्तरालुलितास्तिष्ठन्ति पाथःकणाः पूर्वोत्खातविशुष्कपल्वलगतः पोत्री च मुस्ताशनः ॥

The lion sits idle, unable to move his feet, albeit the elephant is just near him. The antelope, as a rule, doth not take his mouthful of tender grass even at noon. The calf, with its neck inert, is unable to suck its mother's teat. Even the Brāhmaṇas are loth to apply the hands to the mouth while performing the morning rites (1. 54). The female swan feels great pain when a piece of lotus-stalk is put in her mouth (by her mate). The she-elephant languishes, resting the trunk on the ground, with her full breasts benumbed with cold. The Śabara woman, taking some fruit juice in her hands, piteously weeps when she sees in the winter morning the inert face of her child (1. 56). Even at noon the elephants drink only wave-splashed water from the banks of rivers. Even though the lion is athirst, water doth not come down his throat from the tip of the tongue. Drops of water remain rolling between the lips of antelopes. The boar resorts to the dry pond previously dug up, and feeds on Musta grass there (1.57).

The love life of animals in the spring is described in the following verse;

हंसो यत्र मृणालिनीकिसलयैर्गण्डूषतोयैर्गजः कोकश्चुम्बनचेष्टितैः परिपतन् पारापतः कूजितैः ।
एणः शृङ्गाविघर्षणैर्मृगपतिर्गाढं पुनः श्लेषणैः शृङ्गारप्रसरप्रसादिहृदयः स्वां स्वां प्रियां सेवते ॥

In springtime the animals, their hearts gladdened by the surge of love, caress their mates, each his own; the swan with offerings of tender leaves of water-lilies, and the elephant with mouthfuls of water; the red goose with strenuous kissings, and the flying dove with cooings; the antelope with gentle scratchings with the horns; and the lion with close embraces ever and anon (3. 442).

Geographical names are sometimes used to add a zest to natural descriptions:

आमन्दं पल्लवीनां रतिरभसभरप्रासकेलीविनोदाः सामोदं केरलीनां मुखकमलवनामोदपानप्रगल्भाः ।
आशैत्यं कुन्तलीनां कुचकलशरसावासकाराः समीराः काले वान्ति स्म तस्मिन् किल मलयलतानर्तिनो दाक्षिणात्याः ॥

The breezes of the south, which make the creepers on the Malaya mountain dance, blew at the time, soft, fragrant and cool. Verily these breezes delight in the vehement gaiety of love, in which the Pallava women indulge; avidly imbibe the fragrance of the lotus mouths of the women of Kerala; and linger on the perspiration on the high bosoms of the women of Kuntala (2. 69).

Morning scenery is described in 3. 3-22, and moonrise in 3. 479-489.

उत्कल्लोलो जलधिरजडं नीलनीरेजमेतन्मारः स्फारः प्रमदहृदयोदारचाराश्चकोराः ।
सौधोत्सङ्गाः सपदि विहितक्षीरपूराभिषङ्गा यस्योल्लासे स जयति जनानन्दनश्चन्द्र एषः ॥

वृद्धिर्वर्धेर्विजयसमयः पुष्पकोदण्डपाणेः क्रीडानीडं रतिरसविधेः प्राणितं पञ्चमस्य ।
स्त्रीणां लीलावगमनिगमः कामिनां केलिहेतुः स्रोतःसूतिर्निजमणेभुवां देव चन्द्रोदयोऽयम् ॥

Yonder Moon thrives in glory, causing delight to men. When he joyously rises, the ocean surges with waves; the blue lotus comes to life, the god of love waxes strong; the Cakora birds move freely about with delighted hearts; and the surface of palaces is forthwith flooded with milk! (3. 481). Sire, this moonrise causes the ocean to swell. It is the hour of the flowerbowed Cupid's triumph. It is the pleasure resort of the sentiment of love and the life-breath of the fifth note of the gamut. It is the science that teaches women their graceful movements; the occasion for the sports of lovers; and the source of the oozing of moonstones (3. 484).

Descriptions of mountains and the Siprā river occur in Book. V. The following verse is addressed to an ancient tree:

पान्थैः पल्लवलुण्टनं करटिभिः स्कन्धस्य संघट्टनं संबाधो हरिभिः शकुन्तनिकरैः क्षोदस्तु किं वर्ण्यते ।
किं चान्यत्तव देवदेहसदृशस्त्रैलोक्यमान्यस्थितेरात्मीया इव यस्य याचकजनैः स्वच्छन्दसेव्याः श्रियः ॥

Travellers pluck thy leaves; elephants shake thy trunk; monkeys harass thee; and how can the pecking by bevies of birds be described? What else can be said? Divine and universally honoured as thou art, thy riches can be enjoyed at will by suppliants as if they were all their own! (Book V, p. 177).

Apart from the glimpses of animal life in the account of the seasons, a considerable number of verses is devoted to the description of animals in our work. Verses in praise of horses and elephants are recited by the bards on the occasion of the presentation of the royal horse and the royal elephant to Yaśodhara on the eve of his coronation. Elephants receive the first tribute of praise (2. 167–190). For example,

भयेषु दुर्गाणि जलेषु सेतवो गृहाणि मार्गेषु रणेषु राक्षसाः ।
मनःप्रसादेषु विनोदवेधसो गजा इवान्यत् किमिहास्ति वाहनम् ॥ 2. 176.

Another series of verses is recited by the keepers on the occasion of the sports of elephants witnessed by Yaśodhara (3. 291–318). The poet often succeeds in presenting a life-like picture of the animal.

उत्तम्भीकृतकर्णतालयुगलः प्रत्यस्तपांसुक्रियः प्रत्यादिष्टकरेणुकेलिरमणः प्रत्यर्पिताम्भोघटः ।
पातुः प्रार्थनया चिराय विधृतानिक्षून् गृहीत्वा करे तिष्ठत्यन्यकरीन्द्रसंचरमनाः कोपव्यथाकीलितः ॥

The elephant stands, holding in his trunk the sugarcanes ere long seized at the instance of the keeper. He is rooted to the ground by the frenzy of wrath, his mind fixed on a rival; and the flat ears stand firm and erect. He hath given up playing with dust and renounced the joy of sports with his mate and repelled the pot of water set before him (3. 293).

Horses receive their share of praise in 2. 191–208. For example,

कदनकन्दुककेलिविलासिनः परबलस्खलने परिघा हयाः ।
सकलभूवलयेक्षणदृष्टयः समरकालमनोरथसिद्धयः ॥

Perhaps more interesting are certain individual verses on other animals. A simple yet faithful description of a dog occurs in Book V:

निर्मांसास्यः कपिलनयनः स्वल्पतीक्ष्णाग्रकर्णः कुक्षिक्षामः पृथुलजघनः पूर्णवक्षःप्रदेशः ।
दुग्धस्निग्धप्रवृत्तुदशनः सारमेयो महीशामाखेटाय प्रजवचरणः किंचिदाभुग्नवालः ॥

The same Book contains the following vivid picture of a huge buffalo:

रक्तप्रान्तविलोललोचनयुगः प्रोथप्रतिष्टाननः प्रोत्कूणाग्रविषाणभीषणवपुर्नीलाञ्जनाद्रिप्रभः ।
उत्कर्णः पृथुकन्धरो गुरुखुरः स्थूलत्रिकोरःस्थलः सा मृत्वा कमनीयबालधिरभूच्छागी पुनः कासरः ॥

The she-goat, after death, was reborn as a buffalo with a fine hairy tail. His eyes were nimble and fringed with red, and the mouth firmly based on the snout. He resembled a mountain of blue collyrium with a body made fierce by the horns curved at the extremities. He had erect ears, broad shoulders, massive hooves, and fleshy breast and buttocks (Book V, p. 224).

Epitaphs on animals do not seem to occur in Kāvya poetry, and the following mournful verses on a favourite peacock and a dog, uttered by the king on their death, belong to a type rare in Sanskrit literature.[1]

प्रासादमण्डनमणौ रमणीविनोदे क्रीडावनीधरशिलातलचित्रलेखे ।
को नाम केलिकरतालविधिं वधूनां नृत्तानुगं त्वयि करिष्यति कीर्तिशेषे ॥

(Addressed to the peacock): 'Thou wast the oramental gem of the palace and the joy of the ladies, and gleamed like a picture on the rocks of the pleasure hill. Who will dance to the joyous clapping of hands by the damsels, since thou art dead?'

सिंहः सुखं निवसतादचलोपकण्ठे सोत्कण्ठमेणनिचयश्चरतात् स्थलीषु ।
सत्त्वाः परेऽपि विपिने विलसन्त्वशङ्कं नाकं गतोऽयमधुना ननु विश्वकद्रुः ॥

Verily this dog is gone to heaven. Let the lion now live happily on the mountain slope. Let the deer graze on the fields with zest. Let other animals, too, move about freely in the woods without fear (Book V, p. 192).

The commotion of the animals in the Siprā river, caused by the inroad of an army of fishermen, equipped with boats, nets and spears, is graphically described in the following verse:

उड्डीनाण्डजडिम्भमाकुलभवन्नालीकिनीकाननं कूलोत्तालबिलान्तरालचलनग्लानालगर्दार्भकम् ।
प्रायःपङ्किलगर्तगर्वरमिलद्धौलेयबालं मुहुस्तत्स्रोतः कलुषीबभूव विवशग्राहं विगाहृत्ततः ॥

Then the rolling waters of the river became turbid ever more, with the alligators lying helpless. The young birds flew about, and the waterlilies swayed to and fro. The young water-snakes, briskly moving about on the bank, languished after running into the holes. The young turtles mingled with the buffaloes in the muddy hollows (Book V, p. 217).

III. The Cremation-ground

One of the most elaborate and comprehensive descriptions in *Yaśastilaka* is that of the cremation-ground in the opening chapter, in which the sterner aspects of Nature are brought into play, and the entire description is of a kind not fully met with in Kāvya literature. The reader is at once reminded of the picture of the cremation-ground in *Mālatīmādhava*, but the aim of Bhavabhūti is to evoke horror, while that of Somadeva is to excite pity, and the verses are appropriately put in the

1 Cf. the commemorative inscription mentioned in Chapter V, p. 123. It has been pointed out that the preface to the *Histories* of Orosius (417–18 A. D.) 'has a charm of its own, for it is one of the few places in ancient literature where dogs are mentioned with feeling.' In early Greek poetry we have the epitaph of Simonides on the hound Lycas whose white bones lying in the tomb are still a terror to the wild beasts. The poet refers to the mountain landscape in which the hound ran while alive. "Thy worth is well-known to tall Pelion and far-seen Ossa and the lonely peaks of Cithaeron." Fragment 142, Diehl: *Anthologia Lyrica* V, p. 113.

mouth of the Jaina sage Sudatta.[1] The delineation of the horrid scene is followed by the thoughts provoked by the sight of the decomposing corpse of a young woman, and specially by the contrast between her former beauty and present condition. The decaying body is described limb by limb; and while the description of the scene of desolation shows graphic power, that of the dead woman is overdone, and lapses into wearisome details, although there are some beautiful verses which recount her former charms. Some of the verses in which the cremation-ground is described are cited below:

अर्धदग्धशवलेशलालसैर्भण्डनोद्भटरटद्गलान्तरैः । कालकेलिकरकौतुकोद्यतैर्विश्वकद्रुभिरुपद्रुतान्तरम् ॥
श्येनकुलं घूककुलं द्रोणकुलं श्वकुलभण्डनाड्डीतम् । शवपिशितप्राशवशाद्दिवि भुवि च समाकुलं पुरतः ॥

The place is overrun by dogs eager to devour the fragments of half-burnt bodies. They are busy fighting and loudly bark and indulge in a pastime delightful to the god of death. And in the foreground, flocks of hawks, owls and ravens, scared away by the fighting of the dogs, throng in disorder on the earth and in the sky in the hope of feeding on the flesh of the corpses (1. 13-4).

गृध्राघ्रातसमांसकीकसरसस्रावोत्पथाः पादपाः प्रेतोत्प्रान्तपतत्पतत्रिपरुषप्रायाः प्रदेशा दिशः ।
एते च प्रबलानिलाश्रयवशाच्छीर्यच्छिखाः सर्वतः संसर्पन्ति जरत्कपोतरुचयो धूमाश्रिताचक्रजाः ॥

The trees are polluted by the oozings from the fleshy bones swallowed by the vultures, and the topmost branches are blown away by violent gales. The environs are made repulsive by the birds flocking round the dead, and on every side spreads the smoke of funeral pyres, resembling in colour age-worn doves (1. 85).

कालाग्निरुद्रनिटिलेक्षणदुर्निरीक्षाः कीनाशहोमहुतवाहविरुक्षवीक्षाः ।
दाहद्रवच्छववपुःस्फुटदस्थिमध्यप्रारब्धशब्दकठिना दहनाश्रितानाम् ॥

The flames of the funeral pyres are hard to look at, like the eye on Śiva's forehead at the time of the universal fire of destruction, and present a gruesome sight, like a ceremonial fire in which oblations are offered to the god of death. They are harshly loud with the sound produced within the cracking bones of the dead bodies dissolved by the fire (1. 86).

भ्रश्यच्छरीरशवशीर्णशिरोजसारः कुथ्यत्कलेवरकरङ्कहतप्रचारः ।
दग्धार्धदेहमृतकाग्निमयप्रबन्धो वातः करोति ककुभोऽशुभगन्धबन्धाः ॥

The wind fills the regions of the sky with a noxious smell. It is laden with the falling hair of decomposing dead bodies, and checked in its onrush by the skeletons of putrid corpses, and fans the flames clinging to the halfburnt bodies of the dead (1. 88).

1 A brief description of a cremation-ground occurs in Kṣemeśvara's *Caṇḍakauśika* Act IV.

यान्युत्सवेषु कृतिनां कृतमङ्गलानि वाद्यानि मोदिजनगेयनिरर्गलानि ।
तान्येव शोकवशबन्धुरवोद्धुराणि नर्दन्ति संस्थितवतां विरसस्वराणि ॥

Those very musical instruments, which on festive occasions accompany, unimpeded, the songs of joyous crowds, and prove auspicious to the lucky, sound harsh when they mourn the dead, loud as they are with the wailings of kinsmen stricken with grief (1. 89).

दन्तोत्कीलितशुष्ककीकसकलाकीलोद्दलत्तालुकाः कण्ठान्तःप्रविलग्नशल्यशकलोद्गालस्खलत्कुक्षयः ।
प्रेतप्रान्तपुराणपादपपतत्पत्रप्रदुष्यद्दृशः प्रभ्राम्यन्त्यविशङ्कफेत्कृतिक्षीबाः शिवाः सोद्धवाः ॥

The jackals roam about, full of joy and maddened by their own fearless howls. Their palates are pierced by the nail-like fragments of the dry bones stuck fast in the jaws, and their bellies quiver as they spit out pieces of bones sticking in the throat; while their eyes are troubled by the leaves falling from the age-worn trees alongside of the corpses (1. 94).

Sudatta then gives vent to his feelings at the sight of the dead body of the woman, apparently a courtesan:

या पूर्वं स्मरकेलिचामररुचिः कर्णावतंसोत्पलश्लिष्टेन्दिन्दिरसुन्दरद्युतिरभूद्गण्डस्थलीमण्डनम् ।
सेयं कुन्तलवल्लरी पितृवने वातेरिता सांप्रतं धूलीधूसरिता दधाति विसरत्संमार्जनीचेष्टितम् ॥

This lock of hair used to adorn her cheeks and looked like a fly-whisk during the sports of love and beautifully gleamed like bees clinging to lotus ear-ornaments. Driven along by the wind and grey with dust, it now does the work of a moving broom in the cremation-ground! (1. 95).

कस्तूरिकातिलकपत्रविचित्रितश्रीर्योऽभून्मृगाङ्कसमकान्तिरयं कपोलः ।
सोऽद्यच्छविं वहति वायसबालभुक्तः कोथप्रदीर्णतनुतुम्बफलोपमेयाम् ॥

The cheek that was gaily embellished with ornamental designs of musk paint, and gleamed like the moon, is now pecked by young crows, and looks like a gourd lacerated by disease! (1. 99).

या कौमुदीव सरसीव मृणालिनीव लक्ष्मीरिव प्रियसखीव विलासिनीव ।
तैस्तैर्गुणैरजनि सा सुतनुः प्रजाता प्रेतावनीवनवशा विवशा वराकी ॥

By dint of manifold merits, the fair maid was like the light of the moon, like a pool of water, like a water-lily, like the goddess of wealth, like a beloved friend, like an elegant lady. She is now wretched and forlorn, lying helpless in the wilderness of the cremation-ground (1. 113).

यामन्तरेण जगतो विफलाः प्रयासा यामन्तरेण भवनानि वनोपमानि ।
यामन्तरेण हतसंगति जीवितं च तस्याः प्रपश्यत जनाः क्षणमेकमङ्गम् ॥

आश्लिष्टं परिचुम्बितं परमितं यद्रागरोमाञ्चितैस्तत्संसारसुखास्पदं वपुरभूदेवंदशागोचरम् ।
शीर्यच्चर्मचयं पतत्पलभरं भ्रश्यच्छिरापञ्जरं व्यस्यत्संधिबलं गलन्नलकुलं कुथ्यत्स्नसाजालकम् ॥

Without her, the toil of the world seems to be in vain. Without her, the houses look like the woods. Without her, life loses its meaning.

Ye folks, behold her body for a moment. The source of mundane joys, her body used to be clasped, kissed and enjoyed by men thrilled with passion. But it is now reduced to such a plight. The skin is torn to shreds, the flesh is falling off, and the network of veins is loosening. The strength of the joints is gone, the bones are crumbling to pieces, and the sinews are putrescent (1. 121-122).

With the above pictures may be compared that of Amṛtamati, stricken with a fell disease after her crime. Somadeva depicts the gruesome to excite our pity.

अलिकुलमिदं लूतातन्तुप्रतानविधूसरं मनसिजधनुर्जातं जीर्यत्तनुस्थिति पिञ्जनम् ।
कुवलयवनं धत्ते दैन्यं दवाग्निसमाश्रयं घुणदरभरभ्रस्यत्स्तम्भप्रभावमभूद्वपुः ॥

The hair, once dark as a swarm of bees, has turned grey as the threads of a cobweb. The eyebrows, once like Cupid's bow, resemble a dilapidated bow for cleansing cotton. The eyes, once blue lotus blossoms, look miserable, as if within grasp of a forest fire; and the body resembles a worm-eaten pillar, about to crumble[1] (Book V, p. 223).

IV. Other Descriptions

Somadeva's power of portraying the terrible is illustrated in the picture of Caṇḍamārī, which looms large in the opening chapter of the work. Sound echoes the sense in the powerful description of the goddess in 1. 137.

उत्सर्पद्दर्पसर्पाकुलविकटजटाजूटबिभ्यद्विधूनि प्रान्तप्रेङ्खत्कपालावलिचलनरणद्दण्टखट्वाङ्ककानि ।
दैत्यध्वंसप्रमोदोद्धुरविधुतकराभोगखर्वद्रिरीणि स्फाराघाताङ्घ्रिपातोच्छलदुदधिजलान्युद्धतोद्वेल्लितानि ॥

The impetuous movements of the goddess are such that the waters of the ocean are splashed by the heavy impact of her feet; and the moon (on her forehead) is terrified by the horrid mass of her matted hair, entwined with madly excited serpents; while the bells of her club ring out as the human skulls, swaying at her side, move to and fro; and the mountains are laid low by her massive hands as she vehemently waves them in an outburst of joy at the destruction of the demons.

Among other descriptions may be mentioned those of the city of Ujjayinī (2. 14–29) and of king Yaśorgha (2. 31–53). There is a good description of child life in 2. 82–90, which testifies to Somadeva's accurate observation and love of children, and is all the more interesting, as such descriptions are by no means common in Kāvya literature.

अम्बां तात इति ब्रवीति पितरं चाम्बेति संभाषते धात्रीपूर्वनिवेदितानि च पदान्यर्धोक्तितो जल्पति ।
शिक्षालापविधौ प्रकुप्यति धृतो नास्ते स्थिरोऽयं क्वचिद् व्याहूतो न शृणोति धावति पुनः प्रत्युत्थितः सत्वरम् ॥

1 Lit.: pillar crumbling owing to the accumulation of worm-holes.

The child addresses the mother as 'daddy' and the father as 'mammy'. He half utters the words first taught by the nurse. He becomes angry when an effort is made to teach him, and nowhere keeps still when held. He never listens when summoned. He slips and rises quickly and runs again (2. 90).

तद्गेहं वनमेव यत्र शिशवः खेलन्ति न प्राङ्गणे तेषां जन्म वृथैव लोचनपथं याता न येषां सुताः ।
तेषामङ्गविलेपनं च नृपते पङ्कोपदेहैः समं येषां धूलिविधूसरात्मजरजश्चर्चा न वक्षःस्थले ॥

Verily the house where no children play in the courtyard is a jungle. Futile is their birth who have seen no children of their own. Beauty-paint, o king, is like a smearing of mud for those whose bosoms are not bedaubed with the dust transmitted by their children, grey with dust (2. 88).

Descriptions of female beauty, so common in Kāvya poetry, are few and far between in *Yaśastilaka* owing to the very nature of the plot. We may here cite two of the verses spoken by Vāriṣeṇa, unable to forget his young wife even after he has renounced the world:

अलकवलयरम्यं भ्रूलतानर्तकान्तं नवनयनविलासं चारुगण्डस्थलं च ।
मधुरवचनगर्भं स्मेरबिम्बाधरायाः पुरत इव समास्ते तन्मुखं मे प्रियायाः ॥
लीलाविलासविलसन्नयनोत्पलायाः स्फारस्मरोत्तरलिताधरपल्लवायाः ।
उत्तुङ्गपीवरपयोधरमण्डलायास्तस्या मया सह कदा ननु संगमः स्यात् ॥

The watersports of young women in the Siprā river are described in the following verse in Book V:

भ्रश्यत्कर्णवतंसकाः सरलितप्रान्तप्रलम्बालकाः शीर्यत्कज्जललोचनाः परिगलद्गण्डस्थलीचन्दनाः ।
उत्कम्पस्तनमण्डलाः प्रविलसल्लीलाब्जबाहाकुलाः क्रीडन्ति स्म पुराङ्गनाः प्रियतमैरासेव्यमाना इव ॥

A graceful picture of women adorned with floral decorations occurs in the description of the summer in Book III:

विकचविचकिलालीकीर्णलोलालकानां कुरबकमुकुलस्रक्तारहारस्तनीनाम् ।
दरजरठदलाग्रैः पल्लवैश्चूतजातैर्नृप किमपि कषायं योषितां चुम्ब वक्त्रम् ॥

Kiss, o king, the mouths of women redolent with mango shoots with slightly hardening tips. The agile curls of their hair are studded with fullblown Vicakila blossoms, and wreaths of Kurabaka buds and radiant pearlstrings adorn their bosoms (3. 379).

A number of playful verses occurs in connection with the description of moonrise on the subject of the conventional *viraha* of young women such as are frequently found in the Mahākāvyas, and it is interesting to find that the Jaina monk proves himself an adept in dealing with such topics. The following verses contain what is known as *dūtīvākya*, but are attributed in our work, as in so many other cases, to bards attached to Yaśodhara's court.

ग्रीष्मस्थलाब्जिलमितं श्वसितं नितान्तमुद्यानसारिणिसमस्तुतिरश्रुपूरः ।
आनर्तितस्तनतटास्तव कान्त कोपात्कण्ठे च मारुतलवाः सरवाः प्रियायाः ॥

The sighs of thy beloved, o lover, are utterly like desert winds; her tears flow like a garden rivulet; and owing to her wrath her sobs are loud and shake the bosom (3, 496).

भ्रातस्त्वद्विरहेण संज्वरभरादस्याः सरःसंगमे पाथःक्वाथविधेर्यदद्भुतमभूदेतत्तदाकर्ण्यताम् ।
उड्डीनं मुहुरण्डजैस्तिमिकुलैस्तीरे स्थितं दूरतः शीर्णं शैवलिमञ्जरीभिरभितः क्षीणं क्षणाच्चाम्बुजैः ॥

Listen, o brother, to the miracle of how the waters boiled when she entered the waters of the pool, suffering from grievous heat owing to her separation from thee! The birds flew off again and again; the fish kept to the shore at a distance; the offshoots of the moss were torn to shreds all around; and the lotus blossoms withered in a moment! (3. 497).

तव सुभग वियोगात् पञ्चषैरप्यहोभिर्मनसिजशरदीर्घाः श्वासधाराः सुदत्याः ।
स्मरविजयपताकास्पर्धिनी वक्त्रकान्तिस्तनुरतनुधनुर्ज्यातानवं चातनोति ॥

Beautiful lover, in less than a week, owing to her separation from thee, the fair maid's sighs lengthened like Cupid's arrows; the complexion turned white as Cupid's triumphal banner; and the body became lean as Cupid's bowstring! (3. 498).

क्वेदं कार्श्यं क्व च मनसिजस्फारबाणप्रहारः क्वायं तापः क्व च निरवधिर्बाष्पपूरप्रचारः ।
क्वैषा मूर्च्छा क्व च कुचपटप्रेङ्खणश्वासकल्पः क्वासौ लज्जा क्व च मृगदृशश्चित्रमेष प्रजल्पः ॥

What a great contrast between the emaciation of the fair maid's body and the continuous hitting by Cupid's arrows! Between her heat and the unceasing flood of her tears! Between her swoon and the sighs that shake her robe! Between her bashfulness and the words uttered at random! Strange it is all! (3, 502)

बन्धुप्रार्थनतस्त्वयि स्मृतिनिशावेशात्तया मुग्धया दत्तश्चक्षुषि यावकः कृतमिदं बिम्बाधरे कज्जलम् ।
कण्ठे काञ्चिगुणोऽर्पितः परिहितो हारो नितम्बस्थले केयूरं चरणे धृतं विरचितं हस्ते च हिञ्जीरकम् ॥

Begged by her friends (to decorate herself), the foolish girl, owing to the concentration of the night-like train of her thoughts on thee, applied red lac paint to the eyes and collyrium to the ruddy lips;[1] wore the girdle round the neck and the neck-lace on the hips; and fastened the bracelets to the feet and the anklets to the hands! (3. 503).

कामस्यैतत्परमिह रहो यन्मनःप्रातिकूल्यं तस्मादेष ज्वलति नितरामङ्गमाधुर्यहेतुः ।
कामं कान्तास्तदनु रसिकाः प्रीतये कस्य न स्युस्तत्रास्वादः क इव हि सखे या न पक्वा मृणाल्यः ॥

Love's great secret it is on earth: it blazes up on account of disappointment of hopes, lending grace to women's physical charms. Fair women then become subject to intense passion, and who would not delight in them? 'What is their flavour like, o friend?' 'They are just tender water-lilies!' (3. 506).

---

1 Red paint is applied to the lips and collyrium to the eyes.

VI. Didactic Verses

As in other Kāvya works, didactic verses are interspersed in *Yaśastilaka*, and occasionally contain balanced expression of the wisdom of life and bring into relief human traits with remarkable fidelity and insight. The specimens cited here are classified according to the subject dealt with by them.

THE GODDESS OF WEALTH

तातस्तावज्जडनिधिरभूत् सोदरः कालकूटः कृष्णे यस्याः प्रणयपरता पङ्कजाते रतिश्च ।
लक्ष्म्यास्तस्याः सकलनृपतिस्वैरिणीवृत्तिभाजः कः प्रेमान्धो भवतु कृतधीर्लोकविप्लाविकायाः ॥

What wise man will blindly fall in love with the subversive goddess of wealth, a harlot kept by all the kings? The Ocean ('the abode of waters', also 'the abode of folly') is her father, and the Kālakūṭa poison her brother. She loves Kṛṣṇa, the Black, and is fond of the mud-born lotus (2. 160).[1]

असल्लोकानुरोधेन सल्लोकोपेक्षणेन च । व्यालशैलान्तरालाङ्गी कुरङ्गीवाक्षमा रमा ॥

The goddess of wealth is helpless, like a hind placed between a wild elephant on one side and a mountain on the other, because she favours the wicked and neglects the good (3. 177).

TRANSIENT CHARACTER OF LIFE AND ITS JOYS

मायासाम्राज्यवर्याः कविजनवदनस्पर्धिमाधुर्यधुर्याः स्वप्नाप्तैश्वर्यशोभाः कुहकनयमयारामरम्योत्तराभाः ।
पर्जन्यागारसाराश्चिदिवपतिधनुर्बन्धुराश्च स्वभावादायुर्लावण्यलक्ष्म्यस्तदपि जगदिदं चित्रमत्रैव सक्तम् ॥

It is strange that the world is attached to life, beauty and wealth. They are but magnificent as a phantom empire, supremely sweet as the words of poets, beautiful as treasure obtained in dreams, charmingly resplendent like a magic garden, lovely as a mansion of clouds, and, by nature, delightful only as a rainbow (1. 124).

मायारामसमा रमा सुखमिदं दुःखावलेखोन्मुखं स्वप्नालोकनयः सुहृत्परिचयः कान्ताः कृतान्ते हिता ।
उत्साहोऽपि च देहगेहविषयो यः सोऽप्यनित्योदयस्तत्त्वालोकविलुप्तचित्ततमसां पुंसां भवेदुत्सवः ॥

Prosperity is like a magic garden, and pleasure is liable to be marred by pain. Friendship is like the vision of a dream, and a beloved woman is but an aid to Death. Even the zeal for the mansion of the body has merely transient results. Joy is for those who have destroyed the darkness of their minds with the light of the Truth (Book V).

PROPER USE OF WEALTH

लब्धा अपि श्रियो यान्ति पुंसां भोक्तुमजानताम् । अबद्धाः कुञ्जरेन्द्राणां पुलाका इव हस्तगाः ॥

Riches, even though acquired by men who know not how to enjoy them, are lost for ever, like the loose grains of boiled rice seized by mighty elephants with their trunks (3. 78).

---

1 The reference is to the legend of Lakṣmī emerging during the churning of the ocean. *Jaḍanidhi* is purposely used for *jalanidhi*. Kṛṣṇa stands for Viṣṇu, the consort of Lakṣmī. Somadeva rarely uses such devices in his verse.

THE CURSE OF DEPENDENCE

सत्यं दूरे विहरति समं साधुभावेन पुंसां धर्मश्चित्तात् सह करुणया याति देशान्तराणि ।
पापं शापादिव च तनुते नीचवृत्तेन सार्धं सेवावृत्तेः परमिह परं पातकं नास्ति किंचित् ॥
सौजन्यमैत्रीकरुणामणीनां व्ययं न चेद्भृत्यजनः करोति ।
फलं महीशादपि नैव तस्य यतोऽर्थमेवार्थनिमित्तमाहुः ॥

No greater sin is there on earth than earning one's livelihood by serving others. Truth with honesty wanders far away from such men, and piety with compassion departs elsewhere from their hearts; while their sin increases with meanness, as if under a curse. Unless the servants of a king barter away the gems of courtesy, good will and kindness, they are never rewarded by him, for, as is said, money alone begets money[1] (1. 130-131).

THE USE OF POETS

राजन्नशेषविषयातिशयप्रसूतौ येषां महाकविकृतौ न मनीषितानि ।
तेषां श्रुती च रसनां च मनश्च मन्ये वाग्देवताविहितशापमिवेश्वराणाम् ॥

Sire, Sarasvatī's curse, I ween, is on the ears, tongues and minds of those kings, who evince no desire for the works of great poets, which create supreme beauty in an infinite range of themes (3. 275).

ELOQUENCE

यथास्त्ररहिते पुंसि वृथा शौर्यपरिग्रहः । तथोपन्यासहीनस्य वृथा शास्त्रपरिग्रहः ॥
स्फुरन्त्यपि मनःसिन्धौ शास्त्ररत्नान्यनेकशः । वचोगुणविहीनानि भूषयन्ति न सन्मनः ॥
विद्यानां स्फुरितं प्रीत्यै स्त्रीणां लावण्यवद्बहिः । अन्तर्भवतु वा मा वा किं विचारैरतीन्द्रियैः ॥

The bravery of a person without weapons is useless; just so the mastery of the Śāstras is futile in the case of a person without eloquence. The gems of learning may flash in plenty in the ocean of one's mind, but, without eloquence, they can never edify the minds of the wise. Like the beauty of women, the outward manifestation of learning causes delight. The inner existence of either matters little. What is the use of investigating things beyond the range of the senses? (3. 372–78).

FIVE GREAT SINS

स्वामिद्रोहः स्त्रीवधो बालहिंसा विश्वस्तानां घातनं लिङ्गभेदः ।
प्रायेणैतत्पञ्चकं पातकानां कुर्यात् सद्यः प्राणिनः प्राप्तदुःखान् ॥

Hostility to one's master, killing a woman, injury to children, killing those who have been assured of safety, and divulgation of secrets: these five sins nearly always bring swift misery to sentient beings (Book V).

THE RAISON D'ÊTRE OF AHIṀSĀ

यत्परत्र करोतीह सुखं वा दुःखमेव वा । वृद्धये धनवद्दत्तं स्वस्य तज्जायतेऽधिकम् ॥

---

1 The idea seems to be that unless the employees of a king bring him money by fair means or foul, they are never rewarded by him.

The pleasure or pain which a man causes to others in this life is like money lent on interest: it becomes his in a greater measure (Book VII, section 24).

VALUE OF DIRECTING POWER

स्वयं विषमरूपोऽपि संघातः कार्यकृद्भवेत् । अधिष्ठातुः प्रयत्नेन यथा हस्तोऽसमाङ्गुलिः ॥

Like the hand which has unequal fingers, a combination of things, although composed of unequal elements, proves effective by dint of the master's effort (3. 120).

VALUE OF CO-OPERATION

असहायः समर्थोऽपि न जातु हितसिद्धये । वह्निर्वातविहीनो हि बुसस्यापि न दीपकः ॥

Even an able man can never do any good without the help of others Fire, without air, cannot burn even chaff (3. 228).

THE PROPER ATTITUDE TOWARDS ENEMIES

अनुनयत वदत मधुरं यत्कार्यं तदपि मानसे कुरुत । रौति कलं हि मयूरः सविषं च भजङ्गमं दशति ॥
मूर्ध्ना वहति लोकोऽयं यथा दग्धुमिहेन्धनम् । अनुशील्य क्षयं नेयस्तथारातिर्महात्मना ॥
प्रायः सरलचित्तानां जायते विपदागमः । ऋजुर्याति यथा छेदं न वक्रः पादपस्तथा ॥

Conciliate thy enemy and speak to him sweet words, but at the same time carry out what thou hast planned in thy mind. The peacock sings sweetly, but feeds on venomous serpents. Just as fire-wood is carried by. men on their heads in order to burn it, similarly, in the world, a high-spirited person should first conciliate an enemy and then destroy him. It is, as a rule, straightforward people who fall into danger. It is not possible to cut a crooked tree with the same ease as a straight one (Book IV).

VALUE OF Ṛeport

अबुधेऽपि बुधोद्गारे प्राज्ञानुज्ञा विजृम्भते । संस्कर्तुः कौशलादेति यतः काचोऽपि रत्नताम् ॥
आत्मनि विवेकविकलः प्रसिद्धिमात्रेण रज्यते सकलः । कैरव इव कमलेऽपि हि न श्रीः पूज्यं तथाप्यब्जम् ॥

Even if a fool is called wise by all, the wise concur therein. Even glass becomes jewel owing to the craftsman's skill. All men, lacking in discernment, like a thing, simply because it is reported to be good. The goddess of wealth abides neither in the day-lotus nor in the night-lotus; yet the day-lotus is honoured (because it is said to be her abode) (3. 181–82).

A SECRET OF SUCCESS

कार्यार्थिनो हि लोकस्य किमन्याचारचिन्तया । दुग्धार्थी कः पुमान्नाम गवाचारं विचारयेत् ॥

It is useless for people who seek to gain their ends to study the ways of others. Who ever investigates the ways of cows in need of milk? (3. 231).

WHAT IS NOT PROFITABLE TO PHYSICIANS AND MINISTERS

यौ स्वास्थ्याय समीहेते व्याधितस्य नृपस्य च । स्वार्थसिद्धिनिरोद्धारौ धिग्धिक् तौ वैद्यमन्त्रिणौ ॥

Fie, fie on the physician and the minister who strive for the health and well-being of a patient and a king respectivly, since they thereby stand in the way of their own profit! (3. 187).

THE RIGHT THING IN THE RIGHT PLACE

तेजस्तेजस्विनां स्थाने धृतं धृतिकरं भवेत् । कराः सूर्यांश्मवद्भानोः किं स्फुरन्ति हताश्मनि ॥

The might of the mighty produces happy results when exerted in the proper place. The rays of the sun do not flash on gravel as they do on sunstones (3. 178).

THE USE OF OPPORTUNITIES

अज्ञानभावादथवा प्रमादादुपेक्षणाद्वात्ययभाजि कार्ये । पुंसः प्रयासो विफलः समस्तो गतोदके कः खलु सेतुबन्धः ॥

All one's efforts are useless, once an opportunity is lost owing to ignorance or error or negligence. What is the use of a bridge after a flood has subsided? (Book IV).

ENDURANCE

मार्दवाधिकतरं कलधौतं तापताडनसहं च निसर्गात् । एवमेव वपुरुत्तमपुंसां संपदां च विपदां च सहिष्णु ॥

Gold is extremely soft, and yet, by nature, capable of bearing heat and pounding. Likewise, the bodies of the ablest men are capable of enduring privation as well as ease (Book V).

CHARACTERISTICS OF YOUTH

यस्मिन् रजः प्रसरति स्खलितादिवोच्चैरान्ध्यादिव प्रबलता तमसश्च कास्ति ।
सत्त्वं तिरोभवति भीतमिवाङ्गजाग्नेस्तद्यौवनं विनय सज्जनसंगमेन ॥

In youth ill-fame spreads far and wide as if from sin; deep-rooted ignorance reigns as if from blindness; and patience vanishes as if frightened by Cupid's fire. Control thy youth by association with the good (2. 161).

A THIEF SUSPECTS ALL

आत्मनीव परत्रापि प्रायः संभावना जने । यदस्तेनादपि स्तेनः स्वदोषात् परिशङ्कते ॥

People, as a rule, suppose others to be just like themselves. A thief, on account of his own wickedness, suspects another, even though he is not a thief (3. 121).

CONJUGAL FIDELITY IS RARE

सुरतरहस्यं पुंसां यदि भवति स्वासु देव योषासु । किमिति श्रीरतिमन्दो गोविन्दो बल्लवीलोलः ॥

Sire, if the inmost eortic desires of men were confined to their own wives, why should Kṛṣṇa, averse to Lakṣmī's love, run after cowherd maids? (3. 204).

ADVICE TO OTHERS

विचक्षणः किं नु परोपदेशे न स्वस्य कार्ये सकलोऽपि लोकः । नेत्रं हि दूरेऽपि निरीक्षमाणमात्मावलोके त्वसमर्थमेव ॥

All men are expert in giving advice to others, but not in doing their alloted work. The eye can see even distant objects, but not itself (Book IV).

FATAL TEMPTATION

किं नास्ति पलं सलिले येन तिमिः सादरो गलाहारे । प्रायेण हि देहभृतां तत्रासक्तिर्यतो मृत्युः ॥

Is there no other food in the waters that a fish eagerly swallows the bait? Creatures are, as a rule, attached to objects that cause their death (3. 231).

FORCE OF ASSOCIATION

पूज्यमब्जं श्रियः सङ्गाज्ज्येष्ठायाश्च न कैरवम् । प्रायो जनेऽन्यसंसर्गाद्गुणिता दोषितापि च ॥

The day lotus is esteemed for its association with the goddess of wealth, but not the night lotus for its association with the goddess Jyeṣṭhā[1]. Merit and blemish among men depend invariably upon the company they keep (3. 118).

संसर्गेण गुणा अपि भवन्ति दोषास्तदद्भुतं नैव । स्थितमधरे रमणीनाममृतं चेतांसि कलुषयति ॥

It is not strange that even merits turn into blemishes owing to the force of association. The nectar that is in women's lips corrupts the hearts of men (1. 79).

REASON

ईर्ते युक्तिं यदेवात्र तदेव परमार्थसत् । यद्भानुदीप्तिवत्तस्याः पक्षपातोऽस्ति न क्वचित् ॥

Whatever in this world conforms to Reason is really true, for, like the rays of the sun, Reason is partial to none (Book VI, p. 270).

VII. Attacks on Women

Numerous attacks on women occur in *Yaśastilaka* in prose and verse, and this is explained partly by the very nature of the plot and partly by the fact that such attacks are frequent in Jaina literature owing to the stress laid on asceticism and abstention from pleasures. Attacks in verse occur in works like Guṇabhadra's *Ātmānuśāsana*, Śubhacandra's *Jñānārṇava*, Amitagati's *Subhāṣitaratnasaṁdoha* (both censure and praise), and in Hemacandra's commentary on his *Yogaśāstra* 2. 105. A notable instance of such attacks in Jaina canonical literature is found in Taṇḍula-Veyāliya, one of the Paiṇṇas, wherein women are decried in prose and verse. It should, however, be noted that the character of women is sometimes painted in dark colours in non-Jaina works as well, for example, in the Mahābhārata (Anuśāsanaparva, chap. 38).

---

1 For Jyeṣṭhā see Chap. XV.

Specimens of Somadeva's depreeatory verses on women are cited below[1]:

स्त्रीषु साक्षाद्विषं दृष्टौ न सर्पेष्विति मे मनः । तद्दृष्ट एव लोको हि दृश्यते भस्मतां गतः ॥

Verily there is poison in the eyes of women, I ween, and not in the eyes of serpents. Men, indeed, are seen to be reduced to 'ashes' as soon as they are looked at by women (Book IV).

देवैर्मनुष्यैरथ राक्षसैर्वा निसर्गतो गूढतरप्रचारा । ईदृक्तया ज्ञातुमियत्तया वा न शक्यते स्त्रीजनचित्तवृत्तिः ॥

Neither gods nor men nor demons are able to ascertain or fathom the naturally inscrutable working of a woman's mind. Ibid.

यथोच्छिखण्डा मण्डूक्यो लोकविप्लवहेतवः । तथा स्त्रियः स्वभावेन भर्तृव्यसनतत्पराः ॥

Just as crested tadpoles bring calamity to men, similarly women, by nature, set themselves to cause disaster to their husbands. Ibid.

The irresistible temptation offered by women and the bewildering effect of their charms are emphasized in the following verses:

क्षीणस्तपोभिः क्षपितः प्रवासैर्विध्यापितः साधु समाधितोयैः ।
तथापि चित्रं ज्वलति स्मराग्निः कान्ताजनापाङ्गविलोकनेन ॥

The fire of passion is weakened by austerities, attenuated by travelling, and effectively quenched by the waters of meditation. Yet, strange it is, it flares up at the sight of women's glances (1. 72).

तावत्तपो वपुषि चेतसि तत्त्वचिन्ता कामं हृषीकविषये परमः शमश्च ।
यावन्न पश्यति मुखं मृगलोचनानां शृङ्गारवृत्तिभिरुदाहृतकामसूत्रम् ॥

The body undergoes austerities, and the mind meditates on the Truth, and perfect calm prevails over the senses, only so long as a man does not behold the visage of fair women, which, by its amorous play, illustrates the lessons of the science of love (1. 73).

श्रोत्रं श्रुतो हरति वीक्षणमीक्ष्यमाणश्चित्तं स्मृतः कृतसमागतिरङ्गकानि ।
प्राणान् पुनः प्रणयवान् वियुतो रतिं च लोके तथापि वनिताजन एव यत्नः ॥

Women, when heard of, deprive one of the faculty of hearing. Looked at, they deprive one of the power of seeing. Remembered, they captivate the mind; and embraced, they disable the limbs. When in love, they take away one's life; and when separated, they take away one's joy. Yet women are the goal of all efforts in the world (1. 74).

---

1 Somadeva's reasoned views on the subject present an entirely different picture. See Chap. V. Misogynistic traits appear also in other literatures of a bygone age, and have been inspired by different motives. In Italian Renaissance literature, for instance, 'the current abuse of women, in which Petrarch no less than Alberti and Boccaccio indulged, seems to have been a scholastic survival of the coarse and ignorant literature of the medieval clergy'. Symonds: *Renaissance in Italy*, Vol. IV, p. 184 (1937 ed.).

तावद्गुरवो गण्यास्तावत् स्वाध्यायधीरतं चेतः । यावन्न मनसि वनितादृष्टिविषं विशति पुरुषाणाम् ॥

Teachers are obeyed, and the mind is prone to study, only so long as the poison of women's glances does not enter into the hearts of men (1. 76).

तावत् प्रवचनविषयस्तावत् परलोकचिन्तनोपायः । यावत्तरुणीविभ्रमहृतहृदयो न प्रजायेत ॥

The scriptures maintain their jurisdiction, and it is possible to ponder on the other world, only so long as a man's heart is not enthralled by a maiden's charms (1. 7).

VIII. Metres

No attempt is made here to analyse the metres used by Somadeva in his verses. He uses, as a rule, the ordinary metres employed in Kāvya poetry, and it will be sufficient to point out a few special features, the most notable of which is the adaptation of certain Prākrit metres to the requirements of Sanskrit poetry.

Duvaī or Dvipadī is a Prâkrit metre, of which each foot consists of one *gaṇa* of six *mātrās*, five *gaṇas* of four *mātrās*, and one long syllable at the end; the second and sixth *gaṇas* may be *gurumadhya* (⏑–⏑) or *sarvalaghu* (⏑⏑⏑⏑). The metre is frequently used in Apabhraṁśa poetry, and Somadeva employs it in several verses of *Yaśastilaka* (1. 167, 169; 3. 9, 17, 18, 313, etc). For example,

पूर्वं सरसकरजरेखाकृतिरधररुचिस्ततो रविस्तदनु च घुसृणपिण्डखण्डद्युतिरब्जचयच्छविस्ततः ।
पुनरयमरुणरत्नमुकुरश्रीरुदयति रागनिर्भरैः कुर्वन् ककुभि ककुभि बन्धूकमयीमिव सृष्टिमंशुभिः ॥ 3. 17

शतमखधामहेमकुम्भाकृतिरिन्द्रसमुद्रविद्रुमस्तम्बस्तिमितकान्तिरहरुत्सवसमयसुवर्णदर्पणः ।
उदयति रविरुदारहरिरोहणरुचिरुचिरोत्करैः करैर्दिग्दयितामुखानि पिञ्जरयन्नरुणितजलधिमण्डलः ॥ 3. 18

सुरगिरिरमरसिन्धुरम्भोनिधिरवनिरनूरुसारथिः फणिपतिरमृतरोचिरमराश्च दिशो दश यावदम्बरम् ।
तावदशेषभुवनचिन्तामणिचरित परं महोत्सवैरुत्सवचरितचन्द्र जय जीव विराज चिराय नन्द च ॥ 1. 167

शतमख दहन काल गुह वरुण समीरण धनद चन्द्रमः प्रथितैकैककुम्भिविभवास्तदिभानवत प्रयत्नतः ।
इत्युग्रदेष्टुकाम इव हस्तमुदञ्चति वियति वारणो नो चेदिभविहीनरचना भवतां भविता पताकिनी ॥ 3. 313

It is certain that Somadeva is not the first writer to employ the Duvaī metre in Sanskrit verse. The following verse occurring in *Daśabhakti*, a collection of Jaina devotional compositions in Prākrit and Sanskrit, is, for instance, composed in the Duvaī metre; and the Sanskrit *Bhaktis*, it should be noted, are attributed to Pūjyapāda.

जातिजरोरुरोगमरणातुरशोकसहस्रदीपिताः दुःसहनरकपतनसंत्रस्तधियः प्रतिबुद्धचेतसः ।
जीवितमम्बुबिन्दुचपलं तडिदभ्रसमा विभूतयः सकलमिदं विचिन्त्य मुनयः प्रशमाय वनान्तमाश्रिताः ॥

The Dvipadī or Duvaī, or Doai, as it is also called in the *Prākṛta Paiṅgala*, is, properly speaking, a metre with two *pādas*, and appears as such in

Apabhraṁśa works; but the Prākrit example of Dvipadī given in Hemacandra's *Chandonuśāsana* contains four feet; and the combined definition and example of the metre in the *Prākṛta Paiṅgala*, although apparently given in two verses of two feet each (1. 152, 153), is taken by some to represent one verse of four feet.[1] Somadeva's Sanskrit verses in the Dvipadī metre consist of four feet.

Mayaṇāvayāra or Madanāvatāra[2] is another Prākrit metre used by Somadeva in a group of lyrical verses, in Book V, which describe the Karahāṭa country. Each foot of this metre consists of four *gaṇas* of five *mātrās*, as pointed out by Hemacandra in his *Chandonuśāsana*, Chap. 4. Nanditāḍhya in his *Gāthālakṣaṇa*[3] calls the metre Caṁdāṇaṇa. The verses in question are cited below (p. 162):

सस्यसंपत्तिसंक्षिप्तसीमाभुवः प्रचुरपथिकप्रियापणितपथिवस्तवः ।
सत्रवापीप्रपारामरम्योदयाः पद्मिनीखण्डताण्डविततोयाशयाः ।
श्रीविलासोत्सवस्खलितसुरसमितयः फुल्लफलपल्लवोल्लासिवनवृत्तयः ।
पिकवधूरुतमनोहारिसर्वर्तवः सकलसंसारसुखसेवितागन्तवः ।
समरभरभागिभटभाववादोत्कटाः खेलदुन्मदवृषोत्खाततटिनीतटाः ।
त्यागभोगप्रभावाद्भुतख्यातयः शुद्धवर्णाश्रमाचरितविगतेतयः
प्रवणशरणागतोद्धरणकुलकीर्तयः सन्ति धर्मार्थकामेषु समनीतयः ।
सुकृतफलभूमयो ग्रामविनिवेशिकाः कामिताचासिविजितामरोद्देशकाः ॥

Prākrit metres are also used in the three lyrical panegyrics, two in honour of king Māradatta in Book I (verses 175-212) and one in honour of the Arhat in Book VIII, section 37, consisting of 28 verses. Somadeva's scheme consists of an opening verse or verses in Āryā metre which he calls Varṇa; one verse in Mātrā[4] metre consisting of one line of 41 *mātrās* and

---

1 'इदं च वृत्तं द्विपादमेव न चतुष्पादं, उदाहरणानुरोधादिति केचित्। अन्ये तु यदीदं द्विपादमेव तर्हि लक्षणं पादचतुष्टयेन कथं कृतमिति इदं चतुष्पादमेव, न चोदाहरणविरोधस्तस्य चरणद्वयेनापि संभवात्'। See Comm. on verse 154 in प्राकृतपैङ्गलम् (B. I.).

2 It will be seen that each verse has four feet and each foot twenty *mātrās*. Somadeva seems to follow Apabhraṁśa models. The metre is known also as Kāminīmohana and occurs in the Apabhraṁśa poem *Saṁdeśarāsaka* (verses 82, 83, 85). For example, वयण णिसुणेवि मणमत्थसरवट्टिया, मयउसरमुक्क णं हरिणि उत्तट्ठिया। मुक्क दीउन्ह नीसास उससंतिया, पढिय इय गाह णियणयणि वरसंतिया ॥ 83. The metre is discussed by Bhayani in his Introduction to the poem, p. 58, Singhi Jain Series, Bombay 1945. *Saṁdeśarāsaka* has been attributed to the twelfth century A. D.

3 Edited by Prof. Velankar in *ABORI*, Vol. XIV, pp. 1–38.

4 There are five feet, and Somadeva's scheme is 15 + 11 + 15 + 12 + 15. The Mātrā is an Apabhraṁśa metre and employed in *Saṁdeśarāsaka* (verses 18, 19, 24, 25 etc). In Apabhraṁśa poetry a Mātrā verse is often followed by a Dohā, and the whole is called Raḍḍā. The *Prākṛta Paiṅgala* describes seven varieties of Raḍḍā, that is,

another of 27; one or more verses with four feet of sixteen *mātrās* each, called by him Catuṣpadī; several verses in Paddhatikā or Pajjhaṭikā metre consisting of four feet of sixteen *mātrās* each, and each foot rhyming with the other and ending with a *ja-gaṇa* (⏑ – ⏑) or sometimes four *laghus*; and a concluding verse called Ghattā. It may be noted that the Pajjhaṭikā is a popular metre in Apabhraṁśa poetry. It is, for instance, the prevailing metre of *Karakaṇḍacariu* of Kanakāmara; while it has been pointed out that of the three hundred and fifty-four Kaḍavakas (verse-groups) in Dhanapāla's *Bhavisayattakahā*, almost all with the exception of about seventeen are either in Pajjhaṭikā or in Alillaha metre, which is really a variety of Pajjhaṭikā.[1] As regards the Ghattā verse, in all narrative poems in Apabhraṁśa the concluding couplet of a Kaḍavaka is almost always called Ghattā. Piṅgala recognises a Ghattā metre of 62 *mātrās* (31+31), and Śrutasāgara saya in his commentary on 1. 212 that there are twentyseven varieties of Ghattā, and it may consist of 60 *mātrās* and sometimes of 62 *mātrās*. Of the three Ghattās in our work, two (1. 187 and 8. 37) consist of 60 *mātrās*, and in each half the first two sections of 10 and 8 *mātrās* each have a caesura and rhyme with each other, so that each half of 30 *mātrās* corresponds to a *pāda* of the Caupaiā described and illustrated in *Prākṛta Paiṅgala* (1. 97 and 98). The remaining Ghattā (1. 212) is a two-foot Dvipadī with 28 *mātrās* (6+4+4+4 4+6) in each half.[2] A reference to Apabhraṁśa poetry shows that a variety of metres may be used for the Ghattā verse.

As regards Somadeva's scheme of arrangement, it seems to be based on Prākrit models. An arrangement similar to his is, for instance,

---

of Mātrā; and the composition of some of these resembles that of Somadeva's verse. For instance, the scheme of the Cārusenī variety is 15+11+15+11+15; that of Bhadra is 15+12+15+12+15; and that of Rājasenā is 15+12+15+11+15. Somadeva's scheme represents a slight variation of the Rājasenā variety in respect of the number of *mātrās* in the second and fourth *pādas*, the total number of *mātrās* (68) being the same. The following example of the metre is from *Saṁdeśarāsaka* (verse 25): फुसइ लोयण रुवइ दुक्खत्त, धम्मिल्लउमुक्कमुह, विज्जंभइ अरु अंगु मोडइ। विरहानलि संतविअ, ससइ दीह करसाह तोडइ ॥. This is followed by two lines of Dohā. The scheme followed here is 15+11+15+11+15 corresponding to the Cārusenī of *Prākṛta Paiṅgala*. The Rājasenā scheme of 15+12+15+11+15 is also found in *Saṁdeśarāsaka*, as pointed out by Bhayani (op. cit.), p. 67. The Mātrā is believed to be a very old Apabhraṁśa metre, as it was known to Virahāṅka (*Vṛttajātisamuccaya*, *JBBRAS*, 1929, p. 87) who describes four different varieties of it, Cārunetrī, Rāhusenī etc. See Velankar: *Apabhraṁśa Metres*, *Journal of the University of Bombay*, November 1933, p. 50.

1 See Introduction to Gune's edition in G. O. S., p. 28.

2 See first definition of Dvipadī in *Prākṛta-Paiṅgala*.

found at the beginning of Dhavala's *Harivaṁśapurāṇa* composed in Apabhraṁśa verse, as can be seen from the extracts from that work given in Hiralal's *Catalogue of Sanskrit and Prākrit Manuscripts in C. P. and Berar* (pp. 716 and 763). We have here a group of eulogistic verses beginning with a Vaṇṇī (i. e. Varṇa I. 188–90) followed by a Mātrā (I. 191) and other verses (Catuṣpadī I. 192, Paddhatikā I. 193, 210–11) ending with a Ghattā (I. 212). One of the panegyrics addressed to Māradatta is reproduced below to illustrate the above scheme of arrangement followed by Somadeva. As we have already pointed out (see Chap. I), there was a considerable output of Apabhraṁśa poetry in and before Somadeva's time; and he has clearly borrowed Apabhraṁśa metres and applied them to Sanskrit verse for the sake of novelty.

वर्णः ॥ लक्ष्मीरामानङ्गः सपत्नकुलकालविक्रमोत्तुङ्गः । कीर्तिविलासतमङ्गः प्रतापरङ्गश्चिरं जयतु ॥
उत्सारितारिसर्पः शरणागतनृपतिचित्तसंतर्पः । लक्ष्मीललामकूर्पस्तपतु चिरं नृपतिकन्दर्पः ॥
भुवनाब्जसरस्तरणिर्धर्मामृतहरणिरुदयतरुधरणिः । श्रीरमणीरतिसरणिर्मण्डलिकशिखामणिर्जीयात् ॥

मात्रा ॥ कुवलयोत्सवचन्द्र नृपतीन्द्र लक्ष्मीवर कीर्तिसरदमृतवृष्टिपल्लवितबुधवन ।
आभुवनमभिमानधन धैर्यसदन जय विहितसद्वन ॥

चतुष्पदी ॥ नृप महति भवति किंचिद्गिरापि वक्तुं गुणमखिलं नोत्तरामि ।
दीप्तिर्द्युमणेरवनीश यत्र का शक्तिः काचमणेर्हि तत्र ॥

पद्धतिका ॥ जय लक्ष्मीकरकमलातपत्र सारस्वतरसनिष्यन्दपात्र ।
धर्मार्थकामसमवृत्तचित्त तीर्थार्थिमनोरथवर्तिवित्त ॥

केरलमहिलामुखकमलहंस वङ्गीवनिताश्रवणावतंस ।
चोलस्त्रीकुचकुड्मलविनोद पल्लवरमणीकृतविरहखेद ॥

कुन्तलकान्तालकभङ्गनिरत मलयाङ्गनाङ्गनखदाननिरत ।
वनवासियोषिदीक्षणविमुग्ध कर्णाटयुवतिकैतवविदग्ध ।
कुरुजाङ्गलललनाकुचतनुत्र कम्बोजपुरन्ध्रीतिलकपत्र ॥

घत्ता ॥ नृपनृपतीश्वर भूरमणीश्वर यदिदमखिलगुणसंश्रय ।
उक्तं किंचित्त्वत्स्तुतिकृतिचित्तच्चित्रं न महोदय ॥

Among comparatively rare Sanskrit metres employed by Somadeva may be mentioned the Mattebhavikrīḍita used in 2.229. The metre of the following verse (1. 127) is uncertain.

न दैन्यात् प्राणानां न च हृदयहरिणस्य रतये न दर्पादङ्गानां न च करणकरिणोऽस्य मदनात् ।
विधावृत्तिः किं तु क्षतमदनचरितश्रुतविधेः परे हेतौ मुक्तेरिह मुनिषु न खलु स्थितिरियम् ॥

The verse is composed in a metre corresponding to the Krīḍā metre described by Hemacandra in his *Chandonuśāsana*, chap. 2, but in that metre the 12th and 13th syllables are heavy, whereas they are light in Somadeva's verse.

IX. Ardhasamasyā and Nāndī verses

An interesting example of an Ardhasamasyā verse, of which the first half is spoken by a court poet and the other half by the king, occurs in the description of sunrise in Book III.

अर्धकाव्यकविः—

अरुणकिरणमध्ये विद्रुमस्तम्बबिम्बः क्षितिप किमिव शोभां भानुरुद्यन् बिभर्ति ।

राजा—

बुध युधि मम शत्रोः शोणितापूरितायां प्रतरदुपरि कोपात् पाटलं यद्वदास्यम् ॥ 3. 19

(The poet): "Sire, the Sun with its coral orb rises amid crimson rays. What is its lustre like?" (The king): "Wise one, it resembles my own face, red with fury, emerging above the battlefield overflowing with the foeman's blood." Other examples of Ardhasamasyā verses are found in later Kāvya literature. There is, for instance, a series of them in *Naiṣadhacarita* 4. 102–9 and in Utprekṣāvallabha's *Bhikṣāṭana Kāvya* (Paddhati 9).

Nāndī verses are imitated in 3. 122–124. As explained in the *Nāṭyaśāstra* 5. 109 ff., Nāndī consists of one or more benedictory verses recited by the stage-manager before the commencement of a dramatic performance; and a Nāndī verse may contain eight or twelve *padas* or phrases (*avāntara-vākyas*, according to Abhinavagupta). In certain satirical verses on ministers of kings, attributed to a poet named Taruṇīlīlāvilāsa, the evil ways of a minister are represented as a drama, and three appropriate Nāndī verses are added as a prelude.

तत्र तावत्तरुणीलीलाविलासस्य—

नमो दुर्मन्त्रिणे तस्मै नृपाङ्घ्रिपमहाहय । यद्दशान्नार्थिसंप्रार्थ्यस्तच्छायाश्रमविश्रमः ॥

अष्टपदा नान्दी ।

यस्य शिष्टघटोच्छेदि मन्त्रसूत्रं विजृम्भते । सांपालपाचिने तस्मै नमो दुर्मन्त्रिचक्रिणे ॥

इयं च ।

और्वायापूर्वरूपाय तस्म दुर्मन्त्रिणे नमः । अजडा अपि शोष्यन्ते येन पत्युः श्रियः पराः ॥

इयं च द्वादशपदा । ततश्च–

चञ्चापञ्चजनाकृतिः क्षितिपतिर्यत्राभवन्नायकः... तद्दुर्मन्त्रिदुरीहितं विजयते सूक्तोत्कटं नाटकम् ॥

X. Style

As we have already remarked, Somadeva employs in his verse a simpler and more lucid style than in his prose; and his poetry is, on the whole, free from the intricate and involved ideas and expressions that characterise his prose. He tells us in one of the opening verses of his romance (1. 27) that neither Vakrokti (ornate speech) nor Svabhāvokti (natural expression) alone pleases the wise who delight in a combination of both; and this may be taken as a fair description of the principle underlying his own poetical style. Yet it should be remembered that Somadeva liberally uses the resources of the Kāvya style, and his verses are sometimes marked by the complexities and conventionalism associated with that style.

A few examples will suffice to illustrate the artificial conceits occasionally employed by Somadeva. In 1. 168 a king is told that his Fame, although it is an old eunuch, goes up to enjoy the starry Heaven, after enjoying all the Regions of the sky ('fame' being neuter and 'heaven' and 'regions' feminine in Sanskrit)[1]. The description of battle scenes in 3. 438 ff. is full of far-fetched and exaggerated conceits, and the picture of 'the violent battle' in 3. 436 is made unreal by the poet's anxiety to compare it to the rainy season. An instance of how an otherwise beautiful verse is spoilt by an artificial conceit is provided by the following description of a young woman, which ends by figuring her as an enclosure for capturing Cupid, the elephant (Book VII, section 31):

एषेन्द्रियद्रुमसमुल्लसनाम्बुवृष्टिरेषा मनोमृगविनोदविहारभूमिः ।
एषा स्मरद्विरदबन्धनवारिवृत्तिः किं खेचरी किममरी किमियं रतिर्वा ॥

Conceits like these are a common feature of the Kāvya style in its later phases, and it must be said to the credit of Somadeva that he often shows laudable restraint and discrimination in the use of the many artifices resorted to by the poets of his age.

Citrālaṁkāras are absent in our work, and even *śleṣa* or word-play, which adds to the intricacy of Somadeva's prose, is but rarely used in his verse; and only a few examples of it can be recorded. There is a pun on *kharadaṇḍa* in 3. 430, and the expression *sadāna* has four meanings in 3. 312. The epithets in the verse quoted below (1. 174) are simultaneously applied to three different things: dancing, dalliance with women and the royal court.

चञ्चत्कुन्तलचामरं कलरणत्काञ्चीलयाडम्बरं भ्रूभङ्गार्पितभावमूरुचरणन्यासाखनानन्दितम् ।
खेलत्पाणिपताकमीक्षणपथानीताङ्गहारोत्सवं नृत्यं च प्रमदारतं च नृपतिस्थानं च ते स्तान्मुदे ॥

Elaborate Rūpakas are sometimes met with; for example, in 3. 380, 381, wherein the women companions of Yaśodhara in his summer sports are successively figured as 'rows of woodland groves' and 'pools of water'.

अलककिसलयानां भ्रूलताश्लाघिनीनां नयनमधुलिहानां चारुगण्डस्थलीनाम् ।
कुचकुसुमचयानां स्त्रीवनश्रेणिकानामवनिषु कुरु केलीः किं नृपान्यैर्वनान्तैः ॥

1 उपभुज्य यद्दिशस्ते नपुंसकं वृद्धमपि यशः सर्वाः । द्यामुपभोक्तुं यातं तरलिततारां तदाश्चर्यम् ॥

लसदलकतरङ्गाः कान्तनेत्रारविन्दाः प्रचलभुजलतान्ताः पीनवक्षोजकोकाः ।
अतनुजघनकूलाश्चारुलावण्यवारस्तव नृप जलकेलिं कुर्वतां स्त्रीसरस्यः ॥

A typical Rūpaka is *jarā-rajakī*, Old Age fancied as a laundress whitening the hair[1], reminding one of *rajanī-rajakī* in *Naiṣadhacarita* 22. 113.

A practical example of Samāsokti occurs in connection with the satire on ministers. We are told that certain wise people, being unable to express their sentiments regarding the ministers of a king openly, do so with the help of a Samāsokti.[2]

प्रतीक्षे जातास्थः सुकृतसुलभं तद्दिनमहं यतो यातारोऽमी प्रलयमहयश्चन्दनतरोः ।
अमीषां पापानामिह हि वसतामेष महिमा कदाप्येतच्छायामभिलषति यन्नाध्वगजनः ॥ 3. 168

'With confidence I await the auspicious day when the serpents on the sandal tree will go to ruin. Thanks to those wicked creatures living on the tree, no wayfarer ever seeks its shade.'

An important feature of Somadeva's style is the occasional but deliberate effort to attain lyrical effect and the occasional use of rhyme (2.220, 3.428 etc.). He may be regarded to some extent as a precursor of the lyrical style which reached its full development in Jayadeva's *Gītagovinda*; of this there is interesting evidence in the use of Apabhraṁśa metres in the three lyrical panegyrics considered in Section VIII (see above). Rhyme is also used in isolated verses for lyrical effect (2. 75, 76 226 etc.). Repetition of the last letter in a series of epithets is sometimes practised to give a lyric tone to a verse.

भास्वद्भास्वति दाहवाहिमरुति ज्वालोल्बणाशाकृति etc.
उन्मार्गाम्भसि मेघमन्दनभसि च्छन्नांशुमत्तेजसि etc.
इक्षूल्लासिनि सस्यशालिनि खरं शेफालिकोत्फुल्लिनि etc.

Alliteration is freely used in many verses interspersed in the work, and the quick movement of such verses is invariably in keeping with their lyrical qualities. Good use of onomatopoeia is made in the following description of elephants (3. 304):

तडत्तडिति बन्धनं त्रुटति कन्धरोल्लासने खणत्खणिति वल्लिका गलति विक्रमारम्भिणि ।
मडन्मडिति भज्यते तरुगणः कृताघट्टने खडत्खडिति वारणः पतति चात्र युद्धैषिणि ॥

---

1 'कृष्णच्छविः साद्य शिरोरुहश्रीर्जरारजक्या क्रियतेऽवदाता' 2. 102.

2 तदुक्तं कैश्चिद्विपश्चिद्भिरेतदेव हृदयस्थमपि जिह्वास्थं कर्तुमतरीद्भिः समासोक्तिमिषेण ।'

CHAPTER VIII

Philosophical Doctrines

A considerable number of philosophical doctrines is mentioned and discussed by Somadeva in *Yaśastilaka.* The first section (Kalpa) of Book VI is interesting as a summary of the theories of salvation propounded by different schools of thought, followed by critical remarks on the opinions recorded by the author. The section is called *Samasta-samaya-siddhāntâva-bodhana*, 'Elucidation of the doctrines of all the schools', and important as a collection of philosophical tenets current in the tenth century. Another set of opinions is recorded in Book V in the episode of Caṇḍakarman and Sudatta, in which the former and his companions give an exposition of the doctrines followed by them, while the latter criticizes and tries to refute all of them. If we add to these the various Jaina doctrines explained and discussed in *Yaśastilaka,* it will not be an exaggeration to describe the work as serving the purpose of a veritable compendium of the philosophical speculations of the age. The principal doctrines summarized in the romance are here grouped together according to the system to which they belong.

VAIŚEṢIKA DOCTRINES

Somadeva refers to two classes of Vaiśeṣika thinkers: the Tārkika Vaiśeṣikas and the Saiddhānta Vaiśeṣikas. The main difference between the two schools of Vaiśeṣika philosophy is that the Saiddhāntas were Śaivas or worshippers of Siva[1] and laid stress on faith; while the Tārkikas were followers of the Vaiśeṣika system proper and laid stress on knowledge. The Saiddhāntas held that salvation is the outcome of faith as manifested in initiation into the cult revealed by the omniscient Śiva in his two aspects, corporeal and incorporeal[2]. It may be mentioned in this connection that, according to Haribhadra's *Ṣaḍdarśanasamuccaya* (vv. 13,59), both the Naiyāyikas and Vaiśeṣikas were worshippers of Śiva. Guṇaratna mentions in his commentary four sects among the followers of Śiva: Śaivas, Pāśupatas and two others, and adds that the Naiyāyikas were called Śaivas, while the Vaiśeṣikas were called Pāśupatas. There was, however, a distinct school of Pāśupatas with doctrines of their own, and these do not seem to have been

1 The Siddhāntas or the Śivasiddhāntas are the Śaiva scriptures, and the Śaivas were often called Saiddhāntikas, e. g. in the Gurgi inscription of Prabodhaśiva (मधुमती धाम सैद्धान्तिकानाम्). See Chap. XIII for this inscription.

2 'सकलनिष्कलाप्तप्राप्तमन्त्रतन्त्रापेक्षदीक्षालक्षणाच्छ्रद्धामात्रानुसरणान्मोक्षः इति सैद्धान्तवैशेषिकाः ।' Vol II, p. 269.

directly connected with the Vaiśeṣika system. Somadeva himself, as we shall see, mentions their view of salvation separately.

The Tārkika Vaiśeṣikas, who do not seem to have been Śaivas, held that salvation results solely from the knowledge of the categories based on an understanding of their similarities and dissimilarities; and the categories are Substance, Quality, Action, Generality, Particularity, Inherence and Non-existence.[1] Strictly speaking, this is not an accurate presentation of the Vaiśeṣika view. According to that system, salvation is the result of Dharma and knowledge of the categories is only a means to that end inasmuch as such knowledge produces Dharma, of which the essence is *nivṛtti* or renunciation; and this cannot be realised unless the nature of all objects, external and internal, is comprehended and the evils inherent in them grasped. Besides, Dharma cannot bring about salvation unless it is supported by the will of God. This is the interpretation of Śrīdhara in his *Nyāyakandalī*.[2] Udayana says in his *Kiraṇāvalī* that salvation results from the realisation of the ultimate truth, revealed by the continuous practice of Dharma or renunciation according to the principles laid down in the Veda and other sacred texts, the knowledge of the categories being a preliminary discipline.[3]

It is interesting to note that Somadeva, like Śivāditya, the author of *Saptapadārthī*, definitely includes Abhāva or Negation among the categories. It is wellknown that Kaṇāda recognised only six categories, but from about the tenth century onwards writers on the Vaiśeṣika system such as Śrīdhara and Udayana have emphasized the importance of Ābhāva;[4] and others have given it its legitimate place among the categories.

Somadeva attempts to define with precision the nature of salvation propounded by the Vaiśeṣika system. He says that the followers of Kaṇāda hold salvation to be the absolute cessation of the nine attributes of the Soul, namely, knowledge, pleasure, pain, desire, aversion, effort, virtue, vice and

---

1 'द्रव्यगुणकर्मसामान्यसमवायान्त्यविशेषाभावाभिधानानां पदार्थानां साधर्म्यवैधर्म्यावबोधतन्त्रात् ज्ञानमात्रात् इति तार्किकवैशेषिकाः ।' Ibid.

2 The *Praśastapāda Bhāṣya* says 'निवृत्तिलक्षणः केवलो धर्मः परमार्थदर्शनजं सुखं कृत्वा निवर्तते। तदा निरोधात्'······(see below). Śrīdhara says 'तन्निःश्रेयसं धर्मादेव भवति द्रव्यादितत्त्वज्ञानं तस्य कारणत्वेन निःश्रेयससाधनमित्यभिप्रायः। तत्त्वतो ज्ञातेषु बाह्याध्यात्मिकेषु विषयेषु दोषदर्शनाद्विरक्तस्य समीहानिवृत्तावात्मज्ञस्य तदर्थानि कर्माण्यकुर्वतः तत्परित्यागसाधनानि च श्रुतिस्मृत्युदितानि असंकल्पितफलान्युपाददानस्यात्मज्ञानमभ्यस्यतः प्रकृष्टविनिवर्तकधर्मोपचये सति परिपक्वात्मज्ञानस्य आत्यन्तिकशरीरवियोगस्य भावात्।·········धर्मोऽपि केवलं तावत् न निःश्रेयसं करोति यावदीश्वरेच्छया नानुगृह्यते तेनेदमुक्तम्–ईश्वरचोदनाभिव्यक्तात् धर्मादेवेति ।'

3 'शास्त्रेण पदार्थान् विविच्य श्रुतिस्मृतीतिहासपुराणोपदिष्टयोगविधिना दीर्घकालादरनैरन्तर्यसेवितान्निवृत्तिलक्षणाद्धर्मादेव तत्त्वज्ञानमुत्पद्यते यतोऽपवृज्यते ।·········धर्मस्यैव प्राधान्यम् ।'

4 Udayana says 'अभावस्तु स्वरूपवानपि पृथक् नोद्दिष्टः। प्रतियोगिनिरूपणाधीननिरूपणत्वात्। न तु तुच्छत्वात्.' Śrīdhara says 'अभावस्य पृथगनुपदेशः भावपारतन्त्र्यात् न त्वभावात्'.

mental impressions.[1] Somadeva illustrates this statement by quoting a verse which tells us that, according to the sage Kaṇāda, the nature of an emancipated being is the same as that of the soul, as it may be supposed to exist outside the body. तदुक्तम्—

बहिः शरीराद्यद्रूपमात्मनः संप्रतीयते । उक्तं तदेव मुक्तस्य मुनिना कणभोजिना ॥

This is in conformity with what we know of the Vaiśeṣika conception of salvation, which is also described as a quiescent condition comparable to a fire that has burnt up its fuel.[2] The actual number of the attributes of the soul given by Somadeva is immaterial, since the Bhāṣya of Praśastapāda enumerates as many as fourteen of them.[3] The vital point is the complete loss of attributes in the state of emancipation. Śrīdhara says that salvation does not consist in eternal bliss but in the continued existence of the soul in its own pristine condition, divested of all specific attributes.[4] He meets the objection of Maṇḍana that this kind of salvation is nothing but annihilation, by contending that the cessation of specific attributes does not amount to annihilation in the case of the eternal soul.[5] Nevertheless, the view that salvation consists in the eradication of specific attributes is rejected in philosophical texts of diverse schools, e. g. in *Sāṁkhyasūtras* 5. 75, *Bhojavṛtti* on *Yogasūtras* 4. 33 and Bhāsarvajña's *Nyāyasāra*.[6]

Somadeva makes some statements criticizing the Vaiśeṣika views on salvation. He criticizes the Saiddhānta Vaiśeṣikas by saying that faith alone cannot lead to salvation; the Udumbara fruit never becomes ripe on account of the faith of a hungry fellow. Further, if Mantras or mystic texts brought about the purification of the Self, no one would undergo the hardship imposed by self-discipline. Dīkṣā or initiation, too, cannot bring about salvation, as it is seen that the worldly blemishes which existed before initiation persist even after the completion of the rite.[7] As regards the Tārkika Vaiśeṣikas, Somadeva criticizes their view that knowledge leads to salvation. Knowledge, he says, helps one to comprehend things, but

---

1 'ज्ञानसुखदुःखेच्छाद्वेषप्रयत्नधर्माधर्मसंस्काराणां नवसंख्यावसराणामात्मगुणानामत्यन्तोन्मुक्तिर्मुक्तिः इति काणादाः ।'

2 'तदा निरोधात् निर्बीजस्यात्मनः शरीरादिनिवृत्तिः पुनः शरीराद्यनुत्पत्तौ दग्धेन्धनानलवदुपशमो मोक्ष इति' *Praśastapāda Bhāṣya.*

3 'तस्य गुणाः बुद्धिसुखदुःखेच्छाद्वेषप्रयत्नधर्माधर्मसंस्कारसंख्यापरिमाणपृथक्त्वसंयोगविभागाः ।'

4 'नास्त्यात्मनो नित्यं सुखं तदभावान्न तदनुभवो मोक्षावस्था किंतु समस्तात्मविशेषगुणोच्छेदोपलक्षिता स्वरूपस्थितिरेव ।'

5 'यदुक्तं मण्डनेन विशेषगुणनिवृत्तिलक्षणा मुक्तिरुच्छेदपक्षान्न भिद्यते इति । विशेषगुणोच्छेदे हि सति आत्मनः स्वरूपेणावस्थानं नोच्छेदो नित्यत्वात् ।'

6 See *Naiṣadhacarita*, trans., Appendix I, p. 497.

7 श्रद्धा श्रेयोऽर्थिनां श्रेयःसंश्रयाय न केवला । बुभुक्षितवशात् पाको जायेत किमुदुम्बरे ॥ पात्रवशादिवन्मन्त्रादात्मदोषपरिक्षयः । दृश्येत यदि को नाम कृती क्लिश्येत संयमैः ॥ दीक्षाक्षणान्तरात् पूर्वं ये दोषा भवसंभवाः । ते पश्चादपि दृश्यन्ते तन्न सा मुक्तिकारणम् ॥ Pp. 270–271.

not to acquire them; the mere perception of water, for example, does not slake one's thirst.[1]

Somadeva offers some further criticism on the kind of salvation set forth by the Vaiśeṣikas. The purport of what he says is: it may be readily admitted that there is no knowledge or bliss of a worldly character in salvation, but if it is assumed to be a condition in which knowledge is totally absent, what would be the character of the emancipated soul? There cannot be a soul without knowledge, just as there cannot be fire without heat.[2] The opinion of the Yoga system of Patañjali is cited to show that knowledge exists in the state of salvation. Somadeva argues that such beings as Sadāśiva or Īśvara cannot be held to be worldly entities since they are omniscient, and if they are not worldly entities, they must be held to be emancipated beings. Now, Patañjali tells us that Īśvara, who is untouched by worldly ties such as the Kleśas, Karman and its effects, and impressions, possesses omniscience in an unlimited degree.[3] The example of Śiva or Īśvara, emancipated yet omniscient, thus shows that knowledge can co-exist simultaneously with salvation. Somadeva reinforces his argument by quoting a verse from Avadhūta,[4] addressed to Śiva, in which *universal knowledge* is attributed to the Exalted One, besides irresistible power, aversion to pleasure, contentment, self-control, supreme bliss and unimpeded energy. On these grounds Somadeva, like many other thinkers, rejects the Vaiśeṣika view of salvation as a colourless condition devoid of attributes.

BUDDHIST DOCTRINES

a) As in the case of the Vaiśeṣika doctrines, Somadeva makes three different statements defining Buddhist views on salvation. First, he seems to say that final release results from the practice of *bhāvanā* based on the realisation of *nairātmya*,[5] both of which are well-known Buddhist concepts. Nairātmya is non-existence of the self; man, according to the Buddhists, is a compound of material and spiritual aggregates known as *skandhas*. "Just as the word 'chariot' is but a mode of expression for axle, wheels and other

---

1 ज्ञानादवगमोऽर्थानां न तत्कार्यसमागमः । तर्षापकर्षयोगि स्याद्दृष्टमेवान्यथा पयः ॥ P. 271.

2 बोधो वा यदि वानन्दो नास्ति मुक्तौ भवोद्भवः । सिद्धसाध्यतयास्माकं न काचित् क्षतिरीक्ष्यते ॥ न्यक्षवीक्षाविनिर्मोक्षे मोक्षे किं मोक्षिलक्षणम् । न ह्यग्नावन्यदुष्णत्वाल्लक्ष्म लक्ष्यं विचक्षणैः ॥ P. 272. Ms. A remarks: समस्तपदार्थावलोकन-विनाशलक्षणे (मोक्षे).

3 "किं च सदाशिवेश्वरादयः संसारिणो मुक्ता वा । संसारित्वे कथमाप्तता । मुक्तत्वे 'क्लेशकर्मविपाकाशयैरपरामृष्टः पुरुषविशेष ईश्वरस्तत्र निरतिशयं सर्वज्ञबीजम्' इति पतञ्जलिजल्पितम्, 'ऐश्वर्यमप्रतिहतं सहजो विरागस्तृप्तिर्निसर्गजनिता वशितेन्द्रियेषु ।' इत्यवधूताभिधानं च न घटेत ।" P. 272.

4 For the verse from Avadhūta see Chap. XVIII.

5 'नैरात्म्यादिनिवेदितसंभावनातो भावनातः इति दशबलशिष्याः'. P. 269. See next Chapter for further details.

constituent members, placed in a certain relation to each other; but, when we come to examine the members one by one, we discover that, in an absolute sense, there is no chariot;..........in exactly the same way, the words 'living being' and 'ego' are only modes of expression for a complex of bodily and non-bodily constituents."[1] Bhāvanā is meditation or cultivation, the highest of the three stages of spiritual training recognised by the Buddhists, the other two being *śraddhā* (faith) and *darśana* (sight, personal inquiry). As Poussin says, "That is Faith, adhesion to the word of the Master. To ascertain this statement by personal inquiry is what is called Sight. Finally, to ponder over it until it becomes not only familiar, but actually always present to the mind, that is Cultivation."[2]

Somadeva ridicules the doctrine of *bhāvanā* as a means to salvation. Anything and everything may flash across the mind in the course of *bhāvanā* or meditation; if salvation were to result from meditation, any swindler would obtain it.[3] Somadeva in this connection quotes a verse which describes an imprisoned thief as declaring that he can clearly see his beloved's face (by force of meditation), even though his eyes are closed and the prison locked up and it is pitchy dark inside.[4]

The doctrine of *nairātmya* is set forth also in the episode of Caṇḍakarman (Book V) by the Buddhist Sugatakīrti, one of the interlocutors. He maintains that the belief in a Self is nothing but 'the certain blindness of a great delusion', and quotes two verses which declare the notion of the Self to be the source of all evils:

यः पश्यत्यात्मानं तस्यात्मनि भवति शाश्वतः स्नेहः । स्नेहात्सुखेषु तृष्यति तृष्णा दोषांस्तिरस्कुरुते ॥
आत्मनि सति परसंज्ञा स्वपरविभागात्परिग्रहद्वेषौ । अनयोः संप्रतिबद्धाः सर्वे दोषाः प्रजायन्ते ॥

"Whoso believes in a Self conceives lasting affection for it; from affection arises desire for pleasures, and desire hides all blemishes. Once there is the notion of the Self, there arises that of the not-Self, and from the distinction between one's own self and others arise attachment and hatred. All evils originate, dependent on these two." Vol. II, p. 252.

Sugatakīrti goes on to define the Buddhist view of salvation and calls it *nirodha* or cessation. He quotes a verse which says that, just as the flame of a lamp goes out without leaving any trace when the oil is used up,

---

1 *Visuddhimagga* cited in Poussin: *The Way to Nirvāṇa*, p. 42.

2 Ibid. p. 159.

3 सर्वं चेतसि भासेत वस्तु भावनया स्फुटम् । तावन्मात्रेण मुक्तत्वे मुक्तिः स्याद्विप्रलम्भिनाम् ॥ P. 271.

4 'तदुक्तम्—पिहिते कारागारे तमसि च' etc. See Chap XVIII.

similarly a man becomes calm without attachment, when passion is destroyed. तदाह—

यथा स्नेहक्षयाद्दीपः प्रशाम्यति निरन्वयः । तथा क्लेशक्षयाज्जन्तुः प्रशाम्यति निरन्वयः ॥ Ibid.

Such being the ultimate end of man, Sugatakīrti comes to the conclusion that all forms of religious austerities are nothing but self-torture.[1] He goes on to quote a verse which enumerates the five emblems of folly: the authority of the Vedas, the theory of a Creator, bathing for religious purposes, the pride of caste, and self-mortification. तदुक्तम्—

वेदप्रामाण्यं कस्यचित् कर्तृवादः स्नाने धर्मेच्छा जातिवादावलेपः ।
संतापारम्भः क्लेशनाशाय चेति ध्वस्तप्रज्ञानां पञ्च लिङ्गानि जाड्ये ॥ Ibid.

Certain other verses are cited by Sugatakīrti in support of sensual enjoyment;[2] and the object of Somadeva is to show Buddhism in an unfavourable light, the theory of *nairātmya* being represented as leading to materialism. The doctrine comes in for further criticism in Sudatta's reply to Sugatakīrti. The Buddhist monk recognises his alms-bowl, the houses of the donors, and himself as recipient of the alms: how can he then believe in the non-existence of the Self?[3] If a man becomes extinct without leaving any trace, there can be no continuity of life,[4] and such a unique being cannot be compared to anything else, for example, a lamp. Further, if an individual is liable to destruction at each successive moment (for, in the Buddhist view, man is not the same for two consecutive moments), how does he hold together a compact group like that of the sense organs? How can impressions abide in something that is in a state of flux? Somadeva, therefore, declares that the Buddhist doctrine is devoid of all proof, and as such cannot provide a basis for the regulation of *dharma* and *adharma*.[5] The Buddhist, after denying the existence of the visible Self, might vociferously maintain the existence of some unseen principle (for example, the *skandhas*), but his position would be no better than that of the potter who asserted that his donkey had two horns, but his neighbour's ox had none![6] Sudatta then attacks the Buddhist doctrine that there is rebirth but no transmigration of a soul.

1 'एवं च सति केशोल्लुञ्चनतप्तशिलारोहणकेशदर्शनाशनविनाशब्रह्मचर्यादयः केवलमात्मोपघातायैव ।'

2 'पयोधरभरालसाः····' 'स्त्रीमुद्रां झषकेतनस्य····.' See Chap. XVIII.

3 सोऽहं तदेव पात्रं तान्येतानि च गृहाणि दातृणाम् । इति नित्यं विदुषोऽपि च दुराग्रहः कोऽस्य नैरात्म्ये ॥ Vol. II, p. 256.

4 The Jaina critic misunderstands the significance of Nirodha, and wrongly interprets it as annihilation without any sequel (निरन्वय). See next Chapter for the correct meaning of Nirodha.

5 संतानो न निरन्वये विसदृशे सादृश्यमेतन्नहि प्रत्यासत्तिहते कुतः समुदयः का वासना वास्थिरे । तत्त्वे वाचि समस्तमानरहिते ताथागते सांप्रतं धर्माधर्मनिबन्धनो विधिरयं कौतस्कुतो वर्तताम् ॥ P. 257.

6 दृष्टात्ययात्तत्त्वमदृष्टमेष प्रसाधयेच्चेद्वचनासरालः । तदा खरोक्ष्णोः श्रुतितो विषाणे विधन्निषेधंश्च जयी कुलालः ॥ Ibid.

नाहं नैव परो न कर्मभिरिह प्रायेग बन्धः कचिन्नोक्ता प्रेत्य न तत्फलस्य च वदेदित्थं स बौद्धो यदि ।
कस्मादेष तपःसमुद्यतमनाश्चैत्यादिकं वन्दते किं वा तत्र तपोऽस्ति केवलमयं धूर्तैर्जडो वञ्चितः ॥

"The Buddhist maintains that neither 'I' nor any one else exists nor does bondage, as a rule, result from *karman* in this life nor does a man reap the consequences of his actions after death. If so, why does a monk, bent on austerities, worship shrines and the like? Or, perhaps, there is no scope for austerities here. The fool is simply deluded by cheats." (Vol. II, p, 257)

b) The ancient Buddhist doctrine of Nirvāṇa is also mentioned by Somadeva. He states that, according to the Buddhists, emancipation consists in the emergence of a detached frame of mind,[1] and quotes two verses in illustration of the doctrine:

दिशं न कांचिद्विदिशं न कांचिन्नैवावनिं गच्छति नान्तरिक्षम् ।
दीपो यथा निर्वृतिमभ्युपेतः स्नेहक्षयात् केवलमेति शान्तिम् ॥
दिशं न कांचिद्विदिशं न कांचिन्नैवावनिं गच्छति नान्तरिक्षम् ।
जीवस्तथा निर्वृतिमभ्युपेतः क्लेशक्षयात् केवलमेति शान्तिम् ॥

"The flame of a lamp, when the oil is used up, goes not to any of the four quarters nor to any point between nor earthwards nor skywards. Ceasing to burn, it simply becomes extinct. Just so a sentient being, when his passion is destroyed, goes not to any of the four quarters nor to any point between nor earthwards nor skywards. Becoming calm, he simply attains peace." (Vol. II, p. 270)[2]

The end of passion (*kleśa*) is often represented as *nirvāṇa* in early Buddhist texts. The *kleśas* are *moha* 'delusion', *rāga* 'lust' and *dosa* 'hatred or malice'. We read, for instance, in the *Saṁyuttanikāya* XXXVIII. I: *yo kho āvuso rāgakkhayo dosakkhayo mohakkhayo idaṁ vuccati nibbānaṁ ti*. The end of lust, hatred and delusion is here called Nirvāṇa. The nature of Nirvāṇa is discussed in the *Milindapañha*[3] which describes it as a condition in which no evil dispositions can grow.[4] Nirvāṇa is supreme bliss, in which the burning heat of the threefold fire (lust, malice and delusion) is totally absent.[5] As water allays the thirst of men and beasts, so does Nirvāṇa allay the thirst of craving after lusts, craving after future life, and

---

1 'निराश्रयचित्तोत्पत्तिलक्षणो मोक्षः इति मोक्षावसरास्ताथागताः ।' P. 270. See next Chapter for another reference to this definition by a Jaina writer and its interpretation.

2 See also Chap. XVIII.

3 See *The Questions of King Milinda*, trans. by Rhys Davids, Part II, pp. 190, 195, 197, 203.. The extracts in Pāli are from the Devanāgarī edition of the text, Bombay 1940.

4 'निब्बानं सब्बकिलेसानं अविरूहनं'

5 'ब्यपगततिविधग्गिसन्तापं परमसुख निब्बानं'

craving after worldly prosperity.[1] Nirvāṇa is thus "a state of mind to be realised and enjoyed by a man here, on this earth, in this life, and in this life only".[2] If grounded in virtue, and mentally alert, "the man who orders his life aright, wheresoever he may be, will realise Nirvāṇa."[3] It is *peace* beyond compare.[4]

In the Buddhist view, it is immaterial to ask what becomes of the emancipated saint after he has passed away. In the Aggi-Vacchagotta-sutta of the *Majjhimanikāya*, Vacchagotta is asked by the Buddha whether he can tell in what direction an expiring fire goes, whether to east, west, north or south. The reply is *na upeti*, the question does not apply. The fire has simply gone out for lack of fuel to sustain it. Similarly, it is pointed out, everything by which the emancipated saint might be denoted, has passed away, has been completely extirpated; 'reborn does not apply to him nor not reborn nor any combination of such terms'.[5]

Nirvāṇa is in a sense freedom from rebirth. The man who sees the peril in the cycle of births (*pavatta*), says the *Milindapañha*, realises that it is all "burning, and blazing, full of pain and of despair", and yearns for a state in which there is no becoming (*appavatta*), and concentrates his mind on it; and, after mighty endeavour, having gone far beyond the cycle of existence, attains freedom from *saṁsāra*.[6] "And when he has gained that, the man who has ordered his life aright has realised Nirvāṇa."[7]

The only criticism which Somadeva offers in respect of the Buddhist view of Nirvāṇa is that the soul which remains imperishable through a long succession of births cannot become extinct in the state of salvation.[8] Somadeva's criticism is, however, beside the mark, as Nirvāṇa is not salvation to be enjoyed by an imperishable soul after death. As Rhys Davids says, "the parts and powers of the perfect man will be dissolved, and no new being will be born to sorrow. The wise will pass away, will go out like the flame of a lamp, and their Karma will be individualized no longer...........................

---

1 'उदकं किलंततसितपिपासितघम्माभितत्तानं जनपसुपजानं पिपासाविनयनं; एवमेव'''निब्बानं कामतण्हाभवतण्हाविभवतण्हापिपासाविनयनं ।'

2 Ibid. p. 181. f. n. 1.

3 'यथ कत्थचि पि ठितो सम्मापटिपन्नो निब्बानं सच्छिकरोति ।'

4 Cf. 'अनुत्तरं योगक्खेमं निब्बानं' 'अनुत्तरं सन्तिवरपदं परियेसमानो' *Ariyapariyesana Sutta, Majjhima-Nikāya* (26).

5 See *Further Dialogues of the Buddha*, Vol. I, pp. 343, 344.

6 'पवत्तं समतिक्कमित्वा अप्पवत्तं ओक्कमति ।' See Rhys Davids: *Pali-English Dictionary* under *pavatta*.

7 *The Questions of King Milinda* (op. cit.), p. 201.

8 अनेकजन्मसंततेर्यावदद्याक्षयः पुमान् । यद्यसौ मुक्त्यवस्थायां कुतः क्षीयेत हेतुतः ॥ P. 272

So the living, moving body of the perfect man is visible still, though its cause has ceased to act: but it will soon decay and die and pass away; and as no new body will be formed, where life was, will be nothing".[1]

Nirvāṇa corresponds in fact to *jīvanmuktatā*, and this interpretation seems to have been well-known in the tenth century. Utpala, a writer of the Kasmir school of Śaivism, who lived about this time, defines Mokṣa as *jīvanmuktatā*, and quotes in illustration a Buddhist verse, among others, which says that *saṁsāra* consists in a state of mind sullied by lust and other impurities; while freedom from such a condition constitutes Mokṣa.[2]

c) The third important reference to Buddhist doctrine is that to the Mādhyamika theory of Void (*śūnyatā*), which Somadeva attributes to "certain Buddhists who are regular cheats, and have invented the pervasive darkness of *śūnyatā*".[3] The following definition of *śūnyatā* is quoted in *Yaśastilaka* VI. I (p. 269):

नैवान्तस्तत्त्वमस्तीह न बहिस्तत्त्वमञ्जसा । विचारगोचरातीतेः शून्यता श्रेयसी ततः ॥

The purport of the verse is that there is no reality external or internal; hence the realisation of Void is the highest good, transcending as it does the range of the intellect. It is doubtful whether Somadeva fully appreciates the significance of the theory of *śūnyatā* as interpreted by Nāgārjuna and Candrakīrti in the *Madhyamakakārikās* and the *Prasannapadā* commentary respectively. The sum and substance of the doctrine is that *śūnyatā* is nothing but the law of causation known as *pratītya-samutpāda*, that is, whatever is subject to cause and condition is really unborn, has no real origination, and is hence called *śūnya* or void.[4] All objects have only a relative existence like a mirage or a magic show or a dream; and the doctrine of *śūnya* is called *madhyamaka* or the middle doctrine, because it avoids the two extremes of existence and non-existence.[5] The doctrine is such that it

---

1 *Buddhism*, p. 114 (S. P. C. K, 1903).

2 'बौद्धे च—रागादिमलिनं चित्तं संसारस्तद्विविक्तता । संक्षेपात् कथितो मोक्षः प्रहीनावरणैर्जिनैः ॥' *Spandapradīpikā* p. 7 (Vizianagram Sanskrit Series).

3 'पश्यतोहराः प्रकाशितशून्यतैकान्ततिमिराः शाक्यविशेषाः'

4 यः प्रतीत्यसमुत्पादः शून्यतां तां प्रचक्ष्महे । सा प्रज्ञप्तिरुपादाय प्रतिपत् सैव मध्यमा ॥ *Madhyamakakarikā* 24. 18. Candrakīrti says: 'योऽयं प्रतीत्यसमुत्पादो हेतुप्रत्ययानपेक्ष्याङ्कुरविज्ञानादीनां प्रादुर्भावः स स्वभावेनानुत्पादः । यश्च स्वभावेनानुत्पादो भावानां सा शून्यता ।'. Also 'यः प्रत्ययैर्जायते स ह्यजातो न तस्य उत्पादु स्वभावतोऽस्ति । यः प्रत्ययाधीनु स शून्यु उक्तो यः शून्यतां जानति सोऽप्रमत्त ॥ इति भगवतो गाथावचनात् । एवं प्रतीत्यसमुत्पादशब्दस्य योऽर्थः स एव शून्यताशब्दस्यार्थः न पुनरभावशब्दस्य योऽर्थः शून्यताशब्दस्यार्थः ।'

5 'मायास्वप्नगन्धर्वनगरादिवत्तु लौकिकाः पदार्थाः निरुपपत्तिका एव सन्तः सर्वलोकस्याविद्यातिमिरोपहतमतिनयनस्य प्रसिद्धिमुपगताः इति परस्परापेक्षयैव केवलं प्रसिद्धिमुपगता बालैरभ्युपगम्यन्ते' (Chap. 7). 'तदेवं मध्यमकदर्शन एवास्तित्वनास्तित्वद्वयदर्शनस्याप्रसङ्गो न विज्ञानवादिदर्शनादिष्विति विज्ञेयम्' (Chap. 15). Cf. अस्तीति शाश्वतग्राहो नास्तीत्युच्छेददर्शनम् । तस्मादस्तित्वनास्तित्वे नाश्रीयेत विचक्षणः ॥ *Madhyamakakārikā* 15. 10.

must be realised in one's own heart, and hence described as unexplained by speech and beyond the range of mental comprehension.[1] Nirvāṇa, according to the Mādhyamika school, is nothing but the realisation of *śūnyatā*, which consists in the cessation of the complex of worldly notions known as *prapañca*.[2]

Somadeva has a fling at the doctrine of void, when he says that if a follower of the Śūnya theory tries to establish it by means of independent proofs, he will be contradicting his own theory that *everything* is *śūnya* 'void' 'non-existent.'[3] The Mādhyamikas are, however, careful to point out that what they maintain is not *abhāva*, non-existence, but the relative existence of things: they recognise neither eternalism nor annihilationism.[4]

SĀṀKHYA DOCTRINES

There are two statements defining the Sāṁkhya view of salvation in *Yaśastilaka* VI. 1. The first is that salvation results from discrimination between Matter (Prakṛti) and the Self (Puruṣa).[5] The second is that salvation is the condition in which the Self subsides in the pristine state (of pure consciousness) after the cessation of intellect, mind and egoism, resulting in the destruction of the sense organs.[6] The expression, *tadā draṣṭuḥ svarūpe'vasthānam*, is borrowed from the *Yogasūtras* 1. 3. The idea of the soul abiding in itself after the cessation of all mental and intellectual processes occurs in *Sāṁkhyasūtras* 2. 34.[7]

In the episode of Caṇḍakarman (Book V), Sāṁkhya doctrines are represented by Āsuri who quotes the following verse on the Sāṁkhya conception of the Self (p. 250):

अकर्ता निर्गुणः शुद्धो नित्यः सर्वगतोऽक्रियः । अमूर्तश्चेतनो भोक्ता पुमान् कपिलशासने ॥

---

1 Candrakīrti (18. 9) says: 'विकल्पश्चित्तप्रचारः तद्रहितत्वात् तत्तत्त्वं निर्विकल्पम् ।'

2 'शून्यतैव सर्वप्रपञ्चनिवृत्तिलक्षणत्वान्निर्वाणमित्युच्यते' Candrakīrti on *Madhyamakakārikā* 18. 5. Properly speaking, salvation results from the destruction of *Karma* and the *Kleśas*, but the latter spring from *Vikalpas* or fanciful ideas, and these again from *prapañca*, which is eradicated only on the realisation of *Śūnyatā*. Nāgārjuna says: कर्मक्लेशक्षयान्मोक्षः कर्मक्लेशा विकल्पतः । ते प्रपञ्चात् प्रपञ्चस्तु शून्यतायां निरुध्यते ॥ 18. 5. Candrakīrti says: 'ते च विकल्पा अनादिमत्संसाराभ्यस्तात् ज्ञानज्ञेयवाच्यवाचककर्तृकर्मकरणक्रियाघटपटमुकुटरथरूपवेदनास्त्रीपुरुषलाभालाभसुखदुःखयशोऽयशोनिन्दाप्रशंसादिलक्षणाद्विचित्रात् प्रपञ्चादुपजायन्ते। स चायं लौकिकः प्रपञ्चः निरवशेषः शून्यतायां सर्वभावस्वभावशून्यतादर्शने सति निरुध्यते ।'

3 शून्यं तत्त्वमहं वादी साधयामि प्रमाणतः । इत्यास्थायां विरुध्येत सर्वशून्यत्ववादिता ॥ P. 272.

4 See above.

5 'प्रकृतिपुरुषयोः विवेकमतेः ख्यातेः इति सांख्याः ।' P. 269.

6 'बुद्धिमनोऽहंकारविरहादखिलेन्द्रियोपशमावहात्तदा द्रष्टुः स्वरूपेऽवस्थानं मुक्तिः इति कापिलाः ।' P. 270.

7 'तन्निवृत्तावुपशान्तोपरागः स्वस्थः'

Āsuri explains that Prakṛti contaminates the Self, even though composed of bliss, like a piece of crystal, with such manifestations as intellect, egoism and the like, which bring in their train pleasure, pain and illusion. When the Self comes to realise the nature of Prakṛti, its connection with the latter, comparable to that of fire with an iron ball, comes to an end; and the Self attains *Kaivalya* which means the cessation of all connection with knowledge and objects of knowledge.[1] Āsuri then declares that since salvation results simply from discrimination between Prakṛti and the Self, it is useless to perform religious austerities; and one should therefore eat, drink, and be merry, and follow ones' inclination:

अनुभवत पिबत खादत विलसत मानयत कामितं लोकाः । आत्मव्यक्तिविवेकान्मुक्तिर्ननु किं वृथा तपत ॥

This looks like a satire on the Sāṁkhya theory of salvation, but similar views are expressed in an authoritative text like the *Māṭharavṛtti* on the *Sāṁkhyakārikās* (37), where it is stated that, according to Kapila, a man has no prescribed duties; and final beatitude results solely from the *knowledge* of the twentyfive principles recognised by the Sāṁkhya system. The *Māṭharavṛtti* then quotes a verse very similar to that put in the mouth of Āsuri:

हस पिब लल मोद नित्यं विषयानुपभुञ्ज कुरु च मा शङ्काम् । यदि विदितं ते कपिलमतं तत्प्राप्स्यसे मोक्षसौख्यं च ॥

Sudatta criticizes some of the Sāṁkhya tenets in his reply to Āsuri. If, as the Sāṁkhyas hold, bondage and salvation, pleasure and pain, and activity and retirement belong to Prakṛti, what is the use of postulating the existence of a Self?[2] Further, the Sāṃkhya doctrine involves a number of self-contradictions. The Self never acts, yet it enjoys the fruits of action; it is devoid of action, yet adopts an attitude of indifference; it is eternal, yet comes into temporary association with Prakṛti; it is bound up with Prakṛti, yet separates itself from the latter; it is pure, yet it is connected with the impure body; and it is called bliss, though it has no attributes.[3] Besides, if the Self is eternal and without any form, it can have no connection with actions producing their results, just as the sky can have no connection with binding ropes.[4]

In VI. 1 also there is some criticism of Sāṁkhya views. Somadeva asks how it is possible to discriminate between the Prakṛti and the Self, both

---

1 'स यदा······स्फाटिकाश्मानमिवानन्दात्मानमप्यात्मानं सुखदुःखमोहावहपरिवर्तैर्महदहंकारादिविवर्तैः कलुषयन्त्याः······ प्रकृतेः स्वरूपमवगच्छति, तदायोमयगोलकानलतुल्यवर्गस्य बोधवद्बहुधानेकसंसर्गस्य सति विसर्गे सकलज्ञानज्ञेयसंबन्धावैकल्यं कैवल्यमवलम्बते तदा द्रष्टुः स्वरूपेऽवस्थानमिति वचनात् ।' P. 250.

2 बन्धमोक्षौ सुखं दुःखं प्रवर्तननिवर्तने । यद्येष प्रकृतेर्धर्मः किं स्यात् पुंसः प्रकल्पनम् ॥ P. 253.

4 अकर्तापि पुमान् भोक्ता क्रियाशून्योऽप्युदासिता । नित्योऽपि जातसंसर्गः सवर्गोऽपि वियोगभाक् ॥ शुद्धोऽपि देहसंबद्धो निर्गुणोऽपि शमुच्यते । इत्यन्योन्यविरुद्धोक्तं न युक्तं कापिलं वचः ॥ P. 253.

4 नित्येऽमूर्ते सदा पुंसि कर्मभिः स्वफलेरिभिः । कुतो घटेत संबन्धो यथाकाशस्य रज्जुभिः ॥ P. 254.

eternal and pervasive.[1] He seems also to criticize the Sāṁkhya theory that the self continues to exist without any knowledge or mental process after the cessation of its connection with the material world.[2] He points out that the Self is bound to have unlimited knowledge even in its pristine state, once the impurity of Karma is removed, in the same way as the Self has knowledge of things in dreams that come true.[3] The analogy of dream consciousness is continued; and Somadeva contends that even a blind man can see things in a dream, and it is therefore wrong to suppose that the emancipated Self can have no knowledge, being without any sense organs.[4] It is but natural that the intellect should reveal the entire range of objects, like the rays of the sun, once the screen of Karma is destroyed.

VEDĀNTA DOCTRINES

There are two references to Vedānta doctrines in *Yaśastilaka* VI. 1. First, it is stated that, according to the Vedāntins, salvation takes place when Nescience, which brings about the cognition of endless divergences, is destroyed as the result of the realisation of the Absolute.[6] Secondly, all living creatures are merged in the Absolute after the final annihilation of the body, just as the space enclosed within a jar is merged in universal space after the breaking up of the jar.[7]

Somadeva criticizes the above doctrines thus. First, if all divergence is dismissed as Nescience, how can the varied character of the world be explained, with its palpable manifestations of birth, death, pleasure and the like?[8] Secondly, if the Absolute alone exists and nothing else, why is there no cessation of the waves of worldly phenomena? Why is the universe distinctly seen? Why is it not merged in the Absolute, just as the space enclosed within a jar is merged in universal space?[9] The Vedāntins also say that the Supreme Soul is one, though it abides in each individual: it is seen both as one and many, like the moon and its reflections in water. The

---

1 अव्यक्तनरयोर्नित्यं नित्यव्यापिस्वभावयोः। विवेकेन कथं ख्यातिं सांख्यमुख्याः प्रचक्षते ॥ P. 271.

2 See above.

3 बाह्ये ग्राह्ये मलापायात् सत्यस्वप्न इवात्मनः। तदा द्रष्टुः स्वरूपेऽस्मिन्नवस्थानममानकम् ॥ P. 272. Ms. A says: कर्मक्षयात् केवलेन ज्ञानेन बाह्ये पदार्थे ग्राह्ये अवलोकिते सति द्रष्टुरात्मनः स्वस्वरूपेऽवस्थानं स्थितिर्भवति। मानरहित-मनन्तं ज्ञानं स्यादित्यर्थः।

4 यत्र नेत्रादिकं नास्ति न तत्र मतिरात्मनि। तन्न युक्तमिदं यस्मात्स्वप्नमन्धोऽपि वीक्षते ॥ P. 272

5 तदावृतिहतौ तस्य तपनस्येव दीधितिः। कथं न शेमुषी सर्वं प्रकाशयति वस्तु यत् ॥ P. 273.

6 'परमब्रह्मदर्शनवशादशेषभेदसंवेदनाविद्याविनाशात् इति वेदान्तवादिनः।' P. 269.

7 'यथा घटविघटने घटाकाशमाकाशीभवति तथा देहोच्छेदात् सर्वः प्राणी परे ब्रह्मणि लीयते इति ब्रह्माद्वैतवादिनः।' P. 270.

8 भेदोऽयं यद्यविद्या स्याद्वैचित्र्यं जगतः कुतः। जन्ममृत्युसुखप्रायैर्विवर्तैर्मानवर्तिभिः ॥ P. 272.

9 ब्रह्मैकं यदि सिद्धं स्यान्निस्तरङ्गं कुतश्च न। घटाकाशमिवाकाशे तत्रेदं लीयतां जगत् ॥ P. 273.

comparison is, however, fallacious, because the moon is seen as one in the sky and as many elsewhere in the form of reflections; but the undifferentiated Absolute is nowhere seen apart from the diversities of the visible world.[1]

JAIMINĪYA DOCTRINES

Somadeva refers to the Jaiminīyas or the followers of Jaimini, who declare that the mind is by nature impure like charcoal and collyrium, and can never be purified.[2] This opinion is expressed also by Dhūmadhvaja in the episode of Caṇḍakarman and Sudatta, and he deduces from it a sensualist conception of life. He maintains that just as charcoal, though rubbed, never becomes white, similarly the mind, impure by nature, never becomes pure.[3] Further, there is no heaven in the guise of another world for which it is worth while to perform religious austerities; the real heaven is the ardent mutual love of a maiden of twelve and a youth of sixteen![4] Dhūmadhvaja goes on to ridicule those who forsake the pleasures of the senses and strive for pain rather than pleasure.

The opinions of Dhūmadhvaja are controverted by Sudatta. If the mind or the inner faculty is impure, why does Kumārila in offering salutation to Śiva describe him as being composed of pure knowledge?[5] Sudatta then cites a verse which declares the existence of the eternal soul: it is interwoven with all things, yet not in contact with anything, and its nature is ever pure as the sky. कथं चेदं वचनमजर्यम्—

समस्तेषु वस्तुष्वनुस्यूतमेकं समस्तानि वस्तूनि यन्न स्पृशन्ति ।
वियद्वत् सदा शुद्धिमद्यस्स्वरूपं स सिद्धोपलब्धिः स नित्योऽहमात्मा ॥ P. 254

The sage concludes by saying that just as a gem tarnished by impurities can be cleansed with effort, and ore turned into gold by a process of manufacture, similarly the Self can be liberated from passion by those who are well-meaning and resort to the canon of the Arhats.[6]

---

1 अथ मतम्—एक एव हि भूतात्मा देहे देहे व्यवस्थितः । एकधानेकधा चापि दृश्यते जलचन्द्रवत् ॥ तदयुक्तम् । एकः खेऽनेकधान्यत्र यथेन्दुर्वेद्यते जनैः । न तथा वेद्यते ब्रह्म भेदेभ्योऽन्यदभेदभाक् ॥ P. 273.

2 'अङ्गाराञ्जनादिवत् स्वभावादेव कालुष्योत्कर्षप्रवृत्तस्य चित्तस्य न कुतश्चिद्विशुद्धचित्तवृत्तिः इति जैमिनीयाः ।'

3 घृष्यमाणो यथाङ्गारः शुक्लतां नैति जातुचित् । विशुध्यति कुतश्चित्तं निसर्गमलिनं तथा ॥ P. 250.

4 'न चापरमिषस्ताविषः समर्थोऽस्ति यदर्थोऽयं तपःप्रयासः सफलायासः स्यात् । यतः द्वादशवर्षा योषा षोडशवर्षोचितस्थितिः पुरुषः । प्रीतिः परस्परमनयोः स्वर्गः स्मृतः सद्भिः ॥' P. 251.

5 'घृष्यमाणाङ्गारवदन्तरङ्गस्य विशुद्ध्यभावे कथमिदमुदाहारि कुमारिलेन—विशुद्धज्ञानदेहाय...... । ......नमः सोमार्धधारिणे ॥' See Chapter XVIII.

6 मलकलुषतायातं रत्नं विशुध्यति यत्नतो भवति कनकं तत्पाषाणो यथा च कृतक्रियः । कुशलमतिभिः कैश्चिद्धन्यैस्तथाप्तनयाश्रितैरयमपि गलत्क्लेशाभोगः क्रियेत परः पुमान् ॥ P. 254.

The Jaiminīya doctrine is criticised also in VI. 1. Somadeva says that removal of impurities involves transformation of character, and this can be brought about through the operation of the appropriate causes as in the case of gems and pearls.[1]

CĀRVĀKA DOCTRINES

Somadeva refers to the Bārhaspatyas or the followers of Bṛhaspati and calls them the leaders of all the Nāstikas or materialists, popularly known as the Cārvākas. According to them, *dharmas* or qualities may be said to exist only if we can be sure of the existence of a Dharmin, 'one who possesses *dharmas*', that is, the Self. Similarly, there is no other world than this, because no one lives after death. The question of salvation thus does not arise.[2] The Bārhaspatyas then regard emancipation as a myth.

In the episode of Caṇḍakarman and Sudatta, the former sets forth Cārvāka doctrines. He declares that those who believe in the rebirth of a dead man, those who believe in a Dharma whose result is unseen, and those who believe in a soul apart from the body are people who 'see blues and yellows'.[3] The four elements, constituting the body, and moved by the five breaths, produce consciousness,[4] just as substances like flour-water, molasses, and the Dhātakī creeper possess intoxicating properties, and just as the combination of lime, betel and areca-nut produces a red colour. Consciousness lasting from birth to death never reemerges, once it has reached its term, like a leaf fallen from the tree. Since there is no life after death,[5] and the living creatures are like bubbles of water, all painful efforts (such as religious austerities) are futile.[6] "One should therefore live

---

1 स्वभावान्तरसंभूतिर्यत्र तत्र मलक्षयः । कर्तुं शक्यः स्वहेतुभ्यो मणिमुक्ताफलेष्विव ॥ P. 271.

2 'सति धर्मिणि धर्माश्चिन्त्यन्ते ततः परलोकिनोऽभावात् परलोकाभावे कस्यासौ मोक्षः इति समवाप्तसमस्तनास्तिकाधिपत्या बार्हस्पत्याः ।' P. 269.

3 पश्यन्ति ये जन्म मृतस्य जन्तोः पश्यन्ति ये धर्ममदृष्टसाध्यम् । पश्यन्ति येऽन्यं पुरुषं शरीरात् पश्यन्ति ते नीलकपीतकानि ॥ P. 252.

4 Empedocles likewise taught that "it is by these (elements) men think and feel pleasure and pain". Thought, like sense-perception, is only a function of the body, which is composed of the elements (fire, air, water and earth). Burnet: *Early Greek Philosophy*, p. 247; Zeller: *Outlines of the History of Greek Philosophy*, p. 57. In his religious teaching, however, Empedocles laid stress on the doctrine of transmigration of souls.

5 The important Jewish sect of the Sadducees denied 'the survival of the soul—it perishes with the body—and the rewards and punishments in Hades.' Moore: *Judaism*, Vol. II, p. 317.

6 'प्राणापानसमानोदानव्यानव्यतिकीर्णेभ्यः कायाकारपरिणतिसंकीर्णेभ्यो वनपवनावनिपवनसखेभ्यः पिष्टोदकगुडधातकीप्रमुखेभ्य इव मदशक्तिः, पर्णचूर्णक्रमुकेभ्य इव रागसंपत्तिस्तदात्मगुणकार्यस्वभावतया चैतन्यमुपजायते । तच्च गर्भादिमरणपर्यन्तपर्यायमतीतं सत् पादपात् पतितं पत्रमिव न पुनः प्ररोहति । तथा च परलोकाभावे जलबुद्बुदस्वभावेषु जीवेषु

merrily as long as one lives: no one can escape death, and the body, burnt to ashes and extinct, never returns."

Sudatta while criticizing the above doctrines tries to establish the existence of the Self and continuity of births. He cites three factors in favour of his contention. First, a new-born child, just after his birth, sucks his mother' s breast, which cannot be explained otherwise than by supposing the continuity of impressions acquired in a previous birth.[1] Secondly, it is seen that certain persons become evil spirits after death. Thirdly, there are people who can remember their previous lives.[2] Fourthly, no sentient being ever originates from the elements. Hence the conclusion that the Self exists, eternal, and conscious of the manifestations of Matter.[3] Further, it is seen that the body, the sense organs, and the intellect exist only so long as the Self exists, and decay as soon as the Self departs. The Self might be supposed to be non-exisent if the body and the sense-organs continued to exist even after death, but as this does not take place, the dependence of the body upon the Self must be accepted as true.[4] The fact is that the Self is not composed of the elements; it possesses qualities different from theirs. Besides, if the Self were composed of the elements, the latter would also cease to exist when the former ceased to exist.[5] The Self has characteristic qualities such as knowledge, pleasure and pain; and the elements, too, for example, earth, air and fire have their own distinctive qualities: upholding, impelling and burning respectively.[6]

Some are of opinion that a bilious constitution produces among other things intelligence and intellect, but the theory cannot be accepted as valid. Increase or decrease of intelligence may be due to a corresponding excess or

---

मदशक्तिप्रतिज्ञाने किमर्थोऽयं लोकस्यात्मसपत्नः प्रयत्नः ।' P. 253. It will be seen that the Cārvāka here recognises only four elements: water, air, earth and fire. See also next Chapter (section on the Bārhaspatyas).

1 Sallustius, a Greek writer of the fourth century A. D., employs a similar argument in support of transmigration of Souls. "The transmigration of souls can be proved from the congenital afflictions of persons. For why are some born blind, others paralytic, others with some sickness in the soul itself?" Sallustius: *On the Gods and the world*, Eng. trans. in Murray: *Five Stages of Greek Religion*, pp. 241–267.

2 Empedocles likewise speaks (fr. 129) of a man of rare knowledge, believed to refer to Pythagoras, who could remember what happened ten or twenty generations before. Burnet (*op. cit.*), p. 224.

3 तदहर्जस्तनेहातो रक्षोदृष्टेर्भवस्मृतेः । भूतानन्वयनाज्जीवः प्रकृतिज्ञः सनातनः ॥ P. 271.

4 पुंसि तिष्ठति तिष्ठन्ति शरीरेन्द्रियबुद्धयः । यान्ति यातेऽन्यथैतासां सत्त्वे सत्त्वं प्रसज्यताम् ॥ P. 257.

5 विरुद्धगुणसंसर्गादात्मा भूतात्मको न हि । भूजलानलवातानामन्यथा न व्यवस्थितिः ॥ Ibid.

6 विज्ञानसुखदुःखादिगुणलिङ्गः पुमानयम् । धारणेरणदाहादिधर्माधारा धरादयः ॥ Ibid.

deficiency of bile, just as fire waxes and wanes in proportion to the quantity of fuel consumed, but the sharpness of intellect is always seen to be due to study and learning at the feet of a teacher: to deny this is to contradict what is self-evident. In any case, there cannot be any causal relation between bile and intelligence, because there might be plenty of intelligence even when bile is totally absent.

It follows therefore that the mind cannot be a product or attribute of the body nor can it be identical in composition with the body.[1]

PĀŚUPATA DOCTRINES

Somadeva tells us that, according to the Pāśupatas, ritual alone leads to salvation, meaning thereby the system of ritual prescribed in the religious texts of the Pāśupatas. The chief Pāśupata practices mentioned by him are smearing the body with ashes in the morning, at noon and in the evening, adoration (of the idol or the phallus of Śiva or Paśupati), ceremonial offering of water-pots (probably before the idol), circumambulation from left to right, self-humiliation and other processes.[2]

Somadeva does not explain any of the practices mentioned above, but we can understand most of them with the help of the commentary on the *Gaṇakārikā* of Bhāsarvajña, who flourished about the middle of the tenth century, and was probably a contemporary of Somadeva.[3] It may be noted that the *Gaṇakārikā* is one of the very few works on the Pāśupata system so far published, and both the text and the commentary thereon have been quoted in the brief account of the Pāśupata school in the *Sarvadarśana-saṁgraha*. Passing references to Pāśupata doctrines are found also in the commentaries and sub-commentaries on the *Vedāntasūtras* 2. 2. 37 and specially in the *Āgamaprāmāṇya* of Yāmunamuni, the teacher of Rāmānuja; but perhaps the best extant account of the system is found in the commentary called *Ratnaṭīkā* on Bhāsarvajña's *Gaṇakārikā*.[4]

As regards the religious practices of the Pāśupatas mentioned by Somadeva, the *Ratna* commentary refers not only to the smearing of the

---

1 अथ मतम्—पित्तप्रकृतिर्धीमान् मेधावी क्रोधनोऽल्पकामश्च । प्रस्वेद्यकालपलितो भवति नरो नात्र संदेहः ॥ तन्न प्रवर्हेम् । वृद्धिहानी यथाग्नेः स्तामेधोत्कर्षापकर्षतः । पित्ताधिकोनभावाभ्यां बुद्धेः संप्राप्नुतस्तथा ॥ गुरूपासनमभ्यासो विशेषः शास्त्रनिश्चये । इति दृष्टस्य हानिः स्यात्तथा च तव दर्शने ॥ कुतश्चित् पित्तनाशेऽपि बुद्धेरतिशयेक्षणात् । कुतः प्रभवभावोऽत्र स्याद्बीजाङ्कुरयोरिव ॥ × × × × एवं च सतीदं न किंचित् । देहात्मिका देहकार्या देहस्य च गुणो मतिः । मतत्रयं समाश्रित्य नास्त्यभ्यासस्य संभवः ॥ P. 258.

2 'त्रिकालभस्मोद्धूलनेज्यागडुकप्रदानप्रदक्षिणीकरणात्मविडम्बनादिक्रियाकाण्डमात्राधिष्ठानादनुष्ठानात् इति पाशुपताः' P.269.

3 See also next Chapter.

4 The *Pāśupata Sūtras* with the *Bhāṣya* of Kauṇḍinya has recently been published in Trivandrum Sanskrit Series.

body with ashes, three times a day, but to the habit of sleeping on such ashes in the shrine of the deity, and mentions also the custom of ceremonial circumambulation in the course of the devotions.[1] Ijyā is 'worship', 'adoration', the word being found in the *Ratna* commentary in connection with the worship of the phallus of Śiva.[2] Ātmaviḍambana or self-humiliation refers to a group of curious and ludicrous practices calculated to bring the devotee into contempt.

The *Ratna* commentary says that these practices are designed to create a feeling of disrespect (*apamāna*) in the minds of the people in order that the devotee may suffer humiliation, *apamāna* being compared to a forest-fire and regarded as something desirable, probably because it destroys one's pride and teaches one to be meek and mild.[3] This is no doubt a very curious method of inculcating humility; and we are also told that the devotee should indulge in certain antics in full view of a crowd, like an actor on the stage.[4] The practices in question are *krāthana* or pretending to be asleep while awake; *spandana* or shaking the limbs like one suffering from an epileptic fit; *mandana* or walking like a lame man; *śṛṅgāraṇa* or indulging in amorous gestures as if at the sight of a beautiful young woman; *apitatarana* or acting in a disgraceful manner like one devoid of commonsense; and *apitadbhāṣaṇa* or uttering incoherent and meaningless words.

---

1 E. g., 'प्रागादित्योदयात् घटिकाद्वयं पूर्वाह्नसन्ध्या ।..............भगवन्तं प्रणम्य त्वदाज्ञां करोमीत्यभिसंधाय जपन्नेवा-पादतलमस्तकं यावत् प्रभूतेन भस्मनाऽङ्गं प्रत्यङ्गं च प्रयत्नातिशयेन निघृष्य निघृष्य स्नानमाचरेदित्येवं मध्याह्नापराह्न-सन्ध्ययोरपीति..........अथायतनसन्धिनं भूप्रदेशं दिवा..............भस्मनैव शुचि कुर्यात् । तदनु तत्रोपविश्य विध्यभिनिविष्टस्तावत्तिष्ठेद्यावदतिनिद्राभिभूतः श्रान्तश्च भवति । ततः पुनरुत्थाय विवेचयेत् । तदनु मन्त्रैः संस्कृत्य भस्म प्रभूतं प्रस्तरेत् । ततस्तत्र पंच मन्त्रानावर्तयन्नेव स्वपेत् ।' '......निष्क्रम्येशं प्रणम्य प्रणामान्तं प्रदक्षिणत्रयं जपन्नेव शनैः कुर्यात्' etc. This is mentioned prior to the nightly vigil in the shrine of the god (p. 19). See under verse 7.

2 'मूर्तिशब्देन यदुपहारसूत्रे महादेवेज्यास्थानमूर्ध्वलिङ्गादिलक्षणं व्याख्यातम्' etc. Ijyā may also be equivalent to Yāga, a technical term of the Pāśupatas. The entire ritualistic process is called Caryā which is the means to Dharma. Caryā is composed of Dāna, Yāga and Tāpa. Dāna is self-surrender to the deity accompanied by salutations. Yāga is the proper execution of the prescribed ritualistic acts such as smearing the body with ashes. Tāpa is patient endurance of suffering in the discharge of one's religious duties. See *Ratnaṭīkā* under verse 7. Caryā is called also Vidhi and defined as भस्मस्नानादिर्गूढान्तः क्रियासमूहः with which may be compared the definition of Vidhi cited in next Chapter (*section* on Pāśupatas). Caryā is described also as twofold: *vrata* and the *dvāras*. Smearing the body with ashes, sleeping over them, offerings, *japa* and *pradakṣiṇa* constitute *vrata*. The *dvāras* are the practices known as *krāthana*, *spandana* etc.

3 'न चैषां क्रमो नियम्यते । किन्त्वपमानादिनिष्पादकत्वं येन परिभवं गच्छेदित्युपदेशाद्दवाग्नितुल्यत्वेनापमानादेरिष्टतमत्वा-दिति ।'

4 'रङ्गवदवस्थितेषु जनेषु मध्ये नटवदवस्थितो विवेच्य विवेच्य क्राथनादीनि कुर्यात् ।'

Salvation, according to the Pāśupatas, is not only cessation of pain but the acquisition of unlimited supernatural powers; but as far as can be judged from the scanty literature available on the doctrines of the Pāśupatas, salvation in their view does not solely depend upon ritual, as alleged by Somadeva. Caryā or ritual[1] is no doubt a very important factor in the Pāśupata system, but nevertheless it is only one among the five *upāyas* or means of attaining perfection in the religious life.[2] It is, however, possible that Somadeva may be referring to contemporary Pāśupatas, who, like all followers of ritualistic systems, may be supposed to have laid particular emphasis on Caryā or Vidhi as a means of emancipation.

Caryā, also called *cari* and *vidhikriyā*, is fully explained in Kauṇḍinya's commentary on the *Pāśupata Sūtras* 2, 13; 3, 2; 4, 2 etc. It comprises the entire range of Pāśupata practices which are of two kinds: public and private. The public practices are the peculiar ones mentioned above, and the devotee who undertakes them in the presence of all is called *vyaktācāra*. The private observances are those which he carries out unseen by others and known as *vrata*; hence he is called *gūḍhavrata*.

The practices of *krāthana*, *maṇḍana*[3] and the rest are designed to hold up the devotee to ridicule and make him accustomed to humiliation, insults and censure. They are calculated to promote indifference to the world; and there is also the curious belief that the devotee thereby acquires the religious merit of the onlookers who insult him, and transfers his own sins to them.[4] The Pāśupata devotee who is totally devoid of worldly ties is enjoined to go about like a man not in his senses, even like a mad man, whose true nature remains unrevealed to the people at large.[5] The indignities which he willingly suffers appear to take the place of the austerities recognised by other schools. The *Pāśupata Sūtras* 3. 18, 19 declare, for instance, that while undergoing humiliation, the devotee, conversant with the truths, achieves the full measure of austerities. The inculcation of humility is no doubt the main purpose of

---

1 'धर्मस्योपायः चर्या'

2 वासश्चर्या जपध्यानं सदारुद्रस्मृतिस्तथा । प्रसादश्चैव लाभानामुपायाः पञ्च निश्चिताः ॥ *Gaṇakārikā* (7). The five recognised means of attainnig the *lābhas* or ways of perfection are ***vāsa*** or intellectual discipline including the thorough comprehension and realisation of the tenets of the school and the effort to carry them into practice; *caryā* or ritual; religious meditation; concentration of the mind on Śiva as a regular and constant process; and the favour of the deity. See also next Chapter.

3 Kauṇḍinya uses the form *maṇṭana*.

4 3. 3–9.

5 4. 6, 8.

these practices; as we are told that lack of pride born of caste and social standing is superior to all the *Yantras*, by which are meant sacrificial rites and privations such as prolonged fastings.[1] It may be noted that the Pāśupatas, unlike the later Vīraśaivas, recognise the caste-system. The devotee is invariably referred to as a Brāhmaṇa, and it is forbidden to talk to a Śūdra.[2] But the devotee must discard pride of birth; and the Pāśupata way of life, characterized by a complete disregard for personal and social decorum, is designed to result in eradication of caste rules and intensification of *vairāgya*.[3]

The private practices known as *vrata* are resorted to in the *āyatana*, that is, any place sacred to Śiva where the devotee may choose to reside.[4] He must 'bathe' himself with ashes three times a day, sleep over a bed of ashes, and cleanse himself when necessary with the holy ashes (*anusnāna*). He may not wear a wreath of fresh flowers, but take up only such flowers as have been offered to the idol of Śiva. As part of his devotions, he does mental obeisance to the deity (*namaskāra*), meditates on the sacred formulas, and resorts to certain practices which are again peculiar to the Pāśupata sect. In the shrine of the deity, he breaks out into loud laughter, sings songs in Sanskrit or Prākrit in honour of Śiva, and indulges in dancing. He makes also a sound called *ḍuṁḍuṁkāra* (called also *huḍukkāra* in later texts) resembling the bellowing of a bull and produced by joining the tip of the tongue to the palate.[5] Singing and dancing as a medium of religious fervour are well-known in the history of religion. We may refer, for instance, to the early Christian sect of the Euchites, or Massalians, who, like the Pāśupatas, were quietists, lived on alms and had no possessions. They spent all their time in prayers, and indulged in frenzied dancing.[6] Sects like the Massalians had no organisation, but appear to have led a loosely knit communal life. The Pāśupata devotions, on the other hand, were individual and carried out in seclusion.

Ijyā, as explained above, is adoration; and the worship of Śiva is no doubt the central feature of the Pāśupata cult. But *ijyā* properly means *yāga* 'sacrifice'; and the Pāśupatas have their own interpretation of what sacrifice is. Kauṇḍinya says that Yāga is *bhāvanā* or mental concentration on

1 Kauṇḍinya 4. 9.

2 1. 13.

3 Kauṇḍinya 3. 11 saya: सर्वसंस्कारवर्जितेन भवितव्यम्। अतो वर्णाश्रमव्युच्छेदो वैराग्योत्साहश्च जायते.

4 'ग्रामे वा यदि वारण्ये पुण्यस्थानं हि शूलिनः। आवासो धर्मतृप्तानां सिद्धिक्षेत्रं हि तत् परम्॥' quoted by Kauṇḍinya 1. 7.

5 Details in Kauṇḍinya 1. 8.

6 The Massalians who have been called 'Christian fakirs' first appeard on the borders of Syria and Armenia in the latter half of the fourth century, and spread to Syria and Asia Minor. Kidd: *A History of the Church*, Vol. II, p. 373.

Maheśvara to the exclusion of any other deity.[1] Further, we have the doctrine of *atiyajana* or higher sacrifice in contrast to *kuyajana* or the inferior sacrificial rites of the Vedic religion, so called on account of *hiṁsā* and other defects inherent in them. The *atiyajana* is, however, nothing more than the Pāśupata scheme of discipline comprising the religious practices collectively known as *Caryā*.[2]

The Pāśupatas had, as a matter of fact, no elaborate ritual like that of the Śaivas, who had their *Agamas, Tantras* and *Paddhatis* dealing with the subject. They worshipped Śiva, the *liṅgam* or any other image of the god, *Vṛṣadhvaja, S'ūlapāṇi, Nandi* or *Mahākāla*. An important proviso laid down in the Pāśupata Sūtras is that the worshipper should have in view the Dakṣiṇāmūrti of Śiva, that is, he should stand on the southern side of the deity, turning his face towards the north.[3] Stress is also laid on the meditation of the Praṇava; and the devotee repeats various holy *mantras* which invoke the different aspects of Maheśvara.[4] The Sādhaka no doubt worships the image of Śiva, but his attention is directed to the incorporeal aspect of the deity. Pāśupata worship is really self-surrender (*atidāna*) to the Supreme Being, who is without any sense organ, beyond the senses, pervasive and self-existent; who sees without eyes and hears without ears; has no intellect, but has nothing outside the scope of His knowledge; and knows all, but has no knower.[5]

Somadeva criticiizes the Pāśupatas by pointing out that religious acts are useless without knowledge and faith. He opines that if a man is devoid of knowledge, his action is barren of result: the blind may enjoy the shade of a tree, but not the beauty of its fruits. Further, knowledge is useless in the case of one who is lame, that is, unable to act, and so is action in the case of a blind unbeliever; it is the combination of knowledge, action and faith that leads to the realisation of the summum bonum.[6] Somadeva

---

1 Kauṇḍinya 2. 9 says: यष्टव्यो भगवान् महेश्वरः। यजनं भावना. Cf. गच्छंस्तिष्ठन् शयानो वा जाग्रच्चैव स्वपंस्तथा। शङ्करे भावनां कुर्याद् यदीच्छेद् योगमात्मनः॥ quoted by Kauṇḍinya on *Pāśupata Sūtras* 2. 20: नान्यभक्तिस्तु शङ्करे.

2 Kauṇḍinya 2. 15 says: अतियजनं नाम यदायतने लोके वा। तत्रायतने स्नानहसिताद्या लोके च क्राथनस्पन्दनाद्या विधिक्रिया.

3 1. 9.

4 For example, 'वामदेवाय नमो ज्येष्ठाय नमो रुद्राय नमः', 'कालाय नमः', 'कलविकरणाय नमः' 'बलप्रमथनाय नमः', 'मनोऽमनाय नमः'. The last *mantra* sums up the Pāśupata conception of God.

5 2. 15, 27.

6 ज्ञानहीने क्रिया पुंसि परं नारभते फलम्। तरोश्छायेव किं लभ्या फलश्रीर्नष्टदृष्टिभिः॥ ज्ञानं पङ्गौ क्रिया चान्धे निःश्रद्धे नार्थकृद्द्वयम्। ततो ज्ञानक्रियाश्रद्धात्रयं तत्पदकारणम्॥ P. 271.

concludes his remarks by quoting a verse, the purport of which is that knowledge without action is useless as is action without knowledge; a blind man, if he runs, comes to grief and so does a lame man, even though he has the power of seeing. उक्तं च—

हतं ज्ञानं क्रियाशून्यं हता चाज्ञानिनः क्रिया । धावन्नप्यन्धको नष्टः पश्यन्नपि च पङ्गुकः ॥ Vol.II, p. 271

THE KULĀCĀRYAS AND TRIKAMATA

Somadeva tells us that, according to the Kulācāryas, that is, Tāntrikas, salvation results from unhesitating indulgence in all kinds of food and drink, forbidden or otherwise.[1] It may be noted that another Jaina writer, Yaśaḥpāla, the author of the allegorical drama *Moharājaparājaya*, written two centuries later, gives about the same definition of the views of the Kaulas or Kulācāryas. The Kaula in this play declares that one should daily take meat and drink heavily, that being the religion taught by him, allowing free scope to one's desires.[2]

The views of the Kulācāryas are identified by Somadeva with Trikamata. According to this system, one should, after indulging in meat and drink, worship Śiva with wine in company with a female partner sitting on one's left during the rites: the worshipper is to play the rôle of Śiva united with Pārvatī and exhibit the Yonimudrā.[3] This is, generally speaking, a more or less accurate picture of Tāntric ritual as elaborated in texts like *Kulārṇavatantra* and *Kulacūḍāmaṇitantra*, although many of the details are unintelligible and obscure. The use of wine and meat is a conspicuous feature of the cult. As regards relations with the other sex, the *Kulacūḍāmaṇitantra*, for instance, gives a colourful description of the worshipper setting about the mystic rites at night in company with his partner, perfumed and dressed in red and richly adorned with gold ornaments; she sits on a cushion to his left and he gracefully clasps her around with his arm.[4] It should, however, be remembered that ceremonial worship of women of all castes without any distinction is an important feature of Tantric ritual;[5] but the use of meat and wine for religious purposes and freedom of association with women must have led to abuses, and Somadeva

---

1 'सर्वेषु पेयापेयभक्ष्याभक्ष्यादिषु निःशङ्कचित्ताद्वृत्तात् इति कुलाचार्यकाः ।' The term कुलाचार्य is met with in Tāntrik texts, e. g. in *Kulārṇavatantra*, chap. II.

2 खज्जइ मंसं अणुदिणु पिज्जइ मज्जं च मुक्कसंकप्पं । अणिवारियमणपसरो एसो धम्मो मए दिट्ठो ॥ IV. 22

3 'तथा च त्रिकमतोक्तिः—मदिरामोदमेदुरवदनस्तरसरसप्रसन्नहृदयः सव्यपार्श्वविनिवेशितशक्तिः शक्तिमुद्रासनधरः स्वयमुमामहेश्वरायमाणः कृष्णया शर्वाणीश्वरमाराधयेत् इति ।' P. 269.

4 Chap. 3. See also *Kulārṇava*, chap. 10 (भृगुवारे कुलेशानि कान्तामारूढयौवनाम् etc.).

5 Ibid. 3. 16, 17. Cf. *Kulārṇava*, chap. 11–या कचिदङ्गना लोके सा मातृकुलसंभवा ।

has no doubt based his definition of Kaula views on what he saw and heard in his own days. The *Kulārṇavatantra* (Chap. 9) says, like Somadeva, that the Kaulikas do not observe any restriction with regard to food and drink,[1] and goes on to declare that for them exists no injunction or prohibition, virtue or vice, heaven or hell.[2] But the Kaula devotee is described also as a man free from desires, ever content, impartial and chaste, without any striving and desire for heaven, and conversant with the highest truths.[3] The Kaula mystics go about the world in different guises, doing good to men, inscrutable and unperceived by others.[4] The Kaula ideal is, it is true, to eat, drink and be merry, but it is also one of concord and amity, for the Kaula is enjoined not to make any distinction between "You" and "I".[5] Salvation, according to the Kaula system, seems to be union with Śiva to be attained by knowledge, ignorance being destroyed by the performance of one's religious duties[6]. Somadeva's definition of Kaula views does not take into consideration this aspect of the cult; and he criticizes the Kaula standpoint by asserting that if salvation was the outcome of reckless living, it would sooner come to the *thugs* and butchers than to the Kaulas.[7]

Somadeva, as we have seen, treats the Kaula doctrine as identical with Trikamata, to which there is another reference in Book I. We are told that the young prince Māradatta considered his body to be divine like one initiated into the Trika doctrine.[8] The commentary of Śrutasāgara takes Trikamata to mean Śaiva doctrine; and the divine character of the body seems to be a tenet common to the Śaiva and Tāntrika systems. The *Kulārṇavatantra* (Chap. 9) says, for instance, that the body is the abode of the gods, while the Self is Lord Sadāśiva himself.[9] The doctrine is found in a more developed form in the *Sūtasaṁhitā* (belonging to the *Skandapurāṇa*), a comprehensive work of the Advaita school of Śaivism. The *Sūtasaṁhitā* says among other things that the various organs are presided

1 अपेयमपि पेयं स्यादभक्ष्यं भक्ष्यमेव च । अगम्यमपि गम्यं स्यात् कौलिकानां कुलेश्वरि ॥

2 न विधिर्न निषेधः स्यान्न पुण्यं न च पातकम् । न स्वर्गो नैव नरकः कौलिकानां कुलेश्वरि ॥ Ibid.

3 निःस्पृहो नित्यसंतुष्टः समदर्शी जितेन्द्रियः । स्वर्गहीनोऽप्रयासी च योगी परमतत्त्ववित् ॥ Ibid.

4 योगिनो विविधैर्वेशैर्नराणां हितकारिणः । भ्रमन्ति पृथिवीमेतामविज्ञातस्वरूपिणः ॥ Ibid. The expression कुलयोगी is frequently used.

5 पिबन् मद्यं वमन् खादन् स्वेच्छाचारपरायणः । अहं त्वमनयोरैक्यं भावयेन्निवसेत् सुखम् ॥ Ibid.

6 कर्मणोन्मूलितेऽज्ञाने ज्ञानेन शिवतां व्रजेत् । शिवैक्यस्यैव मुक्तिः स्यादतः कर्म समापयेत् ॥ Ibid.

7 निःशङ्कात्मप्रवृत्तेः स्याद्यदि मोक्षसमीक्षणम् । ठकसूनाकृतां पूर्वं पश्चात् कौलेष्वसौ भवेत् ॥ P. 271.

8 'सकलजनसाधारणेऽपि स्वदेहे त्रिकमतदीक्षितस्यैव देवभूयेनाभिनिविशमानस्य'. Vol. I, p. 43.

9 'देहो देवालयो देवि जीवो देवः सदाशिवः'.

over by various deities; for example, the sun is the deity of the eye, Varuṇa that of the tongue, Fire that of speech and so on. Moreover, five deities are said to abide in the body composed of the five elements; Brahman in the earthy portion, Īśvara in the airy portion, Viṣṇu in the watery portion, Rudra in the fiery portion, and Sadāśiva himself in the portion of the body composed of ether. For this reason the body, whether one's own or that of another, should be honoured as having a divine character (*devatāmaya*); no one should de despised even by mistake, and even a fool or a villain should be respected as possessing a body that is divine.[1] Similar views are expressed in the *S'ivapurāṇa* (*Sanatkumāra-saṁhitā*, Chap. 39).[2]

A passing reference to Tantric doctrine as Mantravāda dealing with the mystic diagrams or Yantras occurs in Book I.[3]

ŚAIVA DOCTRINES

Śaiva doctrines are prominently dealt with in the episode of Caṇḍakarman in *Yaśastilaka*, Book V (pp. 251, 254 ff.); and the discussion is of particular interest in view of the struggle of Jainism against the rising tide of Śaivism in certain parts of India in the age of Somadeva and after. Haraprabodha, one of the companions of Caṇḍakarman, is a Śaiva and declares that Lord Śiva has two ways of doing good to the world: the Dakṣiṇa Mārga or the Righthand Path and the Vāmamārga or the Lefthand Path.[4] Of these the Righthand Path is meant for general usage,[5] and two verses are quoted to illustrate its principles (Vol. II, p. 251):

प्रपञ्चरहितं शास्त्रं प्रपञ्चरहितो गुरुः । प्रपञ्चरहितं ज्ञानं प्रपञ्चरहितः शिवः ॥
शिवं शक्तिविनाशेन ये वाञ्छन्ति नराधमाः। ते भूमिरहिताद्बीजात् सन्तु नूनं फलोत्तमाः ॥

To these may be added another verse quoted in VI. 19 (Vol. II, p. 317):

अद्वैतान्न परं तत्त्वं न देवः शंकरात् परः । शैवशास्त्रात् परं नास्ति भुक्तिमुक्तिप्रदं वचः ॥

The first verse declares that the Śāstra, the Teacher, the true knowledge, and Śiva himself are without any connection with *prapañca* or worldly phenomena. The second verse emphasizes the organic connection between Śiva and Śakti, and declares that to accept Śiva without accepting Śakti is like expecting a harvest from seeds without the intermediary of earth.

---

1 *Yajñavaibhavakhaṇḍoparibhāga*, *Sūtagītā* 4. 22 ff. and 7. 3 ff. Cf. अतश्च भोगमोक्षार्थी शरीरं देवतामयम् । स्वकीयं परकीयं च पूजयेत्तु विशेषतः ॥ Ibid. 7. 28 etc.

2 'इदं शरीरं विप्रेन्द्र सर्वदेवमयं शृणु' etc.

3 'मन्त्रवादोक्तिष्विव विविधयन्त्रश्लाघिनीषु'. Vol. I, p. 39.

4 'भगवतो हि भर्गस्य सकलजगदनुग्रहसर्गो दक्षिणो वामश्च ।' P. 251.

5 'तत्र लोकसंचरणार्थं दक्षिणो मार्गः ।' For the Dakṣiṇa Mārga see also Chap. XIII.

The third verse declares that there is no truth higher than non-duality, no god higher than Śiva, and no science more capable of guaranteeing happiness as well as liberation than the Śaiva doctrine.

The three verses quoted by Somadeva may be said to sum up the doctrines of the Advaita school of Śaivism, as propounded in texts like the *S'ivapurāṇa*, the *Sūtasaṁhitā*,[1] and the *Iśvaragītā* incorporated in the *Kūrmapurāṇa*. The doctrines represent a Śaiva adaptation of the views of Advaita Vedānta, whose doctrine of non-duality is mentioned with approval in the *S'ivapurāṇa* (*Jñānasaṁhitā*).[2] The latter text, in one place, uses the significant expression *advaita-śaiva-veda* to denote the Śaiva system and its antagonism to the conception of *dvaita* or duality.[3] The Śaiva doctrine, as developed in the aforesaid texts, postulates absolute non-duality and denies the reality of *prapañca* and *saṁsāra*, that is, worldly phenomena and the course of mundane life.[4] Śiva alone exists self-luminous; and the universe being an outcome of his own Power, nothing exists apart from the Supreme Deity.[5] Śakti, the inherent and conscious Power of Śiva, creates the universe according to his will; and this Power, without beginning and end, is called Māyā, the cause of the material world.[6] No relationship is possible between the visible phenomena and the Supreme Soul, just as there cannot be any connection between darkness and light;[7] but the universe is ultimately merged in Śiva, just as foam and waves rise from the ocean and are merged in the ocean.[8] 'Knowledge free from worldly phenomena' (*prapañca-rahitaṁ*

---

1 Published in three Volumes in Ānandāśrama Series.

2 See Chapter 78 (परं वेदान्तिनो नित्यमद्वैतप्रतिपादिनः etc.)

3 'अद्वैतशैववेदोऽयं द्वैतं न सहते क्वचित्'. *Sivapurāṇa* (*Kailāsasaṁhitā* 10. 166). The expression शिवाद्वैत occurs in verse 96.

4 Cf. एकः स भिद्यते भ्रान्त्या मायया न स्वरूपतः । तस्माद्द्वैतमेवास्ति न प्रपञ्चो न संसृतिः ॥ *Sūtasaṁhitā* (*Jñānayogakhaṇḍa* 20. 4). स्वस्वरूपतया स्वयमेव स प्रस्फुरत्यमलः परमेश्वरः । न प्रपञ्चविभासनमस्त्यतः कस्यचिच्च न बन्धनमोचने ॥ Ibid. (*Yajñavaibhavakhaṇḍa* 15. 30).

5 अतश्च संक्षेपमिमं शृणुध्वं जगत्समस्तं चिदचित्प्रभिन्नम् । स्वशक्तिक्लृप्तं शिवमात्रमेव न देवदेवात् पृथगस्ति किंचित् ॥ Ibid. 12. 29.

6 माया माहेश्वरी शक्तिः सत्त्वादिगुणभेदतः । जीवमाक्रम्य संसारे भ्रामयत्यनिशं द्विजाः ॥…अतो मायामयः साक्षात् संसारः सर्वदेहिनाम् etc. Ibid. 2. 42 ff. आद्या सैका परा शक्तिश्चिन्मयी शिवसंश्रया ।…सैका परा च चिद्रूपा शक्तिः प्रसवधर्मिणी । विभज्य बहुधा विश्वं विदधाति शिवेच्छया ॥ सा मूलप्रकृतिर्माया त्रिगुणा त्रिविधा स्मृता । *Śivpurāṇa* (*Vāyavīyasamhitā* 5. 13 ff.)

7 यथा प्रकाशतमसोः संबन्धो नोपपद्यते । तद्वदेव न संबन्धः प्रपञ्चपरमात्मनोः ॥ छायातपौ यथा लोके परस्परविलक्षणौ । तद्वत् प्रपञ्चपुरुषौ विभिन्नौ परमार्थतः ॥ *Iśvaragītā* 2. 10, 11 (*Kūrmapurāṇa*, *Uparibhāga*).

8 यथा फेनतरङ्गादि समुद्रादुत्थितं पुनः । समुद्रे लीयते तद्वज्जगन्मय्येव लीयते ॥ *Sūtasaṁhitā* (*Jñānayogakhaṇḍa* 20. 20). It is stated in the same Chapter (verse 5) that just as the *ākāśa* is called *ghaṭākāśa* and *mahākāśa*, similarly the One Soul is called by the ignorant both Jīva and Īśvara.

jñānam) seems to refer to the state of *samādhi*, in which the devotee no longer perceives the objects of the world and becomes united with the Supreme Soul.[1] 'The Teacher free from worldly phenomena' (*prapañca-rahito guruḥ*) is the religious preceptor, who is identified with Śiva, and, in the ultimate resort, Śiva himself.[2] The indispensable and inseparable connection between Śiva and Śakti, set forth by Haraprabodha, is frequently emphasized in Śaiva texts and forms a fundamental dogma of the Śaiva system.[3]

The Vāmamārga or the Lefthand Path devised by Śiva is described as leading to pleasure as well as salvation,[4] and corresponds to the grosser aspect of the Tantric cult. The following verse is cited by Haraprabodha to illustrate the Vāmamārga (Vol II, p. 251):

अग्निवत् सर्वभक्षोऽपि भवभक्तिपरायणः । भुक्तिं जीवन्नवाप्नोति मुक्तिं तु लभते मृतः ॥

'One who is devoted to Śiva obtains pleasure in life and release on death, even though he is omnivorous like Fire.'

The verse quoted from the poet Bhāsa[5] as a further illustration of the Vāmamārga advocates the pleasures of love and wine, and completes the picture of the Path as one of gross sensualism combined with devotion to Śiva. It goes without saying that the Advaita school of Śaivism condemns the Vāmamārga as non-Vedic and hindering the rise of true knowledge.[6] The former school glorifies *bhakti*, and asserts that it is Śiva, united with Śakti, that vouchsafes joy as well as liberation, and shines in the hearts of those who are sincerely devoted to him.[7]

Śudatta's reply to Haraprabodha provides a good example of Jaina polemic against Śaivism, and enables us to have an idea of the chief points at issue between the two schools of thought. The following verse quoted by

---

1 यदा सर्वाणि भूतानि समाधिस्थो न पश्यति । एकीभूतः परेणासौ तदा भवति केवलः ॥ Ibid. (verse 25). Also सदा साक्षिस्वरूपत्वाच्छिव एवास्मि केवलः । इति धीर्या मुनिश्रेष्ठ सा समाधिरिहोच्यते ॥ Ibid.

2 सविकारान् राजसादीन् गुणान् रुन्धे व्यपोहति । गुणातीतः परशिवो गुरुरूपं समाश्रितः ॥ *Śivapurāṇa* (*Vidyeśvarasaṁhitā* 16. 84). The conception of Śiva as Ācārya occurs in Bhoja's *Tattvaprakāśa* 1. 15 (योजयति परे तत्त्वे स दीक्षयाचार्यमूर्तिस्थः).

3 Cf. न शिवेन विना शक्तिर्न शक्तिरहितः शिवः । उमाशंकरयोरैक्यं यः पश्यति स पश्यति ॥ *Sūtasaṁhitā* *Yajñavaibhavakhaṇḍa* 13. 30). एवं परस्परापेक्षा शक्तिशक्तिमतोः स्थितिः । न शिवेन विना शक्तिर्न शक्त्या च विना शिवः ॥ *Śivapurāṇa* (*Vāyavīyasaṁhitā* 5. 12). शक्तिशक्तिमदुत्थं तु शाक्तं शैवमिदं जगत् । Ibid. (verse 37).

4 'भुक्तिमुक्तिप्रदस्तु वाममार्गः परमार्थः' (Printed text reads परमार्थतः) P. 251.

5 See Chap. XVIII.

6 वामपाशुपतादीनामश्रौतानां परिग्रहः । पाञ्चरात्राश्रयश्चापि ज्ञानानुत्पत्तिकारणम् ॥ *Sūtasaṁhitā* (*Muktikhaṇḍa* 6.12).

7 भक्तियुक्तजनचित्तपङ्कजे भुक्तिमुक्तिफलदः पुरातनः । शक्तियुक्तपरविग्रहः शिवः सत्यमेव सततं प्रकाशते ॥ *Yajñavaibhavakhaṇḍa* 26. 39. The chapter in question deals with *Śivabhakti*.

Somadeva and put in the mouth of Sudatta (P. 254) records the Jaina objections to the theory of Śiva being the source of scriptural knowledge. तदुक्तम्—

वक्ता नैव सदाशिवो विकरणस्तस्मात् परो रागवान् द्वैविध्यादपरं तृतीयमिति चेत्तत् कस्य हेतोरभूत् ।
शक्त्या चेत् परकीयया कथमसौ तद्वानसंबन्धतः संबन्धोऽपि न जाघटीति भवतां शास्त्रं निरालम्बनम् ॥

The idea of the verse is that Sadāśiva cannot be the expounder of a system, since he is incorporeal nor can this rôle be attributed to the deity in his corporeal aspect, for example, to Śiva as the consort of Pārvatī, because as such he is subject to passion, which makes him unfit for the task. A third alternative is lacking; and it cannot be urged that he expounds the system by means of an extraneous Śakti or Power, because he cannot be supposed to possess any such Power owing to the absence of any integral relationship between the two. It follows therefore that the *śāstra* of the Śaivas is without any authoritative foundation.[1] This dismisses another claim of the Śaivas that a very rare *śāstra* originated from Śiva in the form of Nāda or Sound.[2]

Sudatta then points out certain inconsistencies in the Śaiva doctrine resulting from the two mutually conflicting conceptions of Śiva, the corporeal Rudra and the incorporeal Sadāśiva. The Jaina sage argues that if Rudra is regarded as omniscient, even though he is subject to passion and similar affections, that will contradict Patañjali's definition of Īśvara or the Supreme Being as one untouched by passions, acts, consequences and impressions, and hence possessing the highest degree of omniscience. It is a fallacy to associate omniscience and passion with the same person; and a conception of Rudra, worldly yet omniscient, contradicts also the assertion that Śiva possesses the qualities of freedom from passion, self-control, and omniscience besides irresistible might, contentment, supreme bliss, and untrammelled energy.[3]

Sudatta continues the argument and shows that the conception of the incorporeal Sadāśiva also involves similar contradictions. The poet Grahila,[4] for instance, in his hymn to Sadāśiva, speaks of the phallus of the god and the inability of Brahman and Viṣṇu to find out its limit, and refers also to the burning of the three cities of the demons by Śiva when the earth became his chariot, Indra his charioteer, the sun and the moon the chariot-wheels and so on.[5] Further, there is another aspect of Sadāśiva which is not in keeping with the character of an incorporeal being. Sudatta quotes in this

1 For another attack on the Śaivaśāstra see Chap. X.

2 'एवं च सतीदं न संगच्छते—अदृष्टविग्रहाच्छान्ताच्छिवात् परमकारणात् । नादरूपं समुत्पन्नं शास्त्रं परमदुर्लभम् ॥' Vol. II, p. 255.

3 "रागादिभिरुपद्रुतस्यापि रुद्रस्याप्ततायां 'क्लेशकर्मविपाकाशयैरपरामृष्टः पुरुषविशेष ईश्वर' इति, 'ऐश्वर्यमप्रतिहतं सहजो विरागः'…इति च विरुध्यते." For the verse in question see Chap. XVIII.

4 See Chap. XVIII.

5 For the verse in question see Chap. XVIII.

connection a verse, which says that a living creature is steeped in ignorance and not a master of his own destinies, and goes to heaven or hell, as *directed by Īśvara or S'iva* (Vol. II, p. 255):

अज्ञो जन्तुरनीशोऽयमात्मनः सुखदुःखयोः । ईश्वरप्रेरितो गच्छेत् स्वर्गं वा श्वभ्रमेव वा ॥

It may be noted that the verse is cited in many texts[1] as an illustration of the supreme power of God, and incorporated in the *S'ivapurāṇa*[2] to show that a sentient being is nothing but a plaything in the hand of Śiva.[3] What is important is that the Śaiva system regards Śiva as the *preraka* or *prerayitā*, the great moving or directing force of the universe.[4] Bhoktā or the Self, Bhogya or Matter and Prerayitā or the Mover are, as a matter of fact, three fundamental concepts of the Śaiva system;[5] and the moving power is known also as the Kriyāśakti of Śiva.[6] The Jainas, however, regard this as inconsistent with the conception of Śiva as the incorporeal Sadāśiva. Sudatta contends that it is impossible for the ethereal Sadāśiva to move others; and it is also doubtful whether one who is himself never moved by others should be able to move any one else.[7]

The Jainas attack also the conception of Śiva as the creator of the universe.[8] Sudatta begins his argument by quoting a verse in which Śiva is addressed as the primeval architect of the universe (P. 255):

भोग्यामाहुः प्रकृतिमृषयश्चेतनाशक्तिशून्यां भोक्ता नैनां परिणमयितुं बन्धवर्ती समर्थः ।
भोग्येऽप्यस्मिन् भवति मिथुने पुष्कलस्तत्र हेतुर्नीलग्रीव त्वमसि भुवनस्थापनासूत्रधारः ॥

The sense of the verse is that the Bhoktā or the Soul in bondage cannot evolve any change in unconscious Matter, called Bhogyā or Prakṛti; and the interaction of the two is entirely due to the initiative of Śiva, who sets in motion the process of cosmic evolution.[9] The Jainas, however, do not admit the existence of a personal creator of the universe; and Sudatta utters the following verse which sums up the Jaina objection (P. 256):

कर्ता न तावदिह कोऽपि धियेच्छया वा दृष्टोऽन्यथा कटकृतावपि स प्रसंगः ।
कार्यं किमत्र सदनादिषु तक्षकाद्यैराहृत्य चेत् त्रिभुवनं पुरुषः करोति ॥

The idea of the verse is that no one who creates the world by intellect or will

---

1 See *Naiṣadhacarita*, Trans., Appendix I, p. 509.

2 *Vāyavīyasaṁhitā*, chap. 4.

3 'लीलासाधनभूतोऽयमीश्वरस्येति सूरयः' Ibid. (verse 62).

4 Cf. माया प्रकृतिरुद्दिष्टा पुरुषो माययावृतः । संबन्धो मलकर्मभ्यां शिवः प्रेरक ईश्वरः ॥ *Śivapurāṇa* (*Vāyavīyasaṁhitā*, 1. 4. 18). सर्वेषामेव भावानामन्तरा समवस्थितः । प्रेरयामि जगत् कृत्स्नं क्रियाशक्तिरियं मम ॥ *Īśvaragītā* 6. 5.

5 भोक्ता भोग्यं प्रेरयिता मन्तव्यं त्रिविधं स्मृतम् । नातः परं विजानद्भिर्वेदितव्यं हि किंचन ॥ *Śivapurāṇa* (op. cit verse 73).

6 *Īśvaragītā* (op. cit.).

7 आकाशकल्पस्य सदाशिवस्य परंप्रति प्रेरकता न युक्ता । स्वयं पराप्रेषित एष शंभुर्भवेत् परप्रेरयितेति चिन्त्यम् ॥ P. 255.

8 Cf. *Śivapurāṇa* (*Vāyavīyasaṁhitā* I. 4. 65 ff.).

9 Cf. 'क्षोभयामि च सर्गादौ प्रधानपुरुषावुभौ' *Īśvaragītā* 6. 8. प्रकृतिः क्षरमित्युक्तं पुरुषोऽक्षर उच्यते । ताविमौ प्रेरयत्यन्यः स परः परमेश्वरः ॥ *Śivapurāṇa* (op. cit, verse 16).

has ever been seen; and if an invisible creator is postulated, even the making of a mat might be attributed to him. Further, if there is really some one who builds up the universe, there will be nothing left for carpenters and others to do![1]

Further, Sudatta contends that the conception of Īśvara is redundant, because what is called Īśvara is only another name for Karma. He quotes a verse which records the synonyms of Purākṛta or Karma done in previous births, and among these Īśvara is also included (p. 256):

विधिर्विधाता नियतिः स्वभावः कालो ग्रहश्चेश्वरदैवकर्म ।
पुण्यानि भाग्यानि तथा कृतान्तः पर्यायनामानि पुराकृतस्य ॥

It cannot be urged that Karma, being insentient, is powerless to serve as an agent for the enjoyment or suffering of others.[2] Insentient objects like jewels, magnet and wind are known to have the power of acting upon other objects, and the same is true of Karma.[3] Sudatta in this connection quotes a verse from a work named *Ratnaparīkṣā*[4] in order to prove the miraculous efficacy of jewels in counteracting evils even from a distance. However that may be, the rôle of shaping the destinies of creatures is assigned exclusively to Karma; and the position of God, even if he exists, is reduced to that of a servant.[5] The Jaina doctrine of Karma is calculated to exalt the Self and inculcate self-reliance, since each individual has to solve the problem of existence and liberation by his personal effort. The emphasis is always upon Karma; and Sudatta concludes his sermon by quoting a verse, which declares that the Self by itself acts and reaps the consequences of its deeds, by itself it passes through worldly existence, and by itself is liberated from its bonds (p. 256):

स्वयं कर्म करोत्यात्मा स्वयं तत्फलमश्नुते । स्वयं भ्रमति संसारे स्वयं तस्माद्विमुच्यते ॥

It should be noted that the universe in the Jaina view is uncreated, eternal and endless,[6] hence the objection to the theory of a personal creator, God or Śiva. It will also be seen that the controversy between Jainism and Śaivism centering round the problem of creation resolved itself into one between the theories of Karma and God; and the identifica-

---

1 The verse occurs in *Yaśastilaka* 2. 139. The theory of creation is also ridiculed in a verse in Book VIII, section 37, which says that Śiva creates the mountains and the earth as well as pots and huts! धरणीधरधरणिप्रभृति सृजति, ननु निपगृहादि गिरिशः करोति, Vol. II, p. 388.

2 'कथमचेतनं कर्म परोपभोगार्थं प्रवर्तत इति चेत्तन्न ।' P. 256.

3 रत्नायस्कान्तवातादेरचितोऽपि परं प्रति । यथा क्रियानिमित्तत्वं कर्मणोऽपि तथा भवेत् ॥ P. 256.

4 See Chap. XVIII.

5 विष्टिः कर्मकरादीनां चेतनानां सचेतनात् । दृष्टा चेष्टा विधेयेषु जगत्स्रष्टरि सास्तु वः ॥ P. 256. Ms. A remarks हरे चेष्टा भवतु वो युष्माकं स्रष्टा वृथा । सर्वेषां दास एवेति भावः ।

6 See Chap. X.

tion of Śiva with God was facilitated by the fact that the word *Īśvara* means both Śiva and God.

Another point at issue between Śaivism and Jainism is the question of omniscience; and it must be said to the credit of Somadeva that he fully reproduces the Śaiva point of view in the course of his exposition of Jaina doctrines.[1] The Śaivas point out, with reference to the Jaina conception of Tīrthaṁkara or Supreme Teacher, that the Jainas regard a human being as *āpta* or omniscient, despite the fact that it is extremely difficult for a human being to attain omniscience. Even supposing that a Tīrthakara is omniscient, it will be necessary to find out his teacher, because no man can acquire knowledge by his own effort without the help of a teacher. If it is said that the teacher of a Tīrthakara is another Tīrthakara, one will have to discover the teacher of the latter as well and so on, until we are faced with the absurdity of an endless series of Tīrthakaras and their teachers. The only way to avoid such a situation is to accept either Sadāśiva or Śiva, the consort of Pārvatī, as the teacher of a Tīrthakara; and the Śaivas in this connection cite the authority of the *Yogasūtras* 1. 26, which declare Īśvara to be the eternal teacher of all primeval teachers.[2] The Śaivas also assert that a very rare *śāstra* arose from the incorporeal and quiescent Śiva in the form of Sound, the implication being that such a Being is fit to be the *guru* of a Tīrthakara.[3] Further, they contend that there should only be one Āpta or Omniscient Being. There cannot be a multitude of *āptas* like that of other creatures; and there is no reason why there should be only twenty-four of them, that being the number of Tīrthakaras recognised by the Jainas.[4]

Somadeva replies that a Tīrthakara who possesses three kinds of supernatural knowledge is not the person to require the help of a teacher,[5] and tries to meet the Śaiva objections by showing that the Tīrthakaras are not the only persons who have attained knowledge of the highest truths by their own initiative. As an illustration of this, Somadeva cites a legend concerning the rise of the Vaiśeṣika system of philosophy, according to which the knowledge of the six categories spontaneously dawned upon the

---

1 *Yaśastilaka*, Book VI, section 2.

2 'अथैवं प्रत्यवतिष्ठासत्र:—भवतां समये किल मनुजः सन्नाप्तो भवति तस्य चाप्ततातीव दुर्घटा ।······मनुष्यस्याभिलषित· तत्त्वावबोधो न स्वतस्तथादर्शनाभावात् । परश्चेत् कोऽसौ परः । तीर्थकरोऽन्यो वा । तीर्थकरश्चेत्तत्राप्येवं पर्यनुयोगे प्रकृतमनुबन्धे तस्मादनवस्था । तदभावमाप्तसद्भावं च वाञ्छद्भिः सदाशिवः शिवापतिर्वा तस्य तत्त्वोपदेशकः प्रतिश्रोतव्यः । तदाह पतञ्जलिः—स पूर्वेषामपि गुरुः कालेनानवच्छेदात् ।' Vol. II, p. 276.

3 'अदृष्टविग्रहाच्छान्ताच्छिवात्·········' (see above). The verse is quoted twice, in Books V and VI. 2, pp. 255, 276.

4 'तथाप्तेनैकेन भवितव्यम् । न ह्याप्तानामितरप्राणिवद्गणः समस्ति । संभवे वा चतुर्विंशतिरिति नियमः कौतस्कुत इति······'

5 तत्त्वभावनयोद्भूतं जन्मान्तरसमुत्थया । हिताहितविवेकाय यस्य ज्ञानत्रयं परम् ॥ दृष्टादृष्टमवैत्यर्थं रूपवन्तमथावधेः । श्रुतेः श्रुतिसमाश्रेयं क्वासौ परमपेक्षताम् ॥ P. 277.

sage Kaṇāda in Benares; and Śiva, in the form of an owl, exhorted him to communicate the divine revelation to the Brāhmaṇas.[1] Somadeva does not mention the source of his story, but it seems to be a variation of the popular legend that Śiva, assuming the shape of an owl (*ulūka*), communicated the Vaiśeṣika philosophy to Kaṇāda, whence the name *Aulūkya* given to that system.[2] The crucial point, however, is that even the highest truths can be known by one' s own efforts without instruction by a teacher; it is therefore futile to foist an imaginary preceptor upon the Jaina Tīrthakaras. As regards their number, there is nothing abnormal about it, since there are many things in the world of which a considerable number is known to exist, for instance, lunar days, stars, planets, oceans, mountains and the rest.[3]

It may be noted that the controversy between the Śaivas and the Jainas on the subject of omniscience is at the bottom a contest between two rival conceptions, the S'aivas reserving the term *sarvajña* 'omniscient' for Śiva and the Jainas doing the same for each one of their Tīrthakaras. The Jaina standpoint will be clear from their definition of Āpta.[4] As regards Śiva, he is consistently called *sarvajña* in Śaiva texts,[5] and omniscience is one of the five *śaktis* attributed to him.[6]

The Jainas attack also the doctrine of Śiva and Śakti, to which prominence is given in Śaiva works. Somadeva attempts to prove that the relationship between Śiva and Śakti is a fiction, because the supposed connection can be described neither as *saṁyoga* 'conjunction' nor as *samavāya* 'inherence'. He points out that, according to the Yauga doctrine, that is, the Nyāya theory,[7] *saṁyoga* or conjunction is possible only between two substances; but *śakti* or potency is not a substance, hence there can be no *saṁyoga* between Śiva and Śakti. Nor can *samavāya* or inherence be supposed to be the basis of relationship between Śiva and Śakti. According to the Vaiśeṣika theory, *samavāya* or inherence is the permanent relation between two things which are not known to exist separately, for example, a quality and the qualified. Śakti is, however, known to exist and operate

---

1 'कथमन्यथा स्वत एव संजातषट्पदार्थावसायप्रसरे कणचरे वाराणस्यां महेश्वरस्योलूकसायुज्यसरस्येदं वचः संगच्छेत— ब्रह्मतुला नामेदं दिवौकसां दिव्यमद्भुतं ज्ञानं प्रादुर्भूतमिह त्वयि तद्वत्स विधत्स्व विप्रेभ्यः।' Vol. II, p. 277.

2 Cf. *Naiṣadhacarita* 22. 36 (औलूकमाहुः खलु दर्शनं तत्).

3 नियतं न बहुत्वं चेत् कथमेते तथाविधाः। तिथिताराग्रहाम्भोधिभूभृत्प्रभृतयो मताः॥ P. 277.

4 See Chap. X.

5 Cf. *Sūtasaṁhitā: Yajñavaibhavakhaṇḍa* 22.6; *Śivamāhātmyakhaṇḍa* 2.7; *Muktikhaṇḍa* 2.10.

6 सर्वकर्तृत्वरूपा च सर्वज्ञत्वस्वरूपिणी। पूर्णत्वरूपा नित्यत्वव्यापकत्वस्वरूपिणी॥ शिवस्य शक्तयः पञ्च संकुचद्रूपभास्कराः। *Śivapurāṇa* (*Kailāsasaṁhitā* 10. 158).

7 On the use of the expression *Yauga* in this sense see G. N. Kaviraja in Sarasvati Bhavana Studies, Vol. III, p. 84.

separately from Śiva; so there can be no *samavāya* relationship between the two.[1]

There is no doubt that Somadeva gives a fairly comprehensive account of the philosophical controversies of the Śaivas and the Jainas current in his own age. The Śaivas attacked the Jaina theory of Arhat or the Perfect Saint and tried to establish the superiority of Siva to any such finite personality, whether called Arhat or Tīrthaṁkara. Somadeva, as we have seen, sums up some of the Śaiva objections; and we find a similar attack on the Jaina conception of the Arhat also in the *Īśāna-śivagurudevapaddhati*,[2] a comprehensive work on Śaiva doctrine and ritual, which records the teachings of a line of Śaiva Yogins, who were influential in many parts of India during the ninth, tenth and eleventh centuries.[3] The rivalry of these two important sects covering a considerable period lends more than an academic interest to their controversies in the field of speculative thought.

Somadeva condemns certain fundamental concepts of the Śaiva and Tāntric systems in *Yaśastilaka* VIII. 39.[4] They are chiefly *Jyotiḥ*, *Bindu*, *Nāda*, *Kuṇḍalī*, and *Nirbījīkaraṇa*. *Jyotiḥ* '*Light*' is one of the mystic names of Śiva. In Sanskrit the word is neuter, and it is usual to designate the Śiva-tattva as masculine and feminine and neuter to denote its comprehensive and transcendental character.[5] The Praṇava or Om syllable, which is the expression of Śiva, is also called Jyotiḥ.[6] Kalā is one of the thirty-six principles of the Śaiva system, and denotes the agency which unfolds the power of human beings to act.[7] In other words, Kalā is the source of the limited power of action possessed by the Paśus or creatures in bondage.[8]

Nāda and Bindu are two concepts always mentioned together, but not specifically recognised by certain texts, as pointed out by Rāghavabhaṭṭa in his commentary on *S'āradātilaka* 1. 7. The *S'ivapurāṇa*[9] says that, at the beginning of creation, Śakti, the latent energy of Śiva, becomes manifest by the will of Śiva; and when Śakti is stirred up by the creative urge of Śiva,

1 'संबन्धो हि सदाशिवस्य शक्त्या सह न भिन्नस्य संयोगः। शक्तेरद्रव्यत्वात्। द्रव्ययोरेव संयोग इति योगसिद्धान्तः। समवायलक्षणोऽपि न संबन्धः शक्तेः पृथक्सिद्धत्वात्। अयुतसिद्धानां गुणगुण्यादीनां समवायसंबन्धः इति वैशेषिकमैतिह्यम्।' Vol. II, p. 277.

2 See *Kriyāpāda* 1. 39 ff. See also next Chapter and Chap. XIII.

3 See Introduction to Part II. (Trivandrum Sanskrit Series).

4 ज्योतिर्बिन्दुः कला नादः कुण्डलीवायुसंचरः।...See below.

5 The comm. on *Tattvaprakāśa* 1. 3 says: एकमेव शिवतत्त्वं पुंलिङ्गस्त्रीलिङ्गनपुंसकलिङ्गशब्दैर्व्यवह्रियते, and remarks: तदुक्तं बृंहण्याम्—शिवो देवः शिवा देवी शिवं ज्योतिरिति त्रिधा। अलिङ्गमपि यत्तत्त्वं लिङ्गभेदेन कथ्यते॥

6 Rāghavabhaṭṭa says in his comm. on *Śāradātilaka* 1. 11: गोरक्षसंहितायामपि "इच्छा क्रिया तथा ज्ञानं गौरी ब्राह्मी तु वैष्णवी। त्रिधा शक्तिः स्थिता यत्र तत् परं ज्योतिरोमिति॥"

7 *Tattvaprakāśa* 3. 6. says 'व्यञ्जयति कर्तृशक्तिं कलेति तेनेह कथिता सा'.

8 'किञ्चित् कर्तृत्वहेतुः' *Śivapurāṇa* (*Kailāsasaṁhitā* 10. 161).

9 Ibid. *Vāyavīyasaṁhitā* 5. 18 ff.

there arises Nāda whence emerges Bindu. From Bindu arises Sadāśiva, from the latter Maheśvara, and from the latter again Vidyā, the expressive energy of Śiva consisting of the letters of the alphabet. The foregoing account adds Nāda and Bindu to the five usually accepted Śuddhatattvas, viz. Śiva, Śakti, Sadāśiva, Īśvara or Maheśvara and Vidyā. The *Tattvaprakāśa* of Bhoja, for instance, recognises only these five, and remarks that Nāda and Bindu are included in the Śivatattva.[1]

It is in some of the Tantras that we find an exhaustive treatment of Nāda and Bindu.[2] Roughly speaking, Nāda represents the awakening and Bindu the active aspect of Śakti.[3] According to *S'āradātilaka* 1.7, from Siva emerges Śakti, from Śakti Nāda, and from Nāda Bindu.[4] The *Prapañcasāratantra* (1. 42, 43), explaining the next stage of evolution, says that the Bindu splits up into three portions: Bindu and Nāda (different from the first two) and Bīja, of which Bindu represents Īśvara or consciousness and Bīja unconscious matter, while Nāda represents Puruṣa or the Self, the blend of consciousness with unconscious Matter. While the original Bindu is in the process of disintegration, there arises an indistinct sound, and this is known as Śabdabrahma, the consciousness abiding in the creatures of the universe[5] and the basic foundation of sounds and their meanings. According to Rāghavabhaṭṭa, Nāda and Bindu represent the indistinct, undifferentiated and pervasive sound emerging at the beginning of the process of cosmic evolution initiated by Śiva, and it is this sound that is known as Śabdabrahma.[6] There are also other interpretations, but there is no doubt that Nāda and Bindu were fundamental concepts of the Śaiva system in Somadeva's time.

Although Śabdabrahma is universal and all-pervading, it abides in the form of Kuṇḍalī, better known as Kuṇḍalinī.[7] Kuṇḍalinī is the stored up energy inherent in each individual and the force that produces all forms of sound from the primitive inarticulate murmur to organised literary speech.

---

1 'नादो बिन्दुः सकलौ सदा शिवं तत्त्वमाश्रितौ कथितौ' 2. 11

2 See, for example, *Śāradātilaka*, Chap. 1 and the citations in Rāghavbhaṭṭa's commentary thereon.

3 Rāghavabhaṭṭa (op. cit.) says (1. 7)—तदुक्तं प्रयोगसारे—"नादात्मना प्रबुद्धा सा निरामयपदोन्मुखी। शिवोन्मुखी यदा शक्तिः पुंरूपा सा तदा स्मृता"·········अन्यत्रापि "अभिव्यक्ता परा शक्तिरविनाभावलक्षणा।·········प्रयाति बिन्दुभावं च क्रियाप्राधान्यलक्षणम्" इति।

4 "·········परमेश्वरात्। आसीच्छक्तिस्ततो नादो नादाद्बिन्दुसमुद्भवः॥"

5 Cf. 'चैतन्यं सर्वभूतानां शब्दब्रह्मेति मे मतिः' *Śāradātilaka* 1. 13.

6 'सृष्ट्युन्मुखपरमशिवप्रथमोल्लासमात्रे अखण्डोऽव्यक्तो नादबिन्दुमय एव व्यापको ब्रह्मात्मकः शब्दः शब्दब्रह्मेत्यर्थः' (1. 12).

7 Ibid. 25. 35. Mādhavācārya in his comm. on *Sūtasaṁhitā* (*Śivamāhātmyakhaṇḍa* 5. 9) says 'स एव शब्दब्रह्मात्मको रवो जगदुपादानं बिन्दुतादात्म्येन सर्वगतोऽपि प्राणिनां मूलाधारेऽभिव्यज्यत इत्युक्तम्—स तु सर्वत्र संस्यूतो मूले व्यक्तस्तथा पुनः। आविर्भवति देहेषु प्राणिनामर्थविस्तृतः॥ (*Prapañcasāra* 1. 63) देहेष्विति मूलाधारप्रदेशे·········'

The seat of Kuṇḍalinī is the plexus known as Mūlādhāra,[1] and it is described also as being enclosed within the Suṣumṇā artery.[2] Kuṇḍalinī is visualised as a coiled up (*kuṇḍalībhūta*) serpent; but Rāghavabhaṭṭa, commenting on *S'āradātilaka*, 1. 51[3] points out that there is an artery shaped like a coiled up serpent in the *mūlādhāra*, and this, propelled by nerve-force (Vāyu), travels to all parts of the body. This movement of Kuṇḍalinī under the action of Vāyu is called *guṇana*,[4] and this is what Somadeva means by *kuṇḍalī-vāyu-saṁcara* in *Yaśastılaka* VIII.39. Lastly, Nirbījīkaraṇa is a Yogic process aimed at complete mastery over the body.[6]

In addition to the doctrines outlined above, stray allusions to philosophical topics are occasionally found in *Yaśastilaka* in the course of descriptions, often in artificial comparisons based on word-play. They are of lesser importance and belong to a type common in Kāvya literature.[7]

---

1 'गुदमेढ्रमध्योऽपि मूलाधारः ।' See Padmapāda's comm. on *Prapañcasāra* 2. 43.

2 'मूलाधारे विसरति सुषुम्नावेष्टनी मुहुः' Ibid. 2. 51.

3 'तत्र मूलाधारे कुण्डलीभूतसर्पवन्नाडी वर्तते । तन्नुमध्ये वायुवशादस्याः सञ्चरणमेव गुणनम् ।' *Śāradātilaka* 1. 57 says 'गुणिता सर्वगात्रेषु कुण्डली परदेवता'.

4 For the significance of Vāyu see Introduction to *Prapañcasāratantra* in *Tantrik Texts*, ed. Avalon.

6 A marginal note in Ms. A on a verse in *Yaśastilaka*, Book VI, section 10, p. 296, explaining the expression विज्ञान ('ज्ञानविज्ञानयोस्तेषां विपश्चिन्न च विभ्रमेत्'), tells us that विज्ञान refers to Nirbījīkaraṇa, which is a process of expelling the seminal fluid through the eyes, navel etc. A similar note on the relevant verse in Book VIII, section 32, says the same thing, and adds that the process in question helps one to conquer death by dint of constant practice. Somadeva says: ज्योतिर्बिन्दुः कला नादः कुण्डलीवायुसंचरः । मुद्रामण्डल-चोद्यानि निर्बीजीकरणादिकम् ॥ नाभौ नेत्रे ललाटे च ब्रह्मग्रन्थौ च तालुनि । अग्निमध्ये रवौ चन्द्रे लूतातन्तौ हृदङ्कुरे ॥ मृत्युंजयं यदन्तेषु तत्तत्त्वं किल मुक्तये । अहो मूढधियामेष नयः स्वपरवञ्चनः ॥ *Yaśastilaka* Vol. II, p. 393. Ms. A says नेत्रनाभिप्रमुखमार्गेण शुक्रनिष्कासनकर्म मृत्युंजयं भवति साधनाभ्यासेन । नासिकायामग्नितत्त्वं वर्तते । रवौ दक्षिणनाड्यां चन्द्रे वामनाड्याम् । लूतातन्तौ लिङ्गविषये । हृदये छिद्रं विनापि तदा काले मेदसदृशग्रन्थिः स्यात्. It will be seen that Somadeva uses symbolic terms of the Tantra, and the process of Nirbījīkaraṇa has in view various openings of the body. The Jaina author condemns such Yogic practices.

7 For example, '**सुगतागमा** इवाविकल्पप्रधानाः'; '**सांख्या** इव समाश्रितप्रकृतयः'; '**पारिपुङ्गः** (i. e. बौद्ध) इवानात्मनीनवृत्तिः' Book I, pp. 12, 13, 41; '**समीक्षासिद्धान्तः** (Sāṁkhya doctrine) इव कपिलकुल-कान्तः'; '**मीमांसेव** निरूप्यमाणनियोगभावनादिप्रपञ्चा'; '**पिटकत्रयपद्धतिरिव योगाचार**गोचरा'; '**अमरगुरुभारतीव** निवारितपरलोकदर्शना'; '**योगस्थितिरिव** विहितवृषभेश्वरावतारा' Book V, pp. 170, 246. A marginal note in Ms A explains योगस्थिति as referring to the Yaugas or the followers of the Nyāyā–Vaiśeṣika school, who were generally Śaivas. The Vaiśeṣika theory of salvation comes in for further criticism in a verse occurring in Book VIII, section 37, wherein it is stated that he who does not admit the existence of knowledge and other attributes in the emancipated self cannot postulate the existence of the Self at all, because there cannot be a Self without attributes, just as there cannot be fire without heat विज्ञानप्रमुखाः सन्ति विमुक्ति न गुणाः किल यस्य नयोऽत्र वाञ्छि । तस्यैष पुमानपि नैव तत्र दाहादृहनः क इहापरोऽत्र । *Yaśastilaka*, Vol. II, p. 388. Ms. A explains विमुचि as मुक्तजीवे, and remarks: उष्णत्वं विना यथाग्निर्नास्ति तथा विज्ञानादिगुणान् विना आत्मापि नास्ति. नय is taken as referring either to Śaiva or Kaṇāda.

CHAPTER IX

Schools of Thought

In the preceding chapter we have summarized the doctrines of the various non-Jaiña systems recorded or discussed by Somadeva in *Yaśastilaka*; and we may here enumerate the different systems mentioned by the author and bring together some additional information bearing on the character and historical position of certain of these schools of thought. Towards the beginning of Book VI Somadeva mentions the following schools: Saiddhānta Vaiśeṣikas, Tārkika Vaiśeṣikas, Followers of Kaṇāda; Pāśupatas; Kulācāryas;[1] Sāṁkhyas, Kāpilas; Buddhists mentioned separately as (1) the Disciples of Daśabala, (2) Tāthāgatāḥ, and (3) those who preach the doctrine of the Void; Jaiminīyas; Bārhaspatyas or the followers of the Lokāyata system; Followers of the Vedānta philosophy mentioned twice as Vedāntavādins and Brahmādvaitavādins.

It will be seen that some of the schools of thought are mentioned more than once by way of demonstrating different aspects of the views held by them. In addition to these, Somadeva records Śaiva doctrines and the views of those who believed in the efficacy of Vedic sacrifices. The followers of these schools of thought were obviously contemporaries of Somadeva and so prevailed in the tenth century. It is interesting to compare the non-Jaina systems described in *Yaśastilaka* with the non-Buddhist systems recorded in the ancient Tamil Buddhist Kāvya *Maṇimēkhalai*. Chapter XXVII of that work considers ten such systems: (1) the Pramāṇavāda of the Vaidika systems, (2) Śaivavāda (3) Brahmavāda (4) Nārāyaṇīya or Vaiṣṇavavāda (5) Vedavāda (6) Ājīvaka (7) Nirgrantha i. e. Jaina (8) Sāṁkhya (9) Vaiśeṣika and (10) Bhūtavāda or the Lokāyata system.[2] If we compare the two lists, we shall find that Vaiṣṇavavâda is a notable omission in Somadeva's summary, while the latter makes only a passing reference to the Ājīvikas without mentioning anything about their doctrines.

It may also be pointed out that Somadeva makes a general reference to the four systems (Samayas) in *Yaśastilaka*, II. 32 and the four systems and the six schools of philosophy (Darśanas) in Book IV.[3] Śrutasāgara in his commentary on II. 32 explains the four Samayas as the Jaina, Śaiva, Vaidika,

1 It is not clear why Somadeva connects Trika-mata with the doctrines of the Kulācāryas. The Trika system usually refers to the Kashmir School of S'aivism.

2 Aiyangar: *Manimekhalai in its historical setting*, p. 189 ff.

3 चत्वार एते सहजाः समुद्रा यथैव लोके ऋतवोऽपि षड्‌ च । चत्वार एते समयास्तथैव षड्‌ दर्शनानीति वदन्ति सन्तः ॥ Vol. II, p. 114.

and Bauddha systems; while in his commentary on Book IV he takes them to mean the Jaina, Jaiminīya, Buddhist and Śaiva systems, and explains the six Darśanas as these four plus the Sāṁkhya and Lokāyata systems. It is difficult to say how far this interpretation is correct; but the six Darśanas referred to by Somadeva seem to be identical with the six Tarkas enumerated by Rājaśekhara in *Kāvyamīmāṁsā* (Chap. 2), viz. the Jaina and Buddhist Darśanas and the Lokāyata forming one group, and the Sāṁkhya, the Nyāya, and the Vaiśeṣika forming another group.[1] It is probable that this classification of the Darśanas was popular it the tenth century, the age of Rājaśekhara and Somadeva. It may be noted in this connection that the Darśanas seem to have been variously classified at different epochs: for example, in *Vāyupurāṇa* 104. 16 the six Darśanas are stated to be Brāhma, Śaiva, Vaiṣṇava, Saura, Śākta, and Ārhata i. e. Jaina.[2] Similarly, in *Jñānārṇavatantra* 16. 131–134 we find mentioned the Śaivadarśana, Śāktadarśana, Brāhmadarśana, Vaiṣṇavadarśana, Sūryadarśana, and Bauddhadarśana. Certain points relating to some of the systems criticized by Somadeva require further elucidation.

SAIDDHĀNTA VAIŚEṢIKAS

The mention of two distinct schools of Vaiśeṣika philosophy, Saiddhānta and Tārkika, in *Yaśastilaka* is a noteworthy feature; and, as we have seen, the former school laid stress on the worship of Śiva and faith in him, while the latter represented the orthodox school with emphasis on Dharma and the knowledge of the categories. We do not know when the Saiddhānta school came into being, but the followers of this school seem to be the same as the Vṛddha Vaiśeṣikas mentioned by Vidyānanda (9th century) in his *Āptaparīkṣā*, wherein he remarks that they propound the existence of Maheśvara or Śiva in reality, just as they believe in the reality of Substances, Qualities, Actions, Generality, Particularity, Inherence etc., that is, the categories recognised by the Vaiśeṣika system as such.[3] The same work tells us that a certain section of the Vaiśeṣikas (unlike the orthodox school) postulates the existence of consciousness even in the liberated soul:[4] it is not the pure and infinite consciousness of the Self recognised by the Sāṁkhyas, but *jñānaśakti* or intellectual power;[5] and Maheśvara, like the liberated soul,

---

1 'द्विधा चान्वीक्षिकी पूर्वोत्तरपक्षाभ्याम्। अर्हद्भदन्तदर्शने लोकायतं च पूर्वः पक्षः। सांख्यं न्यायवैशेषिकौ चोत्तरः त इमे षट् तर्काः।'

2 ब्राह्मं शैवं वैष्णवं च सौरं शाक्तं तथार्हतम्। षड् दर्शनानि चोक्तानि स्वभावनियतानि च ॥

3 'यथैव हि महेश्वरस्य स्वरूपतः सत्त्वं वृद्धवैशेषिकैरिष्यते तथा पृथिव्यादिद्रव्याणां रूपादिगुणानामुत्क्षेपणादिकर्मणां सामान्यविशेषसमवायानां च प्रागभावादीनामपीष्यत एव' (under verses 59-76).

4 'ज्ञानशक्तिस्तु निःकर्मणोऽपि कस्यचिन्न विरुध्यते चेतनात्मवादिभिः कैश्चिद्वैशेषिकसिद्धान्तमभ्युपगच्छद्भिर्मुक्तात्मन्यपि चेतनायाः प्रतिज्ञानात्' (under verse 11).

5 The orthodox Vaiśeṣika view of salvation is of course far different. See preceding Chapter.

possesses this power, although he is incorporeal and untouched by Karmas.[1] This school of Vaiśeṣikas which holds that the soul is ever conscious and has the power of knowledge even in the state of liberation, and seems also to believe in Śiva, might be allied to the Saiddhānta Vaiśeṣikas mentioned by Somadeva.

Guṇaratna tells us in his commentary on *Ṣaḍdarśanasamuccaya* (Chap. 2) that the Naiyāyikas are Śaivas and the Vaiśeṣikas are Pāśupatas. The Pāśupatas were a Śaiva sect, but it is impossible to rely on Guṇaratna's statement for the purpose of determining the religious affiliation of the Vaiśeṣika centuries earlier than his time. Somadeva's reference to the Tārkika Vaiśeṣikas shows that there were adherents of the system who were not worshippers of Śiva or Paśupati. Among the medieval exponents of the Vaiśeṣika system Vyomaśiva and Udayana were Śaivas; while Śrīdhara pays homage to Brahmā, Viṣṇu and Śiva separately or conjointly in the opening verses of the different sections of his *Nyāyakandalī*. Apart from the personal beliefs of individual thinkers, Vyomaśiva distinctly says in his commentary on the *Praśastapāda Bhāṣya* in the section on Viparyaya (P. 543) that the Supreme Śiva is different from the worldly souls, and His worship leads to beatitude: this, he says, is the salutary teaching of the Vaiśeṣikas.[2] It would thus appear that the views of Vyomaśiva were closely allied to those of the Saiddhānta Vaiśeṣikas, who held that faith in Śiva was an essential means to final release. Further, while commenting upon the opening verse of the *Praśastapāda Bhāṣya*, Vyomaśiva, unlike Udayana and Śrīdhara, explains the term *Īśvara* in the phrase *praṇamya hetumīśvaram* as Maheśvara, that is, Śiva.[3] Considering the devotion to Śiva evinced by Vyomaśiva in his commentary, it will not be wrong to associate him with the Saiddhānta school of Vaiśeṣika philosophers. As regards the term *Maheśvara*, it occurs even in the *Praśastapāda Bhāṣya*, but here it means the Supreme Lord or the great God who initiates the process of creation. Udayana, for example, explains Maheśvara as *mahān īśvaraḥ* in the relevant section of his commentary on the Bhāṣya, and takes it to mean Parameśvara.[4]

---

1 'चेतना च ज्ञानशक्तिरेव न पुनस्तद्व्यतिरिक्तचिच्छक्तिरपरिणामिन्यप्रतिसंक्रमादर्शितविषया शुद्धा चानन्ता च यथा कापिलैरुपवर्ण्यते तस्याः प्रमाणविरोधात्। तथा च महेश्वरस्य कर्मभिरस्पृष्टस्यापि ज्ञानशक्तिरशरीरस्यापि च मुक्तात्मन इव प्रसिद्धा।'

2 'यदि वा संसार्यात्मनां नानात्वं परमशिवश्चैतेभ्यो भिन्नस्तदाराधनाच्चास्मदादेः श्रेयो भवतीत्येवं हितमुपदिशत्सु वैशेषिकेषु अहितमिति ज्ञानं विपर्ययः।'

3 "ईश्वरशब्दश्च अन्यत्र वर्तमानोऽपि ज्ञानप्रस्तावात् महेश्वर एव वर्तते। 'शंकरात् ज्ञानमन्विच्छेत्' इति वचनात्।"

4 "अन्ये हीश्वरा जगदेकदेशपतय इन्द्रवरुणयमादयः। स पुनः कृत्स्नस्यैव जगतः अतो महानीश्वरः" P. 91. 'परार्थप्रवृत्तेन परमेश्वरेणाधिष्ठितैः पृथिव्यादिभिर्विश्वमारभ्यते' P. 97.

BUDDHISTS

The Buddhist doctrines of salvation mentioned by Somadeva have been explained in the preceding chapter with reference to ancient texts, but it is more likely that Somadeva derived his information from later works prevalent in his time. He says, for instance, '*nairātmyādi-nivedita-saṁbhāvanāto bhāvanātaḥ*' which seems to refer to what is called Nairātmya-bhāvanā in later Buddhist texts. Śāntarakṣita, for example, who belongs to the eighth century, deals fully with the doctrine of Nairātmya in *Tattvasaṁgraha* (vv. 3488 ff). He tells us that the notions of 'I' and 'mine', known as *sattvadṛṣṭi*, are the source of endless suffering, and the only antidote against *sattvadṛṣṭi* is the realisation of Nairātmya (non-existence of the Self); suffering ceases when the conception of 'I' and 'mine' ceases to exist, and when suffering ends there is no more birth. Final release is the outcome of absolute freedom from rebirth, and the realisation of Nairātmya is the peerless gateway to the supreme beatitude. Because, liberation takes place only when egoism comes to an end; and egoism never comes to an end so long as one believes in a Self.[1]

Śāntarakṣita declares that the Buddha is omniscient, because it is he who for the first time propounded the doctrine of Nairātmya, and that is also why he is supreme among the founders of religious systems.[2] Mere realisation of Nairātmya, however, does not lead to the desired goal. What is essential is fervent and constant contemplation (Bhāvanā), ranging over a long period, in the course of which the knowledge of all objects flashes across the mind: it is all-comprehensive Nairātmyabhāvanā of this type that is cultivated by the kind-hearted devotee who desires to do good to the world. For we are told that there are two hindrances to the realisation of the truth, *kleśāvaraṇa* and *jñeyāvaraṇa*: the first is nothing but the *kleśas* (lust, hatred and delusion) that obstruct the vision of the truth, and the second consists in the inability to recognise and comprehend the nature of the true and the false. Direct realisation of Nairātmya does away with *kleśāvaraṇa*, but *jñeyāvaraṇa* cannot be got rid of without fervent, constant and prolonged cultivation of the principle of Nairātmya. The Bhāvanā is practised by some in anxiety for their own release from the sufferings of the world and

1 आत्मात्मीयदृगाकारसत्त्वदृष्टिः प्रवर्तते। अहं ममेति माने च क्लेशोऽशेषः प्रवर्तते ॥ सत्त्वदृक् प्रत्यनीकं च तन्नैरात्म्यनिदर्शनम् । अभ्यासात् सात्म्यमायाते तस्मिन् सा विनिवर्तते ॥ तन्मूलक्लेशराशिश्च हेत्वभावात् प्रहीयते। तस्मिन्नसति तद्धेतुर्न पुनर्जायते भवः ॥ तदत्यन्तविनिर्मुक्तेरपवर्गश्च कीर्त्यते। अद्वितीयशिवद्वारमतो नैरात्म्यदर्शनम् ॥ सर्वेषामपि तीर्थ्यानामहङ्कारनिवर्तनात् । मुक्तिरिष्टात्मसत्त्वे च नाहङ्कारो निवर्तते ॥

2 एतच्च सुगतस्येष्टमादौ नैरात्म्यकीर्तनात्। सर्वतीर्थकृतां तस्मात् स्थितो मूर्ध्नि तथागतः॥ v. 3340.

the cycle of births; while others, philanthropic by nature, are moved to pity by the miseries of the world, and without taking thought of their own interest, consider all worldly beings as their own selves and strive for the salvation of all: kindness is the motive which prompts such men to betake themselves to Nairātmya-bhāvanā. All this will be clear from the following extracts from the commentary of Kamalaśīla on *Tattvasaṁgraha*:

या सादरनैरन्तर्यदीर्घकालविशेषणा भावना सा करतलायमानग्राह्यावभासमानज्ञानफला तद्यथा कामातुरस्य कामिनीभावना···सर्वाकारसर्वमतनैरात्म्यभावना कारुणिकस्येति स्वभावहेतुः । (v. 3339) क्लेशज्ञेयावरणप्रहाणतो हि सर्वज्ञत्वम्, तत्र क्लेशा एव रागादयो भूतदर्शनप्रतिबन्धभावात् क्लेशावरणमुच्यन्ते । दृष्टस्यापि हेयोपादेयतत्त्वस्य यत् सर्वाकारापरिज्ञानं प्रतिपादनासामर्थ्यं च ज्ञेयावरणम् । तत्र क्लेशावरणस्य नैरात्म्यप्रत्यक्षीकरणात् प्रहाणिः । ज्ञेयावरणस्य तु तस्यैव नैरात्म्यदर्शनस्य सादरनिरन्तरदीर्घकालाभ्यासात् ।·········ये तावज्जात्यादिदुःखोत्पीडितमानसाः संसारादुत्त्रस्तमनसस्तदुपशममात्मनः प्रार्थयन्ते, तेषां······संसाराद्भयमेव नैरात्म्यभावनार्थित्वनिमित्तम् । ये तु गोत्रविशेषात् प्रकृत्यैव परहितकरणैकाभिरामाः संस्कारादिदुःखत्रितयपरिपीडितं जगदवेक्ष्य कृपापरतन्त्रतया तद्दुःखदुःखिनः स्वात्मनि व्यपेक्षामपास्य सकलानेव संसारिण आत्मत्वेनाभ्युपगतास्तत्परित्राणाय प्रणिदधते तेषां करुणैव भावनाप्रवृत्तिनिमित्तम् । (v. 3339)

Among non-Buddhist writers earlier than Somadeva, Jayanta gives a clear and succinct account of the theory of Nairātmya as part of the Buddhist argument in *Nyāyamañjarī* (chap. 7), and his remarks may be compared with the statements of Śāntarakṣita reproduced above and the views cited by Somadeva in *Yaśastilaka*, Book V.[1] Jayanta says:

तस्मादुत्सृज्यतामेष मूर्धाभिषिक्तः प्रथमो मोह आत्मग्रहो नाम । तन्निवृत्त्या चात्मीयग्रहोऽपि विरंस्यति अहमेव न किं ममेति । तदिदमहंकारममकारग्रन्थिप्रहाणेन नैरात्म्यदर्शनमेव निर्वाणद्वारमालम्ब्यताम् । तस्य स मार्गः क्षणिकपदार्थनिश्चयः । क्षणिकेषु हि सर्वभावेषु निराश्रयेषु ज्ञानस्याप्याश्रयविरहात् कुतस्त्यमात्मकल्पनमिति ।

Somadeva, as we have seen, criticizes the Buddhist doctrine of Bhāvanā in *Yaśastilaka* VI. 1.[1] An earlier criticism of the doctrine is that of Vidyānanda in *Tattvārtha-śloka-vārtika* 1. 71:

भावनाप्रकर्षपर्यन्तस्तत्सिद्ध्युपाय इति चेत् न, भावनाया विकल्पात्मकत्वेनातत्त्वविषयायाः प्रकर्षपर्यन्तप्राप्तायास्तत्त्वज्ञानवैतृष्ण्यस्वभावोदयविरोधात् । न हि सा श्रुतमयी तत्त्वविषया श्रुतस्य प्रमाणत्वानुषंगात् । ··· सर्वथा भावनायास्तत्त्वविषयत्वायोगात् । तत्त्वप्रापकत्वाद्वस्तुविषयत्वमिति चेत्, कथमवस्त्वालंबना सा वस्तुनः प्रापिका ।

Somadeva gives the following definition of the Buddhist view of salvation in *Yaśastilaka* VI. 1: *nirāśraya-cittotpatti-lakṣaṇo mokṣaḥ* and quotes the two verses ending with *kleśa-kṣayāt kevalam eti śāntim.*[1] The medieval interpretation of this is found in Vādideva Sūri's *Pramāṇa-naya-tattvālokālaṁkāra* 2. 26:

सौगतास्तु केचिन्निराश्रयचित्तसंतानोत्पत्तिर्मोक्ष इत्याचक्षते । तत्राविद्यातृष्णारहितं चित्तं निराश्रयमित्यभिधीयते । अविद्या रागद्वेषाभिलाषः । तृष्णा तु भाविभोगाभिलाषः ।

1 See preceding Chapter.

It will be seen that *nirāśraya* is explained as free from *avidyā* (lust and hatred) and *tṛṣṇā* (craving); and the emergence of a stream of consciousness free from these impurities is described as Mokṣa. This is similar to the ancient teaching that Nirvāṇa is nothing but the end of *kleśas* (lust, hatred and delusion).

In *Yaśastilaka*, Book V, Somadeva gives another definition of the Buddhist view of salvation. Mokṣa is here described as Nirodha consisting in the emergence of a state of mind free from the *āśravas* following the destruction of the notion of the Self.[1] Āśrava is an irregular Buddhist Sanskrit form of the Pāli Āsava, there being four *āsavas*: *kāmāsava*, *bhavāsava*, *diṭṭhāsava* and *avijjāsava* (sensuality, lust for life, speculation and ignorance).[2] Freedom from the Āśravas, which are generally taken to mean the cravings that produce an intoxicating effect on the mind, constitutes the the Buddhist ideal of salvation, known also as Nirodha or cessation. Haribhadra says in *Ṣaḍdarśana-samuccaya* (verse 7) that *nirodha* is *mokṣa*; and Guṇaratna in his commentary thereon explains it as a mental state free from the *kleśas*, that is, lust, hatred and delusion. We thus come back to the old conception of the destruction of the *kleśas*; and it is obvious that the two definitions of the Buddhist view of salvation given by Somadeva do not materially differ from each other.

In Buddhist literature, Nirvāṇa is defined as Nirodha (cessation) in *Milindapañha* III. 6. It is said that inasmuch as the wise man neither takes pleasure in the senses and in the objects of sense nor continues cleaving to them. "in him craving ceases, and by the cessation of craving grasping ceases, and by the cessation of grasping becoming ceases, and when becoming has ceased birth ceases, and with its cessation old age and death, grief, lamentation, pain, sorrow and despair cease to exist." In this way the cessation of all that aggregation of pain is brought about. "Thus is it that cessation is Nirvāṇa."[3] The end of cravings, the absence of passion, Nirodha and Nirvāṇa are mentioned together.[4]

---

1 'विगलिताग्रहे चात्मग्रहे निराश्रवचित्तोत्पत्तिलक्षणो निरोधापरनामपक्षो मोक्षः स्वलक्षणेक्षिणामक्षूणः ।' *Yaśastilaka*, Vol. II p. 252. This is followed by the verse यथा स्नेहक्षयाद्दीपः प्रशाम्यति निरन्वयः। तथा क्लेशक्षयाज्जन्तुः प्रशाम्यति निरन्वयः ॥ See preceding Chapter.

2 See Rhys Davids: *Pali-English Dictionary* under *āsava*.. cf. भिक्षोः क्षीणाश्रवस्य *Divyāvadāna*, p. 542.

3 'तस्स तं अनभिनन्दतो अनभिवदतो अनज्झोसाय तिट्ठतो.तण्हा निरुज्झति, तण्हानिरोधा उपादाननिरोधो, उपादाननिरोधा भवनिरोधो, भवनिरोधा जातिनिरोधो, जातिनिरोधा जरामरणसोकपरिदेवदुक्खदोमनस्सुपायासा निरुज्झन्ति । एवमेतस्स केवलस्स दुक्खक्खन्धस्स निरोधो होति । एवं खो महाराज निरोधो निब्बानं'ति ।' See also *The Questions of King Milinda*, p. 106. *Sacred Books of the East*, Vol. XXXV.

4 'तण्हक्खयो विरागो निरोधो निब्बानं'ति ।' Ibid. IV, 8, 90.

There seem to have been at least two conceptions of Buddhist salvation current in the medieval period. The first is the emergence of a stream of consciousness free from all impurities, and corresponds to the view recorded by Somadeva. Kamalaśīla says in his commentary on *Tattavasaṁgraha* (verse 151) that the practice of Yoga brings about the disappearance of Avidyā followed by the rise of an undefiled stream of consciousness leading to Apavarga or final release:

तस्याश्चाविद्याया योगाभ्यासादसमर्थतरतमक्षणोत्पादक्रमेण व्यपगमात् परिशुद्धज्ञानसन्तानोदयादपवर्गप्राप्तिरित्यतो बन्धमोक्षव्यवस्था युक्तिमती ।

This view is recorded also by Vyomaśiva in the introduction to his commentary on the *Praśastapāda Bhāṣya*, wherein he says that, according to some, the supreme beatitude consists in consciousness, free from the passions, emerging as a result of meditation on Nairātmya and the momentary character of things:

अन्ये तु अस्थिरादिभावनावशात् रागादिवियुक्तज्ञानोत्पत्तिः निःश्रेयसमिति मन्यन्ते । तथाहि सर्वं क्षणिकमिति भावयतो विषयेषु आसक्तिर्व्यावर्तते ······ । तथा सर्व निरात्मकमिति भावनायां नाहं परः न ममायमिति परिग्रहद्वेषाभावे भवत्येव विशुद्धचित्तसंतानोत्पत्तिरिति ।

The second view of Buddhist salvation prevalent in the medieval period, although not recorded by Somadeva, is that Mokṣa is nothing but the complete annihilation of the stream of consciousness, comparable to the going out of a lamp. Vādideva Sūri (op. cit.) mentions this view as that of a certain section of Buddhists along with the former doctrine. He says:

अपरे पुनः प्रदीपनिर्वाणवत् सर्वथा चित्तसन्तानोच्छेदो मोक्ष इति संगिरन्ते ।

Vyomaśiva (op. cit.) explains it along with the other view:

तथा च पटाद्यर्थस्य प्रतिषेधात् सर्वं शून्यमिति च । एवं हि दुःखस्य समुदयनिरोधमार्गेषु विशिष्टज्ञानं निःश्रेयसकारणमिति । तथाहि दुःखं रूपादिस्कन्धपञ्चकं तस्य समुदयः कारणम् ।··· तयोर्निरोधो विनाशः तस्योपायो मार्गः इत्येषु विशिष्टज्ञानवशात् शुद्धचित्तसंतानतदुच्छेदो वा निःश्रेयसमिति युक्तम् ।

The opinion is recorded also by Bhāskara in his *Brahmasūtra Bhāṣya* 2. 2. 18:

ग्राह्यग्राहकाकारविमुक्ता संवित्संततिर्निर्वातस्थप्रदीपवदासंस्कारक्षयात् क्षणपरंपरयावतिष्ठते । संस्कारक्षये सा प्रदीपवदेव निर्वाणमृच्छति । सेयमभावप्राप्तिरपवर्ग इति मन्यन्ते । अपरे तु सन्तत्यविच्छेदमिच्छन्ति ।

Siddharṣi (*Upamiti-bhava-prapañcā kathā*, Book IV) and Guṇaratna (comm. on *Ṣaḍdarśana-samuccaya*, v. 11) attribute the doctrine in question to the Sautrāntika school of Buddhism:

सौत्रान्तिकमतं पुनरिदम् । रूपवेदनाविज्ञानसंज्ञासंस्काराः सर्वशरीरिणामेते पञ्च स्कन्धा विद्यन्ते । न पुनरात्मा । त एव हि परलोकगामिनः । तथा क्षणिकाः सर्वे संस्काराः······सन्तानोच्छेदो मोक्ष इति ।

Both the views are mentioned together by Jayanta in *Nyāyamañjarī* (chap. 9):

निर्वाणादिपदाख्येयमपवर्गं तु सौगताः । सन्तत्युच्छेदमिच्छन्ति स्वच्छां वा ज्ञानसन्ततिम् ॥

VEDĀNTISTS

The school of Vedānta prevalent in Somadeva's time was the Advaita school; and he records the views of the Vedāntavādins or the Brahmādvaitavādins. He refers to Śaṁkarācārya, asserting that the Buddha's doctrine was imitated by the latter[1]. The allegation that the great philosopher was a Buddhist in disguise seems to have been widely current by the middle of the tenth century. Somadeva appears to have been acquainted with the writings of the school of Śaṁkara; and his statement of the ultimate goal according to the Brahmādvaitavādins runs thus: 'यथा घटविघटने घटाकाशमाकाशीभवति तथा देहोच्छेदात् सर्वः प्राणी परे ब्रह्मणि लीयते ।' This reminds one of the following verses of Śaṁkara's *Sarva-vedānta-siddhāntasāra-saṁgraha*:

घटाभावे घटाकाशो महाकाशो यथा तथा । उपाध्यभावे त्वात्मैष स्वयं ब्रह्मैव केवलम् ॥ 695
यत्र यत्र मृतो ज्ञानी परमाक्षरवित् सदा । परे ब्रह्मणि लीयेत न तस्योत्क्रान्तिरिष्यते ॥ 1000.

Sureśvarācārya says in his *Naiṣkarmyasiddhi* II. 68:

यथा विशुद्ध आकाशे सहसैवाभ्रमण्डलम् । भूत्वा विलीयते तद्वदात्मनीहाखिलं जगत् ॥

The doctrine of the Vedānta recorded by Somadeva is summed up also in the following verse quoted in the *Māṭharavṛtti* on *Sāṁkhyakārikā* (39):

देहे मोहाश्रये भग्ने युक्तः स परमात्मनि । कुम्भाकाश इवाकाशे लभते चैकरूपताम् ॥

ŚAIVAS

An interesting feature of Somadeva's treatment of Śaiva doctrines is the light thrown by it on the controversy between the Śaivas and the Jainas on the subject of omniscience and creation.[2] The first is claimed by the Śaivas for Śiva or Maheśvara, while it is reserved by the Jainas for their Arhat; and as for creation, attributed by the Śaivas to Śiva, it is altogether denied by the other sect. The roots of this controversy go to earlier times, and that it is older than the middle of the tenth century is certain. Vidyānanda who belongs to the ninth century tries to refute *S'aṁkara-mata*, Śaiva doctrine, in his *Āptaparīkṣā*[3], and rejects the claim of Maheśvara to be regarded as the creator of the universe and the omniscient author of a system teaching the way to salvation (*mokṣa-mārga*). It will be out of place to analyse his argument; but in dealing with this topic Vidyānanda and Somadeva supplement each other and record valuble information on the

---

1 'द्वैताद्वैताश्रयः शाक्यः शंकरानुकृतागमः' VI. 2. Vol. II, p. 276.

2 See preceding Chapter.

3 'सांप्रतं शंकरमतमाशंक्य दूषयन्नाह' etc.

subject. Vidyānanda's views are partially referred to by Anantavīrya in his commentary on Māṇikyanandi's *Parīkṣāmukhasūtra* (Pratyakṣoddeśa);[1] and it may be pointed out that most of our knowledge of the Śaiva-Jaina controversy is derived from Jaina works.

The background of the controversy between the Śaivas and the Jainas mentioned above is provided by Kumārila's well-known attack on the conception of an Omniscient Being; and the questions involved are part of a larger issue which brought several schools of thought into the arena of philosophical controversy. Kumārila regarded omniscience as something impossible; and instead of positing an omniscient author of the Vedas, he maintained that they were eternal and not the composition of a personal author. Kumārila's views may be studied in *S'lokavārtika* (*Codanāsūtra*) and specially in the verses quoted from him by Śāntarakṣita in the last section of *Tattvasaṁgraha*, many of them being not found in the extant *S'lokavārtika*. It is important to note that Kumārila in the course of his argument insisted on the absurdity of the Buddhist and Jaina notions that the Buddha and the Arhat respectively were Omniscient Beings. The Buddhist reply to this is elaborately given by Śāntarakṣita in *Tattvasaṁgraha*; and the earliest Jaina reply to Kumārila is probably that of Akalaṁka (8th century) in his *Nyāyaviniścaya* (chap. 3). Kumārila, for example, had written in *S'lokavārtika* (2. 141, 142):

एवं यैः केवलं ज्ञानमिन्द्रियाद्यनपेक्षिणः । सूक्ष्मातीतादिविषयं जीवस्य परिकल्पितम् ॥
नर्ते तदागमात् सिध्येन्न च तेनागमो विना । दृष्टान्तोऽपि न तत्रान्यो नृषु कश्चित् प्रवर्तते ॥

Akalaṁka replied to this as follows in *Nyāyaviniścaya* (vv. 412, 413):

एवं यत् केवलज्ञानमनुमानविजृम्भितम् । नर्ते तदागमात् सिध्येन्न च तेन विनागमः ॥
सत्यमर्थबलादेव पुरुषातिशयो मतः । प्रभवः पौरुषेयोऽस्य प्रबन्धोऽनादिरिष्यते ॥

Not only Akalaṁka but other Jaina scholars have tried to refute Kumārila's views, and this explains the large number of quotations from Kumārila found in later Jaina philosophical literature, e. g., in Vidyānanda's *Aptaparīkṣā*, *Aṣṭasahasrī* and *Tattvārtha-śloka-vārtika* (under *sūtra* 1. 29), Abhayadeva's commentary on *Sammatitarka*, *Nyāya-kumuda-candra* and other works. The bitterness of the Jainas against the Mīmāṁsā school for attacking their fundamental doctrine of the Omniscient Being is shown in Siddharṣi's *Upamiti-bhava-prapañcā-kathā* (chap. 4), which declares that the Mīmāṁsā is not a philosophical system at all; and after enumerating six non-Jaina systems including the Mīmāṁsā, Siddharṣi excludes the latter from the field of speculative thought, although he finds room for the materialistic

---

1 'यच्च महेश्वरस्य क्लेशादिभिरपरामृष्टत्वं निरतिशयत्वमैश्वर्याद्युपेतत्वं तत् सर्वमपि गगनाब्जसौरभव्यावर्णनमिव निर्विषयत्वादुपेक्षामर्हति ।'

Lokāyata system.[1] There is no trace of any such bitterness against the Mīmāṁsā in Somadeva's *Yaśastilaka*, as we find here the Śaivas replacing the Mīmāṁsakas as adversaries of Jaina doctrines.

The controversy about omniscience was further complicated by the Naiyāyikas entering the lists in defence of the doctrine. Like the Buddhists and the Jainas, they upheld the theory of omniscience as against the Mīmāṁsakas; and we find, for instance, Jayanta quoting and criticising Kumārila's views in his *Nyāyamañjarī* (chap. 2) and establishing the theory that the adepts in Yoga possess the unhampered faculty of pure and universal knowledge.[2] The Naiyāyikas, however, declare God to be the omniscient creator of the universe and the author of the Vedas. Vātsyāyana, indeed, attributes the authorship of the Vedas to 'trustworthy persons' (Āptāḥ) in his Bhāṣya on *Nyāyasūtras* 2. 1. 68, and does not say that God is their author. Uddyotakara in his *Nyāyavārtika* calls the author of the Vedas a superior individual (Puruṣa-viśeṣa), which might mean God, this being the designation applied to God in *Yogasūtras* 1. 24. The later exponents of the Nyāya system, Jayanta, Vācaspati and Udayana, however, maintain that the omniscient God is the creator of the universe as well as the author of the Vedas. Jayanta, for example, says in his *Nyāyamañjarī* (chap. 4):

कर्ता य एव जगतामखिलात्मवृत्तिकर्मप्रपञ्चपरिपाकविचित्रताज्ञः ।
विश्वात्मना तदुपदेशपराः प्रणीतास्तेनैव वेदरचना इति युक्तमेतत् ॥

The Mīmāṁsā objections to the Nyāya conception of an omniscient Creator are fully stated in Maṇḍana's *Vidhiviveka* (P. 210 ff.).[3] A later writer Śālikānātha, an authoritative exponent of the Prābhākara school of Mīmāṁsā, tries to refute the theory of the omniscience of God in *Prakaraṇapañcikā* (chap. 7). He argues that it is the cycle of tradition (*vṛddha-paramparā*), without any beginning, that fixes the meaning of words and not the significance supposed to be attached to them by God at the beginning of creation. Further, the idea of personal authorship is not compatible with the authoritative character of the Veda which deals with supernormal things.[4] Śālikānātha probably belongs to the tenth century,[5] but in this century the position of the Nyāya-vaiśeṣika school was so strong that

1 अर्वाक्कालिकमेतद्धि मीमांसकपुरं मतम् । तेन दर्शनसंख्यायामेतल्लोकैर्न गण्यते ॥

2 तदेवं क्षीणदोषाणां ध्यानावहितचेतसाम् । निर्मलं सर्वविषयं ज्ञानं भवति योगिनाम् ॥

3 Cf. Handiqui: *Naiṣadhacarita*, Appendix I, p. 505.

4 'न चेश्वरस्य सर्वज्ञानमपि सिध्यति ज्ञानहेत्वभावेन ज्ञानाभावनिश्चयात् । तेनानादिरेव वृद्धपरम्परा शब्दार्थावगमे हेतुर्न सृष्ट्यादावीश्वरकृतः सङ्केतः । ········एवं पुरुषस्य धर्मप्रतीतिं प्रति शब्दमन्तरेणोपायाभावान्न, पौरुषेयत्वे वेदस्यापूर्वात्मके वेदार्थे प्रामाण्योपपत्तिरित्यपौरुषेयत्वाश्रयणम् ।'

5 G. N. Kaviraja: Introduction to *Kusumāñjalibodhanī* (*Sarasvati Bhavana Texts*).

Mīmāṁsā theories were not likely to wield any great influence. Be that as it may, having established the existence of an Omniscient Being, the Naiyāyikas turn against the Buddhists and the Jainas, and deny that the Buddha or the Arhat can ever be called omniscient; and their attitude, on the whole, is one of hostility towards the non-Brahmanical systems. Vācaspati says in his *Nyāyavārtika-tātparya-ṭīkā* that Buddha and Ṛṣabha are known to be the authors of the Buddhist and Jaina scriptures respectively; but as they are not the creators of the universe, like God, how can they be regarded as omniscient?[1] In his commentary on the *Yogasūtra Bhāṣya* also (1. 24, 25) he rejects the claims of the founders of systems like the Buddha, the Arhat, Kapila and others to be regarded as omniscient beings. Further, the Naiyāyikas just mentioned give a new turn to the old Nyāya theory that the Vedas are authoritative, because they are the utterances of a trustworthy person (Āpta); and argue therefrom that the Vedas are the utterances of a Trustworthy Being, because they are accepted by the majority of the people (*mahājana*), and what is not declared by a Trustworthy Being is not accepted by the majority of the people. This is exactly what Udayana says in the *Kiraṇāvalī* commentary on the Praśastapāda Bhāṣya.[2] Jayanta also says that it is possible to speak of anything as being declared by a Trustworthy Being (Āpta) only when it is well-known among and accepted by the majority of the people.[3] He explains Mahājana i. e. the great mass or the majority as those who follow the Varṇāśrama order prevalent in the Aryan country, that is, the Vedic order of society founded on the division of castes and the stages of life, and makes a distinction between Mahājana and Vṛnda, the group or the minority, such as the Buddhists. The latter might claim their *vṛnda* to be the *mahājana* in order to establish the authoritative character of their scriptures, but it is not possible to raise a minority (Vṛnda) to the status of a majority (Mahājana), and the latter always avoids and never approves any scriptures that are opposed to the Vedas.[4] Jayanta therefore concludes that scriptures other than the Vedas cannot be regarded as being composed by a trustworthy individual, because they lack support among the large mass of the people.[5]

---

1 'तत्र शाक्याद्यागमानां बुद्धर्षभादयः प्रणेतार इति स्फुटतरमस्ति स्मरणं न तूक्तलक्षण ईश्वरस्तेषां कर्त्तेति। न चैते शौद्धोदनिप्रभृतयः तनुभुवनादीनां कर्त्तारो येन सर्वज्ञा इति निश्चीयेरन्।'

2 'आप्तोक्ता वेदाः महाजनपरिगृहीतत्वात्। यत् पुनर्नाप्तोक्तं न तत् महाजनपरिगृहीतम्।'

3 'महाजनप्रसिद्ध्यनुग्रहे हि सति सुवचमाप्तोक्तत्वं भवति नान्यथा' *Nyāyamañjarī*, Book IV.

4 'बौद्धादयो बुद्धादीनाप्तान् स्वागमप्रामाण्यसिद्धये वदन्ति ते महाजनमपि निजं तत्सिद्धये वृन्दादिकं वदेयुरेव कस्तत्र प्रतीकारः, उच्यते, चातुर्वर्ण्यं चातुराश्रम्यं च यदेतदार्यदेशप्रसिद्धं स महाजने उच्यते..........चातुर्वर्ण्यचातुराश्रम्यरूपश्चैष महाजनो वेदप्रथमप्रवृत्तः..........अत एव न निजो महाजन उत्थापयितुं शक्यते वृन्दकादिः किं त्वयमेव चातुर्वर्ण्यादिमहाजनः स चैष महाजनो वेदविरुद्धमागमं परिहरत्येव नानुमोदते' Ibid.

5 'अत एवंविधाया महाजनप्रसिद्धेरागमान्तरेष्वदर्शनान्न तेषामाप्तप्रणीतत्वम्।'

Similarly, Vācaspati in his *Tātparyaṭīkā*, makes a sharp distinction between the Vedas and the scriptures of the Buddhists, the Digambara Jainas and others, and observes that no scriptures other than the Vedas are accepted by the majority of the people and mentioned as being composed by God. The Vedas alone, composed by God as they are, maintain the entire social order and provide instruction in the means to attain the good and shun the evil. On the contrary, the teachings of the Buddha and others do not uphold the social order, nor are they accepted by the great mass of the people. Owing to this general reproach, they are followed only by a few barbarians, vilest among men and just like animals, and hence it is impossible to regard such teachings as being propounded by any trustworthy individual.[1]

It will be seen that the arguments of the Naiyāyikas are not only directed against the non-Brahmanical systems as such but against the Jaina conception of the Arhat as the omniscient and trustworthy guide. They seem to put forward a rival Āpta theory to discredit that of the Jainas, and thus reinforce the Śaivas in their attack on the fundamental Jaina doctrine of the omniscient Arhat. It is difficult to determine the chronological relations of the Śaivas and the Naiyāyikas, but they might represent a parallel movement: Vācaspati and Jayanta belong to the ninth century and Udayana to the tenth, and we have seen that the Śaiva-Jaina controversy recorded by Vidyānanda and Somadeva falls in the same period. Further, as Haribhadra tells us in *Ṣaḍdarśanasamuccaya*, the Naiyāyikas were generally Śaivas; and we know, in fact, that the leading Nyāya-Vaiśeṣika philosophers of the period of revival, Bhāsarvajña, Jayanta, Udayana, and Vyomaśiva were all Śaivas. It is also noteworthy that the Naiyāyikas often identify God (Īśvara) with Śiva or Maheśvara. Jayanta does so in *Nyāyamañjarī* (chap. 3);[2] while Bhāsarvajña says in *Nyāyasāra* that salvation is the outcome of the vision of Śiva.[3] The verse *sarvajñatā tṛptiranādibodhaḥ......ṣaḍāhuraṅgāni Maheśvarasya* cited by the Śaivas to illustrate the greatness of Śiva is quoted by Udayana in *Nyāyakusumāñjali* (Book V) in support of the argument for the existence of God; and Udayana's own lines at the end of Book I

देवोऽसौ विरतप्रपञ्चरचनाकल्लोलकोलाहलः ।
साक्षात् साक्षितया मनस्यभिरतिं बध्नातु शान्तो मम ॥

---

1 'न चान्य आगमो लोकयात्रामुद्वहन् महाजनपरिगृहीत ईश्वरप्रणीततया स्मर्यमाणो दृश्यते ।......वेदा एव सकललोकयात्रामुद्वहन्तो हिताहितप्राप्तिपरिहारोपायमुपदिशन्त ईश्वरप्रणीता इत्यवगच्छामः ।...............बुद्धादिवाक्यानि तु न लोकयात्रामुद्वहन्ति । न च तत्र लौकिकानामविगानं.........तस्माद्विगानात् कैश्चिदेव म्लेच्छादिभिर्मनुष्यापसदैः पशुप्रायैः परिग्रहात् नैतेषामाप्तोक्तत्वसंभवः' 2. 1. 68.

2 'रागादयः कथं ते स्युर्नित्यानन्दात्मके शिवे'; 'यस्येच्छयैव भुवनानि समुद्भवन्ति, तिष्ठन्ति यान्ति च पुनर्विलयं युगान्ते। तस्मै समस्तफलभोगनिबन्धनाय, नित्यप्रबुद्धमुदिताय नमः शिवाय ॥' etc.

3 'शिवदर्शनान्मोक्ष इति'.

may be compared with some of the doctrinal verses of the Śaiva school quoted in the preceding chapter. The identity of Śiva with Īśvara seems to have been an accepted fact; and as late as the twelfth century Vādideva Sūri freely uses the term Śiva and its equivalents in his detailed criticism of the Nyāya conception of God in *Pramāṇa-naya-tattvālokālaṁkāra* 2. 26. But in spite of the affinities between the Śaivas and the Nyāya school, the former had an independent system with doctrines of their own; and while the Nyāya school maintained that God was the author of the Vedas, the Śaivas attributed their Śāstras to the omniscient Śiva, and claimed that the Vedas, too, were created by him. It is noteworthy that the *Īśānaśivagurudeva-paddhati* (Kriyāpāda, chap. I) quotes various Śaiva texts to prove that Śiva is not only the author of the Śaiva Āgamas but of the Vedas.[1] The claim was not probably repugnant to the Naiyāyikas who were, generally speaking, Śaivas; and the interconnection of the two schools accounts for the fact that the *Īśānaśivagurudevapaddhati* (op. cit.) quotes a well-known verse of Jayanta's *Nyāyamañjarī*,[2] declaring Parameśvara (God) to be the author of the Vedas, in support of the Śaiva claim that Śiva was their author.

SĀṀKHYAS

We have reproduced Somadeva's criticism of Sāṁkhya doctrines in the preceding chapter, and may here cite another criticism of Sāṁkhya views by a Jaina writer, Devasena, a senior contemporary of Somadeva, who wrote his *Darśanasāra* at Dhārā in 933 A. D.[3] He says in his *Bhāvasaṁgraha* that according to the Sāṁkhya system, Prakṛti does everything and the Self is subject to neither virtue nor sin: this is a negation of moral responsibility and leads to vice and corruption. The Sāṁkhyas, according to Devasena, are addicted to worldly pleasures, consummate drunkards, and devoid of compassion for living creatures; they are given to stealing, reject virtue, and indulge in evil practices.

जीवो सया अकत्ता भुत्ता ण हु होइ पुण्णपावस्स । इय पयडिऊण लोए गहिया वहिणी सधूया वि ॥ १७९ ॥
एए विसयासत्ता कग्गुम्मत्ता य जीवदयरहिया । परतियधणहरणरया अगहियधम्मा दुरायारा ॥ १८० ॥

With this view of Sāṁkhya philosophy may be compared that of Āsuri in the episode of Caṇḍakarman in *Yaśastilaka* towards the end of Book

---

1 E. g., अत्र किरणे—"पुंसामनुग्रहार्थं तु परोऽप्यपरतां गतः । कृत्वा मन्त्रात्मकं देहं वक्ति तन्त्राण्यनेकधा ॥" × × × स्वायम्भुवे—"पुनः स्वेच्छावतारेषु तन्त्रं पाशुपतं तथा । वाकुलं सोमतन्त्रं च जगाद परमेश्वरः ॥ × × × तस्मादत्यन्तमाप्तेन शिवेन श्रुतयोऽखिलाः । प्रणीताः सर्वकर्त्रेति प्रमाणं जायते सताम् ॥" × × × तद्यथा—"ब्रह्मा भूत्वा जगत् सर्वं सदेवासुरमानुषम् । यत् सृजत्यम्बुमध्यस्थं तस्मै ब्रह्मात्मने नमः ॥" इति । एतस्मादपि वेदानां वक्ता ज्ञेयो महेश्वरः ॥ ६१ ॥

2 तथा च न्याये—"वेदस्य पुरुषः कर्ता नहि यादृशतादृशः । किंतु त्रैलोक्यनिर्माणनिपुणः परमेश्वरः ॥" *Nyāya-mañjarī*, Chap. III.

3 See Introduction to नयचक्रसंग्रहः p. 12 (*Māṇikacandra Jaina Granthamālā*).

V.[1] The evidence of Devasena and Somadeva points to the fact that there may have been some degeneration in the moral tone of the Sāṁkhyas in their time, but the ethical ideal of the Sāṁkhya school is manifest from the conception of the Sāttvika form of Buddhi, as propounded in *Sāṁkhyakārikā* (23). As regards the charge that the Sāṁkhyas are devoid of compassion for living creatures, it is belied by their view that animal slaughter in Vedic sacrifices is productive of sin, a point elaborated in the *Māṭharavṛtti*. It is noteworthy that the Jaina Guṇaratna Sūri tells us in his commentary on Haribhadra's *Ṣaḍdarśanasamuccaya* (chap. 3) that the Sāṁkhyas are spiritualists averse to the Vedic cult involving killing of animals, and he mentions in this connection certain devices adopted by them to avoid injury to living creatures, similar to those used by the Jaina monks. Somadeva, on the other hand, classes the Sāṁkhyas with the Buddhists, the Cārvākas, and the adherents of the Vedic, Śaiva, and medical systems, and advises people to abstain from flesh-eating by rejecting the views of all these schools (*Yaśastilaka* VII. 24. Vol. II, p. 331):

तच्छाक्यसांख्यचार्वाकवेदवैद्यकपर्दिनाम् । मतं विहाय हातव्यं मांसं श्रेयोऽर्थिभिः सदा ॥

Obviously the systems mentioned above permitted the eating of animal food; and the Sāṁkhya attitude towards flesh-eating may have been similar to that of the Buddhists, in spite of the repugnance to the slaughter of animals, common to both schools.[2] Somadeva, as we shall see, condemns the Buddhists for eating flesh, and this is probably the reason why Devasena likewise describes the Sāṁkhyas as devoid of compassion for living creatures.

BĀRHASPATYAS

The Bārhaspatyas, as we have seen, are called Nāstikas by Somadeva; and in *Yaśastilaka*, Book V, Caṇḍakarman who expounds their views is described as an exponent of Lokāyata doctrines.[3] Siddharṣi says in his *Upamiti-bhava-prapañcā kathā* that the Bārhaspatyas are the inhabitants of the Lokāyata City.[4] That the Lokāyata was a prominent system in the tenth century and thereabouts is certain. Siddharṣi includes it among the principal non-Jaina systems described by him in his allegorical romance (Book IV); and in the Kudlur Plates of the Ganga king Mārasiṁha, dated 963 A. D., a famous Jaina teacher is described as *Lokāyata-loka-sammata-matiḥ*, 'one whose talents are appreciated by the adherents of the Lokāyata system.' The

---

1 See Chap. VIII.

2 See Chap. XIII. The Pāśupata views on the subject are very similar. See below.

3 'प्रयुक्तलोकायतमतधर्मा' Vol. II, p. 259.

4 लोकायतमिति प्रोक्तं पुरमत्र तथापरम् । बार्हस्पत्याश्च ते लोका ये वास्तव्याः पुरेऽत्र भोः ॥ Book IV.

views of the Bārhaspatya school are discussed by Vimuktātman in *Iṣṭasiddhi* VII. 18,[1] a work composed between 850 and 1050 A. D.[2]

In spite of frequent references to the Lokāyatikas or the Cārvākas, as they are popularly called, in Indian philosophical literature, no systematic work of this school has come down to us, which we can point out as the source of the statements of Somadeva and other scholars who have dealt with Lokāyata doctrines. That there was a work called the *Bārhaspatya Sūtra* seems certain and possibly it was quite brief. Bhāskara in his *Brahmasūtra Bhāṣya* 3. 3. 53 refers, like Śaṁkara, to the Lokāyatikas, and quotes some aphorisms of the Bārhaspatya school. He says:

तथा बार्हस्पत्यानि सूत्राणि—पृथिव्यप्तेजो वायुरिति तत्त्वानि, तत्समुदाये शरीरेन्द्रियविषयसंज्ञा, तेभ्यश्चैतन्यं, किण्वादिभ्यो मदशक्तिवद्विज्ञानमिति ।

The first three of the aphorisms cited above are reproduced also in Vidyānanda's *Tattvārtha-śloka-vārtika* 1. 104 with slight variations:

पृथिव्यापस्तेजो वायुरिति तत्त्वानि, तत्समुदायः शरीरेन्द्रियसंज्ञाविषयः, तेभ्यश्चैतन्यम् ।

Bhāskara and Vidyānanda are assigned to the ninth century, and it may be assumed that the Bārhaspatya Sūtras were current in their time. In addition to the Sūtras quoted by them, the following Lokāyata aphorisms and dicta are cited in Kamalaśīla's commentary on Śāntarakṣita's *Tattvasaṁgraha* (vv. 1858, 1872):

तथाहि तस्यैतत् सूत्रम्—'परलोकिनोऽभावात परलोकाभावः' इति । तथाहि—'पृथिव्यापस्तेजो वायुरिति चत्वारि तत्त्वानि, तेभ्यश्चैतन्यम्' इति । तत्र केचिद्वृत्तिकारा व्याचक्षते—उत्पद्यते तेभ्यश्चैतन्यम्, अन्ये अभिव्यज्यत इत्याहुः । (Under v. 1858).

× × × × × × × × × ×

यथोक्तम्—'एतावानेव पुरुषो यावानिन्द्रियगोचरः' तथा 'पुनरुक्तदेशान्तरं कालान्तरमवस्थान्तरं वा परलोक' इति । (Under v. 1872).

Śāntarakṣita quotes a Lokāyata aphorism in verse 1864 and attributes it to Kambalāśvatara:

कायादेव ततो ज्ञानं प्राणापानाद्यधिष्ठितात् । युक्तं जायत इत्येतत् कम्बलाश्वतरोदितम् ॥

Kamalaśīla remarks: तथा च सूत्रम्—कायादेवेति । कम्बलाश्वतरोदितमिति. As pointed out by G. N. Kaviraj,[3] *S'āṁkara Bhāṣya* on the *Vedāntasūtras* 3. 3. 53 cites the following Lokāyata aphorisms: 'तेभ्यश्चैतन्यम्' 'मदशक्तिवद्विज्ञानम्' 'चैतन्यविशिष्टः कायः पुरुषः', and Sadānanda in *Advaita-brahma-siddhi* cites two more: 'काम एवैकः पुरुषार्थः' 'मरणमेवापवर्गः'. It will be seen that the followers of the Lokāyata school recognise four elements only, but Guṇaratna tells us in his commentary on the relevant

---

1 अत्राहुर्बार्हस्पत्याः—भेदेऽभेदेऽप्ययुक्तत्वान्मुक्तेः पुंसोऽप्यदर्शनात् । देहाद्येवास्ति दृष्टत्वान्नात्मा मुक्तिश्च नेति चेत् ॥

2 See Introduction to the work in *Gaekwad's Oriental Series.*

3 *Sarasvati Bhavana Studies*, Vol. III, p. 68.

section of Haribhadra's *Ṣaḍdarśana-samuccaya* that certain among them include Ākāśa as the fifth element. In *Yaśastilaka* VIII. 37[1] Somadeva mentions only four elements in connection with the system of Bṛhaspati, who is described as attributing consciousness to earth, air, water and fire, but not to the Self.[2]

Apart from aphorisms, a collection of verses containing Lokāyata doctrines seems to have long existed, and such verses are occasionally met with in Indian philosophical literature. One such verse, namely,

एतावानेव पुरुषो यावानिन्द्रियगोचरः । भद्रे वृकपदं ह्येतद् यद्वदन्ति बहुश्रुताः ॥

is cited by Candrakīrti (6th century) in his commentary on Nāgārjuna's *Mūla-madhyamaka-kārikās* (Chap. 18); while this as well as an accompanying verse[3] is quoted in Haribhadra's *S'aḍdarśanasamuccaya* (vv. 81, 82). A Lokāyata verse is quoted also by Somadava in *Yaśastilaka*, Book V, p. 253:

यावज्जीवेत् सुखं जीवेन्नास्ति मृत्योरगोचरः । भस्मीभूतस्य शान्तस्य पुनरागमनं कुतः ॥

It is an oft-quoted verse and cited among earlier writers by Jayanta in *Nyāyamañjarī* (Chap. 7).

Among early works the famous Mahāyāna text *Saddharma-puṇḍarīka*, prior to the third century A. D., alludes to the Lokāyata system at least twice;[4] while the interesting summary of Lokāyata views in Vātsyāyana's *Kāmasūtra* is reproduced by Somadeva in *Yaśastilaka*, Book IV, P. 92.[5] Bāṇa in his *Kādambarī* refers to the teachings of the system as promoting sinful tendencies;[6] while in *Harṣacarita*, Book VIII, the Lokāyatikas are mentioned among the adherents of diverse schools of thought who studied and taught in the hermitage of Divākaramitra in the Vindhya forest.

Somadeva's discussion of Lokāyata views in *Yaśastilaka*, Books V and VI, is an important contribution to our knowledge of the subject.

---

1 भूपवनवनानलतत्त्वकेषु धिषणो निगृणाति विभागमेषु । न पुनर्विदि तद्विपरीतधर्मधाम्नि ब्रवीति तत्तस्य कर्म ॥ Vol. II, p. 388. Ms. A says (विभागं) विभेदनं ज्ञानम् । विदि आत्मनि । See also preceding Chapter (*section* on Cārvāka doctrines).

2 Ajita Kesakambalī, who was a contemporary of Buddha and professed the doctrine of annihilation (*ucchedavāda*), held that a human being is composed of four elements (earth, water, air and fire). 'चातुम्महाभूतिको अयं पुरिसो.' See the *Sāmañña-phala Sutta* in *Dīghanikāya*.

3 पिब खाद च चारुलोचने यदतीतं वरगात्रि तन्न ते । न हि भीरु गतं निवर्तते समुदयमात्रमिदं कलेवरम् ॥

4 'अन्येषु सूत्रेषु न कदापि चिन्ता लोकायतैरन्यतरैश्च शास्त्रैः' III. 148; 'न च तेषां लोकायते रुचिर्भविष्यति' Chap. XXVI.

5 See Chap. XVIII.

6 'लोकायतिकविद्ययेवाधर्मरुचेः'.

Among his literary predecessors Haribhadra gives an interesting exposition of the doctrines of the school in *Samarāicca-kahā*, Book III, in the dialogue between the Jaina teacher Vijayasiṁha and a Nāstikavādin.[1] Similarly, in a story in *Vasudevahiṇḍi*, Book IV, a king named Kurucandra is introduced as a Nāstikavādin, whose views are briefly described.[2] Jayanta says in *Nyāyamañjarī* (chap. 4) that the Lokāyata is mere casuistry and not an authoritative system, as it does not inculcate any duty;[3] but he takes care to expound the tenets of the school at the beginning of Chap. 7, and towards the end of the same chapter calls the Cārvākas '*suśikṣita*, well-trained, describing and refuting their views.

NAIYAYIKAS

While enumerating the theories of salvation put forward by the different schools of thought, Somadeva does not refer to the Naiyāyikas, obviously because their view of *mokṣa* does not differ from that of the Vaiśeṣikas which is defined by him as the complete cessation of the specific attributes of the soul.[4] Somadeva says: 'ज्ञानसुखदुःखेच्छाद्वेषप्रयत्नधर्माधर्मसंस्काराणां नवसंख्यावसराणामात्मगुणानामत्यन्तोन्मुक्तिर्मुक्तिः' इति काणादाः । With this may be compared the statement of Jayanta defining the Nyāya conception of salvation in *Nyāyamañjarī* (Chap. 9): नवानामात्मगुणानां बुद्धिसुखदुःखेच्छाद्वेषप्रयत्नधर्माधर्मसंस्काराणां निर्मूलोच्छेदोऽपवर्ग इत्युक्तं भवति । Jayanta goes on to say:

> इच्छाद्वेषप्रयत्नादि भोगायतनबन्धनम् । उच्छिन्नभोगायतनो नात्मा तैरपि युज्यते ॥
> × × × × × × × × ×
> ननु तस्यामवस्थायां कीदृगात्माऽवशिष्यते । स्वरूपैकप्रतिष्ठानः परित्यक्तोऽखिलैर्गुणैः ॥

Somadeva seems to refer to the Nyāya theory of salvation in a verse addressed to the Arhat in *Yaśastilaka* VIII. 39 (Vol. II, p. 396):

> खसुप्तदीपनिर्वाणे प्राकृते वा त्वयि स्फुटम् । खसुप्तदीपनिर्वाणं प्राकृतं स्याज्जगत्त्रयम् ॥

The verse refers to three types of salvation: *kha-nirvāṇa*, sky-like salvation, *supta-nirvāṇa*, sleep-like salvation, and *dīpa-nirvāṇa*, salvation like the going out of a lamp. According to a marginal note in Ms. A, *dīpa-nirvāṇa* refers to the Buddhist view; *supta-nirvāṇa* to the Sāṁkhya view (because, according to that system, the emancipated Self, although conscious, perceives nothing); and *kha-nirvāṇa* to the Nyāya view, because, as we have seen, the Naiyāyikas believe *mokṣa* to be a

---

1 P. 164 ff. 'एत्थन्तरम्मि .... नाहियवादिणा भणियं ....'

2 'सो या राया णाहियवादी, 'इंदियसमागमभेत्तं पुरिसकप्पणा, मज्जंगसमवाए मयसंभव इव, न एत्तो परभवसंकमणससीलो अत्थि, न सुकयदुक्कयफलं देवनेरइएसु कोइ अणुभवइ'त्ति ववसिओ ....'

3 न हि लोकायते किंचित् कर्तव्यमुपदिश्यते । वैतण्डिककथैवासौ न पुनः कश्चिदागमः ॥

4 See preceding Chapter.

colourless condition like that of the sky, in which the Self exists bereft of all attributes.[1]

It may be noted that there is another conception of salvation different from the usual Nyāya view, and associated with the name of Bhāsarvajña, an important writer of the Nyāya school, assigned to about the middle of the tenth century. It is probable that Somadeva, like Śrīharṣa, who also refers to the Nyāya doctrine of salvation in *Naiṣadha-carita* 17. 75, was either not acquainted with the views of Bhāsarvajña or perhaps ignored them in his treatment of the current theories of salvation.[2]

PĀŚUPATAS

Somadeva describes and criticises the procedure recommended by the Pāśupatas for the attainment of salvation, but he does not tell us anything about the kind of *mokṣa* contemplated by them. The Pāśupata conception of salvation, according to certain writers, is not different from that of the Nyāya school. This requires some explanation.

Śaṁkara in his *Bhāṣya* on the *Vedāntasūtras* 2. 2. 37 criticises the doctrines of the Pāśupatas, but he refers to them simply as Māheśvaras, followers of the system propounded by Śiva.[3] The Pāśupatas were a Śaiva sect, and we know that there were four Śaiva sects in the ninth century, as both Vācaspati and Bhāskara refer to them, the former in his *Bhāmatī* and the latter in his *Brahmasūtra Bhāṣya* 2. 2. 37. The four sects are Śaivas, Pāśupatas, Kāpālikas and Kāruṇika-siddhāntins, the latter being called Kāṭhaka-siddhāntins by Bhāskara. The four-fold division of the Śaiva sects is found also in Yāmunācārya's *Āgamaprāmāṇya* (latter half of the eleventh century), but here the names given are Śaivas, Pāśupatas, Kāpālikas and Kālāmukhas. This classification is followed in Rāmānuja's *S'rībhāṣya*.

---

1 Applied to the Arhat, the epithet is explained as रागद्वेषमोहरहितत्वात् आकाशवत् शून्यं योग-निद्रायां सुप्तं दीपवत् केवलज्ञानेन द्योतकम्.

2 See the English translation of *Naiṣadhacarita* of Śrīharṣa, Appendix I, P. 497 ff.

3 According to Śaṁkara, the Māheśvaras believe in five categories: *Kārya*, *Kāraṇa*, *Yoga*, *vidhi*, and *duḥkhānta*, which are all Pāśupata tenets. Cf. Āgamaprāmāṇya: तत्रैषा पाशुपतप्रक्रिया ।········तत्र पञ्च पदार्थास्तु व्याख्याताः कारणादयः । कारणं कार्यं विधिर्योगो दुःखान्तः ॥ Vācaspati in *Bhāmatī* explains Māheśvaras as referring to the four Śaiva sects including the Pāśupatas, but his interpretation of *yoga* and *vidhi* is based on Pāśupata texts. He says योगोऽप्योंकारादिध्यानधारणादिः । विधिस्त्रिषवणस्नानादिर्गूढचर्यावसानः, with which may be compared the following Pāśupata *sūtras*: भस्मना त्रिषवणं स्नायीत । 1. 2; गूढव्रतः गूढपवित्रवाणिः 4. 2. 3; ओंकारमभिध्यायीत, हृदि कुर्वीत धारणाम् । 5. 24, 25.

We learn from Bhāskara (op. cit.) that the Pāśupatas and the Kāpālikas hold the same view of salvation as the Vaiśeṣikas and the Naiyāyikas, that is, suppose the emancipated Self to be divested of all specific attributes, resembling a block of stone.[1] As for the Śaivas, their conception of *mokṣa* is said to be identical with that of the Sāṁkhyas, that is, according to them, the emancipated Self subsists in a pristine condition of pure consciousness. Bhāskara says: पाशुपतवैशेषिकनैयायिककापालिकानामविशिष्टाः मुक्त्यवस्थायां पाषाणकल्पा आत्मानो भवन्तीति । सांख्यशैवयोश्च विशिष्टा आत्मानश्चैतन्यस्वभावास्तिष्ठन्तीति ।. Yāmunācārya, who gives an account of the Śaiva sects in his *Āgamaprāmāṇya*, offers the same interpretation of the Pāśupata conception of salvation as Bhāskara. He explains *duḥkhānta*, one of the fundamental tenets of the Pāśupata system, as absolute cessation of pain, and states that the Pāśupatas regard this as *mukti*, a condition characterized by the annihilation of the entire range of the specific attributes of the Self: आत्यन्तिकी दुःखनिवृत्तिर्दुःखान्तशब्देनोक्ता तामेव निःशेष-वैशेषिकात्मगुणोच्छेदलक्षणां मुक्तिं मन्यन्ते ।. Duḥkhānta is in fact the apex of the Pāśupata system. As explained in the Ratna commentary on the *Gaṇakārikā* (p. 9), in a negative sense, *duḥkhānta* is absolute cessation of all pain; while, in a positive sense, it corresponds to *siddhi* or the possession of supernatural power like that of Śiva. Siddhi is of two kinds: *jñānaśakti* or the potency of knowledge and *Kriyāśakti* or the potency of action, which has three aspects: extraordinary speed, the power to assume shapes at will, and boundless might with the body and the organs intact. The attainment of the twofold *siddhi* is followed by ten other *siddhis* or miraculous powers:[2] for example, absolute freedom, irresistible knowledge, freedom from risk to life, complete fearlessness, freedom from the effects of old age and from the pangs of death, lack of all hindrances, overlordship etc. The Pāśupata system thus lays great stress on the attainment of supernormal powers; but *siddhi* does not stand alone, as it belongs to a group of five *lābhas* or ways of perfection recognised by the school, the others being *jñāna*, *tapas*, *nityatva* and *sthiti*. Jñāna is knowledge of the truths. Tapas is *dharma* or discipline produced by the observance of practices such as *bhasmasnāna*. The Ratna commentary declares that the devotee is misled from the right path by the thief Adharma and protected by Dharma acting

---

1 For a different view of the Kāpālika ideal of salvation see Chap. XIII. For a discussion of the Nyāya view see *Naiṣadhacarita* 17. 75 and the English Translation, Appendix I (op. cit.).

2 'सर्वदुःखापोहो दुःखान्तः । स द्विविधोऽनात्मकः सात्मकश्चेति । तत्रानात्मकः सर्वदुःखानामत्यन्तोच्छेदः, सात्मकस्तु महेश्वरैश्वर्यलक्षणा सिद्धिः। सा द्विरूपा ज्ञानशक्तिः क्रियाशक्तिश्चेति । तत्र ज्ञानमेव शक्तिर्ज्ञानशक्तिः।······क्रियाहेतुः शक्तिः क्रियाशक्तिः सा त्रिविधा मनोजवित्वादिभेदा। तत्र निरतिशयं शीघ्रकारित्वं मनोजवित्वं,······संभृतकायेन्द्रियस्यापि निरतिशयैश्वर्यसंबन्धित्वं विकरणधर्मित्वं चेति । यदा चेयं द्विरूपा सिद्धिः प्राप्यते तदा दश सिद्धिलक्षणान्यवश्यत्वादीनि पतित्वान्तानि भवन्ति ।'

like a city magistrate (*purapāla*). The power of Dharma (*dharmaśakti*) is revealed in the devotee's strength of mind which is not perturbed even by the songs and music of a Rambhā. Nityatva is constant devotion to the deity. Sthiti is firm concentration of the mind free from impurities on Rudra. The Pāśupata seems to have been a system of religious discipline rather than a school of speculative thought.

Kauṇḍinya's commentary on the Pāśupata Sūtras gives a fuller picture of the moral discipline of the Pāśupata school at an early stage of its evolution. It is based on the *yamas* or modes of self-restraint, viz., *ahiṁsā*, *brahmacarya*, *satya*, *asaṁvyavahāra*, *śauca*, *āhāralāghava* and *apramāda*.

Ahiṁsā is non-injury which is almost as comprehensive as that of the Jainas. Even the lighting of fire is forbidden to avoid hurting sentient beings. Water should be filtered before use through a cloth or a strainer to keep out tiny creatures. Edible vegetable-stalks, growing bulbs and ripe seeds are to be shunned for similar reasons.[1] Ahiṁsā, in short, is avoidance of injury to all forms of life by any process, mental, vocal or physical. The Bhāṣya of Kauṇḍinya quotes the following verse, which declares *ahiṁsā* to be superior to the gift of the golden mount of Meru or the entire earth or the ocean full of jewels:

यो दद्यात् काञ्चनं मेरुं कृत्स्नां चैव वसुंधराम्। समुद्रं रत्नपूर्णं वा न तुल्यं स्यादहिंसया ॥

It is interesting to note that Somadeva has a verse on the same subject in *Yaśastilaka*, Book IV (p. 97), which appears to be a variation of the verse cited above:

यो दद्यात् काञ्चनं मेरुं कृत्स्नां चापि वसुंधराम्। एकस्य जीवितं दद्यात् फलेन न समं भवेत् ॥

Brahmacarya or chastity does not require any explanation. Satya is speaking the truth. Kauṇḍinya quotes in this connection a verse which declares that even a falsehood uttered in mercy to all creatures leads to heaven, but not the truth, which being spoken results in the destruction of the good.[2] Asaṁvyavahāra is keeping aloof from commercial transactions and the royal court. Asteya is abstention from stealing which includes *anadhikāra-pratigraha* (acquisition of property) and *anupālambha* (swindling money out of others). Akrodha is forbearance. Guruśuśrūṣā is serving one's teacher with devotion. Śauca is purity, physical, mental and spiritual. Physical impurities are removed by the use of holy ashes. More important is *bhāvaśauca* or purity of thoughts. Ātmaśauca or spiritual purity is effected

1 Flesh food is permitted provided it does not involve killing, and is lawfully acquired. It is permissible to eat, for instance, the flesh of wild boars and buffaloes. See Kauṇḍinya on *Pāśupata Sūtras* 5. 16.

2 स्वर्गमनृतेन गच्छति दयार्थमुक्तेन सर्वभूतानाम्। सत्येनापि न गच्छति सतां विनाशार्थमुक्तेन ॥

by submission to humiliation, insult and opprobrium. Āhāralāghava is temperance in eating which follows from the injunction to live on alms. Apramāda is constant vigilance in the practice of self-restraint.

The early Pāśupatas appear to have led an austere life without any fixed abode and worldly ties. According to the Pāśupata Sūtras, the devotee lives in a deserted house or a cave or even on a cremation ground (5. 9, 30). He wears a single piece of cloth and, if possible, dispenses with clothing altogether as a token of renunciation of all possessions (1. 10, 11). It is, however, doubtful if in later times such rules were strictly followed. The Pāśupata mendicant is enjoined to live on alms; and according to Kauṇḍinya, even the holy ashes should be obtained by begging. This appears to be conditioned by the rule of *ahiṁsā* which prohibits the kindling of a fire.[1] The Pāśupata contempt for Vedic sacrifices was a natural consequence of the principle of *ahiṁsā*.[2]

Yoga is preliminary to emancipation. Kauṇḍinya frequently defines *yoga* as connection of the individual soul with Īśvara; and the Pāśupata system, in fact, inculcates a process of Yogic discipline (*yogavidhi*), as mentioned in the opening Sūtra. The devotee assiduously observes the essential religious practices,[3] adores Mahādeva with wholehearted and constant devotion, and cultivates the *yamas* or the different kinds of self-restraint. He contemplates the sacred formulas and practises meditation: this is *kriyāyoga*. With his mind diverted from the objects of sense, he is ripe for the real *yoga*, that feeling of the self as the self, directed towards Maheśvara as the ultimate goal.[4] Supernatural powers of vision, hearing, thought-reading and knowledge come to the Siddha who has attained perfection in Yoga. The Siddha attains supernormal qualities like omniscience, speed like that of the mind etc.; and these are called *guṇadharma*, the possession of supreme faculties like those of Maheśvara obtained through His favour.[5] The Siddhis or supreme attainments, which are also *guṇas*, are finally acquired by the devotee. All creatures come under his control, but he is not subject to the control of any; he dominates the minds of all, but he is not subject to similar domination; he has the power of life and death over others, but he is not subject to any such power;

1 Kauṇḍinya 1. 2 says: भैक्ष्यवत् भस्मार्जनं कर्तव्यम्······अहिंसकत्वात्.

2 Kauṇḍinya 2. 15 says: संग्रहप्रतिग्रहहिंसादियुक्तेन श्रवेणाभिनिर्वृत्तिदर्शनात्............अनित्यसातिशयसंकीर्णफलत्वाच्च कुयजनान्यग्निष्टोमादीनि.

3 See Chapter VIII.

4 Kauṇḍinya 1. 20 says: अध्ययनध्यानादिलक्षणः क्रियायोगश्चरतः प्रवर्तत इत्यर्थः।.........विषयेभ्यः प्रत्याहृतचित्तस्य.........योऽयमात्मन्यात्मभाव स महेश्वरे प्रवर्तत इत्यर्थः.

5 Kauṇḍinya 1. 21-26.

he is free from fear, and his power suffers no diminution; he conquers old age and death. Endowed with the Siddhis, the aspirant becomes the Mahāgaṇapati or the associate of Mahādeva.[1]

Fervent devotion to Rudra in this life and intimate association with Him in the life beyond is the goal set before the Pāśupata devotee. The highest Yoga is absorbed concentration on the supreme Rudra, discarding shape and form. This aspect of the deity is called *vāgviśuddha* 'one that transcends the range of speech'.[2] The devotee, in his turn, becomes *dharmātman* or the embodiment of *dharma* as revealed in the process of discipline starting with the *yamas* and culminating in *māhātmya* or that constancy of soul which enables him to devote himself to the religious life.[3] Thus endowed, he attains *rudra-sāyujya* or direct association with Rudra.[4] It is clear that the devotee does not merge his identity in the godhead, as we are told that, 'having gone *near* Rudra' by the prescribed method, the Brāhmaṇa never returns; that is, he is released from the cycle of births.[5] But, before such a consummation is reached, it is essential to destroy the root cause of the *doṣas* or evils. The evils are the various forms of sense experience which lead to lust, wrath, greed, desire, hatred and the rest. Further, the objects of worldly endeavour are also evils on account of the misery caused by their acquisition, preservation and loss, the discontent produced by the insatiabale desire for more and more of them, and injury to others involved in their acquisition and enjoyment. The root cause of the evils is stated to be *adharma*, which causes mental distraction and makes the devotee incapable of living the full religious life.[6]

Once the mind, free from the *doṣas*, is established in its pristine purity and concentrated on Rudra, the devotee reaches the next higher stage. Dharma and Adharma have ceased to operate, and actions and the means thereof are practically non-existent; the Sādhaka stands alone (*eka*) above the physical plane with his mind fixed on Rudra. Adharma, the chief obstacle to Yoga, is no longer active, and the Sādhaka, free from

1 Kauṇḍinya 1. 27–38.

2 5. 27. Kauṇḍinya quotes the following verse: आकृतिमपि परिहृत्य ध्यानं नित्यं परे रुद्रे । येन प्राप्तं योगे मुहूर्तमपि तत्परो योगः ॥ The commentary on *Gaṇakārikā* says: नित्यानागन्तुकैश्वर्ययुक्ते परमकारणे । यत्र वाचो निवर्तन्ते वाग्विशुद्धः स कीर्तितः ॥

3 5. 31; 2. 14.

4 Kauṇḍinya 5. 33 says: साक्षाद् रुद्रेण सह संयोगः सायुज्यम् ।......योगस्य सम्यक्त्वं सायुज्यमिति योगपर्यायोऽवगम्यते.

5 4. 19, 20.

6 See Kauṇḍinya on *Pāśupata Sūtras* 5. 35.

the *doṣas*, stands like a man who has traversed a forest; he is *kṣemin* with his mind concentrated on Rudra. All actions have ceased, and he is devoid of activity; he is *sat* with his mind firmly devoted to Rudra. All thoughts relating to pursuits of good and evil have ceased; and the Sādhaka is now *vītaśoka*, free from anxious thoughts.[1]

Having reached this stage, the unerring devotee comes to the end of all forms of pain and misery through the grace of Maheśvara.[2] This is *duḥkhānta*, but it is not a negative condition, as pointed out by Kauṇḍinya. For emancipation is not merely absolute cessation of all forms of misery but the attainment of *guṇas* or excellences, that is, the supernormal powers which figure so prominently in the Pāśupata system.[3]

It will be seen that the interpretation of the Pāśupata view of salvation as a condition devoid of the specific attributes of the soul, put forward by later writers like Bhāskara and Yāmuna Muni, finds no support in the Pāśupata Sūtras and Kauṇḍinya's commentary. The latter clearly states that, while in the Sāṁkhya-Yoga view the emancipated beings abide in a condition similar to a swoon without the knowledge of self and others, the Mukta in the Pāśupata view is fully endowed with knowledge.[4] The Pāśupatas were, however, a very widely spread sect; and it is possible that there were adherents of the school who held views similar to those recorded by Bhāskara and Yāmuna Muni.

The Pāśupata system is honourably mentioned along with the Vedas, Sāṁkhya, Yoga, and Pañcarātra in the following verse cited by Aparāditya (12th century) in his commentary on *Yājñavalkya Smṛti* 8. 7: सांख्यं योगः पाञ्चरात्र वेदाः पाशुपतं तथा । अतिप्रमाणान्येतानि हेतुभिर्न विचारयेत् ॥ इति अदूष्यत्वेन हेत्वविचारणीयत्वेम च देवीपुराणयोगयाज्ञवल्क्ययोरदूष्यत्वेन तस्य स्मरणात्.

There is no doubt that the Pāśupatas continued to be an influential sect till as late as the twelfth century. They as well as the Śaivas regarded God (i. e. Śiva or Paśupati) as the efficient cause of the universe, unlike the Bhāgavatas or Pāñcarātras who regarded Vāsudeva, the Supreme Soul, as both the efficient and the material cause of the universe, as pointed out by Śaṁkara in his *Bhāṣya* on the *Vedāntasūtras* 2. 2. 37, 42. Aparāditya

1 Kauṇḍinya 5. 39.

2 5. 40.

3 Kauṇḍinya says: संहारं प्राप्तस्य निगळमुक्ताधिकारवन्मुक्तावतिशयितगुणप्राप्त्यर्थम् उच्यते-गच्छेद् दुःखानामन्तम् । दुःखानामत्यन्तं परमापोहो गुणावाप्तिश्च परं भवतीति । तदुभयमपि इत एव भवतीति.

4 'अथ सांख्ययोगमुक्ताः किं न विशेषिताः । उच्यते—विशेषिताः । कथम् । तद्ज्ञानातिशयात् कथम् । सांख्ययोगमुक्ताः' कैवल्यगताः स्वात्मपरात्मज्ञानरहिताः संमूर्छितवत् स्थिताः । अस्य तु ज्ञानमस्ति ।' (5. 39) 'एवं यत् सांख्यं योगश्च वर्णयति असगादियुक्ताः मुक्ताः शान्ति प्राप्ता इति, तदविशुद्धं तेषां दर्शनम् ।' (5. 8).

(op. cit.) gives the following definition of the theistic conception of the Śaivas and the Pāśupatas, and calls it *bhedeśvara-vāda*: तथा च शैवाः— प्रधानपुरुषयोरधिष्ठाता केवलं निमित्तकारणमीश्वर इतरेतरविलक्षणाः प्रधानपुरुषेश्वरा इति भेदेश्वरवादिनः। ....पाशुपताः पुनः कार्यकारणयोगविधिदुःखान्ताः पञ्च पदार्थाः पशुपतिनेश्वरेण पशुपाशविमोचनार्थमुद्दिष्टा इति भेदेश्वरवादमेवाङ्गीकुर्वन्ति.

The Pāśupatas as a Śaiva sect were in conflict with the Jainas. They are, for instance, mentioned along with Śaivas, Kāpālikas, Sāṁkhyas and Buddhists in the Śravaṇa Belgola epitaph of Malliṣeṇa of 1129 A. D. or thereabouts, engraved on a pillar of the temple of Pārśvanātha on the Candragiri hill, which describes a Jaina teacher named Vimalacandra as having publicly challenged all of them to controversy (verse 26).[1] Another Jaina reference to the Pāśupatas is in Hemacandra's *Yogāśāstra* 4. 102 wherein he describes a number of Pāśupata practices (vv. 26–22),[2] which can be better understood by referring to the account of the system in the Ratna commentary on *Gaṇakārikā*. The Pāśupatas, it may be noted, indulged in ceremonial singing and dancing and made various kinds of what to them were auspicious sounds. Hemacandra, however, presents them in an unfavourable light, as liars and quacks and of loose morals. His remarks should be taken with a grain of salt as the relations between the Jainas and the Śaiva sects were not very cordial.[3]

It will be seen that we have an almost unbroken record of Pāśupata tenets form about the eighth to the twelfth century. The Pāśupata school seems to have undergone a sort of revival in the tenth century. The brief but authoritative text *Gaṇakārikā* was composed in this century; and not only Somadeva but Udayana, as stated below, refers to the system. A Mysore inscription, dated 943 A. D., states that Lakulīśa, the traditional founder of the Pāśupata system, became incarnate as a sage named Cilluka to preserve the continuity of his name and doctrines, which points to a revival of Pāśupata teachings in the Mysore country in the latter half of the tenth century; and the sect, in fact, wielded considerable influence in that region for nearly two centuries after this. An inscription found in the temple of Harṣanātha in the Sikar principality of Jaipur State mentions a scholar named Viśvarūpa who was a teacher of the Pañcārtha-Lākulāmnāya, that is, the sacred book of Lakulin, called Pañcārtha.[4] The inscription is dated 957 A. D., and Viśvarūpa was thus a contemporary of Somadeva.[5]

---

1 More about this inscription in Chap. XIII.

2 Hemacandra says जटापटलभस्माङ्गरागकौपीनधारिणाम्। अर्कधत्तूरमालूरैर्देवपूजाविधायिनाम्॥ कुर्वतां गीतनृत्यादि पुतौ वादयतां मुहुः। मुहुर्वदननादेनातोद्यनादविधायिनाम्॥ असत्यभाषापूर्वं च मुनीन् देवान् जनान् घ्नताम्। विधाय व्रतभङ्गं च दासीदासत्वमिच्छताम्॥ गृह्णतां मुञ्चतां भूयो भूयः पाशुपतं व्रतम्। भेषजादिप्रयोगेण यूकालिक्षं प्रणिघ्नताम्॥

3 See Chap. XIII

4 For references see Bhandarkar: *Vaiṣṇavism, Śaivism and Minor religious systems*, pp. 170–173. Poona edition, 1928.

5 For the early history of the Pāśupata sect and its expansion see Chap. XIII.

RÉSUMÉ

Roughly speaking, Somadeva in his *Yaśastilaka* considers certain doctrines of the Sāṁkhya, Buddhist, Vedānta, Nyāya-Vaiśeṣika, Lokāyata, Jaiminīya, Śaiva, Pāśupata and Kaula systems. Early in the tenth century Siddharṣi records the doctrines of the Nyāya, Vaiśeṣika, Sāṁkhya, Lokāyata, Buddhist and Mīmāṁsā systems in his *Upamiti-bhava-prapañcākathā* (Chap. 4), and describes in this connection the views of the four schools of Buddhist thought: Vaibhāṣika, Sautrāntika, Yogācāra and Madhyamaka. Late in the century Udayana mentions several schools of thought at the beginning of his *Nyāyakusumāñjali*: the Aupaniṣadas or the Vedāntins, the Kāpilas or Sāṁkhyas, the Pātañjalas, the Mahāpāśupatas,[1] the Śaivas, the Vaiṣṇavas, the Paurāṇikas, the Yājñikas, the Digambara Jainas, the Mīmāṁsakas, the Naiyāyikas and the Cārvakas. A comparison of this list with the systems described by Somadeva, who seems to have been an elder contemporary of Udayana, shows that the Jaina writer does not mention the opinions of the Paurāṇikas as such nor does he refer to Vaiṣṇava doctrines or the Pāñcarātra system. As regards the Yājñikas, Somadeva mentions the Yāgajñas, 'Experts in sacrificial lore', along with the Buddhists and the Nāstikas in a verse occurring in *Yaśastilaka* VIII. 43.[2] That the opinions of the Yājñikas still prevailed in the tenth century is shown by Somadeva's attack on Vedic sacrifices in the dialogue between Yaśodhara and his mother in Book IV. The Yājñikas are mentioned also by Vidyānanda in *Tattvārthaśloka-vārtika* 1. 20 (verse 38), but here they appear to be identified with the Mīmāṁsakas.[3]

---

1 According to Varadarāja and Śaṁkara Miśra, the Mahāpāśupatas were those Pāśupatas who practised Mahāvrata, which usually means the Kāpālika cult. See G. N. Kaviraja in *Sarasvati Bhavana Studies*, Vol. II, p. 176. A Pāśupata appears in the farce *Mattavilāsaprahasana* composed early in the seventh century, and in it occurs the expression Mahāpāśupata (p. 26) which seems to refer to the Kāpālika figuring in the play. As has already been stated, the Pāśupatas aimed at the acquisition of supernatural powers, and so did the Kāpālikas (see Chap. XIII). It is probable that there was some affinity between the Mahāpāśupatas and the Kāpālikas. It is, however, doubtful if the Māhāvratī mentioned in *Prabodhacandrodaya* 2.3 refers to the Pāśupata system, as explained in the *Prakāśa* commentary which says महाव्रतं पाशुपतव्रतं तत्संबन्धिनी माहाव्रती पाशुपतशास्त्रसंहतिः. The verse in question refers to various exponents of the Mīmāṁsā system; and it is noteworthy that the *Candrikā* commentary takes the expression as referring to the work of a writer of the Bhāṭṭa school of Mīmāṁsa, named Mahāvrata. The verse in the play says: सूक्तं नापि महोदधेरधिगतं महाव्रती नेक्षिता. The *Candrikā* says महाव्रतो नाम भट्टमतानुवर्ती महोदधिप्रतिस्पर्धी. See below for more about the verse.

2 'शाक्यनास्तिकयागज्ञजटिलाजीवकादिभिः' Vol. II, P. 406.

3 'कर्तुरस्मरणं हेतुर्याज्ञिकानां यदीष्यते'

In the same work (1. 32 under verse 15) the Yājñika is said to reject Jaina notions such as those concerning Saṁvara, Nirjarā and Mokṣa.[1]

Statements such as those of Somadeva and Udayana help us to understand the character of the schools of thought current in their age. It may be added that Udayana refers also to the Tautātitas or the adherents of the Bhāṭṭa school of Mīmāṁsā at the beginning of his commentary on the *Praśastapāda Bhāṣya* and to the Prābhākaras in *Nyāyakusumāñjali* (Chap. 3), mentioning in this connection a Gauḍa Mīmāṁsaka, who is identified with the Pañcikākāra in Varadarāja's commentary *Kusumāñjalibodhanī*. The Pañcikākāra is Śālikānātha, the wellknown author of *Prakaraṇapañcikā*, an important work of the Prabhākara school of Mīmāṁsā; and to judge from Udayana's sarcastic remarks about him, he might be the former's contemporary and, if so, lived in the tenth century.[2] Udayana refers also to Bhāskara's interpretation of the Vedānta in *Nyāyakusumāñjali* (chap. 2),[3] showing that Bhāskara's *Brahmasūtra Bhāṣya*, now almost forgotten, was current in his time. Going back a few years earlier than the tenth century, we come across Jayanta's *Nyāyamañjarī*, which also reveals a world of thought full of variety and covering a comprehensive range of intellectual activity Jayanta refers to contemporary sects like Śaivas, Pāśupatas, Kaulas, Pāñcarātras, and Saṁsāramocakas (chap. 4); and throughout his work he records and criticises the views of diverse schools of thought such as Bhāṭṭas, Prābhākaras, Vedāntists, Buddhists, Sāṁkhyas and Cārvākas, and noteworthy doctrines like Jñānakarma-samuccayavāda, Śabda-brahmavāda etc.

Apart from the schools of thought enumerated by Somadeva and Udayana, the tenth century saw also a revival of Nyāya and Vaiśeṣika studies, as witnessed by the works of Bhāsarvajña,[4] Vyomaśiva,[5] Udayana

1 'संवरे निर्जरायां मोक्षे च तदसत्त्ववचनं याज्ञिकस्य विपर्ययः'

2 See Introduction to *Kusumāñjalibodhanī*, ed. G. N. Kaviraja. Varadarāja remarks: गौडो मीमांसकः पञ्चिकाकारः। गौडो हि वेदाध्ययनाभावाद् वेदत्वं न जानातीति गौडमीमांसकस्येत्युक्तमिति, p. 123. Varadarāja has been assigned to about the eleventh century. Śālikānātha is referred to in a verse of the allegorical play *Prabodhacandrodaya* of Kṛṣṇamiśra composed towards the end of the eleventh century: नैषाश्रावि गुरोर्मतं......तत्त्वज्ञानमहो न शारिकगिरां...... सूक्तं नापि महोदधेरधिगतं......Act 2, verse 3. The author of the Candrikā commentary on the play states that Mahodadhi was a fellow student with Śālikānātha and a writer of the Prabhākara School: महोदधिर्नाम शारिकनामा(थ)सहब्रह्मचारी गुरुमते निबन्धनकर्ता. See N. S. edition.

3 'ब्रह्मपरिणतेरिति भास्करगोत्रे युज्यते'

4 See S. C. Vidyabhusan: *History of Indian Logic*, p. 358.

5 Vyomaśiva's date is *circa* 950 A. D. See Hindi Introduction to Pt. Mahendra Kumāra's edition of न्यायकुमुदचन्द्र, P. 120.

and Śrīdhara; and we may include in the list even Jayanta who wrote towards the end of the preceding century.[1] Bhāsarvajña wrote *Nyāyasāra* on which there are numerous commentaries. Vyomaśiva wrote the *Vyomavatī* commentary on the *Praśastapāda Bhāṣya*. Udayana, who tried to fuse together Nyāya and Vaiśeṣika tenets,[2] wrote *Nyāyakusumāñjali, Ātmatattva-viveka, Nyāya-vārtika-tātparya-pariśuddhi* (commentary on Vācaspati's *Tātparyaṭīkā*), *Kiraṇāvalī* (commentary on the *Praśastapāda Bhāṣya*), and *Lakṣaṇāvalī* (984 A. D.), a manual of Vaiśeṣika definitions.[3] Śrīdhara wrote *Nyāyakandalī* (991 A. D.), a commentary on the *Praśastapāda Bhāṣya*. It should also be noted that the expansion of Nyāya and Vaiśeṣika studies not only led to an intensive study of these systems but to the interpretation, criticism and refutation of the doctrines of the other schools, especially those of the Mīmāṁsā, Buddhist and Sāṁkhya systems. It is not rare to find in the writings of the period diverse doctrines of other schools fully and clearly stated before they are subjected to criticism or any attempt is made to refute them. This is particularly true of Jayanta's *Nyāyamañjarī*, and we have already referred in this connection to Udayana's *Nyāyakusumāñjali*. For other examples we need refer only to the accounts of the Buddhist theory of Ideas (with illustrative quotations), the Mīmāṁsā theory of the self-validity of cognitions (with citations from Kumārila), and the Sāṁkhya theory of cognition in *Vyomavatī* (pp. 524 ff., 579 ff., 521 ff.); the summary of Sāṁkhya doctrines in *Nyāyakusumāñjali* (chap. 1); and the discussion of the Prābhākara theory of error, and the clear presentation of Sphoṭavāda and other tenets in Śrīdhara's *Nyāyakandalī* (Pp. 180 ff,, 268 ff.). The latter work quotes, besides, various authors and works, e. g. *Tantravārtika* and *Ślokavārtika* (P. 257),[4] Maṇḍana's *Sphoṭasiddhi* (P. 270) and *Vidhiviveka* (P. 274), the Buddhist logician Dharmottara (P. 76) etc. The interrelation of the various schools is outside the scope of our discussion; but it is evident that there was considerable activity in the sphere of speculative thought, and the doctrines put forward by the different systems formed the basis of the intellectual movement of the century. It is perhaps the mutual conflict of so many schools of thought that led certain thinkers of the age to suggest the way to a synthesis, or proclaim the common ultimate goal of all systems and schools. In a remarkable passage of *Ātmatattvaviveka*, Udayana "attempts to show that in its gradual ascent

---

1 See G. N. Kaviraja in *Sarasvati Bhavana Studies*, Vol. III, p. 104.

2 Ibid. p. 110.

3 Udayana wrote also a commentary on Gotama's Sūtras (न्यायपरिशिष्ट) and प्रबोधसिद्धि, an original treatise on Nyāya. See G. N. Kaviraja in *Sarasvati Bhavana Studies*, Vol. III, p. 112 ff.

4 Cf. Jha's Translation, p. 549.

along tbe path of Mokṣa the soul is confronted with views which broaden out more and more. The different schools of philosophy representing the varied views thus obtained in passing are conceived to form a graduated series, arranged according to an ascending scale of spiritual realisation, and in such a scheme the lower is always supposed to be a stepping stone to the higher and is to be superseded by it."[1] Even more explicitly and with greater catholicity does the Jaina writer Siddharṣi declare the essential unity underlying all faiths and systems of philosophy ih his *Upamiti-bhava-prapañcā kathā* Book VIII (Pp. 1220–1227). The sum and substance of what he says is that the Supreme Soul is one. He is endowed with pure intelligence, and delivers the world with His infinite power. The true religion (Dharma) is also one and consists of such qualities as forbearance, kindness, purity, self-control, truth, chastity, honesty, sacrifice etc. Further, the Ultimate Truth, which is the way to final deliverance, is in reality one, although it may be expressed in different ways; and it is for the realisation of this Truth concerning tho Supreme Lord that people undertake austerities, meditation and vows. Mokṣa is the subsistence of the soul in its pristine condition characterized by infinite intelligence, conation, joy and power, and known by such names as Supreme Attainment, Bliss, Peace, the endless Good, the Deathless State, Brahma, Nirvāṇa etc. The Doctrine that reveals the One God, the One Dharma and the One Truth, and propounds such a state of final deliverance is alone authoritative and commands universal jurisdiction. It is the purport of this Doctrine that men learn with special care and enunciate in varieties of expression. Call it Vaiṣṇava, Brāhmanical, Śaiva, Buddhist or Jaina, it is all the same: the difference in name does not count so long as the meaning remains the same. Such assertions as 'I am right and you are wrong', 'my system is right and yours is wrong' are only a manifestation of jealousy and nothing more. Siddharṣi's sublime conception of the spiritual unity of man is no doubt much in advance of his age.

Somadeva's review of the tenets of the different schools of thought is important as illustrating the Jaina standpoint, and much of what he says is no doubt cogent and valuable even as an independent effort in philosophical criticism. As a matter of fact, he belongs in this respect to a line of Jaina scholars who have discussed, criticised and attempted to refute the doctrines of other schools of thought both before and after the tenth century; for example, Haribhadra, Akalaṅka, Vidyānanda, Anantavīrya, Prabhācandra, Hemacandra, Vādideva, Malliṣeṇa and others. It should, however, be pointed out that, so far as the Brahmanical schools are concerned, the reaction to the impact of

1 G. N. Kaviraja in *Sarasvati Bhavana Studies*, Vol. III, p. 112.

Jaina thought and criticism is surprisingly small; and except for isolated comments and criticism, the vast literature of the Brahmanical systems hardly takes any adequate notice of Jaina tenets and objections. Among noteworthy criticisms of Jaina doctrines may be mentioned those of Śaṁkara in his Bhāṣya on *Vedānta Sūtras* 2. 2. 33–36 and of Kumārila in *S'lokavārtika* (*Codanāsūtra*, v. 141 ff; *S'abdanityatādhikaraṇa*, v. 106 ff. etc.); but, generally speaking, it may be said that Brahmanical writers from Śaṁkara to Udayana have directed their polemical energies against Buddhist rather than Jaina doctrines. To confine ourselves to the Jaina conception of Mokṣa, which it is the intention of Somadeva to contrast with the non-Jaina theories on the subject, it is recorded and criticized as follows by Vyomaśiva in the introductory portion of his commentary on the *Praśastapāda Bhāṣya*:

अन्ये त्वनेकान्तभावनातो विशिष्टप्रदेशेऽक्षयशरीरादिलाभो निःश्रेयसमिति मन्यन्ते। ......तथा घटादिः मृदादिरूपतया नित्यः सर्वावस्थासूपलम्भात्। घटादिरूपतया चानित्यस्तदपायात्। एवमात्माप्यात्मरूपतया नित्यः सर्वदा सद्भावात्। सुखदुःखादिपर्यायरूपतया चानित्यः तद्विनाशात्। ....तदेतदसांप्रतम्, मिथ्याज्ञानस्य निःश्रेयसकारणत्वेन प्रतिषेधात्। अनेकान्तज्ञानं च मिथ्यैव बाधकोपपत्तेः। तथाहि नित्यानित्ययोः विधिप्रतिषेधरूपत्वात् अभिन्ने धर्मिण्यभावः, एवं सदसत्त्वादेरपीति। यच्चेदं घटादिर्मृदादिरूपतया नित्य इति, असदेतत् मृद्रूपतायास्ततोऽर्थान्तरत्वात्। तथाहि घटादर्थान्तरं मृद्रूपता मृत्त्वं सामान्यम्। तस्य तु नित्यत्वेन घटस्य तथाभावः ततोऽन्यत्वात्। घटस्य तु कारणाद्विलक्षणतयोपलब्धेः अनित्यत्वमेव। ....न चानेकान्तभावनातो विशिष्टशरीरादिलाभेऽस्ति प्रतिबन्धः। न चोत्पत्तिधर्माणां शरीरादीनामक्षयत्वं न्याय्यम्। तथा मुक्तावप्यनेकान्तो न व्यावर्तते इति मुक्तो न मुक्तश्चेति स्यात्। एवं च सति स एव मुक्तः संसारी चेति प्रसक्तेः॥ एवमनेकान्तेऽप्यनेकान्ताभ्युपगमे दूषणम्।

Jayanta who devotes so much space to the doctrines of other systems, makes only a passing reference to the Jaina conception of the Self, and summarily rejects certain Jaina tenets as absurd in his *Nyāyamañjarī* (Chap. 9);[1] and it is noteworthy that although he discusses in that chapter the theories of salvation of diverse schools of thought, he has only a fling at certain practices of the Digambara Jaina monks and the absurdity of the notion that such practices lead to salvation. He declares that these monks expect to attain final release by plucking out their hair and going about naked: if they were right, bald persons would attain *mokṣa* straightway, and so would the animals, because they, too, are unclad! Such criticism, of course, does not rise above the level of comic satire of the type found in plays like *Mattavilāsaprahasana* and *Prabodhacandrodaya*.

---

1 कचनिलुञ्चनदिक्पटधारणक्षितिपराक्रमणक्रमपूर्वकम्। क्षपणकास्त्वपवर्गमुशन्त्यमी अतितरां परमार्थविदस्तु ते॥ लोम्नां नित्यमसंभवात् खलतयो मोक्षं क्षणात् प्राप्नुयुस्संसारोपरमो दिगम्बरतया सद्यस्तिरश्चां भवेत्। मुक्ताः स्युर्गिरिशृङ्गयायिन इमे शश्वत्तदारोहणाज्जन्तूनामपवर्गवर्त्म निकटं केनेदृशं दर्शितम्॥

CHAPTER X

Jaina Dogmatics and Moral and Spiritual Discipline

Apart from the fact that one of the aims of *Yaśastilaka* is to illustrate the doctrine of *ahiṁsā*, the work is designed to be a comprehensive manual of Jaina doctrines, and the object of Somadeva is to provide entertainment as well as religious instruction, and help forward the propagation of the Jaina faith. Books VI, VII and VIII of *Yaśastilaka*, divided into fortysix *kalpas* or sections, are styled Upāsakādhyayana or Readings for laymen, and deal elaborately with *samyaktva* or right faith and its various aspects as well as the different vows, which are viewed as the mainstay (*upabṛṁhaka*) of right faith. Somadeva's treatment of these topics is wider than that of many professed manuals on the subject, and what is more remarkable, illustrated in some cases by elaborate stories, which, although not original, are narrated in a manner peculiarly his own. In addition to the contents of Books VI–VIII, there are brief expositions of Jaina doctrines in Books IV and V, while the Anuprekṣās are treated in an elaborate body of verse in Book II. It is true that the Jaina canon and its doctrines had been fixed long before the tenth century, but the age of Somadeva was an era of systematization and interpretation; and judged from this standpoint, his comprehensive review of the salient topics of Jaina dogmatics has a definite place in the literature of Jainism in Sanskrit.

I) Only a brief outline of Somadeva's exposition of Jaina dogma can be attempted in this chapter, and we may start with an interesting summary of the teachings of Jainism contained in a group of verses occurring in the dialogue between Yaśodhara and his mother in Book IV. The summary is in the form of question and answer, and purports to report a conversation between Yaśodhara and a Digambara saint on the tenets of the Jaina religion. It is somewhat as follows: "What is Dharma? That which inculcates kindness to all creatures. Who is Āpta? He who is free from worldly blemishes. What is the means to know him? A *śāstra* free from contradictory statements. What constitutes religious austerities? Extermination of all desire for worldly objects. What is *jīva*? That which possesses self-experienced attributes such as the intellectual faculty. How does the incorporeal *jīva* come into contact with the body? It is bound to the body by its own actions, just as the sky comes into contact with the dust raised by wind; and by its own actions it is subjected to birth in order that it may suffer their consequences, just as a learned Brahmin is made to tumble over an unclean substance by intoxicating drugs. How can Dharma be acquired? By observing the vows to the best of one's ability. What is a vow? The extermination of desire preceded by the acquisition of faith. What is faith? Reasoned belief in the categories (recognised by Jainism). What are the categories? They are the agencies which uphold the universe".[1]

The great discourse on Samyaktva or Right faith in Book VI opens with a further definition of Dharma, which is described as the factor causing human advancement resulting in supreme beatitude. It consists of *pravṛtti* and *nivṛtti,* and applies to householders as well as monks. Pravṛtti is endeavour to attain salvation, while Nivṛtti is abstention from all that leads to worldly bondage.[2] Faith, knowledge and conduct are the causes of salvation; while worldly bondage is caused by false doctrine, non-abstention (from injury, theft etc.), passions (anger, pride, greed and deceit), and *yoga* or the activity of body, mind and speech. Samyaktva or faith is concentration on things that conform to reason; knowledge is that which is free from ignorance, doubt and error; and right conduct is complete cessation of all activity that leads to the acquisition of *Karma.*[3] We are also told at the end of Book VI that Samyaktva is faith in the fundamental principles; knowledge is determining the nature of the fundamental principles; and conduct is complete detachment, devoid of all action whatsoever.[4] Right faith, right knowledge and right conduct are the most important factors in the Jaina view of liberation. As Kundakunda says in *Samayasāra* (verse 162), Samyaktva is faith in the soul and the other categories; the comprehension of their nature is (right) knowledge; and the renunciation of desire, passions etc. is (right) conduct, the three constituting the path to salvation.[5] It may be noted that Somadeva does not discourse on knowledge and conduct, but expounds Samyaktva in detail.

---

1 को भगवन्निह धर्मो यत्र दया भूप सर्वसत्त्वानाम् । को नामाप्तो यत्र हि न सन्ति सांसारिका दोषाः ॥ तज्ज्ञाने क उपायः शास्त्रं यच्चैकवाक्यतायातम् । तर्हि तपः किं विषयव्यासंगविनिग्रहो यत्र ॥ जीवः को यत्रैते भवन्ति बुद्ध्यादयः स्वसंवेद्याः । तस्यामूर्तस्य सतः शरीरबन्धः कथं भवति ॥ स्वकृतैः कर्मभिरेष प्रयाति जीवः शरीरबन्धं वा । वातेरितैः परागैर्भवति यथा संगमो नभसः ॥ तैरेव गर्भवासे स नीयते निजफलोपभोगार्थम् । अशुचिनि मदनद्रव्यैर्निपात्यते श्रोत्रियो यद्वत् ॥ अस्मादृशां स धर्मः कथं तु निजशक्तितो व्रतग्रहणात् । किं व्रतमिह वाञ्छाया यो दर्शनपूर्वको नियमः ॥ किं दर्शनमिदमाहुर्या श्रद्धा युक्तितः पदार्थेषु । के पुनरमी पदार्था यैरेतद्वर्तते जगच्चक्रम् ॥ P. 103.

2 यस्मादभ्युदयः पुंसां निःश्रेयसफलाश्रयः । वदन्ति विदिताम्नायास्तं धर्मं धर्मसूरयः ॥ स प्रवृत्तिनिवृत्त्यात्मा गृहस्थेतरगोचरः । प्रवृत्तिर्मुक्तिहेतौ स्यान्निवृत्तिर्भवकारणात् ॥ P. 268.

3 सम्यक्त्वज्ञानचरित्रत्रयं मोक्षस्य कारणम् । संसारस्य च मीमांस्यं मिथ्यात्वादिचतुष्टयम् ॥ सम्यक्त्वं भावनामाहुर्युक्तियुक्तेषु वस्तुषु । मोहसंदेहविभ्रान्तिवर्जितं ज्ञानमुच्यते ॥ कर्मादाननिमित्तायाः क्रियायाः परमं शमम् । चारित्रोचितचातुर्याश्चारुचारित्रमूचिरे ॥

4 रुचिस्तत्त्वेषु सम्यक्त्वं ज्ञानं तत्त्वनिरूपणम् । औदासीन्यं परं प्राहुर्वृत्तं सर्वक्रियोज्झितम् ॥ P. 326.

5 जीवादीसद्दहणं सम्मत्तं तेसिमधिगमो णाणं । रागादीपरिहरणं चरणं एसो दु मोक्खपहो ॥

II) The whole of Book VI, after a preliminary discourse on the doctrines of other schools of thought, is devoted to the interpretation of Samyaktva, 'the great tutelary deity of man' (*narāṇāṁ mahatī puruṣa-devatā*). Samyaktva or Right Faith depends upon a certain attitude of mind produced by the realisation of the nature of the categories, just as gold is said to be produced by the mere contact of fire with specially treated mercury. It is not necessary to master the scriptures or subject the body to austerities or journey elsewhere or wait for the lapse of time for acquiring Samyaktva. It is the prime cause of salvation; just as the foundation is the mainstay of a palace, good luck that of beauty, life that of bodily enjoyment, royal power that of victory, culture that of nobility, and policy that of government.[1]

Samyaktva is primarily faith in Āpta, Āgama and the Padārthas or Categories. It may be produced in two ways, has eight components, and is characterised by *praśama* and other qualities, and free from erroneous beliefs (*mūḍhatva*). Before considering the various aspects of Samyaktva, Somadeva explains in detail the nature of Āpta, Āgama and the Padārthas (VI. 2, 3.).

III) The Āpta, as the Jaina Tīrthaṁkaras are generically called, is defined as omniscient and free from all blemishes; he is the lord of the universe and the benefactor of all creatures.[2] He extricates the world from the ocean of suffering by *teaching the fundamental truths*, and is therefore to be regarded as the lord of the universe, whom the three worlds obey.[3] He is pure and free from the eighteen defects common to all living creatures such as hunger, thirst, fear, passion, birth, old age, disease, death, anger, sorrow, sleep etc., and is endowed with infinite knowledge, and is the only source of words of wisdom.[4] Passion, hatred and ignorance are the cause of telling a lie, but as the Āpta is free from these, he has no occasion for uttering a falsehood.[5] He resembles in shape the heterogeneous creatures (i. e. men), is a mirror unto the universe, and the master of the worlds.[6]

---

1 'तस्मादधिष्ठानमिव प्रासादस्य, सौभाग्यमिव रूपसंपदः, प्राणितमिव भोगायतनोपचारस्य, मूलबलमिव विजयप्राप्तेः, विनीतत्वमिवाभिजात्यस्य, नयानुष्ठानमिव राज्यस्थितेरखिलस्यापि परलोकोदाहरणस्य सम्यक्त्वमेव ननु प्रथमं कारणं गृणन्ति गरीयांसः।' P. 274.

2 सर्वज्ञं सर्वलोकेशं सर्वदोषविवर्जितम्। सर्वसत्त्वहितं प्राहुराप्तमाप्तमतोचिताः॥

3 यस्तत्त्वदेशनाद्दुःखवार्धेरुद्धरते जगत्। कथं न सर्वलोकेशः प्रह्वीभूतजगत्त्रयः॥ P. 274.

4 क्षुत् पिपासा भयं द्वेषश्चिन्तनं मूढतागमः। रागो जरा रुजा मृत्युः क्रोधः खेदो मदो रतिः॥ विस्मयो जननं निद्रा विषादोऽष्टादश ध्रुवाः। त्रिजगत्सर्वभूतानां दोषाः साधारणा इमे॥ एभिर्दोषैर्विनिर्मुक्तः सोऽयमाप्तो निरञ्जनः। स एव हेतुः सूक्तीनां केवलज्ञानलोचनः॥

5 रागाद्वा द्वेषाद्वा मोहाद्वा वाक्यमुच्यते ह्यनृतम्। यस्य तु नैते दोषास्तस्यानृतकारणं नास्ति॥ P. 274.

6 उच्चावचप्रसूतीनां सत्त्वानां सदृशाकृतिः। य आदर्श इवाभाति स एव जगतां पतिः॥

For various reasons such as subjection to passion, Brahmā, Viṣṇu, Śiva, the Sun-god, or the Buddha cannot claim to be the Āpta. Brahmā is attached to the nymph Tilottamā, and Viṣṇu devoted to Lakṣmī, while Śiva has Pārvatī forming half his body, and yet they are called Āptas! Vasudeva was the father of Kṛṣṇa, and Devakī was his mother, and he himself fulfilled the duties of a king; yet, strangely enough, he is called a god! Further, if the universe exists in his stomach, and he himself is omnipresent, how can he be subject to birth and death?[1] As regards Śiva, being subject to worldly blemishes like passion in his corporeal form, he lacks the authority to propound a religious code; while, in his incorporeal form, Sadāśiva, he lacks the capacity to do so. Besides, with his five mouths, he teaches mutually contradictory doctrines, of which it would be impossible to ascertain the meaning. It is said that a portion of Sadāśiva becomes incarnate in Rudra in every age; but in that case there would be no difference between the two forms of the deity (the one incorporeal and the other endowed with physical form), just as there cannot be any difference between gold and a fragment of it. It is also strange that the deity should indulge in such freaks as begging, dancing, nudity, the destruction of the Three Cities, the killing of Brahmā and the carrying of a human skull in his hands.[2] The Śaiva system, its principles and the nature of its Omniscient deity constitute, therefore, a strange medley of contradictions in respect of the basic doctrine, methods of proof, poetical representation and actual practice.[3]

With regard to Sun-worship, it is strange that the sun alone should be worshipped and not the moon, although the latter also is a planet: the cult surely represents the thoughtless activity of people who have never examined the Truth.[4] As for the Buddhist, he favours indulgence and continence as well as unrestrained indulgence, and is addicted to wine and flesh: how can he be respected by the wise?[5] It seems to be the object of

---

1 द्रुहिणाधोक्षजेशानशाक्यसूरपुरःसराः। यदि रागाद्यधिष्ठानं कथं तत्राप्तता भवेत्॥ अजस्तिलोत्तमाचित्तः श्रीरतः श्रीपतिः स्मृतः। अर्धनारीश्वरः शम्भुस्तथाप्येषां किलाप्तता॥ वसुदेवः पिता यस्य सवित्री देवकी हरेः। स्वयं च राजधर्मस्थश्चित्रं देवस्तथापि सः॥ त्रैलोक्यं जठरे यस्य यश्च सर्वत्र विद्यते। विमुत्पत्तिविपत्ती स्तां कच्चित्तस्येति चिन्त्यताम्॥

2 कपर्दी दोषवानेष निःशरीरः सदाशिवः। अप्रामाण्यादशक्तेश्च कथं तत्रागमागमः॥ परस्परविरुद्धार्थमीश्वरः पञ्चभिर्मुखैः। शास्त्रं शास्ति भवेत्तत्र कतमार्थविनिश्चयः॥ सदाशिवकला रुद्रे यथायाति युगे युगे। कथं स्वरूपभेदः स्यात् काञ्चनस्य कलास्विव॥ भैक्षनर्तननग्नत्वं पुरत्रयविलोपनम्। ब्रह्महत्याकपालित्वमेताः क्रीडाः किलेश्वरे॥ P. 275.

3 सिद्धान्तेऽन्यत् प्रमाणेऽन्यदन्यत् काव्येऽन्यदीहिते। तत्त्वमाप्तस्वरूपं च विचित्रं शैवदर्शनम्॥ P. 276.

4 ग्रहगोत्रगतोऽप्येष पूषा पूज्यो न चन्द्रमाः। अविचारिततत्त्वस्य जन्तोर्वृत्तिर्निरङ्कुशा॥

5 द्वैताद्वैताश्रयः शाक्यः शंकरानुकृतागमः। कथं मर्नाषिभिर्मान्यस्तरसासवशक्तधीः॥ P. 276. Ms. A says गम्यागम्ययोः प्रवृत्तिपरिहारशुद्धिः द्वैतम्। सर्वत्र प्रवृत्तिनिरङ्कुशत्वमद्वैतम्। Cf. *Nyāyakusumāñjali*, chap. II: नापि भक्ष्यपेयाद्यद्वैतरागः. Varadarāja says in his commentary–भक्ष्यस्य पेयस्य वा भक्षेण पेयेन च सह द्वैतं नास्ति किंतु सर्वं भक्ष्यं च पेयं चैकत्वमेवेति कामयमाना इति.

32

Somadeva to show that lack of passion or renunciation is an essential condition of Āpta-hood, and no faith which does not inculcate absolute renunciation can be said to have an Āpta or trustworthy spiritual overlord. It may also be noted that the question of Āpta was an important controversial issue between the Śaivas and the Jainas, and their respective arguments, which Somadeva here analyses, have been summarized in Chap. VIII.

IV) Āgama or a religious code can be pure only if the Āpta is pure, just as children are pure when their parents are of pure descent.[1] An Āgama, which does not conform to reason owing to contradictory statements, is like the raving of a mad man, and can have no authority.[2] The true Āgama is so called because it makes us comprehend (*gamayan*) things relating to the present, past and future by occupying itself with the problems of religious virtue, material prosperity, desires and liberation, and pointing out what is to be shunned and what accepted.[3]

The Jaina Āgama deals with five categories: the self, the non-self, the constitution of the universe, and bondage and liberation with their causes.[4] The Self is the knower and the seer, great and subtle, and acts and suffers. It is coextensive with the body, and ascendant by nature.[5] It is endowed with knowledge and discernment, without which it would be in no way different from a lifeless object. On the other hand, if it be regarded as pure knowledge, it would not have any definite idea, like the painted figure of a man that is neither friend nor foe.[6] Karma is directed by the Self and the Self is directed by Karma; they are like the boat and the boatman and have no one else[7] to direct them.[8] The Self is, by nature, endowed with unlimited power, although it is confined within the body, like a mystic formula circumscribed by the letters of which it is composed.[9]

Ajīva or the non-self comprises Dharma, Adharma, Space, Time and Pudgala or Matter. Dharma is the underlying principle of motion, Adharma that of rest, Space that of non-resistance, and Time that of

1 पित्रोः शुद्धौ यथापत्ये विशुद्धिरिह दृश्यते । तथाप्तस्य विशुद्धत्वे भवेदागमशुद्धता ॥ P. 278.

2 पूर्वापरविरोधेन यस्तु युक्त्या च बाध्यते । मत्तोन्मत्तवचःप्रख्यः स प्रमाणं किमागमः ॥ P. 279.

3 हेयोपादेयरूपेण चतुर्वर्गसमाश्रयात् । कालत्रयगतानर्थान् गमयन्नागमः स्मृतः ॥

4 आत्मानात्मस्थितिर्लोको बन्धमोक्षौ सहेतुकौ । आगमस्य निगद्यन्ते पदार्थास्तत्त्ववेदिभिः ॥

5 ज्ञाता द्रष्टा महान् सूक्ष्मः कृतिभुक्त्योः स्वयं प्रभुः । भोगायतनमात्रोऽयं स्वभावादूर्ध्वगः पुमान् ॥

6 ज्ञानदर्शनशून्यस्य न भेदः स्यादचेतनात् । ज्ञानमात्रस्य जीवस्य नैकधीश्चित्रमित्रवत् ॥

7 प्रेर्यते कर्म जीवेन जीवः प्रेर्येत कर्मणा । एतयोः प्रेरको नान्यो नौनाविकसमानयोः ॥

8 See also Chapter VIII.

9 मन्त्रवन्नियतोऽप्येषोऽचिन्त्यशक्तिः स्वभावतः ।

change; while Pudgala or Matter is endowed with form, touch, taste, smell and colour.[1]

Bandha or bondage is due to the mutual infiltration of Karma and the Self, and their relation is like that of gold and rust. Bondage has no beginning, but has an end.[2] There are four different aspects of bondage according to *prakṛti* or the nature of *karma*, of which there are eight varieties,[3] *sthiti* or the duration of each kind of *karma* in contact with the soul; *anubhāga* or the consequences of *karma*; and *pradeśa* or the number of karmic molecules that enter the soul.[4] It may be noted that Somadeva merely enumerates the different aspects of Bandha which is treated in detail in the *Tattvārthādhigamasūtra*, chap. VIII.

Mokṣa or liberation is the coming of the Self into its own after shedding all inner impurities. Liberation is not non-existence nor lack of consciousness.[5] Somadeva gives two other definitions of the Jaina view of liberation. In VI. 1 he defines *mokṣa* as a state characterised by supreme joy, knowledge, power, potency and subtleness in the highest degree.[6] In VIII. 39 *mokṣa* is defined as the state in which the Self acquires its own characteristics.[7]

The Three jewels (Right faith, Right knowledge and Right conduct) are the causes of salvation, while bondage is caused by false views, lack of self-restraint and other factors such as passions and *yoga* or the vibrations produced in the soul by the activities of mind, body and speech.[8] Lack of faith in Āpta, Āgama and the Padārthas, error and doubt constitute Mithyātva or false views.[9] Taking only one aspect of a matter into consideration, doubt, lack of discrimination, erroneous notions, equal respect for all deities and faiths: these five also constitute Mithyātva, as they contribute towards worldly bondage.[10] It may be noted that Somadeva seems here to

---

1 धर्माधर्मौ नभः कालः पुद्गलश्चेति पञ्चमः। अजीवशब्दवाच्याः स्युरेते विविधपर्ययाः ॥ गतिस्थित्यप्रतीघातपरिणाम-निबन्धनम्। चत्वारः सर्ववस्तूनां रूपाद्यात्मा च पुद्गलः ॥ P. 280.

2 अन्योन्यानुप्रवेशेन बन्धः कर्मात्मनोर्मतः। अनादिः सावसानश्च कालिकास्वर्णयोरिव ॥

3 ज्ञानावरणीय Knowledge-obscuring, दर्शनावरणीय Conation-obscuring, मोहनीय Deluding, अन्तराय Obstructive, नाम Body-forming, गोत्र Family-determining, वेदनीय Feeling, आयुः Age. See *Tattvārthādhigamasūtra*, chap. VIII.

4 प्रकृतिस्थित्यनुभागप्रदेशप्रविभागतः। चतुर्धा भिद्यते बन्धः सर्वेषामेव देहिनाम् ॥

5 आत्मलाभं विदुर्मोक्षं जीवस्यान्तर्मलक्षयात्। नाभावो नाप्यचैतन्यं न चैतन्यमनर्थकम् ॥ P 280.

6 आनन्दो ज्ञानमैश्वर्यं वीर्यं परमसूक्ष्मता। एतदात्यन्तिकं यत्र स मोक्षः परिकीर्तितः ॥ P. 273.

7 See Section XII (d).

8 बन्धस्य कारणं प्रोक्तं मिथ्यात्वासंयमादिकम्। रत्नत्रयं तु मोक्षस्य कारणं संप्रकीर्तितम् ॥

9 आप्तागमपदार्थानामश्रद्धानं विपर्ययः। संशयश्च त्रिधा प्रोक्तं मिथ्यात्वं मलिनात्मनाम् ॥

10 एकान्तसंशयाज्ञानं व्यत्यासविनयाश्रयम्। भवपक्षाविपक्षत्वान्मिथ्यात्वं पञ्चधा स्मृतम् ॥

follow Pūjyapāda's commentary on *Tattvārthasūtra* VIII. 1. Absence of vows, carelessness, cruelty, lack of contentment, and subservience to the dictates of the senses are collectively called Asaṁyama or lack of self-restraint.[1] The four passions, anger, pride, deceit and greed, with their four varieties, plunge the creatures into the sea of transmigration; and activities connected with the mind, speech and the body, according as they are good and bad, are the factors which attach virtues and vices to the Self.[2]

The next Padārtha is the universe, which is, in the Jaina view, without foundation or support, uncreated and free from destruction: it is situated in the midst of space, and rests on air (that is, on the three atmospheres of dense liquid, gross air and thin air).[3] Somadeva records the criticism of this theory by other schools of thought. The Jainas, they say, do not regard the universe with the earth, mountains and oceans as being fixed anywhere nor do they believe that it is upheld by a fish or a tortoise or a serpent or a boar (as in Brahmanical mythology): so they fancy air as upholding the unsupported universe, an absolutely foolhardy proposition. How can air that cannot uphold even clods of earth, wood and similar substances uphold the universe? Somadeva tries to refute this objection by pointing out that the clouds which inundate the universe with rainwater are kept aloft in the sky solely by the force of air.[4]

V) Somadeva goes on to say that those who hold false opinions, not being able to find fault with the conception of Āpta, Āgama and the Padārthas, censure Jaina (Digambara) ascetics for abstaining from bath and ablutions and going about naked and eating their food standing.[5] He tries to defend each of these practices, and says with regard to bathing that it is useless for ascetics, who observe chastity, and are bent on a spiritual way of life. Besides, they do take a bath to avoid pollution caused by contact with Kāpālikas, women in their periods, Cāṇḍālas and Śabaras.[6] Similarly, wholesale ablutions are superfluous on the ground that it is necessary to wash only the limb which

---

1 अव्रतित्वं प्रमादित्वं निर्दयत्वमतृप्तता। इन्द्रियेच्छानुवर्तित्वं सन्तः प्राहुरसंयमम्॥

2 कषायाः क्रोधमानाद्यास्ते चत्वारश्चतुर्विधाः। संसारसिन्धुसंपातहेतवः प्राणिनां मताः॥ मनोवाक्कायकर्माणि शुभाशुभविभेदतः। भवन्ति पुण्यपापानां बन्धकारणमात्मनि॥

3 निराधारो निरालम्बः पवमानसमाश्रयः। नभोमध्यस्थितो लोकः सृष्टिसंहारवर्जितः॥

4 निराधारो निरालम्बः पवमानसमाश्रयः। नभोमध्यस्थितो लोकः सृष्टिसंहारवर्जितः॥ अथ मतम्—नैव लग्नं जगत् क्वापि भूभृद्भाम्भोधिनिर्भरम्। धातारश्च न युज्यन्ते मत्स्यकूर्माहिपोत्रिणः॥ एवमालोच्य लोकस्य निरालम्बस्य धारणे। कल्प्यते पवनो जैनैरित्येतत् साहसं महत्॥ यो हि वायुर्न शक्तोऽत्र लोष्टकाष्ठादिधारणे। त्रैलोक्यस्य कथं स स्याद्धारणावसरक्षमः॥ तदसत्। ये प्लावयन्ति पानीयैर्विष्टपं सचराचरम्। मेघास्ते वातसामर्थ्यात् किं न व्योम्नि समासते॥ P. 281.

5 अमज्जनमनाचामो नग्नत्वं स्थितिभोजिता। मिथ्यादृशो वदन्त्येतन्मुनेर्दोषचतुष्टयम्॥

6 ब्रह्मचर्योपपन्नानामध्यात्माचारचेतसाम्। मुनीनां स्नानमप्राप्तं दोषे त्वस्य विधिर्मतः॥ संगे कापालिकात्रेयीचाण्डालशबरादिभिः। आप्लुत्य दण्डवत् सम्यग्जपेन्मन्त्रमुपोषितः॥

gets actually soiled; no one, for instance, cuts off the nose when a finger is bitten by a serpent.[1]

As regards nakedness, it is urged that the wise hate what is artificial, but not the observance of what is natural. Nakedness is natural: where is the ground to hate it?[2] Further, it would be impossible for the ascetics to observe the vows of non-possession and non-injury if they desired to wear robes made of barks or deer-skins.[3] As for the custom of taking food standing, Somadeva says that its observance does not lead to heaven nor does the failure to observe it lead to hell. The custom merely marks a certain resolution of an ascetic: I will take food only so long as it comes to the hollow of my palm and I am able to take it standing; otherwise I will abstain from food altogether.'[4]

VI) After dealing with the essential Jaina doctrines and the custom of the Digambara *munis*, Somadeva enumerates a large number of religious practices, repugnant to Jainism, and collectively called Mūḍha or Stupid customs and beliefs, from which Samyaktva or Right faith must be absolutely free. They are sun-worship; bath during eclipses; giving away money on *saṁkrānti* days; the morning and evening ablutions; fire-worship; the worship of edifices; ceremonial bathing in rivers and the ocean; adoration of trees, *stūpas*, and sacred offerings of boiled rice; religious suicide by falling from a precipice; bowing at the tail of a cow and taking cow's urine; and the worship of jewels, conveyances, weapons, the earth, Yakṣas and mountains.[5] Association with heretics of other faiths and the adherents of the Vedas also comes within the scope of Mūḍha of which there are many varieties.[6] To attribute divinity to what is not divine, to adopt as a vow what is not really a vow,

---

1 यदेवाङ्गमशुद्धं स्यादद्भिः शोध्यं तदेव हि । अङ्गुलौ सर्पदष्टायां न हि नासा निकृत्यते ॥

2 विकारे विदुषां द्वेषो नाविकारानुवर्तने । तन्नग्नत्वे निसर्गोत्थे को नाम द्वेषकल्मषः ॥

3 नैष्किंचन्यमहिंसा च कुतः संयमिनां भवेत् । ते संगाय यदीहन्ते वल्कलाजिनवाससाम् ॥

4 न स्वर्गाय स्थितेर्भुक्तिर्न श्वभ्रायास्थितेः पुनः । किं तु संयमिलोकेऽस्मिन् सा प्रतिज्ञार्थमिष्यते ॥ पाणिपात्रं मिलत्येतच्छक्तिश्च स्थितिभोजने । यावत्तावदहं भुञ्जे रहाम्याहारमन्यथा ॥ P. 282.

5 सूर्यार्घो ग्रहणस्नानं संक्रान्तौ द्रविणव्ययः । संध्यासेवाग्निसत्कारो गेहदेहार्चनो विधिः ॥ नदीनदसमुद्रेषु मज्जनं धर्मचेतसाम् । तरुस्तूपाग्रभक्तानां वन्दनं भृगुसंश्रयः ॥ गोपृष्ठान्तनमस्कारस्तन्मूत्रस्य निषेवणम् । रत्नवाहनभूयक्षशस्त्रशैलादिसेवनम् ॥ P. 282.

6 समयान्तरपाखण्डवेदलोकसमाश्रयम् । एवमादि विमूढानां ज्ञेयं मूढमनेकधा ॥ Mūḍha or Mūḍhatā corresponds to what is called 'alien cultus' in Judaism, covering heathenism and all that it implies, the worship or acknowledgement of any deity except the true God, veneration of images, and all the customs associated with heathen religions. 'Alien cultus' or heathenism is one of the three deadly sins in Judaism, the others being unchastity in all its forms and homicide. Moore: *Judaism*, vol. I, p. 466; vol. II, p.267. Jainism, on the other hand, appears to treat heathenism as an error of judgment, and keeps it distinct from the cardinal sins envisaged by the Aṇuvratas.

and to accept as the truth what is not a truth at all constitute Mithyātva or falsehood, which has to be renounced.[1] Somadeva defines in this connection the attitude of Jainism towards novices. If a convert to Jainism cannot altogether renounce all his false beliefs, he ought to be given a mixed reception, but it is not advisable to discard him altogether.[2] On the other hand, persons who are wicked by nature should not be induced to accept the Jaina doctrine, but proper consideration should be shown to those who voluntarily adopt the faith[3] (VI. 4).

VII) Somadeva next deals with the *aṅgas* or auxiliaries of Samyaktva, but it will be convenient to summarize first the different aspects of the doctrine enumerated in the concluding section of Book VI.

First, Samyaktva or Right faith may be realised naturally i. e. by intuition with but little effort or acquired from external sources with great effort.[4] Samyaktva is said to be naturally produced[5] when faith in the fundamental principles of Jainism comes into being 'without the suffering attendant on mental wanderings in the wilderness of deliberation', as a result, for instance, of remembering previous births, or hearing religious discourses, or meditating on the image of a Jaina Tīrthaṁkara, or witnessing great religious festivals, or any other similar cause. Samyaktva is said to be acquired[6] when faith in the *tattvas* comes into being after a long time, as a result of great efforts made in thoroughly investigating all the scriptural texts,[7] which can only be understood with the help of methodical instruction by a wise teacher.

Secondly, Samyaktva may be of two, three and ten kinds according to the standpoint from which it is viewed, but faith in the fundamental principles is the common feature of all its phases.[8]

a) Samyaktva may be of two kinds, *sarāga* or accompanied by desire and *vītarāga* or free from desire. It is *sarāga* up to the eleventh *guṇasthāna* or stage of spiritual development; it is *vītarāga* in the last three stages. Sarāga Samyaktva has certain fundamental characteristics such as *praśama* etc., while Vītarāga Samyaktva is characterised by the absolute purity of the soul.[9]

---

1 अदेवे देवताबुद्धिमव्रते व्रतभावनाम् । अतत्त्वे तत्त्वविज्ञानमतो मिथ्यात्वमुत्सृजेत् ॥

2 तथापि यदि मूढत्वं न त्यजेत् कोऽपि सर्वथा । मिश्रत्वेनानुमान्योऽसौ सर्वनाशो न सुन्दरः ॥

3 न स्वतो जन्तवः प्रेर्या दुरीहाः स्युर्जिनागमे । स्वत एव प्रवृत्तानां तद्योग्यानुग्रहो मतः ॥

4 निसर्गोऽधिगमो वापि तदाप्तौ कारणद्वयम् । सम्यक्त्वभाक् पुमान् यस्मादल्पानल्पप्रयासतः ॥ P. 322.

5 'निसर्गात् संजातमित्युच्यते'.

6 'अधिगमादाविर्भूतमित्युच्यते'.

7 'यदा............समस्तेष्वैतिह्येषु परीक्षोपक्षेपादतिक्लिश्य.........चिरेण तत्त्वेषु रुचिः संजायते'.

8 द्विविधं त्रिविधं दशविधमाहुः सम्यक्त्वमात्महितमतयः । तत्त्वश्रद्धानविधिः सर्वत्र च तत्र समवृत्तिः ॥ P. 322.

9 सरागवीतरागात्मविषयत्वाद् द्विधा स्मृतम् । प्रशमादिगुणं पूर्वं परं चात्मविशुद्धिभाक् ॥ Ms. A remarks. एकादशगुणस्थानपर्यन्तं सरागं द्वादशादि वीतरागम्.

Somadeva observes that just as the virility of a man, which cannot be perceived with the senses, can be ascertained from his relations with women, or the generation of children, or his fortitude in danger, or the execution of his designs; similarly, the existence of the Jewel of Right Faith, although extremely subtle owing to its being a condition of the soul, may be inferred from the qualities of Praśama, Saṁvega, Anukampā and Āstikya.[1]

Praśama is restraining the mind from passions and other evil tendencies.[2] Saṁvega is fear caused by worldly existence, the source of all kinds of sufferings, and fleeting like a dream or a magic show.[3] As Hemacandra observes in his *Yogaśāstra* 2. 15, Saṁvega is man's longing for liberation. Anukampā is kindness to all creatures; it is the fundamental basis of *dharma*.[4] Āstikya is a believing attitude of the mind towards the Āpta, the scriptures, the vows and the fundamental principles.[5] Somadeva concludes by saying that long is the worldly bondage of the man who is subject to the fury of the passions, devoid of vows, cruel and unbelieving.[6] It may be added that some writers mention another characteristic of Samyaktva, *nirveda* or indifference to the world.[7]

b) Samyaktva may be of three kinds according as it is accompanied by the destruction of the *karmas* or their abatement or the process of partial abatement and destruction.[8] Somadeva does not treat the topic in detail, but it may be noted that Samyaktva, viewed from this standpoint, is classified into *kṣāyika*, *aupaśamika* and *kṣayopaśamika*, the characteristics of which are explained in detail in Pūjyapāda's commentary on *Tattvārthasūtra* II. 3–5. Briefly speaking, Kṣāyika Samyaktva is caused by the destruction of seven particular kinds of *karma*; Aupaśamika Samyaktva is caused by the mitigation of the four passions and the three kinds of *darśanamoha*; and Kṣayopaśamika Samyaktva is caused by the mitigation of the existing four passions and *mithyātva* and *samyaktvamithyātva* and the destruction of their germs.

c) Samyaktva may also be of ten kinds according to the sources from which it is derived. These sources are *ājñā*, the command of the scriptures

---

1 'यथा हि पुरुषस्य पुरुषशक्तिरियमतीन्द्रियाप्यङ्गनाजनाङ्गसंभोगेनापत्योत्पादनेन च विपदि धैर्यावलम्बनेन वा प्रारब्धवस्तुनिर्वहणेन वा निश्चेतुं शक्यते, तथात्मस्वभावतयातिसूक्ष्मयत्नमपि सम्यक्त्वरत्नं प्रशामसंवेगानुकम्पास्तिक्यैरेकवाक्यैराकलयितुं शक्यम् ।'

2 यद्रागादिषु दोषेषु चित्तवृत्तिनिबर्हणम् । तं प्राहुः प्रशमं प्राज्ञाः समस्तव्रतभूषणम् ॥

3 शारीरमानसागन्तुवेदनाप्रभवाद् भवात् । स्वप्नेन्द्रजालसंकल्पाद् भीतिः संवेग उच्यते ॥ P. 323.

4 सत्त्वे सर्वत्र चित्तस्य दयार्द्रत्वं दयालवः । धर्मस्य परमं मूलमनुकम्पां प्रचक्षते ॥

5 आप्ते श्रुते व्रते तत्त्वे चित्तमस्तित्वसंस्तुतम् । आस्तिक्यमास्तिकैरुक्तं मुक्तियुक्तिधरे नरे ॥

6 रागरोषधरे नित्यं निर्व्रते निर्दयात्मनि । संसारो दीर्घसारः स्यान्नरे नास्तिकनीतिके ॥

7 Hemacandra (op. cit.) says: निर्वेदो भववैराग्यम्.

8 कर्मणां क्षयतः शान्तेः क्षयोपशमतस्तथा । श्रद्धानं त्रिविधं बोध्यं गतौ सर्वत्र जन्तुषु ॥ P. 323.

composed by the exalted and omniscient Arhat or Tīrthaṁkara; *mārga*, the investigation of the Three Jewels of Right Faith, Right knowledge and Right conduct; *upadeśa*, listening to the life-stories of the great men of old such as the Tīrthaṁkaras, the Cakravartins etc.; *sūtra*, the code regulating the conduct and behaviour of the ascetics; *bīja*, a clue to the understanding of all sections of the doctrine; *saṁkṣepa*, summary knowledge of the main topics of the system, Āpta, *sūtra* or the sacred canon, the vows and the categories; *vistara*, comprehensive knowledge of the vast canonical literature consisting of the twelve Aṅgas, the fourteen Pūrvas and the Prakīrṇas; *artha*, personal conviction in matters connected with the sacred lore; *avagāḍha*, profound knowledge of some part of the threefold Canon; and *paramāvagāḍha*, the conviction of a man possessing the three kinds of supernatural knowledge, viz., *avadhi*, *manaḥparyaya* and *kevala*.[1] Samyaktva is thus tenfold according to the source from which it is derived, and we have therefore ten types of Samyaktva: *mārgasamyaktva*, *sūtrasamyaktva*, *arthasamyaktva* and so on.

In early literature the above ten aspects of Samyaktva are dealt with in *Uttarādhyayanasūtra* XXVIII. 16 ff., although some of the sources are differently given: 'Faith is produced by 1. nisarga, nature; 2. upadeśa, instruction; 3. ājñā, command; 4. sūtra, study of the sūtras; 5. bīja, suggestion; 6. abhigama, comprehension of the meaning of the sacred lore; 7. vistara, complete course of study; 8. kriyā, religious exercise; 9. saṁkṣepa, brief exposition; 10. dharma, the Law'.[2] The Sūtra defines each of these factors in detail, and later writers explain them in their own way. The following verse, quoted by Somadeva in *Yaśastilaka* VI. 21, being enumeration of the ten kinds of Samyaktva, occurs in Guṇabhadra's *Ātmānuśāsana*.

आज्ञामार्गसमुद्भवमुपदेशात्सूत्रबीजसंक्षेपात् । विस्तारार्थाभ्यां भवमवपरमावादिगाढं च ॥

Guṇabhadra clearly explains the ten kinds of Samyaktva in the following verses (ibid. 12–14):

आज्ञासम्यक्त्वमुक्तं यदुत विरुचितं वीतरागाज्ञयैव त्यक्तग्रन्थप्रपञ्चं शिवमममृतपथं श्रद्दधन्मोहशान्तेः ।
मार्गश्रद्धानमाहुः पुरुषवरपुराणोपदेशोपजाता या संज्ञानागमाब्धिप्रसृतिभिरुपदेशादिरादेशि दृष्टिः ॥
आकर्ण्याचारसूत्रं मुनिचरणविधेः सूचनं श्रद्दधानः सूक्तासौ सूत्रदृष्टिर्दुरधिगमगतेरर्थसार्थस्य बीजैः ।
कैश्चिज्जातोपलब्धेरसमशमवशाद् बीजदृष्टिः पदार्थान् संक्षेपेणैव बुद्ध्वा रुचिमुपगतवान् साधु संक्षेपदृष्टिः ॥
यः श्रुत्वा द्वादशाङ्गीं कृतरुचिरथ तं विद्धि विस्तारदृष्टिं संजातार्थात् कुतश्चित् प्रवचनवचनान्यन्तरेणार्थदृष्टिः ।
दृष्टिः साङ्गाङ्गबाह्यप्रवचनमवगाह्योत्थिता यावगाढा कैवल्यालोकितार्थे रुचिरिह परमावादिगाढेति रूढा ॥

1 Somadeva says: भगवदर्हत्सर्वज्ञप्रणीतागमानुज्ञासंज्ञा आज्ञा, रत्नत्रयविचारसर्गो मार्गः, पुराणपुरुषचरितश्रवणाभिनिवेश उपदेशः, यतिजनाचरणनिरूपणपात्रं सूत्रम्, सकलसमयदलसूचनाव्याजं बीजम्, आप्तश्रुतव्रतपदार्थसमासालापाक्षेपः संक्षेपः, द्वादशाङ्गचतुर्दशपूर्वप्रकीर्णविस्तीर्णश्रुतार्थसमर्थनप्रस्तारो विस्तारः, प्रवचनविषये स्वप्रत्ययसमर्थोऽर्थः, त्रिविधस्यागमस्य निःशेषतोऽन्यतमदेशावगाहालीढमवगाढम्, अवधिमनःपर्ययकेवलाधिकपुरुषप्रत्ययप्ररूढं परमावगाढम्। P. 323.

2 Jacobi: *Jaina Sūtras*, Part II, p. 154.

VIII) Somadeva enumerates twentyfive hindrances to Samyaktva, known as *dṛgdoṣāḥ*: the three kinds of *mūḍha* or *mūḍhatā*, the eight *madas*, the six *anāyatanas*, and the eight defects, *śaṁkā* etc.[1] He does not explain any of these except the group of eight defects. The three kinds of *mūḍha* are *lokamūḍha* consisting of stupid popular customs such as dips in sacred water; *devamūḍha* or the worship of false deities, ghosts, spirits and the like; and *samayamūḍha* or following the lead of those who profess false doctrines such as astrology, magic lore etc. The eight kinds of *mada* or pride are pride of birth, family, beauty, wealth, intellect, knowledge of the scripture, honour and power respectively, as explained in the Bhāṣya on Tattvārtha-sūtra IX. 6. What is not *āyatana* or abode (of right faith) is *anāyatana*. The six *anāyatanas* are a false deity subject to passion and hate; the followers of such a deity; false austerities; those who practise such austerities; false scriptures; and the followers of such scriptures.[2] The group of eight defects consists of *śaṁkā, kāṁkṣā, vicikitsā, mūḍhadṛṣṭi*, lack of *upagūhana*, lack of *sthitikāra*, lack of *vātsalya* and lack of *prabhāvana*. These will be explained later.

After enumerating the twentyfive hindrances to Samyaktva, Somadeva points out that a man of right conduct, who possesses right faith, and is conversant with the fundamental truths, attains salvation, even though he is devoid of vows; while a man without faith can never attain salvation, even though he observes the vows.[3] External functions and external *karma* are mere agencies: when the three Jewels (Right Faith, Right Knowledge and Right Conduct) are mature, the soul becomes impregnated with them.[4] Right knowledge is not derived from the senses nor right faith from delusion nor right conduct from the body: when the soul attains the supreme bliss of liberation, it simply becomes one with those three.[5] It will be seen that right faith, right knowledge and right conduct are regarded as conditions of the soul, which is, in the ultimate resort, identified with them. Nemicandra puts the idea clearly in his *Dravyasaṁgraha* (verse 39) when he says that, from the ordinary point of view, right faith, knowledge and conduct are the causes of salvation, but in reality one's own soul is the cause of liberation, consisting as it does of those three.[6] Among early writers Kundakunda says in

1 मूढत्रयं मदाश्चाष्टौ तथानायतनानि षट् । अष्टौ शङ्कादयश्चेति दृग्दोषाः पञ्चविंशतिः ॥ P. 324.

2 See Brahmadeva's commentary on *Dravyasaṃgraha*, verse 41.

3 निश्चयोचितचारित्रः सुदृष्टिस्तत्त्वकोविदः । अव्रतस्थोऽपि मुक्तिस्थो न व्रतस्थोऽप्यदर्शनः ॥ P. 324.

4 बहिष्क्रिया बहिष्कर्म कारणं केवलं भवेत् । रत्नत्रयसमृद्धः स्यादात्मा रत्नत्रयात्मकः ॥

5 अक्षाज्ज्ञानं रुचिर्मोहाद्देहाद्वृत्तं च नास्ति यत् । आत्मन्यस्मिञ्शिवीभूते तस्मादात्मैव तत् त्रयम् ॥

6 सम्मद्दंसण णाणं चरणं मोक्खस्स कारणं जाणे । ववहारा णिच्छयदो तत्तियमइओ णिओ अप्पा ॥

Samayasāra (verse 19) that a saint should always resort to (right) belief, knowledge and conduct; these three are in reality nothing but the soul itself.[1] The same author says in *Niyamasāra* (verse 96) that the soul is to be meditated upon as consisting of pure knowledge, pure faith, joy and pure consciousness.[2]

As has already been said, Somadeva deals only with Samyaktva or Samyagdarśana, Right faith, and regards it as the corner-stone of the entire system of Jaina religion and ethics. After dealing with the various aspects of Samyaktva, he sums them up in the following verse occurring in *Yaśastilaka* VIII. 35.

तत्त्वेषु प्रणयः परोऽस्य मनसः श्रद्धानमुक्तं जिनैरेतद्द्वित्रिदशप्रभेदविषयं व्यक्तं चतुर्भिर्गुणैः ।
अष्टाङ्गं भुवनत्रयार्चितमिदं मूढैरपोढं त्रिभिश्चित्ते देव दधामि संसृतिलतोल्लासावसानोत्सवम् ॥

The different kinds of Samyaktva, two, three and ten, as the case may be, and its four characteristics, referred to in the verse, have already been explained. Samyaktva should also be free from the three types of *mūḍha*, that is *lokamūḍha*, *devamūḍha*, and *samayamūḍha* (see above). Besides, it has eight *aṅgas* which are elaborately explained and illustrated by Somadeva in *Yaśastilaka* VI. 5–20.

IX) The eight *aṅgas* or auxiliaries of Samyaktva are freedom from *śaṁkā*, freedom from *kāṁkṣā* or *ākāṁkṣā*, freedom from *vicikitsā* or *vinindā*, freedom from *anyaślāghā* or *mūḍhatā*, *upagūha*, *sthitikāra*, *prabhāvana* and *vātsalya*. Conversely, *śaṁkā*, *kāṁkṣā*, *vicikitsā*, *mūḍhatā* and lack of *upagūha*, lack of *sthitikāra*, lack of *prabhāvana* and lack of *vātsalya* form a group of defects which hamper the growth of *Samyaktva*, and are included among the twentyfive *dṛgdoṣāḥ*. Somadeva's account of the *aṅgas* of Samyaktva are summarised below.

S'aṁkā, *ākāṁkṣā*, *vinindā* and *anyaślāghā* are the four obstacles to the growth of Samyaktva or Right Faith. *S'aṁkā* is fear or hesitation, which causes lack of resolution and the consequent inability to follow in a steadfast manner the chosen doctrine or vow. The story of the fickle sage Jamadagni is meant to illustrate this failing, while Jinadatta and Padmaratha represent the type of devotees who do not flinch from their vows even in the face of death.[3] Freedom from *śaṁkā* enabled even a criminal like Lalita to attain success in the difficult mystic rites, which the pious Dharasena had commenced but failed to accomplish owing to his fear and indecision.

1 दंसणणाणचरित्ताणि सेविदव्वाणि साहुणा णिच्चं । ताणि पुण जाण तिण्णिवि अप्पाणं चेव णिच्छयदो ॥

2 केवलणाणसहावो केवलदंसणसहावसुहमइओ । केवलसत्तिसहावो सोहं इदि चिंतए णाणी ॥

3 See Chap. XVI for the stories.

S'aṁkā is, properly speaking, the fear of a man that he is alone and has no protector in the three worlds; it is the fear born of the ills of world and death.[1] Śaṁkā is also lack of decision, that is, inability to choose between one doctrine and another, one vow and another, and one divinity and another.[2]

Ākāṁkṣā is the desire for worldly happiness, which hampers constancy of faith and the practice of vows. To preserve the purity of one's faith one must renounce the desires and aspirations born of this and the other world, and those encouraged by other faiths based on erroneous doctrines.[3] One must not, for instance, aspire to become a god or a Yakṣa or a king as a result of one's devotion to Right Faith.[4] To exchange Samyaktva or Right Faith for the joys of the world is like exchanging a ruby for butter-milk, and nothing but self-deception.[5] Equanimity of mind (*anākulā cittavṛttiḥ*) in matters of religion is the sure basis of all prosperity and bliss. To develop right faith one must, therefore, be free from attachment to the world; and the chaste maiden Anantamati is praised for rejecting her chance of worldly happiness for the sake of her vow.

Vinindā or Vicikitsā is doubt or hesitation in the exercise of piety as inculcated by one's faith. One must, for instance, have no hesitation in succouring the poor and the sick, however loathsome the object of one's pity may be, because one is required to do so by one's religion. King Auddāyana was praised by Indra, because he personally tended helpless, old and diseased ascetics without scruple or hesitation.[6] It is one's own fault if one is unable to follow the course of conduct prescribed by one's religion or grasp its meaning. It is the fault of the eye if the clear and luminous sky appears to be dark.[7] He who neglects the teachings of one's religion at the sight of physical defects is like a man who rejects gold at the sight of rust on iron.[8] The good who view the teachings of the scriptures and the nature of the body in their proper perspective feel no scruples of any kind in carrying out the tenets of their faith.[9]

---

1 अहमेको न मे कश्चिदस्ति त्राता जगत्त्रये । इति व्याधिव्रजोत्क्रान्तिभीतिं शङ्कां प्रचक्षते ॥ P. 283.

2 एतत्तत्त्वमिदं तत्त्वमेतद्व्रतमिदं व्रतम् । एष देवश्च देवोऽयमिति शङ्कां विदुः पराम् ॥

3 तत् कुदृष्ट्यन्तरोद्भूतामिहामुत्र च संभवाम् । सम्यग्दर्शनशुद्ध्यर्थमाकाङ्क्षां त्रिविधां त्यजेत् ॥ P. 291.

4 स्यां देवः स्यामहं यक्षः स्यां वा वसुमतीपतिः । यदि सम्यक्त्वमाहात्म्यमस्तीतीच्छां परित्यजेत् ॥

5 उदश्वितेव माणिक्यं सम्यक्त्वं भवजैः सुखैः । विक्रीणानः पुमान् स्वस्य वञ्चकः केवलं भवेत् ॥

6 बालवृद्धगदग्लानान् मुनीनौद्दायनः स्वयम् । भजन् निर्विचिकित्सात्मा स्तुतिं प्रापत् पुरंदरात् ॥ P. 296.

7 स्वस्यैव हि स दोषोऽयं यन्न शक्तः श्रुताश्रयम् । शीलमाश्रयितुं जन्तुस्तदर्थं वा निबोधितुम् ॥ P. 294.

8 दर्शनाद्देहदोषस्य यस्तत्त्वाय जुगुप्सते । स लोहे कालिकालोकान्नूनं मुञ्चति काञ्चनम् ॥

9 तदैतिह्ये च देहे च याथात्म्यं पश्यतां सताम् । उद्वेगाय कथं नाम चित्तवृत्तिः प्रवर्तताम् ॥

Anyaślāghā or Mūḍhatā is attachment to the dogmas of other faiths, which a devout Jaina must avoid. The Vedic, Buddhist, and Śaiva scriptures are dismissed by the author as favouring the use of honey, meat and wine, as also the Vedic religion which prescribes sacrifices as a means to salvation. Such practices as purification with earth etc., ceremonial bathing, sprinkling of water, ablutions, and the worship of the Manes and the Fire; the use of deceitful speech, holy ashes, cowdung plasters and Kuśa seats; the wearing of matted hair, ceremonial cloth and girdle; the carrying of clubs and bamboo baskets, and mystic poses of the fingers: all these are described as the stock-in-trade of those who are ignorant of the inner truth.[1] The erroneous dogmas of other systems are attractive in outward appearance but dangerous in their inner significance; they are like the *kimpāka* fruit, and should never be relied upon.[2] A follower of the Jaina faith should neither praise nor become acquainted with such doctrines nor be misled by the knowledge and science of other schools of thought.[3] The devout lady Revatī is accordingly praised for the utter indifference to divinities not recognised by the Jaina scriptures.

Somadeva then describes the four attributes which contribute to the growth of Samyaktva. They are *upagūha, sthitikāra, prabhāvana* and *vātsalya*. Upagūha or Dharmopabṛṁhana is guarding the reputation of one's religion by suppressing or concealing such faults of one's co-religionists as may lower it in the estimation of others. It is, of course, one's duty to enhance the prestige of one's faith by the cultivation of such virtues as forbearance, truthfulness, purity, mercy and honesty, and by the practice of austerities, self-control and charity.[4] At the same time, if any of one's co-religionists commits an offence by chance or error, 'one should conceal it with the wealth of one's own virtues' as does a mother that of her children.[5] This seems to mean that one should establish the innocence of the culprit, even if the attempt should entail personal loss or damage. When, for instace, the bogus Jaina ascetic was arrested by the police for stealing the merchant's Jewel, the latter, being a good Jaina, declared that he had himself given it to the thief, because the conviction of a Jaina ascetic for theft would have lowered the prestige of Jainism among the populace

1 भर्भिभस्मजटावोटयोगपट्टकटासनम् । मेखलाप्रोक्षणं मुद्रा वृसीदण्डः करण्डकः ॥ शौचं मज्जनमाचामः पितृपूजानलार्चनम् । अन्तस्तत्त्वविहीनानां प्रक्रियेयं विराजते ॥ P. 296.

2 अन्तर्दुरन्तसंचारं बहिराकारसुन्दरम् । न श्रद्दध्यात् कुदृष्टीनां मतं किंपाकसंनिभम् ॥

3 तत्संस्तवं प्रशंसां वा न कुर्वीत कुदृष्टिषु । ज्ञानविज्ञानयोस्तेषां विपश्चिन्न च विभ्रमेत् ॥

4 क्षान्त्या सत्येन शौचेन मार्दवेनार्जवेन च । तपोभिः संयमैर्दानैः कुर्यात् समयबृंहणम् ॥ P. 302.

5 सवित्रीव तनूजानामपराधं सधर्मसु । दैवप्रमादसंपन्नं निगूहेद्गुणसंपदा ॥

who were not acquainted with the real facts.[1] Somadeva goes on to say that a religion cannot be sullied by the misdemeanour of a weakling among its adherents, just as the ocean does not become foul on account of a frog dying in its waters.[2] This is, of course, true of all religions, but the Jainas seem to be prepared, under certain circumstances, to ignore occasional infractions of the moral code if they can thereby save their religion from any possible opprobium or disgrace.

Sthitikāra is the strengthening of the conviction of those among one's co-religionists who may be faltering in their loyalty to the faith, and show signs of breaking away from the fold. A person initiated into the Jaina religion may be wavering in his allegiance owing to the rigour of the vows and insufficient knowledge of the scriptures, and it is the duty of the faithful to hearten him and strengthen his loyalty to the faith.[3] A novice must not be discarded on account of a single lapse, and the aim of a good Jaina should be *gaṇavardhana*, 'the advancement of the community', to be accomplished by constant efforts to win back waverers and sceptics and restore their allegiance.[4] The ends of religion can be served only by the efforts of various types of men, and each one should be assigned the rôle for which he is fit.[5] Any negligence of this principle deprives men of access to the truth, prolongs the cycle of births, and contributes to the decay of the faith.[6] The story of Vāriṣeṇa illustrates this aspect of one's obligations to one's religion.

Prabhāvana is propagation of the faith by the installation of images and the establishment of temples and the institution of worship and festivals as well as by the diffusion of knowledge and the practice of manifold austerities.[7] We are also told that it is one's duty to enhance the prestige of the faith, without any motives of worldly gain, by means of charity and diverse forms of knowledge and science and the celebration of grand festivals and ceremonies.[8] The story of Vajrakumāra shows that a good Jaina must be prepared to defend his religion against the encroachments of rival sects.

Vātsalya is helping one's co-religionists in distress, as illustrated in the story of the sage Viṣṇu. Connected with *vātsalya* are certain kindred virtues

---

1 See Chap. XVI.

2 अशक्तस्यापराधेन किं धर्मो मलिनो भवेत् । न हि भेके मृते याति पयोधिः पूतिगन्धताम् ॥

3 परीषहव्रतोद्विग्नमजातागमसंगमम् । स्थापयेद् भ्रस्यदात्मानं समयी समयस्थितम् ॥ P. 304.

4 नवैः संदिग्धनिर्वाहैर्विदध्याद्गणवर्धनम् । एकदोषकृते त्याज्यः प्राप्ततत्त्वः कथं नरः ॥

5 यतः समयकार्यार्थी नानापञ्चजनाश्रयः । अतः संबोध्य यो यत्र योग्यस्तं तत्र योजयेत् ॥

6 उपेक्षायां तु जायेत तत्त्वाद्दूरतरो नरः । ततस्तस्य भवो दीर्घः समयोऽपि च हीयते ॥

7 चैत्यैश्चैत्यालयैर्ज्ञानैस्तपोभिर्विविधात्मकैः । पूजामहाध्वजाद्यैश्च कुर्यान्मार्गप्रभावनम् ॥ P. 309.

8 तद्दानज्ञानविज्ञानमहामहमहोत्सवैः । दर्शनद्योतनं कुर्यादैहिकापेक्षयोज्झितः ॥

which a Jaina layman ought to cultivate. They are *vinaya*, *vaiyāvṛtya*, and *bhakti*. Vinaya is respect for one's teacher, fellow-student, and the community, and for the study of the scriptures and the ideal of self-control.[1] Vaiyāvṛtya is efficient service rendered to the miserable and the sick.[2] Bhakti is pure and sincere devotion to Jina, the Jaina scriptures, and Jaina religious teachers distinguished for their austerities and learning.[3]

X) Somadeva next deals with the salient features of Jaina religious and moral discipline in detail. In Book VII he defines Vrata as the mainstay of Samyaktva, and it is of two kinds according as it is based on the Mūlaguṇas and Uttaraguṇas. The Mūlaguṇas are eight, consisting as they do of abstention from wine, meat, honey and five kinds of fruits such as Udumbara, Aśvattha, Plakṣa and Nyagrodha, which are the breeding ground of various living organisms, visible and invisible.[4] A number of stories is told to illustrate some of the *mūlaguṇas*, and it is asserted that flesh-eaters have no kindness, drunkards never speak the truth, and people who take honey and the Udumbara fruit feel no pity.[5]

Drinking is condemned by saying that it is the root of all evils, since it completely deludes the mind, and is therefore the greatest of all sins. Owing to the loss of the power of discrimination men commit all kinds of sins, which lead to their wandering in the wilderness of worldly existence.[6] It is well-known that wine was the cause of the ruin of the Yādavas, just as gambling was the cause of that of the Pāṇḍavas[7]. Somadeva records also a curious belief that some persons, after a long succession of births and rebirths, are in the course of time transformed into wine to delude the minds of men. The number of sentient beings transformed into a single drop of wine is large enough to fill the universe ![8]

With regard to the prohibition of meat-eating, Somadeva wonders how people who seek their own welfare hope to increase their own flesh

---

1 स्वाध्याये संयमे संघे गुरौ सब्रह्मचारिणि । यथौचित्यं कृतात्मानो विनयं प्राहुरादरम् ॥ P. 316.

2 आधिव्याधिनिरुद्धस्य निरवद्येन कर्मणा । सौचित्यकरणं प्रोक्तं वैयावृत्यं विमुक्तये ॥

3 जिने जिनागमे सूरौ तपःश्रुतपरायणे । सद्भावशुद्धिसंपन्नोऽनुरागो भक्तिरुच्यते ॥

4 मद्यमांसमधुत्यागाः सहोदुम्बरपञ्चकाः । अष्टावेते गृहस्थानामुक्ता मूलगुणाः श्रुते ॥ P. 327. × × × × × × अश्वत्थोदुम्बरप्लक्षन्यग्रोधादिफलेष्वपि । प्रत्यक्षाः प्राणिनः स्थूलाः सूक्ष्माश्चागमगोचराः ॥ P. 330.

5 मांसादिषु दया नास्ति न सत्यं मद्यपायिषु । आनृशंस्यं न मर्त्येषु मधूदुम्बरसेविषु ॥

6 सर्वदोषोदयो मद्यान्महामोहकृतेर्मतेः । सर्वेषां पातकानां च पुरःसरतया स्थितम् ॥ हिताहितविमोहेन देहिनः किं न पातकम् । कुर्युः संसारकान्तारपरिभ्रमणकारणम् ॥ P. 327.

7 मद्येन यादवा नष्टा नष्टा द्यूतेन पाण्डवाः । इति सर्वत्र लोकेऽस्मिन् सुप्रसिद्धं कथानकम् ॥

8 समुत्पद्य विपद्येह देहिनोऽनेकशः किल । मद्यीभवन्ति कालेन मनोमोहाय देहिनाम् ॥ मद्यैकबिन्दुसंपन्नाः प्राणिनः प्रचरन्ति चेत् । पूरयेयुर्न संदेहं समस्तमपि विष्टपम् ॥

with the flesh of others.[1] Just as one's own life is dear to one, similarly the life of another is dear to him; and one should therefore refrain from destroying animal life.[2] The objection to honey is based on the ground that it is pressed out of 'the young eggs in the womb of bees', and resembles the embryo in the first stage of its growth.[3] It is forbidden to eat or drink in the house of those who take wine, meat and honey, and even to use any utensils belonging to them.[4] Further, one who observes the *mūlaguṇas* should always avoid water brought in waterskins, oil kept in leather flasks, and women who are not in a fit state for vows.[5]

In connection with the taboo on meat, we are told that some object even to the eating of beans and pulses, as these, too, according to them, are flesh, being endowed with life like the bodies of camels, sheep and other animals. Somadeva, however, rejects this view, and cites a verse to the effect that flesh may constitute the body of an animate object, but the body of any animate object is not necessarily composed of flesh; just as the Neem is a tree, but any tree is not Neem.[6]

The Uttaraguṇas are twelve in number, and comprise the five Aṇuvratas, the three Guṇavratas and the four Śikṣāvratas. The Aṇuvratas are treated in detail and fully illustrated with elaborate stories in VII.26–32. They consist of limited vows to renounce severally injury, stealing, falsehood, lust and greed.[7]

---

1 तत् स्वस्य हितमिच्छन्तो मुञ्चन्तश्चाहितं मुहुः। अन्यमांसैः स्वमांसस्य कथं वृद्धिविधायिनः॥

2 स्वकीयं जीवितं यद्वत् सर्वस्य प्राणिनः प्रियम्। तद्वदेतत्परस्यापि ततो हिंसां परित्यजेत्॥ P. 330.

3 मक्षिकागर्भसंभूतबालाण्डविनिपीडनात्। जातं मधु कथं सन्तः सेवन्ते कललाकृति॥

4 मद्यादिस्वादिगेहेषु पानमन्नं च नाचरेत्। तदमत्रादिसंपर्कं न कुर्वीत कदाचन॥

5 दृतिप्रायेषु पानीयं स्नेहं च कुतपादिषु। व्रतस्थो वर्जयेन्नित्यं योषितश्चाव्रतोचिताः॥

6 तदाह—मांसं जीवशरीरं भवेन्न वा मांसम्। यद्वन्निम्बो वृक्षो वृक्षस्तु भवेन्न वा निम्बः॥ P. 331.

7 हिंसास्तेयानृताब्रह्मपरिग्रहविनिग्रहाः। एतानि देशतः पञ्चाणुव्रतानि प्रचक्षते॥ P. 333. The Aṇuvratas or lesser vows are intended for laymen and distinguished from the same vows in their more rigorous form, known as Mahāvratas or great vows, which are prescribed for monks and ascetics. The vices against which these vows are directed cover a wide field, being classified into different categories. Theft, for example, includes misappropriation of deposits, as shown by the story of Śrībhūti and Bhadramitra (see Chap. XVI). It is noteworthy that the early Christians, too, included this among the more serious violations of the moral law. Pliny who was sent as legate to Bithynia in 111 A. D. reports in his ninety-sixth letter to the Emperor Trajan that the Christians 'bound themselves with an oath, not for any crime but not to commit theft or robbery or adultery, not to break their word, and *not to deny a deposit when demanded*'. Kidd: *A History of the Church*, Vol. I, p. 325; Bindley: *The Apology of Tertullian*, Appendix, p. 148 ff.

Dealing with the question of injury, Somadeva enunciates a positive view of *ahiṁsā* and defines *hiṁsā* as destruction of living creatures through error of judgement, and *ahiṁsā* as the protection afforded to them.[1] It follows, therefore, that animals must not be killed for the purpose of worshipping the gods or the Manes, or entertaining one's guests, or in any mystic rites, or for medicinal purposes or out of fear: this constitutes the the vow of *ahiṁsā*.[2]

All liquids should be strained through a cloth before use to avoid any possible injury to living creatures, and one should for the same reason give up also eating at night.[3] Rice-gruel (or pickles), syrups, unhusked paddy, flowers, fruits, roots and leaves, being the breeding ground of living organisms, should not be acquired for use nor anything that is frequented by the latter.[4] Hollow stalks and reeds should be avoided as well as creepers and bulbs resorted to by diverse creatures.[5] Herbs or vegetables should be taken when no longer raw, after splitting them into two sections, and all kinds of pulses and beans which are cooked entire should also be avoided.[6]

Somadeva then enumerates certain qualities which should be cultivated to realise the ideal of *ahiṁsā*. They are *maitrī*, *pramoda*, *kāruṇya* and *mādhyasthya*. Maitrī is the disposition not to cause suffering to any one by any physical act or thoughts or words.[7] Pramoda is affection coupled with respect for men eminent for their virtues and religious austerities.[8] Kāruṇya is the will to help the poor, while Mādhyasthya is an equitable attitude, free from pleasure and displeasure, towards those who are devoid of any merit.[9] The supreme quality of kindness is emphasized by declaring that virtue is light and sin darkness, and sin cannot abide in a person crowned with the rays of kindness.[10] Ahiṁsā is thus a positive virtue, and resolves into *jīvadayā* or compassion for living creatures, which by itself is as efficacious as all works combined. The effect of the latter is like the result of agricultural labour, while that of the former is like the miraculous results produced by the Cintāmaṇi gem.[11]

---

1 यत् स्यात् प्रमादयोगेन प्राणिषु प्राणहापनम् । सा हिंसा रक्षणं तेषामहिंसा तु सतां मता ॥ P. 33

2 देवतातिथिपित्रर्थं मन्त्रौषधभयाय वा । न हिंस्यात् प्राणिनां सर्वानहिंसा नाम तद्व्रतम् ॥

3 देवद्रव्याणि सर्वाणि पटपूतानि योजयेत् । × × × × × × × × निशायां वर्जयेद्भुक्तिमिहामुत्र च दुःखदाम् ॥

4 संधानं पानकं धान्यं पुष्पं मूलं फलं दलम् । जीवयोनि न संग्राह्यं यच्च जीवैरुपद्रुतम् ॥

5 यदन्तःशुषिरप्रायं हेयं नालीनलादि तत् । अनन्तकायिकप्रायं वल्लीकन्दादिकं त्यजेत् ॥

6 द्विदलं द्विदलं प्राश्यं प्रायेणानवतां गतम् । सिद्धयः सकलास्त्याज्याः साधिताः सकलाश्च याः ॥

7 कायेन मनसा वाचा परे सर्वत्र देहिनि । अदुःखजननी वृत्तिर्मैत्री मैत्रीविदां मता ॥ P. 335.

8 तपोगुणाधिके पुंसि प्रश्रयाश्रयनिर्भरः । जायमानो मनोरागः प्रमोदो विदुषां मतः ॥

9 दीनाभ्युद्धरणे बुद्धिः कारुण्यं करुणात्मनाम् । हर्षामर्षोज्झिता वृत्तिर्माध्यस्थ्यं निर्गुणात्मनि ॥

10 पुण्यं तेजोमयं प्राहुः प्राहुः पापं तमोमयम् । तत् पापं पुंसि किं तिष्ठेद्दयादीधितिमालिनि ॥

11 एका जीवदयैकत्र परत्र सकलाः क्रियाः । परं फलं तु पूर्वत्र कृषेश्चिन्तामणेरिव ॥ P. 337.

Speaking of theft, Somadeva difines it as taking possession of another's property, not being given by the owner, with the exception of such things which may be used by all.[1] It is permissible to take possession of ungiven property only at the death of one's kinsmen; in case of the living, specific permission for the purpose is necessary.[2] Those who take the vow of non-stealing must not take anything that is the property of others 'whether in a house or in the street or on water or in the woods or on the hills'.[3] With regard to objects of unknown ownership, the king alone has the right to acquire them so that the produce of mines, large and small, belongs to none but the king.[4] Falsification of measures, abetment of theft, receiving of stolen property, and the accumulation of wealth in war time are obstacles to the vow of non-stealing.[5]

Somadeva mentions various degrees of truth and falsehood. Firstly, that which is to some extent true, though on the whole false, as when we say in common parlance, 'he cooks food or weaves cloths'.[6] Secondly, what is to some extent false, though on the whole true, as when a man, after promising to give something at the end of a fortnight, gives it after a month or a year. Thirdly, that which is in all respects true. Fourthly, that which is completely false, as when a man promises to give something which he does not possess.[7] The fourth item should always be avoided, but the transactions of everyday life are founded on the other three, and sometimes even a false statement ceases to be false if it pleases one's preceptor and others. Divulging[8] of secrets, slander, backbiting, forgery and perjury are obstacles to truth.[9] One should not also talk about the wives of others nor speak against the king nor indulge in anti-social talks: one should take care

---

1 अदत्तस्य परस्वस्य ग्रहणं स्तेयमुच्यते । सर्वभोग्यात्तदन्यत्र भावात्तोयतृणादितः ॥ P. 344.

2 ज्ञातीनामत्यये वित्तमदत्तमपि संमतम् । जीवतां तु निदेशेन व्रतक्षतिरतोऽन्यथा ॥

3 मन्दिरे पदिरे नीरे कान्तारे धरणीधरे । तन्नान्यदीयमादेयं स्वापतेयं व्रताश्रयैः ॥

4 रिक्थं निधिनिधानोत्थं न राज्ञोऽन्यस्य युज्यते । यत् स्वस्यास्वामिकस्येह दायादो मेदिनीपतिः ॥ Ms. A remarks यो व्ययीकृतः क्षयं न याति स निधिः । यद् व्ययीकृतं सत् क्षयं याति तन्निधानमल्पमित्यर्थः ॥

5 पौतवन्यूनताधिक्ये स्तेनकर्म ततो ग्रहः । विग्रहे संग्रहोऽर्थस्यास्तेयस्यैते निवर्तकाः ॥ The last item appears as विरुद्धराज्यातिक्रम in *Tattvārthādhigamasūtra* VII. 27, which means 'Contraband trade with a hostile or prohibited country'. Siddhasena says in his commentary—अन्यतर. राज्यनिवासिन इतरस्य राज्यं प्रविशन्तीतरराज्यनिवासिनो वाऽन्यतरराज्यमभिगच्छन्तीति विरुद्धराज्यातिक्रमः· Pūjyapāda hints at profiteering from this source—विरुद्धराज्येऽतिक्रमः । तत्र हि अल्पमूल्यलभ्यानि महार्घ्याणि द्रव्याणीति प्रयत्नः ।

6 Properly speaking, one cooks rice etc. and weaves yarn.

7 असत्यं सत्यगं किंचित् सत्यमसत्यगम् । सत्यसत्यं पुनः किंचिदसत्यासत्यमेव च ॥ अस्येदमैदंपर्यमसत्यमपि किंचित् सत्यमेव यथान्धांसि रन्धयति वयति वासांसीति etc. P. 349.

8 तुरीयं वर्जयेन्नित्यं लोकयात्रा त्रये स्थिता । सा मिथ्यापि न गीर्मिथ्या या गुर्वादिप्रसादिनी ॥

9 मन्त्रभेदः परीवादः पैशुन्यं कूटलेखनम् । मुधासाक्षिपदोक्तिश्च सत्यस्यैते विघातकाः ॥

not to make any unfounded statement.[1] Exaggeration, fault-finding and indecent speech must be avoided, and one should always speak words that are 'noble, beneficial and concise'.[2] One should not praise oneself nor calumniate others: one should not be jealous of the merits of others when they really exist and describe those of oneself which do not exist at all.[3]

Somadeva appears in certain cirumstances to attach greater importance to self-preservation and philanthropic considerations than to speaking out the truth. He opines that the truth must not be spoken if it is likely to endanger others and bring inevitable ruin to oneself.[4] This can only mean that the truth need not always by revealed, if by so doing one can stave off one's own ruin and that of others. Somadeva, however, points out that the effective power of truthful speech is based on the inherent validity of truth itself, and what a truthful man says is on all occasions valid.[5]

It is evident that Somadeva lays as much emphasis on doing good to others as on speaking the truth, if not more. Doing good to others seems to him to be the most natural thing to do, and he fails to understand why people are bent on making others unhappy, since to make others happy is to make oneself happy.[6] To harbour evil thoughts against others is to injure oneself, and Somadeva expresses the idea by saying that 'even while the mind spreads darkness over others, it injects streams of darkness into its veins'.[7] One should accordingly be always merciful and always devoted to the good of others, be of pleasant nature and pleasant manners, do what is pleasant and speak what is pleasant.[8] It is also a sin to withhold spiritual knowledge from any one who asks for it.[9]

Somadeva then discusses the question of *brahman* or chastity, and defines it as regarding all women except one's wife or concubine as one's

---

1 परस्त्रीराजविद्विष्टलोकविद्विष्टसंश्रयाम् । अनायकसमारम्भां न कथां कथयेद्बुधः ॥

2 अत्युक्तिमन्यदोषोक्तिमसभ्योक्तिं च वर्जयेत् । भाषेत वचनं नित्यमभिजातं हितं मितम् ॥

3 न स्तूयादात्मनात्मानं न परं परिवादयेत् । न सतोऽन्यगुणान् हिंस्यान्नासतः स्वस्य वर्णयेत् ॥ P. 350.

4 तत् सत्यमपि नो वाच्यं यत् स्यात् परविपत्तये । जायन्ते येन वा स्वस्य व्यापदश्च दुरास्पदाः ॥ P. 349. cf. Hemacandra: न सत्यमपि भाषेत परपीडाकरं वचः । लोकेऽपि श्रूयते यस्मात् कौशिको नरकं गतः ॥ *Yogaśāstra* 2. 61. The sage Kauśika was famous for speaking the truth, but went to hell because accurate information given by him led to the capture and killing of a band of robbers, who had concealed themselves in a wood close to his hermitage.

5 सत्यवाक् सत्यसामर्थ्याद्वचःसिद्धिं समश्नुते । वाणी चास्य भवेन्मान्या यत्र यत्रोपजायते ॥ P. 350.

6 यत् परस्य प्रियं कुर्यादात्मनस्तत् प्रियं हि तत् । अतः किमिति लोकोऽयं पराप्रियपरायणः ॥

7 यथा यथा परेष्वेतच्चेतो वितनुते तमः । तथा तथात्मनाडीषु तमोधारा निषिञ्चति ॥

8 प्रियशीलः प्रियाचारः प्रियकारी प्रियंवदः । स्यादानृशंसधीर्नित्यं नित्यं परहिते रतः ॥ P. 349.

9 मोक्षमार्गं स्वयं जानन्नर्थिने यो न भाषते । मदापह्नवमात्सर्यैः स स्यादावरणद्वयी ॥

mother, sister or daughter (according to their age).[1] It is also defined as something, the maintenance of which leads to the growth of qualities like *ahiṁsā* or non-injury.[2] In the Realm of Dharma[3] men are by nature temperate in their sexual desires, and one should therefore remain content with one's married wife, and leave alone the wives of others, female relations, and nuns.[4] Study, meditation and the practice of virtue are out of the question so long as the fire of sexual desire burns in the mind.[5] Worldly pleasures should be enjoyed in moderation, like food, to satisfy only physical needs so as to avoid excessive longing for them.[6] The vow of chastity is spoilt by illicit relation with women, unnatural methods of sexual enjoyment, arrangement of other people's marriages and preoccupation with the art of love.[7] Wine, meat, gambling, music with song and dance, personal decoration, intoxication, libertines and aimless wandering: these ten are concomitants of sexual passion.[8] One should be careful not to excite oneself by erotic acts, aphrodisiac potions and erotic literature.[9] It should be remembered that men are never satiated with worldly pleasures, just as fire is never satiated with sacrificial oblations or the ocean with the influx of waters.[10]

Parigraha, the subject of the fifth Aṇuvrata, is attachment to worldly objects, and it should always be curtailed. The attachment may be to both outer and inner objects, the former being ten and the latter fourteen. The outer objects are arable land, corn, money, habitation, clothing and the like, couch and seat, servants, cattle and household articles. The inner objects are false doctrines; the three kinds of inclinations (feminine inclinations, mesculine inclinations and inclinations common to both the sexes): the six kinds of feelings, viz., the sense of the laughable, pleasure, displeasure, sorrow, fear and disgust; and the four passions: anger, pride,

1 वधूवित्तस्त्रियौ मुक्त्वा सर्वत्रान्यत्र तज्जने । माता स्वसा तनूजेति मतिर्ब्रह्म गृहाश्रमे ॥ P. 359.

2 रक्ष्यमाणे हि बृंहन्ति यत्राहिंसादयो गुणाः । उदाहरन्ति तद्ब्रह्म ब्रह्मविद्याविशारदाः ॥

3 Explained in Ms. A as आर्यखण्ड.

4 धर्मभूमौ स्वभावेन मनुष्यो नियतस्मरः । यज्जात्यैव पराजातिर्बन्धुलिङ्गिस्त्रियस्त्यजेत् ॥ Ms. A remarks स्वजात्या परिणीतया सह संभोगः कार्यः । परा चासौ अजातिः पराजातिः परकीयजातिः स्त्री ।

5 स्वाध्यायध्यानधर्माद्याः क्रियास्तावन्नरे कुतः । इन्धे चित्तेन्धने यावदेष कामाशुशुक्षणिः ॥ P. 360.

6 ऐदंपर्यमतो मुक्त्वा भोगानाहारवद्भजेत् । देहदाहोपशान्त्यर्थमभिध्यानविहानये ॥

7 परस्त्रीसंगमानङ्गक्रीडान्योपयमक्रियाः । तीव्रता रतिकैतव्ये हन्युरेतानि तद्व्रतम् ॥

8 मद्यं द्यूतमुपद्रव्यं तौर्यत्रिकमलंक्रियाः । मदो विटा वृथाट्येति दशधानङ्गजो गणः ॥ Ms. A explains अलंक्रिया as यन्त्रलिङ्गलेपादिप्रयोगः

9 मदनोद्दीपनैर्वृत्तैर्मदनोद्दीपनै रसैः । मदनोद्दीपनैः शास्त्रैर्मदमात्मनि नाचरेत् ॥

10 हव्यैरिव हुतप्रीतिः पाथोभिरिव नीरधिः । तोषमेति पुमानेष न भोगैर्भवसंभवैः ॥

deceit and greed.[1] The transient character of the body and the objects of the world, property, wife and children, ought to convince us of the vanity of our desires. Wretched and miserable is the man who uses his wealth for selfish enjoyment and not for the cultivation of virtue, and supremely wealthy are those who do not desire to acquire what they have not got nor rejoice when they have acquired it.[2] Nothing but sin results from the concentration of the mind on wealth, and acquisition through greed of more than one's legitimate share of wealth or property destroys the vow to renounce *parigraha*.[3] The man, who is free from desire for both the outer and inner objects of attachment, is fit to obtain the bliss of heaven and salvation.[4]

XI) The three Guṇavratas are next described (VII. 33), but they are not illustrated with stories, like the five Aṇuvratas. The Guṇavratas are Digvirati, Deśavirati and Anarthadaṇḍavirati. The first two consist of vows to restrict one's movements to a fixed point in a particular direction or in a particular place, preparatory to restraining the mind from external objects by renouncing injury, greed, indulgence and similar propensities.[5] These vows constitute a scheme of preliminary self-restraint designed to secure moral purity and establish mental equilibrium with regard to the objects of the world.

The third Guṇavrata is abstention from the Anarthadaṇḍas, which comprise all accessories of violence and all agencies and means of injury leading to slaughter, capture or confinemet, and are so called because they contribute to the prevalence of strife and discord. The Anartha-daṇḍas include birds and animals like cocks, hawks, peacocks, cats, vicious elephants and ichneumons, and such means of injury as poison, spears, arms, fire whips, nooses and tethers. The person who takes a vow to observe this particular Guṇavrata should not therefore keep noxious animals nor use any implement designed to cause injury or loss of life. The Anarthadaṇḍas cover a wide field and include also sinful gossip, evil thoughts, sports involving loss of life, futile occupations, doing harm to others, jealousy, and all acts that

1 क्षेत्रं धान्यं धनं वास्तु कुप्यं शयनमासनम्। द्विपदाः पशवो भाण्डं बाह्या दश परिग्रहाः ॥ समिथ्यात्वास्त्रयो वेदा हास्यप्रभृतयोऽपि षट् । चत्वारश्च कषायाः स्युरन्तर्ग्रन्थाश्चतुर्दश ॥ P. 366.

2 स श्रीमानपि निःश्रीकः स नरश्च नराधमः। यो न धर्माय भोगाय विनयेत धनागमम् ॥ प्राप्तेऽर्थे ये न माद्यन्ति नाप्राप्ते स्पृहयालवः। लोकद्वयश्रितां श्रीणां त एव परमेश्वराः ॥ P. 367.

3 कृतप्रमाणाल्लोभेन धनादधिकसंग्रहः । पञ्चमाणुव्रतज्यानिं करोति गृहमेधिनाम् ॥

4 यस्य द्वन्द्वद्वयेऽप्यस्मिन् निःस्पृहं देहिनो मनः । स्वर्गापवर्गलक्ष्मीणां क्षणात् पक्षे स दक्षते ॥

5 दिक्षु सर्वास्वधःप्रोर्ध्वंदेशेषु निखिलेषु च। एतस्यां दिशि देशेऽस्मिन्नियत्यैवं गतिर्मम ॥ दिग्देशनियमादेवं ततो बाह्येषु वस्तुषु। हिंसा लोभोपभोगादिनिवृत्तेश्चित्तयन्त्रणा ॥ P. 370.

cause grief and mourning to one's fellow creatures.[1] It will be seen that the third Guṇavrata is designed to supplement the great vow of Ahiṁsā, and Somadeva goes on to say that, by renouncing the Anarthadaṇḍas, the devotee earns the friendship of all creatures and becomes their lord.[2] Deception and violence practised at the instance of others, the overloading of beasts of burden, and causing excessive suffering to them amount to violation of this vow.[3]

XII) The four Śikṣāvratas are treated in detail in Book VIII, which practically brings to an end Somadeva's masterly discourse on the Jaina religion. They are *sāmāyika* or customary worship, *proṣadhopāsana* or religious fasting, *niyama* or limitation of worldly enjoyment, and *dāna* or charity.

We have in our work a comprehensive treatment of *sāmāyika* or the Jaina system of worship, which primarily resolves itself into the worship of Arhats, that is, the all-holy and omniscient Tīrthaṁkaras or Patriarchs. The worship is of two kinds according as it is done with or without the use of idols.

a) The kind of worship in which idols are dispensed with is regulated by what is known as *samaya-samācāra-vidhi*, which prescribes the adoration of certain entities, concrete and abstract, held sacred by Jainism. They are the Five Parameṣṭhins or Exalted Beings and the Three Jewels (Right Belief, Right Knowledge and Right Conduct). All these should be visualized on a piece of birch bark or cloth or wooden board or a slab of stone or on sand or the earth or in the air or in one's heart.[4] The salutations and hymns accompanying the votive offerings are composed by Somadeva himself in ornate prose and verse, and they rank high in Jaina devotional literature.

The Five Parameṣṭhins are adored first. They are, according to Somadeva's interpretation, the Arhat, that is, one of the Tīrthaṁkaras or Patriarchs endowed with superhuman qualities; the Siddha or one who has realised within himself the luminous presence of the Infinite Soul; the Ācārya or the teacher who regulates the social order according the principles of Jainism; the Upādhyāya or the learned preceptor who has mastered

---

1 शिखण्डिकुक्कुटश्येनबिडालव्यालबभ्रवः । विषकण्टकशस्त्राग्निकषापाशकरज्जवः ॥ पापाख्यानाशुभाध्यानहिंसाक्रीडावृथा-क्रियाः । परोपतापपैशुन्यशोकाक्रन्दनकारिता ॥ वधबन्धनसंरोधहेतवोऽन्येऽपि चेदृशाः । भवन्त्यनर्थदण्डाख्याः संपराय-प्रवर्धनात् ॥ पोषणं क्रूरसत्त्वानां हिंसोपकरणक्रि याम् । देशव्रती न कुर्वीत स्वकीयाचारचारुधीः ॥

2 अनर्थदण्डनिर्मोक्षादवश्यं देशतो यतिः । सुहृत्तां सर्वभूतेषु स्वामित्वं च प्रपद्यते ॥

3 वञ्चनारम्भहिंसानामुपदेशात् प्रवर्तनम् । भाराधिक्याधिकक्लेशौ तृतीयगुणहानये ॥

4 भूर्जे फलके सिचये शिलातले सैकते क्षितौ व्योम्नि । हृदये चैते स्थाप्याः समयसमाचारवेदिभिर्नित्यम् ॥ P. 373.

the sacred lore; and the Sādhu or the devotee bent on salvation and engaged in rigorous austerities in the face of insuperable obstacles. It may be added that the doctrine of the Parameṣṭhins is a cardinal feature of Jainism, which offers to some extent to be a cult of the superman in the sphere of religion, and reserves its highest honours for the best of men who uphold religion and society according to the tenets of the Jaina faith.

The Parameṣṭhins as well as the Three Jelwes are invoked in our work in elaborate, long-winding prose salutations, each followed by a supplementary verse, some of which will be found reproduced in Chapter IV. Somadeva refers in this connection to the eightfold worship of the Parameṣṭhins and the Three Jewels.[1]

The prose invocations are followed by a considerable number of verses in praise of Right Faith, Right Knowledge, and Right Conduct, the Arhat, the Siddha, the Ācārya, and Śāntinātha, one of the the Jinas or Tīrthaṁkaras. Most of these eulogies are couched in an elevated style and will be found in the chapter on Somadeva's verse.

b) The worshipper may also use an image of the Arhat, and such worship consists of six items, viz. bathing and adoration of the idol, hymns, silent prayer (*japa*), meditation, and the adoration of the presiding goddess of the scriptures (Śrutadevatā). The first two items, ceremonial bathing and adoration of the idol, are closely interconnected, and illustrated by Somadeva with a series of highflown verses in praise of Jina, designed to accompany each successive stage of the ritual. The various stages of the worship proper are *prastāvanā* (prelude), *purākarma* (preliminary arrangements), *sthāpanā* (placing the idol on the altar), *saṁnidhāpana* (formal installation of the idol), *pūjā* (obeisance and offerings), and *pūjāphala* (declaration of the results accruing from the worship of Jina). The idol is bathed with fragrant water, clarified butter, and the juice of vines, dates, sugarcanes, old myrobalans, areca-nuts, and Piyāla fruits as well as coconut-milk,[2] and anointed with various pastes and compounds made from sandal, aloe wood, cardamoms, cloves and Kaṁkola berries.[3] Four pitchers filled with water and decorated with flowers and leaves are kept ready for the bathing ceremony.[4] The sacred Nandyāvarta and Svastika emblems,

---

1 For example, 'भगवतोऽर्हत्परमेष्ठिनोऽष्टतयीमिष्टिं करोमीति स्वाहा'. 'The eightfold worship is defined as fiollows in Hemacandra's *Yogaśāstra* 3. 120: यदाह । गन्धैर्माल्यैर्विनिर्यद्बहलपरिमलैरक्षतैर्धूपदीपैः सांनाय्यैः प्राज्यभेदैश्चरुभिरुपहृतैः पाकपूतैः फलैश्च । अम्भःसंपूर्णपात्रैरिति हि जिनपतेरर्चनामष्टभेदां कुर्वाणा वेश्मभाजः परमपदसुखस्तोममाराल्लभन्ते ॥

2 द्राक्षाखर्जूरचोचेक्षुप्राचीनामलकोद्भवैः । राजादनाम्रपूगोत्थैः स्नपयामि जिनं रसैः ॥ P. 383.

3 एलालवङ्गकङ्कोलमलयागरुमिश्रितैः । पिष्टैः कल्कैः कषायैश्च जिनदेहमुपास्महे ॥

4 पाथःपूर्णान् कुम्भान् कोणेषु सुपल्लवप्रसूनार्चान् । दुग्धाब्धीनिव विदधे प्रवालमुक्तोल्बणांश्चतुरः ॥

fruits, flowers, unbroken rice, water, handfuls of Kuśa grass, and earthen vessels are revolved in a circular fashion before the idol: this being the ceremony known as nīrājanā.[1] After a final bath (*avabhṛthasnāna*),[2] the worshipper should present to the idol Kalama rice, *havis*, lights, incense, flowers and fruits. White parasols, fly-whisks and mirrors are among the articles used in the worship of the idol.

The following are some of the verses composed by Somadeva to mark the different stages in the worship of Jina.

पाथःपूर्णान् कुम्भान् कोणेषु सुपल्लवप्रसूनार्चान् ।
दुग्धाब्धीनिव विदधे प्रवालमुक्तोल्बणांश्चतुरः ॥ (पुराकर्म) p. 383.
तीर्थोदकैर्मणिसुवर्णघटोपनीतैः पीठे पवित्रवपुषि प्रतिकल्पितार्थे ।
[3]लक्ष्मीश्रुतागमनबीजविदर्भगर्भे संस्थापयामि भुवनाधिपतिं जिनेन्द्रम् ॥ (स्थापना)
सोऽयं जिनः सुरगिरिर्ननु पीठमेतदेतानि दुग्धजलधेः सलिलानि साक्षात् ।
इन्द्रस्त्वहं तव सवप्रतिकर्मयोगात् पूर्णा ततः कथमियं न महोत्सवश्रीः ॥ (संनिधापनम्)

The following verses among others are meant to be recited while worshipping the idol with diverse offerings:

योगेऽस्मिन् नाकनाथ ज्वलन पितृपते नैगमेय प्रचेतो वायो रैदेशशेषोडुपसपरिजना यूयमेत्य ग्रहाग्राः ।
मन्त्रैर्भूःस्वःस्वधाद्यैरधिगतवलयः स्वासु दिक्षूपविष्टाः क्षेपीयः क्षेमदक्षाः कुरुत जिनसवोत्साहिनां विघ्नशान्तिम् ॥ P.383
अमृतकृतकर्णिकेऽस्मिन् निजाङ्कबीजे कलादले कमले ।[4] संस्थाप्य पूजयेयं त्रिभुवनवरदं जिनं विधिना ।

The glory of the bathing ceremony is proclaimed in another verse:

लक्ष्मीकल्पलते समुल्लस जनानन्दैः परं पल्लवैर्धर्मारामफलैः प्रकामसुभगस्त्वं भव्यसेव्यो भव ।
बोधाधीश विमुञ्च संप्रति मुहुर्दुष्कर्मधर्मक्लमं त्रैलोक्यप्रमदावहैर्जिनपतेर्गन्धोदकैः स्नापनात् ॥ P. 385

'Owing to the bathing of Lord Jina with perfumed waters that delight the universe, thou Wishing Creeper of Prosperity, blossom forth with leaves, bringing joy to men; thou Garden of Religious Merit, ever beautiful with fruits, be thou the resort of the faithful; and, thou Soul, shake off now the langour caused by the seat of recurring sins?'

The benign influence of the worship of Jina is expressed in the following benediction:

धर्मेषु धर्मनिरतात्मसु धर्महेतोर्धर्मादवाप्तमहिमास्तु नृपोऽनुकूलः ।[5]
नित्यं जिनेन्द्रचरणार्चनपुण्यधन्याः कामं प्रजाश्च परमां श्रियमाप्नुवन्तु ॥ P. 386.

---

1 नन्द्यावर्तस्वस्तिकफलप्रसूनाक्षताम्बुकुशपूलैः । अवतारयामि देवं जिनेश्वरं वर्धमानैश्च ॥ P. 384.

2 यज्ञैर्मुदावभृथभाग्भिरुपास्य देवं etc. As Ms. A says, यज्ञैः means पूजाभिः. P. 386.

3 Refers to the mystic formula श्रीं. Ms. A says पीठस्यापि पूर्वमर्घो दीयते । अक्षतैः श्रीकारो लिख्यते न तु गन्धेन.

4 Ms. A explains अमृत as पवर्ण and says: पकारेण कर्णिका क्रियते तन्मध्ये स्वकीयं नाम निक्षिप्यते। षोडशदलेषु अकारादयः स्वरा लिख्यन्ते ।

5 Ms. A reads धर्महेतौ for धर्महेतो and explains it as चैत्यालयमुनिशास्त्रसंघेषु.

'Let a king, having acquired glory by dint of virtue, be for the sake of Virtue, favourable to the practice of the virtues and those who are devoted to Virtue. Let the people, too, obtain at will the highest prosperity, ever blessed with the religious merit accruing from the worship of Lord Jina's feet.'

c) The ritual of worship is followed by the singing of hymns in praise of Jina. The next item is Japa or the repetition of the famous Pañcaparameṣṭhi-mantra consisting of thirtyfive letters:

"णमो अरहंताणं, णमो सिद्धाणं, णमो आयरियाणं, णमो उवज्झायाणं, णमो लोए सव्वसाहूणं ।"

This is the *sarvākṣara-mantra.* Somadeva refers also to the *nāmākṣara* formula consisting only of the names of the five Parameṣṭhins,[1] the *mukhyākṣara* formula consisting of the initial letters of the names of the Parameṣṭhins,[2] and formulas consisting of a single letter such as *Om*[3] or अ, but he prefers the one consisting of thirtyfive letters as the most authoritative.[4] The counting of the letters is to be done with a rosary composed of lotus seeds or golden beads or sunstones or gems, and the counting may also be done with flowers or on the finger-joints.[5] The formula is to be repeated in full, very clearly, with stress on the final *anusvāras.*[6] The repetition of the *mantra* may be vocal or mental, the latter method being the more efficacious. Great mystic value is attached to this formula which is eloquently praised by our author.

d) Japa is followed by *dhyāna* or meditation. The thirtyninth section of Book VIII deals with this important subject, and belongs, in fact, to a type of Jaina mystic literature represented by such works as Kundakunda's *Mokkhapāhuḍa* and *Niyamasāra, Samādhiśataka,* Yogīndu's *Paramātmaprakāśa,* Śubhacandra's *Jñānārṇava* and Devasena's *Ārādhanā-sāra.* There are different kinds of *dhyāna,* but the fundamental basis of the Jaina system of meditation is the contemplation and realisation of the true nature of the Self. It is necessary to remember at the outset that Jaina doctrine recognises three kinds of Self: *bahirātmā* or the outer

1 "अर्हत्सिद्धाचार्योपाध्यायसर्वसाधुभ्यो नमः।" Ms. A says अरहंत सिद्ध इत्यादि.

2 "अ सि आ उ सा"

3 See Section (d).

4 सर्वाक्षरनामाक्षरमुख्याक्षराद्येकवर्णविन्यासात्। निगिरन्ति जपं केचिदहं तु सिद्धक्रमैरेव॥ P. 390. See also *Dravya-saṃgraha,* verse 49 and Brahmadeva's comm. thereon. पणतीस सोल छप्पण चदु दुगमेगं च जवह झाएह। परमेट्ठिवाचयाणं अण्णं च गुरूवएसेण॥

5 पुष्पैः पर्वभिरम्बुजबीजस्वर्णार्ककान्तरत्नैर्वा। निष्कम्पिताक्षवलयः पर्यङ्कस्थो जपं कुर्यात्॥

6 'संपूर्णमतिस्पष्टं सनादमानन्दसुन्दरं जपतः।'

Self, *antarātmā* or the inner Self, and *paramātmā* or the higher Self. Kundakunda says in his *Mokkhapāhuḍa* that the external Self consists of the sense organs; the inner Self is the consciousness that the soul is distinct from the body; and the higher Self is the emancipated soul free from the impurities of *Karma*.[1] The *paramātmā* or the higher Self is the sole object of meditation, and it is essential to note that it is not the universal Soul of Vedānta, but the pure and all-knowing soul in each individual, circumscribed and obscured for the time being by the hindrances of *karma*. Jaina meditation is not merely contemplation but realisation of the Self, which is the same thing as liberation or the emancipated existence of the individual soul. As Kundakunda says, the Yogin by contemplating the *paramātmā* divests himself of sin-producing greed and acquires no new *karma*: firm in right conduct and right faith, he contemplates the Self and reaches the supreme goal (ibid. verses 48, 49).[2]

Somadeva begins by saying that the prescribed process of meditation should be sedulously practised by one who desires to contemplate the Supreme Light and attain 'that eternal abode', that is, the abode of the emancipated souls at the top of the universe, as conceived by Jainism. The Supreme Light (*paraṁjyotiḥ*) is the higher Self or *paramātmā*, and the expression is often used in this sense in Jaina literature, e. g., in *Jñānārṇava* 31. 8,[3] 41;[4] 32. 35[5] etc.

Somadeva mentions two broad divisions of meditation, *sabījadhyāna* and *abījadhyāna*. In *sabījadhyāna* the mind is like a lamp, unshaken by the gusts of external and internal delusion, and cheers up at the sight of the Truth.[6] In *abījadhyāna* the mental current reaches a stage when it becomes devoid of conscious thought, and the Self sparkles within itself.[7] In other words, the mind is at work in *sabījadhyāna*, but ceases to function in *abījadhyāna*, leaving the Self to discover itself. The latter is the higher kind of contemplation, of which Somadeva describes the main characteristics. He says that when the five senses sink into themselves and the mind is submerged, the Light dawns on the inner Self. Meditation consists in mental concentration; the Self meditates and reaps the consequences; the

1 अक्खाणि बाहिरप्पा अंतरअप्पा हु अप्पसंकप्पो । कम्मकलंकविमुक्को परमप्पा भण्णए देवो ॥

2 परमप्पय झायंतो जोई मुच्चेइ मलद्लोहेण । णादियदि णवं कम्मं णिद्दिट्ठं जिणवरिंदेहिं ॥ होऊण दिढचरित्तो दिढसम्मत्तेण भावियमईओ । झायंतो अप्पाणं परमपयं पावए जोई ॥

3 'परमात्मा परंज्योतिः'

4 'परंज्योतिस्त्राता परमपुरुषोऽचिन्त्यचरितः'

5 'यो विशुद्धः प्रसिद्धात्मा परंज्योतिः सनातनः'

6 बहिरन्तस्तमोवातैरस्पन्दं दीपवन्मनः । यत्तत्त्वालोकनोल्लासि तत् स्याद् ध्यानं सबीजकम् ॥ P. 391.

7 निर्विचारावतारासु चेतःस्रोतःप्रवृत्तिषु । आत्मन्येव स्फुरन्नात्मा भवेद्ध्यानमबीजकम् ॥

Light of the Self is the object of meditation; and the subjugation of the senses is the means to accomplish it. Lack of strength does not remove obstacles nor does lack of stamina lead to eternal life: one should therefore contemplate the higher Self (*paraṁ brahma*) without any sense of weakness.[1] Two points may be noted in this connection. First, while there cannot be meditation without mental concentration, the destruction of the senses and specially the activity of the mind is the primary condition of self-realisation. Devasena's *Ārādhanāsāra*, which elaborates the point, remarks, for instance, that the Self *ātmā* becomes the higher Self (*paramātmā*) when the activity of the mind is destroyed.[2] Yogīndu in his *Paramātmaprakāśa* (verse 31) describes the higher Self as mindless (*amaṇu*), and the devotee is asked to meditate on the infinite and divine Self by suppressing the mind.[3] Super-mental consciousness is the goal aimed at, and the vision of the Light is said to appear only when the senses are subdued and the mind is at a standstill. Pūjyapāda says in his *Samādhiśataka* (verse 30) that what one visualizes for a moment after controlling all the senses, with the inner Self motionless and calm, is the reality underlying the higher Self.[4] Somadeva says in a mystic verse, which, if we understand it correctly, seems to mean that when the swan of the mind (i. e. the inner Self) is bereft of mental activity and the swan of the soul (i. e. the higher Self) is steady in every respect, the swan of knowledge becomes the swan of the lake of visible phenomena in their entirety.[5] There seems to be here a reference to what Yogīndu calls *haṁsācāra* (2. 170), which is explained as the passionfree purity of the soul concomitant with infinite knowledge and other attributes.[6]

Secondly, the use of the expression *paraṁ brahma* in the sense of the higher Self is another instance of Jaina adaptation of Vedantic terminology. Somadeva uses the expression several times,[7] and other examples are frequently found in Yogīndu's *Paramātmaprakāśa*.[8]

Meditation is always difficult. Just as gems, though found in the earth, are not found everywhere; similarly, meditation, though it depends upon

---

1 चित्तस्यैकाग्रता ध्यानं ध्यातात्मा तत्फलप्रभुः । ध्येयमात्मागमज्योतिस्तद्विधिर्देहयातना ॥ नाक्षमित्वमविज्ञाय न क्लीबत्वममृत्यवे । तस्मादक्लिश्यमानात्मा परं ब्रह्मैव चिन्तयेत् ॥ P. 391.

2 'णिग्गहिए मणपसरे अप्पा परमप्पओ हवइ ।'

3 'चित्तु णिवारिवि झाहि तुहुँ अप्पा देउ अणंतु। 2. 172.

4 सर्वेन्द्रियाणि संयम्य स्तिमितेनान्तरात्मना । यत् क्षणं पश्यतो भाति तत्तत्त्वं परमात्मनः ॥

5 निर्मनस्के मनोहंसे पुंहंसे सर्वतः स्थिरे । बोधहंसोऽखिलालोक्यसरोहंसः प्रजायते ॥ P. 392.

6 Brahmadeva says in his commentary: हंसाचारु संशयविभ्रमविमोहरहितानन्तज्ञानादिनिर्मलगुणयोगेन हंस इव हंसः परमात्मा तस्य आचारं रागादिरहितं शुद्धात्मपरिणाममिति ।

7 See below.

8 बंभु मुणेविणु 1. 109. Comm. says ब्रह्मशब्दवाच्यनिर्दोषिपरमात्मानं मत्वा ज्ञात्वाः; बंभु पवंचहिं जो रहिउ 2. 171 etc.

individual effort, is not possible for everybody.[1] The duration of *dhyāna* is only an *antarmuhūrta*; and it is difficult to attain a state of mind, steadfast in meditation and free from vibration.[2] But *dhyāna*, though it lasts only for such a short time, firm in the soul, totally destroys one's accumulated *karma*, just as a stroke of lightning rends asunder a hill in a moment.[3] There are five factors which contribute towards Yoga or meditation: indifference to the world, maturity of knowledge, lack of attachment, a steadfast mind and ability to endure the privations of hunger, thirst, grief, swoon, old age and death.[4] The obstacles to Yoga are mental suffering, disease, error, carelessness, idleness, confusion, lack of success, attachment and fickleness.[5] He who practises meditation should be free from anger and pleasure, and remain indifferent, like a clod of earth, both to one who pierces him with thorns and one who smears him with sandal-paste.[6] He should maintain a uniform attitude towards gain and loss, home and woodland, friend and foe, the pleasant and the unpleasant, happiness and misery.[7] He should be deeply learned in sacred lore regarding the higher Self, endowed with fortitude, goodwill, and maintain constant silence except for words pleasant and true.[8]

Somadeva then refers to the four kinds of *dhyāna* mentioned in *Tattvārthasūtra*, ch. IX: *ārta, raudra, dharmya* and *śukla*. Ārtadhyāna is of four kinds: contemplation of the presence of an unpleasant object and the anxiety to get rid of it; contemplation of the loss of a pleasant object and the anxiety to regain it; constant thought of pain or disease and the desire to remove it; and the anxiety to enjoy unattained objects of pleasure. Raudradhyāna is also of four kinds according as it is preoccupied with thoughts of injury, falsehood, theft and the preservation of the means of enjoyment. Ārtadhyāna and Raudradhyāna should be avoided by all means: they are, as it were, gates barring the entry of the Three Jewels and effective barriers in the path of liberation; steps leading to hell and wings obscuring the vision of the truth. The tree of rebirth prodigiously grows as long as even a vestige of these two *dhyānas* remains in the mind.[9]

---

1 भूमौ जन्मेति रत्नानां यथा सर्वत्र नोद्भवः । तथात्मजमिति ध्यानं सर्वत्राङ्गिनि नोद्भवेत् ॥ P. 392.

2 तस्य कालं वदन्त्यन्तर्मुहूर्तं मुनयः परम् । अपरिस्पन्दमानं हि तत् परं दुर्धरं मनः ॥

3 तत्कालमपि तद्ध्यानं स्फुरदेकाग्रमात्मनि । उच्चैः कर्मोच्चयं भिन्द्याद्वज्रं शैलमिव क्षणात् ॥

4 वैराग्यं ज्ञानसंपत्तिरसंगः स्थिरचित्तता । ऊर्मिस्मयसहत्वं च पञ्च योगस्य हेतवः ॥

5 आधिव्याधिविपर्यासप्रमादालस्यविभ्रमाः । अलाभः सङ्गितास्थैर्यमेते तस्यान्तरायकाः ॥

6 यः कण्टकैस्तुदत्यङ्गं यश्च लिम्पति चन्दनैः । रोषतोषाविषिक्तात्मा तयोरासीत लोष्टवत् ॥

7 लाभेऽलाभे वने वासे मित्रेऽमित्रे प्रियेऽप्रिये । सुखे दुःखे समानात्मा भवेत्तद्ध्यानधीः सदा ॥ P. 393.

8 परे ब्रह्मण्यनूचानो धृतिमैत्रीदयान्वितः । अन्यत्र सूनृताद्वाक्यान्नित्यं वाचंयमी भवेत् ॥

9 जन्तोरनन्तसंसारभ्रमैनोरथवर्त्मनी । आर्तरौद्रे त्यजेद्ध्याने दुरन्तफलदायिनी ॥ बोध्यागमकपाटे ते मुक्तिमार्गार्गले परे । सोपाने श्वभ्रलोकस्य तत्त्वेक्षावृतिपक्ष्मणी ॥ लेशतोऽपि मनो यावदेते समधितिष्ठतः । एष जन्मतरुस्तावदुच्चैः समधिरोहति ॥
P. 393.

Somadeva then deals with Dharmyadhyāna and Sukladhyāna. He who practises Dharmyadhyāna should ponder over the fundamental principles of Jainism, carefully considering the authoritative means of knowledge, and the various standpoints and aspects.[1] Dharmyadhyāna is of four kinds: *ājñāvicaya* or discerning the truth on the basis of absolute faith in the scriptures composed by Jina; *apāyavicaya* or pondering on the means of making people abstain from wrong belief, knowledge and conduct; *vipākavicaya* or pondering over the consequences of the eight kinds of *karma*; and *saṁsthānavicaya* or pondering over the nature and constitution of the universe. Somadeva gives examples of all the varieties of Dharmyadhyāna. For instance, the devotee may reflect on *ājñā* in the following manner: 'Just as there is no mystery in the world about pure gold and its working, similarly it is the desire of the wise that there should be no mystery about authoritative scriptures. But the scriptures (of other faiths) fail to convince even persons of scanty intelligence like myself. How can they help the creatures sinking in the ocean of worldly existence?'[2] Apāya may be contemplated as follows: 'Alas, the darkness of false doctrines makes men's minds blind to the acceptance of the Three Jewels, even though such a step shines with the rays of reason. Let us hope for the day when, casting off sins, men will see the Truth that puts an end to misery.'[3] After reflecting on the constitution of the universe, the devotee should ponder over the consequences of *karma*: 'There in the universe, upwards, downwards, and athwart, the creatures incessantly wander, like dust, impelled by the gust of their own *karma*.'[4] It is asserted that he who thus practises Dharmyadhyāna, with his senses and mind subdued, has his darkness dispelled, as if at the rise of the sun.[5]

The next step is Śukladhyāna which is the highest form of meditation. The four stages of this *dhyāna* are briefly mentioned by Somadeva (P. 394.):

भेदं विवर्जिताभेदमभेदं भेदवार्जितम् । ध्यायन् सूक्ष्मक्रियाशुद्धो निष्क्रियं योगमाचरेत् ॥

The first stage, called by Somadeva 'diversity devoid of unity', is *pṛthaktva-vitarka-vīcāra*, wherein the devotee is absorbed in the meditation of the Self, but unconsciously allows its different attributes to replace one another. The second stage, called by our author 'unity devoid of diversity', is *ekatva-vitarka-*

1 प्रमाणनयनिक्षेपैः सानुयोगैर्विशुद्धधीः । मतिं तनोति तत्त्वेषु धर्मध्यानपरायणः ॥ P. 394.

2 अरहस्ये यथा लोके सती काञ्चनकर्मणी । अरहस्यं तथेच्छन्ति सुधियः परमागमम् । यः स्खलत्यल्पबोधानां विचारेष्वपि मादृशाम् । स संसारार्णवे मज्जज्जन्त्वालम्बः कथं भवेत् ॥ (इत्याज्ञा) P. 394.

3 अहो मिथ्यातमः पुंसां युक्तिद्योतैः स्फुरत्यपि । यदन्धयति चेतांसि रत्नत्रयपरिग्रहे ॥ आशास्महे तदेतेषां दिनं यत्रास्तकल्मषाः । इदमेते प्रपश्यन्ति तत्त्वं दुःखनिबर्हणम् ॥ (इत्यपायः)

4 अकृत्रिमो विचित्रात्मा मध्ये च त्रसराजिमान् । मरुत्त्रयीवृतो लोकः प्रान्ते तद्धामनिष्ठितः ॥ (इति लोकः) रेणुवज्जन्तवस्तत्र तिर्यगूर्ध्वमधोऽपि च । अनारतं भ्रमन्त्येते निजकर्मानिलेरिताः ॥ (इति विपाकः)

5 इति चिन्तयतो धर्म्यं यतात्मेन्द्रियचेतसः । तमांसि द्रवमायान्ति द्वादशात्मोदयादिव ।

vīcāra, wherein the Yogin concentrates on a particular aspect of the Self without any change or variation.[1] These two stages of Śukladhyāna are followed by the destruction of the 'destructive' *karmas*, and the third stage is known as *sūkṣma-kriyā-pratipāti*, wherein the absorption of the soul in itself still leaves room for minute vibratory movements in the soul. The fourth stage is *vyuparata-kriyā-nivarti*, called by Somadeva *niṣkriya yoga*, wherein vibration or activity of any kind is totally absent. Transcending the body, the Yogin now loses all connection with the mind, and his vital breaths come to an end, while he attains the supreme goal and perfect knowledge.[2] This is the stage in which the Self becomes the higher Self, and this is *mokṣa* or liberation, characterized by the destruction of both 'destructive' and 'undestructive' *karmas*,[3] and free from the limitations of birth, a condition in which the Self attains its own qualities.[4] As Kundakunda says in his *Samayasāra* (verse 196), one who is full of faith and knowledge, and meditates on the Self with undivided attention, soon attains the higher Self, free from *karmas*;[5] and liberation is nothing but the attainment or realisation of the higher Self, as pointed out by Yogīndu in *Paramātmaprakāśa* 2. 10.[6]

One who practises meditation should also contemplate the path of the Three Jewels, the rules of conduct, the Anuprekṣās, and the seven fundamental principles of Jainism, and the personality of Lord Jina.[7] But the contemplation of the Self is the supreme object of *dhyāna*, and the devotee should reflect within himself that he knows the truth and devotedly believes in the scriptures, and will renounce all external activity and merge the Self in the (higher) Self.[8] As explained in *Jñānārṇava* 40.19, the person engaged in meditation should unite the Self with the higher Self, inspired solely by the nature thereof, and impregnating the Self with the qualities of the higher Self.[9]

The realisation of the (higher) Self by the Self by means of the (inner) Self, that is, knowledge, is a mode of expression frequently used in

---

1 See *Tattvārthādhigamasūtra* IX. 39 (ed. Jaini, p. 190).

2 विलीनाशयसंबन्धः शान्तमारुतसंचयः । देहातीतः परं धाम कैवल्यं प्रतिपद्यते ॥ The verse is omitted in the printed text of *Yaśastilaka*, p. 394.

3 The 'destructive' (घातिन्) Karmas are ज्ञानावरणीय, दर्शनावरणीय, मोहनीय and अन्तराय. The 'undestructive' (अघातिन्) Karmas are वेदनीय, नाम, गोत्र and आयुः. See Section IV.

4 प्रक्षीणोभयकर्माणं जन्मदोषैर्विवर्जितम् । लब्धात्मगुणमात्मानं मोक्षमाहुर्मनीषिणः ॥ P. 394.

5 अप्पाणं झायंतो दंसणणाणमइओ अणण्णमणो । लहदि अचिरेण अप्पाणमेव सो कम्मणिम्मुक्कं ॥

6 जीवहँ सो पर मोक्खु मुणि जो परमप्पयलाहु । कम्मकलंकविमुक्काहँ णाणिय बोल्लहि साहू ॥

7 मार्गसूत्रमनुप्रेक्षाः सप्ततत्त्वं जिनेश्वरम् । ध्यायेदागमचक्षुष्मान् प्रसंख्यानपरायणः ॥ P. 395.

8 जाने तत्त्वं यथैतिह्यं श्रद्दधे तदनन्यधीः । मुञ्चेऽहं सर्वमारम्भमात्मन्यात्मानमादधे ॥

9 तद्गुणग्रामसंपूर्णं तत्स्वभावैकभावितः । कृत्वात्मानं ततो ध्यानी योजयेत् परमात्मनि ॥

Jaina mystic literature with peculiar and almost redundant emphasis. Somadeva, for instance, says that when the Self realises the Self within itself by means of the Self as a result of the attainment of the Three Jewels, it attains itself (that is, its own true qualities) along with the higher Self (P. 395):

आत्मायं बोधिसंपत्तेरात्मन्यात्मानमात्मना । यदा सूते तदात्मानं लभते परमात्मना ॥

The idea is expressed in similar language in several other texts, e. g., *Samayasāra* 196; Pūjyapāda's *Iṣṭopadeśa* 22; *Jñānārṇava* 32. 41; *Paramātmaprakāśa* 2. 174:

अप्पाणं झायंतो दंसणणाणमइओ अणण्णमणो । लहदि अचिरेण अप्पाणमेव सो कम्मणिम्मुक्कं ॥
संयम्य करणग्राममेकाग्रत्वेन चेतसः । आत्मानमात्मवान् ध्यायेदात्मनैवात्मनि स्थितम् ॥
आत्मन्येवात्मनात्मायं स्वयमेवानुभूयते । अतोऽन्यत्रैव मां ज्ञातुं प्रयासः कार्यनिष्फलः ॥
एहु जु अप्पा सो परमप्पा कम्मविसेसें जायउ जप्पा । जामइँ जाणइ अप्पें अप्पा तामइँ सो जि देउ परमप्पा ॥[1]

Somadeva declares that the Self meditates, the Self is the object of meditation, the Self is meditation, and the Self composed of the Three Jewels is the result of meditation (P. 395):

ध्यातात्मा ध्येयमात्मैव ध्यानमात्मा फलं तथा । आत्मा रत्नत्रयात्मोक्तो यथा युक्तिपरिग्रहः ॥

The absolute identity of the Self with the higher Self so that there remains no distinction between the subject and object of meditation and meditation itself is proclaimed also in other texts: Pūjyapāda's *Iṣṭopadeśa* 25; Devasena's *Ārādhanāsāra* 11; *Jñānārṇava* 31. 37–8:

कटस्य कर्ताहमिति संबन्धः स्याद् द्वयोर्द्वयोः । ध्यानं ध्येयं यदात्मैव संबन्धः कीदृशस्तदा ॥
आराहणमाराहं आराहय तह फलं च जं भणियं । तं सव्वं जाणिज्जो अप्पाणं चेव णिच्छयदो[2] ॥
अनन्यशरणीभूय स तस्मिन् लीयते तथा । ध्यातृध्यानोभयाभावे ध्येयेनैक्यं यथा व्रजेत् ॥
सोऽयं समरसीभावस्तदेकीकरणं स्मृतम् । अपृथक्त्वेन यत्रात्मा लीयते परमात्मनि ॥

Somadeva has a number of verses which contain the reflections of the devotee engaged in meditation (P. 395):

सुखामृतसुधासूतिस्तद्द्वेरुदयाचलः । परं ब्रह्माहमत्रासे तमःपाशवशीकृतः ॥
यदा चकास्ति मे चेतस्तद्ध्यानोदयगोचरम् । तदाहं जगतां चक्षुः स्यामादित्य इवातमाः ॥
आदौ मधवमधु प्रान्ते सर्वमिन्द्रियजं सुखम् । प्रातःस्नायिषु हेमन्ते तोयमुष्णमिवाङ्गिषु ॥
यो दुरामयदुर्देशे बद्धग्रासो यमोऽङ्गिनि । स्वभावसुभगे तस्य स्पृहा केन निवार्यते ॥
जन्मयौवनसंयोगसुखानि यदि देहिनाम् । निर्विपक्षाणि को नाम सुधीः संसारमुत्सृजेत् ॥
अनुयाचेत नायूंषि नापि मृत्युमुपाहरेत् । भृतो भृत्य इवासीत कालावधिमविस्मरन् ॥
महाभोगोऽहमद्यास्मि यत्तत्त्वरुचितेजसा । सुविशुद्धान्तरात्मासे तमःपारे प्रतिष्ठितः ॥
तन्नास्ति यदहं लोके सुखं दुःखं च नाप्तवान् । स्वप्नेऽपि न मया प्राप्तो जैनागमसुधारसः ॥
सम्यगेतत् सुधाम्भोधेर्बिन्दुमप्यालिहन् मुहुः । जन्तुर्न जातु जायेत जन्मज्वलनभाजनः ॥

'I am the higher Self, the moon of the nectar of bliss, and the mountain

---

1 एष यः आत्मा स परमात्मा कर्मविशेषेण जातः जाप्यः । यदा जानाति आत्मना आत्मानं तदा स एव देवः परमात्मा ॥

2 आराधनमाराध्यं आराधकस्तथा फलं च यद् भणितम् । तत् सर्वं जानीहि आत्मानं चैव निश्चयतः ॥

whence rises the sun of bliss. Overpowered by the fetters of ignorance, I am confined within the body. But when my mind shines under the influence of the contemplation of the higher Self, I will be the eye of the universe, like the sun free from darkness. All pleasures of the senses are sweet at the outset, but bitter at the end, like water in the winter, which at first proves warm to bathers at dawn. Death is ready to swallow even a creature afflicted with a fell disease: who can check his greed for one that is beautiful by nature ? If life, youth, association and the joys of creatures were permanent, what wise man would desire to avoid the cycle of births ? One should neither long for life nor invite death, but remain like a servant maintained with wages, not forgetting the limit of one's term. Paramount happiness is mine today, standing as I do on the farther shore of darkness, the inner Self thoroughly purified by the light of faith in the fundamental truths. No pleasure or pain is there in the world which I have not experienced, but never have I tasted the nectar of Jaina lore even in a dream. No living creature ever becomes subject to the flames of rebirth if he takes, rightly and often, even a drop of that ocean of nectar !'

The devotee should also contemplate the nature and glory of Jina, 'who appears to shine in person in the lights of meditation'. Somadeva describes in a series of verses the various aspects of the Exalted One's sacred majesty, as a guide to the devotee's own contemplation of the true character of Jina. Portions of the *dhyāna* are reproduced below (P. 397):

देवं देवसभासीनं पञ्चकल्याणनायकम् । चतुस्त्रिंशद्गुणोपेतं प्रातिहार्योपशोभितम् ॥
निरञ्जनं जनाधीशं परमं रमयाश्रितम् । अच्युतं च्युतदोषौघमभवं भवभृद्गुरुम् ॥
प्रभवं सर्वविद्यानां सर्वलोकपितामहम् । सर्वसत्त्वहितारम्भं गतसर्वमसर्वगम् ॥[1]
स्तूयमानमनूचानैर्ब्रह्मोद्यैर्ब्रह्मकामिभिः । अध्यात्मागमवेधोभिर्योगिमुख्यैर्महर्द्धिभिः ॥
निरूपं रूपिताशेषमशब्दं शब्दनिष्ठितम् । अस्पर्शं योगसंस्पर्शमरसं सरसागमम् ॥
अतावकगुणं[2] सर्वं त्वं सर्वगुणभाजनः । त्वं सृष्टिः सर्वकामानां कामसृष्टिनिमीलनः ॥
त्रयीमार्गं त्रयीरूपं त्रयीमुक्तं त्रयीपतिम् । त्रयीन्यासं त्रयीतत्त्वं त्रयीचूडामणिस्थितम् ॥[3]
जगतां कौमुदीचन्द्रं कामकल्पावनीरुहम् । गुणचिन्तामणिक्षेत्रं कल्याणागमनाकरम् ॥
प्रणिधानप्रदीपेषु साक्षादिव चकासतम् । ध्यायेज्जगत्त्रयार्चार्हमर्हन्तं सर्वतोमुखम् ॥

Somadeva then explains the Jaina view of gods. He tells us that the Jaina scriptures have imagined the existence of various deities for the protection of the faith, but whoever considers them equal in matters

---

1 न सर्वं गच्छति इति शरीरप्रमाणमित्यर्थः—Ms. A.

2 यद् वस्तु तत् सर्वम् अतावकगुणं त्वत्स्वरूपं न—Ms. A.

3 According to Ms. A, त्रयी means successively (1) रत्नत्रय (2) सत्ता, सुख and चैतन्य (3) राग, द्वेष and मोह (4) the three forms of knowledge (मति श्रुत and अवधि) (5) अतीत, अनागत and वर्तमानकाल (6) उत्पाद, व्यय and ध्रौव्य (7) and the three worlds.

of worship to Lord Jina, 'the eye of the three worlds', is bound to go to the lowest hell, although it is permissible to honour them as well by allotting to tham a portion of the ceremonial offerings. These deities including Indra show favour of their own accord to those who are solely devoted to the Jaina creed, possess right faith, and carefully observe the vows.[1]

The contemplation of Lord Jina mentioned above is an attempt to visualize the diverse aspects of the saviour's personality, and is generally known as *rūpastha dhyāna.*[2] The worshipper may contemplate also the mystic formula signifying the five Parameṣṭhins, namely the *Arhaṁ mantra*, 'the eternal foundation of all branches of knowledge'. While contemplating it the devotee should use the *mandara-mudrā* and mentally locate the *mantra* on his forehead.[3] We are told that sages contemplate this *mantra* after studying all the scriptures and performing the greatest austerities, and that any one who mentally repeats it attains all kinds of prosperity whether he is pure or impure, happy or miserable.[4] It may be noted that this kind of meditation is known as *padastha dhyāna,* explained in *Jñānārṇava* (chap. 38), which describes diverse mystic formulas including the *Arhaṁ mantra.*[5]

The above forms of meditation are called by Somadeva transcendental (*lokottara*), and he makes also certain observations which he calls popular or general (*laukika*). The devotee, for instance, should contemplate the *Oṁkāra* formula, mentally locating it on the tip of the nose and concentrating the mind on space between the eyebrows.[6] He should arouse the mystic lotus inside his navel and move the connected artery, and then direct the four 'winds' or subtle breaths relating to earth, water, fire and air towards the mind.[7] It may be noted that the process referred to here

---

1 'ताः शासनाधिरक्षार्थं कल्पिताः परमागमे' etc.

2 See *Jñānārṇava*, chap. 39.

3 ध्यायेद्वा वाङ्मयं ज्योतिर्गुरुपञ्चकवाचकम् । एतद्धि सर्वविद्यानामधिष्ठानमनश्वरम् ॥ ध्यायन् विन्यस्य देहेऽस्मिन्निदं मन्दरमुद्रया। सर्वनामादिवर्णार्हं वर्णाद्यन्तं सबीजकम् ॥ P. 398. MS. A says मस्तकोपरि हस्तद्वयेन शिखराकारः कुड्मलः क्रियते स एव मन्दरः।

4 'अधीत्य सर्वशास्त्राणि विधाय च तपः परम्' etc.

5 उक्तं च—अकारादि हकारान्तं रेफमध्यं सबिन्दुकम्। तदेव परमं तत्त्वं यो जानाति स तत्त्ववित् ॥ *Jñānārṇava* (op. cit.)

6 पञ्चमूर्तिमयं बीजं नासिकाग्रे विचिन्तयत्। निधाय संगमे चेतो दिव्यज्ञानमवाप्नुयात् ॥ It may be noted that the Jaina *Om* is composed of the first letters of the name of the five Parameṣṭhins. अ (अरहन्त) + अ (अशरीर i. e. सिद्ध) + आ (आचार्य) + उ (उपाध्याय) + म् (मुनि i. e. साधु) = ओम् or ॐ See Brahmadeva's commentary on *Dravyasaṃgraha*, verse. 49.

7 पद्ममुत्थापयेत् पूर्वं नाडीं संचालयेत्ततः। मरुच्चतुष्टयं पश्चात् प्रचारयतु चेतसि ॥ Ms. A says नाभौ स्वभावेन स्थितं कमलं चालयेत् पश्चात् नालाकारेण नाडीं, नाड्या कृत्वा मरुतः हृदयं प्रति प्रापयेत्। (मरुच्चतुष्टयं) पृथ्वी-अप्-तेजोवायुमण्डलानि नासिकामध्ये सूक्ष्मानि स्थितानि तानि चेतसि आत्मविषये प्रचारयतु योजयतु।

is employed in *prāṇāyāma*, and the devotee has to master the control and regulation of each of the four kinds of vital air, believed to be located, each in its own centre, inside the nostrils. The topic is treated in detail in *Jñānārṇava* 29. 15 ff.

Somadeva goes on to say that just as a person, holding a lamp in his hand, looks at something and then puts the lamp aside, similarly the devotee, after having seen the object of knowledge with the help of knowledge, should renounce knowledge (that is, mental action) altogether.[1] Concentration in meditation takes place only when the inflow of all sinful *karma* ceases, and there can be no question of *dhyāna* for those whose minds are corrupted by sin.[2] Milk turned into curds never becomes milk again: similarly, one whose soul has been purified by the knowledge of the truth is not contaminated by sins again.[3]

In conclusion, no real difference exists between the individual Self and the blissful higher Self: the former is so called when in bondage, and becomes the blissful higher Self again when it is released from bondage. There is, however, a great difference between the body and the Self, the former extremely impure and the latter extremely pure, and the Self should always be meditated upon after isolating it from the body.[4] Just as oil remains separate in water, similarly the Self remains apart within the body.[5] Those who know the truth should by proper means isolate the Self from the body in spite of their long association, just as clarified butter is ingeniously separated from curds.[6] The relation between the body and the Self, the one with form and the other without form, is like that of a flower and its fragrance, a tree and its shade, and a face and its reflection.[7]

Somadeva's elaborate discourse on *dhyāna* ends with a definition of *āsanas* or Yogic postures viz. *padmāsana*, *vīrāsana* and *sukhāsana*, and a few hints on the method of acquiring concentration during meditation.

e) The next item of Sāmāyika is the worship of Śrutadevatā or the presiding goddess of the Jaina scriptures, also called Sarasvatī, like her Brahmanical counterpart. Somadeva, following his usual method, gives a

---

1 दीपहस्तो यथा कश्चित् किंचिदालोक्य तं त्यजेत् । ज्ञानेन ज्ञेयमालोक्य पश्चात्तं ज्ञानमुत्सृजेत् ॥ P. 398.

2 सर्वपापास्रवे क्षीणे ध्याने भवति भावना । पापोपहतबुद्धीनां ध्यानवार्तापि दुर्लभा ॥

3 दधिभावगतं क्षीरं न पुनः क्षीरतां व्रजेत् । तत्त्वज्ञानविशुद्धात्मा पुनः पापैर्न लिप्यते ॥

4 जीवः शिवः शिवोर्जः किं भेदोऽस्त्यत्र कश्चन । पाशबद्धो भवेज्जीवः पाशमुक्तः शिवः पुनः ॥ अत्यन्त मलिनो देहः पुमानत्यन्तनिर्मलः । देहादेनं पृथक्कृत्वा तस्मान्नित्यं विचिन्तयेत् ॥

5 तोयमध्ये यथा तैलं पृथग्भावेन तिष्ठति । तथा शरीरमध्येऽस्मिन् पुमानास्ते पृथक्तया ॥

6 दध्नः सर्पिरिवात्मायमुपायेन शरीरतः । पृथक्क्रियेत तत्त्वज्ञैश्चिरं संसर्गवानपि ॥

7 पुष्पामोदौ तरुच्छाये यद्वत् सकलनिष्कले । तद्वत्तौ देहदेहस्थौ यद्वा लपनबिम्बवत् ॥ P. 399.

series of verses, composed by himself, to accompany the various offerings made to the goddess. The following verses are addressed to the goddess at the time of offering water, lights and incense respectively (P. 401):

यस्याः पदद्वयमलंकृतियुग्मयोग्यं लोकत्रयाम्बुजसरःप्रविहारहारि ।
तां वाग्विलासवसतिं सलिलेन देवीं सेवे कविश्रुतरुमण्डनकल्पवल्लीम् ॥

एकं पदं बहुपदापि ददासि तुष्टा वर्णात्मिकापि च करोषि न वर्णभाजम् ।
सेवे तथापि भवतीमथवा जनोऽर्थी दोषं न पश्यति तदस्तु तवैष दीपः ॥

चक्षुः परं करणकन्दरदूरितेऽर्थे मोहान्धकारविधुतौ परमः प्रकाशः ।
तद्धामगामिपथवीक्षणरत्नदीपस्त्वं सेव्यसे तदिह देवि जनेन धूमैः ॥

The following verses mark the conclusion of the worship of Śrutadevatā (P. 401):

कलधौतकमलमौक्तिकदुकूलमणिजालचामरप्रायैः ।
आराधयामि देवीं सरस्वतीं सकलमङ्गलैर्भावैः ॥

स्याद्वादभूधरभवा मुनिमाननीया देवैरनन्यशरणैः समुपासनीया ।
स्वान्ताश्रिताखिलकलङ्कहरप्रवाहा वागापगास्तु मम बोधगजावगाहा ॥

'I worship Goddess Sarasvatī with all-auspicious objects comprising golden lotuses, silken scarves studded with pearls, bejewelled curtains and fly-whisks. Like an elephant entering the waters of a river, may my intellect plunge into the River of Speech, whose current cleanses the mind of all its impurities, (the River) that rises from the Mount of Syādvāda doctrine, is worthy of the veneration of the sages, and fit to be adored by the gods, having no other refuge!' The adoration of Śrutadevatā brings to a close the Sāmāyika or customary worship, and Somadeva concludes this section with a devout prayer to Jina (P. 402):

दृष्टस्त्वं जिन सेवितोऽसि नितरां भावैरनन्याश्रयैः स्निग्धस्त्वं न तथापि यत्समविधिर्भक्ते विरक्तेऽपि च ।
मच्चेतः पुनरेतदीश भवति प्रेमप्रकृष्टं ततः किं भाषे परमत्र यामि भवतो भूयात् पुनर्दर्शनम् ॥

XIII) The second Śikṣāvrata is Proṣadha or religious fasting on four days of the month (the eighth and fourteenth lunar days in each fortnight). He who observes this *vrata* should refrain from all sinful actions and practise self-control; and abstaining from bath, perfumes, bodily decoration, ornaments and women, observe fast and devote himself to religious meditation in a temple or on a hill or at home or in the woods.[1] The inner spirit cannot become pure without the mortification of the body: what else but fire can purify gold?[2] Failure to examine and sweep the ground before use, evil

1 स्नानगन्धाङ्गसंस्कारभूषायोषाविषक्तधीः । निवृत्तसर्वसावद्यक्रियः संयमतत्परः ॥ देवागारे गिरौ चापि गृहे वा गहनेऽपि वा । उपोषितो भवेन्नित्यं धर्मध्यानपरायणः ॥ P. 402.

2 विशुध्येन्नान्तरात्मायं कायक्लेशविधिं विना । किमग्नेरन्यदस्तीह काञ्चनाश्मविशुद्धये ॥

actions, evil thoughts and abstention from the Āvaśyakas or obligatory duties[1] destroy the efficacy of the Proṣadha vow.[2]

XIV) The third Śikṣāvrata is the limitation of worldly enjoyment. Enjoyment is of two kinds. Food and other objects which can be used only once are called *bhoga*, and objects such as ornaments which can be used again and again are known as *paribhoga*.[3] Both kinds of enjoyment should be kept within bounds to prevent 'mental obsession', and one should voluntarily practise abnegation when everything needed comes into one's possession.[4] Abnegation may be of two kinds, *yama* and *niyama*, the former being for life and the latter for a limited period.[5] Flowers and vegetables containing various living organisms, e. g., onions, Ketakī and Nimba flowers, and Sūraṇa roots should be forsaken for life.[6] One should also avoid ill-cooked and prohibited food as well as food that has come in contact with or got mixed up with living organisms, and food that has not been prepared under one's own supervision.[7]

XV) The fourth Śikṣāvrata is *dāna* or charity.[8] That which contributes towards one's own welfare and promotes the cultivation of the Three Jewels in others and brings relief to one's kinsmen as well as others is called *dāna*.[9] Some practise charity with a view to attaining bliss in the next world, others to get it in this world, and there are also those who practise charity because it is proper to do so.[10]

Dāna or charity is of four kinds, namely, gift of *abhaya* or protection, gift of food, gift of medicine and gift of sacred lore.[11] Of these *abhaya* is the highest gift, and the wise should always give the first place to affording protection to all living creatures.[12] Next comes the gift of food, and it is the duty of a householder to feed Jaina *sādhus* or holy men

---

1 (1) Sāmāyika, avoidance of sin leading to equanimity; (2) praise of the twenty-four Arhats; (3) Vandanā, homage to those having the mūla and uttara-guṇas; (4) Pratikramaṇa, repentance; (5) kāyotsarga, cure of spiritual faults by meditation; (6) pratyākhyāna, determination to avoid sin.

2 अनवेक्षाप्रतिलेखनदुष्कर्मारम्भदुर्मनस्काराः । आवश्यकविरतियुताश्चतुर्थमेते विनिघ्नन्ति ॥

3 यः सकृत् सेव्यते भावः स भोगो भोजनादिकः । भूषादि परिभोगः स्यात् पौनःपुन्येन सेवनात् ॥

4 परिमाणं तयोः कुर्याच्चित्तव्याप्तिनिवृत्तये । प्राप्ते योग्ये च सर्वस्मिन्निच्छया नियमं भजेत् ॥

5 यमश्च नियमश्चेति द्वौ त्याज्ये वस्तुनि स्मृतौ । यावज्जीवं यमो ज्ञेयः सावधिर्नियमः स्मृतः ॥

6 पलाण्डुकेतकीनिम्बसुमनःसूरणादिकम् । त्यजेदाजन्म तद्रूपबहुप्राणिसमाश्रयम् ॥ P. 403. Compare *Ratnakaraṇḍa-śrāvakācāra* III. 39: अल्पफलबहुविघातान्मूलकमार्द्राणि शृङ्गवेराणि । नवनीतनिम्बकुसुमं कैतकमित्येवमवहेयम् ॥

7 दुष्पक्वस्य निषिद्धस्य जन्तुसंबन्धमिश्रयोः । अवीक्षितस्य च प्राशस्तत्संख्याक्षतिकारणम् ॥

8 यथाविधि यथादेशं यथाद्रव्यं यथागमम् । यथापात्रं यथाकालं दानं देयं गृहाश्रमैः ॥ P. 403.

9 आत्मनः श्रेयसेऽन्येषां रत्नत्रयसमृद्धये । स्वपरानुग्रहायेत्थं यत् स्यात्तद्दानमिष्यते ॥

10 परलोकधिया कश्चित् कश्चिदैहिकचेतसां । औचित्यमनसा कश्चित् सतां वित्तव्ययस्त्रिधा ॥

11 अभयाहारभैषज्यश्रुतभेदाच्चतुर्विधम् ।

12 अभयं सर्वसत्त्वानामादौ दद्यात् सुधीः सदा ।

according to the nine-fold canon of hospitality consisting of reception, offering of a high seat, washing of the feet, adoration, salutation, affable speech, affable manners and affable temperament, and, lastely, purity of food.[1] Particular attention should be paid to the quality and purity of the food, which should be seasonable and prepared at home and not brought from another locality nor purchased from the bazar.[2] Food that has been touched by wicked people or consecrated to gods and Yakṣas as well as offerings brought for mystic rites should not be given to the *sādhus* to eat.[3]

He who observes the Three Jewels, that is, the cardinal principles of Jainism, is the most deserving of those who are entitled to charity, and anything given to one who is not a follower of the Three Jewels is like seeds sown on barren soil.[4] In fact, charity practised in favour of those who are attached to false doctrines and wrong conduct leads to evil consequences, like the feeding of serpents with milk.[5] If one wishes to be charitable towards such people out of pity or from a sense of propriety, one should give them a residual portion of food to be taken away and not feed them in one's house.[6] Even the sight of them during the reception of Jaina holy men leads to pollution, just as even pure water is contaminated by a vessel containing poison.[7] One must not live or talk with or accord hospitality to Buddhists, Nāstikas, Sacrificers, ascetics wearing matted hair (Śaivas), Ājīvaka mendicants and others of similar persuasion.[8] Conversation with people ignorant of the fundamental truths, and corrupted by evil propensities, leads only to a free fight in which the parties belabour each other with sticks and pull each other's hair.[9]

There are five classes of people who are entitled to hospitality: the *samayin*, the *śrāvaka*, the *sādhu*, the *sūri* and the *samayadīpaka*. The *samayin* is an adherent of the Jaina faith and may be a layman or a monk. The *śrāvaka* is one who has an expert knowledge of astrology, incantations, omens and unseen things in general as well as the art of healing. The time for religious functions such as initiation, festivals and installation of idols cannot be fixed without his help, and Somadeva naively asks how the Jaina

---

1 प्रतिग्रहोच्चासनपादपूजाप्रणामवाक्कायमनःप्रसादाः । विधाविशुद्धिश्च नवोपचाराः कार्या मुनीनां गृहसंश्रितेन ॥ P. 404.

2 ग्रामान्तरात् समानीतं मन्त्रानीतमुपायनम् । न देयमापणक्रीतं विरुद्धं वा यथर्तुकम् ॥

3 'न देयं दुर्जनस्पृष्टं देवयक्षादिकल्पितम् ।' '..................मन्त्रानीतमुपायनम् ॥'

4 तदुत्तमं भवेत् पात्रं यत्र रत्नत्रयं नरे । ....यत्र रत्नत्रयं नास्ति तदपात्रं विदुर्बुधाः । उप्तं तत्र वृथा सर्वमूषरायां क्षिताविव ॥ P. 406.

5 मिथ्यात्वग्रस्तचित्तेषु चारित्राभासाभागिषु । दोषायैव भवेद्दानं पयःपानमिवाहिषु ॥

6 कारुण्यादथवौचित्यात्तेषां किञ्चिद्दिशन्नपि । दिशेदुद्धृतमेवान्नं गृहे भुक्तिं न कारयेत् ॥

7 सत्कारादिविधावेषां दर्शनं दूषितं भवेत् । यथा विशुद्धमप्यम्बु विषभाजनसंगमात् ॥

8 शाक्यनास्तिकयागज्ञजटिलाजीवकादिभिः । सहावासं सहालापं तत्सेवां च विवर्जयेत् ॥

9 अज्ञाततत्त्वचेतोभिर्दुराग्रहमलीमसैः । युद्धमेव भवेद्गोष्ठ्यां दण्डादण्डि कचाकचि ॥

faith will progress if one has to ask the followers of other religions for information about these matters.[1] The *sādhu* is one who has accomplished religious austerities combined with the observation of the Mūla and Uttaraguṇas, that is, the entire range of the Jaina religious vows.[2] The *sūri* is the leader of society in the sphere of knowledge as well as the practice of religion, and should be worshipped like a god, since he is like a boat for crossing the ocean of existence.[3] The *samayadīpakas* are men who advance the cause of the Jaina faith by their knowledge of the world, poetical faculties and other powers as well as eloquence and skill in disputation.[4]

It is useless to test the purity of monks for the purpose of giving them food: whether they are good or bad, the householder is purified by the mere act of giving.[5] Besides, householders are in the habit of spending mony on so many things that it is not wise to consider the pros and cons of a gift too much.[6] The greater the merits of a monk, the greater should be the respect shown to him; but those who are wealthy should use their money, acquired through luck, to help any follower of the Jaina faith, since a monk, conforming to the standard laid down by the scriptures, may or may not be available for the purpose of charity.[7] The creed established by the great Jaina seers is professed by men of diverse faculties, and does not depend upon any single individual, just as a house does not rest on a single pillar.[8]

Dāna is of three kinds: *rājasa*, *tāmasa* and *sāttvika*. Charity accompanied by self-glorification, momentary, casual and lacking in conviction is known as *rājasa*.[9] Charity practised through the agency of servants and slaves without any respect for the recipient or familiarity with him, and without any consideration of merit, is *tāmasa*.[10] Charity is *sāttvika* when hospitality is spontaneous and the recipient worthy, and when the giver has certain qualities, namely, faith, contentment, reverence, knowledge, liberality, forbearance and ability.[11] The *sāttvika* form of charity is the best, the *rājasa* comes next, and the *tāmasa* is the worst. Somadeva says in this connection

---

1 ज्योतिर्मन्त्रनिमित्तज्ञः सुप्रज्ञः कायकर्मसु। दीक्षायात्राप्रतिष्ठाद्याः क्रियास्तद्विरहे कुतः। तदर्थं परपृच्छायां कथं च समयोन्नतिः॥ P. 407.

2 मूलोत्तरगुणश्लाघ्यैस्तपोभिर्निष्ठितस्थितिः। साधुः साधु भवेत् पूज्यः पुण्योपार्जितपण्डितैः॥

3 ज्ञानकाण्डे क्रियाकाण्डे चातुर्वर्ण्यपुरःसरः। सूरिर्देव इवाराध्यः संसाराब्धितरण्डकः॥

4 लोकवित्त्वकवित्वाद्यैर्वादवाग्मित्वकौशलैः। मार्गप्रभावनोद्युक्ताः सन्तः पूज्या विशेषतः॥

5 भुक्तिमात्रप्रदाने हि का परीक्षा तपस्विनाम्। ते सन्तः सन्त्वसतो वा गृही दानेन शुध्यति॥

6 सर्वारम्भप्रवृत्तानां गृहस्थानां धनव्ययः। बहुधास्ति ततोऽत्यर्थं न कर्तव्या विचारणा॥

7 दैवाल्लब्धं धनं धन्यैर्वप्तव्यं समयाश्रिते। एको मुनिर्भवेल्लभ्यो न लभ्यो वा यथागमम्॥

8 उच्चावचजनप्रायः समयोऽयं जिनेशिनाम्। नैकस्मिन् पुरुषे तिष्ठेदेकस्तम्भ इवालयः॥

9 यदात्मवर्णनप्रायं क्षणिकाहार्यविभ्रमम्। परप्रत्ययसंभूतं दानं तद्राजसं मतम्॥ P. 408.

10 पात्रापात्रसमावेक्ष्यमसत्कारमसंस्तुतम्। दासभृत्यकृतोद्योगं दानं तामसमूचिरे॥

11 आतिथेयं स्वयं यत्र यत्र पात्रनिरीक्षणम्। गुणाः श्रद्धादयो यत्र दानं तत् सात्त्विकं विदुः॥

that the statement (made by Brahmanical writers) that what is given in this life is recovered by the donor in the next life[1] is entirely false. Cows, for instance, are in the habit of eating water and grass, but they produce milk, something quite different.[2]

It is the duty of householders to remedy the ills of monks and saints, which may be of three kinds: physical ailments, mental worries and external troubles such as the rigours of cold and wind.[3] If the laity neglect the sufferings of the monks, the latter cannot maintain their spiritual concentration, and the former will render themselves guilty of impiety.[4] While the monks are engaged in expounding and studying the sacred texts, they should be comforted with lodging, food, books and other amenities. The holy texts—the Aṅgas, Pūrvas, Prakīrṇas, Sūktas and the utterances of the Kevalins—would entirely become extinct, if those who know the scriptures thoroughly were to perish on account of neglect.[5] One should therefore help the monks to master the scriptures by sheltering and encouraging them and contributing to their joy, and by providing them with materials necessary for their study.[6] It should be remembered that men, capable of physical labour, for instance, the carrying of arms, are easily available, but those who are endowed with real knowledge are rare like heroes.[7] Knowledge alone can control the mind, like a spear controlling an elephant: without knowledge, physical labour is nothing but labour that is lost.[8] One who concentrates on knowledge succeeds in external austerities without any effort, but, as a matter of fact, external activities no longer take place when the soul is immersed in knowledge.[9] It is doubtful if a man without knowledge can destroy his *karma* even after ages, but a man who is endowed with knowledge and *yoga* is sure to destroy his *karma* in a moment.[10] The man whose speech is not refined by the science of words, and whose intellect is not purified by right principles, is like a blind person labouring according to the convictions of others.[11]

---

1 Cf. *Naiṣadhacarita* 5. 92—दानपात्रमधमर्णमिहैकग्राहि कोटिगुणितं दिवि दायि। साधुरेति सुकृतैर्यदि कर्तुं पारलौकिककुसीदमसीदत् ॥

2 यद्दत्तं तदमुत्र स्यादित्यसत्यपरं वचः। गावः पयः प्रयच्छन्ति किं न तोयतृणाशनाः॥ P. 408.

3 शारीरमानसागन्तुव्याधिसंबाधसंभवे। साधुसंयमिनां कार्यः प्रतीकारो गृहाश्रितैः॥ P. 409.

4 मुनीनां व्याधियुक्तानामुपेक्षायामुपासकैः। असमाधिर्भवेत्तेषां स्वस्य चाधर्मकर्मता॥ (added from MSS.)

5 सौमनस्यं सदाचर्यं व्याख्यत्सु च पठत्सु च। (added from MSS.) आवासपुस्तकाहारसौकर्यादिविधानकैः॥ अङ्गपूर्वप्रकीर्णोक्तं सूक्तं केवलिभाषितम्। नश्येन्निर्मूलतः सर्वं श्रुतस्कन्धधरात्यये॥

6 प्रश्रयोत्साहनानन्दस्वाध्यायोचितवस्तुभिः। श्रुतवृद्धान् मुनीन् कुर्वञ्जायते श्रुतपारगः॥

7 अस्त्रधारणवद्ग्राह्ये क्लेशे हि सुलभा नराः। यथार्थज्ञानसंपन्नाः सौडीरा इव दुर्लभाः॥

8 सृणिवज्ज्ञानमेवास्य वशायाशयदन्तिनः। तदृते च बहिःक्लेशः क्लेश एव परं भवेत्॥

9 बहिस्तपः स्वतोऽभ्येति ज्ञानं भावयतः सतः। क्षेत्रज्ञे यन्निमग्नेऽत्र कुतः स्युरपराः क्रियाः॥

10 यदज्ञानी युगैः कर्म बहुभिः क्षपयेन्न वा। तज्ज्ञानी योगसंपन्नः क्षपयेत् क्षणतो ध्रुवम्॥

11 शब्दैतिह्यैर्न गीः शुद्धा यस्य शुद्धा न धीर्नयैः। स परप्रत्ययात् क्लिश्यन् भवेदन्धसमः पुमान्॥

Somadeva mentions at the end of this section the various factors which destroy the value of charity. They are 'instructions to others' to make a gift on one's behalf, that is, lack of personal attention; jealousy at the liberality of others; lack of punctuality (in serving a guest); the practice of depositing food on sentient objects such as lotus leaves or covering it with same.[1]

XVI) The custom of *sallekhanā* or fasting unto death is dealt with in VIII. 45. Somadeva says that the practice is to be followed when the body is about to perish, like a dry leaf or a lamp without oil.[2] The hour of this last act of life comes when everyday the body loses strength and power of enjoyment, and is beyond remedy.[3] Self-restraint, study, austerities, worship, and charity all become useless if the mind is not pure at the last hour of life.[4] Just as the training of a king, who has learnt the use of weapons for twelve years, becomes useless if he faints on the battlefield; similarly the past conduct of a saint is of no avail if his mind is impure at the end.[5] One should renounce one's affection for friends, infatuation with riches and illwill towards enemies, and then take proper steps (that is, resort to *sallekhanā*) after confessing all sins before the head of the congregation.[6] Food should be gradually given up and then beverages, both sweet and pungent; and one should thereafter abstain from everything with one's mind fixed on the five Parameṣṭhins.[7] There are five factors that destroy the efficacy of *sallekhanā*: the desire to live longer, the desire to die to avoid suffering, longing for friends, recollection of past happiness and the desire for happiness in the next life.[8]

XVII) In *Yaśastilaka* VIII. 44 Somadeva interprets from the Jaina point of view a number of Brahmanical terms, which illustrates certain salient features of the Jaina outlook in religious matters. For instance, a Dīkṣita is not one who kills goats and other animals in sacrifices, but one whose daily sacrifice consists in friendliness towards all creatures.[9] A Śrotriya is not one who has external purity, but one who has nothing to do with wicked deeds and wicked men, and is kindly disposed towards all creatures.[10] A Hotā is not one who kindles the external fire, but one who

1 सार्धं सचित्तनिक्षिप्तवृताभ्यां दानहानये । अन्योपदेशमात्सर्यकालातिक्रमणक्रियाः ॥ P. 410.

2 तरुदलमिव परिपक्वं स्नेहविहीनं प्रदीपमिव देहम् । स्वयमेव विनाशोन्मुखमवबुध्य करोतु विधिमन्त्यम् ॥ P. 413.

3 प्रतिदिवसं विजहद्बलमुज्झद्भुक्तिं त्यजत् प्रतीकारम् । वपुरेव नृणां निगिरति चरमचरित्रोदयं समयम् ॥

4 यमनियमस्वाध्यायास्तपांसि देवार्चनाविधिर्दानम् । एतत् सर्वं निष्फलमवसाने चेन्मनो मलिनम् ॥

5 द्वादश वर्षाणि नृपः शिक्षितशस्त्रो रणेषु यदि मुह्येत् । किं स्यात्तस्यास्त्रविधेर्यथा तथान्ते यतेः पुराचरितम् ॥

6 स्नेहं विहाय वन्धुषु मोहं विभवेषु कलुषतामहिते । गणिनि च निवेद्य निखिलं दुरीहितं तदनु भजतु विधिमुचितम् ॥

7 अशनं क्रमेण हेयं स्निग्धं पानं ततः खरं चैव । तदनु च सर्वनिवृत्तिं कुर्याद्गुरुपञ्चकस्मृतौ निरतः ॥

8 जीवितमरणाशंसे सुहृदनुरागः सुखानुबन्धविधिः । एते सनिदानाः स्युः सल्लेखनहानये पञ्च ॥

9 अद्रोहः सर्वसत्त्वेषु यज्ञो यस्य दिने दिने । स पुमान् दीक्षितात्मा स्यान्न त्वजादियमाशयः ॥ P. 421.

10 दुष्कर्मदुर्जनास्पर्शी सर्वसत्त्वहिताशयः । स श्रोत्रियो भवेत् सत्यं न तु यो बाह्यशौचवान् ॥

casts the fuel of good deeds in the spiritual fire with the formulas of kindness.[1] A Sacrificer is defined as one who adores the deity with the flowers of pure thoughts, the mansion of the body with the flowers of vows, and the fire of the mind with the flowers of forbearance.[2] The Veda that pleases the wise is not the one which causes the destruction of all creatures in sacrifices, but the one which clearly makes known the difference between the body and the soul.[3] The Threefold Lore (i. e. the Veda) is called Trayī, because it destroys the triad of birth, old age and death, the cause of transmigration.[4] A Brāhmaṇa is not one who is blind with the pride of birth, but one who does not destroy life, observes salutary vows, has knowledge, and is without desires and acquisition.[5] The true Pañcāgnisādhaka (one who performs austerities amid five fires) is he who has controlled the five fires: lust, anger, pride, deceit and greed.[6] Knowledge is Brahma, kindness is Brahma, and the destruction of lust is Brahma: when the soul rests securely on these, a man is called Brahmacārin.[7] A Paramahaṁsa is not an ascetic who eats anything and everything like fire, but one who can (like a *haṁsa*, swan) distinguish between *karma* and the soul, intermingled like water and milk.[8]

XVIII) The 46th section of Book VIII, called Prakīrṇaka, which deals with certain miscellaneous topics, brings to a close Somadeva's elaborate discourse on the Jaina religion. It describes chiefly the six daily duties of a householder:[9] worship of the *deva* i. e. Jina, adoration of the teacher, *svādhyāya* or study of spiritual lore,[10] *tapas* or physical and mental activities leading to the purification of the soul by removing external and internal impurities,[11] *saṁyama* or control of the passions and the senses, and the observance of the vows,[12] and *dāna* or charity. Kaṣāya (passion) is derived thus (P. 416):

'कषन्ति संतापयन्ति दुर्गसंगतिसंपादनेनात्मानमिति कषायाः क्रोधादयः । अथवा यथा विशुद्धस्य वस्तुनो नैयग्रोधादयः कषायाः कालुष्यकारिणः, तथा निर्मलस्यात्मनो मलिनत्वहेतुत्वात् कषाया इव कषायाः ।'

XIX) Stray allusions to Jaina tenets occur occasionally in the course of Utprekṣās and similes. For example, मनुष्यरूपेण परिणतं धर्मद्वयमिव Book I,

---

1 अध्यात्माग्नौ दयामन्त्रैः सम्यक्कर्म समिच्चयम् । यो जुहोति स होता स्यान्न बाह्याग्निसमेधकः ॥
2 भावपुष्पैर्यजेद्देवं व्रतपुष्पैर्वपुर्गृहम् । क्षमापुष्पैर्मनोवह्निं यः स यष्टा सतां मतः ॥
3 विवेकं वेदयेदुच्चैर्यः शरीरशरीरिणोः । स प्रीत्यै विदुषां वेदो नाखिलक्षयकारणम् ॥
4 जातिर्जरा मृतिः पुंसां त्रयी संसृतिकारणम् । एषा त्रयी यतस्त्रय्याः क्षीयते सा त्रयी मता ॥
5 अहिंसः सद्व्रतो दानी निरीहो निष्परिग्रहः । यः स्यात् स ब्राह्मणः सत्यं न तु जातिमदान्धलः ॥
6 कामः क्रोधो मदो माया लोभश्चेत्यग्निपञ्चकम् । येनेदं साधितं स स्यात् कृती पञ्चाग्निसाधकः ॥ P. 411.
7 ज्ञानं ब्रह्म दया ब्रह्म ब्रह्म कामविनिग्रहः । सम्यगत्र वसन्नात्मा ब्रह्मचारी भवेन्नरः ॥
8 कर्मात्मनोर्विवेक्ता यः क्षीरनीरसमानयोः । भवेत् परमहंसोऽसौ नाग्निवत् सर्वभक्षकः ॥ P. 412.
9 देवसेवा गुरूपास्तिः स्वाध्यायः संयमस्तपः । दानं चेति गृहस्थानां षट् कर्माणि दिने दिने ॥ P. 414.
10 अनुयोगगुणस्थानमार्गणास्थानकर्मसु । अध्यात्मतत्त्वविद्यायाः पाठः स्वाध्याय उच्यते ॥
11 अन्तर्बहिर्मलप्लोषादात्मनः शुद्धिकारणम् । शारीरं मानसं कर्म तमः प्राहुस्तपोधनाः ॥
12 कषायेन्द्रियदण्डानां विजयो व्रतपालनम् । संयमः संयतैः प्रोक्तः श्रेयः श्रयितुमिच्छताम् ॥

p. 136. This is a reference to the Sāgāradharma, the Rule of life prescribed for the householders, and the Anagāradharma, the Rule of life prescribed for the monks. प्रदर्शितात्मरूपं प्रमाणद्वितयमिव Ibid. The two Pramāṇas recognised by Jaina doctrine, Pratyakṣa and Parokṣa, are referred to. बहिःप्रकटव्यापारं शुभध्यान-युग्ममिव Ibid. The two pure Dhyānas, Dharmadhyāna and Śukladhyāna (see above), are meant. नयनविषयतां गतं नययमलमिव Ibid. A reference to the two types of Naya, the method of comprehending things from a particular standpoint. While the Pramāṇas convey the whole truth, the Nayas reveal only partial truths. Broadly speaking, they are of two kinds: *dravyārthika,* which has in view the substance in its permanent aspect, and *paryāyārthika,* which takes note of the modes of the fluctuating aspect of the substance and its qualities. नयपद्धतिरिव स्याद्वादस्य Book II, p. 223. Naya is also classified into five or rather seven kinds: *naigama,* the non-analytical; *saṁgraha,* the collective; *vyavahāra,* the practical; *ṛjusūtra,* the straight or immediate; and *śabda,* the verbal or nominal. *S'abda* is subdivided into *samabhirūḍha,* the subtle, and *evaṁbhūta,* the actual.[1] According to Malliṣeṇa (*Syādvādamañjarī* under verse 28), the Nyāya and Vaiśeṣika systems follow the Naigama-naya: the Advaita Vedānta and the Sāṁkhya are guided by the Saṁgraha-naya; the Cārvāka school comes under the Vyavahāra-naya; the Buddhists accept the Ṛjusūtra-naya; and the Grammarians and others take their stand on the Śabda-naya.[2] The method of comprehending things from such diverse standpoints is what Somadeva calls *nayapaddhati,* and the doctrine of Syādvāda, known as *saptabhaṅgīnaya,* is represented as being based on the Naya method.[3] The Syādvāda doctrine itself is set forth as follows: (1) May be, it is; (2) may be, it is not; (3) may be, it is and it is not; (4) may be, it is indescribable; (5) may be, it is and yet indescribable; (6) may be, it is not and it is also indescribable; (7) may be, it is and it is not and it is also indescribable.[4] The doctrine of Syādvāda is claimed to be a great synthesis comprehending all the Nayas without any distinction. Malliṣeṇa says in his *Syādvādamañjarī* (under verse 30) that, just as disputants cease from their quarrels after resorting to an impartial judge, similarly the other Nayas, though mutually hostile, are reconciled in the system of the Arhat, their differences being smoothed over by the use of the expression *Syāt, 'may be'.*[5] नयनीतिरिव नवभूमिका Book V, p. 246. This is another refe-

1 For an explanation of these terms see S. C. Vidyabhushana: *A History of Indian Logic*, p. 170, and specially Dhruva: *Syādvādamañjarī* of Malliṣeṇa, Notes, p. 279 ff.

2 'नैगमनयदर्शनानुसारिणौ नैयायिकवैशेषिकौ । संग्रहाभिप्रायप्रवृत्ताः सर्वेऽप्यद्वैतवादाः सांख्यदर्शनं च । व्यवहारनयानुपाति प्रायश्चार्वाकदर्शनम् । ऋजुसूत्राकूतप्रवृत्तबुद्धयस्ताथागताः । शब्दादिनयावलम्बिनो वैयाकरणादयः ।'

3 Śrutasāgara remarks: यथा नयपद्धतिः स्याद्वादस्य मूलं भवति. He explains नयपद्धतिः as नैगमादिनयाना मार्गः.

4 Vidyabhushana (op. cit.), p. 167.

5 'यथा हि समीचीनं मध्यस्थं न्यायनिर्णेतारमासाद्य परस्परं विवदमाना अपि वादिनो विवादाद्विरमन्ति एवं नया अन्योन्यं वैरायमाणा अपि सर्वज्ञशासनमुपेत्य स्याच्छब्दप्रयोगोपशमितविप्रतिपत्तयः सन्तः परस्परमत्यन्तं सुहृद्भूयावतिष्ठन्ते ।'

rence to the Nayas. A marginal note in MS. A on *navabhūmikā* says नैगमादयः, but the ninefold classification of Naya is rather unusual. Perhaps the two broad divisions of *dravyārthika* and *paryāyārthika* and the seven varieties of Naya are meant: of these *naigama, saṁgraha* and *vyavahāra* come under *dravyārthika-naya,* while *ṛjusūtra, śabda, samabhirūḍha,* and *evaṁbhūta* are subdivisions of *paryāyārthika-naya.* Somadeva may have in mind also the nine divisions of Naigamanaya mentioned in certain texts.[1]

क्षपकश्रेणिरिव तपःप्रत्यवायरहितक्षोणिः Book I, p. 133. The reference is to the 'ladder' known as *kṣapakaśreṇi* mentioned in connection with the fourteen Guṇasthānas or stages on the way to emancipation. There are, in fact, two ladders, *upaśama* and *kṣapaka,* for the suppression and destruction of Cāritra-mohanīya-karma or Right-Conduct-Deluding Karma, and they emerge in the eighth Guṇasthāna. Briefly speaking, the Jīva ascends the *kṣapakaśreṇi* and devotes himself to the destruction of Karma, the last vestige of Cāritra-mohanīya-karma being destroyed in the tenth Guṇasthāna, whence he passes to the twelfth Guṇasthāna.[2] Interesting references to Kṣapakaśreṇi occur in Hemacandra's *Triṣaṣṭiśalākāpuruṣacaritra,* e. g. "She mounted at once the *kṣapakaśreṇi,* and, the eight Karmas being destroyed, she attained omniscience at once from the eighth Guṇasthāna." "As he was reflecting rightly in this way, having ascended the *kṣapakaśreṇi* and having attained pure meditation, omniscience becomes manifest from the destruction of the destructive Karmas, like the light of the sun from the removal of a mass of clouds."[3] A reference of the final stage of religious apprenticeship occurs in the following statement in Book I, p. 135:

'जिनरूपग्रहणायोग्यत्वाच्चरमाचारवशामुपासकदशामाश्रितवदलं मुनिकुमारकयुगलम्'

Śrutasāgara takes this to mean the eleventh Pratimā or stage in the life of a layman, known as *uddiṣṭatyāga-pratimā,* wherein he begs his food and refuses what is specially prepared for him. Abhayaruci and Abhayamati are describ-ed as being in this stage of religious apprenticeship, as they were too young to lead the rigorous life of Digambara monks.

References occur also to the twenty-two Parīṣahas[4] and other miscellaneous topics. The three kinds of Karmandins or monks are mentioned in Book I,[5] and Śrutasāgara explains the term as referring to Ācārya, Upādhyāya and Sarvasādhu.

---

1 पर्यायनैगम, द्रव्यनैगम, द्रव्यपर्यायनैगम etc. See Dhruva (op. cit.), p. 298.

2 For a detailed exposition of the Guṇasthānas see Johnson's English Trans. of Hemacandra's *Triṣaṣṭiśalākāpuruṣacaritra,* Vol. I, Appendix III. See also *Pravacanasāroddhāra* I, p. 196 ff. for a discussion of क्षपकश्रेणि.

3 Johnson's *Trans.* (op. cit.), pp. 197, 378.

4 'आपातदुःसहैर्महापरीषहैरिव' Book I.

5 'त्रिविधस्यापि कर्मन्दिवृन्दस्योत्पादितप्रीतिः' Ibid.

CHAPTER XI

The Anupreksās and Jaina Religious Poetry

Jaina religious poetry, as far as it is represented in *Yaśastilaka*, comprises verses on the Anuprekṣās, hymns, and what may be loosely called religio-ethical verses. Of these the Anuprekṣā verses are the most important not only from the standpoint of subject-matter, but on account of the place they occupy in Jaina literature and relgious thought.

In order to appreciate Somadeva's treatment of the Anuprekṣās, it will be convenient to explain their religious background, and enumerate the principal literary attempts to define and interpret them before and after his time. The Anuprekṣas are, roughly speaking, topics of meditation, twelve in number, and cover a wide range of the cardinal teachings of Jainism. They are in the form of reflections on the transient character of things (*anityānuprekṣā*), helplessness (*aśaraṇānuprekṣā*), the cycle of rebirth (*saṁsārānuprekṣā*), loneliness (*ekatvānuprekṣā*), the distinction between the self and the not-self (*anyatvānuprekṣā*), the impurity of the body (*aśucyanuprekṣā*), the inflow of Karmas (*āsravānuprekṣā*), stoppage of the inflow of Karmas (*saṁvarānuprekṣā*), the shedding of Karma (*nirjarānu-prekṣā*), the constitution of the universe (*lokānuprekṣā*), the difficulty of attaining the Right Path consisting of the Three Jewels (*bodhidurlabhānu-prekṣā*), and the Law expounded by the Arhat (*dharmasvākhyātatvānuprekṣā*). It may be noted that the Anuprekṣās are known also as Bhāvanās, specially in Śvetāmbara texts.

Anuprekṣā means *anucintana* 'pondering', 'reflection'. Pūjyapāda in his commentary on *Tattvārthasūtra* 9. 2 explains Anuprekṣā as 'pondering on the nature of the body and other substances'.[1] *Svāmikārtikeyānuprekṣā* (verse 97) defines it as 'pondering on the right principles' (*sutacca-ciṁtā aṇuppehā*). The word is used also in connection with Svādhyāya or study of sacred lore, of which *anuprekṣā*, pondering on what one has learnt, is an important factor. Pūjyapāda says in his commentary on *Tattvārthasūtra* 9. 25: *adhigatārthasya manasā abhyāsaḥ anuprekṣā*. The word is used in this sense also in *Uttarādhyayanasūtra* 29. 22, wherein *anuppehā*, explained as *cintanikā* in Nemicandra's commentary, is one of the factors of *sammatta-parakkama*, 'exertion in righteousness', mitigating the power and duration of practically all the Karmas.

The Anuprekṣās are designed to serve as aids to spiritual progress, produce detachment, and lead the devotee from the realm of desire to

---

1 'शरीरादीनां स्वभावानुचिन्तनमनुप्रेक्षा'

the path of renunciation. The Bhāṣya on *Tattvārthasūtra* 9. 7 says that the devotee, after reflecting on the transient character of worldly objects and relationships, loses all attachment to them: this is the purpose of *anityānuprekṣā*. He reflects on the fact that there is no escape from death and misery, and the sense of helplessness makes him indifferent to the things of the world and inclines him towards the teachings of the Arhat; this is the purpose of *aśaraṇānuprekṣā* and so on. Similarly, Pūjyapāda, in his commentary on the same *sūtra*, says in connection with *aśucitvānuprekṣā* that the body is impure, and its impurity cannot be removed by bath, perfumes, incense and other means; whereas the contemplation of Right Faith and other principles leads to absolute purity: thinking like this in all earnestness amounts to *aśucitvānuprekṣā*. Thus reflecting, the devotee becomes indifferent to the body and concentrates his mind on 'crossing the ocean of births'. In this way the object of each Anuprekṣā is minutely explained, but the general purpose of the Anuprekṣās is to make the aspirant averse to the world and concentrate his mind on the Self and its emancipation. The *Maraṇasamāhī*, a Jaina canonical text, says that contemplation of the Bhāvanās, that is, the Anuprekṣās leads to *vairāgya* or disgust for the world and seems to sum up the Bhāvanās as *vairāgya-bhāvanā* (verses 636 and 638),[1] and describes them also as producing a strong desire for liberation (verse 571).[2] The idea of the Anuprekṣās being the cause of *vairāgya* is stressed also in *Mūlācāra* 8. 73;[3] and we are told that he who always edifies himself with their help becomes free from Karmas, and being pure, attains the Abode of Purity.[4] Śubhacandra in his *Jñānārṇava* 2. 5, 6 recommends the Bhāvanās for the attainment of the purity of thoughts (*bhāvaśuddhi*) and the growth of *saṁvega* (desire for salvation), *vairāgya*, *yama* (self-control) and *praśama* (extinction of the passions). Hemacandra says in *Yogaśāstra* (4 40, 45, 49, 55) that one should vanquish love and hate for the attainment of mental purity which alone shows the way to *nirvāṇa*; and love and hate can be conquered by means of *samatva* or equanimity, which again is produced by *nirmamatva* or lack of selfish desires; and one should resort to the Bhāvanās for the purpose of cultivating *nirmamatva*. Hemacandra concludes by saying that he who ceaselessly preoccupies the mind with the Bhāvanās becomes indifferent to all objects and maintains an even attitude free from love and hate.[5]

---

1 जइ जह दढप्पइण्णो समणो वेरग्गभावणं कुणइ । तह तह असुभं आयवहयं व सीयं खयमुवेइ ॥ बारस वि भावणाओ एवं संखेवओ समत्ताओ । भावेमाणो जीवो जाओ समुवेइ वेरग्गं ॥

2 'दढसंवेगकरीओ'

3 'बुहजणवेरग्गजणणीओ'

4 अणुवेक्खाहिं एवं जो अत्ताणं सदा विभावेदि । सो विगदसव्वकम्मो विमलो विमलालयं लहदि ॥

5 भावनाभिरविश्रान्तमिति भावितमानसः । निर्ममः सर्वभावेषु समत्वमवलम्बते ॥ 4. 110.

The Anuprekṣās have other aspects as well. In *Tattvārthasūtra* 9. 2 they are mentioned among the agencies that cause Saṁvara or stoppage of the influx of Karmas, the others being Gupti, Samiti, Dharma etc. The Anuprekṣās are also brought into special connection with Dharmya-dhyāna, one of the two forms of spiritual contemplation prescribed by Jaina doctrine. In a number of verses quoted by Siddhasena in his commentary on *Tattvārtha-sūtra* 9. 38 the Anuprekṣās are prominently mentioned among the preliminaries to Dharmya-dhyāna.[1] According to Śubhacandra (*Jñānārṇava* 41. 3) the Anuprekṣās are the leading cause of Dharmya-dhyāna, and the devotee is asked to determine the nature of the Self by implanting them in his mind.[2] Śivārya in his *Bhagavatī Ārādhanā* (verse 1714) goes one step further, and definitely recommends the contemplation of the Anuprekṣās as a sort of supplementary discipline in the stage of Dharmya-dhyāna known as Saṁsthānavicaya, consisting in meditation on the constitution of the universe according to the Jaina conception.[3] A similar yet different standpoint is met with in Cāmuṇḍarāya's *Cāritrasāra.* It mentions two kinds of Dharmya-dhyāna, *bāhya* and *ādhyātmika,* and classifies the latter into ten varieties including Saṁsthānavicaya, which is, however, explained as 'investigation of things as they are' (*yathāvasthita-mīmāṁsā*) and completely identified with the twelve Anuprekṣās.

The Anuprekṣās are thus viewed from different standpoints, but their wider aspect can hardly be mistaken. They are in the nature of reflections on the fundamental facts of life, and remind the devotee of the teachings of the Master on the subject of rebirth, Karma and its destruction, equanimity and self-control, the glory of the Law and the final goal. They are no doubt designed to develop the contemplative faculty of the Yogin, and may be called the starting point of *dhyāna.* But they have also a great moral significance inasmuch as they are meant to develop purity of thoughts and sincerity in the practice of religion. Kundakunda, for instance, in his *Bhāvaprābhṛta* (verse 94) exhorts the devotee to contemplate the Anuprekṣās and the twentyfive Bhāvanās, and asks: what is the use of external symbols without inner conviction?[4] The catholic character of the Anuprekṣās is shown by the fact that they are recommended to monks and laymen alike for contemplation (*Maraṇasamāhi,* v. 571). In our work king Yaśorgha ponders on them on the eve of his abdication and retirement from the world. Somaprabha tells us in his *Kumārapālapratibodha* that Kumārapāla, after

1 Vol. II, P. 272.

2 अनुप्रेक्षाश्च धर्म्यस्य स्युः सदैव निबन्धनम् । चित्तभूमौ स्थिरीकृत्य स्वस्वरूपं निरूपय ॥

3 अह तिरियउड्ढलोए विचिणादि सपज्जए ससंठाणे । इच्चेव अणुगदाओ अणुपेहाओ वि विचिणादि ॥

4 भावहि अणुवेक्खाओ अवरे पणवीसभावणा भावि । भावरहिएण किं पुण बाहिरलिंगेण कायव्वं ॥

receiving instruction in the twelve Bhāvanās, experienced a feeling of indifference to the world and used to reflect on them while looking after the affairs of the kingdom.[1] Amitagati in his *S'rāvakācāra* 14. 82 says in conformity with earlier texts that he who meditates on the Anuprekṣās constantly with devotion comprehends all the fundamental facts and attains liberation, after getting rid of his Karma.

The human and spiritual appeal of the Anuprekṣās accounts for their popularity, as evinced by the numerous attempts made to describe and interpret them in Prākrit and Sanskrit verse and occasionally also in prose. A more or less extensive literature may be said to have grown up on the subject, as will be seen from the short sketch given below.

The famous Digambara authority Kundakunda, who is assigned to the beginning of the Christian era, is perhaps the earliest writer to deal with the Anuprekṣās as an independent subject, being the author of a treatise called *Bārasa Aṇuvekkhā*, 'The twelve Anuprekṣās', containing 91 verses in Prākrit (Jaina Śaurasenī). The treatment here is simple yet authoritative, and has influenced later writers on the subject. Connected with this work is the account of the Anuprekṣās in *Mūlācāra* (Chap. 8) in 76 verses in Prākrit. The work is attributed to Vaṭṭakera who is sometimes identified with Kundakunda himself.[2] While these may be the earliest metrical efforts to offer a systematic exposition of the Anuprekṣās, there is an exhaustive treatment of them in a canonical text called *Maraṇasamāhi*, one of the Paiṇṇas, which devotes 70 verses (569-639) to the Bhāvanās. While enumerating the Bhāvanās, it mentions Uttama Guṇas instead of Dharma (v. 573), obviously meaning thereby Uttama Kṣamā, Uttama Mārdava etc., being the characteristics of Dharma.

The three ancient works mentioned above are composed in a more or less similar style, and there is also occasional similarity in thought, and the subject of their inter-relationship requires critical investigation (Mūlācāra 8. 13; Maraṇasamāhi, verse 590; Bārasa Aṇuvekkhā, verse 22; Maraṇasamāhi, verse 588):

मिच्छत्तेणोच्छण्णो मग्गं जिणदेसिदं अपेक्खंतो । भमिहदि भीमकुडिल्ले जीवो संसारकंतारे ॥
हा जह मोहियमइणा सुग्गइमग्गं अजाणमाणेणं । भीमे भवकंतारे सुचिरं भमियं भयकरम्मि ॥
अण्णो अण्णं सोयदि मदो त्ति मम णाहगो त्ति मण्णंतो । अप्पाणं ण हु सोयदि संसारमहण्णवे बुड्डं ॥
सोअइ अण्णजणं अन्नभवंतरगयं तु बालजणो । नवि सोयइ अप्पाणं किलिस्समाणं भवसमुद्दे ॥

---

1 इय बारह भावण सुणिवि राउ, मणमज्झि वियंभियभवविराउ । रज्जु वि कुणंतु चिंतइ इमाउ, परिहरिवि कुगइकारणु पमाउ ॥

2 A. N. Upadhye: *Pravacanasāra, Intro.*, p. 26.

The next important treatise to deal with the subject is *Svāmikārttikeyānuprekṣā* of Kārttikeya, who devotes the entire work of 489 verses in Prākrit to the elucidation of the Anuprekṣās. It is a work of considerable merit, but the treatment of the subject is disproportionate inasmuch as more than 350 verses deal only with Lokānuprekṣā (115-283) and Dharmānuprekṣā (302–486). This is due to the fact that Kārttikeya includes in his work many heterogeneous details not usually incorporated in the discussion of the Anuprekṣās. The date of the author is not certain, but he is assigned to the early centuries of the Christian era.

A comprehensive exposition of the Anuprekṣās occurs also in Śivārya's *Bhagavatī Ārādhanā*,[1] a devotional work in Śaurasenī Prākrit containing more than 2000 verses, of which (1715–1872) deal with the Anuprekṣās. Śivārya is an important writer and said to be a disciple of Samantabhadra. He may be identified with Śivakoṭi who is mentioned in Jinasena's *Ādipurāṇa* 1. 49. That he is considerably earlier than the tenth century is shown by the fact that his *Ārādhanā* was translated into Sanskrit verse by the wellknown writer Amitagati who flourished towards the end of the tenth century and the beginning of the eleventh. Śivārya's style is simple and lucid, and he uses a large number of interesting similes to illustrate his ideas. For example,

रत्तिं एकम्मि दुमे सउणाणं पिंडणं व संजोगो । परिवेसो व अणिच्चो इस्सरियाणाधणारोग्गं ॥ 1720
धावदि गिरिणदिसोदं व आउगं सव्वजीवलोगम्मि । सुकुमालदा वि हायदि लोगे पुव्वण्हछाही व ॥ 1723
जह आइच्चमुदितं कोई वारंतओ जगे णत्थि । तह कम्ममुदीरंतं कोई वारंतओ णत्थि ॥ 1740
ससगो वाहपरद्धो बिलं ति णाऊण अजगरस्स मुहं । सरणं ति मण्णमाणो मच्चुस्स मुहं जह अदीदि ॥ 1781
तह अण्णाणी जीवा परिद्धमाणा छुधादिवाहेहिं । अदिगच्छंति महादुहहेदुं संसारसप्पमुहं ॥ 1782
सरिसीए चंदिगाए कालो वेस्सो पिओ जहा जुण्हो । सरिसे वि तहा चारे कोई वेस्सो पिओ कोई ॥ 1808
छंडिय रयणाणि जहा रयणद्दीवा हरिज्ज कट्ठाणि । माणुसभवे वि छंडिय धम्मं भोगे भिलसदि तहा ॥ 1829
पावपयोगासवदारणिरोधो अप्पमादफलिगेण। कीरइ फलिगेण जहा णावाए जलासवणिरोधो ॥ 1837

Strings of Rūpakas are also used occasionally:

एवं पिणद्धसंवरवम्मो सम्मत्तवाहणारूढो । सुदणाणमहाधणुगो झाणादितवोमयसरेहिं ॥ 1853
संजमरणभूमीए कम्मारिचमू पराजिणिय सव्वं । पावदि संजयजोहो अणोवमं मोक्खरज्जसिरिं ॥ 1854

It is not known when Sanskrit verse was first employed to describe the Anuprekṣās, but Somadeva's account of them in *Yaśastilaka*, Book II in 53 verses composed in the Vasantatilakā metre may be regarded as one of the earliest attempts to expound them in Sanskrit instead of Prākrit verse. His treatment of the Anuprekṣās is weighty and compact and full of spiritual fervour; and his verses on the subject are unique in the sense

1 For a detailed note on the *Bhagavatī Ārādhanā*, see A. N. Upadhye: *Bṛhat-kathākośa* Intro. pp. 50 ff.

that they are composed by a writer who is not only a learned theologian but a religious poet of no mean order.

Far more comprehensive in treatment and simpler in style is the exposition of the Anuprekṣās in Śubhacandra's *Jñānārṇava*, which calls them Bhāvanās and devotes more than 190 verses to the subject. Śubhacandra may be assigned to about the eleventh century, and his *Jñānārṇava* is an authoritative work on Yoga.[1] Although the author disclaims poetical pretensions (1. 19), he handles Sanskrit verse with remarkable felicity and sometimes employs elaborate metres. The following verses from the section on Anitya-bhāvanā will illustrate his style:

गीयते यत्र सानन्दं पूर्वाह्णे ललितं गृहे । तस्मिन्नेव हि मध्याह्ने सदुःखमिह रुद्यते ॥
गगननगरकल्पं संगमं वल्लभानां जलदपटलतुल्यं यौवनं वा धनं वा ।
सुजनसुतशरीरादीनि विद्युच्चलानि क्षणिकमिति समस्तं विद्धि संसारवृत्तम् ॥

Śubhacandra concludes his exposition with an eloquent verse in praise of the Bhāvanās:

एता द्वादशभावनाः खलु सखे सख्योऽपवर्गश्रियस्तस्याः संगमलालसैर्घटयितुं मैत्रीं प्रयुक्ता बुधैः ।
एतासु प्रगुणीकृतासु नियतं मुक्त्यङ्गना जायते सानन्दा प्रणयप्रसन्नहृदया योगीश्वराणां मुदे ॥

Amitagati, whose *Subhāṣitaratnasaṁdoha* and *Dharmaparīkṣā* are wellknown works, wrote also a *S'rāvakācāra* 'Duties of laymen', of which the fourteenth chapter deals with the Anuprekṣās in 84 verses composed in a variety of metres (Rathoddhatā, Dodhaka, Upajāti, Puṣpitāgrā, Vasantatilakā etc.). The following verses may serve as specimens:

यौवनं नगनदीस्यदोपमं शारदाम्बुदविलासजीवितम् ।
स्वप्नलब्धधनविभ्रमं धनं स्थावरं किमपि नास्ति तत्त्वतः ॥ 14. 1
पातकमाश्रवति स्थिररूपं संभृतिमात्मवतां न यतीनाम् ।
वर्मधरान्न नरान् रणरङ्गे क्वापि भिनत्ति शिलीमुखजालम् ॥ 14. 53

Vādībhasiṁha, who flourished in the early years of the eleventh century and wrote the poem *Kṣattracūḍāmaṇi* and the prose romance *Gadyacintāmaṇi*, devotes more than fifty verses to the Anuprekṣās in the former work (11. 28–80). The verses are rather pedestrain in style and composed in the Śloka metre. In the last verse the Self is exhorted to have abiding faith in the exquisitely pure Jaina religion:

तवात्मन्नात्मनीनेऽस्मिन् जैनधर्मेऽतिनिर्मले । स्थवीयसी रुचिः स्थेयादा मुक्तेर्मुक्तिदायिनी ॥

After Vādībhasiṁha we may mention Hemacandra, who flourished in the twelfth century. He deals with the Anuprekṣās, called by him

1 Śubhacandra wrote between 959 A. D., the date of composition of *Yaśastilaka*, which is quoted by him in *Jñānārṇava*, and 1227 A. D., the date of one of the manuscripts of his work. See Chap, I and Pt. Nathuram Premi's *Jaina Sāhitya aura Itihāsa* p. 440.

Bhāvanās, in his *Yogaśāstra* 4. 55-110, besides devoting a large number of supplementary verses (*antaraślokāḥ*) to the topic in his own commentary on the work. There are, for instance, only three main verses in the text on Saṁsāra-bhāvanā, while there are 90 supplementary verses in the *svopajña* commentary, containing an imaginative description of the grief and despair of the gods at the prospect of their fall from heaven (vv. 69-89). The following striking verse also occurs in the commentary (Verse 53, op. cit.):

स्याच्छैशवे मातृमुखस्तारुण्ये तरुणीमुखः । वृद्धभावे सुतमुखो मूर्खो नान्तर्मुखः क्वचित् ॥

Hemacandra eloquently describes the universal discipline and equilibrium maintained by the sustaining power of Dharma in the verses on Dharma-svākhyāta-bhāvanā (4. 96 ff.):

आप्लावयति नाम्भोधिराश्वासयति चाम्बुदः । यन्महीं स प्रभावोऽयं ध्रुवं धर्मस्य केवलः ॥
न ज्वलत्यनलस्तिर्यग् यदूर्ध्वं वाति नानिलः । अचिन्त्यमहिमा तत्र धर्म एव निबन्धनम् ॥ etc.

After Hemacandra comes Siddhasena Sūri who wrote his Sanskrit commentary on Nemicandra's Prākrit work *Pravacanasāroddhāra* in 1192 A. D.[1] In this commentary Siddhasena devotes more than 130 verses to the Bhāvanās, some of them being composed in elaborate metres. Siddhasena's exposition is not without literary merit, as will be seen from the following specimens:

सुमतिरमतिः श्रीमानश्रीः सुखी सुखवर्जितः सुतनुरतनुः स्वाम्यस्वामी प्रियः स्फुटमप्रियः ।
नृपतिरनृपः स्वर्गी तिर्यङ् नरोऽपि च नारकस्तदिति बहुधा नृत्यत्यस्मिन् भवी भवनाटके ॥
यत् प्रोद्दाममदान्धसिन्धुरघटं साम्राज्यमासाद्यते यन्निःशेषजनप्रमोदजनकं संपद्यते वैभवम् ।
यत् पूर्णेन्दुसमद्युतिर्गुणगणः संप्राप्यते यत् परं सौभाग्यं च विजृम्भते तदखिलं धर्मस्य लीलायितम् ॥

Among later accounts of the Anuprekṣās one of the most noteworthy is that of Āśādhara in his *Anagāradharmāmṛta* 6. 57–82. He wrote this work about the middle of the thirteenth century and added to it a *svopajña* commentary after the manner of Hemacandra. He employs elaborate metres, and a good specimen of his style is furnished by the following verse on the rarity of Bodhi or the attainment of the Right Path.

दुष्प्रापं प्राप्य रत्नत्रयमखिलजगत्सारमुत्सारयेयं नो चेत् प्रज्ञापराधं क्षणमपि तदरं विप्रलब्धोऽक्षधूर्तैः ।
तत् किंचित् कर्म कुर्यां यदनुभवभवत्क्लेशसंक्लेशसंविद्बोधेर्विन्देय वार्तामपि न पुनरनुप्राणनास्याः कुतस्त्याः ॥

A brief but interesting exposition of the Bhāvanās in Apabhraṁśa verse is found in Somaprabha's *Kumārapālapratibodha* written in 1184 A. D.[2] on the conversion of king Kumārapāla of Gujarat to Jainism and his instruction in that religion by Hemacandra. The work is written in Prākrit, but certain

1 The date is mentioned at the end of the work: करिसागरविसंख्ये श्रीविक्रमनृपतिवत्सरे चैत्रे । पुष्यार्कदिने शुक्लाष्टम्यां वृत्तिः समाप्तासौ ॥ The Vikrama Saṁvat is 1248.

2 Winternitz: *History of Indian Literature*, Vol. II, p. 571.

portions are in Sanskrit and in Apabhraṁśa, among them the verses on the Bhāvanās towards the end of the third chapter. The following two verses are cited as specimens:

राया वि रंकु सयणो वि सत्तु जणओ वि तणउ जणणि वि कलत्तु ।
इह होइ नडु व्व कुकम्मवंतु संसाररंगि बहुरूवु जंतु ॥
एक्कल्लउ पावइ जीवु जम्मु एक्कल्लउ मरइ विढत्तकम्मु ।
एक्कल्लउ परभवि सहइ दुक्खु एक्कल्लउ धम्मिण लहइ मुक्खु ॥

We are not concerned with the various comments on the Anuprekṣās in prose, but it may be pointed out that they are elaborately expounded in the Bhāṣya on *Tattvārthasūtra* 9. 7 and Pūjyapāda's commentary thereon. The Anuprekṣās are dealt with in detail also in Cāmuṇḍarāya's *Cāritrasāra* written in prose in the eleventh century.[1] This account is based on that of Pūjyapāda who is sometimes copied verbatim, but the description of the Āsravānuprekṣā is interesting as containing a reference to the story of Yaśodhara and Amṛtamati. A detailed interpretation of the Anuprekṣās is found also in Brahmadeva's commentary on Nemicandra Siddhāntacakravartin's *Dravyasaṁgraha* (verse 35). Brahmadeva has been assigned to the thirteenth century.[2]

Despite the extent of the literature on the Anuprekṣās, we do not find in it much originality of thought, as the prevailing characteristics of the various literary attempts to deal with them are rather elaboration and illustration designed to elucidate the cardinal teachings of the Jaina faith. Every writer on the subject seeks to express himself in as striking a manner as possible; and both in point of style and ideas Somadeva's exposition ranks high among the metrical compositions on the twelve Anuprekṣās. Most of his verses on them are translated below.

1. Anityānuprekṣā

(Thoughts on the Transient Character of Things)

उत्सृज्य जीवितजलं बहिरन्तरेते रिक्ता विशन्ति मरुतो जलयन्त्रकल्पाः ।
एकोद्यमं जरति यूनि महत्यणौ च सर्वंकषः पुनरयं यतते कृतान्तः ॥

These (five) life-breaths draw the water of life, like a water-wheel, and leaving it outside, enter the body empty.[3] Death, the destroyer of all, acts with equal effort on old and young, great and small (2. 105).

1 Winternitz: *History of Indian Literature*, p. 587.

2 A. N. Upadhye: *Paramātmaprakāśa*, Introduction, p. 72.

3 The process of breathing is represented as a sort of gradual exhaustion of the vital force, bringing death nearer and nearer.

उच्चैः पदं नयति जन्तुमधः पुनस्तं वात्येव रेणुनिचयं चपला विभूतिः ।
श्राम्यत्यतीव जनता वनितासुखाय ताः सूतवत् करगता अपि विप्लवन्ते ॥

Unstable Prosperity raises a man high and brings him low again, as a whirlwind does a heap of dust. People strive hard for the pleasure afforded by lovely women, but the latter slip away, like mercury, even when securely possessed (2. 107).

शूरं विनीतमिव सज्जनवत् कुलीनं विद्यामहान्तमिव धार्मिकमुत्सृजन्ती ।
चिन्ताज्वरप्रसवभूमिरियं हि लोकं लक्ष्मीः खलक्षणसखी कलुषीकरोति ॥

The goddess of wealth forsakes the valiant and the humble, the good and the highborn, the learned and the pious. A moment's friend, like a villain, she is a source of the fever of anxiety and corrupts the world (2. 108).

वाचि भ्रुवोर्दृशि गतावलकावलीषु यासां मनः कुटिलतास्तटिनीतरङ्गाः ।
अन्तर्न मान्त इव दृष्टिपथे प्रयाताः कस्ताः करोतु सरलास्तरलायताक्षीः ॥

Who can render women sincere, women with large and nimble eyes? The crookedness of their minds seems to overflow their hearts, like the waves of a river, and comes into view in their words, eyebrows and eyes, in their gait, and in the curls of the hair (2. 109).

संहारबद्धकवलस्य यमस्य लोके कः पश्यतोहरविधेरवधिं प्रयातः ।
यस्माज्जगत्त्रयपुरीपरमेश्वरोऽपि तत्राहितोद्यमगुणे विधुरावधानः ॥

Who in the world hath ever passed beyond the range of Death that acts like a robber, ready to clutch and destroy? Even Jina, the overlord of all the three worlds, is powerless against Death when the latter exerts himself (2. 110).

इत्थं क्षणक्षयहुताशमुखे पतन्ति वस्तूनि वीक्ष्य परितः सुकृती यतात्मा ।
तत् कर्म किंचिदनुसर्तुमयं यतेत यस्मिन्नसौ नयनगोचरतां न याति ॥

Thus seeing on all sides the things falling into the destructive fire of Death, the virtuous self-restrained man should strive to pursue that line of conduct wherein Death appears nevermore (2. 111).

2. Aśaraṇānuprekṣā

(Thoughts on one's Helplessness)

दत्तोदयेऽर्थनिचये हृदये स्वकार्यें सर्वः समाहितमतिः पुरतः समास्ते ।
जाते त्वपायसमयेऽम्बुपतौ पतत्रेः पोतादिव द्रुतवतः शरणं न तेऽस्ति ॥

When thy wealth is on the increase and thy heart bent on spending,[1] everybody stands to attention before thee. But, like a bird flying from a ship on the sea, thou hast none to save thee at the hour of death (2. 112).

बन्धुव्रजैः सुभटकोटिभिरासवर्गैर्मन्त्रास्त्रतन्त्रविधिभिः परिरक्ष्यमाणः ।
जन्तुर्बलादधिबलोऽपि कृतान्तदूतैरानीयते यमवशाय वराक एकः ॥

1 Śrutasāgara says 'स्वकार्यें धनकार्यें हृदये चित्ते वर्तमाने सति'.

Even when a man is stronger than an army, being protected by multitudes of kinsmen, millions of warriors, and trusty followers with all the resources of counsel, arms and troops, he is brought under the sway of Death by the latter's messengers— miserable and all alone (2. 113).

संसीदतस्तव न जातु समस्ति शास्ता त्वत्तः परः परमवाप्तसमग्रबोधेः ।
तस्यां स्थिते त्वयि यतो दुरितोपतापसेनेयमेव सुविधे विधुराश्रया स्यात् ॥

Good-natured one, once thou hast attained the full measure of Bodhi (right knowledge, conduct and faith), thou hast verily no protector other than thyself in thy ills. The army of Sins and Sufferings is helpless so long as thou art devoted to Bodhi (2 114).

3. Saṁsārānuprekṣā

(Thoughts on the Cycle of Transmigration)

कर्मार्पितं क्रमगतिः पुरुषः शरीरमेकं त्यजत्यपरमाभजते भवाब्धौ ।
शैलूषयोषिदिव संसृतिरेनमेषा नाना विडम्बयति चित्रकरैः प्रपञ्चैः ॥

In the ocean of existence, the transmigrating soul leaves one body, the result of Karma, and resorts to another. The cycle of existence, like an actress, deludes the soul with many a marvellous show (2. 115).

दैवाद्धनेष्वधिगतेषु पटुर्न कायः काये पटौ न पुनरायुरवाप्तवित्तम् ।
इत्थं परस्परहतात्मभिरात्मधर्मैर्लोकं सुदुःखयति जन्मकरः प्रबन्धः ॥

When by chance wealth is acquired, health is absent. When there is health, longevity attended by wealth is lacking. Thus the process of birth and rebirth inflicts misery on the world with its mutually contradictory attributes (2. 116).

आस्तां भवान्तरविधौ सुविपर्ययोऽयमत्रैव जन्मनि नृणामधरोच्चभावः ।
अल्पः पृथुः पृथुरपि क्षणतोऽल्प एव स्वामी भवत्यनुचरः स च तत्पदार्हः ॥

Let alone the mighty ups and downs in the births to follow; even in this life men are subject to rise and fall. The small becomes great and in a moment the great becomes small. The master becomes servant and the latter attains the former's rank (2. 117).

वैचित्र्यमित्थमनुभूय भवाम्बुराशेरातङ्कवाडवविडम्बितजन्तुवारेः ।
को नाम जन्मविषपादपपुष्पकल्पैः स्वं मोहयेन्मृगदृशां कृतधीः कटाक्षैः ॥

Thus realising the varied moods of the ocean of existence, whose waters, to wit, the creatures, are oppressed by the submarine fire of deadly disease, what wise man will let himself be bewitched by fair women's glances that seem to be the flowers of the poison tree of life? (2. 118)

4. Ekatvānuprekṣā

(Thoughts on one's Loneliness)

एकस्त्वमाविशसि जन्मनि संक्षये च भोक्तुं स्वयं स्वकृतकर्मफलानुबन्धम् ।
अन्यो न जातु सुखदुःखविधौ सहायः स्वाजीवनाय मिलितं विटपेटकं ते ॥

Thyself thou undergoest birth and death, all alone, to suffer the consequences of thy own deeds. Thou hast no companion in happiness or misery. Only a crowd of parasites gathers round thee to make their living (2. 119).

बाह्यः परिग्रहविधिस्तव दूरमास्तां देहोऽयमेति न समं सहसंभवोऽपि ।
किं ताम्यसि त्वमनिशं क्षणदृष्टनष्टैर्दारात्मजद्रविणमन्दिरमोहपाशैः ॥

Let alone thy external possessions, even the body, coeval with thee, will not accompany thee at death. Why dost thou suffer evermore from such fetters of delusion as wife and children and wealth and home, appearing and disappearing in a moment? (2. 120).

संशोच्य शोकविवशो दिवसं तमेकमन्येद्युरादरपरः स्वजनस्तवार्थे ।
कायोऽपि भस्म भवति प्रचयाच्चिताग्नेः संसारयन्त्रघटिकाघटने त्वमेकः ॥

Whelmed with grief, thy relatives will mourn thy death only a day, but on the morrow they will be eager only for thy wealth, and the body will be reduced to ashes by the flames of the funeral pyre. Alone thou pliest the water-wheel of life! (2. 121).

एष स्वयं तमचलैर्ननु कर्मजालैर्लूतेव वेष्टयति नष्टमतिः स्वमेकः ।
पुण्यात् पुनः प्रशमतन्तुकृतावलम्बस्तद्धाम धावति विधूतसमस्तबाधम् ॥

Alone and erring, verily a sentient being is enmeshed, like a spider, in the rigid network of Karma, of his own free will. But by dint of religious merit he advances to that state of bliss, free from all pain, threading his way with the aid of spiritual calm (2. 122).

5. PṚTHAKTVĀNUPREKṢĀ

(Thoughts on the Distinction between the Body and the Self)

देहात्मकोऽहमिति चेतसि मा कृथास्त्वं त्वत्तो यतोऽस्य वपुषः परमो विवेकः ।
त्वं धर्मशर्मवसतिः परितोऽवसायः कायः पुनर्जडतया गतधीनिकायः ॥

Never imagine that thou art composed of the body, because the body is utterly different from thee. Thou art all consciousness, an abode of virtue and bliss; whereas the body, because it is inert, is an unconscious mass (2. 123).

आसीदति त्वयि सति प्रतनोति कायः क्रान्ते तिरोभवति भूपवनादिरूपैः ।
भूतात्मकस्य मृतवन्न सुखादिभावस्तस्मात् कृती करणतः पृथगेव जीवः ॥

The body exists and grows so long as thou art in existence. When thou art dead, it disappears in the form of earth, air and the like. Composed of the elements, it is devoid of feelings such as joy, like a corpse. Hence the blissful self is surely different from the body (2. 124).

सानन्दमव्ययमनादिमनन्तशक्तिमुद्द्योतिनं निरुपलेपगुणं प्रकृत्या ।
कृत्वा जडाश्रयमिमं पुरुषं समृद्धाः संतापयन्ति रसवद्दुरिताग्नयोऽमी ॥

The Self is by nature deathless and without any beginning, endowed with bliss and infinite power, and luminous and pure. The powerful flames of sinful Karma heat it, like mercury, after lodging it in the body (2. 125).

कर्मासवानुभवनात् पुरुषः परोऽपि प्राप्नोति पातमशुभासु भवावनीषु ।
तस्मात्तयोः परमभेदविदो विदग्धाः श्रेयस्तदादधतु यत्र न जन्मयोगः ॥

Under the intoxicating power of Karma, even a man of superior merit goes reeling down to unhappy births. Se let the wise, who know the cardinal difference between the body and the Self, strive for the bliss that is free from rebirth (2. 226).

6. Aśucitvānuprekṣā

(Thoughts on the Impurity of the Body)

आधीयते यदिह वस्तु गुणाय कान्तं काये तदेव मुहुरेत्यपवित्रभावम् ॥
छायाप्रतारितमनिर्मलरन्ध्रबन्धं किं जीव लालयसि भङ्गुरमेतदङ्गम् ॥

Whatever is beautiful becomes unclean in a moment, when applied to the body to lend it charm. Deluded by the complexion, why dost thou, o soul, cherish this perishable frame, beset with cavities of dirt? (2. 127).

योषिद्भिरादृतकरं कृतमण्डनश्रीर्यः कामचामररुचिस्तव केशपाशः ।
सोऽयं त्वयि श्रवणगोचरतां प्रयाते प्रेतावनीषु वनवायसवासगोऽभूत् ॥

This thy lock of hair, beautiful as the fly-whisk of the god of love, and elegantly dressed by ladies with careful hands, will, on thy death, find itself in the haunt of wild ravens on cremation-grounds! (2. 128).

अन्तर्बहिर्यदि भवेद्वपुषः शरीरं दैवात्तदानुभवनं ननु दूरमास्ताम् ।
कौतूहलादपि यदीक्षितुमुत्सहेत कुर्यात्तदाभिरतिमत्र भवाञ्शरीरे ॥

If by any chance the interior of the body were visible outside, and thou couldst bring thyself to look at it even out of curiosity, contact being out of the question, then thou wouldst indeed delight in the body! (2. 123).

तस्मान्निसर्गमलिनादपि लब्धतत्त्वाः कीनाशकेलिमनवाप्तधियोऽचिराय ।
कायादतः किमपि तत् फलमर्जयन्तु यस्मादनन्तसुखसस्यविभूतिरेषा ॥

So let men, having learnt the truth even from the body, unclean by nature, and without taking thought of death, attain before long that inexpressible goal which yields a rich harvest of infinite joy! (2. 130).

7. Āsravānuprekṣā

(Thoughts on the Influx of Karma)

अन्तः कषायकलुषोऽशुभयोगसंगात् कर्माण्युपार्जयसि बन्धनिबन्धनानि ।
रज्जूः करेणुवशगः करटी यथैतास्त्वं जीव मुञ्च तदिमानि दुरीहितानि ॥

With thy heart contaminated by passions, thou dost acquire Karma, the cause of bondage, owing to thy assiduity in evil activities; just as an elephant forgetting himself in the company of his mate, earns for himself the ropes that bind him. Renounce, therefore, o sentient being, all thy misdeeds (2. 131).

संकल्पकल्पतरुसंश्रयणात्त्वदीयं चेतो निमज्जति मनोरथसागरेऽस्मिन् ।
तत्रार्थतस्तव चकास्ति न किंचनापि पक्षे परं भवसि कल्मषसंश्रयस्य ॥

Thy heart is submerged in the ocean of desire, because it clings to the all-giving tree of imagination. Thou dost thereby gain really nothing, but only followest the path to sin (2. 132).

सेर्ष्यं विभूतिषु मनोषितसंश्रयाणां चक्षुर्भवत्तव निजार्तिषु मोघवाञ्छम् ।
पापागमाय परमेव भवेद्विमूढ कामात् कुतः सुकृतदूरवतां हितानि ॥

Thy mind, o fool, absorbed in its hankerings and frustrated in its desires, jealously contemplates the splendour of the objects of desire, but only paves the way to sin. How can those who are remote from virtue acquire joys by merely yearning for them? (2. 133).

दौर्विध्यदग्धमनसोऽन्तरुपात्तभुक्तेश्चित्तं यथोल्लसति ते स्फुरितोत्तरङ्गम् ।
धाम्नि स्फुरेद्यदि तथा परमात्मसंज्ञे कौतस्कुती तव भवेद्विफला प्रसूतिः ॥

Thy birth would never be futile, if thy heart delighted in the Light called the Supreme Self,[1] in the same way as it cheers up, heaving with the waves of desire, when thou thinkest of imaginary pleasures, thy mind consumed by penury (2. 134).

8. Saṁvarānuprekṣā

(Thoughts on the Stoppage of the Influx of Karma)

आगच्छतोऽभिनवकार्मणरेणुराशेर्जीवः करोति यदवस्खलनं वितन्द्रः ।
सत्तत्त्वचामरधरैः प्रणिधानहस्तैः सन्तो विदुस्तमिह संवरमात्मनीनम् ॥

The watchful Soul stops the oncoming dust of ever-new Karmas, with the helping hand of meditation, upholding the banner of right doctrines. The good in the world call this *saṁvara* (stoppage) that benefits the soul (2. 135).

नीरन्ध्रसंधिरवधीरितनीरपूरः पोतः सरित्पतिमपैति यथानपायः ।
जीवस्तथा क्षपितपूर्वतमःप्रतानः क्षीणास्रवश्च परमं पदमाश्रयेत ॥

Like as a boat without holes and joints safely traverses the ocean, defying the surge of waters; similarly, the soul, with the expanse of earlier Karma destroyed, and the influx of new ones stopped, reaches the Supreme Goal (2. 137).

9. Lokānuprekṣā

(Thoughts on the Universe)

मध्याधरोर्ध्वरचनः पवनत्रयान्तस्तुल्यः स्थितेन जघनस्थकरेण पुंसा ।
एकस्थितिस्तव निकेतनमेष लोकस्त्रस्यन्निकीर्णजठरोऽग्रनिषण्णमोक्षः ॥

Composed of the upper, the middle and the lower regions, and bounded by

---

1 For the Jaina idea of the *paramātman* see Chap. X.

the three atmospheres[1], and surmounted by the abode of liberated souls, the universe resembles a man in standing posture (with outstretched legs), with the hands resting on the hips. Ever in the same position, it is thy abode, its womb filled with living creatures[2] (2. 138).

त्वं कल्मषावृतमतिर्निरये तिरश्चि पुण्योचितो दिवि नृषु द्वयकर्मयोगात् ।
इत्थं निषीदसि जगत्त्रयमन्दिरेऽस्मिन् स्वैरं प्रचारविधये तव लोक एषः ॥

When thy mind is beset with sin, thou art born in hell, or as some lower animal. Thou art born in heaven, when thou hast religious merit, and among mankind as a result of virtue and sin. Thus thou livest in the three worlds. The universe exists for thy wanderings at will (2. 140).

अत्रास्ति जीव न च किंचिदभुक्तमुक्तं स्थानं त्वया निखिलतः परिशीलनेन ।
तत् केवलं विगलिताखिलकर्मजालं स्पृष्टं कुतूहलधियापि न जातु धाम ॥

No place is there in the entire universe, o soul, which thou hast not repeatedly enjoyed and left.[3] But not even out of curiosity hast thou ever approached the place whence all Karma is banished (2. 141).

10. Nirjarānuprekṣā

(Thoughts on the Shedding of Karma)

आपातरम्यरचनैर्विरसावसानैर्जन्मोद्भवैः सुखलवैः स्खलितान्तरङ्गः ।
दुःखानुषङ्गकरमर्जितवान् यदेनस्तत्त्वं सहस्व हतजीव नवप्रयातम् ॥

Suffer, o miserable being, the consequences of the pain-bringing, ever-new sins thou hast committed, led astray by the pleasures of life, charming in the beginning and unpleasant at the end (2. 142).

कालुष्यमेषि यदिह स्वयमात्मकामो जागर्ति तत्र ननु कर्म पुरातनं ते ।
योऽहिं विवर्धयति कोऽपि विमुग्धबुद्धिः स्वस्योदयाय स नरः प्रवरः कथं स्यात् ॥

Verily it is due to thy ancient Karma that thou, with desire inbred in thee, makest thyself impure in this life. How can the fool that nourishes a serpent achieve his own success? (2. 143).

आतङ्कपावकशिखाः सरसावलेखाः स्वस्थे मनाङ्मनसि ते लघु विस्मरन्ति ।
तत्कालजातमतिविस्फुरितानि पश्चाज्जीवान्यथा यदि भवन्ति कुतोऽप्रियं ते ॥

Thou sentient being, when thy mind is a little at ease, the keenly felt flames of suffering are quickly forgotten. But if the resolve (to practise virtue), taken at the moment of suffering, is subsequently kept in mind, how can sorrow ever be thine? (2. 144).

---

1 घनवात (gross air), अम्बुवात (vapour), and तनुवात (thin air). See *Tattvārthasūtra* 3. 1 and Pūjyapāda's comm. thereon. Also Jaini's trans. and notes.

2 Śubhacandra gives another picture of the universe according to the Jain conception in his *Jñānārṇava* (Lokabhāvānā): वेष्टितः पवनैः प्रान्ते महावेगैर्महाबलैः । त्रिभिस्त्रिभुवनाकीर्णो लोकस्तालतरुस्थितिः ॥ × × अधो वेत्रासनाकारो मध्ये स्याज्झल्लरीनिभः ॥ मृदङ्गसदृशश्चाग्रे स्यादित्थं स त्रयात्मकः ॥

3 i. e. in the course of transmigration.

11. DHARMĀNUPREKṢĀ

(Thoughts on Dharma or Religious Virtue)

श्रद्धाभिसंधिरवधूतबहिःसमीहस्तत्त्वावसायसलिलाहितमूलबन्धः ।
आत्मायमात्मनि तनोति फलद्वयार्थी धर्मं तमाहुरमृतोपमसस्यमाप्ताः ॥

Intent on faith, and discarding. external activities, the Self, desirous of the twin results, heaven and salvation, cultivates within itself Dharma (Religious Virtue), laying its foundation with the water of the knowledge of the fundamental principles. The wise call Dharma a plant with the properties of nectar (2. 145).

मैत्रीदयादमशमागमनिर्वृतानां बाह्येन्द्रियप्रसरवर्जितमानसानाम् ।
विद्याप्रभाप्रहतमोहमहाग्रहाणां धर्मः परापरफलः सुलभो नराणाम् ॥

Religious virtue, productive of salvation as well as worldly joys, can easily be attained by men who delight in the exercise of good will, kindness, self-control and forbearance; whose minds are free from sensual cravings; and who have destroyed the spectre of ignorance with the light of knowledge (2. 146).

इच्छाः फलैः कलयति प्ररुणद्धि बाधाः सृष्टेरसाम्यविभुरभ्युदयादिभिर्यः ।
ज्योतींषि दूतयति चात्मसमीहितेषु धर्मः स शर्मनिधिरस्तु सतां हिताय ॥

A treasure-house of bliss, may Dharma confer benefit on the good! It crowns one's desires with success and wards off all evils and wields unrivalled power over the creation by reason of its vouchsafing prosperity and other results. It sends forth the Lights of supersensuous knowledge as messengers to evoke the aspirations of the Self! (2. 147).

देहोपहारकृतपैः स्वपरोपतापैः कृत्वाध्वरेश्वरमिषं विदलन्मनीषाः ।
धर्मैषिणो य इह केचन मान्द्यभाजस्ते जातजीवितधियो विषमापिबन्ति ॥

Unintelligent men, who desire to attain Dharma, by worshipping Śiva with vociferous texts,[1] recommending animal sacrifices and causing suffering to their own followers and others, are fools that take poison with the idea of preserving their lives (2. 148).

येऽन्यत्र मन्त्रमहिमेक्षणमुग्धबोधाः शर्वैषिणः पुनरतः शिवतां गृणन्ति ।
ते नावि तारणदृशो दृषदोऽवलम्ब्य दुष्पारमम्बुधिजलं परिलङ्घयन्ति ॥

Those of other faiths, who are befooled by the sight of the efficacy of mystic formulas, and adore Śiva and declare salvation to be his gift, are men who seek to traverse the impassable waters of the ocean by supporting themselves on blocks of stone, fancying that they are crossing by boats (2. 149).

---

1 Śrutasāgara says in his commentary कुतपास्तूर्याणि वेदवचनानि इत्यर्थस्तैः

अज्ञस्य शक्तिरसमर्थविधेर्निबोधस्तौ चारुचेरियममू तुदती न किंचित् ।
अन्धाङ्घ्रिहीनहतवाञ्छितमानसानां दृष्टा न जातु हितवृत्तिरनन्तराया ॥

The strength of one who lacks knowledge and the knowledge of one who is unable to act as well as the strength and knowledge of one who has no faith accomplish nothing, because the lack of faith renders knowledge and strength futile. The salutary endeavour of the blind or the lame or those who have lost all hope hath never been seen to be free from obstacles (2. 151.).

चार्व्यां रुचौ तदुचिताचरणे च नृणां दृष्टार्थसिद्धिरगदादिनिषेवणेषु ।
तस्मात् परापरफलप्रदधर्मकामाः सन्तस्त्रयावगमनीतिपरा भवन्तु ॥

Men are seen to attain their object in acts like the taking of medicine for health, when they have right knowledge and faith and observe the right procedure. So let the good, who aspire after Dharma that gives worldly happiness and final release, devote themselves to the way of realising the triad of right knowledge, conduct and faith (2. 152).

12. BODHYANUPREKṢĀ

(Thoughts on Bodhi or the Acquisition of Three Jewels)

संसारसागरमिमं भ्रमता नितान्तं जीवेन मानवभवः समवापि दैवात् ।
तत्रापि यद्भुवनमान्यकुले प्रसूतिः सत्संगतिश्च तदिहान्धकवर्तकीयम् ॥

Unceasingly wandering on the ocean of transmigration, a sentient creature is born as a human being by chance. Even then birth in a family respected by the world and association with the good are as rare as the coming of a quail within a blind man's grasp (2. 153).

कृच्छ्राद्वनस्पतिगतेश्च्युत एष जीवः श्वभ्रेषु कल्मषवशेन पुनः प्रयाति ।
तेभ्यः परस्परविरोधिमृगप्रसूतावस्याः पशुप्रतिनिभेषु कुमानवेषु ॥

Released from birth in the plant world, after much suffering, a sentient being is again born in the hells on account of his sins, then in the genus of animals, mutually hostile, and then again among uncouth men resembling animals (2. 154).

संसारयन्त्रमुदयास्तघटीपरीतं सातानतामसगुणं भृतमाधितोयैः ।
इत्थं चतुर्गतिसरित्परिवर्तमध्यमावाहयेत् स्वकृतकर्मफलानि भोक्तुम् ॥

Thus, in order to reap the consequences of one's deeds, one has to ply the water-wheel of transmigration, bounded by the vessels of prosperity and adversity, and overflowing with the waters of suffering, and furnished with the expansive cords of sin, with the hub of the wheel rotating in the river of the four conditions of existence[1] (2. 155).

---

1 Hellish, sub-human, human and celestial. See *Tattvārthasūtra* 2. 6.

आतङ्कशोकभयभोगकलत्रपुत्रैर्यः खेदयेन्मनुजजन्म मनोरथाप्तम् ।
नूनं स भस्मकृतधीरिह रत्नराशिमुद्दीपयेदतनुमोहमलीमसात्मा ॥

He who wastes his human birth, obtained after cherished desire, with thoughts of disease, sorrows, fear, pleasures, wife and children, might as well consign a heap of jewels to the flames for the sake of the ashes. Verily his soul is blackened by mighty ignorance (2, 156).

बाह्यप्रपञ्चविमुखस्य शमोन्मुखस्य भूतानुकम्पनरुचः प्रियतत्त्ववाचः ।
प्रत्यक्प्रवृत्तहृदयस्य जितेन्द्रियस्य भव्यस्य बोधिरियमस्तु पदाय तस्मै ॥

May Bodhi (the acquisition of the Three Jewels[1]) lead the man with faith to that exalted state, namely, Liberation, the man that is averse to worldly phenomena and eager for spiritual calm, self-controlled, and kind to all creatures, and fond of the truth, his heart devoted to the Inner Self! (2. 157).

The Hymns

The next category of Jaina religious poetry, the hymns, as far as they are represented in *Yaśastilaka*, consist mostly of verses in praise of the Arhat, the five Parameṣṭhins (Arhat, Siddha, Ācārya, Upādhyāya and Sādhu), and the three Jewels (Right Faith, Right Knowledge and Right Conduct). Most of these verses occur in Book VIII, section 35, while another series of verses accompanying various items in the worship of Jina is found in Section 36. Section 37 of the same Book contains a long hymn in honour of Jina in the lyrical metres described in Chap. VII. Reference may also be made to the *dhyāna* (hymn for mental recitation in the course of meditation) in section 39, extracts from which will be found in Chap. X. Verses in honour of the Jaina Sarasvatī, the presiding goddess of the Scriptures, occur in Section 40, which deals with her worship.[2] While most of these eulogistic and devotional verses occur in connection with Sāmāyika or the customary worship of Jina described in Book VIII, isolated verses in his honour are also found elsewhere in the work usually at the beginning and the end of a chapter.

The verses which we have called hymns are composed in elaborate metres in elevated style, as may be expected in a Kāvya poet like the author of *Yaśastilaka*. They are in the nature of a tribute to moral, intellectual and spiritual grandeur, and glorify the sublime in the sphere of religion, asceticism and spiritual culture. The ideal of omniscient and immaculate sainthood, the utter disregard of the body and worldly aspirations, self-control, altruism and universal good-will, right knowledge and faith and conduct: these form the keynote of the eulogies, the abstract

---

1 i. e. Right Faith, Right Knowledge and Right Conduct.

2 See Chap. X.

character of which may be contrasted with the concrete descriptions of many Brahmanical hymns. At the same time the sectarian character of some of the verses is all too apparent, as their purpose is to glorify Jaina dogmas and tenets, specially the Syādvāda doctrine. Nevertheless, these little hymns or prayers breathe an atmosphere of saintly purity, and proclaim the triumph of Light over Darkness, of the all-pure Self over the obstacles of matter.

The scheme of arrangement of the devotional verses in Book VIII, sections 35–37, is worthy of notice. Somadeva starts with elaborate and complicated prose invocations of the five Parameṣṭhins and the three Jewels,[1] followed by groups of verses styled Bhaktis in the following order: Darśanabhakti (Addressed to Jina), Praise of Right Faith (three verses); Jñānabhakti, Praise of Right Knowledge (three verses); Cāritrabhakti, Praise of Right Conduct (three verses); Arhadbhakti, Praise of the Arhat (seven verses); Siddhabhakti, Praise of the emancipated saints (three verses); Caityabhakti, Praise of the Shrine (one verse); Pañcagurubhakti, Praise of the five teachers, that is, the Parameṣṭhins (one verse); Śāntibhakti, Praise of the Tīrthaṁkara Śāntinātha (one verse); and Ācāryabhakti, Praise of the Preceptor Saints (ten verses). It may be noted in this connection that the use of the term Bhakti in the sense of 'a devotional prayer or hymn' is much earlier than Somadeva, who was no doubt influenced to some extent by the Bhaktis attributed to Pūjyapāda and Kundakunda.[2] The Bhaktis in our work are followed by a description of the ceremonial worship of Jina, dealt with in Book VIII, Section 36, which contains the devotional verses (including a prose passage) recited in the various stages of the ritual. This is followed by the lyrical hymn in Section 37, which is meant to be sung after the formal worship is over. Somadeva's arrangement of the verses is designed to conform to ceremonial requirements, but their independent value as notable specimens of Jaina religious poetry can be easily recognised. The following specimens are mainly from the verses classified above.

DARŚANABHAKTI

ते कुर्वन्तु तपांसि दुर्धरधियो ज्ञानानि संचिन्वत्ं वित्तं वा वितरन्तु देव तदपि प्रायो न जन्मच्छिदः ।
एषा येषु न विद्यते तव वचःश्रद्धावधानोद्धुरा दुष्कर्माङ्कुरकुञ्जवज्रदहनद्योतावदाता रुचिः ॥

Those who possess no faith, ardent with devotion to thy teachings, O Lord,

1 See Chap. IV for specimens.

2 See दशभक्तिः edited by Pt. Jinadāsa Pārśvanātha with the commentary of Prabhācandra. It contains Siddhabhakti, Śrutabhakti, Cāritrabhakti, Yogibhakti, Ācāryabhakti, Pañcagurubhakti etc. in Sanskrit and Prākrit. The work is anonymous, but Prabhācandra remarks at the end of the comm. on Siddhabhakti that the Sanskrit Bhaktis were composed by Pūjyapāda and the Prākrit ones by Kundakunda.

(faith) blazing like lightning fire in consuming the grove of sprouting sins, cannot destroy the cycle of births, even if they, with mighty resolve, perform austerities or acquire knowledge or give away wealth in charity.

संसाराम्बुधिसेतुबन्धमसमप्रारम्भलक्ष्मीवनप्रोल्लासामृतवारिवाहमखिलत्रैलोक्यचिन्तामणिम् ।
कल्याणाम्बुजखण्डसंभवसरः सम्यक्त्वरत्नं कृती यो धत्ते हृदि तस्य नाथ सुलभाः स्वर्गापवर्गश्रियः ॥

The splendour of heaven and final release, O Lord, is easily attained by the meritorious man who possesses the Jewel of Right Faith in his heart. It serves as a causeway for traversing the ocean of worldly wanderings, and acts like a cloud, showering nectar for the lusty growth of the garden of prosperity, of incomparable extent. It is a wishing gem for the entire universe and a lotus pool of mundane bliss.

यद्देवैः शिरसा धृतं गणधरैः कर्णावतंसीकृतं न्यस्तं चेतसि योगिभिर्नृपवरैराघ्रातसारं पुनः ।
हस्ते दृष्टिपथे मुखे च निहितं विद्याधराधीश्वैरस्तत् स्याद्वादसरोरुहं मम मनोहंसस्य भूयान्मुदे ॥

May the lotus of Syādvāda doctrine delight the swan of my mind! It is cherished by the ascetics in their hearts, and its rich perfume is inhaled by mighty kings. The Vidyādhara chiefs keep it in their hands and mouths and under their eyes.

मिथ्यातमःपटलभेदनकारणाय स्वर्गापवर्गपुरमार्गनिबोधनाय ।
तत्तत्त्वभावनमनाः प्रणमामि नित्यं त्रैलोक्यमङ्गलकराय जिनागमाय ॥

Ever do I bow to the Doctrine preached by Jina, applying my mind to the contemplation of its fundamental principles: the Doctrine that dispels the enveloping gloom of false tenets, reveals the way to the cities of Heaven and Salvation, and does good to the universe.

CĀRITRABHAKTI

ज्ञानं दुर्भगदेहमण्डनमिव स्यात् स्वस्य खेदावहं धत्ते साधु न तत्फलश्रियमयं सम्यक्त्वरत्नाङ्कुरः ।
कामं देव यदन्तरेण विफलास्तास्तास्तपोभूमयस्तस्मै त्वच्चरिताय संयमदमध्यानादिधाम्ने नमः ॥

Salutation to thy Rule of conduct, the abode of self-control, self-restraint, meditation and other attributes! Without it, O Lord, knowledge is a burden, like the decoration of an ugly body. Without it the Jewel of Right Faith, a germinating plant, doth not bear fruit in plenty, and the fields of austerities remain ever barren.

यच्चिन्तामणिरीप्सितेषु वसतिः सौरूप्यसौभाग्ययोः श्रीपाणिग्रहकौतुकं कुलबलारोग्यागमे संगमः ।
यत् पूर्वैश्चरितं समाधिनिधिभिर्मोक्षाय पञ्चात्मकं तच्चारित्रमहं नमामि विविधं स्वर्गापवर्गाप्तये ॥

For the attainment of heaven and final release, I venerate that fivefold Rule of Conduct,[1] varied in character, which was practised by

---

1 The five kinds of Right Conduct (सम्यक्चारित्र) are, roughly speaking, सामायिक (equanimity), छेदोपस्थापना (recovery of equanimity), परिहारविशुद्धि (absolute cessation from injury). सूक्ष्मसाम्पराय (all but complete freedom from passion), and यथाख्यात (passionless conduct). See Jaini: *Tattvārthādhigamasūtra* 9. 18. For details see the commentaries of Pūjyapāda and Siddhasena on the *sūtra*.

the sages of old for the attainment of salvation. It is a wishing gem in granting one's desires, an abode of beauty and luck, a ceremonial wristlet for the wedding of the goddess of prosperity, and a meeting-place of family glory, might and health.

ARHADBHAKTI

ध्यानावलोकविगलत्तिमिरप्रताने तां देव केवलमयीं श्रियमादधाने ।
आसीत् त्वयि त्रिभुवनं मुहुरुत्सवाय व्यापारमन्थरमिवैकपुरं महाय ॥

When thou wast assuming the glory of infinite knowledge, O Lord, and the expanse of Darkness was receding before the Light of thy meditation, the entire world stood motionless, ready for continuous rejoicings, like a city preparing for a festival.

त्वं सर्वदोषरहितः सुनयं वचस्ते सत्त्वानुकम्पनपरः सकलो विधिश्च ।
लोकस्तथापि यदि तुष्यति न त्वयीश कर्मास्य तन्ननु रवाविव कौशिकस्य ॥

Thou art free from all blemishes, thy words are well-principled, and all thy acts are inspired by compassion for sentient beings. If the world still doth not delight in thee, O Lord, its action is verily like that of the owl in regard to the sun.

मिथ्यामहान्धतमसावृतमप्रबोधमेतत् पुरा जगदभूद्भवगर्तपाति ।
तद्देव दृष्टिहृदयाब्जविकासकान्तैः स्याद्वादरश्मिभिरथोद्धृतवांस्त्वमेव ॥

In times of yore the world, without enlightenment, was enveloped in the cimmerian darkness of false belief, and submerged in the ravine of worldly existence. It is thou who saved it, O Lord, with the rays of the Syādvāda doctrine, delightful by reason of their opening the lotus blossoms of men's eyes and hearts.

SIDDHABHAKTI

सम्यग्ज्ञानत्रयेण प्रविदितनिखिलज्ञेयतत्त्वप्रपञ्चाः प्रोद्धूय ध्यानवातैः सकलमघरजः प्राप्तकैवल्यरूपाः ।
कृत्वा सत्त्वोपकारं त्रिभुवनपतिभिर्दत्तयात्रोत्सवा ये ते सिद्धाः सन्तु लोकत्रयशिखरपुरीवासिनः सिद्धये वः ॥

May the emancipated saints inhabiting the crest of the three worlds grant ye success! With the three kinds of perfect knowledge,[1] they have comprehended the entire range of the knowable truths, and attained omniscience by sweeping away all dust of sins with the breeze of meditation. The lords of the universe celebrate festivals in their honour on the completion of their mission of doing good to all living creatures.

दानज्ञानचरित्रसंयमनयप्रारम्भगर्भं मनः कृत्वान्तर्बहिरिन्द्रियाणि मरुतः संयम्य पञ्चापि च ।
पश्चाद्गीतविकल्पजालमखिलं भ्रश्यत्तमःसंतति ध्यानं तत् प्रविधाय ये च मुमुचुस्तेभ्योऽपि बद्धोऽञ्जलिः ॥

I fold my hands in obeisance to those who attained final deliverance, after

---

1 अवधि (direct knowledge of matter), मनःपर्यय (direct knowledge of another's mental activity) and केवल (omniscience).

they had completed the entire range of meditation, free from all doubts, all darkness gone, having controlled the internal and external sense organs and the five vital breaths, and concentrated their minds on the application of the law of charity, knowledge, conduct and control of the self.

इत्थं येऽत्र समुद्रकन्दरसरःस्रोतस्विनीभूनभोद्वीपाद्रिद्रुमकाननादिषु धृतध्यानावधानर्द्धयः ।
कालेषु त्रिषु मुक्तिसंगमजुषः स्तुत्यास्त्रिभिर्विष्टपैस्ते रत्नत्रयमङ्गलानि दधतां भव्येषु रत्नाकराः ॥

Thus did they attain the height of absorption in meditation, in places like the ocean, mountain caves, pools of water, rivers, the earth and the sky, islands, mountains, groves of trees and the woods. Emancipated in all the three categories of time,[1] they are worthy of praise by all the three worlds. Oceans[2] as it were, may they confer on the faithful the blessings of the Three Jewels!

PAÑCAGURUBHAKTI

समवसरणवासान् मुक्तिलक्ष्मीविलासान् सकलसमयनाथान् वाक्यविद्यासनाथान् ।
भवनिगलविनाशोद्योगयोगप्रकाशान् निरुपमगुणभावान् संस्तुवेऽहं क्रियावान् ॥

ŚĀNTIBHAKTI

भवदुःखानलशान्तिर्धर्मामृतवर्षजनितजनशान्तिः । शिवशर्मास्रवशान्तिः शान्तिकरः स्ताज्जिनः शान्तिः ॥

ĀCĀRYABHAKTI

दूरारूढे प्रणिधितरणावन्तरात्माम्बरेऽस्मिन्नास्ते येषां हृदयकमलं मोदनिस्पन्दवृत्ति ।
तत्त्वालोकावगमगलितध्वान्तबन्धस्थितीनामिष्टिं तेषामहमुपनये पादयोश्चन्दनेन ॥

With sandal paste I adore their feet! The hold of Darkness on them vanishes at the sight of the light of the Truth, and their lotus hearts are benumbed with joy, when the sun of meditation climbs high in the firmament of their inner souls.

येषामङ्गे मलयजरसैः संगमः कर्दमैर्वा स्त्रीबिब्बोकैः पितृवनचिताभस्मभिर्वा समानः ।
मित्रे शत्रावपि च विषये निस्तरङ्गोऽनुषङ्गस्तेषां पूजाव्यतिकरविधावस्तु भूत्यै हविर्वः ॥

May the ceremonial offerings made in the course of their worship make ye thrive! It is all the same to them whether their bodies come into contact with liquid sandal or mud, or the amorous caresses of women or the ashes of funeral pyres on cremation grounds; and their mental attitude is calm in regard to friend and foe.

योगाभोगाचरणचतुरे दीर्णकन्दर्पदर्पे स्वान्ते ध्वान्तोद्धरणसविधे ज्योतिरुन्मेषभाजि ।
संमोदेतामृतभृत इव क्षेत्रनाथोऽन्तरुच्चैर्येषां तेषु क्रमपरिचयात् स्याच्छ्रिये वः प्रदीपः ॥

May the votive lamp bring ye prosperity on account of its being presented (before their images) in succession! Their inner souls intensely

---

1 The past, the present and the future.

2 Lit: abodes of jewels.

rejoice, as if filled with nectar, when their hearts, skilled in the practice of expansive meditation, having destroyed the insolence of the god of love, approach the lifting of the Darkness and experience the dawning of the light.

येषां ध्येयाशयकुवलयानन्दचन्द्रोदयानां बोधाम्भोधिः प्रमदसलिलैर्भाति नात्मावकाशे ।
लब्ध्वाप्येतामखिलभुवनैश्वर्यलक्ष्मीं निरीहं चेतस्तेषामयमपचितौ श्रेयसे वोऽस्तु धूपः ॥

May this incense burnt in the course of their worship bring ye good! They are as moonrise in delighting the lotus hearts of the faithful.[1] The ocean of their consciousness overflows with the waters of joy in the expanse of their souls, and their hearts are serene, even after acquiring the riches of the entire world.

देहारामेऽप्युपरतधियः सर्वसंकल्पशान्तेर्येषामूर्मिस्मयविरहिता ब्रह्मधामामृतास्तेः ।
आत्मात्मीयानुगमविगमाद्वृत्तयः शुद्धबोधास्तेषां पुष्पैश्चरणकमलान्यर्चयेयं शिवाय ॥

Their actions pay no heed to the pleasures of the body owing to the extinction of all desire, and are free from physical cravings and pride owing to their having attained the deathless state in which the Self abides, and are inspired by pure thoughts owing to the absence of all sense of 'I' and 'mine'. May I worship their lotus feet with flowers for my good!

LYRICAL HYMN TO JINA

नमदमरमौलिमण्डलविलग्नरत्नांशुकरगगनेऽस्मिन् । अरुणायतेऽङ्घ्रियुगलं यस्य जीयाज्जिनो देवः ॥
सुरपतियुवतिश्रवसाममरतरुस्मेरमञ्जरीरुचिरम् । चरणनखकिरणजालं यस्य स जयताज्जिनो जगति ॥ वर्णः ॥
दिविजकुञ्जरमौलिमन्दारमकरन्दस्यन्दकरविसरसारधूसरपदाम्बुज । वैदग्धीपरमपद प्रासत्वादजय विजितमनसिज ॥ मात्रा ॥

यस्त्वाममितगुणं जिन कश्चित् सावधिबोधः स्तौति विपश्चित् ।
नूनमसौ ननु काञ्चनशैलं तुलयति हस्तेनाचिरकालम् ॥
... ...
... ... ॥ चतुष्पदी ॥

सुरमतिविरचितसंस्तव दलिताखिलभव परमधामलब्धोदय ।
कस्तव जन्तुर्गुणमघहरणचरण प्रवितनुतां हतनतभय ॥

जय निखिलनिलिम्पालापकल्प जगतीस्तुतकीर्तिकलत्रतल्प ।
जय परमधर्महर्म्यावतार लोकत्रितयोद्धरणैकसार ॥
जय लक्ष्मीकरकमलार्चिताङ्ग सारस्वतरसनटनाद्यरङ्ग ।
जय बोधमध्यसिद्धाखिलार्थ मुक्तिश्रीरमणीरतिकृतार्थ ॥
... ...
... ... ॥ पद्धतिका ॥

इति तदमृतनाथ स्मरशरमाथ त्रिभुवनपतिमतिकेतन ।
मम दिश जगदीश प्रशमनिवेश त्वत्पदनुतिहृदयं जिन ॥ घत्ता ॥

---

1 A marginal note in Ms. A explains ध्येय as भव्यजन.

VERSES ADDRESSED TO JINA

भक्तिर्नित्यं जिनचरणयोः सर्वसत्त्वेषु मैत्री सर्वातिथ्ये मम विभवधीर्बुद्धिरध्यात्मतत्त्वे ।
सद्विद्येषु प्रणयपरता चित्तवृत्तिः परार्थे भूयादेतद्भवति भगवन् धाम यावत्त्वदीयम् ॥

Constant devotion to Jina's feet, goodwill towards all living creatures, a sense of ability to accord hospitality to all, realisation of the truth of the Self, love of those who possess the true learning, and the application of the mind to the good of others: may all this be mine, O Exalted One, as long as thy splendour lasts!

अमरतरुणीनेत्रानन्दे महोत्सवचन्द्रमाः स्मरमदमयध्वान्तध्वंसे मतः परमोऽर्यमा ।
अदयहृदयः कर्मारातौ नते च कृपात्मवानिति विसदृशव्यापारस्त्वं तथापि भवान् महान् ॥

Thou art a carnival moon in delighting the eyes of celestial maidens, but known to be a mighty sun in destroying the darkness of frenzied passion. Thou art pitiless in regard to Karma, thy enemy, but merciful to the humble. Thou dost thus indulge in opposites, yet art thou great in thy glory!

जगच्चेत्रं पात्रं निखिलविषयज्ञानमहसां महान्तं त्वां सन्तं सकलनयनीतिस्मृतगुणम् ।
महोदारं सारं विनतहृदयानन्दविषये ततो याचे नो चेद्भवसि भगवन्नर्थिविमुखः ॥

If thou art not averse to suppliants, O Exalted One, I beg of thee superabundant wealth of joy for my reverent heart. Thou art the eye of the world and the repository of the light of omniscience; thou art great and good, and thy virtues are declared by all schools and systems.[1]

मनुजदिविजलक्ष्मीलोचनालोकलीलाश्चिरमिह चरितार्थास्त्वत्प्रसादात् प्रजाताः ।
हृदयमिदमिदानीं स्वामिसेवोत्सुकत्वात् सहवसतिसनाथं छात्रमित्रे विधेहि ॥

Thanks to thy favour, my longing for the graceful glances of the goddess of human and celestial prosperity hath long been fulfilled. Make now this heart of mine, owing to its eagerness to serve its master, dwell with thee, the friend of disciples!

VERSES INVOKING THE BLESSINGS OF JINA.

ध्यानज्योतिरपास्ततामसचयः स्फारस्फुरत्केवलज्ञानाम्भोधितटैकदेशविलसत्त्रैलोक्यवेलाचलः ।
आनम्रेन्द्रशिखण्डमण्डनभवत्पादद्वयाम्भोरुहः श्रीनाथ प्रथितान्वयस्य भवतो भूयाज्जिनः श्रेयसे ॥[2]

O Lord of prosperity, may Jina bring good to thee, of renowned dynasty! He hath dispelled the expanse of darkness with the light of his meditation. The universe, like a coastal mountain, stands only on a part of the shore of the ocean of his perfect knowledge, extensive and refulgent! His lotus feet adorn the crown of Indra, bowing in salutation to him! (1. 219).

Most of the benedictory verses occur at the beginning or end of chapters. For example (4.2, 2.245):

तद्ध्यानत्विषि जातकल्मषमुषि प्रादुर्भवज्ज्योतिषि त्रैलोक्यक्षुभि दत्तयात्र ककुभि स्वर्गिस्मृतानुष्टुभि ।
यस्मिन्नच्युति सर्वलोकमहति स्तोत्रोन्मुखश्रीकृति श्रेयोभाजनतां जनः परमगात् स स्ताच्छ्रिये वो जिनः ॥
वित्तेश त्वरतां पुरः सुरतरूद्यानैः समं मातले तूर्णं सज्जय सामजं कुरु गुरो यानोचितां वाहिनीम् ।
आसीदित्थमशेषकल्मषमुषि प्रादुर्भवत्केवले यस्मिन् स्वर्गपतेर्महोत्सवविधिः सोऽव्यात् त्रिलोकीं जिनः ॥

---

1 A marginal note in Ms. A explains the phrase नयनीति ~~as~~ समयसिद्धान्त.

2 The verse is addressed to Māradatta.

The inferiority of the principal Brahminical deities to Jina, who is not, strictly speaking, a deity but a world teacher and saint of superhuman status and universal power, is declared in the following verse:

लक्ष्मीपतिप्रभृतिभिः कृतपादसेवः पायाज्जगन्ति स जयी जिनचन्द्रदेवः ।
साम्यं त्रिविष्टपधृतिस्थितविक्रमस्य दंष्ट्राधृतावनितलस्य हरेर्न यस्य ॥ 3.2

Verses in honour of the Śrutadevatā, the presiding goddess of sacred lore, the Jaina Sarasvatī, occur in connection with her worship, which is described immediately after the discourse on meditation (*dhyānavidhi*).[1] One of these verses is cited below:

चक्षुः परं करणकन्दरदूरितेऽर्थे मोहान्धकारविधुतौ परमः प्रकाशः ।
तद्धामगामिपथवीक्षणरत्नदीपस्त्वं सेव्यसे तदिह देवि जनेन धूपैः ॥

Thou art our sole eye in the perception of objects made inaccessible by the abyss of the senses. Thou art the supreme light in destroying the darkness of ignorance. Thou art a jewel lamp showing the path to the abode of beatitude. Thou art, therefore, O goddess, worshipped by men on earth with offerings of incense (Vol. II, p. 401).

Religio-Ethical Verses

THE WAY OF SAGES

न दैन्यात् प्राणानां न च हृदयहरिणस्य रतये न दर्पादङ्गानां न च करणकरिणोऽस्य मदनात् ।
विधावृत्तिः किं तु क्षतमदनचरितश्रुतविधेः परे हेतौ मुक्तेरिह मुनिषु न खलु स्थितिरियम् ॥

The sages take nourishment not owing to the frailty of the vital forces nor for the gaiety of the antelope-like heart nor for the vigour of the limbs nor for the exhilaration of the elephant-like senses; but for the supreme object of salvation as propounded in the canon of Jina, who hath destroyed the sway of passion. Is this not the customary practice of sages on earth? (1. 127)

USELESS STRENGTH

श्रुताय येषां न शरीरवृद्धिः श्रुतं चरित्राय च येषु नैव । तेषां बलित्वं ननु पूर्वकर्मव्यापारभारोद्वहनाय मन्ये ॥

Verily the strength of those whose physical growth does not lead to the study of the Scriptures and whose study of the Scriptures does not lead to right conduct, is meant, I ween, for merely bearing the burden of the Karma done in previous births (1. 128).

WHEN DEATH IS WELCOME

जीवस्य सद्दर्शनरत्नभाजश्चारित्रयुक्तस्य समाहितस्य । आशंसितो मृत्युरुपप्रयातः परं प्रमोदस्य समागमाय ॥

Death when it comes is welcome and certainly a cause of joy to a man who possesses the Jewel of Right Faith, is endowed with Right Conduct, and practises pure meditation (1. 140)

THE USE AND ABUSE OF HUMAN LIFE

पर्याप्तं विरसावसानकटुकैरुच्चावचैर्नाकिनां सौख्यैर्मर्मसदुःखदावदहनव्यापारदग्धात्मभिः ।
इत्थं स्वर्गसुखावधीरणपरैराशास्यते तद्दिनं यत्रोत्पद्य मनुष्यजन्मनि मनो मोक्षाय धास्यामहे ॥

1 See Chap. X.

यस्तु लब्ध्वापि जन्मेदं न धर्माय समीहते । तस्यात्मकर्मभूमीषु विजृम्भन्तां भवाङ्कुराः ॥

'No more of celestial joys, uneven and bitter on account of their unpleasant sequel, and spoilt by the conflagration of mental anguish!' Thus do the gods, despising celestial happiness, look forward to the day when, born as men, they will be able to say: 'We will concentrate our minds on final release!' Let the sprouts of future births shoot forth in the field of Karma of the man, who does not strive to cultivate piety, even after attaining this human existence (1. 142-3).

KARMA

सुखदुःखानुभवार्थं निजकर्मगलग्रहात् सुदूरोऽपि । जालावलम्नतिमिवज्जन्तुर्यमसमयमायाति ॥

Like a fish caught in a net, a living being, owing to the stranglehold of his own Karma, comes under the law of Death even from afar, in order to experience pleasure and pain (in another birth'). Book V.

HOW MAN BECOMES LIABLE TO REBIRTH

नवं वयश्चारुतरास्तरुण्यो रम्याणि हर्म्याणि शिवाः श्रियश्च ।
एतानि संसारतरोः फलानि स्वर्गः परोऽस्तीति मृषैव वार्ता ॥
दोषस्त्वमीषां पुनरेक एव स्थैर्याय यन्नास्ति जगत्युपायः ।
तत्संभवे तत्त्वविदां परं स्यात् खेदाय देहस्य तपःप्रयासः ॥
बालस्य मौग्ध्यान्न तपोऽधिकारो युवा तपस्येद्यदि तत्र दण्डः ।
कुटुम्बभाराधिकृतश्च मध्यो वृद्धः पुनर्वृद्धिसहाय एव ॥
परोपरोधादयमेवमात्मा मिथ्याग्रहग्रस्तमनःप्रतानः ।
स्वयं विजानन्नपि दैवदूतैराकृष्य नीयेत भवभ्रमाय ॥

Early youth, charming young women, beautiful mansions and salutary wealth: these are the fruits of the tree of life. That there is heaven other than these is definitely untrue. But they have one defect. No means is there in the world to ensure their permanence. If that were possible, the assiduity in religious austerities of those who are conversant with the truth would merely amount to exhaustion of the body. A child is not fit for austerities owing to his ignorance, and a youth is liable to penalty if he should undertake them; while a middle-aged man is responsible for the support of his family, and an old man just manages to subsist. Under the influence of others, a sentient being, although he knows the truth, has his mind in the grip of the demon of false belief, and is dragged along by the messengers of Fate for undergoing the cycle of births (Book IV, P. 94).

DESIRE FOR RELIGIOUS MERIT

महदपि पापं विलयति पुण्याभिमनोरथः सुतुच्छोऽपि । किं नाल्पो रविरेष त्रिभुवनमात्रं तमो हन्ति ॥

Even an insignificant desire for the acquisition of religious merit destroys an enormous quantity of sins. Does not the sun, though limited in extent, destroy the darkness reigning in all the three worlds? (Book V).

CHAPTER XII

A Controversial Dialogue

One of the most interesting episodes of *Yaśastilaka* is the animated dialogue in Book IV between Yaśodhara and his mother Candramati on the subject of animal sacrifice, the former being a convert to Jainism, and the latter a champion of the Brahmanical faith. Certain tenets of the Vedic religion are attacked by Yaśodhara in the course of his argument, and he also attempts to establish the ancient and authoritative character of the Jaina faith by citing various texts from what are apparently non-Jaina sources. A dramatic character is given to the dialogue by the use of parenthetic indications resembling stage directions, and but for the numerous quotations, the dialogue is cast in a form that could easily be adapted to the stage. Another, and perhaps more striking, example of a dramatic dialogue occurs in our work in the story of Padmā in Book VII.[1]

The controversy between Yaśodhara and his mother starts from the point where the latter asks him to sacrifice all kinds of animals before the tutelary goddess, and then perform an appropriate rite to counteract the effect of his evil dream. While making the request, she asserts on the authority of Manu that animals may be legitimately killed in sacrifices and the worship of the gods and the Manes, and, as a matter of fact, a Brāhmaṇa, killing animals on such occasions, ensures for himself as well as the victims a state of bliss after death. Further, the killing of animals in sacrifices is not killing at all, since animals have been created by Brahman himself for the purpose of sacrifices, and sacrifices are meant for the good of all.

Yaśodhara, closing his ears and heaving a sigh, expresses surprise at the amount of evil that can be done by delusion and its cause ignorance, and entreats his mother to allow him to speak a few words. After a preliminary discussion on Cārvāka views, which mother and son agree in repudiating, Yaśodhara admits the desirability of a rite for counteracting the effect of an evil dream, but firmly objects to the expedient of sacrificing animals before the goddess, as suggested by his mother. The protection of living creatures, he argues, is the primary duty of Kṣatriyas, and it would be a repudiation of that duty if he killed harmless animals. A king, in fact, takes up arms only against an armed foe on the battlefield or a malefactor of his kingdom, but never against those who are wretched or lowly or well-meaning. 'How then, mother', asks Yaśodhara, 'can I strike living creatures with weapons, myself pure in my conduct in relation to this life and the life beyond?' Further,

1 See Chap. XVI.

has she forgotten that only the previous day the minister's son Nītibṛhaspati had, at her instance, taught him certain significant verses on the subject?

> न कुर्वीति स्वयं हिंसां प्रवृत्तां च निवारयेत् । जीवितं बलमारोग्यं शश्वद्वाञ्छन् महीपतिः ॥
> यो दद्यात् काञ्चनं मेरुं कृत्स्नां चापि वसुंधराम् । एकस्य जीवितं दद्यात् फलेन न समं भवेत् ॥
> यथात्मनि शरीरस्य दुःखं नेच्छन्ति जन्तवः । तथा यदि परस्यापि न दुःखं तेषु जायते ॥

'A king who constantly desires longevity, strength and health must do no injury to living creatures himself nor allow it to take place when planned by others. One may give away the Meru mountain of gold as well as the entire earth. The result will not be equal to that of saving the life of a single sentient being. Suffering will cease to exist among living creatures if they no longer wish to cause physical pain to others, just as they do not wish to cause it to themselves.'

Yaśodhara points out that there are many commendable expedients other than the killing of animals for propitiating the Brāhmaṇas and the gods, and sustaining the body. Why do honest people then commit the sin of killing? Besides, animal flesh is full of impurities: if it pleased the gods, we would rather worship the tigers!

> संतर्पणार्थं द्विजदेवतानां पुष्ट्यर्थमङ्गस्य च सन्त्युपायाः ।
> अन्येऽपि लोके बहवः प्रशस्ताः सन्तः कुतः पापमिहाचरन्ति ॥
> शुक्रशोणितसंभूतमशुचीनां निकेतनम् । मांसं चेत् प्रीणयेद्देवानेतद्व्याघ्रानुपास्महे ॥

Yaśodhara declares the current opinion that the gods are pleased with animal sacrifices to be false, and says

> हताः कृपाणेन वनेऽपि जन्तवो बाढं म्रियन्ते गलपीडनाच्च ।
> अदन्ति चैतान् स्वयमेव देव्यो व्याघ्राः स्तवार्हाः परमत्र सन्तु ॥
> कृत्वा मिषं दैवमयं हि लोको मद्ये च मांसे च रतिं करोति ।
> एवं न चेद्दुर्गतिसंगमिः स्याद्दुष्कर्मणां कोऽपर एव मार्गः ॥

'Animals surely perish in the woods, killed with swords, or strangled to death, and there are goddesses who of their own accord devour them. But the tigers alone are worthy of praise (for they themselves kill and eat unlike the gods who make others kill). People are addicted to wine and flesh on the pretext that these serve to please the gods. But if the wicked do not go to hell in this way, what other way thitherward is open to them?' Further, if Dharma is really based on the killing of animals, why is hunting called *pāparddhi*, 'progress in sin'? Why is it customary to bring in flesh under cover? Why is flesh called *Rāvaṇaśāka*, 'Rāvaṇa's herb'? Why is it shunned on sacred days? Yaśodhara terminates this part of his argument by quoting a number of authoritative texts in support of abstention from killing.

Hearing these words, Yaśodhara's mother says to herself:

माता—(स्वगतम्) अहो मदीये सुते सांप्रतं जैनजनवात इव लग्नः प्रतिभासते। विषमश्च खलु भवत्ययं जनः। यस्माच्चिरं समयान्तरोपरचितप्रतीकाराण्यप्यन्येषां मनांसि प्रायेण पश्यतोहर इव हरत्यार्हतो लोकः। तद्वासनावासितं हि चेतो न ब्रह्मणापि शक्यतेऽन्यथाकर्तुम्। दुश्चिकित्स्यश्च खलु करिणां कूटपाकल इव प्राणिनां क्षपणकोपनोतश्चित्तस्याभिनिवेशः।

'Ah, now the Jaina wind seems to have taken possession of my scn. These Jainas are difficult people to deal with, because like thieves, they beguile the minds of men, though long protected by the doctrines of other schools. Once the mind is imbued with their ideas, Brahman himself cannot divert it to other channels. The cast of mind produced in men by the Jainas is indeed beyond remedy, like the fever of elephants.' Candramati then recollects the priest's son Śivaśarman having told her that the king had met a Digambara Jaina ascetic living under a tree, and for a long while discussed religious topics with him. She remarks that her son has since evinced a dislike for wine, meat, hunting and animal sacrifice, and demonstrated his hostility to the injunctions of the Vedas and the Law-books.

Then addressing herself to the councillors, and calling them monsters and destroyers of her son and the kingdom, and despoilers of the people, she gives vent to her wrath and censures them for allowing her immature son, despite her instructions to the contrary, to come into touch with the Digambara Jainas, who are, like magicians, habitually skilled in bewitching the world. She addresses her son in a menacing tone, and calling him a raw Cārvāka, tells him that she has understood him well, and can herself give him a suitable reply. She asks him how he can ever have any leaning towards the religion of the Digambaras, which makes no provision for the gratification of the gods, the Manes and the Brāhmaṇas, and for dips in sacred waters as well as oblations in the fire; a religion outside the jurisdiction of the Vedas and the Law-books. None but him would care to talk with those heretics, who speak ill of the gods and the Brāhmaṇas, eat standing like brutes, and are devoid of all sense of shame and personal hygiene. Besides, their system came into being only in the Kali Age, and not even their name was known in earlier times. They hold quite unreasonably that men become gods and the gods are many.[1] To speak the truth, the Veda is the sole authority in the matter of religion, and there is no god other than the Veda. He who does not know the Veda well does not know the regulations of the four castes and the four stages of life. Then if Yasodhara has any devotion

1 The reference is to the twenty four Tīrthaṁkaras or Apostles worshipped as divine beings.

to the gods, let him worship Śiva or Viṣṇu or the Sun. When they are pleased, they transport their worshippers in a moment to their respective cities, and when gratified, vouchsafe even a kingdom.

न तर्पणं देवपितृद्विजानां स्नानस्य होमस्य न चास्ति वार्ता ।
श्रुतेः स्मृतेर्बाह्यतरे च धीस्ते धर्मे कथं पुत्र दिगम्बराणाम् ॥
उद्भाः पशूनां सदृशं प्रसन्ते ये लज्जया शौचगुणेन हीनाः ।
स्वत्तः परस्तैः सह को हि गोष्ठीं करोतु देवद्विजनिन्दकैश्च ॥
नामापि पूर्वं न समस्त्यमीषामभूत् कलौ दर्शनमेतदीयम् ।
देवो मनुष्यः किल सोऽप्यनेकस्त एवमिच्छन्ति च निर्विचारम् ॥
धर्मे प्रमाणं खलु वेद एव वेदात् परं दैवतमत्र नास्ति ।
यो वेद सम्यङ् न हि वेदमेनं वर्णाश्रमाचारमसौ न वेद ॥
अथास्ति भक्तिस्तव दैवतेषु हरं हरिं वार्चय भास्करं वा ।
नयन्ति हृष्टाः स्वपुरीं क्षणेन तुष्टाः प्रयच्छन्ति च राज्यमेते ॥

Hearing these words, Yaśodhara reflects within himself that even washing with nectar cannot cleanse a heart that is by nature black as charcoal. Yet he recognises that his opponent in the debate is his own mother, 'the presiding deity of the kingdom', and she is at liberty to speak as she likes to him. Then addressing his mother and entreating her to pardon him for what he is going to say, he replies to the charges brought by her against the Jaina religion, and in so doing severely criticizes certain aspects of the Brahmanical faith.

Speaking of Śrāddha, Yaśodhara argues that if it is true that the Pitṛs have betaken themselves to earthly existences or celestial abodes as a result of their good deeds, they cannot have any need for annual offerings of rice-balls, which are actually taken by Bṛāhmaṇas and crows:

मर्त्येषु चेत् सद्मसु नाकिनां वा विधाय पुण्यं पितरः प्रयाताः ।
तेषामपेक्षा द्विजकाकभुक्तैः पिण्डैर्भवेद्वर्षकृतैर्न क्वापि ॥

Further, the ancients prescribed Śrāddha and other rites by way of religious observances, because religion has to be practised by all decent people, desirous of their own good, in one form or another; and no one, as a rule, practises religion unless there is an occasion for it:

येनापि केनापि मिषेण मान्यैर्धर्मो विधेयः स्वहितैकतान्यैः ।
अनेन कामेन कृतः पुराणैर्मार्गोऽयमात्माभ्युदयप्रवीणैः ॥
निर्निमित्तं न कोऽपीह जनः प्रायेण धर्मधीः । अतः श्राद्धादिकाः प्रोक्ताः क्रियाः कुशलबुद्धिभिः ॥

Similarly, the observance of Amāvāsyā, pilgrimage, reception of guests, Śrāddha rites, and observances connected with particular days, occasions and stars have been declared by the ancients to be conducive to the religious merit of those who are unable to practise constant charity:

पर्वतीर्थातिथिश्राद्धवारवासरतारकाः । नित्यं दातुमशक्तानां पुण्यायोक्ताः पुरातनैः ॥

It is not true to say that the Jainas do not gratify the Twice-born. They do worship the Munis (Jaina ascetics), who are 'Twice-born', being once actually born, and born a second time at the time of initiation into the religious vows. Nor is it true to say that Jainism does not recognise ceremonial baths, because the Jaina householder is enjoined to take a bath before worshipping the Arhat or studying the Sacred Books or devoting himself to meditation. One must not, however, think that a mere dip in a river or a pool of water or a tank or the ocean leads to any religious merit, for in that case it is the aquatic animals that would go to heaven first. It has been rightly said that those who are maddened by passion, hate and pride, and addicted to women, are never purified even by bathing at hundreds of sacred sites:

जन्मैकमात्माधिगमो द्वितीयं भवेन्मुनीनां व्रतकर्मणा च ।
अमी द्विजाः साधु भवन्ति तेषां संतर्पणं जैनजनः करोति ॥
स्नात्वा यजेताप्तमथवागमं वा पठेद्यदि ध्यानमुपाचरेद्वा ।
स्नानं भवेदेव गृहाश्रितानां स्वर्गापवर्गागमसंगमाय ॥
सरित्सरोवारिधिवापिकासु निमज्जनोन्मज्जनमात्रमेव ।
पुण्याय चेत्तर्हि जलेचराणां स्वर्गः पुरा स्यादितरेषु पश्चात् ॥

तदाह—रागद्वेषमदोन्मत्ताः स्त्रीणां ये वशवर्तिनः । न ते कालेन शुध्यन्ति स्नानात्तीर्थशतैरपि ॥

As regards Homa, it is impossible that the gods who feed on nectar and live in luxury in heaven should ever partake of oblations made in the fire. The expression *agnimukhāḥ*, as applied to the gods, means 'those who have faces bright as fire', just as *candramukhī kanyā* means 'a moon-faced girl'; but it does not mean, as is usually supposed, 'those who have Fire for mouth'.

Yaśodhara then refutes the charge that Jainism is a modern creed unknown to the Vedas and the Law Books, by citing a number of texts supposed to contain references to Jaina ascetics, images and doctrines.[1] It is, accordingly, concluded that just as there are four oceans and six seasons, similarly there are four schools of thought and six systems of philosophy including, of course, the system of the Jainas.[2]

चत्वार एते सहजाः समुद्रा यथैव लोके ऋतवोऽपि षट् च ।
चत्वार एते समयास्तथैव षड् दर्शनानीति वदन्ति सन्तः ॥

The speaker next defends the custom of Jaina ascetics who eat standing and that of the Digambara ascetics, who wear no clothing owing to their determination not to possess anything. As for personal hygiene,

1 See Chapters XIII and XVIII.

2 See Chapter IX.

they carry a water-pot with them, and cleanse any particular limb that might be soiled. Surely, when a man is bitten by a snake on one of the fingers, he cuts off the finger and not the nose:

यावत् समर्थं वपुरुद्धतायां यावच्च पाणिद्वयमेति बन्धम् ।
तावन्मुनीनामशने प्रवृत्तिरित्याशयेन स्थितभोजनास्ते ॥
बालाग्रकोटावपि यत्र संगे निष्किंचनत्वं परमं न तिष्ठेत् ।
मुमुक्षवस्तत्र कथं नु कुर्युर्मतिं दुकूलाजिनवल्कलेषु ॥
शौचं निकामं मुनिपुंगवानां कमण्डलोः संश्रयणात् समस्ति ।
न चाङ्गुलौ सर्पविदूषितायां छिनत्ति नासां खलु कश्चिदत्र ॥

Yaśodhara emphasizes the purity of the Jaina religion:

वदन्ति जैनास्तमिहाप्तमेते रागादयो यत्र न सन्ति दोषाः ।
मद्यादिशब्दोऽपि च यत्र दुष्टः शिष्टैः स निन्द्येत कथं नु धर्मः ॥

'The Jainas call him an Āpta who is free from passion and such other blemishes. How can the cultured censure a religion wherein even terms like wine are condemned'? The Arhat, free from passion, is contrasted with a Brahmanical god. The latter is blind with rage in dealing with enemies, and loves his wives: if such an individual is a god, the universe is full of gods:

परेषु योगेषु मनीषयान्धः प्रीतिं दधात्यात्मपरिग्रहेषु ।
तथापि देवः स यदि प्रसक्तमेतज्जगद्देवमयं समस्तम् ॥

Yaśodhara then condemns the use of wine, flesh and honey; and recounts the evil consequences of drinking.

लज्जा न सज्जा कुशलं न शीलं श्रुतं न पूतं न वरः प्रचारः ।
मद्येन मन्दीकृतमानसानां विवेकनाशाच्च पिशाचभावः ॥

'Those who are stupefied with drink have no sense of shame nor propriety of conduct nor knowledge of sacred lore nor commendable activities; they are as ghosts owing to the loss of the power of discernment.'

The authority of the Veda is next attacked. The speaker contends that the injunctions of the Veda are guided by the instincts of the crowd, and often self-contradictory. No sure clue is to be found in the Veda as to what is to be done and what avoided, and the Veda can in no sense be an authority for the world.

यथाजनाकूतमयं प्रवृत्तः परस्परार्थप्रतिकूलवृत्तः ।
विधौ निषेधे च न निश्चयोऽस्ति कथं स बेदो जगतः प्रमाणम् ॥

An instance of how the Veda follows the instincts of the crowd is found in the fact that the common people desire to take meat, and the Veda sanctions meat-eating by prescribing certain rules for it, e. g., meat is to be taken after ceremonially sprinkling it with water in accordance with the desire of the Brāhmaṇas, and it is also permissible to take it after worshipping the Manes and the gods.[1] Similarly, the Veda legitimizes the lewd desires of certain people by sanctioning incest in the Gosava

1 तथा हि मांसं चेदाचरितुमिच्छसि आचर । किं तु विधिपूर्वकमाचरितव्यम् । तदाह—प्रोक्षितं भक्षयेन्मांसं ब्राह्मणानां तु काम्यया ।···अर्चयित्वा पितॄन् देवान् खादन् मांसं न दुष्यति ॥

sacrifice[1], and there are also other instances in which the injunctions of the Veda follow the inclinations of the populace.[2] This explains the universal popularity of the Veda, for no one who obeys the desires of the people is ever disliked. But men by nature lack the power of discrimination, and covet one another's wives and wealth, and what are we to think of a Scripture that sets itself to conform to their wishes?

प्रसिद्धिरत एवास्य सर्वसाधारणी मता। को हि नाम भवेद् द्वेष्यो लोकच्छन्दानुवर्तनः॥

हिताहितावेदि जगन्निसर्गतः परस्परस्त्रीधनलोलमानसम्।

तत्रापि यद्यागम एष तन्मनोवशेन वर्तेत तदा किमुच्यते॥

Instances of self-contradiction are found in the Veda. There is a Vedic injunction against the drinking of wine and the killing of a Brāhmaṇa, but wine is nevertheless prescribed in the Sautrāmaṇī sacrifice, and a Brāhmaṇa may be sacrificed to Brahman.[3] Similarly, the Veda, after prohibiting a Brāhmaṇa from serving a Śūdra or accepting food or the means of livelihood from him, asks the former to accept for sacrificial purposes the flesh of animals killed by Cāṇḍālas, dogs, tigers and others.[4] Even in worldly affairs a person who is consistent in what he says is alone trusted, and who can have any respect for a scripture containing such conflicting statements?

प्रमाणं व्यवहारेऽपि जन्तुरेकस्थितिर्मतः। को नामेत्थं विरुद्धार्थे सादरो निगमे नरः॥

Yaśodhara points out that independent discussion of the injunctions of the Veda, just as one discusses the scriptures composed by a known author, is held to be a great sin.[5] But he asserts that it is absurd to say that a man is liable to sin as great as that of killing a Brāhmaṇa if he questions the authority of the statements of Manu, Vyāsa and Vasiṣṭha, based on the Veda.[6]

Yaśodhara ridicules the suggestion that he should worship Śiva or Viṣṇu or the Sun.

उमापतिः स्कन्दपिता त्रिशूली संध्यासु यो नृत्यति चर्मवासाः।

भिक्षाशनो होमजपोपपन्नः कथं स देवोऽन्यजनेन तुल्यः॥

'How can Śiva be a god? He is just like other people. He is simply the husband of Pārvatī and the father of Kārtikeya, carries a trident, and dances in the evening twilight. He is dressed in skins, and lives by begging and practises fire-oblation and mutters prayers.'

हरिः पुनः क्षत्रिय एव कश्चिज्ज्योतिर्गणैस्तुल्यगुणो रविश्च।

देवौ स्त एतौ यदि मुक्तिमार्गौ पृथुश्च सोमश्च कुतस्तथा न॥

---

1 मातरि स्वसरि वा चेत् प्रवर्तितुमिच्छसि प्रवर्तस्व। किं तु विधिपूर्वकं प्रवर्तितव्यम्। यदाह—गोसवे etc. For the Gosava sacrifice see Chap .XIV.

2 एवमन्येऽपि सन्ति यथालोकाभिप्रायं प्रवृत्तास्ते ते विधयः।

3 See Chap. XIV.

4 शूद्रान्नं शूद्रशुश्रूषा शूद्रप्रेषणकारिणः etc. See Chap. XVIII.

5 अथ पौरुषेयागमवच्चोदनायां विचारे महत् पातकम्।

6 तदाह—मानवं व्यासवासिष्ठं वचनं वेदसंयुतम्। अप्रमाणं तु यो ब्रूयात् स भवेद् ब्रह्मघातकः॥"'इत्येतन्मुखभाषितम्।

'Viṣṇu again is just a Kṣatriya, and the Sun has characteristics similar to those of the other planets. If those two are gods leading men to salvation, why is it that the Kṣatriya Pṛthu and the moon, too, are not called gods?'

अशेषमेतद्वपुषा बिभर्ति दशावतारेण स वर्त्तते वा ।
शिलाप्लवादप्यतिविस्मयाहं मातः कथं संगतिमञ्चतीदम् ॥

'Viṣṇu is said to sustain the entire universe within his body, and described also as existing in ten different Incarnations. This is far more astonishing than the floating of a stone on water. How can it, mother, be reconciled with facts?'

स्वयं स कुष्ठी पदयोः किलार्कः परेषु रोगार्तिहरश्च चित्रम् ।
अजा परेषां विनिहन्ति वातं स्वयं तु वातेन हि सा म्रियेत ॥

'It is strange that the Sun should be able to exterminate the suffering of others caused by disease, himself stricken with leprosy in the feet! (On the same principle) a she-goat, who (with her flesh) cures the gout of others, would herself die of gout!'

Speaking of the Arhats, the omniscient world-teachers worshipped by the Jainas as divine beings, Yaśodhara explains that the virtues of the Arhat are known from the Scripture composed by himself.[1] The chain of emancipated Arhats and Scriptures is without beginning or end, like the cycle of creation, existence and destruction, or that of the seasons: winter, summer and the rains. Further, it is not absurd to hold that just as there are past, present and future kings, conversant with the three worlds, similarly there are present and future Āptas or Arhats; and plurality of this sort is surely found also in other faiths.

सर्गस्थितिप्रत्यवहारवृत्तेर्हिमातपाम्भःसमयस्थितेर्वा ।
आद्यन्तभावोऽस्ति यथा न लोके तथैव मुक्तागममालिकायाः ॥
भूता भविष्यन्ति भवन्ति चान्ये लोकत्रयज्ञाः क्रमशः क्षितीशाः ।
यथा तथाप्ता यदि को विरुद्धो बहुत्वमन्यत्र च बाढमस्ति ॥

Yaśodhara's mother, on hearing these words, says to herself that the time is gone when her son could be compelled to carry out her wishes by argument or threat or even a box in the ear. Addressing herself to her son, she extols his wisdom and learning, and appeals to him again to offer animal sacrifices to the tutelary goddess for counteracting the effect of the evil dream and preserving his own life. After citing some instances of sages and others who are known to have killed various living creatures for their own good,[2] she asserts that a king, pure in his motives, can never incur any sin, just as lotus leaves cannot be drenched with water or the sky bedaubed with mud. She then declares thus:

विषं विषस्यौषधमग्निरग्नेरियं प्रसिद्धिर्महती यथैव ।
पुण्याय हिंसापि भवेत्तथैव सर्वत्र हे पुत्र न षड्ढलानि ॥

1 गुणाः कुतस्तस्य भवन्ति गम्याः, शास्त्रात् प्रणीतात् स्वयमेव तेन ।

2 See Chapter XVII.

'It is very wellknown that poison is the remedy for poison, and fire for fire. On similar grounds, even destruction of life may lead to religious merit. The number of ploughs is not six on every plot, my child.'[1]

Further, a person in the habit of probing a matter too much with minute investigation gains thereby nothing, and it is advisable to do as the world does, since the path followed by the many is the true path.

न कापि पुंसः पुरुषार्थसिद्धिः सूक्ष्मेक्षयातीवपरीक्षकस्य ।
जगत्प्रवाहेण तु वर्तितव्यं महाजनो येन गतः स पन्थाः ॥

Candramati goes on to praise the joys of wine and flesh-eating.

विलासिनीविभ्रमदर्पणानि कन्दर्पसंतर्पणकारणानि ।
क्रियाश्रमच्छेदकराणि हातुं मधूनि को नाम सुधीर्यतेत ॥
मताः समा मन्मथतत्त्वविद्भिर्मृताः स्त्रियो मद्यविवर्जिताश्च ।
ये भुञ्जते मांसरसेन हीनं ते भुञ्जते किं नु न गोमयेन ॥

'What wise man would attempt to give up wine, the mirror of the graceful gestures of fair women, wine that excites love and removes fatigue? Women who abstain from wine are as good as dead in the opinion of adepts in erotic lore. And those who eat without the flavour of meat verily eat with that of dung.'

Yaśodhara's mother concludes her appeal by citing a number of Smṛti verses on the subject of meat-offerings to the Manes. But the son remains unconvinced, and after a brief soliloquy makes his final declaration on the points at issue.

रजस्तमोभ्यां बहुलस्य पुंसः पापं सतां नैव निदर्शनाय ।
नाप्येनसामसजतामपेक्षा जातौ कुले वा रजसामिवास्ति ॥
जातिर्जरा मृत्युरथामयाद्या नृपेषु चान्येषु समं भवन्ति ।
पुण्यैर्जनेभ्योऽभ्यधिकाः क्षितीशा मनुष्यभावे त्वविशेष एव ॥
यथा मम प्राणवधे भवत्या महान्ति दुःखानि भवन्ति मातः ।
तथा परेषामपि जीवहानौ भवन्ति दुःखानि तदम्बिकानाम् ॥

'The sin committed by a man overpowered by evil propensities and delusion is no example for the good[2] nor does supervening sin, like dust, make any distinction of family or caste. Birth, old age and death and disease and the like are common to kings and others. But kings are superior to other men in religious merit; no difference exists so far as the human aspect is concerned.[3] Mother, just as thou wouldst feel profound sorrow if I were killed, similarly the mothers of others would be aggrieved if their sons were to lose their lives.'

---

1 The speaker means to say that there is no hard and fast rule that *hiṁsā* in every case will lead to sin.

2 The reference is to the sin of men like Gautama and Viśvāmitra who are said to have killed living creatures for preserving their own lives.

3 Yaśodhara refers to the religious responsibility of kings, which makes them uphold the principle of *ahiṁsā*.

Further, if it had been possible to save one's own life by taking the life of another, the kings of old would never have died; and if the *śāstric* injunction sanctioning flesh-eating were to be applied universally, one would have to eat even the flesh of dogs and crows!

परस्य जीवेम यदि स्वरक्षा पूर्वे क्षितीशाः कुत एव मन्त्रुः ।
शास्त्रं तु सर्वत्र यदि प्रमाणं श्वकाकमांसेऽपि भवेत् प्रवृत्तिः ॥

Yaśodhara then attacks the belief that the sacrifice of animals leads to heaven:

लोलेन्द्रियैर्लोकमनोऽनुकूलैः स्वाजीवनायागम एष सृष्टः ।
स्वर्गो यदि स्यात् पशुहिंसकानां सूनाकृतां तर्हि भवेत् स कामम् ॥
मन्त्रेण शस्त्रैर्गलपीडनाद्वा वेद्यां बहिश्चापि वधः समानः ।
स्वर्गो यदि स्यान्मखहिंसितानां स्वबान्धवैर्यज्ञविधिर्न किं तु ॥

'This Vedic lore was created by sensual persons, favourable to the inclinations of the populace, in order to make their own living; and it is the butchers who would mostly go to heaven if that was the destination of those who killed animals in sacrificial rites. Killing is the same whether it is done at the altar or outside, whether it is accompanied by Vedic formulas or brought about by strangulation or weapons. If the animals killed in sacrifices go to heaven, why is it that one's kinsfolk are not sacrificed?'

Yaśodhara illustrates his point further by a story in which a goat, about to be sacrificed, is represented as saying to the priest:

नाहं स्वर्गफलोपभोगतृषितो नाभ्यर्थितस्त्वं मया संतुष्टस्तृणभक्षणेन सततं हन्तुं न युक्तं तव ।
स्वर्गं यान्ति यदि त्वया विनिहता यज्ञे ध्रुवं प्राणिनो यज्ञं किं न करोषि मातृपितृभिः पुत्रैस्तथा बान्धवैः ॥

'I am not eager to enjoy the bliss of heaven nor have I asked thee for it. I am ever content with the eating of grass; it is not right for thee to kill me. Verily, if the animals slain by thee in sacrifices go to heaven, why dost thou not sacrifice thy parents, children and friends?'

Yaśodhara's mother makes no further attempt to argue with her son, and falling at his feet, in spite of his remonstrances, entreats him to accept a compromise in the matter of sacrificing a cock at the altar of Caṇḍikā and partaking of its flesh. Yaśodhara agrees most unwillingly, and the debate comes to an end.

The discussion between Yaśodhara and his mother belongs to a long series of texts wherein Jaina writers have attacked various tenets and practices of the Brahmanical religion, especially those connected with the sacrifice of animals in Vedic rites. There is in fact a whole literature of such attacks interspersed in Jaina writings in Sanskrit and Prākrit, but there are few as systematic and comprehensive as that in our work, not to speak of the dramatic realism which characterizes the dialogue.

CHAPTER XIII

JAINISM AND OTHER FAITHS

POPULAR JAINISM

The period of Rāṣṭrakūṭa hegemony in the Deccan was perhaps the most flourishing epoch of Jainism. Not only in the Rāṣṭrakūṭa empire but in the feudatory Ganga kingdom (Mysore), the religion of the Arhat enjoyed royal patronage and esteem and the support of the people, especially of the commercial classes. The ninth and tenth centuries mark, in fact, an era of great expansion of Jaina culture in that part of India in the sphere of religion, philosophy and literature. Somadeva's *Yaśastilaka*, a contemporary record of documentary value, throws considerable light on the position of Jainism and its relation to other religions during an important period of Indian history.

In the Deccan of the tenth century Jainism was, as it has always been, the religion of an influential and ambitious minority, and nowhere in Jaina literature is the propagandist note more clearly heard than in Somadeva's *Yaśastilaka*. It would appear that, as late as the tenth century, the charge of being an upstart religion lacking in the prestige of antiquity was levelled against Jainism; and Somadeva tries to prove the ancient origin of the faith by citing the authority of a number of texts and authors, supposed to contain, according to him, appreciative references to the Jaina creed and Jaina monks.[1] Unfortunately some of the authorities cited by him do not seem to be very old, while there are others of a dubious character, if not altogether spurious; and they do not, on the whole, carry him very far in defending his thesis. For example, Somadeva claims to find a reference to the expedient of worshipping a Jaina monk for the cure of illness caused by his wrath in a verse of the Jyotiṣa Vedāṅga,[2] but the verse in question is not found in the latter work and seems to be a quotation from a later astrological text. Similarly, in another text, cited anonymously, Bṛhaspati is represented as expounding before Indra the Syādvāda doctrine.[3] The quotations from *Citrakarman* and *Ādityamata* relating to portraits and idols respectively of Jaina Tīrthaṁkaras[4] are no doubt authentic and genuine, but the two works cited by Somadeva cannot be very old, although earlier than the tenth century,

1 *Yaśastilaka*, Book IV.

2 कथं नाम ज्योतिषाङ्गे वचनमिदमुक्तम्–समग्रं शनिना दृष्टः क्षपणः कोपितः पुनः । तद्भक्तस्तस्य पीडायां तावेव परिपूजयेत ॥ Ibid.

3 'सांख्यं योगो लोकायतं चान्वीक्षिकी । तस्यां च स्यादस्ति स्यान्नास्तीति नग्नश्रमणक इति बृहस्पतिराखण्डलस्य पुरस्तं समयं कथं प्रत्यवतस्थे ।' Ibid.

4 See Chap. XVIII.

while Varāhamihira, from whom Somadeva quotes a verse containing a reference to the cult of the Jinas practised by the naked ascetics, fourished only about four centuries earlier than the composition of *Yaśastilaka*.[1] Somadeva then quotes a verse from a work called *Nimittādhyāya*, which describes the visit of 'ascetics free from worldly ties' as auguring prosperity to a place,[2] and he obviously takes the expression *nirgranthāśca tapodhanāḥ* to mean Jaina monks. The date of this work is unknown, but it seems to be referred to by Śāntarakṣita in *Tattvasaṁgraha* (vv. 3511 ff.). He says that if Vedic authority is required as proof of the omniscience of the Buddha, reference should be made to the Nimitta Śākhā of the Veda wherein the Exalted Buddha, the Omniscient sage, is clearly mentioned by the learned Brāhmaṇas.[3] The Nimitta Śākhā of the Veda seems to be a fiction and is probably the same as the *Nimittādhyāya* cited by Somadeva, which might be supposed to contain a reference to the Buddha. That the Nimitta Śākhā was not a Vedic school is shown by the statement of Śāntarakṣita that the hostility of the Brāhmaṇas to the Buddha was responsible for the fact that this particular Śākhā was not included among the Vedic schools, although the text concerned, obviously the same as the *Nimittādhyāya*, could be converted into a Vedic text at will by adding the necessary accents.[4] However that might be, the citation from the *Nimittādhyāya* does not further to any great extent Somadeva's argument in support of the antiquity of the Jaina religion. Similarly, after citing the texts mentioned above, he goes on to enumerate a large number of poets including Bhāravi, Bhavabhūti, Kālidāsa and Māgha, and claims that the Jaina faith enjoys a great reputation in their works.[5]

The anxiety of Somadeva to establish the antiquity of Jainism illustrates the desire of a member of a minority community to enhance the prestige of his faith, so essential for its propagation. The duty of a pious Jaina to his religion is clearly formulated in connection with the *aṅgas* or components of Samyaktva;[6] and one of his sacred obligations seems to be *gaṇavardhana*, expansion of the community, to be carried out by appropriate methods explained by Somadeva in detail.[7] The evidence of Somadeva

1 See Chap. XVIII.

2 निमित्ताध्याये च—पद्मिनी राजहंसाश्च निर्ग्रन्थाश्च तपोधनाः । यं देशमुपसर्पन्ति सुभिक्षं तत्र निर्दिशेत् ॥

3 किंतु वेदप्रमाणत्वं यदि युष्माभिरिष्यते । तत् किं भगवतो मूढैः सर्वज्ञत्वं न गम्यते ॥ निमित्तनाम्नि सर्वज्ञो भगवान् मुनिसत्तमः । शाखान्तरे हि विस्पष्टं पठ्यते ब्राह्मणैर्बुधैः ॥

4 अथ शाखान्तरं नेदं वेदान्तर्गतमिष्यते । तदत्र न निमित्तं वो द्वेषं मुक्त्वाऽवधार्यते ॥ स्वरादयश्च ते धर्माः प्रसिद्धाः श्रुतिभाविनः । कर्तुमत्रापि शक्यास्ते नरेच्छामात्रसंभवात् ॥

5 '......राजशेखरादिमहाकविकाव्येषु ......कथं तद्विषया महती प्रसिद्धिः' Book IV. For the poets in question see Chap. XVIII

6 Book VI.

7 See Chap. X.

clearly shows that while the Jainas were eager to propagate their religion, they were definitely opposed to the admission of undesirable elements to the fold of Jainism, and preferred to welcome those who had voluntarily adopted the faith. At the same time there was a tendency to show considerable latitude to those converts who were unable to forgo completely their former customs and beliefs. As Somadeva says, a person of this category should be given a mixed reception, since the total loss of a new adherent is by no means desirable.[1]

As we have already pointed out, Somadeva defends certain Jaina practices which seem to have provoked adverse comment in non-Jaina circles.[2] The nudity of the Digambara monks was one such example, and there is an interesting episode in *Yaśastilaka* Book V, wherein another attempt is made to justify it. Prince Yaśomati is disgusted at the sight of the Jaina monk Sudatta in the garden of the Sahasrakūṭa temple, and the companion of the prince explains to the merchant Kalyāṇamitra that the king's displeasure is due to his having seen the inauspicious nude fellow before him. Kalyāṇamitra who is a good Jaina makes a spirited reply, in the course of which he asserts that nudity is natural and it is clothing that is artificial: one is nude at birth and during childhood and at the time of enjoying physical comforts; Śiva is nude and so is the recluse who cuts off the tuft of hair on his head. If nudity is objectionable, why is the cow honoured every day ? It is sinful and harmful objects that are inauspicious; if sages, devoted to the good of all sentient beings, and purified by knowledge, meditation and austerities, are an inauspicious sight, what else can be auspicious in the world ?[3] The frequency with which Somadeva defends the nudity and other practices of the Digambara monks seems to suggest that these were considered to be unattractive features of the Jaina creed in the eyes of non-Jainas, and it was accordingly deemed necessary to remove all misconceptions in regard to them in order that there might not be any obstacles in the path of the propagation of Jainism among the masses.

Jaina propaganda seems to have been subtle and effective. In *Yaśastilaka*, Book IV, Yaśodhara's mother describes the Jainas as weaning away the people from other systems, like thieves, and calls the Digambaras magicians expert in fascinating the world.[4] It was also part of Jaina

1 For the relevent verses see Chap. X, section VI.

2 See Chap. X.

3 सुखानुभवने नग्नो नग्नो जन्मसमागमे। बाल्ये नग्नः शिवो नग्नो नग्नश्छिन्नशिखो यतिः॥ नग्नत्वं सहजं लोके विकारो वस्त्रवेष्टनम्। नग्ना चेयं कथं वन्द्या सौरभेयी दिने दिने॥...ज्ञानध्यानतपःपूताः सर्वसत्त्वहिते रताः। किमन्यन्मङ्गलं लोके मुनयो यद्यमङ्गलम्॥

4 See Chap. XII.

propaganda to hold up the tenets of other faiths to ridicule and dilate on the excellence of Jainism. Somadeva, for instance, indulges in unbridled criticism of contemporary non-Jaina faiths and lays emphasis on the essential purity of the Jaina religion. He says among other things that the Omniscient and trustworthy Guide postulated by the Jainas is free from all blemishes such as the passions, and Jainism condemns even the use of words signifying wine and similar objects : how can the wise ever decry a religion like this?[1] Further, it may be noted that Jaina writers often indulge in what is called *dharmaparīkṣā* or the examination of the relative merits of different religions with a view to demonstrating the superiority of Jainism to the others. Somadeva, for instance, examines in his romance various religions and systems, and enumerates the different theories of salvation held by the non-Jaina schools of thought by way of contrasting them with the Jaina view of Mokṣa, which by implication is claimed to be superior to the rest. Amitagati, who is somewhat later than Somadeva, wrote in 1014 A. D. a treatise called *Dharmaparīkṣā* to establish the superiority of Jainism to the Brahmanical religion by pointing out the fallacies and weak points of the Purāṇic mythology. It is noteworthy that *Dharmaparīkṣās* were composed also in Prākrit, Apabhraṁśa and Kanarese. Vṛttavilāsa (*c.* 1160 A. D.) produced a Kanarese version of Amitagati's Sanskrit work : "it tells how two Kṣatriya princes went to Benares, and in successive meetings with the Brāhmans there, exposed the vices of the gods as related in the sacred books."[2] Hariṣeṇa wrote a *Dharmaparīkṣā* in Apabhraṁśa in 988 A. D., and this again is based on a *Dharmaparīkṣā* composed by Jayarāma in Prākrit.[3] Lesser in scope but earlier than these is the episode of *Dharmaparīkṣā* in Uddyotana's Prākrit romance *Kuvalayamālā* Book IV.[4] Here we find that the tutelary goddess Śrī presents king Dṛḍhavarman with a mysterious document, inscribed on a gold plate in Brāhmī characters, and containing what turns out to be the fundamental tenets of the Jaina religion. The next day the king summons an assembly of learned men of different communities and asks them to expound their religious tenets to see whether they correspond to those recorded in the inscription. The Jaina Sādhus alone declare that the doctrines set forth in the document constitute the true faith. Jainism is

---

1 For the verse in question see Chap. XII.

2 Rice: *Kanarese Literature*, p. 37. Brahma Śiva (*c.* 1125) is another Kanarese writer, who in his controversial work *Samaya-parīkṣe* "points out the defects of rival creeds, and justifies the Jaina position."

3 See Dr. Upadhye's article in *The Jaina Antiquary*, Vol. IX, p. 21.

4 See Ratnaprabha's Sanskrit version, p. 202: तदाकर्ण्य राजा धर्मपरीक्षार्थं देवतागृहे कुलदेवतां श्रियमाराधयामास etc.

accordingly declared to be the best of religions, and the king decides to adopt the Jaina faith and enter the monastic order.[1] The shortcomings of other religions and the excellence of Jainism form the sum and substance of Jaina propaganda, reminding one of a certain type of Missionary literature of modern times. Dogmatic assertions declaring the supremacy of the Jaina religion are, as is to be expected, frequent in medieval Jaina literature. Vādībhasiṁha, for instance, invites the ambitious man, desirous of the supreme beatitude, to betake himself to the sacred Jaina faith, 'a lion in destroying the elephants, the wrong creeds:' (*Kṣatracūḍāmaṇi* 11. 105):

> एवं निर्मलधर्मनिर्मितमिदं शर्म स्वकर्मक्षयप्राप्तं प्राप्तुमतुच्छमिच्छतितरां यो वा महेच्छो जनः ।
> सोऽयं दुर्मतकुञ्जरप्रहरणे पञ्चाननं पावनं जैनं धर्ममुपाश्रयेत मतिमान्निःश्रेयसः प्राप्तये ॥

Nothing could be more incorrect than to assume that the success of medieval Jainism was due solely to subtle and successful propaganda. The latter was no doubt an important factor, but the progress made by the faith and the royal patronage enjoyed by it under the Cālukyas, the Rāṣṭrakūṭas, the Gangas, and the Hoysalas as well as under certain feudatory rulers should be attributed rather to the zeal of a succession of saintly Jaina teachers and the confidence inspired by the intellectual eminence of scholars and writers like Akalaṁka, Vīrasena, Jinasena, Guṇabhadra, Pampa, Ponna, Puṣpadanta, Vādirāja, Prabhācandra and others. Such men could be expected to hold their own and maintain the prestige of their faith in a world of thought dominated by the leaders of the Brahmanical revival from Śaṁkara and Kumārila to Udayana and Rāmānuja.

The old philanthropic ideals of Jainism seem to have been upheld in the tenth century. In a remarkable verse of *Yaśastilaka* Somadeva gives expression to the religious ideal of the true Jaina: devotion to Jina, good will

---

1 The recently published *Dhūrtākhyāna* of Haribhadra throws further light on the character and composition of the Dharmaparīkṣā texts. Haribhadra's *Dhūrtākhyāna*, composed in Prākrit verses in the eighth century, is a lively satire on the Puranic legends, and as such allied to the *Dharmaparīkṣās* of Amitagati and others, but it is free from the theological bias and the propagandist tone of the latter. Jayarāma's *Dharmaparīkṣā* is no longer extant, but that of Hariṣeṇa is available in manuscripts. Hariṣeṇa says that the *Dharmaparīkṣā* which was formerly composed by Jayarāma in Gāthā metre is now composed by him in Paddhaḍiyā metre. A comparison of the *Dhūrtākhyāna* and the *Dharmaparīkṣā* of Amitagati reveals considerable similarities; and it is probable that Jayarāma, who is so far the earliest known among the Dharmaparīkṣā writers, utilized Haribhadra's work for sectarian purposes. See Dr. A. N. Upadhye's Introduction to Haribhadra's *Dhūrtākhyāna* edited by Ācārya Jinavijayaji in the Singhi Jain Series No. 19. See also Dr. Upadhye's paper 'Hariṣeṇa's *Dharmaparīkṣā* in Apabhraṁśa' in the Silver Jubilee Number of the *Annals of the B. O. R. I.*, vol. XXIII, pp. 592–608.

towards all creatures, hospitality to all and an altruistic disposition.[1] The four gifts of protection, food, medicine and religious instruction, which constitute the groundwork of Jaina charity, are duly emphasized by Somadeva in connection with the customary vows of a Jaina householder.[2] It is, however, necessary to point out a certain parochial attitude noticeable in the matter of according hospitality and rendering charitable assistance to persons who were not adherents of the Jaina faith. Somadeva distinctly says that those who do not possess the Three Jewels, that is, do not believe in the fundamental Jaina dogmas of Right Faith, Right Knowledge and Right Conduct, are not eligible for gifts; and that charity practised in favour of those who hold wrong views and indulge in wrong conduct, that is, all who are outside the pale of Jainism, leads only to evil consequences, like the feeding of serpents with milk. Hospitality towards such people should be limited to a residual portion of food to be taken away, as a Jaina layman is forbidden to entertain them in his house. He is also asked to keep at arm's length members of other communities such as the Buddhists, the Śaivas and the Brāhmaṇas who perform sacrifices lest familiarity with them should lead to friction and disputes ending in violence.[3] Isolation rather than amity based on free social intercourse was the object aimed at in inter-communal relations.

Jaina writers often attack the Hindu caste system, and we need refer only to the strictures of Jaṭāsiṁhanandi on the theory of castes in his *Varāṅgacarita* 25. 2 ff. It is, however, well-known that the caste system is prevalent among the present-day Jainas almost to the same extent as among the Hindus; and it has been said that 'in practice the modern Jaina is as fast bound as his Hindu brother in the iron fetters of caste.'[4] Evidence recorded by Somadeva in *Yaśastilaka* goes to show that conditions were not far different in the tenth century. He says, for instance, that the three higher castes are alone eligible for religious initiation, while all the four including the Śūdras are fit to receive gifts of food.[5] The status of

1 See Chap. XI.

2 See Chap. X, section XV.

3 For the relevant verses see Chap. X, section XV.

4 In Dharwar, for example, Jain Kshatriyas have disappeared, but Jain Brāhmans, Vaiśyas and Śūdras remain. Jain Śūdras are also called Jain Caturthas [?]. There are various restrictions on interdining. 'If Karnatak Jains go to Gujarat they do not dine with Gujarat Jains, nor, when they come to Dharwar, do Gujarat Jains dine with local Jains'. *Bombay Gazetteer*, Vol. XXII, p. 117.

5 'दीक्षायोग्यास्त्रयो वर्णाश्चत्वारश्च विधोचिताः' *Yaśastilaka*, Book VIII, section 43. A marginal note in Ms. A says: शूद्रजैनानामपि विधा आहार उचितो दीयते इत्यर्थः.

the Jaina Śūdras does not appear to have been more favourable than that of their brethern in Hindu society.

It was impossible for Jainism to remain unaffected by the influences of local customs, beliefs and cults. Ample testimony is borne to this by diverse religious customs such as the burning of the dead and the offering of rice-balls to the crows on the tenth day, the belief in ghosts and spirits, and the worship of various deities, like Padmāvatī.[1] Cakreśvarī, Padmāvatī, Ambikā and Siddhāyikā are, in fact, well-known goddesses of popular Jainism.[2] Of these Somadeva mentions Siddhāyikā as 'a city goddess who has inspired faith in many people' and refers to the pleasance dedicated to her as a refuge for all creatures, in *Yaśastilaka*, Book I.[3]

Medieval Jaina religious Canon seems to have sanctioned, or at least not to have opposed, the observance of local customs and practices. Somadeva says, for instance, that the religion of Jaina householders is of two varieties, *laukika* and *pāralaukika*: the former is based on popular usage and the latter on the scriptures.[4] The castes, he continues, are without a beginning and so are their observances; it is immaterial whether the Jaina Scriptures or *any other S'āstras* are accepted as an authoritative guide with regard to them.[5] Somadeva sums up by observing that it is legitimate for Jainas to follow any custom or practice sanctioned by popular usage so long as it does not come into conflict with the fundamental principles of the Jaina faith or the moral and disciplinary vows.[6] Such views no doubt

---

1 Sharma: *Jainism and Karnataka Culture*, p. 145 ff. The Dharwar Jains are said to have as their family gods Cakreśvara, Dharaṇendra and his wife Padmāvatī, Lakṣmī-Nārāyaṇa [?], and Kṣetrapāla, whom the head of the family daily worships. They go on pilgrimage to the shrine of Padmāvatī at Hombas in Mysore. *Bombay Gazetteer* (op. cit.), p. 118.

2 For Ambikā see *Journal of the University of Bombay*, Vol. IX. Part 2, p. 147 ff. She is represented in sculpture, painting and religious texts with two children and a lion as her vehicle. The latter feature makes her akin to the Brāhmanical goddess Ambikā or Durgā, although the mythological background is altogether different. Nevertheless she too has a grim aspect, and is invoked in Jaina Tantric texts as Śivā, Caṇḍikā, Aghorā etc. Ambikā is still worshipped in Jaina temples in various parts of the country. There was a temple of Ambikā famous as a place of Jaina pilgrimage at Kodinār in South Kāthiāvāḍa. *Bombay Gazetteer*, Vol. I, part I, p. 182.

3 'तदेवमनेकलोकोत्पादितप्रत्ययायाः पुरदेव्याः सिद्धायिकायाः सर्वसत्त्वाभयप्रदावासरसं स्मरसौमनसं नामोद्यानम्'. P.107.

4 द्वौ हि धर्मौ गृहस्थानां लौकिकः पारलौकिकः । लोकाश्रयो भवेदाद्यः परः स्यादागमाश्रयः ॥ Book VIII, Section 34.

5 जातयोऽनादयः सर्वास्तत्क्रियापि तथाविधा । श्रुतिः शास्त्रान्तरं वास्तु प्रमाणं कात्र नः क्षतिः ॥ Ibid.

6 सर्व एव हि जैनानां प्रमाणं लौकिको विधिः । यत्र सम्यक्त्वहानिर्न यत्र न व्रतदूषणम् ॥ Ibid.

imply a recognition of well-established facts and the unescapable influence of social environment rather than any liberalism in the Jaina religious outlook. Further, as we have already pointed out, Jaina religious opinion was lenient in regard to those adherents of the faith who could not wholly discard their former beliefs and practices, and this, too, seems to have facilitated the infiltration of non-Jaina elements into Jaina social and religious usage. Moreover, co-existence with Brahmanism for centuries appears to have influenced Jaina religious practice in various other directions. Somadeva describes, for instance, the five Yajñas for the Jaina householder, and these are clearly modelled on the five Brahmanical Mahāyajñas, although by *Yajña* he seems to mean *dāna*, as explained in a marginal note in Manuscript A.[1] It has also been pointed out that certain Rāṣṭrakūṭa documents, viz. the Konnur inscription of Amoghavarṣa I and the Surat plates of Karkka, which record grants made for Jaina establishments, make provision *inter alia* for such typically Hindu religious rites as *balicarudāna*, *vaiśvadeva*, and *agnihotra*.[2] It is no doubt surprising to find provision made for these rites in grants allocated to Jaina temples and monasteries, but there seems to be no reason to suppose that the rites in question were 'introduced in these records by the oversight of the imperial secretariat'. Considered in the light of Somadeva's observations cited above, the rites mentioned in the two inscriptions could perhaps be legitimately performed by Jainas so long as they did not involve any animal sacrifice, and we seem to find here another instance of Jaina adaptation of non-Jaina practices. With regard to *agnihotra*, the Jainas were no doubt opposed to the Brahmanical rite, but evidence furnished by South Indian Jaina literature clearly shows that the Jainas were not opposed to fire ritual, as such. In a learned note published in the *Jaina Antiquary* Vol. VI, No. II, p. 64, we are told that in Tamil the term *Velvi* is always used to denote fire ritual, while the expression *Veda-Velvi* is used in ancient Tamil literature in the sense of Vedic sacrifice. "Whenever the term *Veḷvi* is used alone, it merely means fire ritual without involving animal sacrifice. Such a fire ritual has never been codemned by Jains, while they were staunchly opposed to Vedic sacrifice on the ground of Ahimsa. Even now among the Tamil Jainas fire ritual is a common thing. During their marriages they do have the characteristic marriage Homam with all its necessary details. Even in temple worship it is a common practice among the south Indian Jainas. Hence it is entirely erroneous to conclude that fire ritual is foreign to Jainas and that it could not be performed or attended by a Jaina". We are also told that the term in the Tamil

---

1 आवेशिकाश्रितज्ञातिदीनात्मसु यथाक्रमम् । यथौचित्यं यथाकालं यज्ञपञ्चकमाचरेत् ॥ Book VIII, section 43.

2 Altekar: *The Rāṣṭrakūṭas and their times*, p. 314.

epic *S'ilappadikāram* for such a rite is "*Arravelvi*, fire sacrifice, according to the doctrine of Ahimsa"

The process of infiltration of non-Jaina elements in Jaina religious practice must have set in before the tenth century, and the gradual transformation of Jainism was already at work when Somadeva formally recognised it and tried to bring it into harmony with the orthodox position of the faith.

Other Faiths

Somadeva attacks various non-Jaina faiths in *Yaśastilaka* which not only throws light on the religious conflict in the tenth century but on the different sects prevalent at the time. The main attacks are directed against Śaivism and its different forms, popular Brahmanism, Vedic sacrifices, the Buddhists and the Ājīvakas.

Śaivism—Dakṣiṇa Mārga

The relations between Śaivism and Jainism are of paramount importance in view of the prolonged conflict of the two religions particularly in the Tamil country and the Deccan. The main doctrinal points at issue between the two systems have been discussed in previous Chapters; and we may here deal with the place of Śaivism in the religious life of the country in the tenth century and thereabouts. Somadeva, as we have seen, speaks of two broad divisions of Śaivism, the *Dakṣiṇa Mārga* and *Vāma Mārga*. The latter *mārga* represents the grosser form of Śaivism or rather Tantricism; while the former may be said to constitute Śaivism proper.

The Śaiva system recognises three fundamental concepts: Pati, Paśu and Pāśa. Pati is Śiva himself, the lord of the Paśus or creatures who are bound by the Pāśas or fetters. These are five or rather four: Mala (nescience or mental darkness), Karma, Māyā and the world produced by it, and the obscuring power of Śiva.[1] The latter has the power both to bind and release, but release cannot be had without undergoing the consequences of one's Karma. Śiva, accordingly, creates the world to enable the creatures to serve out the full term of their Karma. Ever merciful, he assumes the rôle of a preceptor (*ācārya*), and accords initiation (*dīkṣā*), preliminary to final release, to those who have destroyed their

1 'मलं कर्म च माया च मायोत्थमखिलं जगत्। तिरोधानकरी शक्तिरर्थपञ्चकमुच्यते ॥' quoted in comm. on *Tattvaprakāśa* 1. 5. 'मलोऽज्ञानं पशुत्वं च तिरस्कारकरस्तमः। अविद्या ह्याकृतिर्मूर्छा पर्यायास्तस्य वाचकाः॥ quoted from *Kiraṇa*. Ibid. 1. 17.

Karma.[1] Emancipation consists in union with or absorption in Śiva (*S'ivasamānatā, sāyujya*)[2].

The Dakṣiṇa Mārga, as interpreted by Somadeva, seems to represent a sort of monistic system under the influence of Vedāntic ideas. Śiva is regarded as the sole ultimate reality, but the system postulates also thirty-six Tattvas or Principles which last till the dissolution of the creation.[3] They are Śiva, Śakti, Sadāśiva (the volitional aspect of Śiva), Īśvara (the active aspect of Śiva) and Śuddha-vidyā (the omniscient aspect of Śiva); Māyā, Kāla, Niyati (the law regulating the nature of things), Kalā (the urge to activity in creatures), Vidyā (intuition), Rāga (desire including the higher impulse) and Puruṣa; and Prakṛti, Buddhi, Ahaṁkāra, Manas, the ten Indriyas, the five Tanmātras and the five elements. It is important to note that Māyā is the constituent material which Śiva stirs into action with his Śaktis in order to create the universe.[4] The universe is accordingly compared to a magic show,[5] and Śiva is spoken of as identical with Māyā and its product, the universe.[6] In the ultimate resort Śiva is declared to be the sole Reality[7] and the Supreme Principle, in which is reflected the universe composed of the thirty-six Principles, just as a town or a village is reflected in a large mirror.[8] Śiva is the supreme, deathless Absolute (Brahma), the one and the true, subject to no change or modification, self-luminous and beyond the range of mind and speech. He is accompanied by Māyā, and Māyā is at the root of the creation; it is the indestructible germ of the universe, and inspired by Śiva.[9] The principle

1 *Tattvaprakāśa* 1. 15; 6. 2.

2 Ibid. 2. 16.

3 आप्रलयं तिष्ठति यत् सर्वेषां भोगदायि भूतानाम्। तत् तत्त्वमिति प्रोक्तं न शरीरघटादि तत्त्वमतः ॥ *Tattvaprakāśa* 6. 3. In 5. 7 it is stated that Māyā, Puruṣa and Śiva continue to exist after the dissolution of the Tattvas, and creation starts again.

4 असत् स्वतः सदाभासमिन्द्रजालं यथा तथा। तां मायां शक्तिभिः स्वाभिर्विक्षोभ्य परमेश्वरः॥ स्वकर्मानुगुणं सृष्टिं करोति करुणानिधिः। *Īśānaśivagurudevapaddhati* (*Kriyāpāda*) 1. 87, 88. Cf. *Tattvaprakāśa* 3. 3.

5 इत्थं मायादिपृथ्व्यन्तैर्मिथो नातिविलक्षणैः। अशुद्धाध्वनि निष्पन्नमिन्द्रजालोपमं जगत्॥ *Īśānaśivagurudevapaddhati* (*Kriyāpāda*), p. 15.

6 The comm. on *Tattvaprakāśa* 1. 18 says: ज्ञानस्वभाव एवायमात्मा शिवः मायातत्कार्यात्मनावभासते। ततः स एव तदुभयमिति। ...तदुक्तमीश्वरगीतायाम्—स एव मूलप्रकृतिः प्रधानः पुरुषोऽपि च। विकारा महदादीनि देवदेवः सनातनः॥

7 तत्त्वं वस्तुत एकं शिवसंज्ञं चित्रशक्तिशतखचितम्। *Tattvaprakāśa* 2. 13.

8 सर्वविकल्पविहीनं शुद्धं शान्तं व्ययोदयविहीनम्। यत् परतत्त्वं तस्मिन् विभाति षट्त्रिंशदात्म जगत्॥ दर्पणबिम्बे यद्वन्नगरग्रामादि चित्रमविभागि। भाति विभागेनैव च परस्परं दर्पणादपि च॥ Quoted from a शतककार in Śrīkumāra's comm. on *Tattvaprakāśa* 1. 18.

9 Cf. कूटस्थममृतं ब्रह्म सत्यमेकमविक्रियम्।...सदात्मकं स्वयंज्योतिरवाङ्मनसगोचरम्। मायासहायं तत् प्राहुः शिवतत्त्वं मनीषिणः॥ Quoted from सिद्धान्तहृदय in comm. on *Tattvaprakāśa* 2. 5. Also 'मायातत्त्वं जगद्बीजमविनाश्यं शिवात्मकम्' quoted from स्वायंभुव in *Īśānaśiva* (*Kriyāpāda*), chap. 2.

of Advaita is, on the whole, consistently maintained; and when Śiva is described as appearing in the form of Māyā and its product, the universe, it is to be understood that the transformation is apparent and not real. The Śaiva system recognises *vivarta* and not *pariṇāma*.[1]

The Śaiva doctrines corresponding to the *Dakṣiṇa mārga* mentioned by Somadeva are formulated in Bhoja's *Tattvaprakāśa* and the *Īśānaśivagurudevapaddhati*, an encyclopedic treatise, which quotes Bhoja's work, Jayanta's *Nyāyamañjarī* and numerous other Śaiva works and authors, and may be assigned to the latter half of the eleventh century or thereabouts. It is noteworthy that the kind of Śaivism represented in the latter compilation is of the ritualistic and mystic type, due importance being given to *Mantradīkṣā* and *Kriyācaryā* or ritual. The history of medieval Śaivism is yet to be written, but it is this form of Śaivism that seems to have been prevalent in Somadeva's time. The quotations and references in the *Īśānaśivagurudevapaddhati* show that there was a vast amount of Śaiva religious literature extant in the tenth and eleventh centuries. The *Svāyaṁbhuva Tantra* quoted in the *Paddhati* enumerates twentyeight Tantras or Āgamas which expound the doctrines of the Śaiva system, there being two groups of ten and eighteen. The first group consists of *Kāmika, Yogaja, Acintya, Kāraṇa, Ajita, Dīpta, Sūkṣma, Saharṣa, Aṁśumat*, and *Suprabhedaka*, collectively known as the *S'ivabheda Tantras*. The second group of Āgamas or Tantras includes *Vijaya, Niḥśvāsa, Prodgīta, Pārameśvara, Āgneya, Mukhabimba, Svāyaṁbhuva, Raurava, Mākuṭa, Kiraṇa, Lambita, Candrajñāna, Vīrabhadra, Siddha, Sāntānika, S'arvodgīta, Vimala* and *Vātūla*, collectively known as the *Rudrabheda Tantras*. A further quotation from the *Svāyaṁbhuva* mentions a four-fold division of the Śaiva scriptures into *S'aiva Tantra, Pāśupata, Vā (Lā) kula* and *Somatantra*:[2] and it is stated that Śiva delivers the pure among the creatures from misery by means of these four varieties of Tantras with the help of proper ritual knowledge and Yoga[3]. The element of Yoga was important in the Śaiva system, and involved intense faith in and devotion to Śiva, in other words, *bhaktiyoga*, which was no doubt the mainspring of popular Śaivism. The emotional appeal of *bhakti* is illustrated in the fervent hymn to Śiva

---

1 Śrīkumāra (op. cit.) says न च...शिवस्य परिणामित्वमिति वाच्यं विवर्तवादाश्रयणात्·

2 The Śaiva Tantra represents the Śaiva system proper. The Pāśupata and Lākula, if this is the correct reading, may be regarded as variations of the Pāsupata system. Somatantra seems to be same as Somasiddhānta or the Kāpālika system.

3 दीक्षादिसत्क्रियाचर्याज्ञानयोगैर्महेश्वरः। दुःखपङ्काद् भवाम्भोधेस्तारयत्यमलानणून्॥

composed by the Cedi king Yuvarājadeva II, which is preserved for us in the Bilhari inscription of the rulers of Cedi.[1]

The Śaiva system proclaimed the paramount character of the Dharma propounded by Śiva. There was a notable revival of Nyāya-Vaiśeṣika studies in the ninth and tenth centuries,[2] and the Vaiśeṣika system laid great stress on the cultivation of Dharma. The idea appealed to the Śaiva teachers who admitted the necessity of Dharma for the attainment of salvation, but contended that the Śaiva creed, and not the various other Dharmas propounded by the different scriptures, constituted the paramount Dharma. The *Īśānaśivagurudevapaddhati* (*Kriyāpāda*, 1. 4 ff.) quotes the first of the Vaiśeṣika sūtras and says:

> **अथातो धर्ममित्यादिसूत्राद् वैशेषिकादतः । धर्मप्रयोजनं मोक्षः प्रोक्तश्चाभ्युदयो महान् ॥**
> **धर्मा बहुविधाः ख्यातास्तत्तदागमचोदिताः । न हि ते मुख्यधर्माः स्युर्मुख्यधर्माः शिवोदिताः ॥**
> **मायाविकारहीनेन विशुद्धेनामलात्मना । सर्वकर्त्रा शिवेनोक्तं शास्त्रं मुख्यं हि सर्वथा ॥**

ŚAIVA MAṬHAS AND TEACHERS

The Śaiva system was expounded and taught in the *Maṭhas* or monasteries many of which were in existence in central and western India in the tenth century or thereabouts. The Karhad plates of Kṛṣṇa III issued in 959 A. D. record the grant of a village to a teacher named Gaganaśiva, described as a great ascetic proficient in all the *Śivasiddhāntas*. He was the pupil of the Ācārya Īśānaśiva, the head of the Valkaleśvara Maṭha in Karahāṭa (modern Karhāḍ in the Satara district);[3] and the purpose of the grant was the maintenance of the ascetics who lived at the place. It may be assumed that the Valkaleśvara Maṭha was large and important enough to have attracted the notice of the Rāṣṭrakūṭa emperor.

A teacher named Gaganaśivācārya, described as an ornament to the spiritual lineage of the sage Durvāsas, is mentioned in a Kanarese inscription issued by Dattālpendra Srīmāra, a king of the Ālupa family which ruled for many centuries in the Tuḷuva country corresponding to the modern district of South Kanara and part of North Kanara. The subject of the record is the grant of a plot of land in Kārkala in favour of the Maṭha

---

1 समदकरिघटाभिः किं किमङ्गाङ्गनाभिर्मदनशयनलीलां भावयन्तीभिराभिः । कनकतुरगवासोरत्नजातैर्न कृत्यं न हि भवति भवानीवल्लभस्यार्चनं चेत् ॥ Verse 74. (किमिह) बहुभिरुक्तैर्नाथ सर्वस्य हेतुर्भवतु भवति नित्यं **भक्तियोगो** ममैकः । सकलसुखविशेषाद् यत्र पीयूषवर्षः स्वयमनुभवगम्यो जायते त्वत्प्रसादात् ॥ Verse 76. Yuvarājadeva II reigned about the last quarter of the tenth century A. D.

2 See Chapters VIII and IX.

3 'करहाटीयवल्कलेश्वरस्थानपति'.

to which Gaganaśiva belonged.[1] If the Gaganaśiva mentioned in the inscription, which is not dated, is the same as the teacher named in the Karhad grant of Kṛṣṇa III, it may be presumed that the Valkaleśvara Maṭha had a branch in South Kanara, of which Gaganaśiva was the head. It is noteworthy that Gaganaśiva is called in the Karhad grant not the abbot of Valkaleśvara, but a disciple of the abbot Īśānaśiva. It is possible that the latter was the head of the maṭha in Karahāṭa and the former of the branch in Tuḷuva. It may be added that the Ālupa kings were Śaivas, and Śaivism was the predominant religion in Tuḷuva from about the seventh to the thirteenth century, when the Vaiṣṇava movement initiated by Ānandatīrtha came to the fore.[2]

A few years after the Karhad grant of Kṛṣṇa III we find an ascetic named Prabodhaśiva founding a Śaiva Maṭha in central India, at Chandrehe in Rewa State, then within the dominions of the Cedi kings of Tripurī. The relevant inscription is dated in the Kalacuri year 724 corresponding to 972 A. D., and engraved on slabs built into a wall of the monastery, the remains of which still exist at Chandrehe.[3] The edifice is of considerable size and partly two-storeyed, but the upper storey has for the most part collapsed. Still it is 'a very favourable specimen of Hindu civil or domestic architecture' with spacious rooms and smaller chambers.

Two other Śaiva monasteries built during the rule of the Cedi kings, those of Vaidyanātha and Nauhaleśvara or Nohaleśvara, are earlier than the one at Chandrehe. According to the Bilhari inscription of the rulers of Cedi,[4] the Vaidyanātha-maṭha was presented to a teacher named Hṛdayaśiva by Lakṣmaṇarāja who ruled about the middle of the tenth century, being the son and successor of Yuvarājadeva I, who has been assigned to the first half of the same century. The Nauhaleśvara Maṭha was also accepted by Hṛdayaśiva, but made over by him to his disciple Aghoraśiva (vv. 57–8). As noted towards the end of the inscription, the *praśasti* seems to have been put up at the Nohaleśvara Maṭha by Aghoraśiva; and the monastery no doubt existed at Bilhari, in the Jubbalpore district, where the inscription is said to have been found. The Maṭha derived its name from Nohalā, the queen of Yuvarājadeva I, and was obviously attached to the Siva temple caused to be built by her, as stated in the inscription (v. 40).

1 Saletore: *Ancient Karnataka*, Vol. I, p. 388.

2 Saletore (op. cit.), Chapter V.

3 See R. D Banerji: *The Haihayas of Tripuri and their monuments.*

4 *Ep. Ind.* Vol. I, p. 251.

The Bilhari inscription of Prabodhaśiva at Chandrehe and another record of his discovered at Gurgi,[1] in Rewa State, throw light on an influential order of Śaiva monks known as the Mattamayūra family, who propagated the faith in many parts of western and central India from about the ninth to the eleventh century. Prabodhaśiva who founded the Chandrehe monastery was a disciple of Praśāntaśiva. The latter built a hermitage (*āśrama, siddhasthāna*), on the banks of the Śoṇa river at the foot of the Bhramara mountain, and a retreat for the practice of austerities (*tapahsthāna*) on the Ganges, which was held in high esteem by the people of Benares who were devout worshippers of Śiva. Praśāntaśiva is called the ornament of the Mattamayūra family in the Gurgi inscription, and was the disciple of Prabhāvaśiva. The latter was induced to settle in the Cedi country by Yuvarājadeva I and was presented with a Maṭha built at an enormous cost (*ananta-dhana-pratiṣṭham*). Similarly, Lakṣmaṇarāja, who gave the Vaidyanātha monastery to Hṛdayaśiva, is described as having brought the sage 'by manifesting his devotion to him by means of presents sent through honest messengers.' The services of the Mattamayūra monks appear to have been freely requisitioned by the Cedi kings, who placed rich maṭhas at their disposal for the propagation of the Śaiva faith.

Prabhāvaśiva was the disciple of Śikhāśiva or Cūḍāśiva, who, according to the Chandrehe inscription, was the disciple of Purandara of the holy Mattamayūra family, 'the preceptor of kings'. The latter may be said to have initiated the activities of the Mattamayūra organisation; and to judge from the succession of teachers and disciples, he must have lived not later than the end of the ninth century. An inscription found at Ranod or Narod in Gwalior State, about half-way between Jhansi and Guna, and assigned on palaeographic grounds to the end of the tenth or the beginning of the eleventh century, gives some information about this distinguished teacher.[2] A king named Avantivarman, who visited Purandara at Upendrapura (Uṇḍor), and was initiated by him in the Śaiva faith, persuaded the sage to migrate to his kingdom; and there in the city of Mattamayūra, Purandara founded a Matha and another establishment at Raṇipadra, identified with Ranod. Raṇipadra seems to have been a religious centre as it is called a *tapovana*, also a *Yatyāśrama* in the Ranod inscription (vv. 15, 17 59.). There still exists an old building at Ranod, with an open cloister in front of it with rooms at each end, which most probably served the purpose of

1 The inscriptions of Prabodhaśiva are edited and translated in Banerji (op. cit.), App. C.

2 *Ep. Ind.* Vol. I, p. 351 ff.

a Maṭha or residence for monks. It is noteworthy that there are two tanks close to each other outside the courtyard; and one of them might be the tank elaborately described in the Ranod inscription, and said to have been excavated by a teacher named Vyomaśiva. The latter seems to have lived about the middle of the tenth century, as there is a succession of three teachers between him and Purandara: Kavacaśiva, Sadāśiva and Hṛdayeśa. Of them Sadāśiva is said to have practised austerities at Raṇipadra (v. 17). The town and the Maṭha seem to have fallen on evil days at a later date; and it was Vyomaśiva who restored the town to its former prosperity, repaired and improved the dilapidated monastery, installed images of Śaiva divinities, and founded the tank with temples and gardens attached to it (vv. 29, 30, 43, 44).

Madhumatī, in Mālava, was another important Śaiva religious centre in the tenth century. In the Gurgi inscription of Prabodhaśiva, Madhumatī is described as the abode of the Saiddhāntikas or Śaivas; and it was in fact one of the centres of the Mattamayūra monks. Cūḍāśiva or Sikhāśiva, who was, as already mentioned, a disciple af Purandara, is called Madhumatī-pati, 'Lord of Madhumatī', in the Chandrehe inscription. Hṛdayaśiva, who accepted monasteries from Lakṣmaṇarāja, and one of whose predecessors is stated to be Mattamayūranātha in the Bilhari inscription,[1] is described therein as having enhanced the reputation of the *Mādhumateya-vaṁśa* or the family of the Madhumatī monks (v. 55). All this shows that the monks of Madhumatī represent a younger branch of the Mattamayūra line of Śaiva teachers.

The Ranod inscription gives the names of the predecessors of Purandara, the founder of the Mattamayūra lineage. They are Kadambaguhādhivāsin 'Resident of Kadambaguhā'; after him Śaṅkhamaṭhikādhipati 'Master of Śaṅkhamaṭhikā'; then Terambipāla 'Protector of Terambi'; and lastly, Āmardakatīrthanātha 'Lord of Āmardakatīrtha'. Terambi has been identified with Terahi, five miles to the south-east of Ranod, and Kadambaguhā with Kadwaia or Kadwāha, about six miles south of Terahi, and where there are even now some old temples and the ruins of many others. Kadambaguhā seems to have been an early centre of Śaivism where lived a long line of saints (*Siddhasantati*), according to the Bilhari inscription. The sage Rudraśambhu was their revered leader and his disciple was Mattamayūranātha 'The lord of Mattamayūra', who brought spiritual enlightenment to king Avantivarman.[2] This is a clear reference to Purandara,

1 The spiritual pedigree is given as Rudraśambhu–Mattamayūranātha–Dharmaśambhu–Sadāśiva–Mādhumateya–Cūḍāśiva–Hṛdayaśiva–Aghoraśiva.

2 Verse 49. See Kielhorn's re-interpretation of the verse in *Ep. Ind.*, Vol. I, p. 353.

but in the Ranod inscription his immediate predecessor is said to be Āmardakatīrthanātha.

The town of Mattamayūra made so famous by the distinguished line of ascetics named after it has not been identified; but, as suggested by Kielhorn, it must have been somewhere in Central India. As already mentioned, most of the Maṭhas of the Mattamayūra sect were established in various parts of Central India, in the regions corresponding to Malwa, Gwalior State, Central Provinces and Rewa State. But the Mattamayūra monks appear to have gone further afield, and established a branch in Southern Konkan, as shown by the Kharepatan plates of Raṭṭarāja, dated in Śaka 930 = 1008 A. D.[1] Raṭṭa was a prince of the Śilāhāra family of Southern Konkan, a feudatory of the Cālukyan king Satyāśraya, the successor of Taila II. The inscription records the grant of certain villages to a learned teacher named Ātreya for the upkeep of the shrine of Avveśvara, for providing food and raiment to the resident ascetics and for the benefit of pupils (*Chātra*), learned men and guests. There was obviously a Maṭha attached to the shrine. Now, the donee Ātreya was a disciple of an ascetic named Ambhojaśambhu who belonged to the Karkaroṇī branch of the Mattamayūra family; and it is also stated that the yield of the villages granted was for the use of the learned Brahmacārins and Ācāryas of the said branch of the Mattamayūra line of ascetics.[2]

Another important Maṭha of the tenth century was the Golaki Maṭha in the Cedi country, but it does not appear to have been connected with the Mattamayūra line. Golaki or Golagi is said to be a contraction of Goḷagiri, and the Maṭha seems to have been in the neighbourhood of Tripurī, the Cedi capital (modern Tewar within six miles of Jubbalpur). According to the Malakāpuram pillar inscription of the Kākatīya queen Rudra Mahādevī, dated 1261 A. D., the Maṭha was founded by a Śaiva teacher named Sadbhava Śambhu who was patronized by Yuvarājadeva I of Tripurī, who, as mentioned above, ruled in the first half of the tenth century A. D.[3] The inscription mentioned above speaks of another teacher of the same line, named Soma Sambhu, who composed a work called *Somaśambhupaddhati*, and had thousands of disciples, but his exact date cannot be determined, as it is not known how many generations separated him from the founder of the Maṭha. We are inclined to identify him with

1 *Ep. Ind.* Vol. III, p. 292 ff.

2 '*Mattamayūrānvaya-Karkaroṇī-Saṁtati*'; '*Mattamayūrānvayāntargata-**Karkroṇi**-santāna.*'

3 Cf. Mirashi: ***Yuvarājadeva I of Tripurī*** in ***ABORI***, Vol. XI, p. 362.

the Soma Śmbhu quoted several times in the *Īśānaśivagurudevapaddhati* (*Kriyāpāda*), specially as the verses cited from him deal with ritual; and the *Somaśambhupaddhati*, to judge from the title, must have been a work on ritual. If our identification of the two authors is correct, Soma Śambhu may be assigned to the latter half of the tenth or the first half of the eleventh century. It may be added that the succession of teachers at the Golaki Maṭha seems to have continued unbroken till 1261 A. D., the date of the Malakāpuram pillar inscription, which records the grant of a village to a celebrated Śaiva teacher named Viśveśvara Śambhu. The ramifications of the great Maṭha have, as a matter of fact, been traced, beyond the thirteenth century and the geographical limits of Tripurī, to the Tamil and Telugu lands.[1]

A very old Śaiva establishment, much earlier than the tenth century, and associated with the Pāśupata sect, appears to have existed at Kāyāvarohaṇa, also called Kārohaṇa and Kāravaṇa, identified with Kārvān in Dabhoi *tāluka* in Baroda State. The place is known also as Kāyāvataraṇa or Kāyāvatāra. Kauṇḍinya states in the introduction to his *Bhāṣya* on the *Pāśupatasūtras* that the Lord, assuming the form (*kāya*) of a Brāhmaṇa, became incarnate at Kāyāvataraṇa, went on foot to Ujjain, and taught his doctrine to Bhagavat Kuśika. The reference here is to the tradition that the Pāśupata doctrine was revealed by Nakulīśa or Lakulīśa, the last of the the twenty-eight incarnations of Śiva.

The various incarnations of Śiva are mentioned in *Vāyupurāṇa* (chap. 23), *Liṅgapurāṇa* (chap. 24), *S'ivapurāṇa* (*Vāyavīya-saṁhitā* II, chap. 10) and in Kūrmapurāṇa in the last chapter of the first part. The Avatāras begin with Śveta and end with Lakulin; and they are called *Yogācāryas* in the *S'ivapurāṇa*. The *Vāyu* and *Liṅga-purāṇas*, which give the more detailed account, mention Kāyārohaṇa or Kāyāvatāra as the place where Lakulin manifested himself, along with such famous sites as the Kālañjara mountain and the Prabhāsa Tīrtha where certain other Avatāras of Śiva are said to have revealed themselves. The *Liṅgapurāṇa* makes in this connection particular mention of Pāśupata Vrata, and declares its superiority to Sāṁkhya or the Pañcarātra discipline. Kārohaṇa is glorified also in the *Kāravaṇa-māhātmya*, a work of unknown date, which declares it to be a Tīrtha as sacred as Benares and Prayāga; and tells us that Lakulin here merged

---

1 For the Golaki Maṭha see Saletore: *Ancient Karṇāṭaka*, Vol. I, p. 362 ff. In a record found in the Madras Presidency, the Kalacuri king Yuvarājadeva is stated to have donated three lakhs of villages to Sadbhava Śambhu, the head of the Golaki Maṭha. See *Amodā Plates of the Haihaya king Pṛthvīdeva* in *Ep. Ind.* Vol. XIX, p. 75 ff.

himself in the Brahmeśvara Liṅga.[1] The characteristic emblems of Lakulin, a staff in the left hand and a citron in the right, are mentioned in this work.[2]

An interesting link between Kārvān and the ancient founder of the Pāśupata system is provided by two *liṅgas* with the figure of Lakulin sculptured in front: one of them is in the temple of Nakleśvar, and the other in that of Rājrājeśvar, both at Kārvān.[3] Liṅgas with one or four faces of Śiva carved against the liṅga pillar are quite common, and were installed in temples dedicated to Śiva. It appears, however, that *liṅgas* with the figure of Lakulin carved on them were also installed, evidently by members of the Pāśupata sect.

The Purāṇic texts mentioned above assign four disciples to each of the twenty-eight Avatāras of Śiva. Those of Lakulin are stated to be Kuśika, Garga, Mitra and Kauruṣya. Important light on the date of Lakulin and Kuśika is thrown by the Mathura Pillar Inscription of Candragupta II dated in Gupta era 61 = 380–81 A. D.[4] The inscription records the installation of two *liṅgas* called Kapileśvara and Upamiteśvara by a Śaiva teacher named Uditācārya whose pedigree is given. He is described as fourth in succession from Bhagavat Parāśara and tenth from Bhagavat Kuśika. Upamita and Kapila are two other teachers mentioned in the record. Bhagavat Kuśika is no doubt the same as the first disciple of Lakulin mentioned in Kauṇḍinya's *Bhāṣya* on the *Pāśupatasūtras* and the Purāṇic texts. If Uditācārya (380-81 A. D.) is tenth in succession from Kuśika, the pupil of Lakulin, and we allot a certain number of years to each succeeding teacher, Lakulin and Kuśika cannot possibly be later than the second century A. D. The Pāśupata centre at Kārvān was thus established sometime in the second century A. D., and Uditācārya's inscription shows that Pāśupata teachers carried on their activities at Mathura in the fourth century A. D. The epigraph tells us that Uditācārya installed

1 The *Kāravaṇa-māhātmya* is printed as an appendix to *Gaṇakārikā* (G. O. S.). 'Kārvān seems to have suffered great desecration at the hands of the Musalmans. All round the village, chiefly under pipal trees, images and pieces of sculpture and large *liṅgas* lie scattered. To the north and east of the village on the banks of a large built pond called Kāśikuṇḍa are numerous sculptures and *liṅgas*. *Bombay Gazetteer*, Vol. I, Pt. I, p. 83.

2 स्थितः स भगवान् तत्र कायरूपी महेश्वरः। येन कायावतारोऽसौ तेमेदं कायरोहणम्॥ असिदण्डधरो वामे दक्षिणे बीजपूरकम्। ब्रह्मलिङ्गे महादेवि अहमपि लय गतः॥

3 See D. R. Bhandarkar: *Mathura Pillar Inscription of Candragupta II* in *Epigraphia Indica*, Vol. XXI.

4 Ibid.

the *lingas*, Upamiteśvara and Kapileśvara, obviously named after the teachers Upamita and Kapila, in a place called *gurv-āyatana*, which seems to mean a 'Teachers' shrine', where such memorial *lingas* appear to have been placed for worship. It is possible that such shrines belonging to the Pāśupata sect existed at other places besides Mathura.

Uditācārya, as stated above, traces his descent to Kuśika, the first disciple of Lakulin. Another line of teachers who trace their descent to Garga, the second disciple of Lakulin, is mentioned in the Cintra Praśasti of the reign of Sārangadeva of Gujarat, composed in 1287 A. D. at Somanāthapattana, or Prabhāsa, the famous Śaiva Tīrtha, in Kathiawar.[1] It is stated that Śiva became incarnate as Bhaṭṭāraka Lakulīśa, the reputed founder of the Pāśupata system, at Kārohaṇa in the Lāṭa country. He had four pupils named Kuśika, Gārgya, Kauruṣa and Maitreya who set themselves to practise particular Pāśupata vows. From them originated four branches or families of ascetics, and to the line established by Gārgya (*gārgyagotra*) belonged the abbot (*sthānādhipa*) Kārttikarāśi, his disciple Vālmīkirāśī and the latter's disciple Tripurāntaka. These teachers lived in the thirteenth century, but they belonged to an ancient line of Pāśupata ascetics, and were apparently abbots in succession of some Maṭha in Gujarat.

The tradition recorded above appears to be mentioned also in an inscription of the reign of Naravāhana, king of Mewar, the ancient Medapāṭa, dated 972 A. D.[2] The inscription is mutilated, but there are clear references to Kāyāvarohaṇa and Śiva with a *lakula* (staff) in his hand, that is Lakulin or Lakulīśa, and Kuśika and other sages. The object of the inscription seems to be to record the building of a temple of Lakulīśa[3] somewhere in Mewar. It is engraved on a slab built into the wall of a temple called Nāthā's Mandir near Ekalingaji's temple, a few miles north of Udaipur. It is obvious that temples of Lakulīśa existed in the tenth century; and an old temple of Lakulīśa is found also at Badāmi, as mentioned below.

The Pāśupata, as noted in Chapter IX, was an influential school of thought in the tenth century, and Pāśupata teachers played an important part in the religious life of Mysore in the eleventh and twelfth centuries.[4]

1 *Ep. Ind.*, Vol. I, p. 271.

2 *A Collection of Prakrit and Sanskrit Inscriptions* published by the Bhavanagar Archaeological Department, p. 70.

3 'लकुलीशवेश्म हिमवच्छृङ्गोपमं कारितम्'

4 See below.

The influence of Pāśupata teachers and Maṭhas can also be traced elsewhere in the country. Kalhaṇa tells us in *Rājataraṅginī* 5. 404 that the king of Kashmir Cakravarman (935 A. D.) constructed a lodge for the Pāśupatas called the Cakra-maṭha, which, being half built at the time of his murder, was completed afterwards by his widow. Turning to the south, we find that, a few years later, an inscription of the thirtysixth year of the reign of the Cola king Parāntaka I (907-953 A. D.) records a grant of land for the maintenance of certain attendants and offerings in a temple, and for feeding the Śivayogins and the Māheśvaras on the seven festival days beginning with the asterism of Mūla.[1] Here the Sivayogins obviously refer to the Śaivas, and the Māheśvaras appear to be Pāśupatas, as Śaṁkara in his Bhāṣya on the *Vedāntasūtras* II. 2. 37 refers to the latter as Māheśvaras.

An inscription of the reign of Kumārapāla of Gujarat, dated 1169 A. D., throws interesting light on the career of a distinguished Pāśupata teacher named Bhāva-Bṛhaspati *alias* Gaṇḍa. The inscription is engraved on a large stone in the side wall near the door of the temple of Bhadrakālī at Somanāthapaṭṭana, and tells us that he was a native of Benares and belonged to the Gārgeya-vaṁśa, that is, to the spiritual lineage of Gārgya, one of the original founders of the Pāśupata sect. Bhāva-Bṛhaspati left Benares on a tour of pilgrimage and came to Dhārā, and the Paramāra kings are said to have become his disciples. He practised austerities in Mālava and Kanauj and efficiently managed Maṭhas.[2] Subsequently he came to Gujarat where he cultivated the friendship of the reigning king Jayasiṁha Siddharāja. The great achievement of Bhāva-Bṛhaspati was the restoration of the famous temple of Somanātha under the patronage of the next king Kumārapāla, who richly rewarded him for rebuilding the dilapidated edifice.[3]

A Pāśupata Maṭha, much earlier than the thirteenth century, existed on Mount Abu in Rajputana. An inscription, dated Saṁvat 1342 (1285 A. D.), which records the genealogy of the Sisodia kings of Chitore, tells us that the Maṭha on the hill-top was repaired by Rājā Samarasiṁha who also equipped it with a golden flag-staff at the request of a Śaiva ascetic named Bhāvaśaṁkara. The latter was a disciple of Bhāvāgni, a Pāśupata ascetic who was formerly the abbot (*sthānādhīśa*) of the Maṭha.

1 N. K. Sastri: *The Colas*, Vol. I, P. 434.

2 'सम्यक्मठाः पालिताः'

3 *A Collection of Prakrit and Sanskrit Inscriptions* (op. cit.), p. 186.

The establishment was considered very old at the time of the inscription which calls it *anādi.*[1]

The active influence of a faith is best illustrated by the temples devoted to its cultus; and of no other faith is this so true as of S'aivism during several centuries in India. Some of the most important shrines may be casually enumerated here: Somanātha at Somanāthapaṭṭana in Kathiawar, Acaleśvara at Abu, Ekaliṅgajī near Udaipur, Mahākāla at Ujjain, Nīlakaṇṭheśvara at Udayapura near Bhilsa, Oṁkāreśvara in the Nimar Dt. of Central Province, Viśvanātha etc. at Khajuraho, Virāṭeśvara at Sohagpur, Paraśurāmeśvara etc. at Bhuvaneśvara in Orissa, Saṁgameśvara at Badami, (Kailāsa) Īśvara at Ellore, Tārakeśvara at Hangal (Dharwar Dt.), Madhukeśvara at Banavasi, Rājasiṁheśvara at Conjeevaram, etc. A study of the geographical distribution of these Śaiva temples shows the influence and popularity of Śaivism in vast areas of early medieval India until about the 12th century A. D.[2]

ŚAIVISM AND JAINISM: THE LAST PHASE

The struggle of the Jaina faith with Vīraśaivism came in the latter half of twelfth century. In the tenth century Jainism still occupied a privileged position under the patronage of the ruling dynasties in Mysore and the Deccan; and it was about this time that it was in conflict with the prevailing Śaivism of the age. Sectarian controversy was the order of the day; and Somadeva seems to echo contemporary Jaina theological opinion when he denounces Śaivism as a strange medley of mutually contradictory doctrines.[3] Others, besides him, appear to have entered the lists against Śaivism. The Malliṣeṇa Praśasti tells us that the Jaina teacher Vimalacandra challenged the Śaivas, Pāśupatas and Kāpālikas as well as Bauddhas and Kāpilas to argument; while another teacher Hemasena is declared to have vanquished Śiva himself, like Arjuna (vv. 25, 36)! The Praśasti was composed in honour of the Jaina saint Malliṣeṇa who died by fasting at Śravana-Belgola in 1129 A. D., and these two scholars are mentioned in a list of Digambara teachers who preceded Malliṣeṇa.[4] Hemasena is mentioned just before Dayāpāla and Vādirāja, both of whom lived in the first quarter of the eleventh century, and just after Matisāgara, the *guru* of Dayāpāla. Hemasena may possibly be assigned to the end of the tenth century. Then, there are six teachers between Matisāgara and

1 Ibid., p. 84.

2 See Appendix III.

3 See Chapters VIII and X.

4 *Ep. Ind.*, Vol. III, p. 184.

Vimalacandra, who may have lived in the first half of the tenth century, and was perhaps a contemporary of Somadeva.

Similar claims of Śaiva teachers triumphing over their Jaina opponents are occasionally met with. The Ranod inscription states that a celebrated teacher named Vyomaśiva silenced among others the Jainas who are contemptuously likened to jackals (v. 39). Vyomaśiva was a native of Central India, and as already mentioned, he may be assigned to about the middle of the tenth century. Another distinguished opponent of Jaina teachers was Vādi-Rudraguṇa of whom we shall speak later.

One of the points at issue in the Śaiva-Jaina controversy was the position of the Arhats as superhuman universal teachers. The Śaivas contended that the Jaina conception of the Arhat was wholly inadequate: if he was an omniscient teacher, we must ask who his teacher was, and if he was a saint devoted to austerities, there must be some one to vouchsafe the result of his efforts. In either case, it was necessary to postulate a superior Being, self-existent and without a beginning, and He was no other than Maheśvara or Śiva. The Śaiva contention that Śiva was the *guru* of the Jaina Tīrthaṁkaras is recorded by Somadeva in *Yaśastilaka*;[1] while the claim that He confers on the Arhat, who is conditioned in time, the reward of the Latter's religious austerities is put forward in *Īśānaśivagurudevapaddhati* (*Kriyāpāda* 1. 39 ff.).[2]

Jainism began to lose ground from about the eleventh century following the subversion of the Rāṣṭrakūṭa empire and the Ganga kingdom, which were its principal mainstay. Śaivism, on the other hand, continued to make fresh conquests under the Cālukyas of Kalyani, while the Colas, who conquered Mysore early in the eleventh century, were its most ardent champions. Interesting light on the prestige and eminence of the Śaiva teachers of the age is thrown by an inscription of the reign of the Cālukya king Jayasiṁha II, dated 1036 A. D., which records certain grants of land made to a Śaiva scholar named Vādi-Rudraguṇa Lakulīśvara Paṇḍita for the repairs of the temple of Pañca Liṅga, at Baḷḷigāve, 'the royal city of Banavase 12000'.[3] Vādi-Rudraguṇa, described in the inscription as a falling star to the Digambara speakers, defeated in argument a number of eminent

1 See Chap. VIII.

2 तत्कारणं सधीरस्तीत्येषणीयो महेश्वरः। देहप्रमाणमात्मानं नित्यानित्यविशेषणात् ॥ ब्रुवतां जैनसाधूनां महर्षिस्तादृगेव हि। अहिंसादितपोयोगादर्हत्त्वं तस्य तन्मते ॥ सिद्धमित्यादिमान् सोऽपि तपसा परवान् यतः। तत्तपःफलदातान्यस्तैरुत्सृज्येह मत्सरम् ॥ स्वतन्त्रोऽनादिमान् कर्ताध्येयणीयो महेश्वरः।

3 *Epigraphia Carnatica*, Vol. VII. *Inscriptions in the Shimoga District.* **Part I** (No. 126).

Jaina teachers including the famous scholar and poet Vādirāja. The Pañca Liṅga temple was an important educational centre of the Kālāmukha order of Śaiva ascetics, being called 'the Kālāmukhi Brahmacāri-sthāna of Baḷḷigāve'; and the grants in question were made not only for the upkeep of the temple and the worship of the god but for the provision of food and clothing for the students and ascetics. The Kedāra Maṭha of Baḷḷigāve was even a more important Śaiva religious and educational institution. An inscription of the reign of Bijjaḷa, dated 1162 A. D., gives a remarkable picture of the great establishment, called in the record 'Koḍiya Maṭha, the place of the Southern Kedāra', while the deity worshipped in the temple is referred to as 'Dakṣiṇa Kedāreśvara of the Koḍiya Maṭha'.[1] The Maṭha was not only a place of worship but a great centre of learning and a well-organised charitable institution for the destitute and the sick. It is described in the inscription as "the place appointed for the performance of the rites of devotee Brahmacāri-Śivamunis; the place for the recital of the four Vedas with their Aṅgas; the place for commentaries on the Kaumāra, Pāṇinīya, Śākaṭāyana, Śabdānuśāsana and other grammars; the place for commentaries on the Nyāya, Vaiśeṣika, Mīmāṁsā, Sāṁkhya, Bauddha and (other systems); the place for commentaries on the Lākula-siddhānta, the Pātañjala and other Yoga-śāstras; the place for the eighteen Purāṇas, the Dharma-śāstra, all poems, dramas, comedies and every branch of learning; the place where food is freely distributed to the poor, the destitute, the lame, the blind, the deaf.............................; the place for the treatment of the diseases of destitute sick persons; a place of security from fear for all living things". 'The Southern Kedāra' is described also as "the means of the absolution of sin, the very presence of Śiva manifested to all the citizens........." A celebrated Śaiva teacher Vāmaśakti Paṇḍita, designated as Rājaguru, was the head of the Maṭha at the time; and Bijjaḷa, washing the feet of the *guru*, made various grants of lands "for the decoration of the god Dakṣiṇa Kedāreśvara, for gifts of food to the ascetics, for gifts of learning, for repairs of the temple...........". On the same occasion he made grants to two other Śiva temples, those of Somanātha and Brahmeśvara at Abbalūr.[2] Bijjaḷa may have had Jaina leanings, but there is no doubt that he was a patron of Śaivism. It is hardly necessary to point out that it was during his reign that the aggressive Vīraśaiva cult came into prominence and imposed serious handicaps on the further progress of the Jaina faith in South-Western India. Vīraśaivism weaned away the commercial classes

1 Ibid., Inscription No. 102. Baḷḷigāve or Baḷḷigāme is in the Shimoga District of Mysore State.

2 Ablūr in Dharwar District.

who were the chief supporters of Jainism; and whole clans, like the Caṅgāḷvas were converted from Jainism to the Vīraśaiva faith.[1] The influence of the new sect is illustrated by the fact that an important Jaina centre like Bankapur, in the Dharwar district, which had five religious colleges of the Jainas in 1055 A. D., came to have a Hindu population, the greater part of whom were Lingāyats.[2] It is also said that Lingāyats appropriated a large number of Jaina temples in the Kanarese districts and installed in them the *liṅga* as the object of worship.[3] Prior to this, Jaina temples appear to have suffered considerable damage during the Cola invasions of the Cālukyan dominions in the eleventh century. The 'base Cola' (Rājādhirāja I who was killed in the battle of Koppam in 1054 A. D.) is said to have burned down many temples and defiled and damaged Jaina sanctuaries in the Beḷvola province during the reign of Someśvara I. The damage seems to have been repaired to some extent by Lakshma, the governor of Beḷvola, who, in 1071 A. D., restored the Jaina temple at Annigeri, in the Dharwar district, which had been burned down by the Cola invader.[4]

Among the Śaiva sects the Pāśupatas appear to have been very influential in the Mysore country in the eleventh and twelfth centuries. The name of Lakulīsa, the founder of the system, occurs very often in the Mysore inscriptions, and the creed is referred to as the Lākulāgama, Lākulāmnāya and Lākula-samaya. An inscription of 943 A. D. says that Lakulīsa, fearing lest his name and works of merit should be forgotten, became incarnate as the *munināṭha* Chilluka. As mentioned above, a grant was made in 1036 A. D. in favour of Vādi-Rudraguṇa, styled as Lakulīśvara Paṇḍita. An inscription of about 1078 and two others of 1094 and 1103 mention respectively Vālmīki-muni, Śrīkaṇṭha-paṇḍita and his son Someśvara-paṇḍita, all of them distinguished exponents of the Lākula creed.

1 Rice: *Coorg Inscriptions*, Vol. I, p. 13. 1914. The Caṅgāḷvas ruled in West Mysore and Coorg.

2 *Bombay Gazetteer*, Vol. XXII, p. 653.

3 Cousens (op. cit.).

4 See *Two Inscriptions from Gawarwad and Annigeri*, *Ep. Ind.*, vol. XV, p. 337 ff. Also Sastri: *The Colas*, Vol. I, p. 311. Beḷvola is an old Kanarese word meaning a field of standing corn. The name was given to the fertile district near the centre of which are Dambal, Gadag and Lakkundi, in the Dharwar district. *Bombay Gazetteer*, Vol. XXII, pp. 392, 718. There still exist a number of old Jaina temples in this area, at Aminbhāvi (near Dharwar town), Annigeri (between Dharwar and Gadag), Chabbi (about eight miles south of Hubli), Lakkundi (about seven miles south-east of Gadag), Mulgund (about twelve miles south-west of Gadag), and Soratur (about ten miles south of Gadag). *Bombay Gazetteer* (op. cit.), chap. XIV.

The latter is said to have caused the Lākula-siddhānta to blossom. Further, two inscriptions of 1168 and 1179 compare the *rājaguru* Vāmaśakti with Lakulīśvara or Nakulīśvara. Another record mentions a succession of *gurus* of the Agastyeśvara Maṭha at Śrīparvata, all whose names end in *śakti*. The Lākula or Pāśupata system is generally mentioned in the Mysore inscriptions in connection with the Kālāmukha sect;[1] and there is no doubt that the Pāśupatas were known as Kālāmukhas in the Kannaḍa country. The technical expression *Kālam Karcci* (laving the feet) used in Kannaḍa inscriptions on the occasion of making a gift to the teachers of this sect is an indication of the high respect shown to them[2]. These Kālāmukha Pāśupatas were not certainly identical with the Kālāmukhas mentioned by Yāmuna Muni and Rāmānuja in their enumeration of Śaiva sects, as the latter were no better than Kāpālikas.

The mantle of the Pāśupatas appears to have fallen on the Vīraśaivas to a very great extent in the Kannaḍa country. Many of the great Kālāmukha Maṭhas seem to have been transformed into Vīraśaiva Maṭhas. The Kālāmukha Maṭha at Pūvalli, the modern Hūli in the Belgaum District of Bombay Province, which had many branches and a succession of influential abbots, as recorded in a number of inscriptions, is now a Vīraśaiva Maṭha, and provides a striking illustration of the process of transformation[3].

Vīraśaivism represented a mass movement, and was a more serious rival of Jainism. It was also a movement of social reform, and at variance with orthodox Hinduism in several respects. The rapid expansion of this powerful, hostile sect had an adverse effect on the subsequent history of Jainism in the South. Vīraśaivism gathered momentum under the inspiring leadership of Basava, the minister of Bijjala (1162-67 A. D.) who had taken possession of the Cālukyan throne. Kalyāṇa (now in Bidar District, Hyderabad State), the capital of the later Cālukyas, became the centre of direction of the new religious movement. The devotional literature of the Vīraśaivas known as the Vacanaśāstras composed in Kanarese prose goes back to the eleventh century A. D., about a century earlier than the age of Basava; but the literary and religious movement reached its climax about the middle of the twelfth century during the

---

1 See Rice: *Mysore and Coorg from the Inscriptions*, p. 205. Also Bhandarkar: *Vaiṣṇavism, Śaivism and minor religious systems*, p. 171. Poona ed. In an inscription of 1177 A. D., for example, certain ascetics are called upholders of the Lākulāgama-samaya and adherents of the Kālāmukhas.

2 Nandimath: *A Handbook of Vīrśaivism*, p. 9.

3 Nandimath (op. cit.), p. 10.

period of the activities of Basava and his contemporaries. Jeḍara Dāsimayya, one of the early Vacana writers, is believed to have been a contemporary of the Cālukya king Jayasiṁha I whose reign covers the greater portion of the first half of the eleventh century A. D. The principal writers and leaders of the movement, however, belong to the latter half of the next century. Among the contemporaries of Basava may be mentioned Ekāntada Rāmayya, a vigorous propagandist who is said to have destroyed Jaina temples; Prabhudeva who was the head of the Virakta-maṭha at Kalyāṇa, the pontifical seat known as Śūnya-siṁhāsana 'The throne of the void'; Cennabasava who seems to have led the movement after Basava; Siddharāma who is known as Śivayogin, and several others.

The doctrines and social practices of the Vīraśaivas are beyond the scope of our discussion. It may, however, be noted that the apostles of Vīraśaivism laid great stress on intense devotion (*bhakti*) to Śiva, and owed a good deal to the teachings of the great Śaiva saints of the Tamil land. 'Indeed the Vīraśaiva saints claimed the Tamilians as their own; and the Kannada Vīraśaiva literature teems with accounts of the Tamil Śaiva saints.' More important for us is the fact that Vīraśaivism 'spread like wild fire over a considerable portion of the Deccan and southern India.' It enjoyed extensive patronage and privileges under the Vijayanagara kings. It was the religion of the Keḷadi or Ikkeri chiefs who ruled a considerable portion of the Vijayanagara empire. The ancestors of the present rulers of Mysore were Lingāyats till the 18th century.[1] Of all the rivals of Jainism Vīraśaivism seems to have been the most potent, and still continues to play an important rôle in the social and religious life of South-western India.

Apart from the rise of Vīraśaivism, the loss of royal patronage following the overthrow of the Rāṣṭrakūṭas and the Gaṅgas placed Jainism at a disadvantage in its encounter with rival creeds. The reorganisation of Vaiṣṇavism by Rāmānuja and the conversion of the Hoysala king Biṭṭideva (Viṣṇuvardhana) by the latter at the end of the eleventh century was another blow to the prospects of Jainism in the south. Most of the Jaina centres in Karṇāṭaka (Paudanapura, Hanasoge, Humcca, Baḷḷigāme etc.) ceased to be strongholds of Jainism, and "in the centres which fell into the hands of the non-Jainas, only mutilated Jaina images and broken slabs bear silent testimony to the once prosperous condition of Jainism in the country".[2] It has been said of Baḷḷigāme that, like many a great

1 For a brief but authoritative account of Vīraśaivism see Dr. Nandimath's book cited above.

2 Saletore: *Medieval Jainism*, p. 184.

Jaina centre, it today possesses no traces of Jaina worship except broken Jaina images.[1] Still when we speak of the decline of Jainism in Karṇāṭaka we should think in terms of a setback rather than any progressive decay or deterioration. It has been rightly pointed out that Jainism did its best work in the best days of the Rāṣṭrakūṭas in the Southern Maharatta country and Mysore. "These are the portions of South India that happen to be great Jaina centres even now, and in that region Jainism flourished even in the age of the great Colas............Jainism continued to flourish under the Cālukyas and under the Hoysalas at a later time and even in the age of Vijayanagar."[2] It has indeed been said of the Hoysalas that, though they were Jainas first, and later changed over to Vaiṣṇavism, they still built temples dedicated to Tīrthaṅkaras, Śiva and Viṣṇu, and were patrons of all sects alike.[3]

Any talk about the conflict of Śaivism and Jainism during the period under consideration might be misleading if we failed to point out that the two faiths existed side by side, generally speaking, in an atmosphere of toleration and amity in various parts of the country. This is proved by the existence of imposing Jaina temples in such important centres of Śaiva worship as Khajurāho in Bundelkhand or Un in southern Indore. At Khajurāho where the temples were mostly built during the reigns of Yaśovarman and Dhanga (*c.* 930–1000 A. D.), we have the large and fine temple of Jinanātha, which has an inscription of 954 A. D., and was built in the beginning of Dhanga's reign. The Ghanṭai Jaina temple, so called from the bells carved on the pillars, has been partially rebuilt from older materials. The original temple is believed to have been erected in the tenth century A. D.[4]

1 Saletore: *Medieval Jainism*, p. 204.

2 Aiyangar: *Some contributions of South India to Indian Culture*, p. 291.

3 *Mysore Archaeological Report* for 1924, p. 7.

4 Vincent Smith (op. cit.) in *IA*, 1908, P. 133. There are several other Jaina temples at Khajurāho. No. 26 in Cunningham's list is an ancient temple 'restored with plaster and old stones and called Setnāth, which is most probably the original name, as the principal statue enshrined is a colossal standing figure of Ādinātha, 14 feet in height with the title of Setnâth. 'On the pedestal of this statue Cunningham found on his first visit an inscription dated in Saṁvat 1085, or A. D. 1028. No. 27 in his list is a small ancient Jaina temple now dedicated to Ādinātha. There are many Jaina statues, both whole and broken, collected about these temples, with dated inscriptions. One of them is inscribed on a pedestal of a colossal seated statue, and records that the image was dedicated in Saṁvat 1215 (A. D. 1158) during the reign of Madanavarman. *Archaeological Survey of India*, Vol. II, p. 412 ff.

The Un group of temple has been assigned to the eleventh and twelfth centuries. Here we have a large Jaina temples, Chaubara Dera No. 2, 'which in spite of the loss of its *śikhara* still remains one of the most beautiful monuments at Un.' The building has a very large porch in front of the *maṇḍapa*. The second Jaina temple at Un is very well-preserved and popularly known as Goaleśvara. The floor of the *garbhagṛha* is about ten feet lower than that of the *maṇḍapa*, and one has to descend a series of steps. Inside the sanctum stand three huge Digambara Jaina images, one of which measures twelve and a half feet in height. The images bear short inscriptions which give 1206 A. D. as the date of their dedication. Several other large Jaina images have been found at Un, one of which bears the date 1125 or 1135 A. D.[1]

Jaina religious edifices are also found in close proximity to the island of Māndhātā in the Narmadā, in the Nimar District of Central Provinces. 'On the island itself, every temple is dedicated to Śiva or his associate deities; but the north bank of the river opposite, in addition to Śivaite ruins, contains several old structures devoted to Viṣṇu, and a whole group of Jaina temples.' 'The Jaina temples stand on an elevation overlooking, but a little retired from the river. The largest building raised on a plinth of basalt blocks five feet high was perhaps a monastery. It consisted of a quadrangle 53 feet by 43 feet, surrounded by four rows of pillars about 10 feet high. The eastern wall is still complete, decorated with geometrical figures rudely carved in yellow sandstone. On each side of the doorway is a figure carved on slabs about 2 feet high, with Śivaite and Jaina emblems curiously intermix-ed. To the north stood the temple proper, built in a pyramidal shape, with numerous smaller spires. The porch is still erect, but the shrine has been buried beneath the ruins of the dome. The third building was a smaller temple raised on a pyramid of basalt blocks about 25 feet high.'[2]

Interesting sidelight on Śaiva-Jaina relations is provided by the religious history of Mount Abu, which was an early and famous seat of Śaiva worship. The Abu region was subjected by Bhīma I of Gujarat early in the second quarter of the eleventh century A. D.; and the Jaina Vimala Sāha, the first great exponent of marble architecture in India, was sent out as the governor of Abu. It appears that Jaina religious edifices had not existed on the sacred mountain before his time. The magnificent marble temple of Ādinātha was built at Delwara (Devalwada) on Mount Abu by Vimala Sāha in

1 *Progress Report of the Archaeological Survey of India, Western Circle*, 1919, pp. 62-64.

2 *Imperial Gazetteer* of India, Vol. IX, p. 296.

1031 A. D.; and there is a significant tradition associated with the building of the shrine. It is said that the site on which the edifice now stands was formerly occupied by Brahmanical temples, but 'this devout Jaina offered to cover with silver coins as much ground as was required for his temple in return for the permission to erect it. This munificent offer was accepted.'[1]

It is not necessary to mention the existence of Jaina cave temples at Ellora, the home of stupendous rock-cut temples dedicated to Śiva, as the caves here have been assigned to the Rāṣṭrakūṭa period, which coincided with the heyday of Jainism in the Deccan and Mysore. Apart from occasional acts of vandalism, Śaiva-Jaina relations do not appear to have been marred by anything more serious than theological disputes or religious controversies.[2]

ŚAIVISM—VĀMA MĀRGA

The Vāma Mārga, as defined by Somadeva, may be said to represent the grosser form of the Śaiva and Tāntric cults and includes sects like the Kaulas and the Kāpālikas. We have already discussed Somadeva's account of the practices of the Kaulas who are represented as avowed sensualists

---

1 Commissariat: *History of Gujarat*, Vol. I, p. lxii.

2 Jaina temples are said to have been demolished during the invasion of Gujarat by the Paramāra king Subhaṭavarman early in the thirteenth century A. D. Ganguly : *History of the Paramāra Dynasty*, p. 197. As against this, we may point to the flourishing condition of Jaina culture and religion in Malwa from the latter part of the tenth century onwards, which will bear comparison in its own way with the efflorescence of Jainism during Rāṣṭrakūṭa hegemony in the Deccan, or under the Solankis in Gujarat. The harmonious relation of the various faiths in medieval Mālava is shown also by the co-existence of Jaina and Vaiṣṇava temples at several places in Northern Indore. At Kohala, six miles from Bhanpura, to the east of the temple of Lakṣmī-Nārāyaṇa, there are two Jaina temples side by side and known by the popular name of *sas-bahu-ki mandir* or the temples of the mother-in-law and the daughter-in-law, one of which is used for worship even now. At the village of Sandhārā, not far from Bhanpura, the remains include an old temple of Viṣṇu and a Jaina temple called *Tamboli-ka-mandir* or the temple of the betel-seller as well as two other Jaina temples, which have been partly rebuilt at a later date. These two temples are dedicated to Ādinātha and belong to the Digambara community, and regular worship is carried on in both. Two old temples, one dedicated to Viṣṇu and the other to Pārśvanātha, stand in the centre of the village of Kukdesvar, ten miles to the west of Rampura in the northern part of Indore State. It is noteworthy that the Jain temple contains a large bas-relief representing scenes from the life of Kṛṣṇa, which has been built into the south wall of the *maṇḍapa*. For details see *Progress Report of the Archaeological Survey of India, Western Circle, for the year ending 31st March, 1920.*

and worshippers of Śiva.[1] It is related in *Skandapurāṇa, Prabhāsakhaṇḍa* (Chap. 119 of *Prabhāsakṣetra-māhātmya*) that when the great goddess of the Prabhāsakṣetra killed the demons Bala and Atibala and their army, some of the demons who escaped became Kaulas, addicted to meat, wine and women. This seems to be in accord with current description of the Kaulas, but it is an irony that the Purāṇa should have stated also that certain of the demons became Jainas, who were bitterly hostile critics of the former sect. Jayanta in *Nyāyamañjarī* (chap. 4) hints at the objectionable practices of the Kaulas aimed at the attainment of superhuman powers; but as, in this context, he records the views of certain thinkers that all religious systems are authoritative in their own way, he is inclined to put Kaula ritual on a par with such malevolent Vedic rites as the Śyena performed for the purpose of destroying one's enemies.

That the Kaula cult was prevalent in the tenth century is shown not only by the evidence furnished by Somadeva but by that of Rājaśekhara and Devasena, both of whom belong to the first half of the century. In Rājaśekhara's play *Karpūramañjarī* 1. 22 ff. the master magician Bhairavānanda declares that he is an adherent of the Kaula way, drinks wine and enjoys women and so goes forward to salvation. He describes the Kaula religion as charming to all, as its only requirements are a hot strumpet for wife, plenty of meat and wine, alms and a pelt to serve as bed; and opines that while gods like Hari and Brahmā prescribe meditation, the study of the Vedas, and sacrifices as leading to final release, Śiva has the sole credit of having devised a way to salvation consistent with the pleasures of love and wine. The Jaina Devasena gives a similar picture of the Kaula cult in his *Bhāvasaṁgraha* (verses 182-3). Rājaśekhara's verse (*Karpūramañjarī* 1. 23):

रण्डा चण्डा दिक्खिआ धम्मदारा मज्जं मंसं पिज्जए खज्जए अ ।
भिक्खा भोज्जं चम्मखण्डं च सेज्जा कोलो धम्मो कस्स णो भाइ रम्मो ॥

may be compared with Devasena's description of the Kaula religion in *Bhāvasaṁgraha*:

रंडा मुंडा थंडी सुंडी दिक्खिदा धम्मदारा सीसे कंता कामासत्ता कामिया सा वियारा ।
मज्जं मंसं मिट्ठं भक्खं भक्खियं जीवसोक्खं च कउले धम्मे विसये रम्मे तं जि हो सग्गमोक्खं ॥

It is also noteworthy that Devasena, while describing Cārvāka doctrines in the above work (verses 172-76), attributes them to Kaulācārya or the teacher of Kaula doctrines. The Cārvākas or Lokāyatikas were no doubt distinct from the Kaulas, but the insistence of the latter on rank sensualism seems to have led Devasena to identify them with the Cārvākas.

1 Chap. VIII.

Hemacandra says in his commentary on his *Yogaśāstra* 4. 102 that the disciples of the Kaulācāryas are known as Yogins.[1] It may be noted that in *Karpūramañjarī* the Kaula Bhairavānanda is often referred to as *joisara* (Yogīśvara), the great Yogin or adept in mystic rites. Kaula *dīkṣā* is likewise referred to in a *double entendre* in *Nalacampū* (chap. 2).[2]

The Kaulas were akin to the Kāpālikas, and both the Kaula and the Kāpālika cults were anathema to the Jainas. In *Yaśastilaka* VI. 3 Somadeva prescribes a bath for Jaina monks when they happen to come in contact with a Kāpālika.[3] We learn from Yāmunācārya's *Āgamaprāmāṇya* (about 1050 A. D.) that the characteristics of the Kāpālikas were the sacred thread, the smearing of the body with ashes, a crest jewel, various ornaments for the ears and the neck, a human skull and a club. According to them, he who realises the true significance of the six symbols (sacred thread, ashes, crest-jewels, *karṇikā*, *kuṇḍala* and *rucaka*), and meditates on the Self, mentally locating it on the female organ, attains the supreme beatitude.[4] Additional information about the Kāpālika sect is furnished by Kṛṣṇamiśra's allegorical play *Prabodhacandrodaya*, Act III, which introduces a Kāpālika who recounts his beliefs and practices. He wears a garland of human bones, lives on cremation grounds and uses a skull as a dish. Describing his religion, he declares that it consists of the worship of the Mahābhairava form of Śiva with human sacrifices: human flesh is offered as an oblation in the fire, and the worshipper drinks wine from a skull. Not only Mahābhairava but his consort (Mahābhairavī) is worshipped with blood along with a host of goblins called up to the beating of drums. As regards his beliefs, the Kāpālika declares that the world, full of diversities, is not different from Śiva.[5] The Kāpālika ideal of salvation is to become incarnate in a form like that of Śiva and enjoy the pleasures of love with a consort beautiful as Pārvatī. This doctrine is said to have been revealed by Śiva himself, as there can be no happiness without mundane joys; and a state of salvation in which the Self subsists in its pristine condition, like a block of stone, without any consciousness of joy, cannot be a desired goal.[6] This is the sum and

---

1 भक्ष्याभक्ष्ये पेयापेये गम्यागम्ये समात्मनाम् । योगिनाम्ना प्रसिद्धानां कौलाचार्यान्तेवासिनाम् ॥ Verse 33.

2 'विटकौलदम्भदीक्षाभिरिव कुचरूपलोभितलोकाभिः..........कर्णाटचेटीभिः'. The comm. remarks शाक्तदम्भदीक्षासु कुत्सितेन चरुणा मांसादिनोपलोभितलोकाः.

3 संगे कापालिकात्रेयीचाण्डालशबरादिभिः । आप्लुत्य दण्डवत् सम्यग्जपेन्मन्त्रमुपोषितः ॥

4 तथाहुः । मुद्रिकाषट्कतत्त्वज्ञः परमुद्राविशारदः । भगासनस्थमात्मानं ध्यात्वा निर्वाणमृच्छति ॥ तथा । कर्णिकारुचकं चैव कुण्डलं च शिखामणिम् । भस्म यज्ञोपवीतं च मुद्राषट्कं प्रचक्षते ॥ कपालमथ खट्वाङ्गमुपमुद्रे प्रकीर्त्तिते । आभिर्मुद्रितदेहस्तु न भूय इह जायते ॥

5 पश्यामि योगाञ्जनशुद्धचक्षुषा । जगन्मिथोभिन्नमभिन्नमीश्वरात् ॥ 3. 12.

6 दृष्टं क्वापि सुखं विना न विषयैरानन्दबोधोज्झिता, जीवस्य स्थितिरेव मुक्तिरुपलावस्था कथं प्रार्थ्यते । पार्वत्याः प्रतिरूपया दयितया सानन्दमालिङ्गितो, मुक्तः क्रीडति चन्द्रचूडवपुरित्यूचे मृडानीपतिः ॥ 3. 16.

substance of the Kāpālika doctrine, called also *Mahābhairavānuśāsana*, *Parameśvara-siddhānta*, and *Somasiddhānta* in Kṛṣṇamiśra's play. Like Bhairavānanda in Rājaśekhara's *Karpūramañjarī*, the Kāpālika in *Prabodhacandrodaya* puts forward exaggerated claims of miraculous powers, and one of the avowed objects of the Kāpālika cult is the attainment of the supernatural Yogic powers known as the *Siddhis*.[1] It is noteworthy that the Kāpālika is once addressed in the play as Kulācārya[2], which shows that, although the Kaula and the Kāpālika cults were distinct from each other, Kāpālikas were sometimes confused with Kaulas owing to certain resemblances in their practices. The Kaulas are not, as a rule, associated with human sacrifices; yet it is at the instance of a Kulācārya that Māradatta orders preparations for a human sacrifice in the Mahābhairava temple in *Yaśastilaka*, Book I. Members of both sects would seem to have indulged in objectionable practices, but it was the Kāpālikas who were more prominently connected with rites involving the sacrifice of human beings.

In the fourth Act of Kṣemīśvara's *Caṇḍakauśika*, composed in the first half of the tenth century, Dharma appears in the guise of a Kāpālika, armed with a club, and carrying a skull in his hand; and decorated with ashes and human bones. He declares that he is about to attain certain magical powers: control over a goblin who has entered into a corpse, possession of a thunderbolt and magic pills and paints, union with a demoness, and the knowledge of alchemy (*dhātuvāda*) and the elixir of life (*rasāyana*). There is no doubt that the Kāpālikas were charlatans and adepts in black magic, but those who sought to discover the elixir of life and practised alchemy were not necessarily Kāpālikas.

That the Kāpālika cult is much earlier than the tenth century is shown by the wellknown episode in Bhavabhūti's *Mālatīmādhava*, Act V, in which the Kāpālika Aghoraghaṇṭa attempts to sacrifice Mālatī before the goddess Karālā or Cāmuṇḍā.[3] This episode is based on the story of Vidūṣaka in *Kathāsaritsāgara* 3. 4. 158 ff., or rather on Guṇāḍhya's *Bṛhatkathā*, of which the former work is a summary. Although the fanatic, who attempts to sacrifice king Ādityasena's daughter before the idol of

1 अत्रानुज्झितचक्षुरादिविषयासंगेऽपि सिद्ध्यन्त्यमूरत्यासन्नमहोदयाः प्रणयिनाप्यष्टौ महासिद्धयः। etc. 3. 22.

2 'क्षपणकः—अले कापालिअ·········कुलाचालिअ।'

3 A drunken but otherwise innocent Kāpālika appears in the *Mattavilāsaprahasana* of the Pallava King Mahendravikramavarman (first quarter of the 7th century A. D.). About the same time Hsüan-tsang met the first Hindu ascetics of his journey at Kāpiśī, north of Kabul: they had their bodies smeared with ashes and wore a chaplet made of skulls. They were no doubt Śaiva ascetics, but probably not Kāpālikas. Grousset: *In the footsteps of the Buddha*, p. 93.

Kātyāyanī in the story of Vidūṣaka, is called a Pravrājaka or Parivrājaka, there is no doubt that he is a Kāpālika. In another story in *Kathāsaritsāgara* 18. 2 a Kāpālika draws a married woman named Madanamañjarī to a cremation ground for an evil purpose by force of magic formulas and oblations in the fire, but is foiled in his attempt by the intervention of the great king Vikramāditya. In Haribhadra's *Samarāiccakahā*, Book IV, the gambler Maheśvaradatta becomes a Kāpālika and an expert in *gāruḍa-mantra*, mystic formulas for curing snake-bites. The machinations of a Kāpālika and his grim ritual are vividly portrayed in the eighth Act of Rāmacandra's *Kaumudīmitrānanda*. Makaranda in the play allows Kaumudī and Sumitrā to take shelter in a subterranean chamber as a protection against the alleged designs of a Vidyādhara. Meanwhile the Kāpālika offers oblations of human intestines in the fire and attempts to revive what is apparently a corpse which rises and strikes him. The Kāpālika and his accomplices manage to disappear, but Makaranda finds no trace of the chamber or the ladies concealed therein. The episode throws light on certain nefarious tactics of the Kāpālikas as seen by a writer of the twelfth century.

Kāpālikas were known also as Mahāvratins. Jagaddhara in his commentary on *Mālatīmādhava*, Act I, explains the term *Kāpālikavrata* as *Mahāvrata*, and Caṇḍapāla in his commentary on *Nalacampū* (Chap. 6) explains Mahāvratikas as Kāpālikas. In *Kathāsaritsāgara* 5. 2. 81 a Mahāvratin is described as Kapālin ('furnished with a human skull'), wearing matted hair, and white with ashes. In *Yaśastilaka* 1. 115 Death is pictured as a Mahāvratin or a Kāpālika, and the skeleton of a beautiful woman as his club.[1] In the description of the shrine of Caṇḍamārī in *Yaśastilaka*, Book I, Somadeva mentions 'Mahāvratin heroes selling for a price flesh cut from their own bodies.'[2] The uncanny practice of selling human flesh, one's own or that of a corpse, to goblins for the purpose of gaining a desired object is often referred to in Sanskrit literature, and seems to have been resorted to not only by Kāpālikas but by others in desperate circumstances. The love-sick Mādhava appears on the cremation ground in *Mālatīmādhava*, Act V, with a lump of human flesh for sale to the goblins. The practice is referred to in at least two stories of *Kathāsaritsāgara* (5. 2. 180 ff. and 18. 2. 53 ff.). In the first story the brave Aśokadatta goes to a cremation ground on the fourteenth night of the dark half of the month, and offers to the goblins a corpse for sale, the price being a marvellous anklet required

1 'सा कालमहाव्रतिना खट्वाङ्गकरङ्कतां नीना'

2 'कच्चिन्महाव्रतिकवीरक्रयविक्रीयमाणस्ववपुर्लूनवल्लूरम्'

by the king of Benares. In the second story a gambler, who has promised to supply human victims to two Brahmarākṣasas, is at a loss to find them, and repairing to a cremation ground at night, offers to sell human flesh to a goblin in return for a temporary loan of the latter's form and powers wherewith to procure the required victims from among his enemies. In Bāṇa's *Harṣacarita* (Chap. 5) the sale of human flesh (to goblins) by princes is mentioned among the various rites performed for the recovery of Prabhākaravardhana in the latter's capital.[1] The same work (chap. 6) records the story of a prince, apparently of Ujjayinī, who was killed by a goblin, being over-zealous in the matter of selling human flesh on the occasion of the festival of the Mahākāla Śiva.[2] Another reference to the sale of flesh occurs in the third chapter of *Harṣacarita*.[3]

As pointed out by R. G. Bhandarkar, a copper-plate charter of Nāgavardhana, nephew of Pulakesin II, records a grant of a village near Igatpuri in the Nasik District for the worship of the god Kapāleśvara and the maintenance of the Mahāvratins residing in the temple. This shows that the Kāpālika sect existed in Mahārāṣṭra about the middle of the seventh century.[4] The practice of carrying a skull and a club is mentioned among the religious customs of non-Buddhist sects enumerated in *Lalitavistara*, chap. 17.[5] This is a clear reference to the Kāpālika sect in an important work of Buddhist Sanskrit literature composed before, probably long before, the ninth century. It is evident from Bhavabhūti's statements in *Mālatīmādhava*, Act I, that in his time (eighth century) Śrīparvata, a holy mountain in Kurnool District (Madras Presidency) on the Kistna river, was a centre of the Kāpālika cult.[6] There is a reference to a Maṭha of the Mahāvratins in an inscription from Ramnad District (Madras Presidency) of the reign of Vīra Pāṇḍya, showing that the Kāpālikas were well-established in that part of South India in the second half of the tenth century. It is stated in another record issued by a chieftain named Vikramakesari, a contemporary of Vīra Pāṇḍya, that the former presented a big Maṭha to a certain Mallikārjuna of Madura,

1 'अपरत्र प्रकाशनरपतिकुमारकक्रियमाणमहामांसविक्रयप्रक्रमभम्'

2 'महाकालमहे च महामांसविक्रयवादवातूलं वेतालस्तालजङ्घो जघान जघन्यज प्रद्योतस्य पौणकिं कुमारं कुमारसेनम् ।'

3 'महामांसविक्रयक्रीतेन मनःशिलापङ्केनेव'

4 Bhandarkar: *Vaiṣṇavism, Śaivism etc.* (Poona ed.), p. 168.

5 '..............कपालखट्वाङ्गधारणैश्च शुद्धिं प्रत्यगवच्छन्ति संमूढाः'

6 An earlier reference to Śrīparvata is in Subandhu's *Vāsavadattā*: श्रीपर्वत इव संनिहितमल्लिकार्जुनः. Mallikārjuna is the Śivaliṅga worhipped on the hill. The *Padmapurāṇa* (Uttarakhaṇḍa, chap. 19) describes Śrīparvata as the abode of Mallikārjuna. Shivajī visited the sacred site in 1677. For a later description of the temple of Mallikārjuna and its enclosure see Sarkar: *Shivaji*, p. 297.

who was the chief ascetic of the Kālamukha sect.[1] The latter community was akin to the Kāpālikas and both sects indulged in similar practices. The Kālamukhas are in fact included among the Mahāvratikas or Kāpālikas in Trivikrama Bhaṭṭa's *Naḷacampū* composed early in the tenth century (Chap. 6)[2]. The Kāpālikas are accused of cannibalism in Yaśaḥpāla's *Moharājaparājaya* 4. 23, an allegorical drama composed during the reign of Ajayapāla of Gujarat (1172-1176 A. D.).[3]

BRAHMANISM

Somadeva's strictures on the beliefs and practices of popular Hinduism have been summarized in Chapters X and XII. The chief attacks are directed against the Purāṇic traits of the principal Brahmanical deities, the funeral rites (Śrāddha), bathing at sacred sites, and diverse religious practices collectively designated as *mūḍha* or *mūḍhatā*, 'stupid customs.'[4] These attacks while throwing light on the religious conflict in the tenth century are not peculiar to Somadeva, and should rather be regarded as forming part of the customary Jaina polemics against the Brahmanical faith. Such polemics are scattered throughout Jaina literature of all periods, and we may cite here only a few examples bearing on the topics criticized by Somadeva. Jaṭā-siṁhanandi's *Varāṅgacarita*(circa 7th century A. D.) has a Canto called *Mithyāśruti-vighātaka* (XXV), which criticises among other things the caste system, the Brahmans dependent upon the patronage of kings, and the Śrāddha rites, and explains, like Somadeva, why Brahmā, Viṣṇu and Śiva cannot be regarded as trustworthy beings (*āpta*). The author asks in this connection: what are the dacoits like, if the great gods be armed with weapons, trident, thunder, discus, bow, mace, lance, sword and club (25. 80)? Similarly, Devasena in *Bhāvasaṁgraha* (op. cit.) criticizes bathing in sacred waters, Śrāddha, and adoration of cows, and scoffs at the exploits of Brahmā, Viṣṇu and Śiva, who are ridiculed also in *Pātrakesaristotra*. The *Sūtrakṛtāṅga*, a canonical work, ridicules ceremonial bathing thus: "........if perfection could be obtained by contact with water, many beings living in water must have reached perfection: fishes, tortoises, aquatic snakes, cormorants, otters, and demons living in water................. If water did wash off the impure Karman, it must take off merit too." Similarly, the morning and evening oblations in the sacred fire are declared to be meaningless: "Those who, lighting fire in the morning and evening, contend that perfection is obtained through fire (are easily

1 Nilakanta Sastri: *The Pāṇḍyan Kingdom*, p. 116.

2 'कलियुगशिवशासनस्थितिमिव महाव्रतिकान्तःपातिभिः कालमुखैर्वा नरैः संकुलाम्

3 Poussin (op. cit.), p. 145.

4 See Chap. X.

refuted). For if thereby perfection could be obtained, mechanics also, who use fire, would be liberated (1. 7. 14-18)."[1] The same work condemns also the feeding of Brāhmaṇas (2. 6. 43, 44).

In regard to the Jaina attacks on Śrāddha, it is said that the present-day Jainas 'burn the dead, throw the ashes on the third day into a river, and even *offer rice-balls to the crows* on the tenth day, and feed relatives and caste-fellows on the twelfth and thirteenth days."[2] These customs seem to have grown up in later times under Hindu influence. Somadeva, on the other hand, states in *Yaśastilaka*, Book IV, that if the Pitṛs have gone to earthly or celestial abodes, they can have no need of annual offerings of rice balls, which are actually eaten by Brāhmaṇas and *crows*. His statement may be compared with that of Jaṭā-Siṁhanandi in *Varāṅgacarita* 25. 64:

द्विजैश्च काकैर्यदि भुक्तमन्नं मृतान् पितॄंस्तर्पयते परत्र ।
पुरार्जितं तत् पितृभिर्विनष्टं शुभाशुभं तेन हि कारणेन ॥

The Jaina attack on Śrāddha reminds one of the satire of the Greek writer Lucian (second century A. D.) on the custom of making offerings to the dead. In his *Charon, or the Inspectors*, Charon the ferryman conveying souls to Hades exclaims 'What, *they* eat and drink, when their skulls are dry as tinder?.........I should be in a fine predicament, Hermes, and should have no end of trouble if I were obliged not only to bring them down but to bring them up to drink!"[3]

The group of 'stupid customs' mentioned by Somadeva in *Yaśastilaka* VI. 4 and 10 reminds one of those enumerated in *Lalitavistara*, chap. 17, and described as being followed by the misguided adherents of the non-Buddhist sects. Somadeva's list has been reproduced elsewhere;[4] that recorded in the Buddhist text is more comprehensive, and where there are resemblances provides additional details. Among later Jaina writers Hemacandra enumerates a large number of 'stupid customs' followed by diverse non-Jaina communities in his commentary on his *Yogaśāstra* 4. 102, and some of them are undoubtedly mentioned with reference to popular Brahmanism.[5]

---

1 Jacobi: *Jaina Sūtras*, Part II, p. 294.

2 Sharma: *Jainism and Karṇāṭaka Culture*, p. 161.

3 Trans. in *Loeb Classical Library*.

4 See Chap. X.

5 E. g., गूथाशिनीनां च गवां स्पर्शतः पूतमानिनाम् । जलादिस्नानमात्रेण पापशुद्ध्यभिधायिनाम् ॥ वटाश्वत्थामलक्यादि-द्रुमपूजाविधायिनाम् । वह्नौ हुतेन हव्येन देवप्रीणनमानिनाम् ॥ भुवि गोदोहकरणाद् रिष्टशान्तिकमानिनाम् । योषिद्विड-म्बनाप्रायव्रतधर्मोपदेशिनाम् ॥ Verses 23-25.

Somadeva cites the Smṛti injunction that the Veda and the Dharmaśāstras, composed by sages like Manu, Vyāsa and Vasiṣṭha, should be regarded as mandatory and authoritative in all matters, and on no account should their authority be called in question by means of argumentation: in fact, the Brāhmaṇa, who censures the Veda and despises the S'ruti and the Smṛti, should be ostracized as a *nāstika*. These views are summarily rejected by Somadeva. In *Yaśastilaka*, Book IV, he quotes the relevant verses:

मानवं व्यासवासिष्ठं वचनं वेदसंयुतम् । अप्रमाणं तु यो ब्रूयात् स भवेद्ब्रह्मघातकः ॥
पुराणं मानवो धर्मः साङ्गो वेदश्चिकित्सितम् । आज्ञासिद्धानि चत्वारि न हन्तव्यानि हेतुभिः ॥,

and calls them fanciful or absurd utterances (*mukhabhāṣitam*). It may be noted that the Buddhist S'āntarakṣita also quotes the second verse and makes a similar remark in *Tattvasaṁgraha* (verses 3584-5).[1] In *Yaśastilaka* VI. 2 Somadeva quotes the following verses:

श्रुतिं वेदमिह प्राहुर्धर्मशास्त्रं स्मृतिर्मता । ते सर्वार्थेष्वमीमांस्ये ताभ्यां धर्मो हि निर्बभौ ॥
ते तु यस्त्ववमन्येत हेतुशास्त्राश्रयाद् द्विजः । स साधुभिर्बहिः कार्यो नास्तिको वेदनिन्दकः ॥

and remarks that the opinion expressed therein is unsound. He points out that a disputant, who depends entirely upon the Scriptures and never resorts to reasoning, while seeking the truth, is not likely to triumph; as the good appreciate merit, but not a thing whose character has not been ascertained: a jewel is placed on the head, but a stone (unobserved while walking) is kicked away with the foot.[2]

समस्तयुक्तिनिर्मुक्तः केवलागमलोचनः । तत्त्वमिच्छन्न कस्येह भवेद्वादी जयावहः ॥
सन्तो गुणेषु तुष्यन्ति नाविचारेषु वस्तुषु । पादेन क्षिप्यते ग्रावा रत्नं मौलौ निधीयते ॥

The infallibility of the Veda and the Dharmaśāstras was the cornerstone of Hindu orthodoxy, and it was natural for non-Brahmanical writers to challenge the theory that the authority of the Śruti and the Smṛti must be unquestioningly accepted. We have already seen that in the controversial dialogue between Yaśodhara and his mother in *Yaśastilaka*, Book IV, the latter represents the orthodox view and the former the standpoint of the heretics. Yaśodhara's mother declares to her son: Discard Śruti, Smṛti, Itihāsa, and Purāṇic lore if thou hast no use for

1 पुराणं मानवो धर्मः साङ्गो वेदश्चिकित्सितम् । आज्ञासिद्धानि चत्वारि न हन्तव्यानि हेतुभिः ॥ मन्ये तेनैव दत्तेयं जडेभ्यस्तैर्विभीषिका । आज्ञासिद्धत्वमन्यत्र वाङ्मात्रात्किं नु वा भवेत् ॥

2 Cf. Shakespeare, *Measure for Measure*, II. I:
The jewel that we find, we stoop and take it
Because we see it; but what we do not see
We tread upon, and never think of it.

thy soul![1] This is a noteworthy assertion of the Hindu orthodox ideal as it appeared to a Jaina writer of the tenth century.

Somadeva's criticism of Hindu beliefs and practices is not without some historical importance, as it shows that the popular Hinduism of the tenth century was not far different from the religion as it exists today. Somadeva justifies his own attitude towards the Brahmanical religion by asserting that no one who speaks out the truth in regard to the Brahmanical deities and other concepts, exercising his own judgment, can be called a slanderer; otherwise the sun, and even the lamp, which reveal things as they are, would be slanderers, too (Book IV):

देवेषु चान्येषु विचारचक्षुर्यथार्थवक्ता किमु निन्दकः स्यात् ।
एवं न चेत्तर्हि यथार्थदर्शी भानुः प्रदीपोऽपि च निन्दकः स्यात् ॥

It will be however fair to suppose that the real motive underlying Jaina criticism of Brahmanical tenets and practices was propaganda aimed at showing the latter religion in an unfavourable light, and bringing into relief the relative merits of the Jaina faith. Brahmanical writers do not appear to have taken any serious notice of attacks on their religion by hostile critics, but in Śrīharṣa's *Naiṣadhacarita* (Canto XVII) we find a systematic attempt not only to bring together the different charges levelled against the Brahmanical faith by the Jainas and the Buddhists but to formulate an elaborate reply to them from the orthodox standpoint. The aim of the author of *Naiṣadhacarita* is to demonstrate the triumph of Hindu orthodoxy over the heretics, while that of Somadeva is to portray its discomfiture in a religious controversy between a tenacious Jaina and a zealous champion of orthodox Brahmanism.

VAIṢṆAVISM

It is a noteworthy feature of *Yaśastilaka* that, although it discusses or mentions so many philosophical and religious tenets of different schools, it is practically silent upon the Pañcarātra system and Vaiṣṇava doctrine. This is all the more strange, because about the time when Somadeva wrote there was a large mass of Pañcarātra literature extant in Kashmir, as shown by the citations in Utpala's *Spandapradīpikā*, a commentary on Kallaṭa's *Spandakārikā*. Utpala wrote in the tenth century,[2] and quotes in his work *Pañcarātraśruti*, *Pañcarātropaniṣad*, and the three wellknown Saṁhitās *Jayā, Sātvatā* and *Pauṣkarā*. He quotes also the *Viṣṇuyāmala* and two

1 'श्रुतिस्मृतीहासपुराणवाचस्त्यजात्मना चेन्न तवास्ति कार्यम् ॥'

2 Utpala quotes Ānandavardhana and is very probably earlier than Abhinavagupta. Chatterji: *Kashmir Shaivism*, part I, p. 13 ff.

texts called *Saṁkarṣaṇasūtras* and *Jābālisūtras*, which, to judge from the citations, are clearly works dealing with Vaiṣṇava doctrine.[1] It would seem that while works dealing with Pañcarātra or Vaiṣṇava doctrines were widely prevalent in Kashmir in the tenth century, they had not so far become current in the Deccan; otherwise it would be difficult to explain the absence of any reference to Pañcarātra tenets in so encyclopaedic a writer as the author of *Yaśastilaka*.

The Bhāgavatas are casually mentioned by Somadeva in a simile in *Yaśastilaka*, Book I, and spoken of as resorting to Kṛṣṇabhūmi, explained in the commentary as referring to Dvārakā.[2] Another reference occurs towards the end of Book V, wherein Āsuri, one of the interlocutors of the sage Sudatta, in the episode of Caṇḍakarman, is described as a Bhāgavata; but in the discussion that follows he figures as an exponent of Sāṁkhya views. The silence of Somadeva on Vaiṣṇava doctrine seems to be an indication that Vaiṣṇavism was not a force to reckon with in the Deccan in the tenth century; and, in any case, it does not evoke any criticism in his work.

Certain characteristics of Viṣṇu are, it is true, criticized in *Yaśastilaka*. Somadeva, for instance, criticizes the belief in the Incarnations of Viṣṇu, of which he gives the number as ten.[3] He refers also to Rādhā's relations with Nārāyaṇa,[4] and Kṛṣṇa's love for the cowherd maids.[5] But, on the whole, the deity appears in his work rather as a mythological character than as the central figure of a religious system. A passing reference to the idea that the universe is pervaded by Viṣṇu occurs in a description of evening scenery, in Book IV.[6]

The paucity of references to the cult of Viṣṇu, as contrasted with the prominence given to that of Śiva, in Somadeva's work, seems to suggest that, while Vaiṣṇavism existed during the period of the Rāṣṭrakūṭas, it was Śaivism that wielded the greater influence, and formed the principal target of Jaina attacks. It is, however, necessary to go back much earlier to obtain a correct perspective of the relative position of the Vaiṣṇava and Śaiva faiths in the Deccan. The early Cālukyas were mostly, if not all, followers of the Vaiṣṇava cult. The Vaiṣṇava cave at Badami was excavated

1 A definition of Viṣṇu is quoted from the *Saṁkarṣaṇasūtras*; while the citation from the *Jābālisūtras* declares Vāsudeva to be the supreme Soul.

2 'भागवता इव प्रतिपन्नकृष्णभूमयः' p. 13.

3 See Chap. XII.

4 See Chap. XVII.

5 गोविन्दो बल्लवीलोलः । 3. 204.

6 'सर्वं विष्णुमयं जगदिति सत्यतां नयतीव' p. 10.

in 578 A. D. under Kīrtivarman I. In it was installed the image of Viṣṇu and provision made for *nārāyaṇabali* or offering to Nārāyaṇa.[1] Still more significant is the fact that most of the early and archaic-looking temples at Aihole, in the south-eastern portion of the Bijapur district, were originally dedicated to Viṣṇu, the usual cognizance being the figure of Garuḍa upon the dedicatory block over the shrine door.[2] The earliest of these temples are that of Lāḍ Khān and the Kontguḍi group, ascribed to the beginning of the sixth century A. D. The temple of Lāḍ Khān[3] is square in plan and remarkable for its cave-like characteristics: the flat roof, and its want of elevation, the great massiveness of the pillars unusual in structural temples and the total absence of anything like a *śikhara* or tower, except for a small square shrine over the central portion of the roof. The temple has great lattice windows, beautifully finished, in the north and south sides; 'but the most decorated part of the temple is the front porch, the pillars of which have life-sized images upon them in bold relief'. The Kont-guḍi temple is of the same type as the last, and, like it, square in plan. It is smaller in size, 'but, except for the pillars, it is hardly less massive in construction'. 'The roof in them idle, above the four pillars, is flat, and it slopes away from this square space, all around, to the four walls.' Upon the flat central portion of the roof is the first storey of an unfinished tower, with an image niche on each of its four sides. That on the west contains an image of the Varāha *avatāra* of Viṣṇu; while, on the east, is the Vāmana *avatāra*. By the side of Kont-guḍi is another early temple, of an unusual type. The edifice is, in plan, more like an early Muhammadan mosque than a Hindu temple, being in the from of a long open verandah, with three rows of columns in its depth. 'The shrine is just where the *Mihrāb* would have been, being formed by enclosing the space between the central pair of back pillars and the back walls, the doorway being between the pillars'. The pillars are of the same type as those at Lāḍ Khān's and upon the front of one of the pillars is an image of Narasiṁha. Close to this temple is another of the same class, 'built upon the same open verandah plan', somewhat smaller in size.

One of the most remarkable buildings at Aihole is that known as the Durga temple, which, in plan, closely resembles the Buddhist Caitya caves. As in these cathedral caves, the end of the temple is round or apsidal,

1 Bhandarkar: *Vaisnavism, Saivism* etc., Poona edition, p. 61.

2 See Cousens: *Chalukyan Architecture of the Kanarese Districts*, p. 32 ff.

3 So called, because a Muhammadan of that name, not long ago, lived in the deserted building.

and it has a central nave and two side aisles separated by two rows of columns. The central roof is flat and lofty, and that of the side aisles low and sloping. Perhaps the most conspicuous feature is the pillared verandah, outside, surrounding the temple, and projecting in front to form an open pillared hall, or porch. Garuḍa presiding above the shrine door shows that the temple was dedicated to Viṣṇu.

A characteristic common to the temples mentioned above is that the shrine is not a separate compartment from the hall, as is usual in Brahmanical temples, but is formed within the hall itself by enclosing the required space between one of the walls and the nearest pillars. In the *caitya*-like Durga temple, the shrine is in the place where the *dagoba* would be. Even apart from the peculiar shrine, these early temples have many unusual characteristics and stand in a class by themselves, both as regards age and style. In addition to them, there are certain other temples at Aihole, also dedicated to Viṣṇu, which are considered to be earlier than the seventh century A. D., judging by the general style and 'more cyclopean-looking masonry.'

It will be thus seen that Vaiṣaṇavism came to be associated with a very early type of architecture at Aihole, which must have been an important centre of the Viṣṇu cult during the sixth and seventh centuries A. D. But towards the beginning of the eighth century, the centre of gravity shifts to Paṭṭadakal, where we find massive temples being erected in honour of Śiva, and what looks like a change over to Śaivism takes place. Certain old shrines, for example, the Mālegitti-Śivālaya, which were originally dedicated to Viṣṇu, seem to have been converted to Śaiva worship at a later date.[1] On a pillar in the Durga temple at Aihole is a short inscription in letters of the 8th or 9th century, which reads "Śrī-Basa-mayya, the *bhaṭṭa* of Kisuvoḷal." Paṭṭada Kisuvoḷal is the ancient name of Paṭṭadakal, and the presence of the *bhaṭṭa* from that centre of Śaivism 'may be connected with the time when these temples were restored for Śaiva worship.'[2] There is another factor pointing to such conversion of Viṣṇu temples to Śaiva worship. A circular panel of carving representing the *tāṇḍava* dance of Śiva is found, for example, on the front of most of the old temples at Aihole. But the slab often lies loosely against the tower instead of being built in with it; and in the earliest temples the sculpture is of inferior quality compared with that on the other parts. It is probable that the slab bearing representation of the *tāṇḍava* is a later addition made when the temples were first converted to Śaiva worship.[3]

1 See above.

2 Cousens (op. cit.), p. 39.

3 Cousens (op. cit.), p. 40.

Vaiṣṇavism appears to have been a secondary cult under the Rāṣṭrakūṭas. The great cave temples at Ellora were, with a few exceptions, excavated for the worship of Śiva, if we exclude the Buddhist and Jaina caves. The two-storied Daśāvatāra cave is no doubt an exception, and contains sculptures representing Viṣṇu resting on Śeṣa; Viṣṇu, six-armed, holding up the Govardhana hill; and the Varāha, Vāmana and Narasiṁha incarnations. The shrine was excavated about the middle of the eighth century A. D. in the reign of the Rāṣṭrakūṭa king Dantidurga, whose triumphs are recorded in an inscription upon the cave.[1] But Śaiva sculpture preponderates even in the Daśāvatāra cave. Some of them illustrate the Bhairava aspect of Śiva[2]; and there is another of particular interest, designed to prove the superiority of Śiva to Brahmā and Viṣṇu who fail to discover the top and the base respectively of the great *liṅga*.[3] There is another Vaiṣṇava cave at Ellora (No. XXVII), known as the Milkmaid's cave, 'but the style of it says but little for the wealth or influence of the sect in the days when it was executed.'[4]

As already stated, if temple architecture is any index to the influence and popularity of a religion, Śaivism was the more important faith during the rule of the Cālukyas of Kalyāni. There exist a comparatively few examples of later Cālukyan temples dedicated to Viṣṇu. Vikramāditya VI constructed a large temple of Viṣṇu, and had a tank dug in front of it.[5] An inscription slab, in the court-yard of the temple of Dakṣiṇa-Kedāreśvara, records a grant, in 1075 A. D., of a village to the Vaiṣṇava temple of Narasiṁha at Baḷigāve, or Balagāmve, now a small village in Mysore territory, fourteen miles south-west of Hira-Kerūr in the Dharwar district.[6] The Basti or Kalla-Guḍi at Degāmve, about twenty-five miles south-east from Belgaum, is a decorated medieval temple consisting of 'a long pillared hall in front of three shrines on the west side, the middle one projecting forward into the hall in advance of the other two'. The central shrine contains an image of Lakṣmī-Nārāyaṇa. An inscription in the temple records the building of the shrines of Kamalānārāyaṇa and Mahālakṣmī; while another records a grant by Kamalādevī, queen of the Kādamba chief of Goa, to Brāhmaṇas of the village of Degāmve, in 1175 A. D.[7] Standing at right

1 Cousens (op. cit), p. 9.

2 Burgess: *A Guide to Elura Cave Temples*, p. 27.

3 See Chap. XVII.

4 Burgess (op. cit.), p. 46.

5 *Vikramāṅkadevacarita* XVII. 15 ff.

6 Cousens (op. cit.), p. 106.

7 Ibid, p. 119.

angles to the temple of Siddheśvara at Hāveri, in the Dharwar district, is a smaller Vaiṣṇava temple dedicated to Narasiṁha, a large image of the deity being found in the shrine. Mahādeva, the general of Vikramāditya VI, who built the great Śiva temple at Ittagi towards the end of the eleventh century, built also the temple of Nārāyaṇa, which might be identified with the smaller temple, built in granite, upon the south side of the main temple. 'It occupies very much the same position with regard to the main temple as the Vaiṣṇava shrine of Narasiṁha does to the temple of Siddheśvara at Hāveri.'

Of the later Cālukyan temples in the Bellary district of Madras Presidency, there appear to be few that are dedicated to Viṣṇu. Notable exceptions are the temple of Veṇugopālasvāmin at Māgalā and that of Keśavasvāmin at Huvinahaḍgalli.[1]

It is apparent, on the whole, that more elaborate provision seems to have been made for the organised worship of Śiva than for the cult of Viṣṇu under the ruling dynasties of the Deccan. There is also the important fact that, in the history of the Deccan, during seven centuries, Vaiṣṇavism has nothing so imposing and grand to show as the temple of Virūpākṣa at Paṭṭadakal or Kailāsa at Ellora or Mahādeva at Ittagi.

The situation is not far different in the northern part of the Deccan where, architecturally, the most important templeis the great shrine of Śiva at Ambaranātha, built in the eleventh century A. D. The temple of Lakṣmī-Nārāyaṇa at Pedgaon, near Srigunda in the Ahmadnagar district, is 'a perfect little gem', but its date is not known.[2] Far more important for the religious history of the Deccan is the celebrated Vaiṣṇava temple of Viṭhobā, or Viṭṭhala, at Paṇḍharpur in the Sholapur district, on the banks of the Bhīmā. The present temple is of little interest from an architectural point of view; but there is no doubt that it succeeded an older one to the same deity, as an inscription upon a pilaster of a former temple, now used as an overhead beam in the present, informs us that the Hoysala king Vīra-Someśvara presented a gift of gold to the god Viṭṭhala in Saṁvat 1159 (1237 A. D.).[3] Viṭhobā is perhaps the most popular deity in the Deccan, but the temple dedicated to him is not known to have existed before the thirteenth century. The

1 See Rea: *Chalukyan Architecture*, 1896.

2 Cousens: *Mediaeval Temples of the Dakhan*, p. 56.

3 Ibid. p. 64. For another reference see Bhandarkar: *Vaisnavism, Saivism etc.*, Poona edition, p. 124.

cult itself must have existed before this, and probably goes back to a much earlier date, but it is difficult to determine its extent and influence during the period under consideration.

While speaking of the relative position of Vaiṣṇavism and Śaivism in the Deccan, it is necessary to point out that there appears to have been no sharp division between the two cults in those early days. On the other hand, a certain amount of syncretism is apparent in the religious thought of the time. The popularity of the conception of *trimūrti* is an illustration of this. An inscription of the reign of the Cālukya king Vijayāditya says that images of Brahmā, Viṣṇu and Maheśvara were installed in Vātāpipura (Badami) in the third year of his reign, that is, in 699 A. D. The images of these three deities occur also in the panels of the ceilings of several of the oldest temples at Aihole. For example, in the temple beside that of Kont-guḍi, there are finely carved images of Brahmā, Viṣṇu and Śiva in each of the three central bays of the ceiling, Śiva being placed in the centre.[1] There was a temple at Salotgi in the Bijapur district, in the 10th century, for the joint worship of Brahmā, Viṣṇu and Śiva.[2] No less significant is the impartial mixture of Śaiva and Vaiṣṇava sculptures in the early temples of the Deccan. For example, on the exterior walls of the temple of Pāpanātha at Paṭṭadakal, there are images of Śiva in various attitudes, Viṣṇu, Mahiṣāsura-mardinī, Gaṇapati, Narasiṁha, Varāha, the Vāmana *avatāra*, and Kṛṣṇa, upholding the Govardhana hill. Among the sculptures on the walls of the temple of Virūpākṣa, are found Ardhanārī, the Vāmana *avatāra* and Viṣṇu upon the east face of the edifice; Śiva and Pārvatī, the *tāṇḍava* of Śiva, Harihara, Bhairava and Varāha on the north side; Śiva and Viṣṇu in various forms on the west wall; and Lakulīśa, Śiva in different forms, Viṣṇu and Narasiṁha among those on the south wall. Similarly, there is 'an impartial mixture of Śaiva and Vaiṣṇava subjects in the image groups, representing Narasiṁha, Mahiṣāsura-mardinī, Varāha, Viṣṇu, Ardhanārī and Śiva, in the niches around the walls in the outer verandah of the Durga temple at Aihole. Among the sculptures on the pillars in the Śaiva temple of Mallikārjuna or Trailokyeśvara at Paṭṭadakal are depicted scenes from the life of Kṛṣṇa. He is seen, for example, killing Kaṁsa's great elephant, then the demon Keśin who is in the shape of a horse, and, at the end, Ariṣṭa who attacked him in the shape of a savage bull.[3]

1 Cousens: *Chalukyan Architecture of the Kanarese Districts*, p. 37, Fig. 3.

2 Altekar: *The Rāṣṭrakūṭas and their times*, pp. 275, 403.

3 Cousens (op. cit.), pp. 38, 64, 66, 70.

It will be seen that, among the incarnations of Viṣṇu, Varāha, Vāmana and Narasiṁha are the most frequent in the sculptural representations of that deity in the early temples of the Deccan. At Ellora, as in the Daśāvatāra cave, they are found also in the Kailāsa temple, in the corridor surrounding the back half of the court.[1] The ten incarnations of Viṣṇu are found sculptured on a huge rock at Badami, close behind the Bhūtanātha group of temples. Upon the south side of this rock is a sculpture of Nārāyaṇa reclining upon Śeṣa, with the ten *avatāras* in a row above him, some on one side and some on the other side of Brahmā.[2] The sculpture in question is no doubt much earlier than the reference to the ten *avatāras* in Somadeva's *Yaśastilaka*. The number of the *avatāras* came, as a matter of fact, to be fixed at ten long before the tenth century A. D. A verse inscription in Pallava-Grantha characters of about the eighth century A. D., found in the rock-cut temple of Varāha-Perumāl at Mahābalipuram, enumerates the ten incarnations as follows: the Fish, the Tortoise, the Boar, the Man-Lion, the Dwarf, Rāma, Rāma (Paraśurāma), Rāma (Balarāma), Buddha and Kalkin.[3] The reference to the ten *avatāras* in Somadeva's work is, however, of some importance as showing that they were well-known, and probably worshipped, in the Deccan in the tenth century. The image of Nārāyaṇa with the ten *avatāras*, on the rock at Badami, is still worshipped, and a small shrine has been built for the purpose in front of the rock.[4]

The close contiguity of Śaiva and Vaiṣṇava shrines at Hāveri, and probably also at Ittagi, is an indication of the harmonious co-existence of the two cults. Interesting examples of Śaiva and Vaiṣṇava shrines standing in close juxtaposition to one another have been found in Mysore State, at Marale in the Chikmangalur Taluk, and at Mosale, a village about eight miles to the south of Hassan. The twin temples at Mosale are ornate structures standing side by side, a few feet apart, and belong to the Hoysala style of architecture. They are identical in size and workmanship, and have been assigned, on architectural grounds, to the twelfth century A. D., when most of the ornate temples in Mysore State came into being. One of the shrines is dedicated to Śiva styled as Nāgeśvara, while the other contains a Viṣṇu image called Channakeśava.[5]

---

1 Burgess (op. cit.), p. 32.

2 Cousens (op. cit.), p. 57.

3 Sastri: *Two statues of Pallava Kings and Five Pallava Inscriptions. (Memoirs of the Archaeological Survey of India).* p. 5.

4 Cousens (op. cit.), p. 57.

5 *Annual Report of the Mysore Archaeological Department for 1924*, p. 6.

As Purāṇic deities, Śiva and Viṣṇu were equally reverenced in the Deccan, as elsewhere, a trend reflected in sculpture as well as literature. Among the few non-Jaina writers of the Rāṣṭrakūṭa period, Trivikrama Bhaṭṭa, the author of *Nalacampū*, who lived in the early years of the tenth century, under Indra III, was a staunch adherent of the Śaiva faith. The work is described in the colophons as 'imprinted with the lotus feet of Śiva', and the concluding verse of each chapter contains a phrase expressive of devotion to Śiva. The sixth chapter of *Nalacampū* contains, however, a fervent hymn to Viṣṇu; and this also reminds us of the fact that the opening verse of Rāṣṭrakūṭa grants offers salutation to Viṣṇu as well as Śiva. Devotion to both the deities was part of the religious syncretism of the time, and shows the popularity and ascendancy of the Purāṇic religion as a whole. But the evidence furnished by architecture and literary sources shows that, as an organised cult, Vaiṣṇavism occupied a subsidiary position in the Deccan, and seems to have prevailed there in the shadow of Śaivism for several centuries, say, from the eighth to the twelfth. The Vaiṣṇava cult was hardly a rival of Jainism in the Deccan; and we find, accordingly, Jaina attacks levelled chiefly against Śaivism, which was its greatest rival even before the rise of the Liṅgāyats.

BUDDHISTS AND OTHER SECTS

The Jainas had nothing but contempt for those communities who had no objection to taking flesh and wine. In *Yaśastilaka* VI. 10 the Veda and the Buddhist and the Śaiva scriptures are described as favouring the use of honey, flesh and wine.[1] The Buddhists are particularly decried for not observing any restrictions in regard to food and drink. In *Yaśastilaka* VI. 2 Somadeva asks: How can the wise respect the Buddhist who is addicted to flesh and wine?[2]

In another verse the Buddhist appears to be described as a votary of what is called *advaita* pure and simple. Somadeva seems to say that, excepting the Jaina doctrine, all other systems favour either 'the path of duality' (*dvaita*) or 'that of non-duality' (*advaita*); and he illustrates his remarks by saying that the Mantrin or the Śaiva mystic follows the *Vāmamārga* and the *Dakṣiṇamārga,* and the Brahmanical Scriptures lay stress on Karma and Jñāna, while those of the Buddhists merely prescribe

---

1 'श्रुतिशाक्यशिवाम्नायः क्षौद्रमांसासवाश्रयः' p. 296.

2 'कथं मनीषिभिर्मान्यस्तरसासवशक्तधीः' p. 276.

flesh-eating.[1] In *Yaśastilaka* VII. 24 the Buddhists are mentioned first among certain communities who recommend the eating of flesh.[2]

The quarrel of the Jainas and the Buddhists over the question of using flesh as an article of food goes back to very early times. "In the time of Buddha there was in Vaiśāli a wealthy general named Sīha who was a convert to Buddhism. He became a liberal supporter of the Brethren and kept them constantly supplied with good flesh food. When it was noised abroad that the bhikshus were in the habit of eating such food specially provided for them the Tīrthikas made the practice a matter of angry reproach." The Master thereupon announced to the Brethren "the law that they were not to eat the flesh of any animal which they had seen put to death for them, or about which they had been told that it had been killed for them, or about which they had reason to suspect that it had been slain for them. But he permitted to the Brethren as 'pure' (that is, lawful) food the flesh of animals the slaughter of which had not been seen by the bhikshus, not heard of by them, and not suspected by them to have been on their account. In the Pali and Ssu-fen Vinaya it was after a breakfast given by Sīha to the Buddha and some of the Brethren, for which the carcase of a large ox was procured, that the Nirgranthas reviled the bhikshus and Buddha instituted this new rule declaring fish and flesh *pure* in the three conditions. The animal food now permitted to the bhikshus .... was tersely described as '*unseen, unheard, unsuspected*' ...." Two more kinds of animal food were later "declared lawful for the Brethren, viz. the flesh of animals which had died a natural death, and that of animals which had been killed by a bird of prey or other savage creature."[3] This was the Hīnayānist position

---

1 जैनमेकं मतं मुक्त्वा द्वैताद्वैतसमाश्रयौ । मार्गौ समाश्रिताः सर्वे सर्वाभ्युपगमागमाः ॥ वामदक्षिणमार्गस्थो मन्त्री-तरसमाश्रयः । कर्मज्ञानगतो ज्ञेयः शंभुशाक्यद्विजागमः ॥ The Ms. A remarks मन्त्रेण सर्वान् वशीकरोति शैवः । मांसमाशयति बौद्धः । जीवहोमादिक्रियाज्ञानप्राप्तो विप्रः ।

2 'तच्छाक्यसांख्यचार्वाक' etc. A little further on, Somadeva says that a king named Śaurasena, although he had taken a vow to abstain from flesh-eating, became addicted to it, being misled by the doctrines of the Veda, medical lore and the Advaita doctrine (वेदवैद्याद्वैतमतमोहितमतिः). The Advaitamata obviously refers to the Buddhist view of flesh-eating.

3 Watters: *On Yuan Chwang's Travels in India 629–645 A. D.*, Vol. I, p. 55. Manichaeism, which prohibited the slaughter of animals, permitted the Hearers, as distinguished from the Elect, to eat flesh food when it had been slain by others. Cf. Wand: *A History of the Early Church*, p. 141. The Manichaean Elect and Hearers corresponded pretty well to monks and seculars. Babylon was the birth-place of Manichaeism, and Manes, the founder of the new religion about the middle of the third century, was brought up in the sect of the Mugthasila, who laid special stress on abstinence from flesh, wine and women. Kidd: *A History of the Church*, Vol. I, p. 506.

in regard to the use of flesh as an article of food. The Mahāyānist rule, on the other hand, prohibited "the use of flesh of any kind as food by the 'sons of Buddha'", and "some Mahāyānists were strict in abstaining, not only from all kinds of flesh food, but also from milk and its products."[1] In Yuan Chwang's time, for instance, there were three Buddhist monasteries in Karṇasuvarṇa (in Bengal) "in which in accordance with the teaching of Devadatta milk products were not taken as food."[2] So far as Jaina criticism is concerned, the writers do not make any distinction between Hīnayānists and Mahāyānists and condemn the Buddhists as a class for partaking of animal food. That there was considerable laxity in matters of food and drink among the Buddhists in the tenth century and thereabouts seems extremely probable, and charges of soft living were in fact occasionally levelled against them. Devasena, who wrote about twentyfive years earlier than Somadeva, severely criticizes Buddhist doctrine, in his *Bhāvasaṁgraha*, and remarks that the Buddhist regards whatever falls into his begging bowl as pure, eats flesh and shamelessly drinks wine, but if it were possible to go to heaven by eating flesh and drinking wine, it is the drunkards and the huntsmen that would go thither.[3] Similarly, Udayana, who wrote a few decades after Somadeva, says that the absence of any restrictions in the matter of food and drink, eating at all hours of the day, and lightness of religious duties are among the causes that induce men to become Buddhists.[4] Hemacandra says in his commentary on his *Yogaśāstra* 4. 102 that the practice of austerities is impossible for the Buddhists who eat day and night, and make no distinction between lawful and forbidden food. Further, he remarks in an interesting verse that the religion of the Buddha is excellent indeed, its essentials being a soft bed, rice-gruel in the morning, boiled rice at noon, drinking bouts in the evening, and sugarcandy at night.[5] The Buddhists, on the whole, gave offence to the Jainas by their indulgence in food and drink which the latter abhorred.

In *Yaśastilaka* VIII. 43 Somadeva advises his co-religionists to have nothing to do with the Buddhists, the Nāstikas, the Adepts in sacrifices, the Jaṭilas (that is, the Śaivas) and the Ājīvakas.[6] There is no doubt that a

1 Watters (op. cit.), p. 57.

2 Watters, Vol. II, p. 191.

3 पत्तपडियं ण दूसइ खाइ पलं पियइ मज्जु णिल्लज्जो। इच्छइ सग्गगमणं मोक्खगमणं च पावेण॥ असिऊण मंसगासं मज्जं पिविऊण गम्मए सग्गं। जइ एवं तो सुंडय पारद्धिय चेव गच्छंति॥ Verses 68–9

4 'संभवन्ति चैते हेतवो बौद्धाद्यागमपरिग्रहे। तथाहि भूयस्तत्र कर्मलाघवमित्यलसाः।········ भक्षाद्यनियम इति रागिणः।··············· सप्तघटिकाभोजनादिसिद्धेर्जीविकेत्ययोग्याः। *Nyāyakusumāñjali*, chap. 2.

5 दिवसे च रजन्यां च मुखमापृच्छय भक्षताम्। भक्ष्याभक्ष्याविवेकानां सौगतानां कुतस्तपः॥ मृद्वी शय्या प्रातः पेया मध्ये भक्तं सायं पानम्। द्राक्षाखण्डं रात्रेर्मध्ये शाक्योपज्ञः साधुर्धर्मः॥ Verses 9 and 10.

6 शाक्यनास्तिकयागज्ञजटिलाजीवकादिभिः। सहावासं सहालाभं तत्सेवां च विवर्जयेत्॥

certain amount of communal hatred existed between the Jainas and the Buddhists, and mutual recriminations are occasionally found in the religious literature of both the communities. The Jainas contended that since the Buddhists denied the existence of the Self, all their talk of compassion and philanthrophy was meaningless. The Buddha is accordingly called 'ferocious and merciless' (!) in Jaṭāsiṃhanandi's *Varāṅgacarita* 25. 84.[1] On similar grounds Akalaṅka accuses the Buddha of criminal propensities such as injury to others, falsehood, theft and unchastity![2]

The Buddhists are likewise in the habit of giving expression to their contempt for the Jainas and their habits and customs. The celebrated Mahāyāna work *Saddharma-puṇḍarīka* (earlier than the third century) says, for instance, that the Bodhisattva 'must avoid such monks as follow the precepts of the Arhat, and immoral men (chap. XIII)'.[3]

The practice of nudity (*nagnabhāva*) mentioned in the *Lalitavistara* (chap. XVII) among the stupid customs followed by the adherents of the non-Buddhist systems obviously refers to the Digambara monks. In the first half of the seventh century, the great Chinese traveller Hsüan-tsang (the name is variously spelt), a philosopher of Mahāyāna Buddhism, ridicules Jainism as a sort of caricature of the Buddhist religion. "These sectarians", writes Hsüan-tsang, "give themselves up to extreme austerities. Day and night they display the most ardent zeal without a moment's respite. The law expounded by their founder (Mahāvīra) has been largely stolen from the books of Buddha, and on this he guided himself when laying down his precepts and rules. In their religious observances and exercises, they follow almost entirely the rule of the Buddhist monks............ The statue of their teacher, by a kind of impertinent imitation, resembles that of Buddha." Here is a picture of the Digambara monks drawn by the Chinese pilgrim: "The Jainas think they gain distinction by leaving their bodies entirely naked, and they make a virtue of tearing out their hair. Their skin is all broken, and their feet are horny and cracked; they are like those rotten trees that are found close to a river."[4] In similar but less dignified language, certain Digambara practices are held up to ridicule in the *Dohākoṣa* of Sarojavajra (Saraha) written in an Apabhraṁśa dialect sometime between the eighth and twelfth ceuturies.[5] Saraha, who was a Buddhist Tantric writer, says that if it were possible to attain salvation by going about naked, the dogs and the jackals would surely attain it. As

1 'बुद्धस्तु रौद्रो निरनुग्रहश्च'।

2 सिद्धहिंसानृतस्तेयाब्रह्मचर्यप्रवृत्तितः। स प्रत्यस्तमिताशेषदोषो नेति प्रतीयते॥ *Nyāyaviniścaya*, verse 390.

3 *Trans.* Kern, p. 265 (*S. B. E.*)

4 Grousset: *In the footsteps of the Buddha*, pp. 197–8.

5 Ed H. P. Sastri in बौद्ध गान ओ दोहा, Introduction, p. 6.

regards the practice of plucking out the hair, he says something positively indecent. Then he says that if the carrying of peacock's feathers led to salvation, the horses and the elephants who are decorated with them were bound to obtain it![1] Recriminations of this type point to theological hatred, but there is no reason to suppose that there was any deep-seated hostility between the Jainas and the Buddhists. As pointed out by S. C. Vidyabhusan, 'there was no bitter rivalry' between the two communities. According to the same scholar, the Jaina writers Rabhasa Nandi (circa 850 A. D.) and Kalyāṇacandra (about 1000 A. D.) appear to have written commentaries on the Buddhist logician Dharmakīrti's *Saṁbandha-parīkṣā* and *Pramāṇa-vārtika* respectively; while the Jaina Mallavādin (about 962 A. D.) wrote a commentary on *Nyāya-bindu-ṭīkā* of Dharmottara.[2]

The Ājīvakas whom Somadeva mentions among the communities to be shunned by the Jainas were an ancient sect founded by Maṅkhaliputra Gośālaka, a contemporary of Mahāvīra, and the present reference to them shows that members of this sect were still to be found in the tenth century. The Jainas disliked the Ājīvakas, as their founder Gośālaka was a bitter rival and opponent of Mahāvīra, and the former is, as a matter of fact, represented as something of an impostor in early Jaina literature.[3] Nor were the Ājīvakas liked by the Buddhists. Just as Somadeva asks the Jainas to keep aloof from Ājīvakas, Buddhists, Nāstikas and others, similarly the *Saddharma-puṇḍarīka* (Chap. XIII) declares that the Bodhisattva never associates with Carakas, Parivrājakas, Ājīvakas and Nirgranthas (Jainas).[4] The Ājīvakas had certain peculiar doctrines, e. g. the Niyativāda, an extreme form of fatalism propounded by Gośālaka, and seem to have flourished in South India for centuries after the age of Mahāvīra, as their doctrines are included among the contemporary philosophical systems described in detail in the Tamil epic *Maṇimekhalai*, assigned to the early centuries of the Christian era. In another Tamil epic of the same age, the *S'ilappadikāram*, the father of the heroine Kaṇṇaki is said to have distributed his wealth among the Ājīvaka friars. "This is a very important

1 जइ णग्गा विअ होइ मुत्ति ता, ता शुनह शिआलह, लोमोप्पाट्टने अच्छ सिद्धिअ, ता जुवइ णिसम्वह, पिच्छीगहणे दिट्ठि मोक्ख, ता करिह तुरङ्गह ।

2 *A History of Indian Logic*, pp. 194, 198.

3 See Gopani: *Ājīvika sect—A new interpretation* in *Bhāratīya Vidyā*, Vol II, part II.

4 *Trans.* Kern, p. 263 (*S. B. E.*). In ancient Buddhist texts the Ājıvakas are regarded as the worst of the sophists. 'As the sect is thrice mentioned in the Asoka Edicts as receiving royal gifts, it is certain that it retained an important position for several centuries at least.' Rhys Davids: *Dialogues of the Buddha*, Part I, p. 71.

reference inasmuch as the religion of the Ājīvakas, if it could be so described, was undoubtedly practised in South India at the time".[1] It should be noted in this connection that Somadeva, contrary to his usual practice, does not mention any doctrines of the sect so that we cannot tell how far any well-defined Ājīvaka system prevailed in his time. All that the reference to the Ājīvaks in *Yaśastilaka* proves is the existence of the sect in the tenth century.

In *Yaśastilaka* VII. 24 Somadeva seems to refer to another sect, although it is not explicitly mentioned. He says that such is the peculiarity of things that the cow's milk is pure but not the flesh, just as the gem supposed to be on the hood of a snake counteracts poison, while snake-poison itself causes death. Again, milk may be taken, but not the cow's flesh; just as the leaves of a poisonous plant may be taken for the cure of disease, while its roots are sure to cause death.[2] Somadeva seems here to reply to an argument that if it was permissible to take milk there was no reason why one should not take beef. Exactly this opinion is put in the mouth of the leader of the Rahamāṇa sect in the Jaina allegorical play *Moharāja-Parājaya* written about two centuries later, wherein he declares that just as one takes cow's milk, similarly one may take also cow's flesh without incurring sin. Rahamāṇa says further that according to Dhanika, Dharma consists in the killing of Brāhmaṇa ascetics.[3] We do not know anything about this Rahamāṇa who appears in the play along with the Kaula and the Kāpālika, but the views attributed to him might very well represent those of the Muslims. It is not clear whether Somadeva had in mind the views of any particular sect or community while making the statements cited above, but it was not impossible for him to have been acquainted with Muslim customs, since the contact between Indian and Muslim cultures goes back to a date at least two centuries earlier than the composition of his *Yaśastilaka.*

The conflict of religions in the Deccan in the tenth century should not blind us to the general spirit of toleration prevailing in the age. Much important evidence has been adduced by scholars to prove the existence of concord and harmony in the sphere of religion, and we have referred elsewhere[4] to isolated attempts at a synthesis of divergent philosophical and religious views in the century.

---

1 Aiyangar: *Maṇimekhalai in its historical setting*, pp. 57, 193.

2 शुद्धं दुग्धं न गोर्मांसं वस्तुवैचित्र्यमीदृशम् । विषघ्नं रत्नमाहेयं विषं च विपदे यतः ॥ अथवा, हेयं पलं पयः पेयं समे सत्यपि कारणे । विषद्रोरायुषे पत्रं मूलं तु मृतये मतम् ॥

3 रहमाणः—(साटोपम्) जह पिज्जइ गोच्छीरं पलासणे तह य नत्थि सो दोसो । इत्थ य लिंगियवहणे धम्मो दिट्ठ त्ति धणिएण ॥ 4. 24.

4 See Chap. IX.

CHAPTER XIV

JAINA CRITICISM OF VEDIC SACRIFICES

Apart from the criticism of popular Hinduism, Somadeva denounces the Vedic sacrificial system for sanctioning animal slaughter in the controversial dialogue between Yaśodhara and his mother in *Yaśastilaka*, Book IV. As examples of Vedic rites involving the killing of animals he mentions Rājasūya, Vājapeya, Gosava, Aśvamedha, Kārīrī and Puṇḍarīka (in which an elephant is said to have been sacrificed),[1] and condemns also the Sautrāmaṇī sacrifice in which it was customary to drink wine.[2] Vedic sacrifices are represented as sinful also in Buddhist texts, for example, in the *Mahāvastu* (Vol. II, p. 237) wherein Māra instigates the Bodhisattva to perform certain sacrifices for the attainment of heaven and religious merit, viz. Aśvamedha, Puruṣamedha, Somaprāsa, Nirargaḍa (?), Paduma and Puṇḍarīka.[3] References like these are of a literary character and do not always point to contemporary conditions. In any case Somadeva's criticism of Vedic sacrifices and citations from sacrificial texts do not prove that Vedic rites were common in his time, as Vedic sacrifices seem to have gone out of vogue and become obsolete by the tenth century. The Smārta religion reigned supreme; and it has been pointed out, for instance, that there are only two Rāṣṭrakūṭa inscriptions which record grants made to enable Brāhmaṇas to perform Vedic sacrifices like Rājasūya, Vājapeya and Agniṣṭoma. "In all other cases the grants were made for discharging purely Smārta duties connected with *bali, caru, vaiśvadeva.*" Further, "Alberuni was informed that the Vedic sacrifices were rarely performed and practically abandoned because they presupposed a long life.........".[4] It may be added that the decline of Vedic sacrifices must have set in long before the tenth century or even the Rāṣṭrakūṭa period. Śaṁkara in his *Bhāṣya* on the *Vedānta Sūtras* 3. 1. 25, indeed, speaks of Vedic rites as if they were still being performed by cultured people in his time.[5] But it is important to note that the *Praśastapāda Bhāṣya*, which belongs to the early centuries of the Christian era, while laying down the religious duties of a householder in connection with

1 'तथा वेदेऽप्यात्मश्रेयोर्थमशेषविघ्नोपशमनार्थं च राजसूयपुण्डरीकाश्वमेधगोसववाजपेयादिषु वर्षिकामेष्टिकारीरीत्यादिषु च यज्ञेषु प्रवृत्तोऽयं प्राणिवधः स च वधो न भवति।' The object of the Kārīrī sacrifice was to bring rain. For references see Handiqui: *Naishadhacarita*, Vocabulary (*sub voce*).

2 See, for example, the first story of Book VII, summarized in Chap. XVI.

3 'महायज्ञानि च यजाहि अश्वमेधं पुरुषमेधं सोमप्रासं निरर्गडं पदुमं पुण्डरीकं च। एतानि यज्ञानि यजित्वा प्रेत्य स्वर्गेषु मोदिष्यसि बहु च पुण्यं प्रसविष्यसि'।

4 Altekar: *The Rāṣṭrakūṭas and their times*, p. 279.

5 'तस्माद्विशुद्धं कर्म वैदिकं शिष्टैरनुष्ठीयमानत्वादनिन्द्यमानत्वाच्च।'

the Vaiśeṣika scheme of spiritual discipline, prescribes in the first instance Smārta rites such as the five Mahāyajñas and the Pākayajñas, and then mentions the Śrauta sacrifices: the Haviryajñas (Agnyādheya, Darśapaurṇamāsa etc.) and the Somayajñas (Agniṣṭoma, Ukthya etc.), to be undertaken *if one has the capacity to do so.*[1] Udayana who wrote in the last quarter of the tenth century says in his *Nyāyakusumāñjali,* chap. 2, that Vedic rites such as Rājasūya and Aśvamedha were dying out in his time, as they were no longer performed, and that in his age Dharma rested only on one foot, charity, owing to the decline of the Vedic sacrifices.[2] The Nyāya theory of *śākhoccheda*, the dying out of the Vedic schools, was, in fact, more in conformity with the process of history than the Mīmāṁsā view which refused to believe in any such decay.

It may, however, be readily admitted that Vedic sacrifices continued to be sporadically perfomed till quite recent times; and contemporary evidence of the performance of such rites is not rare. The Aśvamedha, in particular, attracted many kings of the ruling dynasties. For example, the Ikṣvāku king Vāsiṣṭhīputra Cāṁtamūla I, who reigned in the Andhra country about the second quarter of the third century A. D., is said to have performed the Aśvamedha and Vājapeya sacrifices.[3] Several inscriptions of the Vākāṭaka kings, who ruled in Central Provinces and Berar, state that Pravarasena I who reigned about the end of the third century A. D. performed four Aśvamedhas besides several other Vedic sacrifices such as Agniṣṭoma, Āptoryāma, Ukthya, Ṣoḍaśin, Atirātra, Vājapeya, Bṛhaspatisava and Sādyaskra. The inscriptions of the Vākāṭakas frequently mention their kinsmen, the Bhāraśivas, who seem to have established themselves on the banks of the Ganges, and are said to have celebrated as many as ten Aśvamedhas.[4] In Gupta records Samudragupta (circa 330–375 A. D.) is stated to have revived the Aśvamedha which had long been in abeyance, evidently in North India; for it seems to have been quite popular in the South. The Pallava king Śivaskandavarman, who has been assigned to about the beginning of the fourth century A. D., is reported to have performed the Agniṣṭoma, Vājapeya and Aśvamedha sacrifices.[5] Dahrasena, the Traikūṭaka king of Northern Deccan, who ruled in the second half of the

---

1 'पञ्चानां महायज्ञानां सायंप्रातरनुष्ठानम् एकाग्निविधानेन पाकयज्ञसंस्थानां च नित्यानां, शक्तौ विद्यमानायामग्न्याधेयादीनां च हविर्यज्ञसंस्थानामग्निष्टोमादीनां सोमयज्ञसंस्थानां च ।'

2 'वैदिका अप्याचारा राजसूयाश्वमेधादयः समुच्छिद्यमाना दृश्यन्ते । यत इदानीं नानुष्ठीयन्ते ।' 'पूर्वं चतुष्पाद्धर्म आसीत् ....संप्रति जीर्यति यज्ञे दानैकपात् ।'

3 Sarkar: *The Early Pallavas*, p. 17.

4 'पराक्रमाधिगतभागीरथ्यमलजलमूर्धाभिषिक्तानां दशाश्वमेधावभृथस्नातानाम्'

5 Sarkar (op. cit.), p. 38.

fifth century, and the Kadamba king Kṛṣṇavarman I, who ruled in West Mysore and Kanara about the end of the fifth century A. D., are also credited with the performance of the Aśvamedha.[1] In the sixth century A. D. the Cālukya Pulakeśi I is mentioned as having performed a great many sacrifices including the Aśvamedha.[2] A much later instance is that of the Cola king Rājādhirāja I, who is known to have performed the Aśvamedha about the middle of the eleventh century.[3] The Yādava king Kṛṣṇa (1247-1260 A. D.) is said to have performed a great many sacrifices and 'brought fresh strength to the Vedic ceremonial religion which in the course of time had lost its hold over the people.'[4] Cāṇḍūpaṇḍita, the author of a learned commentary on Śrīharṣa's *Naiṣadhacarita*, performed a large number of important sacrifices, showing that Vedic ritual was not extinct in Gujarat in the last quarter of the thirteenth century.[5] The Vājapeya was performed in the sixteenth century for the Vijayanagara kings Nṛsiṁha and Kṛṣṇa-Rāya.[6] The Aśvamedha was performed by Sevai Jayasing of Amber as late as the first half of the eighteenth century.[7]

Somadeva while condemning animal slaughter for religious purposes combats the theory that killing in Vedic sacrifices is not, properly speaking, killing, as it ensures to the victim life in heaven.[8] The subject is more systematically dealt with by Malliṣeṇa (1292 A. D.) in his *Syādvādamañjarī* (under verse 11). He tries to show that the killing of animals even for the purpose of Vedic sacrifices is a grievous sin, and quotes in support of his thesis the views of certain Brahmanical thinkers, Sāṁkhyas and Vedāntins and Vyāsa, who abhorred the practice of animal slaughter in Vedic ritual.

तथा च पठन्ति पारमर्षाः । यूपं छित्त्वा पशून् हत्वा कृत्वा रुधिरकर्दमम् । यद्येवं गम्यते स्वर्गे नरके केन गम्यते ॥[9]

वेदान्तिका अप्याहुः । अन्धे तमसि मज्जामः पशुभिर्ये यजामहे । हिंसा नाम भवेद्धर्मो न भूतो न भविष्यति ॥

व्यासेनाप्युक्तम् । ज्ञानपालिपरिक्षिप्ते ब्रह्मचर्यदयाम्भसि । स्नात्वातिविमले तीर्थे पापपङ्कापहारिणि ॥
ध्यानाग्नौ जीवकुण्डस्थे दममारुतदीपिते । असत्कर्मसमित्क्षेपैरग्निहोत्रं कुरूत्तमम् ॥
कषायपशुभिर्दुष्टैर्धर्मकामार्थनाशकैः । शममन्त्रहतैर्यज्ञं विधेहि विहितं बुधैः ॥
प्राणिघातात्तु यो धर्ममीहते मूढमानसः । स वाञ्छति सुधावृष्टिं कृष्णाहिमुखकोटरात् ॥

---

1 *ABORI*, Vol. XXVI, p. 28 and Sarkar (op. cit.), p. 20.

2 Bhandarkar: *Early History of the Dekkan*, 3rd ed., p. 103.

3 Sastri: *The Colas*, Vol. I, pp. 293, 312.

4 Bhandarkar (op. cit.), p. 197.

5 See the English trans. of *Naishadhacarita*, Introduction, p. III.

6 Rice: *Mysore and Coorg from the Inscriptions*, p. 210.

7 See P. K. Gode's papers in *Poona Orientalist*, Vol. II, pp. 166-180 and *Mimansa Prakash*, Vol. II, pp. 43-46.

8 See Book IV and Chapter XII of this book.

9 Cited in the Māṭharavṛtti.

The views of Vyāsa are quoted also by Somadeva, and it is interesting to find Jaina writers drawing on Brahmanical sources to reinforce the doctrine of *ahiṁsā* (*Yaśastilaka*, Book IV):

होमस्नानतपोजाप्यब्रह्मचर्यादयो गुणाः । पुंसि हिंसारते पार्थ चाण्डालसरसीसमाः ॥ इति...व्यासोक्तिः ।
यावन्ति पशुरोमाणि पशुगात्रेषु भारत । तावद्वर्षसहस्राणि पच्यन्ते पशुघातकाः ॥ इति पौराणिकी श्रुतिः । Ibid.

Somadeva's views on the killing of animals in Vedic sacrifices are recorded in the aforesaid dialogue between Yaśodhara and his mother. Malliṣeṇa sums up by saying that just as a cruel man may try to obtain a kingdom by killing his own son, but cannot escape the ignominy and sin resulting therefrom, even if he attains his object, similarly, even though the gods may be gratified by the slaughter of animals sanctioned by the Veda, the sin caused by such killing can never be averted.[1]

The attacks on the authority of the Veda and its religion which we come across in *Yaśastilaka* belong to a class of recriminatory literature directed against Vedic rites by Jaina writers since long before the tenth century. Although the Vedic religion had been obsolete for centuries, it was considered worth while to attack the Veda, since it was the bed-rock on which the superstructure of Brahmanism was claimed to have been built up beyond the ravages of time. Among the many stories invented for the purpose of discrediting the Vedic religion, there are at least three which deserve notice as illustrating the Jaina attitude and mentality in regard to the Brahmanical Scriptures. The earlier version of the story of Sagara, Sulasā, Nārada, Parvata and Vasu related in Jinasena I's *Harivaṁśapurāṇa* (cantos 17 and 23) and Somadeva's *Yaśastilaka*, Book VII, occurs in the comprehensive Jaina Prākrit romance *Vasudevahiṇḍī*, Chap. V (circa sixth century A. D.). This story is interesting as recording the Jaina allegation that the Veda and its religion were the work of a demon named Kālāsura. The latter is also called Mahākāla, e. g. in *Vasudevahiṇḍī* wherein he is described as a most reprobate god, the minister of Yama.[2] Even a sober philosophical writer like Vidyānandi declares in his *Tattvārthaślokavārtika* 1. 20. 36 that the followers of Kaṇāda attribute the authorship of the Veda to Brahman, while the Jainas attribute it to Kālāsura. Similarly, in an outrageous story preserved in *Vasudevahiṇḍī* (Chap. III), Pippalāda, the reputed author of the Atharvaveda, is described as

---

1 'यथा किल कश्चिद्विपश्चित् पुरुषः परुषाशयतया निजमङ्गजं व्यापाद्य राज्यश्रियं प्राप्तुमीहते न च तस्य तत्प्राप्तावपि पुत्रघातपातककलङ्कपङ्कः क्वचिदपयाति एवं वेदविहितहिंसया देवतादिप्रीतिसिद्धावपि हिंसासमुत्थं दुष्कृतं न खलु पराहन्यते ।'

2 'जमस्स लोगपालस्स अमच्चो परमाहम्मिओ महाकालो नाम देवो जाओ ।'

being born of the illicit union of the nun Sulasā and the ascetic Jannavakka. He is deserted by his parents as soon as he is born, but grows up to be an eminent Vedic scholar. In the course of time he comes to know the circumstances of his birth, and invents the Atharvaveda and its black magic in order to take revenge upon his parents. He severs the tongue of his father with a knife, and after reminding him of the crime of desertion of his own child, hacks him to pieces and offers the limbs as oblations in the sacrificial fire. A similar treatment is meted out to his mother. This is the Jaina version of the origin of the magic rites of the Atharvaveda. Another interesting but far from disgusting story about Vedic rites occurs in the eleventh canto of Raviṣeṇa's *Padmacarita* (seventh century A. D.), which contains also a slightly different version of the Parvata story. The story in question describes the destruction of Marutta's sacrifice by Rāvaṇa, represented as a patron of Jainism in Raviṣeṇa's work, which contains a Jaina version of the story of the Rāmāyaṇa. The Jaina sage Nārada argues with the officiating priest about the authority of the Veda and the advisability of performing sacrifices, and tries to convince him of the sinful character of animal slaughter. Some of his sentiments are not unlike those expressed by Yaśodhara in *Yaśastilaka*; the following two verses, the first from *Yaśastilaka*, Book IV and the second from *Padmacarita* 247, may be compared:

शुक्रशोणितसंभूतमशुचीनां निकेतनम् । मांसं चेत् प्रीणयेद्देवानेत व्याघ्रानुपास्महे ॥
शुक्रशोणितसंभूतममेध्यकृमिसंभवम् । दुर्गन्धदर्शनं मांसं भक्षयन्ति कथं सुराः ॥

The assembled Brāhmaṇas are enraged at the interference of Nārada, and attack him with kicks and blows. The news is brought to Rāvaṇa who hastens to the sacrificial site with his soldiers, and there follows a tumultous scene in which the animals kept for the sacrifice are set free and sacrificial posts broken, and the Brāhmaṇas receive a good hammering. The description of the Brāhmaṇas as "huntsmen with the sacred thread round their necks" sums up the Jaina attitude towards the Vedic religion.

Considering the theological hatred of earlier times, it is not surprising to find Jaina writers inventing or giving currency to stories calculated to discredit the Vedic religion and culture. The Jainas had, however, no direct knowledge of Vedic literature, and their criticism of Vedic rites is often disfigured by gross exaggerations, misunderstanding and misstatements. A few examples may be given to show that even a deeply learned scholar like Somadeva is not wholly free from this charge.

In *Yaśastilaka,* Book IV, Somadeva quotes a Vedic phrase ब्रह्मणे ब्राह्मणमालभेत, and opines that the Veda sanctions the killing of a Brāhmaṇa in spite of the general injunction that a Brāhmaṇa should not be killed.[1] We are not here concerned with the question of whether traces of human sacrifice are found in the Vedic age, but the phrase cited by Somadeva belongs to the ritual of the Puruṣamedha which is wrongly supposed by him to be a human sacrifice. The Puruṣamedha was a symbolic rite, and the human victims, men as well as women, who were actually tied to the sacrificial posts, were set free, one and all, after the *paryagnikaraṇa* or carrying of a firebrand round the victims. These are enumerated in the *Vājasaneyisaṁhitā* XXX. 5–22 and the *Taittirīya Brāhmaṇa* III. 4, while the *S'atapatha Brāhmaṇa* (XIII. 6. 2. 12, 13) says: ".........Now, the victims had the fire carried round them, but they were not yet slaughtered. Then a voice said to him, 'Purusha, do not consummate (these human victims): if thou wert to consummate them, man (purusha) would eat man! Accordingly, as soon as fire had been carried round them, he set them free, and offered oblations to the same divinities.................."[2] The *Kātyāyana S'rauta Sūtra* XXI. 1. 12 clearly says that the Brāhmaṇas and the other victims are released, just as the Kapiñjala birds and the other wild animals are set free in the Aśvamedha after the *paryagnikaraṇa* (XX. 6. 9). It is true that there are two Śrauta Sūtras, Vaitāna (XXXVII. 10 ff.) and Śāṅkhāyana (XVI.10 ff.), which set forth a form of Puruṣamedha in which a man is to be sacrificed, but these Sūtras lack Brāhmaṇa authority for what they prescribe; and as Eggeling points out, the Puruṣamedha described therein "is nothing more than what Śāṅkhāyana appears to claim for it, viz. an adaptation, and that a comparatively modern adaptation, of the existing Aśvamedha ritual." Further, "the very fact that, in both Sūtra works, this sacrifice is represented as being undertaken, not for the great object of winning immortal life, but for the healing of the Sacrificer's bodily infirmities, might seem sufficient to stamp the ceremony as one partaking more of the nature of the superstitious rites of the Atharvan priests than of that of the great sacrifices of the traditional Śrauta ritual."[3] According to Keith, the ritual prescribed in the versions of Śāṅkhāyana and the *Vaitāna* "is a mere priestly invention to fill up the apparent gap in the sacrificial system which provided no place for man."[4] Hillebrandt gives too much importance to the version of Śāṅkhāyana and remarks that the

---

1 See Chap. XII.

2 Eggeling's *Translation*, Part V, p. 410.

3 Eggeling: *Śatapatha Brāhmaṇa*, *Trans.*, Part V, Introduction, p. xliv.

4 *Taittirīya Saṁhitā*, *Trans.*, Introduction, p. cxxxviii.

Puruṣamedha is a relic of a barbaric age,[1] but the statement is vague, and there are no reliable data which might enable us to determine the limits of this 'barbaric age'. The evidence of the Śatapatha Brāhmaṇa, a far more ancient text, is of greater value than that of the two Sūtra texts, and the fact remains that as early as the age of the Śatapatha Brāhmaṇa no human victims were sacrificed in the Puruṣamedha. More generally speaking, the legend of Śunaḥśepa "is enough to show that human sacrifice was for the Brāhmaṇa period a horror beyond words".[2] It is also noteworthy that the Puruṣamedha is not mentioned at all in the Saṁhitās of the Black Yajurveda: the *Taittirīya*, the *Maitrāyaṇī* and the *Kāṭhaka* nor in the comprehensive *Baudhāyana S'rauta Sūtra*.[3]

Another misleading statement made by Somadeva in *Yaśastilaka*, Book IV, concerns the Gosava sacrifice. He opines that this rite was devised to sanction incest with one's mother and sister.[4] The Gosava was an *ekāha* or one-day sacrifice and usually performed by a man of position of the Vaiśya caste, who might be honoured by the king and the people. The man who performed the Gosava was therafter called Sthapati, an honorific term. According to some, this rite was exclusively meant for the Vaiśya caste, and one of its impostant features was that fresh milk was poured over the Sacrificer while seated on the bare ground to the south of the Āhavanīya fire. This is roughly the account of the Gosava given in the *Kātyāyana S'rauta Sūtra* XXII. 11. 6-11. The prescribed sacrificial fee of a myriad oxen shows that the rite was performed by a wealthy man, and according to the Śāṅkhāyana Śrauta Sūtra XVI. 15. 1 it should be undertaken by one who desires cattle. The *Taittirīya Brāhmaṇa* II. 7. 6 and *Tāṇḍya Brāhmaṇa* XIX. 13. 1 connect the Gosava with Svārājya or supremacy as the promised goal, and in any case the rite was meant for a leading man of the community as marking the culminating point in his social rank and position. As pointed out by Hillebrandt,[5] there were certain special sacrifices for particular classes of men, e. g. the Rājasūya for the Kṣatriyas, the Bṛhaspatisava for the Brāhmaṇas and the Sūta-, Sthapati-, Grāmaṇī-, and Go-sava for the other orders of society. Now, the Gosava had a particular connection with the bovine species. The *Taittirīya Brāhmaṇa* (op. cit.) observes that the ox is Supremacy, and the Sacrificer acts like an ox.[6] Sāyaṇa's interpretation

1 *Ritual-Litteratur*, p. 153.

2 Keith: *Taittirīya Saṁhitā* (op. cit.), p. cxl.

3 Ibid., p. cxxxviii.

4 'तदाह—गोसवे ब्राह्मणो गोसवेनेष्ट्वा संवत्सरान्ते मातरमप्यभिलषतीति उपेहि मातरमुपेहि स्वसारमिति ।' Books IV and VII, and section 30.

5 *Ritual-Litteratur*, p. 143.

6 'स्वाराज्यं गौरेव गौरिव भवति । य एतेन यजते ।'

"Just as an ox roams freely in the woods, so does the Sacrificer in the Brahmaloka" does not appear to be accurate in view of the detailed explanation of the rite given in the *Jaiminīya Brāhmaṇa* II. 113.[1] The latter text describes the *vrata* of the Gosava and it consists in imitating the ways of an ox. The Sacrificer is to lie with his mother, his sister, and a woman of his own *gotra*, drink water and eat grass with face downwards, and ease himself wherever he feels the necessity.[2] It is said that Janaka of Videha wanted to perform the Gosava, but when he was told about the procedure, he declared that he was willing to pay the prescribed sacrificial fee, but not to undertake the *vrata*, and did not after all venture to set about the rite. Puṇyakeśa, the king of the Śibis, once undertook the Gosava. He felt like easing himself in the royal assembly, and while uncovering himself for the purpose then and there, exclaimed that the rite was suitable only for old men, and only an old man should undertake it, for 'all this' is permissible to the old. The *Brāhmaṇa* therefore concludes that the Gosava was a *sthavirayajña*, and should be undertaken only at an advanced age.[3] It was thus an apparently innocent sacrifice primarily designed for old people, free from the repulsive significance attributed to it by Jaina writers. It may be noted that the *vrata* described in the *Jaiminīya Brāhmaṇa* is omitted in most of the texts dealing with the Gosava, e. g., in the *S'rauta Sūtras* of Kātyāyana (op. cit.), Śāṅkhāyana 14. 15, Baudhāyana 18. 7 and Āśvalāyana 9. 8, and the *Tāṇḍya Brāhmaṇa* 19. 13; while the *Taittirīya Brāhmaṇa* (op. cit.) seems to make only a passing reference to it: *gauriva bhavati*. Caland shows that there is good reason to believe that the *Jaiminīya Brāhmaṇa* is older than the *Tāṇḍya* or *Pañcaviṁśa Brāhmaṇa*, and he thinks that the latter text omitted certain details, e. g. the of *vrata* the Gosava, perhaps because it found them too 'barbaric'.[4] It is quite probable that the childish procedure of behaving like an ox became soon obsolete, and was excluded from the customary ritual of the Gosava.

Somadeva is not the only Jaina author to make misleading statements regarding Vedic sacrifices. Raviṣeṇa asserts in *Padmacarita* 11. 85 that intercourse with forbidden women is required in the Gosava sacrifice. Devasena who wrote *Darśanasāra* in 933 A. D.[5] says in his Prākrit *Bhāvasaṁgraha* (verses 52-3) that the cow is declared to be

1 *Das Jaiminīya Brāhmaṇa in Auswahl*, p. 157.

2 'उप मातरमियादुप स्वसारमुप सगोत्राम्'

3 'तेन हैतेनोत्तरवयस्ये यजेत ।'

4 *Pañcaviṁśa-Brāhmaṇa*. *Trans.* Caland, Introduction, p. xxi.

5 See Introduction to नयचक्रसंग्रहः (Māṇikacandra Jaina Granthamālā), p. 12.

a goddess (by the Brāhmaṇas) and all the gods are believed to reside in her body; yet they kill her in the Gosava sacrifice and eat the flesh; do they not kill those gods by killing the cow?[1] The Jainas had a tendency to believe that all sacrifices whose names began with the name of a living creature involved its slaughter in the accompanying ritual.

Another example of erroneous statements made by Jaina writers about Vedic rites is found in Raviṣeṇa's *Padmacarita* 11. 87–89:

आशुशुक्षणिमादाय पृष्ठे कूर्मस्य तर्पयेत् । हविष्यजुह्वकाख्याय स्वाहेत्युक्त्वा प्रयत्नतः ॥
यदा न प्राप्नुयात् कूर्मं तदा शुद्धद्विजन्मनः । खलतेः पिङ्गलाभस्य विक्लवस्य शुचौ जले ॥
आस्यदघ्नेऽवतीर्णस्य मस्तके कूर्मसंनिभे । प्रज्वाल्य ज्वलनं दीप्तमाहुतिं निक्षिपेद् द्विजः ॥

These verses containing details, corresponding more or less to particulars found in Vedic texts, might very well deceive an unwary reader not familiar with the Vedic sacrificial system. Among the terms used *juhvaka* is a misreading for *jumbaka*, and *viklava* for *viklidha*. Raviṣeṇa means to say that oblations are offered in the fire on the back of a tortoise, but if one is not available, the offerings are made in a fire kindled on the head of a Brāhmaṇa with certain characteristics, immersed in the water up to the mouth. This is an atrocious misrepresentation of a Vedic rite which took place on the third day of the Aśvamedha towards the end of the sacrifice at the end of the purificatory bath (*avabhṛtha*). What really happened was that an oblation of clarified butter was made on the head of a man of hideous appearance, standing in the water, with the *mantra* 'To Jumbaka hail!' The *mantra* occurs in the *Vājasaneyi-saṁhitā* 25. 9, Jumbaka being a name of Varuṇa as explained, for instance, in the *Taittirīya Brāhmaṇa* III. 9. 15. Among the epithets applied to the man the most frequent are *piṅgala* 'tawny-eyed', *khalati* 'bald-headed', *viklidha*, and *śukla* 'white' or rather 'pale'. As regards *viklidha*, it is variously explained as *dantura* 'with protruding teeth' by Karka on the *Kātyāyana S'rauta Sūtra* XX. 8. 16, Mahīdhara on the *Vājasaneyisaṁhitā* 25. 9, and Harisvāmin on the *S'atapatha Brāhmaṇa* XIII. 3. 6. 5; as *svedanaśīlaśarīra* and *viklinnadeha* 'perspiring' 'clammy' by Sāyaṇa on the *Taittirīya Brāhmaṇa* (op. cit.); and as 'leprous' by Varadattasuta Ānartīya in his commentary on the *S'āṅkhāyana S'rauta Sūtra* 16. 18. The latter text as well as the *Baudhāyana S'rauta Sūtra* 15. 37 uses some other epithets to make the man still more repulsive, and Śāṅkhāyana

1 सुरही लोयस्सग्गे वक्खाणइ एस देवि पच्चक्खा। सव्वे देवा अंगे इमिए णिवसंति णियमेण ॥ पुणरवि गोसवजण्णे मंसं भक्खंति सा वि मारित्ता। तस्सेव वहेण फुडं ण मारिया होंति ते देवा ॥

adds that he should be led to a river and immersed therein, and when the waters flow into his mouth the Adhvaryu priest should make an oblation of horse's blood on the man's head with the *mantra* '*bhrūṇahatyāyai svāhā*'. After the oblation the man is brought out of the water (*niḥṣedhanti* explained in the commentary as *nirgamayanti*), and possibly driven away as a scapegoat. Just as there are no traces of remnants of human sacrifice in this rite, as Weber thought, similarly it did not involve any inhuman practice like lighting a fire on a man's head, as alleged by Raviṣeṇa.

It is hardly necessary to cite other examples of Jaina misstatements regarding Vedic rites. Raviṣeṇa tells us also that in a sacrifice called Mātṛmedha one's mother was killed, while in the Pitṛmedha one's father suffered the same fate (11. 86). Jinasena I states that kings were sacrificed by hundreds and thousands in the Rājasūya, which, according to him, was devised by the wicked god Mahākāla, an enemy of kings. This amazing statement occurs in his *Harivaṁśapurāṇa* written in 783 A. D.[1] Hemacandra mentions a *Gomedha* and a *Naramedha* along with the *Aśvamedha* in a sweeping condemnation of Vedic sacrifices in a verse of his commentary on his *Yogaśāstra* 4. 102.[2] In another amusing verse in the same work (2. 38) he declares that the poor Cārvāka is rather preferable to Jaimini, because the former openly professes atheism, while the latter is a monster disguised as an ascetic citing Vedic texts.[3]

It is evident that much of the information of Jaina writers in regard to Vedic rites was based on hearsay, and the only thing they definitely knew about them was that they involved the sacrifice of living beings, men as well as animals. Their statements are no doubt *mala fide*, misleading and erroneous, but similar inaccuracies are found also in the *Māṭharavṛtti* on the *Sāṁkhyakārikā*.[4] It may be noted in this connection that the following sacrificial verse is quoted, perhaps inaccurately, in both the *Māṭharavṛtti* and Somadeva's *Yaśastilaka* VII. 30:

षट्शतानि नियुज्यन्ते पशूनां मध्यमेऽहनि । अश्वमेधस्य वचनादूनानि पशुभिस्त्रिभिः ॥

---

1 सूयन्ते यत्र राजानः शतशोऽपि सहस्रशः । राजसूयक्रतुस्तेन दर्शितो राजवैरिणा ॥ 23. 142.

2 गोमेधनरमेधाश्वमेधाद्यध्वरकारिणाम् । याज्ञिकानां कुतो धर्मः प्रणिघातविधायिनाम् ॥

3 वरं वराकश्चार्वाको योऽसौ प्रकटनास्तिकः । वेदोक्तितापसच्छद्मच्छन्नं रक्षो न जैमिनिः ॥

4 The *Māṭharavṛtti* misunderstands the significance of the Puruṣamedha and the Gosava. It says पशुवधोऽग्निष्टोमे मानुषवधः गोसवव्यवस्था सौत्रामण्यां सुरापानं······कल्पसूत्रेऽन्यदपि अकृत्यं भूरिकर्तव्यतयोपदिश्यते 'ब्रह्मणे ब्राह्मणमालभेत क्षत्राय राजन्यं मरुद्भ्यो वैश्यं तस्करं नारकाय वीरहणम्' इत्यादि श्रवणात् ।

The verse occurs in a different form in the commentaries of Uvaṭa and Mahīdhara on the *Vājasaneyisaṁhitā* 24. 40:

षदशतानि नियुज्यन्ते पशूनां मध्यमेऽहनि । अश्वमेधस्य यज्ञस्य नवभिश्चाधिकानि च ॥

Among other sacrificial citations, all of which are anonymous, we have already reproduced the dubious statement on the Gosava sacrifice quoted in *Yaśastilaka*, Books IV and VII. 30. The dictum सौत्रामणौ य एवंविधां सुरां पिबति न तेन सुरा पीता भवति quoted in the same context cannot be genuine, because although the reference to wine is correct, the name of the rite (*sautrāmaṇī*) is incorrectly spelt. The word is, in fact, consistently misspelt by Somadeva who writes *sautrāmani* for *sautrāmaṇī*.[1] The following sacrificial verse is cited in VII. 30:

गोसवे सुरभिं हन्याद्राजसूये तु भूभुजम् । अश्वमेधे हयं हन्यात् पौण्डरीके च दन्तिनम् ॥

The verse is clearly spurious, and might even be an invention, as it contains the absurd statement that the king is sacrificed at the Rājasūya. The only reference to human sacrifice in the ritual of the Rājasūya is in the legend of Śunaḥśepa, which is recited by the Hotṛ priest after the anointing of the king, but the story in question is nothing less than a condemnation of the offering of a human victim. Hillebrandt's view that the recitation of the legend is a reminiscence of a possible early connection of the Rājasūya with human sacrifice is clearly far-fetched, and has been rejected by Keith.[2]

The following citation bearing on the Puruṣamedha in *Yaśastilaka* VII. 30 is an example of haphazard quotation or misquotation from sacrificial texts. It reads as follows in Somadeva's work:

ब्रह्मणे ब्राह्मणमालभेत इन्द्राय क्षत्रियं मरुद्भ्यो वैश्यं तमसे शूद्रमुत्तमसे तस्करम् आत्मने क्लीबं कामाय पुंश्चलमतिक्रुष्टाय मागधं गीताय सुतमादित्याय स्त्रियं गर्भिणीम् ।

The passage in question forms part of a longer one found with variations in the *Vājasaneyisaṁhitā* XXX. 5ff., the *Taittirīya Brāhmaṇa* III. 4, and the *S'atapatha Brāhmaṇa* XIII. 6. 2. The ancient text, e. g. that of the *Taittirīya Brāhmaṇa*, reads as follows:

ब्रह्मणे ब्राह्मणमालभते । क्षत्राय राजन्यम् । मरुद्भ्यो वैश्यम् । तपसे शूद्रम् । तमसे तस्करम् । नारकाय वीरहणम् । पाप्मने क्लीबम् । आक्रयायायोगूम् । कामाय पुँश्चलूम् । अतिक्रुष्टाय मागधम् । गीताय सूतम् । नृत्ताय शैलूषम् ।

The principles underlying Vedic injunctions are criticized by Somadeva in the aforesaid controversial dialogue in *Yaśastilaka*, Book

---

1 e. g. निखिलमखशिखामणौ सौत्रामणौ in VII. 22.

2 Hillebrandt: *Ritual-litteratur*, p. 145, and Keith: *Ṛigveda Brāhmaṇas*, p. 62.

IV.[1] Similar objections to the authority of the Veda as a whole are recorded in various Jaina works, e. g. Akalaṅka's *Nyāyaviniścaya* (chap. 3), Anantavīrya's commentary on the *Parīkṣāmukha Sūtra* (chap. 3) etc. Akalaṅka attacks the *apauruṣeya* theory of the origin of the Veda, and says that if the Veda revealed its own truth, it would be unnecessary to study texts like the Āyurveda, which are an integral part of the Veda. Further, if the Veda was eternal, the generations of students who have been studying and explaining it would be like an endless succession of blind men following one another; and if the Veda had really no author, its statements would be like the utterances and customs of barbarians which could not be attributed to any competent authority.[2] Anantavīrya goes further and opines that the Veda cannot be regarded as an authoritative source of knowledge, whether it is supposed to be *apauruṣeya* or *pauruṣeya*. In the former case, supposing there exists an endless sequence of Vedic interpretation current from times without a beginning, this interpretation is bound to go astray in the course of time owing to defects of memory, ineptitude of expression, and dishonest motives, thus destroying the authoritative character of the Veda. Even at the present time those who profess astrology, for instance, are seen to make misleading statements: there are some who know the hidden truth but explain it otherwise for some evil purpose; there are some who know the subject but misinterpret it for lack of the faculty of expression; while there are others who make incorrect statements, having missed a vital link in the sequence of facts. The same is the case with the Veda; hence the divergence of opinions regarding *bhāvanā*, *vidhi*, *niyoga* etc., and disagreement among Manu, Yājñavalkya and others in laying down Smṛti rules in harmony with the true import of the Vedas. Thus the Veda would fail to conform to the truth even if it were based on a tradition without any beginning. The *apauruṣeya* theory therefore does not help to establish the Veda as a reliable and infallible guide, nor is the *pauruṣeya* theory more helpful. There are indeed good reasons for supposing the Veda to be the composition of a certain individual or individuals, e. g. the mention of the names of the sages, *gotras* and *schools*, subject to birth and decay, the arrangement of the sentences according to a hard and fast rule, and the dictum

---

1 See Chap. XII.

2 वेदस्यापौरुषेयस्य स्वतस्तत्त्वं विवृण्वतः। आयुर्वेदादि यद्यङ्गं यत्नस्तत्र निरर्थकः॥ शास्त्रज्ञानं तथैव स्यात् सामग्रीगुणदोषतः। अविरोधेऽपि नित्यस्य भवेदन्धपरम्परा। तदर्थदर्शिनोऽभावान्म्लेच्छादिव्यवहारवत्। अनादिसम्प्रदायश्चेदायुर्वेदादिरागमः॥ *Nyāyaviniścaya*, verses, 416–418.

that 'The Veda is the work of a certain person like the Sūtras of Manu' etc. The fact of the Veda having an author does not, however, give it an authoritative character. Anantavīrya declares: "We do not deny authority to the Veda on the ground that it has no author. The Veda lacks authority because it can never be free from defects owing to its expounders having no knowledge of supersensuous things".[1] The Jainas thus close the door, to their own satisfaction, upon all claims that may be put forward in behalf of the Veda being an authoritative source of human knowledge.

It is extremely doubtful if Jaina attacks on the Veda and the Vedic religion made any impression upon Brahmanical circles if they were at all acquainted with them. The regeneration of the Vedic sacrificial system was out of the question, but renewed and vigorous attempts cotninued to be made to eastablish the authority of the Veda on a firmer and sounder basis. The first great effort towards this end in medieval times was made by Kumārila (seventh century A. D.) and the school of Mīmāṁsā founded by him and thereafter by the distinguished writers of the Nyāya-Vaiśeṣika school who flourished in the ninth and tenth centuries. It was the leaders of the latter school that exercised paramount influence in the intellectual sphere in Somadeva's age. The Naiyāyikas rejected the Mīmāṁsā view that the Veda was eternal, and not composed by any individual, and sought to replace the *apauruṣeya* theory by a more plausible doctrine. Jayanta says in his *Nyāyamañjarī* that the Mīmāṁsakas are incapable of devising an adequate method for maintaining the authority of the Veda: words aided by convention can only have the power to signify; the determination of the shades of meaning must inevitably depend upon the judgment of some one; hence words can have any authoritative character only when they are uttered by a trustworthy person and not otherwise.[2] The Naiyāyikas thus usher in the *pauruṣeya* theory and glorify the Veda as the handiwork of God Himself. Jayanta, for instance, says that He who created the universe composed also the Vedas containing His teachings; and the people believe in the Vedas because they believe in Him, the Trustworthy Guide and the Supreme Lord without a beginning: no wise

1 'नास्माभिर्वक्तुरभावे वेदस्य प्रामाण्याभावः समुद्भाव्यते किन्तु तद्व्याख्यातृणाम् अतीन्द्रियार्थदर्शनादिगुणाभावे ततो दोषाणामनपोहितत्वात् न प्रामाण्यनिश्चय इति ।'

2 'न च मीमांसकाः सम्यग् वेदप्रामाण्यरक्षणक्षमां सरणिमवलोकयितुं कुशलाः' etc. *Nyāyamañjarī*, Book I.

man would have thus believed in the Vedas, had they been without an author (as the Mīmāṁsakas hold).[1]

While emphasizing the fact the Veda is composed by God and accepted by the vast majority of the people, the leaders of the Nyāya-Vaiśeṣika school adopt a rather contemptuous attitude towards the Scriptures of the minorities like the Buddhists and Jainas. Vācaspati in *Nyāya-vārtika-tātparya-ṭīkā* 2. 1. 68 contrasts the Vedas with the Buddhist and Jaina Scriptures composed by mere mortals who are neither Creators nor Omniscient Beings.[2] Śrīdhara says in *Nyāyakandalī* (p. 217) that the Veda is known to be the work of a Superior Being (*puruṣa-viśeṣa*), because its message is unquestioningly accepted by all who belong to the *varṇāśrama* order of society. If it were the work of an ordinary person, like the Scriptures composed by Buddha and others, not all discerning persons would unquestioningly act upon its teachings. That with regard to which there is a universal consensus of opinion (on the subject of its reliability) is bound to be an authoritative source of knowledge, like direct perception and similar means of cognition.[3] Thus while the Vedic sacrificial religion was fast becoming a relic of the past, the authority of the Veda was constantly reaffirmed by Mīmāṁsakas, Smārtas, and Nyāya-Vaiśeṣikas alike. It is noteworthy that even Śaṁkara in his Bhāṣya on the *Vedānta Sūtras* 3. 1. 25 supports in principle the slaughter of animals in Vedic sacrifices, and proclaims the purity of all rites prescribed by the Veda. The voice of Jaina criticism was not likely to be heard in an age characterized by a large-scale revival of Brahmanical thought, say, from about the seventh to the end of the tenth century.

---

1 कर्त्ता य एव जगतामखिलात्मवृत्तिकर्मप्रपञ्चपरिपाकविचित्रताज्ञः । विश्वात्मना तदुपदेशपराः प्रणीतास्तेनैव वेदरचना इति युक्तमेतत् ॥ आप्तं तमेव भगवन्तमनादिमीशमाश्रित्य विश्वसिति · वेदवचःसु लोकः । तेषामकर्तृकतया न हि कश्चिदेवं विस्रम्भमेति मतिमानिति वर्णितं प्राक् ॥ Ibid., Book IV.

2 'न चैते शौद्धोदनिप्रभृतयः तनुभुवनादीनां कर्तारो येन सर्वज्ञा इति निश्चीयेरन् ।' See also Chap. IX.

3 'पुरुषविशेषप्रणीतः सर्वैर्वर्णाश्रमिभिः अविगानेन तदर्थपरिग्रहात् यत्किञ्चनपुरुषप्रणीतत्वे तु वेदस्य बुद्धादिवाक्यवत् न सर्वेषां परीक्षकाणामविगानेन तदर्थानुष्ठानं स्यात्·········यत्र च सर्वेषां संवादनियमः तत् प्रमाणमेव यथा प्रत्यक्षादिकम्। प्रमाणं वेदः सर्वेषामविसंवादिज्ञानहेतुत्वात् प्रत्यक्षवत् ।'

CHAPTER XV

Non-Jaina Cults, Customs and Beliefs

Among the non-Jaina cults mentioned in Somadeva's *Yaśastilaka* the most prominent is, of course, that of Caṇḍamārī, which forms the starting point of the story. As we have already seen, human sacrifice was an essential feature of the worship of that goddess, and a detailed, though to some extent fantastic, description of her appallingly gruesome shrine occurs in Book I. Caṇḍamārī is only another form of Caṇḍikā, whose cult is much earlier than the tenth century, as is evident from the descriptions of the goddess and her blood-stained temple in works like Bāṇa's *Kādambarī* and Haribhadra's *Samarāiccakahā*, Book VI. In the latter work the deity is called also Kātyāyanī and Kādambarī. Subandhu in his *Vāsavadattā* likewise refers to the shrine of Kātyāyanī alias Caṇḍā while describing the city of Kusumapura or Pāṭaliputra.[1] In Bhavabhūti's Mālatīmādhava, Act V, the goddess appears as Karālā or Cāmuṇḍā to whom a human victim is about to be offered by a Kāpālika. In Vākpati's *Gaüḍavaho* she appears as Vindhyavāsinī, to whom a lengthy hymn is addressed by Yaśovarman (vv. 285–338), the goddess being called also Caṇḍī, Sabarī and Nārāyaṇī. The hymn in question refers among other things to the human victim and the custom of selling human flesh, as in our work.[2] The self-torture described by Somadeva as being practised by certain fanatics in the temple of Caṇḍamārī[3] is mentioned in another context in Bāṇa's *Harṣacarita* (Book V), which refers, for instance, to the burning of Guggulu resin on the head while supplicating the Mahākāla Śiva, and the offering of flesh cut out of one's own body as an oblation in the fire.[4] The offering of slices of one's own flesh to Cāmuṇḍā is mentioned in Uddyotana's *Kuvalayamālā* composed in the eighth century.[5] The Chinese traveller Yuan Chwang, in the first half of the seventh century, describes a temple, at Prayāga (Allahabad), where certain devotees committed suicide in the hope of gaining 'the paradise of the gods.'[6]

---

1 'यत्र········भगवती कात्यायनी चण्डाभिधाना स्वयं निवसति'

2 'विससिज्जन्तमहापसुदंसण······'(v. 319); 'सूएन्ति वीरविक्कयविक्कममिह जामिणीमसाणेसु' (v. 327). The comm. remarks देवीश्मशाने वीरा सिद्धये महामांसविक्रयं कुर्वन्तीति कौलागमादिषु प्रसिद्धम्. See Chap. XIII for further details.

3 See Chap. II.

4 'अन्यत्र शिरोविधृतविलीयमानगुग्गुलुविकलनवसेवकानुनीयमानमहाकालम्, अपरत्र निशितशस्त्रोनिकृत्तात्ममांसहोमप्रसक्तापवर्गम्'

5 'किंवा चामुण्डायाः पुरस्तीक्ष्णक्षुरिकाविदारितोरुयुगलसमुच्छललोहितपङ्किलभूतलं मांसखण्डैर्बलिं ददामि' Ratnaprabha's *Sanskrit version.*

6 Watters: *On Yuan Chwang*, Vol. I. p. 362. A similar practice has been traced on the island of Māndhātā in the Narmadā, in the Nimar District of Central Provinces. Here, until recent times, devotees were in the habit of dashing themselves over

The cult of the Devī, who is known under different names, Caṇḍikā, Kātyāyanī, Bhavānī, Durgā etc., seems to have been widely prevalent from about the seventh century onwards. The cult, as ordinarily practised, represents what is known as Sakti worship, and must be distinguished from the abnormal ritual mentioned by Somadeva in *Yaśastilaka.* There are, for instance, two rock-cut temples dedicated to Durgā at Māmallapuram, now the village of Mahābalipuram, known also as the Seven Pagodas, on the sea-coast, about forty miles south of Madras. The excavations at this place date from the second quarter of the seventh century A. D.[1] The temples are locally known, the one as Kotikal Maṇḍapa, and the other as Draupadī's Ratha.[2] The former is a primitive-looking shrine consisting of a hall, about 22 feet long and eight feet wide. The latter is a beautifully carved little shrine with a domical roof, and contains a bas-relief figure of Durgā. In front of the temple is a huge rock-cut figure of Durgā's vehicle, the lion. There are, besides, various sculptural representations of the goddess on some of the other temples and rocks at Māmallapuram. A number of crudely fashioned figures of the goddess and her lion are also carved on some of the isolated rocks near the Shore Temple facing the sea. In the so-called Draupadī's Ratha the bas-relief figure of Durgā is four-armed and portrayed standing on a lotus pedestal with two worshippers kneeling at her feet. These features are also seen in the bas-relief representation of the goddess in one of the large panels on the walls of the temple known as the Varāhamaṇḍapa. Other panels, which represent the goddess with eight arms, and trampling on the head of a buffalo, occur on the facade of the Trimūrti Temple and in the

---

the Birkhala cliffs, at the eastern end of the island, on to the rocks by the river brink, where the terrible god Kāla Bhairava resided. The last such offering to Kāla Bhāirava was witnessed in 1824. It is significant that the shrine of Caṇḍamārī is called Mahābhairava in Somadeva's *Yaśastilaka.* It is said that about the time when a Chauhan Rajput named Bhārat Singh took Māndhātā from Nathu Bhil in 1165 A. D., a priest named Daryāo Nāth used to worship Oṁkāra Śiva on the island. There is a legend that Daryāo Nāth by his austerities shut up Kālī Devī, the consort of Kāla Bhairava, who fed on human flesh, in a cave, for the protection of the pilgrims. The mouth of this cave is still shown. It was also arranged that Kāla Bhairāva should in future receive human sacrifices at regular intervals. The disciples of Daryāo Nāth still enjoy lands on account of the worship of Oṁkāra Śivā. *Imperial Gazetteer of India,* Vol. IX, p. 293 ff. It is difficult to separate fact from fiction in these traditions; but an abnormal variety of Tāntric cult seems to have grown up, evidently at a later time, on the island of Māndhātā, and no doubt represented a debased type of Śaivism or Tāntricism resembling the *Vāmamārga* described in Somadeva's *Yaśastilaka.*

1 See Appendix III.

2 See Longhurst: *Pallava Architecture,* Part II.

interior of the Varāha Temple. The story of Durgā slaying the Buffalo Demon was popular not only in India but in Java; and a remarkable bas-relief showing the fight of the goddess with the demon, regarded as one of the finest specimens of Indian art, is found in the so-called Mahiṣāsuramaṇḍapa. The eight-armed goddess, astride on her lion, is represented as shooting arrows at the demon whose colossal figure is seen slightly receding before her, with one of his followers slain and another apparently wounded.[1] It is also noteworthy that, in the bas-reliefs in the Draupadī's Ratha and the Varāhamaṇḍapa, one of the worshippers is shown as cutting off the tresses of his hair with a sword as a votive offering to the goddess. Such practices are, of course, far different from the various forms of self-torture practised in connection with the cult of Caṇḍamārī, or Caṇḍikā, as described by Somadeva and others. The practices described by Somadeva in *Yaśastilaka* evidently belong to an abnormal variety of the cult, which appealed to the fanaticism of a limited class of worshippers. But the cult of the Devī, in the ordinary sense of the term, had a much wider appeal; and old temples dedicated to the Goddess are found in various parts of India.[2] The cult was, as stated below, popular

1 The scene is represented on a much smaller scale in a beautiful panel discovered near the Śiva temple at Bhumara of the early Gupta period (see Appendix III). The goddess is four-armed with a sword in one hand and a trident in another. She stands with her left foot on the head of the buffalo and grasps his tail with one of her hands. See plate xiv (b) in R. D. Banerji's monograph on the temple.

2 Some of the old temples dedicated to Devī may here be mentioned, many of which have been rebuilt in later times. The temple of Ambā Bhavānī on the summit of the hills of Arasur at the south-western extremity of the Aravalli range is an important centre of pilgrimage, and lays claim to a remote antiquity. The ancient town of Darbhavatī or Dabhoi, about twenty miles to the south-east of the city of Baroda, contains a temple dedicated to Bhadra Kālikā Mātā (Bhadrakālī). It is situated to the right of the famous Hira-Gate at Dabhoi on the east side of the old fort, and stands on the site of an older shrine in honour of the same goddess. It was probably built by Vishaldev Vaghela about 1255 A. D. 'Its dimensions are small, but the whole outer face has been so broken by mouldings, and ornamented by sculptures, large and small, as to render it typical of the rich thirteenth century style in Gujarat.' The temple is, in fact, one of the most important architectural monuments of the pre-Muslim period in Gujarat. Another Devī temple known as Kālkā Mātā or Kālkā Bhawānī stands on the lofty summit of the hill of Pavagadh situated about twenty-five miles north-east of Baroda. The goddess has been worshipped on the rocky peak for many centuries as the guardian deity of the hill. 'The shrine, which is visible from a distance of many miles in the plains below, is no doubt very ancient, being mentioned as a place of pilgrimage under the rulers of Anhilvad Patan.' But the present building is probably of a much later date. Commissariat: *History of Gujarat*, Vol. I, pp. lxi, lxxxvii, 191. An ancient temple of Devī or Caṇḍikā, venerated by Rajputs throughout Malwa and Mewar, exists at the small village of Antri in the Garoth District of Indore State. The present temple is, however, a modern structure built with the materials collected from the ruins of an older shrine.

at royal courts, as it was believed to promote success in warfare. The temples and sculptures at Māmallapuram, which was essentially a royal foundation, prove the popularity of the cult of Durgā, probably for similar reasons, during the rule of the Pallavas in the south from the seventh century onwards. The Pallavas were supplanted by the Colas, and it is noteworthy that Vijayālaya, the founder of the line of the imperial Colas, built a Durgā temple at Tanjore[1] after his conquest of the city about the middle of the ninth century A. D.[2] It may be noted that about this time, in Northern

---

A small temple dedicated to the god Sambā (Śambhu) and Devī stands outside the village of Dighi, six miles due east of Kajgaon Station in the East Khandesh District, a couple of miles from the frontier of Hyderabad (Deccan). 'The temple consists of a porch in front, a *maṇḍapa* on pillars with a high dome, an *antarāla* or passage leading to the sanctum or *garbhagṛha* and the sanctum or shirne itself.' The sanctum contains a small *liṅga* and a large standing image of Devī. A niche on the north wall of the *maṇḍapa* contains a dancing figure of Cāmuṇḍā. She has four hands and an emaciated body, but the scorpion usually to be found in her stomach is absent. She holds a trident, a skull-mace (*khaṭvāṅga*) and a skull-cup (*nara-kapāla*). *Progress Report of the Archaeological Survey of India, Western Circle*, 1920, pp. 75, 99. Close to the island of māndhātā in the Narmadā, a small ravine on the north bank of the river, popularly known as the *Rāwana nālā*, contains 'a prostrate figure 18½ feet in length, rudely carved in bold relief on four basalt slabs laid end to end. It has ten arms, all holding clubs and pendent skulls, but only one head. On its chest is a scorpion, and at its right side a rat, while one foot rests on a smaller prostrate human figure.' The huge image no doubt represents Cāmuṇḍā or Mahākālī, and was evidently intended to be placed in a colossal temple which was never completed. The bed of the ravine is covered with huge basalt rocks, slightly carved in some places, which doubtless had the same destination.' *Imperial Gazetteer of India*, Vol. IX, p. 296.

1 Sastri: *The Colas*, Vol. I, p. 140.

Temples of Durgā appear to have been built in different parts of medieval India. An inscription discovered in the village of Dirghāsi, four miles to the north of Kalingapatam in the Ganjam District, records the erection of a *maṇḍapa* in front of a temple of Durgā at Dīrgharāśi or Dirghāsi in the Śaka year 997 (1075 A. D.), by a Brāhmaṇa chieftain named Gaṇapati in the service of the Eastern Ganga king Rājarāja I of Orissa (1068-1078 A. D.). R. D. Banerji: *History of Orissa*, Vol. I, p. 246. There is a ruined temple of Durgā of about the twelfth century, near the village of Balsana in the West Khandesh District of Bombay Presidency. Inside the shrine stands the mutilated image of the goddess. The temples at Balsana suffered badly at the hands of the Muslim invaders. An inscription on the stone lintel of a ruined temple bears a date corresponding to 1148 A. D. See *Progress Report of the Archaeological Survey of India, Western Circle*, 1919, pp. 46, 56. There is an old temple called the temple of Devī Hinglāj in the village of Baridelchi near Mehidpur Town in Indore State. The edifice has been partially rebuilt, as the *śikhara* and the *garbhagṛha* are modern, but the porch in front has four well-carved medieval pillars. Inside the shrine is an old image which is a very good representation of the killing of the buffalo demon by Durgā (*Mahiṣamardinī*). *Progress Report of ASI, Western Circle*, 1920, p. 102.

India, Durgā or Bhagavatī was fervently worshipped by some of the Gurjara-Pratihāra emperors of Kanauj.[1]

Somadeva is not the only Jaina writer of the tenth century who refers to the cult of Caṇḍikā. A few decades earlier, Devasena in his *Bhāvasaṁgraha* (verse 76) mentions the killing of goats at the altar of Caṇḍikā and the worship of the Kula[2] with wine: while Siddharṣi in his *Upamitibhavaprapañcā Kathā* (Book IV) refers to the worship of Caṇḍikā with wine and describes drinking bouts and merrymaking in the forecourt of the shrine of the goddess with their evil consequences. So far as Somadeva is concerned, the cult of Caṇḍikā is located by him in the city of Rājapura in the Yaudheya country, which has been variously identified as the region between the Sutlej and the Jumna, or Bahawalpur State in the Punjab, south of Multan.[3] If the Yaudheya country is supposed to be the region between the Sutlej and the Jumna, Rājapura may perhaps be identified with Rajpura in Patiala state, now an important junction on the North Western Railway. Somadeva describes Rājapura as full of magnificent temples, and it is obviously the capital of the Yaudheya country, but we cannot be certain about its identification. It may be noted in this connection that a Rājapura is mentioned by Yuan Chwang,[4] and it has been identified with the Rājapurī frequently mentioned in the *Rājataraṅgiṇī*, the modern Rajauri in the province of Jammu in Kashmir. We have no evidence to connect Rājapurī with the Caṇḍikā cult, but the Chinese traveller describes the inhabitants from Lampa to Rājapura as 'of rude violent dispositions' and as 'inferior peoples of frontier (i. e. barbarian) stocks', reminding one of the Sabaras who were in the habit of worshipping the goddess under different names. But few ancient remains have been discovered at Rajauri, and a recent survey revealed nothing except a few architectural fragments belonging to temples similar to those of Kashmir proper.[5] The site of Rājapura is, as a matter of fact, of

1 The Partabgarh inscription of Mahendrapāla II (946 A. D.) has, for instance, two verses in praise of Durgā almost at the beginning. Nāgabhaṭa II (first half of 9th century), Bhoja I (second half of 9th century) and Mahendrapala I (end of 9th and early 10th century) are described as ardent devotees of Bhagavatī or Durgā (*paramabhagavatī-bhakta*). *EI*, Vol. XIV, p. 176 ff.

2 Kula means Śakti. For details see Introduction to *Kulacūḍāmaṇi Tantra* (*Tantrik Texts*).

3 Poussin: *Dynasties et Histoire de l'Inde depuis Kanishka*, p. 44.

4 Watters: *On Yuan Chwang*, vol. I, p. 284.

5 Kak: *Antiquities of Bhimbar and Rajauri* (Memoirs of the Archaeological Survey of India, No. 14).

little importance with regard to the cult of Caṇḍamārī. Somadeva's account is in some respects so graphic and detailed that he seems to write from first-hand knowledge of the cult, as it was practised by certain zealots in his time somewhere in the Deccan.

The Mahāyoginīs are described by Somadeva in *Yaśastilaka*, Book I, in connection with the temple of Caṇḍamārī. The description is rather fantastic, but the author's purpose is to depict the terrific aspect of these deities and represent them as fit companions of Caṇḍamārī. In Book III the spy is declared to have communed with the Mahāyoginīs and acquired supersensuous knowledge.[1] These references are interesting as illustrating the fact that the cult of the Yoginīs was prevalent in the tenth century. It is noteworthy that the circular temple of the sixty-four Yoginīs at Bheraghat, thirteen miles from Jubbulpore, has also been assigned to the tenth century.[2] This peculiar shrine 'consists of a huge thick wall along the outer edge of a circular platform, inside which there is a circular row of pillars and pilasters arranged in two concentric circles'. There is a flat roof supported on the pillars and pilasters. According to Cunningham, the temple of the Sixty-four Yoginīs was originally a simple circular enclosure, containing the images of the Yoginīs, the wall being of the same height as the statues. He concluded that the circular cloister, as it at present stands, is the work of two different periods: the old circular wall, with its inscribed statues, belonging to the tenth century; and the cloister, with its roof, being the work of queen Alhaṇādevī in the twelfth century. The actual number of images in the shrine including various other figures is more than eighty. Most of them are seated, with the names of the deities inscribed on the pedestals in letters of the tenth century. For example, Śrī-Thakiṇī, Śrī-Vīrendrī, Śrī-Phaṇendrī, Śrī-Kṣatradharmiṇī, Śrī-Bhīṣaṇī, Śrī-Ghaṁṭālī, Śrī-Jahā, Śrī-Ḍākinī, Śrī-Lampaṭā, Śrī-Indrajālī, Śrī-Īśvarī, Śrī-Aiṅgiṇī, Śrī-Caṇḍikā, Śrī-Ajitā, Śrī-Piṁgalā, Śrī-Vārāhī, Śrī-Erūḍī, Śrī-Vībhatsā, Śrī-Kāmadā, Śrī-Raṇājirā etc. A beautiful figure of Mahiṣamardinī is called Śrī-Teraṁvā. The existence of a separate temple for the worship of the sixty-four Yoginīs shows the popularity of Tāntric cults in the tenth century. It is interesting to note that, under the lotus on which Śrī-Sarvatomukhī is seated is another fullblown lotus, the calyx of which bears the Tāntric emblem of crossed triangles (*Ṣaṭkoṇa*), with the mystic formula *Hrīṁ* in the centre.[3]

---

1 See Chap. IV.

2 R. D. Banerji: *The Haihayas of Tripuri and their monuments*, p. 69.

3 See the detailed description of the images in Banerji (op. cit.)

Another temple dedicated to the sixty-four Yoginīs exists at Khajurāho in Chhatarpur State in Central India. 'The script of the brief inscriptions on its walls does not indicate a period much, if at all, anterior to 900 A. D.'; and the temple has accordingly been assigned to the first half of the tenth century. Three other temples dedicated to the 64 Yoginīs are known to exist, *viz.*, 1) at Surādā in the Pāṭan or Paṭṭana State, one of the Tributary States of Orissa; 2) at Rāṇīpur-Jurāl in the same State; and 3) in Coimbatore District, Madras. It is a remarkable fact that all the known temples dedicated to the 64 Yoginīs are circular, except the one at Khajurāho, which is 'peculiar in being oblong'.[1]

Somadeva refers to the Mothers in connection with the cult of Caṇḍamārī. In his description of the temple of the goddess, in *Yaśastilaka* Book I, he speaks of the Mātṛmaṇḍala or the group of the Mothers as being worshipped there by certain fanatics, who had torn out their intestines to please those deities.[2] The Seven Mothers are here brought into relation with a horrid and ferocious cult, but they had also a benign aspect, and are well-known as the guardian deities of the early Cālukyas, as stated in their copper-plate grants.[3] Sculptural representations of these deities have been found at Aihole and other places in the Deccan.[4] The Seven Mothers, four-armed, each with a child, figure among the sculptures on the south wall of Cave XIV at Ellora, popularly known as Ravana-ka-kai: each has her cognizance on the base below.[5] There is a very well-executed sculpture representing the Seven Mothers on a stone slab, built into the wall of a step-well, out in front of the temple of Siddheśvara at Haveri in the Dharwar district. 'On most of these slabs each goddess holds a child on her lap to denote motherhood, but they are absent on this; and they are generally flanked by Śiva on one side and Gaṇapati on the other. Next to Śiva, in this case, is Brāhmī or Brahmāṇī, the female counterpart of Brahmā, below her being Brahmā's vehicle, the goose. Next is Māheśvarī, Śiva's counterpart, with his bull *Nandi*, beside whom is Vaiṣṇavi seated over Garuḍa. After her come Kaumārī, counterpart of Kārtikeya, with his peacock; Vārāhī with a buffalo instead of the boar; Indrāṇī or Aindrī with the elephant, and, lastly, Cāmuṇḍā with a dog, but sometimes a dead body. This last Mother is shown as a skeleton with long pendent breasts.

1 For detailed references see *Indian Antiquary*, 1908, p. 132.

2 'कचित्तीक्ष्णपुरुषापकृष्टस्वकीयान्त्रयन्त्रदोलनतोष्यमाणमातृमण्डलम्'. There is another reference to the Mātṛmaṇḍala in Book I. See Chap. IV.

3 Bhandarkar: *Early History the Dekkan*, p. 83. Third edition.

4 Cousens: *Chalukyan Architecture of the Kanarese Districts*, p. 45.

5 Burgess: *A Guide to Elura Cave Temples*, p. 24.

Each goddess has four arms, and in their hands they carry symbols belonging to the gods they represent. The arrangement is not always the same."[1] Various sculptures representing Siva and the Seven Mothers are found in the temples at Un in the southern part of Indore State.[2]

The worship of the goddess Aparājitā is mentioned by Somadeva in Book III as part of the general description of the court life of Yaśodhara. In three verses recited by a bard the blessings of the goddess are invoked for the success of the king in warfare. We are told that Aparājitā, called also Ambikā, grants victory to kings on the battlefield, and is herself incarnate in their arms and weapons. The stars are the pearls on her hair, and the sun and the moon are her eyes: the celestial river is her robe, and the oceans are her girdle, and the Meru mountain is her body. She is worshipped by Indra, Śiva, Brahmā and Viṣṇu.[3] It is clear from the Devīmāhātmya section of *Mārkaṇḍeyapurāṇa* (chap. 88 ff.) that Aparājitā, Ambikā, Durgā, Kātyāyanī, Gaurī, Bhadrakālī etc. are different names of Caṇḍikā; they are to be regarded rather as different forms of Caṇḍikā, and worshipped on different occasions for special purposes. The meditation of Aparājitā is recommended in the medieval Tantric work *Īśānaśivagurudevapaddhati* in the course of the ritual prescribed for the worship of Gaurī;[4] and it is interesting to note that one of the rites is meant for the king and prescribed to ensure his victory in war.[5] The same work treats in detail of the worship of Durgā, who is significantly described as capable of destroying hostile armies.[6] Aparājitā is thus one of those deities whose worship was favoured at the royal court as a means to vanquishing the enemies of the king.

We learn further from *Yaśastilaka* that the worship of Aparājitā took place on the Mahānavamī day, and the occasion is, in fact, more important than the name of the goddess. The Mahānavamī festival is mentioned

1 Cousens (op cit.), p. 87. For some other details see the Vocabulary appended to the English Translation of the *Naiṣadhacarita*, under *Ambikā*.

2 See Appendix III. In the Chaubara Dera temple the sculpture occurs twice on doors. An elaborately carved door bears the Seven Mothers with Śiva in the centre, all dancing. Over a door in the small Śiva temple to the north of the Chaubara Dera we have representations of the Seven Mothers with Śiva playing on a lyre. One of the lintels in the temple of Nīlakaṇṭheśvara represents Śtva as dancing with the Seven Mothers.

3 *Yaśastilaka* 3. 459–461.

4 '......अभयवरकरां धृताङ्कुशपाशिनीं, विधृतशशिकलां स्मरेदपराजिताम् ॥' (Mantrapāda) 23. 51.

5 Ibid. 23. 57

6 'अथवा शत्रुसैन्यादिनिग्रहे परमेश्वरीम्' Ibid. 25. 19

by Somadeva also in Book I, wherein we are told that Māradatta invited the populace to the temple of Caṇḍikā on the pretext of celebrating the festival, although it was not the proper season for it.[1] Śrutasāgara in his commentary defines Mahānavamī as the ninth day of the bright fortnight of the month of Caitra. Another Jaina writer, Udayavīra, in his *Pārśvanātha-carita* (chap. IV) includes the Mahānavamī rites among non-Jaina cults and practices and assigns them to the bright fortnight of Caitra and Āśvina.[2] It was usual to celebrate the festival in the latter month, and Mahānavamī was the ninth day of the bright half of Āśvina, marking the culmination of the Navarātra rites commencing from the *pratipad* of that month. Strictly speaking, the term *mahānavamī* was applied to the eighth lunar day of the bright half of Āśvina when in conjunction with the Mūla constellation, and the eighth as well as the ninth day was appointed for the worship of the goddess Cāmuṇḍā or Durgā.[3] The *Garuḍapurāṇa* (chap. 134) gives a similar definition of Mahānavamī, but mentions a different constellation.[4]

The *Devīpurāṇa* (Chap. XXII) gives a detailed account of the Mahānavamī rites which had a special significance for the king. On the eighth or *aṣṭamī* day nine wooden pavilions were erected, or even one, wherein was installed an image of Durgā made of gold or silver or earth or wood. The goddess could also be worshipped in a symbolic way in a consecrated sword or a spear. The king repeated in silence mystic formulas before the goddess and sacrificed an animal after midnight for obtaining victory, the flesh and blood of the victim being offered to the goblins by repeating the Mahākuśika formula. The king then took a ceremonial bath and hit a paste model of his enemy with a sword and presented it to Skanda and Viśākha. This is a remarkable feature of the Mahānavamī cult and illustrates all the more clearly its connection with the king and his security and military plans.

The corresponding account in *Garuḍapurāṇa* (chapters 134 and 135) gives some additional details. The Durgā image is provided with diverse weapons, and appears to have eighteen hands; the left ones holding

---

1 'अकालमहानवमीमहमिषसमाहूतसमस्तसामन्तामात्यजानपदः'

2 'चैत्राश्विनशुक्लाष्टम्यां महानवम्यां गोत्रदेवताविशेषपूजादि'

3 Cf. पुरुषार्थचिन्तामणि p. 59: हेमाद्रौ भविष्योत्तरे—आश्वयुक्शुक्लपक्षस्य अष्टमी मूलसंयुता। सा महानवमी नाम त्रैलोक्येऽपि सुदुर्लभा॥ कन्यागते सवितरि शुक्लपक्षेऽष्टमी तु या। मूलनक्षत्रसंयुक्ता सा महानवमी स्मृता॥ अष्टम्यां च नवम्यां च जगन्मोक्षप्रदाम्बिकां etc.

4 'शुक्लाष्टम्यामाश्वयुजे उत्तराषाढया युता। सा महानवमीत्युक्ता स्नानदानादि चाक्षयम्॥ नवमी केवला चापि दुर्गां चैव तु पूजयेत्। महाव्रतं महापुण्यं शङ्कराद्यैरनुष्ठितम्॥'

various objects, a skull, a shield, a mirror, a bell, a flag, a noose, a drum etc., and the right ones the weapons, spear, lance, club, dart, bolt, arrows etc. Nine other attendant deities with sixteen hands, Ugracaṇḍā, Caṇḍanāyikā, Caṇḍā, Aticaṇḍikā etc., are also worshipped and a five year old buffalo is sacrificed in the latter part of the night. It is probable that of the two accounts that in the *Devīpurāṇa* records an older version of the Mahānavamī cult.[1]

The ninth day of the bright fortnight of Āśvina was, generally speaking, sacred to the Devī, and nearly always the *navamī* cult is brought into relation with the king and his surroundings. We may refer, for instance, to *Viṣṇudharmottarapurāṇa* (Khaṇḍa II, chap. 158), which prescribes the worship of Bhadrakālī and that of the royal insignia and arms and weapons on that day: the goddess is worshipped by the king in a decorated pavilion near the barracks (*śibira*), and he has to keep awake the whole night. Similarly, the worship of the goddess Cāmuṇḍā on the aforesaid *tithi* is prescribed in *Skandapurāṇa*, *Prabhāsakhaṇḍa* (chap. 242 of *Prabhāsakṣetramāhātmya*). The same text describes a great festival in honour of Yogeśvarī, a form of Durgā, commencing from the fifth night of the bright half of Āśvina, the main feature being the mystic presentation of a sword to the goddess; while on the *ninth day*, after the sacrifice of animals, the king at the head of his army leads a procession with the image of the goddess in a chariot (Ibid. chap. 83). These and similar references help us to understand the nature of the Mahānavamī festival, which may be regarded as a magic rite for the success of the king in warfare, or perhaps as a quasi-military festival celebrated under the patronage of the king, and in which he actively participates. A statement in *Devīpurāṇa* (chap. XXII) seems even to suggest that the Mahānavamī rites were put forward as a kind of substitute for the ancient horse-sacrifice.[2] The allusion to Mahānavamī in Somadeva's *Yaśastilaka*, corroborated by similar references in the Purāṇas, shows its popularity as a

---

1 The Mahānavamī cult survives to some extent in the great Durgā Pūjā festival of Bengal and Assam, celebrated in the bright half of Āśvina on the same *tithis* as those prescribed in the Purāṇic texts cited above. The mytholgical background is different, and the image of the ten-armed Durgā, standing on a lion and piercing the Buffalo demon with a lance, is accompanied on either side by the subsidiary images of Lakṣmī, Sarasvatī, Kārttikeya and Gaṇeśa. The eighth and the ninth are the great days of worship, and animal sacrifices are not entirely absent. Prominence is given to the tenth or the Vijayā Daśamī day when the images are immersed in rivers and streams.

2 अश्वमेधमवाप्नोति भक्तिना सुरसत्तम । महानवम्यां पूजेयं सर्वकामप्रदायिका ॥ 22. 28.

court festival; and it is mentioned also in Bāṇa's *Harṣacarita*, Book VIII, which refers to the sacrifice of buffaloes on the occasion.[1] Somadeva does not indeed speak of animal sacrifices in connection with Mahānavamī; and it is quite possible that they were sometimes omitted, specially when the festival was celebrated under the auspices of a court like that of the Rāṣṭrakūṭas, susceptible to the influence of Jaina ideas.

Mahānavamī is followed by Dīpotsava or the Festival of Lights, corresponding to the modern Diwāli. The short description of it addressed to the king by a bard in *Yaśastilaka* 3. 462–4 refers to the whitewashed palaces and the white flags and the rows of lights on the lofty terraces of the edifices of the city; and speaks of 'the women excited by gambling', the gaiety of courtesans, and the sweet notes of music.[2] According to *Padmapurāṇa* (*Uttarakhaṇḍa*), the Dīpotsava commences on the fourteenth day of the dark half of Kārttika, and importance is given to a ceremonial bath on that day followed by a salutation to Yama. The illuminations take place in the evening; temples, buildings, shrines, assembly-halls, stables and fortifications are decorated with lights as are also river-banks, tanks, gardens and gateways. Next day the king entertains the citizens in a large-scale reception; and the Dīpotasva seems to have provided a suitable occasion for promoting cordial relations between the ruler and the ruled. The king is expected to gratify the various classes of people on the joyous occasion, the good men with courtesy and others with food and drink and the learned with conversation and the inmates of the inner apartments with presents of cloth, betel, flowers, camphor and saffron and various delicacies. The village headmen are rewarded with gifts, and money presents are made to the tributaries; while ornaments are distributed among troops, ministers and kinsmen. Seated on a raised platform, the king witnesses bull-fights, and reviews the assembled clansmen and the troops and the actors, dancers and minstrels. An interesting item is the ceremonial fastening of the Mārgapālī, a wreath of Kuśa and Kāśa grass with numerous streamers, to a pillar of the fort or a tree, under which are assembled the horses, elephants and the cattle to ensure protection against disease. During the night the people indulge in gambling, and at midnight the women of the city cast out Alakṣmī, the goddess of poverty, from their homes to the sound of drums and music. The most important item of the nocturnal festivities is the worship of the

1 'महानवमीमहं महिषमण्डलानाम्'. The citation in पुरुषार्थचिन्तामणि (op. cit.) goes on to say सा पुण्या सा पवित्रा च सुधर्मसुखदायिनी। तस्यां सदा पूजनीया चामुण्डा मुण्डमालिनी॥ तस्यां ये सुपहन्यन्ते प्राणिनो महिषादयः। सर्वे ते स्वर्गतिं यान्ति घ्नतां पापं न विद्यते॥

2 See also Chap. VII.

51

demon king Bali. He is painted in gay colours, with the Vindhya range in the background (?), within a circle on the floor, and worshipped with all kinds of lotus blossoms and with wine, flesh and varieties of food. The king, too, with his ministers and priests, worships Bali for a happy new year, and passes the night without sleep in company with actors, dancers and singers (Chap. 122).

The Dīpotsava depicted by Somadeva in *Yaśastilaka* is a secular festival; and the *Padmapurāṇa*, too, emphasizes the prominent rôle played by the court and its entourage in the festivities. But the details given in the Purāṇa indicate also its religious aspect which it has not entirely lost even today. In Bengal, for example, the goddess Kālī is worshipped on the Diwāli or Dīpānvitā night; while the Jainas celebrate the festival of lights on the new moon of Kārttika as a commemoration of the *nirvāṇa* of Mahāvīra. The Dīpotsava or Diwāli, like the ancient Jewish festival of 'Light', called also Hanukkah 'Rededication,'[1] may be described as a secular festival with a distinctly religious background.[2]

The *Padmapurāṇa* (op. cit.), which calls the festival of lights Dīpāvali or Dīpotsava, designates it also as Kaumudī and gives the derivation of the name.[3] The festival is also called Kaumudī in *Vāmanapurāṇa* 92. 58, which describes how it was instituted in honour of Bali after his imprisonment by Viṣṇu. But the Kaumudī, properly so called, was a festival of the moonlight, and so different from the Dīpotsava or Diwāli. Somadeva refers to the Kaumudī festival in *Yaśastilaka* VII. 27,[4] and it is also mentioned in

1 It was an annual eight-day festival instituted in 165 B. C. to celebrate the re-establishment of worship in the temple after the interruption caused by the persecution under Antiochus IV. The illumination of houses on every one of the eight evenings was a characteristic feature of the celebration. 'The illumination was originally solely domestic; later, lamps were lighted in the synagogues also.' Moore: *Judaism*, Vol. II, p. 50.

2 The earliest festival of lights seems to have been celebrated in Egypt in connection with the cult of the goddess Neith of Sais, the capital of the Kings of the XXVIth dynasty, as recorded by Herodotus, II. 62. He says that, on the night of the sacrifice, lamps were kept burning in the open air round about the houses. These lamps were saucers full of salt and oil, the wick burning all night. The illumination took place not only at Sais but throughout all Egypt. Herodotus travelled in Egypt about 450 B. C.

3 'कुशब्देन मही ज्ञेया मुद हर्षे ततो द्वयम्। धातुत्वे निगमैश्चैव तेनैषा कौमुदी स्मृता। कौ मोदन्ते जना यस्मान्नानाभावैः परस्परम्। हृष्टतुष्टाः सुखापन्नास्तेनैषा कौमुदी स्मृता। कुमुदानि बलेर्यस्यां दीयन्ते तेन षण्मुख॥ अर्घ्यार्थं पार्थिवैः पुत्र तेनैषा कौमुदी स्मृता।'

4 The queen Rāmadattā is described as witnessing the celebration of the Kaumudī festival by the women of the city from a high pavilion (नगराङ्गनाजनस्य......कौमुदीमहोत्सव-समयमालोकमानया तमङ्गोत्सङ्गसमासीनया).

Uddyotanasūri's *Kuvalayamālā* which assigns it to the full moon of the autumn.[1] An earlier reference to the Kaumudī festival occurs in Āryaśūra's *Jātakamālā* (XIII) in the story of Unmādayantī: the city is decorated with flags and the ground bestrewn with flowers; songs, dance and music are in full swing; luxury goods are exposed for sale and the streets thronged by gaily dressed crowds. It is noteworthy that there is no reference to artificial illumination which is a characteristic of the Dīpotsava. The Kaumudī was, in fact, a glorification of the autumnal full moon. It was a popular festival, being also mentioned in *Mudrārākṣasa*, Act III and *Mālatīmādhava*, Act VII, and seems to be identical with the Kaumudījāgara noticed in Vātsyāyana's *Kāmasūtra* 1. 4. 42. According to the Jayamaṅgalā commentary thereon, the latter festival took place on the full moon night of Āśvina, the chief amusements being swings and gambling. The festival is mentioned simply as Kaumudī in *Kāmasūtra* 5. 5. 11, and the commentary here explains it as *Kojāgara*, which is the same as the full moon of Āśvina.[2] It is probable, however, that it was also customary to celebrate the Kaumudī festival on the full moon night of Kārttika.[3]

A hymn to Sarasvatī which is also a benediction addressed to the king occurs in Book III (vv. 261–8), and is described as accompanying the dance that takes place in connection with the preliminary worship of the deities before the commencement of a play. One of the verses runs thus:

मानससरोविनिर्गतसितसरसिरुहस्थितेः सरस्वत्याः । वरवर्णकीर्णकान्तिः पुष्पाञ्जलिरस्तु रङ्गपूजायै ॥

"Let this handful of flowers, radiant with beautiful colours, offered to Sarasvatī, abiding on the white lotus beds emerging on the Mānasa lake, serve the purpose of *raṅgapūjā* or the ceremonial worship preceding a dramatic performance."

---

1 Ratnaprabhasūri's Sanskrit version, p. 133.

2 It is probable that *Kojāgara* is a contraction of *Kaumudījāgara* in spite of the usual derivation *Ko jāgartti*. In Bengal and Assam the Kojāgara or the Kojāgarī Pūrṇimā is definitely associated with the worship of Lakṣmī on the full moon after the Durgā Pūjā celebrations usually in Āśvina. An all-night vigil is recommended in honour of Lakṣmī, and the goddess is believed to ask at midnight: *Ko jāgartti*, 'Who is awake?' See the citations in *Śabdakalpadruma* under *Kojāgara*. For example, आश्विने पौर्णमास्यां तु चरेज्जागरणं निशि । कौमुदी सा समाख्याता कार्या लोकविभूतये ॥ कौमुद्यां पूजयेल्लक्ष्मीमिन्द्रमैरावतं स्थिरम् ।... निशीथे वरदा लक्ष्मीः को जागर्त्तीति भाषिणी । तस्मै वित्तं प्रयच्छामि अक्षैः क्रीडा करोति यः ॥ It will be seen that the full moon of Āśvina is referred to as Kaumudī.

3 See Dhruva's edition of *Mudrārākṣasa*, Act III, *Notes*. In *Mudrārākṣasa*, 3. 10 the Kaumudī is described as a *pārvaṇa vidhi*, which is explained by the commentator Ḍhuṇḍhirāja as taking place on *pārvaṇa* or the full moon of Kārttika. See Telang's edition. Kaumudī is explained as a festival in Kārttika in *Trikāṇḍaśeṣa* 2. 3. 19.

The custom of *raṅgapūjā*, as described in Bharata's *Nāṭyaśāstra* (chap. 3), is a very old one and illustrates the interconnection of art and religion in ancient India. In the *Nāṭyaśāstra*, however, *raṅgapūjā* is an elaborate process involving the worship of a large number of deities in the playhouse with various offerings, and Sarasvatī is merely one among them; but it is probable that in later times Sarasvatī alone was worshipped, and in any case Somadeva does not mention the worship of any other deity in the *nāṭyaśālā*. Further, according to Bharata, the item of *Pūrvaraṅga*, an elaborate musical prelude consisting of songs and dances before the performance of a play, takes place after the *raṅgapūjā* proper is over. Somadeva seems to make a combined reference to both the items when he speaks of *pūrvaraṅgapūjā*, but the distinct mention of *raṅgapūjā* in the verse quoted above shows that he has in mind the customary worship preceding a dramatic performance in the Hindu theatre. In regard to the position of Sarasvatī in *raṅgapūjā*, Somadeva's verses in praise of the goddess in *Yaśastilaka* are mainly in the nature of a benediction addressed to the king; and in the *Nāṭyaśāstra* also, after the formal worship of the deities in which Sarasvatī has her due share,[1] the preceptor of the dramatic art (*nāṭyācārya*) praises and greets the king and the dancing girls, and then utters a benedictory verse for the prosperity of the king, in which the blessings of Sarasvatī and certain allied deities are prominently invoked.[2]

Sarasvatī is represented by Somadeva as white and seated on a white lotus: she is three-eyed (i. e. has an eye on the forehead), and has matted hair on the head, and the crescent for ear-ornament. She has four hands bearing different emblems: the *dhyāna-mudrā* (also called *cintā* or *jñānamudrā*); a rosary of Rudrākṣa beads; a book; and the *varada-mudrā*.[3] Somadeva's description of Sarasvatī roughly corresponds to that found in authoritative texts like *S'āradātilaka*, *Īśānaśivagurudevapaddhati* and *Prapañcasāratantra*, except for minor variations in the distribution and character of the emblems. According to *S'āradātilaka* 6. 4[4] and *Prapañcasāra* 7. 3, for instance, the emblems are *jñāna-mudrā*, a rosary of Rudrākṣa beads, a jar of nectar and a book; while *Prapañcasāra* 8. 41 substitutes

---

1 ब्रह्माणं मधुपर्केण पायसेन सरस्वतीम्। शिवविष्णुमहेन्द्राद्याः संपूज्या मोदकैरथ ॥ *Nāṭyaśāstra* 3. 37

2 Ibid. 3. 88 ff.

3 *Yaśastilaka* 3. 261, 262.

4 ...मुद्रामक्षगुणं सुधाढ्यकलशं विद्यां च हस्ताम्बुजैर्बिभ्राणां विशदप्रभां त्रिनयनां वाग्देवतामाश्रये ॥ Rāghavabhaṭṭa says in his commentary: मुद्रा ज्ञानमुद्रा । अङ्गुष्ठतर्जनीयोगरूपा पार्श्वाभिमुखी । विद्या पुस्तकं तन्मुद्रेत्यर्थः. The "book" is explained as referring to the पुस्तकमुद्रा, which is described as the closed left fist facing oneself (वाममुष्टिः स्वाभिमुखी बद्धा पुस्तकमुद्रिकेति).

a lyre for the *jñāna-mudrā*. According to Īśānaśiva (Mantrapāda 18. 6), the emblems are *varada-mudrā*, a rosary, a lyre and a book.

The cult of Sarasvatī seems to have been prevalent in the Kanarese districts in the age of Somadeva. There is an old temple of Sarasvatī at Gadag, in the Dharwar district, which, though small in size, contains some of the most elaborately carved pillars throughout the whole extent of Cālukyan architecture. It stands close to the eleventh century temple of Trikūṭeśvara, and might possibly be of the same date. Within the shrine is an image of Sarasvatī, seated cross-legged upon a high pedestal, which has a peacock depicted in the central panel below. Unfortunately, the image is mutilated, the four arms being lopped off at the elbows. Otherwise, it is a very finely carved example representing the graceful figure of the goddess, with the pearlstrings around the neck and the jewelled band about the waist. The elaborate pile of curly tresses on the head is surmounted by a six-tiered coronet of jewels. Another image of Sarasvatī, of inferior workmanship, was found in the old Jaina temple at Lakkundi in the Dharwar district. It is a more complete example representing the goddess with four arms. 'In her right upper hand is an elephant goad or *aṅkuśa*. The right lower rests open, palm upwards, upon her knee, with a small petalled flower upon it. In the left upper hand she holds a folded book, while the left lower holds a citron.'[1] While the iconography shows divergence in details, the cult appears to remain the same.

Traces of a temple of Sarasvatī, older than that at Gadag, have been found at Aihole, the home of early temples in the Deccan. Close to the temple (No. 9) in the field to the south of the village, there stood another temple, but all that remains of it now is the shrine doorway and the seat or throne of the image. As in the temple at Gadag, a peacock, with its crest and long tail, is sculptured on the front of the pedestal, which seems to be an indication that the temple was dedicated to Sarasvatī. 'It thus occupies exactly the same position with regard to the temple as the later temple of Sarasvatī does to the temple of Trikūṭeśvara at Gadag.'[2] In northern India, there is 'a famous temple of the goddess Sarasvatī, or Sāradā Devī' at Maihar, now a station on the railway between Allahabad and Jabalpur.[3]

Pilgrimage to the shrine of the goddess Nandā on the Himalayas, evidently on the peak now known as Nandadevi, is mentioned in *Yaśastilaka*

1 Cousens: *Chalukyan Architecture of the Kanarese districts*, pp. 25, 79, 110.

2 Ibid., p. 44.

3 Vincent Smith: *History and Coinage of the Chandel Dynasty* in *Indian Antiquary, 1908*, p. 136.

VII. 31.[1] The cult of this goddess is described in detail in *Devīpurāṇa* (chap. 92-93), and extraordinary merit is said to accrue from the difficult journey to the almost inaccessible shrine. The goddess is clad in white raiment, and has four hands; she is surrounded by numerous beautiful maidens who are eager to marry her devotees. A noteworthy feature of the cult is that respect for women is particularly enjoined on the worshippers of the goddess (ibid. 93. 165 ff.). Nandā-tīrtha is described in *Devīpurāṇa* as a Śaiva *tīrtha*, and, as in *Yaśastilaka*, the goddess is called Bhagavatī Nandā (93. 22-24).[2]

A city-goddess named Siddhāyikā, 'who inspired the confidence of many people', is mentioned in Book I.[3] In Book IV there is a reference to the evil spirit Kṛtyā who kills her own worshippers.[4] It may be noted that, according to *Kathāsaritsāgara* 5. 121-2, Cāṇakya worshipped Kṛtyā with magic rites in order to bring about the death of king Nanda. Krityā is mentioned also in Śivasvāmin's *Kapphiṇābhyudaya Mahākāvya* 3. 24, 28,[5] composed in Kashmir in the ninth century. A reference to the six magic rites of the Tantric cult occurs in a verse in *Yaśastilaka*, Book IV.[6] According to *S'āradātilaka* 23. 122 ff., they are *śānti* or cure of disease and the expulsion of evil spirits such as Kṛtyā; *vaśya* or bringing others under one's control; *stambhana* or paralysing the activity of others; *vidveṣa* or causing enmity between friends; *uccāṭana* or compelling one to abandon hearth and home; and *māraṇa* or killing. Each of these rites has a presiding goddess who is worshipped at the beginning, and the goddess Jyeṣṭhā seems to be connected with the process of *vidveṣa*.[7] A reference to Jyeṣṭhā occurs also in *Yaśastilaka* 3. 118 wherein she is said to be worshipped with white lotus blossoms.[8] Jyeṣṭhā is diametrically opposite to Lakṣmī, being the goddess of adversity (Alakṣmī), and so called, because she is believed to have emerged prior to Lakṣmī during the churning of the ocean. Her legend is related in *Liṅgapurāṇa* (*Uttarabhāga*, chap. 6), and she is particularly associated with sinners and evil-doers and all those who are outside the pale of the Brahmanical religion.

---

1 'नन्दाभगवतीयात्रानुसारित्वात्'

2 यथा गङ्गा नदीनां तु उत्तमत्वे व्यवस्थिता । तद्वद्भगवती नन्दा उत्तमत्वेन संस्थिता ॥

3 'तदेवमनेकलोकोत्पादितप्रत्ययायाः पुरदेव्याः सिद्धायिकायाः········सरसौमनसं नामोद्यानमवलोक्य'. Siddhāyikā appears to be a Jaina goddess. See Chap. XIII.

4 'अन्यथा कृत्याराधक इव ध्रुवं पञ्चजनः पञ्चतामञ्चेत् ।'

5 'अत्युग्रां जपत इव प्रकोपकृत्यां निर्मातुं द्विषदभिचारमन्त्रतन्त्रम'; 'कृत्येव भ्रुकुटिरतिस्फुटा'.

6 'षट्कर्मकार्यार्थमथान्नशुद्धयै' etc.

7 शान्तिवश्यस्तम्भनानि विद्वेषोच्चाटने ततः । मारणान्तानि शंसन्ति षट् कर्माणि मनीषिणः ॥ रोगकृत्याग्रहादीनां निरासः शान्तिरीरिता ।···रतिर्वाणी रमा ज्येष्ठा दुर्गा काली यथा क्रमात् ॥ षट्कर्मदेवताः प्रोक्ताः कर्मादौ ताः प्रपूजयेत् ।

8 'पूज्यमब्जं श्रियः सङ्गाज्ज्येष्ठायाश्च न कैरवम् ।'

The worship of Cupid was celebrated as a court festival in the spring amidst vernal sports, of which we have a lively picture in *Yaśastilaka*, Book III.[1] A further reference to the festivities in connection with the worship of of Cupid, in which the king participates, occurs in Book V.[2]

Certain beliefs and customs belonging to the sphere of popular religion are recorded in *Yaśastilaka*. The moon of the fourth lunar day was believed to cause disputes.[3] A dove alighting inside a house was supposed to forebode its destruction.[4] A number of evil omens described in connection with Yaśodhara's journey to the temple of Caṇḍikā in Book IV, e. g. the trumpeting of a female elephant at the commencement of a journey, the braying of a donkey from behind etc. A shower of crested tadpoles on a house was an evil portent indicating destruction of wealth and prosperity.[5] Elephants were supposed to be possessed by a spirit named Madapuruṣa, of terrible aspect, like lightning fire.[6] Śrutasāgara in his commentary quotes a verse which enumerates the characteristics of Madapuruṣa: he has sixteen hands, four jaws, red eyes and flaming hair.[7]

Among popular customs referred to by Somadeva may be mentioned that of *ājyāvekṣaṇa* or looking into clarified butter in the morning to counteract the effects of evil dreams and obtain other salutary results. It was a practice observed by kings while Brāhmaṇas uttered blessings.[8] The wellknown custom of *nīrājana* or ceremonial waving of lights was observed as part of the evening rites to ensure the well-being of the king. A quantity of salt, thrown into the fire, after whirling it over the king's head, was supposed to counteract the evil eye, and this was also accompanied by the ceremony of offering boiled rice to the goblins on the roadside. This seems to have been followed by the act of *nīrājana* proper, which consisted in revolving lights beside the king.[9] It was also customary to perform the *nīrājana* ceremony in honour of the royal horses and elephants on special occasions like the coronation of the king.[10]

---

1 'मधौ मकरध्वजमाराधयामास'.

2 See Chap. II.

3 See Book III (चतुर्थं चतुर्थीचन्द्रात्') and Śrutasāgara's comm. thereon.

4 'अगारान्तरापतितः कपोत इव निर्वास्य' Book III.

5 गेहे शिखण्डिमण्डूकवृष्टिश्च श्रीच्छिदे द्विषः 2. 72.

6 'ज्वलज्ज्वालवज्रवैश्वानरकरालमूर्तिना मदपुरुषेणाधिष्ठिततया द्विगुणीभूतभीमसाहसनिकाय' Book III.

7 "मयूरग्रीवाभं चपलरसनं रक्तनयनं, चतुर्दंष्ट्राहिंस्रं पृथुकरशिरोमेढ्रजठरम् । चलन्मुक्तं शङ्कुश्रणमदभयं षोडशभुजं ज्वलत्केशं वन्दे मदपुरुषमत्युग्रवदनम् ॥". शङ्कुश्रण seems to be a mistake for शङ्कुश्रव.

8 *Yaśastilaka* 2. 96.

9 Ibid. 3. 476, 477

10 'आचरितगजवाजिनीराजनैः' Book II.

CHAPTER XVI

Jaina Religious and Moral Stories

A considerable number of independent stories occurs in *Yaśastilaka*, Books VI and VII, their purpose being to illustrate diverse tenets of Jaina religion and ethics. The first series in Book VI is meant to illustrate the different aspects of Samyaktva or Right faith, while the second series in Book VII illustrates two of the Mūlaguṇas and the five Aṇuvratas. The stories, on the whole, belong to the sphere of religion and folklore, and form part of the body of Jaina narrative tradition, generally known as Kathānaka literature. Jacobi says: 'The rise of the Kathānaka literature............may be placed about the end of the first century A. D. Its end is indicated by the time of Haribhadra who lived about 750 A. D. For Haribhadra wrote Tīkās on the Āvaśyaka and other Sūtras and Niryuktis: and the Tīkās form the fourth and last layer of the Kathānaka literature.'[1] Generally speaking, the stories incorporated by Somadeva in his work must be considered much earlier than the tenth century, and, as we shall see, several of them are actually found or referred to in earlier texts. Somadeva has thus no originality in respect of these stories, and his turgid prose is hardly suited to the treatment of such simple tales. His great merit is in bringing together so many ancient stories and elaborately narrating them by way of illustrating various teachings of the Jaina religion. He has, in fact, preserved for us a highly interesting collection of stories, which, from the standpoint of religion and folklore, is hardly less important than the story of Yaśodhara. Their literary interest is enhanced by the fact that they form a sort of independent story-book within the framework of the romance.

Some of the stories recorded by Somadeva are based on Brahmanical mythology, and may be called Jaina versions of Hindu tales. The story of the sage Viṣṇu is nothing but a Jaina adaptation of the story of the Dwarf Incarnation of Viṣṇu. Jamadagni and Reṇukā are well-known in Brahmanical mythology; the story of Vasu, as we shall see, is originally a Brahmanical legend. Perhaps the most notable of the stories preserved in *Yaśastilaka* is an early legend, probably the earliest known, concerning the foundation of the once famous Jaina Stūpa of Mathurā.[2] Most of the stories illustrating the Aṇuvratas may be described as folktales. All the stories recorded in Books VI and VII are summarized below in the order in which they occur in Somadeva's work.

---

1 Jacobi: Introduction to *Sthavirāvalīcarita or Pariśiṣṭaparvan*, p. vii.

2 See below (VII) and Chap. XVII.

I) The first story, in three sections, shows that without will-power, it is impossible to attain success in the practice of religion, and hints that ascetics of the Brahmanical faith lack in this essential quality. Two friends Dhanvantari, the son of a merchant, and Viśvānuloma, the son of a priest, were banished by the king of the city of Bhūmitilaka on account of various offences, and in the course of their wanderings they came to Hastināgapura. There Dhanvantari was initiated into the Jaina religion, and devoted himself to meditation under the Jaina discipline; while Viśvānuloma followed the Brahmanical faith and became an ascetic wearing a mass of matted hair. After their death they were reborn as gods under the names of Amitaprabha and Vidyutprabha respectively. One day the latter happened to boast about the superior status of Brāhmaṇa sages like Jamadagni, Mātaṅga and Kapiñjala, and both decided to descend to the earth to ascertain the truth. There in the Badarikā hermitage they saw the sage Jamadagni engrossed in rigorous austerities, his hair and beard white with age, and his body enveloped in a tangled mass of creepers, shrubs and ant-hills. Seeing him, the two gods assumed the form of a pair of birds, and having settled inside his beard, began to talk with each other. One of the birds said to his mate that he would have to go to attend the marriage of the bird-king Garuḍa, but wonld return without the least delay; if he spoke falsely, his sin would be as great as that of 'this' sinner of a sage. Jamadagni was angry to hear these words, and squeezed his beard with a view to punishing the birds, but they flew away and perched on the top of an adjoining tree. The sage recognised the birds to be a couplc of gods in disguise, and asked them respectfully what sin he had committed. The birds cited two verses to the effect that one should renounce the world only after bringing children to the world. The sage was accordingly guilty of infringing the rule laid down in the Law-books, and should, therefore, marry and beget children. Jamadagni, on hearing this, exclaimed, 'That is quite easy', and went off to marry Reṇukā, the daughter of the king of Benares, his uncle, and in the course of time became the father of Paraśurāma.

With the fickle nature of Jamadagni is contrasted the steadfast purpose and resolution of two Jaina devotees. The two gods passed on to Magadha, and there saw Jinadatta, absorbed in meditation in a cremation ground on a dark Caturdaśī night. They commanded him to give up his meditation, and tried to intimidate him by conjuring up terrible scenes of a veritable war of the elements, with bursting rain-clouds, thunder and storm; and at the same time tried to cajole him out of his resolution by offering to grant various boons. Jinadatta, however, remained unmoved, and the two gods showed their appreciation of his courage and determination, by presenting him with a magic formula enabling one to travel through the air. Jinadatta, in his turn, gave the formula to his pupil Dharasena, after having utilized it for the purpose of visiting the Jaina shrines on the Mountain of the gods.

Turning from the veteran Jinadatta, the two gods decided to try their tactics on a novice, recently initiated into the Jaina faith. They happened to see Padmaratha, the king of Mithilā, going to worship the Tīrthaṁkara Vāsupūjya on the very day of his initiation; and immediately began to disturb him by conjuring up various scenes of horror including certain tiger-shaped monstrosities. Unable to strike terror into his heart, they plunged him into a huge expanse of mud, but the drowning prince only said 'Salutation to Lord Vāsupūjya!' The two gods then extolled Padmaratha's courage and fortitude, and took their departure.

The value of intrepid courage and resolution in the practice of religion is further illustrated in a sequel to the main story. Dharasena, who had received the magic formula for aerial travel from Jinadatta, began the perilous mystic rites necessary for its practical application amidst the nocturnal horrors of a cremation ground. The details of the rites are obscure, but the main item seems to have been the suspension of a swing from the branch of a banyan tree over a consecrated ground, bristling with numerous sharp arrows fixed in the earth with upturned points: the devotee was to mount on the swing and cut the arrows to pieces while uttering the magic formula. Meanwhile, Lalita, the misguided son of a king, who had turned thief, having been robbed of his patrimony by relatives, came out in the darkness, on the mission of stealing for his mistress a famous necklace belonging to the chief queen of the lord of Kuśāgrapura. He succeeded in his venture, but could not evade the police owing to the lustre of the necklace being visible in the darkness. So he threw away the ornament, and walking about in the outskirts of the city, came upon the scene of Dharasena's mystic rites. Seeing that Dharasena was hesitating to mount the swing, the thief questioned him about the procedure; and having acquainted himself with the sacred formula, boldly seated himself on the swing and cut off at one stroke the entire mass of arrows. As a result of his bravery, the thief acquired the magic powers longed for by Dharasena, and later became a Jaina ascetic and attained salvation on the mount of Kailāsa.

II) The sacrifice of personal ambition and self-interest for the sake of one's vow is illustrated in the story of Anantamati, the beautiful daughter of the merchant Priyadatta, an inhabitant of Campā. On the eve of his departure for the Sahasrakūṭa shrine for the celebration of the Eight-day rites, the merchant sent for his daughter, and was told that she was playing the bride with her doll, while her maiden friends were singing nuptial songs. When Anantamati appeared before the old man, he asked her in jest to take the vow of chastity rather than harbour thoughts of marriage. The maiden, however, took the vow very seriously. Once in springtime she came out to indulge in the pastime of singing in company with her maiden friends on the day of Cupid's festival, when she was seen by a Vidyādhara, travelling through the air, accompanied by his wife. Wishing to abduct her, the demi-god went back to his home, left his wife there, and then returned and flew away with Anantamati. But his wife was quick to follow, and seeing her in a rage, he hastily dropped the maiden in a forest near Śaṅkhapura. There she was seen by a Kirāta hunter named Bhīma who took her away to his village. Failing to seduce her by persuasion, he decided on violence; but meanwhile, through the intervention of the sylvan deities, who admired the firmness of the girl, the house of the hunter caught fire, and the miscreant, seeing the danger, begged her to forgive him, and then left her on the slope of a mountain on the border of Śaṅkhapura. There she was found by a young merchant who had encamped with his caravan near by; but unable to seduce her with money, he made her over to a bawd in the city of Ayodhyā. The latter, failing to mislead the girl, presented her to the king of that region, who in his turn discarded her, being baffled by her constancy and the opposition of the presiding goddess of the city, who had marked her displeasure by doing harm to many of the king's subjects. Anantamati then came to live in a shrine near the house of Jinendradatta, the husband of her father's sister. After some time her father, while on a visit to his brother-in-law, happened to see her engaged in austerities in the shrine, and proposed to marry her to her cousin Arhaddatta, the son of Jinendradatta. But she firmly rejected the proposal on account of her vow of chastity.

III) Lack of hesitation in the practice of one's religion, for example, in the exercise of piety, is illustrated in the story of king Auddāyana, famous for his philanthropic actions. In order to test his piety, a certain god assumed the form of a religious mendicant, a loathsome leper with stinking and decaying limbs, and came to the king's house and asked for food. The king received him with open arms, and personally waited upon and treated him to a sumptuous meal. Unfortunately the leper felt sick, and as he lay in a mass of vomitted food, the king raised and washed him with his own hands, wiped his body with a silken scarf, and solaced him with soft and kind words. The god then threw off his disguise, and took his departure after praising and honouring the king with divine presents.

IV) Unswerving allegiance to the tenets of the Jaina faith and the lack thereof are illustrated in the stories of Revatī and Bhavasena respectively. A Vidyādhara prince, indifferent to worldly happiness, abdicated in favour of his son, and desiring to visit the Jaina temple at Mathurā, took leave of his *guru* Munigupta at Madura, 'the Mathurā of the south', and departed for the north with a congratulatory message from Munigupta to Revatī, the consort of Varuṇa, king of Mathurā. Arriving at the city by air, the Vidyādhara decided to test the religious conviction of Bhavyasena, a learned Jaina teacher, and of the faithful Revatī. Assuming the form of a young student, he first appeared before Bhavyasena and expressed his desire to study grammar with him. One day while walking with his teacher in the outskirts of the city, the Vidyādhara, by his supernatural powers, covered the ground with young sprouts of corn; and, on Bhavyasena hesitating to walk over them, because in the Jaina scriptures the sprouts of corn were regarded as stationary creatures, the so-called student argued that they had no characteristic of life such as breath, and were merely transformations of earth, very like gems. Bhavyesena believed his words and walked over the sprouts, without questioning the validity of his assertion. Similarly, the Vidyādhara persuaded Bhavyasena to use a clod of earth for cleansing purposes by arguing that it did not contain any living creatures, as maintained by Jaina doctrine. Then he persuaded him to take water without first straining it through a cloth, as required by Jaina practice (in order to eliminate living creatures), his argument being that no such creatures were visible in the transparent water. In this way the Vidyādhara satisfied himself that Bhavyasena lacked inner conviction and tenacity of faith in the religion professed by him; he now realised why the sage Munigupta had neglected to address any message to Bhavyasena.

The Vidyādhara then proceeded with elaborate preparations to test the faith of Revatī, well-known for her whole-hearted devotion to the Jaina faith. He betook himself to the eastern quarter of the city, and there created a sensation by assuming the form of Brahman, seated on a swan, with all his characteristics and paraphernalia. The Vedic verses uttered by the latter were being eagerly listened to by a multitude of sages such as Mātaṅga, Bhṛgu, Bharata, Gautama, Garga, Piṅgala, Pulaha, Puloman, Pulasti, Parāśara, Marīci and Virocana. The Arts incarnate in the form of beautiful maidens were standing by, plying their fly-whisks, and the deep-voiced Nārada was acting as doorkeeper. Revatī heard of this extraordinary phenomenon, but remained indifferent for she knew that Brahman did not figure among the sixty-three Famous Persons recognised by the Jaina scriptures.

The Vidyādhara then appeared in the southern quarter of the city and attracted great attention by assuming the form of Viṣṇu, lying on the coils of the lord of serpents, and wearing a ruby crown surmounted by a large spray of Pārijāta blossoms. Brahman, seated on a lotus emerging from Viṣṇu's navel, was reciting the latter's thousand names; Indra and the goddess of wealth were caressing his feet; the captive wives of demons were waving fly-whisks; and Garuḍa was maintaining order among the assembled gods. The apparition displayed the usual emblems of Viṣṇu: the quoit, the conch, the lotus and the Nandaka sword. Reports of this strange phenomenon were brought to Revatī, but she evinced no curiosity, and said, "There are, indeed, nine Viṣṇus or Vāsudevas known as Ardhacakravartins in Jaina lore, but they are no longer in existence; the one must, therefore, be a magician come to delude the people".

The Vidyādhara appeared next in the western quarter of the city and assumed the guise of Śiva, mounted on a gigantic bull, and accompanied by Pārvatī. The apparition was furnished with the usual equipment of Śiva: the drum, the bow, the sword, the axe, the trident and the club; and attendants such as Analodbhava, Nikumbha, Kumbhodara, Heramba and Bhiṅgiriṭi were paying homage to the deity. News of this strange incarnation of Śiva or Rudra came in due course to Revatī, but she took no notice of it and said, "There are, indeed, some Rudras mentioned in the scriptures as creating obstacles in the path of religious austerities, but they are dead and gone as a result of their actions; so this must be some one else who is disturbing the peace by his magical tricks".

The demi-god then resorted to the northern quarter, and appeared in the form of a Jaina Tīrthaṁkara, seated on his throne in a marvellous audience-hall, furnished with perfumed chambers, pillars, tanks, gates, Stūpas, flags, incense, water-jars, and various other receptacles. There gods and mortals participated in magnificent festivities, and false Jainas like Bhavyasena were also celebrating religious festivals. The show, however, produced no impression on Revatī, who knew that the Jaina scriptures recognised only twenty-four Tīrthaṁkaras, and the latter having attained salvation, the new impersonation must be the work of some adept in magic.

Unable to shake the faith of Revatī by any of these devices, the Vidyādhara at last revealed himself before her, and respectfully delivered Munigupta's message which she received with the utmost veneration and joy.

V) The necessity of guarding the reputation of one's religion is emphasized in the story of the thief disguised as a religious mendicant. Yaśodhvaja, the king of Pāṭaliputra, had a son named Suvīra, who, being without education and moral training, fell into evil company and became addicted to theft and adultery. One day, while on a visit to a pleasure garden, he came across a gang of thieves and gamblers, and announced a rich prize for any one of them who could steal a certain marvellous jewel from a Jaina shrine, located on the top floor of a seven-storied building belonging to the merchant Jinendrabhakta, an inhabitant of the city of Tāmalipti. One of the company, a notorious thief named Sūrya, declaring that it was an easy task for him, immediately started for the kingdom of Gauḍa to carry out his boast. On his arrival there he disguised himself as a religious mendicant, and attracted the attention of all and sundry by the rigour of his fastings and austerities. Gradually he succeeded in winning the love and confidence of Jinendrabhakta; and once when the latter was about to start on a sea-voyage, he invited the so-called ascetic to come and stay in his temple during his absence. After making some pretence of unwillingness, the dissembler accepted the offer, and soon after the departure of the merchant, he stole the jewel and slipped away at the dead of night. But the lustre of the jewel in the darkness attracted the notice of the watchmen; and, pursued by them, the thief entered the camp of the merchant in the outskirts of the city where he was halting for the night. The merchant was awakened from sleep by the shouts of the watchmen, and at once recognised his old acquaintance; but quickly realising that the accusation of theft against a Jaina ascetic would discredit the religion, he solemnly declared before the officials that he had himself given the jewel to the ascetic, a noble soul, who deserved their highest veneration and respect.

VI) The duty of strengthening the loyalty of one's fellowmen to the Jaina faith is illustrated in the story of Vāriṣeṇa, the other-worldly son of Śreṇika, the king of Magadha. Once on a dark night Vāriṣeṇa was absorbed in deep meditation in a desolate cremation ground. Meanwhile, at midnight, a rogue named Mṛgavega stole a costly necklace belonging to a merchant's wife at the instance of his mistress, a courtesan named Magadhasundarī. Pursued by the police, he flung the necklace in front of Vāriṣeṇa and disappeared under cover of darkness. The police, finding the necklace lying near by, suspected Vāriṣeṇa of the theft and reported the matter to the king, who was inexorable in the dispensation of justice, and immediately ordered his son to be punished and tortured as a thief. Vāriṣeṇa calmly suffered the indignities inflicted upon him, eliciting by his fortitude the praise and admiration of the gods, and soon after renounced the world and became an ascetic. Puṣpadanta, the minister's son, was his intimate friend from childhood, and Vāriṣeṇa prevailed upon him to become an ascetic like himself. Puṣpadanta, however, found it difficult to forget his beautiful newly married wife Sudatī in spite of his vow. Twelve years rolled by, and still her memory haunted him day and night. Vāriṣeṇa, fearing that he would one day renounce his vow and return to his wife, hit upon a stratagem, and paid a visit to his mother, the queen Celinī, accompanied by his friend. The queen received both of them cordially, and Vāriṣeṇa asked her to send for her daughters-in law. They were soon ushered to their presence, resplendent in their dress and adornment, and lovely with the fresh beauty of youth. Vāriṣeṇa then requested his mother to send for the wife of his friend Puṣpadanta; but during the long period of her separation from her husband, she had lost her beauty and youth, and when she appeared before them, her ugly, emaciated and worn out figure made a sad contrast to the charming ladies who were standing beside her. The sight was too much for Puṣpadanta to bear, and he asked for leave to depart. In this way Vāriṣeṇa confirmed his friend in the resolution to maintain his vow, and both thereafter continued their austerities together.

VII) The king of Ahicchatra in the Pañcāla country had a learned priest named Somadatta. Once the latter's wife who was expecting the birth of a child expressed a great desire to partake of ripe mangoes at a time when their season had already passed. Somadatta accordingly went in search of mangoes, accompanied by his pupils, and entered the Kālidāsa forest where they saw a large mango tree overloaded with the ripe fruit, as a result of the mystic power of the sage Sumitra who lived under the tree.

Somadatta sent some mangoes to his wife with one of his pupils, but himself remained there spellbound by the teachings of the sage, renounced all worldly aspirations, and became an ascetic. He started austerities on the Nābhigiri mountain in Magadha, and his wife in due course gave birth to a male child and came to her husband with the baby; but finding him utterly indifferent and insensible to family ties, she left the child before him on the rocks and returned home. Meanwhile, a Vidyādhara prince named Bhāskaradeva, who had been ousted from his heritage by his younger brother Purandara, fixed his camp at Balavāhanapura and came with his wife to pay homage to Somadatta, while the latter was engaged in austerities. Taking pity on the child, they adopted him as their own and named him Vajrakumāra. Bhāskaradeva then worshipped the sage and left with the child for Bhāvapura.

Vajrakumāra grew up to be a youth possessing valour and courage, attained the rank of a Vidyādhara and married his uncle's daughter Indumatī.

Once on the Himālayas he rescued Pavanavegā, the wife of a Vidyādhara prince, who was engaged in certain magic rites for attaining the power of assuming a multitude of forms, but was about to be devoured by the Mystic Force in the shape of a huge serpent. Vajrakumāra ultimately married Pavanavegā, and succeeded in restoring his adoptive father to the throne by overthrowing the usurper Purandara. Later on, he visited Somadatta, his real father, who was then practising austerities at Mathurā, renounced the world, and became an ascetic.

About this time at Mathurā there was an orphan girl who, according to a prophecy, was destined to be the chief queen of Pūtikavāhana, the lord of that city. A Buddhist monk, who was acquainted with the prophecy, carefully brought up the girl in a monastery, and she was called in jest Buddhadāsī, 'Buddha's maidservant'. She grew up to be a beautiful young lady, and soon attracted the notice of the king of Mathurā, who won her hand by agreeing to make her his chief queen.

Aurvilā, the first queen of Pūtikavāhana, was in the habit of sending out a ceremonial chariot in honour of the Jaina Saviour on the occasion of the Eight Day's Festival at Mathurā, but the new queen, owing to her Buddhist affinities, used her influence with the king and sought to stop the practice and establish a new festival in honour of the Buddha. Alarmed at the machinations of her co-wife, Aurvilā approached the sage Somadatta and appealed to him to ensure the continuity of the festival of the chariot. Somadatta instructed his son and disciple Vajrakumāra to do the needful.

Vajrakumāra who had attained the supernatural powers of a Vidyādhara went up to the city of the Vidyādharas, and began to descend from the sky with a huge concourse of Vidyādharas, carrying flags and banners, gates, pillars and canopies, mirrors, white parasols and gold jars, and diverse materials of worship. Ladies were singing to the accompaniment of various musical instruments; there was merry-making by dwarfs, hunchbacks, dancers, bards and panegyrists; and charming maidens were carrying lights, censers, perfume and flowers. Decorated cars, chariots, horses and elephants formed part of the company. While the citizens of Mathurā thought that a multitude of gods was coming to take part in the worship of the Buddha, organised by the Buddhist woman, Vajrakumāra with the Vidyādharas took up his residence in the house of Aurvilā, and for eight days caused her chariot to go round the city. Then he erected there a Stūpa marked with the image of the Arhat, and the shrine has ever since been known as "Built by the gods". In this way the designs of the Buddhist woman were foiled and the glorification of the Jaina faith assured through the timely intervention of Vajrakumāra.

VIII) The next story is designed to illustrate the value of sympathy for one's co-religionists, and interesting as a Jaina version of the story of Bali and the Dwarf Incarnation of Viṣṇu. Jayavarman, the king of the city of Viśālā in Avanti, had four ministers headed by Bali, all of whom were heretics. They were Śukra, a Buddhist; Bṛhaspati, a materialist; Prahlādaka, a Śaiva; and their elder brother Bali who was an expert in Vedic lore. Once the Jaina ascetic Akampana, while on a visit to the city, encamped in the public park, and the streets were crowded with citizens going to pay homage to the sage. Seeing this, the king, too, expressed his desire to visit and pay his respects to the sage, but the ministers sought to dissuade him by glorifying their respective faiths. Bali, for instance, extolled the Veda and the Vedic religion, while Prahlādaka emphasized the glory of Śiva and the Śaiva scriptures. Disgusted with the attitude of the ministers, the king mounted on an elephant and betook himself to the camp of the sage. Thereafter offering his salutations, he entered into conversation with the Sūri on religious topics such as the nature of heaven and salvation. Bali who had accompanied the king intervened with the remark that heaven was nothing but the mutual love of a maiden of twelve and a youth of sixteen, and there was no other heaven invisible to the human eye. The sage asked Bali if direct perception was the only proof admitted by him. On his replying in the affirmative, the sage asked him how in that case he would prove the occurrence of the marriage of his own parents or the existence of his forefathers. Bali was very much annoyed at this, and unable to hit upon a plausible reply, he abused the sage in indecent and insulting terms. The king did not say anything then and there for the sake of decency; but returning home, he banished Bali and his brothers from his kingdom on the pretext of some other offence.

Bali with his brothers took refuge in the country of Kurujāṅgala, and he became the chief minister of king Padma of Hastināgapura. There he won the gratitude of the king by vanquishing the latter's enemy Siṁhakīrti who had invaded the city. Bali then obtained the king's permission to set out on an expedition of conquest. Meanwhile, the sage Akampana, accompanied by a huge concourse of monks, had in the course of his wanderings arrived in the vicinity of Hastināgapura, and taken up residence for the rainy season in a large cave of the Hemagiri mountain. Bali, on his return from the expedition, came to know of the whereabouts of his old opponent and decided on revenge. By virtue of a boon conferred upon him by king Padma as a mark of gratitude for the overthrow of Siṁhakīrti, Bali obtained from the prince the entire sovereignty of the kingdom for a certain number of days, during which the king's authority was to be limited to his inner apartments. Bali then began the performance of an Agnihotra sacrifice with intoxicating substances near the camp of Akampana Sūri, with a view to causing annoyance and disturbance to the sage and his followers.

Meanwhile, in the city of Mithilā, a Jaina monk named Bhrājiṣṇu, going out at night, inferred from an observation of the stars that somewhere ascetics were being subjected to maltreatment and oppression. Thereupon the head of the monastery with his supernatural knowledge ascertained the mischief being done by Bali, and asked a devotee named Puṣpakadeva, capable of travelling through the air, to go and request on his behalf the powerful sage Viṣṇu to counteract the evil. The latter, on receipt of the message, immediately proceeded to Hastināpura and appealed to king Padma to give the necessary protection to the oppressed monks, but the king pointed out that Bali, and not he, was reigning at the moment.

The sage Viṣṇu then decided on a crafty manœuvre. Assuming the form of a dwarf, he went to the place where Bali was performing his sacrifice, and began to recite verses of the Veda in a melodious tone. Attracted by his sonorous voice, Bali came out of the sacrificial pavilion and asked him what he desired. The dwarf replied that, having been robbed of his home by his relatives, he wanted only a slice of land measuring three steps, and on hearing this, Bali at once granted his desire. The sage then discarded the guise of a dwarf and began to extend his frame upwards and downwards and athwart, without any limit. He fixed one step on the foundation of the ocean and another in the sky; and not finding room for a third, placed it on Bali and sent him down to the nether regions.

IX) The evil consequences of drinking are illustrated in the following story. A wandering religious mendicant named Ekapād, arriving at the Vindhya forest from the town of Ekacakra on his way to the Ganges, fell in with a crowd of Cāṇḍālas, who were indulging in bouts of drinking and partaking of meat in the company of youthful intoxicated women. The Cāṇḍālas detained the mendicant, and declared that he must, on the pain of death, either drink wine or take meat or become intimate with a woman. The mendicant reflected that the eating of flesh was strictly prohibited in the Law-books, and so was union with a Cāṇḍāla woman, but wine was drunk in the Vedic sacrifice Sautrāmaṇī, and the ingredients of wine such as flour, water and molasses were quite pure. Thus thinking, he preferred to take wine, but under the influence of drink he joined in the merrymaking of the women; and feeling hungry, partook of meat, and soon passion compelled him to desire the company of one of the Cāṇḍāla women.

X) The next story illustrates the advantage of abstention from wine. In the city of Valabhī, a gang of five notorious thieves went out one night during heavy rain, and stole a large quantity of treasure. They, however, fell out while dividing the booty, but soon ceased to quarrel and indulged in drinking bouts. But drink made them quarrel again, and a free fight ensued, resulting in the death of all of them except Dhūrtila. The latter was in the habit of taking a vow of abstention for one day whenever he happened to meet a pious ascetic, and that day he had taken a vow to abstain from wine. Dhūrtila then felt disgusted with the world and shaved his head and became a monk.

XI) The following story is meant to show that even the desire to eat flesh is a sin. Saurasena, the king of the city of Kākandī, had taken a vow of abstention from flesh-eating, but gradually under the influence of the Brahminical faith he became greedy of meat, and secretly employed his cook Karmapriya to procure the flesh of all kinds of animals for his table. Preoccupation with his public duties did not, however, leave him sufficient leisure to satisfy his desire fully.

One day the cook Karmapriya, while in quest of game, died from snake-bite, and after death he became a huge whale in the ocean. The king, on his death, was reborn as a small fish living in the cavity of the whale's ear. The fish noticed that while the whale slept, opening his mouth, large numbers of aquatic animals used to enter the cavity of his throat and go out again. The fish pitied the whale for not being able to devour any of these animals, and said to himself that had he been as big as the whale he would have emptied the ocean of its animals. In the course of time the fish and the whale both died, and were reborn as denizens of hell with the power of remembering their past lives. While in hell the former whale said to the fish: "It was but natural that I should have come here as a result of my sins. But how came you who merely lived upon the filth of my ear?" The fish replied: "On account of my evil thought, more harmful than even the depredations of a whale!"

XII) The next story illustrates the merit of abstention from flesh. There was a Cāṇḍāla named Caṇḍa in the town of Ekānasī in Avanti. One day in the outskirts of the town he put a jar of wine on one side and a plate of meat on the other, and standing in the middle, partook of both in quick succession, while he whirled round a leather thong and struck down birds flying over him. As a result, snake-poison attaching to the beaks of the birds dripped on to the wine, and contaminated the beverage.

Meanwhile two sages possessing the power of travelling through the air descended from the sky to give religious instruction to the people, and the Cāṇḍāla approached and entreated them to assign a suitable vow to him. Thereupon one of the sages asked him to fix a rope in the intervening space between the plate of meat and the jar of wine, and said that the momentary abstention from either that would be caused in going from one extremity to the other would constitute a sufficient vow of abstention for him. The Cāṇḍāla acted accordingly, and after helping himself to the meat, said that he would abstain from it until his return from the other end. He then went towards the wine-jar, drank the wine and died from the effects of poisoning. As a result of the merit accruing even from the momentary abstention from meat, the Cāṇḍāla was reborn as the chief of the Yakṣas in the world of these spirits.

XIII) The following story illustrates the consequences of malevolence: There was a fisherman named Mṛgasena in Śirīṣagrāma in Avanti. One day he entreated a famous sage to assign a religious vow to him, and he was accordingly advised to refrain from killing his first catch on that particular day. The fisherman cast his net and soon caught a huge fish, but remembering the vow assigned to him, let the fish go after attaching to it a strip of cloth for the purpose of recognition. It so happened that he caught the same fish five times in the course of the day, but on each occasion let it go without any harm. His wife Ghaṇṭā was furious to see him return home empty-handed in the evening, and as she shut the door against him, he had to pass the night outside, resting his head on the trunk of a tree. Mṛgasena was bitten by a snake during the night and found dead in the morning. The wife who was now overwhelmed with grief committed suicide by entering the flames on the funeral pyre.

The story now goes on to narrate the rebirth of Mṛgasena. Viśvambhara was the reigning king of Viśālā where lived the merchant Guṇapāla, his wife Dhanaśrī and daughter Subandhu. As ill-luck would have it, the king asked the merchant to give his beautiful and accomplished daughter in marriage to the son of the court jester. Afraid of the disgrace resulting from such a marriage as well as the wrath of the king in case of refusal, Guṇapāla fled with his daughter to Kauśāmbī, leaving his wife, who was with child, in the house of his friend Śrīdatta, a wealthy merchant. The sages Śivagupta and Munigupta happened to see Dhanaśrī in the house of Śrīdatta; and Munigupta having pitied the condition of Dhanaśrī, who was pale and weak and dejected, the other declared that in spite of her present troubles, she would become the mother of a son destined to be a merchant prince and the son-in-law of king Viśvambhara. The merchant Śrīdatta overheard the conversation of the two sages, and, burning with envy, he devised a nefarious plan. No sooner had the child been born than he spread a report that Dhanaśrī had given birth to a dead child. At the same time he secretly summoned a Cāṇḍāla and handed the child to him to be put to death.

The Cāṇḍāla was moved to pity by the beauty of the child, and instead of killing, he left him in a secluded place and went home. The merchant Indradatta, who was the brother-in-law of Śrīdatta, came to know about the child from some cow-boys; and as he was childless, he came to the spot and gave the child to his wife Rādhā to be adopted as their son. Then he celebrated great festivities as if a child had been born unto them.

Śrīdatta heard of the turn things had taken, and devised another plan to kill the child. He went to Indradatta and persuaded him to give him the custody of the child, 'his blessed nephew', whom he would bring up in his own house. Śrīdatta then made over the child to another Cāṇḍāla to be put to death.

The Cāṇḍāla, instead of killing the child, left him in a wood on the bank of a river, and there he was guarded by the cows grazing on the spot. In the evening the cowherds came, and, finding the child, reported the fact to the head of the settlement Govinda, who gave him to his wife and adopted him as his own son. The child grew up to be a handsome youth and was named Dhanakīrti.

One day Śrīdatta happened to come to the place in the course of his commercial transactions, and saw Dhanakīrti in the house of Govinda. He understood everything when he heard the story of the youth, and told Govinda that he had an urgent message to send to his son at home, and requested that Dhanakīrti might be sent as a messenger. Govinda agreed, and Dhanakīrti set out on his journey with Śrīdatta's letter, in which the merchant asked his son Mahābala to kill the youth immediately on his arrival. Dhanakīrti took rest on his way under a mango tree and fell fast asleep. A courtesan named Anaṅgasenā, who was gathering flowers nearby, happened to see the youth and approached him while he was asleep, and seeing a letter suspended from his neck, took it and read it through. Cursing the merchant she substituted for it another letter addressed to his wife and son, in which he was represented as enjoining them to give his daughter Śrīmatī in marriage to Dhanakīrti. The latter woke up after the courtesan's departure; and on arrival at the merchant's house, he delivered the letter to Mahābala and his mother, and was duly married to Śrīmatī.

The strange news reached Śrīdatta who at once returned home and hatched another plot. He posted a hired assassin and a wicked priestess in a desolate shrine of the goddess Durgā in the outskirts of the city, and asked Dhanakīrti to go there at nightfall with some offerings for the idol. Dhanakīrti consented, but Śrīdatta's son Mahābala, seeing him going out alone in the dark, dissuaded him from the visit, as he was a stranger to the place, and offered to go to the shrine himself with the offerings. Dhanakīrti accordingly stayed at home, and Mahābala went and met with death at the assassin's hands in the shrine of Durgā.

Overwhelmed with grief at the death of his son, Śrīdatta communicated the whole story of his conspiracy to his wife, and asked for help to get rid of the unwelcome guest. She promised co-operation, and, taking a number of sweetmeat balls, black and white, mixed the latter with poison, and asked her daughter Śrīmatī to give them to her husband to eat, while the black ones were to be given to her father. She then went away to the river for a bath. Śrīmatī served the sweetmeat balls in her mother's absence, but by mistake gave the poisoned ones to her father, whose death was instantaneous, and followed by that of her mother, who in her grief committed suicide by swallowing some of the poisoned sweets.

Sometime after the death of Śrīdatta and his wife, Dhanakīrti who continued to prosper was one day seen by king Viśvambhara. The latter was struck with the beauty of the young merchant, and decided to give his daughter in marriage to him, thus fulfilling the prophecy made about Dhanakīrtī even before his birth. His father Guṇapāla, hearing reports of his continued luck and prosperity, now came from Kauśāmbī and met his wonderful son. The courtesan Anaṅgasenā also came to see him.

One day the merchant Guṇapāla, accompanied by Dhanakīrti and his family and Anaṅgasenā and Śrīmatī, paid a visit to the sage Yaśodhvaja, and, after obeisance, entreated him to explain the mystery of Dhanakīrti's providential escapes from death and the continued success of his glorious career. The sage pointed out that Dhanakīrti was in his previous birth the fisherman Mṛgasena, and he was now enjoying the fruits of the vow of non-violence which the latter had taken for a day. The courtesan Anaṅgasenā was the fish whose life had been spared by Mṛgasena on the day of his vow, while Śrīmatī was no other than Ghaṇṭā, the wife of Mṛgasena, who had entered the flames after her husband's death. Having heard the story of their previous births, Dhanakīrti, Anaṅgasenā and Śrīmatī, all three, took the vow of renunciation and became ascetics under the Jaina system of discipline, and attained a blessed state after death.

XIV) The following story illustrates the consequences of theft or rather breach of trust. Siṁhasena was the king of Siṁhapura in the land of Prayāga, and Rāmadattā was his chief queen. The learned Śrībhūti who had a great reputation for speaking the truth was his priest, and Śrīdattā was the latter's devoted wife. A young merchant named Bhadramitra, on the eve of a voyage to Suvarṇadvīpa with other merchants, had left seven priceless jewels in the custody of Śrībhūti. Unfortunately, on the return voyage, Bhadramitra suffered shipwreck, but succeeded in reaching the shore by clinging to a floating plank. Having lost his friends and wealth, he was reduced to sore straits, and, arriving destitute at Siṁhapura, went to Śrībhūti and asked for the jewels entrusted to him. But the latter pretended not to recognise him and denied having received any jewels at all. When Bhadramitra persisted in demanding the jewels, Śrībhūti had him dragged to the king's presence, and, accusing him of calumny and defamation, had him repudiated by the king.

Not discouraged in the least, Bhadramitra climbed every night a tamarind tree which stood near the queen's palace, and regularly at dusk and dawn he kept shouting from the top of the tree that Śrībhūti refused to return his jewels, and if the accusation turned out to be false, he (Bhadramitra) might be tortured to death. One evening the queen Rāmadattā, while she was watching the celebration of the Kaumudī festival by the women of the city, heard the plaint of Bhadramitra and devised a plan to test the truth of the charge against Śrībhūti. She invited the latter to a game of dice with her; and, under her instructions, a maidservant went to his wife, and won her confidence by producing certain articles belonging to her husband, which he had lost in the game, and obtained from her the jewels on the pretext that he had sent for them. The ruse succeeded perfectly well and the jewels were immediately taken to the king.

The king mixed up the jewels with those in his treasury and sent for Bhadramitra, and when the latter arrived, he was asked to single out the ones belonging to him. Bhadramitra had no difficulty in finding them, and the king was at once convinced of the guilt of Śrībhūti, and lavishly praised and rewarded the young man for speaking the truth. The king then sent for Śrībhūti, and, after severely reprimanding him for his treachery, ordered that, by way of punishment, he must either swallow a certain quantity of cow-dung or submit to be roughly handled by a number of stalwart wrestlers; otherwise he would have all his property confiscated. Śrībhūti calmly accepted the latter alternative, and was turned out of the city, mounted on an old donkey and wearing a garland of potsherds. As a result of his sins, he was attacked with leprosy, and put an end to his life by entering the flames. He was reborn as a serpent, and after causing the death of many creatures, expired and became a denizen of hell.

XV) The following story illustrates the disastrous consequences of falsehood: Ayodhana was the king of Hastināgapura and his queen was Atithi. Sulasā was their daughter, and she had been betrothed by her mother to Prince Madhupiṅgala of Paudanapura even before her birth. The king, however, decided to hold a Svayaṁvara for her to choose a husband, and issued invitations to a number of princes including Madhupiṅgala and Sagara. The latter was the lord of Ayodhyā and sent a highly cultured nurse named Mandodarī and the priest Viśvabhūti to win over Sulasā before the Svayaṁvara took place. They came to Hastināgapura, and Mandodarī managed to become a teacher of the harem, and influenced Sulasā in favour of Sagara. The priest, on the other hand, ingratiated himself with the king and the queen, and created in their minds a dislike for Madhupiṅgala. When the Svayaṁvara took place and the suitors came, Sulasā under the influence of Mandodarī chose Sagara and not Madbupiṅgala as her husband.

Madhupiṅgala in his grief became an ascetic, and arriving at Ayodhyā in the course of his wanderings, happened to take rest at the gateway of Sagara's palace. The priest Viśvabhūti was at the time giving lessons in prognostics to his disciple Śivabhūti, who observed the mendicant and expressed surprise at the contrast between his physical characteristics and his wretched condition, and spoke disparagingly of the science they were studying. Viśvabhūti, however, explained to his pupil the story of Madhupiṅgala and how he had become an ascetic owing to his failure to win the hand of Sulasā who had preferred Sagara. Madhupiṅgala felt grievously insulted at these remarks of his old enemy, and when, after death, he was reborn as the demon Kālāsura, he vowed vengeance against Viśvabhūti as well as Sagara, and waited for a suitable opportunity to carry out his designs.

Viśvāvasu was the king of the city of Svastimatī and Vasu was his son. The learned Kṣīrakadamba was the priest of the king and Parvata was his son. One day the priest was expounding the ethical principles of the scriptures to his disciples Vasu, Parvata, and Nārada, who was the son of the priest of another king. Two sages Anantagati and Amitagati happened to see them, and while the former expressed his admiration for the teacher and his disciples, the latter remarked that two of them were likely to reverse in practice the teachings of the sacred texts. The priest heard these remarks and interpreted them to mean that two of the group would go to hell and the two others to heaven. He thought it most unlikely that he, a pious man, would go to hell, while he was certain that Vasu would, for that was where princely power led to. He was not sure about the fate of Nārada and Parvata; so with a view to testing their virtue and intelligence, he created by magic two lambs and gave one to each of them, with instructions to kill the animals and eat the flesh at a place where no one could see him. Parvata took his lamb to a secluded enclosure behind the house of his father, killed it and roasted and partook of the flesh. Nārada, on the other hand, pondered over the injunction about a place where no one could see him; and concluding that there could be no place, whether in a town or in a forest, where one could be beyond the range of one's own eyes or the eyes of the gods or the omniscient minds of the great sages, he refrained from killing his lamb and returned it to his teacher.

After this incident, the priest Kṣīrakadamba renounced the world and became an ascetic, and died by fasting. After his death Nārada came on a visit to Parvata, his old friend and companion. One day Parvata was expounding the text *ajair yaṣṭavyam* to some pupils, and interpreted the word '*aja*' as 'goat,' so that the text would mean 'Sacrifices should be made with the flesh of goats'. Nārada intervened and pointed out that their departed teacher had interpreted the word to mean 'grains three years old', and that was the correct explanation. Parvata disputed the truth and accuracy of this statement, and both agreed that they should request prince Vasu to act as umpire, and accept his ruling as final.

Nārada and Parvata then went to Vasu who received them cordially and undertook to give his decision on the morrow. Meanwhile, the widow of the priest Kṣīrakadamba, who was aware that he had interpreted the word in the sense mentioned by Nārada, betook herself to Vasu; and in her anxiety to save her son from disgrace, reminded the prince of a certain boon that he had promised to her, and demanded that he should now fulfil his promise, by bearing testimony to the truth of the interpretation put forward by Parvata. Vasu knew that Parvata's statement was wrong, and that he would go to hell if he supported him, but he was bound by his promise to Parvata's mother and decided to abide by his pledged word. Next morning Vasu came to his court and occupied his famous crystal throne; and on an appeal by Nārada to speak the truth, declared that Parvata's interpretation was the right one. Disaster followed this false declaration, for amid the lamentation of the citizens Vasu, as he was seated on his throne, went down to hell. Even now, at the time of the first oblation of the day, people say "Rise up, Vasu; ascend to heaven."

Nārada was deeply aggrieved at the turn events had taken, and, feeling disgusted with the world, became an ascetic and devoted himself to meditation. The citizens in their fury rushed upon Parvata, to whom they attributed the downfall of their king, and, after pelting him with stones, and mercilessly whipping him, drove him out of the city, half-dead, mounted on a donkey, and compelled to wear a wreath of potsherds round his neck. Parvata took refuge in a dense forest, and there on the bank of a stream he was seen by Kālāsura, who approached him and won his confidence by representing himself to be his father's friend Śāṇḍilya. Parvata told him his story, how after the death of his father he had been addicted to drink, meat and courtesans, and gave a wrong interpretation of the text *ajair yaṣṭavyam* knowing it to be false, down to his dispute with Nārada and its unhappy sequel.

Kālāsura consoled Parvata and asked him to take heart and join him in a new venture. He persuaded Parvata to insert in the Vedic texts injunctions sanctioning various sacrifices involving slaughter of animals, use of wine, and moral laxity and perversion. He then came to Ayodhyā, and in the outskirts of the city assumed the form of the god Brahman, and commenced a vast sacrifice at which Parvata acted as the Adhvaryu or officiating priest. Magic forms of sages like Piṅgala, Manu, Mataṅga, Marīci and Gautama recited Vedic *mantras*, while Parvata propounded the doctrine that the animals were created for sacrifices, and killing at sacrifices was not tantamount to killing, since sacrifices contributed to the good of all. Goats, birds, elephants, horses and other animals were accordingly killed at the sacrifice and their flesh offered as oblations in the fire. Kālāsura by his magic showed the slain animals as going about in heaven in aerial cars, and the phantom sages proclaimed the glory of the phenomenon.

The exploits of Kālāsura created a sensation among the people and attracted the notice of Sagara and Viśvabhūti, who were also induced by him to sacrifice animals and partake of their flesh. Kālāsura then reminded them of the wrong they had done him during his previous birth, and murdered both by throwing them into the sacrificial fire amidst the oblations. Parvata continued to kill numerous animals for sacrificial purposes, but Kālāsura disappeared soon after. Helpless and miserable without his friend, Parvata suffered and died and went to hell.

XVI) The story of Kaḍārapiṅga and Padmā is meant to illustrate the consequences of illicit passion. Dharṣaṇa was the king of Benares and Ugrasena was his minister. Puṣya was the king's priest, and he had a beautiful young wife named Padmā. Kaḍārapiṅga, the son of the minister, was a misguided and dissolute youth, who one day saw Padmā, while walking in the streets with his boon-companions, and was at once enamoured of her. There was an old nurse named Taḍillatā, and she was persistently implored by the young man to help him to fulfil his heart's desire. The nurse thought it advisable to consult Ugrasena about his son's request, but the minister who was in his dotage openly encouraged her in the evil project.

The nurse visited Padmā's house, delighted her with her conversation, and became very intimate with the young woman. One day after some preliminary remarks on free love, she described to her the young man's ardent love for her and the suffering caused by his passion. Padmā pretended to agree to the bawd's proposal, and the chances of the minister's son looked bright indeed.

Meanwhile, the minister Ugrasena who favoured the criminal intentions of his son devised a scheme to ensure the absence of Padmā's husband from the city, on a prolonged mission. He told the king that, in a cave near the Ratnaśikhaṇḍa peak of the Himālayas, there was a marvellous bird called Kiṁjalpa, variegated in colour, and capable of talking like a man, the possession of which had a magic effect on the fortunes of the lucky owner. He further suggested that he and the priest Puṣya who knew the place might be sent in quest of the bird. The king dissuaded the minister from going owing to his great age, and ordered that the priest should undertake the journey alone.

While Puṣya was preparing to start, Padmā explained to him the real motive behind the proposed expedition, and asked him to make a show of departure and return secretly at night and remain concealed at home. He followed the instructions of his wife; and one night, according to a pre-arranged plan, the bawd brought over the minister's son to Padmā's house and introduced the young man to her. She asked both of them to seat themselves on a sofa, cunningly placed over a deep pit; and as soon as they sat down, they fell headlong to the bottom of the pit, and there they remained imprisoned, living on the remains of boiled rice left over by the household.

After some time, Padmā made it known that her husband would arrive in a few days with the Kiṁjalpa bird and the female spirit, its mother. She then caused the young man and the bawd to be put in a cage, after their bodies had been painted with various colours and decked with the feathers of diverse kinds of birds. The cage was then removed to a wood near the city and left in charge of Puṣya, who was dressed in travelling attire, as if he had returned from a journey. Padmā, meanwhile, dressed herself in a manner becoming a woman whose husband was abroad, and set out to receive Puṣya in company with her girl friends, who were all talking about the 'exploit' of her husband. On the following day Puṣya accompanied by his wife, proceeded to the royal palace with the precious load and asked the king to behold the Kiṁjalpa and the mother bird. The king scrutinized the pair, and saying that he could see only Kaḍārapiṅga and the bawd Taḍillatā in the cage, demanded an explanation of the mystery. Padmā then recounted the whole story, and the king praised and honoured her with rich presents, and sent her home in a chariot drawn by Brāhmaṇas, expert in Vedic lore. As for Kaḍārapiṅga and his father Ugrasena, their shameful intrigue was proclaimed before the people, and they were banished from the city. The young profligate, after long suffering the consequences of his sin, died and went to hell.

XVII) The following story is meant to illustrate the sin of unlawful possession. In the city of Kāmpilya in the Pañcāla country there was a merchant named Sāgaradatta who was, in spite of his wealth, a notorious miser, and went to ridiculous lengths in effecting economies and avoiding expenditure. The king of the place, whose name was Ratnaprabha, desiring to build a pavilion for witnessing elephant-races, selected for the purpose the site of a ruined palace belonging to a former king, and ordered the debris to be cleared. The bricks of the delapidated palace were of gold, but as they had lost their lustre, the king took them for ordinary bricks and employed workmen to heap them together in another place for erecting a temple. The workmen while carrying the bricks happened to drop one of them on the roadside, and the miser, finding it there, took it home and put it at the place where he used to wash his feet. The dirt having been removed by the daily friction of his feet, the brick regained its original colour, and the miser, seeing that the bricks were of gold, bribed the workmen and acquired as many of the bricks as he could.

One day the miser had to go to the city of Kākandī where his sister's son had died, but at the time of his departure he gave instructions to his son Sudatta to collect the bricks in his absence in the same fashion as he had done. Sudatta was, however, above such meanness; and when his father, on his return, asked him how many of the bricks he had managed to acquire, he replied that he had done nothing of the kind.

The miser was shocked to hear this, and condemning his own feet which had taken him to the hated town of Kākandī, he mercilessly pounded them with a slab of stone. The king, who had come to know about these happenings, had the bricks scraped by artisans; and convinced that they were of gold, he ordered the confiscation of the miser's property and banished him from the city. Sudatta was, on the other hand, provided with capital to carry on his business, and his ancestral home was returned to him as a reward for his honesty. The miser, who was known as Piṇyākagandha, 'one who smells of oil-cakes,' suffered on account of his sins and went to hell after his death.

Apart from the stories outlined above, there are allusions to certain popular tales in Book IV. The story of Kāñcanikā is cited to illustrate the inscrutable nature of women: she is said to have killed her husband, son and paramour, and then immolated herself on the funeral pyre of her husband[1]. The story of the merchant's wife and Mūladeva, and that of

1 इहैव वात्स्यायनगोत्रजस्य पुत्री भृगोः काञ्चनिकेतिनाम्नी । पतिं च पुत्रं च विटं च हत्वा भर्त्रा तु सार्धं दहनं विवेश ॥

Upādhyāyikā, although they are folktales, are mentioned by Somadeva along with wellknown mythological stories, and will be found in Chap. XVII. The following 'ancient tradition' cited in Book IV forms part of a popular tale related in the commentary:

यदर्थे च मही त्यक्ता जीविताधँ च हारितम् । सा मां त्यजति निःस्नेहा कः स्त्रीणां वल्लभो नरः ॥

The story, as given by Śrutasāgara, is as follows. The daughter of the king of Pāṭaliputra was married by the son of another king, but soon after the marriage the father of the girl fell ill, and the sacrifice of the daughter was recommended by a Tantric teacher as the only means of the king's recovery. Hearing this, the husband of the girl fled with her to a forest where she was bitten by a serpent. The prince was about to commit suicide from grief, but the sylvan deities interfered and told him that his bride would revive if he gave her half of his life-span. He agreed and the bride at once came to life, and they both continued their journey and reached a town. There the prince fell asleep in a hospice, and meanwhile a fellow named Devakeśin enticed the girl away. When the husband woke up, he saw her entering the town with the man, and a quarrel ensued over the possession of the girl, who, however, claimed the stranger as her husband. Thereupon the prince demanded back the portion of the life-span which he had given her, and the wicked woman at once dropped dead. The bystanders having asked for an explanation of these strange happenings, the prince uttered the verse quoted above: 'She for whom I had renounced the earth and given away half my life left me without pity. Who can ever be dear to women?'[1]

As we have already stated, several of the stories summarized above are met with in earlier works. The eight stories in Book VI meant to illustrate the different aspects of Samyaktva are, for instance, stock illustrations, and briefly referred to in Samantabhadra's *Ratnakaraṇḍakaśrāvakācāra* 1. 19, 20,[2] the stories being summarized in Prabhācandra's commentary on the work. They were thus wellknown in Samantabhadra's time, and that they are much earlier than Samantabhadra[3] seems also certain. Kundakunda, who lived about the first century A. D., mentions, for instance, Bhavyasena, one of the principal characters of the fourth story of our collection, in *Bhāvaprābhṛta* (verse 52), the typical instance of a man who failed to become a true monk despite his knowledge of all branches of the Scriptures.[4]

1 For another version of the story see *Pañcatantra*, Book IV.

2 तावदञ्जनचौरोऽङ्गे ततोऽनन्तमतिः स्मृता । उद्दायनस्तृतीयेऽपि तुरीये रेवती मता ॥ ततो जिनेन्द्रभक्तोऽन्यो वारिषेणस्ततः परः । विष्णुश्च वज्रनामा च शेषयोर्लक्ष्यतां गताः ॥

3 Samantabhadra is believed to be earlier than the fifth century A. D. See Pt. Yugalkisore's Introduction (in Hindi) to *Ratna-karaṇḍaka-śrāvakācāra*, p. 142.

4 अंगाइं दस य दुण्णि य चउद्दसपुव्वाइं सयलसुयणाणं । पढिओ अ भव्वसेणो ण भावसवणत्तणं पत्तो ॥

As regards the other stories, there is no doubt that the story of Sagara and Madhupiṅgala with the intermediate one of Vasu, Parvata and Nārada is a very old one. The case of Madhupiṅgala is referred to by Kundakunda in *Bhāvaprābhṛta* (verse 45).[1] The entire story including the episode of Vasu is narrated in detail in *Vasudevahiṇḍī*, a comprehensive Prākrit prose romance earlier than the seventh century,[2] to illustrate the origin of what is politely called the 'non-Aryan' Vedas.[3] The episode of Vasu is as old as the Mahābhārata and appears to be the oldest portion of the legend. It seems to have been incorporated in the Jaina story owing to the lesson of *ahiṁsā* conveyed by it, and provides another instance of Jaina adaptation of Brahmanical stories. The original story as related in the Mahābhārata (Śāntiparva, chap. 335 ff.) is as follows.

"Vasu was a great king of the Satya Age, also known as Uparicara, a disciple of Bṛhaspati and an ardent devotee of Viṣṇu, who worshipped the deity according to the tenets of the Sātvata or Pañcarātra system. An *aśvamedha* performed by him was remarkable for the fact that no animals were killed in the sacrifice, the oblations being made with the produce of the forest. Once while travelling through the sky, he was asked to act as umpire in a debate, which took place between the gods and the sages about the interpretation of the word *aja* in the statement that sacrifices should be performed with *ajas*. The gods maintained that the word meant 'goats', while according to the sages, it meant 'grains of corn'. Vasu out of partiality for the gods, gave the decision in favour of the latter, whereupon the sages cursed and condemned him to a life in the nether regions. While living under the earth, Vasu was nourished by a stream of clarified butter poured for him by the priests as an oblation in sacrifices, which gave it the name of *vasordhārā* 'the stream of Vasu'. Advised by the gods, Vasu continued to worship Viṣṇu even in the nether regions, and favoured by him, he regained his freedom and ascended to Brahmaloka." The story of Vasu is also referred to in the Anuśāsanaparva 6. 34, where it is stated that he went to hell for speaking even a single falsehood. A variation of the story occurs in *Matsyapurāṇa*, chap. 143, where the lesson drawn is not so much the danger of falsehood as that of rash judgment in religious matters.

Jinasena I narrates in his *Harivaṃśapurāṇa* written in 783 A. D. several stories mentioned above: the story of Vasu, Nārada and Parvata in 17. 38 ff. and that of Sagara and Madhupiṅgala in 23. 45 ff., the story of the sage Viṣṇu and Bali in 20. 1 ff. and that of the priest Śrībhūti and and his punishment in 27. 20 ff. Some of these stories are found in the Bṛhat-Kathākośa of Hariṣena written in 931–32 A. D.

---

1 महुपिंगो णाम मुणी देहाहारादिचत्तवावारो । सबणत्तणं ण पत्तो णियाणमित्तेण भवियणुय ॥
2 *Annals of the B. O. R. I.*, Vol. XVI, p. 32.
3 Book V (सोमसिरिलंभो).

A variation of the story of Vajrakumāra occurs in Hemacandra's *Pariśiṣṭaparva* (Canto XII), which, though later than Somadeva's *Yaśastilaka*, used old materials. Here, too, Vajra appears in the role of defender of the Jaina faith against the Buddhist community, although the place and circumstances are different. Somadeva's account is doubtless of greater importance as being connected with a wellknown historical monument, the Jaina Stūpa of Mathurā. It will be interesting to compare it with the version recorded by Hemacandra.

"The king (of Purī) was a Buddhist, and so were part of the inhabitants, while the majority of them were Jainas. As the two rival sects were continually competing with each other, the Jainas, being richer than their rivals, bought up all flowers so that the Buddhists could get none to offer in their temples. But the Buddhists induced the king to issue a strict order that no flowers should be sold to the Jainas. In this calamity the latter entreated Vajra to help them; for the Paryuṣaṇāparvan was drawing near, when the laity used to worship the images of the Arhats with flowers.

Promising his aid, Vajra went through the air to the town of Maheśvara, and entering the park of Hutāśana he met the gardener Taḍit who was a friend of his. Feeling greatly honoured by Vajra's visit, the gardener inquired with what he could serve him, and being told that flowers were wanted, he promised twenty lakhs of flowers. Vajra ordered him to have them ready against his return, and then flew through the air to the Himālaya, and thence to the Padmahrada, the residence of Śrīdevī. There he met the goddess who held in her hand a lotus to worship the gods with, but she gladly gave it to Vajra when he asked for it.

Returning to Hutāśana's park he produced by magic a divine car, in which he placed the lotus given by Śrī and round it the twenty lakhs of flowers brought together by his friend Taḍit. Accompanied by the Jṛmbhaka gods in their cars, whom he had called up to attend him on his journey through the air, he travelled towards Purī. When he and his train were just above the town, the Buddhists believed that the gods descended from heaven to worship the Buddha images. But great was their disappointment when the celestial train landed in a Jaina temple. Never has Paryuṣaṇāparvan been celebrated with such splendour as then at Purī. The miracles just related induced the king and his subjects to embrace the Jaina faith."[1]

The last but one story of the series, that of Padmā, is a tale of the trapping of a libertine by a chaste woman, and resembles the story of Vararuci's wife Upakośā and the plight of her lovers, recorded in *Kathāsaritsāgara*, Canto IV. As we have seen, the story, as related by Somadeva, is in the form of dramatic dialogues linked by narrative passages, and might easily be converted into a little play.[2]

---

1 Jacobi: *Pariśiṣṭaparvan*, p. xcvi.

2 See chap. IV.

CHAPTER XVII

Myths and Legends

JAINA LEGENDS OF MATHURĀ

Of the several legends recorded by Somadeva, that of the famous Jaina Stūpa of Mathurā is of outstanding interest, and narrated in detail in *Yaśastilaka* Book VI, sections 17, 18.[1] It is wellknown that the ruins of the ancient Stūpa were discovered in the course of excavations at the Kaṅkālī Ṭīlā standing in the angle between the Agra and Govardhan roads during the season 1889–90.[2] Somadeva gives an entirely different version of the story of foundation of the Stūpa from that recorded in Jinaprabhasūri's *Tīrthakalpa*, a work of the fourteenth century, and made known by Bühler many years ago. Somadeva is nearly four hundred years earlier than Jinaprabha, and probably records the earliest known version of the legend of the Stūpa, which was regarded as of divine origin as early as the second century A. D. An inscription of the year 79, engraved on the left hand portion of the base of a large standing figure of a Jina found in the Kaṅkālī mound in the season 1890–91, records the fact that an image of the Tīrthaṁkara Aranātha was set up at the Stūpa, "built by the gods" (*thūpe devanirmite*). "The sculpture belongs to the Kushān period, and the mode in which the date is expressed shows that the year 79 must be referred to the era used by the great Kushān kings. This year 79 falls within the reign of Vāsudeva, one of whose inscriptions is expressly dated in the year 80." The important thing to note is that when the inscription in question was executed, "not later than A. D. 157 (79+78)", the Jaina Stūpa of Mathurā was already so old that it was regarded as the work of the gods. "It was probably, therefore, erected several centuries before the Christian era, and may have been at least as ancient as the oldest Buddhist Stūpa."[3] According to Jinaprabha, the Stūpa was built by the goddess Kuberā for two Jaina saints named Dharmaruci and Dharmaghoṣa, and among the idols installed in its precincts the chief was that of Supārśvanātha. The Stūpa was originally of gold, but later encased in brick as a safeguard against pillage. In the eighth century it was repaired by Bappabhaṭṭi Sūri, and at his request provided with a stone dome by King Āma.[4] According to Somadeva, on the other hand, the Stūpa was founded by the saint Vajrakumāra,

---

1 See Chapter XVI.

2 See Vincent Smith: *The Jaina Stūpa and other Antiquities of Mathurā*, Allahabad, 1901.

3 Smith (op. cit.), pp. 12, 13.

4 Introduction to Pandit's edition of *Gaüḍavaho*, p. cliii

Worship of the Stūpa by Kinnaras and Suparṇas, see p. 433.

Procession on its way to the Stūpa, see p. 433.

Exploring the Śiva Linga, see p. 433.
(Rajaputana Musuem, Ajmer)

son of Somadatta, during the reign of Putikavāhana, and there is no reference to its ever being made of gold.

The Jaina Stūpa of Mathurā seems to have existed in Somadeva's time, as is apparent from his statement that "the shrine is still known by the name of *Devanirmita*, "Built by the Gods".[1] It may also be noted in this connection that the colossal image of Pārśvanātha, seated in meditation, found in the Kaṅkālī mound at Mathurā in 1889, and bearing an inscription dated Saṁvat 1036 or 980 A. D.,[2] was possibly built and installed within Somadeva's lifetime. The discovery of another colossal image of a Jina, also seated in meditation, at the same site, and bearing an inscription dated Saṁvat 1134 or 1078 A. D.,[3] gives evidence of the continuity of Jaina religious life at Mathurā sixty years after the sack of the city by Mahmud of Ghazni in 1018 A. D. As Dr. Führer says, "these ancient temples were used by the Jainas during the greater part of the eleventh century, and their destruction happened in very late times".[4] As regards the great Stūpa, its site is at present a bare flat mound without any semblance of an ancient edifice on its surface. But a sculpture on a Toraṇa lintel from the Kaṅkālī Ṭīlā, now preserved in the Lucknow Museum (J 535), shows the Stūpa as being worshipped by Kinnaras and Suparṇas (half birds and half men), and gives us an idea of the general appearance of the monument as it originally stood. The reverse side of the lintel represents a procession probably on its way to the Stūpa (see illustrations). Vincent Smith describes the piece of masonry as the central portion of the lowest beam of a Toraṇa archway in the railing round a Stūpa, and says that it may have belonged to the ancient Stūpa, and is certainly an early work, probably to be dated about 100 or 50 B. C.[5]

The existence of Jaina temples at Mathurā, called Uttaramathurā to distinguish it from Dakṣiṇamathurā or Madura in the Pāṇḍya country, is attested by another reference in *Yaśastilaka* VI. 10.[6] Two temples were, in fact, discovered under the Kankālī Ṭīlā. In the Museum Report for 1890–91 Dr. Führer writes that an inscription, incised on an oblong slab, gives the name

---

1 'अत एवाद्यापि तत्तीर्थं देवनिर्मिताख्यया प्रथते ।' Vol. II, p. 315.

2 Now in the Provincial Museum, Lucknow, J 143. The date is variously read as 1038 and 1036. Smith (op. cit.), p. 4 and Agrawala: *Guide-Book to the Archaeological Section of the Provincial Museum*, p. 13. In the text of the inscription sent to me by Dr. Agrawala the date is given as 1036.

3 J 145, Provincial Museum, Lucknow.

4 Smith (op. cit.), p. 4.

5 Smith (op. cit.), p. 22.

6 'उत्तरमथुरायां जिनेन्द्रमन्दिरवन्दारुहृदयदोहदवर्ती वर्तेऽहम् ।'

of the founder of one of the temples; and as its characters do not differ much from those used in the earliest dated inscriptions of the Indo-Scythic period, he infers that one of the edifices was built before 150 B. C.[1]

The legend of the Jaina Stūpa of Mathurā, as recorded by Somadeva, is also important as throwing light on the rivalry between the Jaina and Buddhist communities at the epoch of the foundation of the Stūpa.[2] It is obvious from the legend that the Buddhist wife of Pūtikavāhana sought to abolish the Jaina Eight-day festival at Mathurā and replace it by a celebration in honour of the Buddha. Her attempt was foiled by Vajrakumāra, and the foundation of the Stūpa bears testimony to the unhindered celebration of the great Jaina festival at Mathurā.

Legends relating to certain pious Jainas of Mathurā occur in *Yaśastilaka.* That of Revatī, wife of king Varuṇa, famous for her unflinching devotion to the Jaina faith, is given in detail in VI. 11.[3] In Book IV Somadeva refers to the story of Arhaddāsa, who, though a householder, showed the resolution of an ascetic, when he continued his meditation unperturbed even at the sight of the sufferings caused to his family by some hostile deities.[4] Aurvilā, the pious Jaina wife of king Pūtikavāhana of Mathurā, who had to contend against the machinations of her young Buddhist co-wife, figures prominently in the legend of the great Stūpa.

OTHER JAINA LEGENDS

In Book IV occurs a reference to the story of the sage Puruhūta of Pāṭaliputra, who was once a king, but had abdicated in favour of his son and become an ascetic: even during his austerities he could not repress his martial spirit when he heard that his son was waging war against his enemies.[5]

In Book I Somadeva refers to the temptation of the monk Rathanemi who gave up his austerities on witnessing the performance of a nautch-girl.[6] Rathanemi was the brother of the great ascetic Ariṣṭanemi, and his story occurs in *Uttarādhyayanasūtra*, chap. XXII; but, in the latter text, he feels tempted at the sight of his brother's discarded bride Rājīmatī at a lonely spot. Śrutasāgara, on the other hand, in his commentary on *Yaśastilaka*, says that Rathanemi was a teacher of the Digambara sect, and married a nautch-girl, a girl of the potter caste, and a princess in succession,

---

1 Smith (op. cit.), p. 3.

2 See Bṛhat-Kathā-kośa of Hariṣeṇa, Story No. 12.

3 See Chap. XVI.

4 'यथा उत्तरमथुरायां निशाप्रतिमास्थितस्त्रिदिवसूत्रितकलत्रपुत्रमित्रोपद्रवोऽप्येकत्वभावनमानसोऽर्हद्दासः ।' p. 137.

5 'कुसुमपुरे चरादाकर्णितसुतसमरस्थितिरातापनयोगयुतोऽपि पुरुहूतदेवर्षिः ।' Ibid.

6 'रथनेमेश्च नटीनर्तनदर्शनात् ।' Vol. I, p. 109.

and took also the religious vow as often. The story, according to Śrutasāgara, is found in a *Kathākośa*.

In Book IV Somadeva refers to the early Jaina legend of the burning of Dvārakā by the sage Dvaipāyana.[1] The episode is clearly mentioned in the *Antagaḍadasāo*, Book V; and the *Harivaṁśapurāṇa* of Jinasena I, composed in 783 A. D., narrates in detail how the city was burnt to ashes by the sage, as a revenge for being assaulted by the Yādava young men under the influence of drink (canto 61). The name of the sage is Dīvāyaṇa in the Ardhamāgadhī text and Dvīpāyana in the Harivaṁśapurāṇa. Two other Jaina legends are cited in Book IV to illustrate the view that the doing of something different from what one resolves or promises to do does not cause any harm, provided it is harmless to others. There is a scriptural tradition (*pravacana*) that a king of Mithilā named Padmaratha once set out on a journey apparently to worship the pontiff Vāsupūjya, but his real object was to become a leader of the Jaina church.[2] Similarly, a young merchant named Sukumāra, who wished to renounce the world, had promised to his mother that he would do so after passing a day with each of his five hundred wives, but carried out his resolution sooner on hearing from a sage that he was not destined to live long.[3]

NON-JAINA LEGENDS

a) Brahmā, Viṣṇu and the Śivaliṅga

The dispute of Brahmā and Viṣṇu about the extent of the Śivaliṅga is mentioned in a verse, quoted by Somadeva from an earlier text in Book V.[4] The story is also referred to in Śrīharṣa's *Naiṣadhacarita* 10. 51 and narrated in detail in *Skandapurāṇa*.[5] It is noteworthy that there are important sculptural representations of the legend. In one of the cave-temples of Ellora,[6] Śiva is depicted 'inside a *liṅga* with flames issuing from the side of it. Viṣṇu is represented below on the right as Varāha the boar-*avatāra*, digging down to see if he can reach the base of the great *liṅga*; having failed to do so, he is also represented as worshipping it. On the other side is Brahmā ascending to discover the top of it, which he also failed to do, and stands as a

---

1 'किं नु खल्वज्ञो द्वैपायनो येन स तादृशं कर्म समाचचार ।' Vol. II, p. 139. See Bṛhat-kathā-kośa of Hariṣeṇa, Story No. 118.

2 See Bṛhat-kathā-kośa, No. 51.

3 'तथा च प्रवचनम्—वासुपूज्यभगवतो वन्दनामिषेण गतो मिथिलानगरीनाथः पद्मरथो बभूव गणधरदेवः । मातुः कानिचिद्दिनानि दन्तारोऽपि पञ्चशतयुवतिरतिमारः सुकुमारश्च साधयामासाभिमतम् ।' See also Śrutasāgara's comm. thereon, p. 72.

4 See Chap. XVIII for the verse in question.

5 See Handiqui: *Naishadhacarita*, Notes, p. 410.

6 Cave XV.

worshipper."[1] Similarly, in a beautiful sculpture preserved in the Rajputana Museum, Ajmer, and assigned to the tenth or eleventh century, Brahmā with a long beard is represented as soaring upwards, and Viṣṇu as diving below, to explore the top and the base of the *liṅga* respectively. After their failure, Brahmā is shown as standing on one side of it and Viṣṇu on the other.[2]

b) 'Necessity knows no law'

In Book IV Yaśodhara's mother, in her plea for animal sacrifices for one's wellbeing, says that 'the great sage' Gautama killed even his benefactor Nāḍījaṅgha to save his own life, and Viśvāmitra killed a dog for the same purpose.[3] Somadeva here tampers with two stories found in the Mahābhārata, Śāntiparva (section on *āpaddharma*). Gautama was really a degenerate Brahman who killed the divine crane Nāḍījaṅgha, perceiving no other means of sustenance, despite the great favours conferred on him by the bird. He is severely condemned in the Mahābhārata for ingratitude. Viśvāmitra, on the other hand, partook of dog's flesh in the house of a Cāṇḍāla, and yet incurred no sin, because he did so for the purpose of self-preservation during a famine. The story of Viśvāmitra feeding on dog's flesh is also referred to in *Manusmṛti* 10. 108. It may be noted that Śrutasāgara in his commentary invents fanciful stories to explain these allusions.

c) Women and the practice of religion

A group of traditional stories (*śruti*) is referred to in the message of Amṛtamati to Yaśodhara in Book IV, bearing on the duty of women to accompany their husbands in the practice of religion. She cites the wellknown instances of Rāma and Sītā, Draupadī and Arjuna, Sudakṣinā and Dilīpa, Lopāmudrā and Agastya, Arundhatī and Vasiṣṭha, Reṇukā and Jamadagni. On the other hand, the danger of women engaging in religious austerities, however rigorous, unaccompanied by their husbands, is illustrated by the little known story of a Brahmin woman named Brahmabandhū, who, although she was fasting unto death, at Prayāga, was associated by scandal with a monk named Govinda.[4]

---

1 Burgess: *A Guide to Elura Cave Temples* (Reprint), p. 28.

2 The sculpture was examined by me during my visit to Ajmer in October, 1941. No catalogue was then available. See the illustration.

3 'किमङ्ग महामुनिर्गौतमः प्राणत्राणार्थमात्मोपकारिणमपि नाडीजङ्घं न जघान । विश्वामित्रः सारमेयम् ।' p. 124.

4 'तथाच श्रुतिः—किल वानप्रस्थभावेऽपि रामस्य सीता सधर्मचारिण्यासीत् । द्रौपदी धनंजयस्य......रेणुका च जमदग्नेरिति । ....यथा प्रयागे प्रायोपवेशनस्थितापि ब्रह्मबन्धूब्राह्मणी गोविन्देन परिव्राजा सह किल परीवादभागिनी बभूवेति ।' p. 149

d) Effect of calumny

The evil that can be done by popular report, however false, is illustrated by another group of traditional stories (*laukikī śrutiḥ*) in Book IV. It is said that the sage Bṛhaspati was once refused admission to Indra's council-chamber owing to a false accusation brought against him by a gambler in the city of Cuṅkāra. A monk named Cakrapāṇi was debarred from entering Benares, because a minstrel named Ṣajaka, having failed to obtain a share in his earnings, spread a report that the monk was in the habit of devouring children. An ascetic named Mārkaṇḍa was excluded from the hermitages of anchorites, because he lived among drunkards, even though he used to drink only water.[1]

e) Wisdom no bar to moral transgression

The above group of legends is followed by another, designed to show that even the wise at times commit offences, regardless of consequences. The crime of the sage Dvaipāyana is mentioned first. We are then told that Rāvaṇa abducted Sītā, even though he was presumably acquainted with the story of Dāṇḍakya in the Nītiśāstras.[2] The latter story occurs in the Rāmāyaṇa, Uttarakāṇḍa, Chap. 80, 81, where it is related how king Daṇḍa and his kingdom were destroyed by the sage Bhārgava as a punishment for violating the latter's daughter Arajā. The legend of Daṇḍa is also treated in detail in *Vāmanapurāṇa*, Chap. 63 ff. and mentioned in *Kāmasūtra* 1. 2. 44.

The wellknown stories of Nahuṣa's insult to the sages and Brahmā's passion for his own daughter are next referred to. Then comes the story of how Vararuci carried a pitcher of wine for the sake of a courtesan.[3] The source of the story is obscure, but it seems to be a variation of a legend recorded in Hemacandra's *Pariśiṣṭaparva* 8. 87 ff., which relates that the poet took to drinking under the influence of a courtesan named Upakośā with fatal results for himself.[4]

f) Legends of female character

A group of legends is cited in Yaśodhara's soliloquy in Book IV to illustrate the fickle character of women, and how they defy all restrictions on their movements. After referring to the mythological stories of Ahalyā

---

1 'तथाच लौकिकी श्रुतिः—किल बृहस्पतिः सदूवृत्तोऽपि चुङ्कारनगरे लोचनाञ्जनहरेण कितवेन मिथ्याप्रवाददूषितः शतक्रतुसभायां प्रवेशं न लेभे। अलब्धांशंनाशेन तु षजकनाम्ना वाग्जीवनेन अयं भिक्षाभ्रमणव्याजेनार्भकान् भक्षयति इत्युपहतश्चक्रपाणिः परिव्राट् वाराणस्याम्। मधुपेषु मध्ये पीतपयाश्च मार्कण्डतापसस्तापसाश्रमेषु।' p. 138.

2 'पौलस्त्यो नीतिशास्त्रेषु नाश्रौषीद्दाण्डक्योपाख्यानम्' etc. p. 139.

3 'वररुचिश्च वृषलीनिमित्तमासवनिपोद्वहनम्' etc.

4 Summarized by Jacobi in his edition of the work, p. lxix.

and Indra; Pārvatī and the Elephant Demon; and Chāyā and the Fire god (the former had been placed by her father in the custody of Yama who vainly put her in his stomach for safety), Yaśodhara cites two little known tales. The first relates to the wife of a merchant, who resorted to the expedient of putting on a single cloth with her, but could not thereby prevent her from committing adultery with Mūladeva. The second story is about a clever adulteress named Upādhyāyikā, the wife of a Brāhmaṇa teacher.[1] According to Śrutasāgara, the name of the husband was Garga and that of the woman Somaśrī.

The temptations offered by women are illustrated in Book I by the legend of how the austerities of Śiva were interrupted by the sight of the water-sports of the daughters of Dakṣa, those of Brahman by the musical performance of the nymph Tilottamā, those of Parāśara by the meeting of the fisherman's daughter, and those of Rathanemi (see above) by the dancing of a nautch-girl.[2]

g) Miscellaneous Stories

The legend of Jīmūtavāhana is referred to in a simile in Book I.[3] The allusion to Rādhā and Nārāyaṇa in Book IV[4] is of particular interest in view of the paucity of early references to the former, and shows that the Rādhā legend must be much earlier than the 10th century. It is noteworthy that both Kṛṣṇa and Rādhā are mentioned in Hāla's Gāthāsaptaśatī 1. 89.[5] A woman named Rādhā appears in the story of Dhanakīrti in *Yaśastilaka* VII. 26. The antiquity of the name is shown by the fact that a woman called Rādhā is also mentioned in *Lalitavistara*, chap. 18, the famous Mahāyāna work, earlier than the ninth century.[6] The ten Incarnations of Viṣṇu are referred to in *Yaśastilaka*, Book IV.[7]

---

1 'तथाहि अनुश्रवः—कृतरक्षाशल्याप्यहल्या किलाखण्डलेन सह संविवेश, हरदेहार्धाश्रितापि गिरिसुता गजासुरेण, यमजठरालयापि छाया पावकेन, एकवसनवैदेहकवधूर्मूलदेवेन, एवमन्याश्चोपाध्यायिकाप्रभृतयो निजपतिसमक्षमुपपतिभिः सहारेभिरे महासाहसानि।' p. 62. A story very similar to that of Chāyā and the fire god occurs in *Milindapañha* iv. 2. 18. A Dānava, to guard his wife, put her into a box, and swallowing it, carried her about in his stomach. That did not prevent a Vidyādhara entering his mouth and enjoying the company of his wife. Rhys Davids: *The Questions of King Milinda*, Vol. I, p. 217.

2 'श्रूयते हि किलालक्ष्यजन्मनो दक्षसुतानां जलकेलिविलोकनात् तपःप्रत्यवायः, पितामहस्य तिलोत्तमासंगीतकात् कैवर्तीसंगमात् पराशरस्य, रथनेमेश्च नटीनर्तनदर्शनात्।' Vol. I, p. 109.

3 'जीमूतवाहनचरितावतारमिव नागवल्लीविभवसुन्दरम्।' p. 95

4 'किं न रेमे···राधा नारायणेन' Vol. II, p. 142.

5 मुहमारुएण तं कह्न गोरअं राहिआए अवणेन्तो। एताणँ वल्लवीणं अण्णाण वि गोरअं हरसि॥ N. S. Press, third edition.

6 'तेन खलु पुनर्भिक्षवः समयेन सुजाताया ग्रामिकदुहितुर्दासी राधा नाम कालगताभूत्।'

7 'दशावतारेण स वर्तते वा'. For the verse in question see Chapter XII.

CHAPTER XVIII

Quotations and References

A remarkable feature of Somadeva's *Yaśastilaka* is that it quotes or refers to a large number of earlier authors and works, many of them otherwise unknown or but insufficiently known. These references have thus a great chronological value, forming as they do a definite landmark in Indian literary history. There are indeed few writers who have enriched Kāvya literature with so great a variety of well-stocked scholarship as the author of our romance.

POETS

In Book IV Somadeva refers to the following poets as Mahākavis, and claims that their *kāvyas* testify to the great reputation of the Jaina religion: Urva, Bhāravi, Bhavabhūti, Bhartṛhari, Bhartṛmeṇṭha, Kaṇṭha, Guṇāḍhya, Vyāsa, Bhāsa, Vosa, Kālidāsa, Bāṇa, Mayūra, Nārāyaṇa, Kumāra, Māgha and Rājaśekhara. These names are followed by a reference to what Somadeva calls 'the *Kāvyādhyāya* composed by Bharata', probably the 17th chapter of Bharata's Nāṭyaśāstra which deals with 'the adornments of poetry' (*kāvyavibhūṣaṇāni*), figures of speech and similar topics.

While some of the above names are well-known, we know practically nothing about the others. Nārāyaṇa may be Bhaṭṭanārāyaṇa, the author of *Veṇīsaṁhāra*, but we cannot be sure about this. Kumāra is very probably Kumāradāsa, the author of *Jānakīharaṇa.* The reference to Guṇāḍhya seems to suggest that the lost *Bṛhatkathā* was extant in the Deccan in the 10th century. The reference to Bhāsa is not clear, and may not have anything to do with the dramatist of that name. In any case, Bhāsa is again mentioned as a Mahākavi in a subsequent chapter (Vol. II, p. 251), and the following verse quoted therein shows that he was a follower of the sensual aspect of the Śaiva cult.[1] इममेव च मार्गमाश्रित्याभाषि भासेन महाकविना—

पेया सुरा प्रियतमामुखमीक्षणीयं ग्राह्यः स्वभावललितोऽविकृतश्च वेषः ।
येनेदमीदृशमदृश्यत मोक्षवर्त्म दीर्घायुरस्तु भगवान् स पिनाकपाणिः ॥

"One should drink wine and gaze at a beloved woman's face and assume a garb that is beautiful by nature and unspoilt.[2] Long live Śiva, the Exalted One, who discovered such a way to salvation." It may be noted that the verse occurs in the Pallava king Mahendravarman's *Mattavilāsaprahasana* where it is declaimed by a drunken Kāpālika, after salutation to Śiva.

---

1 See Chap. VIII.

Ms. A remarks विकाररहितः नग्न एव.

With regard to the other poets mentioned in Somadeva's list no early poet of the name of Kaṇṭha is known, but a writer named Kaṇṭha is cited several times as an authority on Sanskrit roots in Kṣīrasvāmin's *Kṣīrataraṅgiṇī*.[1] Combination of grammar and poetry is not rare in Sanskrit literature, but we do not know whether this Kaṇṭha was also a Mahākavi. As to Urva, two of our Manuscripts (B and C) give the name as Utsavva, but the reading of the printed text is supported by the other two Manuscripts (A and D) which seem to read Ūrva. There seems no doubt that Urva is the correct reading which has also the merit of being adopted in Śrutasāgara's commentary. Urva is probably the same as the poet Aurva cited in Vallabhadeva's *Subhāṣitāvalī* which attributes the following verses to him:

अश्यद्घनान्धकारेऽथ प्राप्ते वर्षानिशाक्षये । शरत् प्राभातवेलेव प्रकाशमनयद्दिशः ॥
रिक्ता विपाण्डुरात्मानो निःशब्दाः प्राप्तलाघवाः । त्वत्सपत्ना इव घना न्यस्तचापा दिशो ययुः ॥

The second verse is evidently addressed to a king, and Aurva seems to have been a court-poet.

Of the remaining poets, Bāṇa is mentioned in another place, the reference being to his *Kādambarī*.[2] Māgha, too, is mentioned twice, Yaśodhara being addressed as a Māgha in poetic appreciation.[3] As regards Bhavabhūti, a reference to the plot of his *Mālatīmādhava* occurs in Somadeva's *Nītivākyāmṛta* (*Yuddhasamuddeśa*).[4] In Book V Somadeva quotes verses from two other poets about whom we know nothing. They are Grahila, who sings the glory of Śiva, and Nīlapaṭa, who heaps scorn on those who deny themselves the charms of women to seek the bliss of salvation. The following two verses are by Grahila:

आस्तां तवान्यदपि तावदतुल्यकक्षमैश्वर्यमीश्वरपदस्य निमित्तभूतम् ।
स्वच्छेफसोऽपि भगवन्न गतोऽवसानं विष्णुः पितामहयुतः किमुतापरस्य ॥ इति,
रथः क्षोणी यन्ता शतधृतिरगेन्द्रो धनुरथो रथाङ्गे चन्द्रार्कौ रथचरणपाणिः शर इति ।
दिधक्षोस्ते कोऽयं त्रिपुरतृणमाडम्बरविधिर्विधेयैः क्रीडन्त्यो न खलु परतन्त्राः प्रभुधियः ॥

इति च ग्रहिलभाषितम् । (Vol. II, p. 55).[5]

The following verse is attributed by Somadeva to Nīlapaṭa (Vol. II, p. 252). इदमेव च तत्त्वमुपलभ्यालापि नीलपटेन—

---

1 Ed. Liebich, Breslau, 1930.

2 See Chap. IV.

3 'सुकविकाव्यकथाविनोददोहदमाघ' Book II.

4 'श्रूयते हि किल दूरस्थोऽपि माधवपिता कामन्दकीयप्रयोगेण माधवाय मालतीं साधयामास ।'

5 The second verse occurs in Puṣpadanta's *Mahimnastotra*. It is possible that Somadeva's remark ग्रहिलभाषितम् might simply mean 'an obstinate utterance,' as the verses in question are cited to illustrate certain alleged contradictions in the conception of Śiva. See Chap. VIII.

पयोधरभरालसाः स्मरविघूर्णितार्धेक्षणाः क्वचित् सलयपञ्चमोच्चरितगीतझङ्कारिणीः ।
विहाय रमणीरमूरपरमोक्षसौख्यार्थिनामहो जडिमडिण्डिमो विफलभण्डपाखण्डिनाम् ॥

Nīlapaṭa seems to be the same as the poet Nīlapaṭṭa cited in *Saduktikarṇāmṛta* which quotes from him the following playful verse on the irony of Śiva's burning the god of love. It would seem that Nīlapaṭa or Nīlapaṭṭa was a poet who laid stress on the pleasures of love.

अयं स भुवनत्रयप्रथितसंयमी शङ्करो बिभर्ति वपुषाधुना विरहकातरः कामिनीम् ।
अनेन किल निर्जिता वयमिति प्रियायाः करं करेण परिलालयन् जयति जातहासः स्मरः ॥

The following verse is attributed in Book IV to Vararuci (p. 99):

प्राणाघातान्निवृत्तिः परधनहरणे संयमः सत्यवाक्यं काले शक्त्या प्रदेयं युवतिजनकथामूकभावः परेषाम् ।
तृष्णास्रोतोविबन्धो गुरुषु च विनतिः सर्वभूतानुकम्पा सामान्यं सर्वशास्त्रेष्वनुपहतविधिः श्रेयसामेष मार्गः ॥

The verse is found in the Nirṇaya Sāgara edition of Bhartṛhari's *Nītiśataka*, but seems to be an interpolation. It is not included in Jīvānanda's edition of the work in *Kāvyasaṁgraha*, vol. II. Somadeva refers to Bhartṛhari in the above list, and must have been acquainted with his work. It is hardly possible that he would have missed the verse in *Nītiśataka* if it had formed part of the text. The verse in question is put in the mouth of Vararuci in a story in Durgasiṁha's Kanarese rendering of the *Pañcatantra*, based on Vasubhāga's Sanskrit version of the work; but as the latter recension is no longer extant, it is difficult to say whether Somadeva borrowed the verse from Vasubhāga.[1]

Two verses of Bhartṛhari are quoted by Somadeva in Book V without mentioning their author, one from *S'ṛṅgāraśataka* and the other from *Nītiśataka*, the printed text of the *S'atakas* showing slight variations:

स्त्रीमुद्रां झषकेतनस्य महतीं सर्वार्थसंपत्करीं ये मोहादवधीरयन्ति कुधियो मिथ्याफलान्वेषिणः ।
ते तेनैव निहत्य निर्दयतरं मुण्डीकृता लुञ्चिताः केचित् पञ्चशिखीकृताश्च जटिनः कापालिकाश्चापरे ॥
नमस्यामो देवान्ननु हतविधेस्तेऽपि वशगा विधिर्विन्द्यः सोऽपि प्रतिनियतकर्मान्तफलदः ।
फलं कर्मायत्तं यदि किमपरैः किंच विधिना नमः सत्कर्मभ्यः प्रभवति न येभ्यो विधिरपि ॥

As pointed out elsewhere,[2] Somadeva quotes a large number of verses on the ministers of kings from various poets, but it is doubtful whether they are historical names. There is a similar reference to a poet named Gaṇapati in the verse quoted below:

वृत्तिच्छेदस्त्रिदशविदुषः कोहलस्यार्थहानिर्मानग्लानिर्गणपतिकवेः शंकरस्याशु नाशः ।
धर्मध्वंसः कुमुदकृतिनः केकटेश्च प्रवासः पापादस्मादिति समभवद्देव देशे प्रसिद्धिः ॥

It is stated in the verse that the wicked minister Pāmarodara insulted the poet Gaṇapati. Śrutasāgara in his commentary takes Tridaśa, Kohala

1 *The Poona Orientalist*, Vol. II, p. 181.

2 See Chap. VII.

and Kekaṭi also as referring to poets, but the verse mentions only Gaṇapati as a poet. We cannot but regard these names as fictitious, but it is noteworthy that there was actually a poet named Gaṇapati earlier than the tenth century. Rājaśekhara praises him in a verse cited in Jalhaṇa's *Sūktimuktāvalī*, which also quotes another verse wherein he is mentioned along with several well-known poets.[1] Verses from Gaṇapati are cited in *Saduktikarṇāmṛta* and *Subhāṣitāvalī*, and he seems to have composed a work named *Mahāmoda*.

The following verse is quoted by Somadeva from an unnamed work on poetics. (3. 274):

त्रिमूलकं द्विधोत्थानं पञ्चशाखं चतुश्छदम् । योऽगं वेत्ति नवच्छायं दशभूमिं स काव्यकृत् ॥

GRAMMARIANS

Somadeva says in Book I that the monks accompanying Sudatta expounded to their disciples the tenets of 'the Aindra, Jainendra, Cāndra, Āpiśala, Pāṇinīya and *many other grammars*'. The grammar of Pāṇini needs no comment, but the others are less familiar, and it is interesting to find that they were in vogue in the tenth century. About a century later, the Mulgund Inscription[2] of the reign of Someśvara I, dated 1053 A. D., refers to the erudition of the Jaina Muni Narendrasena in the Cāndra, Kātantra, Jainendra, Śabdānuśāsana and Aindra grammars, and that of Pāṇini; and these were no doubt the standard grammars of the day. As late as the thirteenth century Bopadeva mentions at the beginning of his *Kavikalpadruma* eight ancient grammarians including Indra, Candra, Āpiśali, Pāṇini and Jainendra, and says that he has composed his work 'after examining their opinions'. Samayasundara in his commentary on the Jaina *Kalpasūtra* 2. 9 includes the Aindravyākaraṇa and the Āpiśalivyākaraṇa among the eighteen grammars mentioned by him; but while it may be assumed that the grammars enumerated by Somadeva were current in the Deccan for a few centuries after his time, it would be rash to draw any conclusion about the popularity of these ancient texts from late references occurring in a writer of the seventeenth century.

No work called the Aindra grammar has come down to us, but the Kātantra system is believed to be derived from the Aindra school, of which the traditional founder is the god Indra, who first appears in the rôle

1 अथो गणपतिं वन्दे महामोदविधायिनम् । विद्याधरगणैर्यस्य पूज्यते कण्ठगार्जितम् ॥ 4. 72; दण्डी बाणदिवाकरौ गणपतिः कान्तश्च रत्नाकरः 4. 111

2 *Epigraphia Indica*, Vol. XVI, Part II.

of a grammarian in the *Taittirīyasaṁhitā*.[1] In later times Indra is mentioned as the author of a grammar in Śrīharṣa's *Naiṣadhacarita* 10. 135; and Cāṇḍūpaṇḍita, who wrote a remarkable commentary on the poem towards the end of the thirteenth century, takes the reference to mean the Aindra grammar.[2]

Tibetan tradition, however, speaks of an Indravyākaraṇa by a grammarian named Indragomin, and it is said to have been prevalent among the the Buddhists of Nepal.[3] The question requires further investigation.

The Āpiśala referred to by Somadeva is the ancient grammar of Āpiśali earlier than Pāṇini who refers to him in the rule *vā supyāpiśaleḥ*. Āpiśali's opinion is cited in connection with another rule in the Mahābhāṣya on Pāṇini 4. 2. 45,[4] and we learn from the same work (4. 1. 14) that a Brāhmaṇa woman who studies Āpiśala, that is, the grammar of Āpiśali, is called Āpiśalā.[5] Occasional references to the tenets of the Āpiśala school are found in the *Kāśikā* and Jinendrabuddhi's *Nyāsa* thereon. For example, we read in *Kāśikā* 6. 2. 36: आपिशलस्यापत्यमापिशलिराचार्यः ।...तेन प्रोक्तमापिशलम् ।...अधीयते येऽन्तेवासिनस्तेऽप्यापिशलाः । ......आपिशलेर्वा छात्रा आपिशला इति......आपिशलपाणिनीये शास्त्रे ।. *Kāśikā* 7. 3. 95 while explaining the rule तुरुस्तुशम्यगःसार्वधातुके says—आपिशलास्तुरुस्तुशम्यमः सार्वधातुकासु छन्दसीति पठन्ति. Jinendrabuddhi remarks—सार्वधातुकास्विति स्त्रीलिङ्गनिर्देशः स्त्रीलिङ्गस्य सार्वधातुकाशब्दस्यापिशलिना संज्ञात्वेन प्रणीतत्वात् ।. Jinendrabuddhi on *Kāśikā* 1. 3. 22 mentions another peculiarity of Āpiśali: सकारमात्रमस्तिं धातुमापिशलिराचार्यः प्रतिजानीते । तथाहि न तस्य पाणिनेरिव अस भुवीति गणपाठः । किं तर्हि । स भुवीति स पठति ।...स त्वागमौ गुणवृद्धी आतिष्ठते । एवं हि स प्रतिजानीत इत्यर्थः । References to Āpiśali's grammar are found also in writers of the Kātantra school, e. g. in Durgasiṁha's comm. on the rule द्वितीयैनेन—आपिशलीयव्याकरणे समयादीनां कर्मप्रवचनीयत्वं दृष्टमिति मतम् ।.

The Cāndra grammar referred to by Somadeva is the work of the Buddhist Candragomin, and has been edited[6] and assigned to the 5th century A. D.[7] The Jainendra is the work of the famous Jaina philosopher and grammarian Pūjyapāda, also known as Devanandin. He is said to have been the tutor of the Ganga king Durvinīta who ruled about the end of the fifth century. But a Jaina scholar named Niravadyapaṇḍita who was a spiritual adviser of the Cālukya king Vinayāditya (680–696 A. D.) is described in an inscription as the house-pupil of Pūjyapāda; and R. G. Bhandarkar has on

1 Belvalkar: *Systems of Sanskrit Grammar*, p. 10.

2 Explaining the phrase ताद्दृक्कृतव्याकरणः, C. P. says ताद्दृक् कृतम् ऐन्द्रं व्याकरणं येन सः.

3 Winternitz: *Geschichte der indischen Litteratur*, Vol. III, p. 398.

4 'तथा चापिशलेर्विधिः' etc.

5 'आपिशलमधीते ब्राह्मणी आपिशला ब्राह्मणी ।'

6 See *Candra-Vṛtti*, Ed. Liebich, Leipzig, 1918.

7 Belvalkar (op. cit.), p. 58.

this ground suggested about 678 A. D. as the date of the grammarian.[1] It is possible, however, that there was more than one Pūjyapāda, and it is usual to assign the grammarian to the latter half of the fifth century. It may be noted that of the two recensions of the Jainendra grammar that preserved in Somadeva's commentary *S'abdārṇavacandrikā* composed in 1205 A. D. is the earlier and more complete.[2]

Somadeva refers to Pūjyapāda again in Book II. The young prince Yaśodhara is described as being proficient in grammar like Pūjyapāda and in the science of logic like Akalaṁka.[3] We shall speak about Akalaṁka a bit later. As regards Pūjyapāda, although he was no less distinguished for his philosophical and other writings, he was regarded as a grammarian *par excellence,* a founder of an independent grammatical system. 'Like Pūjyapāda in grammar, like Akalaṁka in logic' became a sort of proverbial expression among later Jaina writers. The comparison occurs, for instance, in some of the Śravaṇa Belgola inscriptions. An inscription dated Śaka 1037 describes (verse 30) a teacher named Meghacandra as:

षट्तर्केष्वकलङ्कदेवविबुधः साक्षादयं भूतले । सर्वव्याकरणे विपश्चिदधिपः श्रीपूज्यपादः स्वयं ॥

Another teacher, Jinacandra by name, is called जैनेन्द्रे पूज्य(पादः) सकलसमयतर्के च भट्टाकलङ्कः (verse 23) in an inscription of about Śaka 1022. Similarly, in an inscription dated Śaka 1320 a teacher named Śrutamuni is called शब्दे श्रीपूज्यपादः सकलविमतजित्तर्कतन्त्रेषु देवः (verse 40).[4] The grammatical learning of Pūjyapāda is further attested by the citations from the *Mahābhāṣya* occurring in his *Sarvārthasiddhi,* one of the earliest commentaries on the *Tattvārthasūtra.*[5]

A casual reference to the grammarian Patañjali, the author of the *Mahābhāṣya*, occurs in a metaphor based on word-play in Book VI, section 20: 'शस्त्रशास्त्रविद्याधिकरणव्याकरणपतञ्जले बले'.

NĪTIŚĀSTRAS

In Book III Somadeva describes Yaśodhara as having studied the Nītiśāstras of Bṛhaspati, Śukra, Viśālākṣa, Parīkṣit, Parāśara, Bhīma, Bhīṣma, Bhāradvāja and others.[6] None of these ancient works is now extant, but there is no doubt that they were available in the 10th century.

1 *Early History of the Deccan,* Third edition, p. 102.

2 See introduction to Benares edition, and Winternitz (op. cit.), p. 400.

3 'पूज्यपाद इव शब्देतिह्येषु', 'अकलङ्कदेव इव प्रमाणशास्त्रेषु'

4 जैनशिलालेखसंग्रहः, pp. 62, 119, 202 (मणिकचन्द्रदिगम्बरजैनग्रन्थमाला).

5 See Pathak in *Annals* of the B. O. R. I, Vol XIII, p. 32.

6 गुरुशुक्रविशालाक्ष········भारद्वाजादिप्रणीतनीतिशास्त्रश्रवणसनाथं श्रुतिपथम्······P. 471

The opinions of the followers of the schools of Bṛhaspati (*Bārhaspatyāḥ*) and Śukra (*Auśanasāḥ*) are cited several times in Kauṭilya's Arthaśāstra, and these two ancient writers on statecraft are often quoted in the Mahābhārata and other texts.[1] A large number of quotations from Bṛhaspati in verse occurs in Lakṣmīdhara's *Kṛtyakalpataru* (Rājadharmakāṇḍa)[2] composed in the twelfth century; and as late as the fourteenth century, Caṇḍeśvara quotes Bṛhaspati, Bārhaspatya, and the Nīti or Rājanīti of Śukra in his *Rājanītiratnākara,* but the work of Śukra quoted therein is not the same as the extant *S'ukranītisāra,* which is believed to be a later compilation.

Another reference to Śukra occurs in Book II. The young prince Yaśodhara is described as proficient as Śukra in political science and the disposition of troops on the battlefield.[3] The Nītiśāstra of Śukra seems to have paid special attention to the latter topic, as the Mahābhārata (Āśramavāsikaparva 7. 15) refers to the *Vyūhas* known as Śakaṭa, Padma, Vajra and mentions in this connection the *śāstra* of Uśanas.

अथोपपत्त्या शकटं पद्मवज्रं च भारत । उशना वेद यच्छास्त्रं तत्रैतद्विहितं विभो ॥

The subject is treated in detail in Kauṭilya's Arthaśāstra 10. 6, wherein the discussion opens with a reference to the classification of *vyūhas* according to Uśanas and Bṛhaspati.[4]

We know very little about the Nītiśāstras of Parīkṣit, Bhīma and Bhīṣma. With regard to the latter, the opinions of an old writer on politics named Kauṇapadanta are cited several times in Kauṭilya's Arthaśāstra (1. 8. etc.), and as Kauṇapadanta is an epithet of Bhīṣma, the two names might refer to the same author. The Nītiśāstra of Parāśara seems to be different from the Dharmasaṁhitā of the same author. The opinions of Parāśara and the school of Parāśara are quoted several times in Kauṭilya's Arthaśāstra (1. 8, 15 etc.). An opinion of Parāśara is cited also in Kāmandaka's *Nītisāra* 8. 39.[5] An early reference to the Nītiśāstra of Parāśara occurs in the *Tantrākhyāyikā,* the oldest recension of the *Pañcatantra,* which mentions the Nītiśāstra of Manu, Bṛhaspati, Bhṛgu, Parāśara, Sālaṅkāyana and Cāṇakya (Book III).

We know a bit more about Bhāradvāja. The Nītiśāstra of Bhāradvāja has to be distinguished from the Smṛti work attributed to the same

1 See Kane: *History of Dharmaśāstra,* Vol. I, sections 17 and 16.

2 Ed. J. Sastri. Lahore.

3 'कविरिव राजराद्धान्तेषु', 'काव्य इव व्यूहरचनासु'.

4 'पक्षावुरस्यं प्रतिग्रह इत्यौशनसो व्यूहविभागः । पक्षौ कक्षावुरस्यं प्रतिग्रह इति बार्हस्पत्यः ।'

5 द्वे एव प्रकृती न्याय्ये इत्युवाच पराशरः । अभियोक्तृप्रधानत्वात् तथान्यो योऽभियुज्यते ॥

author or possibly some other author of the same name. Most of the available data about Bhāradvāja have been collected by Kane,[1] who points out that he is mentioned as one of the writers on Rājaśāstra in the Mahābhārata (Śāntiparva 58. 3) and that his opinions are cited several times in Kauṭilya's Arthaśāstra. It may be added that the opinion of a Bharadvāja is cited in Kāmandaka's *Nītisāra* 9. 57.[2]

The following verses are quoted by Somadeva in Book IV from a work of Bhāradvāja, called *Ṣāḍguṇyaprastāva.*

अवक्षेपेण हि सतामसतां प्रग्रहेण च । तथा सत्त्वेष्वभिद्रोहादधर्मस्य च कारणात् ॥
विमाननाच्च मान्यानां विश्वस्तानां च घातनात् । प्रजानां जायते लोपो नृपतेश्चायुषः क्षयः ॥

कथमिदमभाषत षाड्गुण्यप्रस्तावे भारद्वाजः । (p. 100).

The purport of these lines is that the king and the citizens of a state go to ruin if the good are dishonoured and the wicked held in esteem, if living beings are injured and injustice prevails, if those worthy of respect are insulted and the faithful killed. The influence of these ideas can be seen from the fact that they are amplified in the following verses of Kauṭilya's Arthaśāstra (7. 5):

अवक्षेपेण हि सतामसतां प्रग्रहेण च । अभूतानां च हिंसानामधर्म्याणां प्रवर्तनैः ॥......
अदण्डनैश्च दण्ड्यानां दण्ड्यानां चण्डदण्डनैः । अग्राह्याणामुपग्राहैर्ग्राह्याणां चानभिग्रहैः ॥......
उपघातैः प्रधानानां मान्यानां चावमाननैः ......। प्रकृतीनां क्षयो लोभो वैराग्यं चोपजायते ॥
क्षीणाः प्रकृतयो लोभं लुब्धा यान्ति विरागताम् । विरक्ता यान्त्यमित्रं वा भर्तारं घ्नन्ति वा स्वयम् ॥

Bhāradvāja seems to have advocated the rule of concord and harmony in the relations of a king and his subjects, and the verses in question are cited by Somadeva in support of the doctrine of *ahiṁsā*. The principle of non-violence is in fact enunciated in another verse of Bhāradvāja quoted in the anonymous commentary on Somadeva's *Nītivākyāmṛta* (Vyasana-samuddeśa).

तथा च भारद्वाजः—

तृणच्छेदोऽपि नो कार्यो विना कार्येण साधुभिः । येन नो सिध्यते किंचित् किं पुनर्मानुषं सहम् (?) ॥

We know nothing about the contents of Bhāradvāja's *Ṣāḍguṇyaprastāva*, but the name suggests that it dealt with the six *guṇas* or principles of foreign policy. It is possible that this was the name of Bhāradvāja's work on politics or *daṇḍanīti*, of which *ṣāḍguṇya*, according to the Mahābhārata, formed the quintessence (Śāntiparva 59. 78, 79).[3]

---

1 *Journal of the University of Bombay*, September, 1942, p. 81.

2 स्वशक्त्युत्साहमुद्वीक्ष्य विगृह्णीयान्महत्तरम् । केसरीव द्विपमिति भरद्वाजः प्रभाषते ॥

3 षाड्गुण्यगुणसारैषा स्थास्यत्यग्रे महात्मसु ।

Somadeva seems to have utilized another verse of Bhāradvāja. Both in *Nītivākyāmṛta* and *Yaśastilaka* (3. 23) he tells us that to confide the care of a kingdom to officials is to entrust cats with the guarding of milk. **नियुक्तहस्तार्पितराज्यभारास्तिष्ठन्ति ये स्वैरविहारसाराः । बिडालवृन्दाहितदुग्धमुद्राः स्वपन्ति ते मूढधियः क्षितीन्द्राः ॥** In *Nītivākyāmṛta* we have: मार्जारेषु दुग्धरक्षणमिव नियोगिषु विश्वासकरणम् ।. There is no doubt that the idea is based on the following verse of Bhāradvāja quoted in the anoymous commentary on *Nītivākyāmṛta* (Amātyasamuddeśa). **तथा च भारद्वाजः—**

मार्जारेष्विव विश्वासो यथा नो दुग्धरक्षणे । नियोगिनां नियोगेषु तथा कार्यो न भूभुजा ॥

We shall now speak a few words about Viśālākṣa. He and Bhāradvāja are mentioned among the writers on Rājaśāstra in the Mahābhārata (Śāntiparva 58. 2, 3). The Mahābhārata (ibid. 59. 80–82) relates a legend, according to which Śiva, otherwise known as Viśālākṣa, abridged a lengthy Nītiśāstra composed by Brahman, and this shorter version containing ten thousand chapters was known as *Vaiśālākṣa* after Śiva. What is certain is that Viśālākṣa was an ancient writer on state-craft whose opinions are quoted several times in Kauṭilya's Arthaśāstra (1. 8, 17 etc.), Kāmandaka's *Nītisāra* 8. 28[1], and Viśvarūpa's commentary on Yājñavalkya 1. 328.[2] He is also mentioned in Caṇḍeśvara's *Rājanītiratnākara*.

The following quotation from Viśālākṣa occurs in *Yaśastilaka*, Book III. **'नैकस्य कार्यसिद्धिरस्ति'** इति विशालाक्षः (p. 453). The maxim is incorporated by Somadeva in his *Nītivākyāmṛta*, chap. 18, without acknowledgment. It is quoted also in Kauṭilya's Arthaśāstra 1. 15 with a slight variation: **'नैकस्य मन्त्रसिद्धिरस्ति'** इति विशालाक्षः ।. A similar idea occurs in a quotation from Yama found in Lakṣmīdhara's *Kṛtyakalpataru* (Rājadharmakāṇḍa 15. 70): नैकः कार्याणि यः कुर्यात् सोऽत्यन्तं पाति मेदिनीम् ॥

The opinions of Viśālākṣa sometimes run counter to those of Bhāradvāja, to judge from the statements preserved in Kauṭilya. Bhāradvāja, for example, contrary to the above maxim, opines that the king should deliberate alone on secret matters of policy: **'गुह्यमेको मन्त्रयेत'** भारद्वाजः ।. Further, while Bhāradvāja recommends submission in the face of a superior enemy, Viśālākṣa recommends fighting with the combined strength of all one's forces, regardless of victory or defeat.[3]

'बलीयसाभियुक्तो दुर्बलः सर्वत्रानुप्रणतो वेतसधर्मा तिष्ठेत् । इन्द्रस्य हि स प्रणमति यो बलीयसो नमति' इति भारद्वाजः । 'सर्वसंदोहेन बलानां युध्येत । पराक्रमो हि व्यसनमपहन्ति । स्वधर्मश्चैष क्षत्रियस्य युद्धे जयः पराजयो वा' इति विशालाक्षः । Kauṭilya 12. 1.

---

1 एतेऽष्टादश चैतेषां शत्रुमित्रे पृथक् पृथक् । चतुष्पञ्चाशत्कमिति विशालाक्षः प्रभाषते ॥

2 एवं च विशालाक्षः—वन्यान् वनगतैर्नित्यं मण्डलस्थास्तथाविधैः । चारैरालोच्य सातत्कुर्याज्जिगीषुर्दीर्घदूरदृक् ॥

3 See also Kane's paper in *Journal of the University of Bombay* (op. cit.)

There is another quotation from Viśālākṣa in Book IV: 'चातुर्मास्येष्वर्धमासिकम्, दर्शपौर्णमासयोश्चातूरात्रिकम्, राजनक्षत्रे गुरुपर्वणि च त्रैरात्रिकम्, एवमन्यासु चोपहतासु तिथिषु द्विरात्रमेकरात्रं वा सर्वेषामघातं घोषयेदायुर्बलवृद्ध्यर्थम्' इति कथमुपनिषदि वदति स्म विशालाक्षः ।. The purport of these lines is that non-injury to all creatures should be proclaimed (by the king) during the four months of rains for a fortnight, during the New and the Full Moon for four nights, on days related to the constellation under which the king was born and on Saṁkrānti days for three nights, and similarly on certain inauspicious lunar days for one or two nights. Viśālākṣa is reported as making this statement in an *Upaniṣad*. The word seems to be used in its wider sense of 'secret doctrine' and *Upaniṣad* might simply refer to Viśālākṣa's Nītiśāstra. We know, for example, that the Mahābhārata (Śāntiparva 103. 40) uses the expression *daṇḍopaniṣad* in the sense of 'secret application of force';[1] and Somadeva himself uses the word *upaniṣad* in the sense of 'secret' or 'mystery' in relation to the teachings of the Arthaśāstra. He says, for instance, 'अर्थशास्त्रविचारपल्लवकलोकप्रकाशितोपनिषत्सु परिषत्सु' (Book III) 'in assemblies where scholars expert in the discussion of the Arthaśāstra revealed the mysteries (of that science)'.

The passage from Viśālākṣa's *Upaniṣad* cited above occurs in Kauṭilya's Arthaśāstra 13. 5 with slight modifications and omissions in connection with the restoration of peace in a conquered country: चातुर्मास्येष्वर्धमासिकमघातं पौर्णमासीषु च चातूरात्रिकं राजदेशनक्षत्रेष्वेकरात्रिकम् । It is possible that the passage is adapted from the work of Viśālākṣa, just as certain verses of Bhāradvāja have also been amplified and incorporated in the text of the Arthaśāstra.[2] In face of this, it is impossible to accept Śrutasāgara's identification of Viśālākṣa with the sage Prabhākara and explanation of *Upaniṣad* as *Vedāntaśāstra.*

Somadeva seems to borrow an idea from another old writer whom he does not mention, but who is cited in the anonymous commentary on his *Nītivākyāmṛta.* Both in *Yaśastilaka* (3. 25) and *Nītivākyāmṛta* he expresses the opinion that the troubles of the master are the opportunity of the servants, and says that just as physicians try to aggravate the illness of wealthy patients, similarly the officials of a king try to add to his troubles.

व्याधिवृद्धौ यथा वैद्यः श्रीमतामाहितोद्यमः । व्यसनेषु तथा राज्ञः कृतयत्ना नियोगिनः ॥

He says in *Nītivākyāmṛta*: वैद्येषु श्रीमतां व्याधिवर्द्धनादिव नियोगिषु भर्तृव्यसनादपरो नास्ति जीवनोपायः. There is no doubt that the above idea is based on the following verse quoted

1 Nilakaṇṭha says रहस्यदण्डः.

2 See above.

from an ancient writer named Raibhya in the commentary on *Nītivākyāmṛta* (Svāmisamuddeśa). तथा च रैभ्यः—

ईश्वराणां यथा व्याधिर्वैद्यानां निधिरुत्तमः । नियोगिनां तथा ज्ञेयः स्वामिव्यसनसंभवः ॥

Similarly, Somadeva seems to have adapted another idea from the ancient writer Atri, well-known as an author of Smṛti works. Somadeva says in *Yaśastilaka* 3. 230:

एकामात्ये महीपाले नालं लक्ष्मीर्विजृम्भते । लतायास्तत्र का वृद्धिः शाखैका यत्र शाखिनि ॥

In *Nītivākyāmṛta* (10. 82) he says: किमेकशाखस्य शाखिनो महती भवति च्छाया ।. The idea is based on the following verse quoted from Atri in the commentary on the above work. तथा चात्रिः—

यथैकशाखवृक्षस्य नैव च्छाया प्रजायते । तथैकमंत्रिणा राज्ञः सिद्धिः कृत्येषु नो भवेत् ॥

The following verse is cited by Somadeva in Book IV without mentioning the source. उक्तं च—

राज्ञि धर्मिणि धर्मिष्ठाः पापे पापाः समे समाः । राजानमनुवर्तन्ते यथा राजा तथा प्रजाः ॥

The verse is quoted in the commentary on *Nītivākyāmṛta* (Svāmisamuddeśa) and attributed to Vyāsa. It is cited from Vṛddha Cāṇakya in Böhtlingk's *Indische Sprüche.*

The following two verses are also cited in *Yaśastilaka* (3.258-9) without mentioning the source.

नेमिमेकान्तरान् राज्ञः कृत्वा चानन्तराक्षरान् । नाभिमात्मानमावच्छेन्नेता प्रकृतिमण्डले ॥
अष्टशाखं चतुर्मूलं षष्टिपत्रं द्वये स्थितम् । षट्पुष्पं त्रिफलं वृक्षं यो जानाति स नीतिवित् ॥

The purport of the first verse is that a king desirous of supremacy should make himself the centre of the Circle of States, making the neighbouring kings and those living beyond his immediate neighbours the circumference of the Circle. Yaśodhara says that while considering the verse in an assembly of learned men, he discussed also the second verse which has a bearing on the composition of the Circle of States, and dealt with the entire system of arrangement and distribution of alien states. The second verse is a sort of synopsis of the various topics of the Nītiśāstras, and from the nature of the reference we should expect to find both the verses in the same text, but actually we find the first verse in Kauṭilya's Arthaśāstra and the second in Kāmandaka's *Nītisāra.* The Arthaśāstra 6. 2 cites the first verse with an important variant, reading *arān* for *narān.* The reading (*spokes*) completes the metaphor of the wheel, but does not materially alter the sense of the verse. As regards the second verse, it occurs in Kāmandaka 8.42, but we cannot be certain that Somadeva took the verse from the latter work, as Śaṁkarārya in his commentary on Kāmandaka cites the verse independently from Auśanas, that is, the Nītiśāstra of Sukra.

The following verses quoted anonymously in *Yaśastilaka* 3.77 and Book VI, section 13, are found in Kauṭilya's Arthaśāstra 10.6 and 3.1 respectively. तदाह—

एकं हन्यान्न वा हन्यादिषुः क्षिप्तो धनुष्मता । प्राज्ञेन तु मतिः क्षिप्ता हन्याद्गर्भगतानपि ॥

दण्डो हि केवलो लोकं परं चेमं च रक्षति । राज्ञा शत्रौ च पुत्रे च यथादोषं समं धृतः ॥

The first verse occurs also in the *Pañcatantra* (*Tantrākhyāyikā*) 3.123. It occurs in a somewhat different form in the Mahābhārata (Udyogaparva 33.47).

एकं हन्यान्न वा हन्यादिषुर्मुक्तो धनुष्मता । बुद्धिर्बुद्धिमतोत्सृष्टा हन्याद्राष्ट्रं सराजकम् ॥

The following verse occurring in *Yaśastilaka* (towards the end of Book IV) is found in Kauṭilya 5.6:

कालश्च सकृदभ्येति यं नरं कालकाङ्क्षिणम् । दुर्लभः स पुनः कालस्तस्य कर्म चिकीर्षतः ॥

The verse is found also in the *Pañcatantra* (*Tantrākhyāyikā*) 3.74, the latter text reading *tena* for *tasya* and *cikīrṣatā* for *cikīrṣataḥ*. The *Pañcatantra* seems to have borrowed the verse from Kauṭilya, as the preceding sentence स्वयमुपगता श्रीस्त्यज्यमानाभिशपतीति लोकप्रवादः is a variation of Kauṭilya's स्वयमारूढा हि स्त्री त्यज्यमानाभिशपतीति लोकप्रवादः. The real author of the verse seems to be Bhāradvāja, as both the verse and the sentence preceding it form part of certain opinions of Bhāradvāja which Kauṭilya here cites and subjects to criticism.

There are also a few verses in our romance which are clearly based on Kauṭilya's Arthaśāstra. The following verse is one of three (3.106-108) which Somadeva represents as containing the essence of all the Arthaśāstras. He says:

स्वस्मान्निजः परोऽन्यस्मात् स्वः परस्मात् परो निजात् । रक्ष्यः स्वस्मात् परस्माच्च नित्यमात्मा जिगीषुणा ॥

The verse is obviously based on the following verse found in Kauṭilya 9. 3:

परे परेभ्यः स्वे स्वेभ्यः स्वे परेभ्यः स्वतः परे । रक्ष्याः स्वेभ्यः परेभ्यश्च नित्यमात्मा विपश्चिता ॥

The following Nīti verse on the risks of hunting is cited in Book V:

स्तेनद्विषद्विषव्यालश्वापदप्रभवं भयम् । शर्मधर्मविरामश्च मृगयायां महीपतेः ॥

The verse seems to be based on Kauṭilya 8. 3: 'स्तेनामित्रव्यालदावप्रस्खलनभयदिङ्मोहाः क्षुत्पिपासे च प्राणाबाधस्तस्याम् ।'. The references of Somadeva to the Arthaśāstra are of a general character, and he does not seem to refer to any particular Arthaśāstra. Two such references have been mentioned above. Another occurs in the following Nīti verse cited in Book IV, which sums up a leading idea of the Arthaśāstra: to outwit one's enemies and not to be outwitted by them (p. 152):

एतदेवार्थशास्त्रस्य नित्यमध्ययने फलम् । यत् परानभिसंधत्ते नाभिसंधीयते परैः ॥

A similar summing up occurs also in Manu 7. 180:

यथैनं नाभिसंदध्युर्मित्रोदासीनशत्रवः । तथा सर्वं संविदध्यादेष सामासिको नयः ॥

The rise of Candragupta to power, though resourceless, through the efforts of a good minister is mentioned in a traditional verse (*śruti*) cited by Somadeva (3. 242). तथाच श्रुतिः—

दुर्योधनः समर्थोऽपि दुर्मंत्री प्रलयं गतः । राज्यमेकशरोऽप्याप सन्मंत्री चन्द्रगुप्तकः ॥

The tradition is also mentioned by Somadeva in his *Nītivākyāmṛta* 10. 4, wherein Viṣṇugupta or Cāṇakya is referred to by name: तथा चानुश्रूयते विष्णुगुप्तानुग्रहादनधिकृतोऽपि किल चन्द्रगुप्तः साम्राज्यपदमवापेति ।. The anonymous commentary on the above work quotes a verse from Śukra which contains the same allusion, *vṛhala* (*vṛṣala*?) apparently referring to Candragupta. तथा च शुक्रः—

महामात्यं वरो राजा निर्विकल्पं करोति यः । एकशोऽपि महीं लेभे हीनोऽपि वृहलो यथा ॥

Somadeva says in the course of a discussion in *Yaśastilaka* 3. 86:

पुष्पैरपि न योद्धव्यं किं पुनर्निशितैः शरैः । तामवस्थां गतानां तु न विद्मः किं भविष्यति ॥

He says also in *Nītivākyāmṛta* 32. 30: पुष्पयुद्धमपि नीतिवेदिनो नेच्छन्ति किं पुनः शस्त्रयुद्धम् । The anonymous commentary cites here the following verse from Vidura. तथा च विदुरः—

पुष्पैरपि न योद्धव्यं किं पुनर्निशितैः शरैः । उपाय......पूर्वं तस्माद्युद्धं समाचरेत् ॥

The verse is not found in the *Viduranīti* incorporated in *Vīramitrodaya* (*Rājanītiprakāśa*). There is, however, no doubt that the verse adapted by Somadeva is an old one. Śrīharṣa's *Naiṣadhacarita* 4. 81 refers to the idea thus:

अहह नीतिरवासभया ततो न कुसुमैरपि विग्रहमिच्छति ।

Nārāyaṇa in his commentary quotes the line पुष्पैरपि न योद्धव्यं etc. and adds: इति नीतिः.

The following verse is quoted in *Yaśastilaka*, Book III, without mentioning the source. तथा चोक्तं शास्त्रान्तरे—

चारो यस्य विचारश्च राज्ञो नास्तीक्षणद्वयम् । तस्यान्धदुग्धवद्राज्यं मन्त्रिमार्जारगोचरम् ॥

A reference to the *Nītiśāstras* in general occurs in Book I: नीतिशास्त्रैरिव प्रकाशितशमयोगतीर्थोद्योगैः. The Tīrthas are the eighteen agencies with whose help a king governs the state. Śrutasāgara says-उक्तं च–'सेनापतिर्गणको राजश्रेष्ठी दण्डाधिपो मन्त्री महत्तरो बलवत्तारश्चत्वारो वर्णाश्चतुरङ्गबलं पुरोहितोऽमात्यो महामात्यश्चेत्यष्टादश राज्ञां तीर्था भवन्ति ।'.

SMRTI WORKS

A considerable number of Smṛti citations occurs in *Yaśastilaka*, but most of them are from Manu as shown below. Manu 3. 267–271 on the offering of various kinds of meat in the Śrāddha rites is quoted in Book IV.

तिलैर्व्रीहियवैर्माषैरद्भिर्मूलफलेन च । दत्तेन मासं प्रीयन्ते विधिवत् पितरो नृणाम् ॥
द्वौ मासौ मत्स्यमांसेन त्रीन् मासान् हारिणेन च । औरभ्रेणाथ चतुरः शाकुनेनैव पञ्च वै ॥
षण्मासांश्छागमांसेन पार्षतेन हि सप्त वै । अष्टावेणस्य मांसेन रौरवेण नवैव तु ॥

दश मासांस्तु तृप्यन्ति वराहमहिषामिषैः । शशकूर्मस्य मांसेन मासानेकादशैव तु ॥
संवत्सरं तु गव्येन पयसा पायसेन वा । वार्ध्रीणसस्य मांसेन तृप्तिर्द्वादशवार्षिकी ॥

All the five verses are quoted also by Hemacandra in his *Yogaśāstra*, Chap. II. Several verses of Manu (5. 39, 41–2) on the eating of meat and the killing of animals in sacrifices and other rites are quoted in Book IV.

यज्ञार्थं पशवः सृष्टाः स्वयमेव स्वयंभुवा । यज्ञो हि भूत्यै सर्वेषां तस्माद्यज्ञे वधोऽवधः ॥
मधुपर्के च यज्ञे च पितृदैवतकर्मणि । अत्रैव पशवो हिंस्या नान्यत्रेत्यब्रवीन्मनुः ॥
एष्वर्थेषु पशून् हिंसन् वेदवेदार्थविद्द्विजः । आत्मानं च पशूंश्चैव गमयत्युत्तमां गतिम् ॥

The above three verses are quoted also by Hemacandra in *Yogaśāstra* (op. cit.) Manu 5. 27, 32 and 56 are also quoted.

प्रोक्षितं भक्षयेन्मांसं ब्राह्मणानां तु काम्यया । यथाविधि नियुक्तस्तु प्राणानामेव चात्यये ॥
क्रीत्वा स्वयं वा क्षुत्पाद्य परोपहृतमेव च । अर्चयित्वा पितॄन् देवान् खादन् मांसं न दुष्यति ॥
न मांसभक्षणे दोषो न मद्ये न च मैथुने । प्रवृत्तिरेव भूतानां निवृत्तिश्च महत् फलम् ॥

The following verse is cited in *Yaśastilaka* Book VII, section 30.

ओषध्यः पशवो वृक्षास्तिर्यञ्चः पक्षिणो नराः । यज्ञार्थं निधनं प्राप्ताः प्राप्नुवन्त्युच्छ्रितां गतिम् ॥

The verse corresponds to Manu 5. 40, but Manu reads *tathā* for *narāḥ*. Somadeva seems to have purposely substituted *narāḥ* for *tathā* to exaggerate the repulsive character of Vedic sacrifices. Certain verses on the duties and character of women are quoted from Manu (5. 155, 154 and 9. 14) in Book IV.

नास्ति स्त्रीणां पृथग्यज्ञो न व्रतं नाप्युपोषितम् । पतिं शुश्रूषयेद्यत्तु तेन स्वर्गे महीयते[1] ॥
विशीलः कामवृत्तो वा गुणैर्वा परिवर्जितः । उपचर्यः स्त्रिया साध्व्या सततं देववत् पतिः ॥
नैता रूपं प्रतीक्षन्ते नासां वयसि संस्थितिः । विरूपं रूपवन्तं वा पुमानित्येव भुञ्जते ॥

The following two verses are cited by Somadeva in Book IV as 'old traditions' (पुरातन्यौ श्रुती):

पौंश्चल्याच्चलचित्तत्वान्नैःस्नेह्याच्च स्वभावतः । रक्षिता यत्नतोऽपीह भर्तृष्वेता विकुर्वते ॥
यदर्थे च मही त्यक्ता जीवितार्धं च हारितम् । सा मां त्यजति निःस्नेहा कः स्त्रीणां वल्लभो नरः ॥

Of these the first is Manu 9. 15. The second is cited also in *Pañcatantra* 4. 47 which reads it somewhat differently:

यदर्थे स्वकुलं त्यक्तं जीवितार्धं च हारितम् । सा मां त्यजति निःस्नेहा कः स्त्रीणां विश्वसेन्नरः ॥

The following two verses on renouncing the world and taking to an ascetic's life are cited from Manu (6. 3, 6. 36), the first in Book IV and the second in Book VI, section 5.

संत्यज्य ग्राम्यमाहारं सर्वं चैव परिच्छदम् । पुत्रेषु दारान्निक्षिप्य वनं गच्छेत् सहैव वा ॥
अधीत्य विधिवद्वेदान् पुत्रांश्चोत्पाद्य युक्तितः । इष्ट्वा यज्ञे यथाकालं ततः प्रव्रजितो भवेत् ॥

The Manu text reads *dharmataḥ* for *yuktitaḥ* and the second line as इष्ट्वा च शक्तितो यज्ञैर्मनो मोक्षे निवेशयेत्. The accompanying verse cited in Book VI, section 5:

अपुत्रस्य गतिर्नास्ति स्वर्गो नैव च नैव च । तस्मात् पुत्रमुखं दृष्ट्वा पश्चाद्भवति भिक्षुकः ॥

1 Here the Manu text reads the second line as पतिं शुश्रूषते येन तेन स्वर्गे महीयते.

is not found in Manu, and seems to be a *subhāṣita*. It is cited in Böhtlingk's *Indische Sprüche* from a *Vikramacarita* and a *Subhāṣitārṇava*.

The precept cited in *Yaśastilaka*, Book IV (आत्मानं सततं रक्षेद्दारैरपि धनैरपि) is the second line of Manu 7. 213. The verse in question occurs also in *Garuḍa-purāṇa* (Pūrvakhaṇḍa 109. 1). The above citations are all anonymous, but a verse quoted in Book IV (p. 100) is definitely attributed to Vaivasvata Manu and found in the *Manusmṛti* (6. 66):

भूषितोऽपि चरेद्धर्मं यत्र तत्राश्रमे रतः । समः सर्वेषु भूतेषु न लिङ्गं धर्मकारणम् ॥

It may be noted here that Kullūka reads *dūṣitaḥ* for *bhūṣitaḥ*. but the latter reading is found in Medhātithi and adopted by Jolly in his edition of Manu. The verse in question is found also in *Agnipurāṇa* 161. 11, which however reads शुद्धभावः for भूषितोऽपि.

The following verse on the sufferings in hell of those who kill animals is cited in Book IV as a Purāṇic tradition (इति कथमियं पौराणिकी श्रुतिः):

यावन्ति पशुरोमाणि पशुगात्रेषु भारत । तावद्वर्षसहस्राणि पच्यन्ते पशुघातकाः ॥

A similar verse occurs in Manu 5. 38:

यावन्ति पशुरोमाणि तावत्कृत्वो ह मारणम् । वृथापशुघ्नः प्राप्नोति प्रेत्य जन्मनि जन्मनि ॥

Somadeva cites the following verse in Book VII, section 30.

महोक्षो वा महाजो वा श्रोत्रियाय विशस्यते । निवेद्यते तु दिव्याय स्रक्सुगन्धनिधिर्विधिः ॥

There is a similar verse in Yājñavalkya 1. 109 (Ānandāśrama ed.), but the second line in it is entirely different.

महोक्षं वा महाजं वा श्रोत्रियायोपकल्पयेत् । सत्क्रियाऽन्वासनं स्वादुभोजनं सूनृतं वचः ॥

The following verses are cited anonymously in Book IV. तदुक्तम्—

विमत्सरः कुचेलाङ्गः सर्वद्वन्द्वविवर्जितः । समः सर्वेषु भूतेषु स पतिः परिकीर्तितः ॥
आपस्नानं व्रतस्नानं मन्त्रस्नानं तथैव च । आपस्नानं गृहस्थस्य व्रतमन्त्रैस्तपस्विनः ॥
न स्त्रीभिः संगमो यस्य यः परे ब्रह्मणि स्थितः । तं शुचिं सर्वदा प्राहुर्मारुतं च हुताशनम् ॥ इति. P. 110

उक्तं च—

तिलसर्षपमात्रं यो मांसमश्नाति मानवः । स श्वभ्रान्न निवर्तेत यावच्चन्द्रदिवाकरौ ॥
संदिग्धेऽपि परलोके त्याज्यमेवाशुभं बुधैः । यदि न स्यात्ततः किं स्यादस्ति चेन्नास्तिको हतः ॥ P. 115

तथा च स्मृतिः—

सप्तग्रामेषु यत् पापमग्निना भस्मसात्कृते । तस्य चैतद्भवेत् पापं मधुबिन्दुनिषेवणात् ॥ P. 116

The following verses are cited in Book IV as an illustration of alleged contradictory statements found in Smṛti texts. The first verse, for example, condemns the acceptance by Brāhmaṇas of food or livelihood from Śūdras, whereas the second verse permits Brāhmaṇas to accept even the flesh of animals killed by Cāṇḍālas, dogs and tigers for use in religious rites.

शूद्रान्नं शूद्रशुश्रूषा शूद्रप्रेषणकारिणः । शूद्रदत्ता च या वृत्तिः पर्याप्तं नरकाय ते ॥
तथा मांसं श्वचाण्डालक्रव्यादादिनिपातितम् । ब्राह्मणेन ग्रहीतव्यं हव्यकव्याय कर्मणे ॥ P. 118

With regard to the first verse, the Smṛtis of Aṅgiras and Āpastamba (Chap. 8) contain a statement very similar in tone.

शूद्रान्नं शूद्रसंपर्कः शूद्रेणैव सहासनम् । शूद्राज्ज्ञानागमः कश्चिज्ज्वलन्तमपि पातयेत् ॥

As regards the second verse, the *Prajāpatismṛti* recommends the acquisition of meat for religious purposes from hunters, who, as a rule, belong to the lower strata of society: व्याधेभ्यो मेध्यमांसानि ग्राह्याणि द्रव्यपर्ययैः (verse 143). Further, the *Bṛhat-Parāśarasaṁhitā* 6. 328[1] holds that the flesh of animals killed by dogs and tigers is pure, and may be used in religious functions.

क्रव्यादैः सारमेयाद्यैर्हतं मृगादिमाहरेत् । एतच्छाकवदिच्छन्ति पवित्रं द्विजसत्तमाः ॥

Somadeva refers in Book III to several ancient writers on Smṛti. The envoy of Yaśodhara is described as surpassing in intellect Pulaha, Puloma, Pālakāpya and Kātyāyana.[2] Of these writers Pulaha and Pulastya are among the ten teachers of Dharma mentioned in a verse of Vṛddha-Yājñavalkya quoted in Viśvarūpa's commentary on *Yājñavalkyasmṛti* 1. 5, and mentioned also in a similar verse in *Vṛddha-Hārītasmṛti* 8. 3. Puloma was a writer on politics, and his opinion is cited in Kāmandaka's *Nītisāra* 8. 21. Kātyāyana was a great jurist.[3] The reading Pālakāpya in the above list is doubtful. It is not clear why a writer on elephants should be mentioned along with celebrated writers on Dharma. Besides, the four Manuscripts used by me read Pālakāvya, and even Śrutasāgara who reads Pālakāpya says that there may be a reference to two different names,[4] so that we have to suppose the mention of two writers, Pāla and Kāvya. The latter is no other than Śukra, the great authority on *rājanīti*, but we know nothing about Pāla as a writer on Dharma or state-craft. It may, however, be mentioned that a writer named Pālaki is quoted in the anonymous commentary on *Nītivākyāmṛta* 22. 2, but the quotation is about the eight weapons of a war elephant, and this Pālaki may turn out to be the same as Pālakāpya. On the other hand, there was an old writer on Dharma named Gopāla, who is mentioned in the *Bṛhat-parāśarasaṁhitā* of Suvrata (1. 14) and the *Rājanītiratnākara* of Caṇḍeśvara.

ELEPHANT-LORE

In Book II Somadeva refers to the treatises on elephant-lore composed by Ibhacārin, Yājñavalkya, Vāddhali (v. r. Vāhali), Nara, Nārada,

---

1 See *Parāśaradharmasaṁhitā*, Vol. III, Part I (*Bombay Sanskrit Series*).
2 'निजप्रज्ञातिशयावहेलितपुलहपुलोमपुलस्तिपालकाप्यकात्यायनमतिजातम्'
3 Kane: *The History of Dharmaśāstra*, Vol. I, p. 213ff.
4 पालकाप्यस्य काव्यस्य वा द्वयं भिन्नम् ।

Rājaputra, Gautama and other sages. The committee of experts appointed to examine and select an elephant for Yaśodhara's coronation is described as having mastered the treatises of these writers. None of their works is now extant, but it is remarkable that so many texts on elephants were available in the tenth century. Some of the names occur in a long list of sages who are represented as attending the court of Romapāda, the king of the Aṅgas, in Pālakāpya's *Hastyāyurveda* (Chap. I), an ancient work of which we have only an imperfect text in the printed edition. These sages are described in Pālakāpya as conversant with the ways of elephants,[1] and we find mentioned among them Gautama, Rājaputra, Bāṣkali (v. r. Vākvali, Vākpati), Yājñavalkya, Nārada and Mātaṅga. The latter name might be our Ibhacārin, as the *Mātaṅgalīlā* of Nīlakaṇṭha, which summarizes this portion of Pālakāpya in the first Paṭala, calls one of the sages Mātaṅgacārin, which is same as Ibhacārin.[2]

The nature of Somadeva's reference leaves no doubt that there were actual treatises on elephants attributed to Gautama, Yājñavalkya and Nārada, but it is not known whether these authors had anything to do with their namesakes in the field of Smṛti literature. As regards Rājaputra, he seems to be the same as the Rājaputra whom we know as a writer on politics from citations in the anonymous commentary on *Nītivākyāmṛta*. According to Kane,[3] Rājaputra is cited also in Ballālasena's *Adbhutasāgara*, but Somadeva's reference to him is about two centuries earlier, and probably the earliest known, if we leave aside the occurrence of the name in Pālakāpya. Among later writers Mallinātha cites Rājaputra's treatise on elephant-lore in his commentary on *Raghuvaṁśa* 4. 39.[4]

In Book II Somadeva describes the young prince Yaśodhara as being proficient in elephant lore like Romapāda,[5] to whom we have already referred. In Pālakāpya's *Hastyāyurveda* (Chap. I) he is stated to be the king of the Aṅgas, and we see him at his court at Campā, attended by a large number of sages, and worried by the problem of catching wild elephants. Then appears the semi-legendary figure of Pālakāpya, the great authority on the diseases of elephants and their cure; and throughout the rest of the work Romapāda is represented as the pupil of the famous teacher. According to the *Hastyāyurveda*, Pālakāpya was the son of a sage named Sāmagāyana and a female elephant who was no other than a nymph metamorphosed by a

1 यूथस्य नयकोविदाः 1. 67.
2 See verse 5.
3 Op. cit., p. 341.
4 'त्वग्भेदाच्छोणितस्रावान्मांसस्य क्रथनादपि । आत्मानं यो न जानाति तस्य गम्भीरवेदिता ॥ इति राजपुत्रीये
5 'रोमपाद इव गजविद्यासु'

curse. The home of the sage was on the side of the Himālayas on the banks of the Lauhitya or the Brahmaputra, which points to north-eastern Assam where the river is still called Luit. From here Pālakāpya wandered to Campā in search of a favourite herd of elephants, which had been driven away by Romapāda and his troops in the absence of the sage. We are further told that, at the request of Romapāda, Pālakāpya decided to settle at Campā, and the king caused a hermitage to be laid out for the sage in the outskirts of the city. The tradition of Pālakāpya and Romapāda as teacher and pupil is recorded also in *Agnipurāṇa*, chapters 286 and 387. Nīlakaṇṭha says in his *Mātaṅgalīlā* 12. 29 that *roman*, according to the old teachers, means a lotus, and Romapāda was so called because his feet were marked with figures of lotuses.

PHILOSOPHICAL CITATIONS

Most of the philosophical citations are anonymous, and occur towards the end of Book V and in Book VI, sections 1 and 2. They have been considered in Chap. VIII and IX, and some of them are reproduced below. There are at least two quotations from the Upaniṣads. "न ह वै सशरीरस्य प्रियाप्रिययोरपहतिरस्ति । अशरीरं वाव सन्तं न प्रियाप्रिये स्पृशतः ।" Book V, p. 254.

एक एव हि भूतात्मा देहे देहे व्यवस्थितः । एकधानेकधा चापि दृश्यते जलचन्द्रवत् ॥ VI. 1

The first is from the *Chāndogya Upaniṣad* VIII. 12. 1. The second occurs in various texts, e. g., *Brahmabindūpaniṣad*, *Amṛtabindūpaniṣad* etc. with slight variations. Śaṁkara in his Bhāṣya on the *S'vetāśvataropaniṣad* 1. 8 quotes the verse from *Vāśiṣṭha Yogaśāstra.*

The following definition of the fundamental doctrine of the Vedānte in *Yaśastilaka* VI. 1, namely, "यथा घटविघटने घटाकाशमाकाशीभवति तथा देहोच्छेदात् सर्वः प्राणी परे ब्रह्मणिलीयते" reminds one of *Avadhūtagītā* 2. 25:

घटे भिन्ने घटाकाश आकाशे लीयते यथा । देहाभावे तथा योगी स्वरूपे परमात्मनि ॥

Somadeva remarks in Book V (P. 254): कथं चेदं वचनमजर्यम्—

समस्तेषु वस्तुष्वनुस्यूतमेकं समस्तानि वस्तूनि यं न स्पृशन्ति ।
वियद्वत् सदा शुद्धिमद् यत्स्वरूपं स सिद्धोपलब्धिः स नित्योऽहमात्मा ॥

The verse occurs in the well-known Vedāntic text *Hastāmalaka*, commented upon by Śaṁkara, which declares the Self to be identical with intelligence. Printed editions usually read the second line as follows:

······शुद्धमच्छस्वरूपं स नित्योपलब्धिस्वरूपोऽहमात्मा ॥

The following verses are cited in Book V (p. 252) in illustration of Buddhist doctrines.

यः पश्यत्यात्मानं तस्यात्मनि भवति शाश्वतः स्नेहः । स्नेहात् सुखेषु तृष्यति तृष्णा दोषांस्तिरस्कुरुते ॥
आत्मनि सति परसंज्ञा स्वपरविभागात् परिग्रहद्वेषौ । अनयोः संप्रतिबद्धाः सर्वे दोषाः प्रजायन्ते ॥

The first verse is quoted also in Haribhadra's *Anekāntajayapatākā* (p. 33) and the second in *Nyāyakandalī* (p. 279). Other Buddhist verses quoted by Somadeva are: तदाह--

यथा स्नेहक्षयाद्दीपः प्रशाम्यति निरन्वयः । तथा क्लेशक्षयाज्जन्तुः प्रशाम्यति निरन्वयः ॥ Book V

तदुक्तम्—

वेदप्रामाण्यं कस्यचित् कर्तृवादः स्नाने धर्मेच्छा जातिवादावलेपः ।
संतापारम्भः क्लेशनाशाय चेति ध्वस्तप्रज्ञानां पञ्च लिङ्गानि जाड्ये ॥

The following verses seem to be quoted from Aśvaghoṣa's *Saundarananda* XVI. 28, 29 wherein the lines appear in a somewhat different order. तदुक्तम्—

दिशं न कांचिद्विदिशं न कांचिन्नैवावनिं गच्छति नान्तरिक्षम् ।
दीपो यथा निर्वृतिमभ्युपेतः स्नेहक्षयात् केवलमेति शान्तिम् ॥
दिशं न कांचिद्विदिशं न कांचिन्नैवावनिं गच्छति नान्तरिक्षम् ।
जीवस्तथा निर्वृतिमभ्युपेतः क्लेशक्षयात् केवलमेति शान्तिम् ॥[1]

The statement of the doctrines of the Laukāyatikas put in the mouth of Yaśodhara's mother in Book IV is taken almost verbatim from the *Kāmasūtra* I. 2. 25–30. Somadeva says "न धर्मांश्चरेत् एष्यत्फलत्वात् संशयितत्वाच्च । को ह्यबालिशो हस्तगतं पादगतं कुर्यात् । वरमद्य कपोतः श्वो मयूरात् । वरं सांशयिकान्निष्कादसांशयिकः कार्षापणः" इति महान् खलु लोके लौकायतिकलोककोलाहलः । (p. 12). It may be pointed out that Vātsyāyana reads *paragatam* for *pādagatam* and simply says इति लौकायतिकाः·

The following verse cited by Somadeva in VI. 1 to illustrate the power of Bhāvanā to represent all things clearly is cited also by Anantavīrya in his commentary on *Parīkṣāmukhasūtra* (*Pratyakṣoddeśa*). तदुक्तम्—

पिहिते कारागारे तमसि च सूचिमुखाग्रनिर्भेद्ये । मयि च निमीलितनयने तथापि कान्ताननं व्यक्तम् ॥

Patañjali's *Yogasūtras* 1. 24–26 are quoted in VI. 1, 2.

'क्लेशकर्मविपाकाशयैरपरामृष्टः पुरुषविशेष ईश्वरस्तत्र निरतिशयं सर्वज्ञबीजम्' इति पतञ्जलिजल्पितम् । तदाह पतञ्जलिः—'स पूर्वेषामपि गुरुः कालेनानवच्छेदात् ।'

The following verse is quoted in Book V and VI. 1 where it is attributed to Avadhūta.

ऐश्वर्यमप्रतिहतं सहजो विरागस्तृप्तिर्निसर्गजनिता वशितेन्द्रियेषु ।
आत्यन्तिकं सुखमनावरणा च शक्तिर्ज्ञानं च सर्वविषयं भगवंस्तवैव ॥ इत्यवधूताभिधानं......

The verse is not found in the Avadhūtagītā. It is quoted and attributed to Avadhūta also in Anantavīrya's commentary on *Parīkṣāmukhasūtra* (op. cit.). A very similar verse is quoted from *Vāyupurāṇa* in Vācaspatimiśra's

1 Aśvaghoṣa reads दीपो यथा निर्वृतिमभ्युपेतो नैवावनिं गच्छति नान्तरिक्षम् । दिशं न कांचिद्विदिशं न कांचित् स्नेहक्षयात् केवलमेति शान्तिम् ॥ etc.; further, he reads एवं कृती for जीवस्तथा·

commentary on the *Vyāsabhāṣya* on Yogasūtras 1. 25. It is cited also in Udayana's *Nyāyakusumāñjali* (Chap. 5), and occurs in *Īśvaragītā* (*Kūrmapurāṇa, Uparibhāga*, 8. 12).

सर्वज्ञता तृप्तिरनादिबोधः स्वतन्त्रता नित्यमलुप्तशक्तिः । अनन्तशक्तिश्च विभोर्विधिज्ञाः षडाहुरङ्गानि महेश्वरस्य ॥

The verse occurs also in *S'ivapurāṇa* (*Vidyeśvarasaṁhitā*) 16. 13 which reads the last two lines thus:

अनन्तशक्तिश्च महेश्वरस्य यन्मानसैश्वर्यमवैति वेदः ॥

Avadhūta seems to have been a Śaiva philosopher. The following verse is attributed to him in Śrīkumāra's commentary on Bhoja's *Tattvaprakāśa* 1. 15. शक्तिद्वयं च भगवतावधूतपादेनोक्तम्—

बध्नाति काचिदपि शक्तिरलुप्तशक्तेः क्षेत्रज्ञमप्रतिहता तव पाशजालैः ।
ज्ञानासिना च विनिकृत्य गुणानशेषानन्या करोत्यभिमुखं पुरुषं विमुक्तौ ॥

Somadeva quotes a number of verses from little known Śaiva texts in Book V (pp. 251, 255). तदाह—

प्रपञ्चरहितं शास्त्रं प्रपञ्चरहितो गुरुः । प्रपञ्चरहितं ज्ञानं प्रपञ्चरहितः शिवः ॥ तदाह—
शिवं शक्तिविनाशेन ये वाञ्छन्ति नराधमाः । ते भूमिरहिताद्बीजात् सन्तु नूनं फलोत्तमाः ॥
अग्निवत् सर्वभक्षोऽपि भवभक्तिपरायणः । भुक्तिं जीवन्नवाप्नोति मुक्तिं तु लभते मृतः ॥
अदृष्टविग्रहाच्छान्ताच्छिवात् परमकारणात् । नादरूपं समुत्पन्नं शास्त्रं परमदुर्लभम् ॥ Quoted also in VI.2
भोग्यामाहुः प्रकृतिमृषयश्चेतनाशक्तिशून्यां भोक्ता नैनां परिणमयितुं बन्धवर्ती समर्थः ।
भोग्येऽप्यस्मिन् भवति मिथुने पुष्कलस्तत्र हेतुर्नीलग्रीव त्वमसि भुवनस्थापनासूत्रधारः ॥

The following controversial verse directed against the central conception of Śaivism is cited twice in Book V and in VI. 2. तदुक्तम्—

वक्ता नैव सदाशिवो विकरणस्तस्मात् परो रागवान् द्वैविध्यादपरं तृतीयमिति चेत्तत्कस्य हेतोरभूत् ।
शक्त्या चेत् परकीयया कथमसौ तद्वानसंबन्धतः संबन्धोऽपि न जाघटीति भवतां शास्त्रं निरालम्बनम् ॥

The following verse quoted by Somadeva in Book V is cited from Lakṣmīdhara's *Kṛtyakalpataru* (*Rājadharmakāṇḍa*) XIV. 160. तदाह—

विधिर्विधाता नियतिः स्वभावः कालो ग्रहश्चेश्वरदैवकर्म ।
पुण्यानि भाग्यानि तथा कृतान्तः पर्यायनामानि पुराकृतस्य ॥

A reference to Kumārila occurs in Book V. कथमिदमुदाहारि कुमारिलेन—

विशुद्धज्ञानदेहाय त्रिवेदीदिव्यचक्षुषे । श्रेयःप्राप्तिनिमित्ताय नमः सोमार्धधारिणे ॥

It is the initial verse of Kumārila's *S'lokavārtika*.

The following verses are quoted from Jaina texts in Book VI, section 21. उक्तं च—

आसन्नभव्यताकर्महानिसंज्ञित्वशुद्धपरिणामाः । सम्यक्त्वहेतुरन्तर्बाह्योऽप्युपदेशकादिश्च ॥

उक्तं च—

अबुद्धिपूर्वापेक्षायामिष्टानिष्टं स्वदैवतः । बुद्धिपूर्वव्यपेक्षायामिष्टानिष्टं स्वपौरुषात् ॥

दशविधं तदाह—

आज्ञामार्गसमुद्भवमुपदेशात् सूत्रबीजसंक्षेपात् । विस्तारार्थाभ्यां भवमवपरमावादिगाढं च ॥

The second verse occurs in Samantabhadra's *Āptamīmāṁsā*. The third verse is from Guṇabhadra's *Atmānuśāsana*, and explained by Somadeva in detail. Another verse from Guṇabhadra's *Atmānuśāsana* is cited in Book VII, section 26. तदुक्तम्—

परिणाममेव कारणमाहुः खलु पुण्यपापयोः कुशलाः । तस्मात् पुण्योपचयः पापापचयश्च सुविधेयः ॥

Guṇabhadra wrote towards the end of the ninth century, and it is remark able that he counted as an authoritative writer by the middle of the tenth century. A reference to the great Jaina logician and philosophical writer Akalaṁka occurs in Book II.[1] He flourished about the eighth century A. D.[2] and wrote *Tattvārtharājavārtikālaṁkāra*, *Nyāyaviniścaya* and other works.

MEDICAL AUTHORITIES

In *Yaśastilaka* 3. 328 Somadeva refers to the opinions of several ancient medical writers about the right time for taking the principal meal of the day. They are Cārāyaṇa, Nimi, Dhiṣaṇa and Caraka.

चारायणो निशि निमिः पुनरस्तकाले मध्ये दिनस्य धिषणश्चरकः प्रभाते ।
भुक्तिं जगाद नृपते मम चैष सर्गस्तस्याः स एव समयः क्षुधितो यदैव ॥

A casual reference to Caraka occurs also in Book VI, section 10: 'अभिनवजनमनोह्लादन-वचनागदप्रयोगचरकभट्टारक'. Nimi is a very ancient authority, being quoted in *Caraka-saṁhitā* (*Sūtrasthāna*, Chap. 26). He is described as the king of Videha: 'सप्त रसा इति निमिर्वैदेहः, मधुराम्ललवणकटुतिक्तकषायक्षाराः ।'. Nimi is quoted also in *Aṣṭāṅgahṛdaya* of Vāgbhaṭa II,[3] Kṣīrasvāmin's commentary on the *Amarakoṣa* 2. 5 28, Ḍalhaṇa's commentary on *Suśrutasaṁhitā*[4] and other works. Cārāyaṇa can hardly be called a medical writer. In Vātsyāyana's *Kāmasūtra* 1. 1. 12 Cārāyaṇa is said to have treated the general section of the *Kāmasūtra* of Bābhravya Pāñcāla in a separate treatise. It is noteworthy that the opinion of Cārāyaṇa referred to by Somadeva is actually found in Vātsyāyana's *Kāmasūtra* 1. 4. 20: 'सायं चारायणस्य'. As explained in the *Jayamaṅgalā* commentary, Cārāyaṇa recommends eating in the forenoon and the evening and not in the forenoon and the afternoon, as advised by Vātsyāyana. A number of verses from Cārāyaṇa is quoted in the anonymous commentary on Somadeva's *Nītivākyāmṛta*, but as they are on Nīti, it is difficult to say whether the two Cārāyaṇas are identical.

---

1 'अकलङ्कदेव इव प्रमाणशास्त्रेषु'

2 Hiralal: *Catalogue of Sanskrit and Prākrit Manuscripts in C. P. and Berar*, p. XXVIII.

3 See list of authors cited in N. S. Edition.

4 See list of authors cited in N. S. edition.

In Book II the young prince Yaśodhara is declared to be well-versed in the art of healing, like Kāśirāja.[1] Kāśirāja is explained by the commentator as Dhanvantari. According to a tradition preserved in the *Harivaṁśa* (Parva I, Chap. 29), in the dynasty of Kāśa king Dhanva had a son named Dhanvantari, said to be an incarnation of the divine physician of that name on account of his knowledge of medical lore. In the same line of kings Divodāsa came two generations after Dhanvantari, and it is remarkable that at the beginning of the *Suśruta-saṁhitā* Suśruta and other sages are described as being instructed in medical lore by Divodāsa Dhanvantari, the king of Benares: अथ खलु भगवन्तममरवरमृषिगणपरिवृतमाश्रमस्थं काशिराजं दिवोदासधन्वन्तरिमौपधेनव...सुश्रुतप्रभृतय ऊचुः। 'Dhanvantari' is here explained by Ḍalhaṇa as 'an expert in surgery,'[2] and it is clear that Divodāsa, like his ancestor, was an expert in the art of healing and had the epithet Dhanvantari attached to his name. Divodāsa is described in the *Harivaṁśa* (op. cit., verse 29) as the king of Benares, and in the Mahābhārata (*Anuśāsanaparva* 30. 16 Cal. ed.) he is said to have founded the city. It appears that an ancient line of kings ruled in the country round about Benares, and both Dhanvantari and Divodāsa belonging to this dynasty were famous as medical authorities and known as Kāśirāja. The *Harivaṁśa* (op. cit., verses 26–7) tells us that Kāśirāja Dhanvantari learnt the Āyurveda from Bhāradvāja, and dividing it into eight sections taught them to his disciples.

तस्य गेहे समुत्पन्नो देवो धन्वन्तरिस्तदा। काशिराजो महाराज सर्वरोगप्रणाशनः॥
आयुर्वेदं भरद्वाजात् प्राप्येह भिषजां क्रियाम्। तमष्टधा पुनर्व्यस्य शिष्येभ्यः प्रत्यपादयत्॥

Dhanvantari is cited as an authority in the *Carakasaṁhitā* (*S'ārīrasthāna* 6. 21), *Aṣṭāṅgahṛdaya*[3] and other works. For a fuller discussion of the problem of Dhanvantari the reader may refer to the learned Sanskrit Introduction to the Nirnayasagar edition of the *Suśrutasaṁhitā*.

WRITERS AND TREATISES ON PAINTING, SCULPTURE, GEMS ETC.

A work on painting called *Citrakarma* ascribed to Prajāpati is quoted in Book IV. प्रजापतिप्रोक्ते च चित्रकर्मणि—

श्रमणं तैललिप्ताङ्गं नवभिर्भित्तिभिर्युतम्। यो लिखेत् स लिखेत् सर्वां पृथ्वीमपि ससागराम्॥

A work on sculpture called *Adityamata* is quoted in the same Book. आदित्यमते च—

भवबीजाङ्कुरमथना अष्टमहाप्रातिहार्यविभवसमेताः। ते देवा दशतालाः शेषा देवा भवन्ति नवतालाः॥

A work on gems called *Ratnaparīkṣā* is quoted in Book V.

1 'काशिराज इव शरीरोपचारेषु'

2 'धनुः शल्यशास्त्रं तस्य अन्तं पारम् इयर्ति गच्छतीति धन्वन्तरिः तम्।'

3 See list of authors cited in N. S. edition.

तदुक्तं रत्नपरीक्षायाम्—

न केवलं तच्छुभकृन्नृपस्य मन्ये प्रजानामपि तद्विभूत्यै । यद्योजनानां परतः शताद्धि सर्वाननर्थान् विमुखीकरोति ॥

The work cited by Somadeva is Buddhabhaṭṭa's *Ratnaparīkṣā*, and the verse is found in the text edited by Finot in *Les Lapidaires Indiens* (Paris, 1896). The work is incorporated in *Garuḍapurāṇa* (*Pūrvakhaṇḍa*, chapters 68-80) without acknowledgement. The verse cited by Somadeva is also found among the verses quoted from *Garuḍapurāṇa* in Bhoja's *Yuktikalpataru* in the section on gems. It may be noted that *Garuḍapurāṇa* as well as the other two texts (with slight variations) read भाग्यैः प्रजानामपि तस्य जन्म for मन्ये प्रजानामपि तद्विभूत्यै recorded by Somadeva. In Book II the young Yaśodhara is described as an expert in the examination of gems, like Śukanāsa, who seems to be an ancient authority on gems.[1]

Reference to writers on elephants has been made in a preceding section. In Book II Yaśodhara is compared to Raivata in the mastery of the science of horses.[2] That there were works on the subject in the tenth century is shown by the reference to the *ācāryapariṣad* 'committee of experts' appointed to select a horse on the occasion of Yaśodhara's coronation in Book II and the use of technical terms. But Raivata is explained in the commentary as the son of the Sun, and appears to be a mythological figure. He is the same as the god Revanta mentioned in *Bṛhatsaṁhitā* 58. 56, according to which his image should be represented as riding a horse, surrounded by a hunting party.

A quotation from *Bṛhatsaṁhitā*, Chap. 60, occurs in Book IV. वराहमिहरव्याहृते प्रतिष्ठाकाण्डे च—

विष्णोर्भागवता मयाश्च सवितुर्विप्रा विदुर्ब्राह्मणां मातॄणामिति मातृमण्डलविदः शंभोः सभस्मा द्विजाः ।
शाक्याः सर्वहिताय शान्तमनसो नग्ना जिनानां विदुर्ये यं देवमुपाश्रिताः स्वविधिना ते तस्य कुर्युः क्रियाम् ॥

A verse from *Nimittādhyāya* occurs in the same Book. निमित्ताध्याये च—

पद्मिनी राजहंसाश्च निर्ग्रन्थाश्च तपोधनाः । यं देशमुपसर्पन्ति सुभिक्षं तत्र निर्दिशेत् ॥

A verse from *Svapnādhyāya* is quoted in Book VI, section I: न चायं सत्यस्वप्नोऽप्रसिद्धः स्वप्नाध्यायेऽतीव सुप्रसिद्धत्वात् । तथा हि—

यस्तु पश्यति रात्र्यन्ते राजानं कुञ्जरं हयम् । सुवर्णं वृषभं गां च कुटुम्बं तस्य वर्धते ॥

There is a *Svapnādhyāya* in thirtyfive verses in *Matsyapurāṇa* (Chap. 242), but it does not contain the above verse which, however, occurs in the *Svapnādhyāya* included in *Agnipurāṇa* (Chap. 229). Two interesting references to *Svapnādhyāya* or the science of dreams occur in *Lalitavistara*. In

---

1 'शुकनास इव रत्नपरीक्षासु'

2 'रैवत इव हयनयेषु'

Chap. 12 it is mentioned among the branches of study in which the Bodhisattva distinguished himself. In chap. 6 we find mentioned a class of people whose vocation seems to have been the interpretation of dreams, being styled as स्वप्राध्यायीपाठक.

A reference to the science of arms occurs in Book III, the *Dhanurveda* being described as occupying the highest place among treatises on the *āyudhasiddhānta*. It is, however, doubtful whether the verse 3. 465 is a citation from the Dhanurveda. Somadeva says

यावन्ति भुवि शस्त्राणि तेषां श्रेष्ठतरं धनुः। धनुषां गोचरे तानि न तेषां गोचरो धनुः ॥
इत्यायुधसिद्धान्तमध्यासादितसिंहनादाद्धनुर्वेदादुपश्रुत्य......

A *Pañcatantra* is mentioned in Book VII, section 31, but it is doubtful whether it has anything to do with the wellknown book of tales: 'पञ्चतन्त्रादिशास्त्रविस्तृतवचन उग्रसेनो नाम सचिवः।' It is noteworthy that a marginal note in Ms. A explains *pañcatantra* as *tarkavyākaraṇādi*.

In the same section of Book VII the following verse is attributed to 'those who are well-versed in the Purāṇas'. वदन्ति पुराणविदः—

विधुर्गुरोः कलत्रेण गोतमस्यामरेश्वरः। संतनोश्चापि दुश्चर्मा समगंस्त पुरा किल ॥

Casual references to the Tripiṭaka and the treatise of Bharata occur in the description of the Jaina temple in Book V. 'पिटकत्रयपद्धतिरिव योगाचारगोचरा', 'भरतपदवीव विधिलयनाट्याडम्बरा'.

Dattaka, an ancient authority on erotic lore, is mentioned in Book II.[1] In Vātsyāyana's *Kāmasūtra* 1. 1. 11 Dattaka is said to have treated the section on courtesans of the *Kāmasūtra* of Bābhravya Pāñcāla in a separate treatise, being employed for the purpose by the courtesans of Pāṭaliputra. It may also be mentioned that a Kāmasūtra is mentioned at least twice by Somadeva, but without any reference to Vātsyāyana or any other author. 'न क्षमश्चिरपरिचितकामसूत्रायाः काकिलादिकरणोदाहरणानाम्' Book I, 'शृङ्गारवृत्तिभिरुदाहृतकामसूत्रम्' 1. 73.

A number of popular or moral verses is quoted by Somadeva without mentioning the source (Book VII, sections 27, 28, 29; Books IV & VII; Book VI, sections 5, 6, 10, 13, 15, 16, 17 and 19):

पादमायान्निधिं कुर्यात् पादं वित्ताय कल्पयेत्। धर्मोपभोगयोः पादं पादं भर्तव्यपोषणे ॥ इति पुण्यश्लोकः[2]
भवति चात्र श्लोकः—अल्पैरपि समर्थैः स्यात् सहायविजयी नृपः। कार्यायान्तो हि कुन्तस्य दण्डस्त्वस्य परिच्छदः॥
भवति चात्र श्लोकः—अस्थाने बद्धकक्षाणां नराणां सुलभं द्वयम्। परत्र दुर्गतिर्दीर्घा दुष्कीर्तिश्चात्र शाश्वती ॥
न व्रतमस्थिग्रहणं शाकपयोमूलभैक्षचर्या वा। व्रतमेतदुन्नतधियामङ्गीकृतवस्तुनिर्वहणम् ॥
भवति चात्र श्लोकः—अतस्तत्त्वविहीनस्य वृथा व्रतसमुद्यमः। पुंसः स्वभावभीरोः स्यान्न शौर्यायायुधग्रहः ॥

1 'दत्तक इव कन्तुसिद्धान्तेषु'

2 Cf. चतुधा विभजे भोगे, सवे मित्तानि गन्थति, एकेन भोगे भुञ्जेय्य, द्वीहि कम्मं पयोजये, चतुत्थञ्च निधापेय्य, आपदासु भविस्सतीति। *Dīgha Nikāya* XXXI. 26.

भवति चात्र श्लोकः—उररीकृतनिर्वाहसाहसोचितचेतसाम् । उभौ कामदुघौ लोकौ कीर्तिश्चाल्पं जगत्त्रयम् ॥
भवति चात्र श्लोकः—जले तैलमिवैतिह्यं वृथा तत्र बहिर्श्रुतिः । रसवत् स्यान्न यत्रान्तर्बोधो वेधाय धातुषु ॥
भवति चात्र श्लोकः—विशुद्धमनसां पुंसां परिच्छेदपरात्मनाम् । किं कुर्वन्ति कृता विघ्नाः सदाचारखिलैः खलैः ॥
भवति चात्र श्लोकः—अन्तःसारशरीरेषु हितायैवाहितेहितम् । किं न स्यादग्निसंयोगः स्वर्णत्वाय तदश्मनि ॥
भवति चात्रार्या—तृणकल्पः श्रीकल्पः कान्तालोकश्चितोचितालोकः । पुण्यजनश्च स्वजनः कामविदूरे नरे भवति ॥
भवति चात्रार्या—पुण्यं वा पापं वा यत्काले जन्तुना पुराचरितम् । तत्तत्समये तस्य हि सुखं च दुःखं च योजयति ॥
भवतश्चात्र श्लोकौ—सम्बसंश्च समावेव यदि चित्तं मलीमसम् । यात्यक्षान्तेः क्षयं पूर्वः परश्चाशुभचेष्टितात् ॥
स्वमेव हन्तुमीहेत दुर्जनः सज्जनं द्विषन् । योऽधितिष्ठेत्तुलामेकः किमसौ न व्रजेदधः ॥

All the verses cited above occur in the two Books of *Yaśastilaka* containing the moral and religious stories. Besides, at the end of each story is quoted a verse containing a summing up of the story in question, and these verses seem to belong to Jaina Kathānaka literature, and are probably quoted from earlier texts. One such verse (Book VII, section 24)

क्षुद्रमत्स्यः किलैकस्तु स्वयंभूरमणोदधौ । महामत्स्यस्य कर्णस्थः स्मृतिदोषादधोगतः ॥

is, for example, found in Jaṭāsiṁhanandi's *Varāṅgacarita* 5. 103. Specimens of summary verses of this type are quoted below (from Books VI & VII):

भवति चात्र श्लोकः—कादम्बताक्ष्यगोसिंहपीठाधिपतिषु स्वयम् । आगतेष्वप्यभूत्रैषा रेवती मूढतावती ॥
भवति चात्र श्लोकः—सुदतीसंगमासक्तं पुष्पदन्तं तपस्विनम् । वारिषेणः कृतत्राणः स्थापयामास संयमे ॥
भवति चात्र श्लोकः—चण्डोऽवन्तिषु मातङ्गः पिशितस्य निवृत्तितः । अत्यल्पकालभाविन्याः प्रपेदे यक्षमुख्यताम् ॥
भवति चात्र श्लोकः सर्वार्थः—

पञ्चकृत्वः किलैकस्य मत्स्यस्याहिंसनात् पुरा । अभूत् पञ्चापदोऽतीत्य धनकीर्तिः पतिः श्रियः ॥

APPENDIX I

Somadeva and the Pratihāra Court of Kanauj

A statement in the anonymous commentary on Somadeva's *Nītivākyāmṛta* appears to show that the work was written at the instance of a king of Kanauj named Mahendradeva or Mahendrapāladeva. The commentator, whose date is unknown, mentions, however, a Jaina monk named Municandra as the author of *Nītivākyāmṛta*, and describes Somadeva as his *guru*.[1] This is, of course, contrary to all that we know about Somadeva who gives a lot of information about himself in the colophons to his *Yaśastilaka* and *Nītivākyāmṛta*.

It has recently been suggested by some scholars[2] that Somadeva may have passed some time at Kanauj: and, during his sojourn there, he was encouraged to compose his *Nītivākyāmṛta* by Mahendrapāla I (circa 893–907 A. D.), or more probably, by Mahendrapāla II who is known to have reigned about the middle of the tenth century A. D. The Partabgarh Inscription of the time of Mahendrapāla II of Kanauj is, for instance, dated *Saṁvat* 1003 = 946 A. D. (*Ep. Ind.* Vol. XIV, pp. 176-188). But the supposed connection of Somadeva with the Pratihāra court of Kanauj can hardly be accepted as a historical fact; as, unlike his association with the Deccan, it is mentioned neither in the colophons to his works nor in the Parbhani inscription.

It has been suggested that the following acrostic verse found at the end of the first Book of *Yaśastilaka* contains a veiled reference to Mahendrapāla.

सोऽयमाशार्पितयशा **म**हेन्द्रामरमान्यधीः । **दे**यात्ते संततानन्दं **व**स्त्वभीष्टं जिनाधिपः ॥

The first letter of each foot of the verse gives, when combined, the name Somadeva, as pointed out in Śrutasāgara's commentary; but it is extremely doubtful if there is any word-play in the expression *mahendrāmara-mānya-dhīḥ* leading to the surmise that *Mahendrāmara* stands for Mahendradeva or Mahendrapāla. Apart from the fact that the commentator is not aware of any such word-play, *Mahendrāmara* might very well refer to Mahendradeva, the elder brother of Somadeva, mentioned in the colophon to his *Nītivākyāmṛta*.

As pointed out elsewhere, Yaśodeva, the spiritual ancestor of Somadeva, belonged to the Devasaṁgha, according to the latter's own statement in *Yaśastilaka*; but, according to the Parbhani inscription, Yaśodeva belonged to the Gauḍasaṁgha. It is possible that the Gauḍasaṁgha was connected with the Gauḍa country, and Yaśodeva may have lived there. It is also possible that the Gauḍasaṁgha, after its migration from Bengal, came to be known as

---

1 'तथा स्वगुरोः सोमदेवस्य च प्रणामपूर्वकं शास्त्रस्य तत्कर्तृत्वं ख्यापयितुं......मुनिचन्द्राभिधानः क्षपणकव्रतधर्त्ता नीतिवाक्यामृतकर्त्ता'

2 See Raghavan in *New Indian Antiquary*, Vol. VI, p. 67 and Pt. Premi in *Jaina Siddhānta Bhāskara*, vol. XI, p. 90.

Devasaṁgha, the name used by Somadeva. The latter was, however, the disciple not of Yaśodeva, but of Nemideva; and except for one solitary reference, he alone is mentioned in all the colophons occurring in *Yaśastilaka* and *Nītivākyāmṛta*. In the present state of our knowledge, there is no reason to suppose that Somadeva or his teacher Nemideva ever migrated from the Gauḍa country to Kanauj and thence to the Deccan.

The term *Gauḍa* in Gauḍasaṁgha is not without some ambiguity. In south Kanara there is a class of people called *Gauḍas* who are farmers and labourers and speak the Tulu or the Kannaḍa language. They are generally Hindus, but some are Jainas. They have a regular system of village government: in every village, for instance, there are two head-men, the *Grāma-Gauḍa* and the *Vattu* or *Gottu Gauḍa*.[1] It will not be surprising if the Gauḍa-saṁgha has something to do with the *Gauḍas*. In the latter sense the word is derived from *gāvuṇḍa* (*farmer*) changing into *gauṇḍa* or *gauḍa*; and it also means the village headman.

The Mysore inscriptions throw further light on the Gauḍas. Some of the petty rulers of Mysore belonged to the Gauḍa caste or community. 'The Āvati-nāḍ Prabhus were Gauḍas or farmers of the Morasu-wokkal tribe, who came from the east in the fifteenth century and settled in the Āvati village'; and 'their immediate descendants became founders of the modern States in eastern Mysore which were subordinate to Vijayanagar. The leader of the Āvati Prabhus was named Baire-Gauḍa, and the inscriptions of the family date from 1428 to 1792.' 'The Yelahanka-nāḍ Prabhu is mentioned even in 1367, but the inscriptions of this Āvati branch run from 1599 to 1713. They generally had the name Kempe-Gauḍa, after the most celebrated of the line. He founded Bangalore in 1537.' The Sugaṭūr-nāḍ Prabhus had the name Tamme-Gauḍa, and their territory included a great part of the Kolar District. Other references to the Gauḍas are also found in the Mysore inscriptions. 'In 1417, when a Gauḍa, who had gone to visit the local governor, fell down dead in his presence, a sort of inquest was held on the body and it was sent back to his home. This was under Vijayanagar rule.' Under Mughal rule 'we find in 1720 a regular magisterial process in the case of a Gauḍa whose village had been taken possession of by some one else during his absence abroad.'[2] It is also noteworthy that an inscription of 1027 A. D. refers to an *agrahāra* named Gauḍa with its 32,000 Brāhmaṇa residents, believed to be an exaggeration.

All this shows that the name *Gauḍa* was quite familiar in the Kanarese country both in the territorial and vocational sense as indicated above; and it is therefore difficult to rule out the possibility of the Gauḍasaṁgha being originally connected with a village settlement of the Gauḍas. We cannot, of course, be certain on the point, but the fact that Somadeva lived and worked in the Deccan inclines us to look for the home of his Saṁgha in

1 Sturrock: *South Canara* quoted in Sharma: *Jainism and Karṇāṭaka Culture*, p. 158. See also Mahalingam: *Administration and Social Life under Vijayanagar*, pp. 80, 236.

2 Rice: *Mysore and Coorg from the Inscriptions*. pp. 165, 176, 177.

3 Saletore: *Ancient Karṇāṭaka*, Vol. I, 332.

Karṇāṭaka rather than in Bengal. It is true that we hear of Jaina Saṁghas in Bengal even at a later date, though the term Saṁgha has a slightly different sense here. The Jaina writer Bālacandra Sūri, for example, tells us, in his *Vasantavilāsa-mahākāvya* (10. 25), that Saṁghapatis from Lāṭa, Gauḍa, Vaṅga and other places came to join Vastupāla, the famous minister of Gujarat, in his grandiose pilgrimage to Śatruñjaya and Girnar in 1220 A. D.[1] But, so far as Somadeva is concerned, his supposed migration from Bengal does not appear to be supported by any reliable evidence so far discovered.

APPENDIX II

The Verses on the Courtezan's Corpse and a Buddhist Legend

The Buddhist antecedents of Sudatta's reflections on the corpse of a courtezan lying in the charnel-field (*Yaśastilaka* 1. 95ff.) have been discussed in Chapter VI. That there was an underlying story going back to ancient times seems certain; and the framework of the original narrative can be seen in the story of Sirimā, as related in the *Dhammapada* commentary composed about the middle of the fifth century A. D. The story occurs in Book XI in connection with *Dhammapada* 147, and is here summarized from Burlingame: *Buddhist Legends,* Part 2, p. 330 (Harvard Oriental Series, Vol. 29). Certain verses of Somadeva on the dead courtezan recall the concluding words of the Teacher in the Buddhist legend.

Sirimā was a beautiful courtezan of Rājagaha, who used to give food to eight monks regularly in her house. A certain monk, hearing of her beauty, went to receive food in her house. She was ill at the time, but the monk was so enamoured of her that he became indifferent to all about him, and was unable to take any food.

"On that very day in the evening Sirimā died. Thereupon the king sent word to the Teacher, 'Reverend Sir, Jīvaka's youngest sister Sirimā is dead.' When the Teacher received that message, he sent back the following message to the king, 'Sirimā's body should not be burned. Have her body laid in the burning-ground, and set a watch, that crows and dogs may not devour it.' The king did so. Three days passed, one after another. On the fourth day the body began to bloat, and from the nine openings of her body, which were like to sores, there oozed forth maggots."

The king then issued a proclamation ordering all to approach to behold Sirimā. He sent a message to the Teacher, asking that the Congregation of Monks presided over by the Buddha might approach to behold Sirimā.

"Now that young monk had lain for four days without touching food, paying no attention to anything anyone said to him; the rice in his bowl had rotted, and his bowl was covered with mildew. The rest of the monks who were his fellows approached him and said to him, 'Brother, the Teacher is

1 Introduction to *Vasantavilāsa Mahākāvya* (G. O. S.), p. xii.

going forth to behold Sirimā.' When the young monk, lying thus, heard the name Sirimā, he leaped quickly to his feet. Someone said to him, 'The Teacher is going forth to behold Sirimā; will you also go?' 'Indeed I will go', he replied. And tossing the rice out of his bowl, he washed it and put it in his net and then set out with the company of monks.

The Teacher surrounded by the Congregation of Monks stood on one side of the corpse; the Congregation of Nuns and the king's retinue and the company of lay disciples, both male and female, stood on the other side of the corpse, each company in its proper place. The Teacher then asked the king, 'Great king, who is this woman?' 'Reverend Sir, it is Jīvaka's sister Sirimā.' 'Is this Sirimā?' 'Yes, Reverend Sir.' "Well! send a drum through the town and make proclamation, 'Those who will pay a thousand pieces of money for Sirimā may have her.'" Not a man said 'hem' or 'hum'. The king informed the Teacher, 'They will not take her, Reverend Sir.' 'Well then, great king, put the price down.' So the king had a drum beaten and the following proclamation made, 'If they will give five hundred pieces of money, they may have her.' But nobody would take her at that price. The king then proclaimed to the beating of a drum that anyone might have her who would give two hundred and fifty pieces of money, or two hundred, or hundred, or fifty, or twenty-five, or ten, or five. Finally he reduced the price to a penny, then to a half-penny, then to a quarter of a penny, then to an eighth of a penny. At last he proclaimed to the beating of a drum, 'They may have her for nothing.' Not a man said 'hem' or 'hum'. Then said the king to the Teacher, 'Reverend Sir, no one will take her, even as a gift.' The Teacher replied, 'Monks, you see the value of a woman in the eyes of the multitude. In this very city men used to pay a thousand pieces of money for the privilege of spending one night with this woman. Now there is no one who will take her as a gift. Such was her beauty who now has perished and gone. Behold, monks, this body diseased and corrupt.' So saying he pronounced the following stanza:

147. *See this painted image, this mass of sores,*
huddled together,
Corrupt, once possessed of many thoughts, but
now possessing neither
strength nor stability."

APPENDIX III

Śaiva Temples and their Geographical Distribution

GUJARAT

The power and influence of Śaivism is reflected in the numerous old temples dedicated to Śiva, which exist in various parts of India, and in many cases, go back far beyond the limits of the tenth century A. D. We may commence our survey with the celebrated temple of Somanātha on the seashore, in south-western Kathiawar, at Somanāthapattana, close to the modern port of Verāval. Somanātha was no doubt earlier than the tenth century, and may have been as early as the Maitrakas of Valabhi (the modern Vala, near Bhavnagar), who held sway over Gujarat and Kathiawar during the sixth, seventh and eighth centuries of the Christian era, and call themselves *parama-māheśvara* or devout worshippers of Śiva in their inscriptions.[1] The great Śaiva temple was built upon fifty-six pillars of teak wood covered with lead, and the glory of its wealth and splendour lives in the pages of Muslim historians.[2] It was sacked and desecrated by Mahmud of Ghazni in 1026 A. D., and subsequently destroyed by a lieutenant of Mahmud; but soon after, it was rebuilt of stone by Bhīmadeva I, the Solanki king of Gujarat (1022–64 A. D.). It was again restored and rebuilt by Kumārapāla in the third quarter of the twelfth century, evidently in consequence of its being again attacked, or of having fallen into ruin. The present ruin represents the rebuilding by Kumārapāla.[3]

Śaivism was paramount in Gujarat during the rule of the Solanki kings who were great builders of temples dedicated to Śiva. Their capital was at Aṇahillapura (Aṇahilavāḍa or Patan), and other important places during their reign were Siddhapur and Vadnagar, now included in Baroda State, to the north of Ahmedabad. The first king Mūlarāja (942–96 A. D.) was a fervent devotee of Śiva in the form of Somanātha or Someśvara; and the temple of Mūleśvara and the Tripuruṣaprāsāda appear to have been built by him in honour of Somanātha.[4] Siddharāja (1094–1143), whose name is still familiar everywhere in Gujarat, built the great Sahasraliṅga tank which derived its name from the numerous *liṅga* shrines on its banks. In the centre of the tank was an island on which stood the temple of Rudreśvara.[5]

---

1 Exceptions are Dhruvasena I (526 A. D.) who is called *parama-bhāgavata*, and his brother and successor Dharapaṭṭa who is styled *paramāditya-bhakta* or a great devotee of the Sun. Guhasena, who was a worshipper of Śiva (558–564), calls himself *paramopāsaka* or a great devotee of Buddha in his grant of 566 A. D. *Bombay Gazetteer*, Vol. I, pt. I, p. 83; Poussin: *Dynasties et Histoire de L'Inde*, pp. 133–139.

2 See *Bombay Gazetteer*, Vol. I, pt. I, p. 165. The ancient temple is stated to have been thirteen storeys high, with its top surmounted by fourteen cupolas of gold which glittered in the sun and were visible from a long distance. The original edifice was built of brick and its floor was made of planks of teak wood with the interstices filled with lead. See Commissariat: *History of Gujarat*, Vol. I, lx. and Nazim: *The Life and Times of Sultan Mahmud of Ghazna*, p. 212.

3 Cousens: *Architectural Antiquities of Western India*, p. 40. Kumārapāla's temple suffered in every subsequent Muhammadan invasion of the place, though it was repaired and restored from time to time. In 1395 it was destroyed by Muzaffar Khan, and again by Ahmad I, after his war with the Rav of Junagadh in 1414. Commissariat (op. cit.), p. lxxiv.

4 'तथा नित्यं नित्यं...श्रीसोमेश्वरपत्तने यात्रायां शिवभक्तितया व्रजंस्तद्भक्तिपरितुष्टः सोमनाथ उपदेशदानपूर्वं मण्डलीनगरमागतः। तेन राज्ञा तत्र मूलेश्वर इति प्रासादः कारितः। तत्र नमश्चिकीर्षोर्हर्षेण प्रतिदिनमागच्छतस्तस्य नृपतेस्तद्भक्तिपरितुष्टः श्रीसोमेश्वरः अहं ससागर एव भवन्नगरे समेष्यामीत्यभिधाय श्रीमदणहिल्लपुरेऽवतारमकरोत्।' See *Prabandhacintāmaṇi*, p. 17 (Singhi ed.).

5 'Hardly a vestige now remains of the Sahasraliṅga tank, the theme of so much legend and song. Its site is still pointed out to the north-west of modern Patan.' Commissariat (op. cit), p. lxvi.

Siddharāja restored and rebuilt also the great temple of Rudramahālaya, which had been founded by Mūlarāja at Siddhapur on the north bank of the Sarasvatī, seventeen miles to the east of Patan. In or around the court were eleven other shrines in honour of the Rudras. This magnificent temple was destroyed by the Muslim conquerors of Gujarat; but the stupendous fragments that still exist give an adequate idea of the grandiose design of the original structure.[1]

Vadnagar (the ancient Ānandapura), situated 19 miles southeast from Siddhapur, was a great religious centre in Gujarat, and noted as the home of the Nāgara Brāhmaṇas who worshipped Śiva. An inscription engraved on a stone slab records the building of the walls of the town by Kumārapāla, the equally famous successor of Siddharāja, in *Saṁvat* 1208 or 1151 A. D. The town had at one time an unusually large number of temples, but the number 3000 mentioned by Abul Fazl at the end of the sixteenth century is no doubt an exaggeration. The chief temple, that of Hāṭakeśvara Mahādeva, is a lofty structure to the west of the town.[2]

It is sad to think that few temples in Gujarat have survived intact; and the only remains now of the Solankis and the Vaghelas are but fragments. Fortunately, the great temples of the Deccan, Bundelkhand, Orissa and South India are still in existence; and we shall in the course of our study enumerate the more important examples as far as they illustrate the progress and influence of the Śaiva faith in those regions.

From Gujarat we may turn to Mount Abu which was a flourishing centre of Śaivism at an early age. The *Prabhāsakhaṇḍa* of the *Skandapurāṇa* has a section on Arbuda or mount Abu, which gives an account of its sacred sites and the legends associated with them. In medieval times the Abu region was ruled by a branch of the Paramāra dynasty of Mālava from the end of the tenth century to the end of the thirteenth under the suzerainty of the Caulukyas of Gujarat. It may be noted that Bhīma I of Gujarat (1022-64 A. D.) brought for a time the Abu territory under his direct control in the second quarter of the eleventh century; and the Jaina Vimala Sāha was deputed as the governor of Abu, who built the famous marble temple of Ādinātha in 1031 A. D.

Among the *liṅgas* worshipped at Abu, Acaleśvara was the most famous. An inscription of Yaśodhavala, one of the Paramāra kings of Abu, dated 1150 A. D., was found in the temple of Acaleśvara. Early in the thirteenth century we hear of the prince Prahlādana, the founder of Palanpur, melting down a Jaina brass image for making a metal bull for Acaleśvara Mahādeva.[3]

---

1 Commissariat, p. lxvii.

2 Ibid. lxxii. It may be noted that, while the main temples in Gujarat were dedicated to Śiva, there were ancient temples devoted to the cult of Kṛṣṇa or Viṣṇu at Dvārakā and the adjoining island of Bet or Śaṅkhoddhāra. They were destroyed by Mahmud Shah I in his expedition of 1473. The existing temples are later structures. Ibid. p. 174.

3 Ganguly: *History of the Paramāra Dynasty*, pp. 304, 319.

The sacred sites of Mount Abu mentioned in the *Arbudakhaṇḍa* of the *Skandapurāṇa* include Kanakhala (chap. 26) and Caṇḍikāśrama (chap. 36), or the hermitage of Caṇḍikā, which appears to have been a shrine of the goddess with an attached monastery. Both Kanakhala and Caṇḍikāśrama are mentioned in the Abu inscription of the Śaiva ascetic Kedārarāśi, which gives a detailed account of his building activities at Kanakhala. The inscription was incised in 1208 A. D. during the reign of Dhārāvarṣa at Abu under the suzerainty of Bhīma II of Gujarat. The record opens with verses in praise of Śiva and Ujjain, and enumerates the succession of teachers of the Capala or Capalīya sect which seems to have been an order of Śaiva monks in Mālava. Altogether eight teachers are mentioned; and the first teacher Tāpasa, a great devotee of Caṇḍīśa or Siva, came from the New Monastery (Nūtana-maṭha) at Ujjain, and became the head of the Caṇḍikāśrama which was, as we have seen, located at Mount Abu. Kedārarāśi, the last teacher to be mentioned must have lived in the last quarter of the twelfth century; and to judge from the succession of teachers and disciples, Tāpasa may have become the head of the Caṇḍikāśrama about the middle of the eleventh century. As regards Kedārarāśi, he carried out an extensive building programme, according to his inscription. He renovated the entire site of Kanakhala with stone-slabs (*uttāna-paṭṭa*), and provided it with an enclosure with lofty walls. He repaired also the temple of Atulanātha, built two new massive temples of Śiva in front of the shrine of Kanakhalanātha, and erected a row of pillars of black stone, in the *maṇḍapa* of the temple of Kanakhalaśambhu. His sister Mokṣeśvarī also built a beautiful temple of Śiva at the place.[1]

The capital of the Paramāra Chiefs of Abu until about the beginning of the 14th century was at Candrāvatī, now a small village at the junction of the Śivālan with the Banās river near the south end of Mount Abu and in the Sirohi State. Here the numerous temples were constructed of white marble, a rare phenomenon in the history of Hindu architecture; and many of them must have been dedicated to Śiva, as Śaivism was the prevailing religion in this area. The evidence of sculptures, scanty though it is, points to the same conclusion. In one of the marble edifices, for instance, the principal figures were a three-headed statue with a female seated on his knee, sitting on a car, with a large goose in front (i. e. Brahmā); Śiva with twenty arms; Bhairava with twenty arms, one holding a human head by the hair, a victim lying beneath, and a female on each side; one drinking the blood falling from the head. Unfortunately Candrāvatī is in ruins, and no idea can be formed of the cults practised in its beautiful temples.[2]

1 *An Abu inscription of the reign of Bhīmadeva II, Indian Antiquary*, Vol. XI, p. 220.

2 Candrāvatī is one of the tragedies of Indian archaeology. Twenty marble edifices of different sizes were still in existence when the spot was first visited by Sir Charles Colville and his party in 1824. Nevertheless, about this time, the petty Chief of Girwar, a few miles to the northwest of Candrāvatī, who regularly sold the marble materials, was called by Colonel Tod 'the depredator and salesman

MEWAR

Śaivism was the prevailing religion in neighbouring Mewar where the worship of Ekaliṅga Siva was the symbol of a national cult and has survived till today. The worship of Ekaliṅga is mentioned in an inscription of Naravāhana, dated 972 A. D., but the cult is earlier than the tenth century as two inscriptions, dated Saṁvat 1331 and 1342 (1274 and 1285 A. D.) respectively, which give the genealogy of the ruling dynasty, place the cult of Ekaliṅga at the beginning of the political history of Mewar.[1] We are told that an ascetic named Hārītarāśi who was a devotee of Ekaliṅga gave a miraculous gold anklet to Bappa, the Brāhmaṇa founder of the dynasty, and helped him to acquire the throne. The cult of Ekaliṅga was thus prevalent at least as early as the ninth century, and the deity is still worshipped at the place now called Ekalingaji, about twelve miles north of Udaipur on the way to Nāthadvāra. The present temple is not later than 1213 A. D., as a date, Saṁvat 1270, is inscribed on a pillar together with the name of Rājā Jaitrasiṁha.[2]

The evidence to be considered further will show that Śaivism represented a vigorous religious movement in a large part of western and central India from Gujarat to Rewa in the tenth century and thereabouts. The expansion of Saivism in western India goes back, however, to a much earlier date, as it was the prevailing religion under the Valabhi kings as early as the sixth century A. D.

MĀLAVA

An early and celebrated focus of Śaivism was in Mālava whose capital Ujjayinī or Avantī was famous through the ages as the seat of the worship of

---

of what time and the ruthless Turk had spared of its relics'. Gustav le Bon, a French archaeologist, writing in 1884, said that he had made a long journey to Candrāvatī to visit a temple among other remains, but was informed that the temple had been recently reduced to fragments by an engineer to pave a road! Cousens who visited the place at a later date reported: "Save portions of the basement of one temple and a few blocks of the back wall of another, nothing now remains of the beautiful shrines discovered in 1822 excepting one solitary column, which by its loneliness accentuates the desolation around it'. The fact is that the temples of Candrāvatī were literally carried off to build railway bridges and culverts and to break up for metalling the permanent way. 'The site of the old city and its extent are still indicated by the mounds of bricks that formed the foundations of these old temples—of which there are great numbers; and on the south side are portions of the ancient city walls which faced the river Śivālan.' 'Judging from such images as still lie about, it would appear that the majority of the temples were Brahmanical, and that they were built of white marble.' See Burgess and Cousens: *Archaeological Survey of Western India (Northern Gujarat), Vol IX*, pp. 96–102.

1 *A Collection of Prakrit and Sanskrit Inscriptions* (op cit.) pp. 75, 85. In the introductory note the date of the inscription is given as 1339, but 1331 appears as the date in the last line. P. 77.

2 Ibid. p. 93.

Mahākāla Śiva. The legends connected with the numerous sacred sites and *liṅgas* of Avantikṣetra, known also as Mahākāla-vana, are narrated in detail in the *Avantyakhaṇḍa* of the *Skandapurāṇa*. Mahākālavana is described here as a *yojana* in extent, and mentioned as one of the most important Śaiva Tīrthas along with Prabhāsa, Puṣkara, Kedāra and Kāyāvarohaṇa. It is possible that the famous temple of Mahākāla existed as early as the fifth century A. D. Kālidāsa, in his *Meghadūta* (vv. 30–7), in the course of the description of Ujjayinī, refers to the sacred abode (*dhāma*) of Caṇḍīśvara, styled also as Mahākāla, on the Gandhavatī river, which is in fact one of the sacred streams of Avantikṣetra mentioned in the *Skandapurāṇa*.[1]

The temple of Mahākāla at Ujjain was as famous as that of Somanātha in Kathiawar. About the middle of the tenth century, Dhanika, a Paramāra chief of Vāgaḍa (the modern Banswara and Dungarpur States in Southern Rajputana, not far from Ujjain), is known to have erected the Śiva temple of Dhaneśvara near Mahākāla.[2] Early in the tenth century, the Rāṣṭrakūṭa emperor Indra III, while leading an expedition to conquer Kanauj, is believed to have stopped with his war elephants at the courtyard of the temple of Mahākāla to pay homage to the deity.[3] The great temple continued to exist for more than two hundred years after the destruction of the temple of Somanātha; but the tragedy was re-enacted in 1233 A. D. when Sultan Īltutmish invaded Ujjain and demolished the ancient shrine during the reign of the Paramāra king Devapāla. According to Firishta, the magnificent temple was built on the same plan as that of Somanātha, and is said to have occupied three hundred years in building: it contained the image of Vikramāditya as well as that of Mahākāla, which the invader caused to be conveyed to Delhi and broken at the door of the great mosque.[4]

The Paramāras of Mālava, who ruled as independent monarchs from about the middle of the tenth century to the end of the thirteenth, and whose dominions, in their widest limits, extended from Gujarat to Central Provinces and from Khandesh to Northern Indore, were devout worshippers of Śiva and great builders of Śiva temples. The Paramāra king Bhoja, the most famous Indian monarch of the eleventh century A. D., built a number of temples dedicated to Kedāreśvara, Rāmeśvara, Somanātha, Suṁḍīra (?) and Kālānala-Rudra.[5] These temples no longer exist, as most of the religious edifices of Mālava were destroyed by the Muhammadans.

---

1 *Āvantyakhaṇḍa*, Chap. I of *Caturaśītiliṅga-māhātmya*.

2 See *Two Paramāra Inscriptions* in *Epigraphia Indica*, Vol. XXI, p. 41; Ganguli: *History of the Paramāra Dynasty*, p. 337.

3 See *Cambay Plates of Govinda IV* (v. 19.) in *Ep. Ind.*, Vol VII. The Kālapriya mentioned in the verse is believed to be identical with Mahākāla.

4 Briggs: Firishta, Vol. I, p. 211; Prasad: *History of Medieval India*, p. 159.

5 See Verse 20 of the *Udepur Praśasti of the kings of Mālvā* in *Epigraphia Indica*, Vol. I, pp. 222–38. Bühler takes Kāla, Anala and Rudra separately. But the reference seems to be to Kālāgni-Rudra, one of the terrible forms of Śiva, mentioned by Somadeva in *Yaśastilaka*, Book I, p. 151.

Of the existing temples of Mālava the Nīlakaṇṭheśvara at Udayapur and the Siddhanātha or Siddheśvara at Nemawar, both dedicated to Śiva, are the most important. The temple of Nīlakaṇṭheśvara at Udayapur, now a village thirty miles to the north of Bhilsa, in Gwalior State, was built by the Paramāra king Udayāditya in 1059 A. D.[1] Built of red sandstone, it is one of the best preserved temples in India, as it somehow eacaped to a very large extent the devastating hand of Muslim vandalism, although there is still a Muhammadan masjid at the back of the temple. A legend says that Aurangzeb, on his return from the Deccan, passed through this place and ordered the demolition of the temple; but Mahādeva appeared to him in a dream, and commanded him on pain of death to desist from his act of sacrilege. The next morning Aurangzeb found himself ill, and stopped the destruction of the temple; but a masjid was ordered to be built at the back of the temple. It is noteworthy that until recent times the temple was 'frequented by both Hindus and Muhammadans and the *liṅgam* within equally reverenced by both.' The *liṅga* is 'now inclosed in a shell of highly polished yellow metal said to be gold.'

The temple 'is singularly beautiful both in plan and in elevation; and although large, the parts are so well-proportioned, that it does not look large, and it is only on measurement that its real size is realized.' 'But it is in excellence of execution of the floral sculptured ornamentation that this temple surpasses all others. They are executed with remarkable fineness and freedom and are not overcrowded so as to destroy effect, but by a judicious interposition of broad plain surfaces worked with exquisite care, the ornamental value both of the flowered bands and of the plain are mutually enhanced. Doubtless a great deal of the beauty of the carvings is due to the superior quality of the stone here used; and the Khajurāho temples, if built of similar materials, would, some of them, have been more beautiful.' 'The great dome is formed of overlapping courses of stones, ranged in successive diminishing circles over each other. Twelve ribs, each rib composed of exquisitely sculptured females, at once adorn and strengthen this beautiful roof; and this roof, thus adorned, and as it were vivified by the sculptures, rests on the massive pillars below, forming a whole of unsurpassed beauty and harmony.'[2]

The richly sculptured temple of Siddhanātha stands right on the bank of the Narmadā at Nemawar in Indore State, twelve miles from Harda station on the G. I. P. Railway. It cannot be later than the 10th century, and consists of a *garbhagṛha* and a *maṇḍapa,* which is open on three sides with an open porch on each side. The *maṇḍapa* appears to be a later addition, and is built of bluish sandstone; while the *garbhagṛha* with its *śikhara* is built of beautiful yellowish grey sandstone. Except for a modern structure which has been added on the top of the maṇḍapa providing access

1 Ganguly: *History of the Paramāra Dynasty*, p. 258. The temple of Maṇḍaleśvara Mahādeva at Pāṇāherā in Banswara State in Southern Rajputana was also built in 1059 A. D. by Maṇḍalīka, a Paramāra chief of the Vāgaḍa branch of the family. See *Two Paramāra Inscriptions* (op. cit.).

2 *Archaeological Survey of India*, Vol. VII, pp. 85–88.

to the chamber immediately above the *garbhagṛha*, the edifice 'has not suffered any damage or structural alteration during the nine hundred years that have elapsed since it was built.' The temple is in use, and worship is still carried on there on an elaborate scale. To the north of the temple of Siddhanātha is an unfinished temple of Viṣṇu, of which only the *garbhagṛha* stands.[1]

The large temple of Bhojeśvara is situated at Bhojpur twenty miles to the south of the city of Bhopal. It appears to be named after the great Paramāra king Bhoja, and has been assigned to the eleventh or twelfth century A. D. In plan the building is a simple square; and an incomplete but richly carved dome is supported by four massive pillars, each of which is 40 feet in height. Inside the building stands a colossal *liṅga*, seven and a half feet high and more than seventeen feet in circumference, on a platform made of three superimposed blocks of sand-stone.[2]

An important group of Śaiva temples, fairly well-preserved, exists in the large township of Un in the Nimar District of Indore State.[3] It has been said that 'with the exception of Khajurāho in central India, there is no other place in Northern India where so many ancient temples are still to be found intact. The carvings on the temples at Un are slightly less elaborate than those on the celebrated temples of Khajurāho, but in all other respects they would compare very favourably with the Khajurāho group.' There are at least seven temples of Śiva of which the largest is called Chaubara Dera. It has an elaborately carved magnificent *maṇḍapa* with a large porch in the front and two small ones on the sides. The *maṇḍapa* is supported by four round carved pillars, and the dome over it is richly carved in the style of the domes of the marble temple of Vastupāla-Tejaḥpāla on Mount Abu. The group of buildings includes a large temple of Śiva called Mahākāleśvara[3] and another of the same name. The Śiva temple of Vallaleśvara appears to have been rebuilt at a later date when a round dome like that of a mosque was built in place of the *śikhara*. A beautifully carved temple of Śiva called Nīlakaṇṭheśvara stands inside the modern village, and close to it is a small underground temple of Śiva called Gupteśvara. 'The shrine, of which only a small underground chamber remains, must have been originally below the ground level, as the level of the floor of the *garbhagṛha* is about thirty feet below the level of the floor of the sanctum in the temple of Nīlakaṇṭheśvara.'

1 *Progress Report of the Archaeological Survey of India, Western Circle, for the year ending 31st March, 1921*, pp. 98–106.

2 Ganguly: *History of the Paramāra Dynasty*, p. 270.

3 *Progress Report of the Archaeological Survey of India, Western Circle, for the year ending 31st March, 1919*, pp. 61–64. Plates. XVIII–XXI.

4 A temple dedicated to Śiva under the name of Mākāleśvara (Mahākāleśvara) also exists in the village of Makla in the Mehidpur District of Indore State. This district lies in the centre of Mālava and is very close to Ujjain. The *maṇḍapa* of the temple has been rebuilt, but the *garbhagṛha* is intact, and provides a good example of Hindu temple architecture of the 11th and 12th centuries in Mālva. *Progress Report of the Archaeological Survey of India, Western Circle*. 1920. p. 101.

A typically Saiva sculpture representing Śiva and the Seven Mothers is found engraved on doors and lintels in some of the temples including the Chaubara Dera. An inscription in the latter temple mentions Udayāditya of Mālava who is known to have reigned in the latter part of the eleventh century. This is no doubt an important clue to the age of the temples at Un. Another inscription in the Chaubara Dera temple engraved on the figure of a serpent exhibits the Sanskrit alphabet and some of the conjugational terminations; and this had apparently an educational purpose. Two similar inscriptions, on a larger scale, are engraved on two pillars in the Bhojaśālā or School of King Bhoja, now the Masjid of Kamal Maula, at Dhar.[1]

The island of Māndhātā in the Narmadā, in the Nimar District of Central Provinces, south-east of Indore, was a seat of Śaiva worship at an early age, probably long before the tenth century. To judge from

---

1 Ibid. p. 46. Remains of old Śiva temples are fairly numerous in Indore State, many of which have been rebuilt in later times. Two or three of these temples may be mentioned. The village of Modi, seven miles to the west of Bhanpura in the north of Indore State, contains the ruins of a number of temples, one of which is still in position. The temple was dedicated to Śiva, but only the *garbhagṛha* is intact. 'The lintel of the door leading to the interior of the sanctum bears the figure of Śiva as Lakulīśa, and some of the large stones of the basement bear inscriptions in characters of the 12th century A. D.' The village of Kukdesvar, ten miles to the west of Rampura in the north of Indore State, contains the temple of Sahasra-mukheśvara. The old temple having collapsed, the present structure was built in its place. But the *liṅga* in the sanctum is very old and a real *sahasra-liṅga*. 'It consists of a huge *liṅga* about three feet in height and twelve to sixteen inches in diameter. The body of the *liṅga* is covered with rows of miniature *liṅgas* of uniform shape and size measuring about an inch and a half in height.'

'The tableland or plateau at the foot of which Bhanpura lies is thickly studded with ancient remains, and shows ample signs of having been at one time a thickly populated locality of ancient Mālava.' The remains on this plateau include those of two old temples at Navali or Naoli. One of these is the temple of Nandikeśvara which stands at the southern end of the village. The temple was partly rebuilt at a later date with the old materials. The *maṇḍapa* has disappeared, but the sanctum still stands. The *liṅga* of Nandikeśvara is octagonal at the bottom and round at the top.

Old Vaiṣṇava temples are found here and there in Indore State. The old village of Kohala, for instance, in the Garoth District in northern Indore, six miles from Bhanpura, contains three temples dedicated to Viṣṇu. The largest is the temple of Varāha which contains one of the finest images of the Boar Incarnation. Of the other two temples that of Lakṣmī–Nārāyaṇa is one of the best preserved monuments in Mālava. 'The *śikhara* is tall and slender, and resembles that of the temple of Mahākāleśvara at Un.' The temple of Caturbhuja is exactly similar in plan, but the *śikhara* is far inferior to that of Lakṣmī–Nārāyaṇa. The temple of Śeṣaśāyin exists at the village of Kethuli which lies at the foot of the plateau on which Navali (see above) is situated. An old temple of Viṣṇu, partly rebuilt, exists at Kukdesvar. 'With the exception of the roof, the porch in front and the *Maṇḍapa* are of the same date as the old *garbhagṛha* on the west, i. e. 12th or 13th century A. D.' The existing Vaiṣṇava temples in Mālava are of uncertain date; and there is apparently no Vaiṣṇava temple which can compare in grandeur and magnitude with any of the outstanding major temples dedicated to Śiva. See *Progress Report of the Archaeological Survey of India, Western Circle*, for 1920.

the evidence of the *Revākhaṇḍa* included in the *Skandapurāṇa*, the banks of the river were studded with holy places beginning from the sacred Amarkantak on the Maikal Range in Central India. All the temples on the island are devoted to the worship of Śiva or his associate deities; but Muslim vandalism has done its work so thoroughly (from about 1400 A. D.) that 'every dome has been overthrown, every figure mutilated.' There are numerous temples ancient and modern; but the age of the older shrines does not appear to have been accurately determined.

The celebrated shrine of Oṁkāra, a form of Śiva, is situated on the island, and that of Amareśvara on the southern bank of the river. These are among the most famous of the ancient Liṅgas in India; and pilgrims who have vowed to visit the twelve Jyotirliṅgas offer their adorations to both Oṁkāra and Amareśvara. References to Oṁkāra and Amareśvara are occasionally found in the inscriptions of the Paramāra kings of Mālava. The Māndhātā plates of Jayasiṁha issued in 1055 A. D. record the grant of a village for the maintenance of the Brāhmaṇas of the *paṭṭaśālā* at the holy site of Amareśvara. An inscription of Arjunavarman issued in 1215 A. D. during his sojourn at Amareśvara says that he granted certain lands to a Brāhmaṇa after having worshipped Oṁkāra, the lord of Bhavānī. Three plates recording a grant of Devapāla in 1225 A. D. were found near the temple of Siddheśvara at Māndhātā. Evidently the Nimar District was included in the dominions of the Paramāras of Mālava in the early part of the thirteenth century A. D. Earlier than this, the famous Paramāra king Vākpati Muñja, who reigned towards the end of the tenth century A. D., is said to have built many temples and embankments at places like Ujjain, Maheśvara and Māndhātā.[1]

'The oldest of the Śivaite temples is probably that on the Birkhala rocks. Unlike the other temples, which present the ordinary shrine and porch, it consists of a courtyard, with a verandah and colonnades supported on massive pillars, boldly carved in rectilineal figures.' 'On the hill stand the ruins of a very fine temple, now called Siddheśvara Mahādeva. To each of the four sides of the shrine was added a projection containing a doorway; and before every doorway was a porch resting on fourteen pillars, elaborately carved and about 14 feet high.' 'The temple of Gaurī Somanātha appears to be an old shrine rebuilt with lime. Somanātha himself is a gigantic *liṅga*, now black, but once white, as his name denotes.' It may be noted that traces of Vaiṣṇavism are not wholly absent in the Māndhātā region. The north bank of the river opposite contains some old structures devoted to Viṣṇu. 'Where the Narmadā bifurcates are the remains of some gateways and a large shapeless building containing twenty-four figures of Viṣṇu and his *avatāras*, carved in good style in a close-grained green stone. Among them is a large Varāha or Boar Avatāra covered with the same panoply of sitting figures as that at Khandwā.'[2]

---

1 Ganguli: *History of the Paramāra Dynasty*, pp. 63, 124, 202, 210.

2 *Imperial Gazetteer of India*, Vol. IX, p. 293 ff.

BUNDELKHAND AND BAGHELKHAND

From Mālava we may pass on to Bundelkhand which was an important centre of Śaivism during the rule of the Chandel kings in the tenth, eleventh and twelfth centuries. The Chandel Kingdom included Khajurāho (now a village in Chhatarpur State, Central India), Kālañjar in Bāndā Dt., U.P. and Mahoba (in Hamirpur Dt., U.P.). Khajurāho is famous for its group of magnificent temples second in importance only to the Bhuvaneśvar group in Northern India. The splendour of Khajurāho reached its climax in the tenth century during the reign of Dhanga (*c.* 950–1000 A. D.), who was a devout Śaiva, and died, according to an inscription, at Prayāga, 'fixing his thoughts on Rudra, and muttering holy prayers.' The northern style of temple architecture found its most perfect expression in the edifices at Khajurāho, which were designed on a grand scale, executed in a fine sandstone, and richly adorned with sculpture. Dhanga's father Yaśovarman (*c.* 930-50 A. D.) built the magnificent Caturbhuj temple completed in 954 A. D.[1]; but the largest building of the Khajurāho group is the great Śiva temple called Kandariyā Mahādeo, believed to have been erected during the tenth century. It is 109 feet in length and 59½ feet in width with a height of 116½ feet above the ground.[2] The temple known as Viśvanātha is no less grand, the steeple being about 100 feet high, and was, according to an inscription, built during Dhanga's reign.[3] 'The temple of Mṛtanga

1 A temple of Nārāyaṇa was built by queen Citralekhā in 955 A. D. at Bayana in Bharatpur State The relevant inscription recording the fact is incised on a slab in the pavement of the Ukhā mosque at Bayana, now transformed into the Ukhā mandir. A portion of an old Hindu temple found inside the Ukhā mandir might represent the remains of the temple of Nārāyaṇa erected by queen Citralekhā. *Progress Report of the Archaeological Survey of India, Western Circle*, 1919, p. 43; 1920, p. 109.

2 The temple contains a marble *liṅga* 4¼ feet in girth. Cunningham counted no less than 226 statues inside the temple, and 646 outside, or 872 statues altogether, of which the greater number are from 2½ to nearly 3 feet in height. 'The richness of the carvings is rivalled by the profusion of the sculptures.' 'The general effect of this gorgeous luxury of embellishment is extremely pleasing, although the eye is often distracted by the multiplicity of the details.'

3 The Viśvanātha temple is 87½ feet long by 46 feet broad. Its plan is similar to that of the Kandariyā temple, 'but it is altogether in better preservation itself, and its five subordinate temples are still standing or traceable at the four corners of its terrace, and in front of the entrance.' Cunningham counted 602 statues of from 2 to 2½ feet in height 'in the different ranges of sculpture of this gorgeous temple.' Inside the shrine there is a *liṅga*. 'Inside the entrance portico of this temple, there are two large inscribed slabs which are dated respectively, in the Saṁvat years 1056 and 1058 or A. D. 999 and 1001.' The earlier inscription records the building of the temple to Śiva and the dedication of a *liṅga* made of emerald (*marakatamayam*) by Rājā Dhanga. The temple itself is said to have been called *Pramathanātha*, but the emerald *liṅga* no longer exists. Facing the entrance of the Viśvanātha temple is a small open temple which contains a colossal recumbent figure of the bull Nandi. 'In plan it is a square of 16 feet with 12 pillars and a small open porch of two pillars on each of the four sides, thus forming an open temple of 20 pillars'. 'It evidently forms part of the Viśvanātha temple, and must be of the same date.'

Mahādeo[1] is remarkable for its large dome of overlapping stones, with a diameter of 22 feet, without extraneous support'. The temples are in more or less satisfactory preservation, which is largely due to the fact that Khajurāho luckily escaped the fury of Muslim vandalism.

There are two more temples on the Kurar Nala to the south of the village, called Nīlkanth Mahādeo and Kunwār Math. The former is a mass of ruins; but inside the sanctum there still exists the *argha* or pedestal of a *liṅga*. A pilgrim's inscription carved on the wall of the sanctum bears the date Saṁvat 1174 (A. D. 1117), and refers to the deity as Gaura or the White God. The temple seems to have been erected in the tenth or eleventh century. The Kunwār Math is also dedicated to Śiva, whose figure occupies the central position over the doorway of the sanctum, between Brahmā and Viṣṇu. It is one of the finest temples at Khajurāho, and 66 feet long and 33 feet broad outside. There is no inscription to fix the date of the temple; but as the word Vasala, a mason's mark, is repeated several times on the stones of both of the Kurar Nala temples, Cunningham infers that they are of the same age, that is, the tenth or eleventh century. At Jatkari, 1½ miles to the south of Khajurāho, there are two dilapidated temples, one of which is dedicated to Śiva whose *liṅga* of marble is enshrined within.

Kālañjar, with its strong fortress, was the military stronghold of the Chandel kings; and from early times the hill was famous as a favourite resort of Śaiva ascetics. The buildings at Kālañjar are not, however, important as architecture. 'The upper gate, leading to the outwork in the middle of the west face, where the great *liṅgam* of Nīlakaṇṭha stands, is attributed by local tradition to king Parmāl or Paramardi (1165–1203 A. D.).' A hymn of praise to Śiva composed by Paramardi is inscribed on a slab at Kālañjar bearing the date 1201 A. D.

At Mahoba there is the Madan Sāgar lake associated with the Chandel king Madanavarman (1128–1165 A. D.). A fairly well-preserved granite temple, equal in size to the largest of the sandstone temples at Khajurāho, stands on a rocky island in the north west corner of the lake. The shrine is known as Kakrā Marh and was dedicated to Śiva. The ruins of a second temple dedicated to Viṣṇu, called Madārī, exist on another islet in the lake. Both the temples are ascribed to the reign of Madanavarman.

The Devī cult is almost everywhere associated with Śaivism; and it is noteworthy that a tribal goddess called Maniyā Deo (Devī) was the tutelary deity of the Chandels. Maniyā Devī appears to be akin to the Goṇḍ deities, and reminds one of Vindhyavāsinī, who was worshipped by the hill tribes of the Vindhya region, as described by Vākpati in his *Gaüḍavaho*. There are

---

1 Called also Mṛtyuñjaya Mahādeva. It is a large square temple enshrining a colossal *liṅga*, 8 feet in height and 3 feet 8 inches in diameter. 'It is 24½ feet square inside and 35 feet square outside, with a projecting porch 18½ feet long and 9¼ feet broad on each side.' 'It is situated 30 feet to the south of the Caturbhuj temple, and is most probably of the same age' (i. e. the middle of the tenth century A. D.).

three known shrines of the goddess, at Mahoba, at Maniyāgaṛh, a large ruined fort, situated on a hill overlooking the town of Rājgaṛh in Chhatarpur State, and at the village of Barel in Hamirpur District. The Devī Jagadāmbī temple at Khajurāho is among the best, and like the others, has been assigned to the tenth century.

There is no doubt that Śaivism was the prevailing religion in Bundelkhand, and the architectural grandeur of Khajurāho rests on the great temples dedicated to Śiva: but the cult of Viṣṇu had also a recognised place, as shown by some of the temples dedicated to that deity.[1] The Baghārī inscription found near Mahoba commemorates the building of temples to both Viṣṇu and Śiva by the ministers of Parmāl or Paramardi in 1195 A. D. We may refer in this connection to the allegorical play *Prabodhacandrodaya*, which was produced during the reign of the Chandel king Kīrtivarman, about the year 1065 A. D.: it refers to shrines of Viṣṇu (v. 5) and glorifies Visṇubhakti (Faith in Viṣṇu), one of the prominent characters in the play. It may, however, be noted that Śiva is glorified in the second verse of the prologue; and we are told in v. 9 that the Absolute is variously designated as Brahmā, Viṣṇu or Śiva.[2]

Śaivism was prevalent not only in Bundelkhand but in other areas of Central India. Jaso, the chief town of the tiny state of that name in Baghelkhand, seems to have been an important place in the middle ages. It contains an old temple of Śiva and a large tank called the Rekra Talav. Two colossal images of Śiva as *Tripurāri* and *Naṭeśa* were found close to the Rekra Talav. The temple of Kumhra Mahādeva is a building in the Khajurāho style of about the eleventh or twelfth century.[3]

---

1 The most important is the Caturbhuj completed in 954 A. D. (see above). 'The temple is 85 feet 4 inches in length and 44 feet in breadth, or almost exactly the same size as Viśvanātha.' Immediately to the east of the Caturbhuj temple is a small open temple containing a colossal statue of the Varāha Avatāra of Viṣṇu No. 17 in Cunningham's list is a large temple situated close to the north end of the village. 'The temple is called Vāmana or the Dwarf Incarnation of Viṣṇu, a name which is certainly not correct; for, although there is a large statue of the dwarf god, 4 feet 8 inches high, enshrined inside, yet there is a small figure of Śiva himself over the centre of the entrance to the sanctum, with Brahmā and Viṣṇu to the right and left.' One or two more temples of Viṣṇu are mentioned by Cunningham.

2 For the Chandel kings and their monuments see Vincent Smith: *History and Coinage of the Chandel dynasty* in *Indian Antiquary*, 1908. 'The remains, more or less complete, of more than thirty temples are traceable at Khajurāho and the neighbouring village of Jatkari.' See also Cunningham: *Archaeological Survey of India*, Vol. II, pp. 412–39. Cunningham writing in 1865 says that Khajurāho is still frequented by pilgrims who assemble in thousands for the celebration of the Śivarātri in the month of Phālgun, at which time an annual fair is held. It may be noted that a similar fair is held at Elephanta on the occasion of the Śivarātri festival every year in February when pilgrims visit the island in large numbers to worship the *liṅga* enshrined in the great cave temple in the western hill. Sastri: *A Guide to Elephanta*, p. 32.

3 *Progress Report of the Archaeological Survey of India, Western Circle, for the year ending 31 st March, 1919*, p. 60.

It may be noted that the history of Śaivism in this region goes back to much earlier times. Seven miles to the south-east of Jaso are the ruins of the ancient city of Nachna Kuthara in Ajaygadh State in Bundelkhand. Some of the oldest known Hindu temples in India have been discovered at this place. The earliest of these is a flat-roofed temple surrounded by a narrow covered veranda on three sides. 'There was a very small *maṇḍapa* or porch in front of the only door of the shrine, which has collapsed entirely.' Over the shrine is a small upper chamber instead of a *śikhara*, with a flat roof slightly raised at the centre. The temple is well-preserved, but without any idol, and has been assigned to the early Gupta period, i. e., 4th - 5th century A. D. To the south-west of this temple there is a large stone-built temple of Śiva with a tall spire, which has been assigned to the later Gupta age. The *maṇḍapa* in front has collapsed, and 'inside the temple there is a huge four-faced *liṅga* (*Caturmukha Mahādeva*) which is certainly earlier in date than the temple itself.' 'To the east of the Gupta temple are the remains of another temple of Mahādeva of which only the foundations and the *liṅga* remain. The ground around is strewn with carved blocks of stone from which it appears that this temple was of the same date as the temple of the four-faced Mahādeva.'[1]

The Nāgod State area, now included in the Baghelkhand Agency of Central India, appears to have been an early focus of Śaivism, and continued as such till medieval times. An ancient temple of Śiva exists at Bhumara, a village twelve miles to the west of the town of Unchehra in Nāgod State. It is flat-roofed and similar in all respects to the early Gupta temple at Nachna except that there is no upper chamber over the shrine. The similarity in size and plan and the nature of the carvings indicates that both the temples belong to the same age, probably the middle of the fifth century A. D. As in the case of the temple at Nachna, the *maṇḍapa* has collapsed, but inside the shrine was found a huge *ekamukha liṅga* measuring a little more than six feet in height.[2]

f In the small hamlet of Sankargadh, in Nāgod State, there is, at the oot of a small conical hill, an ancient tank, now almost silted up, on the banks of which exist a very large collection of Śaiva sculptures and a very small stone temple of the later Gupta period. Two paved foot-paths lead to the door of the temple which stands on a mound, and on both sides of the foot-paths an unusually large number of *liṅgas* have been arranged. The temple consists of a single chamber with one door; and the interior of the shrine is perfectly plain, and contains a very large *liṅga*. The *śikhara* of the temple was added at a later date, perhaps in the 10th or 11th century, sculptures of which period are found scattered around the edifice. 'No inscriptions were discovered at the place, but from the technique the lower part of the temple can be assigned to the sixth century A. D.'. The images gathered around the shrine

---

1 Ibid., pp. 53, 61.

2 R. D. Banerji: *The temple of Śiva at Bhumara* (*Memoirs of the Archaeological Survey of India.* No. 16).

include a very fine image of Śiva and Pārvatī; and it is apparent from the carving that the sculpture belongs to the later Gupta period, i. e. 6th or 7th century A. D. There is besides a very large collection of images of Śiva and Pārvatī at this place, most of which belong to the 11th and 12th centuries A. D. Close by are the ruins of a large medieval temple of Śiva of the 11th or 12th century A. D. 'There must have been other temples also at this place, as in all some 15 or 20 *liṅgas* were discovered within a short area, some of which belong to the earlier periods, as they are natural Phallic symbols of the God of Destruction.'

The villages of Khoh and Majhgawan, in Nāgod State, contain ruins extending over three miles in length, in which the remains of a large and once populous city lie buried. The biggest mound is the Ataria Khera where the remains of a Vaiṣṇava temple were partly excavated by Cunningham, who discovered at the same place a fine image of the Boar Incarnation of Viṣṇu. This area, too, seems to have been a centre of the Śaiva cult. A number of *ekamukha liṅgas* was found in the village and in the mounds surrounding it, and broken images of Mahiṣamardinī were found both at Khoh and Majhgawan. More important is the neighbouring site known as Nakti-ka-Talai, which contains the remains of two fine stone-built temples of the early Gupta period. They are Śiva temples and stand side by side, hidden from view by thick bamboo groves. Here was also found one of the finest known *ekamukha liṅgas*, well-preserved and bearing the bust of Śiva on its western face. Śiva is represented with three eyes, and his crescent is carved in relief on the fore part of the mass of matted hair on the head. 'The face of this bust is a masterpiece of the plastic art of the early Gupta period.'[1]

The evidence of temples and sculptures shows that Śaivism was firmly established in certain areas of Central India in the Gupta period. In the tenth century and after, Śaivism was the prevailing religion in the area corresponding to Rewa State during the rule of the Cedi or Haihaya kings of Tripuri. Here are some important Śaiva monuments which claim our attention.

The territory of the Haihayas of Tripurī in the 10th–12th centuries was the Dāhala country or the modern district of Jubbulpur; but under the more powerful princes the Cedi kingdom included 'that portion of Central India which lies to the south of the river Tons, consisting of the modern States of Nagod, Maihar, the eastern part of Panna and the western part of the northern division of Rewa State.' The existing monuments of the Cedi country consist chiefly of Śaiva monasteries and temples, and are found for the most part in Rewa State and the district of Jubbulpur.[2] We have already referred to

1 For Sankargadh, Khoh etc. see *Progress Report of the Archaeological Survey of India, Western Circle, for the year ending 31st March, 1920.*

2 For details see R. D. Banerji: *The Haihayas of Tripuri and their monuments* (*Memoirs of the Archaeological Survey of India, No. 23*). All the monuments have not been fully explored, and many of them are not in a good state of preservation.

61

the influence of the Śaiva monks of the Mattamayūra line and their monasteries in the Cedi country. As regards temples, the remains are found chiefly in Rewa State: at Chandrehe and Gurgi, not far from Rewa town, and at Bhirpur, Amarkantak and Sohagpur. The Śiva temple at Chandrehe was built about the middle of the tenth century A. D. It is the earliest specimen of the circular type of temples which came into vogue in this part of the country during the tenth century. The ruins of another temple of the same type were found near the village of Masaun in the neighbourhood of Gurgi, twelve miles due east of Rewa Town. Temples of this kind, with circular *garbhagṛhas*, are extremely rare; and it has been suggested that this type of temple architecture was designed by the builders employed by the Śaiva monks of the Mattamayūra sect in the Cedi country. The Gurgi temple appears to belong to the same period as the one at Chandrehe which it closely resembles; and it is probable that it might be the Śiva temple which, according to the Gurgi inscription of Prabodhaśiva, was built by the abbot Praśāntaśiva, close to the very high temple of Śiva built by Yuvarājadeva I, who ruled in the first half of the tenth century. The latter temple seems to have been built on the Gurgaj mound, at Gurgi, where 'the sites of two large temples are now marked by deep pits and the overturned colossal figures which were once enshrined inside'. The figures in question refer to a four-armed Durgā nine feet high, seated on a lion, and a still larger sculpture of Śiva aad Pārvatī lying on its face, the slab being more than twelve feet long by more than five feet broad. 'If the temples which occupied this mound bore any proportion to the size of the colossal figures which they enshrined, they must have been of considerable size, certainly not less than 100 feet in height.'

Among other temples of the Cedi region may be mentioned that of Virāṭeśvara Śiva at Sohagpur, the Karan Mandir at the sacred site of Amarkantak, and the temple of Vaidyanātha Mahādeva at Baijnath, all in Rewa State. The Karan Mandir is a Śiva temple ascribed by local tradition to Karṇa Rāja, the powerful Haihaya king who ruled in the third quarter of the eleventh century A. D. It is a temple of rare design having three separate shrines; but it never was completed. 'The superb magnificence of such a temple with its three tall and profusely sculptured lofty towers of graceful outline can only be realised by actual sight.' Lastly, the Bheraghat inscription of Alhaṇādevī, the widow of king Gayākarṇa, issued in 1155 A. D., records the foundation of a temple of Śiva with a *maṭha* or monastery and a hall of study and gardens around them. 'This temple, or rather the lower part of its *garbhagṛha*, still exists and is known by the name of the temple of Gaurīśaṁkara.' It stands on the summit of a hillock at Bheraghat, better known as the Marble Rocks, thirteen miles from Jubbulpur. The temple is located within the circular enclosure of the shrine of the Sixty-four Yoginīs of which we have spoken.[1]

It will be thus seen that the early monuments of the Cedi country are almost exclusively devoted to the cult of Śiva. It is evident that at the time

1 See Chap. XV.

when Somadeva wrote, Śaivism was predominant in central India as in the south. We may now turn to Orissa.

ORISSA

Early medieval Orissa was an important centre of Śaivism.[1] Bhuvaneśvara in the Puri District is the home of early temples dedicated to Śiva, the oldest being the Paraśurāmeśvara assigned to the eighth century A. D. The temple of Mukteśvara, famous for its sculptures representing scenes of religious life, for example, ascetics and disciples and the worship of Śiva, is somewhat later. The temple of Liṅgarāja, regarded as the most stupendous edifice of its kind in Orissa, is placed about the middle of the tenth century. Close to it is situated the small but exquisitely beautiful temple of Pārvatī, which is probably of the same date as its great neighbour. Other important Śaiva temples at Bhuvaneśvara include the Brahmeśvara (eleventh century), which stands on a platform with four smaller temples at the corners, and thus occupies a position similar to that of the temple of Goṇḍeśvara at Sinar, twenty miles from Nasik.[2] The beautiful temple of Megheśvara situated close to the Brahmeśvara was built towards the end of the twelfth century; while the Śiva temple of Cāṭeśvara was built about the year 1220 A. D. in the village of Krishnapur in the Cuttack District.[3] It may be noted that the only architecturally important Vaiṣṇava temple at Bhuvaneśvara is the Ananta-Vāsudeva said to have been built by Bhavadeva, a minister of king Harivarman of Eastern Bengal.[4] It cannot be much later than the great temple of Liṅgarāja.

Interesting early temples dedicated to Śiva exist also at Khiching, the old capital of the rulers of Mayurbhanj, and in Baudh State on the right bank of the Mahānadī. The twin temples at the village of Gandharāḍi, a few miles from Baudh Town, belong to the same style of architecture as the Paraśurāmeśvara at Bhuvaneśvara. If the Paraśurāmeśvara is assigned to the middle of the eighth century, the Gandharāḍi temples may be placed towards the close of that century. The two temples are exactly similar to each other: the one is dedicated to Siddheśvara Śiva with its *śikhara* surmounted by a Śivaliṅga, and the other is a Vaiṣṇava shrine dedicated to Nīlamādhava, with a wheel of blue chlorite on the top of the *śikhara*. A wheel on the top of the *śikhara* is a common feature of Vaiṣṇava temples, but the location of an entire Śivaliṅga on the top of a temple is something unknown in Orissan architecture.

Next in importance are the three Śiva temples, situated close to the modern temple of Rāmeśvara, in Baudh Town. They have been assigned to the ninth century. Beglar, who saw them in the last quarter of the 19th century,

1 This section is based on R. D. Banerjea: *History of Orissa*, Vols. I and II. Chapters 29 and 30 deal with Architecture and Plastic Art respectively. See also R. D. Banerjea: *Antiquities of the Baudh State in Journal of the Bihar and Orissa Research Society*, Vol. XV.

2 See below.

3 R. D. Banerjea (op. cit.), Vol. I, p. 262.

4 This view is no longer accepted. See *The History of Bengal*, Vol. I, p. 203, published by the University of Dacca.

says: 'though small they are gems of art in their own humble way.' R. D. Banerjea says: 'The decorative motifs and the plastic art of the three temples at Baudh are certainly superior to and older than the great Liṅgarāja-Ananta-Vāsudeva group at Bhuvaneśvara.' A peculiarity of the three temples in Baudh Town is that they have no *Maṇḍapa* or *Jagamohana*, as it is called in Orissa, its place being taken by a porch over the entrance. Unfortunately the porch still exists only in one of the temples. Another peculiarity is that in plan the three temples are eight-rayed stars, and the *arghapaṭṭas* of the Liṅgas are also similar. The Baudh temples are no doubt older than the Liṅgarāja group at Bhuvaneśvara, specially because the large Jagamohana had not yet come into vogue.[1]

Khiching likewise was a prominent centre of Śaiva worship. It is about ninety miles from Bāripada, the present capital of Mayurbhanj, and the site represents the ruins of a large ancient city, which was the home of a people much more civilized than the present aboriginal inhabitants with a sprinkling of Oriya nationals. The principal shrine was that of Cāmuṇḍā known as Kiñcakeśvarī; and the Śiva temples that have survived are the Kutaitundi or Nīlakanṭheśvara and the Candraśekhara which is still intact. The Śaiva sculptures discovered at Khiching (Umā-Maheśvara, the bust of Śiva etc.) bear testimony to the influence of the Śaiva cult in the area dominated by the culture of Khiching.[2] The architecture of the three Śiva temples in Baudh Town and those at Khiching is believed to represent an intermediate stage between such early specimens as the Paraśurāmeśvara and the Mukteśvara at Bhuvaneśvara and the twin temples at Gandharāḍi and the next phase of Orissan art as we find it in the temples of Liṅgarāja, Brahmeśvara and Anantavāsudeva at Bhuvaneśvara. The Candraśekhara temple at Khiching has accordingly been assigned to about 900 A. D. A peculiarity of the temples at Khiching, as in the case of the three temples at Baudh, is that they are without any *Maṇḍapa* or *Jagamohana*. As a matter of fact, there are certain temples at Bhuvaneśvara also, for instance, the Bhāskareśvara, which have no Jagamohana. Some of them are believed to be older than the great temple of Liṅgarāja.

Most of the early Hindu temples in Orissa are thus dedicated to Śiva. The Paraśurāmeśvara at Bhuvaneśvara is the earliest. The Gandharāḍi temples, although one of them is dedicated to Viṣṇu, come next; and the Mukteśvara at Bhuvaneśvara is placed at the end of the early period. All these edifices are characterized by spires or *śikharas* of which the curvature is much less pronounced than that of the *śikharas* of later temples; and in this respect they belong to the same category as such early temples in other parts of India as the later Gupta temple at Nachna Kuthara,[3] the Daśāvatāra temple at Deogarh in Jhansi District and certain other temples at Aihole.[4]

1 *JBORS*, Vol. XV, p. 80.

2 See the plates in R. D. Banerjea: *History of Orissa*, Vol. II.

3 See above.

4 "The Paraśurāmeśvara cannot be very far removed in date from the post-Gupta temple of the Daśāvatāra at Deogadh in the Jhansi District. The low regularly curving outlines of the temples at Gandharāḍi and the Paraśurāmeśvara belong

The predominance of the great Śaiva centre at Bhuvaneśvara, or Āmratīrtha, continued for centuries until it was eclipsed by the final establishment of the cult of Jagannātha at Puruṣottama or Puri. The great temple of Jagannātha at Puri (the *Vimāna* or the sanctum and the *Jagamohana*) was erected by Anantavarman Coḍagaṅga (1078–1148 A. D.) towards the close of the eleventh century, but the architectural style is considered to be degenerate in comparison with the classic examples of Orissan art at Bhuvaneśvara. The Eastern Gaṅgas of Kaliṅga extended their rule over the whole of Orissa in the second half of the eleventh century. But their tutelary deity was Gokarṇasvāmin, or Gokarṇeśvara Śiva, who is so often mentioned in their inscriptions, and whose shrine was located on the top of the Mahendra mountain in Ganjam District. Vajrahasta (1038–68 A. D.), the grandfather of Anantavarman Coḍagaṅga, is called *parama-māheśvara* or a devout worshipper of Śiva in one of his inscriptions. Nevertheless the establishment of the temple of Jagannātha at Puri was a turning-point in the religious history of Orissa. A famous Vaiṣṇava scholar, Naraharitīrtha, a disciple of Ānandatīrtha, the founder of the Mādhva school, was the regent of Orissa for twelve years during the minority of Narasiṁha II (1278–1306 A. D.), and built the temple of Yogānanda-Nṛsiṁha at Sri-Kurmam in Chikakole *Tāluka* of the Ganjam District in 1281 A. D. Other inscriptions recording gifts by Naraharitīrtha have been found in the temple of Kūrmeśvara at Sri-kurmam and that of Lakṣmī-Narasiṁhasvāmin at Siṁhācalam near Waltair. The final triumph of Vaiṣṇavism, or rather Neo-Vaiṣṇavism, in Orissa was not, however, achieved until long after the fall of the Eastern Gaṅgas. The new empire of Orissa extending from Medinipur to Trichinopoly was built up by Kapilendra (1435–70), who liberally patronized the great temple at Puri. His successor Puruṣottama (1470–97) added the Bhogamaṇḍapa to the temple of Jagannātha. It was during the reign of his successor Pratāparudra (1497–1541) that Neo-Vaiṣṇavism became paramount in the religious life of Orissa owing to the long residence of the Bengali saint Caitanyadeva in the country and his powerful influence on the king and the people. Unfortunately, as ably demonstrated by R. D. Banerjea, the supremacy of the new Vaiṣṇavism in Orissa coincided with the political downfall of the country; and "the acceptance of Vaiṣṇavism or rather Neo-Vaiṣṇavism was the real cause of the Musalman conquest of Orissa twenty-eight years after the death of Pratāparudra." So far as the equilibrium of faiths was concerned, the predominance of

---

to the same type as the Śikharas of the Deogadh temple and the later temple at Nachna Kuthara. Sometime during the course of the 9th century A. D., temple types in Orissa began to change and the Śikhara grew taller. It was at this time that the curve of the spire became abrupt near the Āmalaka. The only known examples of this type are the three small temples in Baudh town." JBORS, Vol XV, p. 80. The Daśāvatāra temple at Devagarh on the Vetravatī river is believed to be a monument of the Gupta age (early fifth century A. D.). It was dedicated to Viṣṇu whose image must have been installed in the sanctum. A short inscription in Gupta Brāhmī characters on a big square pillar refers to the gift (*dāna*) of Bhāgavata Govinda, obviously the founder of the temple. See Dr. V. S. Agrawala's paper on the temple in *Art and Thought* (Luzac, 1947), p. 51.

the cult of Jagannātha inevitably led to the decay of the older cults of Śiva at Bhuvaneśvara and elsewhere.

In the tenth century or thereabouts the Śaiva centre at Bhuvaneśvara appears to have been as important as any other centre of Śaiva worship in Central or Western or South India. About this time Bhuvaneśvara was included in the dominions of the Somavaṁśi kings, who at first ruled in the Eastern part of Mahākosala corresponding to the Chattisgarh Division of Central Provinces, and later extended their control over portions of northern and central Orissa. These kings appear to have been Śaivas. Mahābhavagupta Janamejaya who appears to have reigned at the beginning of the tenth century is described in one of his charters as a devout worshipper of Śiva. His successor Mahāśivagupta Yayāti is probably the same as the king Yayāti-Keśarī who, according to Orissan tradition, built the massive temple of Liṅgarāja at Bhuvaneśvara. As we have seen, even on architectural grounds, this edifice has been assigned to the tenth century. Similarly, the temple of Brahmeśvara at Bhuvaneśvara is said to have been built by the mother of Udyotakeśarī, described as seventh in descent from Janamejaya, probably the same as Mahābhavagupta Janamejaya. The temple thus appears to have been erected in the early part of the eleventh century.[1]

Among the kings of earlier dynasties who ruled in different parts of Orissa, Śagguyayyana of the Māna dynasty, who reigned in Southern Tosali or Tosala (the area to the south of the Chilka lake), is described as *paramamāheśvara* or devout worshipper of Śiva in an inscription issued by his feudatory Śivarāja in the Gupta year 283 = 603 A. D.[2] The early Karas who ruled over Central Orissa in the eighth century A. D. were Buddhists. Among the later Karas, the queen Tribhuvana Mahādevī is described as a devout worshipper of Viṣṇu; while the Hindol plate of Śubhakara II records the grant of a village in Northern Tosali or Tosala (the area around Bhuvaneśvara and Puri) for the benefit of the temple of Pulindeśvara and the maintenance of Śaiva ascetics.[3] Among the Bhañja chiefs of Khiñjali[4] who ruled in the eighth and ninth centuries, Śatrubhañja, one of whose grants was issued in 744 A. D., and his successor Raṇabhañja I are described in their inscriptions as worshippers of Viṣṇu; but Netṛbhañja, the son of Raṇabhañja I, is called a devout worshipper of Śiva.[5] The tutelary deity of these Bhañjas was Stambheśvarī who appears to have been a tribal goddess like Maniyādevī of Bundelkhand (see above), or the more famous Vindhyavāsinī Devī worshipped by the Śabaras. The cult of these goddesses was, as a rule, affiliated to the Tantric aspect of medieval

1 R. D. Banerjea (op. cit.), Vol. I, Chap. XIV; Vol. II, pp. 356, 366, 373.

2 Ibid. Vol. I, p. 118.

3 R. D. Banerjea (op. cit.), Vol. I, p. 158.

4 The territory corresponding to the States of Gangpur, Bonai, Bamra, Rairakho, Sonpur, Patna and Karond with a portion of Sambalpur, mostly inhabited by aboriginal tribes, was known as Khiñjali. It was divided into two parts by the river Mahānadī. R. D. Banerjea (op. cit.), Vol. I, p. 6.

5 Ibid. Chap. XII.

Śaivism. It may be added that the existence of prominent centres like Bhuvaneśvara and Khiching provides more conclusive evidence of the prevalence of the Śaiva cult in early medieval Orissa than the religious predilections of individual rulers.

DECCAN

From Orissa we may pass on to the Deccan which was one of the earliest centres of Śaivism in India. Most of the Vākāṭaka kings, who ruled in the area corresponding to Central Provinces and Berar in the fourth and fifth centuries A. D., are described in their inscriptions as *paramamāheśvara* or fervent devotees of Śiva.[1] One of them, Rudrasena I, who reigned in the first half of the fourth century A. D., is described as a devotee of Mahābhairava, which shows that Śiva was worshipped in both his benign and terrible forms.

The Vākāṭakas were related by marriage to the Bhāraśivas who are invariably mentioned in the initial portion of the inscriptions of the former. Gautamī-putra, the son of Pravarasena I, married the daughter of the Bhāraśiva king Bhavanāga; and the issue of this marriage was Rudrasena I. The Bhāraśivas seem to have carved out a principality for themselves on the banks of the Ganges, as they are described as having had their coronation bath with the pure waters of the Ganges acquired by their valour. These Bhāraśivas were staunch Śaivas, as they are described as having pleased Śiva by carrying the *śivaliṅga* on their shoulders,[2] resembling in this respect the Vīraśaivas or Lingayats of later times. It is possible that they originally belonged to the Deccan and later established themselves in North India.[3]

The Vākāṭakas must have built shrines dedicated to Śiva, but none of them is known to have survived. Rudrasena I is said to have built a *dharmasthāna*, probably in honour of Mahābhairava. It is also possible that the ancient flat-roofed temple at Tigowā near Bahuribandh in the Jubbalpur District was dedicated to Śiva, like the flat-roofed temple at Bhumara in Nāgod State.[4]

It may be noted that the cult of Viṣṇu was patronized by two of the Vākāṭaka kings. Unlike his predecessors, Rudrasena II worshipped Cakrapāṇi (Viṣṇu), probably under the influence of his wife Prabhāvatīguptā, the daughter of the Gupta emperor Candragupta II (380-414 A. D.); while Pṛthiviṣeṇa II, the last known king of the elder branch of the Vākāṭaka dynasty, who reigned in the second half of the fifth century A. D., is described

---

1 See, for instance, Mirashi: *Paṭṭan plates of Pravarasena II*, *Epigraphia Indica*, Vol. *XXIII*, pp. 81–88; Kielhorn: *Bālāghāt Plates of Prithiviṣeṇa II*, Ibid. Vol. IX, pp. 267–71; and Mirashi: *The Vakataka Dynasty of the Central Provinces and Berar* in *Annual Bulletin of the Nagpur University Historical Society*, October, 1946.

2 'अंसभारसंनिवेशितशिवलिङ्गोद्वहनशिवसुपरितुष्टसमुत्पादितराजवंशानाम्'

3 See Mirashi: *Pauni Stone Inscription of the Bhāra King Bhagadatta*, *EI*, Vol. XXIV pp. 11 – 15.

4 See above.

as a *parama-bhāgavata* or fervent worshipper of Viṣṇu in the Bālāghāt plates. The sacred hill of Rāmagiri with the footprints of Rāma on its slopes, made famous by Kālidāsa in his *Meghadūta*, was a holy spot in the Vākāṭaka age, and is mentioned as such in the Ṛiddhapur plates of Prabhāvatīguptā which were issued from Rāmagiri.[1] Similarly, the Paṭṭan plates of Pravarasena II (first half of the 5th century A. D.) record the grant of a village called Aśvatthakheṭaka for the maintenance of a charity hall in honour of the foot-prints of Mahāpuruṣa, evidently Viṣṇu or Rāma.[2] It should, however, be noted that Pravarasena II himself is described as a *parama-māheśvara* or a fervent devotee of Śiva in Vākāṭaka inscriptions.

Further light on the prominent position of Śaivism in ancient Deccan is thrown by an inscription of the early Rāṣṭrakūta king Abhimanyu issued at Mānapura. It records the grant of a village called Uṇḍikavāṭikā to a recluse named Jaṭābhāra in honour of the god Dakṣiṇa-Śiva of Peṭhapaṅgaraka. It was formerly thought that Dakṣiṇa-Śiva might be the deity of the great Śaiva shrine in the Māhadeva Hills in the Hoshangabad District of Central Provinces; and Peṭhapaṅgaraka might be Pagāra, the headquarters of the Zamindari of that name. Mānapura could be Mānapura in Malwa, about twelve miles south-west of Mhow, or Mānapura near Bandhogarh in Rewa State. But, as suggested by Prof. Mirashi, it is much more probable that the Mānapura mentioned in the inscription of Abhimanyu is identical with Māṇ, the chief sub-division of the Sātārā District of Bombay Province, through which flows the Māṇgaṅgā, a tributary of the Bhīmā. It is noteworthy that an inscription of Avidheya, another king of the same family, records the grant of a

1 'रामगिरिस्वामिनः पादमूलात्'. Rāmagiri is now Rāmṭek, a wellknown place of pilgrimage near Nagpur. At present the centre of interest is the group of temples on the hill overlooking the town. The temple of Rāmacandra, about 500 feet above the town, is the most prominent. The others are dedicated to Lakṣmaṇa, Kauśalyā, Satya Nārāyaṇa, Lakṣmī Nārāyaṇa, Hanumān etc. The temple of Harihara is popularly known as the Daśaratha temple. There are also two temples with huge idols of Narasiṁha and the remains of a very old temple of the Dwarf incarnation called Trivikrama. One of the temple courts contains a huge image of the Boar Incarnation under a small flat-roofed shrine. An inscription on a wall of the temple of Lakṣmaṇa contains the names of two kings of the Haihaya family who reigned in Mahākośala (modern Chattisgarh) in the latter part of the fourteenth century A. D., and so gives a clue to the age of the building. It is noteworthy that the aforesaid inscription refers to several Śaiva temples, such as Ghaṇṭeśvara, Sudheśvara, Kedāra, Ambikānātha, Dharmeśvara, Muktiśvara etc. Besides, there is a Śivaliṅga called Dhūmreśvara Mahādeva, to whom offerings are made by pilgrims before worshipping Rāma. The *liṅga* is believed to represent Śambuka, the Śūdra ascetic killed by Rāma. The presence of the Śivaliṅga in front of the temple of Rāma and the enumeration of Śiva temples in the inscription mentioned above would seem to indicate the existence of a Śaiva cult prior to the foundation of the existing Vaiṣṇava temples. It may also be noted that the group of temples on the hill includes two temples dedicated to Mahiṣāsura-mardinī; and down the hill is a temple of Caṇḍikā built of massive blocks of hewn stone. For details see *Indian Antiquary*, 1908. p. 202 ff.

2 'महापुरुषपादमूलसत्रोपयोज्यं'.

village called Pāṇḍaraṅgapallī situated on the bank of the Ane river, which is most probably identical with the Yennā, or the Veṇā, which rises on the Mahābaleśvara plateau and falls into a valley to the east of the Mahābaleśvara hill in the Sātārā District. As regards the shrine of Dakṣiṇa-Siva mentioned in the records of Abhimanyu, there are several Śaiva temples on the summit of hills in the Sātārā District, the best known being that of Mahābaleśvara not far from the source of the Kṛṣṇā. Mānapura was no doubt founded by Mānāṅka, the first king of the family, who is mentioned in both the inscriptions; and Abhimanyu and Avidheya were apparently ruling over the territory corresponding to the Sātārā District of Bombay Province. The inscriptions in question have been assigned to the fifth century A. D. on paleographic grounds; and genealogical considerations have led to Mānāṅka being placed in the last quarter of the fourth century and Abhimanyu towards the end of the fifth century A. D.[1] The rulers of Mānapura, or the Rāṣṭrakūṭas of Mānapura, as they have been called, were thus contemporaries of the Vākāṭakas, and appear to have been, like them, worshippers of Śiva. As for the cult of Viṣṇu, it no doubt existed in the Vākāṭaka age, but seems to have occupied a secondary place; and similar conditions appear to be reflected in the subsequent history of the Deccan.

Śaivism played a decisive rôle in the temple architecture of the Deccan[2] and the adjoining countries. The early Cālukyas were mostly followers of the Vaiṣṇava cult. The Vaiṣṇava cave at Badami in the Bijapur district was excavated in 578 A. D. under Kīrtivarman I; while his brother Maṅgalīśa who succeeded him upon the throne is described as a *parama-bhāgavata*. There is also no doubt that some of the ancient temples at Aihole, now a village, about twelve miles due east of Badami, were dedicated to Viṣṇu.[3] But, towards the beginning of the eighth century A. D., the Cālukyas show a decided leaning to Śaivism, and seem to have become worshippers of Śiva. It is about this time that Paṭṭadakal, now a small village, about ten miles east of Badami, emerges as an important religious centre with Śaivism playing a dominant rôle. Three Śaiva temples of considerable size were built here, the oldest being the massive temple of Vijayeśvara, now called that of Sangameśvara built by Vijayāditya (696-733 A. D.). Of the other two, the temple of Virūpākṣa (Lokeśvara) is the largest and the most important of the old temples in the Kanarese districts. It was built by Lokamahādevī, the queen consort of Vikramāditya II (733-746 A. D.), in commemoration of his having thrice conquered Kāñcī or Conjeveram. 'Including the eastern and western gateways, the building measures 250 feet over all, of which the main building occupies a length of 120 feet.' Within the great hall are eighteen heavy square pillars, decorated with sculptures representing scenes from the Rāmāyaṇa and the Mahābhārata. Close to the temple of Virūpākṣa is that of Mallikārjuna, which has been identified with the temple of Trailokyeśvara

1 Mirashi: *The Rāṣṭrakūṭas of Mānapura* in *ABORI*, Vol. XXV, p. 36.

2 For details see Cousens: *Chalukyan Architecture of the Kanarese Districts.* Archaeological Survey of India, Vol. XLII, 1926.

3 See below (section on Vaiṣṇavism).

erected by the younger queen of Vikramāditya II, named Trailokyamahādevī, a sister of Lokamahādevī. The general plan and design are the same as in Virūpākṣa, but many parts of this temple have been left unfinished. The temples of Vijayeśvara, Virūpākṣa and Trailokyeśvara form an imposing group; and an inscription which gives us information about these three temples is engraved upon a great column which stands upon the north side of Virūpākṣa. It was erected by a sculptor, named Śubhadeva, for a Śaiva teacher named Jñānaśiva who had come from a place on the north bank of the Ganges, in 754 A. D., during the reign of Kīrtivarman II. There are certain other old Śaiva temples at Paṭṭadakal, such as those of Kāśīviśvanātha, Galaganātha and Kāḍasiddheśvara, but they are smaller in size, and of uncertain date; and there exist also the remains of two other temples of the same class, namely, Jambhuliṅga and Candraśekhara. Far more important is the large ornate temple of Pāpanātha, which cannot be later than that of Virūpākṣa, but seems to have been dedicated to Viṣṇu, as shown by the Garuḍa emblem over the shrine door. There are, however, indications that it was, at a later date, converted to Śaiva worship.[1]

Śiva temples are found also at Badami, in the south-east corner of the Bijapur district, the former Vātāpi, a capital of the early Cālukyas. The oldest and the best preserved is the Mālegitti-śivālaya, 'the Śaiva shrine of the female Garland-maker,' 56 feet in length, and of the same style as the older temples at Aihole. 'It is a complete Dravidian temple.... All its parts are heavy and massive and well proportioned to one another.' It seems to have been originally dedicated to Viṣṇu, with that deity in the ceiling, and Garuḍa on the lintel of the shrine doorway. Another interesting temple at Badami is the smaller one of Lakulīśa, an incarnation of Śiva, whose image is seated upon the altar in the shrine, and represented nude as usual. Badami possesses yet another old Śaiva temple, that of Virūpākṣa, which is still in use.

In a secluded glen between Paṭṭadakal and Badami is the temple of Mahākūṭeśvara, which may be ascribed to the early part of the sixth century A. D., as an inscription of 601 A. D., engraved on a column found near the temple, records an additional grant made in continuation of a previous endowment of the god Śiva under the name of Makuṭeśvaranātha. Another temple, which, on the grounds of style and 'more cyclopean-looking masonry', is regarded as older than the seventh century A. D., is that of Huchchimalli-Guḍi at Aihole. Unfortunately 'the interior of the shrine has been totally wrecked, portions of the *liṅga* and the paving of the floor lying about in great confusion'. An inscription of 708 A. D., upon the front of

1 'There is a *dvārapāla*, four-armed, on either side of the shrine door......... In the upper left hand of the south figure is a *triśūla*, but it has been made of plaster, evidently after the temple was converted to Śaiva worship.' There is also the *tāṇḍava* sculpture on the face of the tower. On the other hand, 'the *aṣṭadikpāla* ceiling, in the centre of the hall, has Viṣṇu reclining upon Śeṣa as its central panel instead of the *tāṇḍava* of Śiva which is usual in such ceilings found in Śaiva temples.' Cousens (op. cit.), p. 69.

the temple, records a grant of oil to the priest of the temple by the Cālukya king Vijayāditya, the builder of the Vijayeśvara temple.

The Cālukyas were supplanted by the Rāṣṭrakūṭas about the middle of the eighth century A. D. The latter achieved little in the way of building structural temples, but they 'had their own works in hand in the north, notably the great excavations at Elūrā, which extended from the Daśa Avatāra cave to the extensive group of Jaina caves around the Indra and Jagannāth Sabhās.' These included the great monolithic temple of Kailāsa, dedicated to Siva, which appears to have been excavated at Elūrā or Ellora, about fourteen miles northwest of Aurangabad, during the reign of Kṛṣṇa I who ruled between 756 and 775 A. D. He is described as having built many temples of Śiva, resembling the Kailāsa mountain; and, it was under the orders of this monarch that a most marvellous Siva temple, evidently the great Kailāsa temple, is said to have been constructed on the hill at Elāpura (Elūrā).[1] The Kailāsa resembles the temple of Virūpākṣa (Lokeśvara) at Paṭṭadakal in plan and details, although the former is hewn out of the solid rock, and the latter is built in the ordinary way on level ground. There is similarity even in the sculptures on the two temples, representing scenes from the Rāmāyaṇa and the Mahābhārata. 'In Lokeśvara they occur upon the broad bands round the shafts of the great columns of the hall, while on Kailāsa they are sculptured in narrow bands on the wall of the basement below the porch'. 'Another unusual representation is that of the Śiva-*liṅga* with Brahmā and Viṣṇu beside it, which is found, in both cases, on the front of the temple.' The Kailāsa, in spite of its marvellous technique, and the more graceful treatment of its details, thus appears to be modelled on Virūpākṣa; and it is probable that the Rāṣṭrakūṭas copied the Cālukyan building art when they had overthrown the dynasty, just as the Cālukyas themselves had copied the Dravidian architecture of the south when they had carried their victorious arms to Kāñcī or Conjeveram.[2] Unlike other cave-temples, the Kailāsa, once gorgeously painted, stands, isolated from the surrounding rock, 'in a great court averaging 154 feet wide by 276 long at the level of the base, entirely cut out of the solid rock, and with a scarp 107 feet high at the back.'[3] The bewildering amount of labour and technical skill expended on the celebrated temple bears eloquent testimony to the importance which the Śaiva cult had attained in the Deccan in the Rāṣṭrakūṭa age.

The Ellora group of cave temples includes, besides the Kailāsa, other shrines dedicated to Śiva such as the large cave north of Kailāsa (XVII), and Caves XXII (Nīlakaṇṭha), XXIII and XXVI. Far more important is Cave XXI, a lofty Śaiva temple, locally known as Rāmeśvara. 'The hall is 15½ feet high and measures 69 feet by 251 with a chapel at each end, cut off by two cushion-capital pillars.' Cave XXIX is known as Sītā's

1 Bhandarkar: *Early History of the Dekkan.* Third edition, p. 109 ff.

2 For an elaborate comparison between the two temples see Cousens (op. cit.), p. 62.

3 Burgess: *A Guide to Elura cave temples*, p. 31. (Reprinted by the Hyderabad Archaeological Department).

Nahāni, or Dumar Lena. 'The great hall, including the shrine, is 148 feet wide by 149 deep, and 17 feet 8 inches high, but the excavation extends to about 240 feet from north to south.[1]' This cave is remarkably similar to the great Śaiva cave temple at Elephanta, 'but it is larger and in some respects finer; it is also, perhaps, later in age.' The shrine is a small square room containing a *liṅga*, with four doors, each guarded by a pair of gigantic *dvārapālas*.

Elephanta is a small island near Bombay, about seven miles to the north-east of Apollo Bandar; and the great cave temple of Śiva hewn out of the living rock is on the north face of the western hill. The cave consists of a central hall and four vestibules, and measures about 130 feet in length, the breadth being approximately the same. The roof is supported by massive columns varying in height from 15 to 17 feet. These originally numbered twenty-six, of which eight have collapsed. The cave is remarkable for its colossal sculptures representing Śiva in his various forms including Naṭarāja, Gaṅgādhara and Ardhanārīśvara. But the most striking sculpture in the cave is the huge panel consisting of a triple-headed bust of Śiva, which rises to a height of 17 feet 10 inches above a moulded base, nearly 3 feet high. The image stands in a recess 10½ feet deep, 'within which the heads emerge cliff-like from the native rock.'

The triple head represents three aspects of Śiva: Tatpuruṣa (the supreme Mahādeva) in the middle, and Vāmadeva (the Beautiful) and Aghora (the Terrible) on the sides. The image of Mahādeva 'dominates the whole assemblage. It is the concrete form of Śiva whose *liṅga* is worshipped in the adjacent shrine. The plan of the rock-cut temple was thus adjusted to the image; the entire hall is laid out in front of it in its deep recess. The stage is set for that form (*rūpa*) of His who is beyond form, and who pervades the universe, which thus is His visible body.'[2]

The cave-temple at Elephanta has generally been assigned to the latter part of the eighth century A. D., and is probably of the same age as the excavations at Ellora, which fall in the Rāṣṭrakūṭa period. The close resemblance between the Dumar Lena at Ellora and the Elephanta cave has attracted the attention of observers; while pillars with 'compressed cushion capitals' have been found both in Elephanta and some of the cave temples at Ellora. But the simple grandeur of the Elephanta sculptures in striking contrast to the complex and grotesque multiplicity of those at Ellora suggests a somewhat earlier date for the former, possible the seventh century A. D.[3] In the tenth century A. D., Ellora and Elephanta must have been great centres

1 Ibid. p. 47.

2 Stella Kramrisch in *Ancient India*, Number 2, p. 7.

3 See Hirananda Sastri: *A Guide to Elephanta* (published by the Government of India) and Burgess: *The Rock temples of Elephanta or Ghārāpurī*. When the Portuguese occupied the island in 1534, the cave temple must have been in excellent preservation. The Portuguese captain Joao de Castro, who visited the island in 1538, thought that the cave could not be the work of human hands. 'Even Apelles', he says, 'might have learned from the proportion and symmetry of the figures.' 'The

of Śaiva worship, like Somanāthapattana, Ujjain, Khajurāho, and Tanjore.

Apart from the Ellora and the Elephanta cave-temples, there were no doubt other temples dedicated to Śiva in existence during the Rāṣṭrakūṭa period. It was in a Śiva temple that Govinda III (794-814 A. D.) deposited the two statues sent by the king of Ceylon as a token of submission.[1] 'The custom of founding a Śiva temple in commemoration of a dead ancestor, and of naming the deity after the person to be commemorated, had already become prevalent in our period. Hebbal inscription, dated 975 A. D., refers to a temple of Bhujjabbeśvara built to commemorate Bhubbarasi, the grand-mother of the Gaṅga ruler Mārasiṁha II.'[2] It may be noted that Śiva temples existed in Mysore during the Rāṣṭrakūṭa period. The religion of the Gaṅgas was Jainism, but they were liberal in their outlook; and some of the early kings favoured the worship of Śiva, for example, Taḍangāla Mādhava and Avinīta (circa 5th–6th century A. D.). A considerable number of Śiva temples seems to have been built during the rule of the later Gaṅgas who were contemporaries of the Rāṣṭrakūṭas. Notable among these are the shrine of Bhoganandīśvara at the foot of the Nandi hills, Someśvara at Gangavaripalli, Kapileśvara at Manne etc.[3] The construction of so many temples for the worship of Śiva proves the prevalence of Śaivism side by side with Jainism in Mysore, although under the Gaṅgas the latter was the more influential and favoured religion.

Śaiva temples were constructed or maintained, on a wide scale, during the reign of the Cālukyas of Kalyani, as shown by the various grants and endowments recorded in their inscriptions. For example, an inscription of 980 A. D. belonging to the reign of Taila II is the subject of an endowment made for the benefit of the temple of Suvarṇākṣi, a form of Śiva, styled as Śaṁkara-Svayaṁbhū-Suvarṇamahākṣi, at Soval (Sogal in the Belgaum district).[4] An inscription of 1064 A. D.[5] records the grant of an endowment to the temple of Keśaveśvara at Poṭṭiyūr (Hoṭṭūr); another of 1074 A. D.[6] deals with the grant of a town for the maintenance of the sanctuary of Rāmeśvara at Pomballi (Hombli); while the temple of Mahā-Svayaṁbhū-

Portuguese annalist Diogo de Couto writing in the opening years of the 17th century says that the interior of the temple had formerly been covered with a coat of lime mixed with bitumen and other compositions that made the temple bright and very beautiful and worth seeing; and the features and workmanship were such that 'neither in silver or wax could such figures be engraved with greater nicety, fineness or perfection.' Unfortunately it was during Portuguese occupation that the temple was damaged and the figures sadly mutilated. For detailed references see Commissariat-*History of Gujarat*, Vol. I, Appendix, pp. 541–9.

1 Altekar: *The Rāṣṭrakūṭas and their times*, p. 69.

2 Ibid. p. 287.

3 Rao: *The Gangas of Talkad*, p. 232. A systematic study of the early temples of Mysore is a desideratum.

4 *Epigraphia Indica*, Vol. XVI, pp. 2, 6.

5 Ibid. Vol. XVI, p. 82.

6 Ibid. p. 69 ff.

Somanātha, 'the Somanātha of the South', at Purikara (Puligere, the modern Lakshmeshwar), (all in the Dharwar district), is referred to in several inscriptions belonging to the first half of the twelfth century A. D.[1] Further, an inscription of the reign of Soyi Deva, the son of Bijjala, records endowments made in 1172 A. D. for the temples of Śiva-Somanātha (Rāya-Murāri-Somanātha) and Bijjeśvara at Māḷige (Māḍagihāḷ in Jat State, near Bijapur).[2]

Apart from inscriptional evidence, there exists a large number of surviving specimens of later Cālukyan Śaiva temples, ranging from the tenth century to the end of the twelfth, mostly in the Dharwar district and the immediate neighbourhood.[3] In fact, it will be no exaggeration to say that later Cālukyan architecture was almost entirely devoted to the glorification of the Śaiva faith. The advent of the later Cālukyas under Taila II, towards the end of the tenth century, gave a fresh impetus to temple building; and it is from this time that we notice a gradual transformation of the earlier Dravidian style, till what is known as the Cālukyan style came into existence. In the first place, the earlier building material, the rougher grained sandstone, was abandoned in favour of 'the more compact, tractable, and finer grained black stone known as chloritic schist, which dresses down to a much finer surface, and has enabled the sculptors to produce so much of that beautiful, delicate, lacelike tracery which characterises the later work.' In the second place, there was a diminution in the size of the masonry, the heavy cyclopean blocks of the early temples being discarded in favour of much smaller ones. Finally, the storied or horizontal arrangement of the towers, a prominent characteristic of the Dravidian style found in the early temples, became obliterated by a great profusion of ornamental detail, and underwent a process of approximation to the vertical bands up the centre of each face of the Northern tower. The transition from the earlier to this later style, evolved about the tenth and eleventh centuries, is seen in the S'aiva temple of Kalleśvara at Kukkanūr[4] and the Jaina temple at Lakkuṇḍi[5]; while that of Kāśīviśveśvara at the latter place shows a further marked development of the Cālukyan tower. On a beam in the hall of the latter building is an inscription, dated in the thirteenth year of the reign of the later Cālukya king Vikramāditya VI, which corresponds to 1087 A. D.[6] One of the finest of existing Cālukyan temples 'probably the finest temple in the Kanarese districts, after Haḷebīd,' is that of Mahādeva in the small village of Ittagi, in the Nizam's territory, about twenty-two miles due east of Gadag in the Dharwar district. 'It measures, over all, 120 feet by 66 feet,' and consists of a shrine, with its antechamber, a closed and a great open hall at the east end, which was originally supported upon sixtyeight pillars. The temple is mentioned in

1 Ibid. *Three Inscriptions of Lakshmeshwar* by L. D. Barnett.
2 Ibid. Vol. XV, p. 317.
3 See Cousens (op. cit.), p. 74 ff.
4 A village in the Nizam's territory, at a short distance across the border from Gadag in the Dharwar district.
5 Now a small village near Gadag.
6 Cousens (op. cit.), p. 79.

an inscription of 1112 A. D., which tells us that it was founded, as a temple of Śiva, under the name Mahādeveśvara, by Mahādeva, the *daṇḍa-nāyaka*, or general, of Vikramāditya VI (1075-1125 A. D.). He founded also a temple of Nārāyaṇa, and other S'aiva shrines such as those of Caṇḍāleśvara and Bhairava.[1]

One of the largest Śaiva temples of the Cālukyan period, in the Dharwar district, is that of Tārakeśvara, in the town of Hāngal, 'chiefly remarkable for the magnificent dome which covers the central portion of the great hall,' the roof of which is supported upon fifty-two pillars. The temple of Kaiṭhabheśvara at Ānavaṭṭi, in Maisur, just across the border from the Dharwar district, is distinguished by its unusually lofty hall, the pillars being massive in proportion. The temple of Dakṣiṇa-Kedāreśvara at Balagāmve is now shorn of its importance, but it was a great educational centre, of which we have already spoken. Śaiva temples of the Cālukyan period are found also at Chaudadāmpur (*Mukteśvara*), Hāveri (*Siddheśvara*), Haralhalli (*Someśvara*), and Raṭṭehalli (*Kadambeśvara*), all in the Dharwar district.

The temple of Kadambeśvara contains an inscription which records a grant to it in 1174 A. D. for repairing the building. Inscriptions dating from 899 to 1262 A. D. are engraved on several slabs standing beside the temple at Chaudadāmpur, the later ones recording grants and gifts to the god of the temple under the names of Mukteśvara and Muktinātha.

The temple of Madhukeśvara at Banavāsi, a very ancient place, now a village, eighteen miles south by west from Hāngal, belongs to the eleventh century, as one of the inscribed slabs in and around the temple records a grant in the year 1068 A. D. The so-called Temple of the Sixty Columns, now in a ruined state, at Bankapur, and that of Trikūṭeśvara at Gadag, both in the Dharwar district, may also be ascribed to the eleventh century. The former temple contains inscriptions upon either side of the shrine door, recording grants made to the god Nāgareśvara in 1138 and 1091 A. D. Similarly, one of the inscriptions collected together at the temple of Trikūṭeśvara records a grant made in 1062 A. D. in the time of Āhavamalla II.[2] Cālukyan temples are found also in the Bellary district of the Madras Presidency, and most of them are dedicated to Śiva (Kalleśvara, Katteśvara, Bhīmeśvara etc.)[3]. There is no doubt that the inspiration derived from Saivism helped the building art of the Cālukyas and the technical competence of their craftsmen to give a distinctive stamp to Indian culture in the Deccan.

Even in the northern part of the Deccan, outside the sphere of the Cālukyas, we find a preponderance of temples dedicated to Śiva.[4] The most ornate of the temples in the Deccan style is that at the village of Ambarnātha, about four miles south-east of Kalyan, in the Thana district. 'This chef-d'oeuvre of the builder's art' was built for the worship of Śiva

1 Poussin: *Dynasties et Histoire de l' Inde*, p. 211; *Epigraphia Indica*, Vol. XIII, p. 36 ff.

2 Cousens (op. cit.), pp. 84, 96, 104, 112, 128.

3 See Rea: *Chalukyan Architecture*. Archaeological Survey of India. New Imperial Series, Vol. XXI.

4 See Cousens: *Mediaeval Temples of the Dakhan*. Archaeological Survey of India, Vol. XLVIII.

in 1060 A. D., during the reign of the Śilāhāra chief Mummuṇi or Māmvāṇi. The temple measures 89 feet by 73½ feet, and is made up of the sanctum and *maṇḍapa* or hall, the latter being provided with three entrances, each with its own porch. The temples in the Deccan style are not remarkable for their size, that of Gondeśvara or Govindeśvara at Sinnar, twenty miles south of Nasik, being about the largest now standing. It is a *pañcāyatana* temple forming a group of five shrines, the central main temple being dedicated to Śiva, and the four small surrounding shrines to Viṣṇu, Gaṇapati and others. It is supposed to have been built by Rāv Govinda; and 'it is possible it may be named after Govindarāja, one of the Yādava princes, who ruled about the beginning of the 12th century'. Another temple, that of Maheśvara, at Pāṭṇā, ten miles to the south-west of Chalisgaon in Khandesh, was completed by a chief Govana, of the Nikumbha family, who was ruling in that locality under the Yādavas in 1153 A.D.[1]

To sum up, the temple architecture of the Deccan bears testimony to the paramount character of Śaivism in that region from about the eighth century to the end of the twelfth. No other faith, whether Vaiṣṇavism or Jainism, during this period, found so elaborate an expression in the building art of the time.

SOUTH INDIA

From Deccan we may turn to South India properly so called. The classic land of Śaivism was the Tamil country which witnessed one of the greatest epochs of the faith. Śaivism is prevalent in South India even today; and it is said that the Saivas form the bulk of the population in the districts of Tinnevelly, Madura, Trichinopoly, Tanjore, South Arcot, Chingleput, Madras, North Arcot, Salem and Coimbatore, and are also found in large numbers in certain parts of Ceylon, Malabar and Travancore; in short, wherever Tamil is the prevailing tongue.[2] Going back to early times, we find sixty-three cononized saints known as Nāyanmars or Aḍiyārs, who are the real founders of Śaivism in South India. Included among them is Koccenganān, one of the Cola kings mentioned in early Tamil literature. He must have flourished long before the seventh century when he had already become a legendary figure. The importance of Koccenganān lies in the fact that he appears to have been one of the earliest builders of Śiva temples in the Tamil country. The Vaiṣṇava Ālvār Tirumangai, who lived about the middle of the eighth century, says in one of his hymns that the king built seventy beautiful shrines dedicated to Śiva, besides offering worship to Viṣṇu at Tirunaraiyūr. He is also described as having founded other temples to Śiva in the hymns of Sambandar and Sundaramūrti.[3]

---

1 An old temple of Śiva called Mallikārjuna exists at Nagansur in Akalkot State, near Sholapur in Bombay Province. It is built in the Cālukyan style, popularly known as Hemādpanti; and, like all temples built in this style, it has an open porch in front of the *maṇḍapa* which is supported by four elaborately carved pillars. A temple of Śiva, apparently of the later Cālukyan period, was discovered and excavated under the inner wall of the old fort at Sholapur. *Progress Roport of the Archaeological Survey of India, Western Circte*, 1919, p. 59; 1920, p. 74.

2 *Tamilian Antiquary*, No. 3, p. 1. 1909.

3 Sastri: *The Colas*, Vol. I, p. 67.

The chronology of the Aḍiyārs has not been settled in all its details, but the saint Appar and his younger and more influential contemporary Sambandar are known to have lived in the first half of the seventh century A. D. Sambandar was a contemporary of another Śaiva devotee, Siruttoṇḍar, who was the general of the Pallava king Narasiṁhavarman I, and conquered with him Vātāpi, the Chālukyan capital, about 642 A. D.[1] The next important saint, Sundaramūrti, has been assigned to the early part of the ninth century A. D. The saint Śeramān Perumāl was a contemporary of Sundaramūrti.[2]

The hymns composed by Appar, Sambandar and Sundaramūrti form the first seven sections of the Śaiva canonical literature in Tamil. Of the eleven sections of this literature, the first three contain the hymns of Sambandar, and the next three those of Appar; while the seventh is composed of the hymns of Sundaramūrti. These seven sections, or rather collections, constitute the group known as the Tevāram.[3] The eighth section contains the famous Tiruvāśakam of the great saint and poet Māṇikkavāśagar. He has been assigned to various dates, but it is almost certain that he is considerably earlier than the seventh century, as Appar refers to a well-known miracle associated with his life, and mentions a Vācaka who seems to be identical with the saint.[4] The hymns of the Aḍiyārs give fervid expression to intense, self-effacing devotion to Siva, and proclaim absolute faith in His abounding grace and beneficent mission. Their religious fervour and spiritual depth represent an early phase of Śaivism of which the keynote is *bhakti.*

Tamil Śaivism has an important bearing on the religious conflict, to which we have referred in this work. Here, Śaivism was in open conflict with Jainism, and the antagonism was far more deep-rooted than in the Deccan, where the Jaina faith continued to be in a favoured position until long after its discomfiture at Kāñcī and Madura. In the Tamil country Jainism lost effective royal patronage as early as the seventh century A. D. when it had only commenced to obtain royal favour in the Deccan, for example, under Pulakeśi II. The great Pallava king Mahendravarman I was converted from Jainism to the Śaiva faith by Appar in the first quarter of the seventh century A. D. The Śaiva saint had been persecuted by Mahendra; but, after his conversion, the king became an ardent champion of the new faith, and is said to have demolished the Jaina monastery at Pāṭaliputtiram, a seat of Jaina learning in the South Arcot district, and built a Śiva temple on the spot.[5] Appar himself was born a Śaiva, became a Jaina and leader of the Jaina settlement at Pāṭali (now the modern town of Cuddalore), and later reverted to his former religion.[6] Further to the south, Kūn Pāṇḍya of

---

1 Jouveau-Dubreuil: *The Pallavas*, p. 68.

2 Aiyangar: *Some Contributions of South India to Indian Culture*, p. 217.

3 *Tamilian Antiquary* (op. cit.), p. 2.

4 Ibid. No. 4, pp. 1-55. See also Sastri: *The Pāndyan Kingdom*, p. 67.

5 Jouveau-Dubreuil: *Pallava Antiquities*, Vol. I, p. 40; Longhurst: *Pallava Architecture*, Part I, p. 7.

6 Aiyangar (op. cit.), p. 237.

Madura was similarly converted from Jainism to the Śaiva faith by the saint Sambandar; and this king has been identified with Arikesari Māravarman who commenced his reign about the middle of the seventh century A. D.[1] The conversion of Kūn Pāṇḍya and Mahendravarman I may be regarded as a turning point in the history of Śaivism in South India, as it meant practically the elimination of Jainism as a serious rival. But the story of the persecution of the Jainas, eight thousand of whom are said to have been cruelly put to death at Madura at the instigation of Sambandar, is probably an exaggeration for which the Tamil *Purāṇas* are responsible.[2] Sambandar was, however, noted for his anti-Jaina zeal, as he has given vent to his implacable hatred of the Jainas in all his hymns.[3] The rancour against the Jainas lurked in various legends, one of which recounts, for instance, that these heretics once sent an elephant to destroy the city of Madura, but Śiva petrified the beast in the form of the neighbouring Ānamalai hill.[4]

The Śaiva Aḍiyārs as well as the Vaiṣṇava Ālvārs were assiduous in combating heresy in the Tamil land. Māṇikkavāśagar turned against the Buddhists, whom he defeated in argument at Chidambaram and thereafter converted to the Śaiva faith. He was a high officer of the Pāṇḍya king of the time until he renounced the world at the call of Śiva; and it is possible that Pāndyan rule included Chidambaram in his day. The dialectical triumph of Māṇikkavāśagar was repeated by Sambandar at Madura, but his opponents were the Jainas, who refused to adopt the Śaiva faith despite their humiliation.[5] Thus, while the earlier saint was an antagonist of the Buddhists, the efforts of Sambandar were directed against Jainism; and, it may be assumed that the hostility of so influential a leader of religious opinion contributed towards the retrogression of the Jaina faith in the South. The rôle of Appar in this conflict of religions was no less important, as the conversion of Mahendravarman I gave to Śaivism one of its greatest patrons and protagonists. The decline of Jainism in the Tamil country was thus largely due to the loss of royal patronage and popular support brought about by the influence and missionary zeal of the leading Saiva saints. The process of decay, far-reaching as it was, must have been gradual, as references to Jaina temples and images are occasionally found in the records of the succeeding centuries. It is noteworthy that, as late as the first quarter of the tenth century, the Pāṇḍya king Rājasiṁha II is said to have endowed, among others, several Jaina temples. 'It is clear from such facts that Jainism was not overwhelmed so completely as Buddhism by the rising tide of Śaivism and Vaiṣṇavism in the land.'[6]

The paramount influence of Śaivism in the Tamil country is also attested by the temple architecture of the time, as in the case of the Deccan.

---

1 Jouveau-Dubreuil: *The Pallavas*, p. 68.
2 Sastri: *The Pāndyan Kingdom*, p. 97.
3 *Tamilian Antiquary*, No. 3, p. 7.
4 Sastri (op. cit.), p. 4.
5 Sastri (op. cit.), p. 96.
6 Sastri (op. cit.), p. 95.

As stated above, the early Cola king Koccenganān is said to have built many Śiva temples; while the Tevāram saints celebrate a very large number of them in their hymns.[1] But, so far as existing examples are concerned, South Indian architecture may be said to begin with the Pallavas, or more precisely, with the reign of Mahendravarman I in the first quarter of the seventh century A. D. The shrines, before his time, appear to have been built of perishable materials, but he introduced the art of excavating temples in the natural rock in the Tamil country. Almost the first cave temple, 'caused to be built by King Curious-minded, without bricks, without timber and without mortar,' is the one at Māṇḍagappattu in the South Arcot district; and it was dedicated to Brahmā, Viṣṇu and Śiva.[2] Most of the remaining caves, with one exception, were excavated for the worship of Śiva under the form of the *liṅga*; and they are found in the North Arcot, Chingleput, and South Arcot districts of the Madras Presidency. The name Mahendra occurs in inscriptions on the caves at Trichinopoly, Pallāvaram, Mahendravāḍi and Vallam; while one or other of his *birudas* is mentioned in those on the caves at Dalavānūr and Śīyamaṅgalam.[3] Mahendravarman's comic play *Mattavilāsaprahasana* is mentioned in a mutilated inscription on one of the caves at Māmaṇḍūr[4] in the North Arcot district.

One of the inscriptions on the upper cave cut in the rock at Trichinopoly contains a verse, which has been taken to refer to Mahendravarman's former hostility to the Śaiva religion. The verse in question seems to express the hope that, while king Guṇabhara (one of the *birudas* of Mahendravarman I) is a worshipper of the *liṅga* emblem, the *liṅga* enshrined in the temple will proclaim the fact that he has desisted from 'hostile action', that is, his former persecution of the Śaiva faith.[5]

Mahendravarman's conversion gave a new impetus to Śaivism in the Tamil land. Only one of his caves, that at Mahendravāḍi, is dedicated to Viṣṇu. The rock-cut temple at Singavaram in the South Arcot district contains a very large image of Viṣṇu sleeping on the serpent Ananta, and is thought to belong to the epoch of Mahendravarman on architectural grounds. Of the three caves at Vallam (near Chingleput) two are dedicated to Śiva, one of which contains an inscription of Mahendravarman: the third cave is dedicated to Viṣṇu.[6] Reference may be made in this connection to the great rock-cut temple at Undavalli in the Guntur district, situated on the

---

1 *Tamilian Antiquary*, No 4, p. 30.

2 'एतदनिष्टकमद्रुमलोहमसुधं विचित्रचित्तेन निर्मापितं नृपेण ब्रह्मेश्वरविष्णुलक्षितायतनम्' See Jouveau-Dubreuil: *Conjeevaram Inscription of Mahendravarman I.* Trichinopoly, 1919.

3 Jouveau-Dubreuil: *Pallava Antiquities*, Vol. 1, p. 39.

4 Ibid.: *The Pallavas*, p. 39.

5 *South Indian Inscriptions*, Vol. I, 1890, p. 29. The temple is excavated half way up the Trichinopoly rock, and consists of a rock-cut hall measuring 30 feet in length and 15 feet in width. A remarkable sculptural panel, carved in the west wall of the hall, and measuring about seven feet square, represents Śiva with four arms, the right upper arm holding the Ganges issuing from his hair.

6 Jouveau-Dubreuil: *Pallava Antiquities*, Vol. I, pp. 49 53.

south bank of the Kṛshṇā opposite to Bezwada. 'The temple consists of a ground floor and three upper storeys hewn out of the natural rock. It has a frontage of about 90 feet in length and rises to a height of 50 feet from the ground level.' The ground floor and especially the third or top storey are unfinished. The temple may be said in fact to be four-storeyed, but its different storeys are supposed to represent 'three temples of the Mahendra period excavated one above the other in the same rock.' The principal image in the temple is a huge decayed image of Viṣṇu lying on the serpent Ananta found in the second storey. 'A similar figure exists in the shrine attached to the big Śiva temple at Mahābalipuram known as the Shore temple, and it also occurs in a large bas-relief panel in a Śiva temple close to the Lighthouse at the same place.' The colossal image of Anantaśayana and certain Vaiṣṇava sculptures have led to the belief that the rock-cut temple at Undavalli was originally dedicated to Viṣṇu. But, as we have seen, it is not rare to find an image of Viṣṇu, particularly in the form of Anantaśayana, located in a Śiva temple. 'The style of the doorkeepers, panels and niches containing Saiva figures, and the group of rockcut miniature Śiva temples containing *liṅgas* on the hill close by all indicate that Undavalli was a stronghold of the *liṅga* cult in the seventh century in spite of the presence of Vaiṣṇava figures in the big temple.' The origin of the temples at Undavalli and Bezwada is obscure; and 'there is no actual proof that they are the works of the Pallavas, but their architectural style seems to denote that they were excavated by the latter and that they represent their earliest attempts in this direction before the Pallavas were driven south by the Chālukyas and executed similar but better works in the Tamil Country.'[1]

There is an ancient Pallava cave-temple known as the Orukal Maṇḍapa on the east side of the Vedagirīśvara hill bordering the town of Tirukkalukkunram not far from Chingleput. The temple was dedicated to Śiva as the shrine contains a large cylindrical granite *liṅga*. 'The style of its architecture clearly denotes that it was excavated in the reign of Mahendra. The Vedagirīśvara temple on the summit of the hill is likewise an ancient structure, but later than the Orukal Maṇḍapa. Carved on the back wall of the main shrine of this temple is the Somaskanda panel representing Śiva and Pārvatī in the centre with the child Skanda seated between them. It may be noted that the Somaskanda panel is not found in any

---

1 Longhurst: *Pallavà Architecture*, Part I, pp. 5, 22, 27, 29. Jouveau-Dubreuil first pointed out that the Undavalli caves closely resemble those of Mahendravarman, but he thought that they were the work of the Viṣṇukuṇḍins who seem to have reigned on the banks of the Godāvarī and the Krishṇā towards the end of the sixth century A. D., before that country was conquered by the Chālukyas. Further, as the caves of Trichinopoly and Pallāvaram contain certain surnames of Mahendravarman, which are all of Telugu origin, Jouveau-Dubreuil supposed that Mahendravarman I reigned over the Telugu country and imported into the Tamil country the art that existed on the banks of the Krishṇā. *The Pallavas*, pp. 32, 33. Longhurst assumes, on purely architectural grounds, that the Bezwada and Undavalli cave-temples are Pallava monuments of the early part of the seventh century.

shrine of the temples of the Mahendra period. It appears in the reign of Narasiṁhavarman I, e. g. on the back wall of the shrine cell in the Dharmarāja Ratha, and occurs in all the Pallava temples of the Rājasiṁha period.

Mahendravarman I was succeeded by Narasiṁhavarman I in the second quarter of the seventh century A. D. He was the founder of the sea-coast town of Māmallapuram, now the village of Mahābalipuram, on a strip of sand, about 40 miles south of Madras. All his monuments as well as those of his grandson Parameśvaravarman I (about 655–690 A. D.) are mainly found at this place, and consist of cave-temples and the so-called *rathas*. The cave-temples are rock-cut excavations of the same style as those of the Mahendra period, but there is a distinct improvement in design and workmanship. The clumsy pillars with cubical capitals of the Mahendra period are replaced by elegant pillars with bulbous capitals, and the interiors are 'often decorated with sculptural figures in high-relief of great beauty and executed with remarkable skill.' The *rathas* are monolithic free-standing temples, delicately carved, and look like rock-cut models of structural temples.[1] 'A few were dedicated to Vishṇu, but most of them were devoted to the worship of Śiva and his consort Pārvatī, *the latter sometimes in the form of Durgā.* In a few cases, a combined worship of Śiva and Viṣṇu seems to have occurred in the same temple.'

The most remarkable monument at Mahābalipuram is the so-called Dharmarāja Ratha, 'a lofty pyramidal-roofed temple with three storeys of cell-terraces above the ground floor, rising to a small octagonal dome.' The ground floor consists of a hall, about 28 feet square, with a projecting portico facing the west. As an example of marvellous stone-cutting and carving, it is 'quite the most wonderful monument in Southern India. It is also veryi nteresting as the prototype of the lofty structural pyramidal temples of later times.'

It may be definitely stated that the Dharmarāja Ratha and the Gaṇeśa Temple[2], 'quite the most finished and ornate' of all the *rathas*,

---

1 For example, tne so-called Arjuna's Ratha (*these local names have no historical significance*) represents 'a stone model of a small two-storeyed building crowned with an octagonal bell-shaped dome mainly of timber construction.' The Sahadeva's Ratha consists of a ground floor and two upper storeys, with a waggon-headed roof. All three floors are apsidal-ended like Buddhist *caityas* or churches. 'Like all the other so-called *rathas*, it is obviously a stone model of a building mainly of wooden construction.' The Bhīma's Ratha is waggon-roofed: 'it is a stone model of a large barn-like building mainly of timber construction. On plan it measures 42 feet in length, 25 feet in width and is about 25 feet high.' The roof of this so-called Bhīma's Ratha 'would seem to be the prototype of the ordinary waggon roof of all the great *gopurams* or gate-ways of the South Indian temples.' The *ratha* known as the Gaṇeśa temple is an oblong monolithic edifice 'with two upper storeys and a waggon-roof, having two gable end facades with horseshoe bargeboards like Bhīma's Ratha which it closely resembles, although much smaller, being only 20 feet in length from north to south, 11½ feet in width, and 28 feet in height.' See Longhurst: *Pallava Architecture*, Part II.

2 So called, because an image of Gaṇeśa was installed in the temple by the villagers in recent times.

and the cave-temples known as the Dharmarāja Maṇḍapa and the Rāmānuja Maṇḍapa were originally dedicated to Śiva. The name *atyanta-kāma-pallaveśvara-gṛha*, 'the Śiva temple of Atyantakāma Pallava', is inscribed on the east and west sides of the third storey of the Dharmarāja Ratha, and occurs also in a duplicate inscription on the Gaṇeśa temple and the Dharmarāja Maṇḍapa. Further, a verse condemning those who do not worship Śiva occurs in the same inscription, and is found also inscribed on the Rāmānuja Maṇḍapa[1]. As regards *atyanta-kāma*, it seems to have been a *biruda* of both Narasiṁhavarman I and Parameśvaravarman I. The name Śrī-Narasiṁha and the epithet *atyanta-kāma* occur, the former twice, in a string of inscription (Nos. 1-16) engraved in an archaic alphabet on the Dharmarāja Ratha, showing that it was founded by Narasiṁhavarman I. The name Parameśvara and the title Atyantakāma occur in the duplicate inscription on the Gaṇeśa temple and the Dharmarāja Maṇḍapa; and it is probable that the reference is to Parameśvaravarman I.[2] As both these temples are called *atyanta-kāma-pallaveśvara-gṛha*, the title Atyantakāma is here thought to refer to Parameśvaravarman I. But the name *atyanta-kāma-pallaveśvara-gṛha* is inscribed also on the east side of the third storey of the Dharmarāja Ratha (Inscription No. 17), not in the archaic alphabet of Inscriptions 1-16, but in the florid alphabet used in the inscriptions on the Dharmarāja Maṇḍapa and the Gaṇeśa temple. It is therefore supposed that the Dharmarāja Ratha was built by Narasiṁhavarman I, but it was consecrated by Parameśvaravarman I, surnamed Atyantakāma, who gave it the name of Atyantakāmapallaveśvara.[3]

Most of the other temples at Mahābalipuram were devoted to the worship of Śiva. The rock-cut temple near the Durgā shrine is a large five-celled Śaiva temple similar, on plan and in dimensions, to the temple of Mahendravarman at Pallāvaram.[4] The central shrine of the Trimūrti temple was dedicated to Śiva, and 'contains a basrelief carved on the back wall representing a four-armed standing image of Śiva.' The so-called Arjuna's Ratha was also dedicated to Śiva, and contained a head of the deity surmounted by the trident. It is believed that 'these trident heads were set up in the shrine cells in place of the usual Śiva *liṅgas*. The custom appears to have been peculiar to the Pallavas as such images do not seem to have been discovered elsewhere.' The Mahiṣāsura Maṇḍapa is a large triple-celled Śaiva cave-temple: 'a socket hole, cut in the centre of the floor of the cell, points to the fact that it had, or was designed for a Śiva *liṅga*.' A large square panel on the back wall of the shrine chamber contains a bas-relief representing the Sukhāsana group (Śiva, Pārvatī, the child Skanda and the bull Nandi).

1 'धिक् तेषां धिक् तेषां पुनरपि धिग्धिग्धिगस्तु धिक् तेषां । येषां न वसति हृदये कुपथगतिविमोक्षको रुद्रः ॥'

2 अमायश्चित्रमायोऽसावगुणो गुणभाजनः । स्वस्थो निरुत्तरो जीयादनीशः परमेश्वरः ॥ v. 2. अत्यन्तकामो नृपतिर्निर्जितारातिमण्डलः । ख्यातो रणजयः शम्भोस्तेनेदं वेश्म कारितम् ॥ v. 5. Parameśvara in v. 2 primarily refers to Śiva, but seems to refer also to the king of that name.

3 See *South Indian Inscriptions*, Vol. I, 1890, pp. 1–6; Jouveau-Dubreuil: *Pallava Antiquities*, Vol. I, pp. 60–64.

4 Longhurst (op. cit.), p. 13.

The two cave-temples known as the Varāha Maṇḍapa and the Varāha Temple appear to be the only ancient Vaiṣṇava shrines at Mahābalipuram. Carved in bas-relief in four large panels on the walls of the former are remarkable sculptures representing the Varāha Avatāra, the Vāmana Avatāra, Lakṣmī and Durgā. The Varāha Temple contains a large bas-relief, 8 feet high, of the Boar Incarnation, carved on the back wall of the shrine chamber. Vaiṣṇavism seems to have ousted the Śaiva faith from its dominant position at Māmallapuram at a much later date when the *liṅgas* were cast out of the shrines, and some of the Śiva temples damaged and subjected to what has been called Vaiṣṇava vandalism.[1] But there is no doubt that during the Pallava period Māmallapuram was a stronghold of Śaiva worship.

There must have been Śaiva temples at other places besides Māmallapuram during the reigns of Narasiṁhavarman I and Parameśvaravarman I. The Kūram plates issued by the latter, sometime after his victory over the Chālukya Vikramāditya I in 674 A. D., record a grant to the Śiva temple of Vidyāvinīta Pallaveśvara, which has been identified with the dilapidated Śiva temple at Kūram, a village near Conjeeveram.[2] At Melacheri in the South Arcot district there is a cave-temple dedicated to Śiva, which contains an inscription recording the fact that it was built by the emperor Candrāditya. It has been surmised by Jouveau-Dubreuil on paleographic grounds that Candrāditya was a name of Narasiṁhavarman I or Parameśvaravarman I.[3]

The Pallava cave-temples[4] are small in comparison with the stupendous excavations at Ellora, and appear to have gone out of vogue by the end of the seventh century. Parameśvaravarman I was succeeded by his son Narasiṁhavarman II, or Rājasiṁha, who distinguished himself by his piety and devotion to Śiva. About the first decade of the eighth century A. D., he built the central shrine of the Kailāsanātha temple at Conjeeveram, the Shore Temple at Mahābalipuram, and the old Śiva temple at Panamalai in the South Arcot district.[5] The temples of Rājasiṁha possess fluted black stone *liṅgas*,

---

1 Longhurst (op. cit.), Part II, pp. 5, 34, 37. 'The comparatively ruined and desecrated state of the Śaiva shrines, and the dispersion, overthrow and destruction of *liṅgas*, together with the unmolested state of the Vaishnava temples and symbols, suggest strongly the violent overthrow of the Śaiva by the Vaishnava faith' at Māmallapuram. The interior of the so-called Rāmānuja Maṇḍapa was completely wrecked, and one of the pillars of the Mahiṣāsura Maṇḍapa was cut out and removed to the Varāha Temple, presumably, to be used in the construction of the modern *maṇḍapa* erected in front of the old rockcut shrine. 'The few Tamil inscriptions dating from 1073 to 1235 A. D. that have been found at Māmallapuram, indicate that the Vaiṣṇava sect was dominant during that period, and its followers seem to have remained in the ascendant down to the present day. They still occupy the Varāha Temple and the large modern-looking Sthalaśayana Temple in the village and keep up the services of their sect therein.'

2 Jouveau-Dubreuil: *The Pallavas*, p. 45.

3 Ibid.: *Pallava Antiquities*, Vol. I, p. 66.

4 One of the largest, the so-called Mahiṣāsura Maṇḍapa, is '32 feet long from north to south, 15 feet wide and 12½ feet high.'

5 See Longhurst: *Pallava Architecture, Part III.*

and on the back wall of the shrine is carved the Somaskanda panel representing Śiva and Pārvatī, seated, with the child Skanda on the latter's knee. The temple of Airāvateśvara at Conjeeveram is also dedicated to Śiva, and bears all the characteristics of the style of Rājasiṁha, but it is not definitively known whether it was built in his reign.[1]

The Shore Temple is built on the shore within a few feet of the sea at Mahābalipuram. From an architectural point of view, it appears to be earlier than the central shrine of the Kailāsanātha temple, as the latter seems to be mainly a development of the former. The Shore Temple faces the sea on the east side, and at the back facing the west is another Śiva temple, smaller in size, but built in the same style as the main building. 'The stepped tower over the central shrine is divided into three main storeys, like Dharmarāja's *ratha*, and is crowned with the usual umbrella-shaped ornament surmounted by a lofty black stone *Kalaśam* or urn-finial.'

The central shrine of the Kailāsanāth temple at Conjeeveram is called Rājasiṁheśvara in old inscriptions, as it was built by Rājasiṁha; while his son Mahendravarman III seems to have completed the edifice. Mahendravarman III built also a smaller Śiva temple with a waggon-headed roof, now called Nāradeśvara, in front of the Kailāsanātha Temple, and named it Mahendreśvara, or Mahendravarmeśvara, after himself.[2] At a distance of 26 feet to the east, in front of the central shrine of the Kailāsanātha or Rājasiṁheśvara temple, is an old *Maṇḍapa* or pillared hall which seems to have been built about the same time as the temple. It is now connected with the latter 'by an unsightly modern apartment with an entrance on the south side.' 'The pyramidal tower over the central shrine is divided into three main storeys rising to a total height of about 50 feet and is crowned with the usual umbrella ornament surmounted by an urn-finial.'

The provision of procession paths and big enclosures around the temples of the Rājasiṁha period is an entirely new feature, as in the earlier Pallava temples it was not customary to surround the shrine witha circumambulatory passage or procession path, nor was any attempt made to provide walled enclosures or temple-yards around the shrines prior to this period. 'It would appear that, originally, the procession path, or passage around the shrine was open to the sky as in the Shore Temple. In the Panamalai and Conjeeveram temples, we find the passage closed with a flat roof and the interior in total darkness.' 'The style of the temples of the earlier period shows that the Hinduism of those early days was a simple, straight-forward form of worship conducted openly, and free from that secrecy and mysticism which forms such a striking feature of that religion in later times, necessitating the provision of secret passages around the shrine, gloomy interiors and high-walled enclosures, features quite unknown in the earlier examples.' The elaboration of structural details and appendages shows that the cults of the temples and Śaiva ritual in particular tended to become more and more elaborate and complex, say from the eighth century onwards.

---

1 Jouveau-Dubreuil: *The Pallavas*, p. 46.
2 Longhurst (op. cit.), Part III, p. 10.

The temple of Kailāsanātha at Conjeeveram is of considerable historical importance, as it serves as one of the connecting links between the architecture of Southern India and that of the Deccan. The Chālukya Vikramāditya II (733–746 A. D.), who invaded the Pallava dominions (Tuṇḍāka-viṣaya or Toṇḍai-maṇḍalam), defeated the Pallava king Nandivarman and entered Kāñcī or Conjeeveram. But he spared the Pallava capital and seems to have respected and admired its monuments, the Rājasiṁheśvara or the Kailāsanātha temple in particular. It is stated in the Vakkaleri grant that he acquired great religious merit by restoring to the stone temple of Rājasiṁheśvara, caused to be built by Narasiṁha-pota-varman, and to other temples, the gold, which had probably been confiscated by his subordinates without his permission.[1] That Vikramāditya II visited the Kailāsnātha temple seems to be proved by a Kanarese inscription engraved on a pillar of the ancient *Maṇḍapa* in front of the central shrine, which begins with the name of "Vikramāditya Satyāśraya Śrī-Pṛthivī-vallabha", and mentions the temple of Rājasiṁheśvara.[2] As mentioned above, the great temple of Virūpākṣa at Paṭṭadakal was built by the queen consort of Vikramāditya II in commemoration of his conquest of Kāñcī; and the superior technique of that temple, as compared with the shrine of Vijayeśvara built by his predecessor Vijayāditya, has been explained by supposing that Vikramāditya II must have brought with him skilled artisans from the southern capital. That this is not a mere guess is shown by an inscription on the eastern gateway of Virūpākṣa, which speaks of the builder of the Lokeś-vara (Virūpākṣa) temple as 'the most eminent *sūtradhāri* of the *southern* country.' Further, "high up on the front or east face of the temple of Pāpanātha at Paṭṭadakal is an inscription in praise of a certain Chaṭṭara-Revadi-Ovajja who is said to have 'made the southern country', i. e. was the builder of the temples of the southern country. He belonged to the same guild, the Sarvasiddhi-ācāryas, as the builder of Virūpākṣa in the last inscription." It is therefore probable that the old temple of Vijayeśvara at Paṭṭadakal was constructed by local builders, and that of Virūpākṣa by more capable architects from the Pallava capital.[3] It may be assumed that Vikramāditya's conquest of Kāñcī indirectly gave a stimulus to the building art and the Saiva faith in the Deccan, and the temples of Conjeeveram and the shrine of Rājasiṁheśvara in particular seem to have been the main source of inspiration.

Narasiṁhavarman II or Rājasiṁha was succeeded by Mahendravarman III, and the latter by Parameśvaravarman II. Parameśvaravarman II built an important Viṣṇu temple, that of Vaikuṇṭha Perumāl at Conjee-

1 'नरसिंहपोतवर्मनिर्मापितशिलामयराजसिंहेश्वरादिदेवकुलसुवर्णराशिप्रत्यर्पणोपार्जितोर्जितपुण्यः' *South Indian Inscriptions*, Vol. I, p. 146.

2 Ibid. p. 147. The inscription records that the king, having captured Kāñcī and inspected the riches of the temple, gave them again to the god i. e. did not confiscate the property of the temple. *Ep. Ind.*, Vol. III, p. 359.

3 Cousens: *Chālukyan Architecture of the Kanarese Districts*, p. 61.

veram, of which we shall speak later. The Śiva temple of Vīraṭṭaneśvara at Tiruvādi in the South Arcot district contains an inscription belonging to the reign of Parameśvara-Pottaraiyar, and might perhaps be attributed to Parameśvaravarman II.[1]

There was a change in the line of succession after Parameśvaravarman II, and Nandivarman Pallavamalla came to the throne about 720 A. D. The Pallavas reigned for a further period of more than a century and a half, and continued the tradition of building temples in honour of Śiva. These shrines are smaller in size, of which the best examples are the temples of Mukteśvara and Mataṅgeśvara at Conjeeveram. The first may be assigned to about the middle of the eighth century and the second to its end.[2] The temple of Kailāsanātha at Ālambākkam founded by Dantivarman, who succeeded Nandivarman Pallavamalla towards the end of the eighth century A. D., was probably rebuilt during the Cola period. To the later Pallava period also belong the temple of Paraśurāmeśvara at Gudimallam near Renigunta and that of Vādāmallīśvara at Oragadam near Chingleput. It is said that Śiva temples with the name Paraśurāmeśvara are not rare in the South, and they are believed to owe their existence to Paraśurāma. The temple at Oragadam is apsidal-ended, and modelled on the style of the rock-cut temple known as Sahadeva's Ratha at Mahābalipuram. 'Apsidal-ended temples of this type are not uncommon in Southern India, and as a rule are dedicated to Śiva. Perhaps in adopting this style of building from the Buddhists, the Brāhmaṇas saw in its apsidal-ended plan the sacred form of the *liṅga* or phallic emblem of Śiva, and thus considered it an appropriate design for Śaivite temples.'

One of the latest Pallava temples dedicated to Śiva is that of Vīraṭṭaneśvara at Tiruttani, which belongs to the reign of Aparājita, the last of the Pallavas, and was therefore built in the last quarter of the ninth century. 'It is square on plan with a small porch or hall facing the east giving access to a shrine chamber 6 feet square.' 'The tower or *Vimāna* over the shrine chamber is designed like a small model of a Buddhist *caitya* and bears a striking resemblance to Sahadeva's Ratha.'

That Śaivism was the prevailing religion during the Pallava period is shown by the Pallava monuments, most of which are dedicated to Śiva. It has been said of the Pallava capital that 'in the south the honour belongs to one city only and that is Kāñcī. It seems that this position was attained by Kāñcī under the orthodox rule of the Pallavas and mainly by the religion of Śaivism which they propagated and favoured together with the greatness of the Śaiva saints who flourished there. Buddhism and Jainism both found followers in the Pallava empire, but the religion of the ruling family and the people generally was Śaivism. They built a few Viṣṇu temples, but Śiva was their family deity, and Kāñcī is still

1 Jouveau-Dubreuil: *The Pallavas*, p. 46.

2 For the later Pallava temples see Longhurst (op. cit.), Part III and Jouveau-Dubreuil: *Pallava Antiquities*, Vol. II.

the greatest stronghold of Śaivism in the south, and the most devout Śaiva poets and saints belong to that city.[1] The simultaneous existence of Vaiṣṇavism cannot indeed be ruled out, but it seems to have played a subsidiary rôle during the Pallava period and probably long after. The earliest of the Alvārs were associated with Kāñcī, but it is not easy to assign dates or the extent of their influence on contemporary society. Tirumangai, the last of the Alvārs, has been assigned to the eighth century, and he was probably a contemporary of Nandivarman Pallavamalla.[2] Among the great Pallavas, Parameśvaravarman II appears to have been a devout Vaiṣṇava, and the Vaikuṇṭha Perumāl temple built by him at Kāñcī is one of the few large Pallava temples dedicated to Viṣṇu.[3] The Keśava Perumāl temple at Kūram near Conjeeveram is another Pallava shrine dedicated to Viṣṇu. It contains an inscription of the reign of Dantivarman, and there is no doubt that the temple belongs to the latter half of the eighth century.[4] Similar traces of Vaiṣṇavism are found in the Pāṇḍya country where, as we have seen, some of the early triumphs of Śaivism had been achieved. In 770 A. D. Mārangāri or Madhurakavi, a minister of the Pāṇḍya king Varaguṇa Neḍunjaḍayan built a stone temple for Viṣṇu in the Anamalai hill near Madura, and gave a village to some Brahmins apparently on the occasion of the installation of the image of Narasiṁha in the temple. The king, too, built a large temple for Viṣṇu, but though he is called *parama-vaiṣṇavan* in inscriptions, he was liberal in his benefactions to Śaiva temples.[5]

The Pallavas were supplanted by the Colas about the end of the ninth century A. D. when Āditya I defeated Aparājita, the last independent king of the Pallava dynasty. The Colas were ardent Śaivas, and their rule prolonged the domination of the Śaiva faith. They were also great builders of temples, and from an architectural point of view, the later Pallava style merges into the early Cola. According to the Anbil plates, Aditya I (circa 871–907 A. D.) built on both banks of the Kāverī tall stone temples in honour of Siva. After his death, a Sive temple called by the names Ādityeśvara and Kodaṇḍarāmeśvara was founded in his memory by his son and successor Parāntaka I (907–953 A. D.). As already mentioned,

1 Longhurst (op. cit.), Part III, p. 9.

2 Aiyangar (op. cit.), p. 275.

3 Like the Kailāsanātha temple, the pyramidal tower consists of a central shrine on the ground floor and three upper storeys. The one on the ground floor contains a large four-armed image of Viṣṇu in a sitting posture. The shrine of the first floor contains a fairly large image of Viṣṇu in the form of Anantaśayana. The cell on the second floor contains a smaller image of Viṣṇu. The third story of the tower is hollow. The Anantaśayana form of Viṣṇu seems to have been popular in the South. Between the Shore Temple and the small attendant Śiva temple at Mahābalipuram, 'is a third shrine containing a large decayed stone image of Viṣṇu in a recumbent position and representing that deity in the form of Anantaśayana.' It is an oblong cell built up against the back wall of the smaller Śiva temple, and appears to be a later addition. Longhurst (op. cit.), pp. 3, 16.

4 Jouveau-Dubreuil: *Pallava Antiquities*, Vol. II, p. 14.

5 Sastri: *The Pāndyan Kingdom*, p. 63.

the custom of founding such memorial temples dedicated to Śiva was also prevalent in the Deccan in the tenth century. Parāntaka I is known to have covered with gold the Śiva temple at Cidambaram. 'In fact Parāntaka's reign was a great epoch in the history of South Indian temple architecture, and the work of temple-building begun by Āditya was continued vigorously during the best part of his reign.'[1]

South Indian Śaivism may be said to have reached its apogee during the reign of Rājarāja I (985-1014 A. D.). The great literary reorganisation of Tamil Śaivism took place in his time. The hymns and devotional poems of the Śaiva saints were collected and arranged in eleven sections, or Tirumurai, by Nambi Āṇḍār Nambi, a Brahmin priest of Tirunāraiyur in the Tanjore district, under the patronage of Rājarāja Abhaya Kulaśekhara Cola, identified with Rājarāja I.[2] The encouragement of Nambi Āṇḍār Nambi in his great undertaking was not the only service rendered by Rājarāja I to the cause of Śaivism. It was he who built the celebrated Śiva temple at Tanjore, the Rājarājeśvara, perhaps the most magnificent creation of the South Indian building art, with the *vimāna*, or tower, rising 'over the sanctum to a height of nearly 200 feet on a square base of about a hundred feet.' Rājarāja who invaded and conquered Ceylon seems to have built a stone temple to Śiva at Polonnaruwa, the new capital of the island, founded after the destruction of the ancient capital Anurādhapura by the invading armies. It is a small but beautiful structure, and one of 'the few Hindu monuments in Ceylon, which are still in a good state of preservation.' The Śiva temple at Dādāpuram in the South Arcot district bears an inscription of Rājarāja, and is another well-preserved example of the early Cola style of the tenth century A. D.[3] It may also be noted that an inscription of the twenty-fourth year of the reign of Rājarāja I records a sale of land, tax-free, for the *pavitrārohaṇa* ceremony in honour of Mahādeva of the Candramaulīśvara temple by certain residents of Merpāḍi *alias* Rājāśrayapuram.[4] Pavitrārohaṇa or Pavitrāropaṇa is an important Śaiva rite described in detail in *Īśānaśivagurudevapaddhati* (*Kriyāpāda*, chap. XXI).

Rājarāja I was succeeded by his son Rājendra I who reigned till 1044 A. D. The latter is said to have imported Śaivas from the banks of the Ganges and settled them in Kāñcīpura and in the Cola country. The great Śiva temple built by him in his new capital Gangaikoṇḍacolapuram still stands amidst the ruins of the city in the Trichinopoly district. The emphasis on *vimānas* of stupendous height is the outstanding feature of the early Cola style at Tanjore and Gangaikoṇḍa-colapuram.

It is not necessary for our purpose to pursue further the course of Śaivism in South India. The finishing touch to the devotional literature

1 Sastri: *The Colas*, Vol. I, Chap. VII.

2 *Tamilian Antiquary* No. 3, 1909, p. 2.

3 Jouveau-Dubreuil: *Dravidian Architecture*, p. 37.

4 Sastri (op. cit), p. 512.

of Tamil Śaivism may be said to have been given by Śekkilār in the twelfth century, by recounting the lives of the Śaiva saints in his *Periyapurāṇam*, based on the earlier work of Nambi Aṇḍār Nambi. The organisation of Vaiṣṇavism initiated by Nāthamuni in the tenth century and continued by Yāmunācārya was completed about this time by Rāmānuja, who seems to have been an elder contemporary of Śekkilār. The activity of the Vaiṣṇava Acāryas thus falls within the period of the Śaivite Colas. Rājarāja the Great was liberal in his outlook, and though a devout Śaiva, built Viṣṇu temples in Mysore and richly endowed others.[1] But it is significant that Rāmānuja and his followers were persecuted by a Cola king usually supposed to be Kulottuṅga I who commenced his reign in 1070 A. D. There are other instances of the Cola persecution of the Viṣṇu cult ; and, in any case, the initial triumph of Rāmānuja was achieved not in the Cola country, but in Mysore under Biṭṭideva or Viṣṇuvardhana Hoysala who reigned in the first halt of the twelfth century.

APPENDIX IV

The Kālāmukha Sect

In Chapter XIII, p. 350, we have referred to the important Kālāmukha sect and its influence in the Mysore country in the eleventh and twelfth centuries. The Kālāmukhas were influential also in the Cola country from about the tenth century A. D.; and the relevant evidence is summarized by Prof. Nilakanta Sastri in his *Colas*, Vol. II (part I), p. 494. A *maṭha* of the Kālāmukhas existed at Melpāḍi (North Arcot), where Kṛṣṇa III established his camp during his invasion of the Cola kingdom, as recorded in Somadeva's *Yaśastilaka*. Kālāmukha teachers bearing the names Śailarāśi and Jñānarāśi are mentioned in connection with endowments in the temple of Tiruvānaikkoyil (Chingleput) in the years 1127, 1205 and 1231. A Kālāmukha teacher sold some land to the temple at Koyil Tevarāyanpeṭṭai (Tanjore district) in 1123 A. D.

As we have seen, the Kālāmukhas of the Mysore region were Pāśupatas, and are often described as exponents of the Lākula creed; and sometimes a teacher is compared to Lakulīśvara, the founder of the system, or styled as Lakulīśvara-Paṇḍita. Similar evidence is furnished by the Cola inscriptions. The head of the *maṭha* of the Kālāmukhas at Melpāḍi was, for instance, called Lakulīśvara-Paṇḍita. Some of these Kālāmukha teachers are called also *mahāvratin*, 'possessed of the great vow'. An inscription from Jambai (South Arcot) of the reign of the Cola king Vīrarājendra (1063–69 A. D.) mentions a Mahāvratin Lakulīśvara-Paṇḍita in connection with the local temple. An inscription of the twentieth year of the reign of Kṛṣṇa III, i. e. about 959 A. D., describes how a certain man of a noble family,

1 Sastri (op. cit.), p. 224.

a devoted friend of the Cola prince Rājāditya, turned ascetic after the death of the latter on the battlefield (see p. 2), and became a *mahāvratin*, under the name of Caturānana Paṇḍita, and the head of the *maṭha* at Tiruvorriyūr (Chingleput district). It is difficult to explain why the Kālāmukha ascetics are styled here as *mahāvratin*, which is the usual name for Kāpālikas (see p. 358). It is true that the Kālāmukhas are sometimes described as a sect very much akin to the Kāpālikas who were notorious for their evil practices. But the Kālāmukhas of the Mysore and Cola inscriptions were followers of the Pāśupata system, and could hardly have been affiliated to the degenerate Kālāmukha sect mentioned by Yāmuna Muni and Rāmānuja. It is, of course, not impossible that among the members of the Kālāmukha Pāśupata sect there were a few who might have adopted the Kāpālika way of life and figured as the Kālāmukhas stigmatized by the Vaiṣṇava teachers.

The Kālāmukha teachers described in the Cola inscriptions as Mahāvratins might be same as the Mahāpāśupatas mentioned by Udayana in his *Nyāya-kusumāñjali*, which was composed in north India towards the end of the tenth century, about the time when the Kālāmukha Pāśupatas were becoming prominent in the south. We have noted (p. 241) that the commentators on *Nyāyakusumāñjali* explain Mahāpāśupatas as those Pāśupatas who observe *mahāvrata* or the great vow. A certain amount of doctrinal affinity seems to have existed as between the Pāśupatas and the Kāpālikas (see p. 241); but it seems certain that *mahāvrata* did not exclusively mean the Kāpālika cult, and the term *mahāvratin* was applied also to the Kālāmukha Pāśupata teachers of the south.

We learn from Sastri: *Colas* (op. cit.) that a chieftain named Vikramakesari presented a big *maṭha* to a Kālāmukha teacher named Mallikārjuna who was his *guru*, and gave him also eleven villages attached to the *maṭha* for the maintenance of fifty Asita-vaktra, that is, Kālāmukha ascetics. Vikramakesari belonged to Koḍumbālūr (Pudukkottah) and was an ally of the Cola king Parāntaka II who ruled after 953 A. D. On p. 359 we have connected Mallikārjuna with the disreputable Kālāmukha sect; but in the light of the evidence furnished by the Cola inscriptions, it will be more appropriate to suppose that he was one of the Kālāmukha Pāśupata teachers who figure so prominently in the religious life of the south from about the tenth century onwards. These teachers, respected and patronized by kings, and in charge of monastic establishments, could hardly be supposed to have belonged to a sect akin to the Kāpālikas merely on account of the similarity of names.

Index of Geographical Names mentioned in *Yaśastilaka*.

Comm. refers to Śrutasāgara's commentary on *Yaśastilaka*.

Page numbers refer to the N. S. edition of *Yaśastilaka*.

Ahicchatra in Pañcāla, Book VI, section 15. Identified with Ramnagar in Bareilly District, U. P. Sacred to the Jaina Saviour Pārśvanātha. Somadeva says श्रीमत्-पार्श्वनाथपरमेश्वरयशःप्रकाशनामत्रे अहिच्छत्रे.

Aṅga 3. 247 etc. Corresponds roughly to the modern districts of Bhagalpur, Monghyr etc.

Aśmaka, Book III, p. 567: अश्मकवंशवैश्वानरः. Same as Aśmantaka mentioned in 1. 207: अश्मन्तक वेश्म विहाय याहि. Comm. explains Aśmantaka as the Sapādalakṣa mountain. The Barbara mentioned in 3. 112 is also explained by the comm. as the ruler of the hill tract of Sapādalakṣa. Aśmaka, Aśmantaka, the Barbara country, and Sapādalakṣa are thus identical. The capital of Aśmaka was Podana or Paudanapura, identified with modern Bodhan, situated on an affluent of the Godavari in the Nizamabad District of Hyderabad State. See Saletore: *The Southern Aśmaka* in *Jaina Antiquary*, Vol. VI, p. 60. Paudanapura is mentioned in *Yaśastilaka*, Book VII, section 28, where it is located in Ramyakadeśa (रम्यकदेशनिवेशोपेतपौदनपुरनिवेशिनः). According to the Parbhani inscription (see Chap. I of this book), the Cālukya chief Yuddhamalla I ruled over the Sapādalakṣa country, and caused his elephants to be bathed in a tank filled with oil at Podana. अस्त्यादित्यभवो वंशश्चालुक्य इति विश्रुतः । तत्राभूद् युद्धमल्लाख्यो नृपतिर्विक्रमार्णवः ॥ सपादलक्षभूभर्ता तैलवाप्यां स पोदने । अवगाहोत्सवं चक्रे शक्रश्रीर्मददन्तिनाम् ॥. Aśmaka is called Assaka in Pāli literature, and Podana is the same as the ancient Potana, the capital of Assaka, which is one of the seven Kingdoms of India mentioned in a verse cited in the Mahāgovinda Suttanta of the *Dīghanikāya*. In the *Suttanipāta* (verse 977), Assaka is located on the banks of the Godavari. The name appears as Asmaka in the *Mahāvastu*, Vol. 3, p. 208. The Aśmaka country thus corresponds to the Nizamabad District of Hyderabad State and the adjoining territory, and possibly covered in ancient times the southernmost area of Berar as well as the northern part of Hyderabad. See also Sarkar: *The Vākāṭakas and the Aśmaka country* in *IHQ*, Vol. XXII, p. 233 and Mirashi: *Historical Data in Daṇḍin's Daśakumāracarita* in *ABORI*, Vol. XXVI, p. 20.

Ayodhyā, Book VI, section 8 (कोशलदेशमध्यायामयोध्यायां पुरि). Kośala is mentioned in 3.249 (कौशेयैः कोशलेन्द्रः). Comm. explains कोशल as Vinītāpura. Under 1.210 it says विनीतायाः अयोध्यायाः.

Balavāhanapura, Book VI, section 15.

Barbara, see under Aśmaka.

Bhāvapura, Book VI, section 15.

Bhoja country (भोजावनी) 1. 207. Same as Vidarbha or Berar. Bhandarkar: *Early History of the Dekkan*, section III.

Bhūmitilaka, see under Janapada.

Campā, Book VI, section 8 (अङ्गमण्डलेषु......चम्पायां पुरि). Near Bhagalpur. The ancient capital of the kingdom of Aṅga.

Cedi, Book III (चेदिषु नदीशः etc.). The capital of Cedi was Tripurī (Tewar, near Jubbalpur). Under 1.207 comm. explains Cedi as Kuṇḍinapura.

Cerama, Book III. Yaśodhara is described as पल्लवपाण्ड्यचोलचेरमहर्म्यनिर्माणप्रकाश्यमानदिग्विजयवाहिनीप्रचारः. Cerama = Cera = Kerala (Malabar). In 1. 208 the Cera king is addressed thus: चेरम पर्यट मलयोपकण्ठम्. The reading of the printed text, वेरम, is a mistake, as the mss. read चेरम. Kerala is mentioned several times: केरलीनां नयनदीर्घिकाकेलिकलहंसः Book I; 3. 247; 3. 112: केलिं केरल संहर; 1. 210: केरलमहिलामुखकमलहंसः and केरलेषु करालः etc. Book III, p. 431.

Cola, see under Cerama. Also 3. 247. Cf. चोलीनयनोत्पलवनविकास 1. 186; चोलीषु अलतानर्तन.

मलयानिलः Book I. The traditional Cola country is represented by the modern districts of Trichinopoly and Tanjore and part of Pudukkottah State. Comm. on 3.247 calls the Cola country Mañjiṣṭhādeśa, 'The land of madder', also Samaṅgadeśa (under 1. 86), *samaṅga* being same as *mañjiṣṭhā*. Under 1. 208 (चोलेश जलधिमुलङ्घ्य तिष्ठ) comm. identifies the Cola country with Gaṅgāpura, which seems to be an abbreviated Sanskritized form of Gangai-koṇḍa-colapuram, the Cola capital during the eleventh and twelfth centuries, 'at the meeting point of the modern districts of Trichinopoly, S. Arcot and Tanjore.'

Cuṅkāra, Book IV, p. 138. A city associated in a legend with the sage Bṛhaspati.

Dahāla, Book VII, section 29. Same as Ḍāhala or Ḍāhāla identified with the kingdom of Cedi (q. v.). Somadeva describes it as full of sugarcane groves, and says that the city of Svastimatī is in Ḍahālā (अथ कामकोदण्डकारणकान्तारैरिवेक्षुवणावतारैर्विराजितमण्डलायां डहालायामस्ति स्वस्तिमती नाम पुरी).

Das'ārṇa, Book IV, p. 153. Also दशार्णवर्णिनीकर्णपूरः Book III, p. 568. The capital of Daśārṇa was Vidiśā, the remains of which are between the rock of Bhilsa and the hill of Udayagiri. In the midst of this buried city is the hamlet of Besnagar, in Gwalior State. Comm. says दशार्णं नाम नगरं गोपाचलात् गव्यूतिचत्वारिंशति वर्तते. Daśārṇa is identified with East Malwa and the adjoining region with its capital at Vidiśā and the rivers Daśārṇā (modern Dhasan) and Vetravatī (modern Betwa) running through it. *IHQ*, Vol. XXI, p. 61.

Ekacakrapura, Book VII, section 22.

Ekānasī, Book V (explained in comm. as Ujjayinī), p. 226. Mentioned also in Book VII, section 25, and located in Avanti.

Girikūṭa, Book VII, section 29.

Hastināgapura, see under Kurujāṅgala.

Hemapura, Book VI, section 15.

Indrakaccha, Book VI, section 9. The city of Raurukapura, also called Māyāpurī, is located in the Indrakaccha country. The name Raurukapura is omitted in the printed text, and supplied here from the manuscripts. Raurukapura seems to be the Roruka of the Buddhist texts, the capital of Sovīra, an important centre of the coasting trade, apparently on the Gulf of Cutch. Rhys Davids: *Buddhist India*, p. 38. Cf. *Mahāvastu*, Vol. 3, p. 208: सौवीराणां च रोरुकं.

Janapada, Book VI, section 5. The capital of Janapada was Bhūmitilakapura. The place is not identified, but for early coins of Janapada see Rapson: *Indian Coins*, p. 12. Janapada was perhaps near the Kuru country, as in the story in question (See Chap. XVI) two friends, banished from Bhūmitilakapura, come to Hastināgapura in Kurujāṅgala.

Kākandī, see under Kāmpilya.

Kālidāsa, name of a forest, near Ahicchatra, on the Jalavāhinī river (जलवाहिनीनामनदीतटनिकटनिविष्टप्रतनने महति कालिदासकानने Book VI, section 15).

Kaliṅga, Book V. Sudatta is described as the lord of the Mahendra mountain, the home of elephants, in Kaliṅga (कलिङ्गेषु द्विरदमदामोदमन्दकन्दरोदरपरिसरत्पवनपानपरमधुकरालीनीलमणिमेखलाङ्कितनितम्बवसुंधरस्य महेन्द्रमहीधरस्याधिपतिः). The Kaliṅga forest, famous for its elephants, is thus defined in a verse quoted in the comm. on Book II: उक्तं च— 'उत्कलानां च देशस्य दक्षिणस्यार्णवस्य च । सह्यस्य चैव विन्ध्यस्य मध्ये कालिङ्गजं वनम् ॥' The elephants of Kaliṅga are referred to also in *Yaśastilaka* 3. 248.

Kamboja 1. 211 (कम्बोजपुरन्ध्रीतिलकपत्र); कम्बोजीनां नाभिवलभिगर्भसंभोगभुजङ्गः Book I. Comm. on Book II (देवमिव कुलेन काम्बोजम्) identifies Kamboja with Bāhlīkadeśa (modern Balkh in Northern Afghanistan). Under 1. 211 comm. identifies Kamboja with Kashmir and the neighbouring countries, and calls the Kamboja women large-headed: काश्मीरादिदेशस्त्रीणां बृहन्मुण्डानाम्. It explains also कम्बोजीनाम् as बृहन्मुण्डकमनीयकामिनीनाम्. Kamboja was near Gandhāra 'in the extreme north-

Vanavāsi in the North Kanara District." The territories of the Kadambas of Vanavāsi comprised the North Kanara District and parts of Mysore, Belgaum and Dharwar. Somadeva seems to have this area in his mind. See Sarkar in *IHQ*, Vol. XXII, p. 233. Kuntala seems, however, to refer to a wider area. "The following verse which occurs in the Nilgund plate describes the Later Cālukya emperor Jayasiṃha II *alias* Mallikāmoda as ruling over the Kuntala country where flows the famous river Kṛṣṇavarṇā (i. e. the Kṛṣṇā which gets this name after its confluence with the Veṇā near Māhuli, 3 miles east of Sātārā): विख्यातकृष्णवर्णे तैलस्नेहोपलब्धसरलत्वे। कुन्तलविषये नितरां विराजते मल्लिकामोदः॥" The Rāṣṭrakūṭas and the Later Cālukyas are described in contemporary records and Sanskrit works as rulers of Kuntala. The capital of the Rāṣṭrakūṭas was Mānyakheṭa, modern Mālkheḍ in the Gulbarga District of Hyderabad State; while that of the Later Cālukyas was Kalyāṇa, about 50 miles almost due north of Mālkheḍ, near Bidar in the Bidar District in the same State. "Mālkheḍ is about 250 miles, as the crow flies, north by east of Banavāsi and more than 50 miles north of the Kṛṣṇā." The *Udayasundarīkathā* says that Pratiṣṭhāna, modern Paiṭhaṇ on the Godāvarī, was the capital of the Kuntala country. Kuntala thus did not comprise only the North Kanara District of Bombay Province and parts of Mysore, Belgaum and Dharwar Districts, but extended much further to the north so as to include what we now call the Southern Maratha country. See Mirashi in *IHQ*, Vol. XXII, p. 310.

Kurujāṅgala 1. 211 (कुरुजाङ्गलललनाकुचतनुत्र). A portion of the Kuru country, which contained the city of Hastināpura, called by Somadeva Hastināgapura or Hastināpura in Book VI, section 20. Jāṅgaladeśa and Hastināgapura are mentioned also in Book VII, section 28.

Kuśāgrapura in Magadha, Book VI, section 6 (मगधदेशेषु कुशाग्रनगरोपान्तापातिनि). Kuśāgrapura is mentioned by Yuan Chwang, being called the centre of Magadha and its old capital. "The city derived its name from the excellent fragrant reed-grass which abounded there." Watters: *On Yuan Chwang's Travels in India*, Vol. II, p. 148. According to a tradition preserved in Hemacandra's *Triṣaṣṭiśalākāpuruṣacarita*, Prasenajit was king of Kuśāgrapura. Because of frequent fires in Kuśāgrapura Prasenajit ordered that any one in whose house a fire occurred should be exiled from the city. As a fire subsequently occurred in the palace, Prasenajit felt bound by his own edict, left the city, and founded Rājagṛha. See Johnson in *IHQ*, Vol. XXII, p. 228. Rājagṛha, the new capital, is modern Rajgir, south of Patna, near Bihar (town). Rājagṛha, called also Pañcaśailapura, the city surrounded by the five hills, is mentioned by Somadeva in Book VI, section 13 (मगधदेशेषु राजगृहापरनामावसरे पञ्चशैलपुरे).

Kusumapura, Book IV (कुसुमपुरे चरादाकर्णित etc). Same as Pāṭaliputra.

Lampāka, Book III (लम्पाकपुरपुरंध्रिकाधरमाधुर्यपश्यतोहरे......हैमने मरुति). Identified with the modern Laghman. It is the Lan-po of Yuan-chuang, and supposed to represent the *Lambatai* of Ptolemy. Watters: *On Yuan Chwang*, Vol. I, p. 181.

Lāṭa 1. 185 (लाटीमुखाब्जसंभोगहंस). Comm. says लाटीनां भृगुकच्छदेशोद्भवानां स्त्रीणाम्. Bhṛgukaccha, or Bharukaccha, as it is called in Pāli, is modern Broach (District and Town) at the mouth of the Narmadā. Lāṭa corresponds roughly to Eastern Gujarat.

Madra 3. 112 (प्रविश रे मद्रेश देशान्तरम्). Identified with the country about Sākala (Sialkot) in the Punjab between the Ravi and the Chenab.

Māhiṣmatī, Book III (हिमालयमलयमगधमध्यदेशमाहिष्मतीपतिप्रभृतीनामवनीपतीनां बलानि and माहिष्मतीयुवतिरतिकुसुमचापः). Comm. says माहिष्मती नाम नगरी यमुनपुरदिशि पत्तनम्. Supposed to be Maheshwar on the Narmadā in Indore, or

Mandhata, also on the Narmadā, in Nimar District, C. P. Māhiṣmatī was the capital of the early Kalacuris (Kaṭaccūris) who ruled over Mahārāṣṭra between the extinction of the Andhrabhṛtyas and the rise of the Cālukyas. Bhandarkar: *Early History of the Dekkan*, 3rd. ed., Notes, p. 251. Kṛṣṇarāja, the founder of the early Kalacūri dynasty, established himself at Māhiṣmatī about the middle of the 6th century A. D. The capital was later transferred to Tripurī near Jubbulpur. Cf. *IHQ*, Vol. XXI, p. 84.

Mathurā. For references to Mathurā see Chap. XVII of this book. In Book VI, section 10, Uttara–Mathurā, 'Mathurā of the North', is distinguished from Dakṣiṇa–Mathurā, 'Mathurā of the South,' in Pāṇḍyamaṇḍala, i. e. Madura.

Mithilāpura, Book VI, section 20.

Nābhigiri, Book VI, section 15. A mountain in Magadha on the border of the city of Sopārapura (मगधविषये सोपारपुरपर्यन्तधाम्नि नाभिगिरिनाम्नि महीधरे).

Nepāla 3. 249 (मृगमदैरेष नेपालपालः).

Padmāvatī, Book III (पद्मावतीपुरपरमेश्वरः). Comm. explains it as Ujjayinī. Mentioned also in Book VII, section 26. A marginal note in MS. A gives the same explanation.

Padminīkheṭa, Book VII, section 27. Name of a city.

Pallava 1. 207 (पह्लव लघु केलीरसमपैहि); 1. 210 (पह्लवरमणीकृतविरहखेद); and पह्लवीषु नितम्बस्थलीखेलनकुरङ्गः Book I. The Pallava country was the region of Kāñcī (Conjeeveram), the ancient Toṇḍaimaṇḍalam, ruled over by the Pallavas until they were overthrown by the Colas towards the end of the ninth century. The Pallava territory was annexed by the Colas, but the memories of Pallava rule must have been still fresh when Somadeva wrote a little more than half a century later. Further, Pallava chieftains continued to rule here and there under Cola suzerainty. Poussin: *Dynasties et Histoire de l'Inde*, p. 271. Comm. explains Pallava as Pañca-Drāmila, which is rather vague, but there is no doubt that the Drāmila or Drāviḍa or the Tamil country is meant. In Book III Somadeva describes a Drāmila or Tamil or Dravidian Regiment (द्रामिलं बलम्). Apart from the Pallavas, the Kāñci territory is mentioned in Book III (काञ्चिकामिनीकुचकलशकिसलयः). Comm. says काञ्चिर्नाम दक्षिणसमुद्रतटदेशः.

Pañcāla. A king of Pañcāla (modern Rohilkhand, U. P.) figures prominently in Book III. The Pañcālakas are mentioned in 3.112, 247.

Pāṇḍu, Book IV (पाण्डुषु मुण्डीरम्). Same as the Pāṇḍya country. The king of the Pāṇḍyadeśa is mentioned in 3.248.

Pāṭaliputra. The courtesans of Pāṭaliputra are incidentally referred to in Book III (पाटलिपुत्रपण्याङ्गनाभुजङ्गः). Another Pāṭaliputra, located in Surāṣṭradeśa (Kathiawar), is mentioned in Book VI, section 12.

Paudanapura. See under Aśmaka.

Paurava, Book III (पौरवपुरंध्रीरोध्रतिलकः). Comm. says that Pauravapura is Ayodhyā.

Rājapura, capital of the Yaudheya country, described in Book I. "The Yaudheyas have been identified with the modern Johiyas of Bhāwalpur, but in ancient times their territory was more extended." Rapson: *Indian Coins*, p. 14. Rājapura may perhaps be identified with modern Rajanpur in Bahawalpur State, south of Multan. See also Chap. XV of this Book.

S'aṅkhapura, Book VI, section 8. Seems to be not far from Ayodhyā. In the story in question Anantamati is abandoned in the neighbourhood of a mountain bordering on Śaṅkhapura, whence she is taken to Ayodhyā by a merchant who had pitched his camp near by (शङ्खपुरपर्यन्तपर्वतोपकण्ठे परिहृता तत्समीपसमावासितसार्थानीकेन...वणिक्पतिपाकेनावलोकिता सती स्वीकृता च......कोशलदेशमध्यायामयोध्यायां पुरि...समर्पिता).

Siṁhala 1.186, 3.247 etc.

Siṁhapura, Book VII, section 27. Located in the Prayāga country. Not the Siṁhapura mentioned by Yuan Chwang. See Watters (op. cit.), Vol. I, p. 248.

Sindhu 3.248 (तुरगनिवह एष प्रेषितः सैन्धवैः). The Saindhavas mentioned are the princes ruling over the Indus territory.

S'irīṣagrāma, Book VII, section 26. Located in Avanti.

Śopārapura. See under Nābhigiri.

S'rīcandra 3.249 (श्रीचन्द्रश्चन्द्रकान्तैर्विविधकुलधनैर्मागधः प्राभृतैस्त्वां, द्रष्टुं द्वारे समास्ते...). The reference is obscure. Comm. explains Śrīcandra as the lord of the Kailāsa mountain.

S'rīmāla 3. 247. Bhinmal in Jodhpur State. It is the Bhillamāla mentioned in the Praśasti of the Jaina Prākrit romance *Kuvalayamālā* composed in the eighth century. Śrīmāla was the original home of the Jains now inhabiting Rajputana, Western India, the Punjab and the U. P. See Jinavijayaji Muni in *Bhāratīya Vidyā*, Vol. II, Parts I and II.

Sūrasena, Book IV (सूरसेनेषु सुरतविलासम्). The Mathurā country.

Surāṣṭra, Book VI, section 12. Kathiawar. Cf. सौराष्ट्रीषु वलिवाहिनीविनोदकुञ्जरः Book I. Comm. says गिरिनारिसौराष्ट्रियोषित्सु. The first name refers to Girnar Hill near Junagarh in Kathiawar.

Suvarṇadvīpa, Book VII, section 27. Sumatra. In the story in question the young merchant Bhadramitra along with his companions goes on a voyage to Suvarṇadvīpa, and returns after acquiring choice and rare local products in exchange for a huge quantity of merchandise (पुनरगण्यपण्यविनिमयेन तत्रत्यमचिन्त्यमात्माभिमतवस्तुस्कन्धमादाय प्रत्यावर्तमानस्य). See Chap. XVI of this book.

Suvela, Book V. A mountain to the south of the Himālaya. 'हिमालयाद्दक्षिणदिक्कपोलः शैलः सुवेलोऽस्ति लताविलोलः।'

Svastimatī, see under Ḍahālā.

Tāmalipti, Book VI, section 12. Described as being in Pūrvadeśa and Gauḍamaṇḍala. Modern Tamluk in Midnapore District, Bengal.

Ujjayinī. Described with Avanti in Book II.

Valabhī, Book VII, section 23. (अशेषविद्यावैशारद्यमदमत्तमनीषिमत्तालिकुलकेलिकमलनाम्यां वलभ्यां पुरि). Also वलभिरम्भोरुविभ्रमभ्रमरः Book III. Valabhī was the capital of the Maitrakas of Surāṣṭra (Kathiawar), and is now represented by the ruins at Wala, about 20 miles N. W. of Bhavnagar.

Vanavāsi 1. 211 (वनवासियोषिदीक्षणविमुग्ध) and 1. 189. "Situated in the corner between the Ghāṭs, the Tungabhadrā and the Varadā." Bühler's *Introduction to Vikramāṅkadevacarita*. Comm. on 1. 211 says गिरिसोपानगरादिस्त्रीणाम्, that is, the Vanavāsi area contained Girisopā (modern Gersoppa in North Kanara District, Bombay Province) and other cities. It may be noted that under 1. 211 comm. reads गिरिसोपा and not गिरिसोपान, as stated in a footnote on p. 181 of the printed edition. Vanavāsa is mentioned in the *Mahāvaṁsa* XII. 31, and, as pointed out by Geiger, there is a modern town Banavāsi in North Kanara. *Imp. Gaz. of India*, S. V. See under Kuntala.

Vaṅga 3. 247 (अन्यैश्चाङ्गकलिङ्गवङ्गपतिभिः) and वङ्गेषु स्फुलिङ्गः etc. Book III.

Vaṅgāla, Book III: वङ्गालेषु मङ्गलः etc., p. 431. Perhaps the earliest reference to the country of Vaṅgāla in classical Sanskrit literature. For other references see D. C. Ganguly: *Vaṅgāladeśa* in *IHQ*, December, 1943. "In the eleventh century Dacca District was in the country of Vaṅgāla.... In the fourteenth century Sonargaon is definitely known to have been the capital of Vaṅgāla, which extended from Dacca to Chittagong." Others think that the southern part of old Vaṅga came to be known as Vaṅgāla, and identify it with Candradvīpa, i. e. parts of the Buckergunge District and the adjoining region. See D. Sarkar: *The City of Bengals* in *Bhāratīya Vidyā*, Vol. V, p. 36. Vaṅgāla is mentioned in the Tirumalai inscription (1024 A. D.) of Rājendra Cola, while the Ablur inscription of Kalacurya Vijjala (1157-67 A. D.) mentions Vaṅga and Vaṅgāla separately. *Ibid.* Vaṅgāla has also been identified with south-east Bengal including Chittagong. *IHQ*, Vol. XXII, p. 280.

Vaṅgī 1. 210 वङ्गीवनिताश्रवणावतंस; and Book IV: वङ्गीमण्डले नृपतिदोषात् etc., p. 95. Vaṅgī seems to be the Vengi country, being the districts between the Godāvarī and the Kṛṣṇā, where ruled the Eastern Cālukyas. But the comm. in both places identifies Vaṅgī with Ratnapura. On 1. 210 it says वङ्गीवनितानां विनीतायाः अयोध्यायाः पूर्वदिक्स्त्रीणां रत्नपुरस्त्रीणाम्. Ratnapura (modern Ratanpur in Bilaspur District, C. P., to the north of Bilaspur Town) was the capital of Dakṣiṇa Kośala, where reigned a branch of the Cedis of Tripurī.

Vārāṇasī in the Kāśi country (काशिदेशेषु). Book VII, section 31.

Vijayapura in Madhyadeśa, Book VI, section 7.

Viśālā, same as Ujjayinī. अवन्तिविषयेषु सुधान्धः—सौधस्पर्द्धिशालायां विशालायां पुरि, Book VI, section 19. Mentioned also in Book V.

Yaudheya, see under **Rājapura.**

General Index

C

Q

R

T

U

V